How to Cook Everything Vegetarian

Completely Revised Tenth Anniversary Edition

How to Cook *Everything*® Vegetarian

Mark Bittman

Simple Meatless Recipes for Great Food

Photography by Burcu Avsar & Zach DeSart
Illustrations by Alan Witschonke

Houghton Mifflin Harcourt

Boston | New York

2017

For information about permission to reproduce selections from
this book, write to trade.permissions@hmhco.com or to Permissions,
Houghton Mifflin Harcourt Publishing Company, 3 Park Avenue,
19th Floor, New York, New York 10016.

hmhco.com

Library of Congress Cataloging-in-Publication Data is available.

ISBN 978-1-118-45564-7 (hardcover)

ISBN 978-0-544-18694-1 (ebook)

Book design by Kelly Doe and Emily Crawford

Printed in China

SCP 10 9 8 7 6 5 4 3 2 1

Contents

Acknowledgments

Much has changed since the publication of the original *How to Cook Everything Vegetarian,* both in my life and in the world of vegetarian cooking. One thing that's remained constant is my close association with Angela Miller and Kerri Conan; without either of them, none of this would have happened.

The original edition was produced with work, help, and/or support by or from Amanda McDougall, Chris Benton, Kate Bittman, Emma Baar-Bittman, Sean Santoro, Peter Meehan, Linda Funk, Thom Leonard, Susan Hughes, Genevieve Ko, Rita Powell, Alice Kearney, Julia Turshen, Carl Karush, Michael Chessa, Mark Fitzgerald, Alan Richman, Linda Ingroia, Todd Fries, Natalie Chapman, Michael Friedberg, Adam Kowit, Charleen Barila, Rob Garber, Michael Olivo, Jeff Faust, Nick Anderson, Gypsy Lovett, Carrie Bachman, and Serene Jones.

This wonderful and thorough revision was largely and splendidly managed by Pam Hoenig, with some serious help from Kerri and Emily Stephenson. Others on my team included Jennifer Griffin, Perri O. Blumberg, Grace Rosanova, and Kate Bittman. The wonderful, beautiful, I-can't-say-enough-about-it photography is by Burcu Avsar and Zach DeSart, with food styling by Victoria Granof and Burcu Avsar.

And, we have an entire publishing house behind us, in this case HMH, whose How to Cook Everything cohort includes Deb Brody, Bruce Nichols, Rebecca Liss, Jessica Gilo, Melissa Lotfy, Marina Padakis Lowry, Tom Hyland, Kevin Watt, David Futato, and Rebecca Springer. The day-to-day editor—not a fun job, dealing with me, but she handled it brilliantly—was Stephanie Fletcher. Suzanne Fass copyedited.

To my friends and family, thank you, as always. To my kids, I've said it before and I'll keep saying it: You are the best. To my mom: You've seen quite a few of these! Congrats to you too. And to Kathleen, thanks for being there/here during the sometimes tortured and always rewarding hours of producing this monster.

Mark Bittman
New York, 2017

Introduction

I'm not a vegetarian, nor am I invested in you becoming one. I began writing *How to Cook Everything Vegetarian* in 2002, when I realized that our future depended on eating more plant-based foods. I'll get into the "why" of that in a bit, but the book became a fascinating journey of both introspection and revelation: As I explored the world of cooking plants, I continued to recognize how important a skill this was for home cooks, and how it could really be both life- and planet-changing.

It's worth noting that my changed cooking and eating experience in the ten years since *How to Cook Everything Vegetarian* was first published has been largely in sync with that of much of the U.S. population. Yes, Americans continue to outconsume just about everyone when it comes to meat—only the Australians beat us, 205 pounds of meat and poultry per year to our 200.6 pounds in 2015—but there has also been an uptick in the number of Americans who identify themselves as vegetarians (this includes vegans). In a Harris poll conducted by the Vegetarian Resource Group in 2016, more than 35 percent of Americans said they ate a vegetarian meal at least once a week, at home or in a restaurant.

Twenty years ago that number was probably 5 percent. And almost everyone I talk to eats less red meat than they used to.

What encourages me is that the idea of eating meatless meals—the understanding that this is a healthy thing to do and worth aspiring to—has become mainstream. Whether you do it for reasons of health, animal rights, cost (cut back on meat and—especially—processed foods, and watch your food bills drop), or environmental responsibility, abstaining from eggs, dairy, and meat, either as a lifelong choice or as a goal within an omnivore diet (as I do), has become part of the national conversation about food.

It's also a lot easier to be a part- or full-time vegetarian than it was ten years ago. All supermarkets have refrigerated sections for soy products, carrying both block and silken tofu, as well as miso, tempeh, and seitan. And who could have envisioned so many healthy ingredients essentially going viral—quinoa, kale, cauliflower, brown rice, unsweetened yogurt, *chia seeds*?

In addition, interest in how people eat across the globe and the desire to discover and experiment with unfamiliar flavors has led to the mainstreaming of ingredients that were considered exotic ten years ago: smoked paprika, lemongrass, gochujang, harissa, mangoes, sherry vinegar, all manner of seaweed. It's a fantastic time to be a home cook and the perfect time to experiment with meat-free cooking.

How to Cook Everything Vegetarian 2.0

In writing this second edition, I eliminated recipes with flavors that seemed dated and those that, though vegetarian, didn't seem consistent with the goal of good health, and developed new recipes in line with today's more adventurous taste buds. (I'm not antidairy, but taking meat out of food and loading it up with cheese and eggs instead may appeal to people who are ethically vegetarian, but from health and environmental perspectives that may not be much different.) To that end, the desserts chapter has gotten a massive workover, putting the focus more on recipes that include fruits and vegetables (yes, of course, carrot cake and more!), as well as sweetly satisfying desserts that are vegan and/or gluten free. The same goes for the bread chapter, where there are now many more vegan breads.

The first edition included recipes for how to make your own tofu and seitan; in this edition, DIYers will also find from-scratch recipes for nut butters; grain, bean, and nut milks; vegan "cheese"; tofu jerky; soy nuts; and more.

This edition also includes a brand-new chapter on beverages. Take your pick of fresh juice drinks, smoothies (with and without dairy), aguas frescas, and tea- and coffee-based drinks, from brewing a good cuppa (including how to prepare matcha tea) to making your own cold brew coffee.

Finally, the most immediately obvious change in the second edition is the glorious photography. This is in keeping with the changes in attitudes about vegetarian cooking: It's no longer considered austere and ugly, and we're proving that here. And if a photograph ends up inspiring you to make a particular recipe, then it has done its intended job.

How to Use This Book

How to Cook Everything Vegetarian has a handful of features designed to help you use it immediately, no matter how you like to cook.

SERVINGS AND PORTIONS

The majority of recipes make four servings. The notable exceptions are desserts, legume dishes (because I encourage you to cook these from scratch and store leftovers), and sauces and seasonings.

TIME

Each recipe includes an estimation of how long it takes to prepare from start to finish, including any hands-off time. This will vary based on your experience but you don't have to be an expert cook to meet the time estimates.

VARIATIONS, LISTS, AND CHARTS

Hassle-free cooking is all about options, so nearly all of my recipes include variations. The ones that involve changing a technique or substituting several ingredients appear after the main recipe and are also listed in the index. Any lists and charts that follow build on the variations, with more ideas for combining ingredients and flavor profiles. Feel free to use these suggestions as written or as a jumping off point for your own explorations.

THE LEXICONS

These are rundowns of key ingredients (like beans, grains, herbs, and spices) and they appear throughout the book where they are most relevant. The Vegetables, Fruits, Nuts, and Seeds chapter (pages 147 to 304) is essentially one long lexicon with recipes interspersed.

THE INDEX

As comprehensive as it can be, and the fastest way to search for what you want.

Icons

There are four symbols: 🄵, 🄼, 🅅, and 🄾.

🄵 tells you that the recipe is fast, taking 30 minutes or less to prepare.

🄼 indicates that the dish can be made ahead, either in full or to a certain point, and stored for finishing or serving later. (These are excellent dishes for entertaining.)

🅅 means the dish is vegan.

🄾 This icon is new to this edition, and means that with a small tweak, the recipe is vegan—for example, leaving out an optional ingredient or choosing the vegan alternative listed in the ingredients, like using oil when butter or oil is given as a choice.

Getting Started

Even if you're setting up your first kitchen, it's unlikely that your cupboards are entirely bare. You've probably got a few pots, pans, and gadgets, food in your fridge and pantry, an appliance or two; in any case, you have the most important devices: stove, fridge, and sink. Or maybe you cook regularly and are fully stocked. Whatever your situation, I'll help you take inventory and evaluate what you need to make everyday meal preparation hassle free and enjoyable. After that comes a guide to basic food prep and cooking techniques, from knife skills to sautéing and braising. This will become your go-to reference section whenever you have questions about a particular recipe or technique.

SETTING UP YOUR PANTRY

Cooking is more convenient if you always have certain ingredients on hand. Stocking a few key foods in the cupboard and fridge will make it far easier for you to cook when you want to.

With these essentials, you'll be in good shape to cook most everything in this book. You can fill your pantry all at once or gradually, buying a few staples every time you hit the supermarket.

FOR THE CUPBOARD

EXTRA VIRGIN OLIVE OIL Every time I refer to olive oil in this book, I mean extra virgin. It doesn't have to be expensive—though the really good stuff is—but it should be full- and clean-flavored. It helps if you can taste before you buy it; that's easiest in a store that sells it in bulk. Once opened, it keeps for a month or two at room temperature, kept out of direct sunlight, and longer in the fridge (be aware that olive oil will get more viscous when it's chilled; it doesn't affect the flavor but it'll take longer to pour it out of the bottle).

VEGETABLE OIL You need a good-quality, neutral-tasting oil for frying and for those times you don't want the flavor of olive oil to dominate. For more on the options, see pages 626 to 627.

VINEGAR I keep several kinds on hand: white and rice vinegars for neutral acidity; sherry vinegar for the best flavor, generally; balsamic vinegar for something on the sweeter side. White wine and red wine vinegars are useful also. For more on vinegars, see pages 632 to 633.

SALT AND PEPPER When I call for salt, I mean kosher salt. Pepper refers to black pepper. Freshly ground is best at the table, but high-quality preground pepper can save time and is indistinguishable in most cooking applications.

PASTA AND NOODLES The best Italian-style pasta is made in Italy, and the best rice and other Asian-style noodles are usually also imported. Keep a couple of packages of your favorites on hand.

BEANS I almost always cook beans from dried but I understand the need and preference for the convenience of canned. Either way, keep a couple of packages of dried or cans of your favorite beans on hand.

CANNED TOMATOES Essential for tomato sauce as well as a base for soups, stews, and other dishes. I always have a couple of cans of peeled whole and diced tomatoes on hand.

SPICES AND DRIED HERBS Start with those you like best and use most often. A generic starter kit might include dried thyme and tarragon, paprika (smoked and regular), a variety of ground chiles (cayenne, red chile flakes, mild ground chiles), ground cinnamon, cumin and fennel seeds . . . it's hard to know when to stop, but this is your call. I like to grind and mix my own spice blends (see pages 648 to 652) and keep whole spices for those on hand, as do most experienced cooks. Ground spices and dried herbs lose their potency eventually; it's best to replace them annually. Whole spices keep better, but it's still best to buy only what you're going to use within a few months to a year. Keep them a dark, cool place in airtight containers. For more on herbs and spices, see the lexicons on pages 635 to 637 and 642 to 647.

ONIONS AND GARLIC Essential to so many dishes; store away from sunlight to prevent sprouting.

SOY SAUCE A must. Make sure it contains soy and wheat (unless you're gluten-free, then seek out a quality wheat-free brand) as primary ingredients and doesn't include caramel color or artificial flavorings. Keeps indefinitely.

RICE AND OTHER WHOLE GRAINS I always have several varieties of rice on hand, as well as other grains (for more on rice and other grains, see the lexicon on pages 400 to 403). Store away from sunlight at room temperature or in the fridge or freezer, in airtight containers (to keep bugs out).

FLOUR, CORNMEAL, BAKING POWDER, AND BAKING SODA Especially if you like to bake. Store flour and cornmeal away from sunlight at room temperature in airtight containers (to keep bugs out). For more on the different types of flours, see pages 572 to 577.

SWEETENERS Sugar (both white and brown), maple syrup (though it will impart its flavor if added in large enough quantity), and honey (if you're not a vegan) are all options; see pages 682 to 685 for other alternatives. Keep sugar in an airtight container or bag to avoid ants and to keep brown sugar from drying out. Once opened, maple syrup should be refrigerated. Honey can be stored at room temperature; if it crystallizes, that's fine—gently warm it and the crystals will melt.

COCONUT MILK Indispensable for Indian and Southeast Asian cooking and as an alternative to dairy. You can make your own (see page 304), but canned is fine. When selecting a can, shake it; if you don't hear sloshing, put it back. This means the milk has separated and the coconut cream has hardened; once that happens, it's impossible to get the cream to re-emulsify. Always shake a can of coconut milk before opening it unless the recipe instructs you to just use the coconut cream on top. Transfer any leftover to a jar and refrigerate after opening; it will keep for a week or a little longer. You can also freeze it for several months.

FOR THE FRIDGE OR FREEZER

BUTTER Obviously optional if you are a vegan or prefer to use oil. If using, buy unsalted. Keeps forever frozen, for weeks refrigerated.

EGGS My recipes assume large eggs. Store them in their container; otherwise their shells with absorb odors from other items in the fridge. If you can buy local, do so; the freshest eggs have the best flavor and color.

MILK OR NONDAIRY MILK For dairy, use whatever level of fat you prefer, except for the baking recipes, some of which were tested with, and call for, whole milk. For nondairy options to use for cooking, buy whichever type you prefer and buy it plain, with no added flavorings.

TOFU Different types of tofu keep for different lengths of time. You can always freeze it; this changes the texture, but in some ways for the better. See pages 482 to 483 for more on the different kinds and their uses.

TEMPEH Great to have on hand to add to most any kind of dish; it keeps for weeks in the fridge and months in the freezer. For more on tempeh, plus recipes, see pages 512 to 518.

MISO An easy way to add protein and deep umami flavor to most any cooked dish; just stir in a tablespoon of

Vegan Substitutions

Many delicious dishes are naturally vegan. Others might seem tough to adjust with good results, but in reality only a few are actually impossible. In fact, most of the recipes in this book can be prepared successfully with vegan ingredients. The key is to first recognize that some things will never be the same as their nonvegan counterparts. But different doesn't necessarily mean worse, provided you also adjust your flavor expectations. Here are some common substitutions for animal-based foods.

FOR MILK

Almost any nondairy milk works in almost every case, though they have their differences. None is as white as cow's milk, though that doesn't bother me much.

Generally, nut milks are excellent in desserts, grain dishes, and thick soups, where their slightly nutty flavor is most welcome, especially in place of cream. Oat milk is the most neutral tasting, with a nice golden color. Rice milk is also neutral tasting, but almost as thin as water and slightly sweet. Soy milk is high in protein and very strong tasting; it also separates a little less than the others during heating. Coconut milk is delicious and thick and heats well; in dishes where its distinctive flavor is not appropriate but you want that thick creaminess, try Cashew Cream (page 300).

FOR BUTTER

Any oil can be used in place of butter, but there are flavor differences. Because their flavors are quite neutral, grapeseed oil, corn oil, and melted coconut oil work best in baking or any time you don't want the distinctive taste of olive oil. In baking or for pancake or waffle batters, substitute ⅓ cup oil for every ½ cup butter. When a recipe calls for softened or cold butter, measure the oil using this same substitution ratio, then chill it in the freezer or fridge for a couple of hours, until it's really thick. Take it out just before you need it, as it will melt quickly.

FOR HONEY

I like using maple syrup for honey in almost every case, but agave nectar has a flavor similar to honey, making it a better substitution if you don't want to add maple flavor. If you're going to use granulated sugar instead, try a brown sugar for a little more flavor, and add a little more liquid. If you want to get really ambitious, melt the sugar in a small pan with a few drops water to make a syrup.

FOR EGGS

You'll find a lot of vegan variations included in this book that already make substitutions for eggs. If you want to veganize a recipe that includes eggs (aside from dishes that are all about the eggs, like omelets or custards), there are a number of substitutions you can make. Depending on the recipe, you may need to try out several substitutions before hitting on the best one.

For each whole egg, substitute:
- 1 tablespoon ground flaxseed or ground chia seeds soaked in 3 tablespoons water for a couple of minutes until gelatinous
- 2 tablespoons water or nondairy milk, 1 tablespoon oil, and 1 teaspoon cornstarch whisked together until smooth
- ¼ cup silken tofu puréed in a blender or food processor until completely smooth
- ¼ cup banana or avocado purée or unsweetened applesauce mixed with 1 teaspoon baking powder
- ¼ cup good-quality neutral-tasting oil

FOR CHEESE

I'm generally not a fan of commercial vegan substitutes. Though the textures and flavors are completely different, ground nuts or bread crumbs work well on both counts in many recipes in place of cheese, especially gratins and pastas in which you're looking for an accent or contrast. You might have to increase the liquid a bit or toss them with a little oil. In recipes where you want the smooth texture of melted cheese, try silken tofu or crumbled firm tofu. For a cream cheese–like substitute, try Cashew Cheese (page 302).

it, or to taste. Keeps almost indefinitely in an airtight container. For more on the different types, see page 652.

STOCK Homemade is best (see recipes on pages 97 to 100); canned and packaged are not much better than water. Refrigerate stock for up to 5 days or freeze up to 3 months.

NUTS AND SEEDS Add crunch and flavor to salads, noodle dishes, and baked goods. Because their oils can go rancid, they're best stored in the refrigerator, where they'll keep for several months, or the freezer, where they'll keep indefinitely. See pages 297 to 305 for information and recipes.

NUT BUTTERS AND/OR TAHINI You can grind your own; see page 299. If the oil separates, stir it back in before using. Nut butters and tahini will keep for months in the fridge.

SESAME OIL Invaluable for adding intense toasty sesame flavor. Fabulous in stir-fries and other dishes. Will keep indefinitely in the fridge. It sometimes gets sludgy from the cold; just take it out about 15 minutes before you need it.

HOT SAUCE An easy way to add flavor and heat. Keep your favorite(s) on hand. In addition to Louisiana-style hot sauce, consider sriracha, Korean gochujang, Vietnamese garlic-chili sauce, and Indonesian sambal oelek.

OTHER CONDIMENTS Ketchup, Dijon and other mustards, mayonnaise, capers, cornichons, and olives are all good to have on hand.

LEMONS AND LIMES Their zests and juices really lift the flavor of a sauce or dish; keep a couple of each on hand at all times. Don't bother with bottled juice.

FRESH GINGER Not quite essential, but its distinctive flavor and heat are a wonderful addition to all sorts of dishes, savory and sweet.

ALL THE TOOLS YOU NEED

Stocking your kitchen with equipment initially costs more than buying food for the pantry and fridge, but like stocking your pantry, you don't need to do it in one shot. Start with the basics, those things you'll use the most, then add as you have the need and the budget.

Two general rules about pots and pans: Avoid uncoated aluminum, which doesn't heat evenly and makes acidic foods taste and look funny, and make sure whatever you buy is ovenproof—that is, no plastic handles.

THE ABSOLUTE MINIMUM

STOCKPOT WITH A LID It should have a capacity of at least 8 quarts. Mostly used for boiling pasta, making stock, and parboiling vegetables.

LARGE POT WITH A LID Four-quart capacity is fine. The heavier the better for even heat and to avoid scorching. For soups and stews.

SMALL OR MEDIUM SAUCEPAN WITH A LID One- or 2-quart capacity. For making sauces, boiling eggs, reheating small quantities of food.

12- TO 14-INCH SKILLET WITH A LID This will be your go-to pan for everything from pancakes to stir-fries. Cast-iron or nonstick aluminum are my first choices. I replace nonstick pans whenever the coating starts to wear out. Cast-iron lasts for generations.

8- TO 10-INCH SKILLET WITH A LID This size works well for omelets or preparing a dish for one or two portions.

KNIVES Invest in the best you can afford, preferably forged steel that extends all the way through the handle. You really only need three (see opposite).

CUTTING BOARDS Wood or plastic, the choice is yours (plastic can go in the dishwasher). Check out the thin, flexible plastic ones, which are inexpensive and take up nearly no room. To keep a board from sliding on the counter as you work, put a damp towel under it.

VEGETABLE PEELER Either vertical or U-shaped, your choice. The sturdier, the better.

SMALL, MEDIUM, AND LARGE MIXING BOWLS Stainless steel and glass are both good. If they nest for storage, even better.

WOODEN SPOONS OF VARIOUS SIZES They're cheap, so get several—and if you have nonstick pans, they're critical, as you can't use metal.

SPATULAS Get a selection of metal and rubber (silicone is heat resistant) flat, wide ones for turning and tapered plastic ones for scraping out batters and sauces.

POT HOLDERS Choose good thick insulated ones rather than silicone, which are hard to use. Kitchen towels, folded over several times, also work; they must be dry, or you may burn yourself.

KITCHEN TOWELS Cotton, please, for best absorbency.

COLANDER Essential for rinsing produce and draining pasta.

FINE-MESHED STRAINER Any size is fine, though medium and large will be most useful. For rinsing grains and other small foods and for straining out solids, as when making stock.

MEASURING CUPS AND SPOONS One set of metal or plastic dry measuring cups (¼, ⅓, ½, and 1 cup), a 2-cup (or bigger) glass liquid measuring cup with a pouring spout, and a set of measuring spoons (¼, ½, and 1 teaspoon and 1 tablespoon).

TONGS Spring loaded, not the kind that look like scissors. They are critical for grabbing and turning.

The 3 Knives You Need

1. **Chef's Knife.** You'll use it for everything from chopping to slicing. Go with an 8- or 10-inch blade, depending on the size of your hand and what feels comfortable to you. I would counsel against a 6-inch blade unless you have very small hands; it's not as versatile as a larger knife.

2. **Serrated Knife.** A must for cutting bread and other baked goods; good for tomatoes too. Look for one with at least an 8-inch blade.

3. **Paring Knife.** For peeling, trimming, and any precise cutting. I like to have a few of these around.

OTHER HANDY TOOLS

WHISK The balloon kind is the ideal tool for quick hand beating.

LARGE METAL SPOONS For serving, tasting, and stirring.

SLOTTED SPOON Essential for fishing food out of water or oil.

LADLE For soup and more.

BOX AND/OR MICROPLANE GRATER A box grater should have several panels for different tasks—the larger the holes, the bigger the pieces. Use the smallest holes for grating hard cheeses like Parmesan and citrus rind, or use a Microplane grater, which is also great for grating citrus zest.

MANDOLINE If you're slicing vegetables to use in gratins or other dishes, it's invaluable for getting super-thin slices or almost any thickness slice you prefer.

SCALE You can live without it, but some things are far better portioned by weight than by volume.

SALAD SPINNER Get the kind that doesn't have holes in the bottom bowl, so you can use it for storage as well as cleaning the salad. It keeps lettuce fresh in the fridge for several days.

DEEP-FRY THERMOMETER Get one that will clip on the side of the pot.

BRUSHES For brushing foods with oil or sauce. Available with natural bristles or heat-resistant silicone bristles; either works fine.

POTATO MASHER The best for making mashed potatoes; works for other vegetable and fruit purées too.

SKEWERS For grilling or broiling vegetable, tofu, or fruit kebabs. If using bamboo or wood, soak in water for 30 minutes beforehand to keep them from burning. I prefer metal skewers with a flat edge, which keeps the food from spinning when you turn the skewers.

FOOD PROCESSOR OR BLENDER The first is more versatile than the latter—and the best tool for making dough quickly—but each has specific uses. Blenders work great for purées, smoothies, and soups. (An immersion, or stick, blender also works well.) If you're into juicing, a juicer makes sense, though you can make your own vegetable and fruit juices without one (see "Juicing with a Blender" on page 748).

BAKING AND ROASTING EQUIPMENT

13 × 9-INCH ROASTING OR BAKING PAN These can be metal (heavier gauge is better) or glass.

8- OR 9-INCH SQUARE BAKING PAN The go-to size for many of the baking recipes in the book. If you use the larger size, check on it earlier, as the cook time may be a bit shorter. Again, metal and glass are equally good.

LOAF PAN The standard size is 8½ × 4½ inches. Get metal, not glass, if you're going to use only one. Nonstick coatings are helpful.

MUFFIN TIN Regular size (not mini, not giant), 6- or 12-cup, depending on how many muffins you usually make at a time. Nonstick or stainless steel is way better than uncoated aluminum.

LARGE RIMMED BAKING SHEET I also use these for roasting. If you make cookies often, consider purchasing a rimless cookie sheet, though it's not necessary.

9-INCH PIE PLATE I prefer glass.

2-QUART GRATIN DISH For casseroles, gratins (naturally), and baking.

WIRE RACKS For cooling baked goods and draining deep-fried foods.

ROLLING PIN For pizza and pie dough. Beginners should avoid tapered pins, which are a bit trickier to use.

BISCUIT CUTTERS Useful for cutting out biscuits, scones, and rolled cookies.

ELECTRIC MIXER OR STAND MIXER Mostly for mixing up batters and cookie doughs, though a food processor does these well also.

TECHNIQUES

If you're an experienced cook, you can probably skip this section. For novices, though, it's an important one: It contains the nuts and bolts of the cooking techniques used not only throughout this book but in cooking in general.

THE BASICS OF CUTTING

Of paramount importance is to start with a sharp knife. When using a knife with a less than sharp edge, you will find yourself compensating by pushing harder on it. This, I know from experience, will eventually lead to the knife slipping and you cutting yourself.

Hold your knife however you feel most comfortable and secure. Some people "shake hands" with their chef's knife—the knife you'll use for three-quarters of your cutting. But the way to hold one for maximum stability and flexibility is to grip the handle as close to the blade as is comfortable and put your thumb on the inside, against the hilt, with your other fingers wrapped around the other side. You can stretch your forefinger up the back of the blade a little bit for more control.

When you work with a chef's knife, use your other hand to hold the food on the cutting board, curling your fingers and thumb under so your knuckles act as a bumper or guide and keeping the tips of your fingers out of harm's way (some people call this position "the claw"). Almost all cutting skills with a chef's knife are basically variations on a rocking motion, with the tip held steady on the cutting board while you maneuver the handle up and down—think of a paper cutter. If this is new to you, try practicing without any food first and hold your knuckles against the blade so you feel how they work as a guide.

Whether you're chopping an onion, mincing a garlic clove, or slicing big planks of potato to throw on the grill, you want all the pieces to be approximately the same size and thickness. My recipes tell you how big to cut things when size is important, but it's okay if the exact measurement isn't spot on as long as you cut everything in pretty much the same way.

Having said all of that, the chances are you're never going to slice, chop, or mince like a chef, because you aren't one. Neither am I, and my knife skills are pathetic compared to those of a chef. It barely matters. Work with sharp knives, be careful and consistent, try to develop a style based on the descriptions above, and don't think you need to work as fast as a pro.

CHOPPING

This most basic cut results in three sizes: coarsely chopped, chopped, and minced. For all of these, you can forget super-even cutting; truly equal size is unimportant. You generally chop foods that play a

Using a Chef's Knife

STEP 1 You can choose to hold a knife with your hand completely on the handle or with your first finger or two wrapping around the top of the blade. In either case, the position should be comfortable.

STEP 2 To mince herbs or aromatics like garlic, put the tip of the blade on the cutting surface and rock the knife up and down; use your other hand to hold the food on the cutting board, curling your fingers and thumb under to keep the tips of your fingers out of harm's way, so your knuckles act as a bumper or guide.

STEP 3 When the pieces become very small and stable, you won't have to hold them anymore, so you can put your free hand over the point of the blade for greater stability; use a rocking motion to mince the food further.

supporting role in the dish—like onions or other aromatics—or things that are going to cook so long they almost melt away.

COARSELY CHOPPED Chunks that are somewhat uneven, bite-size, or even bigger; you're just passing the food under the knife blade without worrying much. Use this cut before puréeing or mashing or when the texture of the dish is intended to be rustic and chunky. Pieces can be as big as an inch in any dimension.

CHOPPED Pieces ¼ inch to ½ inch in size. Onions, bell peppers, and celery are the most common vegetables to get this treatment, though you might want firm tofu or cabbage cut this way for some dishes. In recipes where I don't specify size and just say "chopped," this is what I mean.

MINCED The tiniest bits you can manage: Once you get things finely chopped, it's just a final burst of short, quick chops to get food to this stage. (Sometimes it helps to steady the tip of the knife blade while you mince, to keep it anchored to the cutting board.) Mince when you want to add lots of flavor in an almost invisible, textureless way with foods like garlic, ginger, shallots, or chiles.

SLICING

To slice with a chef's knife, you still press down, just with a little more precision, and cut into pieces of fairly uniform thickness. You can cut foods crosswise, lengthwise, or on the diagonal. The diagonal slice is probably most attractive and gives you the largest surface area for crisping; it's nice to use in stir-fries. To slice bread, cake, and the like with a serrated knife, grip the handle comfortably and use a gentle sawing motion to work your way through the food. Be sure to hang onto the food in such a way that your hands stay clear but your grip remains in control. A mandoline (see page 17) is handy for getting even slices.

JULIENNE

Translation: Cut into sticks. They can be big like French fries or small like matchsticks. I don't call for julienne often—because I don't do it often—but it's an impressive cut and really not that tough. By hand, first make round foods—let's use zucchini as an example—stable on the cutting board by slicing off a little from one side. Slice the food crosswise into chunks the length you want the final julienne, then evenly slice those chunks lengthwise. Stack the slices into piles of three or so layers, then cut them lengthwise into the same thickness as your first slices. You could also use a food processor disk or mandoline.

Chopping and Mincing

STEP 1 Cut the food into manageable and somewhat even-size chunks.

STEP 2 Chop it into smaller pieces.

STEP 3 If necessary, mince into very small pieces, using a rocking motion.

DICING

When you dice, you cut food into cubes as even in size as possible (without getting too crazy about it). To get dice, first cut the food into julienne, then across into dice.

CHIFFONADE

Translation: Cut into strands or ribbons. Use the chiffonade cut on big leafy vegetables like kale (cut out the heavy ribs first) and small herb leaves like basil; the technique is the same regardless of the size. Make a pile of washed and dried leaves (not too high), roll them from end to end, and slice the roll as thickly or thinly as you like. (See the illustration below.)

PARING, CORING, PEELING, AND OTHER SPECIAL CUTTING TASKS

These are the cutting skills where you hold manageable pieces of food in one hand and a paring knife in the other, and work in a controlled way without a cutting board. You might be coring and peeling an apple, for example, or trimming the eyes from a potato. Often these jobs involve pulling the paring knife toward you, using the thumb on the hand holding the food as the safety guide. If you're not confident working this way, then stick to putting the food on a board and cutting away from you.

THE BASICS OF MEASURING

All of the recipes in this book can be measured with cups and spoons, though I sometimes offer weights when an ingredient is bought by weight. Many experienced cooks eyeball everything in all but the most precise recipes, and though I don't advocate ignoring measurements, with practice you'll get there too. Think about this for starters: Does it matter whether your stir-fry has a heaping cup or a scant cup of chopped carrots?

When measurement matters, however, it really matters, so it pays to learn the right way to do it. When you bake breads, make desserts, or work with eggs in custards and the like, you must measure carefully. It's important to accurately measure grains and beans to be cooked, mostly because I think you'll be surprised by how little a cup really is. And liquids are often critically important to measure.

To measure liquids, set a liquid measuring cup on the counter and fill it to where you think the correct marking is. Then get down at eye level to the cup and double-check. Surface tension causes the liquid to look a little like a concave bubble, and the bottom "line" of that bubble should be even with the line on the cup. Add or pour off some liquid until it is. This sounds ridiculously obsessive, but after you do it a couple times, it will become second nature.

Cutting Chiffonade

STEP 1 Roll up the leaf or stack of leaves.

STEP 2 Cut thin slices of the leaf from top to bottom.

Using a Paring Knife

Before there were vegetable peelers, there were paring knives; as long as you're careful—peel toward yourself, using your thumb to counter the pressure of the knife—they work perfectly.

To measure dry ingredients, follow the "spoon-and-sweep" method: use a spoon to put the ingredient in a dry measuring cup of the size called for in the recipe, heaping it a bit over the top. Then rest the flat side of a knife or spatula on the rim and swipe the excess off the top. Resist the urge to dip the cup in the container holding the ingredient; it does make a difference to how much you get. For measuring spoons, fill them with the ingredient and use the same swiping technique to level it off. Fill measuring spoons to capacity with liquid.

THE BASICS OF COOKING

Cooking is all about harnessing heat. And despite whatever your instincts might tell you, high heat does not automatically lead to burned food. Quite the opposite: Often, unless the pan, oven, pot of water, or grill is hot enough, the food won't cook properly. This holds true for both dry- and moist-heat techniques. Though a few beginning cooks veer toward the other extreme, most are understandably too timid with heat.

If you can master heat, you can become a great cook. Food responds best—meaning it develops a flavorful brown crust or cooks up tender, not mushy—when it suddenly comes into contact with something hot. You almost never want to start with cold ingredients in a cold pan or a cold oven or a cold pot of water. (There are exceptions, yes.)

Measuring Dry Ingredients

To measure flour accurately, use a spoon to overfill the measuring cup, then sweep the top evenly with the flat side of a knife.

Whether you cook with gas or electric doesn't matter; the only difference is that electric stoves take longer to heat up and cool down. So you may need to accommodate the way they respond by working two burners at the same time or by planning ahead and making adjustments a little before they're needed. No big deal.

What counts most is your ability to trust your senses, including smell. Heat has its own aroma, as does food when it's cooking—and burning. You should also listen for the sound of food cooking, and learn to recognize visual signs of doneness like crisping around the edges, dryness, and releasing from the pan or grill. Being observant puts you in control and gives you the confidence to use heat more assertively. And your cooking will instantly improve.

Here's an overview of techniques, with special emphasis on how they apply to vegetarian cooking.

BOILING, PARBOILING/BLANCHING, AND SIMMERING

Few things in cooking are more straightforward than this: You put water in a pot (usually to about two-thirds full), turn the heat to high, and bring it to a rolling boil. Then toss in a large pinch salt and add the food. Boiling works best for dried ingredients like pasta, rice, or legumes, where the food must absorb water as it cooks. Many fresh vegetables are at their best when boiled, and of course boiling is absolutely necessary for stocks and soups.

Parboiling refers to a brief boil before draining and using another cooking technique to finish the cooking. I frequently use this method to prepare vegetables for stir-frying, but it's handy any time you want to partially cook ingredients in advance. Blanching is the same as parboiling, only the food is cooked for less than a minute; this is usually reserved for vegetables, fruits, or herbs either to fix their vibrant color or loosen their skins so they can be peeled more easily. Both parboiling and blanching are usually followed by shocking: The food is drained, then immediately plunged into ice-cold water to stop the cooking.

Simmering is when the liquid bubbles gently, well below the point of a rolling boil.

STEAMING

Since steam is as hot as boiling water (and when it's created in a pressure cooker, it's even hotter), it's an excellent moist-heat method for many vegetables and other foods, like dumplings. The idea is to suspend the food above the boiling water so the steam cooks the food and keeps it moist without letting it become waterlogged. The pot should be large enough to hold the food comfortably and allow the steam to circulate freely. I often choose steaming over boiling because it's usually faster—you don't have to bring a big pot of water to a boil—and the color and texture are often better. Check the food frequently so it doesn't overcook and check the pot to make sure it doesn't boil dry.

You can steam with an inexpensive folding metal basket, sold almost everywhere you can buy kitchen equipment. They're adjustable and convenient. Just open the basket to fit the desired pot, fill with water to just below the basket base, add your food, cover, and steam. Stackable bamboo steamers can be fun, but they're not always easy to use. Better, usually, is to rig your own steamer: Turn a heatproof plate or shallow bowl, two or three ramekins, or a pie plate upside down in a large pot with a tight-fitting lid and put a heatproof plate right side up on top; make sure it's stable and that there's space around it. Fill the pot with just enough water so that it doesn't touch the right-side-up vessel. Put the food in, cover, and turn the heat to high. Once the water starts boiling, lower the heat so it bubbles steadily.

You can also steam tall vegetables—think a bunch of asparagus or a head of cauliflower standing on its stem—by simply popping them into an inch of water and proceeding as usual.

SAUTÉING AND PANFRYING

Sautéing refers to food cooked in a small amount of fat on the stovetop. You can dredge the pieces of food in flour, bread crumbs, or seasonings before sautéing, but it isn't necessary.

The idea is to sizzle the food and create a crust on it so that it's lightly browned outside (caramelized, and therefore tasty) and tender and moist inside. You must follow a few rules to get there: Make sure the fat is hot, almost smoking, before you add the food—oil should shimmer and butter bubble (but not brown). And don't crowd the pan, or the food will steam and never brown. An inch or so between big pieces is fine; smaller pieces require less elbow room. Once everything starts cooking, don't mess with it until the pieces start to brown on the bottom and release easily from the pan. You should be able to hear the food sputtering as it cooks and see the fat bubbling around the edges as they brown. You can adjust the heat and gently swirl the fat around if you like, but let the food itself be.

The related panfrying (also called shallow frying) is like sautéing but with more fat, halfway between sautéing and deep-frying; it works best for flat or cutlet-like vegetables, fruits, batters, or fritters, when you want some serious crisping but don't want to use as much fat as in deep-frying (see page 26). As with sautéing, you can bread or dredge the food, or you can batter it—or do nothing to the food before panfrying, depending on whether you want a coating. Put about ½ inch oil (not

Ways to Rig a Steamer

There are a couple of ways to make a steamer:

You can buy a collapsible metal steaming insert, which will work in any pot.

Or you can use a heatproof plate, slightly smaller than the pot; to raise it off the bottom of the pot, use an upside-down plate, a couple of small ramekins, or whatever else is heatproof and provides a stable base.

butter) in a large deep skillet. When it's hot, add the food. Since the food isn't submerged, you've got to turn it to cook the other side, but because there's more fat than with sautéing, the crust develops better.

There are a couple of other techniques that are not sautéing but use the same kind of pan and a small amount of fat. Sweating, for example, refers to cooking aromatics like garlic or onions: You put a lid on the pan and lower the heat, and let the moisture in the ingredients create steam; the food should not brown. This is also sometimes helpful with thick pieces of food that require more cooking time. However, you won't get the same browned crust. For super-moist foods like mushrooms, you lower the heat a bit, causing the food to first release its water, then dry out without any browning.

STIR-FRYING

Stir-frying is a lot like sautéing except for one crucial thing: the stirring. Instead of letting food sit in the pan and brown, you keep things moving. If you don't have a special burner that holds a wok, it's better to use a large skillet for stir-frying. As with sautéing, you start by heating the pan on the stove over high heat; add oil, and let it get very hot. Then add the food and stir.

5 Tips for a Better Stir-fry

1. The smaller you cut your pieces, the faster they will cook and, to some extent, the more flavor you will get (more browning on more surfaces equals more flavor, up to a point).

2. You can add as many ingredients you like to the final dish, but too many will slow down cooking and muddy the flavor.

3. Use a flat-bottomed skillet (better than a wok for home-cooked stir-fries), the larger the better. Well-seasoned cast-iron is best, and high heat is essential.

4. You may need to parboil and shock those vegetables that won't become tender through direct stir-frying, even if you cut them small; broccoli stems, thick asparagus, and turnips are good examples. If you don't have time for that, cut them small and stir-fry them first before adding any tender, quick-cooking ingredients.

For the most control, remove them from the pan when they're almost done, cook the other vegetables, and return the first batch to the mix for final warming.

5. You need a little liquid in stir-fries. That liquid can be water or something with more flavor, like soy sauce. Add a bit with the vegetables to encourage them to cook more quickly and a little at the end, if necessary, to keep the soy sauce from burning.

DEEP-FRYING

Like sautéing and stir-frying, deep-frying uses hot oil to cook and brown food. You just use a lot more of it, so the oil surrounds the food. The result is either the crispest, most ethereal delights you can imagine—or a soggy, greasy mess. It all depends on having enough good oil at the right temperature, which is almost always between 350° and 375°F.

2 Ways to Deep-Fry

The first: Use a Dutch oven or large saucepan, or a medium saucepan if you want to use less oil and don't mind working in batches. The pot should be deep, with straight sides. A deep-frying thermometer is handy too, clipped to the side of the pan, so you know the exact temperature of the oil.

Put at least 2 inches of oil in the pot. It should fill the pot only partially, with several inches of room left to allow the oil to rise safely without overflowing when the food is added to it. Turn the heat on the burner to medium and wait several minutes before checking the temperature the first time. (Meanwhile, you can prepare the draining setup. I usually use paper towels on a plate, but you can also use wire racks or clean brown paper bags.) If you have a thermometer, use it; all deep-frying recipes give you a specific temperature (or should). If you don't have one, carefully drop a piece of plain bread into the oil. It should bubble, float immediately to the top of the oil, and soon turn golden brown; if it sinks and soaks up oil, wait another 2 to 5 minutes and check the temperature again. If it turns brown too quickly, lower the heat a bit; give the oil a few minutes to readjust, then test again.

It's very important not to overheat the oil because it can spontaneously catch fire (sometimes called "autoignition"); covering the pot while the oil is heating can cause this to occur when the lid is then taken off. If you see the oil start to smoke, turn off the heat or carefully move the pot to a cool burner. If the oil catches fire, do not put water on it and do not try to move it. If you can, turn off the heat and slip a lid over the pan. Or use a kitchen fire extinguisher or smother it with a cup or two of baking soda, flour, or sand.

To start cooking, carefully lower the food into the hot oil with metal tongs or a slotted spoon. Don't add too much food at once; crowding will significantly lower the temperature of the oil and prevent the food from cooking properly. Gently turn the food as it cooks so it browns evenly. If you're new to deep-frying, you might want to take a piece out when it looks done and cut it open to check. There should be a crisp crust surrounding tender, just-done insides. Remove the cooked food with a slotted spoon, drain it, and you're ready to fry another batch. Keep it warm in a 200°F oven while you continue frying.

Alternatively, use a countertop electric deep-fryer. Undeniably the easiest method, but really worth the expense and space only if you deep-fry a lot. Follow the manufacturer's directions.

BRAISING

In this technique, you brown the food first in a little hot oil or butter, then add liquid to the pot, cover, and simmer either on the stovetop or in the oven. As the dish cooks, both the cooking liquid and solid ingredients develop lots of flavor and a luxurious texture. Since the results are often called stews, sometimes people call braising "stewing," though if you want to be super-technical, you don't necessarily brown the food first when you stew.

Braising is frequently used to slow-cook tough pieces of meat, but you can make delicious braised vegetable dishes, and it's a tasty way to cook meat substitutes like tofu, tempeh, and seitan.

ROASTING

Oven heat does all the work here; roasting uses dry heat in a confined environment to crust food on the outside while cooking it through on the inside. All you need is a big shallow pan and a little hot oil or butter to coat the food. Two crucial points: The oven must be very hot, almost always over 400°F. The roasting pan can't be too crowded either; the heat must be able to circulate so that any moisture in the food can easily evaporate, otherwise, you're doing little more than steaming, and you can forget about browning or crispness. You can use seasonings and even a little extra liquid, usually after the food is finished roasting, to make a little pan sauce (see "What's Deglazing?" below).

What's Deglazing?

Deglazing is more a saucing technique than a cooking technique. After panfrying, roasting, or sautéing, you make a sauce out of the tasty browned bits that remain in the pan. Here's how: First transfer the cooked food to a plate or bowl and pour all but a tablespoon or 2 of fat from the pan. Set the pan on a burner (or two if it's a big roasting pan), turn the heat to medium, and add enough liquid to just cover the bottom. You can use water, vegetable stock, juice, wine, beer, or liquor. Use a wooden spoon or spatula to scrape the browned bits up from the bottom and stir until they dissolve. Add more liquid and adjust the heat as needed; it should bubble vigorously.

When all the browned bits are dissolved, keep stirring and cooking until the sauce thickens somewhat. Taste and adjust the seasoning, adding herbs or spices as you like or enriching the sauce with some cold butter, cream, or coconut milk or other nondairy milk. Then you have three choices: Return the food to the pan and toss to coat in the sauce and rewarm. Or put the food on a serving platter. Strain the sauce if you like a less rustic texture. Pour sauce on top of the food or serve it on the side.

BAKING

Like roasting, but usually for a moist food, and at lower heat. Most food that's baked starts as a semiliquid or a fairly wet solid when it goes in the oven; think of cake batter, custard, or bread dough. There may be sauce, water, or other liquid surrounding solids, as in gratins, casseroles, or lasagne. As the heat from the oven warms whatever's in the pan, it causes the moisture to steam and jump-starts all the other chemical reactions needed to raise the dough, melt the cheese, brown the crust, and so on. It's a good idea to have an oven thermometer to verify that your oven's thermostat is accurate, because a glitch of 10 or 15 degrees can make a big difference, depending on what you are baking.

GRILLING

Cooking over fire was our ancestors' original method, and is still a favorite way to prepare food. There's direct-heat grilling, where you put the food on a rack set right over a fire to crisp, brown, and cook through. Or you can grill with indirect heat, with the food off to the side of the fire and the lid on, so the grill works like an oven and cooks the food more slowly.

If you've got a gas grill, preheat the grill by turning all the burners on high, closing the lid, and leaving it for 15 minutes. At that point, readjust the burners to the level of heat called for in the recipe. For indirect cooking, create a cool side by turning off half the burners, which is where you will place the food.

For a charcoal grill, I prefer lump charcoal and use a chimney to get the fire going, but use briquettes if you like, and/or an electric starter. Just stay away from lighter fluid; I think you can still taste it, even after it's supposed to have burned off.

Once the charcoal is going, spread it out for direct grilling or leave it in a pile on one side for indirect grilling. Generally, you want to wait until the coals are covered with ash before you start grilling.

As with deep-frying and baking, I recommend you buy a thermometer if your grill doesn't come equipped with one—and even if it does, it's still a good idea to get one to verify that thermometer is accurate; sometimes they can be way off. If you don't have a thermometer, you're ready to grill when you can hold your hand right above the rack for only a couple of seconds. For less intense grilling, you want to be able to hold your hand above the heat for about four seconds or so. So adjust the distance of the rack from the fire if you can or spread out the coals a bit. Or just wait.

BROILING

If you don't have a grill or don't feel like grilling, broiling is the next best thing. Since the heat source is on top, you'll get browning and even charring like you do on a grill, but you won't get the smoky flavor or the grill marks. All you have to do is turn on your oven's broiler—an open flame or electric heating element—and, while it heats up, prepare the food and put it on a broiler pan or other rimmed baking sheet.

You can broil food anywhere from 2 to 6 inches away from the heat source. It all depends on your broiler, the thickness or density of the food, and the toppings or seasonings (sugar and honey, for example, burn faster than oil or vinegar and so need to be broiled at a greater distance from the heat). Adjust the distance to the broiler as needed; just like with grilling, you want browned, crisp outsides and moist, tender insides. The recipes give you a starting point. But generally, when the food browns and cooks on one side, take the food out and flip it over.

Check your manufacturer's instructions; some electric oven broilers require that the door be open during use. If that's the case, try heating the oven to its highest setting with the door closed, then switch to broil and open the door a crack.

HOW TO HANDLE FOOD SAFELY

Start with good kitchen hygiene: Keep your hands, countertops, utensils, appliances, and tables perfectly clean. Soap and hot water are fine. You can use antibacterial products if you like, but there is some indication that their overuse might actually lower your immunity to infection.

Keep a supply of kitchen towels on hand and change the one you use often; I sometimes go through several a day. And don't let your sponges and dishrags get too dirty, or you'll just spread gunk around your clean kitchen. I boil my sponges for a few minutes every couple of days, or toss them in the washing machine, dishwasher, or microwave. When they get past their prime, I replace them.

All fruits and vegetables should be rinsed well before trimming. If you really want to be careful, wash your cutting board(s) and knives after every task before you use them again. If there's any remaining dirt or bacteria, this keeps it from spreading.

Your refrigerator should run below 40°F (35°F is ideal), and your freezer should stay below 0°F. Cooked food runs into trouble when it's neither hot enough nor cold enough—in a range of temperature known as the danger zone, between 40° and 140°F. So be sure you don't let food hang around at room temperature for more than an hour or so. That means you should cool food down quickly if it's not going to be eaten within an hour, and store in the refrigerator or freezer. Also be sure to reheat leftovers fully. When in doubt, stick in an instant-read thermometer to see what's what; you might be surprised. Reheated food is generally considered safe when its internal temperature reaches 165°F. Thaw foods in the refrigerator or under cold running water. And never put cooked food on a plate that previously held raw food.

Making the Most of Leftovers

In restaurants, chefs call using leftovers "repurposing." They don't just heat up whatever wasn't served the night before. Instead, they reassemble the components differently to make something else altogether.

You can learn this approach too. In fact, you can plan to have leftovers by cooking extra of some ingredients and by doubling or tripling recipes. Throughout the book, I try to provide some specific ideas for how you might do this. You'll come up with even more on your own once you start thinking in terms of components.

Take grilled vegetables, for example: It's a lot of work to light the grill, so you may as well use the fire to cook a big batch. What's left over can fuel meals for days, since they're so versatile. Legumes are another versatile food, and so are grains. Once you get in the habit of keeping extra, already cooked, and on hand, the only trick is to know how to use them. This list, which contains not only recipes but also other lists, should get you started. These recipes and lists are vehicles for purposeful extras—like beans and rice—and leftovers.

Jook (page 424)

Bean Salad, Many Ways (page 71)

The World of Rice Salads (page 76), plus More Rice Salad Variations (page 78)

Fried Rice, with or Without Egg (page 380)

10 Additions to Crunchy Amaranth Griddlecakes (page 406)

Sushi Rice, Sushi Bowls, and Nigiri Sushi (pages 384 to 388)

Bean Croquettes (page 474)

Pasta with Lentils or Other Legumes (page 317)

26 Vegetable and Legume Dishes That Can Be Tossed with Pasta (page 323)

Tips for Dramaticallly Better Asian-Style Noodle Bowls (page 332)

16 Dishes for Stuffing Pasta (page 349)

7 Great Filling Combinations for Flat Omelets (page 530)

8 Great Leftovers to Turn into Quiche Filling (page 539)

22 Unexpected Toast Toppers (page 624)

11 Ideas for Pizza Toppings (page 614)

9 Dishes for Filling Calzones (page 615)

10 Taco and Burrito Ideas (page 621)

Quesadillas (page 620)

REHEATING FOOD

Throughout this book I encourage you to make extra food to store in serving-size containers in the freezer for future use, and to make all or part of dishes hours or even days ahead. This approach to cooking is undeniably efficient and convenient. But until it becomes second nature—and trust me, it will—you might need some tips for reheating.

The best foods for reheating are high in moisture, like soups, sauces, stews, and cooked beans. Crunchy foods usually don't reheat very well, but can be finessed if you heat them, covered, in the oven, then spread them out to dry a bit and crisp. Remember too that not everything must be reheated—many vegetables, pastas, and grains are best eaten at room temperature in salads, or added to another dish in the last minute of cooking.

In general, it's best to reheat food gently, but there are exceptions. You can use a microwave, an oven, or the stovetop. Direct heat on a stovetop burner should generally be low; in a microwave or an oven you can use higher heat. How long something takes to reheat will depend on how much you've got, how dense it is, and the method you choose to reheat it, so until you have some experience, check frequently.

You can reheat frozen food too; it'll just take longer. If you have time, thaw food in the fridge for a day or so. Or thaw in the microwave. For safety reasons, don't let frozen food sit out on the counter to thaw it.

Salads

CHAPTER AT A GLANCE

My mother made me eat a salad a day, and I've tried to stick to that. You might be a salad person, too, but if not you probably will be after diving into this chapter, which includes lots of green, raw, and cooked vegetable salads as well as those based on beans, grains, and pasta. I used to say salads were hard to define, but actually it's easy: any dish that combines fruits, vegetables, or greens and then dresses them in a delicious, slightly acidic sauce. How's that?

Perhaps even more than with most other dishes, the best salads start with the best ingredients, especially since they're often served raw. And it's tough to beat a few slices of fresh-from-the-garden tomato drizzled with oil and sprinkled with salt. But unless you're a fanatic—or a home gardener—you're going to have to compromise if you want to eat salads every day all year long. Fortunately, even at a salad's most basic level, you can take ordinary supermarket ingredients—iceberg lettuce or cabbage, packaged carrots and celery, a few radishes—and with the help of a little extra virgin olive oil and lemon juice or decent vinegar, turn them into something delicious.

THE BASICS OF MAKING SALAD

The simple green salad is just that, but because it has so few ingredients, there's a noticeable difference between good and great. You should, of course, have some delicious olive oil on hand—it's easy enough to come by—as well as decent vinegar or a couple of lemons. However, lettuce should be more than the vehicle for these fine ingredients. On the contrary, the best salads work the other way around: The greens are the star.

The quality of greens in supermarkets has grown tremendously, even since this book was first published. Ditto the options, which is a wonderful thing, because even a little salad of Boston and romaine lettuces, for example, is considerably better than one of either alone. In many ways, the more greens, the merrier; that's why boxes of greens, mixed together,

are so popular. (Well, also because they've virtually done away with washing.)

SALAD GREENS

There are hundreds of edible greens, each with its own personality, from hot mustard greens to sweet chard to bitter radicchio to spicy arugula. And then of course there are lettuces. The fact that now you can buy mixes of these, prewashed and even precut, makes building a "green" salad easier than ever before (although that's no reason to buy the bagged salad kits that contain dressings and all).

While in many instances I find myself buying mixtures of greens, it's still worth understanding the differences among various lettuces and greens. Here's a quick primer.

LETTUCES

There are four basic types:

- **Iceberg** A light-green ball of crisp, super-moist, but not especially flavorful, leaves
- **Romaine** Long, crunchy leaves, still moist but with some bitterness
- **Boston or butterhead** Soft but well-defined heads with tender, very slightly bitter leaves
- **Loose-leaf, bunching, or cutting lettuce (like green and red leaf)** The biggest category of lettuces and the ones that tend to be the most bitter

USING Romaine and Boston lettuces are fine by themselves, though better in mixes because they're so mild. Iceberg needs even more help, though it's good in combination with other vegetables as in Chopped Salad (page 36), or broken into big wedges and used as a vehicle to show off Blue Cheese Dressing (page 674) or the like. Loose-leaf lettuce varies so much in taste and quality that it's hard to generalize, but note that chopped up lettuce can also be thrown into soups and stir-fries.

CHICORY AND ENDIVE

The flavor, texture, color, and versatility of this huge group of greens (which includes radicchio, Belgian endive, curly endive, escarole, frisée, and more obscure greens like Treviso radicchio) is unmatched.

They are all forms of chicory: sharp, crunchy vegetables that vary wildly in appearance but less so in taste and texture. Tight-headed bright red radicchio; long, leafy radicchio (also called curly endive); lettuce-looking, thick-ribbed escarole; the smooth oval Belgian endive; and lacy, frilly frisée all feature a stark bitterness that is readily tamed by cooking or smoothed by olive oil. All are bitter, most are super-crunchy, some are very expensive. (Yet if you can tell the difference with your eyes closed between $5 per pound radicchio and $1 per pound escarole, you have a better palate than I.)

USING Other than endive and frisée, these are almost too bitter to use alone in salads but are great mixed with other greens. Belgian endive can be served like celery, drizzled with olive oil or spread with cream cheese. All of these are delicious braised (for example, try using them in the recipe for Braised and Glazed Brussels Sprouts on page 183), stir-fried as described in Stir-Fried Vegetables (page 154), or brushed with olive oil, sprinkled with salt, and grilled (page 163).

ARUGULA, WATERCRESS, AND DANDELION

These greens are only distantly related, although all are dark green and intensely flavorful. Dandelion greens have the distinction of being among the most vitamin-packed foods on the planet. When young, it is mild flavored; when mature, it is the most bitter of greens. Arugula (also called rocket or rucola) has a distinctive hot flavor, an acquired taste for some. (Baby arugula, which has become more common, is much milder. A shame, really.) And super-peppery watercress—there are other cresses, too, and they're similar—is unjustly used more as a garnish than as a food.

Traditionally these are best in spring and fall, but like almost everything else, they're now available year-round.

USING Arugula is one of the best salad greens there is: Lightly dressed with oil and lemon juice, it's a real treat.

It is also tasty as a bed for grilled vegetables (especially when it wilts a little and absorbs some grilling juices) or in a salad with tomatoes. Watercress makes a fine addition to salads but is also good on sandwiches and in soups—cook with potatoes in broth or water, and purée to make a vichyssoiselike soup. Dandelions can be eaten in salads when young but quickly become too bitter to eat raw; they are then best steamed or stir-fried with soy sauce or garlic and lemon.

SALAD MIXES (MESCLUN)

Mesclun, from the Niçoise dialect for "mixture," is a word originally used to describe a mixture of a dozen or more wild and cultivated greens, herbs, and edible flowers. Now it has come to mean any mix of greens.

Supermarket mesclun (which you are likely to see labeled "spring mix") may not be as interesting as mesclun you make yourself (especially if you're a gardener), but it's undeniably easy to use. Now a year-round staple, sometimes available for as little as $4 or $5 a pound, already mixed mesclun is an incredible bargain when you consider that a pound of greens will serve a substantial side salad to at least six people and probably more like eight.

These mixes are often packaged in plastic, with a special process called Modified Atmosphere Packaging (MAP) that keeps them fresh for a week or longer. (The same is true of other prepackaged salads.) Once opened, however—or if you buy your mesclun loose—use it

Microgreens

Once a reward for diligent home gardeners and a precious garnish for restaurant chefs, microgreens—essentially sprouts—are now increasingly available at farmers' markets and even supermarkets. They're so delicate, they often only need a sprinkle of salt just before eating. Or I sometimes like to drizzle some olive oil into my palm and toss the microgreens gently to coat with my hands.

within a couple of days before it starts to turn even the slightest bit funky.

All of these are prewashed, but I wash them anyway, and I recommend you do too.

THE "OTHER" GREENS

These are the leafy salad greens that don't easily fall into any of the preceding categories. Some, like spinach (see page 248), are available everywhere in many forms. Some, like mizuna and tatsoi (a small-leafed member of the bok choy family), are traditional Asian greens now seen as more or less mainstream in America. Others, like mâche (lamb's lettuce) and its relatives, are quite tender and fragile, with a small window of freshness. Still others are the leafy tops of root vegetables like beets, radishes, and turnips. When they're young and tender these can make excellent salad greens, too.

If you frequent farmers' markets or specialty grocers, you'll run into all of these and more. I encourage you to experiment. Almost all may also be lightly cooked—steamed, boiled and shocked, or stir-fried—though when they're young, fresh, and tender, the best way to eat them is raw.

PREPPING AND STORING SALAD GREENS

TRIMMING For head and whole loose-leaf lettuces, first scoop or cut out the core. (If the head is tight, you'll probably have to use a knife.) Trim away the outer round of leaves and any browned or wilted stems. Tear or cut leaves into smaller pieces, if you like, and rinse.

RINSING Don't skip this process even if the greens come in a bag labeled "prewashed." It's fast and easy and a worthwhile precaution. Put the greens into a salad spinner or in a colander inside a large pot or bowl. Fill the container with water and swirl the greens around. Now lift the salad spinner basket or colander out of the water. Shake out the water. Repeat as necessary until the water

Prepping Salad Greens

You can rinse salad greens up to a day or 2 in advance.

STEP 1 Plunge greens into a salad spinner filled with water or a colander set in a large pot or bowl; swirl the greens around. Lift out the insert or colander and change the water, repeating as many times as necessary to remove all traces of grit.

STEP 2 If you have a salad spinner, spin the greens dry; otherwise, dry them in a towel.

STEP 3 Store, wrapped loosely in kitchen or paper towels, in a loosely closed plastic bag.

contains no traces of sand. Then spin the greens or pat them dry with towels.

STORING Washed, dried salad greens are good to have on hand and keep pretty well. If you have a salad spinner with a bowl, pour the water out after spinning and pop it in the fridge, greens and all. The remaining moisture and ventilated basket provide a good environment for keeping greens fresh for a couple of days or more. If you don't have a salad spinner, line a plastic bag with clean kitchen or paper towels, put the washed greens inside (careful not to pack them too tightly), loosely close the top, and store in the refrigerator (in the crisper, if possible). Greens should always be kept in a cool part of the refrigerator, but not somewhere cold enough to freeze them.

DRESSING AND SERVING SALADS

Few dishes are as pretty as salads, as long as you don't dress them too early or too heavily and end up with wilted greens. But there's no law that says salad must be served in a large wooden bowl with a wooden fork and spoon. Here are some options.

TOSSED SALAD Most of the recipes here call for the leaves to be a manageable size, tossed in dressing. Individual preferences aside, as a general rule ½ cup dressing is about right to dress 4 cups dense vegetables, beans, or grains or 6 to 8 cups salad greens. Once the salad is tossed, you decide whether to divvy it up or serve it from one plate, platter, or bowl at the table.

DRIZZLED WITH DRESSING Thick, chunky, or rich dressings don't always work well for tossing, especially if the vegetables are tender, cooked, or left in large leaves, pieces, or slices. Simply arrange the salad and pour a couple of tablespoons dressing around the top. In cases where the dressing is thick enough to use a spoon, serve it on top or a little to the side of the greens. Think of it more as a dip.

THE WEDGE Retro, and still beloved. Whether you cut a neat pie-shaped slice from a head of iceberg or

8 Crunchy Additions for Any Salad

There are a lot of possibilities to add last-minute crunch to salads—and not just green salads. Here are some of the best:

1. Tofu Croutons (page 497)

2. Toasted Bread Crumbs (page 678)

3. Cubed Croutons (page 679)

4. Seeds like sunflower, sesame, poppy, or pumpkin, raw or lightly toasted (see page 299)

5. Chopped nuts, raw or lightly toasted (see page 299)

6. Any of the crumbles from page 679

7. Bits of panfried or toasted sea greens (see page 650)

8. Popcorn (page 390)

roughly break into the heart of a romaine, the lettuce must be crackling crisp. Then top it with a spoonful of dressing and maybe a sprinkle of something crunchy (see the sidebar above). This is the time to go for thick, creamy dressings like Blue Cheese (page 674).

GREEN SALADS

Given all the options for lettuces and other greens (see pages 32 to 34), this group of salads is only the beginning. Look at "11 Other Ideas for Basic Green Salad" (page 36). Remember to add some crunch (see the sidebar above; the tofu croutons are easy and different). To punch up the flavor you can add the bitter greens, herbs, and flowers that have a long tradition as accompaniments to blander foods. (See the last few recipes in this section for some examples.) Or jazz up your dressing with mustard, roasted garlic, or a fresh herb—but don't overdo it. And remember that green salads are always a good vehicle for leftover simply cooked vegetables, grains, or beans.

Basic Green Salad

MAKES: 4 servings
TIME: 10 minutes
F **V**

A green salad you can eat every day either as a side or use as the base for a main dish.

> 6 **cups lightly packed torn assorted greens (like mesclun, or any lettuce)**
> ¼ **cup olive oil, or more as needed**
> 2 **tablespoons sherry vinegar, or more as needed**
> **Salt and pepper**

Put the greens in a bowl and drizzle with the oil, vinegar, and a pinch each salt and pepper. Toss gently with your hands or two large utensils. Taste, add more oil, vinegar, and/or salt and pepper and toss again. Serve immediately.

GREEN SALAD WITH BALSAMIC DRESSING For a slightly sweeter taste: Replace the sherry vinegar with balsamic vinegar.

NEUTRAL GREEN SALAD Less assertive flavor, perfect alongside dishes with Chinese, Vietnamese, Thai, Indian, or otherwise spicy flavors: Replace the olive oil with 3 tablespoons good-quality vegetable oil; use rice vinegar instead of sherry vinegar.

GREEK SALAD The classic, simplified: Add ⅓ cup crumbled feta cheese and ¼ cup each chopped fresh mint or parsley (or both) and chopped pitted black olives. Use fresh lemon juice instead of vinegar.

LYONNAISE SALAD Very hearty: Use strong-flavored greens like frisée, arugula, dandelions, or radicchio, alone or in combination. Top with 2 Poached Eggs (page 525) or peeled Medium-Boiled Eggs (page 523).

ENDIVE SALAD Elegant and delicious: Combine endive with radicchio, watercress, and other strong-flavored greens. Toss in about ½ cup toasted walnuts or hazelnuts (see page 299) and use nut oil, if you have it.

11 Other Ideas for Basic Green Salad

1. Omit the oil or reduce the vinegar by half for a lighter salad.
2. Substitute any flavorful oil, like walnut, hazelnut, or sesame. (Use less at first, because these are more intensely flavored than olive oil.)
3. Change up the vinegar: red or white wine vinegar, rice vinegar, champagne vinegar, cider vinegar, and many more.
4. Shower the top with freshly grated Parmesan before serving. This is probably the easiest way to enrich any salad.
5. Add chopped raw or lightly cooked vegetables.
6. Add tomatoes: Halve cherry tomatoes or cut large tomatoes into wedges and toss with the greens. The easiest way is to serve the salad on top of thick slices; this prevents the greens from getting soggy.
7. Add a spoonful minced shallot, onion, or scallions, or a pinch minced garlic.
8. Add crumbled blue, feta, or other soft cheese.
9. Add sliced pears, apples, oranges, or other fruit.
10. Add seaweed: Figure about a quarter-ounce, soaked and drained as described on page 53. Or add a sheet or 2 of nori, toasted (see page 244) and crumbled.
11. Add diced roasted red peppers (see page 228; yellow are fine too), capers, or anchovies.

Chopped Salad

MAKES: 4 servings
TIME: 30 minutes
F **V**

Much of the time, I make casual salad dressings right in the bowl. But this vegetable-loaded recipe is ideal for a more complex vinaigrette.

> 2 **celery stalks (preferably from the heart), chopped**
> 2 **carrots, chopped**

1 small to medium red onion, minced

1 cucumber, peeled if you like, seeded, and chopped

1 red or yellow bell pepper, cored, seeded, and chopped

4 cups chopped romaine lettuce (about 1 pound)
Salt and pepper

½ cup any Vinaigrette (page 628), or more to taste

1. Combine the celery, carrots, onion, cucumber, bell pepper, and lettuce in a bowl; sprinkle lightly with salt and pepper and toss.

2. Drizzle with the vinaigrette and toss again. Taste and adjust the seasoning. Serve immediately.

10 Additions to or Substitutions for Chopped Salad

1. Fennel bulb for the celery, trimmed and chopped

2. Avocado (not too ripe), pitted, peeled, and chopped

3. Cabbage, about 1 cup shredded or chopped

4. Haricots verts or other green beans, about 1 cup, cooked briefly and shocked

5. Fresh peas, snow peas, or snap peas, about 1 cup very lightly cooked and shocked (see page 150)

6. Steamed, grilled, or roasted asparagus, chilled and cut into pieces (several spears are all you need)

7. Radishes, ½ cup, chopped

8. New potatoes, about 1 cup, steamed and cut into small chunks

9. Chickpeas (cooked or drained canned), ½ cup or more

10. Nuts like almonds, pistachios, or peanuts, ½ cup chopped into large pieces

Warm Spinach Salad with Tofu Croutons

MAKES: 4 servings
TIME: About 45 minutes
M **V**

Tofu croutons have a crisp appeal all their own, and this slightly sweet soy-based dressing is rich and satisfying.

1 pound fresh spinach leaves, trimmed and rinsed

¼ cup good-quality vegetable oil

1 tablespoon minced fresh ginger

1 tablespoon minced garlic

½ cup sliced scallions

1 tablespoon sugar

2 tablespoons rice vinegar

1 tablespoon soy sauce

2 teaspoons sesame oil
Red chile flakes
Pepper
About 1½ cups Tofu Croutons (page 497)
Salt, if needed

1. Put the spinach in a bowl large enough to comfortably toss the salad.

2. Put the vegetable oil in a skillet over medium-high heat. When it's hot, add the ginger and garlic and cook, stirring constantly, until just soft, about a minute. Add the scallions and cook for another minute, until softened. Stir in the sugar, vinegar, and 2 tablespoons water. When the mixture begins to bubble, turn the heat down to medium-low and cook, stirring occasionally, until it becomes a little syrupy, 2 to 3 minutes.

3. Stir in the soy sauce and sesame oil. Season with red chile flakes and pepper to taste. (You can make the dressing to this point up to an hour or so in advance. Remove it from the heat until you're almost ready to serve, then gently rewarm it.) While the dressing is still warm, pour it over the spinach and toss immediately until well coated. Add the croutons and toss again. Taste and adjust the seasoning, adding a little salt if necessary. Serve right away.

Greens with Fruit, Cheese, and Nuts

MAKES: 4 servings
TIME: 20 to 30 minutes
F **M**

The cheese course—eaten with or without fruit, traditionally before (or instead of) dessert—has gone

Greens with Fruit, Cheese, and Nuts (page 37)

mainstream since the first edition of this book. It's a nice idea, but I stand by translating the concept into a salad, which is lighter, less fussy, and more versatile. However, in keeping with the times, I've added to and adjusted combos in the list that follows; if you're a cheese enthusiast you'll find even more to try.

> About 1 pound any fresh fruit, or 1 cup any dried fruit cut into bite-size pieces
> 1 tablespoon fresh lemon juice
> 4 ounces Gorgonzola or other blue cheese
> ¾ cup walnuts or other nuts
> 6 cups lightly packed mixed greens (like mesclun) torn into bite-sized pieces
> About ½ cup Vinaigrette (page 628; made with olive oil and sherry vinegar)

1. Peel and core the fruit if necessary and remove any seeds or pits. If large, cut the fruit into ½-inch chunks. Toss the fruit with the lemon juice. Cover and refrigerate for up to 2 hours.

2. Crumble or chop the cheese into small bits; cover and refrigerate until needed. Put the nuts in a dry skillet, turn the heat to medium, and toast them, shaking the pan frequently until they are aromatic and beginning to darken in color, 3 to 5 minutes. Transfer to a small bowl.

3. When you're ready to serve, toss together the fruit, cheese, and greens with as much of the dressing as you like. Chop the nuts coarsely, sprinkle them over all, and serve.

10 Fruit, Cheese, and Nut Combos

1. Grapes, Parmesan, pine nuts
2. Oranges, manchego, almonds
3. Apricots, goat cheese, pecans
4. Dried apricots, blue cheese, walnuts
5. Cantaloupe or honeydew, cotija, pepitas
6. Blueberries, Asiago, pistachios
7. Dried plums, feta, hazelnuts
8. Dried pineapple, brie, cashews
9. Peaches, ricotta salata, pecans
10. Plums, fontina, almonds

Balsamic Strawberries with Arugula

MAKES: 4 servings
TIME: 15 minutes
F **V**

In the original *How to Cook Everything*, I featured strawberries in a peppery, slightly sweet compote in the fruit chapter. In Italy, strawberries macerated with balsamic are served as a dessert. Clearly the combination also has legs as a savory salad. To turn the main recipe or any of the variations into a light meal, add crumbled goat cheese or feta, or a couple of handfuls of toasted nuts.

> 3 cups strawberries, hulled and halved or quartered
> 1 tablespoon balsamic vinegar, or more to taste
> Pepper
> 4 cups lightly packed arugula leaves
> Salt
> 2 tablespoons olive oil, or more to taste

1. Toss the strawberries with the vinegar and pepper in a large salad bowl. Let sit for 10 minutes.

2. Add the arugula, sprinkle with salt, and toss again. Drizzle with the oil and toss gently one more time. Taste and adjust the seasoning. Drizzle with more oil if you like and serve.

BALSAMIC FIGS WITH WATERCRESS Use halved or quartered fresh figs instead of the strawberries and watercress instead of the arugula.

BALSAMIC PLUMS WITH RED LEAF LETTUCE Quarter and pit 1 pound plums and use red leaf lettuce instead of the arugula.

BALSAMIC RED GRAPES WITH LACINATO KALE Made this way with sturdier ingredients, the salad can rest in the fridge for up to 2 hours or more: Substitute 3 cups halved grapes for the strawberries and macerate them as described in Step 1, using either dark or white balsamic. While the fruit sits, slice the kale leaves crosswise into thin ribbons and rub them between your hands to "bruise" them a bit before tossing with the grapes.

Bitter Greens with Maple-Onion Dressing

MAKES: 4 servings
TIME: About 1 hour
M **V**

It's so unfortunate that this group of greens is dubbed "bitter." Sure, they're intensely flavored, but in a pleasantly piquant way, especially when dressed with the sweetness of caramelized onions. And they're perfect for winter, when not only do you want something hearty, but the best of these are in season.

 4 tablespoons olive oil
 2 large white or yellow onions, halved
   and thinly sliced
 1 large red onion, thinly sliced
   Salt and pepper
 2 tablespoons maple syrup
 ¼ cup black olives (preferably oil cured),
   pitted
 1 tablespoon sherry vinegar, or more to taste
 4 cups chopped green bitter greens
   (like escarole, chicory, or frisée)
 1 cup chopped radicchio or Belgian endive

1. Put 2 tablespoons of the oil in a large skillet over medium-low heat. When it's hot, add the onions, a sprinkle of salt and pepper, and the syrup. Raise the heat a bit until the mixture sizzles, then adjust the heat so the onions cook steadily without browning. Add the olives and cook, stirring occasionally, until the onions are very soft and deeply colored, at least 30 minutes and possibly up to 60. (You can prepare the recipe up to this point and let the onions sit at room temperature for up to a few hours or refrigerate for longer, then reheat gently.)

2. Add the remaining oil, the vinegar, and 1 tablespoon water and stir to make a dressing. Taste and adjust the seasoning, adding more vinegar or water if you'd like. Put the greens and radicchio in a large bowl, add the onion dressing, toss, and serve.

BITTER GREENS WITH CARAMELIZED FENNEL DRESSING Instead of the onions, use 2 large fennel bulbs. Trim the tops, reserving some of the tender fronds to chop and toss with the salad right before serving. Cut the bulbs in half, core, and thinly slice crosswise. Proceed with the recipe.

CABBAGE SALAD WITH CARAMELIZED ONION OR FENNEL DRESSING Replace the bitter greens and radicchio with 5 cups shredded Napa or Savoy cabbage in the main recipe or the first variation.

Parsley and Herb Salad

MAKES: 4 servings
TIME: About 20 minutes
F **O**

Like Tabbouleh (page 76), this is a salad in which herbs—particularly parsley—play the leading role. I don't agree with the common "wisdom" that flat-leaf (Italian) parsley tastes better than the curly variety, but it is a little easier to handle. You can omit the sweetener if you like, but many people like the way it balances the parsley's bitterness.

 ¼ cup olive oil, or more to taste
 2 tablespoons fresh lemon juice, or more to taste
 1 teaspoon sugar or honey (more or less to taste;
   optional)
   Salt and pepper
 4 cups chopped fresh parsley
 ¼ cup chopped fresh chives or ½ cup chopped
   scallions
 1 tablespoon chopped fresh thyme
 1 teaspoon chopped fresh tarragon

Put the oil, lemon juice, and sugar, if you're using it, in a large bowl, sprinkle with salt and pepper, and whisk to

Bitter Greens with
Maple-Onion Dressing

blend. Add the parsley, chives, thyme, and tarragon and toss to coat. Taste and adjust the seasoning, adding oil or lemon juice as you like. Serve right away.

LETTUCE SALAD WITH PARSLEY A more familiar but almost equally flavorful version: Use 4 cups lightly packed mixed tender greens (mesclun or the like) and reduce the parsley to 1 cup. Keep the other ingredients the same, though you will probably need to add a little more oil and lemon juice.

BASIL AND ROMAINE SALAD Omit the thyme and tarragon. Instead of the parsley, use 2 cups torn basil leaves. Add 4 cups torn romaine lettuce. You will probably need to add a little more oil and lemon juice.

Endive and Blue Cheese Salad

MAKES: 4 servings
TIME: 15 minutes
F M

Each of the major ingredients here can be swapped for something else, and the flavors of the salad can be varied in many ways (see "7 Ways to Vary Endive Salad," right). I like to eat this salad with my fingers; endive leaves are perfect for that.

½	cup crumbled Roquefort, Gorgonzola, Cabrales, or domestic blue cheese
¼	cup olive oil
2	tablespoons sherry vinegar
	Salt and pepper
16–24	trimmed Belgian endive leaves (about 2 endives)
4	ounces enoki mushrooms, left whole
¼	cup chopped fresh parsley or chives for garnish

1. Put the blue cheese, olive oil, and vinegar in a small bowl and sprinkle with salt and pepper. Stir with a fork until only small lumps remain. If you've got time, cover and chill the dressing for up to a day. Taste and adjust the seasoning and stir again before finishing the salad.

2. Spread the endive leaves face-up on a platter and lay a few mushrooms lengthwise on each one. Drizzle the dressing onto the mushrooms, being careful to keep it contained in the leaves if you want to pick them up with your fingers. Garnish with the parsley and serve right away.

7 Ways to Vary Endive Salad

1. For the enokis, substitute slivers of button mushrooms.
2. For the endive, substitute the small inner leaves of romaine or butter lettuce, or radicchio leaves.
3. For the blue cheese, use fresh goat cheese or grated Parmesan or other hard cheese.
4. Add 1 minced small garlic clove and a teaspoon or 2 honey to the oil and vinegar with the blue cheese.
5. Use walnut or hazelnut oil in the dressing and sprinkle the filled leaves with toasted walnuts or hazelnuts (see page 299).
6. Add a small pile of fresh grated radish to the top of each leaf before garnishing.
7. Use 2 tablespoons chopped fresh chervil or tarragon instead of the parsley for garnish.

RAW VEGETABLE SALADS

Many raw vegetables—beets, carrots, artichokes, celery and celery root, mushrooms—make fabulous salads, and without the help of lettuce. The variety of textures, manipulated in large part by whether you grate, chop, or slice, is what makes the options so compelling: For some vegetables the crunch is unsurpassed; others are sublimely tender, almost silky. The flavors range from subtle to stark. And they all stand up to bold dressings.

Spicy No-Mayo Coleslaw

MAKES: 4 servings
TIME: 30 minutes
F M V

You can shred and dress almost any fruit or vegetable and call it slaw. Choose the oil based on the flavors of what else you're serving; substitute cayenne for the fresh chile if it's handier. If you want old-fashioned creamy coleslaw, try the last variation and skip the fresh chile.

 1 tablespoon Dijon mustard, or to taste
 1 tablespoon sherry vinegar, cider vinegar, or fresh lemon juice
 1 teaspoon minced garlic
 1 teaspoon minced fresh chile (jalapeño, Thai, serrano, or habanero), or to taste
 3 tablespoons olive oil or good-quality vegetable oil
 3 cups cored and shredded Napa, Savoy, green, and/or red cabbage
 1 red or yellow bell pepper, cored, seeded, and chopped
 ¼ cup chopped scallions or red onion
   Salt and pepper
 2 tablespoons chopped fresh parsley

1. Whisk together the mustard, vinegar, garlic, and chile in a large bowl. Add the oil a little at a time, whisking all the while, until the dressing thickens.
2. Add the cabbage, bell pepper, and scallions and toss with the dressing. Sprinkle with salt and pepper. Refrigerate until you're ready to serve, tossing once in a while if you can. (It's best to let this rest for an hour or so before serving, to allow the flavors to mellow; the cabbage will also soften a bit and exude some juice. Or let it sit for up to 24 hours if you like, then drain the slaw before continuing.) Just before serving, add the parsley and toss.

CABBAGE AND CARROT SLAW, MEXICAN STYLE Substitute 1 carrot, grated, for the bell pepper, and lime juice for the vinegar. Finish with cilantro instead of parsley, if you like.

APPLE SLAW A little sweeter: Use carrot instead of bell pepper as in the preceding variation. Shred or grate 2 medium or 1 large Granny Smith or other tart, crisp apple and add in Step 2. Lemon juice or cider vinegar are the best choices for the acid here.

SPICY COLESLAW WITH MAYO Creamy without being gloppy or cloying: Reduce the oil to 1 tablespoon and add 2 tablespoons mayonnaise or Vegannaise (page 672) to the dressing in Step 1.

Carrot Salad with Cumin

MAKES: 4 servings
TIME: 15 minutes
F M V

Here's a simple salad in a typically North African style that features the sweetness of fresh oranges offset nicely by the earthiness of ground cumin. For some less traditional ideas using other vegetables the same way, see the variation. Whichever way you go, the salad will keep well, refrigerated, for up to a day after you make it, though it's best served not too cold.

   Juice of 2 oranges
   Juice of 1 lemon
 2 tablespoons olive oil
   Salt and pepper
 1 teaspoon ground cumin, or more to taste
 1½ pounds carrots, trimmed, peeled if you like

1. Whisk together the citrus juices, oil, some salt and pepper, and the cumin in a large bowl.
2. Shred the carrots with the julienne peeler or the grating disk of a food processor. Or slice them crosswise into rounds as thin as you can manage; a mandoline (see page 17) is a helpful tool here. Or shred them using the biggest holes of a box grater. You may need to work in batches. Put the carrots in the bowl with the dressing. Toss, taste, and adjust the seasonings, adding more cumin if you like, and serve.

ROOT VEGETABLE SALAD WITH CUMIN Use any of the following with the carrots, alone, or in any combination: celery root, jícama, Jerusalem artichokes (sunchokes), or kohlrabi. Trim and peel them as necessary.

Brussels Sprout Salad

MAKES: 4 servings
TIME: 20 minutes
F M V

Everyone is surprised when first presented with raw Brussels sprouts, but they're easy to like. The trick is to shred them finely, "bruise" them a bit, and dress them at least an hour before serving. The longer the salad sits, the softer and milder tasting the leaves become.

1½	pounds Brussels sprouts, trimmed
	Salt
⅓	cup olive oil
2	tablespoons fresh lemon juice, or more to taste
1	small red onion, halved and thinly sliced
	Pepper

1. Use the shredding blade of the food processor to shave the Brussels sprouts into thin pieces; you may have to work in batches. Or slice them thinly crosswise by hand.

2. Transfer the sprouts to a large bowl and add a large pinch salt. Gather handfuls of the shreds together, rubbing, lifting, and separating them until the salt is distributed and the shreds soften a bit.

3. Add the olive oil, lemon juice, onion, and a generous sprinkle of pepper. Toss thoroughly and refrigerate for at least 1 hour or up to 6. Taste and adjust the seasoning, adding more lemon if you like, and serve cold or at room temperature.

ESCAROLE SALAD Excellent with a little Parmesan added: Instead of Brussels sprouts, use escarole. Trim the ends and slice each head crosswise into paper-thin shreds. Salt and rub the leaves as described in Step 2. In Step 3, add 1 teaspoon minced garlic.

CHARD SALAD The stems are sweeter than celery and the leaves mellow and become silky: Substitute any color chard for the Brussels sprouts. After trimming, remove the leaves from the stems and slice each separately crosswise into thin pieces. Proceed with Step 2.

KALE SALAD Red kale is especially gorgeous but you can use lacinato or green kale, too: As in the chard variation above, separate the stems from the leaves before slicing.

5 Flavorful Additions to Brussels Sprout Salad or Its Variations

Alone or in combination, just toss them in. In some cases, you'll want to wait to add salt until after tasting.
1. ½ cup grated Parmesan or manchego cheese
2. ½ cup chopped pitted black or green olives
3. ½ cup dried fruit, like raisins or cranberries, or chopped dried apricots, plums, or dates
4. ½ cup chopped nuts, like hazelnuts, almonds, walnuts, or pecans
5. ¼ cup chopped dried tomatoes

Shaved Artichoke Salad

MAKES: 4 servings
TIME: 30 minutes
F

For a real treat, try this salad of shaved baby artichokes layered with Parmesan: It's unbelievable. The same ultra-thin slicing principle applies for this salad as for Brussels Sprout Salad (left).

2	lemons
8	baby artichokes, cleaned (see pages 168–169)
	Parmesan cheese
3	tablespoons olive oil, or more as needed
	Salt and pepper
¼	cup chopped fresh parsley or basil for garnish

1. Squeeze the juice of 1 lemon into a large bowl of ice water. Slice the artichoke hearts, and the bottoms, if they're tender enough, as thin as possible. As you slice them, drop them into the water; this will help keep them from browning.

Brussels Sprout Salad

Shaved Artichoke
Salad (page 44)

2. Shave the Parmesan into thin slices with a vegetable peeler; you want about as many pieces as you have artichoke slices, of about the same size. Zest the second lemon, then juice it.

3. Drain the artichoke slices and pat dry. Dry the bowl and return the artichoke slices to it. Add the olive oil and 1 tablespoon of the lemon juice. Sprinkle with a little salt and a generous amount of pepper and toss gently.

4. Layer the artichokes with the Parmesan on a platter or individual plates. Taste and add more olive oil, lemon juice, salt, or pepper as needed. Garnish with the lemon zest and parsley, and serve right away.

SHAVED MUSHROOM SALAD Really simple: Instead of the artichokes, slice 1 pound white button mushrooms as thinly as possible. No need to drop them into lemony water. Proceed from Step 2.

SHAVED APPLE SALAD Aged white cheddar or Parmesan is equally good here: Use 4 tablespoons cider vinegar instead of the lemons (omit the zest) and substitute about 1½ pounds any crisp apple for the artichokes. Use 3 tablespoons of the vinegar in the soaking water. Core the apples and slice them thin; proceed with the recipe, substituting the remaining tablespoon cider vinegar for the lemon juice in the dressing. Dill or chives are nice alternatives to the parsley or basil.

Soy-Sesame Marinated Celery

MAKES: 4 servings
TIME: 15 minutes, plus 3 hours to marinate
M V

I make this salad all the time as a little something to snack on before dinner, a side dish, or a unusual addition to a picnic spread; it's ten times better than its description. Try the variations, too.

 1 **pound celery stalks, heart, and leaves**
 1 **teaspoon salt**
 4 **teaspoons sugar**

 3 **tablespoons sesame oil**
 1 **tablespoon soy sauce**
 2 **teaspoons rice vinegar or cider vinegar**
 ½ **teaspoon minced garlic**
 1 **teaspoon chili oil (optional)**

1. Trim and string the celery stalks (see page 192), then cut the celery stalks and heart into 2-inch lengths. Chop the leaves and keep them separate. Mix the stalks and heart with the salt and 1 teaspoon of the sugar in a colander and set aside for 10 minutes. Meanwhile, whisk together the remaining sugar, the sesame oil, soy sauce, vinegar, garlic, and chili oil if you're using it in a large bowl.

2. Rinse, drain, and pat the celery dry, then toss with the dressing and the celery leaves. Cover and let sit in the refrigerator for at least 3 hours or up to a day, stirring whenever you think of it. Serve chilled.

GINGER MARINATED CELERY Substitute 1 tablespoon minced or grated fresh ginger for the garlic. Instead of the sesame oil, use any good-quality vegetable oil, and substitute 1 tablespoon fresh lemon juice for the vinegar.

SCALLION MARINATED CUCUMBERS Substitute 2 large cucumbers for the celery and 3 trimmed scallions for the garlic. Peel the cucumbers, halve lengthwise, scoop out the seeds, and cut each half crosswise into thin slices. Salt as described in Step 1. Mince the scallions and add to the dressing in Step 2.

Celery Rémoulade

MAKES: 4 servings
TIME: 20 minutes
F M

Like Caesar salad, rémoulades are named for the dressing: a tangy, mustardy mayonnaise, one that has the potential to make anything it touches taste good. The classic French bistro preparation calls for celery root, but you can use thinly sliced celery or a few other hearty vegetables instead (see the variations).

½ cup Rémoulade Sauce (page 671), or
more to taste
1 large celery root (about 1½ pounds), or
1 pound celery stalks
Fresh lemon juice (optional)
Salt and pepper (optional)
2 tablespoons chopped fresh parsley
for garnish

1. Have the rémoulade sauce ready in a large bowl.

2. Peel and trim the celery root or trim and string the celery stalks (see page 192). Use a food processor to grate the celery root or slice it into matchsticks, or cut by hand. If you're using celery, cut the stalks and hearts crosswise into paper-thin slices; discard the leaves or save to add to soup.

3. Toss the celery root or celery slices and leaves with the rémoulade until coated. Taste and add lemon juice, salt, pepper, or more dressing as you like. Sprinkle with the parsley and serve.

POTATO RÉMOULADE A delicious potato salad: Boil 1½ pounds small waxy potatoes like red, white, or other colored new potatoes or fingerlings until tender. Be sure not to overcook them. When the potatoes are cool enough to handle, halve or quarter them. Toss with the rémoulade sauce while they're still warm. Proceed with Step 3. Enjoy warm, at room temperature, or chilled.

PARSNIP RÉMOULADE Sweeter than celery root but the same ivory color: Trim and peel 1½ pounds parsnips and use instead of celery root.

To Salt or Not to Salt?

The word "salad" comes from the ancient word for "salt," so the technique of salting ingredients to eat raw is rooted in early food preparation. When vegetables with a high water content come into contact with salt—exactly what happens when you dress them—they release their water. This both dilutes the dressing and prevents the greens from absorbing its flavors. If, however, you salt these vegetables before they go into salad, you can extract some of their water beforehand and make them firmer, crisper, and more flavorful. Their appearance also changes and looks almost translucent, partially cooked. These foods in particular benefit from salting:

CABBAGE
When slaws are made with salted cabbage, they are noticeably less watery, and stay crisp and fresh a few days longer. Put sliced cabbage in a colander, sprinkle with salt (about 1 tablespoon for 6 cups cabbage), and set aside to drain. After about an hour, rinse, drain, and gently squeeze dry, then proceed with the recipe.

CUCUMBERS
Supermarket varieties especially benefit from salting. First peel, seed (see page 49), and slice them. Then use the same procedure as for cabbage. For extra crispness, rinse, then wring dry in a towel after salting; otherwise, just pat them dry after rinsing.

RADISHES
Sliced radishes may be salted like cabbage and cucumbers (they become milder and crisper) but only for an absolute maximum of 45 minutes, or they will become limp.

ONIONS
As with radishes, you can make onions milder and crisper by salting them, either directly or in a salt-water bath (about 1 tablespoon salt per quart water). Let sit for a half hour or longer, then rinse and dry before using.

TOMATOES
Lightly salting tomatoes improves their flavor and tightens their flesh, but they are fragile. Use less salt (about 1 teaspoon per pound tomatoes) and leave them for only 15 minutes or so. Put salted chopped tomatoes in a colander (set over a bowl if you want to trap the tomato water for another use, like that on page 98). Salted tomato slices and wedges work best put directly on towels or spread out on wire racks.

LETTUCES AND GREENS
Don't salt—or dress—lettuce and greens until right before serving. They wilt fast and never recover.

KOHLRABI RÉMOULADE The texture is almost like a radish, only less watery: Trim and peel 1½ pounds kohlrabi and cut the leaves into thin ribbons; use instead of celery root.

CHAYOTE (MIRLITON) RÉMOULADE A nice way to use chayotes: Halve and pit 2 chayotes and use instead of the celery root.

Cucumber Salad with Soy and Ginger

MAKES: 4 servings
TIME: 30 minutes, mostly unattended
F V

Simple, versatile, and always delicious. Best, of course, with not-oversized cucumbers in season, but the small, thin "Persian" cucumbers (usually sold in packs of four or six, and grown in Canada) or long, wrapped "English" cucumbers are good substitutes in winter, as are Kirbys, often used for pickling.

1½	**pounds cucumbers**
	Salt
¼	**cup good-quality vegetable oil**
2	**tablespoons rice vinegar**
2	**tablespoons soy sauce, or to taste**
1	**tablespoon minced fresh ginger**
1	**teaspoon sugar**
	Pepper
2	**tablespoons chopped fresh cilantro** **for garnish**

1. If you're using skinny Persian or English cucumbers, just slice them and proceed to Step 2. If you're using conventional supermarket cucumbers, peel them. Cut in half lengthwise, then scoop out the seeds with a spoon. Cut them crosswise into thin slices, sprinkle with salt, put in a colander, and let drain over a bowl or in the sink for about an hour, until you can see moisture beading on the surface. Rinse, drain, and spin or pat dry. (If you want super-crunchy cucumbers, wring dry in a kitchen towel.)

2. Whisk together the oil, vinegar, soy sauce, ginger, and sugar in a large bowl. Add the cucumbers and toss until coated with dressing. Taste and adjust the seasoning. Garnish with the cilantro and serve right away. Or chill for up to 2 hours, then garnish with the cilantro and serve cold.

CUCUMBER SALAD, KOREAN STYLE More assertive: Replace 1 tablespoon of the vegetable oil with sesame oil. Add ½ teaspoon or more minced fresh chile (like serrano, jalapeño, or Thai) and 1 teaspoon minced garlic. Along with the cilantro, garnish with 2 tablespoons toasted sesame seeds (see page 299).

CUCUMBER SALAD WITH SOUR CREAM OR YOGURT For the dressing, in Step 2 whisk together ½ cup sour cream or yogurt, or a combination, 2 tablespoons fresh lemon juice, white wine vinegar, or white balsamic vinegar, ¼ cup chopped fresh dill or parsley, or more to taste, pinch cayenne (optional), and pepper to taste. If you like, you can amp the salad up by adding ½ cup each chopped seeded tomato and red or yellow bell pepper with the cucumbers.

Seeding Cucumbers

Thick cucumbers should almost always be seeded. It takes almost no time at all.

STEP 1 First cut the cucumber in half the long way.

STEP 2 Then scrape out the seeds with a spoon.

Raw Beet Salad

MAKES: 4 servings
TIME: 20 minutes
F M V

Raw beets are as crunchy as carrots, and so sweet that they need a strongly acidic dressing like this one for balance. Tarragon adds a pleasant hint of licorice.

  1½   pounds beets (preferably small)
  2   large shallots, minced
     Salt and pepper
  2   teaspoons Dijon mustard, or to taste
  1   tablespoon olive oil
  2   tablespoons sherry vinegar or red wine vinegar
  ¼   cup chopped fresh parsley (optional)
  1   tablespoon chopped fresh tarragon (optional)

1. Peel and quarter the beets. Grate the beets on the largest holes of a box grater. Put in a large bowl and add the shallots.
2. Sprinkle with salt and pepper and add the mustard, oil, vinegar, and the parsley and/or tarragon, if you're using them. Toss to combine. Taste and adjust the seasoning, toss again, and serve right away. Or cover and chill for up to several hours.

RAW BEET SALAD WITH CABBAGE AND ORANGE Quite nice-looking: Use equal weights beet and cabbage, about 12 ounces each, shredding both. Peel, seed (if necessary), and chop 1 or 2 oranges and add them, including their juice, in Step 2.

RAW BEET SALAD WITH CARROT AND GINGER Ginger and beets are killer together: Use equal weights beet and carrot, about 12 ounces each, shredding both. Substitute peanut oil for the olive oil and lime juice for the vinegar. Add about a tablespoon minced fresh ginger. Use cilantro instead of parsley and omit the tarragon.

RAW BEET SALAD WITH YOGURT DRESSING Creamy but no longer vegan: Replace the olive oil and 1 tablespoon of the vinegar with 2 tablespoons plain yogurt.

Five-Layer Avocado Salad

MAKES: 4 servings
TIME: 30 minutes
F

A festive and traditional salad; if you can find Mexican *crema*, substitute that for the mayonnaise and sour cream.

  ¼   cup mayonnaise (to make your own, see page 670)
  ¼   cup sour cream
  2   tablespoons olive oil
  3   limes
 1 or 2 minced fresh hot chiles (like jalapeño or serrano), or to taste
     Salt and pepper
  2   large fresh tomatoes, each cut crosswise into 4 thick slices
  ½   pound jícama, or daikon or other radishes, peeled if necessary, grated or minced (about ¾ cup)
 3 or 4 small oranges (preferably blood oranges), peeled, thinly sliced crosswise, and seeded if necessary
  1   small red onion, halved and sliced paper-thin
  4   avocados, pitted, peeled, and sliced
  ½   cup chopped fresh cilantro for garnish

1. Whisk together the mayonnaise, sour cream, and oil. Whisk in the juice of 2 of the limes and the chiles and sprinkle with salt and pepper. Taste and adjust the seasoning. Put the dressing in a small pitcher or serving bowl. Cut the remaining lime into wedges.
2. Put the tomatoes in a single layer on a large, deep platter or bowl. Sprinkle the jícama on top, then arrange the orange slices on top, then the onion. Finish with the avocado slices. Drizzle with about ¼ cup of the dressing, garnish with cilantro and lime wedges, and serve, passing the remaining dressing at the table.

SIX-LAYER AVOCADO SALAD WITH MANGOES More is better: Peel, pit, and cube 1 or 2 large mangoes. Add them to the salad on top of the onions and before the avocado.

SIX- OR SEVEN-LAYER AVOCADO SALAD A little more savory: Crumble 4 ounces queso fresco (about 1 cup). For six layers, add it after the avocado and before dressing. For seven, make the mango variation, and add it between the mango and the avocado.

Corn Salad with Tomatoes, Feta, and Mint

MAKES: 4 servings
TIME: 30 minutes

Ⓕ

Fresh raw corn kernels cut from the cob are ideal here, though you can use thawed frozen corn in a pinch. The juice from the tomatoes delivers just the right amount of acidity, so there's no need for vinegar. Eat this as is, or toss it with cooked rice or beans for a more filling salad; you may have to add oil and vinegar accordingly.

2–3 cups raw or cooked corn kernels (from 4 to 6 ears)
1 large or 2 medium fresh tomatoes, seeded and chopped
4 ounces feta cheese, crumbled (about 1 cup)
3 tablespoons olive oil
½ cup chopped fresh mint
Salt and pepper

Put the corn, tomatoes, and cheese in a bowl. Drizzle with the olive oil and toss. Add the mint leaves and toss again. Taste, season with salt and pepper, and serve right away.

PEA SALAD WITH TOMATOES, FETA, AND MINT If the peas are garden fresh, use them raw: Simply substitute peas for the corn.

Improvising Raw Vegetable Salads

All it takes to make your own raw vegetable salad is a willingness to appreciate the flavor of vegetables in their basic form and an understanding of how to put things together.

WHAT DOESN'T WORK RAW

There's a short list of vegetables that I avoid eating raw. Not that many will actually hurt you—there are recipes out there touting their virtues—but they're not particularly appealing. Eggplant, for starters (it's a texture thing), sweet potatoes (raw butternut squash is better), and potatoes (which actually may give you an upset stomach).

THE CUT MATTERS

Almost without exception, raw vegetables are more appealing in thin, small pieces, even foods you couldn't imagine you'd enjoy without cooking. Whether you grate them, cut into matchsticks or shoestrings, make long, noodlelike ribbons, or slice ultra-thin chips affects the way they react with salt, absorb dressings, and feel in your mouth. Cut controls the crispness, too, so remember: The more delicate the cut, the less crunch.

ADD FAT FOR CREAMINESS

I usually prefer that fat come in the form of lighter oils: Extra virgin olive oil, sesame oil, and walnut oil are all good choices. But there's nothing to stop you from using any kind of fresh cream (including unsweetened whipped cream), sour cream, mayonnaise, or yogurt to dress raw vegetables. If you're vegan, you can achieve creaminess with nondairy milks, silken tofu, puréed vegetables, and vegetable fats like coconut oil.

ADD ACIDITY FOR TANGINESS

Vinegar, fresh citrus and other fruit juices, wine, mustard, and even spirits all balance fat with bright, astringent flavors. Each will bring unique character to the salad. For more about vinegars and dressings see pages 632 and 628 to 631.

ASSEMBLE AND TOSS

I usually dress salads right in the bowl, either by whisking together a quick concoction before adding the vegetables. Or, if fat and acid are the only components, I'll pour them right on the salad before tossing. You can always make a dressing separately to drizzle on at the table.

SEA GREENS (SEAWEED) SALADS

Sea vegetables or sea greens—calling them "weeds" shows no respect, though everyone (including me) still does—come in a wide variety of shapes, sizes, and colors (see page 244). Even if you don't eat fish, you'll still appreciate their flavor—which is straight "ocean."

Sea greens work best when used in relatively small quantities to add complexity to a wide range of other ingredients—and served not just with the expected Asian dishes, but in European, American, and even Latin American cooking. The results are approachable, familiar salads with an unexpected twist.

While seaweed salad has become a popular staple in America's Japanese restaurants, many home cooks remain intimidated. Seaweed is an odd ingredient, after all, and if not treated right can be a bit slimy; people also imagine that sea greens are overpoweringly salty. Let the collection here convince you otherwise.

Though occasionally you will see sea greens fresh or frozen, in vacuum-sealed packages, they're most commonly sold dried. To rehydrate, just soak pieces in tap water until they expand—usually to several times their original size—lighten in color, and become pliable. This can take just a few minutes to up to an hour, depending on the type of sea green and how thick and well dried it is. When it's ready, rinse in cold water to remove excess sliminess, squeeze and pat dry if you'd like, and chop or slice as necessary. Generally, rehydrated dried seaweed is brown to olive green or sometimes almost black.

Simplest Seaweed Salad

MAKES: 4 servings
TIME: 20 minutes
F M V

Any sea green will work here, alone or in combination, though wakame is the mildest. (For more information on the different kinds and how to prepare them, see pages 244 to 246.) This will keep well in the fridge for days.

1 ounce wakame or other seaweed
¼ cup minced scallions or red onion
2 tablespoons soy sauce, or to taste
1 tablespoon rice vinegar, or to taste
1 tablespoon mirin or 1 teaspoon sugar, or to taste
1 tablespoon good-quality vegetable oil
2 teaspoons sesame oil, or to taste
Pinch cayenne, or to taste
Salt (optional)
1 tablespoon toasted sesame seeds (see page 299; optional)

1. Rinse the seaweed and soak it in at least 10 times its volume of water until tender, 5 to 10 minutes or more. Drain and gently gather and squeeze the pieces to remove excess water. Pick through the seaweed to sort out any hard bits (there may be none) and chop or cut up (you may find it easier to use scissors) if the pieces are large. Transfer to a bowl.

2. Add the scallions, soy sauce, vinegar, mirin, vegetable and sesame oils, cayenne, and salt to taste, if you're using it, and toss. Taste and adjust the salt or other seasonings. Garnish with the sesame seeds and serve.

10 Additions to Simplest Seaweed Salad

You can add these singly or in combination. I love radishes and cucumber combined here, for example.

1. ½ to 1 pound cucumber, peeled, seeded if necessary (see page 49), thinly sliced, and salted and squeezed to remove excess water

2. Several radishes or a 2-inch piece of peeled daikon or jícama, thinly sliced

3. ½ cup grated carrots or peeled parsnips

4. Grated fresh ginger, about a tablespoon, or more or less to taste

5. 1 or 2 tomatoes, seeded and chopped

6. ½ to 1 cup peeled and chopped Asian pear or Granny Smith apple

7. 1 cup halved green or red grapes

8. 1 to 2 cups cooked or drained canned black or white soybeans

Sea Slaw

9. ½ cup chopped nuts like peanuts, walnuts, almonds, cashews, or pecans
10. 1 to 2 tablespoons Kombu Dashi (page 100) for extra juiciness and flavor

Sea Slaw

MAKES: 4 servings
TIME: 20 minutes, plus time to rest
F M V

The most colorful slaw you've ever seen: The wakame quickly absorbs some of the dressing and plumps up a bit, but remains chewy. (You can use any type of sea green you like, but if you want a really vibrant green, the key is instant wakame.) Serve with any vegetable burger (pages 500 to 508), or as part of an Asian small-plate feast. Toss a cup or 2 with chilled cooked noodles and you've got yourself a crunchy pasta salad.

> ¼ **cup instant wakame or other dried seaweed**
> ¼ **cup Vegannaise (page 672) or mayonnaise**
> 2 **tablespoons rice vinegar**
> 1 **tablespoon soy sauce**
> 1 **teaspoon sugar**
> ½ **cup chopped peanuts**
> 2 **cups chopped cabbage (preferably Napa; about ½ pound)**
> 1 **cucumber, peeled, seeded (see page 49), and thinly sliced**
> 1 **red bell pepper, cored, seeded, quartered, and thinly sliced**
> ½ **cup lightly packed fresh cilantro leaves**
> **Salt and pepper**
> **Red chile flakes (optional)**

1. If using instant wakame, skip to Step 2. If not, rinse the seaweed and soak it in at least 10 times its volume of water until tender, 5 to 10 minutes or more. Drain and gently gather and squeeze the pieces to remove excess water. Pick through the seaweed to sort out any hard bits (there may be none) and chop or cut up (you may find it easier to use scissors) if the pieces are large.

2. Whisk together the vegannaise, vinegar, soy sauce, sugar, and peanuts in a large bowl. Add the wakame or prepared seaweed, the cabbage, cucumber, and bell pepper. Toss to coat in the dressing; refrigerate for anywhere from 15 to 60 minutes, depending on how crunchy you like it; the longer it sits, the less crunchy it becomes. Or cover and refrigerate for up to 24 hours; you may need to drain off excess liquid before proceeding. Add the cilantro, a sprinkle of salt and pepper, and chile flakes to taste, if you're using them. Taste and adjust the seasoning, toss one last time, and serve.

Seaweed Romaine Salad

MAKES: 4 servings
TIME: 30 minutes
F M

We tend to think of seaweed as a strictly Asian ingredient, but the people of the United Kingdom and Canada's Maritimes are also longtime seaweed eaters—and it grows all over the world. Americans are finally catching on. This Mediterranean-flavored salad demonstrates how well seaweed takes to the flavors of any cuisine.

> ½ **cup whole or halved dried tomatoes (about ½ ounce)**
> 4 **cups boiling water**
> 2 **tablespoons olive oil**
> 1 **tablespoon red wine vinegar**
> 2 **tablespoons toasted pine nuts (see page 299)**
> 1 **teaspoon minced garlic**
> ½ **cup chopped roasted red peppers (see page 228)**
> 1 **cup dried fine seaweed (like arame, instant wakame, or chopped dulse; about ½ ounce)**
> 4 **cups lightly packed torn romaine leaves**
> ½ **cup chopped fresh basil**
> ¼ **cup grated Romano, Parmesan, or ricotta salata cheese, plus more for the table**
> **Salt and pepper**

1. Put the tomatoes in a bowl and add the boiling water. Soak until the tomatoes are pliable but not mushy, 5 to 10 minutes. Remove with a slotted spoon and drain, reserving the soaking water. Chop the tomatoes and put them in a large bowl. Add the oil, vinegar, pine nuts, garlic, and roasted bell peppers and stir to combine.

2. If using instant wakame, skip to Step 3. If not, rinse the seaweed and add it to the reserved tomato soaking water. Let sit until tender, 5 to 10 minutes. Drain, rinse, and gently squeeze the pieces to remove excess water. Pick through the seaweed to sort out any hard bits (there may be none).

3. Add the seaweed to the bowl and stir to coat with the dressing. (You can make the salad up to this point, cover, and refrigerate it for up to 2 days.) To serve, add the romaine, basil, and ¼ cup cheese to the salad and toss. Taste and add salt if necessary and lots of pepper. Serve, passing the extra cheese at the table.

BALSAMIC SEAWEED ROMAINE SALAD For a slightly sweeter, deeper taste: Use 2 tablespoons balsamic vinegar instead of the red wine vinegar.

SEAWEED ROMAINE SALAD, PUTTANESCA STYLE Make either the main recipe or the balsamic variation. Add ½ cup chopped pitted black or green olives and 2 tablespoons each capers and minced red onion or shallot along with the tomatoes.

Arame and Bean Threads with Ponzu Dipping Sauce

MAKES: 4 servings
TIME: 30 minutes, plus about 2 hours to chill
Ⓜ Ⓥ

The fine, noodlelike texture of arame and its mild grassy flavor make this more accessible than the title might seem. (It's also dead easy to make.) The ponzu sauce has a bright citrus taste, but if you don't have the right ingredients handy, use about ¾ cup Soy Vinaigrette

(page 631) instead. Serve this salad cold with Grilled or Broiled Tofu (page 486) or as a light meal on a bed of mixed greens.

> 1   2-ounce bundle bean threads
> 1   ounce dried arame (about 2 loosely packed cups)
> 1   recipe Ponzu (page 657)
> 2   teaspoons sesame oil
> ½   cup sliced scallions
> ½   cup minced toasted walnuts (see page 299; optional)
>   Salt and pepper

1. Put the bean threads in a large bowl and cover with boiling water. Soak for about 10 minutes, until soft and clear. Use kitchen scissors or a sharp knife to cut the threads into 2- to 3-inch pieces. (This shouldn't take more than a few cuts.)

Dried Seaweed Sprinkles in Salads

A dash of dried seaweed provides a crunchy counterpoint in any salad. The texture is lighter than seeds or nuts, less cumbersome than croutons, and of course healthier than most other last-minute additions. Think of the flavor as a cross between a dried herb and a fresh one, with a subtle, slightly salty oceanic taste. When left to marinate in a tossed salad for a few minutes, the seaweed will expand and soften, but just a bit.

You can use arame, hijiki, or instant wakame straight from the package, since they are already in wispy threads; cut dulse and kombu into strips with kitchen scissors. (Try to use a knife and watch bits of seaweed fly all over the kitchen.) Or drop a handful into a spice grinder, coffee mill, or food processor. Pulse a few times until you get small pieces; be careful not to pulverize.

Another solution: Keep a jar of Nori "Shake" (page 650) on hand.

2. Add the arame to the water with the bean threads and stir gently to combine. Soak until the arame is crisp-tender, another 10 to 15 minutes. The bean threads will take on the color of the seaweed, only lighter. Drain well in a strainer for a few minutes, then transfer to a clean bowl. Toss with ¼ cup of the ponzu sauce and the sesame oil. Cover and refrigerate until very cold. (You can make the salad in advance to this point, cover, and refrigerate it for a day or 2.)

3. To serve, divide the remaining ponzu sauce among 4 small bowls so diners can dip each bite into the sauce. Toss the salad with the scallions and the walnuts, if you're using them, taste and add salt and pepper if necessary, and serve.

ARAME AND BEAN THREADS WITH FERMENTED BLACK BEANS Substitute Soy Vinaigrette (page 631) for the ponzu. In Step 2, add ¼ cup rinsed fermented black beans to the salad. Sprinkle with red chile flakes to taste. To serve, toss with more dressing if you like and add chopped fresh cilantro along with the scallions.

BEAN THREADS WITH ARAME Reverses the noodle-to-seaweed ratio: Increase the amount of bean threads to two 2-ounce bundles. Reduce the amount of arame to ½ ounce (about 1 loosely packed cup).

TOMATO SALADS

Just because we have access to tomatoes all year doesn't mean they're always good. Some people only eat fresh tomatoes in season, and stick to canned the rest of the year. If you can't hold out, try to find those with at least a bit of tomatoey aroma and some give in the texture when gently squeezed. Let any tomato ripen *at room temperature*, until they are soft and deeply colored. And *never* refrigerate them (this makes them mealy) unless you feel you must chill them down for a salad. If that's the case, no more than an hour, please.

Tomato Salad, Ethiopian Style

MAKES: 4 servings
TIME: 15 minutes, plus time to chill
F V

If you have time to chop tomatoes, you have time to make this salad, which also works as a relish for sandwiches and other salads. The light, fresh-tasting, oil-free dressing features turmeric, which turns the salad a lovely sunset color. Or substitute almost any spice or mix—curry or chili powder, cumin, five-spice, or jerk seasoning.

> 3 tablespoons fresh lemon juice
> ¼ cup chopped red onion
> 1 tablespoon minced jalapeño chile, or more or less to taste
> 1 teaspoon ground turmeric
>   Salt and pepper
> 4 large fresh tomatoes, seeded and chopped

1. Put the lemon juice, onion, jalapeño, and turmeric in a large bowl. Sprinkle with salt and pepper and stir to combine. Add the tomatoes and toss to coat.

2. Chill for up to 30 minutes if you like. Taste, adjust the seasoning, and serve.

Tomato Salad with Hard-Boiled Eggs

MAKES: 4 servings
TIME: 20 minutes
F

Sheer delight, especially if you use a mixture of several different colored tomatoes at the peak of summer. Hard-boiled eggs add a nice chew and heft—and you can always double the quantity to make the dish even more substantial—but I also like the variations, when the runny yolks mingle with the dressing and coat everything with a rich creaminess.

4 eggs
2 shallots, thinly sliced
4 cups lightly mixed greens or all bitter greens
(like dandelion or frisée)
¼ cup Mustard Vinaigrette (page 631), plus
more for drizzling
Salt and pepper
5 or 6 fresh tomatoes (preferably a colorful variety
of heirlooms), cut into wedges
2 cups croutons (to make your own, see page 678)

1. Hard-boil the eggs according to the directions on page 521. When the eggs have cooled to room temperature, peel and quarter them.

2. Put the shallots and greens in a large bowl and toss with the vinaigrette. Season with salt and pepper. Put the dressed greens on individual serving plates or a platter. Top with the tomato wedges, eggs, and croutons. Drizzle with a little extra dressing and serve.

TOMATO SALAD WITH POACHED EGGS Prepare and dress the salad first and put it on individual serving plates or shallow bowls, omitting the croutons. Poach the eggs according to the recipe on page 525. Remove the eggs with a slotted spoon and drain on paper towels. Top each serving of salad with an egg.

TOMATO SALAD WITH FRIED EGGS Prepare and dress the salad first and put it on individual serving plates or shallow bowls, omitting the croutons. Fry the eggs according to the recipe on page 524. Top each serving of salad with an egg.

Cherry Tomato Salad with Soy Sauce

MAKES: 4 servings
TIME: 15 to 30 minutes
F M V

Cherry and grape tomatoes are actually worth eating in winter, so this dish can help quench your cravings until the summertime slicers are back. If you have time, let this salad sit at room temperature for up to 15 minutes to release some of the juice from the tomatoes and create a deeply flavored mahogany-colored glaze.

2 tablespoons soy sauce, or more to taste
Pinch sugar
2 teaspoons sesame oil
4 cups cherry or grape tomatoes, halved
crosswise
¼ cup chopped fresh basil (preferably Thai)
Pepper

1. Combine the soy sauce, sugar, and oil in a large bowl. Add the tomatoes and basil and sprinkle liberally with pepper. Stir gently to coat the tomatoes with the dressing.

2. Let stand at room temperature for up to 15 minutes, stirring once or twice. Taste, add more soy sauce and pepper if you like, and serve.

BALSAMIC CHERRY TOMATO SALAD Use balsamic vinegar—white or dark, as you like—instead of the soy sauce. Substitute 1 tablespoon olive oil for the sesame oil. For the herb, try basil, parsley, or chives.

Watermelon and Tomato Salad

MAKES: 4 servings
TIME: 15 minutes
F

A quintessential summer dish; beautifully ripe tomatoes and sweet, juicy watermelon are musts for this salad. Use variously colored heirloom tomatoes for an outrageous presentation.

3 large fresh tomatoes, thickly sliced
¼ watermelon, seeded, peeled, and cut similarly
to the tomato slices
Salt and pepper
4 ounces fresh goat or feta cheese, crumbled
Extra virgin olive oil as needed

Watermelon and Tomato Salad (page 58)

Alternately stack the tomato and watermelon slices on a large plate or platter, sprinkling each layer with a tiny bit of salt and pepper. Crumble the goat cheese over the top and drizzle with olive oil. Serve immediately.

CANTALOUPE AND TOMATO SALAD WITH ROSEMARY
Replace the watermelon with 1 medium cantaloupe, honeydew, or cassava melon. Omit the cheese and sprinkle with a teaspoon or 2 of minced fresh rosemary leaves. Drizzle with olive oil and serve. **V**

PEACH AND TOMATO SALAD Substitute 3 large ripe peaches, pitted and thickly sliced, for the watermelon. Use blue cheese instead of goat cheese if you like or omit the cheese and sprinkle with chopped fresh basil leaves.

Tomato and Bread Salad

MAKES: 4 servings
TIME: 30 minutes
F **M** **V**

The toasted croutons absorb the tomatoes' juices but stay crunchy. Eat this alone, on a bed of greens, or alongside a generous slice of fresh mozzarella.

> 8 **ounces unsliced bread (any kind; stale is fine) or about 8 ounces Croutons (page 678)**
> ¼ **cup olive oil**
> 2 **tablespoons red wine vinegar or fresh lemon juice**
> 2 **fresh tomatoes, seeded and chopped**
> 1 **small red onion, halved and thinly sliced**
> 1 **teaspoon minced garlic**
> **Salt and pepper**
> ½ **cup chopped fresh basil or parsley**

1. If you're using the croutons, skip to Step 2. If using bread, heat the oven to 400°F. Cut the bread into large cubes and spread on a baking sheet. Bake, turning the cubes once or twice, until golden, 15 to 20 minutes. Set aside to cool. (You can make the croutons ahead to this point and keep them tightly covered at room temperature for up to 2 days.)

2. Put the oil, vinegar, tomatoes, onion, and garlic in a large bowl. Sprinkle with salt and lots of pepper and toss to coat. Add the croutons and basil and toss gently. Taste and adjust the seasoning and serve immediately.

GRILLED BREAD SALAD If you have the grill going: Instead of cutting the bread and oven-toasting it, prepare a charcoal or gas grill for medium-high heat and adjust the rack 4 inches from the heat. Grill the bread briefly on both sides, 3 to 5 minutes total, until browned. Let cool a bit, then cut into large cubes. Proceed with Step 2.

BREAD SALAD WITH GREENS The winter version: Instead of the tomatoes, use 2 cups cooked chopped greens like escarole, kale, or spinach. Add ½ cup currants or raisins and ¼ cup toasted pine nuts (see page 299). You may want to add more olive oil and lemon juice too.

CORN BREAD SALAD The Southwestern twist: Use Corn Bread (page 580) instead of plain bread croutons. In Step 2, add 1 teaspoon chili powder to the tomato mixture and substitute ½ cup sliced scallions for the red onion if you like. Use cilantro instead of basil or parsley.

COOKED VEGETABLE SALADS

Almost anything cooked can be dressed and eaten like salad. These dishes are among the most convenient: All may be made ahead and chilled, ready to pull from the fridge and dress whenever you feel like it. But you can also serve them still warm or at room temperature. (I generally opt for room temperature.)

These are also a great way to give leftovers a second life. Grilled, roasted, sautéed, and fried vegetables all qualify (see "Grilling Vegetables," pages 167 to 168). If they were cooked or served with a little oil the first time around, they might need only a squeeze of fresh citrus or a splash of vinegar and a handful of fresh herbs to become salad. But I encourage you to get in the habit of cooking a little extra and leaving them as plain as possible so you have even more options.

Pan-Roasted Corn Salad with Black Beans

MAKES: 4 servings
TIME: 20 minutes
F M V

Black beans are almost smoky, and roasted corn emphasizes that taste while adding an element of sweetness; acidity and heat keep all the flavors balanced. There's nothing left to do but enrich the salad with the creaminess of avocado—and cheese if you like (see the variations). Use it to fill burritos or tacos, serve as a dip to be scooped with chips, or spoon into a bowl to eat as is.

    2   tablespoons olive oil
        Kernels from 4 ears corn
        Salt and pepper
    1   tablespoon minced garlic
    1½ cups cooked or canned black beans, drained but
        still moist
    1   fresh tomato, seeded and chopped
    1   teaspoon minced jalapeño or other small chile,
        or more to taste
    2   tablespoons fresh lime juice
    1   avocado, pitted, peeled, and chopped
        for garnish
    ½   cup chopped fresh cilantro for garnish

1. Put the oil in a large skillet over high heat. When it's hot but not smoking, add the corn, along with a large pinch salt and some pepper. Cook, shaking the pan or stirring only occasionally, until the corn is lightly charred, 5 to 10 minutes. Add the garlic and cook, stirring, for 1 minute more, until it is fragrant.

2. Combine the corn with the beans, tomato, jalapeño, and lime juice in a large bowl. Taste and adjust the seasoning. Garnish with the avocado and cilantro, and serve. Or cover and refrigerate for up to a couple of hours. (Bring back to room temperature and garnish right before serving.)

PAN-ROASTED CORN AND CANNELLINI SALAD Substitute cannellini beans for the black beans, lemon for the lime juice, fennel for the avocado, and basil for the cilantro.

PAN-ROASTED CORN AND BEAN SALAD WITH CHEESE To the main recipe, add ½ cup crumbled queso fresco in Step 2; to the variation above, add ½ cup grated Parmesan. Toss again—or not—before serving.

Mushroom Salad, Italian-American Style

MAKES: 4 servings
TIME: About 1 hour
M V

A vinegary, almost-pickled mushroom dish that can also be used as a garnish or condiment as well as a topping for green salad. It's also good tossed with chopped Belgian endive (figure 2 heads for this amount of mushrooms) or other bitter greens.

    4   tablespoons olive oil
    1   pound button or other mushrooms, trimmed
        and quartered
        Salt and pepper
    ¼   cup minced onion
    1   tablespoon slivered garlic
    ¼   cup red wine vinegar
    ¼   cup chopped fresh parsley for garnish

1. Put 3 tablespoons of the oil in a large skillet over medium heat. When it's hot, add the mushrooms, sprinkle with salt and pepper, and cook, stirring occasionally, until they give up their liquid and begin to brown,

5 to 10 minutes. Lower the heat a bit and add the onion; cook until the onion softens, another 3 to 5 minutes. Add the garlic and cook, stirring occasionally until fragrant and soft, 1 to 2 minutes more. Turn off the heat.

2. Transfer the mushrooms to a bowl and stir in the vinegar and remaining tablespoon oil. Let cool to room temperature for at least 30 minutes. Garnish with the parsley and serve. Or let sit at room temperature for another hour or 2 before garnishing and serving.

Grilled or Broiled Portobello Salad with Soy Vinaigrette

MAKES: 4 servings
TIME: 40 minutes

Ⓥ

So meaty you won't believe it. Consider doubling the number of mushrooms and serving this as a main course, or use it to stuff sandwiches, burritos, tacos, or enchiladas.

4	large portobello mushrooms, stems discarded
¼	cup good-quality vegetable oil, or more as needed
	Salt and pepper
6	cups lightly packed mixed greens
½	cup Soy Vinaigrette (page 631)

1. Heat a charcoal or gas grill or turn on the broiler for medium heat; adjust the rack to 4 to 6 inches from the heat source. Rub or brush the mushrooms with enough oil to lightly coat them, then sprinkle liberally with salt and pepper. Grill or broil until they shrink and are lightly browned and slightly crisp, anywhere from 2 to 5 minutes per side, depending on your equipment. Brush or drizzle them with more oil if they start to look too dry. Transfer to a cutting board and cut into thick ribbons.

2. Put the greens in a large bowl and toss with ¼ cup of the dressing. Spread the mushroom slices on top and drizzle with their accumulated juices. Drizzle with a little more of the dressing and serve.

GRILLED OR BROILED SHIITAKE SALAD WITH SOY VINAIGRETTE A little more work but always impressive: Instead of the portobellos, remove the stems from 1 pound shiitake mushrooms. Thread the mushroom caps on metal skewers or wooden ones that have been soaked in water for at least 20 minutes. Proceed with the recipe from the beginning of Step 1.

GRILLED OR BROILED PORTOBELLO OR SHIITAKE SALAD WITH BALSAMIC SYRUP Especially good if you use arugula for the greens: Follow the main recipe or variation above, substituting olive oil for the vegetable oil and Balsamic Syrup (page 633) for the dressing.

Cauliflower Salad with Olives and Bread Crumbs

MAKES: 4 servings
TIME: 45 minutes

Ⓜ Ⓥ

Bread crumbs give this crunchy one-skillet dish, which has roots in southern Italy, plenty of body. This is delicious with panfried eggplant (page 161) or grilled zucchini (see page 167). The steam-searing technique is handy for all sorts of vegetables.

4	tablespoons olive oil, plus more as needed
1	tablespoon chopped garlic
1½	cups bread crumbs (preferably fresh, see page 678)
	Salt and pepper
½	cup chopped fresh parsley
1	large cauliflower (1½–2 pounds), cut into bite-sized florets
1	small red onion, halved and thinly sliced
½	cup chopped pitted black olives
2	tablespoons red wine vinegar

1. Put 2 tablespoons of the oil in a large skillet over medium heat. When it's hot, add the garlic and cook, stirring frequently, until it becomes fragrant, about 1 minute. Add the bread crumbs and cook, stirring occasionally, until they're toasted, 3 to 5 minutes. Sprinkle with salt and pepper, stir in the parsley, and transfer the mixture to a small bowl.

2. Wipe out the skillet, return it to medium-high heat, and add the remaining oil. When it's hot, add the cauliflower, sprinkle with salt, add 1 cup water, and quickly cover the pan. Cook, shaking occasionally, until you can barely pierce a floret with a sharp knife, 5 to 10 minutes. Remove the cover, scatter the onion over all, and cook, undisturbed, until the water evaporates and the cauliflower starts to brown, 5 to 10 minutes. Stir once or twice and transfer the vegetables to a large bowl. Let sit for a few minutes to cool.

3. Add the olives, vinegar, and about ½ cup of the crumbs. Toss, taste, and adjust the seasoning, adding more olive oil if you'd like. Toss again and serve, passing the remaining crumbs at the table.

LEMONY CAULIFLOWER SALAD WITH PARMESAN BREAD CRUMBS Omit the olives and vinegar. Zest and juice 1 lemon. In Step 1, add ½ cup grated Parmesan cheese and the lemon zest to the bread crumbs along with the parsley. In Step 3, add the lemon juice to the cauliflower before tossing.

Eggplant Salad with Miso

MAKES: 4 servings
TIME: About 30 minutes
F M V

The typical way to prepare this traditional Japanese salad is to boil the eggplant, and I give directions for doing it that way. But if you have the time and energy, sauté the cubes in a little good-quality vegetable oil, as in Ratatouille Salad (page 66). And grilled eggplant slices (see page 166) are especially delicious. All of these cooking methods work well with the dressing in the main recipe and the variations.

1 eggplant (about 1 pound)
  Salt
⅓ cup white or other miso, or to taste

2 tablespoons good-quality vegetable oil
1 tablespoon soy sauce
1 tablespoon mirin or brown sugar
1 tablespoon rice vinegar or fresh lemon juice
  Cayenne
¼ cup chopped walnuts

1. Bring a large pot of water to a boil and salt it. Trim the eggplant (no need to peel) and cut it into 1-inch cubes. Boil the eggplant until tender but not falling apart, 3 to 5 minutes. Drain well and leave it in the colander to cool. (You can refrigerate the eggplant, covered, for up to 24 hours at this point. Bring it back to room temperature before proceeding.)

2. Pat the eggplant dry with paper towels. Whisk together the miso, oil, soy sauce, mirin, and vinegar in a large bowl. Thin with a tablespoon water if necessary.

3. Add the eggplant to the dressing, sprinkle with just a little salt and a pinch cayenne, then toss. Taste and adjust the seasoning. Top with the walnuts and serve.

EGGPLANT SALAD WITH MISO AND TOFU All you need for dinner: In Step 3, add 1 pound cubed Baked Tofu (page 485) or Tofu Croutons (page 497). Increase the dressing ingredients to ½ cup miso, ¼ cup oil, and 2 tablespoons each soy sauce, mirin, and vinegar.

EGGPLANT SALAD WITH SOY VINAIGRETTE What to do if you don't have miso: Omit the miso, oil, soy sauce, mirin, vinegar, and cayenne. Make either the main recipe or the tofu variation, but instead of the miso dressing, use ½ cup Soy Vinaigrette (page 631). Garnish with 1 tablespoon sesame seeds instead of the walnuts, if you like.

Ratatouille Salad

MAKES: 4 servings
TIME: 30 minutes
F M V

Eggplant, zucchini, onions, and tomatoes are a familiar Mediterranean combination, especially in summer. Too often, however, they're overcooked and mushy. Enter the ratatouille salad, where the vegetables remain distinct even though the ingredients are cooked, and a hint of lemon juice keeps everything tasting fresh. Eat this alone or on a bed of greens. For a heartier salad, toss in cooked rice, white beans, or the pasta of your choice and drizzle with a little more olive oil. A sprinkle of grated Parmesan or ricotta salata is a welcome addition too.

  1 **medium or 2 small eggplants (about 8 ounces total)**
  4 **tablespoons olive oil, or more as needed**
    Salt and pepper
  1 **large zucchini, halved lengthwise and then cut crosswise into thick slices**
  1 **small onion, chopped**
  1 **tablespoon minced garlic**
  2 **tomatoes, seeded and chopped**
  1 **tablespoon chopped fresh thyme**
  1 **tablespoon fresh lemon juice**
  ¼ **cup chopped fresh parsley for garnish**

1. Trim the eggplant (no need to peel) and cut it into 1-inch cubes.

2. Put 2 tablespoons of the oil in a large skillet over medium heat. When it's hot, add the eggplant, sprinkle with salt and pepper, and cook, stirring occasionally until soft and golden, 5 to 10 minutes; add more oil to keep the pieces from sticking if necessary. Remove from the pan and drain on paper towels.

3. Put the remaining oil in the pan and add the zucchini. Cook, stirring occasionally, until just starting to wilt, 2 or 3 minutes. Add the onion and garlic and cook and stir until the onion softens, another 2 to 5 minutes. Add the tomatoes and thyme and adjust the heat so the mixture sizzles. Cook, stirring occasionally, until the tomatoes start to wilt and release their juice, another minute or 2. Remove from the heat, stir in the lemon juice, and sprinkle with salt and pepper.

4. Put the eggplant in a large bowl and add the vegetables and dressing from the pan. Stir to combine. Cool to room temperature, taste and adjust the seasoning, adding

more olive oil if you'd like. Or cover and refrigerate for up to 2 days. When you're ready to eat, add the parsley, toss again, and serve cold or at room temperature.

EGGPLANT AND ZUCCHINI SALAD WITH CINNAMON Just slightly exotic with the warm spices: Instead of garlic, use 1 tablespoon minced fresh chile (like jalapeño, Thai, or habanero), or to taste. Instead of thyme, use 1 teaspoon ground cinnamon. Garnish with chopped fresh mint instead of parsley.

Grilled Eggplant Salad with Garlic and Saffron Mayonnaise

MAKES: 4 servings
TIME: 45 minutes, plus time to chill
Ⓜ

Many grilled vegetables are terrific in salads, but eggplant may be the king of them all: meaty, flavorful, and somehow intrinsically smoky. (You can understand why Middle Eastern and Asian cuisines rely so heavily on it.) Here the eggplant is cooked whole—charred, to tell the truth—before dressing. But you can also use grilled skin-on slices of eggplant (see page 166) for a more intense smoky flavor and crisp texture.

  1½ **pounds eggplants (preferably small)**
   1 **tablespoon minced garlic**
   2 **tablespoons olive oil**
     Salt and pepper
   ½ **cup mayonnaise (to make your own, see page 670) or Greek yogurt**
     Large pinch saffron threads
   2 **lemons, cut into wedges for serving**
   ¼ **cup chopped fresh parsley for garnish (optional)**

1. Heat a charcoal or gas grill or turn on the broiler for medium-high heat; adjust the rack to about 4 inches from the heat source. Cut the eggplants in half lengthwise up to the stem so they're split but still intact. Spread the garlic between the eggplant halves and press the halves back together.

2. Grill or broil the eggplants, turning once or twice, until they are blackened outside and soft inside, 10 to 15 minutes. Let the eggplants cool enough to handle, still closed, then cut off the stems, peel off the skins, and let cool further. Chop into large pieces, reserving any juices, and put everything in a bowl. Drizzle with the olive oil, sprinkle with salt and pepper, and toss to coat.

3. Put the mayonnaise in a small bowl and crumble in the saffron; whisk until the threads dissolve. (You can prepare the salad ahead to this point, cover the bowls, and refrigerate for up to a day. Serve cold or return the eggplant to room temperature.) When you're ready to serve, mound the eggplant on salad plates or a small platter, with the lemon wedges and a spoonful of the saffron mayonnaise on the side. Garnish with the parsley, if you like.

VEGAN GRILLED EGGPLANT SALAD Instead of the mayonnaise use soft silken tofu. Before adding the saffron, whisk the tofu until it's smooth and creamy. And when you add the saffron, include a pinch salt. V

Roasted Broccoli Salad with Tahini Dressing

MAKES: 4 servings
TIME: 30 to 35 minutes
M V

For salads, I often put a different spin on my usual vegetable-roasting technique to ensure a crisp-tender texture and vibrant color. I use a rimmed baking sheet, go a little easy on the oil (so the dressing won't make everything soggy), and crank up the heat. A tangy, nutty dressing makes this salad rich and satisfying enough for a light lunch. Add a handful of beans or serve it over the bean burgers on page 502 and you have dinner.

1½ pounds broccoli, trimmed and cut into large florets
4 tablespoons olive oil
   Salt and pepper
1 small red onion, halved and thinly sliced
⅓ cup tahini (to make your own, see page 305)
¼ cup fresh lemon juice, or more to taste
1 teaspoon minced garlic
1 teaspoon ground cumin

1. Heat the oven to 425°F. Put the broccoli on a large rimmed baking sheet, drizzle with 2 tablespoons of the oil, sprinkle with salt and pepper, and toss with your hands to coat, then spread out the florets in a single layer. Roast, undisturbed, until the color starts to brighten, 5 to 10 minutes.

2. Scatter the onion on top, stir and turn with a spatula to combine the vegetables, and return to the oven. Roast, stirring once or twice more, until the onion has darkened a bit and you can just pierce a piece of broccoli with a thin-bladed knife, 5 to 10 minutes more, depending on how big the florets are. (You can prepare the salad to this point up to several hours in advance and refrigerate. Either return it to room temperature or serve chilled.)

3. Put the remaining oil in a small bowl with the tahini, lemon juice, garlic, cumin, and some salt and pepper. Whisk, adding water 1 tablespoon at a time, until the dressing becomes smooth and coats the back of a spoon. Taste and adjust the seasoning; add more lemon juice if you'd like. (You can make the dressing up to a day in advance, cover tightly, and refrigerate until serving.)

4. Transfer the broccoli to a platter or individual plates, drizzle with the dressing, and serve warm, at room temperature, or chilled.

ROASTED BRUSSELS SPROUTS WITH PEANUT DRESSING
Trim and halve 2 pounds Brussels sprouts instead of the broccoli and use 6 scallions, chopped, instead of the onion. Substitute peanut butter for the tahini and lime juice for lemon juice.

Potato Salad

MAKES: 4 servings
TIME: 30 minutes, plus time to cool

M V

My favorite potato salad is dressed in a mustard vinaigrette. Whatever your preference, the key to the best potato salad is to toss it while the potatoes are still warm, so they absorb some of the dressing. Then, ideally, serve at room temperature.

1½   pounds potatoes (like red, fingerling, Yukon Gold, or even baking potatoes)
      Salt
5   tablespoons olive oil, or more to taste
2   tablespoons sherry, cider, or any wine vinegar, or more to taste
1   tablespoon Dijon or whole-grain mustard, or more to taste
½   cup minced fresh parsley
¼   cup any minced onion (red, white, or yellow, or scallions)
      Pepper

1. Peel the potatoes if you like or wash and scrub well. Cut into bite-sized pieces. Put in a pot with enough water to cover them and add a large pinch salt. Bring to a boil, then lower the heat so the water bubbles gently. Cook the potatoes until tender but still firm and not mushy, 15 minutes or so, depending on the potato. Drain well and let cool just until they're no longer steaming.

2. Whisk together the oil, vinegar, and mustard in a large bowl until combined. Add the parsley and onion and sprinkle with salt and pepper.

3. Fold the still-warm potatoes into the dressing with a rubber spatula or a large fork. Taste and adjust the seasoning; add more dressing ingredients if you like. Serve as is. Or refrigerate for an hour or so to cool the salad down. (You can prepare the salad in advance up to this point; cover and refrigerate for up to a day. Serve cold or at room temperature.)

10 Simple Additions to Potato Salad

Add any of these alone or in combination to taste:

1. Chopped fresh herbs like chives, chervil, dill, oregano, rosemary, or sage

2. Chopped sweet or dill pickles

3. Chopped celery or fennel bulb

4. Chopped red bell pepper, fresh or roasted (see page 228)

5. Capers or pitted and chopped pitted olives

6. Chopped shallot, raw or lightly cooked in olive oil, instead of the onion

7. Cooked fresh peas

8. Minced garlic, about 1 teaspoon

9. Cayenne or minced fresh chile (jalapeño, Thai, serrano, or habanero)

10. Fragrant or Hot Curry Powder (page 649; start with 1 teaspoon)

Which Potato for Salads?

Potatoes are grouped into three types; there's more about them all on page 231. The characteristics of each are especially important in salads. Conventional wisdom dictates a low-starch waxy potato for salad. Many unusual varieties fall into this category, including fingerlings and purple potatoes, which make for stunning salads.

But—at least once—try using starchy (baking) potatoes. They're mealier than waxy potatoes, so the chunks break apart easily after cooking to help bind the dressing with the potatoes. They're not everyone's cup of tea, but if you like thick mashed potatoes, you'll probably go for salads made from these. One tip: To prevent starchy potatoes from waterlogging the salad, drain them well, shaking the colander once in a while. You still want them to be slightly warm for dressing, though.

The other choice is to use an all-purpose potato like Yukon Gold, which will give you a firm potato whose exterior deteriorates just a little. Sweet potatoes (which aren't really in the same family) also make gorgeous potato salads, though they don't require as much cooking and break apart more easily than regular potatoes, especially when overdone.

Roasted Sweet Potato Salad with Red Pepper Vinaigrette

MAKES: 4 servings
TIME: About 45 minutes
Ⓜ Ⓥ

Here's another potato-vinaigrette combo, this time with sweet potatoes. (If it's a more classic recipe you're after, turn to the Potato Rémoulade variation on page 48.) Unlike some potato salads, this one is best served warm or at room temperature, though of course you can refrigerate and serve it up to a day later, as long as you take it out of the refrigerator beforehand to take the chill off.

4	**large sweet potatoes**
8	**tablespoons olive oil**
	Salt and pepper
¼	**cup red wine vinegar or sherry vinegar**
1	**red bell pepper, cored, seeded, and quartered**
2	**teaspoons ground cumin**
1	**tablespoon grated orange zest**
½	**cup sliced scallions**
½	**cup minced fresh mint or parsley**
1 or 2	**fresh minced chiles (like jalapeño, serrano, or habanero), or to taste**

1. Heat the oven to 400°F. Peel the sweet potatoes and cut them into bite-sized pieces. Put them on a baking sheet, drizzle with 2 tablespoons of the oil, and toss to coat. Sprinkle with salt and pepper. Roast, turning occasionally, until crisp and brown outside and just tender inside, about 30 minutes. Remove and keep on the pan until you're ready to dress the salad.

2. Make the dressing while the potatoes roast: Put the remaining 6 tablespoons oil in a blender, along with the vinegar, bell pepper, cumin, and orange zest. Sprinkle with a little salt and pepper. Purée until smooth.

3. Toss the warm potatoes in a large bowl with the scallions, mint, and chiles. Add ½ cup of the dressing and toss to coat, adding more if necessary. Taste and adjust the seasoning. Serve right away or chill for up to several hours.

GRILLED SWEET POTATO SALAD WITH RED PEPPER VINAIGRETTE Instead of roasting the sweet potatoes, grill them according to the directions on page 167.

CRISP SHREDDED HASH BROWN SALAD WITH RED PEPPER VINAIGRETTE Prepare Oven-Roasted Hash Browns (page 238) instead of the sweet potatoes; be careful not to overseason with salt and pepper. While the potatoes are still warm, proceed with Step 2.

BEAN SALADS

This whole family of salads is essential to vegetarian and vegan eating: They're substantial enough to eat as a one-dish meal, especially when they contain greens or vegetables. The variety of flavors, shapes, sizes, and textures keeps you from getting bored. And most can be made hours—if not days—ahead for ultimate convenience.

You can also use a spoonful or 2 as a relish to serve with grilled or roasted vegetables or rice bowls, or even for topping soup. Mash slightly or pulse in the food processor and you have an instant, high-flavored sandwich spread. Or toss ½ cup or so with leftover pasta or grains, and you create a portable meal to eat on your lunch hour or, better still, on a picnic blanket.

Two suggestions specific to salads: Undercooking the beans is key—just slightly, so they are barely tender inside and their skins remain intact. And dress them while still warm, so they absorb the flavors around them.

Bean Salad, Many Ways

MAKES: 4 to 8 servings
TIME: 10 minutes with cooked or canned beans; 1½ to 3 hours from scratch (depending on the bean), mostly unattended
Ⓕ Ⓜ Ⓥ

This is a master recipe, something you can rely on forever. Though you can certainly use canned beans here, if you try this recipe once from scratch, you will be hooked. The number of servings you'll get depends on whether you eat it as a main dish or a side. You can certainly tuck the whole thing into the fridge to eat over the course of several days. To maximize your options, you can also cook a whole batch of beans, freeze half for another use, and cut the rest of the recipe down by half. (For details about selecting, cooking, and storing dried beans, see pages 427 to 428.)

2 cups dried beans, split peas, or lentils, or 4 to 5 cups cooked or canned, drained but still moist
1 tablespoon red wine vinegar, other good vinegar, or fresh lemon juice, or more to taste
¼ cup minced red onion or shallot
Salt and pepper
¼ cup olive oil, or more to taste
¼ chopped fresh parsley

1. If you're cooking beans to make this recipe, follow the directions on page 435, cooking until they're just tender but before their skins split and they become mushy. The exact time will vary depending on the bean variety and the beans' age.
2. While the beans are cooking, or if you're using already cooked or canned beans, stir together the vinegar and onion in a large bowl. Sprinkle with salt and pepper. Stir in the olive oil.
3. Drain the beans, rinse them, and drain again if they are canned. Add to the dressing, preferably while they are still hot if you cooked them yourself. Toss gently until the beans are coated with dressing, adding more vinegar or oil if you like. Let cool to room temperature and/or refrigerate, stirring once or twice to distribute the dressing. Stir in the parsley, taste and adjust the seasoning, and serve.

BEAN SALAD, ITALIAN STYLE A little stronger: Use cannellini or cranberry beans. If you'd like a slightly milder taste, use white wine vinegar. Add 1 tablespoon minced garlic and 1 teaspoon minced fresh rosemary along with the onion, or if you have fresh basil and you'll be serving the salad right away, use ¼ cup or so instead of rosemary.

BEAN SALAD, INDIAN STYLE If you're cooking from dried beans, be sure to allow a little more time: Use chickpeas. Use rice vinegar, and replace the onion with 2 tablespoons minced or grated fresh ginger (or to taste). Instead of olive oil, use 2 tablespoons good-quality vegetable oil and 2 tablespoons coconut milk. Replace the parsley with cilantro.

BEAN SALAD, FRENCH STYLE Use flageolet beans. Use sherry vinegar. Use thinly sliced shallot. Instead of the parsley, stir in 2 tablespoons minced fresh tarragon right before serving.

BEAN SALAD, GREEK STYLE Possibly my favorite: Use dried fava or gigante beans. Use lemon juice. Add 1 tablespoon minced garlic to the vinegar along with the onion. Instead of parsley, use fresh mint.

BEAN SALAD, JAPANESE STYLE A teaspoon of soy sauce at the end is nice here too: Use edamame or adzuki beans. Use rice vinegar and substitute good-quality vegetable oil for the olive oil. Instead of parsley, use 2 sheets nori, toasted and crumbled (see page 244).

BEAN SALAD, CHINESE STYLE The ginger changes everything: Use dried soybeans (black or white) or mung beans. Use Chinese black vinegar or rice vinegar. Instead of onion, use 1 tablespoon each minced fresh ginger and garlic. Replace olive oil with 2 tablespoons sesame oil and 2 tablespoons good-quality vegetable oil. Use soy sauce instead of salt for final seasoning and toss with ¼ cup chopped scallions instead of the parsley.

6 Simple Last-Minute Additions to Bean Salads

Depending on the ingredient, you may need more oil and vinegar or other acidic component. Here's a simple formula: For every tablespoon oil, add a teaspoon of acidity. You will also probably want to add a bit more salt or soy sauce, pepper, and fresh herbs as well.
1. Salad greens: Toss the finished salad with 4 cups bite-sized pieces romaine, arugula, mesclun, frisée, mizuna, or tatsoi.

2. Chopped tomatoes: Spread the dressed beans out on a platter, top with the finishing herb, seaweed, or scallions (according to the recipe or variation), then top with 1 cup chopped fresh tomato. Drizzle with a little more oil and serve.

3. Chopped nuts or seeds: Stir in ½ cup. Some specific ideas: Hazelnuts with white beans in the Italian Style; almonds in the French Style; walnuts in the Greek Style; sesame seeds in the Japanese Style; and peanuts in the Chinese Style.

4. Bean sprouts: Add 1 cup mung or soy bean sprouts to either the Japanese Style or Chinese Style variation.

5. Cooked greens: For a more substantial dish, toss the finished salad with any kind of cooked hearty green like kale, cabbage, escarole, or spinach.

6. Cheese: Toss cubes of paneer or Fresh Cheese (page 568) with the Indian variation; grate or shave Parmesan cheese on the Italian Style variation; crumble blue cheese or goat cheese on the French Style; or crumble feta on the Greek Style.

Lemony Lentil Salad

MAKES: 4 servings
TIME: About 45 minutes
M V

Small dark-green, almost-black lentils—Puy or one of the similar varieties—are my first choice for this bistro-style salad. But use whatever lentils you have handy; the more common brown lentils work well here, as do split peas, for that matter. There's no reason to use canned, since lentils cook relatively fast and will continue to cook as they cool; you will technically be undercooking them. Follow the cues below and you should be fine. If you decide to make this salad ahead, bring it back to room temperature before serving for maximum flavor.

    1   cup dried lentils (preferably Puy or
        other green lentils), sorted and rinsed
    1   bay leaf
    2   cloves garlic, peeled
    2   lemons
    2   tablespoons olive oil
    1   tablespoon capers
    ¼   cup minced fresh chives, shallot,
        or red onion
        Salt and pepper

1. Put the lentils in a pot and cover with water by 1 inch. Add the bay leaf and garlic and bring to a boil. Cover and lower the heat so the lentils bubble gently. Cook until barely tender and not yet burst, 15 to 30 minutes, checking occasionally to make sure there is always enough water in the pot to keep the lentils from burning. (They will continue to cook as they cool.)

2. Squeeze the juice from one of the lemons into a large bowl. Peel the other lemon, remove the outer membrane, and chop the segments into small pieces, taking care to remove any seeds. Add the segments to the juice along with the olive oil, capers, and chives. Sprinkle with a little salt and pepper and stir.

3. Drain the lentils and stir them into the dressing while still hot. Let rest, stirring occasionally to distribute the dressing, to cool for a few minutes. Taste and adjust the seasoning and serve warm. Or cover and refrigerate for up to several days.

Warm Chickpea Salad with Arugula

MAKES: 4 servings
TIME: 20 minutes
F

Chickpeas frequently get the salad treatment throughout the Mediterranean and Middle East. My version is an amalgam of a few recipes I've had and includes ginger, garlic, and cumin. After the seasonings are cooked and the beans warmed, the dressing is finished in the pan, then tossed with arugula leaves to soften them slightly. You can make this a side salad or first course by skipping the egg and serving smaller portions (or halving the recipe). As is, consider it a light meal.

Warm Chickpea Salad with
Arugula (page 73)

3 tablespoons olive oil
1 tablespoon minced fresh ginger
1 tablespoon minced garlic
½ teaspoon cumin seeds
   Salt and pepper
1½ cups cooked or canned chickpeas,
   drained but still moist
1 tablespoon rice vinegar
1 teaspoon honey
4 cups lightly packed arugula leaves
1 small red onion, halved and thinly sliced
4 hard-boiled eggs (see page 521), quartered
   (optional)

1. Put the oil in a deep skillet over medium heat. When it's hot, add the ginger, garlic, and cumin and cook, stirring constantly, until the ginger and garlic are soft and fragrant, 1 to 2 minutes. Sprinkle with salt and pepper, then stir in the chickpeas until hot and coated with the oil and seasonings, 1 to 3 minutes.

2. Remove from heat and stir in the vinegar, honey, and 1 tablespoon water with a fork. Mash a few of the chickpeas as you stir to add texture to the dressing. Put the arugula and onion in a large bowl and toss with the warm chickpeas and dressing. Taste and adjust the seasoning. Garnished with hard-boiled eggs, if you like, and serve right away.

WARM CHICKPEA SALAD WITH ARUGULA AND SOMETHING VEGAN Terrific alternatives: Simply replace the eggs with Tofu Croutons (page 497), Crunchy Crumbled Tempeh (page 512), or even uncooked tofu cubes. Omit the honey. **V**

Edamame Salad with Seaweed "Mayo"

MAKES: 4 servings
TIME: 30 minutes
F M V

Whether you use fresh or frozen here, edamame (young soybeans; see page 433) need to cook for only a couple of minutes. The result is a crisp, fresh-tasting bean with a texture somewhere between limas and favas, perfect for salads. Here I dress them simply, in a briny and richly colored vegan "mayonnaise" based on seaweed. You can also use regular mayonnaise (to make your own, see page 670) or Vegannaise (page 672). For a cold rice bowl meal, serve this with Citrus Rice Salad (page 77) or with plain Sushi Rice (page 384). It's also perfect with crackers or on a bed of greens.

   Salt
4 cups shelled edamame, fresh or frozen
1 red or yellow bell pepper, cored, seeded,
   and chopped
½ cup chopped scallions
½ cup Seaweed "Mayo" (page 673)
   Salt and pepper
1 tablespoon white or black sesame seeds
   for garnish

1. Put a few inches of water in a saucepan, salt it, and bring to a boil. Cook the edamame, stirring occasionally, until heated through and bright green, 2 or 3 minutes. Drain and run under cold water until cool. Drain thoroughly.

2. Toss the edamame in a large bowl with the bell pepper, scallions, and mayo. Season with salt and pepper and garnish with the sesame seeds if serving immediately. Or cover and refrigerate for up to 3 days and garnish just before serving.

GRAIN SALADS

Grain salads are not only delicious and filling; they also provide fiber and protein. You can eat them alone, serve them on a pile of greens, or spike them with beans, tofu, cheese, or eggs to make satisfying and complete meals.

   Various cooking techniques for grains are described on pages 397 to 398, but for salads, I rely mostly on "Cooking Grains, the Easy Way" (page 398). One change is that I often rinse them after cooking to remove some of the starch and keep the grains separate. And as with beans, it's optimal to cook the grains when you want to prepare a salad so you can dress them warm and allow them to absorb flavor as they cool. Likewise it's better to under- than overcook to avoid mushiness.

But you and I both know that if these were all hard-and-fast rules, you wouldn't be eating grain salads very often. The real-life approach is to plan for leftovers whenever you cook a pot of grains by doubling the recipe if necessary. That will ensure that you always have the ingredients for last-minute options at your fingertips.

Tabbouleh

MAKES: 4 servings
TIME: 40 minutes
V

Though bulgur is part of what makes tabbouleh tabbouleh, the real focus is on the herbs: You must include fresh herbs, and lots of them, combined with the ripest tomatoes, to make the best version. It's a wonderful accompaniment to grilled food.

½	cup medium-grind bulgur
⅓	cup olive oil, or more as needed
¼	cup fresh lemon juice, or to taste
	Salt and pepper
2	cups chopped fresh parsley (leaves and thin stems only)
1	cup chopped fresh mint
½	cup chopped scallions
4	tomatoes, seeded and chopped

1. Soak the bulgur in hot water to cover until tender, 15 to 30 minutes. Drain well, squeezing out as much water as possible. Toss the bulgur with the oil and lemon juice and season with pepper.

2. Just before you're ready to serve, add the parsley, mint, scallions, and tomatoes and toss gently. Taste and adjust the seasoning. Serve at room temperature or chill for up to an hour or 2.

TABBOULEH MADE WITH OTHER GRAINS Instead of the soaked bulgur in Step 1, use 1½ cups cooked grains; quinoa, freekeh, farro, and millet all work well. You can use rice, too, but make sure it's at room temperature or even a little warm when you serve it so the kernels aren't too gritty.

BEAN TABBOULEH Skip the grains altogether: Substitute 2 cups any cooked beans (chickpeas are especially good), roughly mashed, for the bulgur.

Rice Salad

MAKES: 4 servings
TIME: About 30 minutes
F M V

There's no reason to eat the same rice salad twice. This master recipe offers enough variations to give you the hang of the way ingredients come together in different cuisines, making rice salad an easy way to experiment with traditional or cross-cultural combinations.

The master recipe here will work for virtually any type of rice. Though I make suggestions for the specific variations, ultimately you should use whatever you like and whatever you have handy. Feel free to try other grains here too.

In my opinion, rice salads should never be eaten directly out of the refrigerator—unless, of course, you're desperately hungry—because the starches in the rice need some time to soften up. But this slight disadvantage also places them among the ultimate make-ahead dishes. If the salad is assembled a few hours in advance, the rice has a chance to soak up flavors, whether in the fridge or out (you usually don't have to refrigerate if it's going to be only a couple of hours). Before serving, just pull the salad out and leave it covered on the counter for a half-hour or so to take the chill off.

3–4	cups cooked long-grain white rice, cooled a bit but not ice cold
½	cup chopped red or yellow bell pepper

½ cup chopped celery

½ cup chopped carrot

¼–½ cup Vinaigrette (page 628), made with olive oil and sherry vinegar or red wine vinegar

½ cup chopped scallions

¼ cup chopped fresh parsley

Salt and pepper

1. Put the rice, bell pepper, celery, and carrot in a large bowl. Drizzle with ¼ cup of the vinaigrette and use two big forks to combine, fluffing the rice and tossing gently to separate the grains.

2. Stir in the scallions and parsley, taste, season with salt and pepper, and moisten with a little more dressing if needed. Serve at room temperature. Or cover and refrigerate for up to a day, bringing the salad back to room temperature before serving.

RICE SALAD, JAPANESE STYLE Use short-grain brown or white rice. Grate the bell pepper, celery, and carrot or pulse them in a food processor with the metal blade. For the vinaigrette use Simple Miso Dipping Sauce (page 653). Add 2 cups cubed firm tofu (preferably baked, see page 485). Instead of the parsley, crumble 2 sheets toasted nori (see page 244) over the salad and sprinkle with 2 tablespoons black or white sesame seeds.

RICE SALAD, INDIAN STYLE Use brown or white basmati rice. When making the vinaigrette, use rice vinegar, replace the oil with coconut milk, and add 1 tablespoon Fragrant Curry Powder (page 649), or more to taste. Instead of the bell pepper, celery, and carrot, add ½ cup each cubed cooked potato, cooked cauliflower florets, and green peas (cooked frozen are fine). Substitute cilantro for the parsley and sprinkle with chopped pistachios, if you like.

CITRUS RICE SALAD Use any rice. For the vinaigrette use citrus juice; choose from lemon, lime, orange, blood orange, tangerine, pink grapefruit, or a combination. Whatever you choose, add 2 tablespoons of the grated zest and 1 tablespoon sugar or honey to the blender when making the vinaigrette. Instead of the bell pepper, celery, and carrot, use 2 cups chopped peeled citrus fruit; substitute red onion for the scallions and mint for the parsley. A handful of chopped almonds or pecans makes a nice addition. ⓞ

TOMATO RICE SALAD Use any kind of long-grain brown or white rice. When making the vinaigrette, omit the vinegar and add 1 chopped tomato to the blender. Instead of the bell pepper, celery, and carrot, add 2 cups chopped fresh tomato. Substitute 1 teaspoon minced garlic for the scallions. Try chopped basil, chives, chervil, or dill instead of parsley. Small cubes of fresh mozzarella—use as much as you'd like—make this a meal.

Farro Salad with Cucumber and Yogurt-Dill Dressing

MAKES: 4 servings
TIME: 30 to 40 minutes

Cool, crunchy, and chewy, this is a perfect summer salad. You can start with any cooked whole grains you might have handy, including pearled barley, which was suggested in the first edition of the book—but the farro cooks relatively quickly so even if you start from scratch you'll still be serving it within an hour. Quinoa and freekeh are also tasty, quicker-cooking options.

1 cup farro

Salt

1½ pounds cucumbers, peeled if necessary, seeded (see page 49), and chopped

2 tablespoons fresh lemon juice, or more to taste

2 tablespoons olive oil

1 cup Greek yogurt

Pepper

½ cup chopped scallions

½ cup chopped fresh dill, mint, or parsley, or a combination

(continued on page 80)

More Rice Salad Variations

To make the huge number of variations on rice salad (page 76) more accessible, I've put them in chart form, where they're broken down by the main recipe's basic components (rice, aromatics and vegetables, dressing, and herbs and garnishes). Just follow the directions in each column for that variation, referring to the main rice salad recipe. (Descriptions of the rice varieties are on pages 365 to 367, and the vinaigrette is on page 628.)

VARIATION	RICE	AROMATICS AND VEGETABLES	DRESSING	HERBS AND GARNISHES
Herbed	Any kind of rice	Omit bell pepper, celery, and carrot but keep scallions.	Vinaigrette; add 1 cup any fresh herbs, alone or in combination, to blender.	None needed
With Olives and Feta	Any kind of rice	Replace bell pepper, celery, and carrot with ½ cup any pitted and chopped olives and 1 cup crumbled feta cheese.	Vinaigrette	½ cup chopped walnuts or hazelnuts, toasted, if you like (optional)
Hippie	Long-grain brown rice	Replace celery and carrot with 3 cups cooked, shocked broccoli florets (see page 150).	Soy or Mustard Vinaigrette (page 631)	¼ cup toasted sunflower seeds
Italian Style	Best with Arborio rice	Replace bell pepper, celery, and carrot with 1½ cups chopped plum or cherry tomatoes, and scallions with thinly sliced red onion. Add 1 teaspoon minced garlic.	Vinaigrette	1 tablespoon chopped fresh rosemary or 1 teaspoon dried and ½ cup grated Parmesan
Pesto	Arborio rice if possible, or anything, really	Omit bell pepper, celery, carrot, and scallions.	¼ to ½ cup Pesto (page 634), thinned with 1 tablespoon red wine vinegar.	No additional herbs needed. Olive oil and grated Parmesan. Wonderful with sliced tomatoes and fresh mozzarella.
With Fermented Black Beans in Lettuce Cups	Long-grain rice; jasmine rice is nice, if you have it	No change	Soy Vinaigrette (page 631); after blending, stir in 1 tablespoon minced fresh ginger and ¼ cup rinsed fermented black beans.	Substitute cilantro for parsley. Serve in large lettuce leaves.

VARIATION	RICE	AROMATICS AND VEGETABLES	DRESSING	HERBS AND GARNISHES
French Style	Any long-grain white rice	Substitute sliced radish for bell pepper and 1 cup chopped cooked green beans (preferably haricots verts) for celery and carrot. Replace scallions with ¼ cup minced shallot. Extra good with 1 cup cooked flageolet beans.	Mustard Vinaigrette (page 631)	Add 2 tablespoons chopped fresh tarragon.
Spanish Style	Medium-grain or Arborio rice	Replace celery with 1 cup cooked green peas (frozen are fine).	Vinaigrette; use sherry vinegar and add a pinch saffron (optional) or smoked paprika.	Sliced almonds (optional) with the parsley
Cuban Style	Long-grain white rice	Replace celery and carrot with 2 cups cooked or canned black beans. Replace scallions with thinly sliced red onion. Add 1 to 2 teaspoons minced garlic.	Lime Vinaigrette (page 631)	No change
Persian Style	Brown or white basmati or jasmine rice	Replace bell pepper and celery with ½ cup chopped cashews and 1 cup chopped pitted dates.	Vinaigrette; replace vinegar with lemon juice; add 1 teaspoon ground cinnamon and 2 teaspoons ground cumin.	Chopped fresh mint
Tropical	Brown jasmine or basmati rice	Replace bell pepper, celery, and carrot with ½ cup each cubed fresh pineapple and mango and chopped macadamia nuts. Replace scallions with toasted coconut.	Vinaigrette; use rice vinegar and good-quality vegetable oil.	Chopped fresh cilantro
Wild Rice	Wild rice	Replace bell pepper, celery, and carrots with 1 cup dried blueberries, cranberries, or cherries and ½ cup chopped almonds.	Lemon Vinaigrette (page 631)	Replace parsley with mint, if you like.

(*continued from page 77*)

1. Rinse the farro and put it in a saucepan with water to cover by at least 2 inches. Add a large pinch salt and cook over medium-high heat, stirring occasionally, until the farro is tender, 15 to 25 minutes from the time the water boils. Drain if necessary and let cool a bit.

2. While the farro cooks, put the cucumber in a colander or strainer and sprinkle with about a tablespoon salt. When the farro is cooling, rinse the cucumbers in cold water and drain well.

3. Whisk the lemon juice, oil, yogurt, and a sprinkle of pepper in a large bowl until combined. Add the scallions, herbs, cucumbers, and farro. Toss, taste and adjust the seasoning, adding more lemon if you'd like, and serve.

FARRO PEA SALAD A tad more colorful: Instead of the cucumber, use 1½ cups blanched and shocked fresh or thawed frozen peas. Or try 1 pound trimmed and chopped sugar snap or snow peas.

FARRO CUCUMBER SALAD WITH WALNUTS Some crunch: Replace 1 tablespoon of the oil with walnut oil, if you'd like. In Step 3, toss ½ cup chopped walnuts into the salad along with the scallions.

WILD RICE SALAD WITH CUCUMBER AND YOGURT Instead of the farro, use wild rice and double the cooking time. Or use 3 cups cooked wild rice (see page 418).

FARRO SALAD WITH CUCUMBER AND VEGAN DILL DRESSING Works with the main recipe or any of the previous variations: Instead of the yogurt, use soft silken tofu. **V**

Quinoa and Sweet Potato Salad

MAKES: 4 servings
TIME: 40 minutes
M **V**

I've made lots of changes to this recipe since the first edition for a better range of colors, flavors, and texture.

The key is stir-fried sweet potatoes. This works with any leftover cooked grain.

- 2½ cups cooked quinoa or other small-kernel grain (see page 398) or 1 cup raw
- 4 tablespoons olive oil
- 1 pound sweet potatoes (1 large or 2 medium), peeled and grated
- 1 large shallot, minced
  Salt and pepper
- 2 tablespoons sherry vinegar or white wine vinegar
- 1 red bell pepper, cored, seeded, and chopped
- ¼ cup chopped fresh chives or parsley for garnish

1. If you're starting with raw quinoa or other grain, cook it according to the directions on page 397. Drain if necessary and let cool a bit.

2. Put 2 tablespoons of the oil in a large skillet over medium-high heat. When it's hot, add the sweet potatoes and shallot, spreading them out as evenly as possible; sprinkle with salt and pepper. Cook, undisturbed, until the mixture sizzles and browns on the bottom, 3 to 5 minutes. Stir with a spatula to turn and separate the potatoes, then cook, stirring like that every 2 or 3 minutes, until they're just tender but not mushy. Transfer to a baking sheet and separate the pieces so the potatoes stop cooking.

3. Whisk together the remaining oil and the vinegar in a large bowl with a sprinkle of salt and pepper. Add the sweet potatoes, quinoa, and bell pepper and toss with two forks, separating the ingredients as you coat them in the dressing. Taste, adjust the seasoning, and garnish with the chives. Serve at room temperature, or cover and refrigerate for up to several hours.

SOUTHWESTERN MILLET AND SWEET POTATO SALAD A little more guts: Substitute millet for the quinoa, lime juice for the vinegar, and cilantro for the chives. When you assemble the salad in Step 3, add 1 avocado (peeled, pitted, and diced), ¼ cup toasted pepitas (pumpkin seeds; see page 299), and ¼ teaspoon cayenne or red chile flakes.

Quinoa Salad with Crunchy Tempeh

MAKES: 4 servings
TIME: 30 minutes
F M V

You'll love the crispness tempeh contributes to this full-bodied salad. The bean sprouts and tomatoes bring even more texture and color to the dish, but you can skip them—or substitute other cooked or raw vegetables—and still have an excellent main-dish salad.

2½ cups cooked quinoa or other small-kernel grain (see page 398) or 1 cup raw
3 tablespoons good-quality vegetable oil
8 ounces tempeh, crumbled (about 2 cups)
1 tablespoon minced fresh ginger
1 tablespoon minced garlic
1 cup mung bean sprouts (optional)
1 cup chopped fresh tomatoes (optional)
2 tablespoons rice vinegar
1 tablespoon sesame oil
1 tablespoon soy sauce, or to taste
Salt and pepper
½ cup chopped scallions for garnish
¼ cup chopped fresh cilantro for garnish

1. If you're starting with raw quinoa or other grain, cook it according to the directions on page 398. Drain if necessary and let it cool a bit.

2. Put the vegetable oil in a skillet over medium heat. When it's hot, add the tempeh and cook, stirring occasionally and breaking it into small pieces, until crisp all over, 5 to 10 minutes. Stir in the ginger and garlic and cook for another minute or 2, until fragrant. Add the

---

15 Salads That Make Great Meals

Almost any of the salads here can be made more filling with the addition of protein or other hearty ingredients. Cooked beans, cheese, hard-boiled eggs, and nuts or seeds are some obvious solutions.

I urge you to try some form of cooked tofu—Grilled Tofu (page 486), Baked Tofu (page 485), or Tofu Croutons (page 497). Crunchy Crumbled Tempeh (page 512) and seitan (page 508) are also good options, and remember that there's not only great flavor but a fair amount of protein in sea greens (pages 244 to 246), cooked whole grains (page 398), and whole grain croutons (page 678).

Another way to expand a salad into a meal is to toss some of the salad with a bowlful of cooked beans, noodles, or grains. All of the recipes in the "Cooked Vegetable Salads" section (page 61), and many of the other all-vegetable salads here, work great with this technique. Just moisten with a little more vinaigrette, dressing, or oil and vinegar.

Other salads in this chapter are hearty enough to make a meal exactly as they are, especially the ones made from beans, grains, and pasta or noodles; you may want to increase the portion size a bit. Here's where to find them:

1. Warm Spinach Salad with Tofu Croutons (page 37)

2. Endive and Blue Cheese Salad (page 42)

3. Arame and Bean Threads with Ponzu Dipping Sauce and its variations (page 56)

4. Bean Salad, Many Ways (page 71)

5. Rice Salad (page 76)

6. Tomato Salad with Hard-Boiled Eggs and its variations (page 57)

7. Farro Salad with Cucumber and Yogurt-Dill Dressing and its variations (page 77)

8. Warm Chickpea Salad with Arugula (page 73)

9. Pan-Roasted Corn Salad with Black Beans (page 62)

10. Quinoa Salad with Crunchy Tempeh (page 82)

11. Quinoa and Sweet Potato Salad (page 80)

12. Tomato and Bread Salad (page 61)

13. Japanese-Style Summertime Pasta Salad (page 85)

14. Wheat Berry or Other Whole Grain Salad with Cabbage and Coarse Mustard (page 83)

15. Nutty and Fruity Wheat Berry or Other Whole Grain Salad and its variations (page 83)

bean sprouts and the tomatoes, if you're using them, stir, and turn off the heat. Stir in the vinegar, sesame oil, and soy sauce and transfer everything to a large bowl.

3. When the quinoa is dry and cooled, toss it with the tempeh mixture. Taste and add salt, if necessary, and lots of pepper. (You can prepare the salad up to this point and let it rest for an hour or so for the flavors to meld, or refrigerate it for up to a couple of hours.) Garnish with the scallions and cilantro just before serving.

QUINOA SALAD WITH LENTILS If you're still leery about tempeh: Instead of the tempeh, use 2 cups cooked or canned lentils, drained as dry as possible.

QUINOA SALAD WITH BEANS Substitute any kind of cooked or canned bean for the tempeh. Drain them well, put them in a shallow bowl, and mash them with the back of a fork to break them up a bit before adding them in Step 2.

Nutty and Fruity Wheat Berry or Other Whole Grain Salad

MAKES: 4 servings
TIME: 20 minutes
F V

Like the green salad with fruit and cheese on page 37, this recipe provides lots of chances for improvisation. So for the fruit and nut components use what you've got and what's in season—in that order.

- 1 navel orange, peeled and separated into sections
- ¼ cup olive oil, or as needed
- 2 tablespoons red wine vinegar or other vinegar
- 1 tablespoon chopped fresh thyme or rosemary
  Salt and pepper
- 2 cups cooked wheat berries or any of the other grains listed on pages 400–403
- ½ cup chopped scallions

- ½ cup dried cranberries or cherries
- ½ cup peanuts

1. Cut the orange segments in half and put the pieces and any accumulated juices in a large bowl. Add the oil, vinegar, and thyme, sprinkle with salt and pepper, and stir to combine.

2. Add the wheat berries and scallions, along with half the cranberries and peanuts. Toss, then taste and adjust the seasoning. Garnish with the remaining fruit and nuts and serve right away.

Wheat Berry or Other Whole Grain Salad with Cabbage and Mustard

MAKES: 4 servings
TIME: 20 minutes
F M V

Dress the sweet earthiness of wheat berries with a sharp counterpoint and you get a hearty salad with memorable flavors.

- 1 pound Savoy or green cabbage
- ⅓ cup olive oil, or more to taste
- 2 tablespoons whole grain mustard, or more to taste
- 2 tablespoons cider vinegar or white wine vinegar, or more to taste
  Salt and pepper
- 1 small red onion, halved and thinly sliced
- 2 cups cooked wheat berries (see page 398)

1. Trim the cabbage and grate it by hand or in a food processor. You should have about 4 cups.

2. Whisk the oil, mustard, and vinegar together in a large bowl. Add a little salt (mustard can be quite salty, so go easy) and a lot of pepper. Separate the onion slices into the dressing and stir until coated.

3. Add the cabbage and wheat berries to the mixture and toss well. Taste and adjust the seasoning, adding more

Wheat Berry or Other Whole
Grain Salad with Cabbage
and Mustard (page 83)

oil, mustard, or vinegar. Serve right away or cover and refrigerate for up to a day.

5 Ways to Vary Wheat Berry Salad with Cabbage and Mustard

1. Try one of the other grains listed on pages 400 to 403.
2. Substitute prepared or grated fresh horseradish for the mustard.
3. Add 1 cup sliced celery.
4. Add 2 cups chopped crisp apples.
5. Add 2 cups cooked or canned cannellini beans, drained but still moist.

PASTA AND NOODLE SALADS

One thing hasn't changed since I wrote this book ten years ago: My idea of a good pasta salad is eating a good noodle dish at room temperature. (See "6 Pastas or Noodles That Are Delicious at Room Temperature" on page 86.) Maybe just before serving you brighten it with some chopped herbs, a squeeze of lemon, or a drizzle of vinegar or toss it with sturdy greens.

To make delicious cold dishes with noodles or macaroni as the main ingredient, you really have to tap the ingredients and techniques of other countries. And then follow this rule:

Make and eat. A couple of hours tops at room temperature does no harm, but don't refrigerate it; the notion that you can make pasta salad the night before to eat ice cold at some point in the future leaves you with a congealed, muted-flavor dish.

Japanese-Style Summertime Pasta Salad

Hiyashi Chuka
MAKES: 4 servings
TIME: 30 minutes
F **V**

A Japanese summertime staple—flexible like a chef's salad, only based on noodles and dressed with a

pleasantly sweet, brothy dressing that pulls everything together. Ramen noodles are traditional here; great fresh ones are more available now than when I first wrote this book, so seek them out. You can also substitute soba, somen, or even spaghetti as long as you adjust the cooking time. I serve this for guests—it's fun to set up a buffet table—or make it as a way to clean out the fridge or gorge on something ripe and in season. (See the list that follows for a start with possible toppings.)

> Salt
> ½ cup Kombu Dashi (page 100) or water
> 3 tablespoons soy sauce, or more to taste
> 3 tablespoons rice vinegar
> 1 tablespoon sugar
> 1 teaspoon sesame oil
> 1 teaspoon minced fresh ginger
> 2 tablespoons wasabi powder, or more to taste
> ¼ cup boiling water
> 12 ounces dried or fresh ramen noodles
> 1 cucumber, peeled if you want, halved, seeded (see page 49), and thinly sliced
> ½ cup lightly packed shredded nori
> ¼ cup pickled ginger (to make your own, see page 207)
> 2 tablespoons toasted sesame seeds (see page 299)
> ¼ cup sliced scallions

1. Put a large pot of water on to boil and salt it. Stir together the dashi, soy sauce, vinegar, sugar, sesame oil, and fresh ginger in a small bowl. Taste, add more soy sauce if necessary, and let sit. Dissolve the wasabi in the ¼ cup boiling water; let cool and thicken for a few minutes. Add a little more powder if it seems too thin.
2. Drop the ramen into the pot of boiling water and cook, stirring occasionally, until tender but not mushy. Start tasting after 1 minute; the cooking time can vary by a few minutes. Drain, rinse in a colander under cold running water, and drain again.
3. For individual servings, divide the noodles among 4 serving bowls, then divvy up the cucumber, nori, and

pickled ginger among them. (In Japan, these ingredients are usually nested in individual piles on top of or around the noodles, though you can just scatter the toppings over the noodles if that seems too fussy.) Top each salad with a pinch toasted sesame seeds and the scallions.

4. Serve the noodles with small bowls of the dressing on the side for diners to dress and toss the salad at the table. Pass wasabi to season the noodles.

12 Toppings for Japanese-Style Summertime Pasta Salad

1. Grilled or sautéed shiitake mushrooms (page 167 or 217)

2. Oven-Dried Tomatoes (page 261)

3. A spoonful or two of Simplest Seaweed Salad (page 53)

4. Spicy Korean-Style Pickles (page 91)

5. Individual poached eggs (page 525)

6. Chopped hard-boiled eggs (page 521)

7. Scrambled eggs

8. A handful of bean sprouts

9. Crunchy Crumbled Tempeh (page 512)

10. Thinly sliced or grated daikon or other radish

11. A spoonful or 2 of silken tofu or Deep-Fried Tofu (page 487)

12. Cooked black or white soybeans (½ cup or so per serving)

---

6 Pastas or Noodles That Are Delicious at Room Temperature

1. Pasta with Garlic and Oil (page 312)

2. Pasta with any version of Fast Tomato Sauce (page 312)

3. Linguini with Raw Tomato Sauce (page 314)

4. Pasta with Broccoli, Cauliflower, or Broccoli Raab (page 322)

5. Pasta with Caramelized Onions (page 320)

6. Pasta with Mushrooms (page 324)

Pearl Couscous Salad

MAKES: 4 servings
TIME: About 30 minutes
F M V

Both pearl (Israeli) and "regular" couscous are actually forms of pasta; the only difference is size. Regular couscous is tiny; pearl couscous is about the size of a plump peppercorn, which makes it better for salads. (I'm especially keen on the whole wheat kind, and on fregola, the toasted kind from Sardinia.) This salad is a balancing act of many strong flavors, and personal preference plays a role here. So taste as you go and adjust the seasonings and condiments as you like.

	Salt
1	pound pearl couscous
¼	cup olive oil
2	tablespoons fresh lemon juice
½	teaspoon ground cumin
⅛	teaspoon ground cinnamon
1	Preserved Lemon (page 286), skin only, sliced as thin as possible, or 1 tablespoon minced lemon zest
2	tablespoons capers
¼	cup currants or golden raisins
	Pepper
½	small red onion, halved and thinly sliced
1	cup cooked or canned chickpeas, drained but still moist
1	pint cherry or grape tomatoes, halved
½	cup toasted pine nuts (see page 299)
½	cup chopped fresh parsley

1. Bring a large pot of water to a boil and salt it. Cook the couscous, stirring occasionally, until tender but not mushy; start tasting after 5 minutes. Drain it well, rinse it briefly with cold running water, and drain again.

2. Put the oil, lemon juice, cumin, cinnamon, preserved lemon, capers, and currants in a large bowl with a generous pinch pepper and whisk to combine. Taste and adjust the seasoning, adding more spices, lemon, or salt as you like.

3. Add the couscous, onion, chickpeas, tomatoes, pine nuts, and parsley and toss once or twice. If possible, let the salad rest at room temperature for an hour, tossing every now and then. Taste and adjust the seasoning and serve.

WHOLE GRAIN SALAD WITH PRESERVED LEMON Heartier (and a little longer to prepare): Instead of couscous, use about 5 cups cooked whole grain like farro, barley, freekeh, or wheat or rye berries.

Couscous Salad with Fennel and Raisins

MAKES: 4 servings
TIME: 30 minutes

F M V

Delicate and fluffy couscous is so quick cooking, this salad can be considered almost last minute. It's worth the extra few minutes to make the vinaigrette since the flavors are absorbed more evenly into the pasta than if you dress with separate oil and lemon juice. This is really good with fregola, the large and heavily toasted couscous from Sardinia.

  2½ **cups cooked couscous, regular or whole wheat, or 1 cup uncooked**
  ½ **cup port or red wine**
  ½ **cup raisins**
  1 **large fennel bulb**
  ¼–½ **cup Lemon Vinaigrette (page 631)**
  1 **teaspoon fennel seeds**
    Salt and pepper

1. If you're starting with raw couscous, cook it according to the directions on page 398. Put the port in a small pot over medium heat and warm until steaming but not boiling. Add the raisins and soak until they're plump and tender, 5 to 10 minutes. When the couscous is ready, fluff it with a fork and let it cool a bit.

2. Trim the fennel, reserving a few of the feathery fronds for garnish. Cut the bulb in half lengthwise, then slice each half thinly.

3. Put the raisins and port in a large bowl with ¼ cup of the vinaigrette and the fennel seeds; whisk to combine. Add the couscous and fennel and toss gently until they're evenly coated. (At this point you can let the salad sit for up to an hour; in fact, it will benefit if you have the time.) Taste and adjust the seasoning, and add more vinaigrette as you like.

COUSCOUS SALAD WITH FRIED HAZELNUTS Omit the vinaigrette. Put ¼ cup olive oil in a skillet over medium heat; when it's hot, add ½ cup chopped hazelnuts. Toast, shaking the pan occasionally and sprinkling with salt and pepper, until lightly browned and blistered,

Prepping Fennel

STEP 1 Trim the hard, hollow stalks from the top of the bulb. Save the fronds for garnish if you like.

STEP 2 Cut a thick slice from one side of the fennel.

STEP 3 Stand the bulb on its side and cut through it vertically.

STEP 4 Or cut it horizontally.

3 to 5 minutes. Let sit for 10 minutes to cool, then add 2 tablespoons lemon juice. Toss the nut mixture into the bowl with the raisins and port in Step 3 and proceed with the salad.

COUSCOUS SALAD WITH OLIVES AND FETA Omit the raisins and port; substitute ½ cup pitted and chopped black olives, preferably marinated. You'll need to use more vinaigrette. When you toss the salad in Step 3, add ½ cup crumbled feta cheese and ¼ cup chopped fresh mint.

PICKLED VEGETABLES

Pickling as a process has been around for thousands of years, sustaining people through winters, expeditions, wars, and famine. Every cuisine has at least a handful of pickled things, and with its variety of salty, sour, sweet, and hot flavors, pickled food is almost universally appealing. Mostly we now pickle not to preserve but because we like the flavor.

Pickling occurs when food is put in an environment that prevents the growth of harmful microbes. There are two basic methods for preserving food this way: by using vinegar (an acid) or by salting (using straight salt or a saltwater brine). Through osmosis, the vinegar replaces water in the food's cells. Salting is a slightly less direct and more complex process, in which the salt draws out the food's natural water and allows just enough bacterial growth to produce lactic acid, which then ferments and pickles the food. (Kimchi, page 93, is a perfect example of this salt-pickling process.) Salt is also used when pickling with vinegar, to draw out water and crisp the vegetables and to keep the vinegar that seeps into the vegetable or fruit undiluted.

The trouble with vinegar is that it's often overwhelmingly strong-tasting, and in order to have a true preservative effect, you need a lot. I'd rather reduce the amount of vinegar and sacrifice longevity so that other flavors are more prominent. So the recipes here deliver pickles that keep for days, not weeks. These are not for canning, or long-keeping; they're pickles for pickle lovers.

There are only a few guidelines here: Use the freshest foods for pickling; produce that has blemishes or soft spots will start with more of the harmful microbes you want to avoid. Also, consider the size and density of the fruit or vegetable; smaller and softer pieces pickle more quickly than larger pieces.

Quickest Pickled Vegetables

MAKES: 4 to 8 servings
TIME: 1 hour or less
[V]

The vegetables here are salted directly rather than brined. But even 15 minutes really changes their texture and flavor, making them both pliable and crunchy. Of course, the thinner you slice the vegetables, the quicker the salt and seasonings can penetrate. Which is why shredding is also a good option to shave off even a few more minutes of salting and pickling time.

Other vegetables you can use: radish, jícama, kohlrabi, celery, fennel, cabbage, asparagus, green beans, or onion.

1 **pound cucumber, zucchini, summer squash, or eggplant**
1 **tablespoon salt**
½ **teaspoon sugar**
1 **tablespoon minced fresh dill or 1 teaspoon dried dill**
2 **teaspoons vinegar**

1. Wash the vegetable well, peel if you like, and slice as thin as possible (a mandoline is perfect for this) or grate them. Put the vegetable in a colander and sprinkle with the salt; toss well. Gently rub the salt into the vegetable with your hands for a minute.
2. Let the colander sit in the sink or in a bowl until the vegetable softens, 15 to 30 minutes depending on the vegetable; toss and squeeze every few minutes. When little or no more liquid comes out of the vegetable, rinse well in cold water. Put in a bowl.
3. Toss with the sugar, dill, and vinegar and serve right away; this pickle does not keep well.

Quickest Pickled
Vegetables (page 89)

This makes a spicy garnish for tacos, rice, beans, and more: Use an assortment of thinly sliced radishes, jícama, cucumber, and red onion. Substitute cilantro for the dill; add a thinly sliced jalapeño if you like (or habanero if you like it mouth-searing); use red wine vinegar.

QUICKEST-PICKLED MANGO OR PAPAYA A perfect use for underripe mangoes or papaya, and it easily moves between Indian, Southeast Asian, Latin, and Caribbean cuisines: Substitute thinly sliced or julienned still-firm mango or papaya for the vegetable and cilantro, mint, or ginger for the dill.

Marinated Garden Vegetables

MAKES: About 8 servings
TIME: About 45 minutes
Ⓜ Ⓥ

Since these crunchy, tangy, Italian-American-style vegetables keep for several weeks, I like to store them prominently in my fridge in a big jar. You can serve them on toothpicks; on top of greens or tossed with salads (using the brine, which works perfectly as a dressing); or tossed with cooked pasta, whole grains, or beans for a quick, hearty salad.

  1 **cup red wine vinegar**
  2 **tablespoons salt**
  2 **sprigs fresh or 2 teaspoons dried oregano**
  2 **bay leaves**
  2 **cloves garlic**
  ¾ **cup olive oil, plus more for drizzling**
  1 **bunch broccoli, cut into florets**
  1 **small head cauliflower, cut into florets**
  2 **zucchini or summer squash, trimmed and sliced crosswise**
  2 **carrots, cut into ½-inch-thick slices or sticks**
  1 **red bell pepper, cored, seeded, and sliced**
  1 **onion, cut into 8 wedges**
  ½ **cup green or black olives, pitted if you like**
     Pepper

1. Put the vinegar, salt, oregano, bay leaves, garlic, olive oil, and 4 cups water in a large nonreactive pot and bring to a boil. Add the broccoli and cauliflower and cook for a minute. Add the zucchini, carrots, bell pepper, onion, and olives, cover, and turn off the heat.
2. Let cool to room temperature in the pot. Serve at room temperature or chilled, drizzled with some of the brine and some olive oil and sprinkled with lots of pepper. Store the mixture in its brine in a covered plastic or glass container in the refrigerator for a month or more.

MARINATED WINTER SQUASH Substitute a 3-pound (or so) winter squash like butternut, pumpkin, Hubbard, or kabocha for the broccoli, cauliflower, zucchini, carrots, bell pepper, and olives. Trim, peel, and seed the squash and cut into 1-inch cubes. Make the brine as directed and bring to a boil. Add the squash to the brine along with the onion in Step 1.

MARINATED ARTICHOKES Fantastic in salads, sandwiches, and on pizza: Substitute 12 or more cleaned raw artichoke hearts or baby artichokes (see page 165) for the broccoli, cauliflower, zucchini, carrots, bell pepper, and olives. Make the brine as directed and bring to a boil. Add the artichokes to the boiling brine in Step 1 and cook for about 10 minutes, then cover and turn off the heat. Proceed with Step 2.

Spicy Korean-Style Pickles

MAKES: 4 to 8 servings
TIME: At least 1 hour
Ⓜ Ⓥ

A dry-ish pickle, based on those traditionally served throughout Southeast Asia in small portions with an assortment of other pickled or fermented items. I love

Crudités

Everyone loves cut-up raw and cooked vegetables served cold with something for dipping. I've adopted the French term *crudités* for this versatile snack but there doesn't need to be anything fancy about them.

Crudités are sold in supermarkets, ready to go. But don't buy those unless you're absolutely desperate. Cutting vegetables for crudités is simple. As long as you keep the vegetables large enough to pick up easily and dip without accidentally dunking your fingers, you'll be in good shape. But they should be small or slender enough to pop into your mouth or bite easily; usually about ½ inch wide is just right. Broccoli and cauliflower florets work best with an inch or so of stem to hold onto; core and seed bell peppers and slice into ½-inch-or-so-wide sticks, cutting the curved ends off, if you like.

You can prepare all the components of a crudité platter, including the dip, in advance. Some, like waxy potatoes—which are excellent—must be cooked first. Others, like asparagus, broccoli, cauliflower, and root vegetables, can be served raw or cooked. It's generally best to cut them up before cooking so you have better control over doneness: Boil or steam them until crisp-tender (one step closer to raw than you might otherwise), then plunge them into an ice bath to shock and stop their cooking and capture the vibrant color. Also consider the possibility of roasted or grilled vegetables as crudités; they're unexpected and a good contrast to whatever you're serving raw. Just be sure not to overcook them: Crispness is key.

Store raw vegetables in ice water to keep them crisp, and cooked vegetables in airtight containers; both will hold for a day or so. Drain raw vegetables well and put them on a kitchen towel or paper towels to dry—dip doesn't stick to wet vegetables. Bring cooked vegetables to room temperature.

12 Easy and Attractive Crudité Preparations

1. Baby carrots (not the nubby kind sold in bags) or larger carrots: cut into sticks

2. Asparagus spears: trimmed, bottoms peeled; raw or steamed

3. Green or wax beans: whole; steamed or roasted

4. Sugar snap peas: whole; raw or steamed

5. Belgian endive: individual leaves

6. Jícama: peeled and cut into sticks

7. Root vegetables: halves, slices, or wedges; steamed or roasted

8. Any waxy potatoes: halves, slices, wedges, or small fingerlings; steamed or roasted

9. Red or white radishes; whole, halves, or wedges, or slices if large

10. Cucumber: cut into spears and seeded

11. Kohlrabi: peeled and cut into thin coins

12. Bell pepper: cored, seeded, and cut lengthwise into sticks

14 Dips to Serve with Crudités

Nearly any salad dressing also works fine.

1. Pesto (page 634)

2. Parsley "Pesto" (page 638)

3. Garlic Mayonnaise or any flavored mayonnaise or Vegannaise (page 671 or 672)

4. The Simplest Yogurt Sauce (page 673)

5. Blue Cheese Dressing (page 674) or Blue Cheese Dip (page 556)

6. Ginger-Scallion Sauce (page 631)

7. Creamy Cilantro-Mint Chutney (page 670)

8. Simple Miso Dipping Sauce (page 653)

9. Nutty Miso Sauce (page 653)

10. Peanut Sauce, Four Ways (page 657)

11. Tahini Sauce (page 306)

12. Hummus (page 463)

13. Any bean dip (pages 462 to 465)

14. Any well-seasoned vegetable purée (page 150)

this super-easy recipe for its hot, salty, slightly sweet flavors—and its versatility.

Other vegetables you can use: radish, jícama, celery, cabbage, kohlrabi, cauliflower, turnips, or summer squash.

 1   **pound Kirby or other thin-skinned cucumbers**
 1   **tablespoon salt**
3–4 **tablespoons chile-garlic paste (to make your own, see page 665)**
 1   **teaspoon sugar**
 2   **tablespoons sesame oil**
 2   **tablespoons soy sauce**

1. Wash the cucumbers well, scrub them if they're spiny, and cut into ¼-inch-thick slices. Put them in a colander and sprinkle with the salt; toss well. Gently rub the salt into the cucumbers with your hands for a minute.

2. Lay a plate over the cucumbers in the colander and weight the plate with whatever is handy—a few cans from the pantry or your teakettle filled with water, for example. Let sit for about 30 minutes; 1 hour is fine. Rinse the cucumbers, then pat dry with towels; transfer them to a bowl.

3. Add the chile-garlic paste, sugar, sesame oil, and soy sauce, toss to combine, and let sit for at least 30 minutes. You can eat the pickle right away. Or put it in an airtight container, packing the cucumbers down into the container so the liquid comes to the surface, cover, and refrigerate for up to 3 weeks.

SALTED CABBAGE WITH SICHUAN PEPPERCORNS
Essentially another spin on Kimchi (right)—a sweet and hot quick pickle: Substitute 6 cups shredded green or Napa cabbage for the cucumbers. Use 1 tablespoon each salt, mirin, soy sauce, and Sichuan peppercorns, and reduce the sesame oil to 1 teaspoon. Skip Step 1. Instead, mix together all the ingredients in a large bowl, toss very well, then press in the bowl with a weighted plate as in Step 2. Do not rinse. Remove the weight, toss again, and serve or cover and refrigerate; it will keep for 5 days or so.

Kimchi

MAKES: 8 servings
TIME: About 2 hours, mostly unattended
M V

You can easily find kimchi in refrigerated jars at supermarkets, but making it yourself gives you far more control over the level of spiciness. Plus some kimchi contains fish sauce and/or fermented shrimp; making your own allows you to keep it vegetarian. Refrigerated, this will keep for about a week.

Other vegetables that work: all scallions (use about 50, total, split in half lengthwise), or 2 to 3 pounds of daikon, black radish, or turnip, peeled and shredded.

 1   **head green, Savoy, or Napa cabbage (about 2 pounds), separated into leaves**
     About ½ cup coarse salt
20   **scallions, including most of the green, chopped**
 1   **tablespoon red chile flakes, or more to taste**
¼   **cup soy sauce**
¼   **cup minced garlic**
¼   **cup sugar**

1. Layer the cabbage leaves in a colander, sprinkling a little salt between layers. Let sit over a bowl for at least 2 hours. When the cabbage is wilted, rinse and dry.

2. Mix the scallions, red chile flakes, soy sauce, garlic, and sugar together in a large bowl. Chop the cabbage and toss with the spice mixture. Serve immediately. Or cover and refrigerate for up to a week; it will become stronger every day.

Miso-Cured Vegetables

MAKES: 4 to 8 servings
TIME: 1 or 2 days
M V

I love this classic Japanese pickle, often served in sushi rolls or alongside rice and noodle dishes. It's intense so a little goes a long way. You can use any type of miso, from the milder white to the robust red. The vegetables pick up the subtle flavors of the miso; saltier, darker misos pickle more quickly. (For more about them all, see page 652.)

Other vegetables you can use (the sturdier the vegetable, the longer it requires in the miso): radish, jícama, celery, kohlrabi, turnips, carrots, eggplant, corn on the cob (cut crosswise into coins), summer squash.

1 pound zucchini or other vegetable from the list above
At least 2 cups white or yellow miso

1. Peel the vegetables if necessary and cut them into slices ¼ inch thick or thinner (a mandoline or food processor is perfect for this).

2. Spread 1 cup of the miso in a shallow bowl, an inch deep, then add the vegetables. Top with the remaining cup miso, plus more if necessary, to bury the vegetables. Cover with plastic wrap and let stand at room temperature for 12 hours.

3. Fish out one of the slices, rinse it off, and sample it; depending on the vegetable and the thickness of the slice, it may require another 12 to 24 hours.

4. To serve, remove the slices from the miso, rinse, and cut them into small pieces. Refrigerate the miso in a clean container; it may be reused several times to make pickles, or for any other recipe using it. These keep for a few days, but they're really at their best right when they're ready.

SWEET MISO-CURED VEGETABLES Add 1 tablespoon mirin or honey to the miso before curing the vegetables.

Soups

CHAPTER AT A GLANCE

Soup is a one-pot course on fundamental cooking techniques—only without the pressure. Making soup can teach you how to use both main ingredients and seasonings, alone and in combination. You practice timing, controlling temperature, and recognizing doneness, all in a comfortable manner. Make a mistake—short of burning the pan—and the results are almost always delicious anyway, since the whole idea is to capture every bit of flavor from a collection of ingredients.

But—and this is a real but—even though soup is a terrific way to use imperfect produce and leftovers like grains or beans, the old saying "garbage in, garbage out" also applies to the pot on the stove. You must stick to the basic principle of using real, good food.

Soup is rarely difficult or even that time consuming. Some of the recipes in this chapter take thirty minutes or less to prepare; if one takes longer, the cooking time is largely unattended. And almost every stock and soup can be made ahead and reheated; some can even be served cold.

On top of that, soup is flexible: It makes an ideal first course for entertaining, the perfect meal to pull from the freezer for a weeknight supper, or an easy lunch to make ahead and pack for school or work. The recipes here will also show you how to vary ingredients so you can use it as a vehicle for pantry items and exploring flavors.

Almost every soup is best when it begins with stock, so if at all possible, begin with one of the stocks on pages 97 to 100. The body and extra flavor provided by this base will improve any soup. If you cannot, though, rather than rely on packaged stock, just begin with water (read "Why Not Use Water?" on page 98), and consider increasing the quantities of aromatic vegetables—carrot, celery, and onion are the basics—to build in some intensity.

VEGETABLE STOCKS

At one time, I believed the best meatless stock began with vegetables roasted in olive oil. I now appreciate the fresh, bright taste of stocks that begin with raw vegetables and even fruit; I've learned how to harness intensely flavored ingredients for lightning-quick infusions; and I'm more than happy to kick-start stocks with juice, beer, wine, coffee, or tea. In other words: Vegetarian stocks can be a lot more—and a lot faster—than roasted vegetables simmered in water.

The main problem with homemade stock is that you never seem to have enough of it. The recipes in this section all make about 2 quarts—a little more than enough for any of the soups in this chapter. Fortunately, making double or even triple-size batches isn't any more difficult than making small ones. Then all you have to do is tuck the stock away for a rainy day.

Here's how: If you store stock in the refrigerator and bring it back to a boil every second or third day, it will keep more or less indefinitely. It's best to store it in an airtight food storage container (I use glass) and transfer to a pot every time you reboil. If you don't reboil it, it will keep for about 5 days.

If you want to save space, boil the stock down to about half its original volume. Now you have concentrate that's easier to cool and store. Add water when you start cooking with it.

To freeze stock, first let it cool completely. (You can

speed things along by setting the pot in ice water in the sink, then transferring it to the fridge.) Then ladle the cooled stock into serving-size containers—plastic bags or containers, or glass (leave a little headroom to allow for the liquid to expand without breaking the glass); quart-size is usually best. Cover tightly and freeze.

Frozen stock will keep for months, though it does deteriorate somewhat in flavor over time. If you remember you have it, however, it's unlikely to last that long. And the cycle will begin again.

The Fastest Vegetable Stock Ever

MAKES: About 1 quart
TIME: 40 minutes, somewhat unattended
Ⓜ Ⓥ

If you don't have all the ingredients listed below, it's fine to substitute, keeping in mind that the stock will taste like whatever vegetables you use. The longer you can simmer the stock, the more intense it will be, up to an hour or so. And if you're planning to use this for a soup that requires 6 cups stock, double the batch and store the leftovers, or make up the difference with 2 cups water.

2	carrots, cut into chunks
1	onion, quartered (don't bother to peel)
1	potato, cut into chunks
1	celery stalk, chopped
2 or 3	cloves garlic (don't bother to peel)
10–20	parsley sprigs
2	tablespoons olive oil
	Salt and pepper

1. Put everything in a saucepan or small stockpot with 6 cups water, using a pinch of salt and a bit of pepper. Bring to a boil, then adjust the heat so the mixture bubbles steadily but gently. Cook for about 30 minutes, until the vegetables are tender.
2. Strain the stock through a fine-meshed strainer, then taste and adjust the seasoning before using or storing.

Vegetable Stock

MAKES: About 2 quarts
TIME: 1 hour, somewhat unattended
Ⓜ Ⓥ

There are a few differences between this and the super-fast recipe. Here you cut the vegetables into smaller pieces, which helps extract more flavor, and you pan-cook them, which browns them a bit and adds an intensity and a little sweetness. The simmering time remains about the same, but if you can spare a few more minutes, all the better.

2	tablespoons olive oil
4	carrots, sliced
4	celery stalks (plus any available leaves), sliced
2	onions, quartered (don't bother to peel)
2	baking potatoes, peeled and cut into chunks
1	head garlic (separate the cloves but don't bother to peel)
1	pound white button mushrooms, trimmed and halved or sliced
	Salt and pepper
10–20	parsley sprigs
2	bay leaves

1. Put the oil in a large pot over medium heat. When it's hot, add the carrots, celery, onions, potatoes, garlic, and mushrooms. Sprinkle with salt and pepper, cover, and cook, undisturbed, until you hear the vegetables sizzle, 3 to 5 minutes. Uncover, stir once or twice, and cook, stirring only enough to prevent burning until the vegetables release their liquid and begin to brown, 15 to 20 minutes. (If you have more time, keep going another 15 to 20 minutes or until they're even darker.)
2. Add 10 cups water, the parsley, and the bay leaves. Bring to a boil, then adjust the heat so the mixture bubbles steadily but gently. Cook until the vegetables are very tender, anywhere from 15 to 60 minutes depending on how much time you can spare.
3. Strain through a fine-meshed strainer. Taste and adjust the seasoning before using or cooling and storing.

Why Not Use Water?

Follow my reasoning: All stocks start with water combined with solids. (Even if you use juice, booze, or some other flavored liquid, they too began with water.) The mixture is boiled to extract flavor from the solids; the stronger the flavors, the quicker the water is flavored. Though stocks are usually made in advance and strained, they're only rarely served clear, as a consommé or broth. In this book, the stocks are designed as a base for fresh vegetables or other ingredients—noodles, rice, eggs, cheese, and so on.

This means you can begin any soup with water instead of stock, as long as you add sufficient vegetables and other seasonings and aromatics and cook the mixture long enough for a flavorful liquid to develop. If you don't have time to make stock, use water; just add wine, extra vegetables, or herbs. Or try one of the super-quick broths that follow. But don't make the mistake of thinking that there is no soup without stock.

12 Ways to Flavor Water

When you don't have time to make stock but want something a little more interesting than water, try one of these. Flavored water is also perfect for cooking grains and as the backdrop to simple bowls of noodles, whole grains, or beans.

To make each of the following: Bring 8 cups salted water to a boil in a large pot. Add the flavoring ingredients, let the liquid return to a boil, then turn off the heat, cover, and let steep undisturbed for 15 minutes. Strain, then use right away or refrigerate for up to a few days.

1. Mushroom Water
Use ½ ounce dried porcini or shiitake mushrooms (about ½ cup). After steeping, reserve the mushrooms to cook later, and strain the water carefully to remove any grit.

2. Sour Water
Start with ¼ cup of vinegar, like balsamic, cider, or rice vinegar. Add more to taste.

3. Herb Water
A mix is best; you can wing it. Use parsley, mint, cilantro, dill, basil, or chives in larger quantities; use oregano, rosemary, thyme, tarragon, sage, or lavender by the sprig or pinch.

4. Juicy Water
If you've got a juicer or powerful blender, this is the way to go: Replace up to half of the water with freshly squeezed fruit or vegetable juice.

5. Tomato Water
Use ½ cup dried tomatoes (not oil-packed).

6. Boozy Water
Replace up to 3 cups of the water with beer, wine, or hard cider.

7. Parmesan Water
You know those rinds of cheese you've been saving in the fridge or freezer? This is how you can put several to excellent use.

8. Nut Water
Add 1 cup of any nut, even unsweetened coconut. If you've got an extra minute to toast the nuts in the bottom of the pot before boiling the water, all the better.

9. Tempeh Water
Nuanced, slightly nutty flavor with just the right amount of tang: Crumble 1 pound of any kind of tempeh into the water.

10. Garlic Water
Roasted Garlic (page 205) is better, but even just adding the unpeeled cloves from a head of raw garlic leaves behind a haunting and surprisingly mild broth.

11. Seaweed Water
A little seaweed will give a pleasant brininess. Try a 3- or 4-inch piece of kelp or a pinch of arame; avoid nori, which disintegrates without adding much flavor. Don't boil the water after adding the seaweed. Heat at a gentle bubble until the seaweed is soft, 10 to 20 minutes, or let it steep like tea as the stock cools for storing.

12. Hot Water
Fresh chiles deliver herbaceous, sometimes sweet heat, while dried add smoky, rich flavors. Remove any stems, and remember the seeds are often hotter than the flesh.

Roasted Vegetable Stock

MAKES: About 2 quarts
TIME: About 2 hours, mostly unattended
M V

Taking the time to roast the vegetables adds more complex flavors that you can only get from dry-heat caramelization. And by using leeks instead of onions and adding a few other ingredients not included in the preceding recipes, you wind up with something really fine.

    3 leeks, trimmed, rinsed well, and cut
       "nto chunks, or 2 onions, quartered
       (don't bother to peel)
    4 carrots, cut into chunks
    2 celery stalks, cut into chunks
    1 parsnip, cut into chunks (optional)
    2 potatoes, peeled and quartered
  6–8 cloves garlic
    1 pound white button mushrooms, trimmed
       and halved or sliced
    ⅓ cup olive oil
       Salt and pepper
       Small bunch fresh parsley leaves, plus
       10 sprigs
 2 or 3 sprigs fresh thyme
    ¼ cup soy sauce, or more to taste
   10 black peppercorns
    ½ cup white wine

1. Heat the oven to 450°F. Put the leeks, carrots, celery, parsnip (if you're using it), potatoes, garlic, and mushrooms in a large roasting pan. Drizzle with the oil, sprinkle with salt and pepper, and stir to coat. Spread the vegetables out in a single layer. Roast, turning the vegetables a couple of times with a spatula to prevent burning, until everything is deeply browned and fairly dry. This will take 30 to 45 minutes; don't rush it.
2. Use a slotted spoon to scoop the roasted vegetables into a large pot; add the herbs, ¼ cup soy sauce, the peppercorns, wine, salt to taste, and 8 cups water. Turn the heat under the pot to high.

3. Put the roasting pan over high heat and add 2 cups water. Bring to a boil, and scrape up all the bits of vegetables that have stuck to the bottom of the pan. Pour the entire mixture into the pot.
4. Bring the stock to a boil, then partially cover and adjust the heat so the mixture sends up a few bubbles at a time. Cook until the vegetables are falling apart and the liquid is deeply colored, 30 to 45 minutes. Strain through a fine-meshed strainer, pressing on the vegetables to extract as much stock as possible. Taste and adjust the seasoning, adding more soy sauce if you'd like, before using or cooling and storing.

Mushroom Stock

MAKES: About 2 quarts
TIME: About 1½ hours, mostly unattended
M V

The combination of fresh and dried mushrooms gives this stock a pronounced mushroom flavor that might compete with other ingredients; for most of the soups in this chapter, you will probably want to use one of the preceding vegetable stocks or plain water. But when there are mushrooms in the soup, or if you plan to use the stock as the foundation for a richly flavored sauce or gravy, this is the recipe to turn to.

    4 tablespoons good-quality vegetable oil
    1 onion or 4 shallots, sliced, or 2 leeks,
       trimmed, rinsed well, and sliced
    4 carrots, chopped
    4 celery stalks, chopped
       Salt and pepper
   1½ pounds white button mushrooms,
        trimmed and chopped
    2 ounces dried shiitake, porcini, or
       other dried mushrooms, or a
       combination, rinsed
 10–20 parsley sprigs
    2 bay leaves (optional)

1. Put 2 tablespoons of the oil in a large pot over medium-high heat. When it's hot, add the onion and cook, stirring occasionally, until soft, 2 to 3 minutes. Add the carrots and celery and sprinkle with salt and pepper. Cook, stirring frequently, until the vegetables are tender, another 5 to 10 minutes. Remove with a slotted spoon and reserve.

2. Add the remaining 2 tablespoons oil and turn the heat to high. When it's hot, add the white mushrooms; sprinkle with salt. Cook, stirring frequently, until they give up their liquid, it evaporates, and the mushrooms begin to brown, 5 to 10 minutes, adjusting the heat as needed to keep them from burning. Add the dried mushrooms and cooked vegetables and stir to combine.

3. Add 10 cups water along with the parsley and the bay leaves if you're using them. Bring to a boil, then reduce the heat so the stock bubbles vigorously. Cook, stirring once or twice, until the vegetables are very soft and the stock has darkened and reduced slightly, 30 to 45 minutes. Strain through a fine-meshed strainer. Taste and adjust the seasoning before using or cooling and storing.

Kombu Dashi

MAKES: About 2 quarts
TIME: 15 minutes
F **M** **V**

Dashi is the building block of Japanese cuisine, and is often flavored with dried bonito, a tuna-like fish; this variation is just as traditional. I sometimes add ginger to my kombu dashi because it adds a nice secondary flavor, but feel free to omit it. If you have this stock around, I guarantee you'll use it for all sorts of things.

1	piece dried kelp (kombu), 4 to 6 inches long
2 or 3	nickel-sized slices fresh ginger (don't bother to peel)

1. Put the kelp, ginger, and 10 cups water in a saucepan over medium heat. Don't allow the mixture to come to a boil. As soon as it is about to, turn off the heat and remove the kelp. (You can use it as a vegetable at this point; see page 244 for some ideas).

2. Let the ginger sit in the dashi for a couple of minutes as it cools, then strain the dashi through a fine-meshed strainer. Use the dashi immediately or refrigerate for up to 2 days.

NO-COOK DASHI Many Japanese cooks believe this to be a superior version (and it saves you time), but it requires some advance planning: Immerse the dried kelp in 8 cups cold water in a bowl on your way out the door in the morning. It will infuse the water with its flavor in 6 to 8 hours (but can sit for longer if you need). Strain and use as you would cooked dashi.

SINGLE-VEGETABLE SOUPS (OR NEARLY SO)

Soups made from just one or two vegetables have clear flavors that range from intense to subtle. This family of soups is also generally faster than most others, so it's a good introduction to the world of soup making, and can help you take the first steps toward understanding ingredient-driven, variable cooking. When you focus on just one vegetable, it's easy to experiment with substitutions.

The recipes in this section also demonstrate the principle that precooking vegetables in a little oil coaxes maximum flavor from them. Though most of the action happens on the stove, a couple of the soups here highlight the benefits of oven roasting, broiling, or even grilling. A bonus: Single-vegetable soups are almost always delicious served chilled, especially when you add a little cream.

Onion Soup

MAKES: 4 servings
TIME: About 1 hour
M **O**

Here, time transforms one of the world's most common ingredients into a spectacularly satisfying soup. You can make stock in a separate pot while the onions cook, but using water also works well: Add two more bay leaves, a stalk of celery, a whole carrot, and a couple of parsley sprigs if you have them, and simmer the soup for 10 to 15 minutes longer; discard whatever you added just before serving. Many variations follow, so be sure to check 'em out.

    4 tablespoons (½ stick) butter or olive oil
    4 large yellow onions, halved and thinly sliced
       (about 6 cups)
       Leaves of 2 or 3 sprigs fresh thyme or
    1 teaspoon dried thyme
    1 bay leaf
    1 whole head garlic, cut crosswise at the
       bottom to reveal the cloves
       Salt and pepper
    5 cups vegetable stock (pages 97–100)
       or water
    2 tablespoons cognac, Armagnac, or brandy
       (optional)

1. Put the butter in a large pot over medium heat. When it foams, add the onions and cook, stirring occasionally, until they're quite soft and begin to brown. This will take 30 to 45 minutes; don't rush it.

2. Add the thyme, bay leaf, and garlic, sprinkle with salt and pepper, and cook, stirring almost constantly for a minute before adding the stock and the cognac if you're using it.

3. Bring to a boil, then adjust the heat so that bubbles occasionally break the surface, and cook, undisturbed, until the onions fall apart and the broth darkens, 30 to 45 minutes. (You can make the soup in advance up to this point. Cool, cover, and refrigerate for up to 2 days.) Remove the garlic and bay leaf, taste and adjust the seasoning, and serve hot.

CLASSIC ONION SOUP WITH CHEESE CROUTONS
Turn the broiler on high and move the rack about 4 inches from the heat source. Cut 4 large, thick slices of crusty bread, and toast them under the broiler, flip them over, rub each with a clove of garlic, and top each with about ¼ cup grated Parmesan, cheddar, or Gruyère cheese or spread with a thin layer of fresh goat cheese. Return to the broiler until the cheese melts, browns, and bubbles. Divide the hot soup among 4 bowls and float a slice of bread in each.

SMOKY ONION SOUP WITH ALMONDS When the soup is done, combine ½ cup almonds, 2 teaspoons smoked paprika, and ½ teaspoon ground cumin in a blender or food processor and turn the machine on. Slowly and carefully add some of the broth, a little bit at a time, until the mixture is as smooth as you can get it. Stir the mixture back into the soup and serve, garnished with chopped parsley.

CARAMELIZED LEEK SOUP Instead of the onions, use about 2 pounds leeks. Trim so the tender green parts remain; rinse well, even between the leaves, then slice crosswise. (You still want about 6 cups.) Proceed with the main recipe or any of the variations.

Freezing Soups

Almost any soup can be frozen for as long as six months. If you are making a soup to freeze it, you're better off holding some ingredients out until after you thaw and reheat the soup. For example, dairy (or dairylike ingredients like soy milk), should be added after the soup is thawed and reheated. The same goes for rice, pasta, and potatoes, all of which will swell and soften to the point of mushiness during freezing. If you know you're going to be freezing a soup, it also pays to undercook the vegetables slightly so they don't become too mushy on reheating.

Finally: When you pour soup into a container, allow an inch or so of space between the top of the liquid and the seal to allow for expansion. Thaw soups in the refrigerator or microwave or gently on the stovetop.

Cauliflower Soup, Italian Style

MAKES: 4 servings
TIME: 40 minutes
V

This two-step technique is how many people cook vegetables in Italy, and it turns almost any vegetable into a soup—or pasta sauce—in a sec. Garlic, pepper, and oil are the distinguishing characteristics, with bread in some form often in the mix. Try the same method on broccoli or broccoli raab, celery, cabbage, winter or summer squash, or Brussels sprouts. Instead of topping it with croutons, try a grated sharp cheese like Parmesan, pecorino Romano, or ricotta salata, a dollop of fresh cheese like ricotta or goat cheese, crumbled feta, or chopped hard-boiled eggs.

- ⅓ cup olive oil
- 1 onion, chopped
- 1 tablespoon minced garlic
- ½ teaspoon red chile flakes, plus more to taste
- 1 large head cauliflower (about 3 pounds), cored and broken or cut into small florets
  Salt and pepper
- 6 cups vegetable stock (pages 97–100)
- 8 large Croutons (page 678), made with olive oil, or 4 ounces any day-old bread torn into chunks
- ¼ cup chopped fresh parsley or basil for garnish

1. Put about half the oil in a large pot over medium heat. When it's hot, add the onion and cook, stirring occasionally, until it softens and begins to brown, 5 to 10 minutes. Stir in the garlic, chile flakes, cauliflower, and some salt and black pepper and continue to cook, stirring, until the cauliflower glistens, 3 to 5 minutes.

2. Add the stock and stir. Bring to a boil over high heat, then adjust the heat so the mixture simmers. Cook until the cauliflower is tender but not falling apart, 10 to 15 minutes.

3. Taste and adjust the seasoning, then stir in the remaining oil. Divide the croutons among bowls, ladle in the soup, garnish with herbs, and serve.

Potato and Leek Soup

MAKES: 4 servings
TIME: 30 minutes
F M O

Potato-leek soup, made from winter staples, can be either rustic or refined, depending on whether you take the extra step to purée it. Use whatever potato you have handy: the sidebar on page 104 will give you an idea what to expect. You can also make this using sweet potatoes or serve it chilled, chunky style or creamy (see variations below).

- 3 tablespoons olive oil or butter
- 1½ pounds potatoes (any type), peeled and cut into small cubes
- 3 large leeks, white and light green parts only, rinsed well and sliced into thin rings
  Salt and pepper
- 4 cups vegetable stock (pages 97–100) or water

1. Put the oil or butter in a large pot over medium heat. When the oil is hot or the butter foams, add the potatoes and leeks. Sprinkle with salt and pepper and cook, stirring frequently, until they're coated and sizzling, 2 to 3 minutes.

2. Add the stock and cook until the potatoes can be easily pierced with a fork and the leeks are silky, 15 to 20 minutes. (You can make the soup in advance up to this point. Cool, cover, and refrigerate for up to 2 days.) Taste and adjust the seasoning and serve.

CREAMY POTATO (OR SWEET POTATO) AND LEEK SOUP
You decide how creamy: Use an immersion blender to purée the soup in the pot. Or let the soup cool a little, carefully purée it in a blender (working in batches if necessary), and return it to the pot. Stir in ½ to 1 cup

cream, sour cream, Greek-style yogurt, or coconut milk and reheat gently; don't let it boil. Garnish with chopped fresh chives.

5 More Ideas for Potato and Leek Soup

1. Cook about 1 cup shredded carrots or cabbage along with the potatoes and leeks and increase the stock by the same volume to keep it from getting too thick.
2. Finish the soup with a topping of other fresh herbs like parsley, basil, or chervil.
3. Grate a little Parmesan cheese over all.
4. Use a different vegetable—asparagus is good, as are peas—in place of a portion of the potatoes.
5. Use assertive seasonings like soy sauce, fermented black beans, sesame oil, or chile paste to intensify the flavor and take the soup in a completely different direction.

Which Potato, Which Soup?

If you want to thicken a soup, starchy baking potatoes are your best choice (see "Giving Soups More Body," page 125).

If you want distinctive, firm chunks of potato in your soup, stick with one of the waxy types like any small red- or white-skinned potato. These can take longer than other kinds of potatoes to become tender, but when they do the texture is creamier and less mealy.

All-purpose potatoes like Yukon Gold or many thin-skinned white varieties will do a little of each, breaking down enough to thicken the soup a bit but also leaving you something to sink your teeth into. Specialty potatoes, like fingerlings and Peruvian purple, generally fall into this category.

Unpeeled potatoes are fine in soup, though after the potato starts to break down, the skin will slip off. The only exceptions are sweet potatoes and yams, which should always be peeled. They also become tender and dissolve faster than regular potatoes.

Roasted Beet Borscht

MAKES: 4 servings
TIME: About 1½ hours, mostly unattended, plus time to chill if desired
Ⓜ Ⓞ

Roasting the beets concentrates their sweet, earthy flavor and turns the soup a deep purple. No, it's not the way my grandmother made her borscht, but I know she would approve because it tastes so good. She wouldn't have used golden or candy-striped Chioggia beets either —she probably never saw them—but feel free; their sunny colors are awesome. Like her version, this borscht and its variations are good hot or cold.

>   About 2½ pounds beets (any kind), peeled and quartered
> 4 tablespoons olive oil
>   Salt and pepper
> 1 large white onion, chopped
> 1 bunch fresh dill, stems and fronds separated
> 4 hard-cooked eggs (optional)
> 1 pound waxy potatoes, boiled until tender and kept hot for garnish (optional)
>   Fresh lemon juice
>   Sour cream or yogurt for serving (optional)

1. Heat the oven to 375°F. Put the beets in a single layer in a large rimmed baking sheet or roasting pan, drizzle with 2 tablespoons of the oil, and sprinkle with salt and lots of pepper. Toss to distribute the oil. Roast, turning the pieces once or twice with a spatula, until a thin-bladed knife pierces a piece with little resistance, 30 to 40 minutes. (You can prepare the beets up to this point. Cool, cover tightly, and refrigerate for up to 2 days before proceeding.) When cool enough to handle, chop the beets as finely as possible by hand or by pulsing in the food processor.
2. Put the remaining 2 tablespoons oil in a large pot and turn the heat to medium-high. When it's hot, add the onion and cook, stirring occasionally until soft, 2 to 3 minutes. Turn the heat to medium-low and continue

cooking, stirring once in a while, until the onion is golden and very tender, 10 to 15 minutes more.

3. Add the beets and stir. Tie the stems of the dill in a bundle with string and add them along with 6 cups water. Bring the soup to a boil, then reduce the heat so it bubbles gently. Cover and cook, stirring occasionally, until the soup is brightly colored and the beets are starting to melt away, 10 to 15 minutes.

4. Chop the dill fronds. Slice or chop the eggs and potatoes if you're using them. Remove the dill stems from the soup and add lemon juice to taste. Taste and adjust the seasoning if necessary. Serve the borscht topped with the chopped dill and any of the garnishes you like, and pass the sour cream at the table if you're using it.

ROASTED MUSHROOM BORSCHT With a deeper, earthy flavor: Start with 1 pound beets and 2 pounds mushrooms like shiitake, cremini, portobello, button, or a mixture of these. Trim the mushrooms but leave them whole and add them to the beets in the pan in Step 1. When the beets and mushrooms are roasted, chop as directed in Step 1 and proceed to Step 2.

VEGAN ROASTED BEET BORSCHT Skip the eggs and sour cream or yogurt. Instead, garnish the soup with roasted or grilled vegetables, cubed raw or baked firm tofu (page 485) or a dollop of soft silken tofu, or a sprinkle of chopped cashews or pistachios. **V**

BORSCHT CONSOMMÉ An elegant and unusual starter: Replace the water with 6 cups vegetable stock or Mushroom Stock (page 97 or 99) and add a bay leaf. In Step 3 continue to cook the vegetables until the beets become very tender and break apart. Strain; discard the solids or save them for another use (along with the mushrooms if you're making that variation). Return the liquid to the pot and add lemon juice, salt, and pepper to taste. Reheat and serve hot, with or without a spoonful of sour cream, garnished with the dill or some chives.

Tomato Soup

MAKES: 4 servings
TIME: 30 minutes
F **M** **V**

Slowly caramelizing late-summer tomatoes makes fresh tomato soup way more intense. To move things even further, I add a little tomato paste, which provides the depth that even good fresh tomatoes sometimes lack. If there are no good tomatoes around—which is the case about nine months of the year—opt for the Wintertime Tomato Soup on page 107.

2	**tablespoons olive oil**
2	**tablespoons tomato paste**
1	**large onion, sliced**
1	**carrot, diced**
	Salt and pepper
3	**cups peeled, seeded, and chopped tomatoes (canned are fine; include their juice)**
1	**tablespoon chopped fresh thyme or 1 teaspoon dried thyme**
3	**cups vegetable stock (pages 97–100), Tomato Water (page 98), or water, plus more as needed**
1	**teaspoon sugar (optional)**
¼	**cup chopped fresh parsley, basil, or dill for garnish**

1. Put the oil in a large pot over medium heat. When it's hot, add the tomato paste and cook, stirring constantly, until it's fragrant and darkens a little, less than a minute.

2. Add the onion and carrot, sprinkle with salt and pepper, and cook, stirring, until the onion begins to soften, 3 to 5 minutes.

3. Add the tomatoes and thyme and cook, stirring occasionally, until the tomato pieces break up, 10 to 15 minutes. Add the stock, stir, and taste. Adjust the seasoning; if the soup is flat tasting, stir in the sugar. (You can make the soup in advance up to this point. Cool, cover, and refrigerate for up to 2 days.)

If the mixture is too thick, add a little more stock or water. Garnish with the herbs and serve.

PURÉED TOMATO SOUP The stuff of your childhood, or close to it: Increase the tomatoes to 4 cups and reduce the stock to 2 cups. When the tomatoes are cooked in Step 3, use an immersion blender to purée the soup in the pot. Or let the soup cool a little, carefully purée it in a blender (working in batches if necessary), and return it to the pot. Or if you've got a food mill, pass it through that. Reheat to a gentle bubble, and garnish as in the main recipe.

CREAM OF TOMATO SOUP No longer vegan, of course: Substitute butter for olive oil and reduce the stock to 1 cup. Follow the directions for the Puréed Tomato Soup variation. While reheating the puréed soup, add 1 cup cream or half-and-half; be careful not to bring it to a rolling boil.

VEGAN CREAM OF TOMATO SOUP Follow the directions for the Puréed Tomato Soup variation but reduce the stock to 1 cup. While reheating the puréed soup, add 1 cup nondairy milk like almond, hazelnut, oat, or coconut (the reduced-fat kind is fine). Be careful not to bring it to a rolling boil.

SILKY TOFU CREAM OF TOMATO SOUP Follow the directions for the Puréed Tomato Soup variation, but instead of the stock use one 12-ounce package soft silken tofu. After puréeing, reheat the soup gently; don't let it boil. You might need to thin it with a little stock, water, or nondairy milk.

Wintertime Tomato Soup

MAKES: 4 servings
TIME: About 1½ hours, mostly unattended
M V

Yes, this is tomato soup from a can, but it's really, really good. The secret is to use canned and dried tomatoes, a powerful combination—especially after you roast the canned tomatoes, which intensifies their taste and improves their texture. The result makes a perfect base for stew: Try adding cooked potatoes, pasta, beans, or vegetables after the tomatoes have melted into the broth, or try the rice-based variation for something a little heartier.

1 cup lightly packed dried tomatoes (about 2 ounces; preferably not packed in oil)
1 28-ounce can whole peeled tomatoes
¼ cup olive oil
1 tablespoon fresh thyme or 1 teaspoon dried thyme (optional)
1 tablespoon chopped garlic
1 carrot, chopped
1 small red onion, halved and thinly sliced
   Salt and pepper
2 teaspoons sugar
4 cups vegetable stock (pages 97–100) or water
¼ cup chopped fresh parsley for garnish

1. Heat the oven to 375°F. Put the dried tomatoes in a heatproof bowl and cover with 2 cups boiling water. Drain the canned tomatoes, reserving the juice. Halve the tomatoes and put on a rimmed baking sheet. Drizzle with 2 tablespoons of the oil and sprinkle with the thyme if you're using it. Roast, turning once or twice with a spatula, until the tomatoes are dry and lightly browned, 25 to 35 minutes.

2. When the tomatoes are roasted, drain the dried tomatoes, reserving the soaking liquid. Pour a little of the soaking liquid onto the baking sheet and scrape up the browned bits from the bottom of the pan with a spatula, breaking up the roasted tomatoes at the same time. Roughly chop the dried tomatoes.

3. Put the remaining oil in a large pot over medium-high heat. When it's hot, add the garlic and cook just until it begins to color, a minute or so. Add the carrot and onion and cook until they start to release their liquid, 1 to 2 minutes more. Sprinkle with salt and pepper, then add the sugar and stir until it melts, just a few seconds.

4. Add the reserved liquids from the canned and dried tomatoes and continue stirring until the liquid mostly evaporates and darkens, 5 to 10 minutes. Stir in the stock, the contents of the roasting pan, and the dried tomatoes. Turn the heat to high and bring the soup to a boil, then lower the heat so it bubbles gently. Cover and cook until the vegetables are very tender, about 30 minutes. Garnish with the parsley and serve.

WINTERTIME TOMATO AND RICE SOUP Add 1 cup short-grain rice, like Arborio, to the pan in Step 4, just after the tomato liquids have cooked. Increase the stock to 6 cups.

CREAMY WINTERTIME TOMATO SOUP Use an immersion blender to purée the finished soup in the pot. Or let the soup cool a little, carefully purée it in a blender (working in batches if necessary), and return it to the pot. Stir in 1 cup heavy cream, sour cream, or crème fraîche and reheat the soup, stirring frequently, without bringing it to a boil.

Mushroom Stew

MAKES: 4 servings
TIME: 45 minutes
◎

I don't often use flour to thicken soups, because there are more flavorful (and nutritious) ways to give them body (see page 125). But there are exceptions, like Corn Chowder (page 121) and this Louisiana-inspired mushroom stew. In both cases the flour is cooked, here in a moderately toasted roux, which gives it a lovely nuttiness.

¼	**cup olive oil or 4 tablespoons butter (½ stick)**
¼	**cup flour**
1½	**pounds shiitake, portobello, cremini, or white button mushrooms or a mixture, trimmed and sliced**
	Salt and pepper
1	**onion, chopped**

2	**celery stalks, chopped**
1	**green bell pepper, cored, seeded, and chopped**
2 or 3	**sprigs fresh thyme or 1 teaspoon dried thyme**
6	**cups Mushroom Stock (page 99), vegetable stock (pages 97–100), or water**
¼	**cup dry sherry for garnish (optional)**

1. Put the oil and flour in a large pot over medium heat. As the mixture warms, stir almost constantly with a wooden spoon or a whisk. The roux should bubble along at first, then start to take on a golden color. If it is smoking or darkening too fast, lower the heat a little. Continue cooking and stirring until the roux turns the color of coffee with cream, 10 to 20 minutes.
2. Turn the heat up to medium-high and add the mushrooms. Sprinkle with salt and pepper. Cook, stirring constantly, until they are coated in the roux and start to release their liquid. Turn the heat down to medium-low and cook, stirring occasionally, until the mushrooms begin to brown, 5 to 8 minutes. Stir in the onion, celery, bell pepper, and thyme. Cook, stirring occasionally, until the vegetables are soft, 3 to 5 minutes.
3. Stir in the stock, turn the heat up to medium-high, and bring to a boil. Lower the heat so the stew bubbles gently but steadily. Cover and cook, stirring occasionally, until the stew has thickened and the vegetables are very tender, 5 to 10 minutes. Fish out the sprigs of thyme if you used them. Taste and adjust the seasoning. Serve, drizzling each bowl with a tablespoon of sherry, if you'd like.

MUSHROOM STEW WITH GREEN BEANS Trim ½ pound green beans and cut them into 1-inch pieces. In Step 3, right after you add the stock, stir in the beans.

EVEN RICHER MUSHROOM STEW Reduce the stock to 5 cups. Add 1 cup cream at the very end. Do not boil after the cream is added.

VEGAN MUSHROOM STEW Use olive oil instead of butter; if you wish to make it richer, substitute 1 cup oat or nut milk for 1 cup of the stock. ⓥ

MIXED VEGETABLE SOUPS

I've built many choices into the following recipes to give you the confidence (and permission, if you need it) to use whatever vegetables you have handy. In many ways, making substitutions when several ingredients are at play is less risky than it is with single-vegetable soups.

You start with a flavorful base and add the best produce you have on hand. Combining two or more vegetables creates a multidimensional broth that may not be quite the same the next time you make it—and that's okay. Make a few of these and you'll get a feel for how mixed vegetable soups are commonly treated in different cuisines and how simple it is to go from one continent to the next just by adjusting seasonings and ingredients.

Minestrone

MAKES: 4 servings
TIME: 45 to 60 minutes
Ⓜ Ⓥ

I've probably made minestrone once a month for years, never the same way twice. Tomatoes of some kind are the only constant; everything else is up for grabs. To facilitate this use-what-you-have approach, the ingredient list groups the vegetable options as "hard" and "soft" and gives a few suggestions, but soon you'll be making this without a recipe. Trust me.

  ¼ cup olive oil, plus more for drizzling
  1 onion, chopped
  1 carrot or parsnip, chopped
  1 celery stalk, chopped
     Salt and pepper
     About 1½ cups chopped hard vegetables like potatoes, winter squash, rutabaga, or turnips, peeled if necessary, in smaller-than-½-inch dice
  2 tablespoons chopped garlic
  1 cup chopped tomatoes (canned are fine; include the juice)

  6 cups any vegetable stock (pages 97–100) or water
     About 1½ cups soft vegetables like green beans, cut into pieces; drained cooked, canned, or frozen shell beans; diced zucchini or summer squash; or chopped fennel bulb
  ½ pound dark, leafy greens like kale, collards, or spinach, stems cut out and discarded, leaves cut across into thin ribbons

1. Put the oil in a large pot over medium heat. When it's hot, add the onion, carrot, and celery. Sprinkle with salt and pepper and cook, stirring, until the vegetables begin to soften, 3 to 5 minutes.

2. Add the hard vegetables and garlic and cook, stirring, for a minute or 2 before adding the tomatoes. Raise the heat so the mixture sizzles. Continue stirring until the tomatoes darken and start to become dry. Add the stock, bring to a boil, and adjust the heat so the soup bubbles gently. Cook, stirring every now and then, until the hard vegetables are fairly soft and the tomatoes have broken up, 10 to 15 minutes. (You can make the soup in advance up to this point. Cool, cover, refrigerate for up to 2 days, and reheat before proceeding.)

3. Add the soft vegetables and adjust the heat so the mixture bubbles enthusiastically. Let them have a 2-minute head start before adding the greens. Cook, still stirring occasionally until all the vegetables are quite tender, a final 10 to 15 minutes. Taste and adjust the seasoning, and serve, passing some olive oil at the table for drizzling.

PISTOU Traditionally you'd use pesto with a lot of garlic here: Stir in ½ cup or more Pesto or any of its variations (page 634).

PASTA E FAGIOLI Use whatever vegetables you like in the main recipe but reduce the quantities by about half. In Step 3 add a total of 2 cups drained cooked, canned, or frozen beans—kidney, white, borlotti, chickpeas, cannellini, lima, or a mixture—with the soft vegetables. When it's time for the greens to go in the pot, add no more than 1 cup small pasta (like tubetti) or larger pasta broken into bits along with another cup water. Continue to cook and stir as in the main recipe until the vegetables are soft and the pasta is tender but not mushy, 5 to 10 minutes.

HERBED MINESTRONE Use what you have on hand, and to taste: For example, in Step 1, add the leaves from a fresh sprig of oregano, marjoram, or rosemary. In Step 3, finish with a few more leaves or 1 cup chopped fresh basil.

PARMESAN MINESTRONE If you have the hard bits from a piece of Parmesan in the refrigerator or freezer, cut it—rind and all—into small pieces and add it along with the first batch of vegetables in Step 2. It'll become chewy during cooking and is not only edible but delicious. Then grate some more Parmesan cheese for serving.

Smoky Eggplant and Zucchini Soup

MAKES: 4 servings
TIME: 1½ hours, mostly unattended
M V

In Spain, a hearty, chunky soup similar to minestrone is likely to begin with roasting summertime Mediterranean vegetables, which yields a more robust flavor (and takes a little more time). Extra smokiness comes from a hit of pimentón—smoked paprika.

1   large eggplant, peeled
2   zucchini or summer squash
2   red bell peppers
1   large onion, chopped
1   head garlic, separated into cloves and peeled
6   tablespoons olive oil
    Salt and pepper
2   large tomatoes, chopped, or 1 15-ounce can
    diced tomatoes
1   tablespoon smoked paprika
1   teaspoon ground cumin

6   cups vegetable stock (pages 97–100)
    or water
¼   cup chopped fresh parsley for garnish

1. Heat the oven to 425°F. Cut the eggplant, zucchini, and bell pepper into 1- to 2-inch chunks, all roughly the same size. Put the vegetables on two rimmed baking sheets or in one large roasting pan. Scatter the onion and garlic on top, drizzle with 4 tablespoons of the olive oil, sprinkle with salt and pepper, and toss to coat all the vegetables. Roast, stirring occasionally, until the vegetables are soft and well browned, 45 to 60 minutes.

2. Meanwhile, put the remaining 2 tablespoons oil in a large pot over medium-high heat. When it's hot, add the tomatoes and cook, stirring constantly, until they start to sizzle and release some of their juices. Lower the heat so the mixture sizzles gently and cook, stirring occasionally, until the tomatoes look jammy, 15 to 20 minutes. Sprinkle with the paprika and cumin and stir until fragrant. Turn off the heat until the roasted vegetables are ready.

3. Add the roasted vegetables to the tomatoes. Put the pan (or if using two pans, work with one at a time) over two burners set on medium-high, and add 1 cup of the stock. Once the liquid starts bubbling, scrape the bottom of the pan to loosen any browned bits. Carefully pour the mixture into the pot with the tomatoes along with the remaining stock.

4. Bring the soup to a boil, then lower the heat so it bubbles gently but steadily. Cook, stirring occasionally, until the vegetables are very soft and the soup comes together, 5 to 10 minutes. (You can make the soup in advance up to this point. Cool, cover, refrigerate for up to 2 days.) Taste and adjust the seasoning, and serve, garnished with the parsley.

SMOKY ROOT VEGETABLE SOUP Instead of the eggplant, zucchini, and bell pepper, use a total of 2 pounds mixed root vegetables like carrot, parsnip, celery root, rutabaga, turnip, and/or sweet potato or other potatoes. Use canned tomatoes instead of fresh. The vegetables will take at least 1 hour to roast.

SMOKY WINTER SQUASH SOUP Pumpkin, butternut, kabocha—all good choices: Figure about 2½ pounds before peeling, trimming, and seeding. Substitute canned tomatoes for the fresh. Squash will take about 1 hour to roast.

Tortilla Soup

MAKES: 4 servings
TIME: About 1 hour
Ⓜ Ⓥ

Tortillas and lots of vegetables—some charred, some not—together in one pot with a liberal dose of Southwest seasonings: It's a little like a taco party in a bowl. There are three cooking techniques in this recipe, but I've streamlined them for efficiency. For the best texture, let the soup sit for five minutes or so after you add the crisp tortillas—that's just long enough for everyone to come to the table and add garnishes from the list on page 112.

	Good-quality vegetable oil for frying
8	corn tortillas (stale are fine), cut into ½-inch strips
	Salt and pepper
1	large onion, halved and sliced
1	poblano chile, seeded and sliced
1	carrot, sliced
3	tablespoons olive oil
2	tablespoons minced garlic
1	tablespoon chili powder
1	teaspoon ground cumin
1	28-ounce can whole tomatoes or 1½ pounds ripe fresh tomatoes, chopped
1	tablespoon chopped fresh oregano or epazote or 1 teaspoon dried
4	cups vegetable stock (pages 97–100) or water
1	cup corn kernels (frozen are fine)
2	limes, cut into wedges, for serving
	Additional toppings as you like (see the list that follows)

1. Turn on the broiler to high and move the rack about 4 inches from the heat source. Put about ½ inch of vegetable oil in a large skillet over medium-high heat. When it's hot (a tortilla strip should sizzle immediately but not turn brown), fry the tortilla strips in single-layer batches, stirring and turning them with a spatula until golden brown and crisp, 2 to 4 minutes per batch. Transfer to paper towels to drain, sprinkle with salt, and repeat until the tortillas are done. (You can prepare the tortillas up to a day ahead; seal in an airtight container and store at room temperature.)

2. Put the onion, poblano, and carrot in a single layer on a rimmed baking sheet, drizzle with 1 tablespoon of the olive oil, sprinkle with salt and pepper, and toss to coat. Spread the vegetables in a single layer again and broil, stirring and turning once or twice with a spatula, until they're lightly charred in places, 5 to 8 minutes total.

3. Put the remaining 2 tablespoons olive oil in a large pot over medium-high heat. When it's hot, add the garlic

Frozen Vegetables in Soup

If you keep frozen vegetables handy, you have no excuses not to make soup, especially the recipes in this section, since you can easily substitute this for that. In cases where I don't make specific suggestions, use your judgment.

I've defended frozen vegetables elsewhere (page 148), but I will add that frozen vegetables I would rarely consider substituting for fresh in other dishes (like broccoli or cauliflower) take well to slow cooking and simmering. Others that are always good replacements, like corn and peas, are a super convenience.

There are two ways to use frozen vegetables in soup, both good: If you're in a hurry, just pour them into the pot straight from the bag. This will cool down your soup a bit, so figure you might need to increase the cooking time. The second method is to start the vegetables in hot fat. Gently browning them as they thaw will release their natural flavors and improve their texture. Then build in the liquid and finish the soup.

and stir constantly until it is just starting to color, about 1 minute. Add the chili powder and cumin and a sprinkle of salt and pepper and keep stirring until they become fragrant. Add the tomatoes, crushing them in the pan with the back of a spoon; then add the charred vegetables, the oregano, and stock and bring to a boil. Reduce the heat so the soup bubbles gently but steadily. Cover and cook, stirring occasionally, until the tomatoes melt into the broth and the vegetables are quite soft, 10 to 15 minutes. (You may make the soup in advance up to this point. Cool, cover, refrigerate for up to 2 days, and gently reheat before proceeding.)

4. Stir in the corn and return the soup to a boil. Taste and adjust the seasonings. Add the tortilla strips (but don't stir) and remove from the heat. Serve within 10 minutes, passing the limes and whatever toppings you'd like at the table.

7 Garnishes for Tortilla Soup

1. 1 cup shredded lettuce or cabbage

2. 1 cup chopped fresh cilantro

3. 1 ripe avocado, pitted, peeled, and sliced

4. Several sliced radishes or 1 cup chopped jícama

5. 1 cup crumbled queso fresco or grated Monterey Jack cheese

6. ½ cup Mexican *crema* or sour cream

7. Salsa and/or hot sauce

Hot and Sour Soup

MAKES: 4 servings
TIME: 40 minutes
V

This is the only soup in which I use cornstarch, because you need it to duplicate the silky texture we're used to from the restaurant version; of course you can skip it. Cooking some of the mushrooms until they're almost completely dry results in two completely different textures, adding some pleasant surprises in every bite. Note that the heat in this comes from ground black (or white) pepper, but you can add some chile flakes too, if you like.

3 tablespoons good-quality vegetable oil
1 pound white button or cremini mushrooms, sliced
½ pound shiitake mushrooms, stemmed, caps sliced
Salt and lots of black or white pepper
1 tablespoon minced garlic
1 tablespoon minced fresh ginger
6 cups vegetable stock (pages 97–100) or water
2 celery stalks, chopped
2 cups chopped green cabbage
¼ cup rice vinegar, or more to taste
1 tablespoon sesame oil
1 tablespoon soy sauce, or more to taste
3 tablespoons cornstarch
1 pound extra-firm tofu, cut into ½-inch cubes
½ cup chopped scallions for garnish
¼ cup chopped fresh cilantro for garnish

1. Put 2 tablespoons of the vegetable oil in a large pot over medium heat. When it's hot, add all the mushrooms, sprinkle with salt and a lot of pepper, and give them a quick stir. Cover, turn the heat down to medium-low, and cook, undisturbed, until you see steam escape, 3 to 5 minutes. Uncover and cook, undisturbed, until the liquid boils off, 3 to 5 minutes. Transfer half the mushrooms to a plate.

2. Raise the heat so the remaining mushrooms sizzle. Cook, stirring occasionally, until they're dry, shrunken, and as crisp as you like them, another 3 to 5 minutes. Transfer the crisp mushrooms to the plate. Return the pot to the heat and add the remaining tablespoon vegetable oil along with the garlic and ginger. Cook, stirring frequently, until they're soft and fragrant, 1 to 3 minutes. Raise the heat to high and stir.

3. Add the stock, celery, and cabbage and bring the soup to a boil, then lower the heat so the soup bubbles steadily. Cook, stirring once in a while, until the cabbage and celery soften and the broth is darkened a bit, 3 to 5 minutes.

4. Whisk together the vinegar, sesame oil, 1 tablespoon soy sauce, ¼ cup water, and the cornstarch to make a smooth slurry. Stir the cornstarch mixture into the soup along with the mushrooms and cook, stirring, until it just begins to thicken, 1 to 2 minutes. Add the tofu. Taste and adjust the seasoning with salt, lots of pepper, soy sauce, and/or vinegar. Garnish with the scallions and cilantro and serve.

HOT AND SOUR EGG DROP SOUP Beat 2 eggs with a little salt in a small bowl. After you add the cornstarch mixture in Step 4, pour the eggs into the soup slowly, whisking all the while, until they form nearly translucent ribbons. Remove from the heat right away, garnish, and serve.

Green Gumbo

MAKES: 4 servings
TIME: About 1 hour
M V

The inspiration here is *gumbo z'herbes* (or *gumbo vert*), a Creole stew frequently served for meatless meals during Lent. If you want to follow the tradition strictly, include a mixture of seven different types of greens for good luck; but I mean really. Using brown rice flour for the roux keeps this gluten-free, but if you don't have any and gluten isn't a problem, whole wheat or all-purpose flour is fine.

- ⅓ cup olive oil
- ⅓ cup brown rice flour
- 1 onion, chopped
- 1 green bell pepper, cored, seeded, and chopped
- 2 celery stalks, chopped
- 2 tablespoons minced garlic
   Salt and pepper
- 6 cups vegetable stock (pages 97–100) or water
- 1 tablespoon fresh thyme leaves or 1 teaspoon dried thyme
- 1 tablespoon chopped fresh oregano or 1 teaspoon dried oregano
- 2 bay leaves
- 1½ pounds spinach, trimmed of thick stems and chopped
- 2 zucchini, chopped
   Cayenne

- 2 cups cooked brown long-grain rice for serving (optional)
   Chopped fresh parsley for garnish

1. Put the oil in a large pot over medium-low heat. When it's hot, add the flour and cook, stirring almost constantly, until the roux darkens to the color of hot chocolate and becomes fragrant, 10 to 15 minutes. Adjust the heat as necessary to keep the mixture from burning.
2. Add the onion, bell pepper, celery, and garlic and raise the heat to medium. Sprinkle with salt and pepper and cook, stirring frequently, until the vegetables have softened, 5 to 10 minutes.
3. Add the stock, thyme, oregano, bay leaves, spinach, zucchini, and cayenne to taste. Bring to a boil, then reduce the heat so the soup bubbles gently but steadily. Cook until the vegetables are very tender, 10 to 20 minutes. (You may make the soup in advance up to this point. Cool, cover, refrigerate for up to 2 days, and reheat before proceeding.) Remove the bay leaves. Taste and adjust the seasoning. Serve ladled over a scoop of rice, if you'd like. Garnish with the parsley.

RED GUMBO Call this a "Creole curry"—completely untraditional but delicious and probably also good luck: Substitute chickpea flour for the rice flour and replace 2 cups of the stock with one 28-ounce can tomato purée. Instead of the spinach, use chard. Instead of the zucchini, use 3 sliced carrots. When the roux is ready in Step 1, add 2 teaspoons smoked paprika and stir until fragrant before proceeding.

Korean-Style Vegetable Soup

MAKES: 4 servings
TIME: 40 minutes
V

One of the simplest and fastest of mixed vegetable soups, but flavorwise the equal of anything, thanks to the intensity of sesame oil and seeds, soy sauce, and plenty of garlic. The fresh red chiles called for here

Korean-Style Vegetable
Soup (page 113)

—sold at all Korean and many other Asian markets—are not super-fiery, but they will add some heat as well as substance. If you can't find them, just add a couple of dried red chiles along with the garlic.

- 2 tablespoons good-quality vegetable oil
- 1 tablespoon sesame oil, plus more for drizzling
- 2 tablespoons minced garlic
- 4 fresh long Korean red chiles, seeded and chopped
- 1 carrot, chopped
- 1 celery stalk, chopped
- 1 cup diced peeled daikon radish or white turnip
- 2 cups chopped green cabbage
  Salt and pepper
- 6 cups vegetable stock (pages 97–100) or water
- 2 tablespoons soy sauce, plus more to taste
- ½ cup chopped scallions for garnish
- 1 tablespoon sesame seeds, toasted (see page 299), for garnish

1. Put the vegetable and sesame oils in a large pot over medium heat. When they're hot, add the garlic. As soon as it begins to sizzle, add the chiles, carrot, celery, daikon, and cabbage; sprinkle lightly with salt and pepper. Cook, stirring occasionally, until the vegetables begin to soften, 3 to 5 minutes. Add the stock and soy sauce and bring to a boil.

2. Adjust the heat so the soup bubbles gently. Cook until all the vegetables are as crisp or tender as you like, anywhere from 10 to 30 minutes. Taste and adjust the seasoning, adding more soy sauce if you'd like. Sprinkle with the scallions and sesame seeds, drizzle with a little sesame oil, and serve.

Peanutty Vegetable Soup

MAKES: 4 servings
TIME: About 45 minutes
Ⓜ Ⓥ

This soup is based on the colorful, chunky peanut ("groundnut") dishes of Senegal. It's filled with vegetables, and a bowlful topped with a scoop of simply cooked millet or almost any other grain easily makes a meal. If you'd prefer something creamy, try the variation.

- ¾ cup roasted peanuts
- 2 tablespoons good-quality vegetable oil
- 1 red onion, halved and thinly sliced
- 1 tablespoon minced fresh ginger
- 1 tablespoon minced garlic
  Pinch cayenne, or more or less to taste
  Salt and pepper
- 6 cups vegetable stock (pages 97–100) or water
  About 1 pound sweet potatoes or yams, peeled and cut into thick slices
- 1 pound plum tomatoes, halved, or 1 28-ounce can whole tomatoes (drain and reserve the liquid for another use)
- 1 pound collards or kale, stems cut out and discarded, leaves cut across into wide ribbons
- ¼ cup chunky peanut butter

1. Use the flat side of a wide knife or cleaver, or use a food processor, to break the peanuts into large pieces.
2. Put the oil in a large pot over medium heat. When it's hot, add the onion, ginger, and garlic and cook, stirring occasionally, until the vegetables are soft, 3 to 5 minutes. Add ½ cup of the peanuts and the cayenne, sprinkle with salt and pepper, and stir for a minute. Add the stock, sweet potatoes, and tomatoes. Bring to a boil, then lower the heat so the soup bubbles gently but steadily. Cover and cook, stirring occasionally, until the potatoes are just tender and the tomatoes break down, 8 to 12 minutes.
3. Stir in the collards and peanut butter. Cover and cook until the collards are tender, 3 to 5 minutes. Taste and adjust the seasoning. Garnish with the remaining peanuts and serve.

CREAMY PEANUTTY VEGETABLE SOUP Like velvet: Omit the collards or kale. In Step 3, along with the peanut butter, stir in 1 cup coconut milk. Use an immersion blender to purée the soup in the pot. Or let the soup cool a little, carefully purée it in a blender (working in batches if necessary), and return it to the pot. Reheat to a gentle bubble without boiling, taste and adjust the seasoning, and garnish with the remaining peanuts.

CREAMY SOUPS

Many people think that for every bowl of smooth, creamy soup on the table there's a worn-out cook in the kitchen—cream soups are so impressive, they must be difficult, right?

To the contrary. While it's true that puréeing adds an extra step, this elegant family of soups is often even better when made in advance, so they're perfect for entertaining. Since creaminess often comes from a simple addition after the soup is cooked, finishing them at the last minute is no big deal.

There are vegan and light options here, too. Vegans will obviously want to use some kind of vegetable oil instead of the butter. But before you reach for the soy milk, check out all of your options in "Creaminess Without Dairy" on page 120.

One more note: Always be careful puréeing hot soup. It's important to let it cool down a bit before putting it in a blender, and to blend it in small batches so it doesn't blow the lid off the blender container (I could tell you a story about blueberry soup on my ceiling if you like). Or, use an immersion blender right in the pot.

Cream of Spinach Soup

MAKES: 4 servings
TIME: About 30 minutes
F M O

This could be called "cream of anything soup" but since spinach is so ubiquitous—and is especially good with cream—consider this a master recipe (and note the variations). Here, you'll learn the simplest technique for smooth and creamy soups that aren't overly thick. (If that's more what you're after, see the sidebar on page 125, or the Mushroom Stew on page 108.) All of these versions are delicious served chilled.

2   **tablespoons butter or olive oil**
1   **onion, chopped**
1   **pound spinach, trimmed of thick stems**
2   **cups vegetable stock (pages 97–100) or water**
2   **cups cream, half-and-half, whole milk, or nondairy milk**
    Salt and pepper

1. Put the butter or oil in a large pot over medium heat. When the butter foams or the oil is hot, add the onion and cook, stirring, until it softens, 3 to 5 minutes.

2. Add the spinach and cook, stirring, until it's coated and beginning to wilt. Add the stock, bring to a boil, then quickly lower the heat to a bubble. Cover and cook, stirring once or twice, until the spinach is tender but still brightly colored, just a minute or 2.

3. Use an immersion blender to purée the soup in the pot. Or let the soup cool a little, carefully purée it in a blender (working in batches if necessary), and return it to the pot. (You can make the soup in advance up to this point. Cool, cover, refrigerate for up to 2 days, and reheat before proceeding.) Stir in the cream and let heat up, stirring frequently, without bringing the soup to a boil. Taste, adjust the seasoning, and serve.

CREAM OF OTHER GREENS SOUP Almost anything you choose will be more assertive than spinach: Instead of the spinach use watercress (my favorite), arugula, kale, escarole, sorrel, or other greens. You may have to increase the cooking time in Step 2 by several minutes.

CREAM OF CELERY SOUP Instead of spinach, chop 1 pound celery and cook it with the onion in Step 1 until thoroughly softened, about 10 minutes. After bringing the stock to a boil in Step 2, let it simmer for 20 minutes before puréeing.

CREAM OF BROCCOLI OR CAULIFLOWER SOUP Substitute 1½ pounds broccoli, florets separated and stems chopped, or 1 head cauliflower, hardest part of the core discarded and everything chopped, for the spinach. Add

it to the pot along with the stock and simmer until very tender, 15 to 20 minutes.

LESS CREAMY CREAM OF SPINACH SOUP If you'd like a little less richness in your "cream of" soup, you can play with the ratio of stock to cream, going with 3 cups stock and 1 cup cream or even 3½ cups stock and ½ cup cream just to add a touch of creaminess at the end. You can also substitute wine for some of the stock; I would keep it to no more than 1 cup.

CHEESY CREAM OF SPINACH SOUP After adding the cream, you can also gently stir in up to 1 cup grated cheese; Parmesan and cheddar are traditional and tasty choices.

Carrot-Coconut Soup

MAKES: 4 servings
TIME: 40 minutes
Ⓜ Ⓥ

Creamy soups don't have to originate in Europe or the United States. This one is based on coconut milk and features Southeast Asian flavors, including a little heat.

 2 tablespoons good-quality vegetable oil
 4 scallions, white and green parts separated and chopped
 3 stalks lemongrass, trimmed, bruised, and cut into 2-inch lengths
 2 tablespoons chopped fresh ginger
 1 tablespoon chopped garlic
 1 or more small fresh hot chiles (like Thai or jalapeño), chopped
    About 1 pound carrots, chopped
    Salt
 4 cups coconut milk (to make your own, see page 304) or 2 14-ounce cans plus a little water
 2 limes: 1 zested and juiced, 1 quartered for serving
 1 teaspoon sugar (optional)
 ¼ cup chopped fresh cilantro for garnish

1. Put the oil in a large pot over medium heat. When it's hot, add the white parts of the scallions along with the lemongrass, ginger, garlic, and chiles. Cook, stirring and turning occasionally with a spatula, until the garlic is golden and the scallions and chiles begin to soften, 3 to 5 minutes.

2. Add the carrots and a large pinch of salt and stir to combine. Add the coconut milk, lime zest and juice, and 2 cups water. Bring the mixture to a boil, then lower the heat so it bubbles gently but steadily. Cook, stirring occasionally, until the carrots are very tender, 10 to 15 minutes.

3. Remove the pieces of lemongrass, then use an immersion blender to purée the soup in the pot. Or let the soup cool a little, carefully purée it in a blender (working in batches if necessary), and return it to the pot. (You can make the soup in advance up to this

10 Ways to Turn Soup into a Meal

If you cook even a couple of times a week, you probably have one or more of these tucked away in the fridge right now. Add up to a cup of any of the following foods, alone or in combination, and your soup becomes far more substantial:

1. Any plain-cooked rice or grain (pages 367 to 368 or 398)

2. Any plain-cooked beans (page 435)

3. Tofu Croutons (page 497)

4. Fried Tofu (preferably cut into cubes, page 487)

5. Baked Tofu (preferably cut into cubes, page 485)

6. Slices of any seitan (pages 508 to 512)

7. Crunchy Crumbled Tempeh (page 512)

8. Any of the burgers (page 502 to 508), crumbled

9. Grated or crumbled cheese (if you want it to melt, put it in the bowl before serving)

10. Torn whole grain bread (a good use for stale loaves)

point. Cool, cover, and refrigerate for up to 2 days.) Reheat the soup until it's hot without letting it come to a boil. Taste and adjust the seasoning, adding the sugar if you think the tanginess and heat need balancing. Garnish with cilantro and green parts of the scallions, and serve with lime wedges.

CURRIED CARROT-COCONUT SOUP This seasoning turns the soup from light and bright to deep and haunting, so I like to play that up with hefty garnishes: When the aromatics are ready in Step 1, add 2 tablespoons sweet or hot curry powder. Cook, stirring, until it darkens and becomes fragrant, no more than a minute. Serve the soup topped with toasted coconut and chopped pistachios along with the other garnishes.

Creaminess Without Dairy

Soups can be made creamy without cream, of course: Just use any of the nondairy "milks" discussed on page 15. Soy, almond, and coconut have the most pronounced flavor; rice and oat milks are more neutral, and more watery. Nut milks taste how you think they would. And soft silken tofu will make the soup thicker without a pronounced beany flavor.

Like cow's milk, nondairy milks tend to separate if boiled. That means vegan milks work best in the company of thoroughly cooked potatoes or beans, and really shine in puréed soups, where there are enough other solids to help control the separation.

Because cream is mostly fat, and vegetable-based milks—and dairy milk and yogurt—are relatively lean, it's nearly impossible to duplicate the same mild, silky texture you get from adding cream to a soup. It helps to incorporate an additional tablespoon or 2 of oil into the recipe to enrich it; this is best done either at the very beginning, while cooking the aromatics; during puréeing (if the soup is puréed); or by passing a full-flavored oil like olive or sesame at the table, as a last-minute drizzle.

Pumpkin (or Winter Squash) Soup

MAKES: 4 to 6 servings
TIME: About 1 hour, mostly unattended
Ⓜ Ⓞ

All of the other members of the hard-skinned squash family (see page 263), from the most common (butternut squash and pumpkin) to the most esoteric (look around: they're everywhere), are great. All of them (except maybe the oversized pumpkins used for jack-o-lanterns, which are not bred for eating, really) deliver incredibly smooth texture when puréed, with or without cream. And since winter squashes are easy to grow and the vines are prolific, this is a soup that's popular almost everywhere, as you'll see from the variations.

3 tablespoons olive oil or butter
1 onion, chopped
3 pounds sugar pumpkin or any winter squash like butternut or kabocha, peeled, seeded, and cut into 2-inch cubes
1 tablespoon chopped fresh sage or rosemary
Salt and pepper
5 cups vegetable stock (pages 97–100) or water
1 cup cream or nondairy milk

1. Put the oil in a large pot over medium heat. When it's hot, add the onion and cook, stirring occasionally, until it begins to soften, 2 to 3 minutes. Add the pumpkin and sage, sprinkle with salt and pepper, and cook until fragrant, another minute or so.
2. Add the stock and bring to a boil, then lower the heat so the soup bubbles gently but steadily. Cover and cook, stirring occasionally, until the pumpkin starts to fall apart, 20 to 30 minutes.
3. Use an immersion blender to purée the soup in the pot. Or let the soup cool a little, carefully purée it in a blender (working in batches if necessary), and return it to the pot. (You can prepare the soup in advance up to this point. Cool, cover, and refrigerate for up to 2 days. Add the cream and serve cold or proceed with the recipe.)

4. Add the cream and gently heat the soup without letting it boil. Taste and adjust the seasoning. Garnish with an extra grinding of pepper if you'd like, and serve.

PUMPKIN SOUP WITH CHIPOTLE A little bit of smoky heat: In Step 1, add 1 tablespoon minced garlic to the onion. When you add the stock in Step 2, stir in 1 or 2 canned chipotle chiles, chopped with a little of their adobo (be careful, these can be hot). Garnish with chopped fresh cilantro and toasted pumpkin seeds (see page 299).

INDIAN-STYLE PUMPKIN SOUP Omit the sage or rosemary and use good-quality vegetable oil or butter instead of olive oil. In Step 1, along with the onion, cook 1 tablespoon minced garlic, 1 tablespoon minced fresh ginger, and 1 tablespoon curry powder. Substitute coconut milk for the cream. If you like, garnish with ¼ cup chopped fresh mint.

Corn Chowder

MAKES: 4 servings
TIME: About 1 hour

This is a creamy, roux-thickened chowder showcasing fresh sweet corn. If you like your chowder even richer, substitute cream for some or all of the milk. And if you have a hankering for this when summer is long gone, use frozen corn, skip Step 1, and use 3 cups vegetable stock (pages 97–100).

You can make this even heartier by adding potato: Peel and cut 1 large baking potato into ½-inch dice. Add it to the chowder in Step 3 five to ten minutes before adding the corn.

>   Kernels from 8 ears corn (about 4 cups;
>   see page 198), cobs reserved
>   Salt and pepper
> 4   tablespoons (½ stick) butter
> 1   cup chopped scallions
> ¼   cup flour

> 4   cups milk
> 2   tablespoons chopped fresh parsley for garnish

1. Put the corncobs and 3 cups water in a large pot over medium-high heat. Sprinkle with salt and pepper. (The cobs won't be submerged but that's fine.) Bring to a boil, then lower the heat so the water bubbles gently. Cover and cook, checking occasionally, until the water is opaque and the cobs soften, 25 to 30 minutes. Discard the cobs and transfer the broth to a bowl.
2. Return the pot to medium-high heat (no need to wipe it out) and add the butter. When the butter foams, add the scallions and cook, stirring occasionally, until they're soft, about 1 minute. Turn the heat down to medium and stir in the flour. Cook, stirring constantly with a whisk or a wooden spoon, until the mixture starts to turn golden and the flour no longer smells raw, 5 to 10 minutes. Add the milk and the reserved broth and turn the heat up to medium-high. Stir or whisk constantly until the flour is dissolved and the soup starts to thicken, 2 to 3 minutes.
3. Add the corn kernels and bring to a boil, then lower the heat so the soup bubbles gently. Cook, stirring occasionally, until the corn is just tender and the soup has thickened even more, 5 to 10 minutes. Taste, adjust the seasoning, garnish with parsley, and serve.

ROASTED CORN CHOWDER Heat the oven to 400°F. Put the corn kernels on a rimmed baking sheet, drizzle with 2 tablespoons olive oil, sprinkle with salt and pepper, and spread out evenly. Roast the corn, stirring and turning frequently with a spatula, until the kernels start to brown, 15 to 25 minutes. Follow the recipe from the beginning, using the roasted kernels and reducing the cooking time in Step 3 to 3 to 5 minutes.

CHEESY CORN CHOWDER In Step 3, along with the corn, add ½ cup grated cheese, like Parmesan, sharp cheddar, or a Mexican cheese like Cotija or Chihuahua.

VEGAN CREAMY CORN CHOWDER Substitute olive oil for the butter. Instead of milk use a grain, soy, or nut milk. V

MANHATTAN CORN CHOWDER Tomato-based and also vegan: Instead of the milk, use 4 cups chopped fresh tomatoes (canned tomatoes also work fine; figure on two 28-ounce cans); add in Step 2 along with the corn-cob broth. 🔽

BEAN SOUPS

Bean soup is really my favorite, and I'm not alone. And, as everyone knows, beans are high in both protein and fiber, which makes them an important component of a plant-based diet.

As an ingredient in vegetable soups, legumes serve many functions. They work as a thickener; they add a wide range of distinct textures and tastes; they can enhance all sorts of soups in often surprising ways. And they're almost universally interchangeable.

Some of these soups call for cooking dried beans in the soup pot so their broth is integral to the soup; others offer the convenience of already-cooked or canned beans. Most recipes and variations explain how to adjust the soup for either method.

I prefer bean soups a tad on the thin side but the consistency is easy enough to adjust if you prefer thicker soup: Either decrease the amount of stock or water in these recipes by a half-cup or so, or add another third-cup of uncooked beans (or a half-cup of cooked) as directed. Or, purée some of the beans with a bit of liquid and stir them back into the soup—or simply mash some of the beans right in the soup.

Frozen Beans and Greens Soup

MAKES: 4 servings
TIME: 30 minutes
F M O

Limas, favas, and edamame are all sold frozen, and are all a bit firmer and chalkier than other legumes; they also have a pleasantly vegetal taste. And yes, go ahead and use frozen spinach if you really want to save time.

¼ cup olive oil
1 onion, chopped
1 tablespoon chopped garlic
   Salt and pepper
   Red chile flakes (optional)
1 15-ounce can tomato purée
2 cups frozen lima beans
3 cups vegetable stock (pages 97–100) or water
1½ pounds spinach, trimmed of thick stems and chopped, or 1 10-ounce bag frozen spinach
½ cup grated Parmesan cheese (optional)

1. Put the oil in a large pot over medium-high heat. Add the onion and garlic, sprinkle with salt and pepper, and cook, stirring frequently, until they soften and become translucent, 2 to 3 minutes. Stir in a pinch of chile flakes if you'd like.

2. Add the tomato purée, beans, and stock. Bring the mixture to a boil, then add the spinach and bring to a boil again. Lower the heat so the soup bubbles gently but steadily. Cook, stirring frequently, until the spinach softens and the soup thickens, 3 to 5 minutes. Taste, adjust the seasoning, and serve, sprinkled with some cheese if you'd like.

FROZEN FAVA–ESCAROLE SOUP Frozen fava beans are increasingly available and are creamier than lima beans: Use them here instead and substitute escarole for the spinach. (You'll only find it fresh; however, you can always substitute another frozen green like mustard or collards.)

FROZEN EDAMAME–BOK CHOY SOUP Some simple swaps: Instead of olive oil, use 2 tablespoons good-quality vegetable oil and 1 tablespoon sesame oil; edamame for the limas; and bok choy for the spinach. (You'll only find it fresh; however, you can substitute another frozen green like mustard or spinach.) In Step 1, go easy on the salt, and add 2 tablespoons soy sauce in Step 2 along with the stock. Instead of the Parmesan, garnish with chopped peanuts if you'd like and pass more soy sauce and sesame oil at the table.

CANNED CHICKPEA AND SAFFRON SOUP If you ever see fresh chickpeas, grab them; figure they'll take 30 to 60 minutes to get tender. Otherwise you can make this soup with canned chickpeas, which share a similar texture with the frozen beans used here. Add a pinch of saffron (or smoked paprika) along with the salt and pepper, and garnish the finished soup with chopped toasted almonds.

Split Pea Soup

MAKES: 4 servings
TIME: About 1½ hours
Ⓜ Ⓞ

Meat eaters automatically associate split peas with ham bones, so many vegetarian versions of split pea soup add a smoky taste through smoked chiles like dried chipotle or ancho. Tossing a piece of toasted seaweed into the soup is another way to add a meaty dimension. I like those options, but I also like a straight, distinctive pea flavor; the choice is yours.

> 2 cups dried green split peas, rinsed and picked over
> 6 cups vegetable stock (pages 97–100) or water
> Salt and pepper
> ¼ cup olive oil or 4 tablespoons (½ stick) butter, melted

1. Put the split peas and stock in a large pot over medium-high heat. Add a large pinch of salt and bring to a boil, then lower the heat so the mixture bubbles gently but steadily. Cover and cook, stirring occasionally, until the peas are so soft they break apart, 45 to 60 minutes.
2. If you'd like, mash the peas with a fork or potato masher. Or for an ultra-smooth soup, use an immersion blender in the pot, or let the soup cool a little, carefully purée it in a blender (working in batches if necessary), and return it to the pot. (You can make the soup in advance up to this point. Cool, cover, and refrigerate for up to 2 days.) Reheat the soup to a boil, adding more stock or water if it's too thick. Taste, adjust the

seasoning, and serve, drizzled with some olive oil or butter and sprinkled with lots of black pepper.

YELLOW OR RED SPLIT PEA SOUP WITH GINGER Believe it or not, each split pea color tastes slightly different; both are a little less earthy-tasting than the green ones: When you set the split peas to boil in Step 1, add 2 tablespoons minced fresh ginger. Use melted butter for the final drizzle, or to keep the soup vegan, drizzle 1 to 2 teaspoons sesame oil over each bowl.

Black Bean Soup

MAKES: 4 servings
TIME: 30 minutes with cooked or canned beans
Ⓜ Ⓞ

Here's a master recipe for whenever you want to start with cooked or canned beans. I like to mash some of the black beans in the pot for a smooth-chunky effect.

> 3 tablespoons olive oil
> 1 large onion, chopped
> 1 tablespoon minced garlic
> 1 tablespoon chili powder
> 1 tablespoon ground cumin
> 2 tablespoons sherry or dark rum (optional)
> 4 cups cooked or canned black beans (page 435), drained
> 3 cups vegetable stock (pages 97–100) or water
> Salt and pepper
> 1 tablespoon fresh lime juice, plus more to taste
> ½ cup sour cream or plain yogurt (optional)
> ¼ cup chopped fresh cilantro for garnish

1. Put the oil in a large pot over medium heat. When it's hot, add the onion and cook, stirring, until it softens, 3 to 5 minutes. Add the garlic, chili powder, and cumin and cook, stirring, until fragrant, another minute or so.
2. Stir in the sherry if you're using it and let it bubble away for a minute. Add the beans and stock, and sprinkle with salt and pepper. Bring the soup to a boil, then reduce the heat so it bubbles gently but steadily. Cook,

stirring occasionally, until the vegetables soften and the soup thickens, 5 to 10 minutes. Turn off the heat.

3. Use a potato masher to purée some of the beans in the pan (or you can use an immersion blender to purée the soup until almost smooth). (You can make the soup in advance up to this point. Cool, cover, refrigerate for up to 2 days, and reheat before proceeding.) Add the lime juice and stir; taste and adjust the seasoning. Garnish with sour cream, if you'd like, and cilantro, and serve.

TANGY ORANGE–BLACK BEAN SOUP Omit the lime juice. In Step 2, replace 2 cups of the stock with 2 cups orange juice (preferably fresh); add 2 teaspoons grated orange zest.

BLACK BEAN SOUP, LATIN AMERICAN STYLE More like a stew: When you add the beans in Step 2, include 2 sweet potatoes, peeled and cut into 1-inch chunks; they'll take about 20 minutes to become tender. Don't purée. Instead, when the sweet potato is ready, add 1 red bell pepper, cored, seeded, and chopped, and 1 cup chopped mango (frozen is fine). Continue cooking until just warmed through before serving.

Giving Soups More Body

You can make any soup thicker (and usually more flavorful) by adding any of these ingredients, alone or in combination.

GRAINS

Grains—especially whole grains like cracked wheat, brown rice, or millet—are more flavorful than potatoes in soup. And they do not melt away, though white rice will become pretty soft. Adding a scoop of cooked grains to the finished soup is one thing. But if you want to increase body and richness, add a small quantity (¼ to ½ cup) of grain at the beginning of the recipe; cook until it's falling apart, then purée.

POTATOES

Starchy or all-purpose potatoes (like baking potatoes or Yukon Golds) add heft and flavor to almost any soup. (Waxy potatoes, like "new" potatoes, have a different effect; see the sidebar on page 104 for more detail.) If you're going to purée the soup after cooking, just peel and dice a potato or 2 (figure about a half pound per batch) and add it at the same time as the broth or water. If you want to thicken a chunky bean or vegetable soup, a spoonful or 2 of leftover mashed potatoes will do the trick. A few minutes before serving, stir them into the soup until completely dissolved and heat until almost boiling.

PASTA

Be sure you have enough extra liquid and room in the pot to accommodate the noodles as they swell, and serve the soup immediately; noodles turn to mush quickly. A more refined option is to cook the noodles separately, put them in each bowl, then ladle the hot soup over them. Store the leftover noodles and soup separately. Figure an ounce or 2 (no more) of dried pasta per serving.

LEGUMES

White beans are neutral, versatile, and creamy, especially when puréed. Cooked legumes can be added to already made soups or cooked along with the other ingredients until tender, then puréed or mashed.

NUT AND SEED BUTTERS OR PASTES

These deliver loads of flavor; use them judiciously so they don't compete with other ingredients. Because they have more fat than other ingredients discussed here, they make the soup richer, with more body. A good example of nuts as a thickener is Peanutty Vegetable Soup (page 115). Other seeds, like chia and hemp, have a tremendous capacity to absorb liquid and can create a silky, gelatinous texture; add them judiciously, no more than 1 tablespoon initially.

EGGS

The classic Greek soup avgolemono is thickened with an egg–lemon juice emulsion. You can add that emulsion to any soup you think it would suit: Whisk together 3 eggs and the juice of 2 lemons. Ladle a bit of hot (never boiling) broth into the egg mixture and stir to combine. Repeat that two more times. Then carefully stir the egg mixture into the soup. Do not boil the soup after the egg is added, or the egg will curdle.

Cannellini (or Any Bean) Soup

MAKES: 4 servings
TIME: At least 1 hour

M V

You can make soup out of any dried beans you like—white or otherwise—but cannellini are among the creamiest; they purée beautifully and have a mild beany flavor that most people like. See "7 Ideas for Cannellini (or Any Bean) Soup," right, for all the directions you can take this.

1½ cups cannellini or other dried beans, rinsed and picked over, and soaked if you have the time (see page 428)

---

16 Whole-Meal Soups

These are the most substantial soups in this chapter.

---

6 cups vegetable stock (pages 97–100) or water, or more as needed
1 onion, chopped
1 large carrot, chopped
1 celery stalk, chopped
2 bay leaves
1 tablespoon fresh thyme leaves or 1 teaspoon dried thyme
Salt and pepper
¼ cup (or more) olive oil for drizzling
Chopped fresh parsley for garnish

1. Drain the beans if you've soaked them. Put them in a large pot with the stock, onion, carrot, celery, bay leaves, and thyme. Bring to a boil, then lower the heat so the mixture bubbles gently but steadily. Cover and cook, stirring occasionally, until the beans are very soft and falling apart, anywhere from 40 to 90 minutes, depending on how dry they were and whether or not you soaked them. Add more liquid as necessary so the mixture remains soupy.

2. When the beans are almost ready, sprinkle with salt and pepper. Fish out the bay leaves and discard. If you like, you can purée the soup at this point: Use an immersion blender to partially purée it in the pot, leaving it a bit chunky. Or let the soup cool a little, carefully purée some or all of it in a blender (working in batches if necessary), and return it to the pot. (You can make the soup in advance up to this point. Cool, cover, refrigerate for up to 2 days, and reheat gently before proceeding; you may need to add a bit of water to help thin it out.) Taste and adjust the seasoning. Drizzle with some olive oil, garnish with parsley, and serve.

7 Ideas for Cannellini (or Any Bean) Soup

As good as basic bean soup is, it can be made even more delicious with a few simple additions. Try any of these, alone or in combination:

1. Tomato paste (about ¼ cup) or a cup or 2 chopped fresh or canned tomatoes, added at the beginning.

2. Nori seaweed, toasted (see page 244) and minced, about ¼ cup, added at the beginning and/or a sprinkle as a garnish. Use sesame oil instead of olive oil for drizzling.

3. Chopped fresh vegetables—carrots, celery, potatoes, shallots, turnips, or whatever you like (1 to 2 cups)—added when the beans are getting tender but still have a little ways to go.

4. Any whole grain, like brown rice, barley, or cracked wheat (½ cup or so), with the beans reduced by the same amount, added at the beginning; or quick-cooking grains (¼ cup), like quinoa, couscous, or bulgur, stirred into the soup when the beans are tender—cover the soup and let it stand off the heat until the grains are tender, 15 to 20 minutes.

5. Minced garlic (at least 1 teaspoon), added about 5 minutes before the end of cooking.

6. Chopped greens, like kale or collards (1 to 2 cups), added during the last 5 minutes of cooking.

7. 4 to 8 Garlic Croutons (page 678), 1 or 2 added to the bottom of each soup bowl before serving.

Coconut-Lentil Soup with Vegetables

MAKES: 4 servings
TIME: 1½ hours, mostly unattended
V

I use regular brown lentils here, but you can use red lentils, which cook faster, or the more traditional split pigeon peas known as tavoor dal (available at most Asian and Indian markets); they're all good. There are so few beans they melt into the background, with the soft vegetables and shreds of coconut left swirling in the complex golden broth. If okra or zucchini isn't your thing, use about 1½ pounds of whatever vegetables you have, in any combination, like winter squash, turnips, or sweet potato, to cauliflower, spinach, eggplant, or green beans.

3 tablespoons good-quality vegetable oil
1 onion, chopped
1 tablespoon minced garlic
1 tablespoon minced fresh ginger
  Salt and pepper
3 tablespoons curry powder (to make your own, see page 649)
1 teaspoon ground turmeric
1 cup chopped fresh tomatoes or 1 15-ounce can diced tomatoes
¼ cup shredded coconut
½ pound okra, trimmed and sliced
1 pound zucchini, trimmed and chopped
½ cup dried lentils or split pigeon peas (tavoor dal), rinsed and picked over
4 cups vegetable stock (pages 97–100) or water
2 cups coconut milk (to make your own, see page 304) or 1 14-ounce can mixed with a little water
12 fresh basil leaves, or fresh curry leaves if they're available, torn

1. Put the oil in a large pot over medium heat. When it's hot, add the onion and cook, stirring occasionally, until soft and translucent, 3 to 5 minutes. Add the garlic and ginger and cook for another minute. Sprinkle with salt and pepper. Cook, stirring occasionally and lowering the heat to prevent burning if necessary, until the vegetables are golden and beginning to melt together, 10 to 20 minutes.

2. Turn the heat to medium-high and add the curry powder and turmeric. Cook, stirring frequently, until darkened and fragrant, just a minute or 2. Add the tomatoes, coconut, okra, zucchini, and lentils. Add the stock and coconut milk and bring to a boil, then reduce the heat so that the soup bubbles gently but steadily.

3. Cook, stirring occasionally, until the lentils and vegetables break apart, 30 to 40 minutes; add water as necessary to keep the mixture brothy. Add the basil leaves, stir once or twice, then taste, adjust the seasoning, and serve.

Lentil Soup

MAKES: 4 servings
TIME: About 1 hour, mostly unattended
Ⓜ Ⓥ

This classic recipe is easy as can be, especially for a dish so filling and nutritious. It's on the thin side, but it's chunky. If you prefer your lentil soup smooth, purée it; for added richness and body, stir in ½ cup cream at the end, or use 1 more carrot and celery stalk at the beginning and mash or purée some of the solids when you're done cooking.

3	tablespoons olive oil
1	onion, chopped
	Salt and pepper
2	carrots, chopped
2	celery stalks, chopped
1	tablespoon chopped garlic
1	tablespoon fresh thyme leaves or 1 teaspoon dried thyme
6	cups vegetable stock (pages 97–100) or water, or more as needed
1	cup dried lentils, rinsed and picked over
1	bay leaf

1. Put the oil in a large pot over medium heat. Add the onion and sprinkle with salt and pepper. Cook, stirring occasionally, until it's soft, 3 to 5 minutes.
2. Add the carrots, celery, and garlic and cook, stirring occasionally, until the vegetables start to soften, another 3 to 5 minutes. Add the thyme and cook, stirring, until fragrant, no more than a minute.
3. Add the stock, lentils, and bay leaf and sprinkle with a little salt and pepper. Bring to a boil, then lower the heat to a steady bubble. Cook, stirring once or twice, until the lentils are tender, 20 to 30 minutes; add more stock a little at a time if the mixture seems too thick. (You can make the soup up to this point, cool, cover, and refrigerate for up to several days.) Fish out the bay leaf, taste and adjust the seasoning, and serve.

ITALIAN-STYLE LENTIL SOUP WITH RICE Substitute fresh or dried oregano for the thyme and increase the amount of stock to 8 cups. Prepare the soup through the beginning of Step 3. After the lentils have cooked for about 10 minutes, add ½ cup short-grain rice (like Arborio or carnaroli) and 1 cup chopped tomatoes (canned are fine). Continue as directed until the lentils and rice are tender but not mushy. Pass grated Parmesan cheese and more olive oil for adding at the table.

LEBANESE-STYLE LENTIL SOUP WITH RICE Similar to the Italian version, with different rice and seasonings: Add 2 teaspoons each sumac and cumin along with the thyme and increase the stock to 8 cups. Prepare the soup through the beginning of Step 3. After the lentils have cooked for about 10 minutes, add ½ cup basmati rice and 1 cup chopped tomatoes. Continue as directed until the lentils and rice are tender but not mushy. Garnish with chopped fresh parsley and pass more olive oil at the table.

NOODLE SOUPS

For the most part, you want to make noodle soup by adding cooked noodles to cooked soup just before serving. This maintains the integrity of each and keeps everything from turning into an undifferentiated, starchy mess. Undercook the noodles slightly (they'll finish cooking in the hot broth); you can even prepare them ahead, rinse them in cold water to stop the cooking and remove the surface starch so they don't stick together, cover, and refrigerate until you're ready to use them.

Often, it's better to cook the noodles right in the soup, to maximize the body-building and flavor benefits. Soups made this way have only a narrow window of time before serving—the noodles start to break down quickly—but I maximize that window by using the sturdiest noodles, or frying them first to make them a little less soluble.

Pho

MAKES: 4 servings
TIME: About 1 hour, depending on garnishes
Ⓜ Ⓥ

Fish and meat often figure prominently in the Vietnamese meal-in-a-bowl soup known as pho, but there are traditional and fine vegetarian options, chief among them this broth made from soy sauce and a blend of spices like star anise and cinnamon. All that's required is a willingness to invest in making the broth and a few additional toppings and you'll be handsomely rewarded.

2	tablespoons good-quality vegetable oil
1	large onion, halved and sliced
1	head garlic, cloves separated but unpeeled
1	2-inch piece fresh ginger, cut into coins
	Salt
	Pinch sugar
3 or 4	star anise pods
1	cinnamon stick
2	bay leaves
2	tablespoons black peppercorns
6	cups vegetable stock (pages 97–100)
¼	cup soy sauce, plus more to taste
1	tablespoon cider vinegar
1	bunch fresh cilantro
½	pound mushrooms (any kind), trimmed
8	ounces thin rice vermicelli
6	cups boiling water
4	scallions, sliced, for garnish
2 or 3	limes, cut into wedges, for garnish
	Additional toppings as you like (see the list that follows)

1. Put the oil in a large pot over medium heat. When it's hot, add the onion, garlic, and ginger. Sprinkle with some salt and the sugar and cook, stirring occasionally, until the vegetables soften, 3 to 5 minutes. Add the star anise, cinnamon, bay leaves, and peppercorns and stir until warm and fragrant, no more than a minute. Add the stock, soy sauce, vinegar, half the cilantro (save the rest for garnish), mushrooms, and 1 cup water. Bring to a boil, then lower the heat so the stock bubbles gently. Cook, partially covered, until you are happy with the concentration of flavor, 30 to 60 minutes.

2. Put the rice vermicelli in a large bowl, sprinkle with salt, and cover with the boiling water. Soak until the noodles are barely tender; start checking after 3 minutes. Drain the noodles, then rinse them and the bowl with cold water to cool down. Return the noodles to the bowl, add enough cold water to cover, and let sit until you're ready to serve.

3. Strain the broth through a fine-meshed strainer, return it to the pot, and keep at a gentle bubble. Taste and adjust the seasoning, adding more soy sauce if you'd like. (You can make the broth to this point, cool, and store it in the refrigerator for several days or the freezer for a few months. Return it to a boil and keep hot until time to serve.)

4. Prepare any additional toppings from the list that follows (or whatever else you'd like) and put them in bowls or platters. Drain the noodles and divide them among big bowls; ladle some broth over the noodles. Garnish with the scallions, limes, and sprigs of the reserved cilantro. Top the soup with other additions as you like.

12 Ways to Enhance Pho

The list here is far from comprehensive, but will give you some idea of different ways to turn a bowl of noodle soup into a meal:

1. Sliced or grated raw daikon or other radishes, carrots, kohlrabi, or turnips

2. Mung bean sprouts

3. Sliced steamed vegetables, like bok choy, Napa cabbage, mustard greens, broccoli or broccoli raab, carrots, green beans, or summer squash

4. Shelled edamame

5. Pickled ginger (see page 207)

6. Tofu Croutons (page 497)

7. Precooked tofu (see pages 485 to 487), diced or very thinly sliced

8. Seitan and Lentil Loaf (page 509) or Pan-Seared Seitan (page 510), diced or very thinly sliced

9. Crunchy Crumbled Tempeh (page 512)

10. Fresh mint or Thai basil sprigs (or any basil)
11. Sliced fresh hot chiles (like Thai, serrano, or jalapeño), chile paste (see page 664), or hot sauce
12. Sesame oil

Green Tea Broth with Udon Noodles

MAKES: 4 servings
TIME: 15 minutes

F V

In Japan, udon noodles are often eaten with their flavorful cooking liquid, which is sometimes water, sometimes stock or broth. Often vegetables are cooked in that liquid before the noodles are added, so it becomes even tastier. Here the starting "broth" is green tea. With its haunting herbaceousness, the resulting soup is elegant in both simplicity and speed; and the list that follows shows the ways to embellish and intensify the flavor. For heat, add a pinch or 2 of cayenne to the broth in Step 1, or serve the soup with a dab of wasabi paste.

½	**cup green tea leaves**
	Salt
12	**ounces udon noodles**
	Pepper
2	**tablespoons mirin or 2 teaspoons sugar (optional)**
	Soy sauce for serving
	Sesame oil for serving

1. Put 10 cups water in a large pot and bring to a boil. Remove from the heat and let rest for a couple of minutes. Stir in the tea leaves, cover, and steep until fragrant and richly colored, 5 to 10 minutes. Strain the broth through a fine-meshed strainer and return the broth to the pot. Discard the tea leaves.
2. Bring the tea to a boil and sprinkle with salt. Stir in the udon. When the broth returns to a boil, add 2 cups of cold water. When the liquid returns to a boil, turn the heat down so that it bubbles gently without overflowing.

3. Cook, stirring occasionally, until the noodles are tender not mushy; start checking after 3 minutes. Taste and add more salt, a few grinds of pepper, and the mirin or sugar, if you'd like. Serve with soy sauce and sesame oil to pass for drizzling at the table.

10 Additions to Green Tea Broth with Udon Noodles

Some of these are garnishes to serve over the noodles; others are cooked in the broth to give it more character. And some can go either way:

1. 1 cup finely chopped fresh tomatoes, added as the broth bubbles
2. ½ cup cubed tofu, added to the broth when the noodles are nearly finished cooking
3. 1 cup cooked small beans, like soybeans, adzuki, edamame, or mung, added when the noodles are nearly finished cooking
4. 4 to 8 scrambled eggs, added when the noodles are nearly finished cooking
5. 1 tablespoon grated fresh ginger, added as the broth bubbles
6. 2 sheets nori, lightly toasted and cut into 1-inch strips (see page 244) or ¼ cup Nori "Shake," (page 650) for garnish
7. 1 tablespoon white or black sesame seeds or 1 teaspoon black mustard seeds, for garnish
8. 2 tablespoons nuts, like pistachios, cashews, or hazelnuts, toasted (see page 299), for garnish
9. A thinly sliced onion, handful of julienned cucumber, or 1 or 2 cups shredded cabbage added as the broth bubbles or for garnish
10. 2 cups mung bean sprouts, added as the broth bubbles or for garnish

GRAIN SOUPS

Whole grains rarely dominate the other ingredients in a soup, but they make great contributors. Unlike beans, they're neutral enough to provide a backdrop for other ingredients, and they bring a nuttier flavor and chewier texture than the more neutral-tasting pasta and noodles. You can't go wrong.

All the grains in the following recipes are cooked directly in the stock or water, which adds body and flavor to the soup. But precooked grains are a valuable last-minute addition to many soups. If you cook extra whenever you make a pot of grains, you'll always have some handy when inspiration strikes.

Mushroom Barley Soup

MAKES: 4 servings
TIME: 45 minutes
V

A classic, delivering hearty texture and lots of flavor. It starts with the key ingredient for intensifying many mushroom dishes, dried porcini (you'll also use their soaking liquid), and builds additional layers of flavor by deeply browning the mushrooms. This technique ups the umami factor, as does the unorthodox addition of soy sauce.

1   ounce dried porcini mushrooms
    (about 1 cup)

2   tablespoons olive oil
1   pound fresh shiitake, cremini, portobello,
    or white button mushrooms, stemmed and
    roughly chopped
3   carrots, sliced
1   cup pearled barley
    Salt and pepper
1   bay leaf
3   cups Mushroom Stock (page 99), vegetable
    stock (pages 97–100), or water
1   tablespoon soy sauce, or more to taste

1. Soak the porcini in 3 cups hot tap water. Put the olive oil in a large pot over medium-high heat. When it's hot, add the fresh mushrooms and carrots and cook, stirring occasionally, until the liquid released by the mushrooms evaporates and they begin to brown, 10 to 15 minutes. Add the barley and continue to cook, stirring frequently, until it begins to toast and become fragrant, 1 to 2 minutes. Sprinkle with a little salt and plenty of pepper and remove from the heat.

2. When the porcini are soft, lift them out of the soaking liquid with your hands or a slotted spoon, reserving the liquid. Sort through the mushrooms

7 Noodle- and Grain-Loving Soups

You can add cooked noodles or grains to dozens of soups, but here are some of my favorites to get you going:

1. Cauliflower Soup, Italian Style
(page 102): Small pasta like shells, orzo, or orecchiette; bulgur, farro, or other wheats.

2. Tomato Soup (page 105): Any of the ideas above will work with the basic recipe (but not the variations); rice is classic in tomato soup but millet is also good.

3. Frozen Beans and Greens Soup
(page 122): Add broken fideo or angel hair (or rice vermicelli to the edamame–bok choy variation) during

the last 3 to 5 minutes of cooking. If you don't want the soup to become too thick, stir in extra water or broth. Brown rice or quinoa is also delicious.

4. Kimchi Soup with Tofu (page 138): Mung bean threads, presoaked and drained (see page 331); hulled or pearled barley is also a good grain choice.

5. Any stock (pages 97 to 100) or broth made from any miso (page 652) with Tofu Croutons (page 497). Try soba or udon or use

any Asian-style rice or wheat noodle; white or brown rice or buckwheat.

6. Tofu and Bok Choy "Goulash"
(page 140): Rice vermicelli, presoaked; or put a scoop of white or sticky rice in the bottom of the bowl before ladling in the soup.

7. Egg Drop Soup, Many Ways
(page 141), but only these variations: Small or tubular pasta in Egg Drop Soup, Italian Style; or thick rice noodles in Egg Drop Soup with Sea Greens.

and discard any hard bits, then coarsely chop them. Carefully pour the reserved soaking liquid into another container, leaving any grit in the bottom of the bowl.

3. Return the pot to medium-high heat, add the porcini, and cook, stirring, for about a minute. Add the bay leaf, the mushroom soaking liquid, and the stock. Bring to a boil, then lower the heat to a gentle bubble. Cover and cook until the barley is very tender, 20 to 30 minutes. Fish out the bay leaf and add the soy sauce. Taste and adjust the seasoning, adding more soy sauce if you'd like, and serve.

WHOLE GRAIN MUSHROOM BARLEY SOUP Pearled barley cooks faster and creamier because it has had most of the fiber removed; using whole grain results in a nuttier, more nutritious soup but takes a little longer: Instead of the pearled barley, use hulled barley, oat groats, or wheat berries. Be prepared to add more stock if necessary to thin the soup as it cooks. Start checking the grains for tenderness after 30 minutes cooking time; depending on what you use, they may take another 10 to 20 minutes.

Barley Soup with Seasonal Vegetables

MAKES: 4 servings
TIME: 45 minutes

V

Use this recipe as a model for enjoying soup year-round: When you let the season dictate your choice of vegetables, the heartiness changes dramatically. The basic recipe calls for just what you want on a cold winter day. Now fast-forward to the summer variation that follows, garnish it with fresh basil, and suddenly barley soup doesn't seem quite so wintry.

2 tablespoons good-quality vegetable oil
1 onion, chopped
1 tablespoon minced garlic
  Salt and pepper
1 cup pearled barley
8 cups vegetable stock (pages 97–100) or water, plus more as needed
  About 2 pounds root vegetables (turnips, parsnips, rutabagas, carrots, celery root, waxy potatoes like Yukon Gold or fingerling,

Adding Cheese to Soups

Contrary to fast food practices, cheese is not a given in food, but it is wonderful in soups, in a variety of ways. The flavor of both cheese and soup will determine whether they'll make a good match. Try to combine mild with mild, for example, or use aged cheese to season sturdy soups that can stand up to more assertive flavors.

Generally, you can stir grated cheese in right before serving or sprinkle it on top for a garnish, as long as it's appropriate. You don't want cheese in most Asian soups, for example, and you have to be careful of adding cheese to bean soups; it doesn't take much before the cheese will bind the beans together like glue.

Soft cheeses like camembert, as well as lighter goat and fresh cheeses, work well as a last-minute garnish for cream soups, because they melt away so quickly. Try putting a small spoonful in each bowl and ladle the steaming soup around it.

Salty, sharp, hard grating cheeses like Parmesan are terrific in many soups but can clump up if cooked too long. They're best used at serving time. The rinds from these hard cheeses are great added to soup during cooking; they enhance both richness and flavor, and you can chomp on them at the table, a wonderful thing.

Use smoked cheeses—judiciously—for a savory flavor reminiscent of smoked meat.

Crumbling cheeses like queso fresco, feta, and blue cheeses take a long time to melt in soup, which make them good if you're looking to create some contrast.

To add both cheese and crunch to brothy soups, spread or melt a small amount of cheese on a thick slice of toasted bread and float it on top of each bowl or pass a plate of cheesy croutons at the table.

alone or in combination), peeled and cut into
1-inch pieces

1 tablespoon chopped fresh sage or 1 teaspoon
dried sage

1. Put the oil in a large pot over medium-high heat. When it's hot, add the onion and cook, stirring occasionally, until it's soft, 3 to 5 minutes. Add the garlic, sprinkle with salt and pepper, and cook, stirring constantly, until fragrant, about a minute more.

2. Add the barley and cook, stirring constantly, until the barley starts to toast and stick, 1 to 3 minutes. Stir in the stock and bring to a boil, then lower the heat so the liquid bubbles gently but steadily. Cover and cook until the barley begins to soften but is still quite firm in the center, 10 to 15 minutes, stirring a few times.

3. Add the root vegetables and return the soup to a boil; add a little more stock if necessary so the solids are just submerged. Lower the heat to a simmer again, cover, and cook until the vegetables and barley are very tender, another 10 to 20 minutes. Stir in the sage, taste, adjust the seasoning, and serve.

BARLEY SOUP WITH SUMMER VEGETABLES No limit to what you can choose here, instead of or along with root vegetables: Use tomatoes, corn, zucchini or other summer squash, peas, okra, or eggplant, either alone or in combination. Wait to add them until the barley is almost completely tender in Step 3, another 5 minutes or so; then reduce the time of the second simmer by about 5 minutes. Substitute 1 cup torn fresh basil leaves for the sage, adding half with the vegetables and using the rest as a garnish.

BARLEY SOUP WITH ROASTED SEASONAL VEGETABLES Heat the oven to 450°F. Peel and chop the root or summer vegetables. Put them in a roasting pan, drizzle with ¼ cup olive oil, sprinkle with salt and pepper, and roast, turning once or twice with a spatula, until browned and tender, 15 to 30 minutes, depending on the vegetables. Meanwhile, cook the soup as directed,

simmering the barley until fully tender, 20 to 30 minutes. Add the roasted vegetables, taste, and adjust the seasoning.

WHOLE GRAIN SOUP WITH WINTER OR SUMMER VEGETABLES To adapt the main recipe and variations for hulled barley, wheat or other grain berries, farro, or oat groats, increase the cooking time in Step 2 by 10 to 30 (or more) minutes, depending on the grain. It should be to the same doneness described at the end of Step 2 before you add the vegetables. (You may need to include more liquid when you do.)

Farro and Bean Soup

MAKES: 4 servings
TIME: About 1 hour

Ⓜ Ⓞ

Farro—and this soup—is most closely associated with Lucca in Tuscany, a spot also famous for its olive oil. So that vegans can enjoy all of the pleasure, too, offer toasted nuts as an alternative to the Parmesan passed at the table.

¼	cup olive oil
1	large onion, halved and sliced
2	celery stalks, chopped
2	carrots, chopped
1	tablespoon minced garlic
	Salt and pepper
1	cup farro
2	cups chopped tomatoes (canned diced are fine; don't bother to drain)
6	cups vegetable stock (pages 97–100) or water, or more as needed
2	cups cooked or canned cannellini or other white beans, drained
¼	cup chopped fresh parsley or basil for garnish
1	cup grated Parmesan cheese and/or ½ cup toasted chopped pine nuts or almonds for serving

Farro and Bean
Soup (page 135)

1. Put the oil in a large pot over medium heat. When it's hot, add the onion, celery, carrots, garlic, a large pinch of salt, and some pepper. Cook, stirring occasionally, until the vegetables are glossy and begin to soften, 5 to 10 minutes.

2. Add the farro, tomatoes, and stock and stir. Bring to a boil, then lower the heat so it bubbles gently but steadily. Cook until the farro is tender but not mushy, 20 to 30 minutes, adding stock or water as necessary if the soup becomes too thick. (You can make the soup in advance up to this point. Cool. cover, and refrigerate for up to 2 days, then reheat before proceeding. If the farro soaks up all the liquid in the soup, add water to thin it out before proceeding.)

3. Add the beans and herbs and cook, stirring occasionally, until the soup is bubbling again. Taste and adjust the seasoning, and serve with the Parmesan and/or nuts passed at the table.

FARRO AND BEAN SOUP WITH MUSHROOMS Before starting the recipe, soak about ½ ounce dried mushrooms in 1½ cups hot tap water until pliable, 15 to 20 minutes. Lift the mushrooms from the soaking water with your hands or a slotted spoon; reserve the liquid. Chop the mushrooms and add them to the vegetables in Step 1. Reduce the stock to 5 cups, and when you add the farro in Step 2, carefully pour in about 1 cup of the reserved soaking liquid, leaving any grit in the bottom of the bowl.

TUSCAN-STYLE WHOLE GRAIN SOUP Instead of farro in either the main recipe or the variation, you can substitute spelt, wheat, or other whole grain kernels, hulled barley, or oat groats. Adjust the cooking time as necessary (see the table on pages 400 to 403 for some guidelines) and keep an eye on the liquid as they cook, adding more as necessary to make sure they never start sticking.

TOFU AND MISO SOUPS

Over the years, tofu converts have told me that soup was their gateway preparation. No wonder: all the things

you think you don't like about bean curd—its blandness and spongy texture—can be advantages in a flavorful bubbling brew.

There are two ways to make tofu soups: The first is to add cubes or slices of tofu after the soup is made. When heated gently, they become a high-protein, mildly flavorful garnish. (See the list on page 138 for ideas about where this works best.) The second way is to feature tofu as a key ingredient. Because tofu soaks up seasonings, it's perfect for adding heft and texture to soup without changing the flavor much. See page 483 for everything you need to know about buying and preparing tofu. Meanwhile, here are a few other tips specific to soup:

CRUMBLED, CUBED, OR SLICED TOFU Right out of the package, this is the easy way. Firm tofu doesn't change much; it just absorbs a bit of flavor (and gets warm, of course). If you handle them carefully, softer tofus swell considerably and firm up a bit.

BAKED FIRM TOFU, CUBED OR SLICED Baking draws a lot of moisture out of the tofu so it can absorb more flavor from the soup. The time in the oven also intensifies the flavor of tofu, like roasted soy nuts.

FROZEN FIRM TOFU, CRUMBLED, CUBED, OR SLICED With its porous texture and lower moisture content, frozen tofu absorbs flavor from the soup quicker than other forms. Plan ahead, though, because tofu needs a day or so in the freezer, and a couple of hours to thaw on the counter (or overnight in the fridge) before it's easy to cut. Before using, put the whole block in a shallow bowl and press down with your palm to squeeze out excess water, then pat it dry.

FRIED THINLY SLICED FIRM TOFU Whether you oven-fry the slices or panfry them, the results are crisp, nutty wafers that are like super-nutritious croutons.

SILKEN (OR SOFT) TOFU When the soup features crunchy ingredients, like Kimchi Soup with Tofu, the creamy texture of silken tofu is a nice foil. In this case, the tofu also helps balance the heat of the spicy cabbage. You can first whisk the tofu until smooth, then stir it in as a creamy addition, or add it as cubes or small pieces.

TOFU SKINS Like pasta, this pleasantly chewy form of bean curd comes in both dried and fresh forms. In soup they're like a cross between noodles and eggs. Cut them into strips before adding to the soup.

MISO This adds wonderful flavor and texture to soup. Feel free to use whatever miso you might have in your refrigerator, but be mindful of this golden rule: Once you've added the miso, don't bring the soup to a boil; it will negatively impact its flavor and health benefits.

Kimchi Soup with Tofu

MAKES: 4 servings
TIME: 25 minutes
F V

Fermentation is enjoying a renaissance moment in this country, in part thanks to kimchi, which is a key component in many Korean soups.

  2   tablespoons good-quality vegetable oil
  1   tablespoon sesame oil
  1½ cups kimchi (to make your own, see page 93), chopped
  1   tablespoon rice vinegar, plus more to taste
  1   tablespoon soy sauce, plus more to taste
  ½   cup short-grain white rice
  12 ounces soft silken tofu, drained
      Pepper
  ½   cup chopped scallions for garnish

1. Put the vegetable and sesame oils in a large pot over medium heat. When hot, add the kimchi and cook, stirring, for just a few seconds. Add 7 cups water along with

the vinegar and soy sauce and bring to a boil, then lower the heat so the mixture bubbles gently but steadily.
2. Add the rice, stir, and once again adjust the heat so the mixture simmers. Cover and cook, undisturbed, until the rice is tender and the broth thickens, 15 to 20 minutes.
3. Add the tofu and stir to break it into pieces with a spoon. Let the soup return to a boil, then remove from the heat. Taste and adjust the seasoning, adding more soy and vinegar if you'd like along with some black pepper. Garnish with the scallions and serve.

KOREAN-STYLE MUSHROOM SOUP WITH TOFU With unfermented vegetables, you've really got to have mushroom stock here instead of water to make the best broth: Instead of the kimchi, use a combination of 1 pound sliced white button mushrooms and ½ pound shiitake mushrooms, sliced (caps only; remove and reserve the stems for stock). In Step 1, when you add them to the hot oil, keep cooking, stirring occasionally, until they release their liquid and the pot becomes dry again; you

7 Soups to Add Tofu To

Tofu is best added to soups at the last minute before serving—so it heats through without falling apart. If you're using silken tofu, try to add it whole and let it break apart naturally as you stir. For firm tofu, press it first if you have time (see page 483) so it absorbs more flavor from the soup.

1. Firm tofu in Coconut-Lentil Soup with Vegetables (page 127)

2. Firm tofu in Peanutty Vegetable Soup (page 115)

3. Firm or silken tofu in Korean-Style Vegetable Soup (page 113)

4. Firm tofu (preferably fried, see page 486)

in Tortilla Soup (page 111)

5. Silken tofu in Mushroom Barley Soup (page 133)

6. Firm or silken tofu, or tofu skins in Pho (page 130)

7. Silken tofu in Egg Drop Soup with Sea Greens (page 142)

can even brown them a bit. When the mushrooms are ready, add 1 to 2 tablespoons gochujang or other chile paste or sauce and 2 tablespoons sesame seeds. Proceed with Step 2.

Tofu and Bok Choy "Goulash"

MAKES: 4 servings
TIME: 30 minutes
F V

Any hearty, piquant soup with bits of ground or chopped beef could fairly be called a goulash. This all-vegetable spin achieves a similar texture and flavor with fried crumbled firm tofu along with ginger, garlic, chiles, and fermented black beans. If you don't have time to freeze or press the tofu, use it straight from the package; the texture will be a little less meaty, but cooking will help the extra moisture evaporate. For a more traditional take on the classic Eastern European goulash, see the variation. Serve this with plain white rice.

 1 **pound firm tofu, pressed (see page 483), frozen (see page 483), or directly from the package**
 3 **tablespoons good-quality vegetable oil**
 1 **tablespoon minced garlic**
 1 **tablespoon minced fresh ginger**
 1 **teaspoon red chile flakes, or to taste**
 2 **tablespoons fermented black beans**
 6 **cups vegetable stock (pages 97–100) or water**
 1 **pound bok choy, stems and leaves separated and chopped**
   Salt and pepper

1. Crumble the tofu with your hands or a fork in a bowl until the pieces are small and uniform. You should have about 2 cups.

2. Put the oil in a large pot over medium-high heat. Add the garlic and ginger and cook, stirring occasionally, until softened and just beginning to color, about 1 minute. Add the tofu. Stir with a wooden spoon, let the mixture sit for a moment or 2, then stir again. Repeat

several times, scraping up any browned bits from the bottom of the pot with the spoon, until the tofu, garlic, and ginger are golden and dry.

3. Add the chile flakes and black beans and cook, stirring and mashing with the spoon until fragrant, 1 or 2 minutes. Add the stock and bok choy stems, scraping up any tofu and seasonings stuck on the bottom of the pan. Bring to a boil, then lower the heat so the liquid bubbles gently but steadily. Cover and cook, stirring occasionally, until the soup thickens, 3 to 5 minutes.

4. Add the bok choy leaves to the soup and return it to a gentle bubble. Cover again and cook, stirring once or twice, until the bok choy is barely tender, another 2 or 3 minutes. Taste and adjust the seasoning, and serve.

MORE-TRADITIONAL GOULASH SOUP WITH TOFU
Terrific over Boiled Potatoes (page 233): Use 1 pound chopped green cabbage (about 4 cups) instead of bok choy. Omit the ginger, red chile flakes, and black beans. Instead, cook ½ cup chopped red onion with the garlic and season the tofu as it cooks. Add 1 tablespoon paprika and 2 tablespoons tomato paste in Step 3. When you add the stock, also add 1 cup diced tomatoes (canned are fine) and the cabbage.

TEMPEH "GOULASH" If you like the stronger flavor of tempeh, replace any or all of the tofu with crumbled or chopped tempeh.

Miso Soup

MAKES: 4 servings
TIME: About 15 minutes
F V

At its simplest, miso soup is like instant tea: miso whisked with water, which you can do in a cup with a fork. With this broth, you choose what to add. Tofu and scallions are traditional, but do what you like: carrots, peas, beans, greens, sea greens, and so on. Several ideas are listed below, but the general idea is light and simple.

Remember: the darker the miso, the more intense the soup.

    4 cups Kombu Dashi (page 100) or water
    ⅓ cup any miso
    12 ounces silken tofu
    ½ cup chopped scallions

1. Heat the dashi or water in a pot until steaming; don't boil it. Turn the heat to low, then whisk together about ½ cup of the liquid with the miso in a small bowl until smooth.

2. Pour the thinned miso back into the hot liquid, add the tofu, and break it up a little. Stir once or twice and keep on the heat just long enough for the tofu to get hot (but don't let it come to a boil). Add the scallions, stir again, and serve.

7 Additions to Miso Soup

1. Add reconstituted seaweed, either the kombu from making the dashi (chopped) or a little steamed hijiki, along with the tofu.

2. Add sliced shiitake mushroom caps, either fresh (simmer briefly in Step 1) or dried (soaked first; see page 217). For extra flavor, sauté the sliced mushrooms in good-quality vegetable oil or butter.

3. Add thinly sliced or minced daikon or other radish; simmer briefly in Step 1.

4. Add a clove of minced garlic in Step 1.

5. Add about ½ package bean thread noodles, soaked (see page 331) and cut, along with the tofu.

6. Add about 1 cup chopped cooked greens, like collards or spinach, along with the tofu.

7. Garnish with grated fresh ginger.

EGG SOUPS

Adding eggs to soup is among the easiest ways to deliver richness, body, and flavor. It's the simplest way to add protein too.

In Egg Drop Soup, Many Ways (right), the technique is to "scramble" beaten eggs into bubbling stock; the result is thin, tender wisps of egg throughout the soup. This is a technique you can do with almost any soup.

If you don't want those obvious egg strands, you must temper the eggs—mix them with a little hot broth before adding to the soup. As the eggs warm, the soup will thicken naturally, as long as you're careful not to boil the soup and curdle the eggs. This is another technique you can use elsewhere.

To poach eggs in soup, gently slip whole eggs into the hot soup, again being careful not to let the liquid boil vigorously. This is a technique I love; you'll see it in the variation Poached Egg Soup (page 142), but again, it's useful in many other instances.

Finally, you can top soup with already cooked eggs, whether they're fried, scrambled, poached, hard-boiled, whatever. See the list on page 142 for the most basic ideas. Or try the Egg "Noodle" Soup with Mushrooms (page 143) for something a little fancier.

Egg Drop Soup, Many Ways
MAKES: 4 servings
TIME: 20 minutes
F

The idea of scrambling eggs into a pot of simmering liquid is not unique to Chinese restaurants. In fact, my starting point is a Colombian dish, enriched with milk and seasoned with cilantro. But if you explore the variations, you'll see how global the notion is, and how valuable.

    1 tablespoon olive oil
    1 tablespoon minced garlic
    4 cups vegetable stock (pages 97–100) or
       water
       Salt and pepper
    2 cups milk
    4 eggs, beaten
    ½ cup chopped fresh cilantro for garnish
    2 scallions, sliced, for garnish

1. Put the oil in a large pot over medium-high heat. Add the garlic and cook, stirring frequently, until golden, about 1 minute. Add the stock along with a pinch of salt and pepper. Raise the heat to high and bring to a boil. Add the milk and heat until it just returns to a boil, then lower the heat so that the liquid bubbles gently but steadily.
2. Add the eggs to the soup in a steady stream, stirring constantly. You want the eggs to scramble, not just thicken the soup, but you don't want them to clump, so keep stirring until the eggs are cooked, 1 to 3 minutes. Taste and adjust the seasoning, garnish with the cilantro and scallions, and serve.

EGG DROP SOUP, MEXICAN STYLE With cheese and chile: Add 1 teaspoon ancho or a mild chili powder to the garlic. Omit the milk and increase the stock to 6 cups. Stir ½ cup crumbled queso fresco or grated cheddar or Jack cheese into the eggs before adding them.

EGG DROP SOUP, ITALIAN STYLE Parmesan makes this superb: After cooking the garlic, add ½ cup chopped tomatoes (canned are fine) and heat through. Omit the milk and increase the stock to 6 cups. Stir ½ cup grated Parmesan cheese into the eggs before adding them. Substitute basil or parsley for the cilantro and omit the scallions.

EGG DROP SOUP WITH SPINACH More substantial: Increase the olive oil to 2 tablespoons. Omit the milk and increase the stock to 6 cups. Stir ½ cup grated Parmesan cheese into the eggs. Add 1 pound fresh spinach, trimmed of thick stems and chopped, along with the stock and cook, stirring occasionally, until it's tender, 2 or 3 minutes, before adding the eggs. Skip the cilantro and scallions. Garnish with additional cheese if you'd like.

EGG DROP SOUP WITH SEA GREENS A lovely Japanese-style soup: Replace the olive oil with good-quality vegetable oil and substitute 1 tablespoon minced fresh ginger for the garlic. Skip the milk and use 6 cups Kombu Dashi (page 100) for the liquid in Step 1. Toast 2 sheets nori (see page 244) and slice into 1-inch ribbons; stir into the eggs. Omit the cilantro.

CURRY EGG DROP SOUP Use butter instead of olive oil and increase it to 2 tablespoons. Add 1 tablespoon minced fresh ginger and 2 tablespoons curry powder along with the garlic. Replace the milk with coconut milk.

POACHED EGG SOUP A little more work, but so wonderful: Choose any of the variations. Bring the soup to the bubbling point in Step 1. Instead of beating the eggs, carefully crack 4 eggs, one at a time, into a small saucer or bowl and slip each into the soup without breaking the yolk. Don't stir. Cover the pot and cook the eggs until the whites are set and the yolks are as runny as you like, 3 to 5 minutes. Carefully scoop the poached eggs into serving bowls and gently ladle in the soup. Top with the garnishes and cheese, if you're using it.

TOFU DROP SOUP, MANY WAYS Gives the soup a remarkable and delightful texture: Use 2 tablespoons sesame oil in Step 1 and fry the garlic until golden and crisp, 1 to 2 minutes. Pour in the stock and sprinkle with salt and pepper; bring to a boil. Combine half a 16-ounce package silken tofu and 2 cups coconut milk in a blender or food processor and blend until smooth. Pour into the simmering stock, then stir the remaining tofu into the soup, breaking it into small pieces. Cook until the tofu is heated through; taste and adjust the seasoning. Garnish as in the main recipe, and drizzle more sesame oil on top if you'd like. Ⓥ

8 More Ideas for Egg (or Tofu) Drop Soup
To make the soup in its sparest form, pare the ingredients down to 6 cups of any stock, salt and pepper, and the eggs. Start by heating the stock to bubbling and proceed with the recipe. Enjoy as is, or try one of these ideas:
1. Before adding the eggs, add 2 cups cooked brown or white rice to the bubbling stock.
2. Before adding the eggs, add any leftover cooked potato to the broth, like Home Fries (page 235), Oven-Roasted Hash Browns (page 238), or even chunks of baked potato.
3. After adding the eggs, stir in 2 cups plain cooked pasta or Asian noodles.

4. After the eggs cook, stir in ½ to 1 cup minced tender and mild but flavorful herbs: chervil, parsley, chives, basil, dill, and/or fennel fronds.

5. Finish the soup with 2 tablespoons chopped olives or Tapenade (page 291).

6. Put a slice of your favorite toasted bread (buttered or brushed with olive oil, if you'd like) in the bottom of each bowl. Pour the soup on top.

7. Stir ½ cup chopped oven-roasted tomatoes (page 258) into the soup before serving.

8. Stir in a pat of butter or a tablespoon or 2 of olive oil just before serving.

Egg "Noodle" Soup with Mushrooms

MAKES: 4 servings
TIME: About 45 minutes
Ⓜ

The "noodles" in this soup are made entirely of beaten eggs, which are cooked in a thin layer until just set. Once the sheets of egg cool down a bit and become pliable, you simply roll them up and slice it crosswise into coils of egg "noodles." These tender ribbons hold up well in soups, adding texture and flavor.

This is also an easy way to add eggs to all sorts of dishes, from salads and sandwiches to rice and pasta, especially since the "noodles" can be made ahead and refrigerated.

4	eggs
3	tablespoons good-quality vegetable oil
8	ounces shiitake mushrooms, stems discarded or reserved for stock, caps thinly sliced
	Salt and pepper
1	tablespoon minced garlic
4	scallions, thinly sliced on the diagonal
1	tablespoon sesame seeds
2	tablespoons soy sauce
2	teaspoons sesame oil
6	cups vegetable stock (pages 97–100) or water
7	ounces firm tofu (½ block), cut into small cubes (optional)
½	cup chopped fresh cilantro for garnish

1. Whisk the eggs with 2 teaspoons water in a small bowl. Add 1 tablespoon vegetable oil to a small nonstick pan over medium heat. When it's hot, pour a small amount of the egg into the pan, tilting it from side to side so the egg completely covers the bottom; it should be very thin. Cook until the top is firm, 1 minute or less; carefully flip it over and cook for another 15 seconds or so. Transfer to a cutting board. Repeat until you use up all the egg, piling them on top of one another. Roll them up and cut across into thin strips.

2. Heat the remaining 2 tablespoons vegetable oil in a large pot over medium-high heat. When it's hot, add the mushrooms, a large pinch of salt, and plenty of pepper. Cook, stirring occasionally, until the mushrooms release their liquid and the pot gets dry again, 5 to 10 minutes. Lower the heat to medium and cook, stirring occasionally, until they're as browned as you like them, 5 to 10 minutes more.

3. Stir in the garlic and cook, stirring frequently, until it's softened, 2 or 3 minutes. Add the scallions and sesame seeds, and cook, stirring constantly, until fragrant,

6 Ways to Use Eggs in Soups

1. Scramble eggs into Cauliflower Soup, Italian Style (page 102).

2. Garnish Creamy Potato and Leek Soup (page 102) with sliced hard-boiled eggs.

3. Set a fried egg atop each bowl of Onion Soup or any of its variations (page 100).

4. Garnish Creamy Spinach Soup (page 116) with chopped hard-boiled eggs.

5. Set a fried egg atop each bowl of Farro and Bean Soup (page 135).

6. Scramble eggs into Pho (page 130).

1 or 2 minutes. Add the soy sauce, sesame oil, and stock, and scrape with a wooden spoon to loosen any browned bits stuck to the bottom of the pan. Raise the heat to high, bring to a boil, then lower the heat so the soup bubbles gently but steadily.

4. Add the egg "noodles" and the tofu if you're using it. Stir once. Taste and adjust the seasoning, garnish with cilantro, and serve.

EGG "NOODLE" SOUP WITH BEAN THREADS Two unusual "noodles," combined: Before starting the soup, soak 2 bundles (4 ounces) bean thread noodles in warm tap water until transparent and pliable (see page 331). Keep in the water until ready to use, then drain and cut with scissors into manageable pieces. Stir into soup just before adding the egg "noodles."

COLD SOUPS

Obviously, summer is the best time to enjoy cold soups, when vegetables like tomatoes, cucumbers, and radishes are in season and hot soup loses its appeal. There are options here designed for year-round eating too. You can expand your repertoire—and make repurposing leftovers a breeze—by chilling hot soups, too. And if it's a sweet soup you're after, see the section in the Desserts chapter, starting on page 681.

Cool Yogurt Soup with Nuts

MAKES: 4 servings
TIME: About 20 minutes, plus time to chill
F M

A savory smoothie, served in a bowl.

    ¼ **cup roasted pistachios or toasted pumpkin seeds**
    2 **cups yogurt**
    ¼ **cup milk**
    1 **cup chopped fresh mint**
        Salt

    1 **small melon like honeydew, cantaloupe, or casaba, peeled, seeded, and grated, shredded, julienned, or finely chopped (about 2 cups)**
    2 **tablespoons fresh orange or lime juice**
    1 **teaspoon chili powder or a pinch cayenne**

1. Use the flat side of a wide knife or cleaver, or a small food processor, to break the pistachios or pumpkin seeds into large pieces.

2. Vigorously whisk together the yogurt, milk, mint, and a sprinkle of salt in a bowl until you smell the mint, just a minute or so. Push the mixture through a fine-meshed strainer. Discard the mint.

3. Put the melon, orange juice, and chili powder in a blender with the yogurt mixture and purée until smooth. Transfer to a storage container, cover, and refrigerate for at least 2 hours, stirring occasionally (the fruit will release liquid, which will become part of the soup). Taste and adjust the seasoning if necessary, then serve with a sprinkle of pistachios.

COOL CUCUMBER-YOGURT SOUP WITH NUTS A bit more savory: Keep the pistachios and mint, but use cucumber and lemon juice instead of the melon and orange or lime juice. Omit the chili powder and add 1 teaspoon curry powder.

YOGURT SOUP WITH FRESH PEAS Instead of pistachios, use cashews; replace the mint with ¼ cup chopped fresh tarragon. In Step 3, omit the melon, juice, and chili powder. Parboil 2 cups fresh peas (or use frozen peas directly from the bag) and add them to the blender along with 1 teaspoon sugar.

Smooth Gazpacho

MAKES: 4 servings
TIME: About 20 minutes
M V

Two tips: If fresh tomatoes aren't ripe or in season, you're better off using whole canned. A blender will give you a smoother soup than a food processor.

2 pounds tomatoes, chopped, or 1 28-ounce can tomatoes (don't bother to drain)
1 cucumber, peeled, seeded (if you'd like), and chopped
2 slices white bread (a day or 2 old is ideal), crusts removed, torn into small pieces
¼ cup olive oil, plus more for drizzling
2 tablespoons sherry vinegar or red wine vinegar, or more to taste
1 clove garlic
Salt and pepper

1. Put the tomatoes, cucumber, bread, oil, vinegar, and garlic with 1 cup water in a blender or food processor. Pulse at first, then let the machine run until the mixture is smooth. If the gazpacho seems too thick, thin it with additional water.

2. Taste and add salt, pepper, and vinegar as necessary. Serve right away, drizzled with olive oil, or refrigerate and serve within a couple of hours; taste and adjust the seasonings if needed, as cold can mute the flavors.

SPICY SMOOTH GAZPACHO Omit the vinegar and add the juice from 1 lemon or lime and 1 seeded fresh chile (like jalapeño or serrano) before puréeing in Step 1. Garnish the finished soup with ½ red or yellow bell pepper, cored, seeded, and chopped; 2 sliced scallions or shallots; and more fresh chile if you'd like.

COLD TOMATO SOUP Substitute an additional pound of fresh tomatoes or 1½ cups canned for the cucumber and fresh lemon juice for the vinegar. Add 1 tablespoon chopped fresh tarragon, chervil, or dill before puréeing in Step 1. Garnish with a dollop of sour cream or crème fraîche and a grind of pepper instead of the olive oil.

Ultra-Fast Avocado Soup

MAKES: 4 servings
TIME: 10 minutes, plus time to chill
F M

This lovely, celadon-colored soup is about as simple as it gets. The subtle, rich flavors of avocado and milk benefit from a hit of acidity, so I add orange or lime juice at the end, but that's about it. You can, however, dress it up for company: A couple of brightly colored cherry tomatoes tossed with oil, salt, and pepper and nestled in the middle of the soup are handsome additions, as are a few cilantro sprigs.

3 or 4 ripe avocados, pitted and peeled
3 cups milk (preferably whole)
Salt and cayenne
2 tablespoons fresh orange or lime juice, plus more to taste

1. Put the avocados in a blender with half the milk, a large pinch of salt, and a small pinch of cayenne, and purée until smooth. Transfer to a storage container and stir in the remaining milk and the citrus juice. Press a piece of plastic wrap directly on the surface of the soup so it doesn't discolor, and cover the container.

2. Chill the soup for at least 2 hours, or up to 6 hours if you have time. Taste and adjust the seasoning if necessary, adding more citrus juice if you'd like, and serve.

VEGAN ULTRA-FAST AVOCADO SOUP Same luxurious texture and richness, minus the dairy: Instead of the cow's milk, use any nut or grain milk, according to the flavor you want. V

COCONUT-AVOCADO SOUP Use coconut milk instead of the cow's milk. Top each serving with a sprinkle of toasted coconut (see page 304) and a little minced fresh hot red or green chile if you'd like. V

Vegetables, Fruits, Nuts, and Seeds

The information in this chapter will help you buy the best-quality produce possible, and prepare it well. By "produce," I mean both fruits and vegetables, the cornerstones of plant-based eating—and as you probably know, the distinction between the two is a bit blurry. We treat a lot of what are technically fruits as vegetables, and they're among the most beloved: tomatoes, eggplant, winter and summer squashes, cucumbers, even corn.

And we don't often cook with the plants we think of as fruits, like stone fruit, apples, bananas, and so on. We think of what we call fruits as sweet and vegetables as savory, so I've separated the two accordingly within the chapter. (You will find many sweet fruit recipes in the Desserts chapter.)

Here, then, is a lexicon of vegetables commonly found in the United States, with details about shopping, storing, basic cooking, and a couple of hundred vegetable-focused recipes (single-vegetable dishes, stir-fries, gratins, pies, and so on). This is followed by a lexicon of fruits, more information, and still more recipes. The chapter ends with information on and recipes for nuts and seeds.

THE BASICS OF BUYING AND HANDLING PRODUCE

The quality of the produce you select is as important as—or perhaps even more important than—how you cook it. This would argue for buying everything straight from the farm, or growing it yourself, but those may not be practical for most people. And cooking, like so much else in life, is about compromise. So there are probably some surprises in my suggestions here.

BUYING

It's not "fresh or nothing": Some frozen vegetables and fruits can have better quality than what passes for fresh, especially in the winter; they're generally inexpensive, too, and the convenience can't be beat.

Most of the time, however, you want to buy fresh produce. And when you do, be picky. In general, most vegetables should be slightly firm and most fruits slightly soft. Needless to say, you should check for damage or rotten spots and make sure the color is right.

Equally important: Consider the season. Virtually all fresh produce is available year-round thanks to imports, but seasonal selections almost always mean higher quality, and are a natural match for season-appropriate styles of cooking. Because of the many climates in the United States, we don't have a "national season" for much produce, so wherever you live, tune in to what's available locally. And be flexible: If you go to the store and something you planned on cooking doesn't look great, reach for an alternative or head to the freezer case. In almost every recipe in this chapter—and throughout the book—I offer substitutions for the main vegetable or other ingredient.

Also, consider the source: If you're concerned about the impact of conventional farming methods on your health and the environment—and you should be—think about buying organic fruits and vegetables. But my feeling is that it's more important to seek out locally or regionally grown produce. If it's organic, so much the better.

STORING AND PREPARING

Mostly, you'll want to refrigerate fruits and vegetables when you bring them home, but that's not always the case; check the individual listings in this chapter for more details.

Don't rinse vegetables and fruits until you're ready to use them. Water may rinse away natural defenses against rotting, and moist produce is more prone to mold and bacteria growth. I wash everything I'm going to eat raw, even when I'm going to peel it, since any bacteria or dirt on the outside can spread to the inside with handling.

A soft brush is a handy tool for cleaning potatoes you don't want to peel, cucumbers with little spines, and other more rigorous jobs. You can also use one of those mildly abrasive dishwashing pads. Washing greens and small vegetables couldn't be easier: Put them in a salad spinner or a colander inside a large pot, fill it with water, swish the veggies around, lift the liner or colander out of the water, and drain. If the vegetables are particularly sandy or muddy, repeat until they're clean.

THE BASICS OF COOKING VEGETABLES

My goal is to help you become more comfortable cooking vegetables instinctively and experimenting with your own favorite ingredients and techniques. I want you to develop an intuition for flavors and substitutions. The recipes throughout this chapter provide a great place for beginners to start and a useful reference for more experienced cooks.

Cooking vegetables can completely change their taste and texture and, for that matter, their nutritional profiles (see "Raw Versus Cooked, Nutritionally"). Some cooking methods—roasting, sautéing, broiling, and grilling, for example—deepen flavor by caramelizing the natural sugars or starches in vegetables, while techniques like steaming and poaching brighten both their taste and their color.

Though there are some exceptions (noted in specific vegetable entries and recipes), I prefer to cook vegetables until crisp-tender (al dente). You're looking for a state in which the vegetables retain a subtle, pleasant crunch but are tender and moist enough to be pierced easily with a skewer or thin-bladed knife—or your teeth! When crisp-tender, vegetables like asparagus and broccoli will be flexible but not flopping over, and their color will be bright. You'll learn to assess crisp-tender doneness by sight after a while, but start by simply taking a bite of the vegetables as they cook to gauge their texture.

Generally, it's important to leave a little elbow room in the pot whenever you cook vegetables. A pot of water will take a long time to return to a boil if you load it with too much—and then the vegetables will probably get mushy. In the microwave, overcrowding keeps vegetables from cooking evenly. Crowding the pan or pot during sautéing or frying causes the vegetables to soak up extra oil instead of starting to cook on contact, and keeps them from browning properly. Bottom line: Have a little patience and work in batches if necessary.

MICROWAVING

The microwave is ideal for steaming veggies with barely any water, providing you know your machine well enough to cook them evenly and take them out before

Raw Versus Cooked, Nutritionally

There have been many studies about the nutrition of vegetables, both raw and cooked, as well as how different methods of cooking fare, nutrition-wise. The results are a mixed bag. Water-soluble nutrients don't take well to heat, vitamin C and B vitamins in particular. On the other hand, cooking breaks down the thick cell walls of vegetables like tomatoes, carrots, asparagus, broccoli, cabbage, and mushrooms, making some nutrients and compounds—especially the antioxidants lycopene and carotenoids—more available for absorption. But it's not that simple: Studies have shown that in some produce, cooking compromises certain compounds thought to fight precancerous cells, while other studies have found that in different produce, heat can create compounds that fight precancerous cells. Finally, there is no consensus regarding which cooking methods are most effective for nutrient retention—some studies say boiling and pressure cooking are the best and others say exactly the opposite—though most agree that frying creates dangerous free radicals.

My recommendation is simply to eat both raw and cooked vegetables, and to cook them in the ways you like best, so you'll enjoy them and eat more of them.

they overcook. Put vegetables on a plate or in a shallow bowl, sprinkle them with a couple of tablespoons of water, then cover them loosely with a vented microwave cooking lid, a paper towel, or a heavy fitted lid. Stir, check, and re-cover the vegetables periodically. Be careful when you uncover them; the steam will be very hot.

STEAMING

Cooking vegetables above—not in—a small amount of simmering water is fast, efficient, and healthy. This method is great for plain vegetables you want to eat right away or marinate in a vinaigrette (page 628) and cool down for salad. (For a specific example, see Basic Steamed Cauliflower on page 188.)

You can buy fancy vegetable steamers, but one of those fold-up baskets that you set into the bottom of a pot works fine, as does a colander or even, in a pinch, a heatproof bowl that fits in the pot (see "Ways to Rig a Steamer," page 25). Fill the basket or bowl with vegetables, set it over an inch or so of water, cover the pot, and turn the heat to high. Once the water comes to a boil, adjust the heat to keep the water bubbling steadily. Check frequently to prevent overcooking and make sure there's still water in the bottom of the pot. If you want to stop the cooking immediately to hold the vegetables for future use, as soon as you remove them, shock the vegetables in a bowl of ice water to cool them quickly.

BOILING/SIMMERING, PARBOILING, BLANCHING, AND SHOCKING

To boil, there are two options: bring a large pot of water to a boil, salt it generously, and toss in the vegetables. Let the water come back to a boil; continue to boil (or turn it down to simmer, just barely bubbling) until the vegetables are just tender, then drain them and continue with the recipe as instructed. The other is put the vegetables in a pot, add water to cover, then bring to a boil and continue to boil/simmer.

Parboiling simply means to boil vegetables until they are only partially cooked; it's usually done for vegetables that you will finish cooking by some other method like stir-frying or sautéing. Parboiling gives those vegetables a head start so that everything can finish at about the same time; it's especially useful for dense vegetables that might not cook all the way through using a faster high-heat method. It's also a good precooking method that can save time later.

Blanching also involves cooking vegetables in boiling water, but very briefly—usually a minute or even just a few seconds. This tenderizes the vegetable only slightly while fixing its bright color. It can also be used to tame the harsh flavor of some vegetables like onions.

With both parboiling and blanching, the vegetables are usually drained and "shocked": dropped into ice water to stop the cooking. As soon as they have cooled, drain again.

Vegetable Purée

MAKES: 4 servings
TIME: 40 minutes
Ⓜ Ⓥ

Purées are all-purpose: They make a perfect bed for burgers, cutlets, "meat" balls, and slices of cooked tofu, tempeh, or seitan. Or use them underneath other vegetables like asparagus, broccoli spears, sliced or cubed eggplant, or roasted chunks of potato.

Vegetable purée can be used as a "sauce" for pasta (you may want to thin it first), rice or risotto, cooked whole grains, baked potatoes, or thick slices of toast. Well-seasoned warm or room-temperature purées are also lovely dips for anything from crudités to dumplings to grilled tofu skewers; thin them, if necessary, with a little stock or other liquid. They make good spreads for sandwiches and fillings for burritos or tacos too.

This recipe is a straightforward template for puréeing almost any vegetable. See the chart on page 152 for more ideas.

To make an impromptu gratin, put the purée in a greased shallow baking or gratin dish, sprinkle with bread crumbs, dot with butter or drizzle with olive oil, and bake in a 375°F oven until hot and bubbly.

Clockwise from left: Golden beet, pea, and butternut squash purées

More Vegetable Purées

These are suggestions for pairing vegetables with seasonings and flavorings. You can mix and match as long as you choose just one ingredient from each column. Make any dairy-based purée vegan by using the cooking water, vegetable stock (pages 97 to 100), silken tofu, juice, or unsweetened soy, coconut, or nut milk as the liquid, and oil for the fat.

VEGETABLE	LIQUID	FAT	SEASONING	GARNISH
2 pounds raw will give you 3–4 cups cooked and chopped	As much as you like or need to reach the desired consistency; usually about ½ cup	2–3 tablespoons	1–2 tablespoons in addition to salt and pepper	As much or as little as you like
Broccoli	Ricotta cheese	Olive oil	Nutmeg	Grated Parmesan cheese
Butternut squash	Coconut milk	Good-quality vegetable oil	Curry powder	Toasted shredded coconut
Carrots	Orange juice	Olive oil	Minced fresh ginger	Grated orange zest
Chestnuts	Heavy cream or crème fraîche	Butter	Honey or maple syrup	Chopped roasted chestnuts
Corn	Sour cream	Butter or olive oil	Chili powder	Queso fresco, chopped fresh tomato, and chopped cilantro
Daikon radish	A bit of the boiling liquid	Sesame oil (a few drops)	None needed	Toasted sesame seeds or Nori "Shake" (page 650)
Eggplant	Silken tofu	Sesame oil (a few drops)	Any miso	Sliced scallions; pass soy sauce at the table
Parsnips	Milk or cream	Melted butter	Seeds from 1 inch vanilla bean, or 1 teaspoon vanilla extract	Chopped hazelnuts
Shell peas	Heavy cream or half-and-half	Melted butter	Chopped fresh tarragon	Dijon mustard
Turnips	Sour cream	Melted butter or olive oil	Chopped red onion	Chopped fresh parsley

About 1½ pounds vegetables (one kind or
a combination)
Salt
2 tablespoons olive oil
Pepper
Chopped fresh parsley for garnish (optional)

1. Peel and trim the vegetables as necessary; cut them into roughly equal-size pieces, 1 or 2 inches in diameter. Put everything in a pot with water to cover and add a large pinch salt. Or put in a steamer above an inch or so of water. Bring the water to a boil and cook until the vegetables are tender, 5 to 15 minutes, depending on the vegetable.

2. Drain the vegetables well, reserving some of the cooking water. (You can prepare the vegetables up to this point, cool, cover tightly, and refrigerate for up to 2 days before proceeding.) Put the vegetables through a food mill placed over the pot, or cool slightly and purée them in a blender or food processor with as much of the reserved cooking water as you need to get the machine going. If the vegetables are very tender, you can mash them with a large fork or potato masher, adding the water as needed.

3. Add the oil and stir, then taste, season with more salt if necessary, and sprinkle with pepper. Serve, keep warm, or allow to cool for reheating later. (Reheat over low heat on the stove, stirring occasionally, or zap in the microwave until hot.) Garnish with parsley, if you like, before serving.

RICH VEGETABLE PURÉE Replace the olive oil with butter and add up to ½ cup heavy cream, sour cream, half-and-half, or whole milk. Proceed with Step 3.

Boiled or Steamed Greens

MAKES: 4 servings
TIME: 10 to 30 minutes
F M V

This is the basic method for cooking greens (or just about any vegetable in the variations). Both work just fine; boiling gives you a little more control, but steaming is faster.

If the leaves and stems are pliable and can be eaten raw—as with spinach, arugula, or watercress—it's a tender green and can be cooked as is. If the stems are as crisp as celery and the leaves a little tough or rubbery—as in bok choy, chard, kale, or collards—it's best to separate the leaves from the stems (see the illustration on page 211) and give the stems a head start.

Other vegetables you can use: any green except sorrel (it will dissolve)

Salt
1–2 pounds greens (like spinach, kale, or chard), washed and trimmed
Fresh lemon juice, olive oil, or butter

1. Rig a steamer (see page 25) or bring a large pot of water to a boil and salt it. If the greens have very thick stems (more than ⅛ inch or so), separate them from the leaves.

2. Add the stems or the stems and leaves to the steamer or pot and cook until bright green and tender, from 3 minutes (for spinach) to 10 (for kale and collards). If you held back the leaves, add them when the stems are just about tender.

3. Drain, then serve, drizzled or topped with whatever you like. Or shock in ice water, drain again, and proceed.

BOILED OR STEAMED TENDER VEGETABLES This will work for broccoli, cauliflower, green beans, asparagus, peas of any type, even eggplant (be careful not to overcook): Cook until the vegetable is just tender, which will vary from about 3 (peas) to 7 (broccoli florets) to 10 or 12 (broccoli stems, some green beans) and up to 25 minutes (for a large whole head of cauliflower). Proceed from Step 3.

BOILED OR STEAMED ROOT VEGETABLES OR TUBERS It's best to follow individual recipes given in this chapter, especially for potatoes and sweet potatoes. But as a general rule, this will work for beets, turnips, radishes, winter squash, and so on: Peel the vegetable or not as you prefer; leave whole if possible to prevent waterlogging. Cook until the vegetable is quite tender and can be pierced easily with a thin-bladed knife, from 10 minutes (radishes, for example) to nearly an hour (large potatoes). Proceed from Step 3.

SAUTÉING

Sautéing means to cook food (any food) quickly in a small amount of hot fat. (Stir-frying is a subset of sautéing.) Set a skillet over medium to medium-high heat and add some oil or butter—1 to 2 tablespoons (more if you like) per pound of food. When the oil or butter is hot, add the vegetables and stir or toss them around in the pan until they're cooked, seasoning as needed. Don't crowd, or the vegetables will steam instead of brown. (For a specific example, see Pan-Grilled Corn with Chile, page 198.)

STIR-FRYING

Stir-frying is one of the best and fastest ways to get an entire meal on the table, and, frankly, is a lot like sautéing, with bite-size pieces of food cooked in a small amount of oil over high heat. You can stir-fry just about any vegetable (and most other things as well): Cut the ingredients into more-or-less bite-sized pieces. If you want to include vegetables that take more than just a couple minutes to cook, like broccoli florets, for instance, they should be blanched first, to cut down on the time they'll need when you start stir-frying. If you plan to serve your stir-fry with rice, have that ready, because the stir-frying itself is the last thing you do: Once you get started, the whole process moves quickly without any down time.

Stir-Fried Vegetables

MAKES: 4 servings
TIME: 30 minutes
F M V

Stir-fries are a fantastic, fast way to use those singleton carrots, celery stalks, and other vegetables sitting in your fridge. One key to a fast stir-fry is the size you cut your vegetables: The smaller you cut them, the quicker they cook.

> 2 **tablespoons good-quality vegetable oil**
> 1 **tablespoon minced garlic**
> 1 **tablespoon minced fresh ginger**
> ½ **cup chopped scallions or onion**
> 1 **large carrot, cut into pieces, thinly sliced, or julienned**
> 2 **stalks celery, cut into pieces, thinly sliced, or julienned**
> ¼ **cup any stock or water, plus more as needed**
> 1 **pound snow peas or sugar snap peas, trimmed (thawed frozen are fine)**
> 2 **tablespoons soy sauce**
> 1 **teaspoon sesame oil**

1. Heat a large, deep skillet over medium-high heat for 3 to 4 minutes. Add the vegetable oil and, almost immediately, the garlic, ginger, and scallions. Cook, stirring, for about 15 seconds, then add the carrot, celery, and stock and raise the heat to high.
2. Stir-fry until the vegetables are tender, about 7 minutes. If the mixture is completely dry, add a couple of tablespoons more liquid. Add the snow peas, soy sauce, and sesame oil; stir and turn off the heat. Serve or store, covered, in the refrigerator for up to a day.

Stir-Fried Vegetables, Vietnamese Style

MAKES: 4 servings
TIME: 30 minutes
F V

Lots of garlic and lots of black pepper are the keys to this simple but flavorful stir-fry.

Normally, when adding broccoli to a mixed vegetable stir-fry, I would blanch it to cut down on its cook time. But because this stir-fry starts with the broccoli, it's not necessary.

Other vegetables you can use: Really, any

assortment you like, provided you cook each vegetable alone to make sure they are all cooked perfectly.

¼ cup good-quality vegetable oil
1 cup broccoli or cauliflower florets, in about 1-inch pieces
2 carrots, thinly sliced
½ cup snow peas or sugar snap peas, trimmed
1 medium to large onion, thinly sliced
2 dried chiles
1 tablespoon minced garlic
2 tablespoons Fishless Fish Sauce (page 656) or soy sauce (or to taste)
1 teaspoon black pepper (or to taste)
Salt

1. Put 1 tablespoon of the oil in a nonstick skillet over high heat. When it's hot, add the broccoli. Cook, stirring occasionally, for about a minute, then add 2 tablespoons water. Continue to cook and stir until the vegetable is crisp-tender, about 5 minutes. Remove from the pan and repeat the process with the carrots, then the snow peas. **2.** Put a little more oil in the pan and add the onion. Cook over high heat, stirring once in a while, until it softens and begins to char, 3 to 5 minutes. Add the chiles and garlic and cook for another 30 seconds. **3.** Add ¼ cup water, the sauce, and the pepper; return the cooked vegetables to the pan. Cook, stirring, until the vegetables are lightly coated. Taste and adjust the seasoning, adding salt if necessary, and serve.

BRAISING

A combination of sautéing and simmering, braising allows you to cook vegetables until they're fully tender and take advantage of their flavor. Root vegetables, cabbages, sturdy winter greens, and alliums (garlic, shallots, leeks, and onions) are all good candidates for braising because they benefit from the extra time.

17 Additions to Stir-Fried Vegetables

Generally, you can add about 1 to 2 cups of any extras to the basic stir-fry. You may need to add a bit more liquid if the pan seems dry at any point.

1. Bamboo shoots, added just before the end of cooking

2. Sliced water chestnuts, added just before the end of cooking

3. Tofu, pressed, fried, or baked and cubed, added with about 2 minutes cooking to go

4. Tofu skins, frozen or reconstituted dried (see page 482), sliced and added with about 2 minutes cooking to go

5. Green beans, preferably blanched (see page 24), added with the carrots and celery; add them whole if thin or cut into 2-inch or so lengths

6. Spinach or watercress, trimmed, added with about a minute to go

7. Mushrooms, fresh or reconstituted dried, trimmed and sliced or chopped, added with the carrots and celery

8. Daikon radish, julienned or shredded, added with about a minute to go

9. Corn kernels, added with about a minute to go

10. Cabbage, trimmed and cut in chiffonade (see page 23), added with the scallions

11. Bok choy, stems separated from the leaves and chopped, leaves cut into chiffonade; add the stems with the carrots and celery and the leaves with the snow peas

12. Asparagus, blanched, added with the snow peas

13. Zucchini or summer squash, cut into slices or chunks, added with the carrots and celery

14. Any color bell pepper, seeded and sliced, added with the carrots and celery

15. Soy or mung bean sprouts, added just before the end of cooking

16. Broccoli or cauliflower florets, blanched, added with the carrots and celery

17. 1 medium to large tomato, halved, seeded, and chopped, added with the carrots and celery

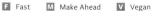

Begin by sautéing. After the vegetables have softened a little and are coated in oil, add liquid—stock, milk, juice, wine, water, more olive oil. Bring to a boil, then lower the heat so the mixture bubbles gently, or put the pot in a 350°F oven. You can cover the vegetables during braising or leave them uncovered, depending on how saucy you want the final dish to be, adding more liquid as needed to keep everything from drying out.

Quick Coconut-Braised Vegetables

MAKES: 4 servings
TIME: 30 minutes
F V

This delicious braise can be varied in a number of ways, all delicious. If you like Thai curries, this is for you.

- 3 tablespoons good-quality vegetable oil
- 1 large white onion, sliced
- 2 tablespoons chopped garlic
- 2 dried chiles; 1 fresh chile, minced; or 1 teaspoon Chile Paste (page 664) or Red or Green Curry Paste (page 666), or to taste
- 3 lime leaves (preferably fresh; dried are okay), chopped, or the grated zest of 1 lime
- 1½ pounds eggplant, zucchini, or summer squash, or a combination, peeled as necessary and cut into chunks
- 1½ cups coconut milk (to make your own, see page 304, or use 1 14-ounce can and a little water)
- 3 tablespoons soy sauce or Fishless Fish Sauce (page 656)
  Salt and black pepper
  Lime wedges

1. Put the oil in a large skillet over medium-high heat. When it's hot, add the onion and cook, stirring occasionally, until it softens a bit, 3 to 5 minutes. Stir in the garlic, chiles, and lime leaves, then add the vegetable(s). Cook, stirring occasionally and adjusting the heat as necessary so the vegetable cooks quickly without burning, until it softens, 10 to 20 minutes (zucchini will cook faster than eggplant).

2. Add the coconut milk and simmer until thickened, about 5 minutes. Add the soy sauce, then taste and add salt and pepper if necessary. Serve hot, with lime wedges.

Ratatouille

MAKES: 4 to 6 servings
TIME: About 1½ hours, mostly unattended
M V

This classic French dish is no more complicated than combining vegetables, herbs, and olive oil in various proportions and braising them on the stove or in the oven until very soft.

Other vegetables you can use: You can pretty much include whatever you want in this kind of oven braise, but potatoes and mushrooms are the most common additions to ratatouille that I haven't included here.

- ½ cup olive oil, plus more for serving
- 2 large onions, sliced
- 1½–2 pounds eggplant (preferably small), sliced ½ inch thick
- 1 pound zucchini, trimmed and cut into large chunks
- 2 red or yellow bell peppers, seeded and sliced
- 4 plum or 2 round tomatoes, chopped (or drained canned in a pinch)
  Fresh herbs, any you can find are good (thyme, marjoram, rosemary, savory, basil, parsley, or chervil), chopped, to taste, plus more for garnish
- 10 cloves garlic, halved
  Salt and pepper

1. Heat the oven to 350°F.
2. Pour a couple of tablespoons of the oil in a casserole or heavy ovenproof skillet. Make a layer of half of the onion, followed by half the eggplant, then half the

zucchini, peppers, tomatoes, herbs, and garlic (the order doesn't matter, just that they're layered) and sprinkle with salt and pepper. Repeat with the remaining vegetables and more herbs. Drizzle with the remaining oil.

3. Braise it in the oven for about an hour, pressing down on the vegetables occasionally with a spatula, until they are all completely tender. Garnish with more herbs, drizzle with a little more oil, and serve hot, warm, or at room temperature.

STOVETOP MIXED VEGETABLES WITH OLIVE OIL This requires a little more attention: Combine all the ingredients in the largest skillet you have (a broad saucepan will also work) and cook, stirring occasionally, over medium heat, adjusting the heat so the mixture simmers in its own juices without browning. Cooking time will be just a little shorter, perhaps 45 minutes or so.

BRAISING AND GLAZING

This technique is less straightforward than the others, but is easy to pick up. The idea is to combine the benefits of steaming—speed and moisture—with the power of sautéing—caramelization and crispness—all in one pot. As an added benefit, when you braise and glaze vegetables, their nutrients don't get left behind in a pot of water. (For a specific example, see Braised and Glazed Brussels Sprouts, page 183.)

Put some oil or butter in a deep skillet and turn the heat to medium. Sauté some garlic, onion, shallot, and/or ginger if you like—just for 30 seconds or so—then add the vegetable (like carrots, broccoli, cauliflower, asparagus, or any root vegetable, sliced or chopped) with a little water and a sprinkle of salt. The longer the vegetable needs to cook, the more water you'll need, but generally just ¼ to ½ cup will do.

Now cover the pan. Cook, uncovering only often enough to stir and check the water level, until the vegetable is just tender, 5 to 15 minutes depending on the vegetable and size of cut. The goal is to keep just enough water in the pan to steam the vegetable until it's cooked without letting the pan go dry. To glaze, uncover and raise the heat to cook out almost all of the remaining water; the combination of the fat and the starches and sugars from the vegetable will create a glossy coating.

FRYING

When it comes to frying vegetables, you've got a few choices, starting with the decision whether or not to coat. Whatever you decide, you can either pan-fry them in shallow oil or deep-fry in enough oil to submerge them.

TO PANFRY Set a deep skillet over medium to medium-high heat and pour in the oil, up to ½ inch deep or so, though ⅛ inch or so is enough if you're panfrying vegetables in a batter. It should be hot but not smoking before you add the vegetables (test a small piece first; the vegetable should immediately sizzle vigorously). Add the vegetables, working in batches if necessary to prevent crowding, and fry as directed in the particular recipe.

TO DEEP-FRY Heat 2 to 3 inches oil in a deep skillet to a temperature between 350°F and 375°F. Be careful to allow enough room in the pot for the vegetables to displace the oil. Add the vegetables, working in batches if necessary to prevent crowding, and fry, stirring a few times for even cooking, as directed in the particular recipe. See "Deep-Frying," page 26, for complete instructions.

Korean Vegetable Pancakes

Pa Jun

MAKES: 6 to 8 servings
TIME: 45 minutes

Ⓜ

These addictive pancakes are almost crêpelike in their crisp and chewy texture. That texture—crisp on the outside, tender and chewy on the inside—is best if you use half rice flour, which is pretty easy to find these days. Serve the pancakes hot or at room temperature with Korean-Style Soy and Sesame Dipping Sauce and

Korean Vegetable
Pancakes (page 157)

Marinade (page 656), or a mixture of soy sauce and vinegar.

Other vegetables you can use: corn kernels, radish (especially daikon), or broccoli

- 2 cups flour (preferably 1 cup all-purpose plus 1 cup rice flour, or use all-purpose)
- 2 eggs, lightly beaten
- 1 tablespoon good-quality vegetable oil, plus more for frying
- 5 scallions (green parts only), cut into 3-inch pieces and sliced lengthwise
- 20 chives (preferably Chinese — "garlic" — chives), cut into 2-inch lengths, or ¼ cup chopped fresh cilantro
- 2 carrots, grated
- 1 small yellow squash or zucchini, grated

1. Mix the flour, eggs, and 1 tablespoon oil with 1½ cups water until a smooth batter is formed. Add the scallions, chives, carrots, and squash and stir to combine.

2. Heat a large nonstick skillet over medium-high heat and pour in about ⅛ inch oil. When it's hot, ladle in a quarter of the batter and spread it out evenly into a circle. Turn the heat down to medium and cook until the bottom is browned, about 5 minutes. Then flip and cook for another 5 minutes. Repeat with the remaining batter, adding more oil if necessary.

3. As the pancakes finish, remove them and, if necessary, drain on paper towels. Cut into small triangles and serve with a soy dipping sauce.

CRISPY KIMCHI PANCAKES Spicy: Use kimchi liquid in place of some or all of the water in Step 1. Add about 1 cup chopped Kimchi (page 93) to the batter.

JAPANESE VEGETABLE PANCAKES (OKONOMIYAKI)
These large pancakes make a spectacular entrée: Use only ½ cup flour and increase the eggs to 6. Use 5 to 6 cups total shredded green cabbage in place of the chives, carrots, and squash. Fry in pan-sized pancakes or smaller-sized. Serve with Chile Mayonnaise (page 671).

Batter-Fried Vegetables

MAKES: 4 servings
TIME: 30 minutes
F

Nearly any vegetable can be battered and fried, with terrific results. Hard vegetables should be thinly sliced, ¼ inch thick or less; tender ones, like zucchini and eggplant, can be cut thicker, up to ½ inch. Green beans, snow peas, and small mushrooms and okra pods can be left whole.

The best way to serve batter-fried vegetables is the moment the morsels come out of the oil and are drained. But if you want to serve them as part of a sit-down meal, keep them warm for a few minutes in a 200°F oven (ideally on a rack). I love this with Garlic Mayonnaise (page 671) or just a squirt of lemon juice.

- Good-quality vegetable oil for deep-frying
- 2 cups all-purpose flour
- 1 teaspoon baking powder
- 1 teaspoon salt
- Black pepper
- 1 egg
- ¾ cup beer or sparkling water
- 1½ pounds vegetables of your choice (all of one type or a combination), cut into pieces (see headnote; depending on how they are cut, you should have 2–4 cups vegetables)
- Coarse salt

1. Put at least 2 inches oil in a deep pan on the stove and turn the heat to medium-high; bring to 350°F (see "Deep-Frying," page 26).

2. Mix together 1 cup of the flour, the baking powder, salt, some pepper, the egg, and beer in a medium bowl until just combined. The batter should be the consistency of pancake batter. It's okay to leave some lumps; you don't want to overmix.

3. Dredge each vegetable piece lightly in the remaining 1 cup flour. Working in batches, dip in the batter to coat, and add to the oil. Do not crowd the vegetables. Cook, turning once if needed, until golden all over, just a few

Different Ways with Breaded and Panfried Vegetables and Fruit

VEGETABLE OR FRUIT	PREPARATION	HOW TO FRY	SUGGESTED ACCOMPANIMENTS
Fennel	Trim; cut crosswise into ¼-inch-thick slices; dredge as directed.	Fry at about 350°F until golden brown on both sides, about 5 minutes total.	Mint or Dill "Pesto" (page 638); Herbed Yogurt Sauce (page 674)
Mushrooms	Small whole button or cremini, shiitake caps work best; clean and trim; dredge as directed.	Fry at about 350°F until breading is golden brown (interior cooks quickly).	Seaweed "Mayo" (page 673); Basil Dipping Sauce (page 654); Simple Miso Dipping Sauce (page 653)
Onions	Trim; cut crosswise into ½-inch-thick slices; separate slices into rings; dredge in flour, egg, and bread crumbs or just flour as directed.	Fry at about 375°F until golden brown, about 3 minutes total. Panfrying small quantities is fine.	Blue Cheese Dressing (page 674)
Squash blossoms	Leave whole; dredge as directed.	Fry at 375°F, just enough to get exterior golden brown, about 4 minutes total.	Avocado Yogurt Sauce (page 674)
Sweet potatoes, yams	Peeling is optional. Cut lengthwise into wedges (no more than ½ inch at thickest part) or ¼-inch-thick slices; dredge as directed.	Fry at about 350°F so interior has time to cook before exterior gets too dark, and flip when one side is golden brown; fry about 8 minutes total.	Ponzu (page 657)
Tomatoes	Cut green tomatoes in ¼–½-inch slices and dredge in a 2:1 mixture of cornmeal and flour seasoned with salt and pepper.	Use about ¼ inch oil and fry at 350°F until golden brown, 2 to 3 minutes per side.	Enjoy traditionally at breakfast as a side to eggs. But also delicious with a little dollop of Garlic Mayonnaise (page 671)
Winter squash	Peel and cut into ¼-inch slices; dredge as directed.	Fry at about 350°F so interior has time to cook before exterior gets too dark, and flip when one side is golden brown; fry about 8 minutes total.	Pesto (page 634); Curry Ranch Dressing (page 672)
Zucchini, summer squash	Cut into bite-size pieces or diagonal slices; dredge as directed.	Fry at about 375°F until golden brown on both sides, about 5 minutes total.	Salsa Cruda (page 660); Real Ranch Dressing (page 672); Fiery Yogurt Sauce (page 674)

minutes. Drain on a rack or paper towels, sprinkle with coarse salt, and serve immediately.

PAKORA-STYLE FRIED VEGETABLES For the batter, use ¼ cup chickpea flour, all-purpose flour, or cornmeal; omit the baking powder and egg, and replace the beer with ¾ to 1 cup water. Add a pinch cayenne if you like and salt and pepper to taste. The batter should be thin. Use chickpea flour or all-purpose flour for dredging. Serve with any chutney (pages 668 to 670). ▣

TEMPURA FRIED VEGETABLES For the batter, omit the baking powder, salt, and pepper. Mix together 1½ cups rice flour or all-purpose flour, 3 egg yolks, and 2 cups ice-cold water (this is really important for the lightest, crispest coating; get the water super-cold with ice cubes); the batter should be thin. Use rice flour or all-purpose flour for the dredging. These are best enjoyed as soon as they come out of the hot oil. Serve this and the Vegan Tempura below with any of the dipping sauces on pages 653 to 659.

VEGAN TEMPURA Sparkling water adds airiness to this two-ingredient batter: Follow the preceding variation, omitting the egg yolks and substituting very cold sparkling water for the ice water. ▣

Breaded and Panfried Eggplant (or Any Other Vegetable)

MAKES: 4 servings
TIME: 1 hour
Ⓜ

Classic for eggplant, this is a good technique to make almost any sturdy vegetable crunchy and tender. Like any fried food, this is best immediately after cooking, so drain briefly, then serve. If you must wait, hold in a 200°F oven for a bit; a wire rack set over a rimmed baking pan is ideal, but any ovenproof platter will work.

Eggplant produces a very substantial "cutlet" when handled this way, but so do many of the other vegetables in the chart opposite. I love them with just lemon juice, sometimes with a little soy sauce or hot sauce.

    4 or 5 small or 2 large eggplant (about 2 pounds total), trimmed
    1 cup all-purpose flour for dredging
    3 eggs
    3 cups dried bread crumbs for dredging
       Salt and pepper
    3 tablespoons butter plus 3 tablespoons olive oil or 6 tablespoons oil, plus more as needed
       Chopped fresh parsley for garnish
       Lemon wedges

1. Cut the eggplant into ½-inch-thick slices. Set out the flour, eggs, and bread crumbs on separate plates or shallow bowls next to each other on the counter. Have a stack of parchment paper or wax paper sheets ready. Beat the eggs in a shallow bowl and season liberally with salt and pepper.
2. Dredge the eggplant slices, one at a time, in the flour, then coat with the egg, then dredge in the bread crumbs, pressing to help the crumbs adhere. Stack the breaded cutlets between layers of parchment and then transfer the stack to the refrigerator to chill for at least 10 minutes and up to 3 hours.
3. When you're ready to cook, heat the oven to 200°F. Put the butter and oil in a deep pan on the stove and turn the heat to medium-high; when it's ready—about 350°F—a pinch flour will sizzle immediately when thrown in. Put in a few of the eggplant slices; cook in batches as necessary, being sure not to crowd the pan.
4. Turn the eggplant slices as soon as they're browned, then cook the other side. The total cooking time should be 5 minutes or less. As each piece is done, transfer it first to paper towels to drain briefly, then to an ovenproof platter; transfer the platter to the oven. Add more oil to the pan between batches, if necessary.
5. Serve as soon as all the pieces are cooked. Garnish with parsley and serve lemon wedges on the side.

CELERY ROOT "SCHNITZEL" This is terrific: Substitute peeled celery root (or potatoes, beets, or rutabaga) for the eggplant, cutting it into ¼-inch-thick slices and cooking for about 10 minutes total.

SESAME-FRIED EGGPLANT Pair this with any soy-based dipping sauce (pages 654 to 659): Use 2 cups bread crumbs and 1 cup sesame seeds for the final dredging. Replace 2 to 3 tablespoons of the oil or butter with sesame oil.

COCONUT-FRIED PLANTAINS A totally tropical appetizer, side dish, or dessert: Substitute 4 or 5 yellow to yellow-black plantains for the eggplant; peel and cut straight or diagonal into about ¼-inch-thick slices. Use 1½ cups bread crumbs and 1½ cups shredded coconut for the final dredging. They'll fry up a bit faster, 2 to 3 minutes per side.

GRAIN-FRIED BUTTERNUT SQUASH Ground grains add a nutty flavor: Substitute about 2 pounds peeled butternut squash sliced ¼ inch thick for the eggplant. Use 3 cups ground oats or barley instead of the bread crumbs for the final dredging.

FRIED ONION RINGS, STREAMLINED A slightly less crunchy onion ring; these make a fantastic garnish too: Substitute 2 thinly sliced onions for the eggplant. Omit the bread crumbs and eggs. Separate the onion slices into rings, dredge the rings in just flour, and fry in oil until golden brown. ⒱

VEGAN BREADED AND PANFRIED EGGPLANT This variation can also apply to any of the variations: Instead of the egg, use soy, grain, or nut milk. For frying, use all oil. ⒱

ROASTING

Roasting vegetables takes longer than other cooking methods, anywhere from 15 minutes for asparagus to an hour for potatoes. But it's a great method for entertaining, because the results can be served right out of the oven or at room temperature. (For a specific example, see Roasted Squash Pieces in the Shell, page 266.) The dry heat of roasting in a hot oven intensifies the flavor of vegetables by cooking out their internal water. The results range from slightly chewy to completely tender on the inside and crisped on the outside, with good color. Roasted vegetables are also wonderful served over greens with vinaigrette as a hearty salad.

In general, tender vegetables roast well at 375°F, and sturdier, slower-cooking vegetables (like potatoes and other root vegetables) can cook at 400°F or higher. Cut the vegetables about the same size to promote

4 Ways to Vary Any Breaded and Panfried Vegetable

1. Change the breading.
For the bread crumbs, try using panko, shredded coconut, finely chopped nuts or seeds, pulverized raw whole grains like rice, rolled oats or barley, or kasha (pulse in the food processor to grind any of these), or part grated Parmesan and part bread crumbs.

2. Season the breading.
Add chili powder, cayenne, lots of black pepper, or pretty much any spice blend imaginable. See "Different Ways with Breaded and Panfried Vegetables and Fruit" (page 160) for ideas.

3. Streamline the process.
Omit the eggs and bread crumbs and simply dredge the vegetables in flour before frying. This works best for vegetables with a decent amount of moisture for the flour to stick to—hard vegetables like carrots or winter squash won't have the same flour coating as onions or zucchini.

4. Change up the garnish.
Use a fancy salt if you've got one. Instead of serving the vegetables with parsley and lemon, try a sprinkle of vinegar and chopped fresh rosemary or thyme. Just make sure your garnishes don't clash with any seasoning in the bread crumbs.

even roasting, toss them in oil or melted butter (1 to 2 tablespoons per pound of vegetables), then spread them out in a large roasting pan or rimmed baking sheet. Use 2 pans if necessary to make sure you don't crowd the pan. Sprinkle with salt and pepper and pop them in the oven.

If you're looking for super-crisp, browned roasted vegetables (especially sturdier vegetables), sear them first to speed the process along: Heat the oven to 450°F with the roasting pan or baking sheet in the oven while you prep the vegetables. Toss the vegetables with oil, salt, and pepper in a large bowl. When you're ready to roast them, carefully pull the hot pan out of the oven, dump the vegetables on, and quickly spread them in a single layer; you'll hear them sizzle. Close the door, turn the oven down to the usual roasting temperature, and proceed with the recipe.

When the vegetables start to brown and release from the pan, shake the pan or use a spatula to toss them around a bit so they brown on all sides, being careful not to break the pieces apart.

Vegetable Crisps

MAKES: 4 servings
TIME: 30 minutes
F V

Delicious and colorful, you can make these with all sorts of root vegetables like beets, carrots, parsnips, rutabagas, turnips, or even kohlrabi.

3–4	tablespoons good-quality vegetable oil, plus more for greasing
1	pound vegetables, trimmed and peeled
	Salt and pepper

1. Heat the oven to 400°F. Lightly grease a couple of baking sheets or line them with parchment paper.
2. Cut the vegetables in half (or in quarters for larger items, like rutabagas), then crosswise into thin slices (⅛ inch or so). You can use a mandoline for this; just don't set it too thin. If the item is small in diameter, like carrots, simply cut them crosswise. Toss the slices with the oil and spread them out on the baking sheets. (It's okay if they're close, but don't let them overlap.)
3. Roast the slices until they begin to brown on the bottom, 10 to 12 minutes. Flip them over and sprinkle with salt and pepper. Keep roasting until they're well browned, another 10 minutes or so. Serve immediately.

7 Ways to Season Vegetable Crisps

When you sprinkle them with the salt and pepper, dust the crisps with any of the following seasonings (to make your own, see pages 648 to 652):
1. Curry powder
2. Garam masala
3. Chili powder
4. Jerk seasoning
5. Five-spice powder
6. Japanese seven-spice mix
7. Za'atar

GRILLING OR BROILING

When you expose the surface of vegetables to intense heat, the outside will cook much faster than the insides. Ideally when grilling you get both browning—or charring—and tenderness, with the added bonus of a bit of smoky flavor. (Broiling, really, is nothing more than upside-down grilling.)

This is the ultimate crisp-tender cooking method, ideal for "meaty" large pieces of sturdier vegetables. Eggplant, onions, mushrooms, squash, corn on the cob, and potatoes are the most obvious candidates to grill or boil, though tomatoes, green beans, and asparagus work great too. You can thread small pieces on skewers or use a perforated grilling basket. Coat everything lightly with a little oil or a marinade and grill or broil about 4 inches away from the heat source. (For a specific example, see Grilled or Broiled Eggplant, page 201, or the chart on pages 167 to 168.)

Serve grilled vegetables (or fruits; see page 273) hot or at room temperature, with almost any dish: grain

Vegetable Crisps
(page 163)

dishes, burgers, or baked, grilled, or broiled tofu. Or serve them simply on their own, with cheese, sprinkled with chopped fresh herbs, or drizzled with olive oil or a flavored oil (see page 627).

Here are a few pointers to perfect your vegetable and fruit grilling technique:

- To prevent sticking, use 1 to 2 tablespoons oil per pound. Any more fat will cause flare-ups.
- Skewer or use a perforated grilling basket for very small foods. If you are not using a basket or skewers, cut the vegetable or fruit into pieces large enough so they won't fall between the grill grates. Slices are fine for many items, like potatoes, squash, eggplant, or apples.
- If you're using wood or bamboo skewers, soak them in water for 30 minutes before using to keep them from burning.
- Make sure to clean the grill grates; your vegetables and fruit will be less likely to stick.
- If you're grilling a variety of vegetables, be sure to start with the ones that take the longest to cook and add the others incrementally, saving the quickest-cooking ones for last. Because grilled vegetables are also great at room temperature, it's okay to pull them off while the others finish.
- Apply barbecue or other sweet sauce or coating toward the end of cooking so it has time to glaze but not burn.

THE VEGETABLE LEXICON

Here, in alphabetical order, is just about everything you need to know about the most common vegetables. Each entry includes basic information, the ideal cooking method, and, in most cases, featured recipes. This section will expand your repertoire of vegetable dishes and help you to develop your own variations and accompaniments. It's designed to foster flexibility, with a line in each recipe and vegetable entry suggesting possible substitutions. If you think of this section as a mini-dictionary, the world of vegetables will become a lot more accessible than you might expect.

ARTICHOKES

Artichokes are the flower buds of a thistle plant. The petals (we call them "leaves") are green, tough, and spiked, and surround a choke of fine, hairlike fibers. The heart is at the base of the bud and is attached to the thick, edible stem, which is best if peeled before cooking.

Round, bulbous globe artichokes are the most common. So-called baby artichokes have more tender leaves and no chokes and can be eaten whole. But know: Not all small artichokes are baby artichokes. The best baby artichokes are fully mature artichokes that grow at the base of the plant; what you see most often are small artichokes that grow on side branches and are simply labeled "baby." These are not as tender and have a semideveloped choke that must still be removed. They're good; but they're not the same thing.

Whole artichokes can be boiled, but I prefer steaming because they don't become waterlogged. You can also parcook them by boiling or steaming, then grill over direct heat.

Eating the leaves is fun: scrape off the flavorful "meat" using your front teeth. The closer you get to the center, the more tender the leaves, which can be eaten in bunches, but avoid the furry choke (it got its name for a reason!). Or trim away the leaves and scrape away the choke with a spoon to get to the delicious heart. Hearts and baby artichokes can be sautéed, braised, fried, roasted, or grilled whole, halved, or sliced.

BUYING AND STORING Artichokes are usually available throughout the year but are best in spring and fall. Look for those that are heavy for their size; they should make a squeaking sound when you squeeze them. Store wrapped loosely in plastic in the refrigerator.

PREPARING Raw artichokes discolor quickly when cut and darken when cooked; rub with half a lemon or drop in a bowl of water with a couple of tablespoons of lemon juice or vinegar immediately after cutting to preserve color.

(continued on page 168)

Grilling Vegetables

VEGETABLE	PREPARATION	HOW TO GRILL
Artichokes	Works best with baby artichokes. Clean as instructed on page 168; halve lengthwise. Pat dry; brush with oil.	Over a medium-high fire until tender when pierced with a skewer and charred in places, 4–5 minutes per side.
Asparagus	Trim and leave whole. Brush or toss with oil.	Over a hot fire, turning occasionally, just until thick part of stalk can be pierced with a skewer or knife tip, 5–10 minutes total.
Avocado	Halve lengthwise, pit, and peel. Brush with lemon or lime juice; oil is optional.	Over a moderate fire until browned in places, 2–5 minutes per side.
Broccoli	Trim and cut into florets. Toss with oil.	Use a perforated grill basket for florets. Grill over a moderate fire, turning occasionally, until crisp-tender and browned in places, 10–15 minutes total.
Cauliflower	Trim; cut into florets or cut from top to bottom into ¾–1-inch-thick "steaks." Toss or brush with oil.	Use a perforated grill basket for florets. Grill over a moderate fire, turning occasionally, until crisp-tender and browned in places, 5–10 minutes total. Grill steaks directly on the grates until tender when pierced with a skewer and well browned (even a bit charred in places), 10–15 minutes per side.
Chayote	Remove the pit; halve, quarter, and cut into thick slices, or cube and skewer. Brush with oil.	Over a moderate fire, turning occasionally, until browned and tender when pierced with a skewer, 10–15 minutes total.
Chiles, bell peppers	Core and seed; leave whole, halve, or cut into squares and skewer. Oil is optional.	Over a moderate fire, turning occasionally, until skin is blistered and dark brown, and flesh is tender, 10–15 minutes total.
Corn	Pull down husks and remove silk; replace or remove husks. Oil is optional when husks are removed.	Over a moderate fire, turning occasionally, until some kernels char a bit and others are lightly browned, 15–20 minutes with husks on, less than half that with husks off.
Eggplant	Peel if you like; cut into ¼–½-inch-thick slices or 1½-inch cubes and skewer. Brush with oil.	Over a moderate fire until tender when pierced with a skewer and browned, 5–7 minutes per side.
Endive, radicchio	Halve or quarter lengthwise, depending on size. Brush with oil.	Over a medium-high fire, turning occasionally, until browned and crisp in places, 2–4 minutes per side.

VEGETABLE	PREPARATION	HOW TO GRILL
Fennel	Trim bulb; halve (if small), quarter, or cut into slices. Brush with oil.	Over a moderate fire until crisp-tender and browned (even charred) in places, 3–5 minutes per side.
Green beans	Trim but leave whole. Toss with oil.	Use a perforated grill basket if you have one. Grill over a hot fire until tender when pierced with a skewer and charred in places, 3–5 minutes; no need to turn.
Jícama	Trim, peel, and cut into ½-inch slices. Brush with oil.	Over a medium-high fire until browned, 7–10 minutes per side.
Mushrooms	Remove stems from portobello or shiitakes; trim small mushrooms; leave whole, slice thickly, or cut into cubes; skewer if small. Brush with oil.	Over a medium-high fire until browned, juicy, and tender when pierced with a skewer, 3–5 minutes per side.
Okra	Trim but leave whole. Toss with oil.	Over a moderate fire until tender when pierced with a skewer, 3–5 minutes per side.
Onions	Halve lengthwise without peeling or peel and cut into wedges or ½–1-inch slices. Brush with oil.	Over a moderate fire, turning once (use a spatula to keep together), until nicely browned and tender when pierced with a skewer, 10–15 minutes per side.
Potatoes, sweet potatoes	Any kind of potato will work. No need to peel. Cut into long wedges or ¼–½-inch-thick slices. Brush with oil.	Over a moderate fire until browned and tender when pierced with a skewer, 4–7 minutes per side.
Scallions	Trim but leave whole. Oil is optional.	Over a medium-high fire, turning occasionally, until deeply browned and tender, 5–10 minutes total.
Tomatoes	Cut into thick slices or leave cherry or grape tomatoes whole. Brush or toss with oil.	Over a moderate fire. Grill slices until soft but not mushy, 3–5 minutes per side. Grill cherry or grape tomatoes in a perforated grill basket until blistered and charred in places, 2–3 minutes per side.
Winter squash	Cut into 4 to 8 wedges, depending on size; seed. Brush cut sides with oil.	Over a medium-high fire, skin side down, until tender when pierced with a skewer, 30–50 minutes. Slice away blackened skin and cut flesh into cubes to serve.
Zucchini, summer squash	Trim; halve lengthwise. Brush with oil.	Over a moderate fire until tender when pierced with a skewer, 3–5 minutes per side.

(continued from page 165)

For whole artichokes: Cut off the pointed tips of the leaves with scissors or cut off the whole top third (a large serrated knife will help you get through the tough leaves, but any heavy knife will do the job). Use a paring knife to cut ¼ inch off the bottom of the stem, then peel the remaining stem up to the base of the artichoke. Pull off the toughest exterior leaves. To remove the choke, halve or quarter the artichoke and scrape it out with a spoon, or cut off the tops of the leaves, pry open the central leaves, and pull and scrape out the choke.

For artichoke hearts, cut off as much of the tops of the leaves as possible or halve the artichoke lengthwise. Use a paring knife to cut ¼ inch off the bottom of the stem, then peel the remaining stem up to the base of the artichoke; scrape out the choke with a spoon.

Small or baby artichokes, if tender enough, can be eaten whole, but sometimes they benefit from having the tops of the leaves and the exterior leaves trimmed. Otherwise, halve, quarter, or slice lengthwise. Remove the choke if necessary.

Most canned and jarred artichokes are already cooked and can be added whole, chopped, or sliced in the last few minutes of cooking. Rinse heavily marinated or brined ones to wash away some of the liquid's flavor.

Thaw frozen artichokes and use as you would fresh, but cut the cooking time roughly in half since they are already partially cooked.

BEST COOKING METHODS Steaming (whole or hearts), sautéing (only for baby artichokes and hearts), braising (only for baby artichokes and hearts)

WHEN ARE THEY DONE? Whole artichokes are ready when the outer leaves pull off easily. Taste one: If the meat comes off easily and is tender, it's done. Artichoke hearts are done when very tender; pierce with a skewer or thin-bladed knife to check, then taste to be sure.

Steamed Artichokes

MAKES: 4 servings
TIME: 45 to 70 minutes
Ⓜ Ⓥ

Artichokes sometimes become soggy when you boil them, so it's better to steam them; just be careful that the pot doesn't boil dry. You can add some gentle seasonings to the steaming water if you like—tarragon or thyme, onion or garlic, lemon juice or vinegar.

Serve the artichokes hot with melted butter, at room

Trimming Artichokes, Version 1

STEP 1 Peel off tough outer leaves.

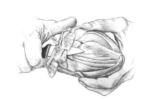

STEP 2 Trim around the bottom of the artichoke.

STEP 3 If you want to cook only the bottom, cut off the top half of the leaves.

STEP 4 Then scoop out the choke. If you want to leave the artichoke whole but remove the choke, force the top leaves open, then use a long spoon to scrape out the choke. (This will take a little while but isn't difficult.)

temperature with vinaigrette, or cold with mayonnaise. Or serve at any temperature with lemon and/or olive oil and salt.

    4   large or 12 small artichokes
        Juice from 1 lemon

1. With scissors or a large knife, trim the top ½ inch or so from the artichokes. Using a paring knife, peel around the base and cut off the bottom ¼ inch. Break off the roughest of the exterior leaves. As you prep each artichoke, put it in a large bowl of water with the lemon juice.
2. Put the artichokes bottom up in a steamer. Cover and cook for 20 to 40 minutes. Sample an outer leaf; when it pulls away easily and its meat is tender, they're done.
3. Drain them upside down for a minute or 2 before serving hot; store upside down if you plan to serve them later. If you like, scoop out the chokes with a teaspoon (see the illustration, left).

Braised Artichoke Hearts

MAKES: 4 servings
TIME: 45 minutes
M **V**

This dish is just as good at room temperature as it is hot; double it and you'll have leftovers to toss with pasta or rice, top pizzas, or mix into frittatas.

    ½   cup fresh lemon juice (3–4 lemons)
        Salt and pepper
    6   large artichokes
    3   tablespoons olive oil
    1   tablespoon minced garlic
        Chopped fresh parsley for garnish

1. Put the lemon juice in a bowl with ½ cup water and sprinkle with a little salt and pepper.
2. Cut the bottoms off the artichokes; don't bother to remove the chokes from them now. Trim the bottoms to reveal the heart. As you finish each artichoke, cut the heart into thick slices and toss them with the lemon water.
3. Put the oil in a large, deep skillet over medium heat. When it's hot, add the garlic and cook, stirring frequently, until it softens, about a minute. Use a slotted spoon or tongs to transfer the artichokes to the pan, saving the liquid in the bowl. Cook, stirring occasionally, until the slices begin to soften a bit, about 5 minutes. Add the reserved liquid, bring to a boil, and cover. Reduce the heat to medium-low and cook for about 10 minutes, shaking the pan every now and then to toss the artichokes. Check for tenderness. If not quite ready, cover and cook until done, another minute or so.
4. Taste and adjust the seasoning. Serve hot or at room temperature; garnish with parsley just before serving.

Trimming Artichokes, Version 2

STEP 1 Use scissors or a sharp knife to cut the pointed tips from the top of the artichoke.

STEP 2 Cut the artichoke in half.

STEP 3 Then cut it into quarters.

STEP 4 Scrape the fuzzy choke out from each of the quarters.

ROASTED ARTICHOKE HEARTS Crisp, with unparalleled flavor: Heat the oven to 425°F. In Step 3, increase the oil to ¼ cup, put it in a large ovenproof skillet or roasting pan, and set it in the oven. When the oil gets hot, transfer the artichoke slices and garlic to the pan and toss to coat in the oil. (Save the lemon water.) Roast until the slices release from the pan, 10 minutes or so, then turn them and continue roasting until tender, another 10 minutes. Transfer the artichokes to a serving platter and set the pan over medium- high heat. Add about a cup of the lemon water and stir up any brown bits from the bottom of the pan. Cook for a few minutes, until the mixture thickens a bit, stir in the parsley, then taste and adjust the seasoning. Pour the sauce over the artichokes and serve immediately or at room temperature.

BRAISED ARTICHOKE HEARTS WITH POTATOES The potatoes will soak up most of the liquid, creating a thick vegetable stew: Peel 2 large waxy potatoes if you like; cut into large chunks and steam or boil until tender (or use leftover cooked potatoes). Increase the olive oil to ¼ cup and the garlic to 2 tablespoons. In Step 3, when you check the artichokes, fold in the potatoes. Re-cover the pan and cook just long enough for the potatoes to reheat.

4 Classic Ways to Serve Cooked Asparagus

Cooked asparagus can be served immediately in any of these ways. These are also good in combination, as you'll quickly discover.

1. Drizzle with olive oil or melted butter. Any Compound Butter (page 676), Flavored Oil (page 627), or Vinaigrette (page 628) is also good.

2. Squeeze lemon or lime juice over it or drizzle with vinegar.

3. Top with mayonnaise (to make your own, see page 670) or Hollandaise Sauce (page 674), both classics.

4. Top with minced or finely crumbled Hard-Boiled Eggs (page 521).

BRAISED FROZEN ARTICHOKE HEARTS Works for the main recipe or any of the variations and is good in a pinch: Use about 3 cups frozen artichoke hearts; no need to thaw them. Proceed with Step 3.

ASPARAGUS

Long, usually green spears of asparagus can range from pencil thin to the thickness of a finger. They are available year-round at supermarkets, though the best are those you find locally and freshly picked in spring. Check out farmers' markets from as early as February in the South through May or June in the North.

There are also white and purple varieties. Purple is indistinguishable from green in flavor, but white asparagus—grown by protecting it from light while it grows, which prevents color from developing—has a distinctive nutty flavor.

BUYING AND STORING Look for plump, unshriveled spears of the thickness you prefer (they're all good) with undamaged tips. Avoid spears that look woody. Store wrapped loosely in plastic in the refrigerator, or stand up in a half inch or so of water. Use as soon as possible.

PREPARING Snap off the bottom of each spear; it will usually break naturally where it becomes too woody to eat. I recommend peeling asparagus (use a vegetable peeler) to remove the fibrous skin from just below the tip to the base; this step isn't necessary if the spears are pencil thin.

BEST COOKING METHODS Steaming, sautéing, roasting, grilling

WHEN IS IT DONE? When you can easily insert a skewer or thin-bladed knife into the thickest part of the stalk. Undercooked asparagus is crisp; overcooked asparagus is mushy.

OTHER VEGETABLES YOU CAN USE In some recipes, you can substitute green beans or sugar snap peas, but really there is nothing like asparagus.

Asparagus, Done Simply

MAKES: 4 servings
TIME: 15 minutes
F M V

Here are five of the most common ways to cook asparagus, with very little prep involved.

1½–2 **pounds asparagus, trimmed and peeled**
    Salt

Whichever method you use, cook just until the thick part of the stalks can be pierced with a knife. Serve hot, or refrigerate to serve later (see "4 Classic Ways to Serve Cooked Asparagus," opposite).

TO BOIL Lay the asparagus in a skillet that can hold the spears without crowding, cover with salted water, cover the skillet, and turn the heat to high.

TO STEAM Stand them up in a pot in an inch of salted water; it's nice, but hardly essential, to tie them in a bundle first. Cover and turn the heat to high.

TO MICROWAVE Lay them in a microwave-safe plate or shallow bowl with about 2 tablespoons salted water; cover with a lid. Microwave on high for 3 minutes, shake the container, and continue to microwave at 1-minute intervals.

TO ROAST Heat the oven to 450°F. Toss the asparagus in a roasting pan with a tablespoon or 2 oil and sprinkle with salt. Roast, turning the spears once or twice, for 10 to 15 minutes.

TO GRILL OR BROIL Prepare a charcoal or gas grill for medium-high direct heat or turn on the broiler for medium-high heat; adjust the rack to about 4 inches from the heat source. Toss the asparagus with a tablespoon or 2 oil and sprinkle with salt. Position on the grill perpendicular to the grates in a single layer; close the lid and grill, turning the spears once or twice, for 5 to 10 minutes. Or lay out on a broiler pan in a single layer and broil, turning once, about the same amount of time.

Simplest Asparagus Gratin

MAKES: 4 servings
TIME: 10 minutes, with cooked asparagus
F M

Cover cooked asparagus with cheese, stick it under the broiler until the top is golden brown and crisp around the edges, and you have a fabulous and elegant dish. You can prepare any of the variations using asparagus instead of the suggested alternative vegetable.

Other cooked vegetables you can use: green or wax beans, artichoke hearts, fennel, eggplant, leeks, spinach, celery root, parsnips, zucchini, winter squash, or sweet potatoes

1 **tablespoon butter or olive oil for the pan**
1½–2 **pounds cooked asparagus**
    Salt and pepper
1 **cup grated Gruyère or Swiss cheese**
¼ **cup Fresh Bread Crumbs (page 678)**
¼ **cup chopped fresh parsley for garnish**
    Pinch paprika (optional)

1. Turn on the broiler; adjust the rack to about 4 inches from the heat source. Grease a shallow medium baking pan or gratin dish with the butter.
2. Put the asparagus in the dish, sprinkle with salt and pepper, cover with the cheese, and sprinkle with the bread crumbs. Broil for 3 to 5 minutes, until the cheese is melted and golden. Sprinkle with a few more grinds pepper, the parsley, and the paprika if you like, and serve.

SIMPLEST ONION GRATIN Sweet and satisfying: Replace the asparagus with about 5 cups lightly pan-cooked onion (see page 221).

MUSHROOM AND ROQUEFORT GRATIN Any mushrooms and any blue cheese will work nicely: Replace

Simplest Asparagus
Gratin (page 171)

the asparagus with about 5 cups sautéed mushrooms (page 217) and use crumbled Roquefort for all or part of the cheese.

ROASTED BEET AND GOAT CHEESE GRATIN A wonderful, familiar combination: Replace the asparagus with about 5 cups sliced peeled roasted beets (page 178) and use crumbled goat cheese for the cheese and thyme leaves instead of parsley. Sprinkle the beets with the thyme leaves, then the goat cheese, and proceed with the recipe.

BROCCOLI OR CAULIFLOWER AND PESTO GRATIN Pesto beyond pasta: Replace the asparagus with about 5 cups chopped boiled or steamed broccoli or cauliflower (page 150) and use Parmesan for the cheese. Omit the parsley. In Step 2, toss the broccoli or cauliflower with a cup or so Pesto (page 634), sprinkle with the Parmesan, and proceed with the recipe.

AVOCADOS

Technically a fruit, the avocado floats between vegetable and fruit status; it's almost always used in a savory manner like a vegetable, but is rarely cooked, so it's treated more like a fruit. Avocado flesh is a pretty light green, ultra-smooth, and creamy, with a rich and subtle flavor. It's perfectly complemented by the acid in citrus fruit or a mild vinegar, but is easily overwhelmed by other flavors. It's loaded with fat, but that fat is mostly monounsaturated.

There are many varieties, from tiny to melon size, but we see mostly Hass and Fuerte in the United States. Hass is pear shaped and has a dark-green to black leathery, wrinkled, and bumpy skin; it's great for eating straight, spreading, or mashing. Fuerte it usually larger and has smooth green skin and firmer flesh that's not as well suited to spreading or mashing but is better for slicing.

BUYING AND STORING Avocados ripen at room temperature, so they are often sold (and best bought) nearly rock hard. Give them a gentle squeeze before buying: you don't want mushy spots or bruises; when one is ripe, it will yield to pressure. To hasten ripening, put them in a paper bag at room temperature for a couple days. Store ripe avocados in the refrigerator for up to a week.

PREPARING Slice avocados lengthwise around the seed and remove the pit; peel off the skin or scoop out the flesh with a spoon. Avocados discolor quickly when cut; sprinkle with citrus juice immediately after cutting to minimize darkening. If you want to store half, wrap it

Preparing an Avocado

STEP 1 Cut through the skin and flesh lengthwise to the pit, then rotate the avocado to cut all the way around it. Twist the halves apart.

STEP 2 A careful, swift, and not-too-forceful strike of the knife will implant it in the pit, which will then lift out easily.

STEP 3 Scoop out the flesh with a spoon.

with the pit intact and refrigerate—the pit helps keep it from turning brown.

BEST COOKING METHOD Best eaten raw, sliced, mashed, or puréed; at most they can be grilled quickly. Delicious simply spread on bread and sprinkled with lemon or lime juice or a mild vinegar and salt.

Crunchy Corn Guacamole

MAKES: 4 servings
TIME: 15 minutes
F M V

A new twist on a traditional guacamole (see the Minimalist Guacamole variation). The corn kernels add texture and flavor.

1	lime
1	cup corn kernels (preferably just stripped from the cobs, but drained thawed frozen is acceptable)
½	teaspoon minced garlic
½	cup chopped scallions
1	serrano or jalapeño chile, stemmed, seeded, and minced (optional)
	Salt
2	tablespoons chopped fresh cilantro
¼	cup chopped toasted pumpkin seeds (see page 299)
3	ripe avocados (preferably Hass)

1. Grate the lime zest, or use a zester to make long strands, and reserve. Cut the lime into wedges. Put the lime zest, corn, and garlic in a food processor; squeeze in the juice of half of the lime wedges and pulse to make a chunky purée.

2. Put the corn mixture in a medium bowl along with the scallions, chile if you're using it, and a large pinch salt and mash until well combined. Add the cilantro and pumpkin seeds and mash a few more times.

3. Cut the avocados in half and remove the pits; reserve the pits if you will not be serving the guacamole right away. Scoop the flesh into the bowl and mash, leaving a few chunks of avocado. Squeeze in lime juice to taste from the remaining lime wedges.

4. Season with salt and serve. Or tuck the pits on top of the guacamole, cover the surface with plastic wrap (this will help keep the guacamole from turning brown), and refrigerate for up to 4 hours. Remove the pits before serving.

MINIMALIST GUACAMOLE More traditional: Omit the corn kernels and pumpkin seeds. Add the grated zest and garlic to the scallions in Step 2 and proceed with the recipe.

GUACAMOLE WITH TOMATOES OR TOMATILLOS For extra flavor, grill, broil, or roast the tomatoes or tomatillos before adding them: Replace the corn and pumpkin seeds with 1 cup chopped tomato or ½ cup chopped husked tomatillos. Add the zest and garlic in Step 2.

BEAN SPROUTS

We most often see mung bean and soybean sprouts in stores, though you can sprout just about any bean—or grain, for that matter—at home (opposite). Mung bean sprouts have pale yellow or green heads with fairly long, semitranslucent, plump tails. They are available fresh in bags or in bulk; also canned, but these aren't worth the tin they're in.

Soybean sprouts—also sold in bags or loose—are larger; their heads are a yellow-colored split soybean, and the white crunchy tails are about 2 inches long. Soybean sprouts are often used in Korean dishes and offer a more substantial crunch than mung bean sprouts.

BUYING AND STORING Shop for bean sprouts in Asian markets if they're not at your supermarket. Look for plump, crisp, fresh-smelling sprouts, avoiding those that are slimy or off-smelling. If they're prepackaged in bags, inspect as best you can. Store wrapped loosely in plastic or in the store's packaging in the refrigerator. Use as soon as possible, but they'll keep for a couple of days.

PREPARING Some people like to trim the tails, but it's not necessary. Rinse and drain the sprouts well.

DIY Bean and Seed Sprouts

MAKES: About 2 cups
TIME: 1 week, mostly unattended
Ⓜ Ⓥ

The most common sprouts are made from mung beans—they're the familiar ones with the pale heads, sometimes sheathed in green, and longish tails—but you can sprout almost any seed or bean, from alfalfa to radish to wheat to lentil. Even herb seeds like basil will sprout, and they're delicious. If sprouting seeds, buy seeds packaged especially for this purpose, to ensure they haven't been chemically treated. With this method you can combine sprouts of different types in the same container. All it takes is time and a little daily routine.

½ cup dried mung beans or other beans, lentils, seeds, or whole grain

1. Rinse the beans with water and drain; pick over to remove any debris, small stones, or damaged beans. Put them in a 1-quart jar, fill the jar with water, and cover with some type of cover that will allow you to drain the water, like cheesecloth secured with a rubber band around the neck of the jar. Set the jar away from sunlight and let soak at room temperature for 6 to 12 hours, until the beans are swollen with absorbed water. (Seeds, fine grains, and lentils will take the shorter time; larger beans and grains take longer.)

2. Rinse and drain the beans two times through the cover, then position the jar upside down at an angle (you'll need to prop it against something) on a rack set on a baking sheet—again, away from sunlight—to allow air to circulate and excess moisture to drain. Rinse and drain the beans this way two to four times a day until they sprout and the sprouts grow to the length you prefer, usually ½ to 1 inch. Depending on what you're sprouting, the entire process can take 2 to 4 days.

3. Rinse the sprouts and drain them well before refrigerating in a covered container with some paper towels

Making Sprouts

You'll need a clean 1-quart jar and some kind of drainable top, like cheesecloth secured with a rubber band at the neck. Rinse the beans (these are mung beans) or seeds well, put them in the jar, cover with water, and let soak for 6 to 12 hours.

STEP 1 Drain, rinse, cover with the top, and prop the jar as shown. Keep it away from sunlight. Continue rinsing and draining at least twice a day, but preferably three or four times.

STEP 2 After a day or so, the beans will open.

STEP 3 A day or two later, they'll start to sprout.

STEP 4 After about 3 days, the beans will have fully sprouted. When the sprouts are the length you want them, rinse one more time and drain well. To get small green leaves, expose them to light for a few hours, then rinse, drain, and refrigerate.

to absorb any remaining moisture. If you place alfalfa or radish sprouts in the sun for several hours, they will develop little green leaves. Rinse again, drain, and refrigerate. Sprouts will keep several days.

Crisp-Fried Bean Sprouts

MAKES: 4 to 6 servings
TIME: 30 minutes
F V

Bean sprouts take well to frying. Here they are lightly coated with a batter and gently stirred in hot oil. If some stick together, fine; if not, that's good too. What you get is something akin to shoestring French fries. This is good without the garnishes, terrific with them; you could also serve it as lettuce wraps, rolled in leaves of Bibb or green leaf lettuce.

Other bean sprouts you can use: soybean or adzuki bean (which you'll probably have to grow yourself; see page 175)

   Peanut or good-quality vegetable oil
   for deep frying
 1 pound bean sprouts (about 4 cups),
   rinsed and drained well
 ¼ cup soy sauce
 2 cups all-purpose flour, rice flour,
   or cornstarch
   Salt and pepper
 1 cup chopped roasted peanuts for garnish
   (optional)
 1 cup chopped fresh cilantro for garnish
   (optional)
   Minced fresh chile (like jalapeño or Thai), red
   chile flakes, or cayenne to taste for garnish
   (optional)
   Lime wedges for garnish (optional)

1. Put at least 2 inches oil in a deep, heavy saucepan over medium-high heat; bring to about 350°F on a deep-frying thermometer. Cover a plate with paper towels, a clean kitchen towel, or brown paper.

2. While the oil is heating, put the bean sprouts in a large bowl, drizzle the soy sauce over them, and toss gently to moisten all. Add the flour, a few spoonfuls at a time, and toss until the sprouts are evenly coated.

3. When the oil is hot, add about 1 cup or so of the bean sprouts. Turn and stir them occasionally with a slotted spoon until crisp and golden on all sides, 3 to 5 minutes. Transfer to the plate to drain. Sprinkle with salt and lots of black pepper while hot. Repeat until all the sprouts are done. Serve immediately, garnished with the peanuts, cilantro, chile, and/or lime wedges as you like.

BEETS AND BEET GREENS

Beets come in an array of colors (from dark red to golden yellow to striped) and shapes and sizes (from the familiar round to long and thin, to tiny). The beet's sweet and earthy flavor is wonderful served hot, cold, or at room temperature. Beets keep for several days once cooked and raw beets keep for weeks in the fridge.

BUYING AND STORING Size doesn't matter when it comes to beets; large ones are almost always just as good as small, and they're easier to handle. One sure sign of freshness is the presence of the greens (which are edible and lovely—small young leaves can be added raw to salad; larger leaves should be sautéed or braised until tender); if the greens are fresh looking, the roots are fresh too. Beets should be very hard when you buy them; avoid any that are soft. Remove all but an inch of the stems (cook the greens as soon as you can) and store the roots wrapped loosely in plastic in the refrigerator.

PREPARING Scrub well; leave on an inch or so of the stems to minimize bleeding. Peel beets after they've cooked. Whole beets are easiest to peel when they're very hot, so use a kitchen towel you don't care about staining (or several paper towels) to protect your hands and slip the peels off.

BEST COOKING METHODS Baking, roasting, braising and glazing. Raw beets are also good.

WHEN ARE THEY DONE? When tender all the way through; pierce with a skewer or thin-bladed knife to check. Slight overcooking is usually preferable to undercooking.

OTHER VEGETABLES YOU CAN USE Turnips, rutabagas, carrots, parsnips

Beets, Done Simply

MAKES: 4 servings
TIME: 15 to 90 minutes
Ⓜ Ⓥ

Like asparagus, you can use a multitude of techniques to cook beets. Peel immediately (use a kitchen towel). Or shock boiled, steamed, or microwaved beets in ice water until cool; drain again and peel.

Other vegetables you can use: turnips, rutabagas, daikon, or parsnips

Salt
4 large or 8 medium beets (1½–2 pounds), washed well and trimmed, with about 1 inch of the stems still on

TO BOIL Bring a large pot of water to a boil; salt it. Put the beets in the water, cover the pot, and turn the heat to medium-low. Simmer until the beets can be pierced with a thin-bladed knife, 30 to 45 minutes. Drain.

TO STEAM Put the beets in a steamer above an inch or 2 salted water. Cover and cook over steadily bubbling water for 30 to 45 minutes (keep an eye on the water level), until they can be pierced with a thin-bladed knife. Drain.

TO MICROWAVE Put the beets in a microwave-safe plate or shallow bowl with about 2 tablespoons salted water; cover with a lid. Microwave on high for 6 minutes, shake the container, and continue to microwave in 2-minute intervals, just until they can be pierced with a thin-bladed knife. Drain.

TO ROAST Heat the oven to 400°F. Wrap the beets individually in foil and put them on a rimmed baking sheet or roasting pan. Roast undisturbed for 45 to 90 minutes, depending on the size, until a thin-bladed knife pierces one with little resistance. They may cook at different rates; remove each one when it is done.

BOK CHOY AND OTHER ASIAN GREENS

The word *choy* in Cantonese basically means "cooking greens," and there are a whole slew to choose from, especially in Asian markets. To keep things simple, only the most common are included here, but don't let that stop you from trying more; almost all can be prepared and cooked the same way.

Bok choy is the Asian green most commonly available in supermarkets. It grows in large, loose heads with wide, crisp white stalks and dark-green flat leaves. Its flavor is mildly cabbagey and fresh, and the stalks take on an almost creamy texture once cooked. The miniature jade-green variety—called Shanghai or baby bok choy—is equally delicious and tender.

Gai lan (aka Chinese broccoli, kale, or mustard greens) is common in Asian markets. It looks similar to broccoli raab; the long, narrow stalks are smooth, thick, and green with dark-green leaves and small clusters of flower buds. The stems retain a lovely crispness when cooked, and the leaves wilt like kale; the flavor is a cross between broccoli and mustard greens but milder than either.

BUYING AND STORING The leaves and stems should be fresh looking and crisp; avoid any with yellowing on the leaves. Bok choy's stems should be unbroken and bright white. Look for unopened flowers on gai lan, but a few open buds are okay. Store wrapped loosely in plastic in the refrigerator.

PREPARING Wash and remove any damaged or yellowing leaves. For bok choy, cut off the root end and the inch or so above it; slice or chop it as you like. If the stems are thick, separate them from the leaves and start cooking them a couple minutes before the leaves. Baby bok choy can remain whole, or you can halve or quarter it through the root end, depending on its size.

To prepare gai lan, trim any dried-out or tough stems, and separate the leaves from the stems (the stems need longer to cook).

BEST COOKING METHODS Steaming, sautéing, stir-frying

WHEN IS IT DONE? When the stems are tender but still crisp (especially for gai lan) and the leaves are wilted

OTHER VEGETABLES YOU CAN USE Cabbage, kale, broccoli

Quick-Cooked Bok Choy

MAKES: 4 servings
TIME: 30 minutes
F V

The fat, thick stems of bok choy become creamy and tender during cooking in a way that you cannot duplicate with other greens. That makes the basic, simple version of this recipe wonderful; the slightly more complicated variations are even better.

Other vegetables you can use: Napa cabbage, white chard (probably the closest in texture, but with different flavor), or broccoli raab

- 1 **head bok choy (about 1½ pounds)**
- 3 **tablespoons good-quality vegetable oil**
  Salt and pepper

1. Cut the leaves from the stems of the bok choy. Trim the stems as necessary, then cut them into roughly 1-inch pieces; rinse everything well. Put the oil in a large skillet over medium-high heat. When it's hot, add the stems and cook, stirring occasionally, until they just

lose their crunch, about 3 minutes. Add the leaves and about ½ cup water or vegetable stock (pages 97 to 100) if you prefer.

2. Cook, stirring occasionally, until the liquid evaporates and the stems become very tender, about 10 minutes more; add a little more liquid if necessary. Sprinkle with salt and pepper and serve immediately.

BOK CHOY WITH CAPERS, OLIVES, AND GARLIC Use olive oil instead of vegetable oil. In Step 2, when the greens are tender, stir in 2 tablespoons drained capers, ¼ to ½ cup chopped pitted olives (preferably oil-cured), and 1 tablespoon minced garlic. Cook for another minute or so, stirring, then add fresh lemon juice or balsamic vinegar to taste (start with 1 tablespoon). Cook for another 5 seconds and serve.

BOK CHOY WITH BLACK BEANS If you like, also add some cubed Baked Tofu (page 485) or Deep-Fried Tofu (page 487) along with the beans for an entrée: While cooking the stems in Step 1, soak 1 tablespoon fermented black beans in 2 tablespoons dry sherry, rice wine, or water. In Step 2, when the greens are tender, stir in the beans and their liquid, along with 2 teaspoons minced garlic and 1 teaspoon minced fresh ginger. Cook for another minute or so, stirring, then add 1 tablespoon soy sauce, or to taste. Cook for another 5 seconds and serve.

BROCCOLI, BROCCOLINI, AND BROCCOLI RAAB

A member of the *Brassica* genus that includes cabbage, mustard, turnips, and more, broccoli is flavorful, easy to prepare, inexpensive, and nutritious. We're most familiar with the dark-green type, but some can have a bit of purple coloring in the buds. Since broccoli is a cool weather crop, it's reliably available year-round, and since it travels well the quality is so good that there's really no reason to buy frozen.

Though a cousin of broccoli, broccoli raab looks quite different, with thick, elongated stems sporting spiky leaves and topped with small flower heads. It's one terrific vegetable: strong tasting, deliciously bitter, and easy to prepare.

Broccolini is a hybrid of broccoli and gai lan (also known as Chinese broccoli or Chinese kale; see the entry for Bok Choy and Other Asian Greens, page 178). Like broccoli raab, it has long, slightly curving stems that terminate in open florets, but no leaves. Its flavor is much more akin to that of broccoli; it possesses none of broccoli raab's bitterness.

BUYING AND STORING For broccoli, look for tightly packed florets with no yellowing, on top of a crisp stem. For broccoli raab and broccolini, look for bright green color and crisp stems; no wilted or yellowing leaves, no yellow flowers blooming from the heads. Store wrapped loosely in plastic in the refrigerator; broccoli will keep for several days, broccoli raab and broccolini should be used as soon as possible.

PREPARING For broccoli, strip the stalk of leaves, if any (these are edible; cook along with the florets if you like). Cut off the dried-out end of the stalk; peel the tough outer skin of the stalk with a vegetable peeler or paring knife as best you can. Break the head into florets and, if you like, cut the stalk into equal-length pieces.

For broccoli raab and broccolini, trim the dry ends of the stems and pull off any yellowing or wilted leaves (in the case of broccoli raab).

BEST COOKING METHODS Steaming, microwaving, braising and glazing, stir-frying. Regardless of method, cook broccoli stalks longer than the florets—just start them a minute or 2 earlier.

WHEN IS IT DONE? Broccoli: It's a matter of taste. When bright green, it's still crisp and quite chewy, and some people like it that way. Cook it for another couple of minutes and it becomes tender; overcook it and it becomes mushy and begins to fall apart (this can be really good). Try cooking until a skewer or thin-bladed knife can easily pierce the stalk. Broccoli raab and

broccolini are done when you can insert a skewer into the thickest part of the stalk without resistance. Undercooked is too crisp; overcooked is mushy.

OTHER VEGETABLES YOU CAN USE Broccoli and cauliflower are almost always interchangeable.

Broccoli or Cauliflower (or Just About Anything Else), Roman Style

MAKES: 4 servings
TIME: 30 minutes

F M V

You see almost everything done this way in Rome, and it's always good. The variation is a little simpler, but requires more judgment.

Other vegetables you can use: almost anything—dark, leafy greens like collards and kale, green beans, carrots, potatoes, turnips, beets

3–4	tablespoons olive oil
1	tablespoon minced garlic
2	dried chiles (optional)
	Salt and pepper
1	pound broccoli or cauliflower (about 1 medium head), trimmed, broken into florets of any size, parboiled and shocked (see page 150), and patted dry
	Grated zest and juice of 1 lemon
	Chopped fresh parsley for garnish

1. Put 2 tablespoons of the oil in a large skillet over medium heat. When it's hot, add the garlic and the chiles if you're using them, and cook, stirring occasionally, until the garlic is golden, a minute or 2. Add the broccoli and raise the heat to high. Cook, stirring only if it sticks—you don't want the vegetable to fall apart—until it begins to brown. Add the lemon zest and cook for another minute or 2.

2. Serve hot or at room temperature. Just before serving, stir in the lemon juice, drizzle with the remaining oil, and garnish with parsley.

BRAISED AND GLAZED BROCCOLI OR CAULIFLOWER (OR JUST ABOUT ANYTHING ELSE) No precooking needed: In Step 1, start with ¼ cup olive oil. Thirty seconds after adding the garlic, add the broccoli and ¼ cup water. Cover the pan. Cook, uncovering and stirring occasionally, until the broccoli is just tender, 10 to 15 minutes. Uncover, raise the heat, and cook out all but a little of the remaining water; by then the vegetables should be turning golden. Proceed with the recipe from Step 2.

Stir-Fried Broccoli

MAKES: 4 servings
TIME: 30 minutes
F V

Broccoli is ideal for stir-fries: You get crunch from the stems (cut them fairly thin so they'll cook quickly) and tenderness from the florets. And you can use broccoli as a main ingredient in just about any stir-fry recipe in this book. If you have leftover cooked broccoli, by all means use it, but stir-fry no longer than it takes to heat the broccoli through.

Other vegetable you can use: cauliflower

2 tablespoons peanut or good-quality vegetable oil
About 1½ pounds broccoli, trimmed, cut into bite-size florets, stems cut into pieces no more than ⅛ inch thick
Salt
1 teaspoon sugar
1 cup vegetable stock (pages 97–100) or water
2 tablespoons soy sauce

Put the oil in a large, deep skillet over medium-high heat. When it's hot, add the broccoli, raise the heat to high, and cook, stirring, until it's bright green and glossy and beginning to brown, about 5 minutes. Sprinkle

with salt and add the sugar and stock. Stir and continue to cook until almost all the liquid evaporates and the broccoli is tender, about 5 minutes more. Stir in the soy sauce, taste and adjust the seasoning, and serve.

Broccoli Raab with Garlic and Pecorino

MAKES: 4 servings
TIME: About 20 minutes
F M

Such a simple preparation but so delicious, with the nutty saltiness of the cheese playing against the bitter of the broccoli raab.

Other vegetables you can use: broccoli, broccolini, gai lan, turnip or mustard greens, asparagus, kale, collards

About 1½ pounds broccoli raab, trimmed and cut up
3 tablespoons olive oil
4 cloves garlic, slivered
Salt and pepper
1 cup grated pecorino cheese

1. Boil or steam the broccoli raab for about 3 minutes, until it is bright green and beginning to get tender. Drain and plunge it into ice water for a few moments and drain again. (You can prepare the broccoli raab up to this point, wrap it well or place in a covered container, and refrigerate for up to 2 days.) Squeeze the excess liquid from the broccoli raab and chop it coarsely.
2. Heat the oil and garlic in a large skillet over medium heat until the garlic is fragrant. Add the broccoli raab and cook, stirring occasionally, until it's heated through, 5 to 7 minutes. Remove from the heat, season with salt and pepper to taste, toss with the cheese, and serve.

BRUSSELS SPROUTS

Believed to have been developed in Belgium (hence the name), these miniature cabbages have enjoyed

Broccoli Raab with Garlic and Pecorino (page 181)

a resurgence in popularity—even though they were always terrific. The small heads grow in vertical rows on long, thick stalks; occasionally they're sold still on the stalk, but that isn't necessarily a sign of freshness.

BUYING AND STORING Brussels sprouts are a winter vegetable and are best from early fall through early spring, though you can find them year-round. Smaller is better; reject any with yellow or loose leaves or those that are soft or not tightly packed. Store wrapped loosely in plastic in the refrigerator.

PREPARING Trim the hard edge of the stem and remove any loose leaves. Cut, slice, or leave whole.

BEST COOKING METHODS Roasting, sautéing, simmering; if shaved very thin, they can be eaten raw.

WHEN ARE THEY DONE? When just tender enough to be pierced easily by a skewer or a thin-bladed knife. Do not overcook.

OTHER VEGETABLES YOU CAN USE Any cabbage

Braised and Glazed Brussels Sprouts

MAKES: 4 servings
TIME: 30 minutes
F M O

When browning Brussels sprouts, I like to leave them whole; they're less likely to overcook, and they look great that way. But you can chop or shred them too; they'll cook more quickly.

Other vegetables you can use: shredded green or red cabbage, or broccoli or cauliflower florets

- 3 **tablespoons olive oil or butter**
- 1 **pound Brussels sprouts, trimmed**
- ½ **cup or more vegetable stock (pages 97–100), white wine, or water, or more as needed**
  Salt and pepper

1. Combine the oil, Brussels sprouts, and stock in a deep skillet with a tight-fitting lid, sprinkle with salt and pepper, and bring to a boil. Cover and adjust the heat so the mixture simmers; cook until the sprouts are just tender, 5 to 10 minutes, checking once or twice and adding liquid as needed.

2. Uncover and raise the heat to boil off all the liquid so that the vegetables become glazed and eventually brown. Resist the urge to stir them frequently; just let them sizzle until golden and crisp, then shake the pan and loosen them to roll over. It's okay if some sides are more well done than others. Taste and adjust the seasoning, then serve hot or at room temperature.

Roasted Brussels Sprouts with Garlic

MAKES: 4 servings
TIME: 45 minutes
M V

Brussels sprouts are ideal, I think, when the exterior is crisp—very, very dark brown, almost burned. This combination of sautéing and roasting does the trick nicely.

Other vegetables you can use: red cabbage (I like it cut into wide ribbons), radicchio wedges

- 1 **pound Brussels sprouts**
- ¼ **cup olive oil**
- 5 **cloves garlic, or more to taste, peeled**
  Salt and pepper
- 1 **tablespoon balsamic vinegar**

1. Heat the oven to 450°F. Trim the hard edge of the stems from the Brussels sprouts, then halve each through the stem end. Put the oil in a large ovenproof skillet over medium-high heat. When it shimmers, arrange the sprouts in one layer, cut side down. Toss in the garlic and sprinkle with salt and pepper.

2. Cook, undisturbed, until the sprouts begin to brown, 5 to 10 minutes, then transfer to the oven. Roast, shaking the pan occasionally, until the sprouts are quite brown and tender, about 30 minutes.

3. Taste and adjust the seasoning. Drizzle with the balsamic vinegar, stir, and serve hot or warm.

CABBAGE

Savoy is the best head cabbage: tender, crinkly, light green, and mild-flavored. The elongated, mostly white, and ruffled-leaved Napa is also tender and lovely used raw. The more common smooth-leaf green and red varieties are also fine, of course, but they tend to be tougher and more strongly flavored than either Savoy or Napa.

Cabbage has a bad reputation for being an unpleasant-tasting vegetable, and when overcooked it can be. If you've been turned off to cabbage, try Buttered Cabbage, opposite; you will be pleasantly surprised.

BUYING AND STORING Look for tightly packed heads that are heavy for their size; avoid any with yellowing or loose leaves. Store in the refrigerator; it'll last a couple of weeks.

PREPARING Remove the first layer or 2 of exterior leaves. Use a thin-bladed knife to cut a cone-shaped section wider than the area of the core out of the stem end. To shred, cut the cabbage into quarters or eighths, depending on size, and cut crosswise into thin strips. Or use a mandoline. Napa cabbage can be cut crosswise whole to shred it.

BEST COOKING METHODS Sautéing, stir-frying, braising. Also fermented, as in sauerkraut and Kimchi (page 93)

WHEN IS IT DONE? When crisp-tender to soft, but not mushy

OTHER VEGETABLES YOU CAN USE Brussels sprouts, collards, bok choy (especially for stir-frying)

Cabbage Stuffed with Lentils and Rice

MAKES: 8 to 12 rolls (at least 4 servings)
TIME: About 1 hour

Ⓜ Ⓞ

Here the stuffed cabbage leaves are steamed; this "wet" cooking method makes for a moist and tender dish. You can also braise the cabbage packages in a sauce—see the variation—or in vegetable stock.

Stuffing Cabbage Leaves

STEP 1 Stuffing a cabbage or other leaf is much like making a burrito: Put a not-too-large amount of filling in the center and fold over the end closest to you.

STEP 2 Fold in the sides.

STEP 3 Roll up the leaf.

Other vegetables you can use: any sturdy cooking green

         2   **tablespoons olive oil, plus more for garnish (optional)**
         ½   **onion, chopped**
         2   **teaspoons minced garlic**
         2   **cups vegetable stock (pages 97–100) or water**
         ½   **cup brown, white, or basmati rice**
         ½   **cup dried lentils**
             Salt and pepper
         1   **head green or Savoy cabbage, cored**
      8–12   **slices Gruyère, fontina, Gouda, or mozzarella cheese, or 8–12 tablespoons (1–1½ sticks) butter (optional)**
             Chopped fresh parsley or chives for garnish

1. Put the oil in a medium pot over medium-high heat. When it's hot, add the onion and cook, stirring occasionally, until it's soft, about 5 minutes. Add the garlic and cook for another minute, then add the stock and bring to a boil.

2. If you're using brown rice, add it to the pot along with the lentils. If you're using white or basmati rice, add the lentils and cook them for 5 minutes, then add the rice. Turn the heat to medium-low so that the mixture bubbles gently, cover, and cook until the lentils and rice are tender and the liquid is mostly absorbed (you don't want it completely dry), 25 to 30 minutes. If there is excess liquid, take the cover off, turn the heat to high, and boil it off, being careful not to burn the bottom. Sprinkle with salt and pepper and transfer the filling to a bowl.

3. While the lentils and rice are cooking, pull off 8 to 12 large, untorn leaves and put them in a steamer above a couple of inches boiling salted water. Cover and cook until the leaves are just flexible enough to bend. Make a V-cut in each leaf to remove the tough central stem.

4. To stuff the cabbage leaves, put a leaf, curved side up, on the counter or a cutting board. Put ¼ cup or so filling in the center of the leaf, near where you cut out the stem. Fold over the sides, then roll up from the stem end, making a little package; you'll quickly get

the hang of it. Don't roll too tightly—the mixture will expand as it cooks. Skewer the rolls with a toothpick or 2 to hold them together or just put them seam side down on a plate. (You can make the stuffed cabbage to this point up to a day or 2 in advance; cover and refrigerate. Bring the rolls to room temperature before proceeding.)

5. Put the cabbage packages in the steamer (add more water if it's low) and cook until the cabbage is tender, 10 to 15 minutes. If you're using the cheese, top each roll with a slice of cheese and run under the broiler until bubbly. Or simply drizzle with olive oil or melt a pat of butter on top. Sprinkle with the parsley and serve.

CABBAGE STUFFED WITH LENTILS AND RICE IN RED WINE SAUCE Make a sauce for braising before making the stuffing: Put a tablespoon olive oil in a deep skillet large enough to hold all the cabbage packages in a single layer over medium-high heat. When it's hot, add ½ onion, minced, and cook until soft, about 5 minutes. Stir in 2 tablespoons tomato paste and cook until it's rusty brown. Add 1 cup red wine, let it cook for a couple of minutes, then add 2 cups vegetable stock and a couple of sprigs fresh thyme. Reduce the heat so the sauce bubbles gently. Proceed with the recipe from Step 1. In Step 5, instead of steaming, put the packages in the simmering sauce, cover, and cook until the cabbage is tender; add more stock if the sauce reduces too much. Omit the cheese, oil, or butter in Step 5. ◾V

Buttered Cabbage

MAKES: 4 servings
TIME: 20 minutes
◾F

This is simply delicious with ordinary green cabbage (and even better with Savoy), largely because you don't overcook it. For extra flavor, melt the butter with a clove of garlic, some minced shallot, or a little good paprika.

Serve this as a side dish or combine with other relatively plain dishes, like Boiled Potatoes (page 233) or

Chickpeas in Their Own Broth with Crisp Bread Crumbs (page 454).

Other vegetables you can use: collards, kale, bok choy, and the like

Salt
2–4 tablespoons butter
About 20 cabbage leaves

1. Bring a large pot of water to boil and salt it well. Put the butter in a medium saucepan over medium-low heat and melt it; if you let it brown a little bit, great, but don't burn it.

2. When the water boils, add the cabbage and cook, stirring every now and then, until it becomes tender, about 5 minutes. Remove with tongs or a slotted spoon and drain well; toss gently with the melted butter and serve.

CARROTS AND PARSNIPS

Carrots are cheap, versatile, and available year-round. But that doesn't mean they're not seasonal—a good November carrot is incomparable. In any case, you can eat carrots raw or cook them almost any way you like. Beyond the usual orange, carrots come in a variety of colors including purple, maroon, yellow, and white. The differences in flavor are subtle (if they exist at all); keep in mind that the colors usually mute during cooking.

Parsnips look like white carrots. They are sweeter than carrots, with a nice earthy flavor, and are (to my knowledge) always cooked.

BUYING AND STORING Bagged carrots are a no-brainer—as long as they're hard and crisp. Carrots with the tops should have bright greens that are crisp and unwilted. Remove the tops before storing, as they draw moisture and nutrients from the carrot itself. (You can chop up the tops and add them to soup.) Avoid any carrot that is soft, flabby, cracked, or growing new leaves. I don't buy the so-called baby carrots (they're actually peeled and cut regular carrots); even though they're convenient, they dry out too quickly. Store wrapped loosely in plastic in the refrigerator. They keep for at least a couple weeks but eventually dry out, crack and lose a lot of their nutrients.

For parsnips, smaller specimens are usually best; larger ones can be woody and rough, though I have had splendid parsnips as thick as a sweet potato. They should be firm and crisp. Store as for carrots or other roots.

PREPARING You can peel carrots, or not, depending on your preference, but you should peel parsnips, which have a tougher skin. Then trim off both ends. Chop, slice, or grate as you like. For large parsnips (more than 1 inch thick at the broad end), it's sometimes best to remove the woody core. Cut the thinner portion off and set aside. Cut the thick portion in half and dig out the core with the end of a vegetable peeler, paring knife, or sharp spoon. Or ignore it; it usually softens sufficiently during cooking.

BEST COOKING METHODS Steaming, braising, braising and glazing, roasting

WHEN ARE THEY DONE? When tender but not soft; taste and you'll know

OTHER VEGETABLES YOU CAN USE Beets, turnips, celery root

Quick-Glazed Carrots or Parsnips

MAKES: 4 servings
TIME: 30 minutes
F M O

One of the most useful recipes ever. Carrots and parsnips cooked this way are terrific hot, warm, or at room temperature (use oil instead of butter if you plan to serve them less than hot) and can take a wide variety of herbs and other simple additions. If you can find real baby carrots—the very thin ones—just trim them quickly, don't even bother to peel them; they'll be super.

Other vegetable you can use: turnips

About 1 pound carrots or parsnips, cut into coins or sticks

2 **tablespoons olive oil or butter**
Salt and pepper
White wine or vegetable stock (pages 97–100; optional)

1 **teaspoon fresh lemon juice (optional)**
Chopped fresh parsley, dill, mint, basil, or chervil for garnish (optional)

1. Combine the carrots, oil, and a sprinkle of salt and pepper in a saucepan no more than 6 inches across. Add about ⅓ cup water, white wine, or stock. Bring to a boil, then cover and adjust the heat so the mixture simmers.
2. Cook, more or less undisturbed, until the carrots are tender and the liquid is pretty much gone, 10 to 20 minutes. Uncover and boil off the remaining liquid. Add the lemon juice if you're using it. Taste and adjust the seasoning. Serve hot or within an hour or 2, garnished with herbs if you like.

QUICK-GLAZED CARROTS OR PARSNIPS WITH ORANGE AND GINGER Not much more work but far more impressive: Add 1 tablespoon minced or grated fresh ginger in Step 1. Use fresh orange juice in place of water. Garnish with a teaspoon or more grated orange and/or lemon zest instead of herbs.

BALSAMIC-GLAZED CARROTS OR PARSNIPS WITH GARLIC Amazing: Use balsamic vinegar in place of the water and add 5 to 10 peeled whole cloves garlic along with the carrots. Proceed as in the main recipe, adding water if the mixture dries out before the carrots are done.

Carrots or Parsnips with Dates and Raisins

MAKES: 4 servings
TIME: 20 minutes
F M V

A quick vegetable dish that's delicious at room temperature, this is perfect for a Middle Eastern–style meal of salads, spreads, and breads or with Stuck-Pot Rice with Potato Crust (page 381) and a dollop of yogurt.

Other vegetable you can use: kohlrabi

2 **tablespoons olive oil**
1 **small yellow onion, halved and thinly sliced**
½ **cup chopped pitted dates**
¼ **cup raisins (preferably golden)**
Large pinch saffron threads (optional)
Salt and pepper
1 **pound carrots or parsnips, cut into ¼-inch-thick slices**
½ **cup chopped pistachios, almonds, or walnuts for garnish (optional)**
Chopped fresh mint for garnish

1. Put the oil in a deep skillet over medium heat. When it's hot, add the onion and stir until soft, 3 minutes or so, then add the dates, raisins, and saffron if you're using it. Sprinkle with salt and pepper and stir until fragrant, about a minute.
2. Stir in the carrots and ¼ cup water. Bring to a boil, cover the pan, and turn the heat down to medium-low. Cook, undisturbed, for 5 minutes.

5 Ways to Jazz Up Quick-Glazed Carrots or Parsnips

1. Add ½ cup or so chopped onion, shallot, scallions, or leeks.

2. Add ½ cup or so chopped pitted dates, raisins, dried currants, or dried tomatoes.

3. Whisk together 1 tablespoon soy sauce and 1 tablespoon miso, then stir this into the carrots just as they're done. (Use sake as the glazing liquid instead of water, if you have it.)

4. Add 1 cup or so shelled peas, snow peas, or sugar snap peas (thawed frozen are fine) along with the carrots.

5. Add a tablespoon or so any mild chile paste (page 664; one made with ancho chiles would be ideal).

3. Uncover and raise the heat a bit. Cook, stirring occasionally, until the liquid has evaporated and the carrots are cooking in the oil, 5 to 10 minutes. Lower the heat and continue to cook, stirring occasionally, until tender, just a minute or 2 more. Taste and adjust the seasoning, then garnish and serve.

ROASTED CARROTS OR PARSNIPS WITH DATES AND RAISINS Wonderful in the dead of winter: Omit the onion and saffron. Cut the carrots into sticks and drizzle with the oil. Sprinkle with salt and pepper. Roast in a 425°F oven until the carrots are tender and browning, about 25 minutes. Add the dates and raisins in the last 10 minutes of roasting. Garnish with the nuts and mint. Serve hot, warm, or at room temperature.

CARROTS OR PARSNIPS WITH DRIED APRICOTS AND CHIPOTLE Sweet, smoky, and hot: Soak 1 or 2 dried chipotle chiles in warm water to cover until soft and pliable, about 20 minutes. Drain well, remove the stem and seeds, and mince the flesh as finely as you can. Omit the raisins and saffron. Instead of the dates, use chopped dried apricots. Proceed with the recipe, adding the chile and apricots in Step 1.

CAULIFLOWER

With its ivory-colored florets, cauliflower is arguably the starkest member of the *Brassica* genus in terms of appearance. Even cooler are the chartreuse-colored broccoflower and the outlandishly spiky, lime-green Romanesco, both of which are hard to identify as either cauliflower or broccoli—broccoflower is a hybrid of the two, and Romanesco is a less-common cousin of cauliflower. There is also a peachy-colored, vitamin A–rich (it contains about twenty-five times the amount that white does) orange cauliflower, as well as purple cauliflower.

BUYING AND STORING Heads should be heavy, beautifully white with no gray or brown spots, and crisp. Ideally, you want one with the leaves still wrapped around the flower. Store wrapped loosely in plastic in the refrigerator and use within a week or so.

PREPARING Remove the outer leaves and, if necessary, scrape off any gray or brown spots. You can cook it whole or separate it into florets before cooking. To separate into florets, begin at the base of the head and cut florets from the core, one after the other. The florets may in turn be broken or cut into smaller pieces if you like.

BEST COOKING METHODS Steaming, braising and glazing, roasting

WHEN IS IT DONE? When just tender enough to pierce with a skewer or thin-bladed knife. Overcooking is not as disastrous as it is with other members of the cabbage family, but it's still not desirable.

OTHER VEGETABLES YOU CAN USE Broccoli and cauliflower are almost always interchangeable; broccoflower, Romanesco

Basic Steamed Cauliflower

MAKES: 4 servings
TIME: About 30 minutes
F M V

You can speed the cooking of cauliflower by cutting it up before cooking, but because it crumbles easily, you'll lose some in the process. It's best to allow enough time to cook the head whole. Serve hot cauliflower with butter, olive oil, and/or lemon juice; garnish with parsley.

1 head cauliflower (about 1½ pounds) trimmed

Put the cauliflower in a steamer above an inch or 2 of salted water. Cover and cook over steadily bubbling water until it is just tender enough to be pierced to the core with a thin-bladed knife—no longer. Because it's large, the cauliflower will retain quite a bit of heat after cooking, so it should still be slightly chewy when you remove it from the steamer. Total cooking time will be 12 to 25 minutes, depending on the size of the head.

Breaded Sautéed Cauliflower

MAKES: 4 servings
TIME: 40 minutes

There are many ways to sauté vegetables with bread crumbs—or nuts; see the variation—for a little added crunch. Whether the bread crumbs stick to the vegetable is not all that important, but for the prettiest presentation, use the optional flour and egg.

Other vegetables you can use: broccoli, though it won't look as nice; whole green beans, Brussels sprouts

1 pound cauliflower (about 1 medium head), cut into florets of any size, parboiled and shocked (see page 150), and patted dry
  All-purpose flour for dredging (optional)
2 or 3 eggs, lightly beaten in a bowl (optional)
1 cup bread crumbs (preferably fresh, page 678) for dredging
4 tablespoons (½ stick) butter or ¼ cup olive oil
  Salt and pepper
  Chopped fresh parsley for garnish
  Lemon wedges (optional)

1. If you're using the egg, roll each piece of cauliflower in the flour, dip in the egg, then in the bread crumbs. If you're not using the egg, just roll the pieces in the bread crumbs, patting to help them adhere.

2. Put the butter or oil in a large skillet and turn the heat to medium. When the butter melts or the oil is hot, add the cauliflower pieces. Sprinkle with salt and pepper and cook, adjusting the heat and turning the pieces so the bread crumbs brown on all sides without burning, 8 to 12 minutes.

3. When the cauliflower is browned and tender, remove from the pan. Garnish and serve, with lemon wedges if you like.

BREADED SAUTÉED CAULIFLOWER WITH ONION AND OLIVES The glossy olives and red pepper give this kick and color: Use olive oil. Before adding the cauliflower, add 1 cup chopped onion (red is nice) and cook, stirring occasionally, until the onion softens, 3 to 5 minutes. Proceed as directed, adding ½ to 1 cup pitted black olives (oil-cured are good here, though you can use whatever you like) and ½ teaspoon red chile flakes, or to taste.

BREADED SAUTÉED CAULIFLOWER WITH GARLIC, VINEGAR, AND CAPERS Quintessentially Mediterranean: Use olive oil. Add 1 tablespoon chopped garlic along with the cauliflower. Just before it's done, add 1 tablespoon red wine vinegar, sherry vinegar, or other vinegar and about a tablespoon drained capers.

Manchurian Cauliflower

MAKES: 4 to 6 servings
TIME: 30 minutes

There are many ways to spin this recipe, which originally came to me courtesy of my friend Suvir Saran. According to Suvir, the original version is closely associated with the Chinatown in Calcutta, where it's a common street food. The two-step process includes deep-frying, but the work goes quickly. And people go nuts for it.

Other vegetable you can use: broccoli

  Good-quality vegetable oil
3 eggs
⅔ cup cornstarch
1 teaspoon black pepper
1 teaspoon salt, plus more as needed
1 large or 2 small heads cauliflower, separated into florets
2 teaspoons minced garlic
1 cup ketchup
½ teaspoon cayenne, or to taste

1. Put at least 2 inches oil in a deep pan on the stove and turn the heat to medium-high; bring to 350°F (see "Deep-Frying," page 26).

2. While the oil is heating, beat together the eggs and cornstarch until well blended in a bowl large enough to hold the cauliflower. Season the batter with the pepper and salt, then add the cauliflower. Use your hands to toss until the florets are coated evenly.

3. Fry the cauliflower in batches small enough not to crowd your pan or fryer and be sure to let the oil return to temperature (350°F) between batches. Fry until the florets take on a pale, sandy color, with a little brown mottling, about 5 minutes; transfer to paper towels to drain.

4. Heat 1 tablespoon oil in a large nonstick pan over medium heat and immediately add the garlic. Cook for a minute or 2, until fragrant but not colored, then add the ketchup. Cook, stirring, for about 5 minutes, until the sauce bubbles, thickens, and starts to caramelize around the edges of the pan. Add the cayenne; taste and add salt as necessary. Toss the cauliflower in the sauce until coated evenly and serve.

ROASTED CAULIFLOWER, MANCHURIAN STYLE Easier, but without the batter: Omit the eggs and cornstarch. Heat the oven to 400°F. Put the cauliflower in a roasting pan or rimmed baking sheet, drizzle with 2 tablespoons oil, and sprinkle with 1 teaspoon each pepper and salt. Toss until well coated. Roast for about 30 minutes, stirring once or twice, until the cauliflower is tender and golden. During the last 5 minutes or so of roasting, prepare the sauce as described in Step 4 and proceed with the recipe. **V**

Whole Roasted Cauliflower with Raisins and Balsamic Glaze

MAKES: 4 servings
TIME: About 1½ hours, mostly unattended
M V

Roasting toughens cauliflower and dries it out a bit—and because cauliflower is often mushy and watery, these are good things. I like to get it nice and brown,

and cooking it with a bit of the dressing deepens its flavor. Toss the remaining sauce with the cauliflower at the last minute, along with the raisins, whose sweetness counters the vinegar beautifully.

Other vegetables you can use: broccoli spears or any root vegetable, cut into cubes and roasted

1	**large head cauliflower, trimmed**
½	**cup olive oil**
	Salt and pepper
½	**cup balsamic vinegar**
½	**cup raisins**
½	**cup chopped fresh parsley**

1. Heat the oven to 400°F. Put the cauliflower in a roasting pan, drizzle with 3 tablespoons of the oil, sprinkle with salt and pepper, and cover with foil. Roast until the cauliflower just starts to soften, about 30 minutes. Remove the foil and continue roasting until the cauliflower is golden brown and a thin-bladed knife inserted meets no resistance, another hour or so.

2. Meanwhile, put the vinegar and raisins in a small saucepan over medium heat and bring to a boil. Lower the heat so the liquid barely bubbles and cook, stirring occasionally, until the raisins are plump and the vinegar is syrupy, 10 to 15 minutes.

3. When you're ready to serve, put the cauliflower on a large serving platter, drizzle over the balsamic and raisins and sprinkle with the parsley. Serve hot, warm, or at room temperature.

ROASTED CAULIFLOWER STEAKS WITH BALSAMIC GLAZE AND RAISINS You can also prepare this cutting the cauliflower into thick "steaks," which will increase the surface area available for developing delicious browning: Cut the cauliflower from top to bottom into ¾- to 1-inch-thick slices. Brush the cut sides with oil and season with salt and pepper. Put on a baking sheet and roast, uncovered, until golden brown and tender, about 30 minutes, turning the steaks once. Finish as directed.

CELERY

You probably eat celery raw with carrots or use it as an aromatic in soups, stews, and stir-fries. Celery is rarely treated as a stand-alone vegetable, which is a shame: Its flavor and texture mellow when you cook it, making it a mildly—but uniquely—flavored vegetable.

BUYING AND STORING Celery should be crisp, a bright pale green, and tightly packed—I like celery with its leaves and use them like a fresh herb. Avoid rubbery, wilted, or yellow celery. Store wrapped loosely in plastic in the refrigerator; celery keeps for about two weeks.

PREPARING Trim the leaves from the celery (reserve for use as a garnish if you like) and cut off the bottom core or remove as many stalks as you need. String the celery (see the illustration below) if it's tough and very fibrous, or just cut it into whatever size pieces you need.

BEST COOKING METHOD Braising, hands down

WHEN IS IT DONE? When good and tender; taste a piece.

OTHER VEGETABLES YOU CAN USE Celery and fennel are almost always interchangeable.

Preparing Celery

STEP 1 Celery is usually best when its "strings" are removed. Grasp the end of the stalk between your thumb and a paring knife.

STEP 2 Pull the strings down the length of the stalk.

Oven-Braised Celery

MAKES: 4 servings
TIME: 30 minutes
F M O

You can cook celery using the basic braise-and-glaze method (see page 157), but because it's more fibrous than most other vegetables, it benefits from slightly longer cooking in more liquid. Cooked this way, celery becomes tender and mellow.

Other vegetables you can use: fennel (which takes quite well to this treatment), celery root

> About 1½ pounds celery, trimmed
> 2 tablespoons olive oil or butter
> Salt and pepper
> 1 cup vegetable stock (pages 97–100) or water
> Chopped fresh parsley or dill for garnish

1. Heat the oven to 375°F. Cut the celery into pieces about 2 inches long. Put the oil or butter in a large, deep ovenproof skillet or flameproof gratin dish over medium heat. When the oil is hot or the butter is melted, add the celery and cook, stirring occasionally, until fragrant, 1 to 2 minutes. Sprinkle with salt and pepper. Add the stock and bring to a boil. Put in the oven.
2. Cook until the celery is very tender, 10 to 15 minutes. If much liquid remains, cook a little longer; in the unlikely event that it dries out before the celery becomes tender, add a little more liquid. Garnish with the herb and serve hot or warm.

BRAISED CELERY WITH TOMATO, OLIVES, AND CAPERS In Step 1, add 2 tablespoons minced onion or shallot along with the celery. In the last 5 minutes of cooking, stir in 1 tablespoon drained capers, ½ cup chopped pitted black olives, and 1 cup chopped seeded tomato (drained canned is fine). Garnish with the herb and serve.

CELERY ROOT (CELERIAC, CELERY KNOB)

This is the large, brown, often oddly shaped, bulbous and knotty root of a type of celery grown only for its root. The flavor is distinctively of celery, but the chameleon-like texture depends on the cooking: It's crunchy when raw, creamy when puréed, crisp and chewy when roasted. It's often used raw in salads (like Celery Rémoulade, page 47), but it's also delicious prepared like any other root vegetable, or with them.

BUYING AND STORING Look for firm, heavy bulbs (covered with some dirt is fine) with no soft spots; the smoother the skin, the easier to peel. As with most root vegetables, celery root keeps for a long time, but its flavor is most intense when it is firm and crisp; don't wait until it becomes flabby to eat it. Store wrapped loosely in plastic in the refrigerator.

PREPARING It's usually peeled (though a whole celery root, washed but unpeeled, rubbed with olive oil and salt before roasting, is impressive and delicious). Use a sharp knife rather than a vegetable peeler and understand that you will lose a good portion of the flesh. If more than a few minutes will pass between peeling the celery root and using it, drop it into acidulated water (1 tablespoon lemon juice or vinegar per cup water) to keep it from discoloring.

BEST COOKING METHODS Boiling, sautéing, braising and glazing, roasting

WHEN IS IT DONE? When it's soft

OTHER VEGETABLES YOU CAN USE Parsnips, turnips

Pan-Roasted Celery Root with Rosemary

MAKES: 4 servings
TIME: 40 minutes
V

If you don't already love celery root, you will now. And you can use any strong-flavored herb instead of rosemary, like thyme, sage, or oregano.

Other vegetables you can use: parsnips, rutabaga, turnips, potatoes, carrots

¼	cup olive oil
2	sprigs fresh rosemary
2	cloves garlic, peeled
2	pounds celery root, trimmed, peeled, and cubed
	Salt and pepper
1	teaspoon minced fresh rosemary

1. Put the oil in a large skillet over medium heat. When it's hot, add the rosemary sprigs and garlic and let sizzle gently until fragrant, about 2 minutes. Don't let the rosemary brown; adjust the heat as needed.

2. Add the celery root; it should be in a single layer in the skillet without overcrowding; work in batches if necessary. Cook, turning the celery root a few times, until it's soft and golden brown on all (or most) sides, about 30 minutes. Remove and discard the rosemary and garlic when they have browned.

3. Sprinkle with salt and pepper and the minced rosemary, stir, and serve.

CHARD

Chard (also called Swiss chard) has beautiful dark green, sometimes ruffled leaves, and stems that may be brightly colored crimson red, orange, yellow, or stark white. It's high in oxalic acid, the same compound found in spinach and rhubarb leaves, but chard's flavor is compounded by sweetness. This makes it lovely in omelets and quiches and on its own. In southern France it's made into a sweet pie. Young and very tender stems and leaves can be tossed into salads, while tougher ones must be cooked. Unfortunately, quite a bit of the vibrant color seeps out of the stems and veins when they're cooked.

BUYING AND STORING Look for undamaged stems—thick or thin are both good—and deeply colored, unwilted leaves. Store wrapped loosely in plastic in the refrigerator; it will last several days.

PREPARING Wash well and tear or chop the leaves. If the stems are very thick, strip the leaves from them before proceeding so you can cook the stems a couple of minutes longer.

BEST COOKING METHODS Steaming, braising, sautéing. Regardless of the method, it often makes sense to cook thick stems longer than the leaves; just start them a minute or 2 earlier. If I'm making a sautéed chard dish with onion, I'll add the chopped stems with the onion at the beginning of cooking.

WHEN IS IT DONE? When wilted and tender

OTHER VEGETABLES YOU CAN USE Chard and beet greens are almost always interchangeable; dandelions, turnip greens, spinach

Braised Chard with Olive Oil and Rice

MAKES: 4 servings
TIME: 50 minutes, mostly unattended
Ⓜ Ⓥ

Simple and delicious. The sweetness of the chard really comes through, and the olive oil garnish adds a nice touch. You can use parboiled brown rice (see page 368) for a heartier option.

Other vegetables you can use: kale, Belgian endive (halved lengthwise), bok choy, leek

> 1 **pound chard, trimmed**
> ⅓ **cup olive oil**
> 2 **small carrots, roughly chopped**
>   **Salt and pepper**
> ¼ **cup white rice**
>   **Juice of ½ lemon**

1. Cut the stems out of the chard leaves. Cut the leaves into wide ribbons and slice the stems; keep the leaves and stems separate.

2. Put all but 1 tablespoon of the oil in a large skillet over medium heat. When it's hot, add the chard stems and carrots, along with a sprinkle of salt and pepper, and cook, stirring occasionally, until the chard is tender, about 15 minutes.

3. Add the chard leaves, a little more salt and pepper, the rice, and 1½ cups water. Cover, adjust the heat so the mixture simmers, and cook for about 30 minutes, until the water is absorbed; the mixture should be moist but not soupy. Serve hot, at room temperature, or cold. (You can cover and refrigerate the dish for a day, and then reheat it.) Just before serving, drizzle with the remaining oil and the lemon juice.

CORN

We know fresh corn as a vegetable, but we also know it has many other forms and uses (see pages 389 to 397). For on-the-cob eating, fresher is better, but the new breeds of corn retain their sweetness well for days.

BUYING AND STORING Corn is still best when just picked, so try to buy it at a farmers' market or the like. Ears should be tightly wrapped in their husks, which should be green and fresh looking, not at all dried out. The silk should be supple and golden or golden brown. The kernels should be tightly packed and plump, and should come to the tip of the cob. Store corn in its husk in the refrigerator. Use as soon as possible; it will decline in sweetness as it ages. Frozen corn is fine to cook with but isn't nearly as good as fresh corn; I don't recommend canned corn or any kind of prepared creamed corn.

PREPARING Shuck corn just before cooking. Always remove the silk from cobs before cooking, even if you're cooking in the husk; the silk burns easily and is harder to remove after cooking. Just peel back the husk, remove the silk, and fold the husk back over the corn. If you want kernels only, cut or scrape them from the cob with a knife (in a bowl is neatest).

BEST COOKING METHODS Steaming, roasting, grilling, stir-frying; raw in salsa and salads

WHEN IS IT DONE? When it's hot; there's no point in cooking it any further. Some people believe in bringing the water back to a boil and cooking it for a few minutes more; I haven't noticed any difference.

OTHER VEGETABLES YOU CAN USE Really, there is no substitute for corn on the cob. For cooked corn kernels: green peas, green or wax beans; for raw corn kernels: diced jícama

Steamed Corn on the Cob

MAKES: 4 servings
TIME: 20 minutes or less
F O

To get the most out of corn, keep it cool, shuck it at the last minute, and cook it just long enough to heat it up. Steaming does a perfect job, and you avoid the hassle of bringing a huge quantity of water to a boil. You can keep the corn warm over the boiling water for a while without a problem; this is not to say you should overcook it, or cook it in advance, but that you can hold four ears in the pot while people are eating the other four.

Use 8 ears if corn will be the main part of your meal, otherwise 4 ears is plenty for a side.

    4 or 8 ears fresh corn, shucked
       Salt and pepper
       Butter (optional)

1. Put the corn in a pot with an inch or 2 of salted water; it's okay if some of the corn sits in the water and some above it. Cover and cook over high heat until it is just hot, 10 minutes or less. If the water is already boiling when you add the corn, the corn is very fresh, and/or your stove is powerful enough to keep the water boiling, the cooking time could be as little as 3 minutes.
2. Serve the corn with salt, pepper, and butter if you like.

Corn on the Cob, Grilled or Roasted

MAKES: 4 servings
TIME: 20 minutes
F O

Grilled corn is unbeatable; I like to blacken the kernels a bit, but you can also peel down the husk, remove the silk, and smooth the husks back in place; this will give you bright yellow corn with attractive, nicely charred husks.

Grilled corn is nice sprinkled with a little chili powder (to make your own, see page 648) too.

Other vegetables you can use: none are quite the same, but you can grill whole zucchini

    8 ears fresh corn, shucked
       Salt and pepper
       Butter (optional)

Heat a gas or charcoal grill until moderately hot; adjust the rack about 4 inches from the heat source. Or turn the oven to 500°F. Grill or roast the corn, turning a few

10 Flavorings for Hot Corn

Add alone or in combination:

1. Grated Parmesan cheese

2. Lemon or lime juice (especially with a few dashes hot sauce)

3. Red chile flakes or cayenne pepper

4. Any spice blend, especially chaat masala or chili powder

5. Minced toasted pumpkin, sunflower, or sesame seeds

6. Minced nuts like hazelnuts, almonds, cashews, or peanuts

7. Minced fresh herbs like parsley, mint, chervil, or chives

8. Mashed Roasted Garlic (page 205)

9. Nori "Shake" (page 650)

10. More butter!

times until some of the kernels char a bit and others are lightly browned, 8 to 15 minutes total. Serve with salt, pepper, and butter if you like.

MEXICAN GRILLED CORN (ELOTE) By far the best use of grilled corn: Stir together 1 teaspoon chile powder and ½ teaspoon cayenne. As soon as the corn comes off the grill, brush each ear with 1 tablespoon mayonnaise, then sprinkle with the chile powder mixture and crumbled Cotija or grated Parmesan cheese (½ cup total for 8 ears). Finish with a squeeze of lime juice.

Corn Pancakes, Thai Style

MAKES: 4 servings
TIME: 30 minutes
F

I have made corn fritters twenty different ways over the years, and these are the best: fresh corn barely bound by eggs, seasoned with soy and chile, cooked in butter.

Other vegetable you can use: shelled peas, preferably fresh

>   2 eggs, separated
>   Salt and pepper
>   ½ cup chopped scallions
>   1 teaspoon minced fresh chile (like jalapeño or Thai) or to taste, or red chile flakes or cayenne to taste
>   2 cups corn kernels (preferably just stripped from the cobs, see page 198; but thawed frozen is acceptable)
>   1 tablespoon soy sauce
>   ¼ cup all-purpose flour
> 3–4 tablespoons butter, or good-quality vegetable oil, as needed

1. In a large bowl, combine the egg yolks, a pinch salt, a good ½ teaspoon or more black pepper, the scallions, chile, corn, soy sauce, and flour; mix well.
2. Beat the egg whites in a medium bowl until stiff peaks form. Melt the butter or heat the oil in a large cast-iron

or nonstick skillet over medium-high heat. Fold the egg whites into the corn batter. When the butter foam subsides or the oil is hot, spoon pancake-sized dollops into the pan, 4 to 6 at a time.
3. Cook until nicely browned on one side, 3 to 5 minutes, then turn and brown the other side. Keep warm in a 200°F oven if necessary while you cook the remaining pancakes, adding additional butter or oil as necessary. Serve as soon as all the pancakes are cooked.

Corn Fritters

MAKES: 4 servings
TIME: 30 minutes
F

These are super-crisp, really good, and among the easiest things to fry.

>   ¾ cup cornmeal (the fresher the better)
>   ½ cup all-purpose flour
>   2 teaspoons baking powder
>   Salt and pepper
>   ¾ cup milk, plus more if needed
>   1 egg
>   2 cups corn kernels (preferably just stripped from the cobs, see page 198; but thawed frozen is acceptable)
>   Good-quality vegetable oil, as needed

1. Combine the cornmeal, flour, baking powder, and some salt and pepper in a large bowl. Beat together the milk and egg, then pour the mixture into the dry ingredients, adding a few tablespoons more milk if necessary to make a thick but smooth batter. Stir in the corn.
2. Put at least 2 inches oil in a deep pan on the stove and turn the heat to medium-high; bring to 350°F (see "Deep-Frying," page 26).
3. Drop the fritters by the ¼ cup or large spoonful into the hot oil; you'll probably need to raise the heat to maintain temperature. Cook the fritters in batches, turning once, until nicely browned on all sides, a total of 4 to 5 minutes per batch. Drain the fritters on paper

Corn Fritters

towels, then eat them as they are finished or keep them warm in a 180°F oven until they are all done.

AREPAS A South American staple, made with cheese: Omit the baking powder. Add 1 cup grated cheese, like cheddar, to the batter along with the milk and egg. Add a little more milk to make a slightly thinner, pancakelike batter. Cook in a shallow skillet with just a few tablespoons butter or oil, as you would pancakes.

Pan-Grilled Corn with Chile

MAKES: 4 servings
TIME: 20 minutes
F M V

This recipe is fast, it's easy, and it's completely different—when browned like this, corn takes on a brand-new flavor. This also makes a tasty addition to the salads on page 52.

Other vegetable you can use: shelled peas

- 6 ears fresh corn, shucked
- 1 tablespoon good-quality vegetable oil
- 1 teaspoon minced fresh chile (like jalapeño or Thai), or to taste, or red chile flakes or cayenne to taste
- 1 teaspoon minced garlic or 1 tablespoon minced shallot or white or red onion
- Salt and pepper
- Chopped fresh cilantro for garnish
- Lime wedges (optional)

1. Use a knife to strip the kernels from the cobs. It's easiest if you stand the corn up in a shallow bowl and just cut down the length of each ear as many times as is necessary; you'll quickly get the hang of it.

2. Put the oil in a large skillet over high heat. When it's hot, add the corn, chile, and garlic; let sit for a moment. As the corn browns, shake the pan to distribute it so each kernel is deeply browned on at least one surface.

3. Remove from the heat, then season with salt and pepper. If you're serving immediately, stir in the cilantro and squeeze a little lime juice over the top; pass some more lime at the table.

PAN-GRILLED CORN WITH TOMATOES This becomes a little stewy: Omit the garlic. In Step 2, cook the corn and chile until brown. Add 2 tablespoons more oil and 1 large onion, chopped; cook until the onion softens, 5 to 10 minutes. Add 2 cups chopped tomatoes (fresh and good, please, but canned will do in a pinch) and cook, stirring occasionally, until the tomatoes break down. Proceed from Step 3.

EGGPLANT

Check out a summer farmers' market for the best and widest variety of eggplants: Green, white, striped, or speckled; long and skinny, round and fat, oblong, egg-shaped, or oval; ranging in size from 2 to 12 inches in length. Each type offers a variation in texture and flavor that might influence what you use it for—some are sweeter, some more bitter, and some have a more delicate flesh or tougher skin. The long and slender type slices up nicely for stir-fries, while the large round type provides large chunks or slices for grilling. If you have the option of choosing different types, then by all means do so, but if the usual dark purple variety is all you can get, don't worry about it.

BUYING AND STORING In general, smaller eggplant contain fewer seeds and are less likely to be bitter. I love the golf ball–sized ones, which do not require any trimming or cleaning. But firmness is the most important aspect when buying an eggplant. Look for undamaged specimens, heavy for their size, with no brown spots. The color of the stems also indicates freshness: The greener and fresher looking they are, the better. Store in the refrigerator and use eggplant as soon as possible; although the outside will not look much different, the inside will become soft and bitter within a few days.

PREPARING Trim the stem end; peeling is optional. Slice crosswise or lengthwise, ½ inch to 1 inch thick, or cube any size.

BEST COOKING METHODS Roasting, grilling, broiling, sautéing, stir-frying

WHEN IS IT DONE? When it's tender—almost creamy—and there are no dry spots.

OTHER VEGETABLES YOU CAN USE Really, there is no substitute, but zucchini or summer squash can sometimes fill in adequately.

Skillet Eggplant

MAKES: 4 servings
TIME: About 40 minutes
V

It takes time and a fair amount of oil to cook eggplant on the stovetop but the results are worth it: creamy and flavorful, like no other vegetable.

Other vegetables you can use: zucchini or summer squash, but the results will not be as satisfying

1½–2	pounds eggplant (preferably small)
	About ⅓ cup olive oil
3	teaspoons minced garlic
	Salt and pepper
	Chopped fresh parsley for garnish

1. Peel the eggplant if the skin is thick; cut it into ½-inch cubes.

2. Put the oil and 2 teaspoons of the garlic in a large skillet over medium heat. Two minutes later, add the eggplant. Stir and toss almost constantly until the eggplant begins to release some of the oil it has absorbed, 5 to 10 minutes.

3. Continue cooking, stirring frequently, until the eggplant is very tender, about 30 minutes (this can vary greatly). About 5 minutes before it is done, add the remaining 1 teaspoon garlic.

4. Sprinkle with salt and pepper. Garnish with parsley and serve.

CURRIED EGGPLANT WITH COCONUT MILK Also good with about a third of the eggplant replaced with small cubes of waxy potato, and served over rice: In Step 2, use 2 tablespoons good-quality vegetable oil and, in addition to the garlic, add 2 teaspoons minced fresh ginger and 1 teaspoon red curry paste, curry powder, or garam masala. After the eggplant begins to get tender, stir in about a cup coconut milk and cook until very soft, about 15 minutes more. Taste and adjust the seasoning. Garnish with cilantro.

SKILLET EGGPLANT WITH TOMATOES In Step 2, add 1 medium or ½ large onion, chopped, along with the garlic. In Step 3, as the eggplant becomes tender, stir in about 2 cups chopped tomatoes (fresh are best, but canned are acceptable). Cook for about 10 minutes more, stirring occasionally, until the tomatoes break up, then add the remaining garlic and proceed with the recipe.

SKILLET EGGPLANT WITH GREENS Use about a pound of spinach, arugula, kale, collards, or any fresh green you find at the farmers' market. If you've got greens with sturdy stems, separate them from the leaves and roughly chop everything; you want 3 to 4 cups total: In Step 3, add the stems (if you've got them) after the eggplant has cooked for about 15 minutes; let them cook together for about 10 minutes, then add the leaves. Tender greens

Grilled Eggplant with
The Simplest Yogurt
Sauce (page 673)

like spinach should go in during the last 5 minutes of cooking the eggplant. Add enough olive oil to keep the mixture moist but not greasy. When everything is tender, stir in ½ cup grated Parmesan cheese if you like. Taste and adjust the seasoning. Serve hot or at room temperature.

Grilled or Broiled Eggplant

MAKES: 4 servings
TIME: 30 minutes
F M V

An ideal room-temperature dish, and so reliably good it almost makes sense to prepare it whenever you've got the grill going. It's especially good with The Simplest Yogurt Sauce (page 673) and fresh mint. In the summer, I can't get enough of this.

    2 **medium or 1 large eggplant (1½–2 pounds)**
    1 **teaspoon minced garlic (optional)**
 4–6 **tablespoons olive oil**
       Salt and pepper
       Chopped fresh parsley for garnish

1. Heat a charcoal or gas grill or the broiler to moderately high heat and put the grill rack about 4 inches from the heat source or the broiler rack 4 to 6 inches from the heat source.

2. Peel the eggplant if the skin is thick. Cut into ½-inch-thick slices. If you like, stir the garlic into the oil. Brush one side of the eggplant slices with the oil. Place, oiled side down, directly on the grill or on a baking sheet. Sprinkle with salt and pepper, then brush with more oil. If you're broiling, put the baking sheet under the broiler.

3. Grill or broil, turning once, until the eggplant has browned and become tender, 5 to 10 minutes per side, brushing with more oil if it looks dry. Transfer the slices to a platter, drizzle with the remaining oil, sprinkle with parsley, and serve hot, warm, or at room temperature.

GRILLED OR BROILED EGGPLANT WITH MISO Shortly before the end of cooking, brush the slices with

Sweet Miso Glaze (page 654) or Nutty Miso Sauce (page 653).

GRILLED OR BROILED EGGPLANT WITH TAHINI SESAME GLAZE In the last few minutes of cooking, brush the slices with Tahini Soy Sauce (page 657).

GRILLED OR BROILED EGGPLANT SALAD WITH YOGURT While the eggplant cooks, mix together 1½ cups yogurt, 2 teaspoons minced garlic, ¼ cup each chopped scallions and fresh mint or cilantro, and a couple of teaspoons fresh lemon juice. Chop the cooked eggplant and mix it into the yogurt dressing with a sprinkle with salt and pepper. Serve at room temperature or chilled, with bread if you like.

Eggplant Slices with Garlic and Parsley

MAKES: 4 servings
TIME: About 45 minutes
M V

When all you can find is large eggplant, cook this recipe. It makes their size an attribute. The results are beautifully creamy and savory.

    4 **tablespoons olive oil**
    2 **medium or 1 large eggplant (1½–2 pounds total)**
    1 **tablespoon minced garlic**
   ½ **cup chopped fresh parsley, plus more for garnish**
       Salt and pepper

1. Heat the oven to 400°F. Grease a baking sheet with 2 tablespoons of the oil.

2. Peel the eggplant if the skin is thick; cut it into 1-inch-thick slices. Cut several slits on one side of each of the eggplant slices and lay them on the baking sheet, slit side up. Mix together the remaining 2 tablespoons oil, the garlic, ½ cup parsley, and a sprinkle of salt and pepper. Spread this mixture on the eggplant slices, pushing it into the slits.

3. Bake without turning until the eggplant is soft, 40 minutes or more. Garnish with more parsley and serve hot or at room temperature.

Eggplant Parmesan

MAKES: 6 servings
TIME: About 1 hour
Ⓜ

As filling as lasagne (though it's equally good, and more traditional, without the mozzarella) and more flavorful. If you use Grilled or Broiled Eggplant (page 201) here, you don't have to sauté the eggplant.

Other vegetable you can use: zucchini (cut lengthwise)

> Olive oil as needed
> 2 medium to large eggplants (2–3 pounds total), peeled and cut into ½-inch-thick slices lengthwise
> All-purpose flour for dredging
> Salt and pepper
> 2 cups Fast Tomato Sauce (page 312)
> 8 ounces grated mozzarella cheese (about 2 cups; optional)
> 1 cup grated Parmesan cheese, plus more if you omit the mozzarella
> About 30 fresh basil leaves

1. Heat the oven to 350°F. Put about 3 tablespoons oil in a large skillet over medium heat. When it's hot (a pinch of flour will sizzle), dredge the eggplant slices, one at a time, in the flour, shaking off the excess. Put in the pan, but do not crowd; you will have to cook in batches. Cook for 3 or 4 minutes on each side, until nicely browned. Season the slices with salt and pepper as they cook. Drain on paper towels. Add more oil to the skillet as needed.
2. Lightly oil a baking dish, then spoon a little of the tomato sauce into it. Top with a layer of eggplant, then a thin layer of each of the cheeses, and finally a few basil leaves. Repeat until the ingredients are used up,

reserving some of the basil for garnish and ending with a sprinkle of Parmesan.
3. Bake until the dish is bubbling hot, 20 to 30 minutes. Chop the reserved basil and sprinkle over the top. Serve hot or at room temperature.

ENDIVE, ESCAROLE, RADICCHIO, AND CHICORY

This group of bitter plants can be confusing, in part because the term "chicory" may be used to describe everything in this category. They are all members of the composite family (like daisies), but chicory and endive are different species.

Chicory has a solidly green, narrow leaf and grows in a loose head. Radicchio is red, white, and head-shaped and related to chicory. There are three types of endive: the pale, spear-shaped Belgian endive; the open and frilly curly endive (often called frisée); and the broad-leafed, lettucelike escarole. If that isn't enough, each of the previous sentences is incomplete; there are variations on the variations—some radicchio, for example, is green and red and long. But proper botany, size, and shape aside, all endive and chicory are bitter, leafy, crisp, and firm; they add texture and distinctive flavor to salads and are among the best greens for cooking.

BUYING AND STORING Look for crisp, unwilted leaves. Belgian endive and all but the very exterior leaves of curly endive should be white to pale yellow in color; green coloring indicates the leaves were exposed to sunlight and will be too bitter. Store wrapped loosely in plastic in the refrigerator; chicory and endive keep longer than most salad greens.

PREPARING Trim and wash as you would any lettuce.

BEST COOKING METHODS Sautéing, braising (Belgian endive and escarole), grilling (endive and radicchio)

WHEN ARE THEY DONE? Sautéed or grilled, when crisp-tender; braised, when soft but not mushy

OTHER VEGETABLES YOU CAN USE Dandelion, turnip, or mustard greens when cooked; any lettuce, arugula, or watercress when raw

Braised Endive, Escarole, or Radicchio

MAKES: 4 servings
TIME: About 1 hour
Ⓜ Ⓥ

Endive makes the tidiest dish, but the other options taste just as good. The croutons add a terrific crunch here, though they're not essential.

Other vegetables you can use: just about any bitter green like romaine lettuce, bok choy, cabbage, or Brussels sprouts, halved or chopped accordingly

    3 tablespoons olive oil
    4 Belgian endives, trimmed at the base
       and damaged leaves removed; 2 heads
       radicchio, trimmed and halved; or about
       1 pound escarole, roughly chopped
    ½ cup vegetable stock (pages 97–100) or
       water
       Salt and pepper
    1 teaspoon fresh lemon juice or white wine
       vinegar
    1 cup Croutons (page 678), chopped up a bit, or
       any of the Crumbles (see page 497 or 679),
       optional

1. Put the oil in a skillet with a lid over medium heat. When it's hot, add the endives and cook, turning once or twice, until they begin to brown, 5 to 10 minutes.
2. Add the stock and sprinkle with salt and pepper. Cover and cook over the lowest possible heat, turning occasionally, until very tender, about 45 minutes. Uncover and turn the heat up a bit to evaporate any remaining liquid.
3. Drizzle with lemon juice, garnish with Croutons if desired, and serve hot, warm, or at room temperature.

BRAISED ENDIVE WITH ORANGE JUICE The orange juice caramelizes beautifully, adding a rich sweetness: Substitute butter for the olive oil if you like, and orange juice for the stock. Add 2 tablespoons brown sugar with the orange juice. Omit the lemon juice or vinegar.

Grilled or Broiled Radicchio with Balsamic Glaze

MAKES: 4 servings
TIME: About 15 minutes
Ⓕ Ⓜ Ⓞ

Balsamic vinegar works miraculously to balance the bitterness of radicchio. This makes a fine alternative to a salad; try some crumbled feta, blue cheese, or grated Parmesan and roasted hazelnuts or almonds on top too.

This is also a useful ingredient: Chop it coarsely and stir it into risotto toward the end of cooking or toss together with freshly cooked pasta with some olive oil and Parmesan. Stir it into Tomato and Bread Salad (page 61) or combine it with sliced steamed green beans or cooked cannellini beans.

Other vegetables you can use: endive, chicory, escarole, or romaine lettuce

    4 small or 2 large heads radicchio (about
       1 pound)
    2 tablespoons olive oil
    ¼ cup balsamic vinegar
    1 tablespoon brown sugar or honey
       Salt and pepper

1. Prepare a charcoal or gas grill or turn on the broiler for moderately high heat; put the rack about 4 inches from the heat source.
2. Halve or quarter the radicchio lengthwise, depending on their size. Rub or brush them with the oil, taking care to keep the wedges intact. Whisk the vinegar and sugar in a small bowl until the sugar is dissolved.
3. Put the radicchio wedges on the grill or on a broiler pan, cut sides toward the heat. Grill or broil for a

Grilled Radicchio with
Balsamic Glaze (page 203)

minute or 2, then carefully turn and brush or drizzle with the vinegar mixture. Cook until just starting to crisp and char around the edges, another couple of minutes. Transfer to a plate or platter and sprinkle with salt and lots of black pepper. Serve hot or at room temperature.

GARLIC

Depending on how you handle it, cooked garlic ranges from assertively strong and delicious to sweet and mild. Roasting whole cloves or even the entire head is one of the best ways to bring out the rich sweetness of garlic; simply spread it on toast or use it to season just about anything. Sautéing garlic in oil or butter to season a dish is also magical: Chop or slice the cloves and add to the hot oil or butter; sauté over medium heat just until it softens.

Dehydrated garlic, garlic salt, and garlic powder are poor substitutes for the real thing, as is the chopped garlic in oil found in some markets, though I am a fan of whole peeled garlic in jars, as long as it's fresh.

To remove the garlic scent from your fingers, rinse your fingers in water while rubbing them on any stainless-steel surface (your sink or faucet will do).

BUYING AND STORING Choose loose heads because you can select the best. Look for hard, unshriveled bulbs that have not sprouted. The color and size of garlic is not especially important, though larger cloves are easier to handle and there's less peeling involved. Store in a dark, cool spot where it's exposed to air. Sprouting is not cause for discarding, though some people cut out the sprout because it's (slightly) bitter; rotted or desiccated cloves should be thrown out.

PREPARING Peeling is easiest when the clove is half-smashed with the flat side of a knife blade. For larger quantities, simmer the garlic in water to cover for 30 seconds, or toast it in a dry pan over medium heat, shaking the pan frequently, for about 5 minutes. Either of these treatments will loosen the skins and make it easy to slip out the cloves. To chop large quantities, add whole cloves to a food processor with a bit of oil; this will keep well in a sealed container for a few days.

BEST COOKING METHODS Roasting, simmering in oil

WHEN IS IT DONE? When very, very tender, almost mushy. Roasted cloves will easily squeeze out of their skins.

OTHER VEGETABLES YOU CAN USE Shallots can sometimes fill in, as can onion, but they just aren't the same.

Roasted Garlic

MAKES: 2 heads
TIME: About 1 hour, mostly unattended
M V

Mellow roasted garlic is invaluable as a side, condiment, or ingredient in sauces and other dishes. I like to use more olive oil than I need, because the oil itself—as long as it's stored in the fridge and used within a few days— is another great ingredient in vinaigrettes or used as a finishing oil.

> 2 whole heads garlic
> 2 tablespoons olive oil, or more as needed
>   Salt

1. Heat the oven to 375°F. Without getting too fussy or breaking the heads apart, remove as much of the papery coating from them as you can. Cut the top pointy part off the head to expose a bit of each clove.
2. Lightly grease a small baking dish with oil and add the garlic. Drizzle with more oil and sprinkle with salt. Cover with foil. Roast until the garlic is soft (you'll be able to pierce it easily with a thin-bladed knife), 40 minutes or longer.
3. When cool enough to handle, squeeze the cloves out of the peels. You can refrigerate in an airtight container

for up to a week. To freeze, spread the cloves in a single layer over a baking sheet and freeze, then transfer to an airtight container and store in the freezer for up to 6 months; this way you can take out just as much garlic as you want.

FASTER ROASTED GARLIC If you're in a hurry: Break the heads into individual cloves, but do not peel them. Spread them in a pan, sprinkle with salt, and drizzle with oil. Bake, shaking the pan occasionally, until tender, 20 to 30 minutes.

Garlic Braised in Olive Oil

MAKES: 40 or more cloves
TIME: 45 minutes or less
Ⓜ Ⓥ

There are many ways to soften garlic, such as in the Roasted Garlic recipe above. This is my favorite, though. Just keep the heat low and take your time.

You can use this garlic in myriad dishes, including vinaigrettes and other sauces; or you can serve it as a vegetable. Use the oil in sauces or for sautéing.

Other vegetables you can use: shallots (use about half as many since they're bigger)

½   cup olive oil
40 cloves garlic, or more (don't peel)
    Salt

1. Put the oil in a small skillet over medium-low heat. When it's hot, add the garlic. Sprinkle with salt. Adjust the heat so the garlic just sizzles.
2. Cook, turning occasionally so the garlic cooks evenly, until it gradually turns golden, then begins to brown. The garlic is done when tender. Let cool, then store refrigerated, in the oil, and peel and use within a few days.

GINGER

This spicy, aromatic, gnarled tropical plant is often called a root but it is actually a rhizome—an underground stem. It's tan colored with papery skin that is usually peeled; the flesh is off-yellow, pungent in flavor and fragrance, and has fibers running the length of it. Typically, the younger the ginger, the less fibrous, pungent, and spicy the flesh and the more translucent the skin; more mature ginger can be downright hot—it contains a substance related to capsaicin, which is what makes chiles spicy. It's used fresh, dried, ground, candied, pickled, and preserved.

BUYING AND STORING Look for a smooth, plump piece that is heavy for its size; pass on anything that feels at all soft. Store wrapped loosely in plastic in the refrigerator for as long as 2 weeks; use it before it shrivels. You can also freeze it, tightly wrapped, for up to several months— already grated, in slices, or a full piece, as you prefer.

PREPARING Scrape off the papery skin with the blunt side of a knife, the edge of a spoon, or a vegetable peeler, or peel it with a paring knife, which is faster, if less economical. If the skin is thin enough, you don't even need to peel it. Grate, julienne, mince , or cut the ginger into coins.

BEST COOKING METHODS In stir-fries and other sautés, soups, and braises; raw in salads; steeped in tea or broth

OTHER VEGETABLES YOU CAN USE Only galangal comes close, but that's hard to find.

Pickled Ginger

MAKES: 4 servings
TIME: At least a day, mostly unattended
Ⓜ Ⓥ

Homemade pickled ginger is far better than the pink-tinted stuff you get in restaurants, especially if you start with young, thin-skinned ginger. Use as a condiment with Sushi Bowls (page 384), noodle dishes, and sandwiches of all kinds.

    1 large piece fresh ginger (about 4 ounces)
    1 tablespoon salt
    ¼ cup rice vinegar, or more as needed
    2 tablespoons sugar, or more to taste

1. Peel and thinly slice the ginger, using a mandoline if you have one. Toss it with the salt and let stand for an hour. Rinse thoroughly, drain, and put in a 1-pint glass or ceramic container with a tight-fitting lid.
2. Combine the vinegar with ¼ cup water and the sugar in a small saucepan. Stir over low heat until the sugar dissolves. Taste and add more sugar if you like. Cool slightly and add to the ginger. If the liquid does not cover the ginger, add more vinegar and water in equal parts. Cover and refrigerate.
3. You can begin eating the ginger within a day, though it will improve for several days. It will keep for up to a couple of weeks.

CITRUS-PICKLED GINGER Add the zest from 1 orange, lemon, or tangerine, 2 limes, or ½ grapefruit to the rice vinegar and sugar mixture.

SPICED PICKLED GINGER Would be wonderful with any number of rice or noodle dishes: Add 1 cinnamon stick and 2 star anise to the vinegar-sugar mixture.

GREEN BEANS

Also known as string beans, these are slender beans with edible pods. We're most familiar with the common green bean; wax beans are identical except for their yellow color; long beans are originally Chinese (though now grown here too) and are anywhere from a foot to a yard long; French haricots verts are skinny and tender.

All of these string beans—which have had the strings bred out of them for the most part—can be eaten raw (best when they're fresh off the vine), barely cooked so they're still crunchy, or completely cooked and melt-in-your-mouth soft. Summer is the best season for green beans, though most varieties are available year-round.

BUYING AND STORING Green and wax beans should be crisp, unshriveled, and snap when bent in half. Long beans and haricots verts are more tender and flexible but should still be crisp and unshriveled. Store wrapped loosely in plastic in the refrigerator; use soon—they lose their fresh flavor quickly.

PREPARING Snap or cut off the stem end; leave whole or cut into any length you like. To "French cut" green beans, slice them in half lengthwise. It's a lot of work but results in an appealing look and texture.

BEST COOKING METHODS Steaming, boiling, microwaving, stir-frying, sautéing, roasting, braising

WHEN IS IT DONE? A matter of personal preference: crisp-tender, just tender, or meltingly soft

OTHER VEGETABLES YOU CAN USE Asparagus, peas, broccoli

Green Beans Tossed with Walnut-Miso Sauce

MAKES: 4 servings
TIME: 20 minutes
F M V

This traditional Japanese dish comes together in minutes, and the results are wonderful. Even better, this sauce is almost universally useful. It works on other vegetables as well as plain rice, noodles, or other cooked grains.

Other vegetables you can use: almost any solid vegetable—peas, snow peas, or sugar snap peas (parboiled and shocked); broccoli or cauliflower (parboiled and shocked); potatoes (boiled or baked); eggplant (sautéed); zucchini (steamed or grilled); and so on.

> 1 pound green beans, trimmed, parboiled, and shocked (see page 150)
> 1 tablespoon grated or minced fresh ginger
> ¼ cup white miso
> ½ cup shelled walnuts
> 1 teaspoon soy sauce, or to taste
> Salt

1. Drain the beans and put them in a serving bowl.
2. Put the ginger, miso, walnuts, 2 tablespoons water, and soy sauce in a blender and blend until smooth, stopping the machine and scraping down its sides if necessary. (You may need to add a little more water or soy sauce if the mixture is too thick.)
3. Toss the green beans in the sauce and serve at room temperature.

Twice-Fried Green Beans

MAKES: 4 servings
TIME: About 30 minutes
F V

I like cashews in this, but Crunchy Crumbled Tempeh (page 512) is also good.

Other vegetables you can use: long beans (cut into 2-inch lengths)

> Good-quality vegetable oil for deep-frying
> 1½ pounds green beans, trimmed and patted dry
> Salt
> ½ cup whole or chopped raw cashews
> 1 tablespoon chopped garlic
> ½ cup chopped scallions
> 1 teaspoon minced fresh chile (like jalapeño or Thai) or to taste, or red chile flakes or cayenne to taste
> 2 tablespoons soy sauce, plus more to taste
> 1 tablespoon sugar

1. While you prepare the ingredients, put about 2 inches oil in a deep pan on the stove and turn the heat to medium-high; bring to 350°F (see "Deep-Frying," page 26).
2. Make sure the beans are well dried. Add them to the oil all at once. Cook, stirring occasionally, until they begin to brown, 5 to 10 minutes. Remove them with a slotted spoon and drain on paper towels. Sprinkle with salt.
3. Add the cashews to the oil and cook, stirring frequently, until they brown nicely, about 3 minutes. Remove with a slotted spoon and drain on paper towels; sprinkle with salt. Turn off the heat.
4. Put 2 tablespoons of the oil in a heavy skillet over high heat. When it's hot, add the garlic, scallions, and chile and cook for 30 seconds, stirring. Add the beans and cook, stirring, for about 2 minutes. Add the soy sauce and sugar, stir, and turn off the heat. Taste and add more salt, chile, or soy sauce if you like. Sprinkle on the fried nuts and serve.

Roasted Green Beans

MAKES: 4 servings
TIME: 30 to 40 minutes
M V

It's not a preparation you often see, but roasted green beans are delightful—tender and sweet.

After about 15 minutes, you can flavor these with balsamic vinegar, sesame oil, or any spice mixture; or mix them with Compound Butter (page 676) right before serving.

Green Beans Tossed with
Walnut-Miso Sauce

1½ **pounds green beans, trimmed**
3 **tablespoons olive or good-quality vegetable oil**
Salt and pepper
1 **tablespoon fresh lemon juice,**
or more to taste
Chopped fresh parsley for garnish

1. Heat the oven to 375°F. Mix the green beans and oil in a large bowl and season generously with salt and pepper.

2. Put the beans in single layer on a baking sheet, making sure not to crowd the pan (you might need to use two baking sheets). Roast for 15 minutes, then stir. Add seasoning if you're using it. Roast for another 15 minutes or to the desired consistency. The beans are done when they are browned in spots and start to collapse. Season with the lemon juice and parsley and serve hot, warm, or at room temperature.

HARISSA ROASTED GREEN BEANS Wonderfully spicy: Toss the green beans with 1 tablespoon Harissa (page 665) and 1 teaspoon minced garlic before roasting.

KALE AND COLLARD GREENS

Kale has been cultivated in Europe for thousands of years, and collards are an essential in Southern cooking and what many Southerners mean when they say "greens." Both have leathery, dark-green leaves with thick, sometimes chalky-looking stems. While they are similar, there are a couple of distinguishing features: Collards' leaves are flat and can be quite big (as much as 8 inches across), whereas kale leaves are ruffled and range in size and color from narrow and very dark green to fat and greenish gray. They can grow in warmer climates, but they're actually best when grown in cool weather—even in the snow. Their peak season is midwinter through early spring, but they're now available year-round.

BUYING AND STORING Look for firm, dark-green leaves with no yellowing or wilting. Young leaves with stems no thicker than a pencil are easier to clean; they'll likely have a better texture when cooked too. Store wrapped loosely in plastic in the refrigerator for a few days; use before they start to turn yellow.

PREPARING Rinse the leaves thoroughly; they can be very sandy. If the stems are thick, strip the leaves, chop the stems, and start cooking them a couple of minutes before the leaves. An easy way to cut the leaves is to roll them up, then cut across the roll.

BEST COOKING METHODS Boiling, steaming, braising. Wonderful added to soups and stews. The leaves are good raw and shredded in salads, all the way to braised for long periods of time.

WHEN ARE THEY DONE? When the stems are tender enough to pierce easily with a skewer or thin-bladed knife, unless—and this is sometimes the case—you want the stems on the crunchy side.

OTHER VEGETABLES YOU CAN USE Cabbage, chard, beet greens

Flash-Cooked Kale or Collards with Lemon Juice

MAKES: 4 servings
TIME: 15 minutes
F M V

Regardless of what green you choose, make sure the stems are ⅛ inch thick or less; strip away and discard thicker stems.

Other vegetables you can use: any dark greens like turnip, mustard, or dandelion, or shredded cabbage of any type

1–1½ **pounds kale or collards, rinsed well**
and patted dry
3 **tablespoons olive oil**
Salt and pepper
⅓–½ **cup fresh lemon juice, wine vinegar,**
or sherry vinegar

1. Separate the leaves from the stems. Chop the stems into 1-inch sections; stack the leaves, roll them up like a cigar, and cut into thin strips (see below).

2. Put the oil in a well-seasoned cast-iron or nonstick large skillet over high heat. When it's very hot but not yet smoking, toss in the stems. Cook, stirring almost constantly, until they begin to brown, 3 to 5 minutes.

3. Add the leaves and continue to cook, stirring, until they wilt and begin to brown. Turn off the heat, season with salt and pepper, and add about ⅓ cup lemon juice or vinegar. Taste, adjust the flavors, and serve immediately or at room temperature.

Kale or Collards with Tahini

MAKES: 4 servings
TIME: 20 minutes
F M V

This rich and filling dish is wonderful spooned over rice, especially basmati.

Other vegetables you can use: broccoli raab, broccolini, gai lan; beet, dandelion, or turnip greens; chard, bok choy, cabbage, or spinach

2	**tablespoons olive oil**
1	**tablespoon chopped garlic**
1	**pound kale or collards with stems under ¼ inch thick, rinsed well, dried, and roughly chopped**
¼	**cup vegetable stock (pages 97–100) or water**
¼	**cup tahini (to make your own, see page 305) Salt and pepper**
2	**tablespoons fresh lemon juice or balsamic vinegar Chopped fresh tomato for garnish (optional)**

1. Put the oil in a large, deep skillet over medium heat. When it's hot, add the garlic and cook, stirring, until golden but not brown, about 3 minutes. Add the greens, stock, tahini, and a good sprinkle of salt and pepper. Cover and cook until the greens are wilted and tender, about 5 minutes.

2. Uncover and continue to cook at a low bubble, stirring frequently, until the greens are very tender, at least 5 minutes more. Add more stock if the pot looks dry; you want some sauce, but not soup. Remove from the heat and stir in the lemon juice. Taste and adjust the seasoning. Serve hot, warm, or at room temperature, garnished with tomato if you like.

KALE OR COLLARDS WITH PEANUT BUTTER Substitute peanut butter for the tahini. Add 1 tablespoon minced fresh ginger with the greens and substitute lime juice for the lemon. Garnish with tomato or fresh cilantro.

COLLARDS OR KALE WITH YOGURT Add or substitute ½ cup yogurt for the tahini, but add it with the lemon juice. Garnish with fresh mint or dill.

Garlicky Kale or Collards with Olives and Pine Nuts

MAKES: 4 servings
TIME: 40 minutes
M V

A super side dish that you can turn into an entrée by tossing with pasta, a bit more oil, and a little of the pasta-cooking water.

Preparing Leafy Greens with Thick Ribs

STEP 1 You may remove the stems if they are very thick. Or just cook them a little longer than the leaves. Cut on either side of them, at an angle.

STEP 2 The easiest way to chop large leaves is to roll them up and cut across the log (see "Chiffonade," page 23).

Other vegetables you can use: spinach, chard, cabbage, bok choy

1½	pounds kale or collards, rinsed well
¼	cup pine nuts
2	tablespoons olive oil
6	cloves garlic, or to taste, sliced
½	cup pitted black or green olives, chopped
½	cup white wine or water
	Salt and pepper

1. Cut the leaves from the stems. Cut the leaves into wide ribbons and slice the stems (on the diagonal if you like); keep the leaves and stems separate.

2. Put the pine nuts in a large skillet over medium-low heat. Toast the nuts, shaking the pan and stirring often, until just starting to turn golden brown, 5 to 10 minutes. Remove the nuts from the pan. Put the oil in the skillet and heat for 1 minute. Add the garlic and cook, stirring, until soft, golden, and fragrant, about 10 minutes.

3. Turn the heat to medium and stir in the stems and olives. Cook, stirring occasionally, until the stems soften a bit, just a minute or 2. Add the leaves, wine, and a sprinkle of salt and pepper. Raise the heat to medium-high and cook, stirring, until the leaves are wilted and most of the liquid has evaporated, about 5 minutes. Stir in the pine nuts and taste and adjust the seasoning. Serve hot or at room temperature.

GARLICKY KALE WITH CAPERS AND ALMONDS Substitute slivered almonds for the pine nuts and 2 tablespoons chopped capers for the olives.

Kale or Chard Pie
MAKES: 4 to 6 servings
TIME: 1¼ hours
Ⓜ

A simple pie with a biscuit-like, no-roll crust that is incredibly versatile: As is, it makes a lovely lunch or elegant side. Or turn the pie into a satisfying entrée with Fast Tomato Sauce (page 312) or The Simplest Yogurt Sauce (page 673). And it's perfect for entertaining, since you can bake it ahead and serve it room temperature or warm; cut it into thin wedges or bite-size squares and pass as an appetizer.

Other vegetables you can use: collards, spinach (squeezed dry and chopped), broccoli, cauliflower, cabbage, mushrooms

2	tablespoons butter, plus more as needed
	About 8 large kale or chard leaves, rinsed well and thinly sliced
1	onion, sliced
	Salt and pepper
¼	cup chopped mixed fresh herbs (like parsley, thyme, chervil, and/or chives)
6	eggs
1	cup whole-milk yogurt or sour cream
3	tablespoons mayonnaise
1¼	cups all-purpose flour
½	teaspoon baking powder

1. Heat the oven to 375°F. Melt the butter in a large skillet, preferably nonstick, over medium heat. After a minute, add the kale and onion. Sprinkle with salt and pepper and cook, stirring occasionally, until the leaves are quite tender, about 10 minutes; do not brown. Remove from the heat, add the herbs, then taste and adjust the seasoning.

2. Meanwhile, hard-boil 3 of the eggs (page 521); shell and coarsely chop them. Add to the cooked kale and let cool while you make the batter.

3. Whisk together the yogurt, mayonnaise, and the remaining 3 eggs in a large bowl until smooth. Add the flour and baking powder and mix until completely incorporated. Lightly butter a 12 × 9-inch or comparble ceramic or glass baking dish. Spread half the batter over the bottom, then top with the kale filling; spread the remaining batter over the kale, using your fingers or a rubber spatula to make sure there are no gaps in the top layer.

4. Bake for 45 minutes, until the crust is shiny and golden brown. Let the pie cool for at least 15 minutes

Chard Pie

before slicing it into as many squares or rectangles as you like. Serve warm or at room temperature.

CABBAGE PIE An Eastern European classic: Replace the kale with 1 head Savoy or green cabbage, cored and thinly sliced, and the mixed herbs with ⅔ cup chopped fresh dill.

MUSHROOM AND KASHA PIE Meaty in flavor and texture and can be made with almost any cooked grain, including wheat and rye berries: Substitute 3 cups chopped or sliced mushrooms for the kale, and add 1 cup cooked kasha (page 398) to the mushroom mixture along with the herbs.

KOHLRABI

Kohlrabi is a member of the cabbage family. The whole plant is edible, but it's the bulbous stem base that's prized for its sweet, slightly piquant flavor and crisp texture—slice it thinly, sprinkle with salt, drizzle with oil, and enjoy. When sold without its stems and leaves, kohlrabi is sphere-shaped with several arched ridges (where the stems were attached); its skin is like that of broccoli stems and can be white, light green, or vibrant purple.

BUYING AND STORING Look for specimens that are firm, crisp, and about the size of a golf ball (larger ones can be woody and tough). Store wrapped loosely in plastic in the refrigerator, where they will keep for up to 2 weeks.

PREPARING Peeling is optional for small kohlrabi and recommended for large ones. Slice or chop as necessary.

BEST COOKING METHODS Steaming, sautéing, roasting

WHEN IS IT DONE? Steamed or sautéed, when tender but still crisp; roasted, when soft

OTHER VEGETABLE YOU CAN USE Turnips

Sautéed Kohlrabi with Horseradish and Cream

MAKES: 4 servings
TIME: 20 minutes

F

Kohlrabi is the ultimate what-the-heck-do-I-do-with-this? vegetable. It can be used in many of the recipes in this chapter, plus slaws and soups. Still, it's nice to have a stand-alone recipe for the vegetable that everyone, at some point, has been stumped by.

Other vegetables you can use: turnips, cauliflower

> 2 tablespoons butter
> 1½ pounds kohlrabi, peeled and cubed, leaves removed and chopped
> 1 onion, sliced
> Salt and pepper
> ¼ cup heavy cream
> 1 tablespoon grated horseradish

1. Put the butter in a large skillet over medium-high heat. When it has melted, add the kohlrabi and onion and sprinkle with salt and pepper. Cook the kohlrabi and onion until almost tender, 10 to 15 minutes. Stir in the leaves and cook until wilted, just a few minutes.
2. Add the cream and horseradish and cook for a minute or 2 to reduce. Taste and adjust the seasoning. Serve immediately.

SAUTÉED KOHLRABI WITH MUSTARD SAUCE Replace the horseradish with a tablespoon Dijon mustard or more to taste. Cook for a little longer so the cream and mustard sauce thickens.

SAUTÉED KOHLRABI WITH CHILE Super over rice: Replace the cream with a ½ cup coconut milk and the horseradish with 1 thinly sliced fresh chile (like jalapeño or Thai). **V**

LEEKS

The leek looks like an enormous scallion; since it's a member of the *Allium* genus—which also includes onions, garlic, and scallions—that isn't surprising. Mild and sweet, silky when cooked, leeks are wonderful. Make sure there is plenty of white on the stalk, since you'll trim off most of the green.

BUYING AND STORING Generally, the smaller the leek, the more tender it is; but big, plump leeks are wonderful too. Avoid those that are slimy, dried out, browning, or mostly green. Store wrapped loosely in plastic in the refrigerator; they will keep for weeks.

PREPARING Trim the root end and any hard green leaves (you can freeze these and use them in stock). Make a long vertical slit through the center of the leek, starting about 1 inch from the root end and cutting all the way to the green end (leaving the root end intact helps keep the leek from falling into pieces when you wash it). Wash well, being sure to get the sand out from between the layers. Or if you're going to chop them anyway, trim, chop, and wash afterward; this is much easier and more efficient, as long as you don't care that the leek is no longer intact.

BEST COOKING METHODS Sautéing, braising, roasting

WHEN IS IT DONE? When soft—almost melting

OTHER VEGETABLES YOU CAN USE Onions, shallots, scallions

Leeks Braised in Olive Oil or Butter

MAKES: 4 servings
TIME: 30 minutes
F **M** **O**

Braised leeks are an unusually fine side dish or, when finished with a vinaigrette, a terrific first course (see the first variation on page 216).

Other vegetables you can use: onions or shallots

 ¼ cup olive oil or butter
 3 or 4 leeks (about 1½ pounds), trimmed, halved, and rinsed well
 Salt and pepper
 ½ cup vegetable stock (pages 97–100) or water
 Fresh lemon juice
 Chopped fresh parsley for garnish

1. Put the oil or butter in a skillet or saucepan large enough to fit the leeks in one layer over medium heat. When the oil is hot or the butter is melted, add the leeks. Sprinkle them with salt and pepper and cook, turning

Preparing Leeks

STEP 1 **Remove the tough green leaves. Cut off the root end.**

STEP 2 **Slice the leek almost in half, almost to the root end.**

STEP 3 **Fan out the leaves and either rinse under cold running water or in a bowl. If you're chopping the leeks for cooking, wash after chopping; it will be easier.**

once or twice, until they're just beginning to brown, about 5 minutes.

2. Add the stock and bring to a boil. Turn the heat to low, cover, and cook until the leeks are tender, about 20 minutes. Uncover; if the leeks are swimming in liquid, raise the heat a bit and boil some of it away, but allow the dish to remain moist.

3. Sprinkle about 1 tablespoon lemon juice over the leeks, then taste and adjust the seasoning. Serve hot, at room temperature, or cold, sprinkled with a little more lemon juice and garnished with parsley.

LEEKS VINAIGRETTE Good with some thyme added to the braising mix: Use oil instead of butter and cook out almost all of the liquid in Step 2. In Step 3, moisten the leeks with any Vinaigrette (page 628), and serve. **V**

BRAISED LEEKS WITH TOMATO A little more substantial and much more colorful: Use oil instead of butter, and in Step 2, use 1 cup chopped tomatoes (preferably fresh), in place of the stock. Proceed with the recipe, finishing with either lemon juice or vinaigrette. **V**

BRAISED LEEKS WITH OLIVES Easy and full of flavor: Use oil instead of butter, and in Step 2, after the liquid comes to a boil, add about 1 cup black olives; best are oil-cured (you can leave the pits in), but any will do and all are good. (You'll need less salt.) **V**

BRAISED LEEKS WITH MUSTARD There is a time-honored and wonderful affinity here: In Step 2, before adding the stock, whisk into it 1 tablespoon Dijon mustard, or to taste.

MUSHROOMS

Countless varieties of mushrooms are grown and foraged worldwide, whether large or small; white, black, yellow, tan, red, or many other colors. Some are bland, some are mind-blowingly delicious. Unless you hunt your own—not advisable without expert knowledge—some of the best are also mind-blowingly expensive. Fortunately, mushrooms are highly inter-changeable, and mixing cultivated mushrooms with wild is a smart way to add flavor to a dish and stretch your dollar.

Here is a brief primer of the mushrooms I like to cook with, in order, loosely, of most to least commonly available:

- **Button or white** The most common and bland cultivated variety; white to tan in color; thick caps and stems with gray to dark brown gills; tender and brown when cooked.
- **Cremini (Baby Bella)** Immature cultivated portobello mushrooms. Tan, with dark brown gills; they're shaped like white mushrooms and a bit more robust in flavor.
- **Portobello** A supermarket staple, these are mature cremini mushrooms; tan to brown, with giant, flat caps, thick stems, and dense, dark brown gills that darken whatever dish they're cooked with unless they're scraped out. The flavor is earthy, and they're excellent grilled.
- **Shiitake** The most flavorful cultivated mushroom, and easily the best. Available fresh and dried; the latter is excellent for stock, with a rubbery but pleasant texture when reconstituted and cooked. Tan, flat caps with off-white gills and tough stems when fresh; brown with fatter-looking caps when dried (usually whole); texture is meaty with a hearty, earthy flavor.
- **Oyster** Available wild and cultivated in some supermarkets. They range in color from gray or white to pink, blue, or yellow, and grow in clusters with thick stems and a round or oval leaflike "cap." They have a mild mushroom flavor and slightly chewy texture.
- **Enoki** A delicate Asian mushroom often used as garnish; white with toothpick-thin stems and tiny round caps; very mild in flavor. Best used raw or barely cooked. Not really in the same class, flavor-wise, as many others.
- **Chanterelle** This (usually expensive) wild mushroom is light to golden yellow and shaped like a fat trumpet with a ruffle-edged bell. The flavor is earthy, nutty, delicious. Also available dried.

- **Morel** This wild (and wildly expensive) mushroom is available fresh in the spring and fall and dried year-round. White or brown, it is cone-shaped with a honeycomb-textured cap and hollow center. It has a wonderful earthy flavor. Be sure to clean thoroughly, as they're usually sandy.
- **Porcini** Available dried (quite common and should be in your pantry) and fresh (not so common, and always expensive). It has the most robust, earthy flavor and the meatiest texture of all mushrooms. Very plump, tan to dark-brown caps and fat, off-white stems when fresh. Buy dried from a reputable dealer in quantities of at least 1 ounce at a time (the ⅛-ounce packages often sold are rip-offs). Once you get into using them, you'll buy 4-ounce quantities or more.
- **King** Also known as king oyster mushroom (it's related to the oyster mushroom) or king trumpet mushroom, it has a freeform trumpet like shape with a thick stem that needs only a little trim at the bottom. A wild mushroom that is now being cultivated in this country and elsewhere, its availability is limited, but if you find it, buy it. It has a firm texture and deep umami flavor. Wonderful sautéed and in stir-fries.

BUYING AND STORING Fresh mushrooms should be unbroken, plump, spongy yet firm, and fresh smelling; avoid any that are slimy, bruised, or foul smelling (especially if wrapped in plastic). Fresh wild mushrooms are in season mostly in fall and spring, but may pop up in shoulder seasons and even in summer. White mushrooms should have closed caps that cover the gills. Store wrapped loosely in wax paper or in a brown paper bag with a moist paper towel in the refrigerator; use wild mushrooms almost immediately, certainly within 24 hours.

PREPARING Rinse fresh mushrooms as lightly as you can (they absorb water like a sponge if they sit in it) or brush them clean; be sure to get dirt out of hidden crevices. It's easier to trim some mushrooms, like portobellos, first. Cut off any hard or dried-out spots—usually just the end of the stem. The stems of most mushrooms are perfectly edible, but those of shiitake should be cut off and discarded or reserved for stock. Clean the stems well, cut them in half if they're large (as are those of portobellos), and cook them with the caps.

TO RECONSTITUTE DRIED MUSHROOMS Soak the mushrooms in hot water until they are soft, 5 to 30 minutes, depending on the size. Lift the mushrooms out of the soaking liquid with your hands or a slotted spoon and reserve the soaking liquid; it has great mushroom flavor. If called for in the recipe, very carefully pour it out of the soaking container, leaving the grit behind, or pour into a storage container and freeze to add later to soups, stews, or sauces. Trim away any hard spots on the mushrooms and use as directed. Chinese dried shiitakes must be soaked in boiling-hot water (you might even have to change the water once to get them soft), and they need to be trimmed assiduously.

BEST COOKING METHODS Sautéing, stir-frying, roasting, grilling

WHEN ARE THEY DONE? When tender, though you can cook them until they're crisp too

OTHER VEGETABLES YOU CAN USE Mushrooms are largely interchangeable, including reconstituted dried mushrooms. Otherwise there is no substitute.

Sautéed Mushrooms

MAKES: 4 servings
TIME: About 20 minutes
F M O

There are two ways you can improve almost any mushroom dish: Use something other than button mushrooms and/or include a portion of reconstituted dried mushrooms, preferably porcini. The affinity between fresh and dried mushrooms is such that dried mushrooms make the tame supermarket ones considerably better.

Start with the basic recipe, then try the additions.

¼ cup olive oil or a mixture of oil and butter
About 1 pound mushrooms (preferably an assortment), trimmed and sliced
A handful of dried porcini mushrooms (optional), reconstituted (see page 217)
Salt and pepper
¼ cup dry white wine or water
1 teaspoon minced garlic
Chopped fresh parsley for garnish (optional)

1. Put the oil in a large skillet over medium heat. When it's hot, add the mushrooms, then sprinkle with salt and pepper. Cook, stirring occasionally, until tender, 10 to 15 minutes.

2. Add the wine and let it bubble away for a minute, then turn the heat down to medium-low. Add the garlic, stir, and cook for 1 minute. Taste and adjust the seasoning. Serve hot, warm, or at room temperature, garnished with parsley if you like.

SPICY SAUTÉED MUSHROOMS In Step 1, use good-quality vegetable oil, start with shiitake mushrooms if possible (discard the stems), add a dried chile or 2 to the mix, and use lots of black pepper. In Step 2, use water; add 1 tablespoon soy sauce or to taste, along with the garlic. Garnish with cilantro instead of parsley. V

6 Additions to Sautéed Mushrooms

1. Use any fresh herb you like, but especially chopped fresh chives (a handful), chopped fresh chervil (a handful), tarragon (a few fresh leaves or a pinch dried), or thyme (a teaspoon or so fresh), along with the garlic.

2. Finish with a teaspoon or more fresh lemon juice or vinegar; sherry vinegar is especially nice.

3. Substitute chopped shallot (¼ cup or so), scallions (½ cup or so), or onion (½ cup or so) for the garlic, cooking for 2 or 3 minutes longer.

4. Finish the dish with ½ cup to 1 cup heavy cream or sour cream, simmering gently (don't let sour cream boil; it will curdle). This is best if you cook the mushrooms in butter from the start and use scallions in place of the garlic.

5. In the Spicy variation, stir in 1 tablespoon Chile Paste (page 664) or red or Green Curry Paste (page 666), or to taste, along with the garlic.

6. In the Spicy variation, stir in 1 tablespoon toasted sesame seeds (see page 299) with the garlic and finish with a teaspoon or more sesame oil.

Portobello "Bacon"

MAKES: 4 servings
TIME: 45 minutes
M V

Essential so you never have to buy weird processed substitutes again. And so good you'll always have some in your fridge.

Other vegetables you can use: zucchini, rutabaga

2 tablespoons olive oil
1½ pounds portobello mushrooms
1 teaspoon smoked paprika
¾ teaspoon salt
½ teaspoon pepper

1. Heat the oven to 400°F and evenly space the two oven racks. Line 2 rimmed baking sheets with foil and grease each with 1 tablespoon oil. Remove the stems from the mushrooms and save for another use. Slice the caps crosswise as thin as you can manage; transfer them to the prepared sheets.

2. Arrange the mushroom slices into a single layer and sprinkle with the paprika, salt, and pepper. Transfer the pans to the oven and roast, undisturbed, until the mushrooms release their water and the pan is almost dry again, 20 to 30 minutes.

3. Lower the heat to 325°F and continue to roast the slices undisturbed until they dry and shrivel a bit and release evenly from the pan, another 5 to 10 minutes. Enjoy hot or at room temperature, or cool completely and store in an airtight container in the refrigerator for up to a week.

EGGPLANT "BACON" Eggplant bacon takes a little longer to prepare but is worth the wait: Use closer to

2 pounds eggplant; don't bother to peel. Halve lengthwise and cut crosswise into thin slices. Proceed with the recipe.

COCONUT "BACON" BITS Very different, but good: Heat the oven to 325°F. Whisk together 2 tablespoons soy sauce or tamari, 1½ tablespoons maple syrup, and ½ teaspoon smoked paprika. Pour the mixture over 1½ cups coconut flakes. Let marinate for 30 minutes. Spread on a baking sheet covered with parchment paper and bake until golden and fragrant, 10 to 15 minutes.

Grilled Mushrooms

MAKES: 4 servings
TIME: About 20 minutes
F M V

The best of the widely available mushrooms for grilling are shiitake, cremini, and portobello. Many wild mushrooms are simply too delicate to grill, although fresh porcini, if you can find—and afford—them, are sensational.

Other vegetables you can use: See the chart on pages 166 to 167.

⅓ cup olive oil
1 tablespoon minced shallot, scallions, onion, or garlic
1 teaspoon fresh thyme leaves (optional)
  Salt and pepper
4 large portobello mushrooms, trimmed and halved down the middle; 12–16 cremini, trimmed and halved or left whole; or 12–16 shiitakes, stems removed (reserve for stock), caps left whole or halved
  Chopped fresh parsley for garnish

1. Prepare a charcoal or gas grill or turn on the broiler for moderate heat and put the rack about 4 inches from the heat source. Mix together the oil,

shallot, thyme if you're using it, and salt and pepper. Brush the mushrooms all over with about half of this mixture.

2. Grill or broil the mushrooms with the tops of their caps away from the heat until they begin to brown, 5 to 8 minutes. Brush with the remaining oil and turn. Grill until tender and nicely browned all over, 5 to 10 minutes more. Garnish and serve hot, warm, or at room temperature.

OKRA

Well-loved in the South but largely underappreciated elsewhere in America, okra is a mainstay in South American, Caribbean, African, and Asian cuisines. It's a green (or sometimes purple) oblong, tapered pod covered with a fine fuzz, and ranges in size. Okra oozes a slimy liquid when cut, which is why many people find it unappealing, but that very mucilaginous quality is useful for thickening stews like gumbo. If you've never tried okra or have had a slimy experience with it, try frying it; I guarantee you'll be a convert.

BUYING AND STORING Look for unblemished, plump, firm pods under 3 inches in length; the biggest specimens, over 3 inches or so, are quite seedy and even tough. Large okra, though it may look just as nice, is too often tough and fibrous and not worth eating. Store wrapped loosely in plastic in the refrigerator for up to a few days.

PREPARING Rinse and cut off the stems. Chop or sliver lengthwise if you like. Larger pods must be cut into ½-inch rounds or smaller.

BEST COOKING METHODS Frying, stewing, roasting, grilling

WHEN IS IT DONE? When tender

OTHER VEGETABLES YOU CAN USE Green or wax beans, asparagus

Fried Okra

MAKES: 4 servings
TIME: 30 minutes

F

A quick soak in buttermilk streamlines the breading process to two steps, while the slime disappears into a relatively thick coating that won't fall off. The result is super-crunchy okra with silky insides.

If you don't work in batches, the slices can clump up, but even that can work in your favor (see the variation). This fried okra needs nothing more than a final sprinkle of salt.

Other vegetables you can use: any winter or summer squash

	Good-quality vegetable oil for deep frying
1	**cup cornmeal**
1	**cup all-purpose flour**
	Salt and pepper
	Pinch cayenne (optional)
2	**cups buttermilk**
1½	**pounds okra, trimmed**

1. Put at least 2 inches of oil in a deep pan on the stove and turn the heat to medium-high; bring to 350°F (see "Deep-Frying," page 26). Combine the cornmeal and flour in a shallow bowl or pie plate; sprinkle with a little salt and pepper, and the cayenne if you like, and stir well. Pour the buttermilk into a large bowl, sprinkle with a little salt, and stir.

2. If the okra is small, cut it in half lengthwise; cut larger okra into thick slices, slightly on the diagonal to reveal more of the interior. Working in batches, put a handful of okra into the buttermilk, then fish out the slices one by one, roll them around in the cornmeal mixture, and drop them into the hot oil, taking care not to overcrowd the pan.

3. Cook the okra, stirring gently to cook them evenly, until they are browned all over, 3 to 5 minutes, depending on size. Remove with a slotted spoon to drain on paper towels. Repeat until all the okra are done. Sprinkle with salt and pepper if you like and serve immediately.

OKRA HUSH PUPPIES Even easier: Cut the okra crosswise into ½-inch slices. In Step 2, put the okra into the buttermilk all at once and stir to coat well and release some slime. Use 2 soupspoons to scoop up a clump of buttermilk-coated okra slices (trust me—they will be both clumpy and coated) and roll it around in the cornmeal mixture to coat evenly. Drop the clumps—now called hush puppies—in the hot oil and fry as described in Step 3 (they might take a minute or 2 longer to cook).

ONIONS

Onions may be white, yellow, or red, and pungent, mild, or sweet—the variety is astonishing.

Sweet onions, including Bermuda, Maui, Vidalia, and Walla Walla, are juicy and have a less pungent flavor.

On the smaller side are pearl or boiling onions, cipollini, and shallots. Pearl onions are up to the diameter of a quarter and are best for boiling, braising, and stewing; their small size allows them to cook through whole. Cipollini can be used the same way as pearl onions, and their flattened shape adds an interesting look to any

Pan-Cooking Onions

COOKING TIME	RESULT TO EXPECT
20 minutes	Ivory, softened, and still oniony tasting
25–30 minutes	Golden, wilted, and sweet, with a slight onion sharpness
40–45 minutes	Browned and starting to melt, onion flavor is replaced with sweetness
60 minutes	The color of maple syrup, with a jamlike texture and flavor

dish. Shallots range greatly in size, and can be cooked whole or used chopped like onion.

Scallions and spring onions with green stems attached are generally milder in flavor and softer in texture. Their small size makes them a wonderful garnish. Scallions in particular are fantastic to use raw as a flavorful oniony garnish on salads and in soups, dips, and other dishes; they're also good grilled.

BUYING AND STORING Onions and shallots should be firm and tightly covered in at least one layer of shiny tan-to-yellow or deep red skins; the outer skin of white onions is more papery. An acrid onion aroma before peeling is an indication of a damaged or rotting onion; such onions should be avoided, as should sprouting onions. Store onions and shallots in a cool, dark, airy spot or in the refrigerator for weeks. Store scallions and spring onions in the refrigerator, up to several days.

PREPARING Cutting an onion results in the combination of enzymes that are stored separately in the onion, which then creates a volatile sulfur compound. When this makes contact with the moisture in your eyes, it forms a weak solution of sulfuric acid—hence the burning sensation. If you're peeling and chopping a lot of onions or shallots, you might consider wearing goggles to prevent crying. Cooking deactivates these enzymes, so after you peel the onion (do this without

cutting into it), drop it into boiling water for 30 to 60 seconds, drain, and then cut. Water absorbs the gas, so you can also rinse the peeled onion before cutting.

Leave the root end on onions or shallots you will cook whole; they'll stay together better. For shallots, break the cloves apart and remove the dry skins; trim the stem end and slice or chop as you would an onion.

BEST COOKING METHODS Sautéing, roasting, grilling

WHEN IS IT DONE? When very tender but not quite falling apart

OTHER VEGETABLE YOU CAN USE Leeks

Caramelized Onions

MAKES: 4 servings
TIME: 25 to 60 minutes
Ⓜ Ⓞ

Because onions are composed primarily of water, the longer they cook, the more they shrink. And their flavor changes as they concentrate, from sharp and pungent to complex and sweet. This process is called caramelization. Let the time you have available and the desired result help you decide how dark to make them. (See the chart on page 221 for guidelines.)

Preparing Onions

STEP 1 Cut off the stem end of the onion.

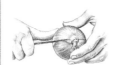

STEP 2 Make a small slit in the skin, just one layer down.

STEP 3 The peel will come off easily.

STEP 4 Cut the onion in half.

STEP 5 Make two or three cuts into the onion, parallel to the cutting board; don't cut all the way through.

Make as much as you like; caramelized onions keep well in the fridge.

Other vegetables you can use: Peel small onions like pearl or cipollini, shallots, or garlic, but keep them whole.

1½–2 **pounds onions (6–8 medium), halved and thinly sliced or chopped (5–6 cups)**
   2 **tablespoons olive oil or butter, plus more as needed**
     Salt and pepper

1. Put the onions in a large skillet over medium heat. Cover and cook, stirring infrequently, until the onions are dry and almost sticking to the pan; this will take about 20 minutes.

2. Stir in the oil and a large pinch salt and turn the heat down to medium-low. Cook, stirring occasionally, until the onions are done as you like them, adding just enough more oil or butter to keep them from sticking without getting greasy. The onions will be ready immediately or after up to another 40 minutes or so, depending on how dark you want them. Taste and add pepper, and more salt if necessary. Serve hot or at room temperature, or cool, cover and refrigerate for up to a week to use in other dishes.

SWEETER CARAMELIZED ONIONS Good with hot, sour, or well-seasoned dishes: In Step 2, add 1 to 2 tablespoons brown sugar along with the oil and salt. Proceed with the recipe, lowering the heat as necessary to prevent sticking or burning.

10 Uses for Caramelized Onions

1. Thicken soups and sauces.
2. Garnish cooked or raw foods.
3. Fill omelets, sandwiches, and burritos.
4. Stir into dips and spreads, or use as a spread by itself!
5. Top a pizza before baking.
6. Toss with pasta or noodles, alone or in addition to sauce.
7. Stir into quiche mixture before baking.
8. Fold into bread doughs and batters.
9. Top breads and rolls before baking.
10. Eat as a side dish.

Roasted Onion Halves

MAKES: 4 servings, plus extra for later
TIME: About 45 minutes, mostly unattended
Ⓜ Ⓥ

You can use any kind of onion you like here, even sweet ones like Walla Walla or Vidalia, though those will be much softer when done. Serve hot, warm, or at room temperature, garnished, if you like, with chopped herbs or nuts. You can use the leftovers as an alternative to raw onion in virtually any dish.

   2 **tablespoons olive oil, plus more for the pan (optional)**
   4 **small onions, halved at the equator, or 1½ pounds shallots, peeled and left whole**
     Salt and pepper
   2 **or 3 sprigs fresh thyme (optional)**

1. Heat the oven to 400°F. Grease a small baking or roasting pan with a little oil or line it with parchment paper. Rub the onions with the 2 tablespoons oil and sprinkle them all over with salt and pepper.

2. Put the onions cut side down in the pan. Roast, undisturbed, until they start to brown, about 20 minutes.

STEP 6 **Now make several cuts down through the top. Again, leave the onion intact at the root end.**

STEP 7 **Cut across to create dice.**

Use a spatula to turn them over. Top with the thyme if you like, then return them to the oven for another 15 to 25 minutes, depending on how tender you want them. Check for doneness by sticking a sharp-tipped knife or skewer into the side of one. Serve hot or at room temperature.

CREAM-ROASTED ONION HALVES Omit the oil. Put ¼ cup heavy cream in a large shallow bowl, roll the onions around in it to coat them all over, and sprinkle with salt and pepper. Let sit for 30 minutes or so, turning every so often, then roast as directed in Step 2 at 350°F.

BALSAMIC-ROASTED ONION HALVES With a complex flavor that's tart and sweet: Follow the Cream-Roasted variation, but use balsamic vinegar instead of cream.

PEAS AND PEA SHOOTS
SHELL PEAS, SNOW PEAS (MANGE-TOUT), SUGAR SNAP PEAS

Peas come in a variety of forms: Shell peas (aka green or English peas) that must be removed from their inedible shells or pods; pod peas like snow peas and sugar snap peas that are entirely edible (pods and all); and field peas, which are nearly always shelled and dried (think black-eyed peas and chickpeas).

Pea shoots are the new growth of the pea vine plus a few leaves, vibrant green in color and delicate; the flavor is incomparable, and delicious. Look for them at farmers' markets or Asian markets.

BUYING AND STORING Fresh shell peas arrive in spring; the pods should be fresh looking and full of medium-size peas. Very large peas are likely to be tough and starchy. To be sure, open one up and taste a couple of peas; if you want to keep eating, buy them. Snow peas and sugar snap peas should be crisp, green, and unshriveled. Again, taste one, and if it's sweet and crisp, buy some. Pea shoots should be tender, fresh-looking, and bright green.

Store peas and pea shoots wrapped loosely in plastic in the refrigerator. Use as soon as possible, as their sweetness is fleeting.

PREPARING For shell peas and field peas, open the pods at the seam and run your finger down the inside to release the peas. To prepare pod peas, remove the little string before cooking. Rinse pea shoots well and trim away any dried-out stems or yellow leaves.

BEST COOKING METHODS Steaming, quick-braising in butter, stir-frying. Peas and pea shoots are always a welcome addition to risotto and stir-fries; you can also add pea shoots raw to salads. Tough peas need to be cooked before being eaten.

WHEN IS IT DONE? As soon as they are hot and bright green, usually less than 5 minutes

OTHER VEGETABLES YOU CAN USE Green or wax beans, asparagus, edamame

Anything-Scented Peas

MAKES: 4 servings
TIME: 20 minutes, if peas need to be shucked
🄵 🄼 🄾

Peas have a delicate flavor that can be enhanced with just a touch of the right ingredient, subtlety being the key. If you've never tasted peas sprinkled with a pinch sugar during cooking, give it a try.

Other vegetables you can use: about 1½ pounds snow peas or sugar snap peas

- 2 **tablespoons olive oil or butter**
- 1 **tablespoon any ingredient from the list on page 226**
- 2 **cups peas (about 2 pounds in the pod; thawed and well-drained frozen are fine)**
  Salt or sugar

1. Put the oil or butter in a large skillet over medium heat. When the oil is hot or the butter is melted, stir in

Anything-Scented Peas
with grated coconut

your ingredient of choice and cook, stirring constantly, until fragrant, just a minute or so.

2. Add the peas and cook for a couple of minutes more, swirling the pan a bit to coat the peas in the pan juices and soften them a bit. Taste, add a sprinkle of salt or sugar as you prefer, and serve hot or at room temperature.

10 Flavor Possibilities for Anything-Scented Peas

1. Grated lemon, orange, or tangerine zest

2. Minced herbs like mint, tarragon, parsley, basil, or chervil

3. Minced fresh ginger or chopped candied ginger

4. Sesame seeds (white or black)

5. Minced garlic

6. Fermented black beans

7. Grated coconut

8. Minced shallot

9. White wine or sake

10. Any miso

PEPPERS AND CHILES

There are literally thousands of varieties of peppers and chiles, ranging from fingernail size to more than six inches long, from sunset orange to fiery red to bright green, varying in flavor and degree of heat from fruity and mild (bell peppers) to mildly hot (poblanos) to I-dare-you blazing hot (habaneros). All are from the genus *Capsicum*. Chiles are available fresh, dried (whole and ground), pickled, and canned.

BUYING AND STORING Avoid peppers and chiles with soft spots or wrinkling. Store fresh peppers and chiles, unwrapped, in your refrigerator's vegetable bin for up to a week or so. When buying dried chiles, look for ones that are still pliable, not dusty or moldy. Store them in an airtight container in a dark, cool place, where they should keep pretty much forever.

PREPARING Unless you're cooking them whole, bell peppers should be cored and seeded before cooking.

If you plan to cut the peppers into strips or dice them, start by cutting the pepper in half; remove the cap and seed mass, along with the wooly ribs, with your fingers. Alternatively, you can cut a circle around the stem and pull it out, along with most of the seeds; rinse out the remaining seeds. Peppers can be peeled, if you like, with a vegetable peeler.

Fresh chiles should be stemmed. Seeding is optional; be aware that the lion's share of a chile's heat (which is caused by a compound called capsaicin) resides in the seeds and ribs. If you want more heat, leave them in; if you want a mellower chile flavor, cut the chile in half lengthwise and scrape out the seeds and ribs with a knife, then cut up as directed. When working with chiles, it is a good idea to wear gloves; unless you wash your hands well with soap and water, capsaicin really stays on your skin for awhile. If you're sensitive, it will burn your skin—but the greater danger is that you'll rub your eye, in which case you're in for a lot of pain.

When working with dried chiles, break them open and shake out the seeds; again, if you want more heat, leave them in. Toast in a dry skillet over medium heat for a couple minutes on each side to develop a bit of smoky flavor. Add them whole or in pieces while cooking, or grind to make your own chile powder. Or you can reconstitute them whole: After toasting, cover them with boiling water and let sit until the chiles are soft, 5 to 30 minutes. Discard skins, seeds, and ribs, if you like. (You can save the soaking water and use that as a flavor agent, too, but it'll likely be quite hot.) See pages 664 to 666 to make your own chile paste.

BEST COOKING METHODS For bell peppers and large mild chiles: roasting, grilling, broiling, sautéing; for smaller, hotter chiles: roasting, adding as seasoning to most any kind of dish

WHEN IS IT DONE? When roasting or grilling, blackened and collapsed. In other cooking, when very tender and soft

Chile Pepper Lexicon (*in descending heat order*)

CHILE	DESCRIPTION	HEAT	FORMS	SUBSTITUTES
Habanero (Scotch Bonnet; not technically the same, but virtually interchangeable)	Round and fairly small, like teeny bell peppers. Neon green to yellow, gold, and orange, depending on maturity and variety. Flavor is fruity, bright, and beautiful but a little goes a long way.	Very hot. Use in tiny amounts, at least until you know you want more.	Fresh and dried	Nothing has the same complex flavor or packs quite the same wallop.
Cayenne	Long, slightly gnarled, and slender. Green to red when mature.	Very hot	Fresh and dried. Available whole and ground into powder	Thai, or use ground
Thai (Thai bird)	Pinky size or smaller. Green to red when mature.	Very hot	Fresh, dried, and sometimes pickled	Cayenne
Serrano	Finger size or smaller. Thin skinned. Red (mature) or green (unripe).	Hot	Fresh and dried	Cayenne or Thai (use less); jalapeño (use more)
Jalapeño	Flavor is slightly herbaceous and grassy. Green mostly, though sometimes red.	Hot to medium	Fresh. Smoked and dried, it's a chipotle, available whole, ground, and canned with adobo sauce	Serrano
Fresno	Like jalapeños only with thinner flesh. Usually red (mature) but sometimes green.	Hot to medium	Fresh	Serrano or jalapeño
Poblano	Like a flatter bell pepper. Dark green or purple; sometimes red (mature). Dried, adds complex flavor without a lot of heat; used in chili powder.	Medium to mild	Fresh. Dried, it's called ancho, available whole or ground	Anaheim or New Mexico
Anaheim	Long, wide, somewhat flat. Green and red (called *chile colorado*).	Medium to mild	Fresh. Dried, it's called a California chile.	Poblano or New Mexico
New Mexico	Similar to Anaheim, only pointed on both ends. Green and red (mature).	Medium to mild	Fresh and dried	Anaheim

Roasted Red Peppers

MAKES: 4 servings
TIME: 20 to 60 minutes
M V

Any bell pepper can be roasted, though red (as well as yellow, orange, and purple) are sweeter than green. This can be done in the oven, in the broiler, or on a grill. Some people do it over an open stovetop flame, but that's really only suitable for one or two at a time.

You can roast as many peppers at once as you like, and the only extra work will be peeling and seeding (which isn't insignificant, unfortunately). But they'll keep for quite a while in the fridge.

> 8   red, yellow, or green bell peppers
> Salt
> Olive oil as needed

1. Cook using one of two methods:

TO ROAST OR BROIL Heat the oven to 450°F, or turn on the broiler and adjust the rack to about 4 inches from the heat source. Put the peppers in a foil-lined roasting pan. Roast or broil, turning the peppers as each side browns, until they have darkened and collapsed, 15 or 20 minutes in the broiler, up to an hour in the oven.

TO GRILL Prepare a charcoal or gas grill until hot and put the rack about 4 inches from the heat source. When the fire is hot, put the peppers directly over the heat. Grill, turning as each side blackens, until they collapse, about 15 minutes.

2. Wrap the cooked peppers in foil (if you roasted or broiled the peppers, you can use the same foil that lined the pan) or put them in a bowl and cover tightly with plastic wrap. Let them cool until you can handle them, then remove the skin (rub it off with your fingers or a paper towel), stems, and seeds. Don't worry if the peppers fall apart.

3. The peppers can be served immediately or cover and store in the refrigerator for up to a few days; bring back to room temperature before serving. When you're ready to serve, sprinkle with a bit of salt and drizzle with oil.

ROASTED POBLANO PEPPERS (RAJAS) A building block of vegetarian Mexican cuisine: Instead of bell peppers, use poblano peppers.

8 Things to Do with Roasted Red Peppers

1. Toss with minced fresh or roasted garlic.

2. Splash with balsamic vinegar.

3. Sprinkle with lots of minced fresh herbs like parsley, mint, basil, or chervil, or a little bit of oregano, thyme, or rosemary.

4. Sprinkle with grated Parmesan, Asiago, Romano, or manchego cheese.

5. Use to fill sandwiches or top bruschetta, pizza, or salads.

6. Scramble with eggs.

7. Purée to make a sauce or spread or to mix with other sauces and spreads.

8. Drizzle in equal parts sherry vinegar and olive oil mixed with a little honey for an antipasto.

My Mom's Pan-Cooked Peppers and Onions

MAKES: 4 servings
TIME: 40 minutes
O

When I was growing up, once a week my mother would make a sandwich of sautéed green peppers and onions, always on a hard roll. It's a great combination, and even better if you add some mushrooms and herbs. In those days olive oil was virtually unheard of outside of Italian families; my mom always used butter.

> ¼   cup olive oil, 4 tablespoons (½ stick) butter, or a combination
> 2   bell peppers (preferably red or yellow),

roasted and peeled if desired, cored, seeded, and cut into strips

2 medium to large onions, halved and thinly sliced

1 cup trimmed and sliced shiitake or button mushrooms
  Salt and pepper

1 teaspoon chopped fresh thyme or marjoram, plus more for garnish (optional), or any fresh herb to taste

1. Heat the oil or melt the butter in a large, deep skillet over medium heat. When the oil is hot or the butter is melted, add the peppers, onions, and mushrooms. Sprinkle with salt and pepper, stir in the thyme, and cook, stirring occasionally and adjusting the heat so the mixture cooks without browning (at least not much), until very tender, at least 20 minutes.

2. Taste and adjust the seasoning, garnish with a bit more thyme if you like, and serve as a side dish or piled into rolls or baguettes.

PAN-COOKED PEPPERS AND ONIONS WITH GINGER
A stir-fry where the vegetables are tender, not crunchy: Instead of olive oil or butter, use good-quality vegetable oil. Go easy on the salt. Instead of thyme or marjoram, use 1 tablespoon minced fresh ginger. In Step 2, use a dash soy sauce and plenty of black pepper for the final seasoning. Serve over Steamed Sticky Rice (page 370) or another plain-cooked rice dish, or toss with Chinese-style egg noodles. Garnish with chopped fresh cilantro. **V**

Creamed Poblanos

Rajas con Crema
MAKES: 4 servings
TIME: 20 minutes
M **F** **O**

This dish is popular in southern and central Mexico, served any time of the day. Enjoy it spooned into a warm corn tortilla, over rice, or as a side dish. You can also top it with the Mexican cheese of your choice, shredded or crumbled.

2 tablespoons good-quality vegetable oil

1 white onion, sliced

2 cloves garlic, sliced
  Salt and pepper

8 poblano peppers, roasted (see page 228), peeled and cut into strips

½ teaspoon ground cumin

⅓ cup heavy cream, Mexican crema, or Cashew Cream (page 300)

1. Put the oil in a large skillet over medium-high heat. When it's hot, add the onion and cook until it softens, 3 to 5 minutes. Add the garlic, season with salt and pepper, and cook for just a minute more.

2. Pour in 1 cup water. Bring to a boil, then turn the heat down so the water bubbles steadily. Cook until the onion is soft and the water has evaporated, 5 to 7 minutes.

3. Add the peppers and cumin and cook until the peppers are heated through, a couple of minutes. Remove from the heat and stir in the cream. Taste and adjust the seasoning if necessary. Serve hot or refrigerate for up to 1 day and reheat gently.

FASTER CREAMED POBLANOS Instead of roasting and peeling the poblanos, simply stem, core, and seed them before cutting into strips.

Chiles Rellenos

MAKES: 4 servings
TIME: 1 hour
M

A fabulous classic: The crisp coating is light and airy, the chiles soft and yielding, and the cheese oozing. You'll never regret the hour it takes to make these—they're that good. If time is an issue, make the chiles through Step 1 up to a day in advance, cover, and refrigerate until ready to batter and cook them.

Chiles Rellenos
(page 229)

4   large or 8 small poblano chiles
3   cups grated or shredded Chihuahua cheese or
    Monterey Jack
    Good-quality vegetable oil for frying
2   egg whites
½   cup all-purpose flour
½   teaspoon salt
1   cup beer or water
    Green Enchilada Sauce (page 664) or
    Salsa Borracha (page 663)
    Crumbled queso fresco for garnish

1. Roast the chiles as directed on page 228; peel off the skins, but leave the stems on. Cut a slit in one side and remove the seeds. Stuff the chiles with the cheese; use toothpicks or a long bamboo skewer to sew them shut.

2. Put at least 3 inches (more is better) oil in a large, deep saucepan. The narrower the saucepan, the less oil you'll need, but the more oil you use, the more chiles you can cook at the same time. Turn the heat to medium-high and heat the oil to about 365°F (a pinch of the batter will sizzle immediately).

3. Whip the egg whites until they hold soft peaks. Whisk together the flour, salt, and beer in a medium bowl. It should be the consistency of thin pancake batter; add flour or beer if necessary. Gently fold the egg whites into the batter; some white streaks remaining are okay.

4. Dip the stuffed chiles into the batter to coat and immediately fry until crisp and golden brown, about 5 minutes. Use the long skewers to help rotate and remove the chiles or use a spatula; drain on paper towels. Remove the picks or skewers and serve immediately with the sauce, sprinkled with queso fresco.

GRILLED CHILES RELLENOS A quicker no-peeling, no-frying variation. The papery skin blisters a bit and can either be eaten or removed by the diners: Skip the roasting and batter and grill the stuffed chiles, turning once or twice, over moderately high heat until the skins are blistered and the flesh is tender. Serve immediately with the sauce.

POTATOES

There are thousands of varieties of potatoes, but when it comes to cooking they fall into three basic categories: starchy, waxy, and all-purpose.

Starchy potatoes are, as the name implies, loaded with starch. They crumble and break easily when cooked, then become dry, fluffy, and mealy in texture. They're best for baking, frying, and mashing. But they're not very good for boiling, unless you want to use their crumbly quality to thicken soups or stews. Russet potatoes, which include Idaho, are the archetypal starchy potato and are often called "baking potatoes." They are large and oval with a light brown "russeted" skin and off-white flesh.

Waxy potatoes, sometimes called "boiling potatoes," have a low starch content; their texture is moister, creamier, and firmer. They usually have smooth, thin skin that ranges from red and purple to yellow or white. They hold their shape well during cooking and are excellent for boiling, steaming, and roasting. Most (but not all) "new potatoes" are waxy.

All-purpose potatoes are in between starchy and waxy potatoes; they're suitable for anything, although not ideal for boiling. For me, Yukon Gold potatoes are the model all-purpose potato with their smooth, golden to brown skins, creamy texture, and yellow flesh.

BUYING AND STORING All potatoes should be firm, unshriveled, and without soft spots, sprouts, or greening. (The green color is an alkaloid called solanine, and comes from sun exposure; it's mildly toxic, but just cut off the affected part—the rest of the potato will be perfectly edible.) Store in a dark, cool, dry spot (not in the fridge) for weeks. Do not store potatoes with onions, as onions release gases that can provoke sprouting in potatoes.

PREPARING Wash and peel if you like; remove any eyes, dark spots, or greening. If the potato is largely green or has rot, discard it.

BEST COOKING METHODS Any

WHEN IS IT DONE? When a skewer or thin-bladed knife inserted in one meets almost no resistance

OTHER VEGETABLE YOU CAN USE Sweet potato

Baked Potatoes

MAKES: 4 servings
TIME: About 1 hour
V

Forget wrapping your baked potatoes in foil or using the microwave, because both techniques will steam them. Keep the oven at 425°F, which is the optimum temperature. You can crank it up to 450°F to gain a little speed, though you'll sacrifice some texture.

Other vegetables you can use: any whole, thick-skinned root vegetable like rutabagas, turnips, or beets, though none will be as starchy and fluffy as a potato

> 4   large starchy potatoes (like Idaho or other russets)
>   Salt and pepper

1. Heat the oven to 425°F. Scrub the potatoes well, especially if you plan to eat the skins. Use a skewer or a thin-bladed knife to poke a hole or 2 in each potato.
2. Put the potatoes in the oven, right on the rack or on a rimmed baking sheet. Bake until a skewer or thin-bladed knife inserted into one meets almost no resistance, about an hour. You can turn them once during baking, though it's not necessary.
3. The potatoes will stay hot for a few minutes. To serve, cut a slit lengthwise into each about halfway into the flesh and pinch the ends toward the middle to fluff, sprinkle with salt and pepper, then top if desired (see the list, opposite, for some ideas).

SALTED BAKED POTATO The skins get a nice crust: After scrubbing, rub each potato with about 1 teaspoon olive oil or butter. Then rub each all over with a fair amount of salt and bake as directed.

BAY- OR ROSEMARY-SCENTED BAKED POTATO Surprisingly dramatic results: After scrubbing the potatoes, cut a deep slit lengthwise into each and sprinkle

Twice-Baked Potatoes

Not only do people love these, but almost all the work is up front, which makes them perfect for entertaining. They're also ideal for single dining and for using up all sorts of leftovers. Bake the potatoes and cool them a bit. Scoop their flesh into a large bowl, leaving the skins intact for a shell. Mash the flesh, adding other ingredients to jazz them up (see the list below), then pile the works back into the skins. Wrap them in foil (or not, as I generally prefer, to get a nice crust), refrigerate them for up to a few hours if you like, and pop them back into the oven shortly before you're ready to eat. At 400°F, most will take only 20 to 30 minutes to reheat.

Here are 11 great add-ins for twice-baked potatoes. Figure a total of about ½ cup extra ingredients for each large potato; they won't hold much more. Mix and match as you like.

1. Chopped fresh herbs

2. Chopped olives, red chile flakes, chopped parsley, and olive oil

3. Grated hard cheese or soft cheese like Brie, goat, or cream cheese

4. Puréed or finely chopped cooked vegetables like eggplant, carrots, broccoli, or spinach, with lots of butter or extra virgin olive oil

5. Any pesto or herb purée (pages 634 to 638)

6. Compound Butter (page 676)

7. Any chutney (pages 668 to 670)

8. Smooth Green Chile Sauce, Indian Style (page 666)

9. Hollandaise Sauce (page 674)

10. Coconut milk and curry powder, garam masala, or chaat masala

11. Fast Tomato Sauce (page 312)

with salt and pepper. Put a couple of bay leaves or 1 sprig rosemary in each slit and drizzle with olive oil, then close them up and set them on a baking sheet. Coat the skins with a little olive oil and sprinkle with more salt and pepper. Proceed with the recipe. Remove the bay leaves or rosemary sprig before serving.

Boiled Potatoes

MAKES: 4 servings
TIME: About 30 minutes
F M V

You can use this technique for starchy, waxy, and all-purpose potatoes, though the results will vary. If boiled potatoes are your ultimate goal, use any red- or thin-skinned waxy variety. It's acceptable to cut potatoes before boiling, for speed, but the results will be a bit waterlogged. So if time is not an issue, cook your spuds whole, then peel them if you wish and cut them after they cool a bit.

> 2 pounds potatoes
> Salt

1. Peel the potatoes before cooking if you like. If you're in a hurry, halve or quarter larger ones. Cut or whole, the idea is to have all the pieces about the same size. Put them in a large, deep pot and cover with cold water. Add a large pinch salt and bring to a boil.

2. Keep the water rolling until the potatoes are done, anywhere from 15 to 30 minutes, depending on the size of the pieces and how tender you want them. The potatoes are done when a skewer or thin-bladed knife inserted into one meets almost no resistance.

3. Drain the potatoes well and let them dry out a bit. If you're peeling them, give them an extra few minutes to cool enough to handle. See the list, right, for serving ideas, or use in another recipe. To store for later, cool, cover tightly, and refrigerate for up to 3 days. Reheat in the microwave or use in any recipe that calls for cooked potatoes.

11 Toppings for Baked Potatoes

1. The classic: butter, sour cream, and/or minced chives

2. Olive oil or any Flavored Oil (page 627)

3. Any cooked or raw salsa

4. Garlic Mayonnaise or other flavored mayonnaise (page 671)

5. Soy sauce or any soy sauce–based dipping sauce (pages 654 to 659)

6. A few dashes hot sauce

7. Worcestershire Sauce, Hold the Anchovies (page 633)

8. Any Vinaigrette (page 628), especially Mustard Vinaigrette

9. Grated cheese like cheddar, Parmesan, Asiago, or Jack

10. Goat cheese, cream cheese, or cottage cheese

11. Baked Beans (page 467)—or any bean dish, really

6 Simple Finishes for Boiled Potatoes

Toss hot potatoes with any of the following ingredients—or a combination—and serve immediately.

1. Butter or olive oil with salt and black pepper

2. Sesame oil, a splash soy sauce, and a sprinkle of sliced scallions or cilantro

3. Miso, a couple of tablespoons

4. Chopped fresh herbs like chives, tarragon, parsley, rosemary, mint, or chervil

5. Chopped roasted nuts, like hazelnuts, almonds, walnuts, or pecans

6. Any Vinaigrette (page 628)

Mashed Potatoes

MAKES: 4 servings
TIME: About 40 minutes
M

Starchy potatoes make the fluffiest mash, but Yukon Gold and other all-purpose potatoes yield a creamy texture. If you like mashed potatoes with the peel included, just scrub them well before cooking. If you like your mashed potatoes lumpy, mash them with a fork or potato masher; if you prefer them smooth and light, use a food mill or ricer. Keep them away from mixers, food processors, and blenders, though, because the potatoes will become gummy.

Some keys to keeping mashed potatoes fluffy: Cook them whole if possible; cook them with the peel on if possible (the peels will slip off easily after cooking, or you can eat them); and refrain from poking them often as they cook. All of these reduce the tendency of the spuds to absorb water, which makes them heavier.

Once the potatoes are mashed and combined with the milk and butter, they will keep for a little while in a double boiler. But it's easier to just boil the potatoes a little ahead of time and let them sit for an hour or so before mashing.

Other vegetables you can use: any vegetable can be mashed; see Vegetable Purée (page 150).

2 pounds starchy or all-purpose potatoes
1 cup milk or buttermilk, plus more
   if needed

4 tablespoons (½ stick) butter
Salt and pepper

1. Boil the potatoes according to the recipe on page 233. (You can prepare the potatoes to this point up to an hour in advance; just leave them in a colander to drain and dry out a bit.)
2. While the potatoes are draining, wipe the pot dry and put it back on the stove over medium-low heat. Add the milk and the butter and sprinkle with salt and pepper.
3. When the butter is almost melted, remove the pot from the heat. Rice the potatoes into the milk mixture, run them through a food mill set over the pot, or add them to the milk mixture and mash with a fork or potato masher. Return the pot to the heat and stir constantly with a wooden spoon to reach the desired consistency, adding more milk if necessary. Taste, adjust the seasoning, and serve.

SMASHED POTATOES Omit the milk. In Step 3, add the potatoes directly to the melted butter in the pan and mash roughly with a fork or masher, leaving lots of lumps. Stir a few times, adding more butter if you like, and serve.

The Many Ways to Flavor Mashed Potatoes

Things to add to the butter as it melts in Step 2:

- Up to ½ cup chopped onion, ¼ cup minced shallot, or 2 teaspoons to 2 tablespoons minced garlic
- 1 to 2 tablespoons minced or grated fresh ginger, or chopped fresh chile (like jalapeño or Thai), red chile flakes, cayenne, or Chile Paste (page 664) to taste

- 1 tablespoon or more curry powder or practically any other spice blend
- 2 tablespoons or more horseradish, grated fresh or prepared

Things to stir into the mashed potatoes as they heat in Step 3 (reduce the milk to ½ cup; you can always add more later):

- Up to 1 cup chopped fresh herbs like parsley, mint, chives, basil, or cilantro
- Up to 1 cup grated melting cheese like Parmesan, Gruyère, cheddar, Jack, or Gouda
- Up to 1 cup fresh goat cheese, cream cheese, or sour cream

- Up to 1 cup Pesto or any herb purée (pages 634 to 638)
- Up to ½ cup miso
- Up to ½ cup chopped nuts or olives
- Up to ¼ cup soy sauce
- ½ cup or so ketchup (trust me; it's delicious) or barbecue sauce
- Up to ¼ cup mustard

VEGAN MASHED POTATOES Works with either the main recipe or the preceding variation: Instead of milk, reserve 1 cup or so water from boiling the potatoes. Or use vegetable stock (pages 97 to 100), silken tofu, a non-dairy milk, white wine, beer, or a combination of these liquids. Replace the butter with olive oil. **V**

Home Fries

MAKES: 4 servings
TIME: About 45 minutes
M **V**

For really crisp home fries, you need two things: waxy potatoes (because starchy ones will fall apart before they get crisp) and patience. If you're short on time, make the first variation. For richer flavor, replace 2 tablespoons of the oil with butter; you can also stir in another tablespoon butter at the end.

Other vegetables you can use: beets, rutabagas, parsnips, or carrots, though they won't get quite as crisp.

> **About 2 pounds waxy potatoes**
> ¼ **cup olive or good-quality vegetable oil, or more as needed**
> **Salt and pepper**

1. Peel the potatoes if you like and cut them into 1-inch chunks. Put the oil in a large skillet, preferably nonstick or cast-iron, over medium heat. When it's hot, add the potatoes and cook, undisturbed, until they begin to brown around the edges and release from the pan, about 10 minutes.

2. Continue cooking until the potatoes are tender and golden brown, about another 20 minutes, turning to brown all the sides without stirring too often. (This is the part that takes the most patience.) Add more oil if needed to prevent the potatoes from sticking. If they are browning too fast, turn the heat down just a tad.

3. When the potatoes are ready, turn the heat up a bit to crisp them up. Sprinkle with salt and pepper and toss

7 Other Vegetables to Mash Along with Potatoes

Mashed potatoes and cooked greens have become one of my favorite side dishes (and the leftovers make fabulous croquettes too). Here are ideas for that, and more: Replace up to 1 pound of the potatoes with any of the following, adding them to the potatoes while they boil or cooking them separately—roasted vegetables are especially nice—and mashing them in later.

1. Cabbage, cut into ribbons or chopped

2. Brussels sprouts, trimmed and quartered

3. Celery root, turnips, or rutabagas, peeled and cubed

4. Carrots or parsnips, peeled and sliced

5. Peas (frozen are fine), added during the last 3 minutes of cooking

6. Winter squash like butternut or pumpkin, peeled, seeded, and cubed

7. Beets, peeled and cubed (they'll turn the mash fuchsia but taste delicious)

to coat. Taste, adjust the seasoning, and serve hot or at room temperature.

LAST-MINUTE HOME FRIES These also use less oil to cook: After cutting the potatoes, boil them in salted water to cover until tender, 10 to 15 minutes. Drain well. Use medium-high heat instead of medium and start with 2 tablespoons oil instead of ¼ cup. Because of the higher heat, watch the potatoes more closely. They will crisp and brown in about half the time.

HOME FRIES WITH ONIONS The classic home-fry combo: In Step 3, when the potatoes are tender and fairly well browned, add 1 cup chopped onion (any kind, including scallions) to the pan. Cook, stirring occasionally, until the onion softens and turns golden, 3 to 5 minutes more.

Oven-Roasted Potatoes

MAKES: 4 servings
TIME: About 1 hour

V

You can oven-roast any kind of potato. Waxy potatoes will form a brown, crisp crust and, as long as you cook them long enough, a creamy interior, while starchy varieties will tend to darken more easily, not become quite as crisp, and turn very, very soft. Both are delicious. You can prepare this with butter instead of oil; if you do, reduce the oven temperature to 375°F.

Other vegetables you can use: any root vegetable, winter squash, or tropical tuber

2   **tablespoons olive oil, plus more as needed**
2   **pounds potatoes**
    Salt and pepper

1. Heat the oven to 400°F. Grease a large roasting pan or rimmed baking sheet with a little of the oil. It should be large enough to hold all the potatoes in a single layer without overcrowding.

2. Scrub the potatoes; peel them if you like. Make sure they're fairly dry. Cut them into chunks of equal size, anywhere from 1 to 2 inches. Put them in the pan, drizzle with 2 tablespoons oil, and toss gently to coat. Sprinkle with salt and pepper.

3. Roast, undisturbed, for 20 minutes before checking the first time. If the potatoes release easily from the pan, stir them a bit or turn the pieces over with tongs. If they look too dry and are sticking, drizzle with a little more oil and toss. Continue roasting, turning every 10 minutes or so, until crisp on the outside and tender inside, another 20 to 30 minutes, depending on the type of potato and how large the chunks are. The potatoes are done when a skewer or thin-bladed knife inserted into a piece meets almost no resistance.

4. Taste, adjust the seasoning with salt and pepper, and serve hot.

OVEN-ROASTED "FRIES" Not as crisp as French Fries (page 242), but close, and much easier and lighter. Use this or any of the other variations to make sweet potato fries: Cut the potatoes, peeled or not, into French fry–style batons. Grease 2 baking sheets or line them with parchment paper. Brush the potatoes with the oil and spread out on the baking sheets without crowding. Proceed with the recipe. Overall cook time will be 30 to 40 minutes.

OVEN-ROASTED COTTAGE "FRIES" So substantial you can eat them like meat: Cut the potatoes, peeled or not, lengthwise into paddles about ¼ inch thick or even a little thicker. Grease 2 baking sheets or line them with parchment paper. Brush the potatoes with the oil and spread out on the baking sheets without crowding. Proceed with the recipe. Overall cook time will be 30 to 40 minutes.

CRISP OVEN-ROASTED COTTAGE "FRIES" WITH GARLIC Follow the preceding variation. Use a combination of butter and olive oil, at least 2 tablespoons of

---

4 Dishes You Can Make with Home Fries or Oven-Roasted Potatoes

1. Patatas Bravas. A Spanish-style dish that's addictive: Dollop potatoes with Garlic Mayonnaise (page 671) and several dashes any hot sauce.

2. Potatoes Benedict. Top each serving of potatoes with a poached egg or 2 (page 525) and a generous spoonful of Hollandaise Sauce (page 674). Garnish with chopped fresh parsley or chervil and a sprinkle of paprika.

3. Crisp Potato Salad. Use panfried or oven-roasted potatoes to make Potato Salad (page 70), or simply toss with about ½ cup or so Vinaigrette (page 628).

4. Potato Tacos. Fill tortillas with potatoes and Creamed Poblanos (page 229). Serve the tacos with shredded cabbage, cilantro, and lime wedges.

Oven-Roasted "Fries"
made with sweet potatoes
and all-purpose potatoes

each. While the potatoes are roasting, mince several cloves of garlic and mix them with a tablespoon or so olive oil. When the fries are nearly done, add the garlic and toss, then return to the oven for a final crisping, which will soften the garlic and turn it golden.

OVEN-ROASTED HASH BROWNS Breakfast potatoes without much fuss: Increase the oil to 3 tablespoons. Peel the potatoes, then shred them on the largest holes of a box grater or with the shredding disk of a food processor. Proceed with the recipe, resisting the urge to mess with the potatoes frequently. When they're tender and crisp on the bottom, use a spatula to turn large portions over and press them down a bit like diner hash browns. Roast until the other side has browned and crisped.

Braised Potatoes, Three Ways

MAKES: 4 servings
TIME: About 40 minutes
Ⓜ Ⓥ

Make this recipe with small heirloom potatoes like fingerlings if you can find them, and be sure to try the variations.

Other vegetables or fruits you can use: any root vegetable, winter squash, or even apples

2	pounds all-purpose or waxy potatoes
3	tablespoons olive oil
	Salt and pepper
1	small onion, chopped
2	cups vegetable stock (pages 97–100) or water
¼	cup chopped fresh parsley for garnish

1. Peel the potatoes. Cut them into large chunks, in half if they're medium-size, or leave whole if they're small.
2. Put the oil in a large pot over medium-high heat. When it's hot, add the potatoes and sprinkle with salt

and pepper. Cook, stirring occasionally, until coated in oil and beginning to turn golden, about 10 minutes. Add the onion and stir a few times until it softens, a minute or 2.
3. Add the stock with enough extra water to barely cover the potatoes. Bring to a boil, stirring once in a while to make sure the potatoes aren't sticking, then turn the heat down to medium-low so that the mixture bubbles gently. Cook, stirring occasionally, until the potatoes get tender, 20 to 25 minutes. Add more liquid if they start to stick. The potatoes are done when a skewer or thin-bladed knife inserted into one meets almost no resistance. Taste and adjust the seasoning, garnish, and serve hot or at room temperature.

BRAISED POTATOES WITH MUSTARD Gorgeous color: When you add the stock in Step 3, stir in ¼ cup any kind of prepared mustard.

CREAM-BRAISED POTATOES Decadent: Use butter instead of olive oil. Instead of stock, use cream, and use milk to finish covering the potatoes in Step 3. When the potatoes are done, stir in 1 tablespoon minced fresh tarragon or chervil if you like, instead of parsley. Serve hot.

Potato and Jerusalem Artichoke Gratin

MAKES: 4 servings
TIME: About 1 hour
Ⓜ

This gratin can be assembled up to 2 days in advance of baking—or even baked 2 days ahead and then reheated before serving. A mandoline gives you slices of consistent thickness—which is the key to even cooking—with little work. You can make this using only potatoes, of course.

Other vegetables you can use: any combination of sweet potatoes, parsnips, celery root, rutabagas, winter squash, burdock, celery, carrots, and/or horseradish (which will mellow while cooking)

2–3   cups heavy cream, half-and-half, or milk
1   pound potatoes, peeled and thinly sliced
1   pound Jerusalem artichokes, peeled and thinly sliced
1½   cups grated Gruyère or Swiss cheese
   Salt and pepper
1   tablespoon chopped fresh thyme

1. Heat the oven to 375°F. Put the cream in a small saucepan and heat over medium heat until it's steaming.

2. Layer the potatoes, Jerusalem artichokes, and cheese—be sure to end with cheese—in a 8-inch gratin or similar ovenproof dish, sprinkling every potato layer with a bit of salt, pepper, and thyme. Pour in enough hot cream to come about three-quarters of the way up the potato layers.

3. Bake, undisturbed, until the potatoes and Jerusalem artichokes are tender (a thin-bladed knife will pierce them with little or no resistance) and the top is nicely browned, 45 to 50 minutes. Serve immediately or keep warm in the oven for up to 30 minutes.

POTATO AND CAULIFLOWER GRATIN WITH CRÈME FRAÎCHE OR SOUR CREAM A little tangy: Substitute cauliflower for the Jerusalem artichokes and crème fraîche or sour cream for the cheese. (Spread it between the layers with a dinner knife.)

SWEET POTATO AND CREAM CHEESE GRATIN An excellent brunch gratin: Substitute 2 pounds sweet potatoes for the potatoes and Jerusalem artichokes and cream cheese for the cheese. Whip the cream cheese with just enough cream to make it spreadable and layer as directed in Step 2. Top the gratin with grated Parmesan, bread crumbs, or chopped pecans. Sprinkle with freshly grated nutmeg just before serving.

SWEET POTATO AND CASHEW GRATIN A vegan version of the proceeding variation: Replace the cream cheese with an equal amount of Cashew Cream (page 300)

of the same consistency. In Step 1, substitute nondairy milk of your choice for the cream. Top with shredded coconut. **V**

Curried Stir-Fried Potatoes

MAKES: 4 servings
TIME: 20 minutes
F **V**

This is an unusual dish—the potatoes remain slightly crunchy—inspired by similar creations from the Sichuan province of China and throughout India. Best with homemade curry powder or garam masala; to make your own, see page 649 or 648. The cumin seeds add a nice bit of crunch, and the cilantro adds a fresh note at the end, but neither is essential.

Other vegetables you can use: cauliflower, broccoli, carrots, turnips, or radishes

3   tablespoons good-quality vegetable oil
1   tablespoon cumin seeds (optional)
1   small red onion, chopped
1½   pounds all-purpose potatoes (like Yukon Gold), peeled and shredded or chopped
1   tablespoon garam masala or curry powder or to taste
   Salt and pepper
   Pinch cayenne, or minced jalapeño or other fresh chile to taste
¼   cup chopped fresh cilantro (optional)

1. Put the oil in a large nonstick or well-seasoned cast-iron skillet over medium-high heat. When it's hot, add the cumin seeds if you're using them and fry for 30 seconds. Add half the onion and all of the potatoes to the oil. Add the garam masala along with salt, pepper, and cayenne. Cook, stirring or tossing, until the onion has caramelized and the potatoes are lightly browned, about 10 minutes; the potatoes need not be fully tender.

Curried Stir-Fried
Potatoes (page 239)

2. Add the cilantro if you're using it, toss once, and transfer to a serving platter. Garnish with the remaining raw onion and serve immediately.

SPICY STIR-FRIED SWEET POTATOES Addictive: Replace the all-purpose potatoes with chopped sweet potatoes. Omit the cumin seeds. Replace the garam masala with 1 tablespoon fresh thyme leaves or 1 teaspoon dried, and ½ teaspoon ground allspice, and increase the cayenne to ½ teaspoon. Reduce the cooking time by a few minutes; the sweet potatoes will cook faster and can burn more quickly. Garnish with juice from 1 lime instead of the cilantro.

STIR-FRIED POTATOES, KOREAN STYLE Great stuff: Omit the garam masala. Use ½ cup chopped scallions instead of red onion. In Step 1, replace the cumin with 1 teaspoon chopped garlic. When you add the scallions and potatoes, also add about a tablespoon minced fresh chile (like jalapeño or Thai), or red chile flakes or cayenne to taste. In Step 2, replace the cilantro with another teaspoon minced garlic and 1 teaspoon minced fresh ginger and cook for 30 seconds or so. Garnish with a tablespoon or 2 toasted sesame seeds (see page 299) and serve.

Potato Nik

MAKES: 4 to 6 servings
TIME: About 40 minutes
M

I love crisp, crunchy potato pancakes (also known as latkes) but they're a pain to cook one by one. Fortunately there's potato nik, my grandmother's clever solution with the mysterious, unexplained name. I figure one nik equals twenty latkes, and you can actually walk away from it for a few minutes while it cooks. Plus, it stays hot for a long time and is delicious warm or at room temperature. For those occasions when you absolutely must have individual latkes, see the first variation.

This is delicious served with your choice of sour cream, applesauce, chutney, or hot sauce.

Other vegetables you can use: sweet potatoes (cook over slightly lower heat for about 5 minutes less per side); a combination of potatoes and sweet potatoes, carrots, or turnips

> **About 2 pounds starchy potatoes (like Idaho or russet), peeled**
> 1 **onion, peeled**
> 2 **eggs, beaten**
> 2 **tablespoons Fresh Bread Crumbs (page 678) or matzo meal**
> **Salt and pepper**
> **Good-quality vegetable oil**

1. Shred the potatoes and onion by hand on the largest holes of a box grater or use the grating disk of a food processor. Drain well in a colander or strainer. Transfer the potatoes and onion to a large bowl and combine with the eggs and bread crumbs; sprinkle with salt and pepper.

2. Put about ⅛ inch oil in a large, deep skillet, preferably nonstick or cast iron, over medium-high heat. When it's hot, pour the batter into the pan and smooth the top. Cook, shaking the pan occasionally, until the bottom is nicely browned, at least 15 minutes, adjusting the heat so the batter sizzles but doesn't burn.

3. To turn, slide the cake out onto a large plate, cover with another large plate, and invert the 2 plates together. Add a little more oil to the pan if necessary and slide the pancake back in, cooked side up. Cook for another 15 minutes or so, until nicely browned. Serve hot or warm, cut in wedges.

LATKES (POTATO PANCAKES) The original: Prepare the potato batter in Step 1 and heat the oil as described in Step 2. When the oil is hot, put large spoonfuls of batter into the pan to form individual pancakes. Cook until browned on both sides, about 10 minutes total per pancake. Drain on paper towels and keep warm in a 200°F oven until all of the latkes are finished.

CHEESY POTATO PANCAKES Not traditional, but irresistible: Add 1 cup grated cheddar, Parmesan, Jack, or Asiago cheese to the batter along with the eggs and crumbs.

French Fries

MAKES: 4 servings
TIME: 30 minutes
F M V

It's a hassle to double-fry French fries, which is the classic (and correct) technique; but it's worth it. Not only will your fries stay crisp longer, but the first step can be done well in advance, leaving you only a quick final frying right before serving. Starchy potatoes are the only option here; waxy potatoes never crisp up quite right.

Purists like to salt the fries and leave it at that, but you can dust them with virtually any spice blend.

Other vegetables you can use: See "7 Other Vegetable Fries," right.

> 2 pounds starchy potatoes (like Idaho or russet)
> Good-quality vegetable oil for deep-frying
> Salt and pepper

1. Scrub the potatoes and peel them if you like. Cut them any way you like—from shoestrings to big batons or chunks—and pat them dry.
2. Put at least 3 inches oil in a deep pan on the stove and turn the heat to medium-high; bring to 300° to 325°F (see "Deep-Frying," page 26).
3. Drop the potatoes into the oil a handful at a time, adjusting the heat as needed to maintain a constant temperature. Fry the potatoes in one batch, stirring occasionally, for 5 to 10 minutes, depending on the cut. The goal of this first frying is to cook them until just tender and beginning to color slightly. Remove with a slotted spoon and drain the potatoes on paper towels or a wire rack. (You can cook the potatoes to this point and keep them on a plate or baking sheet on the counter for an hour or so before proceeding. Be sure to take the oil off the heat.)

4. Heat the oil again, this time to around 350°F. Fry and drain the potatoes a second time—the same way as before—until crisp and deeply colored, just a couple of minutes. Sprinkle with salt and pepper while still hot and serve immediately.

POTATO CHIPS No prefrying is necessary: You'll need a deeper, larger pot and be prepared for the potatoes to absorb more oil. Use a mandoline or a sharp knife to cut the potatoes lengthwise. You want them pretty thin, but not too wispy. Heat the oil to about 350°F. Work in batches and use a slotted spoon or strainer to fish them out of the hot oil as they turn golden. Drain on paper towels or brown bags. Season while hot and serve.

Potato Croquettes

MAKES: 4 servings
TIME: About 25 minutes, made with leftover mashed potatoes

The combination of mashed potatoes inside and crunchy coating outside is irresistible and worth the effort (you can use leftover mashed potatoes if you have them). I

---

7 Other Vegetable Fries

Any starchy vegetable can be French-fried, and it will develop a nice crust without needing to be breaded. Cooking times might vary a bit, so keep close watch the first time using a vegetable and test for doneness early and often. The only trick is to identify what's starchy and what's not. Here's a short list of vegetables that will work:

1. Beets (use slightly lower heat to avoid burning)

2. Carrots (use slightly lower heat to avoid burning)

3. Parsnips (use slightly lower heat to avoid burning)

4. Plantains (use slightly lower heat to avoid burning)

5. Rutabagas

6. Sweet potatoes or yams (use slightly lower heat to avoid burning)

7. Turnips

prefer panfrying croquettes, though you can certainly deep-fry them if you like.

Other vegetables you can use: Jerusalem artichokes

4 **cups mashed potatoes (page 233, made with minimal milk and no butter)**
Salt and pepper
3 **tablespoons olive oil**
1 **onion, chopped**
All-purpose flour for dredging
2 **eggs, lightly beaten in a shallow bowl**
Fresh Bread Crumbs (page 678) for dredging
2 **tablespoons butter or more oil**
Lemon wedges

1. Taste the potatoes and season them with salt and pepper if necessary, taking care not to oversalt. Put 1 tablespoon of the oil in a large skillet over medium-high heat. When it's hot, add the onion and cook, stirring frequently, just until it softens, 3 to 5 minutes. Cool the onion a bit, then stir into the potatoes. Wipe the pan clean. Form the potato mixture into 4 large or 8 small patties.

2. Set out the flour, eggs, and bread crumbs in separate shallow bowls next to each other on the counter. Dredge each patty in the flour, coat with egg, then dredge in the bread crumbs, pressing to help the crumbs adhere; set aside on a plate or a sheet of wax paper.

3. Add the remaining oil to the pan, along with the butter or additional oil, and turn the heat to medium-high. When the oil is hot, cook the patties as you would hamburgers, turning carefully to keep the coating intact as each side browns, about 5 minutes per side. Since all the ingredients are already cooked, the crust is your main concern; the interior will get hot as long as the exterior browns. Drain briefly and sprinkle with more salt and pepper if you like. Serve immediately with lemon wedges on the side.

POTATO CROQUETTES, INDIAN STYLE Vegan and delicious: Start with vegan mashed potatoes and use all good-quality vegetable oil. Use cornstarch instead of

flour and omit the eggs and bread crumbs. As the onion finishes softening in Step 1, sprinkle it with 2 tablespoons curry powder, chaat masala, or garam masala. **V**

POTATO CROQUETTES, JAPANESE STYLE Supercrunchy: Use all good-quality vegetable oil. Replace the onion with ¾ cup chopped scallions and substitute panko for the bread crumbs. To make a simple dipping sauce, combine the juice of 2 lemons with 2 tablespoons soy sauce, or serve with Dashi Dipping Sauce (page 657) or Ponzu (page 657).

POTATO CROQUETTES WITH ROASTED GARLIC AND PARMESAN Omit the onion and 1 tablespoon of the oil. Instead, stir 2 heads mashed Roasted Garlic (page 205) into the potatoes in Step 1, along with 1 cup grated Parmesan. Terrific with Fast Tomato Sauce (page 312).

RADISHES

The more common round or oblong radishes come in an array of colors—bright pink to crimson red, purple, green, and white. We mostly eat them raw, but they are also quite delicious cooked with some butter, especially braised and glazed.

Daikon radish is a little different; it can be as big as your arm and is often sold in cut pieces. Daikon is ivory white in color, with a mild but distinctively radishy flavor. It is common in Asian cuisines, especially Japanese and Korean, and is often pickled (sometimes colored bright yellow).

Black radish is a spicy-hot type of radish with a black skin and white flesh; shred and use it as a garnish or eat with buttered bread.

BUYING AND STORING Radishes with their greens are best; the leaves should be green and fresh looking (the tender leaves can be a spicy addition to salads or stir-fries). The radish should be firm, crisp, and smooth. Large specimens of naturally small radishes can be woody, so watch out for that. Store wrapped loosely in plastic in the refrigerator. Use them before they start to feel soft.

PREPARING Trim and peel if you like (black radishes should always be peeled); slice or chop as necessary. The greens will be sandy, so wash them well.

BEST COOKING METHODS Sautéing in butter, braising and glazing

WHEN IS IT DONE? When crisp-tender to fully tender, but not mushy

OTHER VEGETABLES YOU CAN USE Jícama, water chestnuts if raw; turnips if cooked

SEA GREENS

Sea greens are flavorful and almost always are sold dried. For the most part, they're wild. With the exception of sea beans (samphire), which is sold fresh as branches of a whole plant, we eat primarily the leaves. Most sea greens are protein packed (nori is at the top of the chart with over 30 percent), an outstanding source of calcium (hijiki and wakame contain as much as fourteen times the amount in milk), and high in vitamins (especially A, C, E, and B_{12}, of which there are few vegetarian sources) and minerals (potassium, magnesium, phosphorus, iron, and iodine, which is difficult to obtain from natural sources). And they're delicious enjoyed in salads (pages 53 to 57) and stir-fries, or added to most any kind of dish.

Here are the sea greens you're likely to find in supermarkets, natural food stores, and Asian markets:

- **Arame and Hijiki (Hiziki)** Similar in look and use. Both are slender, almost hairy strands. Arame is finer, milder, and lighter in color; hijiki is black, briny, and expands massively when rehydrated. Use, after soaking, in salads, soups, and stews or add to sautés or stir-fries.
- **Dulse** Dark red, crumpled looking, and relatively soft. It can be eaten straight out of the package or added to salads, sandwiches, or soups. Also available smoked.
- **Kombu (Kelp)** A main ingredient in Kombu Dashi (page 100), kelp contains a substance similar to MSG that enhances flavors. Add it to slow-simmering

foods like beans, grains, soups, and stews; just add a piece to your next simmered dish and see. Sold in large, thick, hard pieces that are dark green and usually coated with a white powder, or as "noodles" for use in Korean cooking. Occasionally sold fresh, especially on the West Coast.
- **Nori (Laver)** The familiar thin, shiny sheets that are used to wrap sushi. Deep greenish purple, almost black; brittle when dry and chewy when moistened. Nori dissolves in liquid and has a mild, nutty flavor. It's excellent toasted (see Nori Chips, page 247) and crumbled into almost anything.
- **Sea Beans (Samphire, Glasswort)** These small, delicate, thin, green "branches" with nubby ends are lovely raw in salads and used as a garnish; they can also be poached for about 30 seconds, which enhances their flavor slightly. That flavor is fresh and "sea-like," and the texture is crisp and delightful. If you see it fresh, buy it; when pickled and sold in jars it's less exciting.
- **Wakame and Alaria** Used interchangeably; the former is harvested in Japan, the latter in North America. Both are dark green when dried and nearly transparent; they turn emerald green when rehydrated. Their flavor is mild; nice in soups and stews, with grains, or added to salads.

BUYING AND STORING You can find dried sea greens pretty easily now, though the best selection will be in Asian markets, natural food stores, and online. Store in a cool, dry spot, where they will keep indefinitely. Fresh sea beans should be crisp and bright green, and smell like the ocean; store them in the refrigerator and use as quickly as possible.

PREPARING Nori requires no soaking; cut it with scissors as needed. It's often toasted to make it sturdier and tastier before use: Put a skillet over medium-high heat. When it's hot, put a single nori sheet in the pan and toast until it shrinks up, about 15 seconds; turn it over and toast the other side for another 15 seconds. Use as directed in the recipe.

Dried dulse

Soaked dulse

Dried hijiki

Soaked hijiki

Soaked wakame

Dried wakame

Use dulse straight out of the package or just give it a rinse in cold water.

For arame, hijiki, wakame, and alaria, rinse once and soak in at least 10 times its volume of water until tender, 5 to 10 minutes or more. Drain and gently gather and squeeze the pieces to remove excess water. Pick through the sea greens to sort out any hard bits (there may be none) and chop or cut up if the pieces are large; you may find it easier to use scissors.

Prepare kombu the same way as arame, but do not rinse first.

Rinse sea beans. Chop only if necessary.

BEST COOKING METHODS For arame, hijiki, alaria, and wakame: boiling, sautéing, stir-frying with other ingredients. For kombu: boiling, braising. For dulse: quickly sautéing, stir-frying. For sea beans: stir-frying (blanch them for 30 seconds first); but they're just as good raw.

WHEN IS IT DONE? When tender

OTHER VEGETABLES YOU CAN USE Most sea greens, with the exception of sea beans and kombu, are interchangeable. Substitute French-cut green beans for sea beans.

Texas Caviar with Sea Greens

MAKES: 4 servings
TIME: 20 minutes with cooked beans
F M O

This vegetarian "caviar" gets close to the real deal, with a briny flavor derived from a glaze seasoned with sea greens. I like it chilled or at room temperature, served with typical caviar accompaniments: minced red onion, crumbled hard-boiled eggs, crème fraîche, sour cream, or yogurt), and chopped cornichons or sweet pickles.

For a little kick, include some minced fresh chile, red chile flakes, or cayenne in the mix. You can also eat these unadorned with Sushi Rice (page 384) or tossed with plain soba or udon noodles.

¼	cup dried dulse, arame, or other mild sea greens
2	tablespoons good-quality vegetable oil
1	shallot, minced
1	cup Kombu Dashi (page 100), sake, or water
2	tablespoons mirin (or substitute 1 tablespoon honey mixed with 1 tablespoon water)
	Salt and pepper
3	cups cooked or canned black-eyed peas, drained as dry as possible

1. Put the sea greens in a clean spice or coffee grinder and pulse until almost ground to a powder.
2. Put the oil in a deep skillet over medium-high heat. When it's hot, add the shallot and cook, stirring constantly, until soft, about a minute. Stir in the sea greens, dashi, and mirin. Sprinkle with a little salt and pepper and let the mixture bubble away until it reduces and thickens into a thin syrup, 5 to 7 minutes.
3. Stir in the black-eyed peas; keep stirring until heated through and coated with the glaze, just a couple of minutes more. Taste and adjust the seasoning. Serve immediately or cool, cover tightly, and refrigerate for up to a week.

Sea Green and Shiitake Stir-Fry

MAKES: 4 servings
TIME: 25 minutes
F V

Fast, nutrient-rich, and delicious. Serve over a whole grain like brown rice, wheat berries, or quinoa, and you're doing even better.

Use any combination of arame, hijiki, dulse, kombu, wakame, and alaria. But note that kombu should either be simmered in water for about 15 minutes first or soaked and sliced very finely; dulse should be added at the last minute.

2 tablespoons good-quality vegetable oil
1 tablespoon minced garlic
1 tablespoon minced fresh ginger
½ cup chopped scallions or onion
½ cup thinly sliced kombu, soaked and simmered in water for 15 minutes, then drained
1 cup sliced shiitake mushroom caps
2 stalks celery, thinly sliced lengthwise or julienned
2 cups soaked, drained, and thinly sliced (if necessary) sea greens (like arame, hijiki, dulse, wakame, and alaria)
¼ cup vegetable stock (pages 97–100) or water, plus more as needed
2 tablespoons soy sauce
1 teaspoon sesame oil

1. Heat a large, deep skillet over medium-high heat for 3 or 4 minutes. Add the oil and, almost immediately, the garlic, ginger, and scallions. Cook, stirring, for about 15 seconds, then add the kombu, mushrooms, celery, sea greens, and stock and turn the heat to high.

2. Cook, stirring constantly, until the vegetables are tender, about 7 minutes. If the mixture is completely dry, add a couple of tablespoons more liquid. Add the soy sauce and sesame oil, stir, and turn off the heat. Serve or store, covered, in the refrigerator for up to a day.

SEA GREEN AND NOODLE STIR-FRY Lo mein, essentially: Bring a large pot of water to a boil and salt it. Cook about 8 ounces fresh Chinese egg noodles, dried Chinese wheat noodles, or spaghetti until they are tender but not mushy, about 4 minutes for fresh noodles, longer for dried, then drain and rinse; toss with a tablespoon or so oil to prevent sticking. Add the noodles to the stir-fry at the end of cooking and stir often, until the noodles are hot.

Nori Chips

MAKES: 2 to 4 servings
TIME: 5 minutes
F M V

These are completely addicting. Eat them as a snack or crumble into popcorn or over a bowl of steamed rice and Kimchi (page 93).

---

5 Ways to Add Sea Greens to Your Daily Cooking

No need to soak sea greens for them to work magic. Here's how to cook with a few in their dried state.

1. Put some in stir-fries. A pinch or 2 of wispy threads like hijiki, wakame, alaria, or arame brings texture, color, and flavor to almost anything in a skillet. For chewiness, add them along with the first vegetables; for crunch add them at the last minute. Just make sure there's a little liquid in the pan for them to absorb.

2. Make sea green seasonings. Pulse hijiki, arame, dulse (or smoked dulse!), or bits of toasted nori in a blender, food processor, or spice grinder until as coarse or fine as you like. Use it like you would spice blends in dressings, sauces, soups, or for the final garnish along with salt and pepper.

3. Toss a piece of kombu into the pot. Add instant brininess to soups, beans, grains, and braises with a strip or 2 of kombu. Keep an eye on the liquid to make sure it doesn't absorb too much. Fish it out before serving.

4. Cook with Kombu Dashi (page 100) instead of water or stock.

5. Put a stack of "grabbers" on the table. Quarter nori sheets and pass them at the dinner table. They're perfect for making mini wraps and scooping up vegetable stir-fries, pilafs, rice bowls, and salads. You can toast them first but I find that as long as they're fairly dry, once you fold a bite of hot food in them, the chewy texture is delightful.

---

6   **sheets nori**
2   **tablespoons sesame oil**
    Salt

1. Put a skillet over medium-high heat. Brush the nori with the sesame oil and sprinkle with salt. Put a single nori sheet in the pan and toast it until it shrinks, about 15 seconds; turn it over and toast the other side for another 15 seconds.

2. Use scissors to cut the sheets into rectangular "chips." Serve within a few hours.

Japanese Egg Crêpes with Nori

MAKES: 5 or 6 crêpes
TIME: 15 minutes

F M

These crêpes are ideal for Sushi Bowls (page 384) and Nigiri Sushi (page 384), and can also be filled with Crisp-Fried Bean Sprouts (page 176) or Stir-Fried Vegetables (page 154). The nori strips add subtle flavor and wonderful visual interest to the crêpes.

2   **sheets nori**
4   **eggs**
2   **teaspoons soy sauce**
1   **teaspoon sugar**
    Pinch salt
1   **tablespoon good-quality vegetable oil**

1. Toast the nori by using tongs to hold the sheets one at a time over a medium-high flame for a few seconds, until they change color. If you have an electric stove, run them under the broiler for 15 seconds to a minute on each side. Use scissors to cut each sheet into 4 or 5 strips; stack them and cut crosswise into thin strips.

2. Put the eggs, soy sauce, sugar, and salt in a bowl and whisk until the sugar and salt are dissolved. Put a small nonstick pan over medium heat. Pour a small amount of the oil into the pan; spread it evenly over the surface with a brush or paper towel. Pour a small amount of the egg mixture into the pan, tilting it from side to side so the eggs completely cover the bottom. The crêpe should be very thin. Sprinkle the top with some of the nori. Cook until the top is firm, a minute or less. To flip the crêpe, use a plastic spatula to lift one edge from the side of the pan, then gently pull up that edge with your fingers, pull up another side with your other hand, and flip the crêpe over. Cook for another 15 seconds or so; remove to a cutting board and repeat, rolling the crêpes into tubes if you like.

3. Let cool to room temperature. Cut the crêpes into thin strips if you're using them for sushi; otherwise, leave whole. Serve or cover and store in the refrigerator, for up to several hours; bring back to room temperature before serving.

SPINACH

Washed spinach is among the most convenient vegetables to prepare. But its price is high and its flavor lacking compared the unwashed, unpicked bunches of spinach that cost much less. Real spinach, locally grown, is best in the spring, but spinach is around all year. In any case, spinach is finally getting its due as a vegetable that is equally wonderful slow cooked, flashed in a pan, or tossed as a green salad. Some people find raw spinach bitter, due to its high amounts of oxalic acid, but most love it cooked.

BUYING AND STORING Buy vibrantly colored green, crisp leaves; those with the pink-hued stem bases are even better (rinse the stems well and cook them with the leaves). Store wrapped loosely in plastic in the refrigerator; use it before it turns slimy or wilts.

PREPARING If it's in a bunch, either chop off all the stems (if you're in a hurry) or untie the bunch and cut off only the tough stems, leaving the tender ones on. Rinse thoroughly in several changes of water, especially if it was bunched, as there may be clumps of mud or sand between the leaves. Chop or slice after cooking.

BEST COOKING METHODS Steaming, sautéing

WHEN IS IT DONE? As soon as it wilts, though you can cook it longer for extra tenderness if you like

OTHER VEGETABLES YOU CAN USE Arugula, beet greens, chard

Spinach with Currants and Nuts

MAKES: 4 servings
TIME: 20 minutes
F M V

A Mediterranean classic, astringent from the spinach, sweet from the currants or raisins, crunchy with nuts, and just as good at room temperature as it is hot. This dish makes a fine dumpling, pie, or pasta filling.

Other vegetables you can use: almost any greens, chopped, though most will take a little longer to cook; broccoli, chard, kale, or collards, cooked until quite tender

¼ cup dried currants or raisins
1 pound spinach, well washed and trimmed of large stems
¼ cup olive oil
1 teaspoon minced garlic (optional)
¼ cup broken walnut pieces or pine nuts, toasted (see page 299)
Salt and pepper

1. Soak the currants in warm water to cover for about 10 minutes while you clean and cook the spinach. Steam or boil the spinach (see page 150) until tender, less than 5 minutes. Let cool.
2. When the spinach is cool enough to handle, squeeze all the excess moisture from it; chop it coarsely. Heat the oil in a large skillet over medium heat. When it's hot, add the garlic if you're using it and cook, stirring occasionally, until golden, about 3 minutes. Add the spinach and raise the heat to medium-high. Cook, stirring occasionally, for about 2 minutes. Drain the currants and add them, along with the nuts.

3. Reduce the heat to medium and cook, stirring occasionally, for another 3 to 4 minutes, until everything glistens. Sprinkle with salt and pepper and serve hot or at room temperature.

SPINACH WITH OVEN-ROASTED TOMATOES Omit the nuts. Replace the currants with 4 or so Oven-Roasted Fresh Plum Tomatoes (page 258), sliced or chopped as you prefer (no need for soaking). Add a handful of black olives, pitted and chopped, if you like.

Spinach with Paneer and Yogurt

Saag Paneer
MAKES: 4 servings
TIME: 30 minutes with premade cheese
F

The chickpea flour "roux" thickens and flavors the yogurt sauce and keeps it from separating, but regular flour works too. If you can't find paneer (an Indian food store is your best bet), substitute mozzarella or feta. Serve this with the basic version of Rice Pilaf (page 372) or Biryani (page 375), with some Raw Onion Chutney (page 668) on the side.

Other vegetables you can use: beet greens, chard, kale

1 pound spinach, rinsed well and trimmed of large stems
¼ cup olive oil
¼ cup chickpea or all-purpose flour
Salt and pepper
2 tablespoons garam masala or curry powder (to make your own, see pages 648–649)
2 cups yogurt (preferably whole milk)
8 ounces paneer, cut into ½-inch cubes (about 1½ cups)

1. Boil and shock the spinach (see page 150); drain well and coarsely chop.
2. Put the oil and flour in a large pot, sprinkle with salt and pepper, and turn the heat to medium-low. Cook,

Spinach with Paneer
and Yogurt

stirring frequently, until the flour darkens a bit and becomes fragrant, about 5 minutes, lowering the heat if necessary to keep it from scorching.

3. Stir in the garam masala, then whisk in the yogurt. Raise the heat a bit and cook, stirring frequently, until the yogurt has heated through and thickened slightly, a couple of minutes. Fold in the spinach and cheese. Cook and stir until hot, another couple of minutes. Taste, adjust the seasoning, and serve.

SPINACH WITH TOFU AND COCONUT MILK Dairy-free: Replace the paneer with cubed extra-firm tofu and the yogurt with 2 cups coconut milk. Proceed with the recipe, covering the pan when you heat the tofu in the mixture so it can warm through. **V**

SUMMER SQUASH

Summer squash are tender and deliciously mild; steamed, with a pat of butter or a drizzle of olive oil and some salt, they can be divine. They're also often found in combination with other summer produce like eggplant and tomato.

Beyond the commonplace yellow squash and zucchini, there is the adorable flying saucer–shaped pattypan with its scalloped edge, bright colors (yellow and light or dark green), and variety of sizes. There's also the chayote, or mirliton as it's called in the South. It looks somewhat like an avocado with its bright-green, wrinkled exterior skin (sometimes covered with spines), and has pale-yellow to white semitranslucent flesh with a texture similar to a melon. The flavor is so mild it picks up that of whatever you cook it with. Use it raw in salads or cooked like any summer squash. Other forms of summer squash—there are many—can be treated the same way as you would zucchini.

BUYING AND STORING Look for smaller, plump, firm, unblemished specimens. Everyone laughs at big zucchini and though those monsters are edible, the small ones are really better; anything over an inch or certainly 2 inches diameter is a candidate for pancakes or bread. For pattypan, select ones under 3 inches in diameter; the older, larger ones, usually white, have bland flesh and tough skin. For chayote, heavy wrinkles usually mean it was left on the vine too long; choose those with the least wrinkled skin. Store wrapped loosely in plastic in the refrigerator; use as quickly as possible, especially if they are fresh from the garden or farm.

PREPARING For yellow squash and zucchini, trim the ends and slice or chop as you like; no need to peel. Leave pattypan whole if tender enough or halve them. Peeling chayote is optional. Halve through the stem end and remove the seed. Leave as halves or chop or slice as you like.

BEST COOKING METHODS Steaming, sautéing, braising (chayote), roasting, frying, grilling

WHEN IS IT DONE? When tender but not falling apart; pierce with a skewer or thin-bladed knife to check.

OTHER VEGETABLES YOU CAN USE Summer squashes are fairly interchangeable.

Summer Squash, Simply Prepared

MAKES: 4 servings
TIME: 20 minutes
F **V**

Here are two basic methods for cooking any kind of summer squash, and both are hard to beat.

- 3 **tablespoons olive oil**
- 1 **tablespoon minced garlic**
- 1½ **pounds summer squash, sliced into rounds**
   Salt and pepper
- 2 **teaspoons fresh lemon juice, or to taste**
   Chopped fresh parsley for garnish

1. Put the oil in a medium skillet over medium heat. When it's hot, add the garlic and cook until it sizzles, about a minute. Add the squash, sprinkle with salt and pepper, and cook, turning occasionally, until the pieces are tender and browned in spots, 10 to 15 minutes.

Steamed Baby Summer
Squash (page 254)

2. Just before serving, sprinkle with the lemon juice, then taste and adjust the seasoning. Garnish with the parsley and serve.

STEAMED BABY SUMMER SQUASH In season, mini squash, an inch or less wide and just a couple of inches long, are becoming increasingly available in supermarkets and certainly in farmers' markets: Substitute baby squash for the full-size squash. Trim, cut them in half lengthwise, and sprinkle with salt and pepper, then steam (see page 150) until tender, about 5 minutes. Transfer to a serving bowl, drizzle with a little olive oil or melted butter instead of lemon juice, toss to coat, and serve.

Zucchini Pancakes with Pesto

MAKES: 4 servings
TIME: About 1 hour, half of that unattended
Ⓜ

Zucchini is the main feature here; the batter just serves to hold things together. You cook these a little more slowly than regular pancakes, to give the squash a chance to soften and the sides to brown.

Other vegetables you can use: yellow squash, carrots, parsnips, celery root, sweet potatoes, or scallions; cooked, squeezed, chopped spinach or other greens

> **About 1 pound zucchini**
> **Salt**
> ½ **onion, grated**
> 1 **egg, lightly beaten**
> 1 **cup flour**
> **Black pepper**
> **Milk, half-and-half, or heavy cream**
> 2 **tablespoons Pesto (page 634)**
> **Melted butter or olive oil for the pan**

1. Grate the zucchini by hand on a box grater or with the grating disk of a food processor. (You should have about 2 cups, packed.)

2. Put it in a colander, sprinkle with 1 teaspoon salt, tossing to mix it in, and let stand for 30 minutes, then transfer to a clean kitchen towel and wring out as much moisture as you can.
3. Mix together the squash, onion, egg, and flour in a medium bowl. Sprinkle with salt and pepper. Add just enough milk so the batter drops easily from a large spoon. Stir in the pesto.
4. Brush some butter or oil in a large skillet or griddle over medium heat. When it's hot, drop in spoonfuls of the batter; use a fork to spread the vegetables into an even layer. (You'll probably have to work in batches.) Cook, turning once, until nicely browned on both sides, about 15 minutes total. If necessary, transfer the pancakes to a baking sheet and keep warm in a 200°F oven until all are finished. Serve hot or at room temperature.

CHEESY ZUCCHINI PANCAKES Substitute olive oil or melted butter for the pesto and add up to 1 cup grated cheese, like cheddar, Parmesan, ricotta salata, or manchego, to the batter, along with the zucchini in Step 3.

BEET PANCAKES Replace the squash with beets. Skip Step 2. Substitute sour cream or goat cheese for the pesto. Add 1 tablespoon chopped fresh thyme to the batter.

BUTTERNUT SQUASH AND HAZELNUT PANCAKES
Use butternut squash and skip Step 2. Replace the pesto with melted butter or olive oil, and add ½ cup chopped hazelnuts to the batter.

SWEET POTATOES AND YAMS
Though they are both tubers and can look very similar, sweet potatoes and yams are different species. Not that it matters much: The names "yams" and "sweet potatoes" are used interchangeably in the South, and canned yams are usually sweet potatoes.

Sweet potatoes are sold year-round in every supermarket. There are two major varieties: One has light tan skin, yellow flesh, a drier texture, and less-sweet flavor; the other type has a reddish-brown skin, bright orange flesh, and is soft and sweet when cooked. Other specialty varieties of sweet potato range in flesh color from purple to rose to white.

Real yams are seldom grown in the United States, nor are they widely available here. When small they are hard to distinguish from sweet potatoes, but they can grow to enormous proportions (over a hundred pounds), and may be sold cut into chunks and wrapped in plastic; look in Latino markets, where they might be called *ñame*. When cooked, the texture ranges from sweet and moist to dry and mealy, depending on type.

BUYING AND STORING Sweet potatoes should be plump, with smooth skin. Avoid any with sprouts. Do not refrigerate; they are best kept in a cool, dark, dry place. They're fairly perishable for a tuber; use within a couple of weeks, sooner if you can.

PREPARING Peel if necessary; slice and chop as you like.

BEST COOKING METHODS Baking, braising, roasting; to make Sweet Potato Fries, follow any of the variations of Oven-Roasted Potatoes on page 236.

WHEN IS IT DONE? When very tender

OTHER VEGETABLES YOU CAN USE Potatoes, carrots, parsnips, any tropical tuber. Many sweet potato recipes are good with winter squash, and vice versa; though the sweet potato generally has denser flesh, the flavors are similar.

Sweet Potatoes, Simply Cooked

MAKES: 4 servings
TIME: 1 hour or less
[O]

For basic use, sweet potatoes can be baked, boiled or steamed, or microwaved. Baked is the best way if you're just going to eat them plain or with butter, but for mashing or use in other recipes, boiling and microwaving are easier.

2 **large or 4 medium sweet potatoes**
   (about 1½ pounds)
   Salt and pepper
   Butter (optional)

TO BAKE Heat the oven to 425°F and line a baking pan with foil. Rinse the sweet potatoes and poke each with a thin-bladed knife in a few places. Put them in the baking pan and bake, turning once, until very tender, about an hour. Serve immediately with salt and pepper, and butter if you like.

TO BOIL OR STEAM Peel the sweet potatoes, cut into large chunks, and cook according to Boiled or Steamed Root Vegetables or Tubers (page 153). They'll probably take 20 minutes or less; be careful not to overcook or they'll fall apart.

TO MICROWAVE Peel the sweet potatoes. Cut into large chunks and put on a plate or in a glass baking dish with a couple of tablespoons water and a little butter if you like. Cover and microwave on high for at least 10 minutes, until soft.

Mashed Sweet Potato Gratin

MAKES: 4 servings
TIME: 25 to 35 minutes with cooked sweet potatoes
[F] [M]

A slightly refined, healthier version of candied yams (which are really sweet potatoes). Mix in some minced fresh ginger for an added kick.

Other vegetables and fruits you can use: apples or pears (sliced, not mashed), any winter squash

4 **tablespoons (½ stick) butter**
   About 1½ pounds sweet potatoes, cooked (left)
   Grated zest of 1 orange
   Salt and pepper
   Freshly grated nutmeg (optional)
½ **cup chopped pecans, walnuts, almonds,**
   or hazelnuts (optional)

1. Heat the oven to 400°F. Grease a gratin dish or 8-inch square baking dish with some of the butter. Mash the cooked sweet potatoes with the remaining butter, the zest, a sprinkle of salt and pepper, and a dash nutmeg if you're using it. Taste and adjust the seasoning. Put the sweet potatoes in the dish, smoothing the surface with a spatula.

2. Sprinkle the top with the nuts if you're using them. Bake until the sweet potatoes are hot and golden on top, 20 to 30 minutes. Serve hot or warm.

MASHED SWEET POTATOES BRÛLÉE You can also prepare this in individual ramekins: In Step 2, after baking, sprinkle the top with ¾ cup brown sugar. Turn on the broiler and adjust the rack to about 4 inches from the heat source. Broil, watching carefully. When the sugar bubbles and browns, it's ready. Let sit for a few minutes before serving.

MAPLE-GLAZED MASHED SWEET POTATOES Follow the preceding variation, but substitute ½ cup maple syrup for the brown sugar; it won't develop a crisp top like the sugar but will thicken and create a rich glaze.

TOMATILLOS

A distant cousin of tomatoes, tomatillos are widely used in Mexican cooking, almost always when firm and green (they're yellow and softer when ripe; there's also a rarer purple variety). Their zingy flavor makes excellent raw and cooked green salsas (see Fresh Tomatillo Salsa, page 660, and Cooked Tomatillo Salsa, page 663). Canned tomatillos are a decent substitute if you can't find fresh.

BUYING AND STORING Best in summer, but available throughout the year. Look for tightly wrapped husks covering firm, unshriveled, and green fruit. Store in a paper bag in the refrigerator; they'll keep for a couple of weeks.

PREPARING Remove the husks and rinse off the sticky resin. No need to core. Slice, chop, purée, or leave whole.

OTHER VEGETABLES YOU CAN USE Green tomatoes or, in a pinch, fresh tomatoes

Stewed Tomatillos and Tomatoes

MAKES: 6 to 8 servings
TIME: About 1 hour, mostly unattended
Ⓜ Ⓥ

Tart green tomatillos play the starring role in this stew, mellowed a bit by the sweetness of fresh tomatoes. The texture is silky and slightly thick. Serve over rice, grits or polenta, or hominy.

Other vegetables you can use: all-green or not-quite-ripe tomatoes

- 2 tablespoons olive oil, plus more for drizzling
- 1 large onion, chopped
- 1 bell pepper or 2 poblano chiles, cored, seeded, and chopped
- 2 cloves garlic, crushed
   Salt and pepper
- 1½ pounds tomatillos, husked and rinsed
- 1 cup vegetable stock (pages 97–100), white wine, or water
- 1½ pounds fresh tomatoes, cut into large chunks
- ½ cup chopped fresh cilantro

1. Put the oil in a large pot or deep skillet over medium-high heat. When it's hot, cook the onion, bell pepper, and garlic until the onion is soft and translucent, 5 to 10 minutes. Sprinkle with salt and pepper.

2. Add the tomatillos and cook until the skins start to break open, 10 to 15 minutes. Pour in the stock and stir. Bring to a boil, then reduce the heat so the mixture bubbles very gently. Cover; cook until the tomatillos are mostly dissolved, about 30 minutes. (You can prepare the dish up to this point, cover, and refrigerate for a day or 2 before proceeding.)

3. Return the heat to medium-high, and when the mixture starts to bubble, stir in the tomatoes. Cook, stirring

occasionally, until the tomatoes wilt, but their skins are still intact. Stir in the cilantro, taste, and adjust the seasoning. Serve hot or at room temperature, drizzled with additional oil.

TOMATOES

The most common tomatoes fall into three basic categories: cherry, plum, and slicing. Cherry and other small tomatoes are sweet and tender, perfect for snacking, tossing whole into salads, and quickly sautéing or roasting with a sprinkle of fresh herbs. Plum (aka roma) tomatoes are medium-size, oval, and meaty. They are available year-round and are best cooked; use for sauces, braises, oven-drying, and stewing. Slicing tomatoes are a broad category of tomato that are typically large and spherical (some flattened, some round). Beefsteaks are one of the most common; they're juicy, flavorful, and delicious raw and cooked. But with the explosion of interest in tomato varieties, most people will see dozens of different varieties between July and October.

Being a delicate fruit, ripe tomatoes do not travel well. The vast majority of supermarket varieties, even in season, are either picked green and ripened off the vine or grown in hothouses; either way, the end result is the same: They don't taste very good. Outside of tomato season, I usually reach for canned tomatoes. In-season, I buy tomatoes at farmers' markets or direct from farmers or gardeners; many years, I grow my own.

BUYING AND STORING Real tomato season is late summer into fall, but you can buy tomatoes any time (see above). The best fresh tomatoes are undamaged, soft—yielding to light pressure but not mushy—and deeply colored. Store all tomatoes at room temperature; refrigeration ruins their texture and flavor.

PREPARING To core tomatoes—an optional refinement, entirely unnecessary in most instances—cut a cone around the core and remove it. To peel—once considered essential, now another optional and unnecessary step—cut a small X in the flower (smooth nonstem) end of the tomato and drop into boiling water for 10 to 30 seconds, until the skin loosens. Plunge into ice water and peel off the skin. To seed, cut a tomato in half through its equator and squeeze and shake out the seeds (you may want to do this over a strainer to save the liquid). The truth is I don't seed tomatoes anymore either (the seeds have real flavor, and their texture is hardly offensive), so unless you care, you can forget about all three of these steps moving forward!

BEST COOKING METHODS You really can't beat a raw ripe tomato during the height of the season. Otherwise, roasting, grilling or broiling, panfrying. And, of course, making tomato sauce (page 312).

WHEN ARE THEY DONE? Whenever you want them to be: They're good from raw to cooked to a mushy sauce.

OTHER VEGETABLES AND FRUITS YOU CAN USE Nothing is the same. In some instances, tomatillos, pineapple, peaches, nectarines, or watermelon

Grilled or Broiled Tomatoes with Basil

MAKES: 4 servings
TIME: 30 minutes
F M O

When you grill a ripe or even semiripe tomato, the high heat caramelizes some of the sugars, dries it a bit, softens the flesh, and removes traces of rawness. The whole process takes just 5 to 10 minutes. Heating the grill, of course, takes longer, but the broiler or a heavy skillet over high heat works just as well. And all of this can be done hours before you intend to use the tomatoes.

You can integrate the cooked tomatoes into a salad or risotto, or simply toss them with pasta. Or you can also serve them as is, drizzled with olive oil and sprinkled with basil.

Other vegetables you can use: eggplant (it will take about twice as long to cook on the grill)

3 or 4 fresh tomatoes
Olive oil as needed
Salt and pepper
⅓ cup torn or chopped fresh basil, or
   more to taste
Grated Parmesan cheese for serving (optional)

1. Prepare a charcoal or gas grill or turn on the broiler for moderate heat; adjust the rack to about 4 inches from the heat source. Cut each tomato into 3 or 4 thick slices. Brush them with oil and sprinkle with salt and pepper.
2. Grill or broil the tomatoes, turning once, until they are soft but not mushy, about 5 minutes total; you should be able to lift them from the grill or broiler pan with a spatula without their falling apart, but only barely. As they cook, use tongs to remove and discard the skins. Transfer the tomatoes to a platter or plates and sprinkle with basil, plus the cheese if you like.

GRILLED OR BROILED TOMATOES AND SCRAMBLED EGGS, CHINESE STYLE Turn grilled tomatoes into an entrée: In Step 1, brush the tomatoes with sesame oil instead of olive oil, then grill or broil as directed; transfer to a plate. Put 1 tablespoon good-quality vegetable oil in a large skillet over medium heat. Add 1 tablespoon minced fresh ginger and 1 teaspoon minced garlic and cook just until they sizzle, about a minute. In a large bowl, beat 6 eggs and stir in the tomatoes, breaking them into pieces. Add the tomato-egg mixture to the pan and cook, stirring almost constantly, until the mixture forms soft curds, 5 to 10 minutes. Stir in 1 tablespoon sesame oil and 2 teaspoons soy sauce. Garnish with chopped scallions and serve.

Broiled Cherry Tomatoes with Herbs

MAKES: 4 servings
TIME: About 5 minutes
F M V

Spread these on Crostini (page 624), drizzle with cream or good olive oil and/or sprinkle with chopped

herbs, toasted bread crumbs, or grated Parmesan. Or eat them alone, one after the other—like candy.

1 pound cherry tomatoes
2 or 3 sprigs fresh oregano, thyme, rosemary, tarragon, or basil
2 tablespoons olive oil
Salt and pepper

Heat the broiler and put the rack about 4 inches from the heat source. Toss the tomatoes with the herbs, oil, and salt and pepper and put on a rimmed baking sheet or in flameproof gratin dish. Broil until the skins brown, blister, and crack, 3 to 5 minutes; check the tomatoes often and shake the pan every so often to roll them around a bit; they can burn quickly. Serve straight from the broiler or warm.

Oven-Roasted Fresh Plum Tomatoes

MAKES: 4 servings
TIME: About 1 hour, mostly unattended
M V

Roasting vastly improves the flavor of supermarket plum tomatoes because the process concentrates the flavor and eliminates any hint of mealiness. Use them immediately in sauces, as a garnish, in pilafs or soups, or in other vegetable dishes. Or store them, tightly covered, in the fridge for up to several days or freeze for several months.

Other fruits or vegetables you can use: peaches, nectarines

2 tablespoons olive oil, plus more for the pan
2 pounds plum tomatoes (about a dozen), halved lengthwise
Salt and pepper

1. Heat the oven to 375°F. Grease a large baking sheet or roasting pan with a little oil.
2. Scoop the seeds out of the tomatoes if you like and put the tomatoes in the pan. Drizzle or brush with

Oven-Roasted Fresh
Plum Tomatoes

2 tablespoons oil and sprinkle with salt and pepper. Roast until they start to char a bit and shrivel (there's no need to turn), 40 to 50 minutes. Tomatoes with seeds take a little longer. Let cool on the pan a bit, then slip the skins off.

OVEN-ROASTED CANNED PLUM TOMATOES An easy way to turn a convenience food into something special and far more useful: Instead of the fresh tomatoes, drain two 28- or 35-ounce cans plum tomatoes, reserving the juice for another use. Omit the salt. Proceed with the recipe.

OVEN-ROASTED EVERYDAY TOMATOES Works for heirloom, beefsteak, or hothouse tomatoes, especially when you want to improve imperfect ones: Core the tomatoes and halve them around the equator instead of lengthwise. Squeeze out the seeds (see page 257). Cut the largest pieces in half again and proceed with the recipe.

OVEN-DRIED TOMATOES Just like the dried tomatoes you can buy in the supermarket: Heat the oven to 225°F. Set a wire rack on top of each of 2 baking sheets (preferably rimmed). Don't season or brush the tomatoes with oil. Put them on the racks, cut side down. Put in the oven and forget about them for 2 hours. Rotate the sheet and check on the tomatoes. If you just want to intensify the tomato flavor and use them immediately, they're done when still soft but somewhat shriveled, 2 to 3 hours total. If you want to keep them for a few days, they're done when they're shriveled and mostly dry, at least 4 hours total (wrap and refrigerate or freeze). If you want to keep them for weeks, they're done when they're dark, shriveled, and dry, 6 or more hours total (wrap and refrigerate, or store in a jar in the pantry).

Tomato Cobbler

MAKES: 6 to 8 servings
TIME: About 1 hour
M

There's nothing quite like a summertime tomato cobbler. The biscuit topping is quickly assembled in a food processor, and you serve it at room temperature, which makes this ideal for a potluck or entertaining.

Other vegetable you can use: tomatillos

	Oil or butter for the baking dish
3	**pounds fresh tomatoes (8–10 medium), cut into wedges**
2	**tablespoons cornstarch**
	Salt and pepper
1	**cup all-purpose flour, plus more if needed**
1	**cup cornmeal**
1½	**teaspoons baking powder**
¼	**teaspoon baking soda**
4	**tablespoons (½ stick) butter, cut into large pieces and very cold**
1	**egg, beaten**
¾	**cup buttermilk, plus more if needed**

1. Grease a 13 × 9-inch baking dish with the oil or butter. Heat the oven to 375°F.

2. Put the tomato wedges in a large bowl and sprinkle with the cornstarch and some salt and pepper. Toss gently to combine.

3. Put the flour, cornmeal, baking powder, and baking soda in a food processor along with a teaspoon salt. Add the butter and pulse a few times until the mixture looks like coarse bread crumbs. Add the egg and buttermilk and pulse a few times more, until the mixture comes together in a ball. If the mixture doesn't come together, add a spoonful or 2 more flour. If the mixture is too dry, add a few more drops buttermilk.

4. Gently toss the tomato mixture again and spread it in the bottom of the prepared baking dish. Drop spoonfuls of the dough on top and smooth a bit with a knife. Try to leave some gaps so the steam from the tomato mixture will have a place to escape as the cobbler bakes. Bake until golden on top and bubbly underneath, 45 to 50 minutes. Cool to just barely warm or room temperature. To serve, scoop portions out with a large spoon.

Stuffed Tomatoes

MAKES: 4 to 6 servings
TIME: 50 minutes with cooked rice
Ⓜ

A simple and delicious dish in which raw tomatoes are stuffed and roasted in a hot oven to maximize caramelization. The tomatoes can be prepared for stuffing in two ways: by slicing off a "lid" to create a container out of the whole tomato or by halving the tomato, scraping out the insides, and stuffing each half (best for large tomatoes or to serve as an appetizer).

Other vegetables you can use: any vegetable that can be hollowed out can be stuffed; the best are mushrooms, small eggplant, zucchini, onions, winter squash, bell peppers

> 4–6 firm fresh tomatoes (about 12 ounces each)
> 1 cup cooked white (page 367), brown (page 367), or wild rice (page 418), or any cooked grain
> 1 cup grated Gruyère, Asiago, manchego, Monterey Jack, or mozzarella cheese
> 1 tablespoon minced garlic
> Salt and pepper
> ½ cup olive oil
> Chopped fresh parsley or basil for garnish

1. Heat the oven to 450°F. Cut a ¼-inch slice from the smooth (flower) end of each tomato (the stem end is typically flatter and makes for a more stable base). Reserve these slices. Use a spoon to scoop out the insides of the tomatoes, leaving a wall about ¼ inch thick. Discard the woody core and seeds and chop the pulp; mix it with the rice, cheese, garlic, and some salt and pepper.

2. Sprinkle the insides of the tomatoes with salt and pepper, stuff them with the rice mixture, and replace the top slices. Spread half the oil in a shallow roasting pan that will allow for a little room between the tomatoes and put them in the pan. Sprinkle all with salt and pepper.

3. Bake the tomatoes for 30 to 40 minutes, until they are shriveled and the stuffing is hot. Test by inserting a metal skewer into the center, removing it, and putting the skewer on your wrist or lip; if it's warm, the stuffing is hot. Serve hot, warm, or at room temperature, drizzled with the remaining oil and garnished with parsley.

BELL PEPPERS STUFFED WITH QUINOA AND GOAT CHEESE Replace the tomatoes with red or green bell peppers, cutting the stem out of the cap and carefully removing the seeds and ribs inside. Use cooked quinoa and goat cheese; mix the herbs into the stuffing if you like.

COUSCOUS-STUFFED TOMATOES WITH HARISSA AND OLIVES Replace the rice with cooked couscous. Omit the cheese. Add ¼ cup chopped tomatoes, 1 tablespoon chopped pitted olives, and 1 tablespoon Harissa (page 665) to the filling. Garnish with parsley. Ⓥ

TURNIPS AND RUTABAGAS

The most common turnips are white and purple on the exterior and solid white inside. Their flavor is mildly cabbagelike (not surprising, since they're in that family) and often a bit sweet. Rutabagas (also called swedes) are usually bigger, with a dark yellow and purple exterior and bright to pale yellow flesh; they can be as large as a cantaloupe, and have a stronger flavor. Other varieties, like Tokyo turnips, may be white throughout. All turnips can be treated pretty much the same.

BUYING AND STORING Look for firm specimens that seem heavy for their size; very large turnips and rutabagas may be woody and have a stronger flavor than small ones. If the greens are attached, they should be fresh looking with no yellowing. Rutabagas are often coated with a thick wax to keep them from drying out. Store wrapped loosely in plastic in the refrigerator; they will keep for weeks.

PREPARING Peel and leave whole (if small enough) or slice or chop as you like; rutabagas must be peeled with a paring knife because of their wax coating.

BEST COOKING METHODS Boiling, braising and glazing

WHEN IS IT DONE? When tender or very soft

OTHER VEGETABLES YOU CAN USE Turnips and rutabagas are interchangeable; parsnips, carrots, radishes, kohlrabi

Braised and Glazed Turnips or Other Root Vegetable

MAKES: 4 servings
TIME: 30 minutes
F O

A basic and valuable technique. Feel free to jazz this up with a few sprigs fresh thyme, a teaspoon curry powder or other spice mix, or simply a couple cloves of garlic.

Other vegetables you can use: anything hard and fibrous, really, alone or in combination: carrots, beets, jícama, parsnips, celeriac, carrots, radishes, rutabagas, waxy potatoes, but not vegetables that easily become mushy, like starchy potatoes and sweet potatoes

 2 **tablespoons olive oil or butter**
 1 **pound turnips or other root vegetable, peeled and cut into chunks**
 ½ **cup or more vegetable stock (pages 97–100), white wine, or water**
  Salt and pepper
  Fresh lemon juice (optional)
  Chopped fresh parsley for garnish

1. Combine the oil, turnips, and stock in a medium saucepan, sprinkle with salt and pepper, and bring to a boil. Cover and adjust the heat so the mixture simmers; cook until the turnips are tender, 15 to 20 minutes, checking once or twice and adding more liquid as needed.
2. Uncover and raise the heat to boil off almost all the liquid, so that the turnips become glazed in the combination of oil and pan juices; this will take 5 to 10 minutes. Taste and adjust the seasoning, add a little lemon juice if you like, garnish with parsley, and serve.

WINTER SQUASH

These squash have tough skins, often unwieldy shapes and sizes, hard and vibrantly colored flesh (yellow to orange to almost red), edible seeds, and a delightfully creamy texture when cooked. There are many varieties, but the most common are butternut, acorn, pumpkin, spaghetti (which is handled a little differently than the others; see page 266), delicata, kabocha, Hubbard, and calabaza. You'll see many more types, particularly at farmers' markets.

Delicata is among the sweetest, and because its skin is edible, requires no peeling; it's the reigning darling of the winter squash family, and rightfully so. Kabocha, similar in size and shape to acorn squash, is also increasingly popular—and available—because of its flavor and edible skin. Among the others, butternut is by far the easiest to peel and cut. But even with butternut, you will waste some of the flesh when peeling; my preference, when appropriate, is to bake or steam squash whole or halved lengthwise, then scoop the flesh away from the peel afterwards.

BUYING AND STORING Winter squash should be firm and heavy; avoid any with soft spots, cracks, or punctures. Store in a cool, dry place (not in the fridge) and use when you can, though often they'll keep for months.

PREPARING Peel with a very sturdy vegetable peeler (I've broken more than a few when peeling winter squash) or a sharp, strong paring knife for butternut and other smooth-skinned varieties. For tougher ridged squashes, set the squash on its flat end or cut off an end to create a flat, stable bottom. Use a sharp knife (the larger the squash, the larger the knife) to cut off slices of the skin starting from the top where the vegetable starts to curve and slice down to the cutting board; cut off strips around the entire vegetable and then chop off the unpeeled ends. Again, you'll waste a lot, but unless you steam or roast the squash whole or halved, there is no way around this.

Use a cleaver or very large, heavy knife to split the

squash in half. Scoop out the seeds and stringy fibers. Discard or roast the seeds (see page 268).

BEST COOKING METHODS Steaming, braising, braising and glazing, roasting

WHEN IS IT DONE? Panfrying or roasting: When very tender and nicely browned; boiling: tender but not waterlogged

OTHER VEGETABLES YOU CAN USE Sweet potato, yam, carrot, waxy potato

Winter Squash, Braised and Glazed

MAKES: 4 servings
TIME: 45 minutes
V

This may become your go-to recipe for winter squash; it will work with any variety. The main recipe, variations, and list of flavorings will get you started, but you'll come up with your own ideas in no time.

Other vegetables you can use: any winter squash except spaghetti, though they will all be more difficult to cut and peel

- 2 tablespoons olive oil
- 1 tablespoon minced garlic
- 1½ pounds butternut or other winter squash, peeled and cut into ½- to 1-inch cubes
- ¼ cup vegetable stock (pages 97–100) or water
  Salt and pepper
  Chopped fresh parsley for garnish

1. Put the oil and garlic in a large, deep skillet over medium heat. When the garlic begins to color, add the squash and stock and sprinkle with salt and pepper. Bring to a boil, cover, and turn the heat down to low. Cook, stirring once or twice, until the squash is tender, about 15 minutes.

2. Uncover the pan and raise the heat to medium-high. Cook, shaking the pan occasionally and stirring less often, until all the liquid is evaporated and the squash has begun to brown, 5 to 10 minutes. Turn the heat back down to low and cook until the squash is as browned and crisp as you like. Taste and adjust the seasoning, garnish with parsley, and serve.

WINTER SQUASH WITH SOY Rich tasting and deeply colored: Use 1 tablespoon minced fresh ginger instead of the garlic, or along with it. Instead of vegetable stock, use 2 tablespoons each soy sauce and water. Garnish with thinly sliced scallions and sesame seeds instead of parsley if you like.

WINTER SQUASH WITH PESTO A terrific dish to toss with pasta: Omit the garlic if you prefer. Increase the stock to ½ cup. In Step 2, when you uncover the pan, stir in ½ cup Pesto (page 634).

WINTER SQUASH WITH COCONUT MILK AND CURRY A saucy dish, perfect with basmati rice: Use 3 tablespoons good-quality vegetable oil instead of the olive oil. Replace the stock with 1 cup coconut milk. In Step 1, add 1 tablespoon minced fresh ginger and 2 tablespoons curry powder with the garlic. Garnish with cilantro instead of parsley if you like.

6 Simple Ways to Flavor Winter Squash, Braised and Glazed

Increase the oil in the basic recipe to 3 tablespoons and stir in any of the following when you uncover the pan in Step 2:

1. ½ cup chopped pitted black olives
2. ½ cup minced fresh herbs like mint, chervil, or basil
3. 1 tablespoon minced fresh herbs like rosemary, oregano, sage, tarragon, or thyme
4. ½ cup chopped nuts (any kind, including coconut)
5. ¼ cup miso
6. Use butter instead of oil and add 2 tablespoons honey or maple syrup, and a pinch cayenne if you like

Roasted Squash Pieces
in the Shell (page 266)

Whole Winter Squash, Roasted

MAKES: variable, depending on the size of the squash
TIME: 1 to 2 hours, again depending size, completely unattended
Ⓜ Ⓥ

Oven roasting is the easiest way to cook any winter squash and extract the flesh, and spares you the daunting task of cutting up a raw squash.

With both methods, the resulting squash will be soft and silky, perfect for purées, soups, or desserts. You can use any quantity or weight of squash; you're only limited by the size of your oven. Expect each pound to yield about a cup of mashed squash or about 1½ cups spaghetti squash strands.

Other vegetables you can use: eggplant, but it will take a lot less time

   **1   or more whole winter squash
        (1–5 pounds)**

1. Heat the oven to 375°F. Rinse the squash. Use a sharp, strong thin-bladed knife, ice pick, or long-tined fork to poke several holes in the top of the squash around the stem.
2. Put the squash on a rimmed baking sheet or shallow roasting pan. Roast, undisturbed, for at least 30 minutes. When the sides start to soften and collapse, move it around or turn it over to promote even cooking. Continue roasting until deeply colored and quite soft. Small squash will take 45 minutes or so, large ones up to 2 hours.
3. Remove the squash from the oven and set it aside to cool almost completely before handling. Cut in half and scoop out the seeds and stringy fiber. Scoop out the flesh, or in the case of spaghetti squash, take a fork and rake it from the bottom up of each half; the flesh will separate into strands. Use immediately or store, tightly covered, in the refrigerator for several days or in the freezer for several months.

ROASTED SQUASH PIECES IN THE SHELL Slightly faster, with most of your time spent preparing the squash: Heat the oven to 400°F. Cover a rimmed baking sheet or shallow roasting pan with foil. Cut the squash as directed on page 263 and seed them if you like (actually, it's easier to remove the seeds once the squash is cooked—plus you get toasted seeds to snack on). You should be left with squash halves or large pieces. Put the squash in the pan, cut side down, and roast until it's starting to get tender, 20 to 30 minutes, depending on the variety. Turn the pieces over and roast until done, another 20 minutes or so. Cool a bit, then scrape out the seeds if you've left them in and scoop out the flesh.

Stuffed Winter Squash with Quinoa, Corn, and Tomatoes

MAKES: 4 servings
TIME: 60 to 75 minutes, mostly unattended
Ⓜ Ⓥ

Acorn squash seems to get all the attention when it comes to stuffing, but there are other varieties that take well to this treatment, including kabocha and small spaghetti squash and pumpkins. Select squash that are 1 to 2 pounds; the smallest spaghetti squash are around 2 pounds. When cutting the squash in half, do it through the equator or the stem, whichever makes more sense for the shape of that particular variety. The squash halves are partially baked, then stuffed and finished to keep the filling from drying out.

**2 or 4   winter squash (depending on
           the variety)**
     **2   tablespoons extra virgin olive oil,
           plus more for brushing and drizzling
           Salt and pepper**
     ¾   cup quinoa
     1   cup chopped cherry or grape tomatoes
     1   cup fresh corn kernels
     2   tablespoons chopped fresh parsley
     2   cloves garlic, minced

1. Heat the oven to 375°F. Cut the squash in half. If necessary, take a thin slice off the uncut side so the squash half sits on the counter without rocking. Remove the seeds and stringy fibers. Brush the interior and cut sides with oil (for varieties with edible skin, also brush the skin) and sprinkle with salt and pepper. Put the squash halves cut side down on a baking sheet and roast for 25 minutes.

2. While the squash is in the oven, put the quinoa in a medium saucepan with 1½ cups water, bring to a boil, reduce the heat to medium, and simmer until the water is just below the surface of the quinoa. Turn the heat off, cover, and let stand until the remaining water is absorbed, 5 to 10 minutes. Stir in the tomatoes, corn, parsley, garlic, 2 tablespoons olive oil, and salt and pepper to taste.

3. After 25 minutes, remove the squash from the oven and turn them cut side up. Divide the stuffing among the squash halves and return to the oven to roast until the squash is fork tender, another 20 to 30 minutes. Serve the stuffed squash drizzled with a little extra olive oil, if you like.

Spaghetti Squash with Fast Tomato Sauce

MAKES: 4 servings
TIME: 75 to 80 minutes, mostly unattended
Ⓜ Ⓞ

A gluten-free alternative to pasta. Cut the squash in half at the equator instead of lengthwise, as is often instructed; the strands wrap around the squash from side to side, not top to bottom, so if you cut it through the middle, you'll end up with longer strands. Make the tomato sauce while the squash is roasting, or earlier in the day or the day before and gently reheat it; add the basil right before serving. The squash can also be roasted the day before and the strands removed. To reheat, microwave on high for 60 seconds or as needed, until piping hot. This also makes a fantastic side dish.

　1　3½- to 4-pound spaghetti squash
　　Olive oil for brushing

Salt and pepper
Fast Tomato Sauce (page 312)
Freshly grated Parmesan cheese for serving (optional)

1. Heat the oven to 400°F. Cut the squash in half through the equator. Use a soup spoon to remove the seeds. Brush the cut sides and interior with oil and sprinkle with salt and pepper.

2. Put the squash on a baking sheet and roast until the interior flesh is fork tender, 45 to 60 minutes; start checking for doneness at 30 minutes. Transfer to a plate. The squash will stay hot in their skin for 10 to 15 minutes.

3. If you have not yet made the tomato sauce, make it while the squash is in the oven. Bring it to a very gentle simmer.

4. Scrape a fork over the interior of the squash from bottom to top to remove the flesh from the skin and tease it apart into long strands. Put in a large serving bowl and toss with the hot tomato sauce to evenly coat the strands. Taste for salt and pepper. Serve hot, with Parmesan if you like.

SPAGHETTI SQUASH WITH FAST TOMATO SAUCE AND CRUNCHY CRUMBLED TEMPEH Add 1 cup Crunchy Crumbled Tempeh (page 512) or more to taste to the simmering tomato sauce to heat through for about 5 minutes before tossing the sauce with the squash strands.

Crisp Squash Seeds

MAKES: 2 cups
TIME: 45 to 60 minutes, mostly unattended
Ⓜ Ⓞ

Don't throw the seeds away when you hollow out your Halloween jack o' lantern or, in fact, when you clean any winter squash. Baked in the oven until crisp, they are a delicious snack. You can omit the cayenne and cumin, if you like; the seeds are delicious seasoned just with salt.

2 cups (approximately) fresh pumpkin seeds
2 tablespoons good-quality vegetable oil
1 teaspoon salt, or to taste
1 teaspoon cayenne, or to taste
½ teaspoon ground cumin (optional)

1. Heat the oven to 350°F.

2. Separate the seeds from the stringy fibers by rinsing them in a bowlful of water. Discard the fibers and dry the seeds between paper towels.

3. Mix the oil, salt, cayenne, and the cumin if you're using it in a medium bowl. Add the seeds and toss until evenly coated. Pour the seeds onto a baking sheet and arrange in a single layer. Bake until the seeds are tan and crisp, 30 to 45 minutes, tossing occasionally. Cool and store in an airtight container at room temperature for up to a week.

MICROWAVE PUMPKIN SEEDS Spread the spice-coated seeds between 2 layers of paper towels and microwave on high until the seeds are tan and crisp, 10 to 15 minutes, stirring every 5 minutes. They will crisp up further as they cool.

THE BASICS OF PREPARING AND COOKING FRUIT

Most of us eat fruit out of hand most of the time, but once you get used to the idea of cooking fruit—and seasoning it in ways both sweet and savory—you have significantly more options.

Fruits are slightly more forgiving than vegetables when it comes to overcooking, but the flesh goes from perfect to mush much faster. That makes slow cooking like poaching, stewing, or roasting most appealing for times you want to walk away from the stove. High-heat methods like grilling and sautéing require more attention because fruits are naturally high in sugars and will burn more easily. So cook fruits at a slightly lower temperature than you would vegetables and keep an eye on them, stirring and turning as necessary.

Firmness is the best way to predict how long a fruit will take to cook: The least fibrous fruits will cook fastest (bananas, strawberries, papaya, and raspberries), while firmer fruits (pineapple, apple, and even citrus) are far more durable.

Like vegetables, fruits will continue to cook as they cool down. So when in doubt, use a fork or a knife tip to judge tenderness and remove the fruit from the heat before it's completely tender. But really, the worst that can happen—provided you don't burn it—is that you'll wind up with a delicious fruit sauce.

Cooked fruit can be incorporated into all sorts of dishes, not just desserts: Think of halved fruit on the grill, and compotes and chutneys. None of these, even the most complex, take more than a few minutes to put together. You'll find many more fruit recipes in the Desserts chapter, as well as instructions for making fruit purées on page 271.

MACERATING

Macerating fruit is simply soaking it in liquid. Juicy fresh fruits like berries, citrus, and peaches often need only a sprinkle of sugar or salt to draw out their juices and create the macerating liquid, while others benefit from added liquid like simple syrup, fruit juice, wine, or brandy. The seasoning can be as simple as a sprinkle of spice, or more complex. Just don't limit yourself to cinnamon and sugar; vinegar, salt, herbs, and all sorts of spices work wonderfully with fruit.

Chop or slice large or medium fruit—small fruits can be left whole—and peel if the skin is tough or if you prefer it peeled. Mix together the fruit, the macerating liquid, and whatever seasonings you're using. Fresh fruits need an inch or so of the liquid, but dried fruits absorb liquid and should be covered by an inch or 2. Cover and set aside at room temperature, or in the refrigerator if your kitchen is warm, stirring every few hours.

Soft and juicy fresh fruits can take as little as 15 to 20 minutes to macerate; denser items, like apple or pineapple, can take 3 to 4 hours; dried fruits require 12 to 24 hours to soften fully. You want the fruit to be tender but not mushy.

Macerating berries

Use macerated fruit as a topping for pancakes, waffles, yogurt, or ice cream, as a filler for crêpes or blintzes, or as a garnish for grains, beans, tofu, tempeh or seitan dishes, and beverages. Or add it to sauces and dressings.

PURÉEING

Puréed fruit makes a light and delicious sauce. Both raw and cooked fruit can be turned into smooth, silky, flavorful purées, and are easy to prepare since nearly any fruit can be puréed. (For a recipe, see Fruit Sauce, Two Ways, page 722, which includes methods for raw and cooked fruit.) Obviously, you want to remove large pits, seeds, thick or tough skin, stems, and other inedible bits.

There are three good ways to purée fruit. The best is to use a blender; it's quick and makes a smooth if not velvety purée. (High-powered blenders are best at achieving super-smoothness.) The food processor is equally quick; it won't make a super-smooth purée with hard fruit like raw apples, but soft or cooked fruit becomes perfectly smooth. The third option is by hand; this works well only for cooked or very soft fruit, and it's more time consuming: Use a fork or potato masher to mash, or use a wooden spoon or the back of a ladle to press the fruit pulp through a fine-meshed strainer set over a bowl, and be sure to scrape the underside of the strainer to remove every last drop of puréed fruit.

For fruits that brown, like raw apples, pears, and bananas, always add a good squeeze or 2 of citrus juice to minimize browning.

Strawberries, raspberries, blackberries, seeded grapes, and other fruits with seeds that you can't easily remove beforehand should be strained after puréeing. So should fibrous fruits, like mangoes. Otherwise, strain as you think necessary to remove unwanted bits of flesh or skin.

POACHING

Pears, apples, pineapple, and quince are good choices, though cherries, grapes, peaches and nectarines, and plums can also all be poached successfully (see Poached Pears, page 718). Dried fruits are also wonderful when poached; see below. It's best to poach fruit in a liquid like seasoned juice, vinegar, or wine; water leaches out too much of the flavor.

Put the prepared fruit in just enough liquid to cover it. Keep the mixture just barely bubbling and cook, turning the fruit once or twice, until a toothpick or skewer barely pierces to the center. A pear might take 20 minutes or so, while cherries will be done in less than 10. Serve with the poaching liquid as is, like a soup, or boil the liquid until it reduces and thickens into a syrupy sauce. Poached fruit keeps well in the fridge for up to a week; cover it tightly so it doesn't absorb other flavors.

STEWING

This is the way to make compote and to cook fruit for jam, and so easy to do: Put cut fruit—either one kind or an assortment—into a saucepan or skillet. Add sugar or

Poaching Dried Fruit

When soaked, dried fruit slowly absorbs the liquid it's soaked in, becoming plump and tender and taking on the liquid's flavors at the same time. You can speed up this process and intensify the flavors by poaching dried fruit in seasoned liquid. The process is the same as for poaching fresh fruit (see Poached Pears, page 718), and the key is to stop before the fruit falls apart. Timing will vary depending on the type of fruit and how dry it was to begin with; usually it'll be in the range of 10 to 30 minutes. So keep an eye on it and be ready to pull the fruit from the pot—use a slotted spoon—as soon as its wrinkles begin to disappear. Then turn up the heat and reduce the poaching liquid until it's syrupy. Cool it a bit and use it as a sauce for the poached fruit, or simply return the poached dried fruit to the syrup for storage.

Refrigerated, poached dried fruit will keep for at least a week. Serve plain or topped with a spoonful of yogurt or sour cream—or if you're feeling indulgent, heavy cream. You can also use it to top cooked grains, cake, or ice cream, or in sauces or chutneys.

another sweetener as directed, cover the pan, and turn the heat to medium-low. Cook, stirring occasionally, until some of the juice is released and the fruit begins to soften, 5 to 20 minutes depending on the fruit. For recipes, see Fruit Compote (page 721) and Fruit Jam (page 722).

You can also "stew" fruit without any cooking at all. See "Macerating" (page 269).

SAUTÉING

Put oil or butter (figure 1 to 2 tablespoons per pound of fruit) in a deep, wide skillet over medium to medium-high heat. When the oil is hot—not smoking—or the butter melts, add the fruit and whatever flavorings you like. Stir or toss the fruit until it's soft and tender and nicely caramelized.

ROASTING OR BAKING

Roasting is one of my favorite ways to cook fruit, because it helps develop deep color and flavor. Just make sure to remove the fruit from the oven before it starts to burn, which can happen quickly. Heat the oven to between 325°F and 350°F, lower than you would for vegetables. Grease a rimmed baking sheet or shallow roasting pan with oil or butter or line it with parchment paper. Add the fruit in a single layer, taking care not to overcrowd it. Drizzle or brush with a little oil or melted butter and season, if you like. Roast, checking occasionally and turning as necessary, until tender and golden, 15 to 45 minutes depending on the density of the fruit. For recipes, see Baked Apples (page 718) or Roasted Figs with Mascarpone (page 720).

FRYING

You can either panfry fruit in shallow oil (½ inch or so) or deep-fry in enough oil to submerge it (2 or 3 inches oil in a deep pot). With few exceptions, fruit should be breaded or battered before deep-frying; the coating not only guards against overcooking but helps control splattering.

TO PANFRY Set a deep skillet over medium to medium-high heat and pour in the oil. It should be very hot but not smoking before you add the fruit. Test a small piece first; it should sizzle immediately and energetically. Add the fruit, working in batches if necessary to prevent crowding, and fry as directed in the particular recipe.

TO DEEP-FRY The oil should reach a temperature between 350° and 375°F (see "Deep-Frying," page 26). Be careful to allow enough room at the top of the pot for the fruit to displace the oil and cause it to rise. Add the fruit, working in batches if necessary to prevent crowding, and fry as directed in the particular recipe.

GRILLING OR BROILING

Grilling is one of the best ways to cook fruit. See the chart, opposite, for how to prep and grill different types of fruit.

Grilled or broiled fruit is great with a green salad, any cooked grain, and a variety of cheeses from fresh cheese, to a soft cheese like Brie, to a hard one like Parmesan. Sweet grilled fruit can be served with ice cream, sorbet, granita, rice pudding, or custard, or next to cake and other drier desserts. Pair it with cream cheese or mascarpone to make a grilled fruit pizza.

DRYING

Unless you have a dehydrator, oven-drying is the way to go. All you need is a baking sheet fitted with a wire rack. Small items like grapes, berries, and cherry tomatoes can be left whole. Medium-size fruits should be halved or sliced. Large and/or very hard fruit like papaya, pineapple, and coconut need to be peeled and sliced. Put the prepared fruit on the rack, cut side down if applicable, and put in a 225°F oven for anywhere from 2 to 12 hours. Rotate the baking sheet every couple of hours and check; the fruit is done when the pieces are as shriveled and dried as you like. Completely dried, brittle fruit can be stored almost indefinitely in an airtight container in your pantry; fruit that's still moist should be wrapped in plastic or put in a container and refrigerated, where it will keep for at least a few days, probably much longer.

Grilling Fruit

FRUIT	PREPARATION	HOW TO GRILL
Apple	Core and slice or cut into wedges; brush with lemon or lime juice and oil or melted butter.	Over a moderate fire, turning occasionally, until browned, 3–5 minutes.
Banana, plantain	Use yellow bananas or ones with just a touch of green; use yellow plantains with a touch of black. Do not peel; cut off ends; slice in half lengthwise; brush cut side with oil or melted butter.	Over a moderate fire, peel side down, until the peel starts to pull away from the flesh, 5–8 minutes. Turn cut side down and grill until browned, about 2 minutes.
Citrus (any)	Do not peel; cut in half along the equator.	Over a moderate fire, cut side up, until heated through, 5–10 minutes. Turn cut side down and brown 1–2 minutes; don't leave too long or the juices will evaporate.
Fig	Leave whole or cut in half; brush with oil or melted butter.	Over a moderate fire until soft, turning once, 5–10 minutes total.
Mango	Peel; cut large slices or wedges off the pit; brush with oil.	Over a moderate fire, turning occasionally, until browned, 3–5 minutes per side.
Melon	Peel or not; cut into wedges or 1½-inch cubes; skewer cubes. Oil is optional.	Over a moderate fire until browned in spots, 3–5 minutes per side.
Papaya	Peel, seed, and cut into wedges or 1½-inch cubes; skewer cubes; brush with oil.	Over a moderate fire, turning occasionally, until browned in spots, 3–5 minutes per side.
Peach, nectarine	Halve or quarter; brush with oil or melted butter.	Over a moderate fire until browned in spots, 7–8 minutes per side.
Pineapple	Peel, core, and cut into slices, wedges, or 1½-inch cubes; skewer cubes; brush with oil.	Over a moderate fire until deeply browned in spots, 4–8 minutes per side.
Plum	Halve or quarter (skewer if you like); brush with oil or melted butter.	Over a moderate fire until browned in spots, 5–8 minutes per side.

Apples, pineapples, coconut, and thin-skinned lemons, oranges, and limes can be thinly sliced and dried until crisp, like chips; use a mandoline for even slices, and squeeze lemon juice over the apple slices to prevent discoloring. Put the slices on a lightly oiled baking sheet, set your oven to the lowest setting (turning it off and on again if the slices begin to brown), and dry the fruit until completely crisp, 2 to 3 hours. Brush the slices with Simple Syrup (page 685) before drying for a sweeter result. Use fruit chips as a garnish on desserts or salads or just as a crunchy snack.

THE FRUIT LEXICON

Here is an alphabetical listing of fruits most commonly available in the United States

APPLES

There are thousands of varieties of apples in every shade of yellow, gold, red, and green, ranging from sweet to tart and mealy to crisp; more than 100 varieties are grown commercially. The U.S. produces over 250 million bushels a year, with Washington, New York, Michigan, and Pennsylvania, in that order, leading in commercial production. One very welcome development since the publication of the first edition of this book is that Americans are choosing flavor over some ideal of the perfect red apple. As a result, you can find many different varieties of apples in the produce section of most supermarkets, in contrast to the days when Red Delicious and McIntosh were king. For unusual heirloom varieties, I urge you to visit orchards in your own area, though even there these local strains are tough to find.

In general, apples are divided into three categories: eating, cooking, and all-purpose. The chart on page 276 lists the apples you are most likely to see in well-stocked supermarkets and their best uses.

BUYING AND STORING All apples should be firm and heavy for their size; avoid any with soft spots. Those that are less than perfectly firm are best suited for cooking. Store in a cool, dry place like a garage or basement, or in the refrigerator; some varieties will keep for weeks. Almost all apples in this country are harvested in the late summer and fall, but wholesalers keep the fruit in reduced-oxygen storage, where they remain in reasonably decent shape for months. But they deteriorate quickly once removed, so use apples quickly in winter and spring.

PREPARING Rinse and take a bite, or peel and cut. To peel, start at the stem or flower end and work in latitudinal strips or around the circumference; a U-shaped peeler is best.

To core, you have several options: You can remove the core and leave the apple whole by digging it out from the stem end with a melon baller and removing it; this leaves the blossom end intact, a nice presentation for baked apples. You can use a corer, which cuts all the way through. Or you can use a slicer-corer that cuts the apple into six or eight slices around the core in one swift motion. Finally, you can quarter the apple and cut out each piece of the core with a paring knife, melon baller, or spoon.

Apples brown quickly once peeled or cut; to prevent

Coring Apples

You can core an apple in several ways. For baked apples, use a melon baller and dig into the stem end, taking out a little at a time until the core has been removed.

For other uses, just cut the apple into quarters and remove the core with a melon baller, paring knife, or spoon.

this, drop them into acidulated water (one part lemon juice to about ten parts water) or white wine, or toss with lemon or lime juice.

BEST COOKING METHODS Baking, stewing, grilling, frying

OTHER FRUIT YOU CAN USE Pears

Applesauce

MAKES: About 2 quarts
TIME: About 1 hour, mostly unattended
Ⓜ Ⓥ

Most people think of applesauce as sweet, but I prefer a neutral approach that allows for savory seasonings. See the list that follows for some ideas.

A food mill is the easiest way to go and produces the best applesauce, because the peels lend both their flavor and color, and there's no need to do the up-front work: If you don't have one, you must core and peel the apples before cooking.

Make as much applesauce as your time and the size of your pot allow by doubling or tripling the quantity. Applesauce freezes well and is handy when packed in small containers.

Other fruits you can use: pear, peach, quince

    5   **pounds apples (preferably a mixture of varieties)**
        Salt

1. Cut the apples in half or, if they're very large, in quarters. If you don't have a food mill, peel and core them. Put about ½ inch water and a pinch salt in a large pot and add the apples. Cover and turn the heat to medium.
2. When the water begins to boil, uncover the pot. Cook, stirring occasionally and lowering the heat if the mixture threatens to burn on the bottom, until the apples break down and become mushy, at least 30 minutes. Let sit until cool enough to handle.

3. If you have a food mill, pass the mixture through it, discarding the solids that stay behind. If not, mash if you like with a fork or potato masher. Freeze or refrigerate.

PEEL-ON APPLESAUCE More fiber, and with red apples, you'll get a slight rosy color, too. Core the apples without peeling in Step 1, then cut them into 1- to 2-inch chunks. Proceed with the recipe, mashing them as described in Step 3.

9 Flavorings for Applesauce

Just put any of the following ingredients into the pot along with the apples. Start with a teaspoon or so per 5 pounds apples, then taste and add a teaspoon at a time as needed.
1. Black pepper
2. Ground cumin, coriander, or caraway seeds
3. Minced fresh chile (like jalapeño or Thai), red chile flakes, or cayenne
4. Chipotle chiles, dried, or canned, with a little of the adobo sauce
5. Chopped fresh ginger (good with savory or sweet)
6. Roasted Garlic (page 205)
7. Any spice blend (to make your own, see pages 648 to 652)
8. Granulated or brown sugar
9. A little grating of nutmeg, or ground cloves or allspice

APRICOTS

Luxuriously sweet and tart with a silky skin, they have a fleshy, succulent interior. Perfectly ripe apricots are hard to find, even if you live where they're grown. Ripe apricots are extremely perishable, so they're picked well before they're ripe. They will ripen some after picking, but rarely develop into the delicious fruit they should be. You can find them that way in some summer farmers' markets.

I think dried apricots are the best dried fruit. Those without sulfur dioxide taste best; those with it have the best color and keep their tender texture longer.

(continued on page 278)

Apple Varieties

In general, apples are divided into three categories: eating, cooking, and all-purpose. This chart lists the most common and some not-so-common—but worth seeking out—varieties, with notes on flavor, texture, and category. But keep in mind that new (and rediscovered older, call them "heirloom") varieties are always coming on the market; plus there are regional varieties that you are likely only to find in farmers' markets. Always be open to trying them and experimenting with their best uses.

APPLE VARIETY	DESCRIPTION	FLAVOR AND TEXTURE	CATEGORY
Braeburn	Red with lighter flecks and a green tinge around the stem; yellow flesh	Sweet, slightly tangy, juicy, crisp	All-purpose
Cortland	Red with bright green patches; white flesh that doesn't turn brown quickly	Sweet, juicy, tender	All-purpose
Empire	Red with lighter flecks and yellowish green patches; cream-colored flesh	Sweet-tart, juicy, very crisp; can also be mushy	All-purpose
Fuji	Red with yellow and green mottling; cream-colored flesh	Sweet, juicy, fairly crisp	Eating
Gala	Red with gold mottling; light yellow flesh	Mild, sweet, crisp	Eating
Golden Delicious	Greenish-gold skin, sometimes with a blush of pink; light yellow flesh	Full-flavored, sweet-tart, juicy, crisp	All-purpose
Granny Smith	Green with light flecks; white flesh	Tart to sweet-tart, juicy, very crisp; holds shape well when cooked	All-purpose
Honeycrisp	Lovely scarlet skin over a yellow backdrop; creamy white flesh	Sweet-tart, juicy, and very crisp; holds shape well when cooked	All-purpose

APPLE VARIETY	DESCRIPTION	FLAVOR AND TEXTURE	CATEGORY
Ida Red	Large and brilliant red; light green flesh with a touch of pink	Sweet, juicy, firm; holds shape well when cooked	Cooking
Jonagold	Red with golden yellow flecks and green streaks; light yellow flesh	Very sweet, juicy, crisp; better than Golden Delicious but harder to find	All-purpose
Jonathan	Red with some bright yellow streaks; off-white flesh	Sweet-tart with a bit of spice, juicy, crisp; does not bake whole well	All-purpose
Macoun	A New England favorite, available late fall only. Red with green patches and mottling; white flesh	Very sweet, juicy, tender	Eating
McIntosh	Bright red with green patches; off-white flesh	Sweet and crisp when very fresh; becomes mushy quickly	All-purpose
Pink Lady	Rosy pink and golden yellow; white flesh that doesn't turn brown quickly	Sweet-tart, juicy, very crisp; lots of flavor	All-purpose
Red Delicious	The most common. Dark red; off-white flesh	Sweet but not complex, often mealy	Eating
Rome	Bright red and round; greenish flesh	Mildly tart, tender	Cooking

(continued from page 275)

BUYING AND STORING Ripe apricots should be deeply colored (even with a speckling of dark orange, almost brown), heavy, and fragrant, and should yield to gentle pressure. Leave unripe fruit at room temperature, in a paper bag if you want to hasten ripening. Store ripe fruit in the fridge for a day or 2, but eat as soon as possible.

Dried apricots should not be too leathery. When you find ones you like—at Middle Eastern and Asian markets—buy in bulk, as they'll keep for a year or more in a cool, dry place, though they do dry out eventually. Soak them if they become too tough.

PREPARING Tear or cut it in half and remove the pit. The kernel inside the pit (crack it like a nut) is similar to almonds and can be eaten, but must be roasted beforehand as it's poisonous raw. To peel apricots, plunge in boiling water for 10 seconds, then slip off the skin.

Dried apricots can be cooked or soaked in liquid to soften.

BEST COOKING METHODS Sautéing, stewing, grilling, baking

BANANAS AND PLANTAINS

Bananas and plantains are the fruits of tropical plants; botanically, they're considered berries. Bananas are usually enjoyed as is, no heat applied. Plantains are always cooked. When they are green, they are very starchy and can be used much like a potato; when ripe, they are sweet enough to be enjoyed as a dessert.

Both bananas and plantains are harvested while still green, and ripen off the plant. The longer they ripen, the softer and sweeter they become. Bananas are yellow when fully ripe, perhaps with some darker spots; as they darken to black, they are considered overripe—but perfect to mash and use in Banana Bread (page 581). When fully ripe, plantains are completely black, but still hold together when cooked.

BUYING AND STORING Bananas and plantains are sold at various stages of ripeness; plantains can take as

long as 2 weeks to ripen from fully green to fully black; bananas ripen within a week. Store at room temperature. Both can be stored in the refrigerator to slow further ripening for weeks; the skins may turn black, but the flesh remains the same.

PREPARING Peel and slice bananas as needed. Plantains require a special peeling technique: Cut off both tips, then cut the plantain into three sections. Make three vertical slits in the skin of each section; peel each piece of the skin off. Trim any remaining skin with a paring knife.

BEST COOKING METHODS Bananas are usually enjoyed raw, but can be sautéed or used in baking. For green plantains, sautéing, and frying. For ripe plantains: braising and stewing. But you can really cook either plantain any way.

WHEN ARE THEY DONE? Bananas are done when caramelized. Green plantains are ready when golden brown and slightly tender. Ripe plantains are done when caramelized and very soft.

OTHER FRUITS OR VEGETABLES YOU CAN USE There is no substitute for raw bananas; in cooking, for ripe bananas substitute ripe plantains. For plantains: When starchy and green, replace with potato, yuca, boniato, or taro; when sweeter and riper, with sweet potato or yam. Green to green-yellow bananas can often fill in for plantains in recipes, as long as they're not too ripe; they cook up similarly.

Sautéed Ripe Plantains

Plátanos Maduros
MAKES: 4 servings
TIME: 20 minutes
`F` `M` `V`

Sweet, but appropriately so. My kids went wild over these when they were young, and still do.

Other fruit you can use: just-ripe bananas (yellow but with only a few black spots)

3   or 4 yellow-black or black plantains, peeled
Good-quality vegetable oil
Salt and pepper
Lime wedges

1. Cut the plantains into 1-inch pieces on the diagonal. Put about ⅛ inch of oil in a large skillet over medium heat. When it's hot, add the plantains, without crowding them, and cook, turning as necessary and adjusting the heat so the plantains brown slowly without burning; you may need to do this in batches. Be especially careful as they near doneness; there is so much sugar in the plantains that they burn easily. The process will take 10 to 15 minutes.

2. Sprinkle with salt, pepper, and lime juice and serve hot.

Fried Plantain Chips

Tostones
MAKES: 4 servings
TIME: 30 minutes
F M V

Easy to make, and as good warm—or at room temperature, as long as they're made not too far in advance—as hot. To me, they need nothing more than salt and maybe a little lime, but some people like them with hot sauce, Chile Paste (page 664), or any salsa (pages 659 to 664).

2   green-yellow plantains or green bananas, peeled
Good-quality vegetable oil
Salt
Lime wedges

1. Cut the plantains into ½-inch rounds. Put about ⅛ inch of oil in a large skillet over medium heat. When it's hot, add the rounds and sprinkle with salt; you'll probably be able to do this in one batch. Brown lightly, about 5 minutes, then turn and brown the other side, another 5 minutes. Transfer the slices to a plate as they're browned. The plantains can be browned an hour

or 2 in advance. Let the oil cool and pour it out; wipe out the pan.

2. When the plantain rounds have cooled a bit, put them between 2 sheets of wax paper and pound with the side of your fist or the palm of your hand until they spread out and just about double in diameter; they will look squashed and might split a little around the edges, which is fine. This can be done an hour or 2 in advance.

3. Put ⅛ inch of fresh oil in the skillet, turn the heat to medium, and again brown the rounds on each side, 5 to 10 minutes total; this time you'll probably have to cook in batches. Serve hot or warm, sprinkled with salt and lime juice.

BERRIES

There are hundreds of types of berries around the world, and they range in color from white to blue to red, orange, yellow, or black. They can be sweet or tart and everything in between, and for the most part are quite perishable. Most are picked well before their prime, which is a problem: They sometimes wind up tasting like cardboard. But if they're shipped ripe, they rot by the time you buy them—another argument for buying and eating seasonally and locally.

BUYING AND STORING All berries should be fragrant, especially strawberries; deeply colored; and soft but not mushy. Eat them as soon as possible—in fact, eat them the day you buy them. Berries really should never be refrigerated, as the cold mutes their flavor. If you find a good deal at a farmstand, you can freeze a large amount of berries on a baking sheet, then transfer to bags to store over the winter.

PREPARING Don't rinse berries until you are about to eat them; it will hasten their deterioration. Because they're so fragile, I usually don't bother rinsing raspberries. To hull strawberries: Pull or cut off the leaves and use a paring knife to dig out the stem and core.

BEST COOKING METHODS Baking, stewing. Strawberries can also be roasted or grilled.

OTHER FRUITS YOU CAN USE Berries are fairly interchangeable when used raw, or use grapes; blueberries, blackberries, and raspberries can substitute for one another in cooked dishes.

CHERRIES

Two types: sweet and sour (tart). Sweet are best for eating raw; sour are too tart to eat raw and best enjoyed cooked. Most supermarket cherries are sweet, deep red, heart-shaped Bing cherries. Sour cherries are more often sold at farmers' markets; they are typically smaller, brighter red, and rounder than sweet varieties.

BUYING AND STORING Look for shiny, plump, firm specimens with fresh-looking green stems. Store wrapped loosely in plastic in the refrigerator; use as soon as possible; they won't last long.

PREPARING Wash and dry for eating out of hand; stem and pit for cooking. A cherry pitter (which also works for olives) is handy.

BEST COOKING METHODS Sautéing, stewing, baking

CRANBERRIES

Cranberries are bright red, round, and too hard and astringent to be eaten out of hand, so they are always cooked or combined with other ingredients. There are many species of cranberry (genus *Vaccinium*), including the Scandinavian lingonberry, but we rarely see any other than Early Black (small and dark red) and Howes (lighter red and more oblong than the Early Black).

BUYING AND STORING Most are sold in plastic bags in the fall and winter. Toss those that are off-color or shriveled. Store in the refrigerator for weeks or in the freezer indefinitely.

PREPARING Nothing to it: Pick over for stems, rinse, and, if necessary, dry.

BEST COOKING METHODS Baking, simmering

OTHER FRUITS YOU CAN USE Dried cranberries, sour or sweet cherries, fresh currants, blueberries

Cranberry Relish with Orange and Ginger

MAKES: About 4 cups
TIME: 10 minutes plus time to marry flavors
M **V**

Tart and complexly flavorful, this uncooked relish partners well with curries, stews, and roasted vegetables. When cranberries are in season, be sure to buy extra to throw in the freezer so you can make this all year long. Stir in ½ cup raisins, pomegranate seeds, and/or chopped walnuts or pecans at the end if you like.

- 1 large navel or other orange
- 4 cups fresh cranberries (about 1 pound), picked over and rinsed, or frozen cranberries, thawed
- ½ cup sugar, or more to taste
- 1 tablespoon minced fresh ginger, or to taste

1. Use a vegetable peeler or paring knife to remove the entire zest of the orange; set aside. Cut away and discard the thick white pith. Cut the orange segments away from their membranes (see page 292).

2. Combine the orange flesh, zest, cranberries, and sugar in a food processor. Process until chunky. Stir in the ginger. Taste and add more sugar if you like. You can serve it right away, but it's best if it sits for at least 30 minutes to allow the flavors to marry. It keeps, refrigerated, for a few days.

CRANBERRY SAUCE WITH ORANGE AND GINGER
Increase the sugar to 1½ cups. Put the cranberries, sugar, and 2 cups water in a medium saucepan over medium-low heat. Cover and cook, stirring occasionally, until the berries pop, the sugar has dissolved, and the sauce is simmering, 10 to 15 minutes. Remove from the heat. Mince the orange zest and add it and the orange flesh and the ginger. Cool to room temperature, then

refrigerate for up to a week. If you prefer your cranberry sauce without the flavor additions, omit the orange and ginger.

DATES

Fresh dates are in season from late summer to the middle of fall. They're sticky-sweet, tender, and juicy; look for them in Middle Eastern or farmers' markets.

Dried dates are intensely sweet and chewy, with a papery outer skin; they're available year-round, with or without the narrow pits. The best varieties are medjool; deglet noor and bread dates (*khadrawy*) are more common but less sweet. Dates work beautifully in both sweet and savory dishes.

BUYING AND STORING Fresh dates should be unblemished and quite moist; they are often sold on the stem. Store at room temperature; for longer storage, wrap loosely in plastic and store in the refrigerator.

Dried dates should be moist and tender; some varieties have a dull, dried-out-looking exterior and others a shiny, succulent appearance; avoid any that have sugar crystals or are stale, shriveled, and hard. Buy organic if you can. Store at room temperature if you're going to eat right away, or for up to 6 months in an airtight container in the fridge.

PREPARING Remove the pits by slicing the fruit lengthwise and pulling the seed out by the tip. Or just squeeze it out.

BEST COOKING METHODS For fresh: stewing, grilling; for dried: stewing, baking

FIGS

Fresh figs are usually available toward the end of summer. Fresh, ripe figs are supple, sweet, and wonderful. The delicate skin is soft, delicious, and easily damaged; the flesh is succulent, gorgeously white and pink, and loaded with tiny edible seeds. Figs range in color from deep purple to brown, reddish orange to green and yellow, and shapes can be round to pearlike. There are many varieties of figs, but we see only a few in fresh form: Black Mission figs and green Calimyrna are the most common.

Dried figs are even sweeter, meaty, and lovely as they are, macerated, or added to braises or stews. Dried are most often black and sometimes brown.

BUYING AND STORING Look for soft, undamaged fruit that's heavy for its size; oozing a bit of sugary syrup is almost a sure sign of perfect ripeness. Hard or dried-out figs will not ripen and are best macerated or poached. Fresh figs are very perishable and should be eaten as quickly as possible; store wrapped loosely in plastic or covered with a paper towel in the refrigerator for a day or 2 at most.

Dried figs should be moist and tender; they're a better deal when purchased in bulk than prepackaged. Store in a cool, dark, dry place.

PREPARING Wash and eat fresh ones.

Dried figs may be eaten, soaked, or cooked as any dried fruit.

BEST COOKING METHODS For fresh: grilling, roasting; for dried: macerating, stewing

GRAPEFRUIT

Two main types, white and red, are differentiated more by flesh color than skin. Red were once sweeter than white, but that's no longer really true.

Pomelo (or shaddock) and ugli fruit (aptly, if cruelly, named) are similar and may be treated like grapefruit.

BUYING AND STORING Look for specimens heavy for their size—the heavier, the juicier. Store in the refrigerator after a day or 2 at room temperature.

PREPARING Cut in half through its equator; use a grapefruit knife to cut the flesh from the skin and then along the sides of the segments to eat from the peel with a spoon. Or peel and separate the segments as you would an orange (see page 292); this is especially useful with smaller specimens.

BEST COOKING METHODS Broiling, grilling

GRAPES

A variety of grapes is usually offered in the late summer to early fall at farmers' markets, like the bluish-purple Concord and the golden green Muscat. Grapes are typically divided into two types: white (also called green) and black (often referred to as red). White grapes are green to greenish yellow in color; black grapes range in color from reddish to deep purple. Generally, table grapes are sweet with a bit of acid, and thin skinned. Americans eat mostly seedless grapes, but breeding out the seeds makes for less flavor.

BUYING AND STORING Ideally you want fresh-looking green stems with only some brown; the grapes should be plump, sweet, and flavorful—taste one.

PREPARING Pesticides are used heavily on grapes, so rinse them very well.

BEST COOKING METHODS Roasting, grilling, sautéing

GUAVAS

Tropical fruit whose skin can be rough and bitter or soft and sweet, depending on the variety. Flesh can be off-white or pink; usually the lighter the flesh, the tarter. Often eaten raw like an apple or sliced and sprinkled with salt or sugar.

BUYING AND STORING Unripe guavas are usually green, turning yellow or maroon when ripe. Look for unblemished fruit and the softest guava you can find; the softer, the sweeter. Underripe fruit can ripen at room temperature. Refrigerate wrapped loosely in plastic and use within a few days.

PREPARING Usually eaten raw

BEST COOKING METHODS Stewing, poaching; cooked into jelly because of its high level of pectin. Can replace tomatoes for a more tropical-flavored savory sauce, like barbecue sauce.

JACKFRUIT

Jackfruit is the largest fruit in the world to grow on trees; each weighs between 10 and 100 pounds. It's the national food of Bangladesh, and here in America it's gaining popularity as a vegan meat substitute, as its texture and taste when simmered and tossed with barbecue sauce are oddly similar to those of pulled pork. The portion of the fruit that is eaten are the seed pods.

When ripe, the flesh is soft and juicy, with a sweet flavor similar to a mango, and is best enjoyed raw; when unripe, it has a meaty, stringy quality. Raw unripe jackfruit is very tannic and must be cooked.

BUYING AND STORING Fresh jackfruit is not common in the United States, but try an Asian or Caribbean market; because the fruit is so big, you're likely to find it sold in hunks. It doesn't keep long, so use within a few days of purchasing; to store, cover with plastic wrap and refrigerate. Increasingly, you can find vacuum-packed jackfruit, and canned (packed in water or brine) is not bad.

PREPARING Rinse canned thoroughly if packed in syrup or brine. For fresh: Cut away the core. Use a paring knife to free individual seed pods from the peel; trim away any white strands, cut the pod open from top to bottom, and remove the pit inside, including its covering. The seeds can be eaten raw, or roasted or boiled like chestnuts (see page 303).

BEST METHODS FOR COOKING For unripe jackfruit: braising, stewing, sautéing.

OTHER FRUITS YOU CAN USE There is no real substitute for jackfruit.

BBQ Jackfruit Sandwiches

MAKES: 4 servings
TIME: 1 hour
Ⓜ Ⓥ

Simmered, then roasted, canned jackfruit tossed with barbecue sauce tastes remarkably like pulled pork. The two steps are key for the best flavor. Simmering softens the jackfruit, allowing you to break it into shreds. Roasting it with barbecue sauce results in caramelization that makes the jackfruit taste like it's come off the grill. Do not prepare this using jackfruit packed in syrup; if you do, you'll have a super-sweet, sticky mess. If you like, top your sandwich with a little coleslaw (page 42).

<table>
<tr><td>1</td><td>cup ketchup</td></tr>
<tr><td>¼</td><td>cup cider vinegar</td></tr>
<tr><td>¼</td><td>cup brown sugar</td></tr>
<tr><td>1</td><td>tablespoon soy sauce</td></tr>
<tr><td></td><td>Salt and pepper</td></tr>
<tr><td>2</td><td>15-ounce cans jackfruit in water or brine</td></tr>
<tr><td>2</td><td>tablespoons good-quality vegetable oil</td></tr>
<tr><td>½</td><td>cup minced onion</td></tr>
<tr><td>3</td><td>cloves garlic, minced</td></tr>
<tr><td>1</td><td>teaspoon smoked paprika</td></tr>
<tr><td>1</td><td>cup vegetable stock (pages 97–100)</td></tr>
<tr><td>4</td><td>ciabatta rolls</td></tr>
</table>

1. Whisk together the ketchup, vinegar, brown sugar, and soy sauce in a small saucepan. Bring to a simmer over medium heat, reduce the heat to low, and let gently bubble for 10 minutes to let the flavors develop. Taste and adjust the seasoning with salt and pepper. Remove from the heat. Continue with the recipe or cool the barbecue sauce, cover, and refrigerate for up to a week; reheat gently over medium-low heat.

2. Rinse and drain the jackfruit in a colander, pressing down to extract as much water as possible from it. Pat dry. Cut and discard the core and any seeds. Heat the oil in a medium saucepan over medium heat. When it's hot, add the onion and garlic and cook, stirring a few times, until softened, 4 to 5 minutes. Add the jackfruit, paprika, and salt and pepper to taste, and stir until well mixed. Add the stock, stir to combine, bring to a simmer, and let continue to simmer, stirring occasionally, until the jackfruit has softened and there is no liquid left in the pan, 10 to 15 minutes. Once it's tender, mash down on it with the back of a spoon or a potato masher to separate the jackfruit into pulled pork–like shreds.

3. While the jackfruit mixture is simmering, heat the oven to 400°F.

4. When the jackfruit is ready, add half the barbecue sauce to the pan and stir to coat well. Transfer the jackfruit to a baking sheet and spread into a single layer. Bake until the jackfruit caramelizes and crisps in places, 15 to 20 minutes.

5. Split the rolls; toast in the oven if you like. Divide the jackfruit among the rolls and serve with the remaining barbecue sauce on the side.

KIWIS

The kiwi's oval shape and fuzzy brown exterior belie its brilliant green and white flesh, stippled with tiny black edible seeds. It's soft, juicy, and sweet-tart when ripe, and more on the tart side when not quite ripe enough. There is also a sweeter yellow-fleshed variety with less fuzz. Kiwis make a nice addition to fruit salads or a garnish.

BUYING AND STORING Most will be fairly hard at supermarkets. Look for unshriveled, unblemished specimens without soft spots. Will ripen at room temperature. When ripe, store in the refrigerator.

PREPARING Peel and slice; cut in half and scoop out the flesh with a spoon.

BEST COOKING METHODS Eat raw.

KUMQUATS

Kumquats look like teeny oval oranges. The entire fruit is edible, but the skin is the best part, thin and sweet, while the flesh is heavily seeded and very tart.

BUYING AND STORING Most often available in winter, frequently still attached to the branch, in specialty or Asian markets. Buy firm, unblemished fruits; store in the refrigerator in a plastic bag.

PREPARING Wash, dry, and slice, chop, or quarter, removing the seeds, or use whole. You can peel them (which is easy) or just eat the skin.

BEST COOKING METHODS Poaching

LEMONS AND LIMES

The lemon is an essential fruit in European cooking, while the lime takes center stage in Asian and tropical cooking; I try to keep both in my kitchen at all times. Be sure to make use of the zest, as it brings the flavor of the fruit without the acid (the zest is only the yellow or green outer portion of the peel; the white pith underneath is bitter). Also keep an eye out for Meyer lemons and key limes—Meyer lemons have a unique floral and piney fragrance; they are a bit less acidic than regular lemons. Key limes are tiny and round and also have a more floral and less acidic flavor than regular limes.

BUYING AND STORING Buy plump specimens, heavy for their size, that yield to gentle pressure; very hard or lightweight fruit will be dry. Store in the refrigerator.

PREPARING Cut into halves, quarters, wedges, or slices and remove the pits (if any) with the point of a knife.

There are a few ways to zest citrus, depending on how you'll use it. A zester is a nifty tool with small sharp-edged holes that cuts off long, thin strips of zest; they are great for garnishing when whole, or can be minced. Another method is to use a vegetable peeler or paring knife to remove the peel in long ribbons. Unless you're really skilled with the knife or peeler, this technique inevitably brings part of the white pith with it; to do a perfect job you should lay the strips down on a cutting board and scrape the white part off with a paring knife, then slice or mince as you like. The third method is using a sharp rasp-type grater (like a Microplane),

which results in tiny flecks of zest that are nearly undetectable in dishes except for their flavor.

OTHER FRUITS YOU CAN USE No real substitute

Preserved Lemons

MAKES: 1 quart
TIME: 20 minutes, plus 2 weeks to cure
Ⓜ Ⓥ

Preserved lemons are a pickle used in North African and Middle Eastern cooking. Chopped up, they can be added to all sorts of pilafs and braised vegetable dishes like Mediterranean Bulgur Pilaf (page 408). Or you can make a refreshing drink by muddling a couple in the bottom of a glass, then filling the glass with ice and sparkling water. They keep in the fridge for months.

> About 3 pounds lemons, washed well and quartered lengthwise
> About ¾ cup kosher salt
> 1 1½-inch cinnamon stick
> 2 or 3 whole cloves
> 1 star anise
> 2 or 3 black peppercorns
> 2 cardamom pods
> 1 bay leaf

1. Fill a 1-quart canning jar with boiling water; soak its lid in boiling water too. Let the water sit while you cut the lemons, then dump the water out.

2. Sprinkle a ¼-inch-deep layer of salt across the bottom of the jar. Nestle a layer of lemon quarters into the bottom of the jar, sprinkle liberally with salt, then repeat, adding the spices as you go. Stop when the jar is about three-quarters full. Squeeze the remaining lemons into the jar—seeds and all—so that the fruit is completely submerged in the lemon juice–salt brine. If you don't have enough liquid, top the lemons off with freshly squeezed juice no later than the following day.

3. Set the jar out on a counter. Vigorously shake it once a day for 7 to 10 days—during this time it will start

to bubble a little. (You'll be surprised at the size of the cloves!)

4. Put the jar in the refrigerator and let the lemons continue to cure for another week before using. When they have cured, unscrew the lid; after a moment, they should smell sweet and citrusy—an ammonia smell means they've gone wrong somewhere along the line and have to be thrown away. The lemons will keep for at least 2 months in the refrigerator.

5. To use in stews, blanch the lemon quarters in unsalted boiling water for 10 seconds, just long enough to leach out a little of the salt. For salads or quick-cooked dishes, scrape the flesh away from the peel, discard the flesh, and blanch the peel in unsalted boiling water.

SHORT-CUT PRESERVED LEMONS If you need preserved lemons in a hurry, dice 2 lemons, removing any seeds. Put in a lidded container, sprinkle with 1 tablespoon each kosher salt and sugar, seal, and shake to combine. Let sit at room temperature for at least 3 hours before using, shaking again every hour or so. Refrigerate if not using right away, for up to a week.

LYCHEES

Lychees are 1½-inch-diameter oval fruits with a brilliant red to pinkish-tan scaly—sometimes prickly—inedible skin that protects the juicy white flesh and a shiny brown inedible seed. The texture is like a fleshy grape; the flavor sweet and one of a kind, akin to that of cherries. (Canned lychees in syrup are mostly just sugary sweet and not worth eating.) They are also available dried (sometimes called lychee nuts).

BUYING AND STORING Summer is peak lychee season; look for them in Asian and farmers' markets. The fruit should be heavy for its size, fragrant, and brightly colored, with flexible—not dried out or brittle—skin. Store wrapped loosely in plastic in the refrigerator; enjoy as soon as possible.

PREPARING Use the stem to break open the skin and gently peel it off; eat the fruit and spit out the seed.

BEST COOKING METHODS Poaching

MANGOES

There are hundreds of varieties of mangoes, ranging in weight from ½ to 1½ pounds; green to yellow, orange, or red; exceedingly tart to syrupy sweet. Both ripe and unripe mangoes are useful: unripe for chutney and pickling, and ripe for eating straight, making salsas and fruit salads, and cooking.

Peeling and Pitting a Mango, Version 1

STEP 1 There are two ways to get the meat out of a mango. The first way begins with peeling, using a vegetable peeler.

STEP 2 Then cut the mango in half, doing the best you can to cut around the pit.

STEP 3 Finally, chop the mango with a knife.

Supermarkets carry the most common yellow and red mangoes year-round, but you'll find a wider selection in Latin, Asian, and Indian markets (my favorite is the creamy Ataúlfo, which arrives here in early spring). In the United States, mangoes are grown in California, Florida, and Hawaii, but the majority are imported from Mexico and farther south.

BUYING AND STORING Color isn't as important as texture; the softer it is, the riper. Some varieties of mango will start to wrinkle a bit at the stem when perfectly ripe. Bought at any stage, however, a mango will ripen if left at room temperature; to hasten ripening, put it in a paper bag. Once ripe, store in the refrigerator.

PREPARING There are a few different ways to go about preparing a mango; how you do it will depend on your knife skills and your patience. (See the illustrations below.) The quick and messy way is to just peel off the skin—a small knife makes quick work of it—and attack. For a neater presentation, trim a piece off the bottom end. Stand the fruit on a cutting board, trim off the skin with a sharp paring knife, then slice the fruit from around the pit.

BEST COOKING METHODS Baking, grilling, sautéing

OTHER FRUITS YOU CAN USE Papaya, cantaloupe or other fleshy orange melon, orange

MELONS

Melons are divided into two categories: muskmelons and watermelons. Muskmelons have either netted skin like the cantaloupe, or smooth skin like the honeydew, and a hollow cavity with seeds; their flesh ranges in color from pinkish orange to lime green to nearly white. Watermelons have smooth skin in varying shades of green, solid or striated, and a watery, sugary sweet flesh that may or may not have seeds embedded throughout; seedless varieties are increasingly common. Their flesh can be the familiar pink or red or, less commonly, yellow, orange, or white.

BUYING AND STORING Selecting the right melon is part skill and part luck. Smell it; if it smells sweet and like a melon, that's a good start. Then shake it; loose seeds are a sign of ripeness for muskmelons; if you gently squeeze the end opposite the stem, it should yield slightly. For watermelons, slap the side and listen for a hollow sound. Eat a ripe melon right away or store it in the refrigerator. An underripe melon can be left at room temperature for a couple of days; how and if it ripens is to some extent a matter of luck.

Peeling and Pitting a Mango, Version 2

STEP 1 Begin by cutting the mango in half, doing the best you can to cut around the pit.

STEP 2 Score the flesh with a paring knife.

STEP 3 Turn the mango half inside out and slice off the flesh.

PREPARING Cut the melon in half and scrape out the seeds of muskmelons with a spoon; continue cutting it into quarters or slices. Use a paring knife to slice off the rind if you like. Watermelons can be served in wedges or slices as is. But if you want or need to seed them, cut into wedges and slice off the top or "heart" to reveal the row of seeds. Remove them with the tines of a fork. Then cut to the desired size.

A melon baller, as you might expect, works well for preparing melons. Or you can simply remove the rind and cut the flesh into pieces. Grated melon is perfect for yogurt sauces and raw salsas; just be sure to grate it over a bowl to save the juices.

Allow chilled melon to come to room temperature before serving; when it's cold, the flavors are muted. Try a squeeze of lemon or lime juice on melon—it adds flavor to an underripe melon and complements a ripe one. A sprinkle of salt is an interesting change of pace, as is a dash of ground chile, or some pepper and lime juice.

BEST COOKING METHOD Grilling

OTHER FRUITS YOU CAN USE Melons are interchangeable with each other; papaya, mango, (sometimes) cucumber, peaches

Grilled Watermelon Steak

MAKES: 4 to 6 servings
TIME: 30 minutes
F V

Grilled watermelon treated like a vegetable with savory seasonings is delicious. Most of the water cooks out, leaving behind a tasty little "steak" with wonderful texture. You can broil it too; just make sure the juices can drain free (not onto your oven floor) so it doesn't steam.

Serve this with a baked potato if you like and something with a little protein, like Grilled or Broiled Tofu (page 486) or Beer-Glazed Black Beans (page 440).

Other fruits or vegetables you can use: any melon, but you'll get smaller slices; any winter squash

1   **small watermelon**
¼   **cup olive oil**
1   **tablespoon chopped fresh rosemary**
    Salt and pepper
    Lemon wedges

1. Prepare a charcoal or gas grill or turn on the broiler for moderate heat; adjust the rack to about 4 inches from the heat source. Cut the watermelon lengthwise in halves or quarters, depending on the size of the melon. From each length, cut 2-inch-thick slices with the rind intact. Use a fork to remove as many seeds from the heart as you can without ruining the shape.
2. Mix the oil and rosemary and sprinkle with salt and pepper. Brush or rub the mixture all over the watermelon slices. Grill or broil for about 5 minutes on each side. The flesh should be lightly caramelized and dried out a bit. Serve with lemon wedges.

CHILE-RUBBED GRILLED WATERMELON STEAK Great as part of any Mexican-style meal: Instead of the rosemary, use 2 tablespoons chili powder. Proceed with the recipe, serving with lime wedges instead of the lemon if you like.

5 Additional Toppings for Grilled Watermelon Steak

Use in place of, or along with, the rosemary:
1. ½ cup crumbled feta or blue cheese
2. ¼ cup chopped fresh basil or mint
3. 1 sliced fresh chile (like jalapeño or Thai)
4. ¼ cup honey mixed with ½ teaspoon cayenne; brush on shortly before removing from the grill
5. ¼ cup chopped black olives

OLIVES

The olive—the fruit, its oil, and the tree itself—has been enormously important to the development of cuisine and even civilization. Originally from the Mediterranean, which is still the world's major producer, olives are now grown in California, Arizona, New Mexico, and much of the rest of the world.

Olives are green when unripe, and darken (eventually turning black) as they ripen. Most olives are picked green for curing; those intended for olive oil are allowed to ripen further; and some are left on the tree until quite dark. The black olives we see in markets either have been turned black by the curing process or are fully ripe olives. Curing olives is essential to making them edible; they contain an extremely bitter-tasting chemical called oleuropein, which is minimized or eliminated by the curing process.

These are the olives most commonly found in markets:

- **Black or Mission** Most often pitted and canned—and tasteless
- **Castelvetrano** Bright green, buttery, mellow, and a little sweet; increasingly popular, and rightly so
- **Kalamata** Usually pretty salty and on the bitter side; dark brown, purple, or black
- **Manzanilla or Spanish** Big, green, rather crisp, and often stuffed with pimientos or garlic cloves
- **Niçoise** Dark red or brown, small but plump, with a slightly sour flavor
- **Oil- or dry-cured** Shriveled, shiny, and jet black; quite bitter, deliciously so
- **Picholine** From France; green, almond-shaped, and crisp

BUYING AND STORING Loose olives should be firm and not dried out (unless oil- or dry-cured, in which case they are shriveled). Taste one before buying, if you can. When ladling out the olives, keep in mind that you're most likely paying by the pound, and any liquid that you include is added weight; however, olives keep longer in liquid. Best policy: Buy only as much as you'll use in a few days. Store in the refrigerator in an airtight container; those in liquid will last weeks if not months. You can also prolong their keeping qualities by covering drained olives in oil; season that oil with herbs, garlic, chiles, and/or citrus rind, and you'll improve their flavor.

PREPARING Remove the pit by slicing the flesh lengthwise and digging it out with your fingers, by crushing it with the side of a knife and picking out the pit, or by using a pitter. It's also totally acceptable to leave the pit in if cooking with olives; just warn the diners. If you like, you can reduce the saltiness of olives by rinsing or soaking them in water for 20 minutes or so, or boiling them for 30 seconds.

BEST COOKING METHODS Grilling, roasting, sautéing

OTHER VEGETABLES YOU CAN USE Caper berries, capers

Tapenade

MAKES: About 1½ cups
TIME: 20 minutes
F M V

A delight from southern France, tapenade was made for spreading on toast, but it's also useful as a sandwich spread, a dip, or—if used sparingly and thinned with olive oil or even water—a sauce.

Good oil-cured olives are best for tapenade as they make a dark, rich paste, but any other kind of flavorful olive will also work well.

> About 1 pound flavorful black olives
> ¼ cup capers, rinsed and drained
> 2 cloves garlic, lightly crushed, or more to taste
> About ½ cup olive oil
> Pepper
> Chopped fresh parsley for garnish (optional)

1. Pit the olives. If you're using oil-cured olives, you can simply squeeze out the pit; with brined olives, you might have to flatten the olive with the side of a knife, which will split it and allow you to remove the pit.
2. Put the olives, capers, and garlic in a food processor or blender, along with about ¼ cup oil. Pulse the machine once or twice. Then, a bit at a time, add enough of the remaining oil (you may not need it all) to make a spreadable and pasty consistency, pulsing after each

addition. Don't keep the machine running; you want a coarse, chunky, uneven blend, as if you had made it with a mortar and pestle (the traditional way).

3. Stir in pepper to taste, then garnish with parsley if you like and serve. Or cover and refrigerate for up to a month.

ORANGES AND TANGERINES

There are three common types of orange: sweet (like the Valencia, navel, or temple); loose-skinned (Mandarin or tangerine); and bitter (Seville). Sweet and loose-skinned oranges are used for eating and juicing, while bitter ones are used only for making marmalades and other cooked products; we don't see them fresh too often in the United States. The outer orange-colored skin (that is, the zest) and interior flesh are edible, while the white pith inside the skin is bitter.

Mandarin oranges are simply a smaller and looser-skinned type of orange. Clementine, Satsuma, and the tangerine are all varieties of Mandarins; they are sweet-tart in flavor and are perfect for eating out of hand. Blood oranges originated as a natural mutation of sweet oranges and, true to their name, have striking red flesh and a sweet-tart juice; most all blood oranges sold in the U.S. (their season is December through April) are imported from Italy.

BUYING AND STORING Oranges are available year-round, although the best are found in fall and winter; tangerines' season is briefer, from late fall through winter. Sweet and bitter oranges should be heavy for their size and yield to gentle pressure but have no soft spots. The color of the skin varies by type, but some "russeting" (brown flecks) or "regreening" (green patches) is perfectly fine. Mandarin oranges should be heavy for their size and without any unusually soft spots, though in general they feel softer than sweet oranges. Oranges generally keep well at room temperature for up to a week; for storage longer than that, refrigerate them in a plastic bag.

PREPARING Sweet oranges are easiest to eat when cut into eighths rather than quarters. To peel, cut four longitudinal slits from pole to pole, through the skin but not into the flesh. Peel each skin segment off. Mandarin oranges can be peeled using your fingers without any difficulty. See the illustrations below for other prep.

BEST COOKING METHODS Baking, grilling, roasting, sautéing

OTHER FRUITS YOU CAN USE Sweet and Mandarin oranges are interchangeable; lemon or lime juice can replace the acidic flavor of bitter oranges

Preparing Citrus Fruits

STEP 1 You can remove citrus zest with a zester, which you just pull across the skin as you would a vegetable peeler.

STEP 2 Before beginning to peel and segment citrus, cut a slice off both ends of the fruit so that it stands straight.

STEP 3 Cut as close to the pulp as possible, removing the peel and pith in long strips.

STEP 4 Cut across any peeled citrus fruit to make wheels.

STEP 5 Or cut between the membranes to separate segments (called "sectioning" or "supreming"), leaving the membrane behind.

PAPAYAS

A tropical fruit that can grow as large as 20 pounds, though most are in the 1- to 2-pound range. Unripe papayas are hard, tart, and solid green; ripe ones have yellow or orange skin, yield to gentle pressure, and are aromatic. When ripe the flesh is soft, melonlike, and deep orange, and the edible seeds are a shiny greenish gray. Papaya is eaten both green and ripe, ideally with a sprinkle of lime.

BUYING AND STORING Available—and good—year-round, especially in Asian and Latin markets. Ripen harder specimens at room temperature. Once ripe, store in the refrigerator in a plastic bag.

PREPARING Wash, peel, cut in half, and scoop out the seeds. Then slice or chop the flesh.

BEST COOKING METHODS Roasting, grilling

PASSION FRUIT

An egg-shaped tropical fruit with purplish-brown skin, it has brightly colored yellow-orange pulp filled with dozens of edible seeds. The flavor is quite tart—almost too tart to eat straight—and the fragrance is wonderful.

BUYING AND STORING Look for deeply colored fruit that's firm and heavy for its size. Ripe passion fruit will have a dimpled or slightly shriveled exterior. When ripe, store in the refrigerator.

PREPARING Cut in half and scoop out the flesh with a spoon. To use just the juice, strain to separate out the seeds; press the pulp to extract as much of the juice as possible.

BEST COOKING METHODS Enjoy raw.

PEACHES AND NECTARINES

Closely related stone fruits, nearly identical in shape and color, but peach skin has soft fuzz and nectarine skin is smooth. The flesh is succulent and juicy. Variations in color don't matter much. There are two broad categories based on how much the flesh clings to the pit: freestone and clingstone. Both are good; freestones are easier to cut up.

BUYING AND STORING Look for plump, gently yielding, fragrant specimens without bruises. Tree-ripened fruit are best, but they do ripen at room temperature—quickly, so keep an eye on them. Put hard fruit in a paper bag to hasten ripening or just ripen on the counter. Don't buy too many at once unless you're planning to cook them; they usually all ripen at the same time.

PREPARING Wash, peel if you like, and eat. To pit, cut in half from pole to pole; twist the halves, which will either come completely free of the pit (freestone) or leave a fair amount of flesh on the pit (clingstone). To peel, drop into boiling water for 10 to 30 seconds, just until the skin loosens; shock in ice water; remove the peel with your fingers and/or a paring knife.

BEST COOKING METHODS Grilling, roasting, sautéing, baking

PEARS

Pears are one of the few fruits that improve after being picked; their flesh sweetens and softens to an almost buttery texture. But eating a perfectly ripe pear can be tricky: their peak is fleeting, so we often end up either with a crunchy fruit with little flavor or a mushy one with no texture.

You're likely to find dozens of varieties beyond the usual Anjou and Bartlett at local farmers' markets and orchards. Here are the most common varieties:

- **Anjou** Green and red types with a broad oval shape; firm flesh (good for poaching); sweet, but not spectacular
- **Asian** Round, apple-shaped with a yellow to russet-gold skin; the flesh is crisp—and is best that way, which is unusual for a pear—and juicy; a delicate apple-pear flavor

- **Bartlett** The most common variety and the only one used for commercial canning and drying. Bell-shaped; green when unripe, yellow with a red blush when ripe, with soft, sweet, and juicy flesh; rarely impressive
- **Bosc** Somewhat tear-shaped with an elongated neck; golden-brown russet skin with a juicy, crisp flesh similar to Anjou but more aromatic. At its best, spectacular, and certainly the best commonly available variety
- **Comice** Squat shape with a stubby neck and stem; green with a bronze blush; very sweet, juicy, soft flesh. Wonderful fragrance—probably the best widely available pear
- **Packham** Imported in winter from the Southern Hemisphere; fat, round, and a bit irregular in shape; green to greenish yellow in color; fairly sweet flesh; rarely great
- **Seckel** Miniature and precious looking (lovely for poaching whole); green with a deep-red blush; spicy flavor. The skin can be tough, but these are worth trying.

BUYING AND STORING Pears ripen best off the tree, so don't be discouraged if all you can find are hard, green fruit. Leave them at room temperature until the flesh yields gently when squeezed and you can smell a nice pear aroma; some varieties will also change color from green to yellow. Asian pears are meant to be firm and crunchy. Store ripe fruit in the refrigerator.

PREPARING Peeling is not necessary, but it's easy with a vegetable peeler. Core by slicing the pear into quarters and then cutting out the core with a paring knife, or halve the pear and dig out the core with a melon baller. Or keep the fruit whole, and dig out the core from the blossom (large) end with a small melon baller. Sprinkle peeled and sliced pears with lemon juice to prevent discoloring if you're not going to use them right away.

BEST COOKING METHODS Baking, poaching, grilling, roasting

OTHER FRUIT YOU CAN USE Apples

PERSIMMONS

Vibrant orange-colored fruit with a sweet, juicy, jellylike interior or a crisp applelike quality, depending on the variety. Heart-shaped Hachiya persimmon—the mushy one—is most common, but the squat Fuyu variety is gaining ground. Hachiya are oblong with a pointed end, and mouth-puckeringly tart when unripe. Fuyu are smaller, tomato shaped, firm, crunchy, and sweet with a subtle cinnamon flavor.

BUYING AND STORING Look for deeply colored fruit; generally the softer, the better for Hachiya, and hard like an apple for the Fuyu. Bought at any stage, however, persimmons will ripen at room temperature, which can take up to a month; put in a paper bag to speed ripening. Once ripe, store in the refrigerator.

PREPARING Eat ripe Hachiyas out of hand—over the sink; they're messy—or cut off the top and scoop out the flesh with a spoon.

Remove the stem from a hard Fuyu (peeling is optional) and slice.

BEST COOKING METHODS For Hachiya: baking; great in desserts, especially in puddings and cakes. For Fuyu: eaten raw, whole, or added to salads or stir-fries

PINEAPPLE

One of the glories of nature, the pineapple is native to Central and South America, and its prickly, diamond-patterned scaly skin ranges from yellow to green to brownish red when ripe. The flesh is juicy, sweet-tart, and acidic. It used to be that pineapples were picked green, and since they don't sweeten much after they are picked, were often disappointing. But the new "gold" hybrids, which now represent nearly 100 percent of many Hawaiian producers' crops, are almost always sweet and juicy, with lovely golden flesh. Which makes the pineapple among the most reliable fruit you can buy.

BUYING AND STORING Look for fruit with a good pineapple aroma and deep-yellow or golden color that yields only slightly to gentle pressure. Underripe pineapples will decrease in acidity if left at room temperature but will not ripen or sweeten (they ripen only on the plant). Eat immediately or store in the refrigerator and use as quickly as possible.

PREPARING There are a few ways to dismember a pineapple: For either one, first cut off the flower (spiky top) and a little skin at the base. Then, with a chef's knife, cut around the perimeter and remove all of the spiny skin. Use a paring knife to dig out any eyes. At that point, cut the pineapple crosswise into round slices, or top to bottom into halves or quarters, then cut out the woody core. Alternatively, you can quarter the pineapple

before removing the skin: Cut straight down from top to bottom with a chef's knife to cut the pineapple in half; then cut each half in half again to make quarters. Use a smaller knife to cut off the woody core from each quarter (at the peak of the triangles) and then use a grapefruit or paring knife to separate the flesh from the skin by cutting between the two; cut the quarter into slices and serve.

BEST COOKING METHODS Grilling, roasting, baking, sautéing

OTHER FRUITS YOU CAN USE Oranges, grapefruit, kiwi, star fruit

Preparing a Pineapple, Two Ways

STEP 1 Cut off the top of the pineapple about an inch below the flower, then slice off the opposite end as well.

STEP 2 Set the pineapple upright. Slice off the skin, working around the pineapple. If necessary, remove any "eyes" with a paring knife.

STEP 3 Cut the pineapple into round slices.

STEP 4 Cut out the core with a paring knife to make rings.

OR STEP 2 Alternatively, stand the pineapple up and cut it into quarters.

STEP 3 Use a grapefruit knife to separate the fruit from the rind and a paring knife to dig out any eyes. Remove the core (the hard edge where the fruit comes to a point), slice, and serve.

PLUMS

Purple, black, red, orange, or green, there are hundreds of varieties of plums, ranging in size, shape, and flavor. They can be syrupy sweet, sweet-tart, or mouth-puckeringly tart.

Plums are divided into two categories, Japanese and European. Japanese types like Santa Rosa or Shiro are larger, sweet, and juicy, making them great for eating out of hand. European plums like Damson are smaller, often used for making prunes (dried plums) and cooking but are equally good eaten fresh.

BUYING AND STORING Available in supermarkets year-round, but the best are the local varieties bought in season, between May and October. Ripe fruit should be soft, even oozing sugary syrup; eat these right away. Avoid plums that are mushy, split, or smell fermented. Underripe fruit will be hard and sour; leave at room temperature to ripen. Once fully ripe, refrigerate them.

Prunes are best bought in bulk at a store with high turnover. They can be stored in an airtight container at cool room temperature. If you have hot, humid conditions, it's best to refrigerate them.

PREPARING Rinse and eat. To peel, drop into boiling water for about 10 seconds, until the skins loosen, then peel with a paring knife.

BEST COOKING METHODS Grilling, roasting, sautéing, stewing, baking

POMEGRANATES

They range in size from an orange to a grapefruit. The exterior skin is leathery and speckled dark red; the edible, potassium-rich seeds contained in inedible white pith are covered with crisp ruby-red flesh. The seeds can be eaten whole, or the juicy flesh sucked off and the seeds discarded.

BUYING AND STORING Pomegranate season is very short—October to November—but the fruit keeps fairly well. Look for unblemished specimens that are heavy for their size, with no soft spots. Keep in a cool, dark spot for a couple of weeks or in the fridge for a little longer. Pomegranate seeds can be frozen for up to several weeks.

PREPARING Cut in half, or cut an inch or so into the top; pry open into segments, then pull the seeds away from the pith. Do this over a bowl to catch the seeds and any juice. Pick out and discard any wooly pith.

BEST COOKING METHODS Eat raw.

QUINCE

Somewhat pear shaped, with smooth, golden skin and a floral fragrance. The flesh is firm, light yellow, and similar to that of a pear, but astringent when raw. When cooked, quince turns dark orange. Their high pectin content makes them a natural for making preserves.

BUYING AND STORING The season is short, from October to December, and it's tough to find them at other times. Look for firm, unshriveled specimens that are golden yellow and fragrant. Store wrapped loosely in plastic in the refrigerator; they will keep for weeks.

PREPARING Peel and core (the seeds are mildly poisonous, not enough to worry about, but don't eat them); chop or slice.

BEST COOKING METHODS Stewing, poaching

RHUBARB

Its stems usually used as a fruit in sweet preparations, rhubarb is actually an extremely tart vegetable. You can take advantage of its tartness or cook it with sugar or sweet fruits, which is why we see it made into pies, preserves, and compotes, often paired with strawberries. Its leaves contain oxalic acid, which can be fatally poisonous if ingested in large enough quantities; at minimum, it will cause gastric distress.

BUYING AND STORING Look for firm and crisp stalks. Store in the refrigerator wrapped in plastic and use as quickly as possible.

PREPARING Rhubarb sold in food stores and farmers' markets is already stripped of its leaves; if you are growing it yourself, trim away all of the leafy parts, leaving only the stem. Although it's not entirely necessary, rhubarb is best if you string it; grab one end between a paring knife and your thumb and pull straight down to remove the celerylike strings that run lengthwise through each stalk.

BEST COOKING METHODS Stewing

WHEN IS IT DONE? When fully tender

STAR FRUIT (CARAMBOLA)

Semitranslucent tropical fruit with five pointed ridges; when sliced crosswise, creates a star shape. Fragrant, juicy, and sweet-tart when perfectly ripe. The skin is edible. It's best enjoyed raw, sliced into salads or used as garnish.

BUYING AND STORING Look for fragrant, yellow, unblemished plump fruit. They will ripen some if left at room temperature. When ripe, store wrapped loosely in plastic in the refrigerator.

PREPARING Rinse, dry, and slice crosswise.

BEST COOKING METHODS Grilling

THE BASICS OF COOKING WITH NUTS AND SEEDS

Nuts and seeds are flavorful and take little or no preparation, placing them among the best ingredients to add texture and flavor to vegetarian dishes. You can sprinkle them into anything from salads to grains to oatmeal to pancake or waffle batters; grind them up into flours to use in batters and doughs; make nut butters to spread on toast or add to sauces or dips; and more. Roasting, toasting, and blanching your own nuts and making your own nut flours and butters take only a bit more effort than buying store-bought, but give you control over consistency and flavor, as well as determining the quality of ingredients you start with.

Generally, nuts and seeds are nutritional powerhouses, packed with protein, (good) fat, fiber, and minerals; they're good sources of B vitamins, potassium, and iron. Walnuts and flaxseeds have omega-3s; almonds, Brazil nuts, and hazelnuts provide calcium. A serving of nuts or seeds has 5 to 11 grams protein, with peanuts, sunflower seeds, and soy nuts at the top.

Nuts are widely interchangeable, with the exception of chestnuts. Choosing is often a matter of taste or simply what you have on hand. Seeds are also fairly exchangeable, though size may also be a factor. I usually always have a good supply of almonds, peanuts, pine nuts, pumpkin seeds (pepitas), sesame seeds, and walnuts or pecans in my freezer; I buy other nuts and seeds in small quantities as I need them for specific uses.

BUYING AND STORING Unshelled nuts should have hard and sound shells, and feel heavy for their size; they don't rattle if you shake them. Look for shelled nuts that are plump, not shriveled, crisp, and fresh smelling. Check the sell-by date on the container if you aren't buying in bulk.

Store all nuts—shelled or unshelled—and seeds in an airtight container in a cool, dark, dry place for up to 4 months, or in the refrigerator or freezer for up to a year. Hazelnuts and Brazil nuts go bad the fastest; pine nuts and sesame seeds also turn rancid quickly, though the freezer slows this process. These more-fragile nuts will keep for only a few weeks.

SHELLING NUTS A nutcracker certainly makes things easier, but a hammer or mallet works too. To minimize the noise and mess of hammering nuts open, cover them, a few at a time, with a towel. Chestnuts must be heated before being peeled (see page 302). Brazil nut shells are very hard to crack, though somewhat easier after roasting.

ROASTING OR TOASTING NUTS AND SEEDS There are generally two methods: roasting in the oven or toasting in a pan on stovetop. To roast, heat the oven to 350°F and put the nuts or seeds in an even layer on a rimmed baking sheet. Roast them until they just start to turn golden brown, 12 to 15 minutes, stirring every so often.

Toasting on the stovetop is better suited to seeds. Heat a pan over medium heat and add the seeds. Toast the seeds, shaking the pan and stirring often, until they just start to turn golden brown, 5 to 10 minutes; pumpkin seeds will puff up slightly and may pop a bit.

In either case, immediately remove the nuts or seeds from the pan before they look perfectly golden brown so that carry-over cooking doesn't overdo it (burned nuts are bitter). They will crisp up as they cool.

BLANCHING NUTS Blanched nuts are nuts with the (sometimes bitter) skins removed. Almonds and hazelnuts are the nuts you're most likely to blanch. Typically this is done by soaking or boiling them, but you can also do it by roasting or toasting, though it's generally not as effective.

To blanch, bring a pot of water to a boil, add the nuts, and turn off the heat; let soak until you see the skins start to loosen, typically a couple of minutes. Drain and pick out the skins. If the skins are stubborn, try rubbing in a towel until the skins loosen.

GRINDING NUTS INTO MEAL, FLOUR, OR BUTTER All you need is a food processor. The only exception is chestnut flour, which you'll have to buy—try Italian or specialty markets—because chestnuts must be dried before milling. Don't overdo it when grinding nuts into meal or flour—it's surprising how quickly nut meal turns into nut butter. Pulse the nuts in a food processor until they are finely ground and look like moist flour; if there are still larger bits of nut, either leave them in for texture or sift them out. If you see any bit of the meal clumping, stop processing before it turns into nut butter. Or keep processing, if nut butter is what you want.

Roasted Nut Butter

MAKES: About 1 cup
TIME: 15 minutes
F M V

It's incredibly simple to make nut butter at home, and roasting the nuts first in the oven enhances their flavors. Try this with any nut you like.

| 1½ | cups unsalted raw nuts |
| | Pinch salt |

1. Heat the oven to 350°F. Spread the nuts on a rimmed baking sheet and roast in the oven until lightly browned and fragrant, 5 to 8 minutes.
2. Let the nuts cool slightly, then transfer to a food processor. Add the salt. Grind the nuts until they are the consistency of coarse meal. Add 2 tablespoons water and process until creamy, 1 to 2 minutes. Add more water as needed, 1 tablespoon at a time, until smooth and spreadable. Taste and adjust the seasoning. Store in an airtight container in the refrigerator for up to a month.

ROASTED NUT AND HONEY BUTTER A touch of sweetness goes a long way: Add 2 tablespoons honey with the water.

Nut or Seed Milk

MAKES: About 2½ cups
TIME: 15 to 20 minutes, plus 8 to 12 hours soaking time
M V

With this recipe and its variations, along with Coconut Milk (page 304) and Cashew Cream (page 300), you've got your vegan dairy replacement needs covered. You'll need cheesecloth to strain the milk, or use a nut bag, which is made for this purpose.

This recipe will work with any kind of nut as well as seeds like hemp and hulled (green) pumpkin. Flax seeds are the one exception, since they need to be ground first, which makes them difficult to strain out. If you like, you can add a touch of sweetness and flavor by including a bit of vanilla extract or agave nectar before puréeing; or dissolve sugar to taste after straining.

This recipe can be doubled, tripled, or more.

1 cup unsalted raw nuts or seeds
¼ teaspoon salt

1. Soak the nuts in generous water to cover for 8 to 12 hours until swollen and soft.

2. Drain and put in a blender with 4 cups fresh water. Process on high until smooth.

3. Line a fine-meshed strainer with 2 layers of dampened cheesecloth so the sides overhang by several inches; set it over a large bowl. Pour in the purée, gather up the ends, and squeeze as much liquid as possible out of the purée. The milk will keep in an airtight container, refrigerated, for 3 to 4 days.

GRAIN MILK You can make this with white or brown rice, rolled or steel-cut oats, buckwheat, or millet; white rice and oats produce milks with the mildest flavor: Substitute the nuts with the grain of your choice and decrease the water in Step 2 to 3 cups.

SOY MILK The results are thicker and richer than commercially made soy milk—more like half-and-half. I like it but if you want something lighter, thin the finished milk with a little cold water. Substitute dried soybeans for the nuts, rinsing first and picking them over for any debris before soaking them. Drain the beans, put them in a pot with enough water to cover, and bring to a boil. Adjust the heat so the liquid bubbles steadily, cover, and cook, stirring once in a while, until just tender, about 1 hour. Drain and add to a blender with 4 cups water; purée. Let sit for a few minutes to cool, then strain as directed in Step 3.

CASHEWS

The cashew is actually a seed, and it grows in quite a remarkable way on the cashew tree, an evergreen native to Brazil but now also grown in Vietnam, India, and Africa. The cashew grows at the end of a cashew apple, a juicy fruit with delicate skin that is enjoyed locally, usually puréed as part of a fruit drink.

The cashew nut has a double shell that contains a resin related to a chemical found in poison ivy that is a powerful skin irritant. For that reason, they are always sold shelled. Shaped like fat commas, cashews are rich tasting and slightly sweet. They have a lower fat content than most nuts and are full of iron and folic acid. When cooked (they are wonderful added to curries and stir-fries), they soften a bit and acquire a somewhat meaty texture.

Cashews are also an excellent choice for making nut butter (see page 299) and nut milk (page 299). When soaked until soft, they can also be turned into a thick cream or you can go thicker still and create something very close in taste and texture to a soft fresh cheese.

BUYING AND STORING When making nut butter, nut milk, or Cashew Cream or Cashew Cheese, start with whole raw cashews. When adding them to another dish, use raw, roasted, or salted roasted as you prefer. Store in an airtight container at room temperature or in the refrigerator.

Cashew Cream

MAKES: 2 cups
TIME: At least 4 hours, mostly unattended
Ⓜ Ⓥ

Turn to cashew cream when you want to add smooth richness to a dish but no dairy. It's a great alternative to coconut milk when you don't want coconut flavor, as its flavor is more neutral. By adjusting the amount of water you add, you can make cashew cream as thin or thick as you prefer.

This can be doubled, tripled, or more, and will keep for a few days in the fridge.

1 cup unsalted raw cashews

1. Soak the cashews in 2 cups water for at least 4 hours, until swollen and soft. Drain; reserve the liquid.

Cashew Cheese
(page 302)

2. Put the cashews in a blender and process on high, adding the soaking liquid a few tablespoons at a time until it reaches the desired consistency.

FAST CASHEW CREAM Ready in 10 minutes: Boil 2 cups water and put ½ cup cashew butter in a small bowl. Turn off the heat, pour ¼ cup of the boiling water into the bowl, and whisk until smooth; whisk in another ¼ cup boiling water, then pour the cashew mixture into the pot and whisk to combine. Return the cream to medium heat and adjust as necessary so the mixture bubbles gently but steadily. Cook, whisking, until the mixture thickens and coats the back of a spoon, 1 to 3 minutes.

CASHEW CHEESE Same principle, only spreadable like cream cheese. Increase the quantity of cashews to 1½ cups. Increase the water in Step 1 to 3 cups. After draining, put them in the blender with 1 tablespoon each lemon juice and nutritional yeast and a pinch of salt; purée until smooth, adding reserved soaking water 1 tablespoon at a time until you reach the consistency you want. Eat as is, or at this point you can add flavors from the list below and pulse until incorporated.

10 Directions to Take Cashew Cheese

Feel free to adjust any of these amounts up or down to suit your own personal taste. And if you can let the cheese sit for a couple hours after seasoning, all the better.
1. Herbed Cheese: Add ½ cup chopped fresh herbs, like chives, parsley, basil, dill, or mint (alone or in combination).
2. Garlic-Mustard Cheese: Add 4 teaspoons Dijon mustard and 1 teaspoon chopped garlic.
3. Chipotle Cheese: Add 1 or 2 minced canned chipotle chiles, plus some of their adobo.
4. Lime-Cilantro Cheese: Add up to ½ cup chopped fresh cilantro and 2 tablespoons fresh lime juice.
5. Sesame-Soy Cheese: Add 1 tablespoon each soy sauce and toasted sesame seeds and 1 teaspoon sesame oil.
6. Lemon-Dill Cheese: Add another tablespoon lemon juice and 1 tablespoon chopped fresh dill. (This is even better the next day.)

7. Ginger-Mint Cheese: Add 1 heaping tablespoon minced fresh ginger and 2 tablespoons chopped fresh mint. (This is even better the next day.)
8. Vanilla-Orange Cheese: Use orange juice instead of lemon juice and add 2 tablespoons grated orange zest and 1 teaspoon vanilla extract.
9. Berry Cheese: Skip the nutritional yeast and add 1 cup mashed berries and 2 tablespoons turbinado sugar.
10. Tangy Cheese: Add 4 teaspoons cider vinegar and 1½ teaspoons white or yellow miso.

CHESTNUTS

Chestnuts are sweet, fairly soft (for nuts), and mealy. Their shells are smooth, dark brown, and rounded, with one flattened side. They have the least amount of protein and the highest starch content of any nut, and are usually roasted or boiled and treated as a vegetable. They are sold fresh in their shells—the best way to get them—in the fall and early winter. Frozen chestnuts are a good substitute when fresh are out of season, as are dried, but canned or jarred ones are usually soggy and break apart easily; they're fine for puréeing or mashing but not much else.

BUYING AND STORING Fresh and in-season is the best; look for them at farmers' markets in the fall. Look for heavy, full, unblemished nuts; they dry out as they age and begin to rattle around in their shells. Store fresh chestnuts wrapped in damp paper towels in a plastic bag in the refrigerator for up to 2 weeks, but use as quickly as you can. Store dried chestnuts in an airtight container at cool room temperature or in the fridge or freezer.

PREPARING Chestnuts must be precooked and their shells and skins removed. The easiest way is to make a shallow X-cut on the flat side, using a sharp paring knife, then to simmer in water to cover or roast at about 350°F until the shells curl and can be peeled off. (You can also deep-fry to take off the shells, always making the shallow cut first.) Remove the inner skin as well, using a paring knife. If the process becomes difficult, reheat the chestnuts.

To reconstitute dried chestnuts, soak them in water to cover overnight, then drain, cover with fresh water, and simmer until they have the consistency you prefer, usually about 45 minutes at a minimum.

BEST COOKING METHODS Boiling is best if you're going to mash or purée; roasting or grilling for eating out of hand; sautéing

WHEN ARE THEY DONE? Depends on what you are using them for; for use in a purée, until soft; for eating out of hand, until nicely chewy

Chestnuts

MAKES: 1 pound (4 to 6 servings)
TIME: About 30 minutes
F M V

Chestnuts must be peeled while they're still warm; use a kitchen towel to protect your fingers as much as you can. They need not be sizzling hot for the skins to slip off, but as you'll see, the hotter the better. If they start to cool and the skins start to stick a bit, reheat and start again.

1 **pound chestnuts, a shallow X-cut made in the flat side**

TO BOIL Put the chestnuts in a pot with lightly salted water to cover and bring to a boil. Turn off the heat after 3 to 4 minutes. Remove a few chestnuts at a time from the water and use a sharp knife to cut off the shell and inner skin. Purée, mash, or use in other recipes.

TO GRILL OR ROAST Prepare a charcoal, wood, or gas grill; adjust the rack to about 4 inches from the heat source. Or turn the oven to 450°F. Put the chestnuts directly on the grill or a perforated grill pan, or on a rimmed baking sheet. Grill with the cover down or roast, turning occasionally, until you can remove the shells easily, about 15 minutes. Eat warm, out of hand. Or remove the shells and skins and sauté in olive oil or butter or use in other recipes.

CHIA SEEDS

These tiny white to black seeds are from the chia plant, which is closely related to sage and a member of the mint family. They are rich in omega-3 fatty acids and antioxidants, an excellent source of protein, and contain a host of minerals, including manganese, phosphorus, and calcium. Because they can absorb up to ten times their own weight in liquid, developing a gel-like texture, whole or ground seeds can be used to thicken soups or pan gravies, as well as to make gelatin-free puddings (see Piña Colada Chia Pudding, page 724).

Also because of its ability to gel, chia can be used as an egg substitute when the egg is being used as a binder: For each egg, substitute 1 tablespoon ground chia seeds mixed with 3 tablespoons water; let it sit until gelled before adding it to the mixture.

BUYING AND STORING Chia seeds can be bought whole or already ground (though you can grind your own easily enough). Store in an airtight container in the refrigerator.

PREPARING Unless they are added to a dish that contains liquid and given a chance to absorb the liquid, the seeds should be soaked until they swell before using.

Chia seeds can also be sprouted to use in salads and stir-fries; see page 175 for directions.

Preparing Chestnuts

STEP 1 Before cooking a chestnut, score the flat side with a sharp knife to make an X.

STEP 2 After cooking, remove both outer shell and inner skin. If the peeling becomes difficult, reheat.

COCONUT

Coconuts grow on tall palm trees in tropical regions around the world. Although the coconut is actually a fruit, it's more helpful to consider it a nut. While fresh whole coconut is wonderful, store-bought shredded fresh and dried coconut are convenient and taste good too. You can use it make your own coconut milk.

BUYING AND STORING Whole coconuts should be uniformly very hard—check the three eyes especially—and you should be able to hear the juice inside when you shake it. Always buy unsweetened shredded coconut. Sometimes you can find shelled fresh coconut; make sure it looks fresh and moist.

Store whole coconuts in a cool, dry spot for up to several months. Store fresh shelled coconut meat in the fridge and use within a few days. Store shredded coconut in the fridge or freezer for up to six months.

PREPARING Use an ice pick, screwdriver, or corkscrew to find the soft eye, then drive the point into the eye and drain out the juice. Put the coconut inside a double layer of plastic grocery or trash bags. Go outside or wherever there is a concrete step or floor; slam the coconut into the concrete as many times as it takes to break it open. Remove the brown shell; just pop it off by inserting a knife blade or aforementioned screwdriver. Chop, slice, or shred the white meat as you like.

BEST COOKING METHOD Shredded coconut develops wonderful flavor when toasted or roasted. Toast for 5 to 10 minutes in a dry skillet set over medium-low heat or roast on a rimmed baking sheet in a 350°F oven until it darkens as much as you want. With either method, keep an eye on it and shake the pan occasionally; it can turn from lightly golden to burnt very quickly.

Coconut Milk

MAKES: About 2 cups (each pressing)
TIME: 20 minutes

F M V

Many recipes include coconut milk in this book, and it is an especially important substitute for vegans and those who are lactose intolerant. It's fine to use canned, but homemade coconut milk is super-easy and much more pure in both flavor and ingredients. All you need is unsweetened coconut.

This recipe gives you a fairly thick milk, akin to canned. Either thin it with water or repeat the process with the used coconut; the second pressing will be thinner.

> 1 cup unsweetened dried shredded coconut meat

1. Combine the coconut with 2 cups very hot water in a blender. Pulse on and off quickly, then turn on the blender and let it work for 15 seconds or so; take care that the top of the blender stays in place. Let sit for a few minutes.

2. Put through a fine-meshed strainer, pressing to extract as much liquid as possible. Discard the solids or repeat with the same amount of hot water. Use the milk immediately or transfer to an airtight container and refrigerate for up to a few days.

FLAXSEEDS

Flaxseeds are harvested from the same plant that produces flax (from which linen is made) and linseed oil. Valued for their nutritional properties, the seeds are packed with protein, fiber, and omega-3 fatty acids. They are small, shiny, flat, and nutty-flavored and range in color from tan to dark brown. Flaxseeds are an easy way to amp up the nutrition of any dish, sweet or savory; just sprinkle a tablespoon over your breakfast cereal, stir it into yogurt or a smoothie, or add it to most any kind of batter or dough. You can also use them to make flaxseed butter (see page 299).

And like chia seeds, flaxseeds can be used as an egg substitute when the egg is used as a binder. The flaxseed must be very finely ground. For each egg, substitute 1 tablespoon ground flaxseed mixed with 3 tablespoons water; let it sit until gelled before adding it to the mixture.

BUYING AND STORING Flaxseeds can be bought whole or already ground (though you can grind your own easily enough). Store in an airtight container in the refrigerator; this is particularly important for ground flaxseed, which can go rancid quickly.

PREPARING Flaxseeds can also be sprouted to use in salads and stir-fries; see page 175 for directions.

HEMP SEEDS

Yes, these white to light-green seeds are from the cannabis plant, but they won't make you high. Though they may be sold as "hemp seeds" (or "hemp hearts"), they aren't the actual seed of the plant, but the tender inner kernel of the seed. They are a good source of protein and omega-3 and omega-6 fatty acids, as well as magnesium and zinc. They have a lovely nutty flavor and can be sprinkled over anything that could benefit from that nuttiness, from savory to sweet dishes. You can also use them to make hemp seed butter (see page 299) or hemp seed milk (page 299). Hemp oil is best used as a drizzling oil, not for cooking.

BUYING AND STORING Hemp seeds can be bought whole or already ground (though you can grind your own easily enough). Store in an airtight container in the refrigerator.

PREPARING Hemp seeds can also be sprouted to use in salads and stir-fries; see page 175 for directions.

SESAME SEEDS

These seeds are small, flat, and oval with a pointed tip, and a light tan (white), rusty red, or black color.

They have a nice nutty, somewhat sweet flavor, especially when toasted. Unhulled white seeds are slightly bitter and harder to digest. You can buy pretoasted sesame seeds (sold as gomasio), but they sometimes have an off flavor. With their rich natural oil and nutty taste, sesame seeds are an important flavoring in the cooking of China, Korea, Japan, India, the Middle East, and Africa; they are also used in Europe and the U.S. and are often lightly toasted before use (see page 299). They are delicious as a coating for fried foods or as a garnish, sprinkled into sauces, dressings, and salads. They are also the basis for tahini.

BUYING AND STORING You can find blends of black and white seeds sold in food stores as "tuxedo mix" (look for them in the Asian food section). Store the seeds in an airtight container in the refrigerator or freezer.

Tahini

MAKES: About 1 cup
TIME: 15 minutes
F **M** **V**

The flavor is so much better than store-bought, which can often taste a bit rancid. If you want to boost the sesame flavor, you can substitute sesame oil for some of the olive oil.

1½ **cups sesame seeds**
4 **tablespoons olive oil, or more as needed**
Pinch salt

1. Put the seeds in a medium skillet over medium heat. Toast them until golden brown and fragrant, shaking the pan often for even browning. It should take 5 to 8 minutes.
2. Immediately pour the seeds into a mini food processor and let cool. Add the salt and grind until they have the consistency of coarse meal. Add 2 tablespoons of

the oil and process 1 to 2 minutes. Add more oil, 1 tablespoon at a time, until the tahini has the consistency you prefer and the right flavor balance; you don't want the olive oil flavor to become more prominent than the sesame. Store in an airtight container in the refrigerator for up to a month.

TAHINI SAUCE Enjoy drizzled over Falafel (page 472), salads, or grilled vegetables: Whisk ½ cup tahini, juice of 1 lemon, 1 minced clove garlic or more to taste, ½ teaspoon ground cumin (optional), and salt and pepper together until smooth. If you like, add olive oil or more lemon juice to taste to thin to the consistency you want.

Pasta, Noodles, and Dumplings

Dried pasta and noodles are cheap, convenient, versatile . . . and beloved. Fresh versions, in which the water is usually replaced by egg, are not difficult to make and are, of course, richer and more flavorful. The egg not only adds flavor but also protein—and fat, which makes the dough easy to handle and gives it a silky, luxurious quality. Fresh pasta dough is used to make other special treats like dumplings and ravioli; these are fun, and can be made in advance. Finally, there are quasi-noodles like gnocchi and spaetzle, which take relatively little time or effort.

Still: For the most part you're going to buy pasta. You can buy "fresh," but know that that's a relative term. At the best markets, they're made regularly and range in quality from fine to terrific. In most supermarkets, "fresh" actually means "stale"; you can live without that stuff; you're better off with dried.

THE BASICS OF DRIED PASTA

This is the pasta you'll buy most often. For most occasions, you want pasta that is 100 percent durum wheat (the flour of which is called semolina), and most of it is, by default. Generally, though the flour comes from the United States or Canada, the best pasta is still made in Italy, but is available everywhere. High

How Much Pasta to Cook?

When I was young, I'd consider it suitable to split a pound of pasta with an equally hungry friend; this, however, is a very large amount of food. And since the first edition of this book, I almost always eat more vegetables (or sauce) with less pasta. Generally, I think a pound of pasta serves three to four as a main course (with other things on the table) or four to six as a starter course or side dish. If you have a scale, try this: 60 grams for a small appetizer serving; 75 for medium, or a small entrée; 100 for a decent-sized entrée; 125 for a hungry person entrée. Adjust accordingly.

quality dried pasta is easier to keep from overcooking and has a deeper, more appealing color and a texture that grabs the sauce better. You can also now find a variety of pastas made from alternative flours (see page 309), if you're interested; I generally stick to the original.

COOKING

With a few exceptions (see One-Pot Pasta, page 314), it's easiest to cook pasta in abundant water. You can get away with less but it means you have to be more vigilant about stirring and keeping an eye on the pot. I use a gallon or so per pound (a little more is even better). Salt the water well: A small fistful is about right—figure 2 tablespoons per gallon of water at least—but taste until you get the knack; you want it "as salty as the sea." (It doesn't matter whether you add the salt to the water before it boils or after, but add it before adding the pasta.) While the pasta cooks, adjust the heat to keep the water boiling and stir frequently, especially at the beginning.

If you have problems with pasta sticking, the problem is likely too little water, too little salt, too little stirring, or all three. (And without enough salt, your pasta will be not only sticky but bland.) Don't add oil to the water—it will keep the sauce from holding on properly later.

If your pot isn't deep enough for spaghetti or other long pasta, either break the pasta in half or hold the noodles by one end and dunk the other. As the bunch softens, swirl the strands around until they bend enough for you to submerge the whole thing. In the long run, get a bigger pot.

Check pasta for doneness by tasting it—*al dente* means "to the tooth"—and you'll never go wrong. (Eventually, you'll be able to tell at a glance and a touch whether it's done.) It's ready when it retains a little bite but is no longer chalky, what I call "tender but not mushy." This holds true for every noodle you make, from fresh egg pasta made in your own kitchen to dried rice noodles from Thailand. Don't trust anyone's recommended pasta cooking times; the box is almost always wrong.

DRAINING, SAUCING, AND TOSSING

There are just a few rules for saucing.

Before draining, dip out and reserve a cup or so of the pasta cooking water. Drain quickly—don't shake the colander compulsively; a quick toss is fine. If your sauce is thick and clumps up on the pasta, just add some of the reserved water (you can also use warmed stock, tomato juice, or the water you cooked your vegetables in), a tablespoon or so at a time, until you achieve the desired consistency. Garnish at the last minute. Serve and eat immediately—pasta is best hot.

WHOLE WHEAT PASTA

Whole wheat pasta tastes a lot better now than it did ten years ago, and is much more widely available. Nutrition-wise, whole wheat pasta has more fiber than regular pasta and a little more protein. Ideally it should be flecked with bits of bran, have a pleasantly nutty flavor, and cook from brittle to tender without instantly turning to mush. As with traditional dried pasta, I prefer Italian brands.

Whole wheat pasta doesn't release as much starch when it cooks, so your final dish won't be as creamy. You can compensate for that with a thick and flavorful sauce. And there are lots of ingredients that are complemented by its nutty flavor: cauliflower, greens, nuts, cheese, garlic, mushrooms, and more. Recipes that are great with whole wheat pasta include:

- Pesto (page 634)
- Pasta with Garlic and Oil and its variations (page 312)
- Fast Tomato Sauce and its variations (page 312)
- Linguine with Raw Tomato Sauce (page 314)
- Any of the pastas with vegetables or legumes (pages 317 to 325)

ALTERNATIVE PASTAS

There's now a staggering array of nonwheat pastas available in supermarkets. They offer the distinctive flavors of their constituent grains, and usually more fiber, vitamins, and minerals than noodles made from refined wheat. And they make it possible for diabetics or anyone with wheat allergies or celiac disease to enjoy a bowl of

---

Do Pasta Shapes Matter?

There are countless dried pasta shapes, not to mention dozens more fresh pasta shapes. Sometimes the shape you use matters, at least a little bit; when you have a sauce with small solid bits or even larger pieces, it's nice to use a shape that will catch them, like shells. For soup, you want small pasta that will fit on a spoon.

But as you probably already know, this is not exactly critical; using an "inappropriate" shape is not quite the same as using salt instead of sugar. So I (as an admitted non-Italian) would argue, as I always have, that you should rarely change the type of sauce you're making because you don't have the "correct" pasta shape. Use what you've got and make what you like. If you have guests from Italy, they might scoff; otherwise no one will care.

---

pasta. (If you have dietary restrictions, check the labels, because some contain wheat or wheat gluten to help them behave more like their traditional counterparts.)

But pasta with little or no wheat (and therefore little or no gluten) will never cook to the tender-yet-firm texture of 100 percent durum pasta, nor result in as creamy a dish. Instead, these noodles tend to go from perfect to mushy in an instant. So check often for doneness and remove from the heat just before it's tender.

The roundup that follows includes the types that are most common, but there are more for you to explore. For more other-than-wheat noodles, see "The Basics of Asian Noodles" (page 331).

BEAN PASTAS You can find high-protein, gluten-free pastas made from chickpeas, black beans, red lentils, green lentils, adzuki beans, and more. They tend to be a bit grainy, and all have a distinctive bean flavor.

BROWN RICE PASTA Perhaps the best of the bunch, this is made from flour derived from rice that has had only the hull removed. It is light to medium brown, with the natural sweetness, nuttiness, and nutrition of brown rice; it also tends to retain a nice bite.

BUCKWHEAT PASTA Gluten-free buckwheat flour, often combined with unbleached white or fine whole wheat flour to lighten the dough. The buckwheat imparts a nutty flavor and brown color to the noodle, whose texture is pleasantly mealy. Soba noodles (see page 331) are made from buckwheat.

CHESTNUT PASTA A traditional pasta of the Mediterranean, made with a mixture of white and chestnut flour. Its subtle, sweet, nutty flavor is best paired with a simple butter sauce or Pesto (page 634). Kinda great, once in a while.

CORN FLOUR AND CORNMEAL PASTAS Wheat- and gluten-free pasta made from different textures of finely ground cornmeal. They taste of corn and are grainier in texture than wheat pasta. They turn mushy quickly, so watch the pot carefully.

QUINOA PASTA The dough of this wheat-free, gluten-free pasta usually combines quinoa and corn. The result is a pasta more assertive in flavor and lighter than traditional durum wheat pastas. But the texture is strangely soft yet gritty.

SEAWEED PASTA Common in Asian cuisines (see page 244), with a variety known as "sea spaghetti" starting to appear as a pasta option in other cuisines. Generally these are better as an addition to a pasta dish rather than an alternative. The briny flavor is pretty strong.

SOY PASTA The kind you find at the supermarkets typically is made with a blend of soy flour and wheat flour, though you may find it made completely from golden, black, or green soybeans at natural food stores. Soy pasta has a relatively high protein content, especially those that are all soy, but the flavor is quite beany and the texture distinctly rubbery. In short: I don't like it.

WILD RICE PASTA You can find pasta made with wild rice flour mixed with semolina flour or with brown rice flour for a gluten-free version. The flavor is strong, and the pasta tends to clump together.

Vegetable Noodles

People have been making "noodles" out of vegetables long before a certain diet craze and you definitely don't need an expensive, single-use machine: a vegetable peeler or a $10 julienne peeler work just fine. Some, like cucumber and zucchini, don't require any cooking. Others might need to be parboiled for 5 minutes or less before saucing. Some vegetables that work well as either pasta or noodle replacements are:

BEETS
Try with goat cheese, pesto, or walnut sauces.

CARROTS
Also takes any sauce. Think tomatoes, cheese, and capers.

TURNIPS OR RUTABAGA
Serve with caramelized onions, butter and sage, or creamy mushroom sauces.

JÍCAMA
Keep it light. Think soy and/or citrus flavors or pasta primavera flavors.

ZUCCHINI OR OTHER SUMMER SQUASH
Goes well with everything, especially tomato sauces.

SWEET POTATOES
Anything that would go well on pumpkin ravioli works here. Try

Gorgonzola with sage and butter.

CHAYOTE
Goes well with garlic and other strong flavors. Try with puttanesca sauce or any chile-based topping.

CELERY OR CELERY ROOT
Cream-based sauces are classic but goes well with anything else from pesto

to classic tomato sauces. By the way, there is no vegetable as easy to turn into a "noodle" as celery; use a regular vegetable peeler.

CUCUMBER
Goes especially well with sauces featuring ginger, soy, garlic, peanut, sesame, and so on. Think Thai.

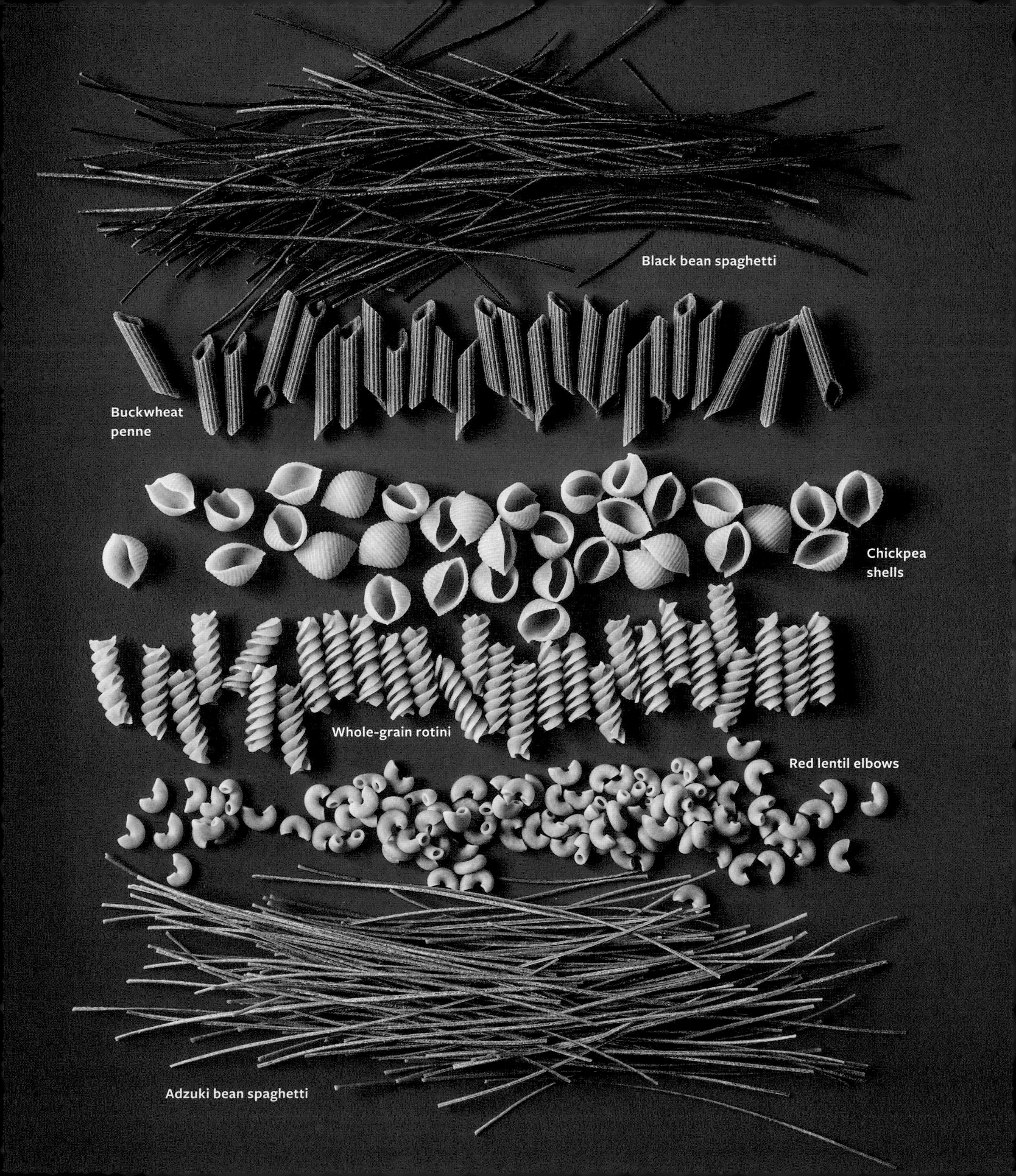

Black bean spaghetti

Buckwheat penne

Chickpea shells

Whole-grain rotini

Red lentil elbows

Adzuki bean spaghetti

Pasta with Garlic and Oil

Pasta Aglio e Olio
MAKES: 4 servings
TIME: 30 minutes
F V

The quintessential late-night Roman dish, great as a snack or even a centerpiece when you want something simple. Needless to say, good olive oil is key. So is not burning the garlic. If you like, you can amp up the fresh herbs, adding up to 1 cup chopped parsley or basil.

> **Salt**
> 1 **pound long, thin pasta, like linguine or spaghetti, or any other pasta**
> 2 **tablespoons chopped garlic**
> 1 or 2 **dried chiles, or to taste (optional)**
> ⅓ **cup olive oil, or more as needed**
> ½ **cup chopped fresh parsley (optional)**

1. Bring a large pot of water to a boil and salt it. When the water boils, add the pasta. Stir occasionally, and start tasting after 5 minutes. Meanwhile, put the garlic, chiles if you're using them, the oil, and a pinch of salt in a small skillet or saucepan and turn the heat to medium-low. Let the garlic sizzle a bit, shaking the pan occasionally, just until it turns golden, then turn off the heat if the pasta isn't ready.

2. When the pasta is tender but not mushy, drain it, reserving about 1 cup of the cooking water. Transfer to a large warmed bowl. Reheat the garlic and oil mixture briefly, if necessary. Dress the pasta with the sauce, adding a little more oil or some of the reserved water if it seems dry; toss with the parsley if you're using it and serve.

PASTA WITH BREAD CRUMBS Crunchy and satisfying: Put the oil in a large skillet over medium heat. When it's hot, add ½ cup Fresh Bread Crumbs (page 678) and cook, stirring frequently, until golden and fragrant, 2 to 3 minutes; remove with a slotted spoon. Turn the heat down to medium-low and stir in the garlic, the chiles if you're using them, and a large pinch of salt. Proceed with the recipe from Step 1, using the bread crumbs as a garnish, stirring them into the pasta at the last moment.

PASTA WITH CHICKPEAS (CECI) Good with cut pasta like ziti, penne, or shells: While you're cooking the pasta, toss about 1 cup cooked chickpeas (drained canned are fine) with the garlic-oil mixture and warm gently.

PASTA WITH TOMATO SAUCES

Pasta and tomatoes seem to have been made for each other, and the combinations are close to infinite. With spices, cheese, butter, or more vegetables, they gain complexity, depth, and flavor. And all the sauces come together in less than 45 minutes (most in half that time); you'll know it's ready because it suddenly goes from looking watery to having that familiar saucy look. Canned tomatoes are by far most convenient, and they're reliable. But in the summer, fresh tomatoes should be your default; chop them up—don't bother to core or seed or peel—and treat them as you would canned.

Fast Tomato Sauce

MAKES: 4 servings; enough for 1 pound of pasta
TIME: 20 minutes
F M O

This is among the most basic and useful pasta sauces and one of those staples, like vinaigrette, that is too easy *not* to make yourself. This sauce works tossed with any pasta or noodle, for pizza (page 613), or as an accent to other simply cooked foods like grains, beans, tofu, eggs, or vegetables. And you can still enjoy spaghetti and meatballs, shaping any of the veggie burger mixtures (pages 502 to 508) into "meat" balls (page 506). It's also a versatile sauce that you can take in many different directions (right).

11 Easy Ways to Tweak Fast Tomato Sauce

Generally, if you're adding ingredients that need to cook, like vegetables, add them to the oil before the tomatoes and sauté for a couple of minutes, stirring. If they don't need extra time, add them along with the tomatoes or after the tomatoes begin to break down.

1. FRESH TOMATO SAUCE
Substitute 2 pounds chopped ripe fresh tomatoes for canned; the cooking time will be about the same. Garnish with lots of Parmesan or chopped fresh parsley or basil.

2. GARLICKY TOMATO SAUCE
Substitute 2 to 10 lightly crushed cloves garlic for the onion, cook over medium-low heat until golden brown, then add the tomatoes and cook as directed.

3. SPICY TOMATO SAUCE (ARRABBIATA)
Substitute 1 tablespoon chopped garlic and 3 to 5 (or up to 10, for that matter) whole dried red chiles for the onion. Cook, stirring, until the garlic is brown, add the tomatoes, and finish as directed. Remove the chiles before serving, if you'd like.

4. TOMATO SAUCE WITH WINE
Add ¼ cup dry white or red wine just before the tomatoes; let it bubble away for a minute before proceeding.

5. TOMATO-MUSHROOM SAUCE
Cook 1 cup sliced mushrooms along with the onion.

6. TOMATO PESTO SAUCE
Use as much or as little pesto as you like: After the sauce has finished cooking, stir in Pesto or one of its variations (page 634). Or after tossing the pasta, top each serving with a spoonful of pesto.

7. RED PEPPER AND TOMATO SAUCE
Add 1 or more chopped roasted red peppers (page 228) along with the tomatoes.

8. PUTTANESCA SAUCE
A Roman classic: Add 2 tablespoons drained capers, red chile flakes to taste, and ½ cup chopped pitted black olives (preferably oil-cured, like Moroccan).

9. CREAMY VODKA SAUCE
About 2 minutes before the sauce is done, stir in ¼ cup each vodka and cream, or to taste. Let simmer for 5 minutes.

10. SPICED TOMATO SAUCE
Unsurpassed as a dipping sauce for Paratha or Chapati (page 592 or 591): Add a couple of teaspoons garam masala or curry powder (to make your own, see page 648 or 649) during the last minute or 2 of cooking. Garnish with cilantro and/or lime wedges.

11. MISO TOMATO SAUCE
Great with udon noodles or brown rice spaghetti: When the sauce is done, remove from the heat and stir in ¼ cup red or dark miso. Garnish with chopped walnuts, if you'd like.

Freezing Tomato Sauce

Since Fast Tomato Sauce (opposite) is so simple, I suggest making double or triple batches and freezing some. Just let the sauce cool; then pack away in freezer bags or tightly sealed containers (small quantities are easiest) and use within 6 months or so. You can thaw it slowly in the fridge or in the microwave or heat gently in a covered pan, stirring occasionally to prevent sticking.

3 tablespoons olive oil or butter

1 onion, chopped

1 24- to 32-ounce can whole tomatoes, drained and chopped

Salt and pepper

Chopped fresh parsley or basil for garnish (optional)

Grated Parmesan or other cheese (optional)

1. Put the olive oil in a large skillet over medium-high heat. When it's hot, add the onion and cook, stirring occasionally, until soft, 3 to 5 minutes. Add the tomatoes and sprinkle with salt and pepper.

2. Cook, stirring occasionally, until the tomatoes break up and the mixture comes together and thickens, 10 to 15 minutes. Taste and adjust the seasoning. Use immediately, garnished with herbs or cheese if you'd like. Or cover and refrigerate for up to several days; reheat gently and add the herbs and cheese just before serving.

FAST TOMATO SAUCE WITH PASTA The Italian—rather than American—way to sauce pasta: Before you start the sauce, put a large pot of water on to boil and salt it. When the tomatoes have been cooking 5 minutes or so and the water comes to a boil, add 1 pound of any pasta to the water and cook, stirring occasionally, until tender but not mushy (start tasting after 5 minutes). Drain the pasta, reserving about 1 cup of the cooking water. Combine the pasta with the sauce (return it to the pot if you want some elbow room) and toss it until coated and steaming, adding enough of the reserved water to keep the pasta from sticking. Garnish with the herbs and/or cheese if you're using them and serve immediately.

One-Pot Pasta

MAKES: 4 servings
TIME: About 20 minutes
F O

Easy and infinitely variable. For a more flavorful sauce, use the liquid drained from canned tomatoes or vegetable stock to replace some of the water. Add up to 2 cups

chopped vegetables: Greens, mushrooms, eggplant, or cauliflower would all work wonderfully.

1 pound linguine or other long pasta

1 pound fresh tomatoes, chopped, or 1 28-ounce can whole tomatoes, drained and chopped

1 onion, sliced

6 cloves garlic, sliced

½ teaspoon red chile flakes, or to taste

3 tablespoons olive oil

Salt and pepper

1 cup fresh basil leaves, chopped

Grated Parmesan cheese, for serving (optional)

1. Put the pasta, tomatoes, onion, garlic, red chile flakes, oil, and 4 cups water in a large skillet over high heat. Sprinkle with salt and pepper. Bring to a boil and cook, stirring and turning the pasta frequently with tongs, until the pasta is al dente and the water has nearly evaporated, about 9 minutes.

2. Season to taste with salt and pepper, stir in three quarters of the basil, divide among 4 bowls, and garnish with the remaining basil and the Parmesan, if you're using it.

CREAMY ONE-POT PASTA Richer: Add ¼ cup mascarpone or cream to the skillet in Step 1.

Linguine with Raw Tomato Sauce

Linguine con Salsa Cruda
MAKES: About 4 servings
TIME: About 30 minutes
F O

A few guidelines: You can use good-quality canned plum tomatoes, as long as you drain them thoroughly first; it won't be the same, but it won't be bad. Do not, however, use dried basil, here or anywhere else. And don't smash the garlic too much or you'll have trouble removing it before serving.

One-Pot Pasta

You can use this sauce on top of soft polenta, as a savory omelet filling, or anywhere you'd use a raw salsa or relish.

> Salt
> 2 cups chopped fresh tomatoes
> 2 tablespoons olive oil
> 2 cloves garlic, lightly smashed
> ¼–½ cup chopped fresh basil
> Pepper
> 1 pound linguine or other long pasta
> Grated Parmesan cheese (optional)

1. Bring a large pot of water to a boil and salt it. Put the tomatoes, oil, garlic, and half the basil in a broad-bottomed bowl. Sprinkle with salt and pepper. Mash together well, using a fork or potato masher, but do not purée. (You can make the sauce an hour or 2 before you're ready to eat and let it rest at room temperature.)
2. When the water boils, add the pasta. Stir occasionally, and start tasting after 5 minutes. Cook the pasta until tender but not mushy. Ladle some of the cooking water into the sauce to thin it out a bit and warm it up. Drain the pasta. Remove the garlic from the sauce. Toss the pasta with the sauce and top with the remaining basil; pass grated Parmesan at the table, if you'd like.

LINGUINE WITH PUNCHIER RAW TOMATO SAUCE Even more flavorful: Add a tablespoon of red wine vinegar (or to taste) to the sauce, plus ½ cup chopped pitted olives. Proceed with the recipe, omitting the cheese. **V**

PASTA WITH DAIRY

Pasta releases starch while it's cooking, which makes it creamy anyway, but when you add cheese, butter, cream, or other dairy products, the dish instantly becomes more substantial and downright luxurious. There are times you can substitute olive oil for butter if you want to make a dish lighter or vegan. And although other cheeses sometimes fill in for Parmesan, if you're going to use Parmesan, make sure it's real Parmigiano-Reggiano.

Pasta with Butter, Sage, and Parmesan

MAKES: About 4 servings
TIME: 30 minutes
F

This is a recipe that demonstrates the value of water in pasta sauces: You can use as little as 4 tablespoons butter here and still make a good sauce, as long as you thin it slightly with some of the pasta cooking liquid. Pecorino Romano, crumbled Gorgonzola, mascarpone, and ricotta salata or fontina are all good here too. Try them alone, with Parmesan, or in any combination.

I just love this, and always have.

> Salt
> 4 tablespoons (½ stick) butter or olive oil
> 20–30 fresh sage leaves
> 1 pound long pasta like linguine or spaghetti, or any other pasta
> 1 cup grated Parmesan cheese, plus more for serving
> Pepper

1. Bring a large pot of water to a boil and salt it. When the water boils, add the pasta. Stir occasionally, and start tasting after 5 minutes.
2. While the pasta cooks, melt the butter in a large skillet over medium heat. Add the sage and cook until the butter browns and the sage sizzles, swirling the butter a few times. Remove from the heat until the pasta is done.
3. When the pasta is tender but not mushy, drain the pasta, reserving about 1 cup of the cooking water. Toss the pasta with the butter and sage in the skillet, adding a little of the reserved water if necessary to thin the sauce. Toss with the Parmesan, sprinkle with salt and pepper, and serve, passing more grated Parmesan at the table.

CACIO E PEPE Omit the sage and heat the butter just until it melts. Use pecorino Romano cheese in place of the Parmesan. In Step 2, add a lot of coarsely ground black pepper; it should be almost assaultive on the palate.

PASTA WITH FRIED EGGS While the pasta cooks, use some of the butter to cook 2 to 4 eggs sunny side up; keep them very runny. When the pasta is done, cut the fried eggs into pieces and toss with the drained pasta along with the remaining melted butter and the Parmesan.

Creamy, Lemony Pasta

MAKES: 4 servings
TIME: 30 minutes
F

This is a pantry meal that seems much fancier than Pasta with Garlic and Oil (page 312) or Pasta with Butter, Sage, and Parmesan (opposite) but is just as easy. Mix in nearly any cooked vegetable before serving for a more substantial dish.

Salt
1 pound any pasta
1 cup soft cheese like mascarpone, ricotta, or goat cheese, or Greek yogurt
Grated zest and juice of 1 lemon
¼ cup chopped fresh chives
Pepper
Grated Parmesan cheese for garnish

1. Bring a large pot of water to a boil and salt it. When the water boils, add the pasta. Stir occasionally, and start tasting after 5 minutes. When the pasta is tender but not mushy, drain the pasta, reserving 1 cup of the cooking water.
2. Return the pasta to the pot, add the cheese, lemon zest and juice, and chives, and turn the heat to low. Stir to coat the pasta, adding the cooking water a little at a time to make a smooth, but not too runny, sauce.

Sprinkle with salt and pepper. Garnish with the Parmesan and serve.

CREAMY PASTA WITH PEAS Almost a one-bowl meal: Add 1 cup peas (thawed frozen are fine) with the pasta in Step 2.

CREAMY PASTA WITH SPINACH A quick and satisfying dinner: Add 1 pound spinach, trimmed of thick stems and chopped, to the pasta for the last minute or 2 of cooking in Step 1. Drain and proceed with the recipe.

PASTA WITH VEGETABLES OR LEGUMES

You can turn just about any vegetable into a pasta sauce as long as you follow some basic rules. Think of tomato sauce, the model for all vegetable-based pasta sauces: aromatics are cooked in fat, vegetables are added and simmered until they're soft. The process can stop there, or you can add cheese or other vegetables; you can purée the sauce; you can add garnishes. The possibilities are endless; look at "26 Vegetable or Legume Dishes That Can Be Tossed with Pasta" (page 323) for more ideas.

Pasta with Lentils or Other Legumes

MAKES: 4 servings
TIME: About 1 hour
M **V**

The intention here is to have the beans, vegetables, and oil create a sauce that's almost meaty. Lentils are ideal but you can make this dish with almost any legume, as long as you cook it until it's soft. (For last-minute cooking, you'll want to start with cooked, canned, or frozen beans, and simply cook them with the vegetables until the vegetables are tender.)

You can also turn this into a more-beans-than-pasta-type dish like Cannellini Beans with Cabbage and Pasta (page 441), or even a soup like Pasta e Fagiole (pasta and bean soup, page 109), simply by adjusting the ingredients and the liquid.

¾ cup dried lentils, rinsed and picked over, or 1½–2 cups cooked small beans
2 carrots, chopped
1 large or 2 medium onions, chopped
2 cups chopped tomatoes (drained canned are fine)
Salt and pepper
1 tablespoon chopped fresh marjoram or oregano or 1 teaspoon dried
3 tablespoons olive oil
½ pound elbows, shells, or other cut pasta
1 teaspoon minced garlic

1. Put the lentils, carrots, half the onions, and water to cover by about 1 inch in a large pot over medium heat. Simmer until the lentils are tender but not mushy, 20 to 30 minutes. (Some lentils may take even longer, but check frequently to avoid overcooking and add water as necessary.) Add the tomatoes, sprinkle with some salt and pepper and half the marjoram, stir, and cook for another 10 minutes or so to let the flavor develop; keep warm over low heat. (You can make the sauce, cover tightly, and refrigerate for a day or 2 or freeze for several weeks. Reheat gently before proceeding.)

2. Bring a large pot of water to a boil and salt it. Put 2 tablespoons of the oil in a skillet over medium-high heat. When it's hot, add the remaining onion and cook, stirring, until it begins to brown and crisp, about 10 minutes.

3. Cook the pasta, stirring occasionally, until it is still quite firm, even a bit chalky in the center. (Start tasting after 5 minutes.) Reserve about a cup of the cooking water and drain the pasta. Stir the pasta into the lentils along with the crisp onions, the garlic, and the remaining marjoram and oil. Add enough of the cooking water to moisten the mixture. Cook for 2 to 3 minutes, until the pasta is tender. Taste, adjust the seasoning, and serve in warm bowls.

Pasta Primavera

MAKES: 4 servings
TIME: 30 minutes
F

You don't have to have a laundry list of specific spring vegetables to make this work; use your judgment about what's in season and which taste good together, and go from there.

Salt
2 tablespoons olive oil or butter
½ teaspoon red chile flakes, or to taste
1½ pounds mixed spring vegetables (like asparagus, spinach or other tender greens, snap peas, snow peas, radishes, baby carrots or turnips, shelled fava beans, or peas), chopped
Pepper
½ cup cream
½ cup grated Parmesan cheese
1 pound any pasta
½ cup chopped fresh chervil or mint for garnish

1. Bring a large pot of water to boil and salt it. Put the oil in a large skillet over medium heat. When it's hot, add the red chile flakes and cook until fragrant, about a minute. Add the vegetables and sprinkle with salt and pepper. Cook, stirring often, until the vegetables are crisp-tender, 3 to 10 minutes, depending on the vegetables (add any vegetables with a much longer cooking time, like root vegetables, 5 minutes before the rest). Add the cream and ¼ cup of the Parmesan, and cook until heated through and thickened, 3 to 5 minutes. Turn off the heat.

2. When the water comes to a boil, add the pasta. Stir occasionally, and start tasting the pasta after 5 minutes. When the pasta is tender but not mushy, drain the pasta, reserving 1 cup of the cooking water. Add the pasta to the vegetables and turn the heat to low. Toss to combine, adding a little reserved cooking water at a time to loosen the sauce, if necessary. Taste and adjust the seasoning. Garnish with the herbs and the remaining Parmesan and serve.

PASTA ESTATE Same idea using summertime vegetables: Use 1½ pounds of mixed seasonal produce like fresh corn kernels, cherry tomatoes, green beans, bell peppers, or zucchini. Use basil for the garnish.

PASTA AUTUNNO Grate or chop any hard vegetables so they cook fast: Use Brussels sprouts, cauliflower, and squash like butternut, spaghetti, or delicata. Garnish with parsley or 1 tablespoon chopped fresh thyme.

PASTA INVERNO A northern Italian spin: Use shredded green or Savoy cabbage and chopped potatoes for the vegetables and fontina in place of the Parmesan. Garnish with toasted walnuts (see page 299).

Pasta with Caramelized Onions

MAKES: 4 servings
TIME: About 1 hour

I found this recipe miraculous when I was introduced to it around 40 years ago. The onions are cooked slowly until they become sweet and incredibly tender.

Many of the ideas found in "8 Ways to Elevate Pasta with Broccoli, Cauliflower, or Broccoli Raab" (page 322) can be used here as well.

5 or 6	medium-to-large onions (about 2 pounds), sliced
⅓	cup plus 2 tablespoons olive oil
	Salt and pepper
1	pound linguine, spaghetti, capellini, fettuccine, or other long pasta
½	cup grated Parmesan cheese, plus more for serving

1. Slice the onions with a mandoline or the food processor's slicing disk (my preference, because this is a lot of onions). Put them in a large dry skillet over medium-low heat and cover. Check and stir every 5 minutes. The onions will first give up lots of liquid, then dry out; after 20 to 30 minutes, when they begin to brown and stick to the pan, remove the cover. Add the ⅓ cup of olive oil, along with a generous sprinkle of salt and pepper. Turn the heat up to medium.

2. Bring a large pot of water to a boil and salt it. Continue to cook the onions until they are uniformly brown and soft, almost pasty, 10 to 20 minutes more. Meanwhile, cook the pasta in the boiling water, stirring occasionally, and start tasting after 5 minutes. When the pasta is tender but not mushy, drain the pasta, reserving 1 cup of the cooking water.

3. Taste the onions and adjust the seasoning. In a warm bowl, toss together the pasta and onions, along with the remaining oil and a little of the cooking water if necessary to allow the mixture to coat the pasta evenly. Toss with the Parmesan and serve, passing more Parmesan at the table.

PASTA WITH SAVORY CARAMELIZED ONIONS The addition of stronger flavors nicely counters the onions' sweetness: In Step 2, add 2 tablespoons capers or chopped pitted black olives (or both) to the onions as they cook. In Step 3, add 1 teaspoon balsamic or other mild vinegar, or vinegar to taste, but don't overdo it.

PASTA WITH CARAMELIZED ONIONS AND YOGURT A heavenly combination: In Step 3, stir in 2 cups Greek yogurt, adding a little of the cooking water if necessary to make a smooth sauce. Replace the Parmesan with Asiago, manchego, or pecorino Romano if you'd like.

PASTA WITH CARAMELIZED ONIONS AND BREAD CRUMBS Even better if you mix the bread crumbs with ½ cup chopped mixed fresh herbs like parsley, mint, and chives: Omit the Parmesan. Toast 1 cup Fresh Bread Crumbs (page 678) or panko in a large dry skillet over medium heat until golden. Sprinkle over the pasta and serve immediately. ◪

PASTA WITH LEEKS AND PARSLEY Silky and rich: Instead of onions, use 1½ pounds leeks, trimmed, rinsed well, dark green tops removed, and sliced. Omit the cheese and garnish with parsley instead. ◪

Pasta with Broccoli, Cauliflower, or Broccoli Raab

MAKES: About 4 servings
TIME: About 40 minutes
Ⓥ

You can use the same water for the vegetable as you do for the pasta. I cook the garlic in the ¼ cup oil listed here, but I usually add a teaspoon or 2 more oil per serving at the table, more for flavor than for moisture. If you like, garnish with grated Parmesan or toasted bread crumbs.

> **Salt**
> **About 1 pound broccoli, cauliflower, or broccoli raab, trimmed and cut into pieces**
> ¼ **cup olive oil, or more as needed**
> 1 **tablespoon chopped garlic, or more to taste**
> 1 **pound penne, ziti, or other cut pasta**
> **Pepper**

1. Bring a large pot of water to a boil and salt it. Boil the vegetable until it's fairly tender, 5 to 10 minutes, depending on the type (broccoli raab is fastest, cauliflower slowest) and the size of your pieces. Meanwhile, put the oil in a large skillet over medium-low heat. When it's hot, add the garlic and cook until it begins to sizzle, about a minute; remove from the heat until you are ready to add the vegetable.

2. Scoop out the vegetable with a slotted spoon or strainer and transfer it to the skillet. Keep the water boiling. Return the skillet to medium-high heat; cook the vegetable, stirring and mashing, until it is hot and quite soft.

3. Meanwhile, cook the pasta, stirring occasionally, and start tasting after 5 minutes. When the pasta is tender but not mushy, drain the pasta, reserving 1 cup of the cooking water. Add the pasta and a couple of tablespoons of the reserved cooking water to the vegetable; toss with a large spoon until well combined.

Sprinkle with salt and pepper, along with more of the cooking water to keep the mixture from drying out. Serve immediately.

PASTA WITH GREENS Here, if you have enough experience to predict doneness, you can cook the greens at the same time as the pasta: Usually you add them to the boiling water during the last minutes of cooking (if using chard, add the stems a few minutes before adding the leaves). But until you're confident, follow the basic recipe, using about 1½ pounds spinach, kale, collard, chard, mustard, or other greens instead of broccoli. For kale and collards, cut away and discard the stems; for spinach, trim and discard any thick stems. For chard, cut the leaves from the stems and cut the stems into 1-inch pieces; for all the greens, chop the leaves. Cook the greens until tender and proceed with the recipe.

PASTA WITH BUTTERNUT SQUASH OR SWEET POTATO Very traditional, quite delicious; you can also purée the soft vegetables with flavorings, which almost always makes a fine sauce: Omit the broccoli. Grate a sweet potato or butternut squash and put it in a saucepan with some water, plus some oil or butter if you'd like. Cook until soft, drain if necessary, then toss it with the cooked pasta and maybe a little chopped sage or nutmeg, butter, and Parmesan.

8 Ways to Elevate Pasta with Broccoli, Cauliflower, or Broccoli Raab

1. Cook 3 or 4 dried chiles along with the garlic or add red chile flakes when you toss the pasta.
2. Add ½ cup or so Pesto (page 634) when you toss the pasta.
3. Stir in 1 cup chopped cherry or regular tomatoes when you combine the pasta and vegetable.
4. Add a couple of tablespoons of Tapenade (page 291) when you toss the pasta.
5. Add 1 cup sliced mushrooms to the oil once the garlic sizzles and continue to cook, stirring occasionally, until you add the vegetable, then proceed with the recipe.

6. Toss in a cup or so of quick-cooking vegetables during the last 30 to 60 seconds of cooking; think pea shoots, shelled fresh peas, or baby arugula.

7. Stir in ½ cup or so puréed roasted red peppers (see page 228) when you toss the pasta.

8. Top with Crunchy Crumbled Tempeh (page 512) or Fried Bread Crumbs (page 678).

Mario Batali's Vegetarian Ragù

MAKES: About 4 servings
TIME: 50 minutes
V

A food processor is essential to get the texture right for this hearty sauce. You can make substitutions as the seasons change, like swapping out the celery root for fennel in spring, eggplant in the summer, parsnips in the fall.

1 onion, chopped
4 large carrots, chopped
8 ounces celery root, peeled and chopped
8 ounces celery, chopped
6 cloves garlic, peeled
8 tablespoons olive oil
1 cup bread crumbs (preferably fresh, page 678) or panko
1 cup tomato paste
1 28-ounce can crushed tomatoes
Salt and pepper
1 pound rigatoni or other cut pasta
½ cup chopped fresh parsley for garnish

26 Vegetable and Legume Dishes That Can Be Tossed with Pasta

If, after saucing, you think the dish needs more moisture, add a little pasta cooking water or extra oil or butter—or both.

1. Braised Artichoke Hearts (page 169)

2. Roasted or Grilled Asparagus (page 171)

3. Buttered Cabbage (page 185)

4. Breaded Sautéed Cauliflower and its variations (page 189)

5. Pan-Grilled Corn with Tomatoes (page 198)

6. Skillet Eggplant and its variations (page 199)

7. Eggplant Slices with Garlic and Parsley (page 201); chop first

8. Braised Endive, Escarole, or Radicchio (page 203)

9. Garlic Braised in Olive Oil (page 206)

10. Leeks Braised in Olive Oil or Butter and its variations (page 215)

11. Sautéed Mushrooms (page 217)

12. Anything-Scented Peas (page 224)

13. Roasted Red Peppers (page 228)

14. My Mom's Pan-Cooked Peppers and Onions (page 228)

15. Spinach with Currants and Nuts (page 250)

16. Sautéed Summer Squash (page 252)

17. Oven-Roasted Fresh Plum Tomatoes and its variations (page 258)

18. Winter Squash, Braised and Glazed, and most of its variations (page 264)

19. Stovetop Mixed Vegetables with Olive Oil (page 157)

20. White Beans, Tuscan Style, and its variations (page 444)

21. Beans and Mushrooms and most of its variations (page 447)

22. Braised Lentils, Spanish Style, and its variations (page 448)

23. Flageolets, French Style, and its variations (page 454)

24. Chickpea Fondue and its variations (page 465)

25. White Bean Purée and its variations (page 459)

26. Tapenade (page 291)

1. Put the onion, carrots, celery root, celery, and garlic in a food processor with 4 tablespoons of the oil. Pulse until the vegetables are ground but not puréed.

2. Put 2 tablespoons of the oil in a large skillet over medium-high heat. Add the bread crumbs and cook until they're crisp, dark brown, and sizzling, 3 to 5 minutes. Transfer the bread crumbs to a paper towel–lined plate.

3. Return the skillet to medium-high heat and add the remaining 2 tablespoons oil. When it's hot, add the vegetables and cook, stirring frequently, until the onion becomes translucent, 3 to 5 minutes. Add the tomato paste, lower the heat, and cook, stirring frequently, until the mixture darkens, 8 to 12 minutes. Add the tomatoes and sprinkle with salt and pepper. Bring to a boil, and then reduce the heat to simmer. Cook, stirring occasionally until the sauce thickens, 15 to 20 minutes.

4. Bring a large pot of water to a boil. When the water boils, salt it and add the pasta. Stir occasionally, and start tasting after 5 minutes. When the pasta is tender but not mushy, drain the pasta, reserving 1 cup of the cooking water. Add the pasta to the sauce in the skillet, raise the heat to medium-high, and cook, stirring constantly until the sauce is steaming, 1 to 2 minutes. If the sauce gets too dry as it heats, add the reserved cooking water, a tablespoon at a time. Taste and adjust the seasoning. Garnish with the parsley and bread crumbs and serve.

Pasta with Mushrooms

MAKES: 4 servings
TIME: 30 minutes
F V

A great use for shiitakes or even ordinary button mushrooms, but otherworldly when made with fresh porcini. A nice option is using half dried mushrooms (porcini, morels, shiitakes; see the variation).

 1 **pound shiitake or other fresh mushrooms**
 ⅓ **cup plus 1 tablespoon olive oil**
 Salt and pepper

 2 **tablespoons minced shallot or 1 tablespoon minced garlic**
 1 **pound any long or cut pasta**
 ½ **cup vegetable stock (pages 97–100; optional)**
 About ½ cup chopped fresh parsley, plus more for garnish

1. Bring a large pot of water to a boil. Remove the stems from the shiitakes (discard them, or save for stock). If you're using wild mushrooms, wipe them clean or rinse them quickly if they are very dirty. Trim of any hard, tough spots. Cut the mushrooms into small chunks or slices.

2. Put ⅓ cup of the oil in a medium-to-large skillet over medium heat. When it's hot, add the mushrooms and sprinkle with salt and pepper. Raise the heat to medium-high and cook, stirring occasionally, until the mushrooms begin to brown, at least 10 minutes. Add the shallot, stir, and cook for another minute or 2, until the mushrooms are tender. Turn off the heat.

3. Meanwhile, when the water boils, salt it and add the pasta. Stir occasionally, and start tasting after 5 minutes. When the pasta is almost done, add the stock or ½ cup of the pasta cooking water to the mushrooms, turn the heat to low, and reheat gently. When the pasta is tender but not mushy, drain the pasta, reserving 1 cup of the cooking water. Add the pasta and the remaining tablespoon oil to the mushrooms, and toss; add a little of the reserved water if the dish seems dry. Stir in the parsley. Garnish with more parsley and serve.

LINGUINE WITH FRESH AND DRIED MUSHROOMS Use button mushrooms or shiitakes. At the start of Step 1, cover ¼ to ½ cup dried porcini mushrooms with hot water and soak for about 10 minutes, until softened. Lift the mushrooms out of the soaking liquid with your hands or a slotted spoon, reserving the liquid, and squeeze out excess moisture. Cut the porcini into bits and cook them with the fresh mushrooms and shallot. Carefully pour the reserved soaking liquid into another container, leaving any grit in the bottom of the bowl. In Step 3, use the soaking liquid to augment or replace the stock or pasta cooking water.

Pasta with Puréed Beans

MAKES: 4 servings
TIME: 2½ hours, mostly unattended
V

Forget fake cheese; this is my dairy-free equivalent of macaroni and cheese. Puréed beans cooked with dried mushrooms make a thick, velvety sauce that clings to pasta; you could not ask more from (vegan) comfort food.

1	**cup dried chickpeas or cannellini beans, rinsed and picked over, and soaked if you have time**
¼	**cup dried porcini or shiitake mushrooms, rinsed**
1	**sprig fresh thyme or 2 bay leaves**
	Salt and pepper
3	**tablespoons olive oil**
1	**tablespoon minced garlic**
½	**teaspoon red chile flakes**
1	**pound cut pasta like fusilli, rigatoni, or farfalle**
1	**cup bread crumbs (preferably fresh, see page 678)**

1. Put the chickpeas in a large pot with the mushrooms and thyme or bay leaves and cover with water; sprinkle with pepper. Bring to a boil over high heat, then reduce the heat so the mixture bubbles steadily. Cook until the chickpeas are tender, up to 2 hours depending on the beans. Drain the cooked beans and mushrooms, reserving the cooking water (you should have about 4 cups) Discard the thyme or bay leaves.
2. Turn the broiler to high and adjust the rack 4 inches away. Bring a large pot of water to a boil and salt it. Put the oil in a large ovenproof skillet over

medium heat. When it's hot, add the garlic and chile flakes and cook until fragrant, about a minute. Add 3 cups of the cooked beans and mushrooms and 1 cup of the reserved water. Sprinkle with salt and pepper and bring to a boil. Purée the mixture in a blender or food processor (working in batches if necessary). Add more of the water a tablespoon at a time until the purée is the consistency of cream. Return the sauce to the skillet.
3. When the water comes to a boil, add the pasta. Stir occasionally, and start tasting the pasta after 5 minutes. When the pasta is tender but not mushy, drain.
4. Add the pasta and the remaining beans and mushrooms to the sauce and turn the heat to medium. Toss the pasta, adding more of the reserved water a little at the time to make a smooth sauce. Sprinkle with the bread crumbs, broil until they are golden and the sauce is bubbling, and serve.

PASTA WITH PURÉED BEANS AND TOMATOES Wonderful with or without the dried mushrooms: Cook the pasta until still chalky in the center. When you combine the pasta, sauce, and beans in Step 4, add 1 cup chopped tomatoes (drained canned are fine). Cook until the tomatoes are heated through. Sprinkle with the bread crumbs. Broil and serve.

PASTA WITH NUT SAUCES

If you think of pasta as a base for a sauce of whatever's available—and remember that pasta is ubiquitous in the Mediterranean—sauces made from nuts doesn't seem like much of a leap.

Remember; you don't want your pasta swimming in a strong-tasting, robust nut sauce, especially if you're using fresh pasta. Use a dollop of any nut butter thinned with some pasta water to add deep flavor and texture (creamy, crunchy, or both).

Other sauces that feature nuts and are delicious with pasta are Pesto (page 634).

Pasta with Walnut Sauce

MAKES: About 4 servings
TIME: 30 minutes

[F]

A rich bread-thickened nut sauce that's especially unbelievable with stuffed pasta, but good in any situation. To make a vegan version of this sauce, use about ½ cup bread crumbs with unsweetened nut milk and omit the Parmesan.

	Salt
1	thick slice Italian bread
½	cup milk
1	cup walnut or pecan halves
2	cloves garlic
½	cup grated Parmesan, plus more for serving
2	teaspoons fresh marjoram or ½ teaspoon dried marjoram
½	cup olive oil
	Pepper
1	pound dried, fresh, or stuffed pasta

1. Bring a large pot of water to a boil and salt it. Soak the bread in the milk. Put the nuts, garlic, cheese, and marjoram in a food processor and turn the machine on. With the machine running, add the oil gradually, using just enough so that the mixture forms a very thick paste. Add the bread and milk and enough water to make a saucy mixture. Sprinkle with salt and pepper.

2. Add the pasta to the boiling water. Cook the pasta, stirring occasionally, until tender but not mushy. Drain the pasta, reserving 1 cup of the cooking water. Toss the pasta with the sauce; if the mixture appears too thick, thin with a little of the reserved water or more olive oil. Taste and adjust the seasoning, then serve with more Parmesan.

PASTA WITH WALNUT-TOMATO SAUCE The acidity in the tomatoes lightens up the sauce a bit: Add 1 tomato, roughly chopped, or ½ cup chopped canned tomatoes; blend with the nuts in Step 1.

PASTA WITH RICH WALNUT SAUCE Add 3 to 4 tablespoons mascarpone, cream cheese, or cream to the food processor in Step 1.

BAKED PASTA

Comfort food at its best. Lasagne is best made with fresh pasta but all the others start with parcooked dried pasta.

Baked Macaroni and Cheese

MAKES: 4 to 6 servings
TIME: About 45 minutes

Use nearly any pasta—tube, corkscrew, or cup-shaped ones work best because they grab the sauce. Just be sure to slightly undercook whatever pasta you use since it will continue to cook in the oven.

For a vegan take on this dish, see Pasta with Puréed Beans (page 325).

	Salt
2½	cups milk (low-fat is fine)
2	bay leaves
1	pound elbow, shell, ziti, or other cut pasta
4	tablespoons (½ stick) butter
3	tablespoons all-purpose flour
1½	cups grated cheese, like sharp cheddar or Emmental
½	cup grated Parmesan cheese
	Pepper
½	cup or more bread crumbs (preferably fresh, see page 678)

1. Heat the oven to 400°F. Bring a large pot of water to a boil and salt it.

2. Put the milk and the bay leaves in a small saucepan over medium-low heat. When small bubbles appear along the sides, about 5 minutes, turn off the heat and let stand.

3. When the water boils, add the pasta. Stir occasionally, until the pasta is at the point where it is almost done but you would still think it needed another minute or 2 to become tender. Drain it, rinse quickly with cold water to stop the cooking, drain again, and put in a large bowl.

4. Melt 3 tablespoons of the butter in a small saucepan over medium-low heat; when it foams, add the flour and cook, stirring often, until the mixture turns golden, about 5 minutes. Remove the bay leaves from the milk and add about ¼ cup of the milk to the hot flour mixture, stirring constantly with a wire whisk. As soon as the mixture becomes smooth, add a little more milk and continue to do so until all the milk is incorporated and the sauce has thickened; it should coat the back of a spoon. Add the grated cheese and whisk gently until it melts.

5. Pour the sauce over the pasta, toss in the Parmesan, and sprinkle with salt and pepper. Use the remaining 1 tablespoon butter to grease a 9 × 13-inch or similar-size baking pan. Put the pasta mixture into it and top with the bread crumbs. Bake until bubbling and browned, about 15 minutes, and serve.

RICH MACARONI AND CHEESE Super-creamy and indulgent: Reduce the milk to ¾ cup. Omit the bay leaves, the first 3 tablespoons butter, and all of the flour. Swap in mascarpone cheese for the grated cheese. Add about 1 cup or so sautéed mushrooms, if you'd like, and 1 tablespoon chopped fresh sage or 1½ teaspoons dried sage. Cook the pasta as directed. Mix together the milk, mascarpone, and Parmesan in a large bowl. Add the cooked pasta and sage, sprinkle with salt and pepper, and combine. Proceed with baking in Step 5.

NUTTY MACARONI AND BLUE CHEESE Use a mild or medium cheddar, and reduce the amount to 1 cup. Substitute 1 cup crumbled blue cheese for the Parmesan. Fold the blue cheese and ¾ cup chopped walnuts into the pasta mixture in Step 5 (melting the blue cheese in the sauce will make it gray).

MACARONI AND GOAT CHEESE WITH CARAMELIZED ONIONS Nice and tangy from the goat cheese, rich and sweet from the onions: Omit the bay leaves. Reduce the grated cheese to 1 cup and substitute 1 cup soft goat cheese for the Parmesan. Proceed with the recipe from Step 1, stirring in 1 cup Caramelized Onions (page 222), ½ cup toasted pine nuts, and 1 tablespoon chopped fresh thyme with the pasta in Step 5.

MACARONI AND CHEESE WITH TOMATOES Add 1½ pounds chopped, drained tomatoes (canned in a pinch, drained) to the sauce in Step 4 when you add the grated cheese. Proceed with the recipe.

MACARONI AND CHEESE WITH GREENS Hearty and filling: Rinse, trim out the stems, and cut across into wide ribbons 1½ pounds greens; kale, collards, escarole, spinach would all work. Wilt in a large skillet with olive oil or butter, then stir in the greens when you combine the pasta and sauce in Step 5.

6 Great Mac and Cheese Combos

Here are some other pastas and cheeses to use. Up the proportions as you like. Some drier hard cheeses, like Parmesan, Asiago, manchego, and some pecorinos, are better when mixed with softer cheeses; similarly, very strong–flavored cheeses are best mixed with mild-flavored cheeses. Try:

1. Pasta shells with ½ cup crème fraîche and 1½ cups pecorino

2. Fusilli or corkscrew with 1½ cups smoked Gouda or mozzarella and ½ cup Parmesan

3. Wagon wheels with 1½ cups goat cheese and ½ cup pecorino Romano

4. Rotini or spirals with 1 cup each Gorgonzola and Bel Paese or fontina cheese

5. Tube pastas like penne, rigatoni, and ziti with 1 cup each manchego and Jack

6. Orecchiette with 1 cup each ricotta and Parmesan or pecorino

Vegetable Lasagne

MAKES: 6 to 8 servings
TIME: 1 hour, with prepared pasta sheets and sauce
Ⓜ

At its simplest, lasagne is a baked dish of layered pasta (each sheet is a "lasagna"; lasagne is plural), sauce, and cheese; adding some cooked vegetables like spinach, zucchini, or mushrooms is a no-brainer. Make your lasagne with fresh pasta whenever you can; it's traditional and completely delicious. However, store-bought noodles are fine, and egg roll wrappers and polenta slices (page 391) work surprisingly well too.

> Salt
> 1 recipe any fresh pasta (page 343), rolled into sheets, or 16 dried lasagne noodles
> 2 tablespoons butter, softened, or olive oil
> 2 recipes Fast Tomato Sauce (page 312), Mario Batali's Vegetable Ragù (page 325), or Tomato-Mushroom Sauce (page 313)
> 3 cups cooked spinach, squeezed dry and chopped, or any other chopped cooked vegetable
> 3 cups ricotta, plus more as needed (substitute shredded mozzarella for half of the ricotta, if you must)
> 2 cups grated Parmesan cheese, plus more as needed
> Pepper

1. Bring a large pot of water to a boil and salt it. Cut the fresh pasta sheets into long, wide noodles approximately 3 × 13 inches or a size that will fit in your baking dish. Cook the noodles (8 at a time for dried noodles) until they are tender but still underdone (they will finish cooking as the lasagne bakes); fresh pasta will take only a minute or less. Drain, then lay the noodles flat on a towel, not touching so they don't stick together.
2. Heat the oven to 400°F. Grease a deep baking dish (9 × 13-inch or similar) with the butter or oil. Add a large dollop of tomato sauce and spread it around. Put a

layer of 4 noodles in the dish, trimming any overhanging edges; top with a layer of tomato sauce, one-third of the spinach, one-fourth of the ricotta (use your fingers to "crumble" it evenly over top), and one-fourth of the Parmesan. Sprinkle some salt and pepper between the layers of tomato sauce and spinach if you'd like.
3. Repeat the layers twice. Top with the remaining noodles, tomato sauce, ricotta, and Parmesan; the top should be covered with cheese; add more ricotta and Parmesan as needed. (You can prepare the lasagne up to this point, wrap it tightly and refrigerate for up to a day or freeze. Bring to room temperature before proceeding.)
4. Bake until the lasagne is bubbling and the cheese is melted and lightly browned on top, about 30 minutes. Remove from the oven and let rest for a few minutes before serving. Or cool completely, cover well, and refrigerate for up to 3 days or freeze for up to a month.

WHITE LASAGNE Decadent: Omit the ricotta and substitute 1 recipe Béchamel Sauce (page 675) for the tomato sauce. If you like, replace the spinach with 2 cups diced cooked butternut squash tossed with 1 tablespoon minced fresh sage and a pinch of nutmeg.

PESTO LASAGNE Alternate layers of pesto and tomato sauce or use all pesto: Substitute Pesto (page 634) for all or half of the tomato sauce.

TOFU LASAGNE Use Eggless Pasta Dough (page 345) or dried lasagne noodles; substitute puréed silken or soft tofu for the ricotta and bread crumbs for the Parmesan. Add basil leaves between the layers if you'd like. Be sure the tomato sauce and spinach are well seasoned. Proceed with the recipe, finishing with a layer of bread crumbs and drizzle with olive oil. Ⓥ

10 Dishes for Layering in Lasagne
Layer any of these dishes (chopped or thinly sliced where appropriate) between your lasagne noodles,

with tomato sauce, Béchamel (page 675), cheese, or nothing.

1. Boiled or Steamed Greens (page 153), particularly spinach
2. Roasted Artichoke Hearts (page 170)
3. Grilled or Broiled Eggplant (page 201)
4. Eggplant Slices with Garlic and Parsley (page 201)
5. Sautéed Mushrooms (page 217)
6. Caramelized Onions (page 222)
7. Roasted Red Peppers (page 228)
8. Oven-Roasted Fresh Plum Tomatoes (page 258)
9. Winter Squash, Braised and Glazed (page 264)
10. Stovetop Mixed Vegetables with Olive Oil (page 157)

Baked Ziti

MAKES: 6 servings
TIME: About 1 hour
Ⓜ

By the time this gets to your mouth, the experience is extremely close to that of lasagne—but it's a lot easier to make. Whatever you do, don't overcook the pasta! It should be too tough to actually eat when you mix it with the sauce, which will make it perfect after baking.

> Salt
> 3 tablespoons olive oil or butter, plus more as needed
> 1 pound any fresh mushrooms, preferably mixed with some reconstituted dried porcini (see page 217)
> 1 large onion, chopped
> 1 tablespoon minced garlic (optional)
> Pepper
> 1 28-ounce can whole tomatoes, chopped, with their liquid
> 1 pound ziti or other large cut pasta
> 1 pound mozzarella (preferably fresh), grated or chopped

About ½ cup grated Parmesan cheese (optional)

1. Bring a large pot of water to a boil and salt it. Heat the oven to 400°F. Put the olive oil or butter in a large skillet over medium-high heat. When the oil is hot or the butter is melted, add the mushrooms and cook, stirring occasionally, until they soften, release their water, and then begin to dry again, about 5 minutes. Add the onion and the garlic, if you're using it; sprinkle with salt and pepper. Lower the heat to medium and continue to cook, stirring occasionally, until the vegetables are soft, 3 to 5 minutes.
2. Add the tomatoes and bring to a boil. Turn the heat down so that the mixture bubbles gently, and continue to cook, stirring occasionally, while you cook the pasta; don't let the sauce get too thick.
3. When the water boils, add the pasta. Stir occasionally and cook the pasta until it's still a bit too underdone to eat. Drain it, but don't shake the colander; allow some water to cling to the noodles. Toss it with the sauce and about half the mozzarella. Grease a large baking dish (9 × 13-inch or similar) and pour or spoon the mixture into it. Top with the remaining mozzarella and the Parmesan if you're using it. Bake until the top is browned and the cheese bubbly, 20 to 30 minutes.

BAKED ZITI WITH RICOTTA Two ways to go: Stir up to 1 cup ricotta into the sauce right before tossing it with the pasta and proceed with the recipe. Or as you're putting the ziti in the baking dish, nestle dollops of ricotta in among the pasta.

BAKED ZITI WITH GARLICKY BREAD CRUMBS Even better with 1 pound spinach, wilted, mixed in: Omit the garlic and cheese in the sauce. Proceed with the recipe, topping the pasta with 1 cup bread crumbs, preferably fresh (page 678), mixed with 1 teaspoon minced garlic and 1 tablespoon olive oil. Bake until the sauce is bubbling and the bread crumbs have browned, 15 to 20 minutes. Ⓥ

THE BASICS OF ASIAN NOODLES

Some noodles from Asia, like fresh Chinese egg noodles, are almost identical to their European counterparts. Others are radically different in taste, texture, and preparation (after all, rice is not the same thing as wheat). Once they're cooked, in a pinch you can substitute one for another, but a familiarity with the noodles of China, Japan, Thailand, and elsewhere will expand your culinary repertoire significantly.

Here's a rundown of the most common varieties of Asian noodles you're likely to encounter, along with preparation tips and cooking times; the list is by no means complete (Asia is a big place, with many different cuisines!), but these are what you're most likely to encounter, and the ones I use most often.

CHINESE EGG NOODLES Long, thin, golden egg noodles made with wheat flour; round or flat, fresh or dried. Cooking time depends on the thickness. The fresh noodles cook quickly, in 3 minutes or so, or you can add them directly to hot soup. Dried take 5 minutes or so; leave them slightly undercooked if you are adding them to soup.

BEAN THREADS (MUNG BEAN THREADS, CELLOPHANE NOODLES, GLASS NOODLES, OR SPRING RAIN NOODLES) These long, slender, translucent noodles are made from mung bean starch and are usually sold in 2-ounce bundles. To prepare, soak the noodles in hot or boiling water until tender, 5 to 15 minutes; you can also cook them for a few minutes in boiling water. Use kitchen scissors to cut them into manageable pieces if necessary. If you're adding them to soup or are deep-frying them, don't bother to soak.

RICE STICKS Mostly from Southeast Asia, these are white, translucent rice noodles that range in width from spaghetti thickness to greater than ¼ inch. Soak in hot water for 5 to 30 minutes, until softened. For a stir-fry, soak the noodles for 15 to 20 minutes, then drain and cook them in the skillet or wok for an additional minute or 2. For soups, add the rice sticks directly to the broth or soak them for 5 to 10 minutes and then drop them into the soup.

RICE VERMICELLI Similar to rice sticks, but long and slender like angel hair pasta. To prepare, soak the noodles in hot water for about 5 minutes or in cold water for 25 to 30. Rinse, drain, and boil for 1 to 2 minutes or stir-fry. If you are adding to soup, boil for only 1 minute after soaking.

UDON Round, square, or flat wheat noodles from Japan, available in a range of thicknesses and lengths; may be fresh or dried. They have a slippery texture and most typically appear in soups and stews, though you can also use them in braised dishes or serve them cold. Boil fresh noodles for a couple of minutes, until tender. For dried noodles, add them to boiling water, allow the water to return to a boil, and then add a cup of cold water. When the water returns to a boil, add another cup of cold water and repeat this process until the noodles are al dente.

SOBA Long, thin, flat Japanese noodles made from buckwheat or a combination of buckwheat and wheat flours. The buckwheat makes the noodles distinctively nutty and light beige to brownish gray, but they are sometimes green because of the addition of green tea. Generally dried, but you may see fresh. Boil the dried noodles for 5 to 7 minutes, the fresh for 2 to 4. If you're serving them cold, rinse thoroughly with cold water after draining.

SOMEN White, round, ultra-thin all-wheat Japanese noodles that cook in just a couple of minutes. They are often eaten cold, especially in the summer.

RAMEN Long, slender, off-white Japanese wheat noodles that appear either crinkled in brick form or as rods; fresh, dried, frozen, or instant. The instant variety is typically deep-fried before being dried and packaged. Boil fresh ramen for just a couple of minutes; dried takes around 5. Prepare instant ramen according to the package instructions; see the variation for Vastly Improved Store-Bought Ramen (page 334).

YUBA (TOFU OR BEAN CURD NOODLES) These are narrow, flat beige noodles, made from pressed tofu; commonly used in salads and stir-fries. They are available fresh, frozen, and dried. Thaw frozen noodles in the fridge, then treat as fresh. Soak dried noodles in warm water for about 15 minutes, then rinse and drain.

Tips for Dramatically Better Asian-Style Noodle Bowls

Start by soaking or cooking the noodles as necessary. When they're tender but still firm, drain and rinse, then put them in a bowl of cold water. This will keep the strands from sticking together while you get everything ready. (This is a handy trick for entertaining.) You get correctly cooked noodles that will keep your soup liquid clear because it's not muddied by the noodles' starch.

Feel free to use water spiked with soy sauce or other flavorings like miso, tamari, Fishless Fish Sauce (page 656), dried mushrooms, ginger, or turmeric, or sautéed aromatics like carrots, celery, scallions, garlic, and onions if you don't have stock or dashi ready.

Thicken the broth by adding any nut butter, smashed Roasted Garlic (page 205) or puréed starchy vegetables like sweet potatoes.

Put a piece of kombu in your broth; remove it before serving or chop it and put it back in.

Take care to not stir the egg if you choose to add one to the broth. Instead, you'll want to stir the noodles over the egg, allowing for it to sit for a minute and poach.

Make sure the broth is boiling hot when you assemble the dish. The noodles will cool it down a bit.

Cold Sesame or Peanut Noodles

MAKES: 2 main-course or 4 side-dish servings
TIME: 30 minutes
F M O

These noodles are easy to prepare; in addition to cucumbers, you can add in other crunchy vegetables like carrots, radish, and peppers. To make it more substantial, add ½ cup or so of small tofu cubes, cooked soybeans, or Crunchy Crumbled Tempeh (page 512). If you use an egg-free pasta, this becomes vegan.

	Salt
1	pound cucumbers
12	ounces fresh Chinese egg noodles or dried (not fresh) long pasta like linguine
2	tablespoons sesame oil
½	cup tahini, peanut butter, or a combination
2	tablespoons sugar
3	tablespoons soy sauce, or to taste
1	teaspoon minced fresh ginger (optional)
1	tablespoon rice vinegar, white wine vinegar, or other vinegar
	Hot chile oil or Tabasco sauce
½	teaspoon pepper, or more to taste
	At least ½ cup chopped scallions for garnish

1. Bring a large pot of water to boil and salt it. Peel the cucumbers, cut them in half, and seed them. Cut the cucumber into shreds (use a grater or a knife, depending on your taste) and set aside.

2. When the water comes to a boil, add the noodles. Cook, stirring occasionally until the noodles are tender but not mushy. (Start tasting after 1 minute for fresh noodles, 5 minutes for long pasta.) While the noodles are cooking, whisk together the sesame oil, tahini, sugar, soy, ginger if you're using it, vinegar, chile oil to taste, and pepper in a large bowl. Thin the sauce with some of the cooking water to about the consistency of heavy cream; you will need ¼ to ½ cup. Stir in the cucumbers.

Improvising Noodle Bowls

This is a mix-and-match chart; you can follow the rows straight across the columns, but you can also use the old "one from column A and one from column B" technique; noodle bowls are like stir-fries in that pretty much anything goes. See the sidebar, opposite, for directions for cooking or soaking the noodles.

NOODLE	BROTH	MAIN INGREDIENTS	GARNISHES (ALONE OR IN COMBINATION)
Udon	Kombu Dashi (page 100)	Spoonsful of silken tofu	Sliced scallions; Nori "Shake" (page 650)
Soba	Kombu Dashi (page 100)	Poached or hard-boiled egg	Pickled Ginger (page 207); Japanese Seven-Spice Mix (page 650)
Somen	Miso	Winter squash cubes, cooked simply (page 150); chopped cooked collards or kale	Chopped toasted walnuts
Rice sticks (thin)	Any	Sesame-Soy Tofu Burgers with Scallions, made into balls (page 505)	Chopped fresh cilantro and minced fresh chile (like jalapeño or Thai), red chile flakes, or cayenne pepper
Rice sticks (medium or wide)	Any vegetable stock (pages 97–100) except Mushroom Stock	Kimchi (page 93); cooked soybeans	Chopped fresh cilantro and shredded carrots
Chinese egg noodles	Mushroom Stock (page 99)	Stir-fried asparagus (page 154) or Sautéed Mushrooms (page 217)	Sesame seeds, cashews, or chopped peanuts
Chinese egg noodles	Vegetable stock (pages 97–100) or soy broth	Spicy Scrambled Tofu (page 489) or Scrambled Eggs (page 523)	Bean sprouts, sliced scallions, and five-spice powder

3. When the noodles are done, drain them and rinse under cold water. Drain again. Toss the noodles with the sauce and cucumbers. Taste, add salt if necessary, then garnish and serve.

COLD FIERY NOODLES Like a salad, really, with lots of crisp vegetables and a light, hot-sweet dressing: Rinse (and trim if you'd like) ½ cup bean sprouts and slice a handful of radishes (any kind). Chop up some cilantro and peanuts for garnish. When you make the dressing, omit the tahini or peanut butter; increase the vinegar to 2 tablespoons and add ¼ cup good-quality vegetable oil. When you stir in the cucumbers in Step 2, add the sprouts and radishes and at least 1 teaspoon Chile Paste (page 664) or minced fresh chile (like jalapeño or Thai). Thin with just 1 tablespoon or so of water. Proceed with the recipe, garnishing each serving with a sprinkle of scallions, cilantro, and peanuts.

COLD GINGER NOODLES Great at any temperature, really: Increase the fresh ginger to 1 tablespoon. When you make the sauce in Step 2, add ½ teaspoon ground ginger and 1 teaspoon honey. Garnish with toasted sesame seeds.

Bean Threads with Coconut Milk and Mint

MAKES: 2 main-course or 4 side-dish servings
TIME: 20 minutes
F V

Noodles and broth are a perfect one-dish meal: easy to prepare ahead, a great vehicle for all sorts of leftovers, and a satisfying combination of textures and flavors. Soupy, but not quite soup; consider these very moist noodle dishes.

> 2 2-ounce bundles glass (mung bean) noodles
> 2 cups coconut milk (to make your own, see page 304) or 1 14-ounce can plus a little water
> ¼ cup soy sauce, or to taste
> 2 tablespoons ketchup

> 1 tablespoon Fishless Fish Sauce (page 656; optional)
>   Salt and pepper
> 8 ounces Crunchy Crumbled Tempeh (page 512)
> ½ cup sliced scallions
> ¼ cup chopped fresh mint
> 2 tablespoons chopped peanuts (optional)
> 1 tablespoon chopped fresh chile (like jalapeño or Thai) or to taste, or red chile flakes or cayenne (optional)

1. Soak the glass noodles in hot water until soft, then cut the strands with kitchen scissors to make manageable lengths. Drain, rinse, and put in a bowl of cold water while you prepare the other ingredients.
2. Bring 4 cups water to a boil and add the coconut milk; stir in the soy sauce and ketchup, and the "fish" sauce if you're using it. Taste and add a little salt if necessary, plus lots of pepper. Keep the broth bubbling.
3. To serve, drain the noodles well and divide them among bowls. Ladle the broth over the noodles and swirl them a bit to make sure they're submerged. Top with the tempeh, scallions, and mint, and the peanuts and chiles to taste if you'd like, and serve.

FASTER NOODLE SOUP Quicker than takeout: Instead of bean threads, boil egg noodles in salted water until tender but not mushy. Drain, rinse, and return to cold water as described in Step 1. In Step 2, omit the coconut milk, bring 6 cups water to a boil, and add the soy sauce and the ketchup. If you like, add 8 ounces firm tofu, cut into small cubes instead of the tempeh. Omit the mint. The peanuts and chiles are optional but recommended.

VASTLY IMPROVED STORE-BOUGHT RAMEN For pocket change, you buy a package of ramen, which is really a serving of noodles with a packet of sodium-laden "broth" concentrate included. Try this: Discard the broth packet. Cook the noodles as in Step 1, then proceed, using as many or as few of the above ingredients as you like. Or cook the noodles as in Step 1, gently dropping an egg into them when they're about half

cooked and reducing the heat to a simmer. When the egg is poached (see page 525), gently stir in 1 tablespoon soy sauce, 1 teaspoon sesame oil, and a dash Tabasco or other hot sauce. Garnish if you'd like with peanuts, tempeh, and/or scallions and serve.

Pad Thai

MAKES: 4 servings
TIME: 30 minutes
F M

Though you probably first fell in love with pad Thai in a Thai restaurant, it's easy to make at home. Cucumber Salad with Soy and Ginger (page 49) or Edamame Salad with Seaweed "Mayo" (page 75) would make a great accompaniment.

12	ounces dried flat ¼-inch-thick rice noodles
5	tablespoons good-quality vegetable oil
3	eggs, lightly beaten
4	cloves garlic, minced
8	ounces pressed tofu (see page 483) or extra-firm tofu, prepared by any of the methods on page 483 or blotted dry, sliced
2	scallions, trimmed and cut into 1-inch lengths
1	cup bean sprouts
2	tablespoons Fishless Fish Sauce (page 656) or soy sauce
2	teaspoons tamarind paste or ketchup
2	teaspoons sugar
¼	cup chopped peanuts
¼	cup chopped fresh cilantro
2	chiles (preferably Thai), seeded, and sliced (optional)
1	lime, cut into wedges

1. Put the noodles in a bowl and pour boiling water over them to cover. Soak until softened, at least 15 minutes; if you want to hold them longer, drain them, fill the bowl with cold water, and return the noodles to the bowl.

2. Put 2 tablespoons of the oil in a large skillet, preferably nonstick, over medium heat. When it's hot, add the eggs and scramble quickly for the first minute or so with a fork almost flat against the bottom of the pan; you're aiming for a thin egg crêpe, one with the smallest curd you can make. Cook just until set, then transfer the crêpe to a cutting board. Cut into ¼-inch-wide strips and set aside.

3. Raise the heat to high and add the remaining 3 tablespoons oil. When it's is hot, add the garlic, tofu, scallions, and half the bean sprouts and cook, stirring occasionally, until the garlic and scallions have softened, 3 to 5 minutes. Transfer with a slotted spoon to a plate.

4. Put the drained noodles, eggs, "fish" sauce, tamarind paste, and sugar in the pan and cook, stirring occasionally, until the noodles are heated through. Add the tofu mixture. Toss once or twice to combine, then transfer to a serving platter. Top with the peanuts, cilantro, chiles if you're using them, and the remaining bean sprouts. Serve with the lime wedges on the side.

EGGLESS PAD THAI Equally satisfying: Omit the eggs and reduce the oil to 2 tablespoons. You can add a tablespoon or 2 of peanut or almond butter in Step 4, if you'd like, for a creamier, filling sauce. V

PAD KEE MAO Another takeout favorite: Omit the eggs, bean sprouts, tamarind paste, peanuts, and cilantro and reduce the oil to 3 tablespoons. Increase the Fishless Fish Sauce to ¼ cup and whisk with 2 tablespoons soy sauce, 1 teaspoon rice vinegar, and the sugar. Crumble the tofu into the skillet with the garlic and chiles and cook until golden and softened, about 5 minutes; remove with a slotted spoon. Cook 1 onion, sliced, and 1 cup sliced red bell pepper until softened, 3 to 5 minutes. Return the tofu mixture, noodles, and sauce to the skillet and cook until heated through, 1 to 2 minutes. Garnish with a handful of holy or Thai basil. V

Soba with Dipping Sauce

MAKES: 4 to 6 servings
TIME: 20 minutes
F M V

Fast, cool, and refreshing. If you can't find soba noodles, substitute all-wheat somen noodles or angel hair pasta, both of which take a few minutes less to become tender.

> 2 cups Kombu Dashi (page 100), chilled
> ½ cup soy sauce
> 2 tablespoons mirin (or 1 tablespoon honey mixed with 1 tablespoon water)
> 2 tablespoons light brown sugar
> Salt
> 8 ounces soba (about three 60-gram bundles)
> 2 scallions, trimmed and chopped
> Wasabi paste for serving (optional)

1. Put the dashi, soy sauce, mirin, and sugar in small bowl. Stir until the sugar dissolves.

2. Bring a large pot of water to a boil and salt it. Add the noodles and cook until tender, 2 to 4 minutes. Drain and rinse under cold running water. (You can prepare the dipping sauce and noodles up to a few hours in advance. Cover and refrigerate the rinsed noodles and sauce separately.)

3. Serve each person a small bowl of noodles set on top of a couple of ice cubes in a larger bowl, with a small bowl with about ½ cup of the dipping sauce scattered with the scallions on the side. Pass a little dish of wasabi, if you're using it, to stir into the dipping sauce.

SOBA WITH SPICY DIPPING SAUCE Packs more of a punch: Omit the mirin and sugar. In a blender, combine 1 tablespoon fresh lemon juice (or to taste), 1 clove garlic, a 1-inch piece fresh ginger, and 1 red chile or 1 teaspoon Chile Paste (or to taste; see page 664), and blend until smooth.

11 Quick Garnishes for Soba with Dipping Sauce

1. Matchsticks of daikon or other radish
2. Matchsticks of peeled and seeded cucumber
3. Minced fresh ginger
4. Chopped pickles, especially Quickest Pickled Vegetables (page 89)
5. Tiny cubes of fresh, pressed, or smoked tofu
6. Minced Hard-Boiled Egg (page 521)
7. Nori "Shake" (page 650) or Nori Chips (page 247)
8. Sesame seeds (black ones look stunning)
9. Finely shredded Napa or other cabbage
10. Chopped walnuts or other nuts
11. Kimchi (page 93)

Stir-Fried Ramen with Vegetables

MAKES: 2 servings
TIME: 25 minutes
F O

Another way to make cheap ramen noodles into a full meal. Of course, you can also use the wide variety of ramen noodles available now, from dried whole grain to fresh.

The vegetables are really just suggestions; you can use cabbage, spinach, celery, mushrooms, green beans, or bok choy. Whatever you use, try to cut the vegetables into shapes that mimic the noodles.

> Salt
> 8 ounces ramen noodles, or 4 packages instant noodles
> ¼ cup soy sauce, plus more for serving
> 1 tablespoon sesame oil
> 1 tablespoon mirin or honey
> 3 tablespoons good-quality vegetable oil
> 2–3 cups quick-cooking vegetables like onion, bell peppers, snow peas, sliced into matchsticks, and/or bean sprouts

1. Bring a large pot of water to a boil and salt it. Add the noodles and cook until pliable but still firm; you don't want to fully cook them. Drain, rinse, and put in a bowl of cold water while you prepare the other ingredients.

2. Whisk together the soy sauce, sesame oil, and mirin in a small bowl. Put the vegetable oil in a large skillet over medium-high heat. When it's hot, add the vegetables, except for bean sprouts, and cook until browned and crisp-tender, 3 to 5 minutes. Pour in the sauce and scrape the bottom of the pan to loosen any browned bits.

3. Drain the noodles and add them to the vegetables along with the bean sprouts if you're using them. Cook, stirring often, until the noodles are tender and hot. Serve, passing the soy sauce at the table.

RICE CAKES

Rice cakes are made by pounding glutinous rice until it forms a smooth, elastic dough, which is then either hand rolled or extruded or molded by a machine. The texture ranges from soft to dense, but good rice cakes are always pleasantly chewy. Most Asian markets sell some form of rice cake, often frozen in plastic packages, and sometimes fresh. They are available in a wide range of flavors, colors, and shapes: savory or sweet; stuffed or plain; pink, green, yellow, or white; round, oblong, crescent, flat as sticks, or thick as ropes. And they can be boiled, stir-fried, braised, steamed, or pan-fried.

Rice Cakes with Sweet Soy Sauce

MAKES: 4 servings
TIME: 30 minutes
F V

These sautéed or stir-fried rice cakes are sweet, salty, spicy, and addicting. There are two kinds of rice cake that work great in this recipe: noodlelike Korean *duk* (aka *dduk* or *deok*) and Chinese New Year cake, which is formed into long, ½-inch-thick white noodles and either sold whole (usually fresh), cut into sticks, or sliced and frozen. Japanese mochi, available in various shapes, also work well.

1 **pound rice cakes**
3 **tablespoons soy sauce**
1 **tablespoon sesame oil**
1 **tablespoon sugar**
3 **tablespoons Korean-Style Chile Paste (page 664) or gochujang, or to taste**
2 **tablespoons good-quality vegetable oil**
  Pepper
  Chopped scallions for garnish
  Toasted sesame seeds (see page 299) for garnish

---

17 Dishes That Can Be Stir-Fried with Rice Noodles

Cook any rice noodles until tender but not mushy, then add them to the pan with the cooked vegetables and toss until heated through. For more moisture, add a little of the noodle-cooking water or vegetable stock; a splash of soy sauce; or a drizzle of sesame oil or good-quality vegetable oil.

1. Stir-Fried Vegetables (page 154)

2. Stir-Fried Vegetables, Vietnamese Style (page 154)

3. Quick-Cooked Bok Choy or Bok Choy with Black Beans (page 179)

4. Grilled or Broiled Eggplant or its variations (page 201)

5. Green Beans Tossed with Walnut-Miso Sauce (page 208)

6. Sautéed Mushrooms (page 217)

7. Pan-Cooked Peppers and Onions with Ginger (page 229)

8. Anything-Scented Peas (page 224)

9. Winter Squash with Soy or with Coconut Milk and Curry (page 264)

10. Agedashi Tofu (page 487)

11. Stir-Fried Tofu with Bell Peppers or Other Vegetables or its variations (page 489)

12. Braised Tofu with Eggplant and Shiitakes (page 491)

13. Braised Tofu and Peas in Curried Coconut Milk or its variations (page 493)

14. Tempeh Chili with Black Beans (page 517)

15. Edamame with Tomatoes and Cilantro (page 436)

16. Hot and Sour Edamame with Tofu or its variations (page 438)

17. Black Soybeans with Soy Sauce (page 457)

Rice Cakes with Sweet Soy Sauce
and Vegetables (page 339)

1. If the rice cakes are frozen, soak them in a large bowl of cold water for a few minutes until they're thawed a bit, then cook them in a pot of boiling water until soft, about 5 minutes, drain, and slice when cool enough to handle.

2. Mix together the soy sauce, sesame oil, sugar, and chile paste in a small bowl and set aside.

3. Put the vegetable oil in a large nonstick or cast-iron skillet over medium-high heat. When it's hot, add the rice cakes, soy sauce mixture, and a sprinkle of pepper; cook until the rice cakes are coated in the sauce, 2 to 3 minutes. If the pan dries out, add a couple of tablespoons of the water. Garnish with scallions and sesame seeds and serve.

RICE CAKES WITH SWEET SOY SAUCE AND VEGETABLES
A quick one-pan dinner: Prepare about 2 cups of any combination of thinly sliced shiitakes, onions, carrots, and/or bell peppers. Add to the hot pan in Step 3; cook until softened, about 3 minutes. Proceed with the recipe, adding more vegetable oil as needed.

RICE CAKES WITH STIR-FRIED GREENS Follow the variation above, substituting 1 pound greens like baby spinach, pea shoots, and/or sliced baby bok choy or Napa cabbage for the vegetables.

CURRIED RICE CAKES Great served with Winter Squash with Soy (page 264): Omit the soy sauce and sugar in Step 2 and add 1 teaspoon curry powder and ¼ cup coconut milk.

RICE CAKES WITH KIMCHI Omit the sesame oil, sugar, and chile paste. In Step 3, add 1 cup or more Kimchi (page 93) a minute or so after the rice cakes.

BRAISED RICE CAKES The rice cakes thicken the liquid as they cook, creating a stick-to-your-ribs dish: Add 3 cups vegetable stock (pages 97 to 100), dashi (page 100), or water and up to 2 cups whatever thinly sliced vegetables you like and/or cubed tofu. Omit the sugar and vegetable oil. Put the stock in a pot and bring to a boil; add the remaining ingredients and cook at a steady

bubble until the rice cakes are soft and the vegetables are cooked. Garnish with scallions and sesame seeds.

RICE OR CELLOPHANE NOODLES WITH SWEET SOY SAUCE If you like, add vegetables as in the first variation: Substitute 8 to 12 ounces rice vermicelli, rice sticks, or cellophane noodles for the rice cakes. Drain the noodles and immediately add them to the pan; you may need additional oil. Proceed with the recipe.

THE BASICS OF FRESH PASTA AND DUMPLINGS

Two basic doughs—one just flour and water enriched with olive oil, the other with egg yolks—form the backbone of a family of dishes shared by cultures around the world. I count cut pasta, ravioli, and gnocchi and pasta-like dumplings like spaetzle in this category.

FRESH PASTA

This section focuses on Italian-style pastas, and the recipes range from rich and eggy to vegan to bright and herby; they're all classic. All-purpose flour is the most convenient and conventional flour to use, though

Making Pasta by Hand

STEP 1 To make pasta by hand, first make a well in the mound of flour and break the eggs into it, then mix to incorporate the flour.

STEP 2 To knead the dough, use the heel of your hand to push into the middle of the dough, fold the dough over, rotate it 90 degrees, and push into it again.

semolina also makes a lovely pasta. But as long as you make some adjustments, you can use any flour for pasta, whether your reason is to change flavor, add nutrients, or avoid gluten; see the table on page 344.

PASTA-MAKING TECHNIQUES

The most traditional way to make fresh pasta is by hand, but it's far easier to start the dough in a food processor, then roll it thin with a pasta-rolling machine.

For *literally* handmade pasta, pile your flour on a smooth, clean work surface (for fresh egg pasta) or in a large bowl (for eggless pasta) and create a well in the middle of the flour. Put your eggs or liquids into the well, then use a fork or wooden spoon to incorporate the flour. Once a dough begins to form, use your hands to fully incorporate the rest of the flour. It'll be messy at first but should start to come together within a couple of minutes. It's at this point, when the dough is still shaggy, that you want to add more liquid (water or olive oil) or flour in small amounts. You'll know which to add by the look and feel of the dough: If it's mushy and sticking to your hands, you need more flour; if it's not coming together and separated into dried-out-looking pieces, you need more liquid.

From this point it's a matter of kneading for a few minutes. Form the dough into a ball and sprinkle it and your work surface with some flour. Use the heel of your hand to push into the middle of the dough; fold the dough over, rotate it 90 degrees, and push into it again. Continue kneading until the dough is completely smooth with some elasticity to it. If you pull off a piece, it should stretch a bit before breaking; if it breaks off immediately, keep kneading. If the dough is sticking to your hands or the work surface, sprinkle it with flour, just enough to keep it from sticking.

Using a food processor is not for purists, but I like it, and the end result is nearly the same as handmade. Put the flour and salt in the processor's bowl and pulse it a couple of times; add the egg and a bit of the liquid you're using and turn the machine on. Gradually add the rest of the liquid(s) until the dough forms a ball. Remove the dough and knead it by hand (see above) or sprinkle it with a good amount of flour and use the pasta-rolling machine to knead it. To use the pasta roller, set the rollers at the thickest setting and work the dough through several times, folding it over after each roll. Slowly work your way down to about the middle thickness setting, then let the dough rest.

USING A MANUAL PASTA MACHINE

You can roll pasta without a machine: Just use a rolling pin, roll from the center out, and keep flouring and turning the dough. But if fresh pasta is something you make or intend to make regularly, a good hand-cranked pasta machine is essential. It will cut down your rolling time by at least half. Most come with a cutter attachment, which will also save you time and give you beautifully cut pasta. These machines are simple to use, easy to maintain, and worth the investment, which is only about $40. (You can also buy an attachment for your stand mixer for considerably more money.)

Secure the machine on a sturdy counter or table-top, making sure the crank handle has clearance and

Using a Pasta Machine

STEP 1 Begin by putting a piece of dough through the thickest setting. Repeat.

STEP 2 Decrease the distance between the two rollers, making the strip of dough progressively thinner. Note that as the dough becomes longer, it will become more fragile. Dust with flour between rollings if necessary.

that there is surface area on both sides of the machine. Sprinkle the machine and surrounding surfaces with flour and set the rollers at the thickest setting (most machines use sequential numbers to indicate settings, but some use letters or just tick marks). Dust a portion of dough with flour and pass it through the machine. Add more flour if the dough sticks.

Decrease the separation of the rollers by one notch and pass the dough through; continue decreasing the thickness one notch at a time and rolling the dough. It's important to roll pasta gradually this way, otherwise the dough will tear. If the dough tears or sticks, ball up the dough and start over. When you get to the thinnest setting, cut the sheet of pasta in half so it's a more manageable length. Roll the sheet through twice more; it's now ready for cutting, stuffing, or freezing.

To clean your pasta-rolling machine, use a clean, dry pastry or paint brush to brush off the flour. Use a dinner knife to scrape off any bits of dough stuck to the rollers and wipe off the exterior with a damp cloth or paper towel. Do not use water; it will gum up any flour in the machine and the gears may rust.

CUTTING PASTA

The fun comes when you cut the pasta into shapes, which can be just about anything. Use the machine's cutting attachment, a knife, or pasta or pizza cutter for the long, flat fettuccine or tagliatelle (basically the same thing; one is just bigger than the other).

To hand-cut fettuccine, pappardelle, lasagne, or similar ribbonlike pasta, dust the sheet of pasta with flour or cornmeal, loosely roll it lengthwise, and cut the roll crosswise as thick or thin as you like. Toss the cut pasta to separate the strands so they don't stick together, adding in a bit more flour or fine cornmeal if necessary. You can leave the noodles in a tangle if you'll be cooking them shortly or hang individually (on a pasta drying rack if you have one but you can also use the backs of chairs or hangers) to dry if not using right away. Homemade fresh pasta is best used the day it is made.

Fresh Egg Pasta

MAKES: 4 servings
TIME: At least 1 hour, somewhat unattended
Ⓜ

Beginners will want to start here. This Emilia-Romagna–style pasta is rich and golden in color from the egg yolks, which also make the dough moist and forgiving.

> **About 2 cups all-purpose flour, plus more as needed**
> 1 **teaspoon salt**
> 2 **eggs**
> 3 **egg yolks**

1. WITH A FOOD PROCESSOR Put the flour and salt in the bowl and pulse once or twice. Add the eggs and yolks all at once and turn the machine on. Process just until a ball begins to form, about 30 seconds. Add a few drops water if the dough is dry and grainy; add a tablespoon flour if the dough sticks to the side of the bowl. Turn the dough out onto a lightly floured work surface.

BY HAND Combine the flour and salt on the counter or large board. Make a well in the middle. Break the eggs into the well and add the yolks. Beat the eggs with a fork, slowly and gradually incorporating a little of the flour at a time. When it becomes too hard to stir with the fork, use your hands until all the flour has been mixed in.

Cutting Noodles by Hand

STEP 1 To make any broad noodle, sprinkle the pasta sheet with cornmeal or flour, roll it up, and cut across the roll at the desired width.

STEP 2 Unroll the noodles, and sprinkle with more flour or cornmeal.

Using Alternative Flours in Fresh Pasta

Some of these choices you can substitute wholly (or you can use less and make up the difference with all-purpose flour); others must be blended with all-purpose flour because they contain no gluten (essential to forming an elastic, easy-to-handle dough) or because their flavor is too strong when used alone.

FLOUR	QUANTITY TO USE WHEN SUBBING FOR 2 CUPS FLOUR
Amaranth	2 cups amaranth
Buckwheat (finely ground)	1½ cups buckwheat and ½ cup all-purpose flour
Kamut	2 cups kamut
Quinoa	1 cup quinoa and 1 cup all-purpose flour
Rye	1 cup rye and 1 cup all-purpose flour
Semolina	2 cups semolina
Spelt	2 cups spelt
Whole durum wheat	2 cups whole durum wheat
Whole wheat	1 cup whole wheat and 1 cup all-purpose flour

2. Knead the dough, pushing it against the board and folding it repeatedly until it is not at all sticky, but smooth, and quite stiff.

3. Sprinkle the dough with a little flour and cover with plastic or a damp towel; let it rest for about 30 minutes. (You can wrap the dough in plastic and store in the refrigerator until you're ready to roll it out, for up to 24 hours.)

4. Clamp a pasta-rolling machine to the counter; sprinkle your work surface lightly with flour. Cut off about one-third of the dough; wrap the rest in plastic or a damp towel while you work. Roll the dough lightly in the flour and use your hands to flatten it into a rectangle about the width of the machine. Set the machine to its thickest setting and crank the dough through. If it sticks, dust it with a little more flour. Repeat. Set the machine to its next-thinner setting and repeat. Each time, if the pasta sticks, sprinkle it with a little more flour, and each time put the dough through the machine twice. Continue to work your way thinner. If at any point the dough tears badly, bunch it together and start again (you will quickly get the hang of it). Use as much flour as you need to, but add in small amounts each time.

5. Pass the dough through the thinnest setting only once. (If it rips repeatedly when you attempt this, pass it through the next-thicker one once.) Flour the dough lightly, cover, and set aside. Repeat the process with the remaining dough.

6. Cut each sheet into rectangles roughly 16 inches long and as wide as the machine; trim the ends to make them neat. Put each rectangle through the machine once more, this time using the broadest (tagliatelle) cutter. Or cut by hand into broad strips to make pappardelle. Cook right away or you can hang the strands to dry for up to a couple of hours.

7. To cook the noodles, drop them into a large pot of boiling salted water, and stir occasionally to prevent sticking. They'll be done when tender, in less than 3 minutes (and probably less than 2). Drain and sauce them immediately and serve.

HERBED PASTA Use 3 whole eggs, no extra yolks. Add 1 tablespoon chopped fresh sage, 1 teaspoon chopped fresh rosemary or thyme, or ¼ cup chopped (minced if mixing by hand) fresh basil, chervil, or parsley when you add the eggs. If using basil, chervil, or parsley, you may need to add about ¼ cup more flour.

SPINACH PASTA Lots of color; the spinach flavor is subtle: Use 3 whole eggs, no extra yolks. Stem, rinse, and steam 8 ounces fresh spinach, or thaw 4 ounces frozen spinach. Drain, squeeze to get as much water out as possible, and chop (mince if mixing by hand). Add the spinach with the eggs, making sure to break up any clumps when mixing. You may need to add about ½ cup more flour.

ORANGE PASTA Neutral-tasting but a stunner: Use 3 whole eggs, no extra yolks. Add 2 tablespoons tomato paste when you add the eggs. Make sure things get thoroughly mixed. You may need to add a little extra flour.

FUCHSIA PASTA Brilliantly hued: Use 3 whole eggs, no extra yolks. Bake 8 ounces beets as in Beets, Done Simply (page 178). When cool enough to handle, peel, chop, and purée in a food processor until smooth. Squeeze out any excess moisture using cheesecloth. Add ½ cup of the well-drained purée with the eggs. You might need to add up to an additional 1 cup flour.

Eggless Pasta Dough

MAKES: 4 servings
TIME: At least 1 hour, somewhat unattended
Ⓜ Ⓞ

Just as simple and easy to work with as the egg pasta; here the hot water replaces the eggs. The pasta will be less rich but still wonderful. You could make up that richness by using butter instead of olive oil, though then it won't be vegan.

- 2 cups all-purpose flour, plus more as needed
- 1 teaspoon salt
- 2 tablespoons olive oil or butter, melted and cooled

1. WITH A FOOD PROCESSOR Put the flour and salt in the bowl and pulse once or twice. Turn the machine on and add ½ cup hot water and the oil through the feed

---

8 Ways to Flavor Pasta Dough

Make sure the added ingredients are thoroughly mixed into the dough.

1. Black pepper Grind about 1 tablespoon into the flour.

2. Saffron Steep a large pinch of crumbled threads in a couple of tablespoons hot water; add along with the eggs or with the hot water. You may need to add more flour.

3. Whole herb leaves This takes a bit more effort but looks spectacular. Parsley, chervil, tarragon, or small basil or sage leaves work best. Roll out the finished dough to the thinnest setting. Place whole stemmed herb leaves randomly on one sheet of pasta, sprinkle with a tiny bit of water, and put another sheet of pasta on top. Roll the sheets together on the thinnest setting possible (essentially pressing the leaves between the layers of dough).

4. Mushroom Grind dried mushrooms into a fine powder in a clean coffee or spice grinder and add to the flour; you need a tablespoon or 2 of powder. Porcini are excellent.

5. Roasted garlic Mash several cloves Roasted Garlic (page 205) to a smooth paste; add along with the eggs or hot water. You may need to add more flour.

6. Pumpkin Add ¼ cup puréed pumpkin along with the eggs. You may need to add more flour.

7. Lemon Add 2 tablespoons grated lemon zest along with the eggs or hot water.

8. Chocolate Mostly for novelty and color: Add a couple of tablespoons cocoa powder to the flour.

tube. Process just until a ball begins to form, about 30 seconds. Add a few drops water if the dough is dry and grainy; add a tablespoon flour if the dough sticks to the side of the bowl. Turn the dough out onto a lightly floured work surface.

BY HAND Put the flour and salt in a large bowl. Make a well in the middle. Add the oil and about ½ cup hot water to the well. Beat the water with a fork, slowly and gradually incorporating a little of the flour at a time. When it becomes too hard to stir with the fork, use your hands until all the flour has been mixed in.

2. Knead the dough, pushing it against the board and folding it repeatedly until it is not at all sticky, but smooth, and quite stiff. Add water ½ teaspoon at a time if the dough is dry and not coming together; add flour if it is sticky.

3. Sprinkle the dough with a little flour and cover with plastic or a damp towel; let it rest for about 30 minutes. (You can wrap the dough in plastic and store in the refrigerator until you're ready to roll it out, for up to 24 hours.)

4. Follow Steps 4 through 8 in the Fresh Egg Pasta recipe (page 343) for rolling, cutting, and cooking the pasta.

STUFFED PASTA

Stuffed pasta is a dumpling, really, and ravioli and tortellini differ from many Asian dumplings (see page 356) only in the nature and flavor of the stuffings. Out of the nearly endless types, I'm focusing on ravioli (squares), tortellini (folded loops), and cannelloni (large open-ended tubes).

Spinach-Ricotta Ravioli

MAKES: 30 to 60 ravioli
TIME: About 1 hour, with prepared pasta sheets
M

A standby stuffed pasta; this stuffing is great in cannelloni, too (see the variation on page 349), and between layers of lasagne (see page 328). Serve with Pesto or any of the variations (page 634) or Fast Tomato Sauce (page 312).

---

5 Simplest Sauces for Fresh and Stuffed Pasta, and Italian-Style Dumplings

Here are a few of my favorite simple sauces that are lovely with any fresh pasta or dumplings and can be made in 30 minutes or less.

1. Butter, Sage, and Parmesan and its variations (page 316)

2. Garlic and Oil (page 312)

3. Fresh Tomato Sauce or Fast Tomato Sauce (page 313 or 312)

4. Walnut Sauce (page 326)

5. Pesto (page 634)

1   egg
½   cup (about 2 ounces) cooked spinach, squeezed dry and chopped
1½   cups ricotta, drained for a few minutes in a strainer
¼   cup chopped fresh parsley
1   teaspoon minced garlic
     A small grating of nutmeg
1   cup grated Parmesan cheese
     Salt
1   recipe Fresh Egg Pasta (page 343) or Eggless Pasta Dough (page 345), rolled into sheets

1. Put the egg, spinach, ricotta, parsley, garlic, nutmeg, and Parmesan in a bowl and mix well. Use immediately or cover and refrigerate for up to a day.

2. Bring a large pot of water to a boil and salt it. Cut each pasta sheet into 4-inch-wide strips and lay them out on the counter. Drop heaping teaspoons of the stuffing in 1½-inch intervals about 1 inch from one long edge of a strip (that is, about 3 inches from the other edge). Set a second strip of pasta on top, pressing with your fingers to seal (you can brush the dough with a little

(continued on page 349)

Making Ravioli

STEP 1 On a counter dusted lightly with flour, cut any length of Fresh or Eggless Pasta dough (page 343 or 345) so that it is 4 inches wide. Place spoonsful of filling evenly on the dough, about 1½ inches apart, about 1 inch from the long sides.

STEP 2 Brush some water between the filling so the dough will stick together. Set a second sheet of pasta on top. Press down to seal between the ravioli.

STEP 3 Cut with a pastry wheel or sharp paring knife. Keep the ravioli separate until you are ready to cook.

Making Tortellini

STEP 1 On a counter dusted lightly with flour, cut any length of fresh pasta dough so it is 4 to 5 inches wide. Cut into 2- to 2½-inch squares.

STEP 2 Brush the dough very lightly with water.

STEP 3 Place a small mound of filling on each square.

STEP 4 Fold into a triangle, pressing tightly to seal the edges.

STEP 5 Fold the widest point toward the filling.

STEP 6 Pick up the triangle and press the two bottom points together. Place your finger inside the newly formed ring and fold over the top of the dough inside the circle. Press to seal.

Spinach-Ricotta
Ravioli (page 346)

(continued from page 346)

water to help it stick). Trim the dough with a sharp knife or fluted pastry wheel, then cut into individual ravioli. (You can prepare the ravioli up to this point in advance. Put them on a parchment paper–lined baking sheet in a single layer, not touching, dust with fine cornmeal or semolina, cover loosely with plastic, and refrigerate for up to a day or freeze. When frozen, transfer to a heavy plastic bag, and keep up to several months. Cook directly from the freezer without thawing.)

3. Cook the ravioli 20 or 30 at a time for just a few minutes, until they rise to the surface. Drain, sauce, and serve immediately.

SPINACH-RICOTTA TORTELLINI Cut the pasta sheets into 2- to 2½-inch squares and brush very lightly with water so they will stick together when you shape the tortellini. Put a rounded teaspoon of stuffing on each square and fold into a triangle, pressing tightly to seal the edges. Fold the widest point toward the stuffing, then pick up the triangle and press the two bottom points together. Put your finger inside the newly formed ring and fold over the top of the dough inside the circle. Press to seal. This will make about 60 tortellini.

SPINACH-RICOTTA CANNELLONI Tomato sauce is best here: Heat the oven to 375°F. Cut the pasta sheets into rectangles at least 4 × 6 inches; boil them for 2 minutes and drain. Lay out the pasta rectangles on the counter. Use a tablespoon to dollop a line of the stuffing along the short edge of each piece of pasta, about an inch or so from the edge; roll the pasta into a tube. Spread a little sauce in the bottom of a 9 × 13-inch baking dish. Add the cannelloni, placing them side by side, seam down and in a single layer; cover with sauce, sprinkle with grated Parmesan, and bake until bubbling, about 20 minutes.

SPINACH-TOFU RAVIOLI This filling also makes a great vegan dip: Use Eggless Pasta Dough (page 345) and omit the egg, ricotta, and Parmesan from the filling. Double the spinach. Put 1 pound firm tofu, 3 tablespoons olive oil, the grated zest of 1 lemon, 2 tablespoons mild miso paste, 2 cloves garlic, ¼ cup chopped fresh parsley, and a sprinkle of salt in a blender or food processor. Blend until smooth and stir in the spinach. Proceed with Step 2. **V**

MUSHROOM-RICOTTA RAVIOLI Use any kind of mushrooms you like: Substitute ¾ cup Sautéed Mushrooms (page 217) for the spinach and reduce the ricotta to 1¼ cups. Drain the mushrooms and finely chop.

BUTTERNUT SQUASH OR SWEET POTATO RAVIOLI For the stuffing, purée 2 cups cooked (preferably baked)

16 Dishes for Stuffing Pasta

Almost anything that would taste good tossed with dried pasta will taste good inside fresh pasta. Drain off excess liquids and mash, crumble, or mince large pieces.

1. Roasted Garlic (page 205)

2. Sautéed Mushrooms (page 217)

3. Caramelized Onions (page 222)

4. Anything-Scented Peas (page 224)

5. Roasted Red Peppers (page 228)

6. Mashed Potatoes (page 233)

7. Spinach with Currants and Nuts (page 250)

8. Oven-Roasted Fresh Plum Tomatoes (page 258)

9. Vegetable Purée (page 150)

10. White Beans, Tuscan Style (page 444)

11. Beans and Mushrooms (page 447)

12. Flageolets, French Style (page 454)

13. Chickpeas in Their Own Broth with Crisp Bread Crumbs (page 454)

14. Fast Nut Burgers (page 507)

15. Oven-Roasted Seitan (page 512)

16. Braised Tempeh, Three Ways (page 513)

butternut squash or sweet potato, then mix with 2 eggs, ½ teaspoon grated nutmeg, and salt and pepper. Taste; if the mixture is not sweet, add a little sugar. Stir in ½ cup grated Parmesan and taste again; adjust the seasoning.

GNOCCHI AND OTHER DUMPLINGS

Gnocchi (pronounced NYO-kee) are Italian dumplings that are boiled and sauced. Getting the dough just right for gnocchi can be tricky, especially the first time around. Don't be discouraged if your gnocchi aren't delicate and fluffy the first time; you'll improve with each batch, and it will get to the point where it's easy enough to quickly make a batch.

This section also explores the world of dumplings outside of Italy; think spaetzle, pierogi, pot stickers, wontons, and others.

Potato Gnocchi

MAKES: 4 servings
TIME: 1½ hours
V

If all the gnocchi you've ever had were hard and chewy, try these. With just a bit of practice you'll soon be making the lightest, fluffiest gnocchi you've ever eaten. Starchy potatoes are a must here (waxy ones will not work), as it's the potatoes' starch, in addition to the gluten in the flour, that holds the dough together.

> 1 pound baking potatoes
>   Salt and pepper
>   About 1 cup all-purpose flour, plus more
>   as needed

1. Put the potatoes in a large pot with water to cover and salt it. Bring to a boil, then adjust the heat so the water simmers and cook until the potatoes are quite tender, about 45 minutes. Drain the potatoes and peel while still hot; use a pot holder or towel to hold the potatoes and peel with a paring knife—it will be easy. Rinse the pot, refill with salted water, and bring to a boil.

2. Use a fork, potato masher, or ricer to mash or rice the potatoes in a bowl, along with some salt and pepper. Add about ½ cup flour and stir; add more flour a little at a time until the mixture forms a dough you can handle. Knead for a minute or so on a lightly floured work surface. Pinch off a piece of the dough and boil it to make sure it will hold its shape; if it does not, knead in a bit more flour. The idea is to make a dough with as little flour and kneading as possible.

Shaping Gnocchi

STEP 1 Start by rolling a piece of the dough into a log. Use flour as needed to prevent sticking, but try to keep it to a minimum.

STEP 2 Cut the dough into approximately 1-inch lengths.

STEP 3 Roll each of the gnocchi off the back of the fork to give it the characteristic ridges.

Clockwise from top: Sweet Potato Gnocchi, Beet Gnocchi, Potato Gnocchi

3. Roll a piece of the dough into a rope about ½ inch thick, then cut the rope into 1-inch lengths. Spin each piece off the tines of a fork to score it lightly. As each gnoccho is ready, put it on a sheet of wax paper; do not allow them to touch.

4. A few at a time, add the gnocchi to the boiling water and stir. A minute after they rise to the surface, the gnocchi are done; remove with a slotted spoon. Put in a bowl and sauce or reheat in butter within a few minutes; these do not keep well.

SPINACH GNOCCHI A lovely green color and subtle spinach flavor: Stem, rinse, and steam 10 ounces fresh spinach, or thaw 5 ounces frozen spinach. Drain the spinach, squeeze to get as much water out as possible, and mince. Add to the potatoes with a pinch of nutmeg if desired.

EGGPLANT GNOCCHI Great with Fast Tomato Sauce (page 312): Add 1 cup mashed roasted eggplant pulp, drained of any liquid, to the potatoes. You may need a little more flour.

CARROT OR BEET GNOCCHI Peel and grate ½ pound carrots or beets. Cook in 2 tablespoons olive oil over medium-low heat, seasoning to taste, until very soft, 20 to 30 minutes. Transfer to a food processor and purée until smooth. Add it to the potatoes (you'll most likely need an extra ¼ cup flour).

Parsnip-Parmesan Gnocchi

MAKES: 4 servings
TIME: 1½ hours

A twist on the usual potato gnocchi, these are loaded with flavor. The Parmesan and extra flour help hold the dough together and make dense, rich gnocchi. Play up their richness even more by browning them in some butter in a pan (see "Browning and Baking Gnocchi," page 352). Serve these gnocchi tossed with Oven-Roasted Fresh Plum Tomatoes (page 258) or with Butter, Sage, and Parmesan (page 316).

>   1   **pound parsnips, peeled and roughly chopped**
>   **Salt and pepper**
> 1½   **cups all-purpose flour**
>   ½   **cup grated Parmesan cheese**
>   **Pinch freshly grated nutmeg (optional)**
>   **Butter for reheating (optional)**

1. Roast, steam, or boil the parsnips until very tender (see page 150). (If boiling or steaming, be sure to drain well before proceeding.) Bring a large pot of water to a boil and salt it.

2. Purée the parsnips in a food processor until smooth; sprinkle with some salt and pepper. Transfer the mixture to a bowl. Add about 1 cup of the flour, the Parmesan, and the nutmeg, if you're using it, and stir. Add more flour until the mixture forms a dough you can handle. Knead for a minute or so on a lightly floured work surface. Pinch off a piece of the dough and boil it to make sure it will hold its shape; if it does not, knead in a bit more flour. The idea is to make a dough with as little flour and kneading as possible.

3. Roll a piece of the dough into a rope about ½ inch thick, then cut the rope into 1-inch lengths; spin each piece off the tines of a fork to score it lightly. As each gnoccho is ready, put it on a sheet of wax paper; do not allow them to touch.

4. A few at a time, add the gnocchi to the boiling water and stir. A minute after they rise to the surface, the gnocchi are done; remove with a slotted spoon. Put in a bowl and sauce, or reheat in butter within a few minutes; these do not keep well.

SWEET POTATO GNOCCHI Substitute sweet potatoes for the parsnips. You might need to add up to ½ cup more flour, depending on your sweet potatoes.

Spaetzle

MAKES: 4 servings
TIME: 30 minutes
F M

Spaetzle is a cross between a dumpling and pasta. It can be seasoned and served, sautéed, tossed with sauce, or added to a broth or soup. I love it put in a gratin dish, topped with grated cheese or bread crumbs, and baked

until bubbling. For something lighter, serve it in Fast Tomato Sauce (page 312).

To shape the spaetzle, you can use a spaetzle maker (it looks like a grater without sharp edges, with an attachment that slides across the top), a colander, a squeeze bottle, or simply a spoon. The spoon and squeeze bottle are the most uncomplicated techniques: load the spoon with about a tablespoon of the batter and let the batter drop into the water. To use a squeeze bottle, squirt small portions of the batter into the water.

Salt
2 cups all-purpose flour
½ teaspoon or more pepper
3 eggs
1 cup milk, more or less
2–4 tablespoons butter or olive oil
Chopped fresh parsley or chives for garnish

1. Bring a large pot of water to a boil and salt it. Combine the flour with the pepper and a large pinch of salt in a bowl. Lightly beat together the eggs and milk in a separate bowl, then stir into the flour. If necessary, add

Tips for Perfect Gnocchi

Use warm, freshly cooked potatoes (leftover baked or mashed potatoes are better for croquettes, page 242, or stuffed pasta, page 349).

Use a ricer or food mill for the potatoes for best results.

Add the flour in small amounts so you don't add too much; use only just

enough flour to make a dough come together.

Don't overknead! Mix and knead the dough gently. It's a delicate dough and you're trying to not develop the gluten at all.

Test-cook a piece of the dough just as it comes together; it will be firmer than you think. If it comes apart in the water, it's not done.

Keep your work surface well floured so the gnocchi don't stick.

Roll the logs out quickly and don't worry too much about getting them perfectly even, which may overwork your dough; they're supposed to look handmade.

Indenting the gnocchi with your finger or rolling them over a fork, cheese

grater, or gnocchi board is optional, but it helps the gnocchi grab the sauce. To indent the dumplings, just flour your thumb and roll it over the gnocchi. Using the fork or board takes some practice; use your thumb to roll the gnocchi over the tines or ridges—your thumb will simultaneously indent the opposite side.

a little more milk to make a batter about the consistency of thick pancake batter.

2. Scoop up a tablespoon or so of the batter and drop it into the water; small pieces may break off, but the batter should remain largely intact and form an uneven disk. Spoon in about one-third to one-fourth of the batter, depending on the size of your pot. When the spaetzle rise to the top, a couple of minutes later (you may have to loosen them from the bottom, but they'll float right up), cook for another minute or so, then transfer with a slotted spoon to a bowl of ice water. Repeat until all the batter is used up.

3. Drain the spaetzle. (At this point you can toss them with a bit of oil and refrigerate, covered, for up to a day.)

4. Put the butter or oil in a large skillet, preferably non-stick, over medium-high heat. When the butter is melted or the oil is hot, add the spaetzle, working in batches, and brown quickly on both sides. Garnish with parsley or chives and serve hot.

HERB SPAETZLE A mix of parsley, chervil, chives, and tarragon is lovely: Stir about 1 cup chopped fresh herbs into the batter.

WHOLE WHEAT SPAETZLE Replace up to half of the all-purpose flour with whole wheat flour and stir about ½ cup chopped fresh oregano or parsley into the batter.

BUCKWHEAT OR CHESTNUT SPAETZLE Add a wonderful nutty flavor: Replace up to half the all-purpose flour with buckwheat flour or chestnut flour.

Vegan Herbed Dumplings for Soup

MAKES: 4 servings
TIME: 1½ hours
Ⓜ Ⓥ

These dumplings work wonderfully in any broth, simple vegetable soup like Onion Soup (page 100) or Pumpkin (or Winter Squash) Soup (page 120), or stew.

  1½ **cups all-purpose flour**
  1½ **teaspoons baking powder**
   3 **tablespoons chopped fresh parsley or chives, or 1 tablespoon chopped fresh rosemary or thyme**
      Salt and pepper
   1 **tablespoon olive oil**
   ⅔ **cup nondairy milk like oat, almond, or multigrain, plus more as needed**

1. Put the flour, baking powder, and herbs in the bowl of a food processor and sprinkle with salt and pepper. Pulse a few times. Pour in the oil and pulse again. With the machine running, pour in half the milk and process

Making Dumpling and Egg Rolls or Wonton Skins

STEP 1 First roll each piece of dough into a log about 1 inch wide on a lightly floured surface.

STEP 2 Cut into 1-inch pieces.

STEP 3 Roll each piece out from the center to form a thin 4-inch circle or square, adding a bit of flour if necessary.

STEP 4 To make larger egg roll wrappers, roll each log into a thin, roughly rectangular shape.

STEP 5 Cut into squares.

just until a dough ball forms. If the dough looks dry, add more milk a tablespoon at a time. Refrigerate the dough for at least 30 minutes and up 2 hours.

2. Bring the broth, soup, or stew that you'll be serving the dumplings in to a boil and adjust the heat so it bubbles gently. Knead the dough on a floured work surface for 1 minute, then roll out to ⅛ inch thick. Cut into 1- to 1½-inch squares or rectangles. Drop the dumplings into the bubbling liquid a few at a time and stir occasionally; cook until the dumplings are no longer raw in the center, 10 to 15 minutes, then serve.

Dumpling Wrappers

MAKES: About 50 wrappers
TIME: 40 minutes
Ⓜ Ⓥ

This versatile wrapper can be used to make all sorts of dumplings, pot stickers, and wontons, plus hand-cut noodles that can be used in European-style recipes as well as Asian. The recipe makes enough for two batches of the stuffing recipes on page 356, so you can pack away half of the wrappers in the freezer, double the stuffing, or make two different kinds of dumplings.

> 2 **cups all-purpose flour, plus more as needed**
> 1 **teaspoon salt**

1. WITH A FOOD PROCESSOR Put the flour and salt in the bowl and add about ½ cup cold water gradually through the feed tube while the machine is running; add as much water as necessary to form a dough ball—the dough should be dry—then let the machine run for about 15 seconds. Finish the kneading by hand, using as much flour as necessary to keep it from sticking.
BY HAND Put the flour and salt in a large bowl and gradually stir in about ½ cup cold water until the dough comes together in a ball. Again, the dough should be quite dry. Turn onto a floured work surface and knead until smooth and elastic, about 5 minutes, sprinkling with flour as necessary to prevent sticking.

2. Shape the dough into a ball, dust with flour, and cover with plastic wrap or a damp towel. Let it rest for 20 minutes to 2 hours. (You can make the dough up to this point, wrap it tightly, and refrigerate for up to a day. Bring to room temperature before proceeding.)
3. Knead the ball for a minute, then cut into 4 pieces. On a lightly floured surface, roll each piece into a 1-inch-wide log, then cut into 1-inch pieces and roll each one out from the center to form a 4-inch round or square, adding a bit more flour if necessary. (You can also roll sheets of dough with a pasta machine, then cut into desired shapes; see page 342.) Use immediately or dust with flour, stack, wrap tightly in plastic, and refrigerate for up to a couple of days or freeze for up to 2 weeks.

WHOLE WHEAT DUMPLING WRAPPERS Use whole wheat flour for all or part of the white flour. You will need to add more water; do so a teaspoon at a time. And the dumplings will need to cook a minute or 2 longer.

EGG ROLL WRAPPERS OR WONTON SKINS You can use these as slightly richer dumpling wrappers or for wontons or egg rolls: Add 1 egg to the flour-salt mix and reduce the water to a little less than ½ cup. Proceed

Store-Bought Wrappers

All sorts of premade dumpling, egg roll, and wonton wrappers are sold in supermarkets. They're undeniably convenient but often contain additives and preservatives, so try to find versions with as few ingredients as possible. You can use store-bought wrappers in any of the recipes in this section; sometimes they're on the thick side and may need to be rolled a bit thinner. Conversely, sometimes they're thinner than ones you might make yourself; adjust the cooking times accordingly and go by visual cues: When the wrapper is slightly puffy and transparent, it's done. Premade wrappers can also be used to make shortcut stuffed pastas (pages 346 to 350).

with the recipe. In Step 3, cut the dough ball into 4 pieces and roll out each one. Cut 3-inch squares for dumpling wrappers or wonton skins, 6-inch squares for egg roll wrappers.

CHINESE-STYLE FRESH NOODLES Make from either the main recipe or either of the preceding variations: In Step 3, after cutting the dough into 4 pieces, roll out each piece into a rectangle. Try to roll the dough as thin as possible without ripping it, preferably to ⅛ inch thick. Lightly dust the rectangles, fold into quarters lengthwise, then use a sharp knife to cut each folded rectangle into thin strips. Alternatively, use a pasta machine: Put the dough rectangles through the thinnest setting, then roll them through the spaghetti cutter. Dust lightly with flour to prevent sticking. Cook in boiling water just until tender, about 3 minutes, then drain, rinse, drain again, and serve immediately.

DUMPLING WRAPPERS FOR PIEROGI Decrease the initial addition of water to ¼ cup and add 2 egg yolks to the flour and salt. If needed, add more water, 1 tablespoon at a time, until the dough forms a ball. The dough will not be as dry as the eggless version.

Steamed Dumplings

MAKES: 24 dumplings; 4 to 6 servings
TIME: 40 minutes
Ⓜ

This is a simplified, streamlined stuffing, but you can get as elaborate as you like; there are few limits to the vegetables you can use in dumplings. The only secret is to include something slightly starchy, or to bind with an egg, so the stuffing doesn't fall out of the wrapper when you take a bite.

As long as your stuffing isn't too moist, you can refrigerate the stuffed dumplings for an hour or so before cooking, or freeze them for up to a few weeks. Dust them with flour first to prevent sticking. But they really are best if you can stuff and cook in one fell swoop.

8	ounces firm tofu
¼	cup chopped scallions
1	cup chopped leeks, Napa cabbage, or bok choy
1	teaspoon minced fresh ginger
1	teaspoon rice wine or dry sherry
1	teaspoon sugar
1	tablespoon soy sauce
1	tablespoon sesame oil
1	egg, lightly beaten
	Salt and pepper
24	round dumpling wrappers (to make your own, see page 355)
	Basil Dipping Sauce (page 654) or Ginger-Scallion Sauce (page 631) for serving

1. Put the tofu in a large bowl and mash with a fork to crumble it. Add the scallions, leeks, ginger, rice wine, sugar, soy sauce, sesame oil, and egg and sprinkle with a large pinch of salt and lots of pepper. Mix gently but thoroughly.

2. Put about 2 teaspoons of the stuffing in the center of a wrapper, then moisten the edge of the wrapper with water and fold over to form a semicircle. Press the seam tightly to seal; it's best if there is no air trapped between the stuffing and wrapper. Set on a lightly floured plate or

Pot Stickers

To panfry these dumplings, put some good-quality vegetable oil in a deep skillet, enough to coat the bottom in a thin layer. When it's hot, put the dumplings in the skillet, seam up, leaving space between them (you will probably have to cook in two batches). Turn the heat to medium, then cover and cook for about 5 minutes. Carefully add ½ cup water to the skillet, then cover and cook for another 2 minutes. Remove the lid, turn the heat to high, and cook until the water has evaporated, about 3 minutes. Remove the dumplings and serve with dipping sauce.

wax paper. (You can make the dumplings to this point, cover tightly, and refrigerate for up to a day or freeze for a couple of weeks; thaw before steaming.)

3. Set up a steamer or put a heatproof plate on a rack above 1 to 2 inches of boiling water in a covered pot (see page 25). Lightly oil the steamer or plate to prevent sticking. Arrange the dumplings in the steamer so they don't touch and steam, working in batches, for about 10 minutes per batch. Serve with dipping sauce on the side.

STEAMED BEAN DUMPLINGS An interesting textural change from tofu: Use 1½ cups cooked adzuki, soy, or black soybeans instead of the tofu and egg. (If you want to make the filling spicy, increase the ginger to 1 to 2 tablespoons and add 1 teaspoon Chile Paste (page 664), or to taste.) In Step 1, put the beans in the bowl and roughly mash. Proceed with the recipe. **V**

STEAMED GYOZA WITH SEA GREENS AND EDAMAME
The Japanese-style dumplings, made with thinner wrappers: Try to find gyoza or wonton wrappers or roll your own as thin as possible. Soak about ½ cup dried wakame or dulse in hot water for 30 minutes. Drain well, and chop. Use 1½ cups edamame instead of the tofu and

mash as described in Step 1; use the chopped wakame instead of the leeks. Serve with Ponzu (page 657), Dashi Dipping Sauce (page 657), or a little soy sauce mixed with a few drops of water.

BEAN THREAD DUMPLINGS Pretty, with a chewy texture: Soak 1 bundle (2 ounces) bean threads in hot water for 5 minutes. Drain and chop into 1-inch pieces. Use the bean threads instead of the egg in the main recipe or any of the variations. **V**

MUSHROOM DUMPLINGS Even better if you use a mix of reconstituted dried and fresh: Omit the egg and sugar. Pulse 8 ounces trimmed mushrooms with the tofu, ginger, rice wine, soy sauce, and sesame oil in the food processor until finely ground. Proceed with the recipe. **V**

SPICY KIMCHI DUMPLINGS This classic Korean combination is best panfried until slightly golden, or you can steam them: Omit the scallions and add ¼ cup kimchi and 1 teaspoon minced fresh chile (like jalapeño or Thai) or to taste.

PEA DUMPLINGS Wonderful in the spring: Replace the tofu with ricotta (or not, if you want them vegan), and

Stuffing and Sealing Half Moon–Shaped Dumplings

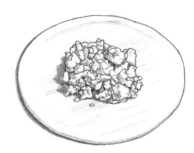

STEP 1 Put a small amount of filling in the middle of a wrapper. Brush the seam lightly (you can use your fingertip) with water or beaten egg yolk.

STEP 2 Bring one edge of the wrapper over the filling to meet the other.

STEP 3 Secure the dumpling with the thumb of one hand, then press the edges closed.

the leeks with 1 cup peas (thawed frozen are fine). Omit the scallions, ginger, rice wine, sugar, soy sauce, and sesame oil and instead add 1 tablespoon grated lemon zest, ½ cup grated Parmesan cheese (optional), and ¼ cup fresh mint leaves, chopped.

Fried Tofu Wontons with Chives and Ginger

MAKES: 30 wontons; 4 to 6 servings
TIME: 30 minutes, with premade wrappers
F V

The best wonton wrappers are super-thin, and some of the store-bought kinds may need a little more rolling to get the signature crisp exterior.

12	ounces silken tofu
½	cup chopped fresh chives (use garlic chives if you can find them) or scallions
1	tablespoon minced fresh ginger
1	teaspoon sesame oil
	Salt and pepper
30	wonton skins (to make your own, see page 355)
	Good-quality vegetable oil, as needed
	Any Asian-style dipping sauce (pages 654–659) or soy sauce mixed with water for serving

Sealing Wontons

To make wontons, put a small amount of filling on a square dumpling wrapper; brush the seam lightly (you can use your fingertip) with water or beaten egg yolk, then press closed.

1. Put the tofu in a food processor and let the machine run until it's smooth. Transfer to a bowl and stir in the chives, ginger, and sesame oil by hand, sprinkle with salt and pepper, and stir again to combine.

2. Put 1 scant tablespoon of the stuffing in the center of each wrapper. Moisten the edges of the wrapper with a few drops of water (use a brush or your finger) and fold into a triangle or semicircle. Press the edges together tightly to seal, making sure no air is trapped between the stuffing and wrapper. If you like, fold the tip of the triangle back and press gently. Set each wonton aside on a floured plate or wax paper.

3. Put at least 2 inches oil in a deep pan on the stove and turn the heat to medium-high; bring to 350°F (see "Deep-Frying," page 26). Working in batches and adjusting the heat as necessary, gently put as many of the wontons into the oil as will fit without crowding. Cook, turning once, until golden brown, less than 5 minutes. Drain for a few moments on paper towels, then serve immediately with dipping sauce.

WONTON SOUP To make the soup more substantial, you can add some shredded cabbage or ribbons of bok choy to the stock while you cook the wontons: Bring about 6 to 8 cups vegetable stock (pages 97 to 100) to a boil. Stuff and seal the wontons as described. Depending on the size of your pot, boil the wontons in the stock in 1 or 2 batches for about 5 minutes per batch. Gently stir occasionally to prevent sticking. Immediately transfer to bowls, ladle the stock over the wontons, and garnish with chopped scallions.

Matzo Balls

MAKES: 6 servings
TIME: At least 2 hours
M

An iconic dumpling most often seen in chicken soup but with uses far beyond. Just be sure to work the dough as little as possible, otherwise they'll be dense and tough.

3 **eggs**
½ **cup vegetable stock (pages 97–100) or Mushroom Stock (page 99)**
¼ **cup chopped or grated onion**
¼ **cup good-quality vegetable oil**
½ **teaspoon salt**
½ **teaspoon pepper**
About 1 cup matzo meal

1. Beat together the eggs and stock in a large bowl. If you prefer light matzo balls, separate the eggs and beat the yolks with the stock. Beat the whites until stiff and set aside.

2. Stir in the onion, oil, salt, and pepper. Add the matzo meal and stir just enough to combine. If you separated the eggs, fold the whites into the dough now. The dough should be quite moist, barely stiff enough to make into balls. If it's too moist, add a little more matzo meal.

3. Cover the dough and refrigerate for an hour or overnight. When you're ready to cook, bring a large pot of water to a boil and salt it. Using wet hands, shape the dough into balls about 1 inch in diameter, again working them as little as possible.

4. Turn the heat under the boiling water to medium-low so that it bubbles gently. Add the matzo balls to the simmering stock and cook until they are expanded and set, about 30 minutes. To serve, put several balls in each bowl and ladle the soup over.

EGGLESS MATZO BALLS A little denser: Omit the eggs and use 8 ounces firm silken tofu. Blend the tofu, stock, onion, and oil in a food processor or blender until smooth, then combine with the remaining ingredients. Proceed with the recipe. Ⓥ

4 Ways to Serve Matzo Balls

Branch out beyond soup. Serve matzo balls with:
1. Melted butter or a drizzle of Flavored Oil (page 627)
2. Pesto (page 634), Parsley "Pesto" (page 638), or any of the variations
3. Caramelized Onions (page 222)

4. Sautéed mushrooms, as in Pasta with Mushrooms (page 324)

Potato-Stuffed Pierogi

MAKES: 24 dumplings, 4 to 6 servings
TIME: About 1 hour
Ⓜ

These dumplings are creamy and savory, cooked in butter and served with cooked onion and sour cream. They can also be boiled and served with melted butter.

About 3 tablespoons butter
1 **large onion, chopped**
Salt and pepper
1 **teaspoon minced garlic (optional)**
1 **cup well-seasoned Mashed Potatoes (page 233)**
24 **round or square dumpling wrappers (to make your own, see page 355)**
1 **egg white, lightly beaten**
Sour cream for serving

1. Put 1 tablespoon butter in a large deep skillet, preferably nonstick or cast iron, over medium heat and add the onion along with a liberal sprinkle of salt and pepper. Cook, stirring occasionally, until the onion softens, then turns brown. This may take as long as half an hour. It's okay if the onion gets a bit crisp on the edges, but lower the heat as necessary so it doesn't cook too fast; basically you want a kind of onion compote.

2. Combine half the onion and the garlic, if you're using it, with the mashed potatoes, then taste and adjust the seasoning. Set the remaining onions aside. There's no need to wipe out the pan. Heat the oven to 200°F.

3. Lay a wrapper on a work surface and put 1 to 2 teaspoons of the stuffing in the center of it. Brush the edge of the wrapper with egg white. If you have cut circles, form half-moons; if you have cut squares, form triangles. Press the seam tightly to seal; it's best if there is no air trapped between the stuffing and wrapper, so press down slightly. Set on a lightly floured plate or wax paper; don't let the dumplings touch. (At this point, you may cover tightly and refrigerate for up to a day or freeze for a couple of weeks; no need to thaw—they'll just take a couple extra minutes to cook.)

4. Bring a large pot of water to boil and salt it. Working in batches, in combination with the frying in Step 5, carefully boil the dumplings until just tender, 3 to 5 minutes. Transfer them with a slotted spoon to the skillet.

5. Put the remaining 2 tablespoons butter in the skillet over medium heat. When the butter melts, add as many boiled dumplings as will fit without crowding and brown them quickly, turning once or twice until the dough is tender, about 10 minutes total. When they are done, transfer them to an ovenproof plate and keep them warm in the oven. Cook the remaining dumplings, adding butter to the skillet as needed. When all are cooked, lower the heat a bit and reheat the reserved onions, then spread them out over the dumplings. Serve hot, passing sour cream at the table.

FRIED CHEESE-STUFFED DUMPLINGS Decadent in an old-fashioned way: Don't bother with the onion, but chop about ¼ cup fresh parsley or dill to use as a garnish. Instead of the potatoes, make a cheese stuffing by draining 1 cup cottage cheese in a fine-meshed strainer for an hour or so, or by mashing 1 cup farmer's or pot cheese. Stir in 1 teaspoon sugar, a pinch salt, 1 egg white, and ¼ cup sour cream.

SAUERKRAUT AND POTATO–STUFFED DUMPLINGS Substitute 1 cup drained sauerkraut for the onion. Mix with mashed potatoes made with olive oil instead of dairy and use Dumpling Wrappers (page 355). Proceed with the recipe, using olive oil or good-quality vegetable oil instead of butter for sautéing. Serve with Caramelized Onions (page 222) or Applesauce (page 275). V

Grains

When I learned to cook, a "grain" was either a break-fast cereal or white rice—usually of the instant variety. Later I was introduced to brown rice and granola. I tolerated the former to be hip; the latter I actually liked, probably because it was sweet.

Eventually, I learned how to cook real rice, and then sushi rice, and then risotto. My grandmother taught me how to make kasha. I produced my own granola, nuttier and less sweet. I experimented with wild rice and bul-gur, and found ways to cook brown rice and wheat ber-ries so they were enjoyable. Quinoa was a revelation, but it was still years before I turned to anything other than white rice as a first choice in grains.

This book changed all that. The more grains I had in my pantry, the more often I cooked them. The more I cooked them, the more I liked them. And in the course of developing this chapter, I made some discoveries that made grain cooking easier and more delicious: I learned to parboil brown rice to use it in place of white rice in any recipe. I learned how easy and smart it was to cook grains in advance, how to use leftover grains as gar-nishes, and that many grains are interchangeable. And I learned that whole grains are among the few foods that are both healthy and filling. In short, I was a convert.

For all of these reasons, I encourage you to try every whole grain you can get your hands on. While the low-carb diet trend continues in various guises—it's all about gluten content now—it has created a market for more interesting grains beyond rice and wheat; you can now buy freekeh (which has more protein than quinoa, and a smoky flavor to boot) and einkorn (an ancient grain that has been cultivated for thousands of years) in supermarkets. And, of course, by going online, you can not only get any of the grains discussed in this chapter delivered to your door, you might be able to find them grown by local farmers.

Stock as many grains as you'll use within a year or so, and that you have room for. (The fridge or even freezer is best, but of course they're fairly shelf-stable; more on that in a bit.) As you work your way through this chapter, you'll see that I often consider many grains interchangeable: "The Grain Lexicon" (see page 400) is arranged by cooking time to help you make easy sub-stitutions. I start with rice recipes and relevant info, since it's still the grain people turn to most often; other grains, including corn and couscous (not exactly a grain, but . . . this is where it belongs) follow.

THE BASICS OF GRAINS

Most grains are members of the grass family. The nota-ble exceptions are buckwheat, quinoa, and amaranth, which are in another category of plants (and distantly related to each other). Even so, all grains have the same basic composition: If you were to look at a single grain and work from the outside in, you would first see the bran, thin but tough layers that protect the interior. Next comes the germ, the "embryo" at the base of the grain, and then the endosperm, which makes up the bulk of the grain and provides food for the germ.

We sometimes eat the bran and germ, which con-tain the most nutrients and fiber, as well as the oil that makes grains perishable, and we always eat the endo-sperm. Most grains are entirely edible, though rice, bar-ley, and oats have an additional protective outer layer, an inedible husk or hull that must be removed before being eaten.

The process of removing parts of grains for con-sumption is called "milling." When the hull—and only the hull—is removed from rice, for example, it retains its bran and germ and is called "brown." Those grains without an outer husk, like wheat, can be eaten "whole," that is, with no milling at all. The less grains are milled, the higher they are in both nutrients and flavor, and the longer they take to cook. This is a trade-off and a choice.

Highly milled grains like white rice, pearled bar-ley, and rolled oats contain just the endosperm—the white or light tan interior of the grain—basically starch and protein. These are the grains with which we're most familiar.

GRAINS AND HEALTH

Whole grains, those that are minimally milled to retain their germ and bran, deliver more fiber than any other food. This is important, since the general consensus is that adults should eat 25 to 30 grams of fiber a day, which is a lot. (Most people average around 5 grams.) A single serving of wheat berries, cracked wheat, or millet can supply up to 25 to 30 percent of that daily recommendation. Eat bulgur or hulled (not pearled) barley and you can get there even faster.

Grains also contain protein in amounts ranging from modest (rice) to substantial (oats, quinoa, freekeh, wild rice). And grains provide, in varying amounts, vitamins, minerals, and phytochemicals—the micronutrients thought to protect us from all sorts of ailments and ills—in quantities that are at least as high as vegetables like broccoli and tomatoes.

BUYING AND STORING

Increasingly, grains are being grown throughout the country and sold locally, often by farmers. These are often the best, but you can buy fresh, good-quality whole grains just about anywhere these days.

All whole grains can spoil, and they're temperature sensitive; the natural oils in the bran and germ turn rancid much more quickly when it's warm. Since you never know how long the package has already been sitting on the store shelf, keep whole grains in the refrigerator or your freezer if you have room. (They need not be thawed before use.) White rice is the least vulnerable of all grains since it has no oils to turn rancid; keep it in a cool, dry spot and it will keep indefinitely. For best flavor and nutrition, and for the fastest cooking times, use grains as quickly as you can—it's better to shop more often than to let them go bad.

RINSING AND DRAINING

Grains are cleaned in the milling process, but most should be rinsed before cooking. Rice may have been coated with talc, quinoa may retain a bit of bitter-tasting, naturally occuring saponin, and any grain may be gritty or have leftover bits of husk or other chaff. Put them in a fine-meshed strainer and rinse under cold running water, shaking and tossing them a bit, or wash in a pot and then drain.

RICE

There are thousands of varieties of rice, but they all fall into just a few categories, so you don't need to know too much.

There are two main groups: indica and japonica. Indica are long-grain rices, which produce generally fluffy and separated grains when cooked. Japonica are medium- and short-grain rices that are sticky and moist when cooked. So long-grain or short-grain is the basic distinction. But it's not the only one.

BROWN RICES

Any rice can be "brown," just as any rice can be milled to be "white." Brown rice has had only its inedible hull removed, leaving the bran and germ intact. The color of the bran varies from light tan to red to deep indigo to black. So *all* of the specialty colored rices—red, black, purple, etc.—are just "brown" rices, with different color brans. Like all whole grains, brown rice is more nutritious than its white counterpart, and deliciously different to boot.

See the sidebar on page 368 for how to use brown rice in place of white rice.

LONG-GRAIN RICES

The indica group of rices have individual grains that are at least three times longer than they are wide. When cooked, they're fluffy and separated; the flavor is neutral to delicately sweet and nutty; all are available brown or white. Different types include:

SOUTHERN LONG-GRAIN The most common long-grain rice in the world and the most widely grown rice in the United States.

BASMATI The best-known and most aromatic rice of South Asia; the premium grade is aged for at least a year. The grains elongate and separate when cooked, and have a distinctly nutty aroma and complex flavor. Worth keeping on hand all the time.

JASMINE Sweetly aromatic Thai rice that is white, smooth, and cooks up slightly sticky. (Broken jasmine rice makes very good sticky rice.)

AMERICAN AROMATICS A group of rices that includes Texmati, Kasmati, Calmati, Jasmati, Della, Wild Pecan, Louisiana Pecan, and Popcorn. They're all knockoffs or hybrids of either basmati or jasmine combined with southern long-grain.

LONG-GRAIN STICKY RICES like Thai, sticky jasmine, glutinous, sweet, or *kao niow* ("sticky rice" in Thai); also called glutinous rice or sweet rice. Generally, these slender, opaque white kernels turn translucent when cooked—except the black variety, which is black or dark purple in color. They're aromatic, with a sweet flavor and very sticky but firm texture (in Thailand and elsewhere, it's formed into small balls and eaten with the hands, like bread). Best steamed (see page 370); black sticky rice is traditionally cooked with coconut milk and palm sugar as a dessert.

RED RICES like California Red, Wehani, Himalayan Red, Thai, and Camargue, are all brown rices that, through breeding or accident, have red bran. They're usually more expensive than standard brown rice but not much different in flavor.

CONVERTED AND INSTANT RICES These rices are pre-processed to reduce cooking time; since rice in general is easy and fast to cook, I don't see any reason in the world to buy them.

SHORT-GRAIN RICES

Varieties in the japonica group—short-grain rices—are fat and rounder than long-grain. They're also stickier and moister, as well as glossy in a most appealing way, when cooked. These are the most common in the United States:

CALROSE The most frequently seen variety, sometimes labeled and sometimes not. Other strains are based on Japanese rices like mochi, Koshihikari, and Akitakomachi, rarely labeled. Most are grown in California. Generally, the kernels are glossy, sticky but firm, moist, and neutral in flavor. They are good, inexpensive substitutes for Arborio and other short- and medium-grain rices in risotto and paella.

RISOTTO RICES like Arborio (most common), Vialone Nano, and Carnaroli, are more expensive. Their center remains firm when cooked (not overcooked, though!), and their starchy outer layers create that creamy risotto texture. *Superfino* is a slightly longer grain than *fino* risotto rice. Use common short- or medium-grain rice as a substitute if you like; the difference is noticeable but only slightly. Paella rices, like Valencia, Bomba, Bahia, and Granza, are similar. Brown varieties can be substituted for white if you follow the directions on page 368.

SHORT-GRAIN STICKY RICES Also called glutinous, sweet, or waxy, these mostly come from China, Korea, and Japan. They're opaque and plump with a slightly sweet flavor and sticky but firm texture. Usually, but not always, these rices are used in desserts and sweet dishes. Mochi is a Japanese sticky rice that's often made into a dough to make rice cakes (see page 339).

AMERICAN BLACK, RED, AND MAHOGANY RICES Aromatic rices with a nutty and spicy flavor. The colors are deeply hued and quite beautiful.

White Rice

MAKES: 4 to 6 servings
TIME: 20 to 30 minutes
F V

It's almost as easy to make pilafs (see page 372) and other slightly more sophisticated rice dishes as it is to make basic rice, but sometimes this is what you're looking for. And needless to say, white rice can be served with almost anything.

1½ cups white rice
Large pinch salt

1. Put the rice in a small saucepan with water to cover by about 1 inch. Add the salt and bring to a boil over medium-high heat, then adjust the heat so the mixture bubbles steadily but not violently. When small craters appear, lower the heat a bit more. When all visible moisture disappears, turn off the heat entirely—this will be 10 to 15 minutes after you started.
2. At this point you can serve the rice (it will be moist but fine) or cover it, with the heat off, and let it sit for 15 or even 30 minutes, during which time it will become a bit drier. See "13 Thirty-Second Ways to Jazz Up Plain Rice," right.

WHITE RICE IN THE MICROWAVE Easy enough, especially for 2 servings: Put 1 cup white rice in a 1-quart measure or bowl and add a large pinch of salt and 1½ cups water. Cover tightly with plastic wrap and cut a slit in the top of the wrap. Microwave for 12½ minutes or until the

grains are plump and tender, then let sit for 5 minutes or so before serving.

Brown Rice

MAKES: 4 to 6 servings
TIME: About 45 minutes
V

Brown rice takes longer to cook than white rice, though by making this the first thing you tackle when you get in the kitchen, you can still prepare a meal in which brown rice plays a role in (usually) less than 45 minutes. You can also parboil it and substitute it for white rice in any recipe (see "The Easy Way to Substitute Brown Rice for

13 Thirty-Second Ways to Jazz Up Plain Rice

1. Stir in a tablespoon or more butter or olive oil.

2. Drizzle with soy sauce.

3. Add lots of pepper.

4. Stir in a couple of tablespoons chopped fresh herbs.

5. Stir in a tablespoon or 2 minced garlic or chopped onion lightly cooked in olive oil or butter.

6. Top with thinly sliced scallions or minced shallot.

7. Stir in a teaspoon or more—just a hint—vinegar.

8. Add fresh lemon juice to taste (great with butter and pepper).

9. Mix in ½ cup or so grated or crumbled cheese, from mild to strong.

10. Mix in ½ to 1 cup cooked beans, with some of their liquid.

11. Top with Fast Tomato Sauce (page 312).

12. Stir in a bit of ground cinnamon, allspice, nutmeg, and/or cloves; exercise restraint and be sure to taste before adding more.

13. Season with any spice mixture.

White," below) or use the method for Cooking Grains, the Easy Way (page 398).

1½ cups brown rice
Large pinch salt

1. Put the rice in a small saucepan with water to cover by about 1 inch. Add the salt and bring to a boil over medium-high heat, then adjust the heat so the mixture bubbles gently. Cover and cook for 30 to 40 minutes, checking occasionally to make sure the water is not being absorbed too quickly; you can add a little more water if necessary. When the liquid has been absorbed, taste and see if the rice is tender or nearly so. If not, add about ½ cup more liquid and continue to cook, covered.
2. When the rice is tender, you can serve it. Or cover it, with the heat off, and let it sit for 15 or even

The Easy Way to Substitute Brown Rice for White

Using brown rice instead of white is easy: Just precook—"parboil"—the same quantity of brown rice first, then substitute that for the raw white rice in any recipe. The techniques after that remain the same—for pilafs, paella, stuck-pot dishes, and, incredibly, even risottos. And the results are terrific. You get the nutty, rich, toasted, satisfying taste of brown rice; perhaps what's most surprising is the texture. Pilafs are still fluffy; risottos are still creamy. In fact, this is one of the most important "discoveries" I made while first researching this book.

Start by bringing a large pot of salted water to a boil. Stir in the brown rice and adjust the heat so that the water bubbles along nicely. Don't stir the rice again; just let it cook for 10 to 15 minutes. (Twelve minutes is about perfect, but it's not that precise, so let's not get nuts about this; you want it slightly tender, not crunchy but far from done.) Drain the rice, then proceed with whatever recipe you choose. You can parboil the brown rice up to an hour or so beforehand or even do it a few days ahead, let cool, then drain and refrigerate.

30 minutes, during which time it will become a bit drier. See "13 Thirty-Second Ways to Jazz Up Plain Rice" (page 367).

Coconut Rice

MAKES: 4 to 6 servings
TIME: 30 minutes
F V

Coconuts grow wild in many rice-growing areas, so the combination is a natural. You can make your own coconut milk (page 304), but canned is easier so it pays to have some around.

3 cups coconut milk or 1½ cups coconut milk plus 1½ cups water
1½ cups rice (preferably short-grain)
Pinch of salt

1. Combine the coconut milk and rice in a saucepan; bring to a boil over medium heat, stirring occasionally. Add the salt, reduce the heat to low, and cover. Cook for 10 minutes, stirring occasionally to make sure the bottom doesn't stick or burn.
2. Uncover and continue to cook, stirring, over low heat until the rice is tender and the mixture is creamy, 10 to 15 minutes. If liquid is absorbed before the rice is done, stir in water about ½ cup at a time, and cook until done.

SPICY COCONUT RICE Delicious: Add 1 tablespoon each minced fresh ginger, garlic, and fresh chile (like jalapeño or Thai) or red chile flakes in Step 1. Garnish with chopped fresh cilantro.

COCONUT RICE WITH COCONUT BITS Crunchier: While the rice is cooking, toast ½ cup shredded coconut in a dry skillet, shaking occasionally, until lightly browned. Stir into the rice just before serving.

COCONUT RICE AND BEANS Make it a meal: Step 1 remains the same. Stir 1 cup cooked kidney, pinto, pink, or black beans with a little of their liquid into the rice when you uncover it.

COCONUT BROWN RICE The main recipe or any of the variations can be made with brown rice: Use 1½ cups coconut milk and 2 cups water. Increase the covered cooking time to 20 minutes and the uncovered time to about 20 minutes, adding more water if necessary. Or start with parboiled brown rice (see "The Easy Way to Substitute Brown Rice for White," opposite) and treat like white rice.

Baked Rice and Black Beans

MAKES: 4 to 6 servings
TIME: About 2 hours, mostly unattended
Ⓜ Ⓥ

This technique—partially puréeing the half-cooked beans and then adding the rice—makes a great case for cooking all rice and bean dishes this way, because the bean flavor really permeates the rice. Throw it in the oven and an hour later you have a one-pot meal with a crisp crust.

2	tablespoons olive oil
1	onion, chopped
1	red or yellow bell pepper, cored, seeded, and chopped
1	tablespoon minced garlic
¾	cup dried black beans, rinsed and picked over, and soaked if you have time
1½	cups long-grain white rice
1	cup chopped tomato; don't bother to drain
	Salt and pepper
½	cup chopped fresh parsley or cilantro

1. Put the oil in a large ovenproof pot over medium heat. When it's hot, add the onion, bell pepper, and garlic and cook, stirring occasionally, until the onion is soft, 3 to 5 minutes. Add the beans and cover with water by 1 inch. Bring to a boil, then turn the heat down to low so that the mixture bubbles gently. Partially cover and cook,

stirring occasionally and adding water if necessary, until the beans are about half-done, softening but still tough in the middle, about 40 minutes or an hour or more if you didn't soak the beans. Heat the oven to 350°F.

2. Remove about half of the beans from the pot. Use an immersion blender or a potato masher to partially purée the beans in the pot—be careful not to overdo it—then return the whole beans to the pot.

3. Stir in the rice, tomato, and a good amount of salt and pepper. If you don't want a crust to develop, cover the pot. Transfer the pot to the oven and bake until the rice and beans are tender, anywhere between 30 and 60 minutes, adding a little water if needed. Taste and season with salt and pepper. Sprinkle with parsley and serve. Or cool, cover, and refrigerate for up to 2 days; reheat and stir in a little water and olive oil just before serving.

BAKED RICE AND WHITE BEANS, TUSCAN STYLE Omit the bell pepper; the onion is optional. Substitute white beans like cannellini, navy, or Great Northern for the black and add 2 to 3 tablespoons chopped fresh sage or just under 1 tablespoon dried sage in Step 1. Proceed with the recipe and drizzle with good olive oil just before serving.

BAKED RICE AND RED KIDNEY BEANS, JAMAICAN STYLE Irresistible with coconut milk: Replace the bell pepper with a fresh hot chile, the black beans with red kidney beans, and the tomato with a 14-ounce can coconut milk. In Step 3, add about 2 teaspoons chopped fresh thyme or ½ to 1 teaspoon dried thyme (to taste).

Rice with Chickpeas

MAKES: 4 to 6 servings
TIME: 30 minutes with cooked chickpeas
Ⓕ Ⓜ Ⓥ

Chickpeas are great with rice; they add richness to the cooking liquid and—provided you don't overcook them—they won't turn to mush. Add more vegetables or firm tofu to any of these recipes (especially the curried variation) and you have a nice one-pot meal.

Other grains you can use: couscous, bulgur, pearled barley, quinoa.

1 tablespoon olive oil

½ onion, chopped

2 cloves garlic, minced

½ bell pepper, any color you like, cored, seeded, and chopped

1½ cups chopped fresh tomato with the juice; don't bother to drain

1¼ cups vegetable stock (pages 97–100) or water

2 tablespoons dry sherry (optional)

1 bay leaf

Salt and pepper

1½ cups long-grain rice

1 cup cooked chickpeas

1. Put the oil in a large saucepan over medium-high heat. When it's hot, add the onion, garlic, and bell pepper and cook, stirring occasionally, until the onion softens, about 5 minutes. Add the tomato, stock, sherry if you're using it, bay leaf, some salt, and plenty of pepper. Bring to a boil.
2. Stir in the rice and chickpeas, cover, and turn the heat down to low so that the mixture bubbles gently. Cook until the liquid is absorbed and the rice is tender, about 20 minutes. Fluff with a fork. Taste and adjust the seasoning. Remove the bay leaf. Serve hot or at room temperature. Or store, covered, in the refrigerator for up to 2 days; reheat or bring back to room temperature and stir in a little olive oil just before serving.

SPICED RICE WITH CHICKPEAS AND ALMONDS Great under grilled vegetables: Omit the bell pepper and sherry. Stir in 1 tablespoon or so of chili powder, garam masala, or curry powder into the cooking onions and proceed with the recipe. Sprinkle with toasted almond slices before serving.

CURRIED RICE WITH CHICKPEAS Richer and spicier: Omit the sherry and replace the stock with coconut milk, if you like. Stir in 1 tablespoon or so of curry powder into the cooking onions and proceed with the recipe.

You can also throw in a handful of peas (fresh or thawed frozen) during the last 5 minutes of cooking.

SAFFRON RICE WITH CHICKPEAS Gorgeous color and lovely flavor: Omit the bell pepper, garlic, and sherry; replace the tomatoes with an additional cup of stock or water. Add ¼ teaspoon crushed saffron threads and 1 teaspoon thinly sliced lemon or orange zest along with the stock in Step 1; proceed with the recipe. Sprinkle with Za'atar (page 652) just before serving.

Steamed Sticky Rice

MAKES: 4 to 6 servings
TIME: About 2 hours, mostly unattended
Ⓜ Ⓥ

This is a one-ingredient wonder, with substance, flavor, and chew; and everyone loves it. It's not difficult to make, as long as you plan ahead a bit.

Buying the right rice is the hard part. It may be called sticky rice, sweet rice, or glutinous rice, but—unfortunately—not all sweet or glutinous rice is sticky rice. Try to buy Thai "sticky rice" or Thai "sweet rice"; also reliable is broken jasmine rice. (There's also black sticky rice, but that's mostly reserved for desserts.) Make sure you buy cheesecloth, too; you'll need it for steaming.

1½ cups sticky rice
Salt and pepper
Soy sauce for serving (optional)

1. Rinse the rice, then soak it in water to cover for at least 1 hour and up to 24 hours.
2. Drain, then wrap in cheesecloth, tying it together at the top, and put in a steamer above boiling water (see page 25). Steam for about 30 minutes, until tender. It's almost impossible to overcook sticky rice, so you can keep it warm over low heat for an hour longer or even more. (You can even cook the rice in advance: Keep it tightly wrapped, refrigerate it, and resteam just before serving.) Season it with salt and pepper and/or soy sauce before serving.

Rice with Chickpeas
(page 369)

Making a good thing better: Toss the cooked rice with 1 cup coconut milk and 1 tablespoon soy sauce. Rewrap and steam (or microwave) for a few minutes to reheat.

STICKY RICE WITH SHALLOTS AND PEANUTS OR COCONUT
This is killer: While the rice is cooking, toast about ½ cup peanuts or shredded coconut in a dry skillet over medium heat until fragrant, about 2 minutes. Chop the peanuts (you don't have to chop the coconut), then toss with ¼ cup each chopped shallot or scallions, chopped fresh cilantro, 1 tablespoon soy sauce, and 2 teaspoons fresh lime juice. Toss with the cooked rice and rewrap and steam (or microwave) for a few minutes to reheat.

STICKY RICE WITH VEGETABLE FILLING Especially nice when wrapped in a lotus or banana leaf, but that step is not necessary: When the rice is done, flatten it into a rectangle. Toss about a cup of any filling you like with a little soy sauce and spread it over the rice. (For example, use Stir-Fried Vegetables, page 154.) Fold the rice over the filling and rewrap and steam (or microwave) for a few minutes to reheat.

Rice Pilaf, Eight Ways

MAKES: 4 to 6 servings
TIME: About 30 minutes, plus a little time to rest
Ⓜ Ⓞ

Pilafs are defined by cooking rice in butter or oil, usually with onion and often with other ingredients, before adding, at the very least, a flavorful liquid like stock. Yellow rice is a form of pilaf, as are biryani and paella; the technique is universal. That first sautéing step is the commonality, and it's what makes pilaf truly one of the great gems of home cooking.

Other than that first step, much is up for grabs: The rice may be long- or short-grain; the liquid may be stock or wine or milk (or even yogurt) or nondairy milk; and the herbs, spices, and solid ingredients can be just about any combination. Brown rice is fair game, too, but the technique is slightly different; see page 368.

You can make this advance: When you're ready to eat, just add a little water, cover it, and heat gently in the microwave, oven, or on the stove.

2–4 **tablespoons butter or olive oil, to taste**
1 **cup chopped onion**
1½ **cups rice (preferably basmati)**
  Salt and pepper
2½ **cups vegetable stock (pages 97–100), warmed**
  Chopped fresh parsley for garnish

1. Put the butter or oil in a large, deep skillet over medium-high heat. When the butter is melted or the oil is hot, add the onion. Cook, stirring, until the onion is soft, 3 to 5 minutes.
2. Add the rice all at once, turn the heat down to medium, and stir until the rice is glossy, completely coated with fat, and starting to color lightly, about 5 minutes. Season well with salt and pepper, then turn the heat down to low and add the stock all at once. Stir once or twice, then cover the pan.
3. Cook for about 15 minutes, until most of the liquid is absorbed. Turn the heat to the absolute minimum (if you have an electric stove, turn the heat off and leave the pan on the burner) and let rest for another 15 to 30 minutes. Taste and adjust the seasoning. Garnish with parsley and serve.

PILAF WITH CURRANTS AND PINE NUTS The Middle Eastern classic: Butter is ideal here, but not necessary. Along with the rice, add ¼ cup currants or raisins, 2 tablespoons pine nuts, 1 teaspoon ground cumin, and ½ teaspoon ground cinnamon.

PILAF WITH CHICKPEAS, PEAS, LIMAS, OR OTHER BEANS
Just before adding the stock, stir in 1 cup cooked chickpeas, raw green peas (frozen are okay, no need to thaw), fresh or frozen limas or edamame beans, or drained cooked or canned (or frozen) pigeon peas or black-eyed peas. Add 1 teaspoon fresh thyme leaves and a bay leaf (remove it before serving).

VERMICELLI PILAF Break enough vermicelli or angel hair pasta into 1-inch lengths to make about a cup. Cook along with the rice until nicely browned. Proceed with the recipe, increasing the stock to about 3 cups.

PILAF WITH SPINACH OR OTHER GREENS Add 2 cups trimmed, rinsed, and chopped fresh spinach, chard, sorrel, watercress, or beet greens along with the onion. Add 1 teaspoon minced garlic just after you stir in the rice, then proceed with the recipe, reducing the liquid to about 2¼ cups.

MEXICAN RICE WITH VEGETABLES In Step 2, just after adding the rice, stir in ⅓ cup each chopped carrot, celery, red or other bell pepper, and green beans or whole peas. Proceed with the recipe, garnishing with parsley or cilantro.

RED OR GREEN RICE PILAF Better known as Arroz Rojo or Verde, these are Mexican pilafs: Use olive or good-quality vegetable oil, and add 1 teaspoon minced garlic just after you stir in the rice. For Arroz Rojo, add about 1 cup chopped tomato (canned is fine; don't bother to drain) just before you add the stock; reduce the stock to 1¾ cups. For Arroz Verde, add about 1 cup chopped roasted and peeled poblano chiles (see page 228). Finish with parsley or cilantro and a squeeze of lemon or lime juice. **V**

KIMCHI RICE Use sesame oil. Don't salt the rice in Step 2. In Step 2, just after adding the rice, stir in ½ cup chopped Kimchi (page 93). Proceed with the recipe, seasoning with soy sauce and garnishing with sliced scallions. **V**

Yellow Rice, the Best Way

MAKES: 4 to 6 servings
TIME: 30 minutes
F O

There is the right way to make this and a number of easy ways, but this version—with saffron, other spices, and a couple of vegetables—is really the ultimate.

2½ cups vegetable stock (pages 97–100) or water
  Large pinch saffron threads
2–4 tablespoons butter or olive oil
1 cup chopped onion
1 red bell pepper, cored, seeded, and chopped
1 tablespoon minced garlic
1½ cups white rice
  Salt and pepper
1 fresh tomato, chopped
⅛ teaspoon ground allspice
2 bay leaves
1 cup fresh or frozen peas
  Chopped fresh parsley for garnish
  Lemon wedges for serving

1. Warm the stock with the saffron in a small saucepan. Put the butter or oil in a large, deep skillet over medium-high heat. When the butter melts or the oil is hot, add the onion and bell pepper and cook, stirring occasionally, until the onion is soft, 3 to 5 minutes.
2. Stir in the garlic and rice, sprinkle everything with salt and pepper, and turn the heat to medium. Stir until the rice is glossy, completely coated with fat, and starting to color lightly, about 5 minutes. Add the tomato, allspice, bay leaves, peas, and stock. Stir, adjust the heat so that the liquid bubbles steadily but not violently, and cover.
3. Cook for about 15 minutes, until most of the liquid is absorbed. Turn the heat to the absolute minimum (if you have an electric stove, turn the heat off and leave the pan on the burner) and let rest for another 15 to 30 minutes. Taste, adjust the seasoning, and remove the bay leaves. Garnish with parsley and serve with lemon wedges.

YELLOW RICE, THE FAST WAY Also great: Omit the red pepper, tomato, allspice, bay leaves, and peas. Bring 3 cups stock or water to a boil. Put 2 tablespoons olive oil in the skillet over medium-high heat. When it's hot, add the onion and a sprinkle of salt and pepper. Cook, stirring occasionally, until the onion is soft, 3 to 5 minutes. Add the rice and cook, stirring occasionally, until

Biryani

glossy. Add the saffron or 1 teaspoon ground turmeric, then the boiling stock. Adjust the heat so it just bubbles and finish cooking as directed.

Biryani

MAKES: 4 to 6 servings
TIME: About 30 minutes
F

India's greatest pilaf, almost always made with basmati rice and butter. Here, tofu is much more convenient than paneer (fresh Indian cheese), but you can use either, or no concentrated protein at all.

> A few saffron threads or 1 teaspoon ground turmeric
> 1½ cups vegetable stock (pages 97–100) or water, warmed
> 2 tablespoons butter (more is better) or good-quality vegetable oil
> 6 cardamom pods or 2 teaspoons ground cardamom
> Pinch ground cloves
> 1 cinnamon stick or ½ teaspoon ground cinnamon
> 2 bay leaves
> 2 cups chopped onion
> 1 tablespoon minced garlic
> 1 tablespoon minced or grated fresh ginger or 1 teaspoon ground ginger
> Salt and pepper
> 1½ cups long-grain rice (preferably basmati)
> 1½ cups yogurt
> 1 pound firm tofu or paneer, cubed (optional)
> Chopped fresh cilantro for garnish

1. If you're using saffron, combine it in a pot with the stock. Put the butter or oil in a large, deep skillet over medium-high heat. When the butter melts or the oil is hot, turn the heat down to medium and add the turmeric if you're using it, cardamom, cloves, cinnamon, and bay leaves. Cook, stirring frequently, until the spices are fragrant, about 2 minutes.

2. Add the onion, garlic, and ginger, along with a large pinch of salt and a sprinkle of pepper, and cook, stirring, until the onion is soft, 3 to 5 minutes. Add the rice all at once and stir until the rice is glossy and completely coated with fat, 2 to 3 minutes. Lower the heat, then add the yogurt and stock and stir. Stir in the tofu. Adjust the heat so the mixture barely bubbles and cover the pan.
3. Cook for 15 to 20 minutes, then check the rice. When the rice is tender and the liquid is absorbed, it's done. If not, cook for 2 to 3 minutes more and check again. Remove the bay leaves and cinnamon stick, if you used it; the cardamom pods are good to eat. Taste and adjust the seasoning, then garnish with cilantro and serve.

Brown Rice Pilaf with Two Mushrooms

MAKES: 4 to 6 servings
TIME: About 1 hour, mostly unattended
O

You can substitute brown rice for white in any pilaf, simply by using parcooked brown rice (see the sidebar on page 368). But cooking raw brown rice in oil alone gives it incredible flavor and decreases the overall cooking time without making the onion mushy. With this technique, you can incorporate any of the variations or suggestions for the white rice pilafs on pages 372 to 373, adjusting the amount of liquid and the time accordingly. If you want to use white rice here, reduce the cooking time in Step 2 to 20 minutes.

Not essential, but cooking the shiitake mushrooms separately makes them crisp and adds a nice contrast.

> ½ cup dried porcini or other mushrooms, rinsed
> 2½ cups vegetable stock (pages 97–100), Mushroom Stock (page 99), or water
> 6 tablespoons olive oil (or half oil and half butter)
> 1¼ cups brown basmati rice
> 1 cup sliced onion
> Salt and pepper
> 1½ cups sliced shiitake mushroom caps (reserve the stems for stock if you like)

1. Combine the dried mushrooms with the stock in a small saucepan over low heat as you begin cooking the rice. Put half the oil (or oil and butter) in a large, deep skillet over medium-high heat. When it's hot, add the rice and cook, stirring occasionally, until it is extremely aromatic and beginning to brown, about 10 minutes.

2. Lift the mushrooms out of the stock with a slotted spoon and add to the rice, reserving the warm stock. Toss the onion into the rice, sprinkle with salt and pepper, and stir occasionally until the onion begins to soften, 3 to 5 minutes. Pour the stock in all at once, carefully; leave any grit in the bottom of the pot. Adjust the heat so that it bubbles very gently, and cover. Total cooking time from this point will be about 40 minutes; check after 20 minutes and again after 30 to make sure there's enough liquid; if not, add about ½ cup water.

3. About halfway through the cooking time, put the remaining oil in a skillet over medium-high heat. When it's hot, add the shiitakes, along with a large pinch salt and some pepper. Cook, stirring occasionally, until the mushrooms brown on the edges, about 10 minutes.

4. When the rice is tender, uncover and cook over medium heat until almost all the liquid is gone. Stir in the browned shiitakes, taste and adjust the seasoning, and serve immediately.

Paella with Tomatoes and Eggs

MAKES: 4 to 6 servings
TIME: 35 to 45 minutes, plus resting time

My vegetarian paella starts with sofrito, a mixture of aromatics, herbs, and tomatoes, sautéed in olive oil until it becomes a thick paste. Saffron is traditional in paella but I also like to add smoked paprika. It's also traditional to serve it with garlic mayonnaise (Aïoli, page 671) but try Chimichurri (page 638) for a deliciously unorthodox alternative. What is not traditional is my addition of eggs, which bake into the savory rice mixture. It's also delicious without, so I have made them optional.

No need for a *paellera* (a two-handled paella pan), but your pan should be wide enough to hold the grains of rice in a thin layer. This will help develop the crusty bits of rice on the bottom of the pan (called *socarrat*) that are the best part of the dish. Since most home cooks don't own such a big pan, I prefer starting paella on the stove in a roasting pan or my largest skillet and moving it to the oven. To properly develop the socarrat, put the pan back on the stove for a couple of minutes before serving.

3½ cups vegetable stock (pages 97–100) or water, plus more if needed
Large pinch saffron threads (optional)
1 pound fresh tomatoes, cored, cut into thick wedges, and seeded
Salt and pepper
4 tablespoons olive oil
1 onion, chopped
1 tablespoon minced garlic
1 tablespoon tomato paste
2 teaspoons smoked or other paprika
2 cups Spanish or other short-grain white rice or parcooked short-grain brown rice (see page 368)
4–6 eggs (optional)
Chopped fresh parsley for garnish

1. Heat the oven to 450°F. Warm the stock in a medium saucepan with the saffron if you're using it. Put the tomatoes in a bowl, sprinkle with salt and pepper, and drizzle them with 1 tablespoon of the olive oil. Toss gently to coat.

2. Put the remaining oil in a large ovenproof skillet over medium-high heat. Add the onion and garlic, sprinkle with salt and pepper, and cook, stirring occasionally, until the onion is soft, 3 to 5 minutes. Stir in the tomato paste and paprika and cook for a minute more. Add the rice and cook, stirring occasionally, until it's shiny, another minute or 2. Carefully add the stock and stir until just combined.

3. Put the tomato wedges on top of the rice and drizzle with the juices that accumulated in the bottom of the

bowl. Use a large spoon to make 4 to 6 indentations in the rice and carefully crack an egg into each. Put the pan in the oven and roast, undisturbed, for 15 minutes. Check to see if the rice is dry and just tender. If not, return the pan to the oven for another 5 minutes. If the rice looks too dry at this point and still isn't quite done, add a small amount of stock, wine, or water. When the rice is ready, turn off the oven and let it sit for at least 5 and up to 15 minutes.

4. Remove the pan from the oven and sprinkle with parsley. If you like, put the pan over high heat for a few minutes to develop a bit of a bottom crust before serving.

PAELLA WITH EGGPLANT Instead of tomatoes and eggs, use 1 pound eggplant, peeled if you like, and cubed. In Step 1, increase the oil to 2 tablespoons. ⓥ

PAELLA WITH MUSHROOM CAPS Instead of tomatoes and eggs, use 1 pound fresh mushrooms like cremini (sometimes called "baby bellas") or shiitake. Trim the stems and save them for another use, but leave the caps whole. Proceed with the recipe, putting the caps on top of the rice, smooth side up. ⓥ

PAELLA WITH SPINACH AND LEMON ZEST You'll have to pile the spinach up on top of the rice, but it will cook down and form a lovely green topping: Instead of tomatoes and eggs, use 1 pound fresh spinach, rinsed, trimmed of thick stems, and chopped. When you put it in the bowl with the olive oil, add 1 tablespoon minced lemon zest. ⓥ

PAELLA WITH FAVA BEANS You could also make this with limas or edamame: Instead of the tomatoes and eggs, use 1 cup shelled and peeled fava beans (frozen are fine). ⓥ

7 Other Toppings for Paella
You can experiment a lot with this dish, and anything that tastes good crunchy and roasted (which is most

things) will be great on top of the paella. Just remember to toss the ingredients in olive oil before adding them. Try:

1. Cooked white beans like cannellini, gigantes, or navy beans

2. Thinly sliced potatoes

3. Thinly sliced lemon

4. Crumbled tempeh tossed with smoked paprika and cumin

5. 1 head roasted garlic cloves, squeezed from the skin

6. Sliced roasted red peppers (page 228)

7. Whole scallions

Risotto with Dried and Fresh Mushrooms

MAKES: 4 to 6 servings
TIME: 45 minutes
Ⓞ

According to the canon, you must use Arborio or one of its relatives to make "real" risotto, but I've long had success with other short-grain rices, and the common varieties cost about a fifth of the usually overpriced Arborio. You can even make it with short-grain brown rice (see "The Easy Way to Substitute Brown Rice for White," page 368). You will lose some creaminess but it's made up for in deep, nutty flavor.

Many people are scared off making risotto, thinking it must be stirred constantly. Yes, the liquid must be added a bit at a time, and yes, the heat must be kept fairly high, and yes, there's a lot of stirring. But that doesn't mean *constant* stirring. That said, once you start the process, you shouldn't leave the stove for more than a minute or so at a time. Remove the rice from the heat when there is still a tiny bit of crunch in the center of the rice kernels and the mixture is moist and creamy.

I always have dried mushrooms on hand; the addition of fresh mushrooms is a bonus. Any vegetable—artichoke hearts, green beans, snow peas, and so on (see the list, opposite)—can be cooked on the side and stirred into the risotto at the last minute, as the shiitakes are here.

½ cup dried porcini mushrooms

5 cups vegetable stock (pages 97–100)

Large pinch saffron threads (optional)

4–6 tablespoons butter or olive oil

1 onion, chopped

1½ cups Arborio or other short- or medium-grain rice

Salt and pepper

½ cup dry white wine or water

1 cup slivered shiitake or portobello mushroom caps

Grated Parmesan cheese (optional)

Making Risotto Vegan

It's easy enough to use oil and skip the cheese but a little trickier to duplicate the creaminess they lend to the dish. Replacing some of the stock or water with rice, oat, or nut milk (specifically hazelnut or almond) will help a lot, though they're all slightly sweet and none is entirely neutral in flavor; soy milk, in fact, is too strong.

1. Rinse the dried mushrooms once or twice, then soak them in a bowl with hot water to cover. Put the stock in a saucepan over low heat; add the saffron if you're using it. Put 2 tablespoons of the butter or oil in a large, deep nonstick skillet over medium heat. When the butter is melted or the oil is hot, add the onions and cook, stirring occasionally, until soft, 3 to 5 minutes.

2. Add the rice and cook, stirring occasionally, until it is glossy and coated with fat, 2 to 3 minutes. Add a little salt and pepper, then the white wine. Stir and let the liquid bubble away. Lift the mushrooms out of the soaking liquid with your hands or a slotted spoon, reserving the

liquid. Chop them, then stir them into the rice. Carefully pour in about half of the soaking liquid, leaving any grit in the bottom of the bowl.

3. Use a ladle to begin to add the stock, ½ cup or so at a time, stirring after each addition and every minute or so. When the stock is just about absorbed, add more. The mixture should be neither soupy nor dry. Keep the heat medium to medium-high and stir frequently. Meanwhile, put the remaining butter or oil (more will make a creamier risotto) in a small skillet over medium-high heat. When the butter is melted or the oil is hot, add the fresh mushrooms and cook, stirring occasionally, until lightly browned and almost crisp, about 10 minutes.

5 Simple Substitutions for Risotto with Mushrooms

Use the dried mushrooms or not, and substitute one of the following for the fresh mushrooms.

1. Fresh peas or cut-up snow peas, sugar snap peas, asparagus, or green beans **Parboil (see page 150) in salted water until bright and just tender (1 to 5 minutes, depending on the vegetable); rinse in cold running water to stop the cooking; drain; stir into the risotto at the last minute.**

2. Broccoli or cauliflower **Cut or break into small florets and parboil very quickly, just until tender; cook in butter for a minute or 2; stir in at the last minute.**

3. Beets, turnips, potatoes, carrots, or other root vegetables **Cut into small cubes and parboil just until tender; cook** quickly in butter until lightly browned; stir in at the last minute. Or use leftovers.

4. Sturdy greens like chard, collards, or kale **Cut out the stems and chop or cut into ribbons; parboil in salted water until bright and just tender (1 to 5 minutes, depending on the** thickness of the leaves); rinse in cold running water to stop the cooking; drain; stir into the risotto at the last minute.

5. Tender greens like arugula, spinach, watercress, or sorrel **Chop (or not) and add instead of the cooked mushrooms in Step 4.**

4. Begin tasting the rice 20 minutes after you add it; you want it to be tender but with a tiny bit of crunch. It could take as long as 30 minutes to reach this stage. When it does, stir in the cooked mushrooms with their butter or oil, and at least ½ cup Parmesan if you're using it. Taste, adjust the seasoning, and serve, passing additional Parmesan at the table if you like.

RISOTTO WITH OTHER GRAINS You can use the same technique (including a very similar cooking time) with other grains: Replace the rice with an equal amount of farro, oat groats, einkorn, or pearled barley. Proceed with the recipe, adding the stock ¼ cup at a time.

Fried Rice, with or without Egg

MAKES: 4 to 6 servings
TIME: 20 minutes with cooked rice
F O

Made just like a stir-fry: You choose your other main ingredients in whatever combination you like—here, vegetables and tofu—and cook them one or two at a time, each in a little bit of oil over high heat (a nonstick or well-seasoned pan is essential), until they are pretty much done, then dump into a bowl. Warm them all together in the pan before serving.

This should be made with leftover or cooked-ahead rice. Warm just-made rice clumps together, but when cooked rice is chilled—even for a few hours—it dries out and separates into individual grains, allowing the rice to be stir-fried with a minimum of oil and to crisp easily. You can use the rice that comes with takeout, but your own basmati—brown or white or both—will give superior results.

- 1 cup fresh or frozen peas
- 3 tablespoons good-quality vegetable oil
- 1 onion, chopped
- 1 bell pepper (any color), cored, seeded, and chopped

- 1½ cups cubed firm tofu
- 1 tablespoon minced garlic, or to taste
- 1 tablespoon minced fresh ginger, or to taste
- 3–4 cups cooked white or brown rice (preferably basmati or jasmine)
- 2 eggs, lightly beaten (optional)
- ¼ cup rice wine, sherry, white wine, vegetable stock (pages 97–100), or water
- 2 tablespoons soy sauce
- 1 tablespoon sesame oil
  Salt and pepper
- ¼ cup thinly sliced scallions or chopped fresh cilantro

1. If the peas are frozen, soak them in cold water to thaw while you begin cooking. Put 1 tablespoon of the vegetable oil in a large skillet over high heat. When it's hot, add the onion and bell pepper and cook, stirring occasionally, until they soften and begin to brown, 5 to 10 minutes. Lower the heat if the vegetables threaten to scorch. Use a slotted spoon to transfer them to a bowl.

2. Add the tofu to the oil and cook, again over high heat, stirring infrequently, until nicely browned, 5 to 10 minutes. Add to the bowl with the vegetables. Drain the peas if necessary and add them to the oil. Cook, shaking the skillet, for about a minute, or until hot. Add them to the bowl.

3. Put the remaining vegetable oil in the skillet, followed by the garlic and ginger. About 15 seconds later, begin to add the rice a bit at a time, breaking up any clumps with your fingers and tossing it with the oil. When all the rice has been added, make a well in its center and break the eggs into it if you're using them; scramble them a bit, then incorporate them into the rice.

4. Return the tofu and vegetables to the pan and stir to integrate. Add the wine and cook, stirring, for about a minute, until everything is hot. Add the soy sauce and sesame oil, then taste and add salt and pepper if necessary. Turn off the heat, stir in the scallions, and serve.

FRIED RICE WITH FROZEN VEGETABLES No apologies; this is good: For the peas, substitute 1 to 2 cups cup frozen vegetables of your choice; there are a lot of interesting mixes now available in supermarket freezers. You can even use frozen bell pepper strips if you like and probably never notice.

FRIED RICE, THAI STYLE In Thailand, they call this Chinese food: In Step 4, stir in a teaspoon or 2 (to taste) red curry paste. Garnish with cilantro and scallions.

PINEAPPLE FRIED RICE Undeniably popular, for good reason: In Step 4, stir in 1½ cups chopped fresh or drained canned pineapple when adding the rice. Adding a chopped tomato at the same time, along with a little ketchup, will give you a more complex flavor.

Stuck-Pot Rice with Potato Crust

MAKES: 4 to 6 servings
TIME: 1½ hours, mostly unattended

This is the first stuck-pot rice I learned to make (with thanks to the late great food writer Paula Peck). Potatoes make the crust here, complemented by the flavors of fennel and saffron. If fennel isn't available or isn't your thing, omit and use celery, or try one of the variations.

Don't worry if the crust at the bottom of the pan comes out in several pieces; that part is often just broken into crisp chunks and served alongside the mound of rice. Be sure to line the pot lid with a cloth towel. This absorbs water so the condensation doesn't drip back into the rice. Normally that doesn't matter, but when you're

---

13 More Tasty Additions to Fried Rice

The list of things you can add to fried rice is longer than the list of things you cannot. But they basically fall into three categories: vegetables; eggs, tofu and the like; and seasonings.

1. Very tender vegetables, or those that can be eaten raw, can be stirred in at the last minute, like 2 cups thinly sliced iceberg or romaine lettuce.

2. Vegetables that will cook in about the same amount of time as the onion or pepper (scallions, shredded zucchini, corn kernels, etc.) should be cooked with or instead of the onion.

3. Harder vegetables—broccoli, cauliflower, eggplant, potato, winter squash—should either be cut into very small pieces, so they will cook in about

the same amount of time as the onion, or quickly parboiled (or deep-fried; see page 157) before incorporating.

4. Cut tomatoes into small wedges and add just after the rice, or you will have tomato sauce.

5. You can also garnish with raw vegetables, like cucumbers made according to the Quickest Pickled Vegetables recipe (page 89), chopped cabbage, or tomato wedges.

6. Any tofu—smoked, pressed, flavored, frozen

and thawed, you name it (see pages 483 to 487)—is great here. Add as you would the tofu in the main recipe.

7. Also good are chopped, cubed, or crumbled tempeh or seitan. I like to fry them in a little oil as if they were a vegetable. You could add chili powder or five-spice powder for a little more flavor.

8. Hard-boiled egg is good option, either chopped or sliced, and added right after the rice.

9. Minced fresh chiles at the beginning, or chile

paste or sauce of any kind at the end; always to taste.

10. Hoisin sauce—or ketchup; they're really not that different—stirred in just after the rice.

11. Basil (preferably Thai), 10 to 15 big leaves, torn up and added at the last moment instead of or in addition to cilantro.

12. Curry powder or almost any other spice mix, stirred in just before you add the rice.

13. Nori "Shake" (page 650) or toasted sesame seeds (see page 299).

Stuck-Pot Rice
with Potato Crust
(page 381)

trying to dry out the bottom of the pan to form a crisp crust, excess water is counterproductive.

Salt
1½ cups white or brown basmati rice
Pepper
Large pinch saffron threads (optional)
4 tablespoons (½ stick) butter, melted, or ¼ cup olive oil
1 large or 2 small waxy potatoes (Yukon Gold or other thin-skinned variety)
1 fennel bulb, trimmed and thinly sliced

1. Bring a pot of water to a boil and salt it. Stir in the rice and return to a boil, then lower the heat so the water bubbles along nicely. Cook undisturbed—white rice for about 5 minutes, brown rice for about 15 minutes. Drain and transfer to a bowl. Taste (the rice will be only partially done), add salt if necessary, and sprinkle with pepper.

2. Stir the saffron if you're using it into 2 tablespoons of the butter. Peel the potatoes and cut them crosswise into thin slices.

3. Put 2 tablespoons plain butter in a large, heavy pot with a tight-fitting lid over medium-high heat. Add the fennel, sprinkle with salt and pepper, and cook, stirring occasionally, until soft, about 2 minutes. Transfer the fennel to a bowl. Turn off the heat (no need to wipe out the pot).

4. Add ¼ cup water and the saffron butter (or the remaining plain butter) to the pot. Carefully cover the bottom of the pot with the potato slices. Add half the rice, then the fennel, and finally the other half of the rice. Wrap a clean kitchen towel around the lid so it completely covers the inside and secure the corners on top so they don't fall anywhere near the stove. Carefully cover the pot. Turn the heat to medium-high. When you hear the water spattering, after about 5 minutes, turn the heat down to very low. Cook, completely undisturbed, for about 45 minutes, until the potatoes start to smell toasty (you will know) but not burned. Remove from the heat and let sit for another 5 minutes.

5. Carefully remove the lid and the towel and turn the pot upside down over a large plate. If the potatoes come out in a single crust, terrific. If not, use a spatula to scrape the pieces out of the pan and put them on top of the rice. Serve, sprinkled with a bit of salt and pepper if you like.

STUCK-POT RICE WITH POTATO CRUST AND LIMA BEANS Use 2 tablespoons chopped fresh dill or 1 tablespoon dried dill instead of the saffron. Instead of the fennel, use 1½ cups frozen lima beans (no need to thaw them). Everything else stays the same.

STUCK-POT RICE WITH POTATO CRUST, LEMON, AND HERBS Brighter in flavor: Use 2 thinly sliced lemons (with peels but no seeds) instead of the fennel. Instead of saffron, use ½ cup chopped fresh mild herbs like parsley, mint, or a combination; 1 teaspoon minced strong herb like tarragon, thyme, or rosemary; or a couple of teaspoons oregano or marjoram, sprinkling them over the layers of potato, lemon, and rice.

STUCK-POT RED RICE WITH POTATO CRUST AND AROMATIC VEGETABLES Instead of brown rice, use red rice. Replace the fennel with 2 carrots and 1 stalk celery, all thinly sliced.

STUCK-POT RICE WITH POTATO CRUST, ALMONDS, AND GINGER Omit the saffron. Instead of the fennel, use ½ cup sliced almonds and 2 tablespoons each sesame seeds and minced fresh ginger. This will take 3 or 4 minutes to soften and get fragrant.

SUSHI

Sushi comes in many forms and I focus on the simplest, which include sushi bowls (*chirashi*), a mound of seasoned sushi rice with tasty hot, cold, or room-temperature ingredients scattered on top, as well as the slightly more involved stuffed rice balls (*onigiri*) and Japanese mixed rice. Rolled sushi (*maki*) is too involved for my taste to do at home but finger sushi (*nigiri*) is sushi rice formed into a small rectangular brick and topped with whatever you choose. (A ribbon of nori can help hold everything together if you like.)

The ingredients for making great sushi rolls or bowls at home are simple, easy to find, and inexpensive: short-grain rice, rice vinegar, a few sheets of nori, and any filling you want. This can be sliced cucumbers, carrots, or avocado, simply cooked edamame, or more elaborate items like Stir-Fried Vegetables (page 154) or Grilled or Broiled Tofu (page 486).

The chart opposite will help you get started with possible ingredient combinations. You can't really go wrong, especially if you pay even the slightest attention to color and texture.

Sushi Rice

MAKES: 4 to 6 servings
TIME: 40 minutes
M V

In Japan sushi rice is considered best slightly warm. In the United States, it's often cool or even cold by the time it's served, but it cannot be made ahead by more than a couple of hours or it loses its great texture. Act accordingly.

1 recipe **White Rice or Brown Rice (page 367)**, **made with short-grain rice**
¼ cup **rice vinegar**
2 tablespoons **sugar**
1 teaspoon **salt**

1. While the rice is cooking, put the vinegar, sugar, and salt in a small saucepan over medium heat and cook, stirring, until the sugar dissolves, less than 5 minutes. Put the saucepan in a bowl filled with ice and stir the vinegar mixture until cool.
2. When the rice is done, put it in a bowl more than twice the size needed to hold the rice—probably the largest bowl you have. Begin to toss the hot rice with

a flat wooden paddle or spoon or a rubber spatula—as if you were folding egg whites into a batter, but much faster and not quite as gently. While you're tossing, sprinkle the rice with the vinegar mixture (if the paddle becomes encrusted with rice, dip it in some water, then shake the water off and proceed). The idea is to cool the rice quickly as it absorbs the vinegar. Sushi rice will not keep for long, but if you cover it with a damp kitchen towel, you can wait a couple of hours to proceed.

Sushi Bowls

Chirashi Sushi
O

Think of chirashi sushi as unstructured sushi (*chirashi* means "scattered"), sushi for when you have a craving but don't feel like making individual rolls. These bowls make perfect one-person meals, they're ideal for using up leftovers, and they also make great party food. All you have to do is set up a colorful buffet of several toppings, condiments, and sauces and let guests have at it.

There is no real recipe for chirashi sushi other than starting with Sushi Rice. Top the rice with anything from Kimchi (page 93) to Sea Slaw (page 55). You can't go wrong. Combine any of the items from the chart opposite, but here are a few classic combos:
1. Stir-fried vegetables and Nori "Shake" (page 650)
2. Cucumbers and carrots marinated in Ponzu (page 657)
3. Sea Slaw (page 55) with toasted sesame seeds.
4. Edamame Salad with Seaweed "Mayo" (page 75) and Cherry Tomato Salad with Soy Sauce (page 58)

Nigiri Sushi

MAKES: 24 to 36 pieces
TIME: 20 minutes with premade rice and topping
F V

Nigiri is hand-shaped sushi. You can use any centerpiece from the "Improvising Sushi Bowls" chart as toppings.

Improvising Sushi Bowls

Pick a centerpiece, drizzle with a spoonful or two from the sauce or marinade column, and finish with as much or as little garnish as you like. Try to pair plain things like simply cooked beans with more complex sauces or marinades and vice versa; you don't want too many complicated components competing with one another.

CENTERPIECE	SAUCE OR MARINADE	GARNISH
Sliced avocado	Sake, mirin, or rice vinegar	Nori "Shake" (page 650)
Stir-Fried Vegetables (page 154)	Ponzu (page 657)	Pickled Ginger (page 207)
Marinated cucumbers, carrots, onions, or radish, using any of the sauces or marinades listed to the right	Ponzu (page 657) Dashi Dipping Sauce (page 657) Strong green tea	Cherry Tomato Salad with Soy Sauce (page 58)
Grilled or Panfried Eggplant (page 201 or 161) or Eggplant Salad with Miso (page 66)	Sautéed Mushrooms (page 217)	Japanese Seven-Spice Mix (page 650)
Cooked small dried beans, like white or black soybeans, adzuki, edamame, or mung (page 435)	Any miso sauce (pages 653 to 654)	Edamame Salad (page 75), with or without the Seaweed "Mayo"
Kimchi (page 93) or Sea Slaw (page 55)	Peanut Sauce, Four Ways (page 657)	Wasabi paste
Tofu skin, frozen or dried, or deep-fried pouches, lightly poached (see page 485), or simple cubes of raw, baked, or fried tofu (pages 484 to 487)	Soy sauce	Chopped shiso leaves
Sea Slaw (page 55)	Korean-Style Soy and Sesame Dipping Sauce and Marinade (page 656)	Kimchi made with daikon (page 93)
Japanese pickles, any kind found in a Japanese market, or Miso-Cured Vegetables (page 93)	Seaweed "Mayo" (page 673) Chile Mayonnaise (page 671)	Thinly sliced scallions

Sushi Bowls shown with, clockwise from top left: smoked tofu, Kimchi (page 93), Seaweed "Mayo" (page 673), Edamame Salad (page 75), Pickled Ginger (page 207), assorted Japanese pickles

Just cut whatever topping you choose into pieces that will fit onto your molded rice.

1 sheet nori, toasted (see page 244; optional)
2 tablespoons rice vinegar or other mild vinegar
1 recipe Sushi Rice (page 384)
¼ cup wasabi paste (optional)
36 small pieces topping (see "Centerpiece" and "Garnish" columns from the chart, page 385)
Pickled Ginger (page 207) for serving
Soy sauce for serving

1. If you're using the nori, cut it into about ½ × 5-inch strips (using scissors is easiest). Mix 1 cup water with the vinegar (this is called "hand water").
2. Put about 2 tablespoons or so of the rice in the palm of your hand; cup your hand and use your other hand to help shape the rice into an oblong piece, about 1 × 3 inches; rinse your hands in the hand water as needed. Smear the nigiri with a dab of wasabi, if using (careful, it's hot), then add your topping.
3. If you like, wrap a strip of nori over the middle of the nigiri, securing the topping in place, and seal the end by dampening it with the hand water. Serve with pickled ginger and soy sauce.

Japanese Rice with Shiitakes, Edamame, and Sea Greens

MAKES: 4 to 6 servings
TIME: 30 minutes
F M V

If you don't already love sea greens, start here. And please use dashi: It adds a complex flavor that can't be replaced and shouldn't be missed.

This can be eaten on its own, but it's wonderful with Stir-Fried Vegetables (page 154) or almost any tofu dish. A few pinches of Japanese Seven-Spice Mix (page 650) or Citrus Sprinkle (page 651) on top boosts flavor.

1½ cups short-grain white rice or parcooked brown rice (see 367)
Kombu Dashi (page 100) as needed (about 2 cups)
4 dried shiitake mushrooms
½ small onion, chopped
1 teaspoon toasted sesame seeds (see page 299)
1 cup shelled edamame (frozen are fine)
½ cup soaked and chopped hijiki, wakame, or kombu (see page 244)
Dash sesame oil
Soy sauce

Forming Nigiri Sushi

STEP 1 Take a small amount of rice, about a quarter of a handful, and gently press it into an oval shape.

STEP 2 Smear with a little wasabi paste if you like.

STEP 3 Top with whatever main ingredient you're using.

STEP 4 Wrap the sushi with a small band of nori if you like.

1. Put the rice in a mediun saucepan and add enough dashi to cover it by about an inch. Bring to a boil, then reduce the heat to low so that it bubbles gently. Cover and cook for about 10 minutes. Meanwhile, soak the shiitakes in hot water to cover. When they're soft, drain (reserve the water) and chop them.

2. Add the shiitakes and their soaking water, onion, sesame seeds, edamame, hijiki, and sesame oil and soy sauce to taste to the rice, cover, and continue to cook until the rice is tender and most of the liquid is absorbed (you don't want it soupy, but not dry either), about 15 minutes. Taste and add sesame oil and soy sauce as necessary. Serve hot or at room temperature. Or cool, cover, and refrigerate for up to 2 days; reheat or bring back to room temperature and stir in a little sesame oil just before serving.

JAPANESE RICE WITH SHIITAKES, TOMATO, AND FERMENTED BLACK BEANS Totally unorthodox and really delicious: Add 1½ cups chopped fresh tomatoes or one 14-ounce can, drained, in Step 2 and substitute ¼ cup rinsed fermented black beans for the edamame.

BLACK THAI RICE WITH COCONUT MILK AND EDAMAME
A savory version of a classic Thai dessert: Use black Thai rice instead of regular white or brown. Substitute coconut milk for the dashi or water and omit the shiitakes, sesame oil, and sea greens but still use the edamame and garnish with sesame seeds.

Mixed Rice, Japanese Style

Kayaku Gohan
MAKES: 4 to 6 servings
TIME: 40 minutes
◎

Kayaku gohan ("mixed rice") is basically Japanese paella; it's far more common in home cooking than sushi. Like paella, you don't need seafood. Like paella, it relies on good ingredients, including rice and stock, and, like paella, it's pretty straightforward to prepare and easy to vary. (Unlike paella, it's made entirely on top of the stove.)

Kayaku gohan uses dashi for the liquid. Dashi can be made in minutes and keeps well.

Nearly any green vegetable can be used in place of the peas; asparagus tips are wonderful, as are edamame or lima beans.

4   cups Kombu Dashi (page 100), or more if needed
5   shiitake mushroom caps (fresh, dried, or a combination; save the stems for stock if you like)
2   tablespoons good-quality vegetable oil
1   onion, chopped
1   burdock root, peeled and julienned or minced (optional)
1   carrot, julienned or minced
1¾ cups short-grain white rice
1   cup fresh peas or thawed frozen peas, or about 1 cup snow peas, slivered
2   tablespoons soy sauce
1   tablespoon mirin or honey
    Salt
1   sheet nori, lightly toasted (see page 244; optional)

1. Warm the dashi in a medium saucepan over low heat (do not boil). If you're using dried shiitakes, add them; remove when they're tender, about 10 minutes. Slice all the mushroom caps.

2. Put the oil in a large, deep skillet or fairly broad saucepan over medium-high heat. Add the mushrooms, onion, burdock if you're using it, and carrot and cook, stirring occasionally, until the mushroom edges are brown, about 10 minutes.

3. Turn the heat down to medium, add the rice, and cook, stirring, until combined. Add the peas and dashi, along with the soy sauce and mirin. Stir, reduce the heat to medium-low, and cover. A minute later, check that the mixture is bubbling gently and adjust the heat if necessary; cook, covered, for 15 minutes.

4. When you remove the cover, the mixture should still be a little soupy. Add a little dashi or water if it's dried out. Raise the heat a bit and cook until the rice is tender and the mixture is still moist but not soupy. Taste and adjust the seasoning with salt or soy sauce. Crumble the nori on top if you're using it and serve.

Rice Balls

Onigiri
MAKES: 4 to 6 servings
TIME: 30 minutes
F M V

There's almost nothing to these: cooked short-grain rice, gently pressed together and shaped with salt-coated hands—they should be quite tender, shaped just firmly enough to hold together—sometimes stuffed with a piece of food, sometimes wrapped with nori, sometimes both, and sometimes neither. Serve as a side dish with Edamame Salad with Seaweed "Mayo" (page 75) or the grilled variation as an appetizer with Simple Miso Dipping Sauce (page 653) or Dashi Dipping Sauce (page 657), or as a snack.

> **Salt**
> 4 **cups cooked white or brown short-grain rice (page 367), still warm**
> **Pickled plums (*umeboshi*), pickled daikon (*takuan*), and/or lightly salted cucumber (page 48) for stuffing (optional)**
> **Soy sauce**
> 4 **sheets nori, lightly toasted (see page 244)**

1. Wet your hands with water and sprinkle a little salt on them. Grab about ½ cup rice and gently shape it into a ball; the rice should hold together easily. If you want to stuff the rice balls, poke a hole in each and put in a bit of any of the fillings. Close up the hole. Wash and dry your hands.
2. Brush each ball lightly with soy sauce.
3. Brush each of the nori sheets with a little soy sauce, then cut each in half (most easily done with scissors). Wrap each ball with a piece of nori, shiny side out. Serve within a few hours.

RICE BALLS WITH SESAME Sprinkle the balls with toasted sesame seeds (see page 299) before wrapping.

CORN

Corn is used as both a vegetable and a grain. For our purposes, in this chapter any dried corn product is considered a grain.

Corn may be dried on its own or processed with something alkaline, which makes it easier to remove the hull and germ. This second category—which gives the kernels that distinctive flavor you immediately associate with warm tortillas—has been around for thousands of years. The earliest American inhabitants discovered that soaking corn along with wood ashes (which contain lime—not the fruit but the chemical product) made the corn more digestible, and therefore more beneficial.

Here are the most common dried corn products and preparations.

CORNMEAL AND CORN FLOUR

Cornmeal is ground dried corn that hasn't been treated with lime. It can be fine, medium, or coarse. You'll find it both processed (usually under heat, so it winds up not tasting like much) and stone ground (the better choice), as well as made from yellow and from white corn. Corn flour is dried corn that has been ground into a fine powder; white and yellow versions are available. Be aware that in the UK "corn flour" refers to cornstarch.

MASA HARINA

This is masa, a dough made from ground hominy that is dried and ground; it has a texture somewhere between flour and fine cornmeal. Masa harina (also sold as masa de harina) is used to make tortillas, tamales, and other Mexican dishes. Most large supermarkets carry masa harina, and some also have the coarsely ground masa harina used for making tamales. Store masa harina for up to 6 months, preferably refrigerated.

HOMINY

Also sold as posole or pozole, this is whole dried corn kernels soaked in lime (calcium hydroxide, called *cal* in Mexico), with the hull and germ then removed. The kernels are big, and may be white, yellow, red, or blue. Dried kernels cook faster if you soak them for a few hours, as you would beans (though this step isn't necessary). Cooked and canned hominy is also sold simply as "hominy." Samp is cracked (not ground) hominy kernels. It is a popular ingredient in some African stews.

Popcorn

MAKES: 4 servings
TIME: About 10 minutes
F O

Forget microwave popcorn. Traditional buttered popcorn doesn't take much more time or effort and contains no weird ingredients. Add butter, sugar, nori, Parmesan cheese, or chopped herbs (see the variations) and it's incredible. Use a compound butter or a good olive oil to add flavor.

> 2 tablespoons good-quality vegetable oil
> ½ cup popping corn

Nutritional Yeast

I didn't love nutritional yeast when it first became trendy among vegetarians back in the seventies, but over the years my position has moderated. So though I still can't advocate using this ingredient gratuitously, nutritional yeast (an inert form that won't leaven foods) can be a valuable condiment and seasoning in vegan dishes and garnishes. Available in powder and flakes, it has a savory, nutty, and, yes, somewhat cheesy flavor. I won't include it in many recipes, but it's nice to have in your pantry for an added boost of umami in vegan foods (especially popcorn). You could try it judiciously where you might otherwise use grated Parmesan cheese, though I would never call it necessary.

> 4 tablespoons (½ stick) butter or olive oil (optional)
> Salt

1. Put the vegetable oil in a very large, deep saucepan (6 quarts or so) over medium heat. Add 3 corn kernels and cover.

2. When the kernels pop, remove the cover and add the remaining corn. Cover and shake the pot, holding the lid on as you do so. Cook, shaking the pot occasionally, until the popping sound stops, about 5 minutes. Meanwhile, melt the butter if you choose to use it.

3. Turn the popcorn into a large bowl; drizzle with the butter and sprinkle with salt to taste while tossing the popcorn. Serve immediately; popcorn is best when hot.

SALTY-SWEET POPCORN You will crave this, and it's great with or without the butter: Sprinkle the popcorn with salt and superfine sugar as soon as it's in the bowl, tossing for even coverage. Taste and add more as needed.

PARMESAN POPCORN Grate Parmesan cheese as finely as possible. Add ¼ cup and toss with the hot popcorn.

HERB POPCORN Lovely with either butter or olive oil: Add ¼ cup minced fresh herbs. Make sure the leaves aren't wet before chopping; press between paper towels to absorb excess moisture. Sprinkle on the herbs as you drizzle with the butter or olive oil.

8 Things to Sprinkle on Popcorn
Some, like cayenne, are more potent than others, so be careful with quantity and toss thoroughly to ensure an even coating.
1. Za'atar (page 652)
2. Citrus Sprinkle (page 651)
3. Japanese Seven-Spice Mix (page 650)
4. Nori "Shake" (page 650)
5. Ground sumac
6. Smoked paprika
7. Cayenne or red chile flakes
8. Nutritional yeast

Polenta

MAKES: 4 servings
TIME: 20 minutes
F O

If you want to make grilled polenta (see the variation), reduce the amount of water slightly or cook it a little longer so the polenta is thick enough to set properly.

You can make polenta with water only, but it's better with some milk in there. You can use nondairy milk if you prefer; opt for oil and skip the cheese, and you'll have vegan polenta. Another nice touch: Stir in about a cup fresh corn kernels when the polenta is just about done.

Other grains you can use: teff (see variation).

½ **cup milk (preferably whole), any nut or grain milk, or water**
Salt
1 **cup coarse cornmeal**
1 **tablespoon butter or olive oil, or more (optional)**
Grated Parmesan cheese (optional)
Pepper

1. Combine the milk with 2 cups of water and a large pinch salt in a medium saucepan over medium heat. Bring just about to a boil, then add the polenta in a steady stream, whisking constantly to prevent lumps from forming. Turn the heat down to low and simmer, whisking frequently, until thick, 10 to 15 minutes. If the mixture becomes too thick, simply whisk in a bit more water. For polenta you're serving right away, you want a consistency like sour cream; for Grilled or Fried Polenta (see the variation), you want something approaching thick oatmeal.

2. Add the butter and/or cheese if you're using them, then taste, add salt if necessary and lots of pepper, and serve. Or prepare it for Grilled or Fried Polenta or Polenta Gratin.

POLENTA WITH HERBS This is also good for Grilled or Fried Polenta, below: Add 1 teaspoon chopped fresh sage or ½ teaspoon dried and 1 teaspoon minced fresh rosemary or ½ teaspoon dried along with the cornmeal. When the polenta is done, stir in ½ teaspoon minced garlic if you like and a tablespoon or 2 of olive oil or butter. Cheese remains optional.

POLENTA GRATIN Immediately after cooking, spoon or pour the polenta into a buttered baking dish of a size that will give you a layer about 1 inch thick. Top with about 1 cup freshly grated Parmesan cheese and broil until the cheese melts and browns slightly. Cut into squares and serve hot or at room temperature.

GRILLED OR FRIED POLENTA A summertime staple: Make sure the polenta is fairly thick when cooked, and omit the butter and cheese. Pour the cooked polenta onto a baking sheet. Let cool for at least 10 minutes, then cut into pieces. When you're ready, brush with olive oil and grill with a little salt and pepper or brown the slices in hot olive oil in a skillet. V

MICROWAVE POLENTA This is more trouble than it's worth but it works, and it's a little faster: Combine the milk, water, salt, and cornmeal in a bowl and whisk until smooth. Cover and microwave for about 2 minutes; whisk. Cover again and repeat the process, microwaving for 1 minute at a time, until the mixture is creamy and smooth. Total time will be around 5 minutes or a little longer. Again, if it thickens too fast, whisk in a little more water. Finish as directed.

ANGÁ BRAZILIAN "POLENTA" Start by cooking 1 cup chopped onion and 1 tablespoon minced garlic in the saucepan with 2 tablespoons olive oil; cook, stirring occasionally, until the onion begins to brown, about 10 minutes. Stir in 2½ cups water, bring just about to a boil, and proceed with Step 1. Omit the cheese. V

PANISSA Basically polenta made with chickpea flour (see page 576), from the Ligurian region of Italy. The results will be less gritty and more prone to lumping, so be sure to stir vigorously: Replace the cornmeal with chickpea flour. In Step 1, put the chickpea flour in a fine-meshed strainer to sift it into the boiling liquid while stirring with your other hand. Proceed with the recipe.

FOOLPROOF TEFF, POLENTA STYLE Cocoa-colored and deeply flavored: Instead of cornmeal, use teff. Cook and stir for a total of 20 to 25 minutes. Add butter and cheese if you like and sauce as you would polenta. Or let cool and slice to fry or grill.

5 Easy Dishes to Serve on Top of Polenta

There are so many dishes in this book that would be great with polenta; here are some you can make in the same amount of time it takes to cook the polenta.

1. Fast Tomato Sauce (page 312)

2. Puttanesca Sauce (page 313)

3. Roasted winter squash (page 266), removed from the shell, cut into bite-size pieces, and tossed with butter and Parmesan

4. Sautéed Mushrooms (page 217)

5. Skillet Eggplant with Tomatoes (page 199)

Polenta "Pizza"

MAKES: 4 to 6 servings
TIME: About 40 minutes
Ⓜ

This is a great way to make polenta, especially if you've got kids eager to get into the kitchen. Just know that you end up with something a lot closer to polenta than pizza, so you'll need a fork.

You can prepare this crust in advance. Make a batch of polenta (make extra, so you can eat some warm) and when it's cool, mix in the oil and spread it on a pan or even a plate. Cover and refrigerate for up to a day or so.

  3 tablespoons olive oil, plus more for the pan
  1 recipe Polenta (page 391, made with 2½ cups water and without butter or cheese), still hot and loose
     Salt and pepper
1½ cups Fast Tomato Sauce (page 312)

1½–2 cups grated mozzarella, Parmesan, Gorgonzola, or fontina cheese or a combination
     Chopped fresh herbs (like basil, parsley, oregano, or marjoram, or a mixture)

1. Heat the oven to 450°F. Brush a thin layer of oil on a pizza pan or baking sheet. Stir 1 tablespoon of the oil into the polenta and pour it onto the prepared pan. Spread it evenly to about ½-inch thickness, working quickly so the polenta doesn't stiffen. Let cool slightly.

2. When the polenta is cool enough to handle, cover it with a sheet of plastic wrap or wax paper. Use your hands to evenly flatten it. Remove the plastic wrap and sprinkle with salt and pepper. Spread the tomato sauce over the polenta, then sprinkle with the cheese and herbs. Drizzle with another tablespoon or so oil.

3. Bake until the cheese is melted and the pizza is hot, 25 to 30 minutes. Cut into slices and serve hot or at room temperature.

BREAKFAST POLENTA "PIZZA" I love this on weekend mornings, especially with leftover polenta (remember to spread on a baking sheet before it cools): Omit the tomato sauce. Make 4 indentations in the polenta crust and crack an egg into each. Top with a grating of cheese (cheddar is fine here) and some snipped herbs (I like sage). Bake until the eggs are set, 10 to 15 minutes.

POLENTA "PIZZA" WITH HERBED TOFU DRIZZLE Instead of the cheese, whisk 12 ounces soft silken tofu with the herbs and an additional 2 tablespoons olive oil until as smooth as possible, or purée the tofu and herbs in a food processor. In Step 2, dollop or drizzle the tofu mixture over the tomato sauce and bake as directed in Step 3. Ⓥ

Posole with Beans

MAKES: 6 to 8 servings
TIME: At least an hour, mostly unattended
Ⓥ

Posole (the ingredient) is made and used everywhere there's corn, and goes by a variety of names, the most

common being hominy. It's got a terrific, corny flavor, but also that distinctively bright, slightly sour taste you probably associate with tortillas.

Posole (the dish) is a soupy stew or hearty soup that takes time to cook, though this time can be reduced greatly if you soak the dried kernels first. The kernels are also sold precooked and canned as pozole or hominy.

> 1 cup dried hominy (preferably soaked as you would beans; see page 428) or about 3 cups cooked or drained canned hominy
> 1 cup dried pink or red beans or black-eyed peas, cooked (see page 435), or 3 cups drained canned beans
>   Salt and pepper
> 1 tablespoon chopped fresh marjoram or oregano or 1 teaspoon dried
> 1 teaspoon (or to taste) minced fresh chile (like jalapeño or Thai), or red chile flakes or cayenne to taste
> 1 tablespoon ground cumin, or to taste
> 1 large onion, chopped
> 1 tablespoon minced garlic
>   Chopped fresh cilantro for garnish
>   Lime wedges for garnish

1. If you're starting with dried hominy, put in a pot, cover generously with water, and cook until nearly tender, at least 1½ hours. Drain, reserving some of the cooking liquid.

2. Put the hominy, beans, salt and pepper to taste, marjoram, chile, cumin, and onion in a saucepan that will hold them comfortably. Add water or some of the hominy-cooking liquid to cover by about an inch and turn the heat to medium-high. Bring to a boil, then adjust the heat so the mixture bubbles steadily. Cook, stirring occasionally, until the beans are quite tender, about 30 minutes, adding a little liquid if necessary; the mixture should be a bit soupy.

3. Stir in the garlic and cook for a few minutes more. Taste and adjust the seasoning. Garnish with cilantro and serve in bowls with lime wedges.

SAMP AND PEAS Sometimes the hominy (called samp, or stampmielies, or stamp, or mealies, in some African dialects and by some African-Americans) here is crushed, which you can do before cooking (put it in a sturdy paper bag and go over it with a rolling pin) or afterward (mash it a bit or use an immersion or regular blender): Use black-eyed peas in place of the beans; omit the marjoram and cumin.

Naked Tamale with Chile-Cheese Filling

MAKES: 4 to 6 servings (or 8 to 12 tamales)
TIME: About 2 hours, mostly unattended
Ⓜ

This cornhusk-free tamale loaf is for the practical cook, not the purist, though you can make the husk-wrapped variation if you want the real thing (see "Cornhusk Tamales," opposite). Forming one large tamale in a pan is easier than shaping individual ones, which means you might make it more often.

Traditional tamales are made with lard or vegetable shortening, because the creamy texture helps make the dough light and fluffy. The first is made from animal products and the second is fine only if you use nonhydrogenated vegetable shortening made from coconut oil and/or palm oil. The best solution, though, is solidified olive oil, which whips up very nicely, has good flavor, and makes for much lighter tamales than those made with butter (another option).

Much of this recipe can be done in advance: Put the oil in the freezer, prepare the onion and pepper mixture or any of the other fillings, and even make the sauce. After that, it'll take only a little over an hour to get the tamales on the table, and most of that time is unattended. To add more flavor to the filling, you can roast both the red peppers and poblanos (see page 228), then peel, seed, and slice, but that's totally optional.

> ⅔ cup olive oil, plus more for greasing the pan
> 2 onions, halved and sliced
> 1 tablespoon sugar

3 red bell peppers, cored, seeded, and sliced

2 poblano or Anaheim chiles, cored, seeded, and sliced

Salt and pepper

2 cups masa harina

1–2 cups vegetable stock (pages 97–100) or water, at room temperature

1 teaspoon baking powder

4 ounces Chihuahua, Monterey Jack, or mild cheddar cheese, grated (about 1 cup)

¼ cup sliced scallions or chopped red onion for garnish

¼ cup chopped fresh cilantro for garnish

2 cups Salsa Roja or Red Enchilada Sauce (page 662 or 663) or Fast Tomato Sauce (page 312), warmed

1. An hour or more before cooking, put ½ cup of the olive oil in the freezer to solidify.

2. Put 2 tablespoons of the remaining oil in a large skillet over medium-high heat. Add the onion and cook, stirring frequently, until soft, about 5 minutes. Stir in the sugar, reduce the heat to medium, and cook, stirring occasionally, until they begin to color, about 5 minutes more. If you're using fresh bell peppers and chiles, add them to the pan now, along with some salt and pepper.

Cornhusk Tamales

Soak 12 dried cornhusks—available in Hispanic grocery stores and even many supermarkets—in warm water for at least 3 hours or overnight. Drain, then separate and clean the husks. Continue to soak in fresh water until needed. Follow the directions for making both the masa and the filling in Naked Tamale with Chile-Cheese Filling (opposite), or the masa and any of the fillings listed on page page 621. To cook: Prepare a large steamer by setting a steamer rack about 2 inches above gently boiling water in a large pot. Put the tamales vertically, open side up, on the rack. Top with another corn husk, cover, and steam until done, 40 to 50 minutes. To test for doneness, remove a tamale and open the husk—the filling should be firm and come away easily from the husk. Let the tamales rest for 15 minutes before peeling. Serve tamales in their husks, passing the sauce on the side.

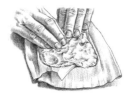

STEP 1 For each tamale, drain a husk and pat dry with paper towels. Put the widest edge closer to you. Put 1 heaping tablespoon masa ½ inch from the widest edge of the husk, then use the back of the spoon to spread the masa into a 4 × 3-inch rectangle along the right edge of the husk, leaving at least ½ inch on each side.

STEP 2 Spoon 2 tablespoons filling lengthwise down the center of the masa rectangle. To wrap the tamales, fold the vertical edges over, bringing them over the dough in the filled center.

STEP 3 Fold up the tapered end (the wider end will remain opened during steaming), and secure the tamale with kitchen string.

STEP 4 Repeat with the remaining masa and filling.

F Fast   M Make Ahead   V Vegan   O Vegan Optional

Naked Tamale with
Chile-Cheese Filling
(page 394)

Cover and reduce the heat to low. Cook, stirring occasionally, until very soft and compact, about 25 minutes. If you're using roasted peppers and chiles, cover and cook the onion as just directed, then add the roasted peppers and chiles after about 15 minutes. Remove from the heat when done. (You can make the filling in advance up to this point. Cool, cover, and refrigerate for up to 2 days. Bring it to room temperature when you're ready to proceed.)

3. Heat the oven to 400°F. Grease a deep 9-inch pie plate, standard loaf pan, or a 10-inch cake pan with a little more oil. Bring a kettle of water to a boil. Put the masa harina in a food processor, turn on the machine, and add the stock ¼ cup at a time until a thick paste forms. (This paste is called a masa, or dough.)

4. Add the frozen oil, the baking powder, and a large pinch salt. Pulse a few times. Then, with the machine running, add stock ¼ cup at a time until the masa is the consistency of thick batter. It should take a little tap to plop off a spoon.

5. Spread half the masa in the prepared pan. Top with the onion-pepper filling and the cheese. Spread the remaining masa on top. Cover the pan with foil and put it in a roasting pan.

6. Carefully pour boiling water into the roasting pan to come halfway up the pie plate or loaf pan. Put the whole thing in the oven and bake until the masa is solid and pulling away from the sides of the pan, about 1 hour. The tamale will keep warm for 15 minutes or so in the water bath. When you're ready to serve, cut into slices or wedges, sprinkle with the scallions and cilantro, and pass the warm sauce at the table.

OTHER GRAINS

Almost all grains are grasses. Beyond that, though, each grain is distinct in terms of flavor, texture, color, and cooking times. Still, most are interchangeable. To help you experiment and make the best use of whatever you have on hand, I've included the line "Other grains you can use" in recipes that work with other options.

---

7 Dishes That Make Great Tamale Fillings

You can use these fillings, with or without cheese:

1. Beer-Glazed Black Beans or any of its variations (page 440)

2. Refried Beans or any of its variations (page 460)

3. Caramelized Onions (page 222)

4. Oven-roasted tomatoes (page 258)

5. Chopped grilled vegetables like eggplant, zucchini, tomatoes, chiles, or squash (see "Grilling Vegetables," page 166)

6. Spicy Scrambled Tofu (page 489)

7. Tempeh Chili with Black Beans (page 517)

By now we've all heard of quinoa, and many of us have tried grains that once seemed exotic. If you haven't given grains like teff or amaranth a try yet, I encourage you to. They taste great, go with nearly any vegetable topping, and are an easy way to add variety to your diet. You'll find all of these in any decent supermarket or health food store, but if you don't, they're just a few keystrokes away.

COOKING GRAINS

If you know nothing about cooking grains, just start with the essential recipe, Cooking Grains, the Easy Way (page 398).

In any case, cooking grains is straightforward: You boil them in water or other liquid. They may be toasted (cooked in a dry skillet) or sautéed (cooked in a skillet with oil or other fat) before further cooking, but for the most part there's not much more to it than this. Don't worry about starting with an exact amount of water; you can always add more, or drain or cook off the excess. (Few experienced cooks actually measure water for grains, because they know it's a little different every time anyway.)

Microwave ovens, pressure cookers, rice cookers, and slow cookers are all fine tools, but the basic recipe is really your best choice. A couple of exceptions worth noting: The microwave works well for quinoa; follow the microwave directions in the variation for White Rice on page 367. The pressure cooker is a bit faster than the stovetop but requires checking for doneness, which is sometimes a hassle. The slow cooker works for long-cooking grains, but you cannot "set it and forget it"; you must check frequently to capture the moment before the grain kernels burst. The rice cooker works well for white rice because white rice is a more consistent product than whole grains. But other grains are too tricky.

Cooking Grains, the Easy Way

MAKES: 4 to 6 servings
TIME: 10 minutes to more than 1 hour, depending on the grain
Ⓜ Ⓞ

I'm providing a recipe for this method, but you don't need it: Put the grains in a pot with water and cook them until they're done the way you like them. Period. The worst thing that can happen is that the inside of the grain will absorb so much liquid its interior bursts through its outer layer. Eventually it will turn to mush, but some people actually prefer their grains burst—the starch released makes the grains creamier.

This recipe can be scaled up and frozen in meal-sized portions for months.

1 cup quinoa, rinsed and drained; barley (any type), oat groats, buckwheat groats, wild rice, cracked wheat, hominy, freekeh, whole rye, farro, teff, spelt, kamut, pearl couscous, or triticale; or 1½ cups wheat berries
Pinch salt
Olive oil, any other oil, or butter for serving

1. Combine the grain with the salt and water to cover by at least an inch in a small-to-medium saucepan. (Use 3 cups water for pearled barley.) Bring to a boil, then adjust the heat so the mixture bubbles gently.
2. Cook, stirring occasionally, until the grain is tender. This will take as little as 7 or 8 minutes with pearl couscous and as long as 1 hour or more for spelt, wheat berries, and other unhulled grains. Add boiling water as necessary for most of the cooking time to keep the grains covered, but, as the grains swell and begins to become tender, keep just enough water in the pot to keep the grains from drying out.
3. The grain is done when it tastes done: Whole grains will always have some bite to them, but milled or cut grains will become mushy if overcooked, so be careful. Ideally, you'll have cooked out all of the water at about the same time the grain is tender, but if any water remains, drain the grain. It can sit in the pot, covered, for 15 minutes to dry it out.
4. Toss the grain with oil or butter to taste if you're serving right away, or see "5 Ways to Enhance Cooked Grains," below. If storing, toss it with a couple of tablespoons oil to keep the grains from sticking together too much, then cool, cover, and refrigerate for up to 3 days or freeze for up to 2 months.

5 Ways to Enhance Cooked Grains

In Step 4, use a large fork to toss any of the following ingredients with the grains and oil or butter:
1. Just-tender cooked vegetables like peas, chopped greens, or broccoli or cauliflower florets, or chopped cooked root vegetables

2. A couple of spoonfuls of a simple sauce, like any Flavored Oil (page 627); any Chile Paste (page 664) or Miso Sauce (page 653); or any of Soy Sauce–Based Sauces on pages 654 to 659

3. ¼ to ½ cup finely grated or crumbled cheese, like Parmesan, feta, any blue cheese, or goat cheese

4. 2 to 3 tablespoons chopped fresh herbs, like chives, parsley, cilantro, or mint

5. 1 to 2 cups of any cooked beans

Precooked Grains with Butter or Oil

MAKES: 4 to 6 servings
TIME: About 10 minutes

🄵 🄾

No matter how you cook grains—I'd suggest following the preceding recipe—you can store them in the refrigerator and reheat them, with flavorings, in a snap. Even if you do nothing more than warm them in olive oil, perhaps with a little garlic, they'll be delicious. And as you can see from the variations, you can take this in plenty of different directions.

3   **tablespoons olive oil, butter, or a combination**
1   **teaspoon minced garlic (optional)**
3–4 **cups any cooked grain**
    Salt and pepper

1. Put the oil and/or butter in a large skillet over medium heat. When the oil is hot or the butter is melted, add the garlic if you're using it, and cook, stirring, for about 30 seconds.

2. Add the grains and cook, stirring occasionally, until hot, 10 minutes at the most. Sprinkle with salt and pepper. Taste, adjust the seasoning, and serve.

PRECOOKED GRAINS WITH ONIONS You can add 1 tablespoon (or to taste) minced fresh chile like jalapeño or Thai, or red chile flakes or cayenne to taste if you like here too: In Step 1, use the garlic or not, as you like. Add about 1 cup chopped onion and cook, stirring occasionally, until it just begins to brown, about 10 minutes. Proceed to Step 2.

(continued on page 404)

Top 9 Grains to Keep on Hand

You can often substitute one grain for another, but not always. Grains are different enough that it's worth keeping a few of them around. These are my favorites, from most commonly available to those you might have to order online or look for in a natural food store:

1. BULGUR **Fast, convenient, versatile; wonderful in summer salads.**

2. COUSCOUS **Ditto for couscous. Keep an eye out for fregola, couscous's Sardinian cousin; it's deeply toasted, delicious, and cooks up the same way.**

3. CORNMEAL **Great flavor, easy to cook in a variety of ways, eminently lovable. A must-have for polenta and corn bread.**

4. WHEAT BERRIES **Slow to cook, but delicious, satisfying, and healthful. Good for breakfast too.**

5. QUINOA **Quick cooking, convenient, delicious, and healthful. No wonder it's so popular.**

6. FREEKEH **Cooks up like quinoa, with its own unique flavor, grassy with an undertone of smokiness. Many stores that carry quinoa now also have freekeh.**

7. ROLLED OATS **Obviously for breakfast but also for use in veggie burgers (page 500).**

8. HOMINY **Hearty and filling. Takes forever to cook from dried, but worth it; canned hominy, on the other hand, is bland and mushy.**

9. FARRO **Among the fastest cooking of the larger whole grains, and delicious. Fabulous in soups.**

A Lexicon of Grains

These are some of the most common and versatile grains (beyond corn and white and brown rice), and my personal favorites, organized by cooking times, from shortest to longest. For more about the flours that come from grains, see page 572.

GRAIN (ALTERNATE NAMES)	COOKING TIME	DESCRIPTION	FORMS AND VARIETIES
Couscous	5 to 15 minutes, depending on the type	Couscous is actually a small pasta traditional to Morocco that seems to be universally thought of as a grain. Israeli couscous is extruded through a round mold and toasted, giving it a larger, pearl-like shape, nuttier flavor, and chewier texture; it's also more forgiving during cooking. Fregola, from Sardinia, is similar to couscous, deeply toasted a golden brown.	Usually made from semolina flour, sometimes in varying colors. Whole wheat couscous is available and very good. Israeli couscous is also known as super couscous, maftoul, pearl couscous, or Israeli toasted pasta; there is a third, slightly larger variety often sold as Lebanese couscous.
Amaranth	10 to 15 minutes	Closely related to quinoa, it is tiny ($\frac{1}{32}$ inch) and round. Can be cooked like porridge, puffed like popcorn, or toasted and used as garnish. Its flavor is mildly nutty and malty. Cooked grains get a bit sticky, and rubbery if cooked too long, but retain a nice crunch.	Whole grains most common; puffed is rare. Usually beige, though other varieties come in shades of tan and brown.
Bulgur (Bulghur, Burghul, Bulger)	10 to 20 minutes, depending on the grind	Wheat kernels, first steamed, then hulled, dried, and ground to varying degrees. Fine grind is ready to eat after soaking in hot water. Its nutty, mild flavor and fluffy, dry texture make it perfect for soaking up liquids and turning into salads. Often confused with cracked wheat (see page 402).	Available in fine, medium, coarse, and very coarse grinds, which are sometimes identified by numbers, from #1 for fine to #3 or #4 for the coarsest.
Rolled Oats (Old-Fashioned Oats)	15 to 20 minutes	Whole oats are toasted, hulled, steamed, and flattened with giant rollers. The quick-cooking variety is cut before steaming and flattening; instant is cut, precooked, dried, steamed, then flattened. Stay away from the latter two if you want any flavor at all. Gluten free but check the package to make sure it was processed in a gluten-free plant.	Raw or quick-cooking rolled oats, instant oats. Some are more heavily processed than others.

GRAIN (ALTERNATE NAMES)	COOKING TIME	DESCRIPTION	FORMS AND VARIETIES
Teff (Lovegrass)	15 to 20 minutes	The smallest grain in the world (less than $\frac{1}{32}$ inch). A staple in Ethiopia, with a mild, slightly sweet, nutty flavor. Cooked teff is soft and a little gummy. When ground into flour, it is used to make the Ethiopian bread injera.	Whole grains: ivory, beige, dark brown, or deep purple-brown, depending on the variety.
Quinoa (Mother Grain, Supergrain)	About 20 minutes	Pronounced KEEN-wa. Indigenous to the Andes, disk shaped, and pinhead size ($\frac{1}{16}$ inch). Nutty and grassy in flavor, with a slightly crunchy but soft texture. Even plain, it's as good as grains get.	Whole grains, white, red, or black. Different colors have very slight differences in taste and degree of crunch. Also made into flakes, which can be used like rolled oats.
Pearled Barley (Peeled Barley, Polished Barley)	About 20 minutes	Barley that has been hulled, steamed, and polished (the bran removed). Creased, oval, dull white-and-tan grains that cook fairly quickly and have a creamy, chewy texture when cooked. A super rice alternative.	This is the familiar barley, sold everywhere and cooked much like rice. You may occasionally see barley flakes, which can be treated like rolled oats.
Steel-Cut Oats (Oat Groats, Whole Oats, Scotch Oats, Irish Oats, Porridge Oats)	20 to 25 minutes	Like rolled oats (with only the outer hull removed), oat groats have a nutty, sweet flavor. Slow cooking and quite chewy. Cut grains cook faster and are often used for breakfast cereal.	Whole or cut grains.
Kasha (Roasted Buckwheat)	20 to 30 minutes	Hulled and roasted buckwheat kernels, brown, triangular, and distinctively nutty. Traditionally toasted again at home in a skillet, sometimes with egg, before liquid is added.	Whole grains.
Buckwheat Groats (Peeled Buckwheat)	20 to 30 minutes	Essentially raw kasha, buckwheat groats are hulled and crushed. Greenish tan, triangular, and fresher tasting than kasha—almost grassy.	Whole grains; also rolled into flakes.

A Lexicon of Grains (cont.)

GRAIN (ALTERNATE NAMES)	COOKING TIME	DESCRIPTION	FORMS AND VARIETIES
Cracked Wheat	20 to 30 minutes	Often confused with bulgur (see page 400), cracked wheat is raw. It offers the same nutty wheat flavor as bulgur and wheat berries, but with a chewier, heartier texture than bulgur and quicker cooking time than wheat berries.	Fine, medium, and coarse grains; most commonly available in medium grind.
Freekeh (Frikeh, Farik)	20 to 30 minutes	Very popular throughout the Middle East. It's roasted green wheat berries with the straw and chaff burned off; what's left is too moist to burn. Has a smoky taste and chewy texture. Has more protein than quinoa and twice as much fiber.	Whole grains.
Millet	20 to 30 minutes	Small, yellow, and beadlike, with a tiny spot at one end (you might recognize it from birdseed). Pleasant tasting, mildly nutty and cornlike. Cooks up fluffy.	Whole grains are most common, meal is available too. Occasionally you may find puffed millet.
Farro (Emmer)	25 to 30 minutes	An ancient wheat-related grain, popular in early Rome, recently "rediscovered" in Tuscany. Tan and oval, not unlike "peeled" whole wheat in appearance. Has a nutty, wheaty flavor. Retains a chewy texture when cooked. With starch similar to short-grain rice, a nice whole grain substitute in risotto. Often confused with spelt.	Whole (pearled and semi-pearled), and crushed or "cracked" grains.
Einkorn	30 to 40 minutes	An ancient form of wheat, first domesticated in what is now Turkey. Has never been crossbred. Contains more protein, potassium, and beta-carotene than modern wheat, and is said to be a more easily digested alternative.	Whole grains.
Wild Rice (Indian Rice, Manomin, Water Oats)	45 to 60 minutes	A marsh grass native to parts of Asia and the Great Lakes region, once a staple for many Native Americans. Long, narrow, deep-brown cylinder-shaped grains that crack open to reveal their white interior when cooked.	Whole grains. There is both farm-raised "wild" rice and truly wild rice, which tends to be less uniform in color, better tasting, and more expensive.

GRAIN (ALTERNATE NAMES)	COOKING TIME	DESCRIPTION	FORMS AND VARIETIES
Hulled Barley (Whole Barley, Pot Barley, Scotch Barley)	45 to 60 minutes	The least processed form of barley, with just the outer hull removed. Takes longer to cook than pearled barley and has a chewier texture, but also a higher nutritional value. Grains are light brown, and oval with pointed ends.	Whole grains and the slightly more processed Scotch or pot barley, which has more of the outer layers removed and is quicker cooking, less chewy, and somewhat less nutritious.
Sorghum	45 to 60 minutes	Part of the grass family and native to Australia, Africa, Asia, and Central America. Has a slightly sweet taste and chewy texture.	Whole grains, popped sorghum (looks like mini popcorn)
Whole Wheat (Wheat Berries)	60 to 90 minutes	Second-largest grain crop in the world (after corn). Unmilled kernels with the bran and germ still intact. Light brown, rounded, oval grain with a nutty flavor and very chewy texture.	Varieties are named for the seasons they are grown in and the traits of their hulls: hard red winter, hard white winter, soft white spring, etc. Whole, cracked (see page 402), and "peeled," which is slightly faster cooking. Flakes are also available and cook in about half the time.
Spelt	60 to 90 minutes	Cultivated for thousands of years, spelt is in the wheat family. Has a pleasant, mild flavor. Appearance is similar to brown rice, though plumper. Sometimes mistakenly labeled farro.	Whole berries and flakes. (Flakes cook in about half the time.)
Whole Rye (Rye Berries)	60 to 90 minutes	Unmilled kernels with bran and germ still intact. The flavor is nutty, the texture firm.	Whole grains and flakes. (Flakes cook in about half the time.)
Kamut (QK-77)	60 to 90 minutes	Pronounced KAH-moot. A modern breed of an ancient variety of wheat. Tan, with kernels two to three times larger than common wheat; also more nutritious, with a sweeter, more buttery flavor.	Whole berries and flakes. (Flakes cook in about half the time.)
Triticale	60 to 90 minutes	Hybrid of wheat (Triticum) and rye (Secale) in both name and biology; a relative newcomer, officially made a viable fertile crop in 1937. Grown primarily in Europe. Rye-flavored, tan grains, a somewhat angular oval.	Whole grains.

(continued from page 399)

PRECOOKED GRAINS WITH ONION AND MUSHROOMS
Reduce the onion in the preceding variation to about
½ cup and add ½ cup sliced shiitake mushroom caps or
other fresh mushrooms. Cook, stirring occasionally,
until both onion and mushrooms brown at the edges,
about 10 minutes. Proceed to Step 2.

PRECOOKED GRAINS WITH NUTS OR SEEDS In Step 1,
use the garlic or not, as you like. Add ½ cup whole or
roughly chopped nuts (cashews or pistachios are good, but
any nut or seed is fine) and cook for 30 seconds (for sesame seeds) to a minute or 2 (for cashews), until the nut or
seed is fragrant but not browned. Proceed to Step 2.

QUICK-COOKING GRAINS

These are the grains that cook in 5 to 20 minutes.
Within this category, they're pretty much interchangeable. So if you don't have one on hand, try any of
the recipes with another that you do. Quick-cooking
grains include:

- Amaranth
- Bulgur
- Couscous
- Pearled barley
- Quinoa
- Rolled oats
- Teff

Making Extra Grains

Whole grains can take some time to cook, but they
will keep in the fridge for days, and in the freezer
for months, so I encourage you to cook 2 or 3 cups
(raw) of any grain at once. You can freeze most of
the cooked grains in meal-sized portions. And with
a batch in the fridge, you can more quickly make
virtually all the recipes in this chapter, plus add a
sprinkle to any number of soups, salads, and vegetable dishes.

Crunchy Amaranth Griddlecakes

MAKES: 4 to 6 servings
TIME: About 20 minutes with cooked amaranth

F

Amaranth works best as an ingredient, not a stand-
alone grain, because even when fully cooked it retains a
super-firm texture. And that's what makes these simple
griddlecakes special. Serve with Beans and Greens (page
444), or as part of any grilled vegetable meal with your
favorite yogurt sauce (page 673).

Since you're starting with cooked amaranth, you can
substitute most any cooked grains, though they won't
be quite as crunchy as amaranth; I would recommend
bulgur, regular or whole wheat couscous, cracked wheat,
kasha, millet, quinoa, wheat berries, or wild rice.

1	egg
1	cup cooked amaranth (page 400)
	Salt and pepper
½	cup all-purpose flour
¼	teaspoon baking powder
	Milk, half-and-half, or cream as needed (no more than ¼ cup)
1	tablespoon chopped fresh thyme
2–3	tablespoons good-quality vegetable oil or butter

1. Heat a heavy skillet or griddle to about 375°F.
2. Whisk the egg in a medium bowl until well beaten.
Whisk in the amaranth and sprinkle with salt and pepper. Whisk in the flour and baking powder. Add enough
milk to make a smooth, medium-thick batter. Whisk in
the thyme.
3. When a drop of water skips across the skillet before
evaporating, it's ready. Brush a little oil or butter on the
pan and let it bubble. Using a large spoon, scoop up a bit
of the batter and drop it in the pan. It should spread about
3 inches. Cook as many griddlecakes as will fit comfortably without running together, turning them after a couple of minutes, when they are brown. Total cooking time
for each batch will run between 5 and 8 minutes. Add a

little more oil to the pan in between batches as needed. Serve immediately, ideally straight from the pan.

CURRIED AMARANTH GRIDDLECAKES When you whisk the egg, add ¼ cup thinly sliced scallions; when you add the amaranth, add 1 tablespoon curry powder. Omit the thyme. Serve the griddlecakes with Raita or Sweet Yogurt Sauce (page 674) or Cilantro-Mint Chutney (page 668).

10 Additions to Crunchy Amaranth Griddlecakes

Whisk these in, either alone or in combination, with the egg before adding the grain.

1. 1 shallot, minced
2. A couple of cloves Roasted Garlic (page 205), squeezed from their skins
3. Horseradish (freshly grated or prepared) to taste
4. 1 tablespoon chopped fresh chives
5. ¼ cup chopped nuts like almonds, walnuts, hazelnuts, or pecans
6. ¼ cup peanut butter, tahini, or other nut butter
7. ¼ cup thinly sliced scallions
8. ¼ cup chopped dried fruit like apricots, cherries, cranberries, or apple
9. ½ cup chopped cooked greens like kale, spinach, or chard, squeezed dry
10. ½ cup corn kernels (thawed frozen are fine)

Pearled Barley Pilaf

MAKES: 4 to 6 servings
TIME: 45 minutes

Here you sauté barley before cooking it with stock (water is fine in a pinch). It's a simple recipe that can be varied in all the same ways as Rice Pilaf (page 372).

> 2 tablespoons butter or olive oil
> ½ cup sliced scallions or chopped onion
> 1 cup pearled barley or other quick-cooking grain (see list on page 404)
> 1 teaspoon chopped fresh tarragon or ½ teaspoon dried, or 1 tablespoon chopped fresh chervil, mint, dill, or parsley
> 3 cups vegetable stock (pages 97–100) or water, plus more as needed
> Salt and pepper
> Chopped fresh parsley for garnish

6 Ideas for Garnishing with Grains

Cooked whole grains, especially the big ones like wheat or rye berries or oat groats, can be used a lot like nuts. A spoonful or 2 adds nutrition, flavor, and body to a wide range of dishes, and once you get in the habit of keeping a batch in the fridge or hanging on to every leftover kernel, you have a bunch of options. Use them straight from the fridge, or toast them in a dry skillet until dry, fry them in a little oil until crisp, or lightly mash them with a fork or give them a quick whirl in a food processor. Once that's done, you're in business. Try:

1. Sprinkling a spoonful or 2 into pilafs, stir-fries, or even scrambled eggs, always toward the end of cooking.

2. Adding them to herb pastes and sauces (pages 634 to 638) and chile pastes (pages 664 to 666) before blending.

The grains will thicken the paste and round out the flavors.

3. Using them as a crunchy garnish on top of pizza, tossed salad, soup, plain cooked or grilled vegetables, devilled eggs, or creamy spreads.

4. Seasoning them with lots of salt and pepper or one of the spice mixtures from pages 648 to 652, or tossing them with chopped fresh herbs like parsley, mint, or cilantro. Then pass them in a small bowl at the table as you would grated Parmesan.

5. Mixing ¼ cup or so into savory batters and doughs. Fritters, griddlecakes, biscuits, and breads can all benefit from the added texture.

6. Folding them into stuffings and fillings.

1. Put the butter or oil in a medium-to-large skillet over medium-high heat. When the butter is melted or the oil is hot, add the scallions and cook, stirring, until soft, 3 to 5 minutes.

2. Add the barley and cook, stirring, for a minute or so, until glossy; add the herb and stock and sprinkle with salt and pepper. Bring to a boil.

3. Turn the heat down to low, cover, and cook for 30 minutes. Check the barley's progress: It's done when tender and all the liquid has been absorbed. Continue to cook if necessary, adding a tablespoon or 2 more liquid if it has all been absorbed and the barley is not quite done. Or if the barley is tender but a little liquid remains, simply cover and turn off the heat; the barley will absorb the liquid within 10 minutes. If any liquid remains that point, drain it off. Sprinkle with parsley and serve.

HULLED BARLEY (OR OTHER LONG-COOKING WHOLE GRAIN) PILAF Double the cooking time for what seems like a completely different grain, with its outer layer of bran—and therefore fiber—intact: Used hulled barley instead of pearled. In Step 3, start checking after 45 minutes and be prepared to add more liquid from there on.

Basic Bulgur or Couscous

MAKES: 4 to 6 servings
TIME: Less than 30 minutes
F **M** **V**

Bulgur is already partially cooked, so it's easier to prepare than other grains. It's also light and fluffy, with a dry texture that's perfect for soaking up butter or oil, pan juices, dressings, and sauces. Couscous cooks up in just the same way and can be used pretty much interchangeably with bulgur.

> 1 **cup bulgur or couscous**

1. Bring a kettle of water to a boil. Put the bulgur or couscous in a bowl and pour 2½ cups boiling water over it. Stir once and let it sit.

2. Fine bulgur will be tender in 5 to 10 minutes, couscous in 10 minutes, medium bulgur in 15 to 20 minutes, coarse bulgur in 20 to 25. If any water remains when the bulgur is tender, squeeze the bulgur in a clean kitchen towel or put it in a fine-meshed strainer and press down on it. For couscous, simply drain it. Season and serve as you like. Use, cover and let sit at room temperature for up to several hours, or cool, cover, and refrigerate for up to 3 days.

Bulgur Pilaf with Vermicelli

MAKES: 4 to 6 servings
TIME: 30 minutes
F **O**

This pilaf is simple but seriously lovable. You can change the flavor profile by adding tomato paste or tossing in some chopped fresh herbs before serving; see the variations and "5 More Bulgur Pilafs" on page 408.

> 4 **tablespoons (½ stick) butter or**
> **¼ cup olive oil**
> 1 **large or 2 small onions, chopped**
> ½ **cup broken vermicelli in 2-inch or shorter**
> **lengths, or small pasta shape**
> 1 **cup bulgur or other quick-cooking grain**
> **(see list on page 404)**
> **Salt and pepper**
> 1 **tablespoon tomato paste (optional)**
> 2¼ **cups vegetable stock (pages 97–100)**
> **or water, heated to boiling**

1. Put the butter or oil in a large skillet or saucepan over medium heat. When the butter is melted or the oil is hot, add the onion and cook, stirring, until soft, 3 to 5 minutes.

2. Add the vermicelli and bulgur and cook, stirring, until coated with the fat. Sprinkle with salt and pepper and add the tomato paste if you're using it. Add the boiling stock. Turn the heat to low, cover, and cook for 10 minutes. Turn off the heat and let sit until the bulgur is tender, 5 to 15 minutes, depending on what grade bulgur it is. Taste, adjust the seasoning, and serve.

BULGUR PILAF WITH GREEN BEANS AND SOY SAUCE
A nice combo: Omit the vermicelli and replace half the butter or olive oil with sesame oil, the onion with 3 chopped scallions, and ¼ cup of the stock with soy sauce. Add 1 tablespoon each minced garlic and fresh ginger with the scallions and 1 cup trimmed and halved green beans along with the boiling stock.

BULGUR PILAF WITH CABBAGE, LEBANESE STYLE Omit
the vermicelli. Along with the onion, add a chopped small leek, 1 cup shredded cabbage, 2 teaspoons or so ground pickling spice, a squeeze of lemon juice, and a dash Worcestershire Sauce, Hold the Anchovies (page 633), if you like.

5 More Bulgur Pilafs
Add all of these in place of the vermicelli:
1. Bulgur and Beet Pilaf: Add 1 cup diced cooked beets, a minced shallot, 2 sprigs fresh thyme, and a tablespoon or two of dry sherry along with the tomato paste.
2. Bulgur Pilaf with Apricots and Pistachios: Stir in ½ cup chopped dried apricots, ½ cup pistachios, and ½ teaspoon cayenne; garnish with a squeeze of lemon juice and some chopped fresh mint after turning off the heat.
3. Bulgur Pilaf with Black-Eyed Peas: Add 1 cup cooked black-eyed peas and ½ teaspoon cayenne, or to taste, along with the tomato paste.
4. Mediterranean Bulgur Pilaf: Add ¼ cup chopped pitted black olives, ¼ cup chopped Preserved Lemon (page 286), and 2 teaspoons chopped fresh oregano or 1 teaspoon dried oregano after turning off the heat. Garnish with crumbled feta cheese.
5. Bulgur Pilaf with Lentils: Add 1 cup cooked lentils and 1 teaspoon each minced garlic, red chile flakes, and ground cumin along with the tomato paste.

Bulgur Chili
MAKES: 6 to 8 servings
TIME: 1 hour, mostly unattended
Ⓜ Ⓞ

Here bulgur takes the place of ground meat, providing body and thickening power. The preparation and cooking are relatively fast and, like most stews, this will taste better the next day.

All sorts of vegetables can be incorporated: corn kernels; chopped zucchini, squash, carrots, celery, and more. Add them in Step 1. Beans are not essential, though they can easily be added (see the first variation).

2	tablespoons olive oil
1	onion, chopped
2	bell peppers (any color), cored, seeded, and chopped
2	tablespoons minced garlic
3	tablespoons tomato paste
2–4	cascabel, guajillo, ancho, or other dried red chiles, soaked, cleaned, and chopped (see page 226)
3	cups chopped ripe tomatoes (about 2 pounds) or canned tomatoes (whole or chopped; don't bother to drain)
4	cups vegetable stock (pages 97–100), chile-soaking liquid, or water, or a combination
2	tablespoons chili powder
	Salt and pepper
1	cup bulgur or other quick-cooking grain (see list on page 404)
	Sliced scallions, chopped fresh cilantro, grated Monterey Jack or cheddar cheese, and sour cream for garnish

1. Put the oil in a large pot over medium-high heat. When it's hot, add the onions, bell peppers, and garlic. Cook, stirring occasionally, until the onions are soft, 3 to 5 minutes. Stir in the tomato paste until it's evenly distributed and begins to color, another minute or 2.

Add the chiles, tomato, stock, chili powder, and a good sprinkle of salt and pepper.

2. Bring to a boil, then turn the heat down so the mixture bubbles gently. Cook, stirring occasionally, until slightly thickened, about 30 minutes. Stir in the bulgur and cook for 10 minutes. Turn off the heat and let sit until the bulgur is tender, about 15 minutes. Garnish as you like and serve hot. Or cover and store in the refrigerator for up to 3 days before reheating gently.

BULGUR CHILI WITH BEANS Add 2 to 3 cups cooked or drained canned kidney, pinto, black, or other beans in Step 2. Omit the cheese and sour cream garnishes. ▼

SMOKY AND HOT BULGUR CHILI Add 2 to 4 chopped canned chipotle chiles, with some of their adobo sauce to taste, in Step 1. Omit the cheese and sour cream garnishes. ▼

ULTIMATE VEGAN CHILI Add as much or as little as you want: Combine the first two variations, adding beans and chipotles to the chili. Add 1 tablespoon chopped fresh ginger in Step 1 for extra spice. In Step 2, add 1 cup fresh or frozen corn kernels or any of the other vegetables listed in the headnote. Omit the cheese and sour cream garnishes. ▼

Pearl Couscous Pilaf with Almonds and Olives

MAKES: 4 to 6 servings
TIME: 20 minutes
F M V

Pearl couscous is so forgiving: It won't turn to mush with too much liquid, it can be served hot or at room temperature, it reheats well, and it's delicious in so many dishes. Highly recommended.

2	tablespoons olive oil
½	onion, chopped

1	cup pearl couscous or other quick-cooking grain (see list on page 404)
3	tablespoons toasted slivered almonds
1	clove garlic, minced
3	tablespoons chopped pitted black olives
1¼	cups vegetable stock (pages 97–100) or water
	Salt and pepper
	Chopped fresh basil, mint, or oregano for garnish

1. Put the oil in a pot over medium-high heat. When it's hot, add the onion and pearl couscous and cook until the couscous is lightly browned and the onion is soft, 3 to 5 minutes. Add the almonds, garlic, and olives and cook for another 2 minutes, until the olives soften a bit.

2. Stir in the stock, sprinkle with a bit of salt (remember, the olives will add salt) and a good amount of pepper, and bring to a boil. Turn the heat to low so it bubbles gently, cover, and cook until the liquid is absorbed and the couscous is al dente, about 10 minutes. Taste, adjust the seasoning, and sprinkle with chopped herbs. Serve hot or at room temperature. Or cool, cover, and refrigerate for up to 2 days. Reheat or bring back to room temperature, stir in a little olive oil, and garnish with the herbs just before serving.

EGGPLANT PEARL COUSCOUS PILAF A bigger, more filling dish: Add about 1 cup eggplant cut into ½-inch or smaller pieces along with the almonds, garlic, and olives. Cook until the eggplant is nearly soft, about 5 minutes.

SPINACH PEARL COUSCOUS PILAF Omit the onion, almonds, and olives. Double the garlic and add about 1 cup chopped cooked spinach, squeezed almost dry, and ¼ cup each pine nuts and raisins in Step 1.

CURRIED PEARL COUSCOUS PILAF Omit the almonds, and olives; add 1 tablespoon each minced fresh ginger and curry powder.

Pearl Couscous Tagine

MAKES: 4 to 6 servings
TIME: 40 minutes
Ⓜ Ⓥ

Tagine refers to both the national dish of Morocco—a stew with vegetables and spices, served with couscous—and the vessel in which it is cooked. The bowl-shaped bottom and conical lid of the pot make sense: The lid is designed to allow just the right amount of steam to escape through the hole in the top and condensation to drip back down into the stew simmering below.

You don't need a tagine to cook a great stew; any deep skillet or pot will do. And pearl couscous isn't the traditional one for this dish, but I like it better. You can use regular or whole wheat couscous if you like; just reduce the simmering time.

2	tablespoons olive oil
1	onion, chopped
2	cloves garlic, minced
1	tablespoon minced fresh ginger
1½	teaspoons ground cumin
2	teaspoons ground turmeric
2	cinnamon sticks
⅓	cup chopped dried apricots, dates, or raisins
1½	cups chopped fresh tomatoes (about 1 pound), or drained canned
2	cups vegetable stock (pages 97–100)
1	cup cooked or drained canned chickpeas
2	carrots, cut into bite-sized chunks
½	head cauliflower, cored, cut into bite-sized chunks
2	zucchini, cut into bite-sized chunks
	Salt and pepper
1	cup pearl couscous or other quick-cooking grain (see list on page 404)

1. Put the oil in a large, deep skillet over medium-high heat. When it's hot, add the onion and cook until soft, 3 to 5 minutes. Add the garlic, ginger, cumin, turmeric, and cinnamon; cook, stirring often, until fragrant, 2 minutes.

2. Add the apricots, tomatoes, stock, chickpeas, carrots, cauliflower, and zucchini, a large pinch of salt, and a good amount of pepper. Bring to a boil. Reduce the heat to a gentle simmer, cover, and cook until the vegetables are just tender. (You can make the tagine in advance up to this point; cool, cover, and refrigerate it for up to 2 days. Bring it to a simmer before proceeding.)

3. Add the couscous and cook until al dente, about 10 minutes. It should have a stewy consistency. Taste and adjust the seasoning. Remove the cinnamon sticks and serve. Or cool, cover, and refrigerate for up to 2 days; reheat gently.

PEARL COUSCOUS TAGINE WITH CARAMELIZED BUTTERNUT SQUASH Replace the apricots with pitted prunes and the chickpeas with ½ cup mixed almonds and chopped Preserved Lemons (page 286). Omit the carrots, cauliflower, and zucchini. Add 1 pound butternut squash, peeled, seeded, and cut into ½-inch slices. In Step 1, cook the butternut squash in the oil until golden brown on both sides, about 10 minutes. Add the onion once you've flipped the squash to cook the other side. Proceed with the recipe.

Roasted Quinoa with Potatoes and Cheese

MAKES: 4 to 6 servings
TIME: 1 hour
Ⓜ

When you boil quinoa for a couple of minutes, then roast it in oil, it develops a crispness similar to toasted nuts. Here the roasted quinoa almost coats the potatoes, and you finish the whole thing off with melted cheese.

If you can find purple potatoes, use them. With a simple green salad—and in summer, sliced ripe tomatoes—this is a perfect lunch or light supper. With scrambled eggs, warm tortillas, and salsa, it's a weekend breakfast. Add any good bean dish and you have a satisfying dinner.

4 tablespoons olive oil

1 pound small waxy potatoes (like fingerling, new red, or Peruvian purple), peeled if you like and cut into 1-inch chunks

2 tablespoons chopped garlic
  Salt

¾ cup quinoa, rinsed and drained, or other quick-cooking grain (see list on page 404)
  Pepper

½ cup sliced scallions

1 or 2 tablespoons minced fresh chile (like jalapeño or Thai), to taste, or red chile flakes or cayenne

6 ounces smoked cheese (like cheddar, Gouda, or mozzarella), grated (about 1½ cups)

¼ cup chopped fresh parsley for garnish

1. Heat the oven to 400°F. Grease an 8 × 10-inch roasting pan with 2 tablespoons of the oil.

2. Put the potato chunks and garlic in a large pot with water to cover, salt it, and turn the heat to high. When the water comes to a boil, stir in the quinoa. Adjust the heat so that the water bubbles rapidly and cook, stirring once or twice, until the potatoes can be just barely pierced with a fork, 3 to 5 minutes.

3. Drain the quinoa, garlic, and potatoes in a fine-meshed strainer, reserving about ½ cup of the cooking water, but leave them fairly wet. Spread them in the prepared pan, sprinkle with salt and pepper, drizzle with the reserved cooking liquid and the remaining 2 tablespoons oil, and gently toss with a spatula. Spread them out again. Roast, undisturbed, for 15 minutes. Gently toss again, scraping up any browned bits from the bottom of the pan, and return to the oven until the potatoes are tender on the inside and golden on the outside, another 10 to 15 minutes.

4. Add the scallions and chile and toss everything one last time. Taste and adjust the seasoning, keeping in mind that the cheese will add some saltiness. Sprinkle the cheese over all and return to the oven until the cheese is melted and bubbling, 5 to 8 minutes. Sprinkle with the parsley and serve.

ROASTED QUINOA WITH SWEET POTATOES AND CHEESE Even more hearty: Replace the potatoes with peeled sweet potatoes. Add 1 roasted red pepper (page 228) in Step 4. Use a mild cheese like mozzarella or queso fresco. Garnish with cilantro instead of parsley.

ROASTED QUINOA WITH SQUASH AND BLUE CHEESE Omit the scallions and chile; use a soft blue cheese like Gorgonzola. Replace the potatoes with 1 pound butternut squash, peeled, seeded, and cut into 1-inch cubes. Proceed with the recipe.

ROASTED QUINOA WITH BROCCOLI Replace the potatoes with 1 pound broccoli, cut into florets and the stem peeled and cut into ¼-inch slices. Reduce the additional cooking time in Step 3 to 5 to 10 minutes. Use sharp cheddar for the cheese.

Baked Quinoa and Beets

MAKES: 4 to 6 servings
TIME: 45 minutes
M O

Here you get the best of quinoa: a hearty, flavorful grain mixed with vegetables, with a crunchy top. This technique works well with lots of vegetables and spice combinations. You could also use carrots, parsnips, or potatoes. Just make sure to shred the vegetables so they cook as fast as the quinoa.

1 cup quinoa or other quick-cooking grain (see list on page 404)

1 pound beets, peeled and shredded

¼ cup olive oil

1 tablespoon minced garlic

1 tablespoon garam masala (to make your own, see page 648)

¼ teaspoon cayenne, or to taste
  Salt and pepper

2 cups vegetable stock (pages 97–100) or water, hot
  Yogurt for garnish (optional)

1. Heat the oven to 400°F. Mix together the quinoa, beets, oil, garlic, garam masala, cayenne, salt and pepper to taste in a large bowl. Taste and adjust the seasoning, adding more cayenne if you'd like it spicier. Transfer to a wide gratin or baking dish or an oven-proof skillet.

2. Pour in the stock and cover the baking dish with aluminum foil. Bake for 20 minutes. Remove the foil and continue baking until the quinoa mixture is mostly dry and the top is browned and crunchy, 15 to 20 minutes. Top with yogurt, if you'd like, and serve hot or warm, or cool, cover, and refrigerate for up to 2 days.

BAKED QUINOA AND BEETS, EASTERN EUROPEAN STYLE
The garlic and caraway are wonderful together: Omit the garam masala and cayenne and use 2 teaspoons caraway seeds.

MEDIUM-COOKING GRAINS

These are the grains that cook in 20 to 45 minutes. Within this category, they're pretty much interchangeable. Medium-cooking grains include:

- Buckwheat groats
- Cracked wheat
- Einkorn
- Farro
- Freekeh
- Kasha
- Millet
- Steel-cut oats

Kasha with Golden Brown Onions

MAKES: 4 to 6 servings
TIME: 45 to 50 minutes
M **O**

This is a classic, delicious Eastern European kasha dish. Many people toss their kasha with an egg before cooking, because it keeps the grains separate. But toasting it in oil accomplishes the same goal, so take your pick. (Without either, the kasha will become mushier, which is fine too.)

3	**cups chopped onion**
3–5	**tablespoons good-quality vegetable oil**
1	**egg (optional)**
1	**cup kasha**
	Salt and pepper
2	**cups vegetable stock (pages 97–100) or water**
1–2	**tablespoons butter (optional)**

1. Put the onion in a large skillet over medium heat. Cover the skillet and cook for about 15 minutes, until the onion is dry and almost sticking to the pan. Add 3 tablespoons oil, raise the heat to medium-high, and cook, stirring, until the onion is nicely browned, another 15 minutes or so.

2. When the onion has been cooking for about 10 minutes, if you're using the egg, beat it, then add the kasha and toss to coat. (If not, proceed to Step 3.) Put in a heavy, large, deep skillet over medium-high heat along with some salt and pepper. Cook, stirring, until the mixture smells toasty, about 3 minutes. Proceed to Step 4.

3. If you're using oil instead of the egg, put 2 tablespoons in a large skillet over medium-high heat. When it's hot, add the kasha, along with some salt and pepper, and cook, stirring, until the mixture smells toasty, about 3 minutes.

4. Turn the heat to a minimum and carefully add the stock to the kasha. (Be careful; it will spatter.) Bring to a boil, reduce the heat so the stock bubbles gently, then cover. Cook until the liquid is absorbed and the grains are tender, 10 to 15 minutes. Turn off the heat.

5. Stir in the onion and the butter if you're using it; taste and adjust the seasoning. Serve or let the kasha sit, covered, for up to 20 minutes. Fluff with a fork just before serving.

KASHA VARNISHKES Cook 1 pound bowtie, shell, or broad egg noodles in boiling salted water until tender but still firm; drain and combine with the kasha and caramelized onion in Step 5.

KASHA WITH PARSNIPS OR CARROTS Replace the onion with about 1 pound parsnips or carrots, peeled and chopped (2 cups or so). In Step 1, put the oil in the pan first, then add the parsnips; cook until the parsnips are golden brown and tender, about 15 minutes. Proceed with the recipe.

KASHA WITH MUSHROOMS Very flavorful and meaty: Replace the onion with 2 cups or so chopped or sliced mushrooms like shiitake, cremini, portobello, button, or a mixture. In Step 1, put the oil in the pan first, then add the mushrooms; cook until the mushrooms are golden brown and soft, about 10 minutes. Proceed with the recipe.

KASHA WITH RADICCHIO OR ESCAROLE For people who love bitter: Replace the onion with 2 cups chopped radicchio or escarole. In Step 1, put the oil in the pan first, then add the greens; cook until softened, about 3 minutes. Add ¼ cup fresh orange juice and a pinch of sugar and cook until the mixture is dark brown and nearly dry, 5 to 8 minutes. Proceed with the recipe.

KASHA PILAF WITH CARAMELIZED ENDIVE Replace the onion with 3 Belgian endives, chopped. In Step 1, put 1 tablespoon oil in the pan first, then add the endive; cook until softened and golden brown, about 10 minutes. Add ¼ cup fresh orange juice and cook until the mixture is golden and nearly dry, 5 to 8 minutes. Proceed with the recipe.

Autumn Millet Bake

MAKES: 4 to 6 servings
TIME: About 1½ hours, mostly unattended
Ⓜ Ⓞ

Though this is perfect for Thanksgiving, you'll probably want to eat it more than once a year. The sweet squash—which makes the dish creamy without adding dairy—is nicely balanced with tart cranberries and the nutty flavor of the millet.

> 4   tablespoons olive oil, plus more for the baking dish
> ¾   cup millet or other medium-cooking grain (see list on page 413)
> 1½ pounds butternut or other winter squash, peeled, seeded, and cut into 1-inch cubes
> 1   cup fresh cranberries
>   Salt and pepper
> 1   tablespoon chopped fresh sage or 1 teaspoon dried sage
> 2   tablespoons maple syrup or honey
> 1   cup vegetable stock (pages 97–100) or water, warmed
> ¼   cup pumpkin seeds or chopped hazelnuts

1. Heat the oven to 375°F and grease a 2-quart casserole, large gratin dish, or 9 × 13-inch baking dish with oil.

2. Put 2 tablespoons of the oil in a small skillet over medium-high heat. When it's hot, add the millet and cook, stirring frequently, until fragrant and golden, about 3 minutes. Spread in the baking dish.

3. Scatter the squash cubes and cranberries on top of the millet. Sprinkle with salt and pepper and the sage and drizzle with the maple syrup. Carefully pour the warmed stock over all. Cover tightly with foil and bake, undisturbed, for 45 minutes.

4. Carefully uncover the baking dish. Turn the oven up to 400°F. Sneak a taste and adjust the seasoning. If it looks too dry, add a spoonful or 2 of liquid. Sprinkle the pumpkin seeds on top, drizzle with the remaining oil, and return the dish to the oven. Bake until the mixture bubbles and the top is browned, another 10 minutes or so. Serve piping hot or at room temperature.

AUTUMN MILLET BAKE WITH CREAM Richer, obviously: Use a mixture of 1 cup heated cream and ½ cup stock, instead of only stock.

Buckwheat Stew with Tofu and Kale

MAKES: 4 to 6 servings
TIME: 50 to 60 minutes

V

Buckwheat groats (or peeled buckwheat, as they're sometimes called) are not the same as kasha, which is pre-roasted. What nonkasha buckwheat has is a grassiness that can be quite refreshing when treated properly. It takes some pan-toasting in oil to bring out its charm, as in this recipe. Unlike kasha, this never turns mushy; the nutty texture remains through the cooking.

¼ cup good-quality vegetable oil

1 onion, chopped

1 potato, peeled and chopped, or
  1 cup broken regular or whole wheat
  vermicelli in 1-inch pieces

½ cup buckwheat groats (not kasha) or other
  medium-cooking grain (see list on page 413)

8–10 cloves garlic, peeled
  Salt and pepper

4 cups chopped kale or collards, stems
  cut away and discarded

8–10 ounces firm tofu, cut into ½-inch cubes
  About 2 cups vegetable stock
  (pages 97–100) or water, or 1½ cups
  plus ½ cup white wine

1 teaspoon Chile Paste (page 664), or to taste

2 tablespoons soy sauce, or to taste

1. Put the oil in a large, deep skillet over medium heat. Add the onion, potato, buckwheat, and garlic and cook, stirring, until everything is pretty much dry and sticking to the pan, 5 to 10 minutes. Sprinkle with salt and pepper.

2. Add the greens and cook, stirring, until they wilt a bit, about 5 minutes. Add the tofu and cook, still stirring, until the tofu browns a little, about 5 minutes more.

3. Add about ½ cup of the liquid (the wine if you're using it), and scrape the pan with a wooden spoon to release all the browned bits on the bottom. Add another cup of the liquid, then adjust the heat so the mixture simmers. Cook, checking and stirring every 5 minutes or so and adding more liquid as necessary, until the buckwheat is just about tender, about 20 minutes.

4. Stir in the chile paste and soy sauce and cook until both the buckwheat and greens are tender, another 5 minutes or so; enough liquid should remain so the mixture is saucy, not soupy or dry. Taste and adjust the seasoning, then serve.

Fluffy Cracked Wheat with Mustard and Tarragon

MAKES: 4 to 6 servings
TIME: About 20 minutes

F O

Don't confuse—as I did for years—cracked wheat, which is raw, with bulgur, which is precooked and dried. If you use bulgur here instead of cracked wheat, you will wind up with mush.

You can use parsley instead of tarragon; dill would be very tasty too.

2 tablespoons olive oil

1 cup cracked wheat or other medium-cooking
  grain (see list on page 413)
  Salt and pepper

¼ cup white wine (optional)

2 teaspoons Dijon mustard

1 tablespoon chopped fresh tarragon
  Butter (optional)

1. Put the oil in a pot over medium-high heat. When it's hot, add the cracked wheat and sprinkle with salt and pepper. Cook, stirring frequently with a fork, until it smells like fresh toast, 3 to 5 minutes.

2. Add the wine if you're using it, stir briefly to combine, and cook until it almost boils off, a minute or 2. If you didn't use the wine, add 1 cup water; if you did add wine, add ¾ cup water. Stir again briefly with the fork, bring to a boil, cover, and reduce the heat to low. Cook, undisturbed, until the liquid is nearly all absorbed, about 15 minutes.

3. Lift the lid and use the fork to stir in the mustard, tarragon, and a pat of butter, if you'd like. Cover again, turn the heat off, and let sit for at least 5 and up to 15 minutes. Taste and adjust the seasoning, fluff one last time with the fork, and serve.

7 Additions to Fluffy Cracked Wheat

Instead of mustard and tarragon, try these combos, with or without the butter; in Step 3, using a fork to combine:

1. Stir in 3 chopped scallions and 2 tablespoons sunflower seeds in Step 3.

2. Stir in 2 tablespoons Chile Paste (page 664) in Step 3.

3. Add 2 tablespoons maple syrup (or less, to taste) and a pinch of cayenne in Step 3.

4. Add ½ cup fresh or frozen peas and ¼ cup chopped fresh mint in Step 3. (A dollop of yogurt goes great with this.)

5. A couple dozen halved seedless grapes and ½ cup chopped toasted almonds, hazelnuts, or pecans, along with lots of pepper, in Step 3.

6. Use sesame oil instead of olive oil in Step 1, and stir in 1 tablespoon or so soy sauce, and ½ cup each chopped roasted peanuts and chopped fresh cilantro in Step 3. **V**

7. Keep the mustard and stir in 2 tablespoons red wine vinegar (or to taste), 1 cup halved cherry tomatoes, and ½ cup chopped fresh parsley in Step 3.

SLOW-COOKING GRAINS

These are the grains that need to cook for over 45 minutes. Within this category, they're interchangeable, so try any recipe with whatever you have on hand. Slow-cooking grains include:

- Kamut
- Rye berries
- Sorghum
- Spelt
- Wheat berries
- Wild rice

Summer Vegetable Stew with Wheat or Rye Berries

MAKES: 4 to 6 servings
TIME: About 20 minutes with cooked grains
F **M** **V**

A stew with wheat berries may bring to mind anything but summer, but a pot of bright, crisp summer vegetables combined with chewy wheat berries is satisfying and won't weigh you down.

Since the wheat or rye berries are added cooked to the stew, you can substitute most any grain, though I would recommend you go with one that has some chew to it, like hominy or hulled barley, so it doesn't get lost in the mix.

> 3 **tablespoons olive oil, plus more for drizzling**
> 1 **leek, including a little light green, rinsed well and thinly sliced**
>   **Salt and pepper**
> 4 **ounces green or wax beans, sliced into 1-inch pieces (1 scant cup)**
> 1 **small zucchini, pattypan, or summer squash, thinly sliced**
> ½ **cup dry white wine, vegetable stock (pages 97–100), or water**
> 2 **cups cooked wheat or rye berries (see page 417) or other slow-cooking grain**
> 2 **fresh tomatoes, cut into wedges**
> ½ **cup chopped fresh basil or parsley**

1. Put the oil in a large saucepan or deep skillet over medium-high heat. When it's hot, add the leek and sprinkle with salt and pepper. Cook, stirring occasionally, until soft, about 2 minutes. Add the green beans and zucchini and stir to coat with the oil. Stir in the wine.

2. Reduce the heat to medium-low, cover, and cook, stirring once or twice, until the vegetables are just starting to get tender, 5 to 7 minutes. Raise the heat a bit and stir in the wheat berries.

3. Cook, stirring frequently, until hot and bubbling, a minute or 2. Stir in the tomatoes, season with salt and pepper, cover, and turn off the heat. After about 5 minutes, add the basil and fluff gently with a fork. Taste and adjust the seasoning. Drizzle with a little more olive oil, if you'd like, and serve. Or let sit for an hour or more and serve at room temperature.

QUICK WHEAT OR RYE BERRY STEW WITH FALL VEGETABLES You can make this through the winter: Instead of the leek, green beans, and zucchini, use 1 yellow onion, a couple of chopped turnips or carrots, and a small (1- to 1½-pound) peeled, seeded, and chopped acorn squash. Increase the cooking time in Step 2 to 15 to 20 minutes. Instead of the tomatoes, cut several green cabbage or chard leaves into ribbons (enough to make a heaping cup) and stir them in. Cook for about 5 minutes more, then finish with a tablespoon chopped fresh sage or 1 teaspoon dried sage in place of the basil.

QUICK WHEAT BERRY STEW WITH SPRING VEGETABLES A celebration: Instead of the leek, green beans, and zucchini, use 2 or 3 scallions, sugar snap or snow peas, and a handful of asparagus spears, sliced into 1-inch pieces. Instead of the tomatoes, use ½ cup fresh peas. Finish with fresh mint in place of the basil.

Basic Wild Rice

MAKES: 4 to 6 servings
TIME: 40 minutes
Ⓜ Ⓞ

You can cook wild rice with brown rice, white rice, or pearled barley (I love this combo) in equal quantities, and integrate its flavor into almost any other rice dish. But beware because it takes almost as long as brown rice to cook, so plan ahead a bit. The easiest way to cook it by itself is with the recipe for Cooking Grains, the Easy Way (page 398), but this is a little more sophisticated.

> 1 **cup wild rice**
> 3 **cups vegetable stock (pages 97–100) or water**
> 1 **bay leaf**
> **Salt and pepper**
> 1 **tablespoon butter or olive oil (optional)**
> **Chopped fresh parsley for garnish**

1. Put the wild rice, stock, bay leaf, and some salt and pepper in a medium saucepan over medium-high heat and bring to a boil.

2. Cover, turn the heat down to low, and cook, undisturbed, for 30 minutes. Check the progress: The rice is done when the grains have plumped up and are quite tender, regardless of whether all the liquid has been absorbed. If the rice is not done, continue to cook, adding more liquid if necessary. If it is done, drain if necessary. Remove the bay leaf. (You can prepare the rice in advance up to this point. Cool, cover, and refrigerate for up to 3 days; reheat gently before proceeding.) Stir in the butter if you like, garnish with parsley, and serve.

WILD RICE WITH BRUSSELS SPROUTS These two work very well together: While the rice is cooking, cook 8 ounces Brussels sprouts according to the recipe for Roasted Brussels Sprouts with Garlic (page 183). Stir them into the rice just as it finishes cooking.

WILD RICE WITH ROASTED WINTER SQUASH Roast about 1 cup chopped butternut or other winter squash (page 266) with butter or olive oil. Stir into the rice as it finishes cooking.

WILD RICE WITH CHESTNUTS Good combined with the Brussels sprouts (above) or mushrooms (next): Roast about 12 chestnuts (see page 299). Peel, roughly chop, then stir into the rice just as it finishes cooking.

WILD RICE WITH MUSHROOMS While the rice is cooking, cook about 1 cup sliced shiitake mushroom caps in 2 tablespoons butter or olive oil until crisp, about 10 minutes. Stir into the rice just as it finishes cooking.

WILD RICE WITH DRIED FRUIT When you add the butter and parsley, stir in ½ cup chopped dried fruit (like apricots, cherries, cranberries, mango, or apple). Put the lid back on for a minute or 2 to warm through and plump.

Summer Vegetable
Stew with Wheat or Rye
Berries (page 417)

GRAINS FOR BREAKFAST

Oatmeal isn't your only whole grain option at the breakfast table. One basic cooking technique can be applied to whatever grain you want to cook for a hot and hearty breakfast cereal.

Fast-cooking grains that are good for hot breakfast cereal include: farina (finely milled wheat cereal), cracked wheat, cornmeal, amaranth, teff, barley flakes, spelt flakes. Slow-cooking grains that are good for hot breakfast cereal include: wheat berries, rye berries, kamut, spelt, barley.

To add even more variety, you can substitute regular milk or soy, nut, or grain milk for half the water, or stir in a bit of the milk, cream, or half-and-half at the end of cooking for a richer breakfast.

Here's how to cook a single serving of grains for breakfast:

1. Combine ½ cup any of the grains listed at left in a small saucepan with a large pinch of salt and water to cover by at least an inch. Bring to a boil, then adjust the heat so the mixture bubbles gently.

2. Cook, stirring occasionally, until the grain is tender. This will take as little as 3 minutes for farina, as long as 20 minutes or more for cracked wheat and teff, or as long as an hour for wheat berries. Add boiling water as necessary to keep the grain covered and to adjust the consistency. Be sure there's enough water in the pot to keep the grain from drying out.

3. The grain is done when it tastes cooked and is as tender as you like it. Stir in some butter or any milk or cream, and add whatever garnishes you like (see "12 Stir-ins for Oatmeal and Other Cooked Grains," left, for ideas).

12 Stir-Ins for Oatmeal and Other Cooked Grains

When feeding a crew, provide an array of garnishes for your guests to dress their own cereals.

1. Ground spices like cinnamon, nutmeg, cloves, allspice, cardamom, or anise

2. Chopped dried fruit

3. Chopped nuts and/or seeds

4. Fresh fruit, chopped or sliced if necessary: apples, bananas, strawberries, apricots, peaches, blueberries, cherries, or raspberries

5. Jam, jelly, marmalade, preserves, or fruit compote

6. Shredded coconut (great when toasted)

7. The Best Granola (page 421)

8. Grated cheese

9. Chopped Hard-Boiled Egg (page 521)

10. Poached Egg (page 525); you can also poach eggs directly in cooking grains, simply by cracking the eggs into the simmering mixture during the last 3 to 5 minutes of cooking.

11. Soy sauce

12. Sautéed greens, especially with soy sauce and a poached egg

Oatmeal or Other Creamy Breakfast Cereal

MAKES: 2 servings
TIME: 15 minutes
F O

Please don't bother with quick-cooking or instant oats; the old-fashioned style takes barely 5 minutes more, and the flavor and texture are far better. This recipe gives you a fairly creamy oatmeal; if you prefer it thicker, use a bit less water. Skip the butter and milk to make this vegan.

Other grains you can use: any kind of rolled or flaked grain—try wheat, rye, quinoa, millet, kamut, or brown rice flakes.

> Dash salt
> 1 cup rolled oats (not quick-cooking or instant)
> Butter (optional)
> Salt, sweetener (maple syrup, sugar, or honey), and/or milk or cream as desired

1. Combine 2¼ cups water, the salt, and the oats in a small saucepan over high heat. When the water boils, turn the heat down to low and cook, stirring, until the water is just absorbed, about 5 minutes. Add butter to taste if desired, cover the pan, and turn off the heat.

2. Five minutes later, uncover the pan and stir. Add other ingredients as desired and serve.

The Best Granola

MAKES: About 8 cups
TIME: 30 minutes
F M O

The technique for making granola is always the same; it's what you add that makes it special. Think of this recipe as guidelines for a basic granola and then customize it in any way you like; there are lots of ideas here. Increase or decrease the other ingredients as you like and toss in others like nut butters, vanilla, or citrus zest. See the "Customizing Granola" chart below for ideas.

Rolled oats are the most common grain, but you can use lots of other rolled and flaked grains like wheat, rye, quinoa, millet, kamut, or brown rice flakes.

6	cups rolled oats (not quick-cooking or instant)
2	cups mixed nuts and seeds (like sunflower seeds, chopped walnuts, pecans, almonds, cashews, and sesame seeds)
1	cup shredded coconut
1	teaspoon ground cinnamon, or to taste
	Dash salt
½–1	cup honey or maple syrup, to taste
1	cup raisins or chopped dried fruit

1. Heat the oven to 300°F.

2. Put a 9 × 13-inch flameproof roasting pan over medium-low heat (put the pan over 2 burners if it's

Customizing Granola

This is not meant to be read by rows. Swap or mix sweeteners, spices, flavorings, nuts, dried fruit, and so forth to get a completely customized granola. The possibilities are nearly endless.

SWEETENERS	FLAVORINGS	FOR CRUNCH AND CHEW
Honey	Spices: cinnamon, nutmeg, cloves, cardamom, anise, coriander, allspice	Nuts: peanuts, almonds, walnuts, pecans, pistachios, cashews, hazelnuts, macadamias
Maple syrup	Vanilla extract or beans	Dried fruits: apricots, dates, cranberries, cherries, blueberries, pears, papaya, mango
Brown sugar	Peanut butter, nut butter, or tahini	Seeds: sesame, sunflower, flax
Molasses	Ginger: fresh, ground, or candied	Chocolate or carob chips
Agave nectar or brown rice syrup	Orange, lemon, or grapefruit zest	Dried, roasted soybeans; toasted amaranth (see page 299)

convenient). Add the oats and cook, stirring occasionally, until they begin to change color and become fragrant, 3 to 5 minutes.

3. Add the nuts and seeds and continue to cook, stirring frequently, for 2 minutes. Add the coconut and cook, stirring, for 2 minutes more. Add the cinnamon, salt, and sweetener, stir, and put in the oven. Bake for about 20 minutes, stirring once or twice, until the nuts, seeds, and coconut are browned and crisp. Remove from the oven.

4. Add the dried fruit, stir, and cool on a rack, continuing to stir once in a while until the granola reaches room temperature. Transfer to an airtight container and store in the refrigerator; it will keep indefinitely.

Puffed Uncooked Grains

MAKES: 1 cup
TIME: 15 minutes
F M V

This is the method to use for small grains, as they don't require water or oil to puff. You can scale this recipe up, but only put 1 tablespoon of grains in the skillet at a time; otherwise they'll just burn and not pop. If your grains don't pop, they probably aren't fresh enough; like popcorn, despite starting with a dried product, you're relying on internal moisture to create pressure on the outer hull. Buy your grains at a store with high turnover and you should avoid this issue.

These are best mixed with Puffed Cooked Grains (right) since you can only make a small amount at a time.

¼ **cup whole dried grains (like millet, sorghum, quinoa, or amaranth)**

1. Heat a large dry skillet over medium-low heat. When the skillet is hot, add 1 tablespoon of the grains and cover. Gently shake the pan often to prevent browning, and listen for the quiet popping (it won't be anything like popcorn). When the grains have puffed, dump them onto a rimmed baking sheet to cool. Repeat with the remaining grains.

2. Let the grains cool completely before transferring them to an airtight container. They'll keep for weeks.

Puffed Cooked Grains

MAKES: 2 cups
TIME: 12 hours, almost entirely unattended
M V

Puffing larger grains takes either industrial equipment, lots of oil, or both, if you want anything like what you buy in the grocery store. This process is healthier, and you shouldn't expect Rice Krispies as the outcome. (Those are actually made with a batter cooked in rice-sized pieces; in other words, they're not puffed rice.) What you get is crunchy, tasty, and healthy. This is the technique to use for any grain that's larger than millet. You're still relying on internal moisture to expand the grain, but here you need to cook the inside a little, then let the grains dry until they have just the right amount of moisture to get the desired result.

This is a multiday process, but it's much easier to scale up than the previous recipe.

1 **cup farro, wheat berries, spelt, rye berries, or rice**
Pinch salt

1. Fill a large pot with water and bring it to a boil over medium-high heat. Add the grains and a pinch salt. Cook halfway (about 20 minutes, but it depends on the grain; see the chart on page 400 for cooking times). Drain the grains and spread on a parchment paper–lined baking sheet, being careful not to crowd the grains. Let them dry overnight.

2. Heat the oven to 500°F. Bake until the grains have puffed, 2 to 3 minutes. Allow to cool completely before storing.

Left to right: Puffed Uncooked
Quinoa, Amaranth, and Millet

Jook

MAKES: 4 to 6 servings
TIME: About 2½ hours
V

Jook—also called congee or rice gruel—is a thinnish Chinese "porridge" typically eaten for breakfast. It is truly astonishing how much flavor a cup of rice can impart to six times its volume of water, but it's the garnishes that really make jook delicious. To me, soy sauce, sesame oil, and scallions are essential, but cilantro and peanuts are also terrific additions.

 1 **cup short-grain rice**
    Salt
 2 **inches fresh ginger, peeled**
 ½ **pound fresh shiitake mushrooms, or about 10 dried**
    Soy sauce
    Sesame oil
 ½ **cup chopped scallions for garnish (optional)**
 ½ **cup lightly packed fresh cilantro leaves for garnish (optional)**
 ½ **cup chopped roasted peanuts for garnish (optional)**

1. Put the rice in a large pot with 6 cups water and a large pinch of salt. Bring to a boil, then lower the heat so the mixture barely bubbles.
2. Slice half the ginger and add it to the pot; mince the remaining ginger and save it for later. If you're using fresh shiitakes, stem them (discard the stems or reserve for stock), slice the caps, and add them to the pot. If you're using dried shiitakes, cover them with boiling water and soak until pliable, then drain, reserving the soaking liquid to use later or for stock; slice the mushrooms and add them to the rice.
3. Partially cover the pot and simmer for 1½ to 2 hours, stirring occasionally to make sure the rice is not sticking to the bottom. If it becomes thick too quickly, turn down the heat and stir in more water or some of the soaking liquid. The jook is ready when it's soupy and creamy,

like the consistency of watery oatmeal. Add the minced ginger, and soy sauce and sesame oil to taste, along with more salt if necessary. Serve with whatever garnishes you choose (see "13 Toppings for Jook," below).

6 Things You Can Cook in Jook

Most of these just need to be added in the last 10 minutes of cooking.
1. Chopped spinach, kale, bok choy, Chinese broccoli, or most greens
2. Shredded Napa cabbage
3. Chopped sweet potato (add in the last 20 minutes)
4. Cubed tofu
5. Fresh or frozen corn kernels (no need to thaw)
6. Dried or macerated fruit (to make your own, see page 269)

13 Toppings for Jook

This should probably just be a list of things you can't put on jook, which isn't much. Almost anything you think of will be good.

1. Poached or hard-boiled egg (page 525 or 521)

2. Toasted sesame seeds

3. Sliced avocado

4. Chile oil or most hot sauces

5. Lightly sautéed spinach

6. Soy sauce, sesame oil, or Fishless Fish Sauce (page 656)

7. Grilled Asparagus (page 171)

8. Stir-Fried Tofu with Scallions (page 490)

9. Fresh or Crisp-Fried Bean Sprouts (page 176)

10. Really Spicy Tofu and Peas in Coconut Milk (page 493)

11. Kimchi, Miso-Cured Vegetables, or Spicy Korean-Style Pickles (pages 93 or 91)

12. Flash-Cooked Kale or Collards with Lemon Juice (page 210)

13. Cilantro or Other Herb "Pesto" (page 638)

Legumes

I love beans and cook them regularly. As I've traveled and as I've experimented with new varieties, I have grown to love them even more.

There was a time when I could barely imagine cooking a pot of beans without "seasoning" it with meat. But beans have tremendous flavor and great texture, and when you play off their natural characteristics, the results can be stunning. Some of my favorite flavorings for beans are the simplest: soy sauce, garlic, smoked or fresh chiles, mushrooms, cheese, and all kinds of greens. Added just after the beans become tender or at the last minute, these ingredients provide dimension and depth. This chapter features legumes in combination with all of these ingredients, as well as simple cooking techniques that will launch you on your own explorations.

Since legumes are largely interchangeable—in terms of both cooking and usage—I've arranged the recipes around the cooking methods. If you've got cooked beans (or, in a pinch, canned beans), pancooked beans (I call them "skillet beans") are the fastest dishes to make. Stovetop bean stews make up the bulk of the chapter, and these dishes cook virtually unattended. Purées and mashes are a tad more elegant, and the baked bean recipes are perfect for entertaining. Remember, too, that some of the most satisfying and interesting ways to eat beans —and to use up leftovers—are in fritters, croquettes, and cakes.

All beans, lentils, and peas belong to the Leguminosae family. These plants produce their seeds in a pod, and it's these seeds we eat. Though you can sometimes find shell beans that have not been dried (see "Fresh and Frozen Shell Beans," page 436), most are sold dried and must be cooked so they rehydrate and become edible. (When both the pods and the seeds are eaten, as in green beans or snow peas, the legumes are commonly categorized as vegetables.) Most commonly, anything in this large plant family that humans eat is called a pulse, but every culture has their own names, and Americans tend to call everything beans, or sometimes legumes or shell beans.

All beans contain about the same amount and types of protein (except soybeans, which are notably higher). They're high in fiber, rich in complex carbohydrates, and relatively low in fat—and the fat they contain is of the

13 Main-Course Legume Dishes

Turning bean dishes into the main feature of a meal is simple: Serve them over rice or just about any grain. To bulk up the dish, add vegetables, Grilled or Broiled Tofu (page 486), Baked Tofu (page 485), Seitan (page 508), or Crunchy Crumbled Tempeh (page 512). You might even sprinkle a handful of Tofu Croutons (page 497) over the top.

Some dishes make great bean tacos, tostadas, or enchilada stuffing, like Beer-Glazed Black Beans (page 440), any of the chilis (pages 455 to 457), or Refried Beans (page 460). Serve with flour or corn tortillas and a spread of toppings: grated cheese, shredded lettuce or cabbage, chopped radishes and scallions, any salsa (pages 659 to 664), hot sauce, Guacamole (page 174), and/or sour cream.

1. Baked Beans (page 467)

2. Baked Brazilian Black Beans (page 469)

3. Baked Pinto Beans, Enchilada Style (page 469)

4. Baked White Bean Cakes (page 477)

5. Bean Croquettes (page 474)

6. Hoppin' John with Smoked Tofu (page 457)

7. Cannellini Beans with Cabbage and Pasta (page 441)

8. Chickpea-Ricotta Gnocchi (page 473)

9. Chickpeas in Their Own Broth with Crisp Bread Crumbs (page 454)

10. Falafel (page 472)

11. Fresh Favas with Eggs and Croutons (page 438)

12. Hot and Sour Edamame with Tofu (page 438)

13. Spicy Red Beans, Indian Style (page 443)

more beneficial unsaturated kind. Given how delicious they can be when handled well, there's no reason not to eat them frequently.

THE BASICS OF COOKING LEGUMES

Beans are an ideal staple: Not only are they easy to store, but once cooked they keep for days in the fridge or months in the freezer, which makes them a perfect make-ahead food.

BUYING AND STORING

Beans rarely go bad, but they do get old. In extreme cases they might taste musty, but more often age simply means they will require more water and time to soften up. Unfortunately, you have little way of knowing when beans were dried, though there are some visual cues; avoid packages with lots of broken beans, imperfect skins, and/or discoloration. Try to buy beans at a place where they're frequently restocked. International groceries and natural food stores offer a great selection, and many specialty and regionally raised legumes are available online.

Store beans in a cool, dry place, not the fridge. Make sure they are tightly sealed, in either their original packaging or a plastic container or glass jar. Some people freeze their dried beans, but as this dehydrates them further, it's not a great idea.

PREPPING

My recipes—and most others—instruct you to wash and pick over beans before cooking. This is because you will sometimes find discolored or bug-eaten beans, or pebbles, twigs, or small dirt clods. (This is especially true if the beans are not overly processed, not necessarily a bad thing.) Just take a minute to put the beans in a strainer or colander, run them under cold water, and swish them around with your hands while you give them a visual once-over.

How Much to Cook?

Most of the recipes here start with 1 pound beans (the size of most bags you buy in the supermarket), which generally yields 5 to 6 cups cooked (each type has a slightly different yield), 6 to 8 servings. I cook more than I need so I can refrigerate or freeze what I don't use immediately (usually about half). Though canned beans are fine in a pinch, I'd much rather eat homemade beans: The flavor and texture are much better. You can, of course, make half the recipe if you prefer.

For the purposes of storage, and because the liquid from cooked beans is a tasty form of stock, I usually like to finish with about an inch of cooking liquid when the beans are done. This is easy enough: Check the pot every half hour or so and add a splash of water if they threaten to dry out. Sometimes you will drain beans before serving, but even then you might save the cooking liquid to cover any leftover beans when storing them, or to enrich soups or stocks. (Chickpea cooking liquid is especially good for this.)

COOKING

Dried beans require a fair amount of water, heat, and time to become edible. How much water they absorb and how long it takes to cook them varies, depending largely on when the beans were harvested and dried. The time difference can be enormous—for example, chickpeas can cook in 45 minutes, or they might need 4 hours. (Soaking can save a little time; see "To Soak or Not to Soak," page 428.)

The best way to cook legumes is at a gentle simmer in just enough water to cover them. Cooked this way, they will maintain their shape, even over long cooking. If you cook legumes at a rapid boil, the skins will tear, causing the beans to start to break down; if you're looking for a creamy consistency, this is an advantage, but if you want intact beans, it's not. The best way to test for doneness is by tasting them (eventually you'll be able to tell at a glance when they're nearly done); take the pot off the heat when they're done the way you want them.

STORING COOKED BEANS

If you get in the habit of cooking a pound or two of dried beans at a time, you'll find that you almost never rely on canned beans. Your own beans, frozen, will keep well, taste better, and cost less.

To store, let the beans cool in their liquid, then put them and their liquid in either large or serving-size plastic containers with tight-fitting lids, whatever makes sense for the way and frequency with which you will use them. Cover and refrigerate for up to 5 days or freeze for up to 6 months.

To reheat from the freezer, either thaw for a day or so in the fridge, thaw in the microwave, or put the block of beans and liquid in a covered pan with a little water and turn the heat to low. Check occasionally to make sure they have enough water but don't stir much or try to break up the ice block, or the beans will break into bits. Heated this way, they generally go from frozen to hot in less than 30 minutes.

USING CANNED BEANS

Canned beans, which are precooked, take no work: You open the can, drain and rinse the beans, and proceed. Elapsed time: a minute. There are, of course, some downsides:

- Although still quite inexpensive, they cost more per serving than dried beans.
- They give you no control over texture. Although many people like the extremely soft texture of canned beans, they come that way and that way only. Should you want less-tender beans, you're out of luck. (There are higher-quality canned beans that are not always overcooked so badly, but they're even more expensive.)
- They range in taste from decent to none: You'd be hard put to tell a canned black bean from a canned white bean with your eyes closed. And some have a decidedly metallic taste.
- They're way more limited in variety than dried beans. You can buy much higher quality dried beans, grown locally, organically, and so on, and a world of different old-school varieties.

I understand the convenience of canned beans, and if using canned beans is the difference between your cooking with and eating beans or not, then by all means use them. But my preference is to make a big batch of beans at my convenience, then freeze them in individual containers, in their cooking liquid (as described on page 427 in "How Much to Cook?"). This way I can thaw what I want in the refrigerator or microwave and proceed.

To Soak or Not to Soak

I cook beans from scratch every week, and it's been years since I have bothered to soak them before cooking. The only benefit to presoaking is that it cuts the final cooking time down, and not insignificantly. But beans are so low maintenance on the stove that letting them simmer for an extra hour is no big deal. (If you're really in a hurry, see "Pressure-Cooked Beans," page 435.) If, however, you prefer to soak, you have two options.

For the long soak method, put the rinsed beans in a large bowl and cover with 2 to 3 inches of water. Let them soak for at least 8 hours and up to 12 hours, then drain, cover with fresh water by 2 inches, add a pinch of salt, and simmer until tender.

For the quick-soak method, put the rinsed beans in a pot and cover with 2 inches of water. Bring to a boil and let boil for 2 minutes. Cover, remove from the heat, and let stand for 2 hours. Add more water to cover by 2 inches, add a pinch of salt, and simmer until tender.

Canary

Kidney

Split peas

Anasazi

Fava

Pinto

Mung

Cannellini

Black
turtle

Black-eyed
peas

The Bean Lexicon

Each of these has a particular appearance, along with (sometimes subtle) differences in flavor and texture. Many are truly interchangeable. You can generally substitute any white bean for another white bean, pink for pink, and red for red. But color isn't the only determining factor: Flavor, texture, and how well a bean holds together during cooking all play important roles. That's why most recipes in this chapter include the line "Other beans you can use." In my judgment, those are the best substitutions, which isn't to say others won't "work," but the results will be more different.

LEGUME	DESCRIPTION	AVAILABLE FORMS
Adzuki beans Aduki	Small, oval, maroon, with a streak of white. Earthy and slightly sweet; dense and creamy. Used in sweet dishes in East Asia.	Dried, canned, fresh, and as sweet red bean paste (used in Asian cuisines)
Anasazi beans Anastazi, Cave, New Mexico cave beans	Mottled with white and burgundy, mild, sweet, and mealy.	Dried, sometimes fresh
Appaloosa beans	Named after the horse for its distinct markings on one end and white to tan coloring on the other. Slender and oval shaped with a creamy texture and rich flavor.	Dried, sometimes fresh, canned
Black beans Turtle beans, Frijoles negros	Medium size, oval, deep black. Taste is rich and earthy, almost mushroom-like. (Don't confuse with Chinese fermented black beans, which are soybeans.)	Dried, frozen, canned
Black-eyed peas Cowpeas	Small, plump, ivory-colored, with a black spot. They cook quickly and absorb flavors well.	Dried, fresh, frozen, canned
Cannellini beans White kidney beans	Large, kidney shaped, off-white, with a nutty flavor and creamy consistency.	Dried, canned
Chickpeas Garbanzo beans, Ceci, Channa dal, Kabli channa	Acorn-shaped, tan (sometimes red or black), with robust, nutty flavor. Take a long time to cook, producing a flavorful cooking liquid.	Dried, fresh, frozen, canned

LEGUME	DESCRIPTION	AVAILABLE FORMS
Cranberry beans Borlotti, Roman, Romano beans	Beautiful dried or fresh; creamy, with bright to deep red dappling; similar in flavor and texture to pinto beans. Delicious fresh.	Dried, fresh, sometimes frozen
Fava beans Broad, Faba, Haba, Fève, Horse, Windsor beans	Large, flattened, wide oval beans, light brown when dried and green when fresh. Need to be peeled. Nutty and creamy when dried, a bit sweet when fresh.	Dried (get split favas, which are already peeled), fresh (in the pod), canned, frozen
Flageolets	Small, kidney-shaped, green-tinged. Quick cooking with an herbal, fresh taste. Cook up creamy while maintaining their shape. Use in soups, stews, and salads.	Dried, fresh, canned
Gigantes Great White, Gigande, Hija beans	Huge, off-white, and sweet, with potato-like texture; popular in Greek, Spanish, and Japanese dishes.	Dried, canned (sometimes with tomato sauce)
Great Northern beans	All-purpose white beans; large, oval.	Dried, frozen, canned
Kidney beans Red beans, Frijoles rojos	Shiny, red, light red or pink, reddish brown, or white (see Cannellini Beans), up to an inch long; hold their shape when cooked and absorb flavors well.	Dried, frozen, canned
Lima beans Butter beans, Butter peas	Generally pale green when fresh and white when dried; flat and kidney shaped, with a hearty texture and buttery flavor. The Christmas lima has pretty reddish purple markings. When fresh, firm pods are best (bulging beans will be starchy). Baby lima beans cook quicker.	Dried, fresh, frozen, canned

The Bean Lexicon (cont.)

LEGUME	DESCRIPTION	AVAILABLE FORMS
Lupini beans Tremocos	Flat, yellow, somewhat square, with a hole at one end. Can be bitter due to a naturally high level of alkaloids, so must be soaked and cooked for a long time, then peeled. Because of this, often sold cooked. To eat, squeeze or suck the sweet, firm beans from the skins.	Dried, canned, jarred (and sometimes pickled), fresh
Mung beans Moong bean, Green gram	A cousin to the urad bean; small, pellet shaped, green when whole and yellow when peeled and split. Slightly sweet.	Dried or peeled and split, or fresh as sprouts
Navy beans Pea, Boston, Yankee beans	Small, round, plump, white, and very useful. Dense and mild flavored with a creamy consistency; great for purées and baked beans.	Dried, frozen, canned
Peas, Dried Split peas, Maquis peas, Matar dal	Small and round; grown specifically for drying. When cooked, starchy and earthy. Green and yellow are nearly the same in all ways but color.	Most commonly sold split, either dried or canned
Pigeon peas Gandules, Congo, Goongoo, Gungo peas, Toovar dal	Tan, nearly round, with one side flattened; sweet, a bit mealy. Many colors: tan, black, brown, red, yellow, spotted.	Usually dried, sometimes split and peeled; also fresh, frozen, canned
Pink beans Chili beans	Interchangeable with pintos. Slightly kidney shaped, rounder, solidly pinkish tan. Common in the Caribbean.	Dried, canned
Pinto beans	Medium size, oval, with a reddish tan and brown speckled exterior. Earthy and creamy. Used to make refried beans.	Dried, frozen, canned

LEGUME	DESCRIPTION	AVAILABLE FORMS
Santa Maria pinquito beans	A cousin of the pink bean, native to the Santa Maria Valley in California. Small; cooks up firm and plump.	Dried, canned
Scarlet runner beans	Black or dark purple with speckles; a popular shell bean in the South. Fat and meaty; keeps its shape when cooked. To enjoy fresh, pick when less than 6 inches long.	Dried; fresh, if you grow your own
Soybeans Edamame (when young and green)	Round, small, yellow or black, and nutty. Edamame are immature soybeans: large, shiny, and usually green; a good substitute for fresh lima or fava beans.	There are hundreds of varieties, available dried, canned, and sometimes fresh or frozen. Edamame are available fresh or frozen, in their pods or already shucked.
Tarbaises Tarbais	Named after a small town (Tarbes) in the foothills of the Pyrenees. Oval, white, sweet, and buttery. Delicious in soups or stews, or added to salads.	Dried
Urad beans Black gram	Indigenous to India. When sold whole (with skins on), known as black gram or black lentils. Called white lentils when sold split (which reveals its white interior); available both with and without their skins. Used in dals.	Dried
Vaquero beans	Dappled white and black. A cousin to the anasazi, can be used as a substitute. Holds its shape and coloring when cooked (and produces a tasty black pot liquor). Used as a chili bean.	Dried
White Coco beans Coco blanc, Haricots cocos	Pretty, almost-egg-shaped, medium-size white bean from France. Creamy texture, mild flavor. Similar to Tarbaises.	Dried, occasionally fresh

Tips for Cooking Beans the Way You Like Them

- Don't add salt until the beans are tender. Adding salt to the water at the beginning will help the beans maintain their shape.
- Cook the beans at a more vigorous simmer or cook them longer, until they start to break down.
- When the beans are done, remove about ½ cup of them, mash them on a plate, and return them to the pot. Or put an immersion blender in the pot and whiz briefly.

- Add a cup or 2 of any milk (dairy or nondairy) to the pot toward the end of cooking. Cow's or goat's milk and coconut, oat, soy, nut, and rice milks are all fair game. Butter or a flavorful oil, like extra virgin olive or a nut oil, will have the same effect; add anytime during cooking.

- Add salt to the cooking water when you start.
- Don't cook the beans at more than a gentle simmer. If you cook beans at a boil, they will bang against each other and eventually fall apart.
- Don't stir the beans any more than is necessary to keep them from burning on the bottom.

6 Simple Additions to Cooked Beans

Talk about making something good superlative—there's nothing easier than this: For every 3 cups hot cooked beans (about 4 servings) add the following ingredients or preparations, either alone or in combination. (The amounts are approximations; really these should be added to taste.)

1. 2 tablespoons butter, extra virgin olive oil, or sesame oil

2. ½ cup chopped fresh parsley, cilantro, mint, or basil

3. 1 tablespoon chopped fresh rosemary, tarragon, oregano, epazote, thyme, marjoram, or sage

4. ½ to 1 cup any chutney (pages 668 to 670) or herb sauce or purée (pages 634 to 638)

5. To room-temperature beans, up to ½ cup any vinaigrette (page 628), mayonnaise (page 670), or yogurt sauce (page 673)

6. A tablespoon or so of any curry powder or spice blend (see pages 648 to 652 for a selection)

4 Flavor Add-ins for a Pot of Basic Beans

If you are going to be using the beans in a recipe that adds different flavors, stick with just salt and pepper. But if you're going to be serving them as is, feel free to add any of these to the pot to change up the taste:

1. A shallot or small onion, chopped, added with the beans

2. Chopped garlic to taste, added with the beans, or Roasted Garlic (page 205) to taste, stirred into the finished beans

3. 1 or 2 dried hot red chiles (dried chipotle will also add wonderful smokiness to the pot), added whole, or 1 hot green chile, like jalapeño or serrano, seeded and chopped, added with the beans

4. 2 to 4 sprigs fresh thyme, oregano, or sage, added with the beans

Basic Beans

MAKES: 6 to 8 servings
TIME: 30 minutes to 4 hours, largely unattended
Ⓜ Ⓥ

When a recipe calls for "cooked beans," this is it (or check out the recipes for making beans using a pressure cooker (below) or slow cooker (right).

1 **pound any dried beans, split peas, lentils, or peeled and split beans, rinsed and picked over**
Salt and pepper

1. Put the beans in a saucepan and cover with cold water by 2 to 3 inches. Add a large pinch of salt if you want your beans to retain their shape. Bring the water to a boil, then reduce the heat so the liquid bubbles gently.
2. Partially cover and cook, stirring occasionally, checking the beans for doneness every 10 or 15 minutes and adding a little more water if necessary.
3. When the beans start to get tender, add several grinds of pepper. As the beans get closer to being finished, they need to be covered with only an inch or 2 of water. Stop cooking when the beans are done the way you like them, adjust the seasoning, and either use or cool and store.

Pressure-Cooked Beans

MAKES: 6 to 8 servings
TIME: Variable
Ⓕ Ⓜ Ⓥ

You cannot beat the pressure cooker for speed; it's really the only way to cook most dried beans in less than an hour, and it's usually way faster than that; presoaking is a waste of time if you use a pressure cooker.

However, there are three disadvantages: First, the timing is imprecise; this means you must open the device and check the progress, usually once or twice. Second, pressure-cooked beans sometimes disintegrate completely (adding salt from the start helps the beans keep their shape). Last, some beans, especially limas, chickpeas, and favas, create a great deal of foam when

Beans, Lentils, and Split Peas in the Slow Cooker

The slow cooker makes cooking beans a hands-free experience. It's important that the beans remain covered with water the entire time—replenish with boiling water if necessary—but otherwise this is a no-brainer; always use the "High" setting to make sure the beans cook fully.

Rinse and pick over 1 pound and put them in the slow cooker; pour in enough water to cover by 2½ inches. Cover and cook on high until the beans are tender. For beans, depending on the type and age this can take 3 to 5 hours; for lentils (including moong and urad dal), 1½ to 2 hours; and for split peas, about 2½ hours.

cooked. If they're crowded into a pressure cooker, this foam can jam the valve and cause problems. As long as you don't fill the pressure cooker more than half full, you need not worry about this.

Don't bother to use the pressure cooker for very fast-cooking beans like lentils or split peas, which can go from done in about 5 minutes to overdone in 6.

1 **pound dried beans (any type except lentils or split peas), rinsed and picked over**
1 **tablespoon any oil**
1 **teaspoon salt (optional)**

1. Put the beans, 6 cups water, the oil, and salt if you're using it in a pressure cooker and lock on the lid. Bring the cooker to high pressure according to the manufacturer's directions. Cook for 25 to 40 minutes (the shorter time for smaller beans like black-eyed peas, the longer for larger beans like chickpeas).
2. Quick-release the pressure, then carefully remove the top and taste a bean. If it is done, let them cool, then store the beans in their liquid, or drain and serve or use in any recipe for cooked beans. If the beans are tender but not quite soft, add more water if necessary, and

simmer the beans without the lid for a few minutes. If they are not yet tender, repeat Steps 1 and 2, cooking for 5 to 10 minutes at a time.

SKILLET BEANS

Precooked legumes make great one-pan dishes, especially when combined with crunchy vegetables, rich oils and condiments, or full-flavored ingredients like mushrooms, garlic, ginger, or onions; tomatoes also can play a wonderful role here.

These dishes couldn't be much easier: Start with a little fat, then layer on ingredients until everything is lightly cooked and hot.

Edamame with Tomatoes and Cilantro

MAKES: 4 servings
TIME: 25 minutes
F V

This simple recipe can take two completely different forms depending on technique: Cook the tomatoes with their juices for a saucy dish, or add them at the last minute for a fresher, more salad-like dish. Other cooked vegetables can be tossed in as well—try corn kernels, cubed eggplant, summer squash, chopped cauliflower, or broccoli.

Other beans you can use: Any fresh shell bean, like lima, fava, or cranberry, will work nicely.

2	**tablespoons olive oil**
1	**small onion or 3 scallions, chopped**
1	**tablespoon minced garlic**
1	**teaspoon ground cumin**
1½	**cups chopped fresh tomatoes (canned are also fine, drained or not)**
2	**cups shelled edamame (fresh or thawed frozen) Salt and pepper**
¼	**cup chopped fresh cilantro for garnish**

1. Put the oil in a skillet over medium-high heat. When it's hot, add the onion and garlic and cook, stirring occasionally, until the onion is soft, about 3 minutes.
2. Add the cumin and tomatoes and cook at a gentle bubble until the tomatoes begin to break apart, about 10 minutes.

Fresh and Frozen Shell Beans

Some shell beans and many heirloom varieties are also available fresh in season, which is June through . . . well, late fall, depending on where you live; some parts of the country see them until past Thanksgiving. Keep your eye out for lima beans, black-eyed peas, pigeon peas, fava beans, edamame, and cranberry beans. You'll find them in farmers' markets, international groceries, and well-stocked supermarkets. (If you're really lucky, you'll see fresh beans, already shelled. Grab 'em when you see 'em.) Here's how to cook them:

FRESH

Shell, then wash fresh beans well and pick through them as you would dried beans, throwing out any that are discolored, misshapen, or broken. Put them in a pot with a tight-fitting lid and enough water to cover by no more than 2 inches. Bring to a boil, lower the heat so they bubble gently, partially cover, and cook for 20 minutes or so before you start testing for doneness. (The exception is edamame; they need only a few minutes in boiling water to become tender.) You can also steam fresh beans over an inch or so of water or microwave in a covered container with a little water. Another alternative is to cook shell beans without shelling, like edamame in a restaurant: Just steam or boil in salted water until a sample bean is tender, then serve hot or at room temperature, drizzled with a little oil (or whatever), for a shell-and-eat treat.

FROZEN

There's no need to thaw frozen beans, which don't come covered in liquid. Just follow the preceding directions for fresh beans; they'll take about the same amount of time.

3. Stir in the edamame and season with salt and pepper. Cook until the edamame are tender, 5 to 7 minutes. Taste and adjust the seasoning, sprinkle with the cilantro, and serve.

EDAMAME WITH TOMATOES AND OLIVES Substitute 8 pitted black olives, sliced, for the cumin and basil for the cilantro.

EDAMAME WITH TOMATOES AND ROASTED CHILES Omit the cumin and add 1 or 2 chopped seeded fresh chiles (like jalapeño or Thai).

EDAMAME WITH DIJON AND WAX BEANS Omit the garlic, cumin, tomatoes, and cilantro. Skip Step 2. In Step 3, add a couple of tablespoons water along with the edamame, cook for a couple of minutes, then add 2 teaspoons chopped fresh tarragon or thyme, 3 tablespoons Dijon mustard, and 1 cup cooked trimmed wax beans cut into pieces. Cook until everything is heated through.

Quick-Cooked Edamame with Kombu Dashi or Soy Sauce

MAKES: 4 servings
TIME: 15 minutes
F **V**

This super-easy and delicious dish cooks up in no time and makes a terrific lunch—hot or cold—on top of soba noodles or rice. If you don't have dashi or stock, use soy sauce as directed; it's even quicker and easier and nearly as good.

Other beans you can use: Any fresh shell bean, like lima, fava, or cranberry, will work.

- 1 **tablespoon good-quality vegetable oil**
- ¼ **cup chopped scallions**
- 1 **tablespoon minced fresh ginger**
- 1 **cup Kombu Dashi (page 100), vegetable stock (pages 97–100), bean-cooking liquid, or ¼ cup good-quality soy sauce mixed with ¾ cup water**
- 1 **small carrot, julienned or chopped**
- ½ **cup snow peas, trimmed and julienned or chopped**
- 2 **cups shelled edamame (fresh or thawed frozen)**
  Salt and pepper

1. Put the oil in a medium skillet over medium heat. When it's hot, add the scallions and ginger and cook, stirring occasionally, until the scallions are soft, about 3 minutes.
2. Add the dashi and bring to a steady bubble. Add the carrot, snow peas, and edamame and sprinkle with salt and pepper. Cook until the vegetables are tender, 5 to 7 minutes. Taste, adjust the seasoning, and serve.

QUICK-COOKED EDAMAME WITH SEA GREENS This is good with almost any sea green, though I like hijiki: Replace the carrot and snow peas with about ½ ounce (⅓ cup) hijiki; soak it in cold water for 10 minutes and drain before adding.

QUICK-COOKED EDAMAME WITH GREEN TEA Replace the scallions with 5 or 6 shiso leaves, chopped, and substitute freshly brewed, not-too-strong green tea for the dashi.

QUICK-COOKED EDAMAME WITH PONZU The zing of the yuzu juice is fantastic: Add the same amount of julienned daikon as carrot and omit the snow peas. Substitute ¾ cup Ponzu (page 657) for the dashi.

QUICK-COOKED EDAMAME WITH FISHLESS FISH SAUCE Replace the ginger with 1 or 2 hot fresh chiles (preferably Thai), minced, to taste, or red chile flakes to taste. Substitute ¾ cup Fishless Fish Sauce (page 656) for the dashi. Proceed with the recipe and add 4 or so chopped fresh basil leaves (preferably Thai) and sprinkle with several tablespoons chopped roasted peanuts before serving.

Hot and Sour Edamame with Tofu

MAKES: 4 servings
TIME: 30 minutes

F V

Fermented black beans provide a briny backbone for the tang of the vinegar and wine and the fresh flavor of the edamame; it's a complex, mouthwateringly delicious dish. Serve with white or brown rice.

¼ cup peanut or good-quality vegetable oil
8 ounces firm tofu, cut into ½- to 1-inch cubes and drained on paper towels
1 onion, chopped
1 tablespoon fermented black beans
1 tablespoon minced fresh ginger
2 teaspoons minced garlic
2 dried hot red chiles, stemmed, seeded, and minced, or red chile flakes to taste
½ cup vegetable stock (pages 97–100) or water, mixed with 2 teaspoons cornstarch
¼ cup rice vinegar or white wine vinegar
⅓ cup Shaoxing wine or dry (fino) sherry
2 tablespoons soy sauce
2 teaspoons sugar
2 cups shelled edamame (fresh or thawed frozen)

1. Put half the oil in a large nonstick skillet over high heat. When it's hot, add the tofu and cook, stirring occasionally, until lightly golden brown, 8 to 10 minutes. Remove from the pan.

2. Put the remaining oil in the hot pan and add the onion. Cook until soft, 3 to 5 minutes, stirring occasionally. Add the black beans, ginger, garlic, and chiles, and cook for another minute, stirring.

3. Stir in the stock mixture, vinegar, wine, soy sauce, and sugar and bring to a boil. Turn the heat down to low and add the edamame and browned tofu. Cook at a gentle simmer until the edamame are tender, 5 to 7 minutes. Taste and adjust the seasoning, adding more soy sauce if necessary, and serve.

HOT AND SOUR EDAMAME WITH VEGETABLES Replace the tofu with about 2 cups any chopped vegetable (or a combination), like bok choy, carrots, celery, daikon, mushrooms, bell pepper, snow peas, green beans, asparagus, broccoli, and/or cabbage.

MA PO EDAMAME WITH TOFU Traditionally a simmered ground pork and tofu dish: Omit the fermented black beans, wine, and vinegar; reduce the oil by half; replace the firm tofu with soft or silken tofu and the onion with ½ cup chopped scallions. Skip Step 1 and proceed with the recipe.

Fresh Favas with Eggs and Croutons

MAKES: 4 servings
TIME: 30 minutes

F

Fresh fava beans are a delicious springtime treat, with a verdant flavor that makes the shucking and peeling worth the effort. Substituting frozen favas or lima beans is perfectly fine out of season or when time is an issue, but the dish won't be the same. Instead of garnishing with the parsley, you can stir in 2 to 3 tablespoons chopped fresh herbs like basil, mint, or chives, or a pesto (to make your own, see pages 634 and 638) right before serving.

Other beans you can use: Just about any fresh or frozen bean, like lima, edamame, black-eyed peas, or cranberry, will be delicious.

¼ cup extra virgin olive oil
8 ounces bread (preferably day-old), cubed
3 cups shelled fresh fava beans (about 3 pounds in the shell), blanched and peeled (see "Preparing Fresh Fava Beans," page 440) or thawed frozen
  Salt and pepper
2 tablespoons fresh lemon juice
2 Hard-Boiled Eggs (page 521), peeled and chopped
  Chopped fresh parsley for garnish

Fresh Favas with
Eggs and Croutons

porters will be rich, and stouts richer still, with deep, caramelized flavors. For a different kind of heat, you can stir in a dollop of Thai-Style Chile Paste (page 664) instead of the chili powder.

Other beans you can use: cooked pinto, pink, pigeon peas, black-eyed peas, appaloosa

2 tablespoons olive oil
1 onion, chopped
1 tablespoon minced garlic
1 cup beer
3 cups cooked or canned black beans, drained but still moist, liquid reserved
1 tablespoon chili powder
1 tablespoon molasses or honey
 Salt and pepper

1. Put half the oil in a large skillet over medium heat. When it's hot, add the bread cubes and cook, stirring frequently, until golden brown, about 5 minutes.
2. Add the remaining oil and the favas and sprinkle with salt and pepper. Cook for about 2 minutes, until heated through. Stir in the lemon juice and eggs, then taste and adjust the seasoning. Garnish with parsley and serve.

1. Put the oil in a large skillet over medium-high heat. When it's hot, add the onion and cook, stirring occasionally, until softened, about 5 minutes. Add the garlic, cook for about a minute, then add the beer, beans, chili powder, molasses, and a good sprinkle of salt and pepper.
2. Bring to a steady bubble and cook until the liquid is slightly reduced and thickened, about 15 minutes. Taste and adjust the seasoning. Serve hot. Or store, covered, in the refrigerator for up to 3 days.

FRESH FAVAS WITH TOFU AND CROUTONS Substitute about ½ cup chopped firm tofu for the eggs; add with the favas. **V**

FRESH FAVAS WITH FETA AND CROUTONS Perfect over hot or even room-temperature orzo: Replace the eggs with ½ cup or more crumbled feta cheese and replace the parsley with chopped fresh marjoram or oregano.

BEER-GLAZED BLACK BEANS AND TOMATOES Any form of tomato—fresh, canned, or paste—is good here: Add 1 cup chopped ripe or canned tomatoes or 1 to 2 tablespoons tomato paste in Step 1.

BEER-GLAZED BLACK BEANS WITH TAMARIND For a bit of tang: Stir in a couple of teaspoons of tamarind paste, and a pinch brown sugar if you like, in Step 1.

Beer-Glazed Black Beans

MAKES: 4 servings
TIME: 20 minutes with cooked beans
F **M** **O**

It's amazing how much flavor you get from adding a cup of beer to black beans, and nearly any beer will work: Lagers and wheat beers yield a lighter and fruitier dish,

BEER-GLAZED BLACK BEANS WITH GINGER AND SOY Add 1 tablespoon minced fresh ginger and 2 tablespoons or so fermented black beans with the garlic in Step 1. Stir in some soy sauce before salting.

Cannellini Beans with Cabbage and Pasta

MAKES: 4 servings
TIME: 30 minutes
🅕 🅞

Serve this piping hot on a cold day or at room temperature when it's warm outside. Flavorful stock is key.

Other beans you can use: It's important to use firm cooked beans, like cranberry, appaloosa, pinto, or chickpeas, that won't break apart when tossed with the pasta.

Salt
½ head cabbage, preferably Savoy, cored and chopped
8 ounces cavatelli, conchiglie, or orecchiette
2 tablespoons olive oil or butter
1 large or 2 medium leeks, including some green parts, rinsed and thinly sliced (about 2 cups)
1 celery stalk, chopped
2 sprigs fresh thyme
¼ cup dry white wine (optional)
1 cup vegetable stock (preferably Vegetable Stock, page 97, or Roasted Vegetable Stock, page 99)
3 cups cooked or canned cannellini beans, drained but still moist
Pepper
Freshly grated Parmesan or pecorino Romano cheese for garnish (optional)

1. Bring a large pot of salted water to a boil over high heat. Add the cabbage and cook until just tender, 3 to 4 minutes. Use a slotted spoon or a small strainer to fish it out; drain and set aside. When the water returns to a boil, add the pasta and cook until tender but firm, 7 to 8 minutes, then drain.

2. Meanwhile, put the oil in a large skillet over medium heat. When it's hot, add the leeks and celery and cook until softened, 5 to 6 minutes, stirring occasionally. Add the thyme and the wine if you're using it, and cook for another minute, until the pan is almost dry. Add the stock, beans, and reserved cabbage. Sprinkle with salt and pepper and cook until the flavors blend and everything is well heated, about 5 minutes more.

3. Add the drained pasta to the skillet and stir gently. Taste and adjust the seasoning, sprinkle with Parmesan if you're using it, and serve.

CANNELLINI BEANS WITH SPINACH AND PASTA Replace the cabbage with 1 pound cleaned and trimmed spinach; no need to parboil it. Add it to the leeks and celery in Step 2 after they have softened. Add a handful of raisins or currants if you like in Step 3.

CHICKPEAS WITH CABBAGE AND PEARL COUSCOUS Replace the cavatelli with 1 cup pearl couscous and the cannellini with chickpeas. Increase the stock to 2 cups. Omit cooking the pasta in Step 1. In Step 2, after adding the stock, chickpeas, and cabbage, bring to a boil and add the couscous. Cover and cook until just tender, about 5 minutes. Stir in a tablespoon or so harissa.

Gigantes with Brussels Sprouts

MAKES: 4 servings
TIME: 20 minutes with cooked beans
🅕 🅞

Extremely versatile; substitute just about any vegetable for the Brussels sprouts. The gigantes are somewhat hard-to-find, but they are worth seeking out. Their potato-like flavor and texture are amazing.

Other beans you can use: any cooked hearty bean like lima (especially large ones), cranberry, pinto, kidney

2 tablespoons olive oil or butter
12 ounces Brussels sprouts, trimmed and halved
1 tablespoon minced garlic
½ cup vegetable stock (pages 97–100) or water
3 cups cooked or canned gigantes, drained but still moist
Salt and pepper
½ cup chopped roasted hazelnuts or almonds
Chopped fresh sage for garnish

Gigantes with Brussels
Sprouts (page 441)

1. Put the oil in a skillet over medium-high heat. When it's hot, add the Brussels sprouts and cook, stirring occasionally, until golden brown, 10 to 12 minutes. Add the garlic and cook for another minute.

2. Add the stock and bring to a boil. Add the beans and a good sprinkle of salt and pepper. Reduce the heat to a steady simmer and cook until heated through, 5 to 7 minutes. Taste and adjust the seasoning, sprinkle with the hazelnuts and sage, and serve.

GIGANTES WITH SHIITAKES Replace the Brussels sprouts with about 2 cups quartered shiitake mushroom caps or other sturdy mushroom.

GIGANTES WITH CHERRY TOMATOES Substitute about 2 cups cherry tomatoes for the Brussels sprouts and pine nuts for the hazelnuts. Garnish with chopped fresh basil or oregano instead of sage.

Spicy Red Beans, Indian Style

MAKES: 8 servings
TIME: About 2 hours
Ⓜ Ⓥ

This freezes well, but if you don't want the leftovers or aren't feeding a crowd, cut the recipe in half.

If you have cooked beans in the fridge or freezer, use them and cut the total time to about 20 minutes; just skip down to Step 2. This doesn't require much of the cooking liquid anyway, since most of the flavor is in the tomato sauce.

Other beans you can use: dried chickpeas (cook time will be closer to 2 hours), black beans

1   **pound dried red beans, rinsed and picked over**
½   **teaspoon cayenne (or to taste)**
     Salt
2   **tablespoons good-quality vegetable oil**
1   **tablespoon minced fresh ginger**
1   **tablespoon minced garlic**
1   **tablespoon ground cardamom**
1   **teaspoon fennel seeds**
1   **teaspoon ground cinnamon**
1   **teaspoon ground turmeric**
     Pinch ground cloves
1   **bay leaf**
2   **cups chopped tomatoes (canned are fine; don't bother to drain)**
1   **tablespoon garam masala or curry powder (or to taste; to make your own, see page 648 or 649)**

1. Cook the beans in water to cover in a medium saucepan with the cayenne and large pinch salt until they are just about tender; this will take 1 to 2 hours, depending on their freshness. Drain the beans, reserving their cooking liquid.

2. Put the oil in deep large skillet over medium heat. When it's hot, add the ginger, garlic, cardamom, fennel, cinnamon, turmeric, cloves, and bay leaf and cook, stirring, for about a minute. Add the tomatoes and cook, stirring occasionally, until they break up a bit, 5 minutes or so.

3. Add the beans to the tomato sauce along with a large pinch salt. Continue to cook until the beans are fully tender, adding a little of the bean cooking liquid if the pan gets too dry. When the beans are done, stir in the garam masala, taste and adjust the seasoning, and serve.

BEAN STEWS

The long cooking times here are deceptive because these recipes are ultra-easy to prepare. With few exceptions, everything goes into one pot and cooks largely unattended. It's also true that almost all of these dishes taste as good or even better rewarmed the next day. And remember that lentils cook in less than 45 minutes.

White Beans, Tuscan Style

MAKES: 6 to 8 servings
TIME: 1 to 2 hours, largely unattended
Ⓜ Ⓥ

An indispensable bean dish that can be enjoyed hot, cold, or at room temperature—one of my kids used to love it as an after-school snack. Serve it with a salad and crusty bread or toss it with a bit of cooked small pasta (like orecchiette) or greens (like cabbage), and you have a fantastic lunch or dinner. It reheats perfectly; just add a bit of water if the beans are too dry.

Other beans you can use: dried gigantes, fava, pinto, cranberry, kidney, appaloosa, anasazi, black-eyed peas, green or brown lentils, soybeans

- 1 pound dried white beans (cannellini, navy, Great Northern, or lima), rinsed and picked over
- 20 fresh sage leaves or 1 tablespoon dried
  Salt and pepper
- 2 teaspoons minced garlic (or more to taste)
- 1 tablespoon olive oil (or more to taste)

1. Put the beans in a large saucepan with water to cover. Turn the heat to high and bring to a boil. Add the sage, turn the heat down so the liquid bubbles steadily but not violently, and partially cover. Cook, stirring occasionally, until the beans are very tender, 1 to 2 hours; add water if the beans dry out.
2. Drain the cooking liquid if necessary, then sprinkle the beans with salt and pepper and stir in the garlic. Taste and adjust the seasoning, stir in the oil, and serve.

FAVAS WITH SCALLIONS Use fava instead of white beans and omit the sage. Use ¼ cup chopped scallions instead of or in addition to the garlic.

CHICKPEAS WITH JALAPEÑOS Substitute chickpeas for the white beans and 1 onion, chopped, for the sage. Add 2 tablespoons minced jalapeño chile with the garlic.

PINTO BEANS WITH RED BELL PEPPER Cilantro stems, loaded with flavor, can withstand longer cooking than the more fragile leaves: Use pinto beans instead of white beans and 2 tablespoons chopped fresh cilantro stems instead of the sage. Sauté 1 cup sliced red bell pepper in 1 tablespoon olive oil over medium-high heat until soft and add with the garlic in Step 2. Garnish with chopped fresh cilantro.

Beans and Greens

MAKES: 4 servings
TIME: 1½ to 3 hours, depending on the bean
Ⓜ Ⓥ

I never tire of this combination, especially since there are so many possible variations. The beans should be somewhat creamy and the greens silky without disintegrating. The secret is to add the greens—and lots of garlic and oil—when the beans are almost done.

- 8 ounces (1 cup) dried chickpeas, rinsed and picked over
  Salt
- 1 medium onion, unpeeled
- 1 bay leaf
- 1 whole clove
- 1 bunch broccoli raab (about 1½ pounds), stems trimmed, coarsely chopped
  Pepper
- 1 tablespoon minced garlic (or more to taste)
- 1 tablespoon plus 1 teaspoon olive oil (or more to taste)
- ½ cup Fried Bread Crumbs (page 678) for garnish

1. Put the chickpeas in a large saucepan with water to cover and a large pinch salt. Turn the heat to high and bring to a boil.
2. Cut a slit in the onion and insert the bay leaf; insert the clove into the onion and add the onion to the chickpeas. Turn the heat down to medium-low so the mixture

Beans and Greens

Other Beans and Greens Combinations

These are some of my favorites, though you can mix and match as you like. The quantities remain the same as in the main recipe, except where noted.

BEAN	GREEN	FAT	GARNISH
Adzuki beans	Bok choy	Sesame oil	Soy sauce and minced fresh chile (like jalapeño or Thai), red chile flakes, or cayenne to taste
Black beans	Kale	Extra virgin olive oil	Chopped toasted Brazil nuts
Cannellini	Escarole	Extra virgin olive oil or melted butter	Grated or shaved Parmesan cheese
Cannellini	1 large or 2 small heads radicchio	Extra virgin olive oil or melted butter	Balsamic Syrup (page 633)
Chickpeas	Chard	Extra virgin olive oil	Chopped toasted almonds
Gigantes or other large white beans	Romaine lettuce (cooked like a green)	Extra virgin olive oil	Crumbled feta cheese
Lentils, brown	Cabbage	Extra virgin olive oil or melted butter	Whole grain mustard
Lentils, green (preferably Le Puy)	Sorrel	Melted butter	Crème fraîche
Lentils, green (preferably Le Puy)	1 large fennel bulb, with fronds, chopped	Extra virgin olive oil or melted butter	Golden raisins, stirred in with the garlic and oil or butter
Navy beans	Broccoli	Extra virgin olive oil or butter	1 cup grated cheddar cheese
Pinto beans	Spinach	Extra virgin olive oil	Fresh Tomato Salsa (page 660) or Fresh Tomatillo Salsa (page 660)
Soybeans, black or white	Mustard greens	Sesame oil	1 tablespoon or so soy sauce and a sprinkle of sesame seeds

bubbles gently, cover partially, and cook, stirring occasionally, until the chickpeas are tender but still intact, about 2 hours. Add water if necessary.

3. Add the broccoli raab and cook until it's tender, 10 to 30 minutes, depending on the thickness of the stems. If you want a soupy mixture, add more water.

4. Remove the onion. Taste and adjust the seasoning with salt and pepper. Stir in the garlic and oil and cook for about 3 minutes. Spoon the chickpeas and greens into individual bowls and garnish with the bread crumbs.

Beans and Mushrooms

MAKES: 4 servings
TIME: 1½ to 2½ hours, depending on the bean
M O

The earthy flavors of beans and mushrooms complement each other perfectly. Use dried or fresh mushrooms, in virtually any combination; see the variations. To emphasize the mushroom flavor, cook the beans in Mushroom Stock (page 99) instead of water or double the amount of mushrooms. You might also garnish this with Sautéed Mushrooms (page 217), using shiitakes if you can and getting them nice and crisp.

Other beans you can use: dried cannellini, navy, gigantes, lima, pinto, kidney, appaloosa, anasazi, green or brown lentils, soybeans

8	ounces (1 cup) dried cranberry beans, rinsed and picked over
	Salt
2	ounces dried porcini mushrooms
1	onion, unpeeled
1	bay leaf
	Pepper
1	tablespoon minced garlic (or more to taste)
1	tablespoon chopped fresh sage or 1 teaspoon dried
¼	cup olive oil or 4 tablespoons (½ stick) melted butter

1. Put the beans in a large saucepan with water to cover and a large pinch salt. Turn the heat to high and bring to a boil. Meanwhile, soak the mushrooms in hot water to cover.

2. Cut a slit in the onion, insert the bay leaf, and add the onion to the beans. Turn the heat down to medium-low so that the liquid bubbles gently, cover partially, and cook, stirring occasionally.

3. When the mushrooms are soft, lift them out of the soaking liquid with your hands or a slotted spoon, reserving the soaking liquid. Squeeze them dry, trim away any hard spots, and chop. Pour the soaking liquid through a paper towel–lined strainer to remove any grit.

4. When the beans begin to soften (30 to 60 minutes, depending on the bean), sprinkle with lots of pepper and stir in the reserved mushroom-soaking liquid. Continue to cook, stirring occasionally, until the beans are tender but still intact; depending on the bean, this will take another 30 to 60 minutes. Add the mushrooms to the beans and continue to cook for 10 to 15 minutes.

5. Remove the onion. Taste and adjust the seasoning. Stir in the garlic, sage, and oil and cook for about 3 minutes. Spoon the beans and mushrooms into individual bowls and serve.

BLACK BEANS WITH DRIED SHIITAKES Substitute black beans for the cranberry beans and dried shiitakes for the porcini. Substitute 2 tablespoons chopped fermented black beans for the sage and sesame oil for the olive oil. Season with soy sauce instead of salt.

CHICKPEAS WITH CREMINIS OR SHIITAKES Add a sprinkle of just about any spice or spice blend if you like: Substitute chickpeas for the cranberry beans and use about 1 pound fresh cremini or shiitake mushrooms, chopped or quartered, instead of the porcini; no need to soak. In Step 3, use 1 cup Mushroom Stock (page 99) to replace the mushroom-soaking liquid. Substitute 2 tablespoons chopped fresh cilantro or parsley for the sage.

Braised Lentils, Spanish Style

MAKES: 4 servings
TIME: 45 minutes

M V

Earthy and slightly smoky; aim for a saucy but not soupy consistency, with just enough liquid to sop up with crusty bread.

Double the recipe if you like, because the leftovers will keep in the fridge for a couple of days and reheat perfectly for lunch or a super-quick dinner.

Other lentils you can use: Earthy-flavored ones work best, like dried Le Puy or black beluga lentils if you can find them.

  2 **tablespoons olive oil**
  ½ **onion, chopped**
  1 **celery stalk, chopped**
  1 **carrot, chopped**
  1 **tablespoon smoked Spanish paprika**
  2 **teaspoons minced garlic**
  ½ **teaspoon crumbled saffron threads (optional)**
  1 **bay leaf**
  ½ **cup dry red wine**
  2 **cups vegetable stock (pages 97–100) or water, plus more as needed**
  1 **cup dried brown or green lentils, rinsed and picked over**
     Salt and pepper
     Chopped fresh parsley for garnish

1. Put the oil in a medium saucepan over medium-high heat. When it's hot, add the onion, celery, and carrot; cook, stirring occasionally, until the onion is soft, 5 to 7 minutes. Add the paprika, garlic, and saffron if you're using it and cook for another minute.
2. Add the bay leaf, wine, stock, and lentils. Sprinkle with salt and pepper and bring to a boil. Turn the heat down to medium-low so that the liquid bubbles gently and cover partially. Cook, stirring occasionally and adding stock or water if necessary to keep the lentils from sticking and burning, until the lentils are tender, 25 to 30 minutes. The lentils should be saucy but not soupy.

Adjust the seasoning, sprinkle with parsley, and serve. Or store, covered, in the refrigerator for up to 3 days.

BRAISED LENTILS, MOROCCAN STYLE A more heavily spiced dish: Double the onion and omit the celery, carrot, paprika, and wine. Add 1 teaspoon each ground turmeric, cinnamon, and cumin. Replace 1 cup of the stock with 1½ cups chopped fresh tomatoes with their juices. Proceed with the recipe. Garnish with chopped fresh cilantro.

BRAISED LENTILS, ETHIOPIAN STYLE Loads of spices and a bit of heat: Omit the celery, carrot, saffron, and bay leaf. Add 1 tablespoon minced fresh ginger and ½ teaspoon each ground allspice, fenugreek, coriander, cardamom, and cayenne. Replace the smoked paprika with 2 tablespoons sweet paprika.

BRAISED LENTILS WITH ROASTED WINTER SQUASH The caramelized roasted squash adds depth: Cut any peeled and seeded medium winter squash (like acorn, butternut, kabocha, or turban) into 1- to 2-inch cubes (about 2 cups); toss it with olive oil to coat and spread on a baking sheet. Roast in a 375°F oven until tender and caramelized (see page 266 for more details on roasting squash). Omit the paprika and saffron and use white wine instead of red. Add the squash to the lentils when they are almost tender.

BRAISED LENTILS WITH CELERY The clean flavor of celery pairs nicely with the earthiness of lentils: Double or triple the amount of celery and omit the carrot, garlic, saffron, and paprika. Use white wine instead of red and stir in 1 teaspoon grated orange zest right before serving.

BRAISED LENTILS WITH PARSNIPS A great fall or winter dish; add a bit of cream for extra richness: Replace the carrot with about 1 cup chopped parsnip and omit the garlic, saffron, and paprika. Use ¼ cup dry (fino) sherry instead of the red wine. Proceed with the recipe, sprinkling with freshly grated nutmeg just before serving.

Types of Lentils

Few foods are eaten as widely eaten as lentils, which, along with barley and wheat, were among the first foods to be cultivated. They're staples in the Middle East and especially India, where they are a vital protein source for the large vegetarian populations. They're also incredibly nutritious, loaded with protein (second only to soybeans), fiber, and other nutrients.

Lentils are classified into three groups, each of which contains a number of varieties; I'm describing only the most popular and widely available here:

BROWN LENTILS

These are the most commonly available, with darker seed coats, ranging from brown to black. Generally, they hold their shape during cooking.

SPANISH BROWN

Spanish Pardina, Continental, Indian Brown, Egyptian, German: Your basic lentil, found in every supermarket. Dull, light brownish green in color, flat, with an earthy, slightly peppery flavor. They may start to split if overcooked.

CASTELLUCCIO

Lenticchia di Castelluccio di Norcia, Lenticchie Umbre, Umbrian: These tiny, nutty-flavored lentils vary in color from light brown to a speckled green. They hold their shape well, making them a good choice for use in salads.

BLACK BELUGA

Beluga, Petite Beluga: Small, rounded, and jet black (they look a little like beads of caviar), they take on a shiny green-black color when cooked. They have a rich earthy flavor, and a soft texture, and hold their shape well, Not unlike lentilles du Puy, right.

GREEN LENTILS

These have glossy dark green to green-brown seed coats and hold up well to cooking but generally take the longest to cook. You're more likely to find these lentils at specialty markets.

LENTILLES DU PUY

Le Puy lentils, French green du Puy: Nicknamed the "poor man's caviar," this lentil is revered for its robust, earthy flavor and ability to hold its shape in cooking. Lentilles du Puy are grown only in Puy, France.

FRENCH GREEN

An American-grown (usually) version of the famed lentilles du Puy, at about half the price. They vary in color from slate to dark green, are rounded, and have an earthy, peppery flavor.

RED LENTILS

The lentils in this category range in color from gold to red and are sold peeled or peeled and split, often under their Indian names, *masoor* or *masoor dal*. They are quick cooking (15 to 30 minutes) and tend to fall apart when tender. Despite their being the world's most popular lentils, you may have to go to an Indian or Middle Eastern market to find them. They are used in many Indian-style dals, like Simplest Dal on page 450.

RED CHIEF

Peeled and varying in color from red to salmon. Quick cooking, with a mild, earthy flavor.

CRIMSON

Petite Crimson: Small, extremely quick cooking. Fall apart completely, making them great for thickening soups and stews.

PETITE GOLDEN

Small, peeled, and golden-yellow in color; rounder in shape and don't fall apart as easily as other red lentils.

CANARY

Sutter's Gold: A hard-to-find peachy-yellow peeled lentil; quick cooking, and if not overcooked can hold its shape.

Simplest Dal

MAKES: 4 servings
TIME: 40 minutes, largely unattended
M O

The most basic dal is flavorful and creamy; if you add butter or oil, the dish becomes more luxurious. In addition to the usual ways of eating dal hot, you can also serve this at room temperature or even cold, to spread on toasted wedges of pita or Paratha (page 592). Leftovers make a terrific sandwich spread.

Other beans you can use: dried yellow split peas, peeled and split mung beans (moong dal)

> 1 cup dried red lentils, rinsed and picked over
> 2 tablespoons minced fresh ginger
> 1 tablespoon minced garlic
> 1 tablespoon mustard seeds
> 1 teaspoon cracked black peppercorns
> 4 cardamom pods
> 2 whole cloves
> 1 ancho or other mild dried chile (optional)
> Salt
> 2 tablespoons cold butter or peanut oil (optional)
> Chopped fresh cilantro for garnish

1. Put the lentils, ginger, garlic, mustard seeds, pepper, cardamom, cloves, and chile if you're using it in a small saucepan and add water to cover by about 1 inch. Cook at a steady simmer until the lentils are quite soft, 20 to 30 minutes, adding salt when the lentils start to soften.

2. Pick out the cloves and cardamom pods. Stir in the butter or oil if you're using it. Taste and adjust the seasoning, then garnish with cilantro and serve.

RED LENTILS AND RHUBARB The rhubarb almost dissolves into this, leaving behind its trademark tart flavor: Add 3 or 4 stalks rhubarb, strings removed, chopped, in Step 1.

RED LENTILS WITH RADISH Crunch and heat: Peel and cut 1 large daikon radish into large chunks (about 2 cups), and add in Step 1. You can also use smaller white or red radishes.

RED LENTILS WITH CELERY ROOT Peel and chop 1 medium celery root (or ⅔ of a large one), and add in Step 1.

RED LENTILS WITH FRESH TOMATOES Really nice color and a little acidity: Cut 4 ripe medium tomatoes into wedges; stir them in during the last 5 minutes or so of cooking.

How to Cook and Eat Dals

Dal is the Indian word used to describe both lentils and beans and the family of stewy dishes made from them. Anyone who has ever eaten in an Indian restaurant has eaten a dal of some kind spooned over basmati rice or served with bread.

Butter, and often lots of it, is the key to the richest dals. (The first time I was in India, I was stunned by the amount of butter people used.) Ghee—clarified butter, which is butter with its milk solids removed, able to withstand high cooking temperatures—is traditional, but whole butter works just fine. Peanut oil and more neutral oils like grapeseed and corn are good alternatives.

I prefer slightly thicker but still soupy dal that you pour over something else—usually rice—and "dry" dal, where the beans remain intact. Thinner dals also make an effective and creamy sauce for simply cooked vegetables like potatoes, eggplant, summer or winter squashes, carrots, and greens. Add more water or stock, or cream or coconut milk, and they become soup. At room temperature or chilled, they're a fine dip for crudités. Dals even make surprisingly good sandwich fillings, especially with lettuce or sprouts and tomatoes.

You can serve dal with plain-cooked basmati or jasmine rice (see page 367) or with Chapati (page 591), pita, or naan (homemade, page 608, or store-bought) for dipping.

RED LENTILS WITH CHAAT MASALA In the main recipe or any of the variations, omit the ginger, garlic, cardamom, mustard seeds, chile, and cloves (all the seasonings other than salt and pepper) and use 1 teaspoon or more chaat masala.

Mixed Whole-Bean Dal with Walnuts

MAKES: 4 to 6 servings
TIME: About 1 hour, largely unattended
M O

Cooking the onion and spice in a little butter and then tomato paste before adding the rest of the ingredients yields a toasty flavor. The adzuki beans add both natural sweetness and creaminess to the dish.

Other beans you can use: Make this a single-bean dal using all dried navy beans or black-eyed peas; black beans, limas, or kidney beans are also good, alone or in combination.

- 2 tablespoons butter or peanut oil
- 1 large yellow onion, chopped
- 1 tablespoon fragrant curry powder or garam masala (to make your own, see page 649 or 648)
- ¼ cup tomato paste
- 1 cup chopped walnuts
- ½ cup dried navy beans, rinsed and picked over
- ½ cup black-eyed peas, rinsed and picked over
- ½ cup adzuki beans, rinsed and picked over
  Salt and pepper
- ½ cup yogurt for garnish (optional)
- ¼ cup chopped fresh parsley for garnish

1. Put the butter or oil in a large saucepan over medium heat. When the butter is melted or the oil is hot, add the onion and cook, stirring occasionally, until soft, about 5 minutes. Stir in the curry powder and keep stirring for a few seconds, until it becomes fragrant. Add the tomato paste and cook, stirring frequently, until it darkens, another couple of minutes.

2. Add the walnuts and stir to coat them in the onion mixture. Cook and stir just long enough for them to warm a bit. Add the beans and enough water to cover by an inch or so.

3. Bring to a boil, then turn the heat down to medium-low so the mixture bubbles steadily but not violently. Cook, stirring occasionally, until the beans are soft, 30 to 45 minutes, adding more water as needed to keep everything moist. Add salt when the beans begin to soften.

4. When the beans are tender and creamy, sprinkle with pepper, then stir well, taste, and adjust the seasoning. Serve garnished with a dollop of yogurt if you're using it and the parsley.

MIXED WHOLE-BEAN DAL WITH CABBAGE AND WALNUTS A little more substantial: Instead of the tomato paste, add 2 cups chopped cabbage. Cook long enough for the cabbage to wilt and color, 5 to 8 minutes, before adding the walnuts and proceeding with the recipe.

MIXED WHOLE-BEAN DAL WITH CAULIFLOWER AND ALMONDS Chop a small head cauliflower and add it instead of the tomato paste. Cook long enough for it to soften a bit, about 5 minutes. Use almonds instead of walnuts and proceed with the recipe.

Lentils and Potatoes with Curry

MAKES: 4 servings
TIME: About 1 hour
M O

You may want to double this recipe so you have some handy in the fridge or freezer, because it reheats beautifully. Don't worry if the potatoes crumble a bit on the second go-round; they will only add body to the dish.

Other beans you can use: dried yellow or green split peas, split mung beans without skins (moong dal); reduce the cooking time by 15 minutes or so

Mung Bean Dal with Apples,
Coconut, and Mint

1 cup dried brown lentils, rinsed and
   picked over
3½ cups water, coconut milk, or vegetable stock
   (pages 97–100), plus more if needed
1 tablespoon curry powder (to make your own,
   see page 649)
2 medium russet potatoes, peeled and cut
   into large chunks
   Salt and pepper
   Yogurt for garnish (optional)
   Minced fresh cilantro for garnish

1. Put the lentils, water, and curry powder in a medium saucepan and bring to a boil over medium-high heat. Turn the heat down to medium-low so that the liquid bubbles gently, cover partially, and cook, stirring occasionally, until the lentils start to absorb the water a bit, about 15 minutes.

2. Add the potatoes and cover the pan completely. Cook, undisturbed, for 10 minutes or so, then stir gently and check to make sure the lentils aren't too dry. If so, add a little more liquid. Add salt when the lentils become tender.

3. Cover and continue cooking until the lentils are soft and beginning to turn to mush and the potatoes are tender at the center, another 5 to 10 minutes; add liquid if necessary. The mixture should be moist but not soupy. Add lots of pepper, stir, then taste and adjust the seasoning. Garnish with yogurt if you're using it and cilantro and serve.

BUTTERY LENTILS AND POTATOES WITH CURRY
A little smoother and more flavorful: When you stir and check the mixture in Step 2, stir in 2 tablespoons cold butter.

CURRIED LENTILS WITH POTATOES, CHICKPEAS, AND SPINACH More substantial: Add 1 cup cooked chickpeas (see page 435) along with the potatoes. When you add the salt in Step 2, also stir in 2 cups baby spinach.

Mung Bean Dal with Apples, Coconut, and Mint

MAKES: 4 to 6 servings
TIME: About 1 hour, largely unattended
Ⓜ Ⓥ

Many dals rely on deep flavors, but here's an example of how fresh, bright ingredients can set off the natural earthiness of the beans. The result is a hearty dish that is also refreshing, even in summer.

Other beans you can use: dried pigeon peas, black-eyed peas, or chickpeas (cook for up to an hour longer)

1½ cups dried mung beans, rinsed and
   picked over
½ cup shredded coconut
2 medium green apples, cored, peeled,
   and chopped
2 tablespoons minced fresh ginger
2 tablespoons minced garlic
   Pinch ground turmeric (optional)
2 cups coconut milk (to make your own, see page
   304, or use a 14-ounce can plus a little water)
¼ cup brown sugar (or to taste)
   Salt and pepper
½ cup chopped fresh mint
½ cup thinly sliced scallions
   Juice of 1 lime

1. Put the beans, coconut, apples, ginger, garlic, turmeric if you're using it, the coconut milk, and brown sugar in a large saucepan. Add enough water to cover. Bring to a boil over high heat, then turn the heat down to medium-low so the liquid bubbles steadily but not violently. Cook, stirring occasionally, until the beans are quite soft, 45 to 60 minutes, adding water or coconut milk as needed to keep everything moist. Add salt when the beans begin to soften.

2. When the beans are tender and the liquid has thickened, sprinkle with pepper and stir in the mint, scallions, and lime juice. Cook for a minute or 2 more. Taste, adjust the seasoning, and serve.

MUNG BEAN DAL WITH CARROTS, CASHEWS, AND THAI BASIL A nice twist: Use whole cashews instead of the coconut. Instead of the apples, use 3 or 4 medium carrots. Add a couple of dried Thai chiles if you like and replace the mint with Thai (or other) basil.

Flageolets, French Style

MAKES: 4 servings
TIME: 1½ to 2 hours, largely unattended

Ⓜ

Once an haute-cuisine standard, this dish features the kidney-shaped flageolet, an immature kidney bean whose lovely color ranges from ivory white to pale green. It is mild tasting and cooks up creamy. To vary the flavor, replace the thyme with tarragon, or garnish with chopped tarragon, chives, or chervil.

Other beans you can use: dried cranberry, navy, or lima

8	ounces (1 cup) dried flageolets, rinsed and picked over
1	medium onion, unpeeled
1	bay leaf
1	whole clove
1	carrot, cut into chunks
4	sprigs fresh thyme or ½ teaspoon dried
	Salt and pepper
2	tablespoons butter
1	tablespoon minced shallot
1	cup cream
	Chopped fresh parsley for garnish

1. Put the beans in a medium saucepan with water to cover. Turn the heat to high and bring to a boil.

2. Cut a slit in the onion and insert the bay leaf; insert the clove into the onion and add the onion to the beans. Add the carrot and thyme. Turn the heat down so the liquid bubbles gently. Partially cover the pot.

3. When the beans begin to soften, after about 30 minutes, season with salt and pepper. Continue to cook, stirring occasionally, until the beans are tender but still intact, about 45 minutes; add water if necessary.

4. Drain the beans and discard the onion and carrot. Put the butter and shallot in a deep skillet large enough to hold the beans. Turn the heat to medium and cook, stirring occasionally, until the shallot softens, about 5 minutes. Add the cream and beans and continue to cook, stirring, until the beans are hot and have absorbed some of the cream, about 10 minutes. Taste and adjust the seasoning, garnish with parsley, and serve.

Chickpeas in Their Own Broth with Crisp Bread Crumbs

MAKES: 4 servings
TIME: 2 to 2½ hours

Ⓜ Ⓥ

Chickpeas and their broth are so flavorful they hardly need anything else to be completely delicious, but a bit of garlic and a good olive oil make this dish spectacular. Cooking your own chickpeas is all but essential here; canned chickpeas just don't have the flavor necessary to carry this; you need that good broth.

1½	cups dried chickpeas
	Salt
1	6-inch piece French or Italian bread (a day or 2 old)
8	tablespoons olive oil
1	tablespoon minced garlic
	Pepper
	Chopped fresh parsley for garnish

1. Put the chickpeas in a large saucepan with water to cover to 2 to 3 inches and a large pinch salt. Turn the heat to high and bring to a boil, then reduce the heat so that the liquid bubbles gently. Partially cover and cook, stirring occasionally, until the chickpeas are tender, 1½ to 2 hours. Add more water if the level gets too low; you want to end up with 2 cups cooking water when the chickpeas are done. (This can be done up to several days ahead; if storing, cool, cover, and refrigerate the chickpeas with 2 cups of their cooking water. Gently rewarm over medium heat before proceeding.)

2. Coarsely chop the bread. Put it in a food processor and pulse until it is shredded, with no chunks larger than a pea but most not much smaller either. Put 6 tablespoons of the oil in a skillet over medium heat. Add the bread and a sprinkle of salt and cook, shaking the pan occasionally, until the crumbs are nicely browned, 5 to 10 minutes. Use a slotted spoon to remove the bread crumbs from the skillet; drain them on paper towels.

3. Stir the garlic into the warm chickpeas and their broth, along with a good sprinkle of salt and pepper. Top with the bread crumbs, garnish with parsley, and serve. Or store the garlicky beans without the parsley and bread crumbs, covered, in the refrigerator for up to 3 days; gently reheat and garnish right before serving.

CHICKPEAS IN THEIR OWN BROTH, CATALAN STYLE
Add a bit of wine and tomato for a slightly more sophisticated dish: After Step 1, cook 1 onion, chopped, with the garlic in 3 to 4 tablespoons olive oil, until soft. Add a splash of white wine and 1 tablespoon tomato paste, then cook for a minute or 2. Add a bay leaf and the chickpeas and continue with Step 2.

CHICKPEAS IN THEIR OWN BROTH, CUBAN STYLE
Loads of garlic and tangy lime juice: After Step 1, cook 1 bell pepper, chopped, along with 2 to 3 tablespoons minced garlic in 3 to 4 tablespoons olive oil until soft. Add 1 teaspoon ground cumin and the chickpeas and continue with Step 2. Sprinkle with lots of fresh lime juice just before serving.

NUTTY CHICKPEAS IN THEIR OWN BROTH Even more toastiness and crunch: After Step 1, pan-roast 1 cup almonds, pine nuts, hazelnuts, or chopped chestnuts in olive oil until aromatic and stir into the chickpeas right before serving.

CHICKPEAS IN THEIR OWN BROTH WITH DRIED TOMATOES The tomatoes finish reconstituting in the chickpea broth, absorbing loads of flavor in the process: Add about ½ cup chopped dried tomatoes, soaked and drained, with the garlic in Step 2 and cook until they are soft, about 10 minutes.

CHICKPEAS IN THEIR OWN BROTH WITH TAHINI A classic combination, just a different form: Add 1 to 2 tablespoons tahini along with the garlic in Step 2. Garnish with a squeeze of lemon juice before serving.

Chili non Carne

MAKES: 6 to 8 servings
TIME: 1½ to 2½ hours, largely unattended
Ⓜ Ⓥ

A straightforward and delicious chili that can be customized to your taste. Increase or decrease just about anything; add pressed tofu, tempeh, or even nuts to bulk up the texture and flavor (see variations). Serve it with lots of garnishes—always great when feeding a crew —like minced onion or scallions, hot sauce, and grated cheese, as well as rice, crackers, or tortilla chips.

Other beans you can use: dried kidney, soybeans, any pink or red bean

> 1   **pound dried pinto beans, rinsed and picked over**
> 1   **onion, unpeeled, plus 1 small onion, minced**
>   **Salt**
> 1   **cup reserved bean-cooking liquid, vegetable stock (pages 97–100), or water**
> 1   **fresh hot chile, seeded and minced, or to taste**
> 1   **tablespoon minced garlic**
> 1   **teaspoon ground cumin (or to taste)**
> 1   **teaspoon minced fresh oregano or ½ teaspoon dried**
>   **Pepper**
>   **Chopped fresh cilantro for garnish**

1. Put the beans and unpeeled onion in a large saucepan with water to cover with a large pinch salt. Bring to a boil over high heat. Turn the heat down so the beans bubble steadily but not violently and cover partially. Cook, stirring occasionally, until the beans are quite tender but still intact, 1 to 2 hours; add water if necessary.

2. Drain the beans, reserving the cooking liquid if you choose to use it. Discard the whole onion. Return the beans to the pot and add the minced onion, reserved liquid, chile, garlic, cumin, oregano, and pepper to taste. Turn the heat to medium and bring to a boil. Cover and turn the heat down to low.

3. Cook, stirring occasionally and adding more liquid if necessary, until the beans are very tender and the flavors have mellowed, about 15 minutes. Taste, adjust the seasoning, garnish with cilantro, and serve. Or let cool and store, covered, in the refrigerator for up to 3 days.

CHILI CON TOFU A great way to add heft: Put 3 table-spoons good-quality vegetable oil in a large skillet over high heat. Add ½ to 1 pound pressed firm tofu or smoked tofu (see page 483 or 482), cubed, and cook, stirring frequently, until browned. Add the tofu to the chili in Step 3.

CHILI CON TEMPEH Add a bit of earthy flavor and more texture: Put 3 tablespoons good-quality vegetable oil in a large skillet over high heat. Add 8 to 16 ounces crumbled or chopped tempeh and cook, stirring frequently, until browned. Add to the chili in Step 3.

CHILI CON NUTS Add about 1 cup chopped walnuts or other nuts in Step 3.

Espresso Black Bean Chili

MAKES: 6 to 8 servings
TIME: 1½ to 2½ hours, largely unattended
Ⓜ Ⓥ

This deep and richly flavored chili has enough caffeine to keep you awake, so bear that in mind when you serve it; use decaffeinated espresso if you or your guests are caffeine sensitive, or save it for lunch. Serve it with rice, a stack of warm tortillas, or tortilla chips, and parsley or cilantro.

Other beans you can use: Earthy-flavored beans that can stand up to the other flavors, like dried pinto, kidney, or soybeans, work best.

   3 **tablespoons good-quality vegetable oil**
   2 **onions, chopped**
   2 **tablespoons minced garlic**
   3 **cups chopped fresh tomatoes (about 1½ pounds whole; canned are fine—don't bother to drain)**
½–1 **cup freshly brewed espresso, 1–2 cups brewed coffee, or 2 tablespoons espresso powder**
   ¼ **cup dark brown sugar or 3 tablespoons molasses**
   2 **tablespoons chili powder (to make your own, see page 648)**
   1 **3-inch cinnamon stick**
   1 **pound dried black beans, rinsed and picked over**
      Salt and pepper

1. Put the oil in a large saucepan with a tight-fitting lid over medium-high heat. When it's hot, add the onions and cook, stirring occasionally, until soft, about 5 minutes. Add the garlic and cook for another minute.

2. Stir in the tomatoes, espresso, brown sugar, chili powder, cinnamon, and beans and add water to cover. Bring to a boil, then lower the heat so the liquid bubbles steadily but not violently. Cover and cook, stirring occasionally, until the beans begin to soften, 30 to 40 minutes. Add a good pinch salt and pepper.

3. Continue cooking until the beans are tender, anywhere from another 45 minutes to 1½ hours. Discard the cinnamon stick. Taste and adjust the seasoning, adding more sugar, salt, or pepper, and serve. Or let cool and store, covered, in the refrigerator for up to 3 days.

SMOKED-TEA CHILI The rich and smoky flavor of Lapsang Souchong—a smoked black tea—is fantastic in this chili with other Chinese flavors: Omit the tomatoes. Add 1 tablespoon minced fresh ginger with the garlic in Step 1. Replace the espresso with 5 to 6 cups freshly brewed Lapsang Souchong tea or any smoked black tea; replace the chili powder with red chile flakes to taste and the cinnamon with 1 teaspoon Sichuan peppercorns; and replace the black beans with dried soybeans. Add water to cover the beans if necessary and proceed with the recipe.

CHOCOLATE CHILI Closer to a deeply flavored Oaxacan mole: Replace the espresso with ½ cup chopped Mexican chocolate or ¼ cup chopped bittersweet chocolate (if you want to keep this vegan, check the label to make sure the chocolate you're using doesn't include milk solids—or lecithin, which can be derived from eggs). Decrease the sugar by half if you're using Mexican chocolate.

Black Soybeans with Soy Sauce

MAKES: At least 4 servings
TIME: 1½ to 2 hours, largely unattended
Ⓜ Ⓞ

A popular side dish in Korea and Japan, this is intensely flavored and delicious, with an unusual and wonderfully firm texture.

8	ounces (1 cup) dried black soybeans or black beans, rinsed and picked over
¼	cup soy sauce
¼	cup sugar (or more to taste)
2	tablespoons mirin or a little more sugar (or substitute 1 tablespoon each honey and water)
2	tablespoons sesame oil
1	tablespoon sesame seeds

1. Put the beans in a medium saucepan with water to cover and bring to a boil over medium-high heat. Partially cover and adjust the heat so the mixture simmers steadily. Cook, stirring occasionally, until the beans are nearly tender and most but not all of the water has evaporated, at least an hour and probably more.
2. Stir in the soy sauce, sugar, and mirin and raise the heat a bit. Continue to cook, stirring frequently, until the beans are glazed and still firm, not quite as tender

as you're used to. Leave them quite moist; the soy sauce will burn if the mixture dries out. Stir in the sesame oil.
3. You can serve the beans hot, at room temperature, or chilled. Just before serving, toast the sesame seeds in a small dry skillet over medium heat, shaking the pan frequently until the seeds color slightly. Sprinkle the beans with the seeds and serve.

Hoppin' John with Smoked Tofu

MAKES: 6 to 8 servings
TIME: About 2½ hours, largely unattended
Ⓜ Ⓥ

Smoked tofu has a slightly dense, chewy texture and strong smoky flavor that makes an excellent substitute for the smoked ham hock traditional to hoppin' John; cooking the tofu whole with the beans, then cutting it up, keeps it moist.

Because hoppin' John is traditionally served with stewed greens for good luck on New Year's Day, I suggest eating this with Boiled or Steamed Greens (page 153) or Sea Slaw (page 55). Add a wedge of Corn Bread (page 580) and you're set.

Other beans you can use: dried pigeon peas

1½	cups dried black-eyed peas, rinsed and picked over
8	cups vegetable stock (pages 97–100) or water
1	14- to 16-ounce package smoked tofu (to make your own, see page 486)
2	medium onions, minced
2	tablespoons minced garlic
1½	cups long-grain white rice
	Salt and pepper
	Tabasco sauce (optional)

1. Put the peas, stock, tofu, onions, and garlic in a large pot with a tight-fitting lid. Bring to a boil, then lower the heat so the liquid bubbles steadily but not violently. Cook, stirring occasionally, until the peas are tender but not mushy, 1 to 2 hours. (You can make the peas

Hoppin' John
with Smoked Tofu
(page 457)

ahead to this point. Cool, cover, and refrigerate for up to 2 days. Reheat gently before proceeding.)

2. When the peas are ready, make sure you have about 3 cups liquid; if you have less, add water to make 3 cups; if you have more, spoon some out. Stir in the rice, sprinkle with salt and pepper, and cover. Reduce the heat to low and cook undisturbed until the rice is tender, about 20 minutes.

3. Remove the lid; if any liquid remains, turn the heat to high for a minute or 2 to boil it off. Remove the tofu, cut it into cubes, and return it to the pot. Use a fork to gently fluff the rice, peas, and tofu. Add a dash or 2 of Tabasco if you like, taste, and adjust the seasoning. Put the lid back on and let the dish rest for at least 5 minutes and up to 15 before serving.

ONE-POT BEAN GUMBO More like a casserole, with the rice and peas all together: When you add the rice in Step 2, stir in 1½ cups chopped tomatoes (canned are fine; don't bother to drain) and 1 cup chopped fresh or thawed frozen okra. When you fluff the rice in Step 3, stir in ½ cup minced red bell pepper.

BLACK-EYED PEAS WITH SMOKED TOFU AND MUSHROOMS Extra earthiness and chew: While the peas are cooking, make 1 recipe Sautéed Mushrooms (page 217). When you fluff the rice in Step 3, stir in the mushrooms along with ½ cup chopped fresh parsley if you like.

BLACK-EYED PEAS WITH SLICED SMOKED TOFU Here the tofu shares the plate with the peas and rice: In Step 3, instead of cubing the tofu and adding it back, remove it and keep warm. When you're ready to serve, thinly slice the tofu and serve it alongside the peas and rice.

PUERTO RICAN–STYLE BEANS AND RICE Substitute pigeon peas for the black-eyed peas. You can omit the tofu, if you prefer. When the peas are tender, stir in 2 tablespoons tomato paste, 1 teaspoon dried oregano, and ½ cup chopped pitted black olives, then stir in the rice. Proceed with the recipe.

PURÉED OR MASHED BEANS

I can't tell you how many times a year I take leftover beans and purée them with olive oil and herbs to make a dip, but it's quite a few. Yet that's only one of the possibilities these dishes present. In a way, they showcase legumes at their most luxurious—creamy, rich, and satisfying. In almost all of the recipes that follow you can use canned beans in a pinch, and for the most part the difference will be minimal.

White Bean Purée

MAKES: 4 servings
TIME: 10 minutes with cooked beans
F M V

One of the most useful bean preparations there is, this purée can serve as a side dish, sauce, spread, or dip. And it is great as an appetizer, served with bread or pita chips and carrot and celery sticks or other sliced vegetables. Best of all, it can be whipped up in no time.

Use it as a spread for Bruschetta (page 623), as a side dish with Seitan and Mushroom Loaf (page 509) or Fast Nut Burgers (page 507), or pool it under Grilled Mushrooms (page 220). For a smoother, richer, more luxurious (but nonvegan) purée, add ¼ cup or so cream to the main recipe or to any of the first three variations and use butter instead of oil.

Other beans you can use: nearly any cooked bean, like cannellini, great Northern, fava, lima, chickpeas, pinto, kidney, appaloosa, anasazi, soybeans, black; or lightly cooked shell beans like fava, edamame, lima

> 3 cups cooked or canned navy or other white beans, drained but still moist, liquid reserved
> Up to 1 cup bean-cooking liquid, vegetable stock (pages 97–100), or water
> 3 tablespoons olive oil
> Salt and pepper
> Chopped fresh parsley for garnish

1. Purée the beans by putting them through a food mill or using a food processor or blender; add as much liquid as you need to make a smooth but not watery purée.
2. Put the purée and oil in a microwave-safe dish or medium nonstick saucepan and stir to mix well. Heat gently until the beans are hot; season with salt and pepper.
3. Garnish with parsley. Serve hot as a side dish or warm or at room temperature as a dip or spread.

BEAN PURÉE WITH ROASTED GARLIC Many kinds of beans work beautifully with roasted garlic: Any white bean, favas, chickpeas, pinto, black-eyed peas, and soybeans are all great. Add 15 to 20 cloves Roasted Garlic (page 205) and 1 teaspoon fresh thyme leaves in Step 1.

GARLICKY PURÉED BEANS Add 1 tablespoon or more minced garlic and a teaspoon fresh rosemary leaves in Step 1. A little grated lemon zest is a nice addition as well—start with 1 teaspoon or so.

CHEESY PURÉED BEANS Stir in ¼ cup finely grated vegan or regular Parmesan, pecorino, fontina, or Gouda in Step 2. Heat until melted, stirring frequently, then proceed with the recipe.

WHITE BEAN AND CELERY ROOT OR PARSNIP PURÉE Even more substantial, and a great substitute for mashed potatoes: Add 1 cup cooked chopped celery root or parsnips in Step 1.

CHICKPEA AND EGGPLANT PURÉE Use chickpeas instead of white beans. Pierce 1 medium eggplant several times with a skewer or small knife. Grill or roast it in a 500°F oven until soft and blackened on all sides, 20 to 30 minutes. Let it cool, then split the skin, scoop out the flesh, and purée it with the beans in Step 1. Add about 3 tablespoons fresh lemon juice (to taste) in Step 3. You can also stir in a tablespoon of tahini, if you like.

LIMA BEAN PURÉE WITH FENNEL AND ORANGE JUICE A terrific spread for Bruschetta (page 623): Use lima beans. Cook 1 medium fennel bulb, trimmed and sliced, in 2 tablespoons olive oil over medium heat until very soft. Add ½ cup fresh orange juice and cook until the liquid is nearly evaporated. Purée the fennel mixture with the beans in Step 1.

BLACK BEAN PURÉE WITH CHIPOTLES Spicy and smoky; perfect with Naked Tamale with Chile-Cheese Filling (page 394) or Chiles Rellenos (page 229): Use black beans. Purée 1 to 2 tablespoons chopped canned chipotle chiles in adobo sauce (to taste) with the beans in Step 1. Proceed with the recipe and garnish with cilantro instead of parsley.

Refried Beans

MAKES: 4 servings
TIME: 20 minutes with cooked beans
F V

Refried beans can be more than just a side dish. Try them as a bed for fried eggs (page 524) or thinned with a little Salsa Roja (page 662) for a hearty enchilada or tamale sauce. Puréed, they make an excellent base for a bean dip (page 462).

For more assertive seasoning, try adding a couple sprigs of epazote (fresh or dried), a bay leaf or 2, and some garlic to the pot as the beans simmer.

> ¼ **cup good-quality vegetable oil**
> 1 **cup chopped onion**
> 1 **tablespoon ground cumin, plus more if desired**
> 3 **cups cooked pinto, red, or black beans, drained but still moist**
> **Salt and pepper**
> ¼ **teaspoon cayenne, plus more if desired**

1. Put the oil in a large skillet over medium heat. When it's hot, add the onion and cook, stirring, until golden brown, 10 to 12 minutes.
2. Add the cumin and cook, stirring, for 1 minute more. Add the beans and mash with a large fork or potato masher. Continue to cook, mashing and stirring, until

the beans are more or less broken up (some remaining chunks are fine).

3. Sprinkle with salt and pepper and add the cayenne and more cumin if you like. Taste, adjust the seasoning, and serve.

CREAMIER REFRIED BEANS For a more velvety texture, use coconut oil instead of vegetable oil.

8 Flavorings for Refried Beans

1. Minced fresh chile, like jalapeño or Thai; add with the cumin

2. Ground ancho or chipotle chile powder; add instead of the cayenne

3. Minced fresh ginger or garlic; add with the cumin

4. Chopped Quickest Pickled Vegetables (page 89); stir in at the end

5. Chopped seeded tomatoes; stir in after mashing the beans and let cook for a minute or 2

6. Chopped fresh cilantro; stir in at the end

7. Chopped black olives; stir in at the end

8. Grated cheddar, Monterey Jack, or Chihuahua cheese, or crumbled queso fresco; sprinkle over the beans before serving

Refried Bean Dip

MAKES: At least 8 servings
TIME: 10 minutes with cooked beans
F **M** **V**

A basic bean dip that's great with tortilla chips, though you could serve it with almost anything: raw sliced vegetables; grilled, broiled, or fried tofu cubes; pita, toast, or crackers—you name it.

Use 3 cups cooked pinto or other beans if you don't have refried beans on hand, but you may want to up the minced chiles and also add ground cumin to taste.

> 1 recipe Refried Beans (page 460)
> Up to 1 cup bean-cooking liquid, vegetable stock (pages 97–100), or water
> ½ cup minced red bell pepper

> ½ cup minced onion
> ½ cup drained diced tomatoes (optional)
> About 1 tablespoon minced fresh chile (like jalapeño or Thai), or cayenne or hot sauce
> 1 teaspoon red wine vinegar or other vinegar
> Salt and pepper

1. Put all but 1 cup of the beans in a food processor or blender and purée until smooth. Add bean-cooking liquid or stock as needed to get the purée going.

2. If needed, lightly mash the remaining beans by hand, using a fork or potato masher; combine with the puréed beans. Stir in the bell pepper, onion, tomatoes if you're using, the chile, and vinegar. Sprinkle with salt and pepper. Taste and adjust the seasonings; thin with more liquid if necessary and serve. Or cover and refrigerate for up to 2 days; bring to room temperature or reheat gently before serving.

FAST BEAN DIP Save a few minutes and some chopping by using prepared salsa: Substitute 1½ cups Fresh Tomato Salsa (page 660) or Fresh Tomatillo Salsa (page 660) for the bell pepper, onion, tomatoes, chile, and vinegar.

CREAMY BEAN DIP Use tofu to keep it vegan, sour cream for a richer dip, or yogurt for a tangy dip: Substitute silken tofu, sour cream, or yogurt for the bean-cooking liquid or stock.

CHEESY BEAN DIP Choose an easy-melting cheese (vegan or regular): After Step 1, gently heat the beans over low heat; stir in about ¾ cup grated cheese, like Cotija, cheddar, or Monterey Jack, until melted. Proceed with the recipe and serve hot or warm.

LAYERED BEAN DIP It may be retro but it's still crazy good: In a serving dish, alternate layers of Refried Bean Dip, grated Monterey Jack or Cheddar, Guacamole (page 174), sour cream, and Fresh Tomato Salsa (page 660). Top with a generous sprinkle of chopped cilantro.

Hummus

MAKES: 4 to 6 servings
TIME: 15 minutes with cooked chickpeas

F M V

Pre-made hummus has become a supermarket standard and, not to put too fine a point on it, it stinks compared to the homemade version of this Middle Eastern classic, which combines the distinctive flavor of chickpeas with the nuttiness of tahini. Make it as nutty, garlicky, lemony, or spiced as you like—I love it with lots of lemon juice. It's also great with a good sprinkling of za'atar (to make your own, see page 652).

If you're serving this as a dip, you may need to add extra chickpea-cooking liquid or water to thin it adequately so that items can be dipped in it. Keep it thick to use as a spread.

2 cups cooked or canned chickpeas, drained but still moist, liquid reserved
½ cup tahini, or more to taste (to make your own, see page 305)
¼ cup olive oil, plus more for garnish
2 cloves garlic, peeled, or to taste
Juice of 1 lemon, plus more as needed
Salt and pepper
1 tablespoon ground cumin or paprika, or to taste, plus more for garnish
Chopped fresh parsley for garnish

6 More Bean Dip Variations

The technique remains the same as in the Refried Bean Dip recipe. Use bean-cooking liquid, stock, or water to thin the purée. The flavorings, like the roasted red peppers or caramelized onions, can be puréed with the beans if you like.

BEANS (3 CUPS COOKED AND DRAINED)	FLAVORINGS	SEASONINGS
Black beans	1½ cups chopped roasted red peppers (page 228) or soaked and drained dried tomatoes, 2 teaspoons minced garlic	1 tablespoon ground coriander
Pink beans	1 cup chopped Caramelized Onions (page 222), ½ cup diced tomatoes	2 teaspoons smoked paprika (pimentón)
Red lentils or yellow split peas (no need to drain)	1 tablespoon minced fresh ginger, 1 tablespoon minced garlic, 1 cup yogurt	1 or 2 tablespoons chaat masala, ¼ cup chopped fresh cilantro
Lima beans	½ cup toasted pine nuts, ½ cup grated Parmesan cheese, 2 teaspoons minced garlic	1 cup chopped fresh basil
Soybeans	½ cup white or yellow miso, ½ cup chopped scallions, 1 tablespoon minced fresh ginger	2 tablespoons rice vinegar
Fava beans	½ cup fruity extra virgin olive oil, 1 tablespoon minced garlic	2 teaspoons grated lemon zest, 2 tablespoons fresh lemon juice, lots of black pepper

Clockwise from top: Beet Hummus (opposite), Hummus (page 463), Edamame Hummus (opposite)

1. Put the chickpeas, tahini, oil, garlic, and lemon juice in a food processor, sprinkle with salt and pepper, and begin to process; add chickpea-cooking liquid or water as needed to allow the machine to produce a smooth purée.

2. Taste and adjust the seasoning, adding more salt, pepper, tahini, garlic, or lemon juice as desired. Serve, drizzled with oil and sprinkled with the cumin and some parsley.

EDAMAME HUMMUS Beautiful green and full of flavor: Substitute cooked edamame for the chickpeas. Omit the cumin or paprika. Substitute cilantro for the parsley if you like.

LIMA HUMMUS Use fresh lima beans if you have them, but frozen are good too: Substitute cooked lima beans for the chickpeas; lime juice for the lemon; and cilantro for the parsley.

BEET HUMMUS Stunningly beautiful: Wrap a small beet in foil and roast in a 400°F oven until very tender, 45 to 50 minutes. When cool enough to handle, rub the skin off with a paper towel. Cut into a couple of pieces and purée with the chickpeas in Step 1.

SRIRACHA CARROT HUMMUS Sweet and hot: Add 1 medium carrot, grated, to the purée. Process just to combine or reduce it to a smooth purée if you prefer. Omit the cumin or paprika and stir in 1 tablespoon sriracha (or to taste) in Step 2.

ROASTED RED PEPPER HUMMUS Roast 1 or 2 red bell peppers (see page 228) and remove the skin, stems, and seeds. Add to the chickpeas in Step 1.

BLACK BEAN HUMMUS Substitute black beans for the chickpeas and lime juice for the lemon juice. Reduce the tahini to ¼ cup. Add ½ cup lightly packed fresh cilantro leaves before puréeing in Step 1. Garnish with chopped cilantro.

Chickpea Fondue

MAKES: 6 to 8 servings
TIME: 20 minutes with cooked chickpeas
F **M** **V**

Throughout the Mediterranean, chickpeas are puréed to make rich sauces, and that's the idea behind this wonderful spin on fondue. This is one place you want to definitely cook your own chickpeas: The fondue will showcase that flavor, combined with that of roasted garlic. The texture is silky smooth—sort of like a warm, smooth hummus, perfect for dipping or as a sauce for everything from pasta or rice to grilled or roasted vegetables.

To serve it traditional fondue style, surround it with things for dipping: cherry tomatoes; cauliflower florets; slices of cucumber and bell pepper; cubes of feta, kasseri, havarti, or fried tofu (page 486); boiled or roasted potato chunks or fingerlings; cubes or slices of roasted or grilled eggplant; or bits of pita or crusty bread.

Other beans you can use: cooked cannellini, great Northern, navy, cranberry

3	**cups cooked chickpeas, drained**
3	**to 4 cups chickpea-cooking liquid**
20	**cloves Roasted Garlic (page 205) or 2 raw cloves (or to taste)**
3	**tablespoons olive oil**
	Salt and pepper
1	**cup vegetable stock (pages 97–100) or water (optional)**
3	**tablespoons fresh lemon juice**
	Chopped fresh parsley for garnish

1. Put the chickpeas with 3 cups of their cooking liquid in a blender and add the garlic and oil; season with the salt and pepper. Let the machine run for a minute or 2, until the purée is very smooth, almost light and fluffy. Add more cooking liquid, stock, or water until the consistency is like a smooth dip or thick soup. Taste and adjust the seasoning, adding more salt, pepper, or garlic as needed.

2. Transfer the purée to a pot over medium heat; heat through while stirring constantly. Stir in the lemon juice. Taste and adjust the seasoning again, adding more salt, pepper, or lemon juice as needed. Serve warm, garnished with parsley.

HUMMUS FONDUE The same delicious sesame flavor: Use the raw garlic instead of roasted. In Step 2 add about 2 teaspoons ground cumin and 2 to 3 tablespoons tahini, to taste.

CHEESY CHICKPEA FONDUE Use a nutty-flavored cheese that melts easily: In Step 2, before heating add ½ cup or more grated cheese, like Parmesan, Gruyère, raclette, Comté, Emmental, or fontina. Or try a blue cheese, like Maytag, Roquefort, or Gorgonzola. Proceed with the recipe, heating the mixture until the cheese is fully melted.

5 Additions to Chickpea Fondue

Stir in any of these just before serving, either alone or in combination.

1. Up to ¼ cup of any herb pesto, herb paste, or sauce, like Pesto (page 634) or Parsley "Pesto" (page 638); omit the garlic if you like

2. A tablespoon or so of any chile paste (pages 664 to 666)

3. A large pinch crumbled saffron threads, steeped in a couple of tablespoons hot water for 10 minutes before adding

4. Up to ¼ cup chopped nuts, like walnuts, almonds, or pistachios

5. A tablespoon or so of any curry powder or similar spice blend (see pages 648 to 652 for a selection)

Mashed Favas

Ful Medames
MAKES: 4 servings
TIME: About 1 hour
Ⓜ Ⓥ

A staple in Egypt and elsewhere, and a true classic, this is a perfect use for favas and a great mashed potato substitute, with lots of possibilities; see the list, right.

I love it for breakfast, with a little raw onion and loads of lemon.

Other beans you can use: dried limas, cranberry

8	ounces (1 cup) dried peeled and split fava beans, rinsed and picked over
1	onion, chopped
1	carrot, chopped
1	celery stalk, chopped
	Salt and pepper
⅓	cup olive oil for serving
2	tablespoons fresh lemon juice for serving

1. Put the beans in a medium saucepan with water to cover. Bring to a boil over high heat, then turn the heat down so the liquid simmers steadily but not violently. Cover partially. When the beans begin to soften, after about 30 minutes, add the onion, carrot, celery, and a good pinch salt and pepper. Continue to cook, stirring occasionally, until the beans are very soft, about 1 hour; add water if necessary.

2. When the beans are done, drain them. Mash the beans and vegetables with a potato masher or wooden spoon, or put them through a ricer or food mill. Adjust the seasoning, then drizzle with the oil and lemon juice and serve.

10 Additions to Mashed Favas

Many of these can be used in combination; lemon zest, shallots, and lemon juice, drizzled with olive oil and sprinkled with parsley, for example, are super.

1. Chopped fresh herbs like parsley, basil, cilantro, chives, tarragon, chervil, dill, or mint

2. Grated lemon zest

3. Sautéed or Roasted Garlic (page 205)

4. Chopped fresh tomatoes

5. Crumbled feta cheese

6. Roasted or boiled potato

7. Chopped steamed broccoli

8. Chopped steamed or roasted cauliflower

9. Cooked and chopped greens like dandelion, escarole, collards, kale, spinach, mustard, or broccoli raab

10. Chopped shallot or mild onion

BAKED BEANS

The dry heat of an oven works magic on beans. When beans are baked covered, as in Baked Beans, you get plump, creamy, individual beans coated in a rich sauce. Bake uncovered, as in Baked Pinto Beans, Enchilada Style (page 469), and you wind up with crunchy crust surrounding tender beans and vegetables; add cheese and you get yet another layer of flavor and texture.

Many of these recipes can be prepared and assembled in their baking dish in advance; cover well with plastic or foil and refrigerate until you're ready, then let them come to room temperature before baking.

Baked Beans

MAKES: 6 to 8 servings
TIME: About 3 hours, largely unattended
Ⓜ Ⓥ

It's tough to find a vegetarian version of baked beans—traditionally made with pork—that captures the dish's creamy texture and delicate balance of sweet and smoky flavors. Enter kelp, also known as kombu (see page 244), the sea green used to make dashi. Kelp contains a natural acid that tenderizes the beans as the seaweed itself melts away, leaving behind a luxurious sauce with complex flavor. If you're looking for extra texture and flavor, try the hearty variation with dulse stirred in at the last minute.

Once you cook the onions and put everything in the pot—which takes about 10 minutes, tops—you can walk away for 2 hours. If you don't have time to soak the beans first (or forgot), the beans will probably take another hour in the oven.

Serve bowls of baked beans with Buttermilk Biscuits (page 587) and Marinated Garden Vegetables (page 91) on the side.

Other beans you can use: dried pinto, pink, great Northern, black, kidney

¼ cup good-quality vegetable oil
2 onions, chopped

¼ cup tomato paste
1 5-inch piece kombu
1 pound dried navy, pea, or other white beans, rinsed and picked over
½ cup molasses (or more to taste)
2 teaspoons dry mustard or 2 tablespoons prepared mustard (or more to taste)
Salt and pepper

1. Heat the oven to 300°F. Put the oil in a large oven-proof pot or casserole with a tight-fitting lid over medium-high heat. When it's hot, add the onions and cook, stirring frequently, until soft and golden, 7 to 8 minutes. Add the tomato paste and stir until deeply colored, another minute or so. Stir in 6 cups water, scraping up any browned bits from the bottom of the pot.
2. Add the kombu, beans, molasses, and mustard. Cover and bake for 2 hours. Stir, add water if needed to keep the beans covered, cover again, and bake until the beans are completely tender, another 30 minutes or more.
3. Sprinkle with salt and pepper, stir well to help break up the kombu, then taste and add more molasses or mustard if you like; also a bit more water if the pot is getting dry. Turn the oven up to 400°F. Return the pot to the oven, uncovered, and bake until the beans are creamy and the liquid has thickened, another 30 minutes or so. Taste, adjust the seasoning, and serve. Or cool, cover, and refrigerate for up to 3 days; reheat gently.

BUTTERY BAKED BEANS Not vegan or even traditional, but rich and luxurious: Instead of using vegetable oil in Step 1, cook the onions in 4 tablespoons (½ stick) butter.

MAPLE–APPLE BUTTER BAKED BEANS Lighter in color and flavor: Replace the tomato paste with ½ cup apple butter and replace the molasses with maple syrup.

HEARTIER BAKED BEANS Closer to bacon-baked beans: Add ½ cup shredded dried dulse (see page 244) after uncovering the pot in Step 3. Make sure there is enough water to cover.

Baked Brazilian
Black Beans

BAKED BEANS WITH A CRACKER CRUMB CRUST After uncovering the beans and raising the oven temperature in Step 3, sprinkle the top of the beans with about 1½ cups crumbled soda or saltine crackers. Return the pot to the oven and cook until the crust is golden, 20 to 30 minutes, then serve.

CURRIED BAKED BEANS Coconut milk adds incredible creaminess: Omit the tomato paste and molasses. After you cook the onions in Step 1, stir in 2 tablespoons curry powder. Reduce the amount of water to 4 cups in Step 1 and add 2 cups coconut milk.

CHIPOTLE BAKED BEANS In Step 2, stir in 2 minced canned chipotle chiles in adobo sauce, or to taste along with the kombu.

Baked Brazilian Black Beans

MAKES: 4 servings
TIME: About 1 hour with cooked beans, largely unattended
Ⓜ Ⓥ

A tropical party dish, one you can make in large quantities ahead of time; it will taste even better the next day. Serve with lots of rice, warm tortillas, and Spicy No-Mayo Coleslaw (page 42), Fresh Tomato Salsa (page 660), or Radish Salsa (page 662).

Other beans you can use: dried black-eyed peas, pinto, kidney, or any medium-size heirloom bean like appaloosa or anasazi

- 2 tablespoons olive oil
- 1 onion, chopped
  About 2 tablespoons minced fresh chile (like jalapeño or Thai), or red chile flakes or cayenne
- 1 tablespoon minced fresh ginger
- 1½ cups chopped fresh tomatoes (about 12 ounces; canned are fine; don't drain)
- 1 large yellow-black plantain or ripe banana, peeled and cut into chunks
- 3 cups cooked or canned black beans, drained but still moist

- 1 cup bean-cooking liquid or water
- 1 tablespoon fresh thyme leaves
  Salt and pepper

1. Heat the oven to 350°F. Put the oil in a skillet over medium-high heat. When it's hot, add the onion and cook, stirring occasionally, until soft, about 5 minutes. Add the chile and ginger and cook for another minute, stirring.
2. Transfer the onion mixture, along with the tomatoes and plantain, to a food processor or blender and purée.
3. Combine the tomato mixture with the beans, bean-cooking liquid, and thyme in an ovenproof dish. Taste and add salt and pepper, then cover and bake until bubbling, about 40 minutes. Serve hot. Or cool and store, covered, in the refrigerator for up to 3 days.

BAKED CURRIED BLACK BEANS Replace the thyme with a couple of fresh or dried curry leaves, adding them with the chile in Step 1. Add 1 tablespoon curry powder before baking in Step 3.

SMOKY BAKED BLACK BEANS Subtly smoky and delicious: Substitute garlic for the ginger, using more if you like. Add 1 to 2 tablespoons smoked Spanish paprika (pimentón) and ½ cup cubed smoked tofu before baking in Step 3.

BRAZILIAN BLACK BEANS AND RICE Simple and more substantial: Stir in 1½ cups long-grain rice and 1 cup vegetable stock (pages 97 to 100) or water in Step 3; bake until the rice is tender, which will take about the same amount of time.

Baked Pinto Beans, Enchilada Style

MAKES: 6 servings
TIME: 40 to 60 minutes with cooked beans
Ⓜ

This dish is dead easy (especially if the beans and salsa have been made ahead) and versatile. Serve with hot tortillas, shredded cabbage, hot sauce, sour cream, and lime wedges—in other words, the works.

Other beans you can use: cooked black, kidney, or any red or pink heirloom bean like appaloosa, cranberry, or anasazi

4 tablespoons extra virgin olive oil
1 recipe Salsa Roja or Cooked Tomatillo Salsa (page 662 or 663, either chunky or puréed as in the variations), warmed
4 cups cooked or canned pinto or pink beans, drained but still moist
  Salt and pepper
1 cup cubed Monterey Jack or Chihuahua cheese
1 cup crushed tortilla chips
½ cup crumbled queso fresco
½ cup chopped fresh cilantro for garnish

1. Heat the oven to 400°F. Use a tablespoon or so of the olive oil to grease a 2-quart soufflé or gratin dish or a 9 × 13-inch baking dish.

2. Spread the salsa over the bottom of the dish and spoon the beans on top. Sprinkle lightly with salt and pepper. Spread the cheese cubes around evenly, pressing them into the beans a bit. Sprinkle with the tortilla crumbs, then the queso fresco, and drizzle with the remaining oil.

3. Bake until the cheese has melted, the sauce is bubbly, and the tortilla chips are browned, 20 to 30 minutes, depending on the size of the baking dish. Remove from the oven, sprinkle with the cilantro and more pepper if you like, and serve.

BAKED PINTO BEANS AND SWEET POTATOES, ENCHI-LADA STYLE Heartier and, well, sweeter: Peel 2 large sweet potatoes and cut them into 1-inch cubes. In Step 2, spread them over the salsa, cover the baking dish with foil, and bake without the beans and other ingredients for 15 minutes. Remove the foil, add the beans and other ingredients, and proceed with the recipe.

BAKED BLACK BEANS AND CORN, ENCHILADA STYLE
Use black beans. Stir 1 cup corn kernels (frozen are fine; don't bother to thaw them) into the beans before adding them to the dish.

FRIED BEANS, BEAN FRITTERS, CROQUETTES, CAKES, AND FRIES

If you eat a lot of beans, variety becomes increasingly important. The recipes in this section turn ordinary legumes into beloved snacks, accompaniments, and main dishes. The transformation is so complete that you might not even recognize the beans anymore, but the results are usually crisp, always tasty, and super-easy, because you usually start with cooked (or canned) beans.

Fried Fava Beans
MAKES: 4 servings
TIME: About 25 minutes, plus overnight to soak the beans
V

I absolutely love the crisp-fried fava beans you can buy as a snack in Spain, Portugal, and Italy. You can find them occasionally on store shelves in this country, but why wait when they are so easy to make yourself? Be warned: These are addictive and won't last till the end of the day.

1 cup dried split fava beans, picked over and soaked in generous water to cover overnight
  Good-quality vegetable oil
  Salt
  Ground chipotle chile powder or smoked paprika (optional)

1. Put the beans in a large bowl, cover with water by 3 to 4 inches, and soak overnight, checking once or twice to see if you need to add more water to keep the

beans submerged. Drain the beans well and pat dry with a kitchen towel or put them in a salad spinner. You don't need to go crazy getting them dry.

2. Pour oil to a depth of at least 2 inches in a large, deep pot. More is better; the narrower the pot, the less oil you need, but the more oil you use, the more beans you can cook at the same time. Turn the heat to medium-high and heat the oil to about 350°F; a single fava bean should sizzle immediately when you drop it in.

3. When the oil is hot, add half the fava beans and cook until golden brown, 8 to 10 minutes, stirring them every minute or so for even cooking and to keep them off the bottom of the pot. Remove from the oil (use a spider or other strainer) and drain on paper towels. Fry the remaining favas in the same way.

4. While they are still warm, sprinkle the beans with salt (I like to salt them pretty generously) and chile powder if you're using it. Enjoy warm or at room temperature. If there are any left over, store in an airtight container at room temperature, though they are best eaten the day they are fried.

SOY NUTS Here we switch up the technique, baking instead of frying to get the crunch: Substitute dried soybeans for the fava beans. Soak, drain, and dry the beans as directed, then toss with 2 tablespoons olive oil or good-quality vegetable oil and some salt and spread in a single layer on a baking sheet. Roast in a 300°F oven, shaking the pan occasionally, until the soybeans are golden brown and crunchy, 1 to 1½ hours. (The lower oven temperature keeps the beans from getting too brown before they develop good crispness.) These will keep in an airtight container for several days.

SHORTCUT ROASTED CHICKPEAS WITH ROSEMARY AND LEMON ZEST Substitute 2 cups cooked or canned chickpeas for the dried favas. Drain and pat dry. Toss with 3 tablespoons olive oil or good-quality vegetable oil and some salt and spread in a single layer on a baking sheet. Roast in a 400°F oven, shaking the pan occasionally, until the chickpeas are brown and crisp, 20 to 30 minutes. After they come out of the oven, toss with 1 tablespoon chopped fresh rosemary, the grated zest of 1 lemon, and more salt if necessary. Best enjoyed the day they are made.

WASABI EDAMAME Substitute a 16-ounce package frozen edamame for the fava beans. Thaw and pat dry. Toss with 2 tablespoons sesame oil. Mix 1 tablespoon wasabi powder into ½ teaspoon salt in a medium bowl, add the edamame, and toss the mixture to evenly coat. Spread the edamame in a single layer on a baking sheet. Roast in a 350°F oven, shaking the pan occasionally, until they are brown and crispy, 45 to 60 minutes. Best enjoyed the day they are made.

Falafel

MAKES: 6 to 8 servings
TIME: 1 hour, plus 24 hours to soak the beans
Ⓜ Ⓥ

One of the things that makes falafel different from other bean fritters is that it's made from uncooked beans. It's best when the beans are soaked for a full day in plenty of water; the result is a wonderfully textured and moist interior with a crisp, browned exterior. The spices and aromatics add to the fabulous bean flavor, and it wouldn't be unheard of to double or even triple the amount of garlic if you like. Serve falafel in pita with lettuce, tomatoes, cucumbers, and other raw vegetables; with a green salad; or on their own, but always with Tahini Sauce (page 306) or any yogurt sauce (page 673); some Harissa (page 665) or other chile paste (page 664) is great also.

Other beans you can use: dried lima; also see the variations

1¾ cups dried chickpeas or 1 cup dried chickpeas and ¾ cup dried split fava beans, rinsed and picked over

1 cup chopped fresh parsley or cilantro

2 cloves garlic, lightly crushed

1   small onion, quartered
1   tablespoon fresh lemon juice
1   tablespoon ground cumin
1   teaspoon ground coriander
    About 1 scant teaspoon cayenne or
    2 teaspoons mild chile powder
1   teaspoon salt
½   teaspoon pepper
½   teaspoon baking soda
    Good-quality vegetable oil for frying

1. Put the beans in a large bowl and cover with water by 3 to 4 inches. (They will triple in volume as they soak.) Soak the beans for 24 hours, checking once or twice to see if you need to add more water to keep the beans submerged.

2. Drain the beans well and transfer to a food processor with the parsley, garlic, onion, lemon juice, cumin, coriander, cayenne, salt, pepper, and baking soda. Pulse until almost smooth, scraping down the side of the bowl as necessary. Add one or 2 tablespoons water if necessary to allow the machine to do its work, but keep the mixture as dry as possible. Taste and adjust the seasoning, adding more salt, pepper, cayenne, or lemon juice as needed.

3. Pour oil to a depth of at least 2 inches in a large, deep pot. More is better; the narrower the pot, the less oil you need, but the more oil you use, the more patties you can cook at the same time. Turn the heat to medium-high and heat the oil to about 350°F; a pinch of the batter should sizzle immediately.

4. Scoop out heaping tablespoons of the batter and shape into balls or small patties. Fry in batches, without crowding, until nicely browned, turning as necessary; total cooking time will be less than 5 minutes. Use a slotted spoon to transfer to paper towels to drain (they can be kept warm in a low oven, if you like, until they are all cooked). Serve hot or at room temperature. Store leftovers in an airtight container in the refrigerator; reheat in a 350°F oven until hot and crisp, about 15 minutes.

SESAME FALAFEL I love this flavor combination: In Step 2, add ¼ cup sesame seeds and 3 tablespoons tahini.

FALAFEL WITH ZA'ATAR Tang from the sumac, nuttiness from the sesame seeds: Use parsley and add ¼ cup Za'atar (page 652) in Step 2.

NUTTY FALAFEL Lots of good texture from the chopped nuts: Replace ½ cup of the beans with walnuts, almonds, peanuts, or hazelnuts (don't soak the nuts). Omit the garlic, cumin, and cayenne. Use parsley, or substitute 1 tablespoon or so fresh thyme leaves for the herb.

MUNG BEAN FRITTERS, ASIAN STYLE Replace the beans with peeled and split mung beans (moong dal; see page 432); soak for 2 to 3 hours. Replace the onion with ¼ cup chopped scallions, the lemon juice with rice vinegar, the coriander with cracked Sichuan peppercorns, and the cumin with minced fresh ginger. Omit the cayenne. Proceed with the recipe. Serve with a dipping sauce made from equal parts soy sauce and rice vinegar or with Korean-Style Soy and Sesame Dipping Sauce and Marinade (page 656).

BLACK-EYED PEA FRITTERS Street food in West Africa and totally addictive: Replace the beans with black-eyed peas, the onion with ½ cup chopped scallions, the coriander with red chile flakes, and the cumin with minced fresh ginger. Proceed with the recipe.

Chickpea-Ricotta Gnocchi

MAKES: 4 servings
TIME: About 1 hour with cooked beans

Like standard potato gnocchi (page 350), these are small boiled dumplings. But since they're based on chickpeas, not potatoes, they're more flavorful and even heartier. Another benefit: The dough is a little easier to handle. In any case, you can treat these exactly as you would gnocchi. Sauce them like pasta, sauce and bake them, or simply toss in butter or oil. See the list that follows for some ideas specific to this recipe.

Using a food mill will produce a finer texture than a food processor, but either gives fine results. The trick is to keep the chickpeas as dry as possible, so resist the temptation to add any extra water. Just keep scraping the side of the work bowl or food mill until you get a smooth and fluffy consistency.

Other beans you can use: cannellini, gigantes

> 3 **cups cooked or canned chickpeas, drained until as dry as possible**
> **Salt and pepper**
> ½ **cup ricotta cheese**
> ½ **teaspoon freshly grated nutmeg**
> **About ½ cup all-purpose flour**
> **Sauce or melted butter for serving**

1. Bring a large pot of water to a boil and salt it.
2. Put the chickpeas and a little salt and pepper in a food mill set over a large bowl and run them through. (Or use a food processor to purée them as smooth as possible, then put them in a large bowl.) You should have about 2 cups. Use a fork to stir in the ricotta and nutmeg. Add ¼ cup of the flour and stir to combine; continue to add and stir in more flour until the mixture forms a dough you can handle, but just barely. Lightly flour a work surface and turn the dough out onto it. Knead for a minute or so. Pinch off a piece of dough and boil it to make sure it will hold its shape; if it does not, knead in a bit more flour.
3. Take a small handful of the dough and roll it between your palms into a rope about ½ inch thick, then cut the rope into 1-inch lengths. (Traditionally, you would spin each of these pieces off the tines of a fork to score it lightly, but you don't need to. What you do need to do is be gentle and handle them as little as possible.) As each gnoccho is ready, put it on a sheet of wax paper; do not allow them to touch.
4. A few at a time, add the gnocchi to the boiling water and stir gently. After they rise to the surface, count to

20 (or so) and remove with a slotted spoon. (Taste one or 2 to make sure your timing is right.) Put in a bowl with a little warm sauce or keep warm in a pan with melted butter. Serve as soon as you have cooked them all; these do not keep well, so enjoy hot.

CHICKPEA-TOFU GNOCCHI Make it vegan: Substitute mashed silken tofu for the ricotta. 🟥

3 Great Ways to Finish Chickpea-Ricotta Gnocchi
1. Toss gently with warm Tahini Sauce (page 306) and sprinkle with grated Parmesan or crumbled feta cheese. Garnish with chopped black olives and parsley if you like.
2. Add a spoonful or 2 Harissa (page 665) to Fast Tomato Sauce (page 312) and sauce them with that.
3. Serve with Spicy Indian Tomato Sauce (page 667).

Bean Croquettes

MAKES: 4 servings
TIME: 20 minutes with cooked beans
🇫 🇲

These are fast, straightforward, and dead easy. Mix in some finely chopped vegetables, spices, or fresh herbs, or change the kind of beans you use—there are tons of variations.

Though this basic recipe needs no coating, it's easy enough to add if you want more crunch: Roll the shaped croquettes in extra cornmeal or bread crumbs, ground rice or lentils, or crushed tortilla chips before frying them in Step 4. For extra crispness, coat the croquettes in beaten egg, then roll them in the coating.

Other beans you can use: any cooked beans you have on hand, including many leftover bean dishes (see the chart, right)

> 2 **cups cooked or canned white or other beans, drained but still moist, bean-cooking liquid reserved**
> **A few tablespoons vegetable stock (pages 97–100) or water (optional)**

½ cup minced onion

¼ cup minced fresh parsley

1 egg, lightly beaten

Salt and pepper

About ½ cup coarse cornmeal or bread crumbs (preferably fresh, page 678)

Peanut or other oil for frying

1. If you want to serve the croquettes hot, heat the oven to 200°F. Mash the beans by putting them through a food mill, or pulse in a blender or food processor. Use a little bean-cooking liquid, stock, or water if the beans are too dry to mash. Do not purée; you want a few bean chunks in this mixture.

2. If you used a blender or food processor, transfer the beans to a medium bowl. Combine the beans with the onion, parsley, and egg and sprinkle with salt and pepper. Add cornmeal by the tablespoon until you've made a dough that is barely stiff enough to handle. You should be able to shape it with your hands without sticking, but it should be quite fragile or the cakes will be dry.

3. Cover the bottom of a large, deep skillet with about ⅛ inch of oil; turn the heat to medium. Shape the bean mixture into patties 2 to 3 inches across or into 1½ × 3-inch logs; when the oil is hot, put them in the skillet. Don't crowd them (you may have to work in batches).

4. Cook the croquettes until nicely browned on all sides, adjusting the heat so that they brown evenly without burning before turning, 7 to 8 minutes total. Keep warm in the oven for up to 30 minutes until you're ready to serve, or serve at room temperature.

SPICY BLACK BEAN CROQUETTES Use black beans and replace the parsley with cilantro. Add 2 teaspoons ground cumin and 2 tablespoons minced seeded jalapeño or other fresh chile or hot sauce to taste in Step 2. Use cornmeal. Serve with salsa.

ADZUKI CROQUETTES An Asian twist: Use adzuki beans. Replace the onion with 2 tablespoons minced scallions. Add 1 tablespoon each minced garlic and fresh ginger in Step 2. Omit the parsley and use crushed Sichuan peppercorns instead of black pepper for seasoning. Dip the croquettes in beaten egg, then roll in panko before frying.

Turning Leftover Bean Dishes into Croquettes

You can make bean croquettes from a variety of leftover dishes, and they're superb; drain them of excess liquid before proceeding. Here are some ideas to get you started:

COMBINE LEFTOVERS FROM	WITH	COAT WITH
Chili non Carne (page 455)	Corn kernels	Crushed tortilla chips
Black Soybeans with Soy Sauce (page 457)	Chopped scallions	Ground rice or panko
Mung Bean Dal with Apples, Coconut, and Mint (page 453)	More diced apple (optional)	Shredded coconut
Buttery Lentils and Potatoes with Curry (page 453)	Peas	Ground lentils or shredded coconut

Baked White Bean Cakes

MAKES: 4 servings (8 cakes)
TIME: 20 minutes with cooked beans
F

If you've got leftover White Beans, Tuscan Style (page 444), you're in luck: Drain them of any liquid and use them here (the sage and the extra garlic will add another layer of flavor). But if you don't, use any cooked white beans, even canned. I eat these hot from the oven, with a sprinkle of cheese and a salad on the side. For a fancier presentation, try warming a little Fast Tomato Sauce (page 312) to serve with them.

Other beans you can use: any cooked white bean like navy or great Northern; see the variations for ideas for other beans

>   3   **cups cooked or canned white beans,**
>   **drained but still moist**
>   2   **eggs**
>   ¼   **cup freshly grated Parmesan cheese**
>   ¼   **cup olive oil or 4 tablespoons**
>   **(½ stick) butter**
>   ¼   **cup minced red onion**
>   2   **tablespoons minced garlic**
>   2   **teaspoons minced fresh rosemary or**
>   **1 teaspoon dried**
>   ¼   **cup all-purpose flour, plus more if needed**
>   ½   **teaspoon baking powder**
>   **Salt and pepper**

1. Heat the oven to 375°F. Put the beans in a large bowl and mash lightly with a fork. Add the eggs and cheese and mix with the fork until combined.

2. Put 2 tablespoons of the oil or butter in a small skillet over medium-high heat. When the oil is hot or the butter is melted, stir in the onion and garlic and cook, stirring frequently, until they are soft, 2 to 3 minutes. Stir in the rosemary and remove from the heat.

3. Add the flour, baking powder, and a sprinkle of salt and pepper (taking into account how well seasoned your beans were to start with) to the beans. Add the onion mixture and stir with the fork until just combined. The consistency should be like thick cookie dough. If not, add a little more flour.

4. Use the remaining oil or butter to grease a baking sheet. Use a large spoon or your hands to form the bean mixture into 8 cakes, not more than ½ inch thick. Put them on the prepared pan. Bake until golden and crisp, about 30 minutes, carefully turning them over after 15 minutes. Serve hot or at room temperature.

CHEESY BAKED RED BEAN CAKES Terrific with salsa: Use red beans instead of white, grated Monterey Jack or cheddar instead of the Parmesan, and epazote or oregano instead of the rosemary.

BLACK BEAN CAKES WITH QUESO FRESCO Great texture, with the cheese staying semifirm: Use black beans instead of white, crumbled queso fresco instead of the Parmesan, and sage or parsley instead of the rosemary. Serve with white rice and Chimichurri (page 638).

BAKED LENTIL CAKES WITH GRUYÈRE Best with Le Puy or other small green lentils, but black or brown lentils are good too: Use lentils instead of the white beans, grated Gruyère or other Swiss cheese instead of the Parmesan, and thyme or tarragon instead of the rosemary. Proceed with the recipe, drizzle with Mustard Vinaigrette (page 628), and serve with Braised Potatoes with Mustard (page 238).

Mung Bean Pancakes

MAKES: 4 to 6 servings
TIME: 40 minutes with soaked beans
M

These highly spiced pancakes (called *bin dae duk* in Korea, where they originate) are easy to love. Make them as large or small as you like and serve with Korean-Style Soy and Sesame Dipping Sauce and Marinade (page 656), or soy sauce mixed with an equal amount of vinegar.

Mung beans come whole, split, and/or peeled. For best texture in this recipe, use split and peeled mung beans, called moong dal in Indian markets. It's also important to soak the beans for at least 2 to 3 hours ahead of time, or they won't purée to the right consistency for the batter.

Other beans you can use: dried split peas, red or brown lentils, channa dal, urad dal

1 cup dried peeled and split mung beans (moong dal), rinsed, picked over, soaked for 2 to 3 hours, or overnight if you have time, and drained
2 eggs
1 tablespoon minced garlic (or to taste)
About 1 tablespoon minced fresh chile (like jalapeño or Thai), or red chile flakes or cayenne
½ cup chopped scallions
1 large carrot, finely julienned or grated
Salt and pepper
¼ cup or so sesame oil, peanut oil, or good-quality vegetable oil

1. Put the mung beans in a blender or food processor and add about ¾ cup water. Purée until a smooth and somewhat thick batter is formed; add more water if necessary.
2. Transfer to a bowl and stir in the eggs, garlic, chile to taste, the scallions, carrot, and a large pinch salt and pepper. The batter should be the consistency of pancake batter.
3. Heat a large skillet over medium-high heat and coat the bottom with oil. Ladle in the batter to form several small pancakes or 1 large pancake. Turn the heat down to medium and cook until the bottom is browned, about 5 minutes, then flip and cook for another 5 minutes.
4. As the pancakes finish, remove them from the pan and, if necessary, drain on paper towels. Repeat with the remaining batter, adding more oil to the pan if necessary. Cut the pancakes into small triangles or serve whole with a dipping sauce.

MUNG BEAN PANCAKES WITH KIMCHI Approaching fiery: Replace the chile and carrot with 1 cup chopped or sliced Kimchi (page 93).

MUNG BEAN PANCAKES, SOUTHEAST ASIAN STYLE Add 1 tablespoon minced fresh ginger and ¼ cup chopped fresh cilantro or Thai basil in Step 2. Cook in vegetable oil. Serve with Fishless Fish Sauce (page 656), Basil Dipping Sauce (page 654), or any of their variations.

BROWN LENTIL PANCAKES A basic lentil pancake that is a fabulous foundation for a delicious yogurt sauce (page 673): Replace the mung beans with brown (regular) lentils and add 1 to 2 teaspoons any ground spice you like (cumin, coriander, caraway, and fennel work nicely) in Step 2. Omit the chile or scallions if you like.

SPICED RED LENTIL PANCAKES Accompanied with just about any chutney (pages 668 to 670), these are utterly fantastic: Substitute red lentils for the mung beans. Add 1 tablespoon minced fresh ginger and 1½ tablespoons or so curry powder, chaat masala, or garam masala in Step 2.

Chickpea Fries
Panelle
MAKES: 4 to 6 appetizer servings
TIME: 45 minutes
M O

Among the best appetizers ever, these fries are crisp, tasty, and satisfying. They're made with chickpea flour (also called besan or gram flour), which can be found in Indian, Middle Eastern, some Asian and health food markets, and often in Italian markets. Like chickpeas themselves, this flour has a robust, nutty flavor. The fries can be made ahead (up to cooking them); flavored in at least a dozen different ways; and cut into all kinds of shapes. Serve them over and over with slight variations in form and flavor, and no one will ever suspect it's all the same basic recipe.

Good-quality vegetable oil for greasing and frying
1 cup chickpea flour, sifted
Salt and pepper
2 tablespoons extra virgin olive oil
Finely grated Parmesan cheese for garnish (optional)

1. Grease a rimmed baking sheet or pizza pan. Bring 2 cups water to a boil in a medium pot. Gradually add the chickpea flour, with a large pinch salt and pepper, whisking constantly to prevent lumps from forming. Reduce the heat to a gentle bubble, stir in the olive oil, and cook for just a minute.

2. Scoop the chickpea mixture onto the prepared pan and spread into an even layer. Let cool for a few minutes, then cover loosely with parchment or plastic. Refrigerate until chilled through, about 30 minutes. (At this point, you can cover the pan tightly and refrigerate for up to a day.)

3. Put enough vegetable oil to come to a depth of at least ⅛ inch (¼ inch is better) in a large skillet over medium heat. Meanwhile, take the chilled the chickpea mixture out of the refrigerator and cut into 3 × ½-inch fries, or into triangles, or rounds (using a cookie cutter). Gently put batches of the fries in the hot oil and fry, rotating them for even cooking and browning on all sides, 3 to 4 minutes total.

4. Drain the fries on paper towels and immediately sprinkle with salt, lots of pepper, and Parmesan if you like. Serve hot or at room temperature with lemon wedges or sauce (see the list below).

PEANUT AND CHICKPEA FRIES The peanut flour adds even more nutty flavor; serve savory, or sweet, sprinkled with confectioners' sugar: Replace half of the chickpea flour with peanut flour. Proceed with the recipe.

11 Fabulous Additions to Chickpea Fries

Most of these are best stirred into the batter just before cooking. Try combinations like chopped parsley with lemon zest and capers; cilantro, green olives, and preserved lemon; or sage and sunflower seeds.

1. Chopped fresh herbs like parsley, basil, cilantro, chives, tarragon, dill, sage, thyme, or rosemary

2. Minced garlic or several cloves Roasted Garlic (page 205)

3. Chopped scallions or shallot

4. Grated lemon zest

5. Chopped or sliced black or green olives

6. Chopped or sliced fresh chiles

7. Chopped dried tomatoes

8. Chopped Preserved Lemon (page 286)

9. Chopped or whole capers

10. Pine nuts, pumpkin seeds, or sunflower seeds

11. Spice mixtures like curry powder, chaat masala, or chili powder

8 Sauces to Serve with Chickpea Fries

1. Fast Tomato Sauce (page 312)

2. Spicy Indian Tomato Sauce (page 667)

3. Chimichurri (page 638)

4. Garlic Mayonnaise (page 671)

5. Ketchup

6. Just about any yogurt sauce or raita (page 673 to 674)

7. Chutney (pages 668 to 670)

8. Tahini Sauce (page 306)

Cutting Chickpea Fries

Spread the chickpea mixture on a rectangular sheet and let it firm up. Then you can cut it into triangles or fries before pan-frying.

Tofu, Burgers, and Other High-Protein Foods

Here is a variety of hearty dishes that offer big flavors and lots of "chew," the role traditionally played by meat, poultry, and fish in most of North America. No doubt you're already familiar with tofu, but I hope and even expect that you'll discover some new flavors and textures in these pages. You might even try making tofu yourself, a dead-easy process that yields delicious results.

This chapter also covers seitan and tempeh, other traditional foods that are seen as meat substitutes. I love seitan: Its meatiness and flavor are incomparable, and it's even better—and considerably cheaper—if you prepare it yourself, and about as difficult as making pancakes. Tempeh—a fermented soy bean cake—is too involved for most people to make at home, but is now sold in supermarkets. You can find it with added grains or seeds, and even marinated, though I usually stick to plain and flavor it myself.

A word about portion sizes: This is the one chapter in the book where the dishes might be considered "main-dish" size, so if you want smaller portions as part of a larger meal or as appetizers or party food, you'll get more. When you're making veggie burgers, just shape smaller patties, or form them into bite-sized "meat" balls (see page 506).

THE BASICS OF TOFU

Though tofu is a relatively recent discovery for Americans, it's been around in China for two thousand years. The word *tofu*, used by most Americans and much of the Western world, is Japanese; it's also called *dofu* in Chinese, and simply means bean curd.

Regardless of terminology, tofu is a nutritional powerhouse. It comes in myriad forms that can be used in just about any way imaginable—fried, stir-fried, baked, grilled, poached, braised, broiled, whipped, blended, included in smoothies or sauces.

Yet this little miracle is nothing more than the simplest nondairy cheese: coagulated soy milk. To make it, an acidic ingredient (even lemon juice works) is stirred into soy milk, which forms curds. For the most common tofu, the curds are drained from the whey, then pressed

in a mold. It's a simple process you can follow at home without much effort or cost (see page 484).

You can find just about any style of tofu from silken to extra-firm at nearly every supermarket, and your local Chinese, Japanese, or Korean market may stock tofu in so many forms that you'll be overwhelmed. I'll stick with the basics here.

BRICK OR BLOCK TOFU The most familiar tofu: brick shaped and sold sealed in plastic with water or in bulk from an open container of water.

To make brick tofu, water is pressed out of the curds to form a dense, crumbly tofu. There are levels of firmness: soft, medium, firm, and extra-firm, determined by water content. In general, this tofu absorbs flavors very well. The firm and extra-firm varieties hold their shape and can be cooked using pretty much every technique; soft and medium tofu may crumble in some dishes.

SILKEN TOFU Also brick-shaped, silken tofu has the texture of custard; it's coagulated without forming curds and is left unpressed. Sold in soft, firm, and extra-firm varieties, it's a great thickener or replacement for eggs or dairy; firm and extra-firm versions can be diced and added to broths and soups, crumbled, deep-fried, or even (gently) stir-fried.

SMOKED TOFU Firm or extra-firm tofu that is completely delicious. I use it in stir-fries, with beans and lentils, and other places. It also makes a great sandwich. If you like, you can smoke your own (see page 486).

FRIED TOFU There are many packaged fried tofus available, including some with pockets that can be filled with sushi rice for Nigiri Sushi (page 384). It's simple enough to fry your own; see Deep-Fried Tofu (page 487).

BAKED TOFU Sold with all sorts of added flavors. I recommend baking your own (see page 485).

TOFU SKINS Super stuff, also sold as dried bean stick, yuba, or bean curd sheets or skins. As with cow's milk, a skin forms on top of warm soy milk as it's coagulating; if you skim that off and dry it, you get tofu skin. It's predominantly used as a wrapper, or sliced and added to stir-fries and soups. Available fresh, dried, and frozen, though you might have to hunt around for it. Reconstitute dried ribbons in water (and fry if you like), unless you're adding it to a soup or broth, which you can do directly. Treat fresh and frozen yuba as you would fresh pasta or egg roll wrappers.

NONSOY "TOFU" If you're in a tofu rut, feeling adventurous, or don't eat soy, there is a group of "tofus" made from other ingredients: sweet "almond" tofu (made from agar and apricot kernels), eaten as a dessert; egg tofu, a combination of soy milk and eggs; Japanese tofus made from sesame seeds or peanuts and a starch; and Chickpea "Tofu" (page 500).

BUYING AND STORING TOFU

Tofu is best when fresh. It has a more defined texture, whether creamy or crumbly, and the flavor is brighter and not at all sour. If you can find locally made tofu, try some soon after it's made; it's a delicacy. And I urge you to try making tofu at home (page 484).

Refrigerated tofu (the kind typically sold in sealed plastic tubs) does not keep for long once opened. Store it in fresh water, and change that water daily; use it within a few days. Tofu has spoiled when it smells and/or tastes sour. For longer storage, tofu can be frozen; see below.

PREPARING TOFU FOR COOKING

Though it's perfectly fine to drain tofu, pat it dry, and use it as is, you can vary the texture of tofu before cooking. Here is a rundown of the techniques called for in the recipes whenever I mention "prepared tofu":

FREEZING Freezing makes the water in tofu expand; when thawed, this water is released, resulting in tofu with a dry, spongy texture that's perfect for grilling, stir-fries, or braised dishes. To freeze, drain the tofu and pat it dry; wrap it in plastic or put in a container and freeze for several hours or until you need it, up to

> ### Making Soy Cheese
> This is so easy to do and makes a great spread. Check out "10 Directions to Take Cashew Cheese" (page 302) for ways to change it up. Purée 14 to 16 ounces firm tofu with 2 tablespoons lemon juice in a food processor until smooth. Add a pinch of salt and 2 tablespoons nutritional yeast, and purée again.

3 months. For extra chewiness, first cut the tofu into cubes, dry them well, and freeze in a freezer bag. Allow enough time to thaw tofu before slicing and cooking.

PRESSING Here you squeeze liquid from brick or block tofu to give it a drier and firmer texture. Cut the tofu in half horizontally and put the halves on four sheets of paper towels, then cover with another four sheets. Set a can of food, heavy cutting board, or a similar weight (about a pound is right; no more than 2) on top so the tofu bulges at the sides slightly but doesn't crack. Wait 20 to 30 minutes, or as time allows; change the towels as they become saturated. The longer you press the tofu, the more liquid it will release and the drier it will become, but even the few minutes it takes you to prepare other ingredients will help. Drier tofu absorbs more flavor, which is especially important for marinating.

Pressing Tofu

Put slices of tofu between layers of paper towels, weight evenly, and let sit for a few minutes, up to a half hour.

PURÉEING Puréed tofu can replace dairy, eggs, or thickeners in smoothies, shakes, sauces, dips, and dressings. The results vary slightly depending on what firmness you use. Running silken tofu in a food processor or blender creates a yogurtlike consistency, while block tofu yields something closer to the consistency of buttercream frosting.

Homemade Tofu

MAKES: 4 to 6 servings
TIME: About 2 hours, mostly unattended
M V

You can buy a tofu kit but the old way is simple enough. All you need are an instant-read thermometer, some cheesecloth (though you can make do with a clean kitchen towel), and a tofu mold, which you can create out of any kind of container you're able to punch a few holes into: a plastic storage container, the plastic tub from store-bought tofu, a loaf pan, or even a strainer. Have a look at "Types of Tofu Coagulants" (below) before starting, but don't worry too much; vinegar and lemon juice work fine.

1 gallon soy milk
2 tablespoons distilled white vinegar, ¼ cup fresh lemon or lime juice, or 2 teaspoons nigari, calcium sulfate, calcium chloride, or Epsom salt, dissolved in ¼ cup warm water

Types of Tofu Coagulants

Different types of coagulants give tofu different textures and flavors. Those most commonly used commercially are calcium sulfate or calcium chloride, magnesium chloride, and/or glucono delta-lactone. But for homemade tofu, alternatives or equivalents are available; here I list them in order from easiest to hardest to find; all work well.

COAGULANT	AKA	DESCRIPTION
Distilled white vinegar		Makes a slightly rubbery tofu (which some people prefer) and may impart a slight vinegar flavor.
Lemon or lime juice		Produces springy tofu with a mild citrus flavor.
Epsom salt	Magnesium sulfate	Available in any drugstore or pharmacy; must be dissolved in a little warm water.
Nigari		Derived from evaporated seawater; makes a smooth, silken-style tofu. Available in health food stores, Japanese markets, and online.
Calcium sulfate or calcium chloride	Gypsum (common name for calcium sulfate)	Makes a more crumbly tofu and adds loads of calcium. Buy food grade, found online.
Magnesium chloride		Produces a smooth tofu. Available in drugstores. Do not use magnesium chloride meant for de-icing sidewalks!
Glucono delta-lactone	GDL	An acid often used to make silken and very soft, almost jellylike tofu; purchase online.

1. Put the soy milk in a large pot over medium-low heat and bring to 140°F, then stir in half of the coagulant. Continue stirring for 5 minutes.

2. Add the remaining coagulant and reduce the heat to low; cook until the mixture begins to form curds, about 15 minutes, then turn off the heat.

3. Line a tofu mold or fine-meshed strainer with a kitchen towel or cheesecloth and ladle or spoon in the curds. Fold the ends of the towel over the top of the curds and put a 3- to 5-pound weight on top (a large can, jar of water on a plate, or something similar is okay). Drain for about 20 minutes, or more for firmer tofu, then remove the tofu from the mold.

4. Put the tofu in a bowl or dish of cold water in the refrigerator for about an hour to let it set. Use or store in water, covered and refrigerated, for up to 5 days, changing the water daily.

Poached Tofu

MAKES: 4 to 8 servings
TIME: 20 minutes
F **M** **V**

Poaching gives tofu a pleasantly swollen and firm texture, and is also the easiest precooking method. Start with silken or regular block tofu. After poaching, use it as you would fried or baked tofu, in stir-fries or other dishes, or serve it simply drizzled with soy sauce, Ponzu (page 657), or any of the suggestions listed in

---

Pressing Homemade Tofu

STEP 1 Put the tofu in a draining container lined with cheesecloth or a not-too-fine towel.

STEP 2 Fold the cloth over the top and weight.

"12 Toppers and Dipping Sauces for Precooked Tofu or Seitan" (page 490).

Salt
1–2 pounds tofu

1. Choose a pot large enough to hold the tofu comfortably. Fill it with water, salt it, and bring to a boil.

2. Carefully add the tofu in one piece (or pieces if you're using more than one block) to the boiling water. Adjust the heat so the water bubbles gently. Cook until the tofu floats, 5 to 10 minutes, but no longer. Remove with a slotted spoon and drain on paper towels. Use or cool, wrap, and refrigerate for up to 3 days.

DASHI- OR KOMBU-BOILED TOFU This is tasty drizzled with plain soy sauce or Ponzu (page 657): If you already have Kombu Dashi (page 100), bring a couple of cups to a slow simmer. Cook the tofu as directed. If you like, serve the tofu with some of the dashi, mixed with a little soy sauce and, if you have it, sake. If you have no dashi, heat a 4-inch piece kombu (kelp) in the salted water, but do not boil. When the water steams, poach the tofu as directed.

Baked Tofu

MAKES: 4 to 8 servings
TIME: About 1 hour
M **V**

Baking tofu gives it a firm, crisp crust, while its interior turns custardy, almost egglike. It's easier, leaner, and less messy than the more common deep frying. Cooled and sliced or cubed, baked tofu can be used anywhere: sandwiches, salads, stir-fries, wherever you'd use deep-fried tofu. To vary its flavor, before putting it in the oven, brush it with soy sauce, miso thinned with the liquid of your choice (sake, stock, water, etc.), barbecue sauce, Teriyaki Sauce (page 659), or Ponzu (page 657).

1–2 pounds firm tofu
Salt

---

1. Heat the oven to 350°F. Dry the tofu with paper towels (just blot off excess water) and sprinkle it with salt. Put on a baking sheet.

2. Bake undisturbed for about 1 hour. The tofu is done when the surface is lightly browned and firm. Use or cool, cover, and refrigerate for up to 3 days.

Crisp Panfried Tofu

MAKES: 4 to 8 servings
TIME: 20 minutes
F M V

Panfrying tofu yields an almost baconlike texture without a lot of extra oil or work. For super-crunchy, chiplike wafers, slice the tofu as thin as you can; if you want a crisp-tender texture, cut thicker pieces. Add it to hot dishes, sandwiches, salads, or serve with a simple sauce (see "12 Toppers and Dipping Sauces for Precooked Tofu or Seitan," page 490).

   2–3   **tablespoons good-quality vegetable oil**
   1–2   **pounds tofu, sliced crosswise ¼ to 1 inch thick (see headnote) and patted dry**
        Salt (optional)

1. Put the oil in a large, deep skillet over medium heat. When it's hot, carefully add the tofu, taking care not to crowd the slices; you'll have to work in batches.

2. Cook until the bottoms are crisp and golden, 3 to 4 minutes, then carefully flip and cook the other side. As they finish, transfer the slices to paper towels and sprinkle with salt if you like. Use or cool, cover, and refrigerate for up to 3 days.

PANKO-CRUSTED PANFRIED TOFU Great on top of pretty much any rice or noodle dish (but not vegan): Put 1 cup all-purpose flour in a shallow bowl; beat 1 egg in another shallow bowl. Dredge tofu slices in the flour, then the egg, then in 2 cups panko bread crumbs. Proceed with the recipe.

Grilled or Broiled Tofu

MAKES: 4 to 8 servings
TIME: 20 to 30 minutes
F V

Cut into slabs, tofu can go directly from the package to the grill or under the broiler, and will become crusty and charred on the outside and warm and custardy inside, with a pleasant bit of chew. For tofu kebabs, cut the slabs into 1- to 1½-inch cubes (one package yields about 24 cubes); the cooking time will be about the same. Before cooking, try brushing the slices with soy sauce, thinned miso, barbecue sauce, Teriyaki Sauce (page 659), or Ponzu (page 657), or sprinkle them with a spice mix.

   1–2   **pounds firm tofu**
        Olive oil
        Salt

1. Prepare a charcoal or gas grill or turn on the broiler for medium heat; adjust the rack to about 4 inches from the heat source.

2. Cut the tofu across into 1-inch slices. Pat dry with paper towels, then lightly brush with olive oil and sprinkle with salt on both sides.

3. Put the tofu on the grill directly over the fire or on a baking sheet under the broiler. Cook until the slices develop a crust and release easily from the grates or pan, 5 to 10 minutes total, turning the slices once. Transfer to a platter and serve or cool, cover, and refrigerate for up to 3 days.

Smoked Tofu

MAKES: 4 to 8 servings
TIME: 35 to 50 minutes, mostly unattended
M V

Smoked tofu adds so much flavor to any dish and it's a snap to make. How much smoke you add is up to you; to my taste, 30 minutes yields great results. If you keep the grill temperature in the medium range, preferably not more than 350°F, you'll end up with a moist, smoky slice, which I think is perfect on a toasted bun with lettuce and tomato. You'll need wood chips for this; no need to soak them, as you'll be smoking for just a short while.

1–2 pounds firm or extra firm tofu
Good-quality vegetable oil for brushing the tofu
Salt and pepper

1. Prepare a charcoal or gas grill for a medium indirect fire, with a hot area and a cool area.

2. Drain the tofu and pat dry with a paper towel. Cut into 1-inch or thinner slices. Lightly brush the slices with oil (this is important; it helps the smoke stick to the tofu) and season with salt and pepper to taste on both sides.

3. Add a couple of handfuls of wood chips to the fire and close the lid of the grill. When the grill is full of smoke, put the tofu on the indirect portion of the grill, away from the fire. Close the lid and cook until the surface has colored nicely, 20 to 30 minutes, or to your taste; I find that tofu has very good smoke flavor when it has turned just the lightest brown, maybe even call it beige. Depending on the proximity of the individual slices to the fire, the edges might get browner and the slices may develop grill marks. Make sure the grill is full of smoke the entire time; you may need to add more chips. Transfer to a plate. Use or let cool, cover, and refrigerate for up to 3 days.

SMOKED TEMPEH Tempeh is a lot drier and denser than tofu, so smoke doesn't penetrate it to the degree it does tofu. For that reason, I cube the tempeh before smoking it, in pieces just big enough that they won't fall between the grates. This also yields more smoke flavor if you use your tempeh crumbled or chopped: Cut two 8-ounce packages of tempeh into 1- to 1½-inch cubes and toss with ¼ cup vegetable oil to coat. (Or, if you prefer to smoke the tempeh whole, brush the pieces with oil; you'll only need about 2 tablespoons.) Grill as directed; taste before taking the tempeh off the grill to make sure it is as smoky as you want it. Time is the same for cubes and whole pieces. Use or refrigerate for up to 10 days.

Deep-Fried Tofu

MAKES: 4 to 8 servings
TIME: 20 minutes
F M V

Deep frying is a standard precooking preparation for tofu, used to produce a nice crust and tender interior. It's faster than baking tofu, but it's a little more complicated. Pat the tofu dry to prevent spattering. Then you have two options: One is to halve it horizontally, which is quick and easy. The other is to cube, slice, or cut it into rectangles or triangles (traditional); this takes a little more effort up front, but it reduces cooking time and gives slightly better results.

Fried tofu can be sauced and served as in the variation, or used later in stir-fries, sandwiches, or salads (see "12 Toppers and Dipping Sauces for Precooked Tofu or Seitan," page 490).

Good-quality vegetable oil for frying
1–2 pounds tofu, halved horizontally, cubed, or sliced (see headnote), and patted dry
Salt (optional)

1. Pour oil to a depth of 2 inches or more in a large, deep skillet or pot over medium heat and heat it to 350°F (see "Deep Frying," page 26).

2. When it's hot, slide in the tofu, in batches if necessary, and fry, turning occasionally, until golden brown and puffy, just a few minutes; do not overcook or the tofu will toughen. Remove with a slotted spoon, drain on paper towels, and sprinkle with salt if you like. Use or cool, cover, and refrigerate for up to 3 days.

AGEDASHI TOFU Best with firm or extra-firm silken tofu: Before frying the tofu, combine 1 cup Kombu Dashi (page 100), 2 tablespoons soy sauce, and 2 tablespoons mirin or 1 tablespoon honey in a small saucepan. Heat until steaming, then keep warm. Cube the tofu, then fry as directed. Put the fried tofu in a bowl and pour the sauce over it, or use the sauce for dipping. Garnish with chopped or shredded scallions, grated daikon,

Deep-Fried Tofu
(page 487)

toasted sesame seeds (see page 299), crumbled toasted nori (see page 244), and/or grated fresh ginger. ◘

Scrambled Tofu with Mushrooms

MAKES: 4 servings
TIME: 20 minutes
F V

Scrambling tofu yields surprisingly scrambled egg–like results, and if you add turmeric it will even be a familiar golden color. The trick is to smooth the tofu out in a food processor before cooking; you can also crumble the tofu with your fingers if you prefer. I like to scramble tofu with cooked vegetables. Vary the vegetables as you like; try chopped broccoli, onion, tomatoes, spinach, beans sprouts, or shredded carrots. You can also play with the proportion of tofu to vegetables if you want a more-vegetable, less-tofu dish.

Eat scrambled tofu as is, or use as a filling for burritos, tacos, or enchiladas; in soups; or tossed with vegetables, grains, or beans.

1	**pound firm tofu, drained, patted dry, and cut into chunks**
	Salt and pepper
½	**teaspoon ground turmeric (optional)**
2	**tablespoons good-quality vegetable oil**
8	**ounces white button or shiitake mushrooms, trimmed and sliced (reserve stems for stock or discard)**
¼	**cup chopped fresh parsley for garnish (optional)**

1. Put the tofu into a food processor and purée until smooth. (This will take a couple of minutes; just let the machine run.) Sprinkle with salt and pepper and add the turmeric if you're using it. Pulse a few more times to mix well.
2. Put the oil in a deep skillet over medium heat. When it's hot, add the mushrooms, sprinkle with salt and pepper, and cook, stirring occasionally, until they are dry and starting to brown.

3. Stir in the tofu and continue cooking and stirring until the tofu is heated through and as dry as you like it, anywhere from 4 to 6 minutes. Taste, adjust the seasoning, and garnish with the parsley if you like.

SPICY SCRAMBLED TOFU Tons of flavor: Purée the tofu and turmeric as directed. Omit the mushrooms and instead sauté 1 tablespoon each minced garlic and fresh ginger, ½ cup chopped scallions, and 1 chopped fresh chile (like jalapeño or Thai). Substitute cilantro for the parsley.

Stir-Fried Tofu with Bell Peppers or Other Vegetables

MAKES: 4 to 6 servings
TIME: 30 minutes
F V

Use firm or extra firm block tofu for stir-fries. You can simply blot it dry before cubing and cooking, further firm it up using the methods on page 483, or change its texture by precooking it (see pages 485 to 487).

Tofu has a tendency not only to stick but also to fall apart, and in most instances you want the tofu to hold together, so it's important to stir-fry in a nonstick or well-seasoned cast-iron pan.

Stir-Frying with Water

Of course, stock or wine adds flavor to stir-fries. But I've seen countless Chinese cooks and chefs work without either, and you can too. Why? Because a stir-fry already has a ton of flavor in it: garlic, ginger, a vegetable or two, the "main" ingredient (like tofu), soy sauce—that's enough flavor for almost anyone. The purpose of liquid in a stir-fry is to loosen the parts of the other ingredients that might stick to the pan, and to create a sauce that binds all the other flavors together. Adding flavor is third on the list of reasons you add liquid. Stock is ideal, but water works fine.

As with most stir-fries, this one is infinitely variable. If you work through the main recipe and then the variations, you'll soon be able to use whatever you have on hand without much more than a glance at these pages.

1½ pounds firm to extra-firm tofu, prepared by any of the methods on page 483 or simply blotted dry

3 tablespoons good-quality vegetable oil

1 large onion, halved and sliced

3 bell peppers (1 each green, yellow, and red, or any combination), cored, seeded, and sliced

1 tablespoon chopped garlic

1 tablespoon chopped fresh ginger

¼ cup rice wine, sherry, sake, white wine, or water

⅓ cup vegetable stock (pages 97–100) or water

2 tablespoons soy sauce

½ cup chopped scallions

---

12 Toppers and Dipping Sauces for Precooked Tofu or Seitan

1. Any raw or cooked salsa (pages 659 to 664)

2. Korean-Style Soy and Sesame Dipping Sauce and Marinade (page 656)

3. Simple Miso Dipping Sauce (page 653)

4. Fast Tomato Sauce (page 312)

5. Peanut Sauce, Four Ways (page 657)

6. Dashi Dipping Sauce or its variations (page 657)

7. Tahini Sauce (page 306)

8. Ginger-Scallion Sauce (page 631)

9. Seaweed "Mayo" (page 673), especially with Deep-Fried Tofu (page 487)

10. Cilantro "Pesto" with Ginger and Chile (page 638)

11. Basil Dipping Sauce (page 654)

12. Any Vinaigrette (page 628)

---

1. Cut the tofu into ½-inch or slightly larger cubes. Put 2 tablespoons of the oil in a large skillet, preferably nonstick, over high heat. When it's hot, add the onion and cook, stirring occasionally, until it begins to soften, a couple of minutes. Add the peppers and continue to cook, stirring occasionally, until the onion and peppers are crisp-tender and a little charred at the edges, about 5 minutes. Remove with a slotted spoon and transfer to a plate.

2. Put the remaining 1 tablespoon oil in the pan, then add the garlic and ginger and cook, stirring, for about 10 seconds. Add the tofu and cook, stirring occasionally, until it begins to brown, a couple of minutes. Add the wine and stock and cook, stirring, until about half of the liquid evaporates. Return the pepper-onion mix to the pan and cook, stirring, for a minute or so to reheat.

3. Add the soy sauce and scallions, cook, stirring, until the scallions becomes glossy, about 30 seconds, and serve.

STIR-FRIED TOFU WITH SCALLIONS Even simpler: Omit the onion and peppers. Cut 1 or 2 bunches scallions into 2-inch lengths, keeping the white and green parts separate. Heat all of the oil; cook the garlic and ginger, then add the tofu and the white parts of the scallions. Cook, stirring occasionally, until the tofu begins to brown, a couple of minutes. Omit the rice wine. Add the stock and cook, stirring, until about half of it evaporates. Add the scallion greens and stir for about 30 seconds. Add the soy sauce, stir, taste, and adjust the seasoning. Garnish with 1 tablespoon toasted sesame seeds (see page 299) if you like, and serve.

STIR-FRIED TOFU WITH PEAS, SNOW PEAS, OR SUGAR SNAP PEAS Use just one or a combination: In Step 1, the onion is optional. Instead of the peppers, add 2 cups peas (frozen are fine, but they should be thawed first if possible) and cook until bright green and just beginning to brown; snow peas and snap peas should not soften too much. Remove and proceed with the recipe.

STIR-FRIED TOFU WITH SHIITAKE MUSHROOMS Any mushroom will work but shiitakes seem to have been made for this: In Step 1, use the onion; you can also use 1 bell pepper if you like. After scooping both out of the pan, cook 2 cups sliced shiitake mushroom caps in 1 tablespoon oil over high heat, stirring, until browned and almost crisp. Remove them with a slotted spoon, then add 1 more tablespoon oil and proceed with the recipe.

STIR-FRIED TOFU WITH BROCCOLI OR CAULIFLOWER Parboiling isn't necessary but saves time and effort: In Step 1, in place of the peppers, use 2 cups bite-sized pieces broccoli and/or cauliflower that have been parboiled for just a minute or 2. Cook, stirring occasionally, until tender but not soft. Remove and proceed with the recipe.

STIR-FRIED TOFU WITH CABBAGE, KALE, COLLARDS, OR OTHER GREENS If you use stems no thicker than ⅛ inch or so, no parboiling is necessary: In Step 1, the onion is optional. Add 3 cups shredded or chopped cabbage, kale, collard, or other greens (mustard, turnip, cress—whatever you like). Cook, stirring occasionally, until wilted and tender, about 5 minutes. Remove and proceed with the recipe.

Braised Tofu with Eggplant and Shiitakes

MAKES: 4 to 6 servings
TIME: 30 minutes
F V

A more-or-less traditional Sichuan preparation, with creamy soft-cooked eggplant and crispy sautéed shiitakes. Substitute green beans for the eggplant if you like.

- 4 **tablespoons good-quality vegetable oil**
- 1 **cup sliced shiitake caps (reserve stems for stock or discard)**
  Salt and pepper
- 1 **tablespoon chopped garlic**
- 1 **tablespoon minced fresh ginger (optional)**
- 1½ **pounds eggplant, trimmed and cut into 1½-inch chunks**
- 1 **tablespoon Chile Paste (page 664), or to taste (optional)**
- ½ **cup vegetable stock (pages 97–100) or water, or more if necessary**
- 2 **tablespoons soy sauce**
- 1 **pound tofu, prepared by any of the methods on page 483 or blotted dry, cut into ¾-inch cubes**
- 1 **tablespoon sesame oil for garnish (optional)**
  Chopped fresh cilantro for garnish (optional)
- 1 **tablespoon toasted sesame seeds (see page 299) for garnish (optional)**
- 2 **tablespoons chopped scallions for garnish (optional)**

1. Put 2 tablespoons of the oil in a large, deep skillet over medium-high heat. When it's hot, add the shiitakes and some salt and pepper and cook, stirring occasionally, until the mushrooms are crisp, 5 to 10 minutes. Transfer with a slotted spoon to a plate.
2. Add the remaining 2 tablespoons oil to the pan and, a few seconds later, the garlic and ginger if you're using it. As soon as the oil sizzles, add the eggplant. Cook, stirring every minute or so, until the eggplant browns, 5 to 10 minutes. Add the chile paste, if you're using it. Add the stock and stir, scraping the bottom of the pan if necessary to release any browned bits of eggplant. Cook until the eggplant is very tender, 10 to 15 minutes more, adding a little more liquid if necessary (unlikely, but possible).
3. Stir in the soy sauce and tofu and cook, stirring occasionally, until the tofu is heated through, about 5 minutes. Stir in the reserved shiitakes and turn off the heat. Taste and adjust the seasoning, then garnish with sesame oil, cilantro, sesame seeds, and scallions, as you like, and serve.

BRAISED TOFU SKINS WITH EGGPLANT AND SHIITAKES Replace the tofu with 8 ounces dried tofu skins: To prepare them for cooking, soak in water until soft, about 30 minutes, then roll the sheets together on a cutting board and slice crosswise to make thin noodle strips.

Braised Tofu and Peas in Curried Coconut Milk

MAKES: 4 to 6 servings
TIME: 40 minutes

V

Braising is a useful technique for tofu because it provides the moist medium that the tofu needs to absorb seasonings. But whereas braised meat dishes take hours, these take minutes, because tofu needs no tenderizing.

If possible, use prepared tofu—fried, pressed, frozen, or whatever method you prefer (see pages 483 to 484) —because it will absorb even more flavor than straight from the package.

This classic Indian technique makes a highly flavored "gravy." I like peas in this recipe, because they're easy (I use frozen except in late spring), and I like the way their bright green color stands out. But you can use almost any vegetable.

Serve over rice or with Chapati or Paratha (page 591 or 592).

3	large onions, quartered
1	28- or 35-ounce can tomatoes, with their juice
2	tablespoons good-quality vegetable oil
	Salt and pepper
2	tablespoons garam masala (to make your own, see page 648) or curry powder, or to taste
1½	pounds firm or extra-firm tofu, prepared by any of the methods on page 483 or blotted dry, cut into ¾-inch cubes
1½	cups peas (frozen are fine; thaw in cold water and drain)
1½	cups coconut milk (to make your own, see page 304)
	Chopped fresh cilantro for garnish

1. Combine the onions and tomatoes in a food processor and purée; depending on the size of your machine, you may have to do this in 2 batches. Put the oil in a large skillet over medium heat. When it's hot, add the onion-tomato purée along with some salt and pepper and the garam masala. Cook, stirring occasionally, until it becomes saucelike, about 10 minutes.

2. Add the tofu and peas and cook for about 5 minutes, until the tofu swells slightly and the peas are tender. Stir in the coconut milk and bring to just about a boil, stirring occasionally. Taste and adjust the seasoning, garnish with cilantro, and serve.

REALLY SPICY TOFU AND PEAS IN COCONUT MILK Add 5 or more peeled cloves garlic and 1 or more seeded fresh chiles (like jalapeño or Thai) to the food processor with the onions and tomatoes. Add 1 tablespoon or more lime juice just before serving.

CREAMY TOFU, PEAS, AND RICE IN COCONUT MILK In Step 1, before you add the onion-tomato mixture to the hot oil, stir in 1 cup any short-grain white rice. Cook and stir until toasted and fragrant, then add the onion-tomato purée, tofu, and coconut milk. Bring to a boil, cover, and reduce the heat to low. Cook for 15 minutes. In Step 2, put the peas on top of the rice mixture, cover again, and remove from the heat. After 5 minutes, stir the peas into the rice along with the cilantro. Taste, adjust the seasoning, and serve.

4 More Ideas for Braised Tofu and Peas in Curried Coconut Milk

Using the main recipe or any of the variations, you can easily turn this into a one-pot stew that will feed a small crowd:

1. Along with the onion-tomato purée, add 2 cups diced (about ½-inch) potatoes, carrots, parsnips, or turnips, alone or in combination. These will cook in about 15 minutes.

2. Along with the tofu, add about 2 cups bite-sized broccoli or cauliflower florets that have been parboiled for a minute or 2.

3. Use fresh or frozen snow or sugar snap peas instead of shell peas.

4. Along with the coconut milk, add about 3 cups shredded spinach, Napa cabbage, bok choy, or other greens; some, like kale, will take a little longer to become tender.

Spicy Ketchup-Braised Tofu

MAKES: 6 to 8 servings
TIME: 20 minutes
F V

Vaguely Chinese, more honestly American, and so delicious. Serve with rice or noodles, or even (gasp!) on bread.

½	cup good-quality vegetable oil
1½–2	pounds firm or extra-firm tofu, cut into 8 slices and pressed lightly (see page 483)
	All-purpose flour for dredging
	Salt and pepper
1	tablespoon minced garlic
1½	cups ketchup
	Cayenne
	Fresh lemon juice

1. Put about ⅓ cup of the oil in a large skillet over medium-high heat. When it's hot, dredge the tofu slices lightly in the flour and add them, one at a time, to the skillet. Do not crowd; you may have to cook in batches. Sprinkle the tofu with salt and pepper as it cooks. As the pieces brown, turn and brown the other side; total cooking time per piece will be 4 to 6 minutes. When the pieces are done, transfer them to a plate. Wipe out the skillet.

2. Put the remaining oil in the skillet over medium heat and immediately add the garlic. Cook for a minute or 2, until fragrant but not colored. Add the ketchup and cayenne to taste (start with about ¼ teaspoon). Cook, stirring and adjusting the heat if necessary, for about 5 minutes, until the sauce bubbles, thickens, and starts to caramelize around the edges of the pan.

3. Return the tofu to the sauce and turn until evenly coated; stir in lemon juice to taste, then taste and adjust the seasoning. Serve.

Marinated Tofu

MAKES: 4 to 6 servings
TIME: 30 minutes, plus time to marinate
M V

You can grill, broil, or pan-cook marinated tofu, and you can use pretty much any marinade you can think of, from Japanese style to Italian style to barbecue sauce.

¼	cup olive oil, plus more for panfrying (optional)
3	tablespoons fresh lemon juice
2	tablespoons chopped or grated onion or shallot
1	teaspoon minced garlic
	Salt and pepper
1½	pounds firm or extra-firm tofu, prepared by any of the methods on page 483 or blotted dry, cut into 12 to 16 slices and pressed lightly
	Chopped fresh parsley for garnish (optional)
	Lemon wedges for serving

1. Combine the oil, lemon juice, onion, garlic, and some salt and pepper in a shallow bowl broad enough to hold the tofu in one layer. Add the tofu, turning to coat it, and marinate, turning occasionally, for 30 minutes or longer (24 hours is okay; cover and refrigerate if it will be longer than 2 hours).

2. TO BROIL Turn on the broiler and adjust the rack so it is about 4 inches from the heat source. Put the tofu slices on a baking sheet and broil until lightly browned on both sides, turning once. Total time will be 10 minutes or less.

TO GRILL Prepare a charcoal or gas grill for moderate heat; adjust the rack to about 4 inches from the flames. Put the tofu on the grate and grill until lightly browned on both sides, turning once. Total time will be 10 minutes or less.

TO PANFRY Put a couple of tablespoons olive oil in a nonstick or well-seasoned cast-iron skillet over medium-high heat. When it's hot, sear the tofu on both sides, for a total of about 5 minutes.

3. Garnish with parsley, if you like, and serve with lemon wedges.

Spicy Ketchup-Braised Tofu

MARINATED TOFU WITH JAPANESE FLAVORS Instead of the olive oil, lemon juice, onion, and garlic, marinate in 3 tablespoons soy sauce, 2 tablespoons sesame oil, 1 tablespoon each mirin and rice vinegar, and 1 teaspoon minced fresh ginger.

MARINATED TOFU WITH SPANISH FLAVORS Add about 1 teaspoon each ground cumin and smoked paprika (pimentón) to the marinade.

CRISP MARINATED TOFU For ultra-crisp and crunchy slices: This technique works for the main recipe or either of the variations. Slice the tofu even thinner, into 18 to 24 slices, and broil, grill, or panfry until the slices are very crisp and dry. (You may have to panfry in 2 batches.)

Pressed Tofu Salad

MAKES: 6 appetizer servings
TIME: 20 minutes, plus 2 hours to marinate
Ⓜ Ⓥ

Be sure to allow the salad to marinate long enough for the tofu to absorb the flavors of the dressing. That part's easy, but requires some planning.

- 1 pound extra-firm or firm tofu, pressed (see page 483)
- 2 medium-to-large carrots, peeled
- 2 large celery stalks, trimmed
- 2 tablespoons soy sauce
- 2 teaspoons Chile Paste (page 664)
- ¼ cup sesame oil

1. Cut the tofu into 2-inch matchsticks, grate the carrots, and very thinly slice the celery. Whisk together the soy sauce, chile paste, and oil in a medium bowl.
2. Toss everything together with the soy mixture, cover, and marinate for at least 2 hours in the refrigerator. Toss again immediately before serving.

Tofu Jerky

MAKES: 4 servings
TIME: About 2 hours, mostly unattended
Ⓜ Ⓥ

Tofu jerky is a flavorful, savory snack, with smokiness from the adobo sauce of canned chipotle chiles, umami from soy sauce, and just a little sweetness from brown sugar. (If you prefer it milder, use tomato paste instead of the adobo.) This recipe makes jerky that's way better than anything you can buy at the store and is, of course, additive-free.

- 1 pound firm tofu
- 2 tablespoons adobo sauce (from canned chipotles in adobo)
- 1 teaspoon brown sugar
- 1 teaspoon soy sauce
- ½ teaspoon salt

1. Heat the oven to 225°F. Line a baking sheet with parchment paper. Halve the tofu horizontally and blot dry. Gently cut each half the long way into 28 slices, about ⅛ inch thick, and lay them on the parchment (it's fine if they're touching). Bake the tofu for 30 minutes.
2. Meanwhile, stir together the adobo sauce, sugar, soy sauce, and salt with 1 tablespoon water in a small bowl. When the tofu has baked for 30 minutes, brush the tops of the slices with a generous amount of the sauce; bake for another 15 minutes. Flip the slices, baste with more sauce, and bake for another 30 minutes. Lightly brush the second side with more sauce and bake for another 15 minutes. You should use up the sauce and the tofu should be chewy (not crunchy) and very pliable.
3. Let the jerky cool completely (the slices will get a bit crisper as they cool). Serve or store in a sealed container in the refrigerator for up to 1 week.

TERIYAKI TOFU JERKY Replace the adobo sauce, sugar, and salt with 2 tablespoons mirin and 1 teaspoon each grated fresh ginger and minced garlic; increase the soy sauce to 2 tablespoons. Glaze the tofu as directed.

SWEET AND SALTY TOFU JERKY Replace the adobo sauce, sugar, and salt with 2 tablespoons maple syrup and increase the soy sauce to 3 tablespoons. Glaze the tofu as directed.

CURRIED TOFU JERKY Omit the adobo sauce, soy sauce, sugar, and salt. Mix together 2 tablespoons ketchup, 1 tablespoon each curry powder and water, and salt and pepper to taste. Glaze the tofu as directed.

Tofu Croutons

MAKES: 4 to 8 servings
TIME: About 1 hour
Ⓜ Ⓥ

Super-crisp and slightly chewy, these nuggets can be used in soups, salads, stir-fries, and noodle dishes or stirred into sauces. You can season them the same way you would regular croutons.

> 1–2 **pounds firm tofu, patted dry and cut into ½-inch cubes**
> 1–2 **tablespoons good-quality vegetable oil**

1. Heat the oven to 350°F. Line a baking sheet with parchment paper, if you like. Put the tofu cubes on the baking sheet and drizzle with the oil. Toss gently to coat.
2. Bake, undisturbed, for about an hour. The croutons will have shrunk quite a bit and be golden. Cool slightly before using (they'll release more easily from the pan) and use or transfer to an airtight container and refrigerate for up to 3 days. Bring to room temperature before using.

Tofu Crumbles

MAKES: 4 to 6 servings
TIME: 30 minutes
Ⓕ Ⓜ Ⓥ

Here's an option if you want something akin to ground meat, without resorting to any of the meat substitutes you can find at the store. (You can also use Crunchy Crumbled Tempeh, page 512, or turn any of the vegetable burger recipes into crumbles, see the sidebar on page 679.)

Season as you like; the ingredient list is just the beginning.

> 3 **tablespoons good-quality vegetable oil**
> 1½ **pounds firm tofu, patted dry**
> **Salt and pepper**
> **Optional additional seasonings: 1 teaspoon chopped garlic; 1 tablespoon ground cumin, ground coriander, chili powder, five-spice powder (to make your own, see page page 649), or any spice mix; up to ¼ cup chopped fresh or rehydrated dried mushrooms, tahini or nut butter, or chopped nuts**

1. Put the oil in a large skillet, preferably cast iron or nonstick, over medium-high heat. When it's hot, crumble the tofu in your desired size pieces straight into the pan. Sprinkle with salt and pepper.
2. Add the additional seasonings, if you're using them. Cook, stirring and scraping the bottom of the skillet occasionally and adjusting the heat as necessary, until the tofu browns and crisps as much as you like, anywhere from 10 to 30 minutes.

ROASTED TOFU CRUMBLES Use this technique with the main recipe or any of the other variations: Heat the oven to 400°F. Crumble the tofu into a bowl and season. Line a baking sheet with parchment paper and spread the tofu in an even layer on the sheet, taking care not to overcrowd (you might need to use 2 baking sheets). Bake until golden and crisp, 40 to 45 minutes, stirring halfway through.

TOFU CHORIZO Use anywhere you want extra spice: Chop 1 onion and 1 tablespoon garlic, and add to the oil when it's hot. Cook, stirring occasionally until the

onion begins to soften, 3 to 5 minutes. Add the tofu and proceed with the recipe. When the tofu is as crisp as you'd like, add 1 tablespoon chili powder, 1 teaspoon ground cumin, and ⅛ teaspoon cinnamon. Cook until the spices are fragrant, about 1 minute. Add 1 teaspoon cider vinegar and scrape up any browned bits from the bottom of the pan. Taste and adjust the seasoning; serve immediately.

TOFU CRUMBLES WITH GINGER Wonderful on top of cold noodles: Put a 2-inch piece peeled fresh ginger, 4 cloves garlic, 1 halved shallot, 2 tablespoons soy sauce, and 1 teaspoon Chili Paste (page 664) or to taste in a food processor and pulse to make a chunky paste. Add the paste right after you crumble in the tofu.

ITALIAN TOFU CRUMBLES I love this served on top of rice with a side of sautéed greens: When the tofu is as crisp as you'd like it, add 1 teaspoon each smoked paprika (pimentón) and fennel seeds and ½ teaspoon red chile flakes (or to taste) and cook until the spices are toasted and fragrant, 1 to 2 minutes.

Tofu Pancakes, Four Ways

MAKES: 4 to 6 servings
TIME: 30 minutes
F M V

These super, unusual, savory (and obviously vegan) pancakes take advantage of tofu's chameleonlike qualities. See the variations for just a few of the flavor combinations you can use.

- 1½ **pounds firm tofu, patted dry**
- ⅓ **cup soy milk or water**
- 3 **tablespoons tahini or any nut butter**
- ½ **cup all-purpose, rice, or whole wheat flour**
  Salt or soy sauce
- ¼ **cup chopped fresh herbs (like parsley, basil, cilantro, dill, or chives; optional)**

- 2–3 **tablespoons sesame or good-quality vegetable oil**

1. Put the tofu, soy milk, and tahini in a food processor and purée until smooth.
2. Transfer to a large bowl and sprinkle with the flour, some salt or soy sauce, and the herbs if you're using them; stir well to combine. The consistency should be like a thick batter; add more liquid or flour to adjust it if necessary. (You can make the batter in advance up to this point; cover and refrigerate for up to a day. You might have to thin it with a bit of soy milk or water before using.)
3. Heat the oil in large nonstick or well-seasoned cast-iron skillet over medium heat. When it's hot, spoon the batter into the pan in whatever size cakes you like, but leave enough room to flip them. Cook, undisturbed, until the bottoms turn golden and release easily from the pan, about 4 minutes. Flip carefully and cook until the other side is golden and cooked through, another 3 minutes or so. Serve.

GINGER-SCALLION TOFU PANCAKES Lovely with any of the soy-based sauces on pages page 654 to 659: Add 2 tablespoons chopped scallions and 1 tablespoon each minced garlic and fresh ginger. Use rice flour, season with soy sauce, and cook in sesame oil.

TOFU PANCAKES, THAI STYLE I like these best served with Peanut Sauce, Four Ways (page 657), but Basil Dipping Sauce (page 654) and Fishless Fish Sauce (page 656) are delicious too: Substitute peanut butter for the tahini. Add 1 tablespoon each minced garlic, fresh ginger, and lemongrass and 1 or 2 Thai chiles, seeded and thinly sliced. Use cilantro for the herb and cook the pancakes in vegetable oil.

TOFU PANCAKES, INDIAN STYLE Perfect with chutney (pages 668 to 670): Substitute 2 tablespoons chaat masala for the tahini and add 1 tablespoon each minced garlic and fresh ginger. Use cilantro for the herb.

Chickpea "Tofu"

MAKES: 3 cups
TIME: 1 day, mostly unattended

Ⓜ Ⓥ

You can use this to replace tofu in many of the recipes in this book, but it's more fragile than soy tofu—somewhere between firm and silken—so it tends to fall apart with lots of agitation, like during a stir-fry. It's delicious in salads or with soups.

1	**cup chickpea flour**
2	**tablespoons plus 1 teaspoon good-quality vegetable oil**
1½	**teaspoons salt**

1. Put the chickpea flour in a large bowl with 5 cups water and stir to combine. Let sit overnight at room temperature.

2. After soaking, carefully remove and discard 2 cups of the water without agitating the chickpea flour slurry too much. Generously grease an 8 × 4-inch loaf pan with 2 tablespoons of the oil. Put the remaining 1 teaspoon oil in a large pot over medium heat. Carefully pour in the remaining water from the slurry, leaving the thick layer of slurry in the bowl. Add the salt to the pot of water and cook, stirring frequently, until it starts to bubble.

3. Stir the slurry into the bubbling water and cook, stirring constantly, until very thick, about 10 minutes. Pour into the prepared pan, cover with plastic wrap or a clean kitchen towel, and let sit at room temperature for 8 hours. Use or cover and refrigerate for up to 5 days.

THE BASICS OF VEGGIE BURGERS

A food processor is almost essential for most of these recipes, because you almost always want to pulse the primary ingredient into small bits. Occasionally you'll want to purée part of the mix, and the food processor does this well too. Yes, you can use a knife or a blender or both in combination, but that's going to be way more time consuming.

There are three keys to cooking these burgers so they develop a crisp outer crust and a tender inside: First, be sure you have enough fat in the pan and that it's hot before adding the burgers. Then let them cook undisturbed until the first side is browned and they release from the pan easily. Finally, don't overcook them. You want them hot but not dried out. You can also broil, bake, or grill some of them; see page page 507.

SHAPING BURGERS

Vegetable burgers are most manageable when they're not too big; ½ to 1 cup each is ideal. They can be on the thick side, but no thicker than an inch or the interior won't get cooked. The recipes here all make 4 to 8 burgers, depending on their size, which is your call.

To shape, cup a little of the mixture in your hand (it helps if they're wet), form it into a ball, then flatten to a patty as gently as possible. You can put the patties on wax or parchment paper to make sure they don't stick to anything, but it's not essential. A spatula can help you move them around without any damage. Particularly if you will be grilling your burgers, I recommend that you refrigerate them for at least 1 hour; this will help them stay together.

You can use these recipes to make loaves, balls, or cutlets. Check out the sidebar on page 506.

SERVING BURGERS

You can slide these onto a bun and dress with the usual fixings like ketchup, mustard, onion, lettuce, or tomato. You can make cheeseburgers. Or go less traditional and top them with virtually any dressing or salsa, or splash with a little soy sauce or hot sauce. You can also make them smaller and pop them into pitas, like falafel.

Or skip the bread entirely and serve the burgers as you would any center-of-the-plate item, with side dishes and whatever sauce you like. Or bread the patties and turn them into "cutlets" (see the sidebar on page 506).

12 Ways to Build Delicious Veggie Burgers

Your options are endless. The basics are to make sure the mixture is neither too dry nor too wet. If you find yourself in the first situation, add a liquid; in the second, add some oats, rice flour, cornmeal, flour, or bread crumbs. For flavoring, try:

1. FRESH HERBS
Add up to ½ cup minced fresh parsley, basil, or dill; somewhat less mint, cilantro, or chervil; 1 tablespoon oregano or marjoram; or 1 teaspoon or so fresh thyme, tarragon, or rosemary.

2. DRIED HERBS AND/OR SPICES
Use by the pinch. To really get the seasoning right, taste and adjust as you go; you can cook a little bit first if you don't want to taste it raw.

3. GARLIC
Add 1 teaspoon or more minced garlic, or 1 tablespoon or more Roasted Garlic (page 205), with a little of its oil.

4. SOY SAUCE OR MISO
Just 1 tablespoon or so soy sauce, but up to ¼ cup any miso.

5. KETCHUP, SALSA, OR MUSTARD
Up to ⅓ cup ketchup or salsa or 1 tablespoon or so Dijon or other mustard.

6. NUTS OR SEEDS
Add ¼ cup or so sesame or sunflower seeds, or up to ½ cup nuts or pumpkin seeds, toward the end of processing the burger mixture.

7. CITRUS ZEST
The slight acidity brightens everything.

8. TOMATO PASTE
A tablespoon or 2 will give the burgers nice color and a more complex flavor.

9. MUSHROOMS
Soak and chop 1 tablespoon or so dried mushrooms, or use up to ½ cup trimmed raw mushrooms; add to the food processor along with the other ingredients.

10. COOKED VEGGIES
Add up to 1 cup cooked vegetables—onions, greens, broccoli, potatoes, sweet potatoes, winter squash, zucchini, whatever you like —along with the other ingredients.

11. COOKED GRAINS
All-grain burgers tend to be mushy and uninteresting, but adding a bit of grains to other burgers results in a terrific light texture. Stir up to 1 cup cooked grains into the burger mixture.

12. CHILES
For heat, you can add cayenne, red chile flakes, or minced canned chipotles or a bit of the adobo sauce. But if you want some texture, you might include ¼ cup or more roasted (or canned) green or red chiles.

Where's the Beef Substitute?

You might notice that there are no recipes here—or anywhere in this book—for cooking with textured soy protein (TSP), Textured Vegetable Protein (TVP), or other soy protein isolates. These are highly processed ingredients that can add protein to a drink or dish; they are used as meat substitutes, mostly in prepared foods at the supermarket: frozen and packaged entrées, crackers and breads, energy bars, and drinks.

Here's why I avoid them: You can get better-tasting protein from whole foods like beans (including soybeans), grains, and eggs. Factor in a few minimally processed high-protein pleasures like cheese, tofu, tempeh, seitan, and dairy or nondairy milks, and there's little reason to stock your pantry with anything so highly processed it can't be made at home.

The Simplest Bean Burgers

MAKES: 4 to 8 servings
TIME: 30 to 40 minutes, plus chilling time
Ⓜ Ⓥ

These burgers are excellent served on a bun with the usual fixings, no matter which bean you use, but I will say that black beans give the best possible result. If you start with well-seasoned, cooked-by-you beans, the results are even better. If you like, replace the oats with rolled rye, wheat, or even soybean flakes. Like almost all veggie burgers, these hold together better if you refrigerate them before cooking.

> 2 **cups well-cooked black, white, or red beans, chickpeas, or lentils, or 1 14-ounce can, drained**
> 1 **onion, cut into chunks**
> ½ **cup rolled oats (not instant), plus more if necessary**
> 1 **tablespoon chili powder or spice mix of your choice (see pages 648–652)**
> **Salt and pepper**
> **Bean-cooking liquid, stock, wine, cream, milk, water, ketchup, etc. (optional)**
> 2 **tablespoons olive oil, or more as needed**

1. Line a baking sheet with parchment or wax paper. Put the beans, onion, oats, chili powder, and some salt and pepper in a food processor. Let the machine run, stopping to scrape down the sides as needed, until the mixture is thoroughly combined but not puréed, about 1 minute. (If you don't have a food processor, put everything in a large bowl and use a potato masher.) Let the mixture sit for 5 minutes. You want a moist consistency that will easily form cakes. If it is too wet, add more oats; if it's too dry, bean-cooking liquid or other liquid. In either case, add the ingredient 1 tablespoon at a time and pulse (or mash) after each addition.

2. Lightly wet your hands and shape the mixture into 4 large or 8 small patties; put them on the baking sheet. Cover and refrigerate for 1 hour or overnight.

3. Put the oil in a large skillet over medium heat. When it's hot, add the patties. Cook, undisturbed, until brown and crisp on one side, 3 to 8 minutes. Add more oil if the pan looks dry, then turn the burgers over carefully with a spatula and cook until they feel firm and are browned on the other side, another 3 to 5 minutes. Serve hot or warm.

BEAN-AND-CHEESE BURGERS Stir ¾ cup freshly grated Parmesan, cheddar, Swiss, Jack, mozzarella, or other cheese into the mixture right before forming into patties.

BEANS-AND-GREENS BURGERS Add 1 cup cooked greens, squeezed dry, to the food processor in Step 1. If mixing by hand, chop before adding.

Forming Veggie Burgers

STEP 1 Gently form the mixture into a ball (it helps if your hands are wet).

STEP 2 Press gently into a patty.

Bulgur Beet Burgers with Ginger

MAKES: 4 to 8 servings
TIME: 45 minutes, plus chilling time
Ⓜ Ⓞ

Dried fruit is the secret ingredient in these rich burgers. You can serve them on a bed of Braised and Glazed Brussels Sprouts (page 183) or any winter green, or for a more casual meal, on a whole grain bun with lots of mustard.

The Simplest
Bean Burgers

Bulgur Beet Burgers
with Ginger (page 502)

1 pound beets, trimmed, peeled, and grated

½ cup packed pitted dates or dried plums (prunes)

½ cup almonds

1 1-inch piece fresh ginger, cut into coins

½ cup bulgur

Salt and pepper

¾ cup red wine or water

1 tablespoon Dijon or other mustard

Cayenne or red chile flakes (optional)

All-purpose flour for binding, if needed

2 tablespoons olive oil or butter

1. Line a baking sheet with parchment or wax paper. Put the beets, dates, almonds, and ginger in a food processor and pulse several times until everything is well chopped but not quite a paste.

2. Put the mixture in a large bowl with the bulgur and a sprinkle of salt and pepper. Bring the wine to a boil and stir it in, along with the mustard, and a pinch or more cayenne if you're using it and cover the bowl with a plate. Let steep for 20 minutes. Taste and adjust the seasoning. Let the mixture rest for a few minutes before shaping it into patties; if it seems too wet, stir in a little flour to help bind it. Lightly wet your hands and shape the mixture into 4 to 8 patties; put them on the baking sheet. Cover and refrigerate for 1 hour or overnight.

3. Put the oil in a large skillet over medium heat. When it's hot, add the patties. Cook, undisturbed, until brown on one side, 3 to 8 minutes. Add more oil if the pan looks dry, then turn them over carefully with a spatula and cook until the burgers feel firm and are browned on the other side, another 3 to 5 minutes. Serve hot or warm.

Sesame-Soy Tofu Burgers with Scallions

MAKES: 4 to 8 servings
TIME: 30 minutes, plus chilling time
Ⓜ Ⓥ

Sea greens add nutrition, taste, and texture to these tofu burgers. For cocktail food, make mini burgers (or "meat" balls; see page 506) to serve on toothpicks and dip in Miso Carrot Sauce with Ginger (page 654) or Fishless Fish Sauce (page 656).

¼ cup arame, kombu, or wakame

1 bunch scallions

1½ pounds firm tofu, patted dry

½ cup panko or bread crumbs (preferably fresh, page 678)

¼ cup sesame seeds

1 tablespoon soy sauce

2 teaspoons sesame oil

Salt and pepper

2–3 tablespoons good-quality vegetable oil

1. Line a baking sheet with parchment or wax paper. Pour boiling water over the arame and soak for 1 or 2 minutes. Drain well.

2. Trim the scallions, put in a food processor, and pulse a few times, until chopped. Transfer to a large bowl. Put about half of the tofu and the arame in the processor (no need to wash it out) and pulse a couple of times, until just crumbled. Add to the scallions. Put the remaining tofu in the processor and let it run until the tofu is smooth. Add it to the bowl along with the bread crumbs, sesame seeds, soy sauce, and sesame oil. Sprinkle with a little salt and lots of pepper and stir well to combine. Lightly wet your hands and shape the mixture into 4 to 8 patties; put them on the baking sheet. Cover and refrigerate for 1 hour or overnight.

3. Put the oil in a large skillet over medium heat. When it's hot, add the patties. Cook, undisturbed, until golden, 3 to 8 minutes. Add more oil if the pan looks dry, then turn them over carefully with a spatula and cook until the burgers feel firm and are golden on the other side, another 3 to 5 minutes. Serve hot or warm.

WALNUT-TOFU BURGERS Rich and silky: Reduce the tofu to 1 pound and omit the sesame seeds. In Step 2, with the first half of the tofu, add ½ cup chopped walnuts (or cashews, almonds, or hazelnuts) and pulse until the mixture is crumbly. When processing the second

Burger Mix as Ground "Meat"

All of the recipes in this section can be cooked without being shaped to make a mixture that's perfect anywhere you'd use ground meat. Prepare the burger mix, but don't form into patties. Heat a little oil or butter in a large deep skillet. When it's hot, add the burger mixture. Resist the urge to stir until it's crisp and brown, then stir and break the pieces apart a bit, continuing to cook until it's as done as you like. Use to fill tacos, burritos, omelets, savory pastries, and sandwiches. Or stir into Fast Tomato Sauce (page 312) for a topping for pizza or pasta.

You can also shape the mixture into loaves, cutlets, or "meat" balls. Think of cutlets as a slightly fancier alternative to a burger. "Meat" balls can be used in the same ways you'd use "real" meatballs—baked or fried, for dinner or for appetizers.

TO MAKE LOAVES

Double any of the burger recipes on pages 502 to 508 and heat the oven to 350°F. Pat the mixture into a greased standard loaf pan and cover with foil. Bake for 30 minutes or so, then uncover and bake until crisp and golden on top, another 20 to 30 minutes. Cool a bit, then slice and serve with ketchup or any of the accompaniments suggested in the recipe.

TO MAKE CUTLETS

Take any burger mixture and shape into small patties about ½ inch thick; chill for at least 1 hour. When you're ready to cook, take three shallow, wide bowls: Beat a couple of eggs in one, put 1 cup flour in another; and put 1 cup bread crumbs (fresh, dried, or panko) in the third. Have another cup of crumbs handy, just in case you need more. Put at least ⅛ inch good-quality vegetable oil in a deep skillet over medium heat. Carefully dip the patties first in the flour, then in the eggs, and finally in the bread crumbs, coating both sides evenly. When the oil is hot, cook the patties, undisturbed, until deeply golden on the bottom, 5 to 7 minutes. Carefully flip and cook the other side until golden. Drain on paper towels. Sprinkle with salt and pepper and serve immediately, with lemon wedges.

TO MAKE "MEAT" BALLS

Line a baking sheet with parchment paper. Roll the mixture relatively small; the balls will cook up fast and crisp that way, without falling apart. Lightly wet your hands. Start with a heaping tablespoon or so and gently squeeze it in one hand, rolling lightly to smooth and even out the surface. Put the balls on the baking sheet as you finish them. They'll take between 15 and 20 minutes to bake at 425°F, depending on the particular recipe. Turn them once or twice for even browning. To fry, film a nonstick or cast-iron skillet with oil or butter and turn the heat to medium. Add the balls to the pan, keeping a little space in between, and cook, undisturbed, until crisp and golden, 3 to 5 minutes. Roll them around a bit to cook the other sides until they're browned all over.

5 Ways to Serve Vegetarian Cutlets

1. Parmesan style (like Eggplant Parmesan, page 202), topped with Fast Tomato Sauce (page 312) and grated mozzarella and Parmesan cheeses

2. With large lettuce leaves and cilantro sprigs for wrapping, and Fishless Fish Sauce (page 656) or Basil Dipping Sauce (page 654)

3. Over plain rice with some mayonnaise whisked with tamari, or any kind of flavored mayonnaise you like

4. With Quickest Pickled Vegetables (page 89) or Spicy Korean-Style Pickles (page 91)

5. On top of any salad of your choosing

half of the tofu, add ¼ cup chopped walnuts and process until smooth.

SESAME-TOFU BURGERS WITH ADZUKI BEANS Nice reddish brown color and meaty texture: Reduce the tofu to 1 pound. In Step 2, with the first half of the tofu, add 1 cup well-drained adzuki beans and pulse a few times until crumbled.

TEMPEH-TOFU BURGERS Deeply flavored: Replace 8 ounces (one-third) of the tofu with 8 ounces tempeh. In Step 2, pulse the tempeh in the food processor along with the sea greens and a little bit of the remaining tofu until crumbly.

Fast Nut Burgers

MAKES: 4 to 8 servings
TIME: 20 minutes, plus chilling time
Ⓜ

If you have a food processor, these take almost no time, and you can make a double batch and freeze them.

> 1   onion, cut into chunks
> 1   cup walnuts, pecans, almonds, cashews, or other nuts (preferably raw)
> 1   cup uncooked rolled oats or cooked short-grain white or brown rice
> 2   tablespoons ketchup, miso, tomato paste, nut butter, or tahini
> 1   teaspoon chili powder or any spice mix you like (to make your own, see pages 648–652), or to taste
>   Salt and pepper
> 1   egg
>   Water, vegetable stock, soy sauce, wine, or other liquid, if needed
> 2   tablespoons olive oil or good-quality vegetable oil

1. Line a baking sheet with parchment or wax paper. Pulse the onion in a food processor until chopped. Add the nuts and oats and pulse to chop, but not too fine.

Baking, Broiling, or Grilling Veggie Burgers

When you're making burgers for a crowd, nothing beats baking or broiling. Baking takes longer, but the slow, relatively high heat results in a nicely textured interior and a magnificent, evenly browned crust. Here's how: Heat the oven to 425°F. Brush a baking sheet with good-quality vegetable oil and line it with parchment paper, or use a nonstick sheet. Put the burgers on the baking sheet and bake until they are deeply colored and release from the pan, about 15 minutes. Flip them and bake for 15 minutes more.

To broil, heat the broiler for at least 5 minutes and adjust the rack so the burgers are about 4 inches from the heat source. Put the burgers directly on a baking sheet. (Don't use parchment; it will burn.) The burgers will take 5 to 10 minutes per side, depending on the kind of burger.

Grilling is a little trickier, only because you need a firmer mixture to start with. Prepare a charcoal or gas grill for medium heat. Make sure the grill grate is clean. Grill for 5 to 10 minutes per side, depending on the kind of burger. If you have a perforated grill pan, use it.

Add the ketchup, chili powder, some salt and pepper, and the egg. Process briefly; don't grind the mixture too fine (the results will not be terrible, but the burgers will be tougher if you do). Add a little water or whatever liquid is handy if necessary; you want a mixture that is moist but not loose. Let the mixture rest for a few minutes. Lightly wet your hands and shape it into 4 to 8 patties; put them on the baking sheet. Cover and refrigerate for 1 hour or overnight.

2. Put the oil in a large skillet over medium heat. When it's hot, add the patties. Cook, undisturbed, until brown, 3 to 8 minutes. Add more oil if the pan looks dry, then turn them over carefully with a spatula, lower the heat a bit, and cook until the burgers feel firm and are brown on the other side, another 3 to 5 minutes. Serve hot or warm.

NUTTIER NUT BURGERS Increase the nuts to 1½ cups and reduce the oats to ½ cup.

NUT-AND-SEED BURGERS Substitute up to ½ cup sesame, sunflower, or pumpkin seeds for half of either the nuts or oats.

VEGAN NUT BURGERS Omit the egg. Use miso or nut butter, not ketchup, and use soy sauce for the liquid. Add 1 sheet toasted nori (see page 244), crumbled, to the food processor. ⓥ

THE BASICS OF SEITAN

If you've ever eaten "mock duck" or "mock chicken" in a restaurant, you've had seitan (pronounced SAY-tan). This tasty meat substitute made from wheat gluten originated in China more than a thousand years ago; the word *seitan*, though, is of Japanese derivation and only started being used in the 1960s. Seitan has a uniquely chewy texture, absorbs flavors extremely well, and can be roasted, panfried, breaded, or even grilled or broiled.

Look for seitan (sometimes labeled "wheat-meat") in the refrigerated section of natural food stores, and most is of acceptable quality. But it can be expensive and is tough to find whole; it's usually cut into small chunks and packaged in its simmering liquid.

MAKING AND USING SEITAN

Making seitan yourself is far cheaper, and allows you to control the seasonings and size of the pieces. All you need is one ingredient: vital wheat gluten flour, also called vital wheat gluten. It's a concentrated high-protein flour that's available in many stores; Bob's Red Mill is the most common brand.

Vital wheat gluten flour is slightly yellow and very fine, almost powdery. It's made after the starch, ash, and other components of wheat flour have been separated and washed away; it is more than 75 percent protein.

When mixed with water, it becomes instantly elastic and rubbery.

Making seitan is a multistep process: Once you've mixed the dough, seitan must be simmered before you can cook with it. You shape the dough into free-form loaves, flavor a little water or stock, and let the seitan gently bubble away in it for an hour or so. As it cooks, the gluten absorbs the liquid and flavor while the loaves triple in size.

Simmering also affects the texture of the seitan. If you prefer a dense texture, turn off the heat after an hour or so. Let it simmer a little longer if you like a lighter, spongier texture. (To check, cut a sliver from a loaf during cooking and taste.) Once the loaves are done, let them cool in the cooking liquid. At that point, you've got several options: You can slice and use the seitan; refrigerate it in the cooking liquid for up to several days; or freeze it in the cooking liquid for up to several months.

Seitan can stand in for tofu in any stir-fry or braised dish; just use equal quantities of seitan and follow the directions as usual.

Seitan

MAKES: 4 to 6 servings (about 1½ pounds)
TIME: 1½ to 2 hours, mostly unattended
Ⓜ Ⓥ

This dough comes together almost instantly, is astonishingly elastic, and is very easy—even fun—to work. It's important to knead it thoroughly, either by hand or by machine, and to let the dough rest before forming and simmering the loaves. You can flavor seitan before adding the water by stirring into the flour up to ¼ cup toasted wheat germ, whole wheat flour, or chopped or pulverized nuts or dried sea greens like kombu, arame, or wakame, as well as any dried herbs or spices to taste.

  1 **cup vital wheat gluten flour**
  ½ **teaspoon salt or to taste**
  1 **recipe Dark or Golden Simmering Liquid for Seitan (pages 509 and 510)**

1. Put the vital wheat gluten flour in a large bowl, a food processor fitted with the short plastic blade, or the bowl of a standing mixer fitted with a dough hook. Sprinkle with the salt.

2. Add ¾ cup water and mix until combined. If loose flour remains, add a couple of drops water, but be careful not to add too much. The dough should be one big, slightly rubbery mass. Continue kneading in the bowl by hand for 5 minutes or so, by mixer for a couple of minutes, or by food processor for just 30 seconds or so, until the dough is a rubbery, elastic mass. Cover the dough with a kitchen towel and let it rest for at least 20 but no more than 30 minutes. Meanwhile, put the simmering liquid in a large pot with a lid over medium heat and bring to a simmer.

3. Pull or cut the dough into 2 equal portions. Stretch, pull, and roll the dough into 2 logs. (I know they look small, but don't worry; they'll plump considerably.) Put them in the simmering liquid and bring the liquid to a boil. It's okay if they aren't submerged.

4. Lower the heat so the liquid bubbles gently and cover the pot. Cook, using tongs to turn the seitan once or twice, for about an hour. Test by cutting a slice off the end with a knife; if you want it a little less dense, cook another 15 to 30 minutes. Cool completely in the liquid before storing or using.

SEITAN AND LENTIL LOAF Once cooled, slice this thin to eat it like pâté with mustard and crackers; chopped, it becomes a tasty addition to Fast Tomato Sauce (page 312): Decrease the vital wheat gluten flour to ¾ cup and add ⅓ cup dried lentils in Step 1. In Step 3, form it into a single oval loaf. Proceed as directed.

SEITAN AND MUSHROOM LOAF Use a spice grinder or mini food processor to pulverize about ¼ ounce dried shiitake or porcini mushrooms. (Don't reconstitute them.) You should have about ⅓ cup powder; it's okay if there are still some small chunks. Decrease the vital wheat gluten flour to ¾ cup. Add the mushrooms to the flour in Step 1. In Step 3, form the seitan into a single oval loaf. Proceed as directed.

Dark Simmering Liquid for Seitan

MAKES: About 6 cups
TIME: 1 minute

F M V

Use this if you plan to use the seitan in Asian-style dishes or with deeply flavored foods like mushrooms, caramelized onions, or root or winter vegetables. The soy sauce colors the seitan a light brown.

Shaping Seitan

STEP 1 Pull or cut the dough into 2 equal portions.

STEP 2 Stretch and pull each ball to lengthen it.

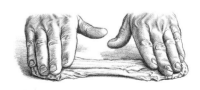

STEP 3 Pat and roll the stretched dough pieces into logs. The dough will be ragged and elastic, so it's okay if they are not perfectly shaped. Each will plump to even out and triple in size during cooking.

If you use oil to further cook or season dark-simmered seitan, use good-quality vegetable oil or sesame oil.

6 cups vegetable stock (pages 97–100) or water
⅓ cup soy sauce

Combine the stock or water and the soy sauce.

GOLDEN SIMMERING LIQUID FOR SEITAN Use this if you want a more neutral color and flavor or plan to use the seitan with spring or summer vegetables. It's best with non-Asian dishes and seasonings. If you use oil to further cook or season golden-simmered seitan, use a good-quality vegetable oil or olive oil: Add 1 tablespoon salt if you are using water, and substitute 1 cup white wine, apple juice, or cider for the soy sauce.

7 Other Seasonings for Seitan Simmering Liquid

Use alone or in combination, with either the dark or golden base.

1. 1 or 2 bay leaves
2. About 1 tablespoon peppercorns, black or Sichuan
3. 6 to 8 cloves garlic, lightly crushed
4. Fresh herb sprigs like rosemary, thyme, sage, oregano, parsley, cilantro, or mint
5. Up to 1 tablespoon tea leaves
6. A pinch asafetida
7. Warm spices like cinnamon (1 stick), cloves (2 or 3), star anise (1 or 2 pods), or cardamom (4 to 6 pods)

Pan-Seared Seitan

MAKES: 4 to 6 servings
TIME: 10 minutes
F V

The simplest way to cook seitan is to cut it in slices and cook in oil. You can also take it further and create a delicious sauce for it right in the pan; I've included a couple of old-school variations that translate beautifully to seitan. Seared pieces of seitan are also great on salads or in soups.

2–3 tablespoons good-quality vegetable oil
1–1½ pounds seitan (page 508), cooled, cut ½ inch thick, and patted dry
Salt and pepper (optional)

Put 2 tablespoons oil in a large nonstick or well-seasoned cast-iron skillet over medium-high heat. When it's hot, add the seitan, taking care not to overcrowd the pan; you will have to work in batches. Cook until the pieces are well browned and release from the pan, 3 to 5 minutes, then flip and cook the other side. Drain on paper towels, taste, and sprinkle with salt and pepper if you like.

SEITAN MARSALA Delicious and satisfying: Use Golden Simmering Liquid to make the seitan and olive oil to pan-sear it. After transferring the seitan to the paper towels, add 1 pound white button or cremini mushrooms, sliced, to the pan, along with another tablespoon oil if the pan is dry, and cook, stirring occasionally, until the mushrooms release their water and most of it evaporates, 5 to 8 minutes. Add ¾ cup each Marsala and vegetable stock (pages 97 to 100) and let simmer until reduced by half. If you want to enrich the sauce, swirl 2 tablespoons butter in it until melted and incorporated. Reduce the heat to low, season with salt and pepper, stir in 2 tablespoons chopped fresh parsley, and return the seitan to the pan, turning to coat the slices with the sauce. Let simmer for 5 minutes to reheat, then serve with the mushrooms spooned over the slices.

SEITAN WITH LEMON-CAPER SAUCE Use Golden Simmering Liquid to make the seitan and olive oil to pan-sear it. After transferring it to the paper towels, if the pan looks dry, add another tablespoon oil. Add ¼ cup chopped shallots and cook, stirring occasionally, until softened, 2 to 3 minutes. Add ½ cup each dry white

Seitan Marsala

wine and vegetable stock and let simmer until reduced by half. Reduce the heat to low, stir in the grated zest of 1 lemon, ¼ cup fresh lemon juice, 2 tablespoons chopped capers, and salt and pepper to taste. Return the seitan to the pan. Let simmer for 5 minutes to reheat, then serve.

Oven-Roasted Seitan

MAKES: 4 to 6 servings
TIME: About 1 hour, mostly unattended
Ⓜ Ⓥ

This is one of my favorite ways to cook seitan; the crust is crunchy and the interior tender. You can slice it thin and eat as you would meat with vegetable and starch side dishes, or added to rice, noodle, or bean dishes. You can add flavor to the loaves by sprinkling them with a spice mix like curry powder or chili powder or smearing with mashed Roasted Garlic (page 205) when you turn them in Step 2.

> 1 recipe Seitan (page 508), cooled and patted dry
> 2 tablespoons good-quality vegetable oil,
>   or more as needed
>   Salt and pepper (optional)

1. Heat the oven to 350°F. Put the seitan loaves on a roasting rack in a large pan and brush with 2 tablespoons oil. Roast, undisturbed, until they start to turn golden, about 30 minutes.

2. Use tongs to turn the loaves over and brush with more oil, if you like. Continue roasting until the seitan is deeply colored, another 15 to 20 minutes. Cool slightly before slicing. Taste and sprinkle with salt and pepper, if you like.

THE BASICS OF TEMPEH

Tempeh (pronounced TEM-pay) originated in Indonesia. Like soy sauce, miso, and vinegar, tempeh is fermented, and has a complex yeasty flavor with a high umami quotient. Like blue cheese, tempeh is inoculated with an edible mold, so it looks pretty wild: an ugly, lumpy, compressed cake of beans (and sometimes grains), usually less than an inch thick. It's more of an acquired taste than many foods, but chances are if you start with Crunchy Crumbled Tempeh (below), you'll love it.

Tempeh is very high in protein, up to 19 percent by weight, which means about 15 grams in a ½-cup serving. Unlike tofu, tempeh is a whole soybean food, so it contains all the nutrients found in whole soybeans, including B vitamins, many amino acids, and fiber.

You can buy tempeh in most supermarkets now, fresh (usually vacuum-sealed for a longer shelf life) or frozen, in many different varieties. All-soybean is the classic and most common, but tempeh can also be made with soybeans and wild rice, brown rice, or other grains. Once you open the package, use it within a few days.

Tempeh can be eaten raw, but it's good steamed, sliced and fried, braised, or baked. I like it best crumbled and crisped in a little hot oil.

Crunchy Crumbled Tempeh

MAKES: 4 servings
TIME: 10 minutes
Ⓕ Ⓜ Ⓥ

My favorite way to use tempeh is crumbling it into other foods, which distributes delicious, crisp bits throughout the dish and makes the most of tempeh's unique flavor. Use it however you like to use bits of cheese: in burritos, salads, grain dishes (especially fried rice, page 380), soups, and so on. It's easy to change up the flavor by adding dried herbs or a spice mix to the tempeh when it's just about done. Start with about 1 teaspoon, then add more to taste if you like. The same goes for chopped fresh herbs; cilantro, parsley, basil, and mint, alone or in combination, will all work. Stir ½ cup in right before taking it off the heat.

> 2 tablespoons good-quality vegetable oil
> 8 ounces tempeh, crumbled (about 2 cups)
>   Salt and pepper

1. Put the oil in a large skillet over medium-high heat. When it's hot, add the tempeh. Cook, stirring frequently and scraping up any browned bits from the bottom of the pan, until the tempeh is deeply colored and crisp on all sides, 5 to 7 minutes.

2. Remove the tempeh with a slotted spoon and drain on paper towels. Sprinkle lightly with salt and pepper and use immediately or cool, cover, and refrigerate for up to 3 days.

Braised Tempeh, Three Ways

MAKES: 4 to 6 servings
TIME: 30 minutes
F V

Tempeh gives any cooking liquid—even water—an added depth that provides a great backdrop for other, more assertive flavors. The recipe gives you three very different dishes with one simple technique. If you add cooked vegetables—virtually any will work; just stir them in with the bean threads—you have a quick one-bowl dinner.

Try replacing the bean threads with 2 or 3 cups cooked rice vermicelli or whole wheat angel hair pasta; both are great.

2 tablespoons good-quality vegetable oil
8 ounces tempeh
1 tablespoon minced fresh ginger
1 tablespoon minced garlic
   Salt and pepper
1 tablespoon curry powder
2 cups vegetable stock (pages 97–100) or water
2 cups coconut milk (to make your own, see page 304)
3 cups chopped cabbage, preferably Napa
4 ounces (2 bundles) bean threads, soaked and cut (see page 331)
½ cup sliced scallions

½ cup chopped fresh basil (preferably Thai), or parsley

1. Put the oil in a large, deep skillet or pot over medium-high heat. When it's hot, use your fingers to crumble the tempeh into the oil. Cook, stirring frequently and scraping up any browned bits from the bottom of the pan, until the tempeh begins to color and gets crisp on all sides, about 5 minutes. Stir in the ginger and garlic and sprinkle with salt and pepper. Keep cooking and stirring until the ginger and garlic soften and the tempeh is deeply colored, another minute or 2. Stir in the curry powder.

2. Add the stock and coconut milk. Turn the heat to high and bring to a boil, then lower the heat so that the mixture bubbles somewhat assertively. Leave uncovered and cook, stirring occasionally, until the liquid thickens a bit, about 10 minutes.

3. Stir in the cabbage and give it a minute or 2 to wilt. Add the bean threads, scallions, and basil. When the mixture just begins to bubble again, taste, adjust the seasoning, and serve.

HOT AND SOUR BRAISED TEMPEH Increase the oil to 3 tablespoons. Along with the ginger and garlic, add 1 tablespoon minced fresh chile (like jalapeño or Thai) or red chile flakes or cayenne to taste. Substitute sugar for the curry powder. Omit the coconut milk and increase the amount of stock to 3½ cups. When you add the liquid in Step 2, stir in ¼ cup each soy sauce and rice vinegar. Proceed with the recipe, using cilantro instead of basil, if you like.

BRAISED TEMPEH WITH SOY AND TOMATO SAUCE Try this with pasta instead of the bean threads, or omit the noodles entirely and spoon it over polenta (page 391): Omit the curry powder. In Step 2, instead of the stock and coconut milk, use 4 cups chopped tomatoes (canned are fine; include the juice) plus ¼ cup soy sauce. You will need to cook the mixture for another 5 minutes or so to thicken it. Use spinach instead of cabbage, if you like. Proceed with the recipe, finishing with basil or parsley.

Tempeh with Rice
and Spinach

Tempeh with Rice and Spinach

MAKES: 4 servings
TIME: About 40 minutes, mostly unattended
Ⓜ Ⓥ

This bright, lemony dish is great for picnics and potlucks because you can serve it at room temperature. It's also delicious made with brown rice; the cook time will be about twice as long.

2	**lemons**
3	**tablespoons olive oil**
8	**ounces tempeh, crumbled (about 2 cups)**
2	**tablespoons minced garlic**
	Red chile flakes or cayenne
	Salt and pepper
1	**cup long-grain white rice (any kind)**
1	**pound fresh spinach, heavy stems discarded**

1. Grate the zest of one of the lemons. Squeeze the juice from both lemons.

2. Put the oil in a deep pot over medium-high heat. When it's hot, add the tempeh and cook, stirring frequently and scraping up any browned bits from the bottom of the pan, until it is deeply colored and crisp on all sides, 5 to 7 minutes.

3. Stir in the garlic, red chile flakes to taste, and the lemon zest, and sprinkle with salt and pepper. Cook and stir for a minute or so, then stir in the rice and toss to coat. Add enough water to cover the rice by an inch and bring to a boil. Adjust the heat so the mixture boils steadily but not violently. When small craters appear in the surface of the rice, lower the heat a bit more. When all visible moisture disappears, 10 to 15 minutes after you started, put the spinach and reserved lemon juice on top of the rice, cover the pot, and turn off the heat. Leave undisturbed for at least 10 minutes or up to 20. Fluff with a fork to combine, then taste and adjust the seasoning, adding lots of black pepper. Serve hot or at room temperature.

TEMPEH WITH RICE AND PEAS Terrific texture, and great with a splash of soy sauce: Substitute 2 cups peas (thawed frozen are fine) for the spinach.

TEMPEH WITH RICE AND MUSHROOMS Especially good with lots of parsley stirred in at the end: Omit the spinach. Use 1 pound mushrooms (one kind or a combination), trimmed and sliced. After cooking the tempeh in Step 2, add the mushrooms and cook, stirring frequently, until they give off their liquid and start to get dry again. Proceed with the recipe from Step 3, skipping the spinach.

Tempeh Hash

MAKES: 4 servings
TIME: About 1 hour
Ⓜ Ⓥ

A twist on an old favorite. You have to cook each of the main elements separately, though you can easily prepare them a couple of hours in advance and assemble the hash at the last minute. All you need with this are some sliced ripe tomatoes or a simple steamed vegetable like carrots or broccoli. A poached egg or two on top would be perfect.

4	**tablespoons good-quality vegetable oil**
2 or 3	**large all-purpose potatoes, peeled if you like, cut into small pieces**
	Salt and pepper
8	**ounces tempeh, crumbled (about 2 cups)**
1	**large yellow onion, chopped**
2	**tablespoons minced fresh ginger**
1	**tablespoon minced garlic**
1	**tablespoon minced fresh chile (like jalapeño or Thai) or to taste, or red chile flakes or cayenne**
1	**tablespoon soy sauce, or more to taste**
1	**tablespoon sesame oil**
1	**teaspoon rice vinegar**
1	**teaspoon sugar**
1	**red bell pepper, cored, seeded, and chopped**
1	**cup chopped fresh cilantro**

Tempeh Hash
(page 515)

1. Put 2 tablespoons of the vegetable oil in a large skillet over medium-high heat. When it's hot, add the potatoes, sprinkle with salt and pepper, and cook, undisturbed, until the edges brown and they release easily from the pan, about 5 minutes. Toss the potatoes gently, scraping up any browned bits from the bottom of the pan, and turn the heat down to medium. Cook, stirring occasionally, until they are crisp and golden on all sides and tender inside, 10 to 15 minutes more. Transfer to a platter or baking sheet.

2. Put 1 tablespoon of the remaining vegetable oil in the skillet and return the heat to medium-high. Add the tempeh and cook, stirring frequently and scraping up any browned bits, until it is deeply colored and crisp on all sides, 5 to 7 minutes. Add the tempeh to the potatoes, but don't stir them together yet.

3. Put the last tablespoon of the vegetable oil in the skillet over medium-high heat. Add the onion, ginger, and garlic and cook, stirring frequently, until they begin to soften, a minute or 2. Reduce the heat to medium-low and cook, stirring occasionally, until caramelized, about 20 minutes. When done, remove from the heat.

4. Meanwhile, whisk together the chile or red pepper flakes to taste, the soy sauce, sesame oil, vinegar, and sugar in a small bowl. (You can prepare the hash in advance up to this point and assemble it up to 2 hours later.)

5. To finish the dish, put the onion mixture over medium heat. Return the tempeh and potatoes to the skillet and stir for a few minutes until hot and sizzling. Add the chile-soy mixture and toss to coat, scraping up any browned bits from the bottom of the pan. Stir in the bell pepper and cilantro. Taste and adjust the seasoning, and serve.

TEMPEH HASH WITH KIMCHI Hot and vinegary: Omit the chile. Coarsely chop 1 cup Kimchi (page 93) and add it to the hash along with the bell pepper and cilantro in Step 5.

Tempeh Chili with Black Beans

MAKES: 4 to 6 servings
TIME: About 2 hours, mostly unattended
Ⓜ Ⓞ

This recipe is a project, but it's the smokiest, most deeply flavored chili in the book. Use canned beans here only if you must; add them after the chili thickens up a bit, during the last few minutes of cooking.

Serve bowlfuls with wedges of Corn Bread (page 580) or use to fill burritos. You might consider making a double batch and freezing some.

2	**heads garlic**
3	**tablespoons olive oil, plus more for coating the garlic**
12	**ounces tempeh, crumbled (about 3 cups)**
2	**onions, chopped**
¼	**cup honey or 2 tablespoons sugar**
3	**carrots, chopped**
2	**tablespoons chili powder**
1	**tablespoon chopped fresh sage or 1 teaspoon dried sage**
2–5	**canned chipotle chiles, chopped, with some of the adobo sauce**
3	**tablespoons tomato paste**
4	**cups chopped fresh tomatoes (about 2 pounds whole; canned are fine—don't bother to drain)**
2	**cups vegetable stock (pages 97–100) or water**
1	**cup dried black beans (preferably quick-soaked; see page 428)**
	Salt and pepper
1	**cup chopped fresh cilantro for garnish**
1	**cup chopped radishes for garnish**

1. Coat the heads of garlic with a little oil and roast according to either of the recipes on page 205.

2. Meanwhile, put 2 tablespoons oil in a large pot with a lid over medium-high heat. Add the tempeh and cook, stirring frequently and scraping up any browned bits from the bottom of the pan, until it is deeply colored and crisp on all sides, 5 to 7 minutes. Transfer with a slotted spoon to a shallow bowl. Return the pot to medium-high heat.

3. Add the remaining tablespoon oil to the pot along with the onions and cook, stirring frequently, until soft, 3 to 5 minutes. Stir in the honey and turn the heat down to medium-low. Cook, stirring occasionally, until the onions are caramelized and deeply colored, about 20 minutes.

4. Add the carrots, chili powder, and sage; cook for a minute or 2, until fragrant. Stir in the chipotles and adobo sauce to taste, followed by the tomato paste, tomatoes, stock, beans, and tempeh. Bring to a boil, then lower the heat so the mixture bubbles gently and cook, stirring occasionally, until the liquid thickens and the beans are tender, about an hour. Add more stock or water if it starts to look dry. Taste, season with salt and pepper, and partially cover.

5. By now the garlic should be done and cool enough to handle. Squeeze the flesh into the pot and stir well. Taste again and adjust the seasoning, adding more chipotle or honey, if you like. Garnish with the cilantro and radishes and serve.

Eggs, Dairy, and Cheese

Eggs moved beyond breakfast long ago, and now we find them poached or fried on top of lunches and dinners in restaurants and, of course, at home. They have recovered from the (unfair) cholesterol scare of earlier decades and are eagerly eaten by people of all dietary persuasions except veganism. Needless to say, they're one of the great building blocks of a vegetarian diet, but they're also among the most versatile ingredients you can eat.

All the basics of egg cooking are here: the common, and some more unusual, ways to cook eggs for breakfast; a broad look at what we think of as traditional breakfast foods (waffles, pancakes, and the like); and a variety of eggs-for-dinner (or lunch, or brunch, or whatever) dishes.

Most of these recipes show off eggs and dairy in a way that wouldn't be quite the same with an egg replacer or vegan cheese. (Still, many vegans will get inspiration for dishes where tofu could be substituted for eggs or cheese, and milk and butter usually have an obvious vegan substitute.) See page 543 for information about "veganizing" pancakes, which can be done, and done well.

Dairy—yogurt, butter, milk, cheese, and products somewhere in between—adds a unique richness to dishes, one that most people adore. While dairy labeling is still confusing, it's easier to find good-quality milk and butter than it was when the first edition of this book came out.

Cheese may be worshipped, fetishized, or taken for granted. Indeed, you can find cheese that is worthy of praise and eat it with nothing more than bread and fruit, or on its own, and you can find cheese that isn't worth eating. Neither of those has a place here: What I've included are ways to use good cheese in great recipes, to produce mostly savory dishes that can be eaten at any time of day. I also provide instructions for making your own fresh cheese, which is easier than making bread. Really.

THE BASICS OF EGGS

Eggs are among our best sources of protein, minerals, and vitamins, not only for vegetarians but for omnivores. (It's one of only a handful of foods with naturally occurring vitamin D.) Recent studies have negated worries about the link between dietary cholesterol (found in food, like eggs) and blood cholesterol (now thought to mostly derive from the saturated fats we consume), and the cholesterol in eggs is even thought to prevent some types of stroke.

BUYING EGGS

If you can get eggs from by a local farmer—or you know someone with chickens—consider yourself lucky. Otherwise, there are so many meaningless and misleading claims that trying to know your way around buying eggs is difficult. In fact, much of the information on egg packages, old and new, can safely be ignored.

Egg sizes are based on weight per dozen and include jumbo, extra-large, large, medium, small, and peewee. Extra-large and large eggs are most common, and most recipes, including mine, assume large eggs, though you can freely substitute extra-large with no ill consequences. The difference between them is only a quarter of an ounce per egg. So in general, unless you're using an extraordinary number of eggs in a single recipe (say a dozen or more), extra-large and large eggs are interchangeable.

It's worth noting that no chickens are (legally) raised using hormones; it's against USDA regulations, so the label "raised without hormones" is as meaningless as the "natural" label for eggs—they all are, or at least they're supposed to be.

There are some labels that are associated with a specific set of voluntary rules and regulations and monitored by third-party auditors:

ORGANIC (OR CERTIFIED ORGANIC)

If you see the USDA Certified Organic stamp, it means the hens are raised without cages and with access to the outdoors; are fed organic, all-vegetarian diets; and are raised without antibiotics, pesticides, and insecticides. It also means the eggs aren't irradiated. "Certified Organic" is the only way to guarantee that your eggs were raised without antibiotics. A new term, "Beyond

Organic," is gaining recognition as being stricter than the USDA Certified Organic standards (though it isn't USDA regulated), but you probably won't see it in a grocery store, which is where you need the most help.

CERTIFIED HUMANE, FREE FARMED, ANIMAL WELFARE APPROVED, AND ANIMAL CARE CERTIFIED

Technically, these are four separate certifications, but they all refer to the animals' living conditions and treatment: guaranteeing a minimum amount of space, access to fresh air, water, and food, and limited stress and/or noise, among other things. Each certification is overseen by an independent association whose inspection regulations are approved by the USDA, but they are not part of a USDA regulatory program. Participation is voluntary. These eggs are not organic, unless separately labeled so.

All other labels you might see on egg cartons are not regulated. Buyer beware.

Always take a quick peek inside the carton to make sure all the eggs are intact. After that, you have to crack open the egg to find out if it's fresh—not something you can do in a supermarket. So go with the pack date. At home, you can look for these four signs of a fresh egg:

- The white is thick and doesn't spread out much.
- The white is a bit cloudy. (This means that the naturally occurring carbon dioxide hasn't had time to fully escape from the egg after laying.)
- The yolk is firm and stands tall.
- The chalazae (the coiled cordlike attachments to the yolk) are prominent.

STORING EGGS

Of course, eggs keep nearly forever (and you'll quickly know when one is bad, by its smell), so although a fresh egg will give you the most amazing fried egg, you can use them in recipes for pretty much as long as you like; they just won't be as delicious as they were when they were fresh.

Eggs should be kept in the refrigerator (in the United States, at least; elsewhere, they're processed differently, which makes room temperature storage just fine), which keeps them fresh and minimizes the growth of harmful bacteria like salmonella. Don't store them in the door of the fridge, which is often too warm, and keep them away from strong-smelling foods; though hard, the shells are porous and eggs easily absorb odors. Use them... well, as quickly as you can. As I said, their quality will decline but they won't go bad for a long time.

Hard-Boiled Egg

MAKES: 1 serving
TIME: About 15 minutes
F M

Hard-boiled eggs are so convenient and versatile that it's worth keeping a few on hand at all times (they keep for a week). They're used in recipes throughout this book, from appetizers to hearty dinnertime dishes. If you have hard-boiled eggs, cooked grains, and some sautéed vegetables in the fridge, you've always got a meal.

I think they're best when cooked for 9 minutes so the yolk is just slightly undercooked and still creamy, not chalky. At 11 minutes (see the variation) the egg is still edible but dry.

If the yolk is green, it's due to a harmless amount of sulfur in the egg, and to not cooling the egg quickly enough. To prevent or minimize it, be sure to immerse the eggs in an ice bath as soon you remove them from the simmering water.

> 1 **egg**
>   **Salt and pepper (optional)**

1. Fill a saucepan about two-thirds full with water and add the egg. Bring to a boil, then turn off the heat and cover. The average large to extra-large egg will be ready 9 minutes later.

2. Plunge into a bowl of ice water for a minute or so, then refrigerate or crack and peel. Sprinkle with salt and pepper if you like and serve.

HARD-BOILED EGGS FOR EGG SALAD The ideal hard-boiled egg for eating as is has a slightly soft yolk, but if

you want the yolk to be completely solid (though a little chalky) so you can chop the egg, leave the egg in the hot water for 11 minutes. Be sure to plunge it into an ice bath immediately so it doesn't overcook.

Soft-Boiled Egg

MAKES: 1 serving
TIME: Less than 10 minutes
F

The egg lover's way to eat a boiled egg: barely cooked, but warm and comforting. Soft-boiled eggs are great stirred into a bowl of reheated leftover grains or a soup or broth.

1 egg
Salt and pepper (optional)

1. Fill a saucepan about two-thirds full with water and bring it to a gentle boil.
2. Use a spoon or some other handy tool to lower the egg into the gently boiling water. Adjust the heat so the water barely bubbles, then cook for 3 to 5 minutes, the lower time if you want the yolk completely runny and the white still slightly liquid, the higher if you want the white very soft but set.
3. Run the egg briefly under cold water, crack the shell, and scoop out the egg. Sprinkle with salt and pepper if you like and serve.

Medium-Boiled Egg

MAKES: 1 serving
TIME: About 10 minutes
F

These are easier than poached eggs and about the same texture: The white is firm and the yolk runny. Use them anywhere you would poached eggs. You can also reheat them after peeling by dipping them in simmering water for about 30 seconds.

1 egg
Salt and pepper (optional)

Easy Peeling

Older eggs peel more easily after boiling than fresh eggs but it does help to immediately plunge them into a bowl of ice-cold water. If you like, leave them in long enough to cool thoroughly—5 minutes or so—then store them in the fridge. They'll be even easier to peel after they come back out, another good reason for making extra.

If you don't want a cold boiled egg, cool them down fast under running cold water so the outside cools enough so you can separate the shell from the egg but the inside stays warm. Just know that this won't completely stop the cooking like an ice bath will.

1. Fill a saucepan about two-thirds full with water and bring it to a gentle boil.
2. Use a spoon or some other handy tool to lower the egg into the gently boiling water. Adjust the heat so the mixture barely bubbles, then cook for 6 to 8 minutes; the shorter time guarantees a cooked but runny yolk, but there may be some undercooked white. With the longer time, the white will be fully cooked, but some of the yolk may have hardened. Try it both ways and see which you prefer.
3. Plunge the egg into an ice bath or cold running water for about 30 seconds, then crack and peel gently, as you would a hard-boiled egg (but more carefully). Sprinkle with salt and pepper if you like and serve.

Scrambled Eggs

MAKES: 2 servings
TIME: 10 minutes
F

You can prepare great scrambled eggs fast. There are only a couple things to keep in mind (besides not overcooking them): Adding a little extra liquid helps prevent overcooking; a tiny squeeze of lemon will make them even more tender, and cream lends a luxurious texture, but even a teaspoon of water helps. And lightly beat the raw eggs with a fork or a whisk, just until the yolks and whites are combined; overbeating will make them tough and watery.

This technique—starting in a cold pan, and making sure that the curds stay small—is the single best way to make creamy, delicious scrambled eggs. See "11 Simple Additions to Scrambled Eggs," below, for more ideas besides cheese.

 4 **eggs**
1–2 **tablespoons butter or olive oil, to taste**
1–2 **tablespoons milk, cream, unsweetened nondairy milk, or water (optional)**
  Salt and pepper

1. Beat the eggs lightly. Pour into a skillet, preferably nonstick, add the butter, and milk if you're using it, and sprinkle with salt and pepper. Turn the heat to medium-high and cook, stirring frequently and scraping the sides of the pan (a heatproof spatula is a good tool here).
2. As the eggs begin to curdle, you may notice that some parts are drying out; whenever you see that, remove the pan from the heat and continue to stir until the cooking slows down a bit. Then return to the heat and continue cooking. The eggs are done when they are creamy, soft, and still a bit runny; do not overcook (unless you like them that way). Serve immediately.

SCRAMBLED EGGS WITH CHEESE Use virtually any kind of cheese you like except for ones that don't melt easily, like feta or queso fresco: As the eggs begin to set, stir in ½ cup grated cheese.

11 Simple Additions to Scrambled Eggs

As in making a flat omelet (page 530) or frittata (page 532), you can add almost anything you want to the beaten uncooked eggs before scrambling; just try to keep the size small:
1. Chopped pickled jalapeños (to taste)
2. Sautéed mushrooms, onions, spinach, or other cooked vegetables, chopped (about ½ cup)

3. Chopped fresh herbs (1 teaspoon stronger herbs like oregano, tarragon, and thyme; 1 tablespoon milder ones like parsley, chives, chervil, basil, and mint)
4. Sour cream, cream cheese cut into bits, or crumbled goat cheese (about ½ cup)
5. Cooked and lightly buttered grains, especially farro, pearled barley, bulgur, or millet (about ½ cup)
6. Any cooked salsa (pages 662 to 664), drained if it's quite moist (up to ½ cup)
7. Chopped tomato (up to 1 cup)
8. Tabasco sauce, Worcestershire Sauce, Hold the Anchovies (page 633), soy sauce, mustard, or other store-bought sauce (to taste)
9. Chopped scallions (up to ½ cup)
10. Chopped roasted red peppers (page 228; up to ½ cup)
11. Any chopped leftover cooked vegetable

Fried Eggs, Sunny Side Up or Over Easy

MAKES: 1 or 2 servings
TIME: 10 minutes

Correctly cooked, fried eggs are nearly as delicate as poached eggs, with tender whites and a barely cooked yolk. Low heat is the easiest way to achieve this, but with practice you can use higher heat and get the same results.

Butter is the most luxurious medium for cooking eggs, and often the most delicious. But it's hardly the only choice: Olive oil lends a delicious flavor (especially with a few sage leaves and a grating of Parmesan), and sesame oil is interesting, especially if you're frying an egg to put on top of Jook (page 424). Good-quality vegetable oil is also acceptable. If you use the smaller amount of fat here, take more care to prevent the eggs from sticking to the pan, or use a nonstick pan.

1 **teaspoon to 1 tablespoon butter or oil**
2 **eggs**
 Salt and pepper

1. Put a skillet, preferably nonstick, over medium heat for about 1 minute. Add the butter and swirl it around the pan. When the foam subsides, about a minute later, crack the eggs into the pan. As soon as the whites lose their translucence (this takes only a minute) turn the heat to low and sprinkle with salt and pepper.

2. Cook the eggs until the whites are completely firm; the last place for this to happen is just around the yolk. If the egg has set up high, rather than spread out thin, there are two techniques to encourage it to finish cooking: The first is to cut through the uncooked parts of the white with a small knife; this allows some of the still-liquid white to sink through the cooked white and hit the surface of the pan, where it will cook immediately. The second is to cover the skillet for a minute or 2 longer to encourage the white to finish cooking. Alternatively, of course, you can flip the eggs over when they're solid enough to be lifted by a spatula. When the eggs are cooked, after about 5 minutes, remove them from the pan and serve.

FRIED EGGS WITH CHEESE Because sometimes you just feel like it: When the eggs just start to set up, sprinkle a tablespoon or 2 of grated cheddar, Monterey Jack, Swiss, Gruyère, or Parmesan on top of each egg.

5 Simple Ideas for Fried Eggs

1. Fresh Herb Fried Eggs. As the butter or oil heats, season it with a few leaves fresh herbs or a smashed clove garlic.

2. Vinegary Fried Eggs. When the eggs have finished cooking, remove them from the pan and pour in 2 tablespoons red or white wine vinegar. Cook to reduce by half, then pour over the eggs.

3. Fried Egg Package. As the white sets, use a butter knife to fold its edges over the yolk, making a little package and further protecting the yolk from overcooking.

4. Super Savory Fried Eggs. Add Worcestershire Sauce, Hold the Anchovies (page 633), or other liquid seasoning like soy sauce or hot sauce, to the white before it sets.

5. Fried Eggs with Tomatoes. Cook ½-inch-thick tomato slices—either ripe or green tomatoes—alongside the eggs (increase the amount of butter slightly).

Poached Eggs

MAKES: 1 or 2 servings
TIME: 10 minutes
F

Poached eggs are wonderful, and my favorite way to turn a bowl of anything into a complete meal: They're sauce and garnish all in one.

Making a poached egg that looks perfect takes a little practice. (In my judgment, it's also overrated; a shaggy poached egg still tastes great. If you want a gorgeous egg in a poached-egg situation, make a medium-boiled egg, page 523, peel it, and reheat it.)

If you want to make more than two eggs, simply use a bigger pan, and be careful to avoid crowding. Or, you can make poached eggs in multiple batches: Keep a separate large pot of water warm over very low heat, and use an instant-read thermometer to make sure the temperature hovers between 145°F and 150°F; adjust the heat accordingly. Cook the eggs in a smaller pot and, as they finish, transfer them to the large pot and cover. Fish them out with a slotted spoon when you're ready to serve.

> 1 teaspoon salt
> 1 teaspoon white vinegar
> 2 eggs

1. Bring about an inch of water to a boil in a small, deep skillet. Add the salt and vinegar and lower the heat to the point where the liquid barely bubbles; if you measure it with an instant-read thermometer, the temperature should be just under 200°F. One at a time, break an egg into a shallow bowl, and gently slip it into the water.

2. Cook for 3 to 5 minutes, just until the white is set and the yolk has filmed over. Remove with a slotted spoon and allow the water to drain off for a couple of seconds. Poached eggs are delicate, so be careful handling them. If you like, drain them briefly on paper towels before putting them directly on the toast or what have you.

5 Great Sauces for Poaching Eggs

You can poach eggs in thicker liquids like sauces, though the technique is slightly different from the one described in the recipe. Make sure the sauce is at least an inch deep in the pan, and heat it only to the gentlest bubble. After you slip in the eggs, cover the pan tightly to steam the eggs. When you're done, you have a deliciously enriched sauce. To make a full meal, simply serve with vegetables and a starch alongside, or over pasta, rice, or toasted bread.

1. Fast Tomato Sauce or any of its variations (page 312)

2. Salsa Roja or any of its variations (page 662)

3. Smooth Green Chile Sauce, Indian Style, or any of its variations (page 666)

4. Cooked Tomatillo Salsa or any of its variations (page 663)

5. Spicy Indian Tomato Sauce (page 667)

Baked ("Shirred") Eggs

MAKES: 2 servings
TIME: 30 minutes

The texture of baked eggs cannot be duplicated by any other method. Plus, you can put all sorts of raw or cooked vegetables, grains, or legumes into the cup before adding the egg, which makes this an easy way to use up leftovers. Try chopped tomatoes, scallions, or herbs; rice pilaf or fried rice; Caramelized Onions (page 222); or cooked mushrooms or greens. You can also top the eggs with bread crumbs, grated cheese, chopped fresh herbs, or a sprinkle of your favorite spice blend—alone or in combination. You may need to cook the eggs a couple of minutes more, depending on the additions.

This is one of the best ways to cook eggs for a crowd, and you can easily scale it up by using a muffin tin.

> Butter or oil, as needed
> About 1 tablespoon cream (optional)
> 2 eggs
> Salt and pepper (optional)

1. Heat the oven to 375°F. Smear a bit of butter or oil in each of 2 custard cups or small ramekins. If you like, put a couple of teaspoons of cream in the bottom of each (a nice touch). Break 1 egg into each cup, then put the cups on a baking sheet. (Or use a muffin tin if you are scaling up the recipe.)

2. Bake until the eggs are just set and the whites solidified, 10 to 15 minutes; the precise time, in a well-calibrated oven on the middle rack, is 12 minutes. Because of the heat retained by the cups, these will continue to cook after you remove them from the oven so it's best to undercook them slightly. Sprinkle with salt and pepper, if you like, and serve.

OVEN-POACHED EGGS Putting the ramekins in a water bath results in ultra-tender eggs: Instead of putting the custard cups on a baking sheet, put them in a deep ovenproof pan. Fill the pan with about an inch of boiling water (partway up the sides of the cups) and cover with foil. Carefully put the pan in the oven and bake to the desired doneness, between 15 and 30 minutes.

BAKED EGGS WITH ONIONS AND CHEESE An impressive, rich brunch dish: Heat the oven to 350°F. In a large, greased baking dish, layer Caramelized Onions (page 222), 1 cup bread crumbs, preferably fresh (see page 678), and 2 cups grated melting cheese like mozzarella or cheddar. Make 8 wells in the cheese mixture and break 1 egg into each. Bake until the cheese has melted and the egg whites are opaque, 15 to 20 minutes. Makes 4 to 8 servings.

Eggs Florentine
(page 528)

Eggs Florentine

MAKES: 4 servings
TIME: 30 minutes

F

You can think of this as vegetarian Eggs Benedict, but I think it's better. And any breakfast that incorporates greens is a plus.

> Salt
> 2 pounds fresh spinach, rinsed well and trimmed of thick stems
> 1 recipe Hollandaise Sauce (page 674)
> 4 English muffins, split, or 8 slices crusty bread
> 2 tablespoons butter
> 8 eggs
> Chopped fresh parsley for garnish (optional)
> Sweet or smoked paprika for garnish (optional)

1. Bring a large pot of water to a boil and salt it. Add the spinach and cook until it is bright green and tender, about a minute. Drain well. When it is cool enough to handle, squeeze the moisture from it and chop.

2. Make or reheat the hollandaise, cover, and keep warm in a double boiler or a bowl set over a pot of simmering water. Toast the English muffins or bread until golden. Butter them and keep warm.

3. When you're ready to serve, poach the eggs following the directions for Poached Eggs (page 525). You may need to work in 2 batches and hold the finished eggs in warm water as described.

4. To assemble: Put a muffin on each plate, open face, or 2 pieces toast. Top each with a mound of spinach, an egg, and a spoonful of hollandaise. Garnish with parsley and/or paprika if you like and serve.

LIGHTER EGGS FLORENTINE Sometimes hollandaise is too much: Replace each English muffin with 2 slices whole wheat bread. Omit the hollandaise. Proceed with the recipe, and garnish each piece of toast with lots of cracked black pepper and a drizzle of balsamic vinegar.

Simplest Omelet

MAKES: 2 servings
TIME: 30 minutes

F

Omelets are, of course, traditional breakfast and brunch dishes, but they also make a wonderful, fast dinner. This is a basic omelet, but it can be filled with almost anything. The variations range from classic (and usually simple) to a bit more complex; some are practically all-in-one meals. See "10 Ideas for Filling Omelets" (page 529).

> 4 or 5 eggs
> 2 tablespoons milk or cream (optional)
> Salt and pepper
> 2 tablespoons plus 1 teaspoon butter or olive oil

1. Beat together the eggs, milk if you're using it, and some salt and pepper in a bowl. Have a clean plate ready near the stove.

2. Put a skillet, preferably nonstick, over medium-high heat and wait a minute. Add 2 tablespoons of the butter; when it melts, swirl it around the pan until its foam subsides, then pour in the egg mixture. Cook, undisturbed, for about 30 seconds, then use a rubber spatula to push the edges of the eggs toward the center. As you do this, tip the pan to allow the uncooked eggs in the center to reach the edges.

3. Continue this process until the omelet is mostly cooked but still quite runny in the center, about 3 minutes. You can cook until the center firms up, if you prefer, another minute or so.

4. Hold the pan at a 45 degree angle so that half of the omelet slides onto the plate, then gently increase the angle of the pan over the plate, allowing the omelet in the pan to fold over onto the first half. Alternatively, you can fold the omelet into thirds (like a letter) using a large spatula, and then slide it out of the pan.

5. Rub the top of the omelet with the remaining teaspoon butter and serve.

CHEESE OMELET Use any grated, crumbled, or soft cheese: Add ½ to ¾ cup cheese to the eggs, in a line along the axis on which you will fold or roll, about a minute before finishing the omelet.

SPANISH OMELET A classic combination of onions and tomatoes: Before cooking the omelet, cook 2 tablespoons chopped scallions or onion in 1 tablespoon butter in a small saucepan over medium heat for 30 seconds. Stir in 1 cup chopped tomato, cook for about 2 minutes, season with salt and pepper, and keep warm. Add the tomato mixture, with a sprinkle of smoked paprika if you like, to the eggs as in the preceding variation.

PANEER AND SPINACH OMELET, INDIAN STYLE Heat ¼ cup yogurt over medium-low heat and add 1 cup lightly packed baby spinach leaves, ½ teaspoon garam masala, and a sprinkle of salt and pepper; cook until the spinach is wilted. Add ½ cup paneer cheese cut into small cubes and the yogurt mixture to the eggs as in the first variation.

10 Ideas for Filling Omelets

You can fill an omelet with just about anything. Here are two lists, the first for more traditional fillings, the second for more substantial fillings that will make your omelet a self-contained meal.

Cooked fillings, like vegetables or grains, should be warm; raw fillings, like cheese, should be finely grated so they melt or heat up quickly. Mix and match any of the fillings, but keep the total quantity to about 1 cup unless otherwise noted.

1. Grated cheese, virtually any kind. Figure about 2 tablespoons per egg. And adding some grated apple at the same time is surprisingly good, too.
2. Chopped fresh herbs. Use 1 teaspoon stronger herbs like oregano, tarragon, or thyme or 1 tablespoon milder ones like parsley, chive, chervil, basil, or mint.
3. Peeled, seeded, and chopped tomato, drained of excess moisture if necessary.
4. Sautéed mushrooms, onions, spinach, or other cooked vegetables, chopped (about ½ cup).
5. Refried beans, or any mashed, puréed, or whole beans, with cheese. Serve with salsa.

6. Cooked grains like bulgur, quinoa, barley, kasha, wheat berries, or farro, with cooked mushrooms and 2 or 3 slices soft cheese like Brie, cream cheese, or any melting cheese.
7. Chopped cooked asparagus and/or roasted red peppers (page 228) with artichoke hearts (drained marinated are fine), and goat cheese.
8. Ricotta mixed with chopped fresh herbs or Pesto (page 634) or any of the variations.
9. Cooked spinach or other greens like kale, chard, or collards (squeezed of excess water), with cubed smoked tofu.
10. Roasted corn (see page 195) sautéed with scallions or sliced onion and fresh chiles, with crumbled queso fresco.

Vegan Omelet

MAKES: 2 servings
TIME: 15 minutes
F **V**

Even if you don't eat eggs, you might crave an omelet. Use this recipe as a template for a "regular" omelet, and fill it with any of the ingredients in any of the recipes or variations.

1   **14-ounce package silken tofu, drained**
2   **tablespoons tahini**
    Salt and pepper
1   **teaspoon cornstarch**
4   **tablespoons olive oil**

1. If you won't be serving the first omelet as soon as it's ready, heat the oven to 200°F. Put the tofu, tahini, a big pinch of salt, some pepper, and the cornstarch in a food processor or blender and process until smooth.
2. Put 2 tablespoons of the oil in a 10-inch nonstick skillet over medium-high heat. When it's hot but not smoking, pour in half of the tofu mixture, using a spatula to evenly distribute it in the pan. Cook until the bottom has browned and the top has set, 5 to 10 minutes. Use a large spatula to loosen one edge of the omelet, lift, and

fold about a third of it toward the center. Slide the spatula under the center of the omelet, lift, and fold it over the opposite edge. Serve immediately or keep warm on an ovenproof plate in the oven. Repeat with the remaining tofu mixture.

Flat Omelet with Cauliflower or Broccoli

MAKES: 4 servings
TIME: 30 minutes

🇫 Ⓜ

All sorts of vegetables can be used here, including fresh, frozen, or cooked leftovers. You can also use cheese (see the first variation), or almost anything you have around.

3	tablespoons olive oil
1½	cups chopped cauliflower or broccoli
½	onion, sliced
1	tablespoon minced garlic (optional)
	Salt and pepper
4 or 5	eggs
	Grated Parmesan cheese for garnish

1. Put 2 tablespoons of the oil in an 8- or 10-inch non-stick or well-seasoned cast-iron skillet over high heat. Add the cauliflower and about ⅓ cup water and cook, stirring occasionally, until the cauliflower is soft and the water evaporated, 5 to 10 minutes. If you're using cooked vegetables, skip the water and cook over medium-high heat until heated through.
2. Add the remaining oil and the onion and the garlic, if you're using it. Sprinkle with salt and pepper and cook until the onion is soft, 3 to 5 minutes more. Turn the heat to low.
3. Lightly beat the eggs with some salt and pepper. Pour the eggs over the cauliflower, using a spoon if necessary to evenly distribute the vegetable. Cook, undisturbed, until the eggs are barely set, 5 to 10 minutes. Sprinkle Parmesan over the top. Serve hot, warm, or at room temperature.

CHEESY FLAT OMELET Make this with or without the vegetables: Sprinkle the cheese on top at the end and melt it in the oven or under the broiler, if you prefer. Or in Step 3, add ¾ cup cheese like cottage cheese, soft goat cheese, ricotta, crumbled blue cheese, or grated Jack or cheddar to the beaten eggs.

7 Great Filling Combinations for Flat Omelets

Just about any vegetable, herb, or cheese can be used in a flat omelet, alone or in combination. About 1½ cups vegetables, ¾ cup cheese, or 1 cup vegetables and ½ cup cheese combined are good starting points.

If you're using leftover cooked vegetables: Let them come to room temperature or give them a quick flash in the pan with some oil or butter, then add the beaten eggs and cook as directed in any of the frittata recipes on pages 530 to 533.

For fresh vegetables: Chop or slice the vegetable into bite-sized pieces. Cook in the skillet with a tablespoon or 2 of oil or butter until tender, adding a little water, as in Flat Omelet with Cauliflower or Broccoli, above, or boil in salted water until tender and drain very well.

For frozen vegetables: Thaw them at room temperature or in the skillet (see the Flat Omelet with Frozen Vegetables variation, right).

1. Sliced potatoes and rosemary (see Home Fries, page 235)

2. Asparagus and Parmesan

3. Summer squash, wheat berries, and ricotta

4. Caramelized Onions (page 222) and blue cheese

5. Spinach and smoked tofu

6. Artichoke hearts, whole wheat or regular pasta, and parsley

7. Roasted red peppers (page 228) and manchego

FLAT OMELET WITH FROZEN VEGETABLES You can perform this magic with almost any frozen vegetable: Substitute 1½ cups frozen vegetables, straight from the bag, for the cauliflower and omit the onion and garlic. In Step 1, cook the vegetables until the pieces separate and are soft; sprinkle with salt and pepper and continue to cook until they begin to brown. Proceed with the recipe.

FLAT OMELET, MEXICAN STYLE Also a great filling for tacos and enchiladas: In Step 1, substitute 3 chopped scallions and about a tablespoon chopped jalapeño for the cauliflower and onion, and cook for just a minute, with no water. In Step 3, add ½ cup crumbled queso fresco and ¼ cup chopped fresh cilantro to the eggs; omit the Parmesan. Serve with salsa and a stack of warm tortillas.

FLAT OMELET, GREEK STYLE Omit the onion, garlic, and Parmesan. Skip Steps 1 and 2. Add ½ cup chopped roasted red peppers (page 228), ½ cup or so crumbled feta cheese, and 1 teaspoon chopped fresh oregano or ½ teaspoon dried oregano to the beaten eggs. Proceed with Step 3.

Spanish Tortilla

Tortilla Española
MAKES: 4 servings
TIME: 40 minutes
Ⓜ

A standard Spanish tapa, also wonderful served in sandwiches with homemade Garlic Mayonnaise (page 671), or, for that matter, ketchup. Don't worry about using so much olive oil, because you'll eventually pour it off; save it in the fridge and use it in regular cooking, or for making another tortilla!

Using a food processor with the slicing attachment will save some prep time here, especially if you double the recipe, which you can do for a crowd.

1   cup olive oil
1¼ pounds waxy potatoes (3 to 4 medium), peeled and thinly sliced

1   onion, thinly sliced
    Salt and pepper
    Pinch smoked paprika (pimentón; optional)
8   eggs

1. Put the oil in a large nonstick skillet over medium heat. About 3 minutes later, add a slice of potato; if bubbles appear, the oil is ready. Add the potatoes and onion and sprinkle with salt, pepper, and the smoked paprika, if you're using it. Turn the potato mixture in the oil with a wooden spoon to coat and adjust the heat so that the oil bubbles lazily.

2. Cook, turning the potato mixture gently every few minutes and adjusting the heat so the potatoes do not brown, until they are tender when pierced with the tip of a small knife. Meanwhile, beat the eggs with some salt and pepper in a large bowl.

3. Drain the potato mixture, reserving the oil. Wipe out the skillet, return it to medium heat, and add back 2 tablespoons of the oil. Combine the potato mixture with the eggs and pour into the skillet. As soon as the edges firm up (this will only take a minute or so), reduce the heat to medium-low and cook, undisturbed, for 5 minutes.

4. Insert a spatula all around the edges of the tortilla to make sure it will slide from the pan. Carefully slide it out—the top will still be quite runny—onto a plate. Cover with another plate and, holding the plates tightly, invert them.

5. Add another tablespoon of the oil to the skillet and use the spatula to coax the tortilla back in. Cook for another 5 minutes, then slide the tortilla from the skillet onto a serving plate. Or you can finish the cooking in a 350°F oven for about 10 minutes. Serve warm (not hot) or at room temperature.

SPINACH TORTILLA Reduce the oil to ¼ cup and omit the potatoes, onion, and paprika. In Step 1, sauté 1 pound fresh spinach in the oil with 1 tablespoon minced garlic, and a pinch red chile flakes if you like. Stir and cook until just softened (only a few minutes). Drain and proceed with the recipe.

TORTILLA PAISANA Reduce the potatoes to 1 pound and add 2 roasted red peppers (page 228), seeded and sliced, and 1 cup peas when you combine the potatoes and eggs.

Vietnamese Omelet

MAKES: 4 servings
TIME: 25 minutes
F M

Perfect with quick-cooking vegetables like bean sprouts and bok choy. Fried or smoked tofu is another fine addition. Serve with Basil Dipping Sauce (page 654) or Peanut Sauce, Four Ways (page 657).

6	eggs
1	tablespoon Fishless Fish Sauce (page 656) or soy sauce, plus more for passing
	Salt and pepper
2	tablespoons good-quality vegetable oil
1	clove garlic, minced
1	shallot, minced
2	scallions, trimmed with only a little of the green part remaining, chopped
2	cups mixed julienned vegetables (like carrots, bean sprouts, mushrooms, or bok choy)
1	fresh chile (like Thai or Serrano), seeded, if you like, and minced
	Chopped fresh cilantro for garnish

1. Lightly beat the eggs with the sauce and some salt and pepper in a medium bowl.
2. Put the oil in a large nonstick or well-seasoned cast-iron skillet over medium heat. When it's hot, add the garlic, shallot, and scallions and cook until fragrant, about a minute. Add the vegetables and chile and cook until they just start to soften, 2 or 3 minutes. Pour in the eggs and swirl the pan to evenly distribute.
3. Cook until the eggs begin to set around the edge, a minute or 2. Cover, turn the heat down to medium-low, and cook until the eggs are just firm, 5 to 7 minutes. (Or, you can put it under the broiler to cook the top.)

4. Slide the omelet out onto a cutting board and let it cool a bit before cutting into wedges. Garnish with cilantro and serve, passing more Fishless Fish Sauce or soy sauce at the table.

Pasta Frittata

MAKES: 4 servings
TIME: 40 minutes
M

This is an instantly lovable and easily varied way to use leftover pasta; if's it sauced, even better. You don't even have to use long pasta; try this with rigatoni for more chew. Or use grains, bread, or potatoes instead of pasta (see the variations). Add whatever fresh herbs you like.

This is great with Fast Tomato Sauce (page 312) or Pesto (page 634) or any of the variations.

2	tablespoons butter or olive oil
5	eggs
	Salt and pepper
1½	cups leftover cooked spaghetti, linguine, fettuccine, or other long pasta, or whatever you have on hand
1	cup grated Parmesan cheese
¼	cup chopped fresh parsley or basil (optional)

1. Heat the oven to 400°F. Put the butter or oil in a large ovenproof nonstick skillet over medium-high heat.
2. Beat the eggs with some salt and pepper in a large bowl. Stir in the pasta with ½ cup of the Parmesan, and the parsley, if you're using it. Pour the mixture into the skillet and immediately turn the heat down to medium-low. Use a spoon if necessary to even out the pasta. Cook, undisturbed, until the frittata firms up on the bottom, 10 to 15 minutes. Transfer to the oven and bake until the top is just cooked, about 10 minutes more. Serve hot or at room temperature with the remaining Parmesan sprinkled on top.

BASIC FRITTATA As easy as it gets: Omit the pasta, add 1 more egg, and add all the Parmesan in Step 2.

FRITTATA WITH GRAINS Substitute 1½ cups or so cooked grains, like farro, wheat berries, rye berries, quinoa, bulgur, or buckwheat, for the pasta.

Breakfast Burritos

MAKES: 4 servings
TIME: 20 minutes with cooked beans
F M

Just about every fast-food joint now sells breakfast burritos, but few will be as good as yours. Fill them as you would tacos, with colorful ingredients like chopped fresh tomatoes, cilantro, black olives, or scallions; chopped fresh chiles; avocado slices or chunks; or small cubes of Home Fries (page 235).

If you're a breakfast-to-go type, double or triple the recipe, wrap the burritos well in plastic or foil, and tuck them away in your freezer. Reheat foil-wrapped burritos in a 350°F oven for 20 minutes or so; or remove the wrapping, drape each burrito with a paper towel, and reheat in the microwave for a couple of minutes when you get to work.

> 2 **cups Refried Beans (page 460), Chili non Carne (page 455), or plain cooked or drained canned pinto or black beans**
> 4 **large flour tortillas**
> 6 **eggs**
> 2 **tablespoons butter or olive oil**
> 1 **cup crumbled Fresh Cheese (page 568) or queso fresco or grated cheddar or Jack cheese**

1. Warm the beans or chili in a small saucepan. To warm the tortillas, wrap them in foil and put in a 300°F oven for about 10 minutes or stack them between 2 damp paper towels and microwave for 30 to 60 seconds.
2. Beat the eggs and cook them in the butter in a large skillet according to the directions for Scrambled Eggs on page 523.
3. When the eggs are nearly done, remove them from the heat and assemble the burritos. Spread the cheese on each tortilla and top with ½ cup or so of beans. Add

the eggs and any sauces (see the list on page 533) or garnishes you like. Roll up (see the illustration on page 622) and serve.

VEGAN BREAKFAST BURRITOS Nice texture: Omit the eggs and butter and skip Step 2. Instead, prepare 1 recipe Scrambled Tofu (page 489) and use that to fill the burritos. Instead of the cheese, use sliced avocado. Proceed with the recipe. V

BEANS AND GREENS BURRITOS Heartier and healthier: In a large skillet, wilt 1 pound chopped kale, spinach, or other greens. Once the greens are cooked down, add the beans and proceed with the recipe.

Huevos Rancheros

MAKES: 2 servings
TIME: 35 minutes
M

For lovers of Mexican food, huevos rancheros are among the best breakfasts ever, especially when served with a salsa (pages 659 to 664), extra beans, avocado slices, shredded lettuce, and/or limes. Mexican *crema* on the side is a nice touch.

If you have the basic components on hand, this is just a matter of assembly, and since the recipe is easily multiplied, it's perfect for entertaining.

7 Sauces for Mexican Breakfast Dishes

1. **Salsa Roja (page 662)**

2. **Cooked Tomatillo Salsa (page 663)**

3. **Fresh Tomato Salsa (page 660)**

4. **Fresh Tomatillo Salsa (page 660)**

5. **Radish Salsa (page 662)**

6. **Bottled hot sauce**

7. **Mexican *crema***

Huevos Rancheros
(page 533)

¼ cup good-quality vegetable oil, plus more
  as needed

4 5-inch corn tortillas

¼ cup Refried Beans (page 460) or any soft,
  well-seasoned beans

4 eggs
  Salt and pepper

½ cup Salsa Roja or Cooked Tomatillo Salsa
  (page 662 or 663) or store-bought salsa

¼ cup crumbled queso fresco or grated
  Monterey Jack or cheddar cheese

¼ cup chopped fresh cilantro or parsley
  for garnish

1. Heat the oil in a small skillet over medium heat. When it's hot, fry the tortillas one at a time until softened and heated through, about 3 seconds per side. Make sure they do not crisp. Drain on paper towels.
2. Spread 1 tablespoon of the beans in the center of each tortilla. (You can prepare the dish to this point up to an hour or so in advance.)
3. Heat the oven to 350°F. Use a little more oil to fry the eggs sunny side up (in a nonstick skillet, if you like), sprinkling with salt and pepper as they cook and following the directions for Fried Eggs on page 524. Put an egg on top of the beans in the center of each tortilla, then top with 2 tablespoons salsa and 1 tablespoon cheese.
4. Carefully transfer the tortillas to a baking dish that holds them snugly. Bake until the cheese is melted, about 5 minutes. Garnish with the cilantro and serve immediately.

SIMPLEST HUEVOS RANCHEROS Omit the tortillas and beans. Scramble the eggs in oil; as they begin to set in the pan, stir in the salsa and cheese. Sprinkle with a little salt and pepper and serve.

HUEVOS RANCHEROS WITH RED MOLE A luxury, but a must if you have leftover sauce: Instead of the salsa, use the Red Mole sauce from the Cheese Enchiladas on page 561. Garnish with chopped tomatoes and scallions, if you like.

Chilaquiles
Scrambled Tortillas
MAKES: 2 servings
TIME: 30 minutes
F

Chilaquiles is an authentic Mexican dish and a personal favorite. It can be prepared many different ways, but in all cases it contains fried tortilla strips cooked in (or under) eggs or sauce. Serve with a little salsa or with garnishes like avocado, chopped tomatoes or scallions, cilantro, sour cream, or queso fresco or Jack cheese— alone or in combination. For a real treat, see the first variation.

6 small corn tortillas (stale are fine)

½ cup olive oil or good-quality vegetable oil

4 eggs

2 tablespoons cream or milk
  Salt and pepper

1. Cut the tortillas in half and then into strips about 1 inch wide. Put the oil in a large skillet over medium-high heat. When it's hot but not smoking, fry the tortilla strips, turning frequently, until golden brown and crisp on both sides, about 3 minutes. (Work in batches to avoid crowding, if necessary.) Use a slotted spoon to transfer them to paper towels. Set the pan with the oil aside.
2. Beat the eggs in a small bowl with the cream and sprinkle with salt and pepper.
3. Pour off all but a tablespoon or so of the oil and put the pan over medium heat. Add the eggs and the tortilla strips and cook, stirring frequently, until the eggs are done how you like them, between 4 and 6 minutes. Taste, adjust the seasoning, and serve.

SAUCED CHILAQUILES Fry and drain the tortillas in Step 1, then cook them with 1 cup Red or Green Enchilada Sauce (page 663 or 664) until the sauce is hot and the tortillas have softened a bit. Fry or poach the eggs (page 524 or 525) and serve them on top of the scrambled tortillas.

SCRAMBLED TORTILLAS WITH SCALLIONS AND CHILES
Sharp and spicy: In Step 3, after pouring off the extra oil and heating the pan, add ½ cup chopped scallions and 1 chopped fresh chile (like jalapeño or Thai), or to taste, or red chile flakes or cayenne to taste. Stir and cook for a minute or 2 to soften the vegetables, then add the tortillas and eggs and proceed with the recipe.

Hard-Boiled Eggs in Quick Tomato Curry Sauce

MAKES: 4 servings
TIME: 30 minutes with cooked eggs

F **M**

This is an awesome recipe (I vividly remember the first time someone made it for me), but it's also a concept that can quickly turn almost any sauce into a meal (see the list on page 538 for more ideas). Similar to poaching eggs in sauce (see page 525), this requires even less effort; the individual ingredients can be prepped ahead of time. And it's a great alternative for people who don't like poached eggs.

To bulk this up, add 2 to 3 cups chopped mixed vegetables like carrots, green beans, potatoes, zucchini, cauliflower, and/or eggplant, along with ½ cup water, to the sauce. Simmer until the vegetables are almost done, then add the hard-boiled eggs. Serve with White Rice (page 367) or Stuck-Pot Rice with Potato Crust (page 381).

> 8 **Hard-Boiled Eggs (page 521)**
> 2 **tablespoons good-quality vegetable oil**
> 1 **cup chopped scallions**
> 2 **tablespoons curry powder (to make your own, see page 649)**
> **Salt and pepper**
> 2 **cups chopped fresh tomatoes (about 1), or drained chopped canned**
> 1 **cup coconut milk (to make your own, see page 304)**
> **Chopped fresh cilantro for garnish**

1. Peel the eggs and set them aside to come to room temperature if cold.
2. Put the oil in a large, deep skillet over medium-high heat. Add the scallions and cook, stirring frequently, until soft, about a minute. Stir in the curry powder and sprinkle with salt and pepper. When the spices are fragrant, add the tomatoes and coconut milk. Bring to a boil, then lower the heat so that it bubbles assertively. Cook, stirring occasionally, until the sauce is thickened, about 20 minutes.
3. When the sauce is ready, add the eggs and cook, stirring once or twice, until the eggs are heated through, about 5 minutes. Taste and adjust the seasoning, garnish with cilantro, and serve.

HARD-BOILED EGGS IN RED CURRY STEW For a Thai flavor that's great with Sticky Rice (page 370): Omit the scallions, curry powder, and tomatoes. Use 2 cups coconut milk, and add 3 cups or so chopped mixed vegetables like red or yellow bell peppers, green beans, carrots, eggplant, or potatoes. Put a pan over medium-high heat, add about 2 tablespoons oil, and cook the vegetables until just tender. Add ¼ cup Red Curry Paste (page 666), stir well, then add the coconut milk. Proceed with Step 3.

POACHED EGGS IN TOMATO CURRY SAUCE Use this technique for any of the sauces in this recipe: Omit the hard-boiled eggs. When the sauce is ready, add another ½ cup water or stock and adjust the heat so that the mixture bubbles gently. One at a time, carefully crack 8 eggs into a saucer and slide into the sauce. When all the eggs are in, cover the pan tightly and cook until the eggs are done to your liking, anywhere from 3 to 7 minutes. To serve, scoop each egg out with a little of the sauce.

SHAKSHUKA Use olive oil instead of vegetable oil and thinly sliced onion in place of the scallions; cook time for them will be a bit longer, 3 to 5 minutes. Replace the curry powder with 1 tablespoon paprika and 1 teaspoon each ground cumin and coriander. Replace the coconut milk with 3 cups chopped fresh or canned tomatoes (no

Hard-Boiled Eggs in Quick
Tomato Curry Sauce

need to drain). Proceed with the above variation, poaching the eggs in the sauce.

8 Sauces for Stewing Hard-Boiled Eggs

Instead of making the quick pan sauce in the main recipe, put any of the following sauces in the pan and add about ¼ cup water to thin it a bit. Heat until bubbling, then proceed with the recipe from Step 3.

1. Smooth Green Chile Sauce, Indian Style (page 666)

2. Nutty Miso Sauce (page 653)

3. Béchamel or any of its variations (page 675); garnish with parsley, if you like

4. Any cooked salsa, like Salsa Roja (page 662) or Cooked Tomatillo Salsa (page 663), or the enchilada sauce variations (page 663 or 664)

5. Spicy Indian Tomato Sauce (page 667)

6. Peanut Sauce, Four Ways or any of its variations (page 657); garnish with cilantro, if you like

7. Fast Tomato Sauce or any of its variations (page 312); garnish with basil or parsley

8. Simplest Dal (page 450) or other any dal recipe (pages 450 to 453)

Cheese Quiche

MAKES: 4 to 8 servings
TIME: About 1½ hours, somewhat unattended

M

Use any good cheese here, or even use bits of several kinds you might have in the refrigerator. If you use a soft cheese like fresh goat, ricotta, or cottage, reduce the cream by ½ cup or so, depending on how wet the cheese is.

Herbs add more flavor, of course: Try ¼ cup chopped fresh basil, parsley, chives, chervil, cilantro, or dill; about 1 tablespoon chopped marjoram or oregano; or 1 teaspoon or so chopped tarragon, thyme, or rosemary.

1	recipe Savory Piecrust (page 710), fitted into a 9-inch deep-dish pie pan, chilled
6	eggs, at room temperature
2	cups grated Emmental, Gruyère, Cantal, cheddar, or other flavorful cheese
2	cups cream, half-and-half, or milk, heated just until warm

How to Use Other Vegetables in Quiche

There are two basic ways to prepare vegetables before adding them to the egg mixture for quiches.

The first is to cook them with butter or olive oil and season with salt and pepper. Most vegetables won't take as long as onions; use your judgment, keeping in mind that they will cook a little more as the quiche bakes.

Or you can cook them briefly in boiling salted water and drain well. Use your judgment about which treatment is right for the vegetable you're using.

In either case, cool the vegetables slightly before adding them to the eggs. And limit the total quantity of extra ingredients—vegetables, cheese, nuts, whatever—to 2 cups. Here are some specific ideas and guidelines to get you started:

BROCCOLI OR CAULIFLOWER Chop into small florets. Boil for a minute or 2.

ASPARAGUS Cook in butter or oil, or boil, until just tender. Great with goat cheese.

ARTICHOKE HEARTS Boil for a couple of minutes. Combine with ricotta and basil.

POTATOES Boil until you can pierce easily with a fork. Season with rosemary or dill.

EGGPLANT Peel if you like and cut into small cubes. Cook in butter or oil until browned and tender, 5 minutes or so. Good with olives, a little tomato, and Parmesan.

BELL PEPPERS Cook until just tender in a little butter or olive oil.

TOMATOES Start with no more than 2 cups chopped fresh or drained canned tomatoes. Cook in butter or oil until quite dry.

GREENS Follow the directions for boiling and shocking greens on page 150. Squeeze out as much water as possible, then coarsely chop them.

½ teaspoon salt
¼ teaspoon cayenne, or to taste

1. Prebake the crust (see "Pre-Baking a Crust," page 708). Start the filling while the crust is in the oven. When the crust is golden brown, set the oven temperature at 325°F and cool the crust slightly on a rack.
2. Beat together the eggs, cheese, cream, salt, and cayenne in a medium bowl until well blended.
3. Put the crust, still in the pan, on a baking sheet and pour in the filling. Bake until almost firm (it should jiggle just a little in the center) and lightly browned on top, 30 to 40 minutes. You may need to reduce the oven heat if the crust's edges darken too quickly. Cool on a wire rack; serve warm or at room temperature.

RICOTTA AND PARMESAN QUICHE Rich and sharp: Substitute 1 cup each ricotta and grated Parmesan for the Emmental and decrease the cream to 1 cup.

QUICHE LORRAINE The deep flavor of caramelized onion and smokiness of tofu take the place of the traditional bacon: Caramelize 3 cups sliced onion (see page 222) and add ½ cup or so chopped smoked tofu in the last few minutes. Combine the onion mixture with the eggs and proceed with the recipe.

Mostly Vegetable Vegan Quiche

MAKES: 4 to 8 servings
TIME: About 1½ hours
Ⓜ Ⓥ

Tofu is the obvious vegan stand-in for many recipes, but here a tart made mostly of vegetables is held together with just a little chickpea batter, which itself is delicious.

  1 recipe Savory Vegan Piecrust (page 710), fitted into a 9-inch deep-dish pie pan, chilled
  2 tablespoons olive oil, plus more for the top

  1 onion, sliced
     Salt and pepper
1½ pounds chopped cooked vegetables (like broccoli, cauliflower, asparagus, mushrooms, corn, potatoes, or a combination)
  1 cup chickpea flour (besan)
2½ cups vegetable stock (pages 97–100), or water
  ¼ teaspoon ground turmeric

1. Prebake the crust (see "Pre-Baking a Crust," page 708). Start the filling while the crust is in the oven. When the crust starts to turn golden, set the oven temperature to 400°F. Cool the crust slightly on a rack.
2. Put the oil in a large, deep skillet over medium heat. When it's hot, add the onion and some salt and pepper. Turn the heat up to medium-high and cook, stirring frequently, until the onion is soft and lightly browned, about 10 minutes; adjust the heat so it doesn't brown too much or crisp up. Add the vegetables, stir, turn off the heat, and let cool slightly.

8 Great Leftovers to Turn into Quiche Filling

Use 2 cups leftovers or 1 cup leftovers combined with 1 cup cheese.

1. Kasha with Golden Brown Onions (page 413)

2. Any cooked grain (see "Cooking Grains the Easy Way," page 398)

3. Beans and Mushrooms (page 447), drained, or any cooked or canned beans, drained

4. Broccoli or Cauliflower (or Just About Anything Else), Roman Style (page 180)

5. Pan-Grilled Corn with Chile (page 198)

6. Eggplant Slices with Garlic and Parsley (page 201)

7. Anything-Scented Peas (page 224)

8. Any Mashed Potatoes (page 233)

Mostly Vegetable Vegan
Quiche (page 539)

3. Whisk together the chickpea flour and 1 cup of the stock in a medium bowl. In a medium saucepan, bring the remaining 1½ cups stock to a boil with the turmeric. Slowly stir in the chickpea flour mixture. Once all the flour mixture has been incorporated, set the heat to low and continue to stir continuously until the mixture becomes thick and glossy, 2 to 3 minutes. Remove from the heat and stir in the vegetables.

4. Put the pie pan on a baking sheet. Spoon the filling (it will be very thick) into the crust. Bake until almost set, 15 to 20 minutes. Remove from the oven, brush with oil, and return to the oven until the top is golden brown, 3 to 5 minutes. Cool on a wire rack; serve warm or at room temperature.

Egg Salad

MAKES: 4 servings
TIME: 15 minutes
🇫 🇲

Egg salad can be as simple as chopped eggs bound with some mayo, but it's better with a squeeze of fresh lemon juice, chopped pickles, and/or chopped fresh herbs stirred in. Although it's way more work, using homemade mayonnaise here makes a huge difference.

Any Deviled Eggs recipe (right) can be made into an egg salad—just add more mayonnaise or the equivalent—and vice versa.

> 6 Hard-Boiled Eggs (page 521), peeled and chopped
> ¼ cup mayonnaise, preferably homemade (page 670), plus more if needed
> 1 tablespoon fresh lemon juice
> 3 tablespoons minced dill pickle or other cucumber pickle (optional)
> 3 tablespoons chopped fresh dill
>   Salt and pepper

Combine the eggs, mayonnaise, lemon juice, pickle (if you're using it), dill, and salt and pepper to taste. Add more mayonnaise if you like it looser. Taste, adjust the seasoning, and serve immediately. Or cover and refrigerate for up to 2 days.

FRENCH-STYLE EGG SALAD Very flavorful: Omit the lemon juice. Add 1 tablespoon Dijon mustard. Use dill pickles or cornichons, and add 1 tablespoon chopped capers. Replace the dill with 1 teaspoon chopped fresh tarragon or chervil.

TOFU "EGG" SALAD Totally vegan, though you wouldn't know it: Substitute 1½ cups chopped medium or firm tofu (page 483) for the eggs and use Vegannaise (page 672) instead of mayonnaise. 🇻

MAYO-LESS EGG SALAD A higher-protein option: Replace the mayonnaise with ¼ cup Hummus (page 463). Drizzle in up to 2 tablespoons olive oil to get the desired consistency.

Deviled (or Stuffed) Eggs

MAKES: 4 servings
TIME: 5 minutes
🇫 🇲

Cayenne, mustard, or anything that provides a bit of bite makes a stuffed egg "deviled." With or without some spice, these eggs are easy to make, great for parties—and the variations are almost limitless.

> 4 Hard-Boiled Eggs (page 521), peeled
>   Salt
> 2 tablespoons mayonnaise (preferably homemade, page 670)
> 1 teaspoon Dijon mustard, or to taste
> ¼ teaspoon cayenne, or to taste
>   Paprika or chopped fresh parsley for garnish

1. Cut the eggs in half lengthwise and carefully remove the yolks.

2. Mash the yolks with a pinch salt, the mayonnaise, mustard, and cayenne in a small bowl. Taste and adjust the seasoning. Spoon the filling back into the whites. (If you are making a lot of deviled eggs and want them to be especially attractive, use a pastry bag with a star tip to pipe them in.)

3. Sprinkle with paprika and serve. Or cover and chill for up to 1 day.

CURRIED DEVILED EGGS Subtly spiced: Substitute yogurt for the mayonnaise, if you like, and Fragrant Curry Powder (page 649) for the mustard. Garnish with cilantro.

JALAPEÑO DEVILED EGGS Make these as spicy as you like: Substitute sour cream for the mayonnaise, 2 teaspoons or more minced jalapeño for the mustard, and ⅛ teaspoon ground cumin for the cayenne. Garnish with cilantro.

VEGETABLE-STUFFED EGGS The key is cutting the vegetables to just the right size so they don't look too chunky but provide a nice texture: Add 1 tablespoon each chopped radish, snow pea, and scallions. Garnish with tarragon or chervil.

---

9 Ways to Flavor Egg Salad or Deviled Eggs

Stir any of these ingredients, to taste, into the filling for deviled eggs or use to season egg salad.

1. Pesto (page 634)

2. Raw Onion Chutney (page 668)

3. Crumbled blue cheese or soft goat cheese

4. Wasabi powder or prepared or grated fresh horseradish

5. Chopped fresh herbs like chives, mint, chervil, parsley, or cilantro

6. Minced garlic

7. Chopped capers or olives

8. Chopped pickles

9. Chopped fresh chiles like jalapeño or Thai

PANCAKES

Pancakes are made from a simple batter of eggs, flour, and liquid, usually with a bit of baking powder for leavening. It's a forgiving batter with lots of room for improvising: beat the egg whites separately and/or use cottage cheese for light and airy pancakes; switch the type of flour; add fruit, nut butter, chocolate chips, or spices. If you like thick pancakes, reduce the liquid; add more liquid for thinner pancakes.

Everyday Pancake batter (below) whips up in no time and can be stored in the fridge for a couple of days, which makes it great for weekdays. You can also mix the dry ingredients to store indefinitely (this, essentially, is Bisquick); just add the eggs and milk when you're ready to cook.

Everyday Pancakes

MAKES: 4 to 6 servings
TIME: 20 minutes

F M O

I cannot tell you how many people have thanked me for this recipe–which is surprising, since it's among the most basic things ever. You gotta learn somewhere, I guess.

You can whip up this batter in the time it takes to preheat the pan; and once you get good at it, you won't need a recipe. (For a small batch, it's all 1s: 1 cup flour, 1 teaspoon sugar, 1 teaspoon baking powder, 1 egg, 1 cup milk. Pinch of salt. Melted butter if you like. A four-year old could remember that.) Store it, covered, in the refrigerator for up to 2 days.

2 cups all-purpose flour, plus more if needed

1 tablespoon sugar (optional)

2 teaspoons baking powder

¼ teaspoon salt

2 eggs

1½–2 cups milk

2 tablespoons butter, melted and cooled (optional), plus butter or good-quality vegetable oil for cooking

1. Heat a griddle or large skillet over medium-low heat while you make the batter. Heat the oven to 200°F if you won't be serving the pancakes immediately.

2. Mix together the dry ingredients in a large bowl. Beat the eggs into 1½ cups milk, then stir in the melted butter if you're using it. Gently stir this mixture into the dry ingredients, mixing only enough to moisten the flour; don't worry about a few lumps. The batter should be pourable, or nearly so; adjust the consistency with either more milk or more flour as necessary.

3. Heat a teaspoon or 2 of butter or oil in a large skillet or griddle. When the butter foam subsides or the oil shimmers, brush it over the surface. Ladle batter onto the griddle, making any size pancakes you like. Adjust the heat as necessary; usually the first batch will require higher heat than subsequent batches. The idea is to brown the bottom without burning it, usually 2 to 4 minutes. Flip when bubbles rise to the surface of the pancakes and the bottoms are cooked; they won't hold together well until they're ready. Cook until the second side is lightly browned. Repeat with the remaining batter, adding another teaspoon or 2 of butter or oil each time you add batter.

4. Serve or keep warm on an ovenproof plate in the oven for up to 15 minutes.

VEGAN PANCAKES Omit the eggs and add 1 tablespoon flaxseed meal to the dry ingredients. Substitute non-dairy milk for the regular and good-quality vegetable oil for the melted butter. Optional ideas for flavor: Replace half of the all-purpose flour with a whole grain flour. Or grind ¾ cup pecans, walnuts, or blanched almonds into the flour (not too long or they will turn into a paste) and substitute for ½ cup of the all-purpose flour. 🆅

BUTTERMILK OR YOGURT PANCAKES Substitute buttermilk or yogurt for the milk; use ½ teaspoon baking soda instead of the baking powder.

GLUTEN-FREE PANCAKES Use any of the gluten-free options discussed on page 574.

BLUEBERRY PANCAKES Just before cooking, stir up to 1 cup fresh or unthawed frozen blueberries into the batter. Turn the heat down a bit on these, as they burn more easily.

BANANA-COCONUT PANCAKES Use one 14-ounce can coconut milk for the milk. Mix the dry ingredients with ½ cup shredded coconut; beat together the eggs and coconut milk in a large bowl. Stir the dry ingredients into the wet until just combined. Gently fold in 2 sliced bananas.

WHOLE GRAIN PANCAKES A bit denser in texture but great grain flavor: Substitute whole wheat, quinoa, amaranth, or teff flour, cornmeal, rolled oats, or a combination for up to 1 cup of the flour.

GINGERBREAD PANCAKES Perfect served with a dollop of whipped cream: Substitute ½ cup molasses for the sugar and add with the milk along with 2 teaspoons minced fresh ginger or ground ginger or 2 to 3 tablespoons chopped candied ginger, 1 teaspoon ground cinnamon, and a pinch ground cloves.

NUT BUTTER PANCAKES Turn the heat down a bit on these, as they can burn easily: Add up to ¼ cup each nut butter or tahini and chopped nuts (ideally the same nuts as the nut butter) or sesame seeds along with the milk.

LEMON–POPPY SEED PANCAKES Substitute ½ teaspoon baking soda for the baking powder. Add 2 tablespoons each lemon juice and poppy seeds and 2 teaspoons grated lemon zest along with the milk.

CHOCOLATE PANCAKES Add ¼ cup cocoa powder and/or a handful of chocolate chips; thin with a little milk or buttermilk if necessary.

ZUCCHINI BREAD PANCAKES Add 1 cup grated zucchini, 1 teaspoon ground cinnamon, and pinch nutmeg.

COCONUT PANCAKES Substitute coconut milk for the regular milk and/or add up to ½ cup shredded coconut.

Vegan Oatmeal Pancakes

MAKES: 4 servings
TIME: 30 minutes with cooked oatmeal
F V

Cooked oatmeal takes the place of eggs here, and makes for a hearty pancake. You can use other grains too: Just make sure they're cooked beyond done—sort of exploded—so the starches help bind. Add up to 1½ cups any chopped fruit if you like.

½ cup all-purpose flour
¼ cup rolled oats (not quick-cooking or instant)
1 teaspoon baking powder
½ teaspoon ground cinnamon
½ teaspoon salt
¾ cup unsweetened nondairy milk, plus more as needed
2 cups cooked oatmeal (made from rolled oats; page 400)
3 tablespoons good-quality vegetable oil

1. Heat the oven to 200°F. Combine the flour, oats, baking powder, cinnamon, and salt in a large bowl. In a separate bowl, stir together the milk and oatmeal until completely blended. Add the oatmeal mixture to the flour mixture and stir gently; don't overmix. The batter should be the consistency of thick pancake batter; if not, add either a little more milk or flour as needed.
2. Put a large skillet or griddle, preferably nonstick or well-seasoned cast iron, over medium heat. When a few drops of water dance on its surface, add 1 tablespoon of the oil and let it get hot; spread it evenly over the surface using a brush or paper towel. Working in batches, spoon the batter onto the skillet or griddle, making any size pancakes you like; spread out the batter a bit so they're not too thick. Cook until bubbles form on the top and pop, 3 to 4 minutes.
3. Carefully flip the pancakes and cook until they're browned on the other side, a couple of minutes more. As they finish, transfer them to a platter in the oven while you cook the remaining batter, adding more oil to the pan as necessary.

Lemon-Ricotta Pancakes

MAKES: 3 to 4 servings
TIME: 20 minutes
F

With ricotta and sour cream or yogurt as their main ingredients, these are quite different from traditional pancakes—light, creamy, and completely delicious.

1 cup ricotta (to make your own, see page 569)
1 cup sour cream or yogurt
3 eggs, separated (see page 546)
2 tablespoons fresh lemon juice
2 teaspoons grated lemon zest
1 cup all-purpose flour
1 tablespoon sugar
½ teaspoon baking soda
   Pinch salt
   Butter or good-quality vegetable oil for cooking

1. Heat a griddle or large skillet over medium-low heat while you make the batter.

6 Tips for Making Perfect Pancakes

1. Use a nonstick griddle or skillet or one of well-seasoned cast iron (it'll need little or no butter or oil).

2. Heat until a few drops of water skid across the surface before evaporating.

3. Ladle the pancakes onto the griddle with enough room in between for flipping.

4. The edges of the pancake will set first; when bubbles appear in the center of the pancake and the bottom is golden brown, it's ready to flip.

5. Serve the pancakes immediately, if possible; that's when they are the best.

6. Melt the butter and gently heat the maple syrup if you're using it (the microwave does a good job here).

Lemon-Ricotta Pancakes

Separating Eggs

STEP 1 Break the egg with the back of a knife or on the side of a bowl.

STEP 2 The simplest way to separate eggs is to use the shell halves, moving the yolk back and forth once or twice so that the white falls into a bowl. Be careful, however, not to allow any of the yolk to mix in or the whites will not rise no matter how much you beat them.

Folding Egg Whites

STEP 1 To fold beaten eggs whites into a batter, first lighten the mixture by stirring a couple of spoonfuls of the whites into it.

STEP 2 Then gently fold the rest of the egg whites in, scooping under the mixture and smoothing over the top. You can use a rubber spatula or your hand, which works equally well.

2. Beat together the ricotta, sour cream, egg yolks, lemon juice, and lemon zest in a large bowl. Combine the dry ingredients in a small bowl. Beat the egg whites with a clean whisk or electric mixer in a medium bowl until they hold fairly stiff but not dry peaks (see opposite).

3. Stir the flour mixture into the ricotta mixture, blending well with a spoon but not beating; don't overmix. Gently fold in the egg whites; they should remain somewhat distinct in the batter.

4. Put about 1 teaspoon butter or oil on the griddle or skillet. When the butter is melted or the oil is hot, spread it evenly over the surface using a brush or paper towel. Add the batter by the heaping tablespoon, making sure you include some of the egg whites in each spoonful. Cook until lightly browned on the bottom, 3 to 5 minutes, then flip and cook until the second side is brown. Add butter or oil to the griddle for each batch until all the batter is used up. Serve immediately; these will not hold.

COTTAGE CHEESE PANCAKES Great with rehydrated raisins or currants: Substitute cottage cheese for the ricotta, decrease the baking soda to ¼ teaspoon, and omit the lemon juice and zest.

WAFFLES

The best waffles are crisp outside and creamy inside. For me, their texture is even more important than what you put in them or on them, so it's crucial to get waffles out of the iron and onto the table quickly. You can keep them warm in the oven for a little while if you absolutely must, but it sort of defeats the whole purpose: Waffles are meant to be eaten immediately—which makes them less than ideal for large groups.

Raised waffles, made with yeast, are unbeatable, and—as long as you remember to make the batter the night before—they're just as easy to make as any other waffles. Buttermilk waffles are almost as good and much more spontaneous. Even the simplest pancakelike waffles, which tend to be thin and crunchy, have their place.

Everyday Buttermilk Waffles

MAKES: 4 to 6 servings
TIME: 15 minutes

F

If you've got buttermilk, sour cream, or yogurt, these are the best waffles you can make right when you want them. Plain milk works too; see the first variation.

You can make these as elaborate as you want; see "12 Things You Can Stir into Any Waffle Batter" on page 548.

2	cups all-purpose flour
2	tablespoons sugar
1½	teaspoons baking soda
½	teaspoon salt
1¾	cups buttermilk, or 1½ cups sour cream or yogurt thinned with ¼ cup milk
2	eggs, separated (see opposite)
4	tablespoons (½ stick) butter, melted and cooled
½	teaspoon vanilla extract (optional) Good-quality vegetable oil for brushing the waffle iron

1. Heat the oven to 200°F if you need to keep the waffles warm for serving. Combine the flour, sugar, baking soda, and salt in a large bowl. In another bowl, whisk together the buttermilk and egg yolks. Stir in the butter and the vanilla, if you're using it.

2. Brush the waffle iron lightly with oil and heat it (check the manufacturer's instructions). Stir the wet ingredients into the dry. Beat the egg whites with a clean whisk or an electric mixer until they hold soft peaks (see below). Fold them gently into the batter.

3. Spread a ladleful of batter onto the waffle iron and bake until the waffle is done (usually 3 to 5 minutes, depending on your iron). Serve or keep warm for a few minutes on an ovenproof plate in the oven.

Beating Egg Whites

Whipping or beating egg whites to a fluffy, bright white foam is easy, especially with an electric mixer. And watching the whites go from clear and slippery to pure white and puffy is pretty spectacular, as their volume increases by seven or eight times.

For equipment, at most you'll need a mixer with a whisk attachment and a spotlessly clean metal or glass bowl; at the least a big whisk, the bowl, and a well-rested arm. Don't use a plastic bowl; its surface is porous, which means it can retain fat molecules, which will interfere with the whites' ability to foam.

There are a couple of potential pitfalls: The first is getting even the tiniest bit of yolk—or any fat—in the whites; even oil residue clinging to the side of a bowl will ruin or seriously impede your whites' ability to whip up. If a bit of yolk does get in the whites, use the tip of a knife to pluck the yolk out or—much safer—start with a fresh egg.

The other mistake when whipping whites is overbeating them. Just like cream (page 701), egg whites can be whipped to various stages:

SOFT PEAKS
The foam will just make a low peak with a tip that readily folds onto itself.

MEDIUM PEAKS
A solid peak, still soft, with a tip that folds over but not onto itself.

STIFF OR FIRM PEAKS
A fairly stiff peak with a tip that hardly bends; dragging your finger through the foam will leave a distinct mark. It should not be clumpy, though.

OVERWHIPPED
The foam will be clumpy, rough looking, and leaking water. There's no fixing overwhipped egg whites; toss 'em.

THE QUICKEST, EASIEST WAFFLES Less air, more crisp, but still good: Instead of the baking soda, use 2 teaspoons baking powder. Use 1½ cups milk instead of the buttermilk. Don't bother to separate the eggs; just whisk them whole with the milk in Step 1. Proceed with the recipe.

WHOLE GRAIN WAFFLES Heartier, healthier, and a little denser, this formula works for both the main recipe and the preceding variation: Substitute up to 1 cup whole wheat flour, cornmeal, rolled oats, or a combination for the all-purpose flour.

WHEATLESS WAFFLES They won't be as fluffy, but they will crisp up nicely: Use any of the gluten-free flour options on page 574 in place of all of the flour.

12 Things You Can Stir into Any Waffle Batter

Add any of these per batch of batter:

1. Ground cinnamon, up to 2 teaspoons

2. Any curry powder, up to 2 teaspoons

3. Minced fresh or ground ginger, up to 2 teaspoons

4. Molasses, substituted for ½ cup milk (excellent with cornmeal)

5. Minced or grated orange or lemon zest, about 2 teaspoons

6. The Best Granola (page 421) or chopped nuts, up to 1 cup

7. Grated cheese like Emmental (Swiss), cheddar, or Jack, about 1 cup, or grated

Parmesan cheese, up to ½ cup

8. Shredded coconut, up to 1 cup

9. Fresh fruit like blueberries, raspberries, or apples, cut into ¼- to ½-inch pieces

10. Dried fruit like apricots, cherries, cranberries, or raisins, up to ½ cup, coarsely chopped

11. Cooked grains, like any rice, millet, wheat or rye berries, couscous, barley, quinoa, or wild rice, up to 1 cup

12. Fresh or thawed frozen corn kernels, up to 1 cup

Overnight Waffles

MAKES: 4 to 6 servings
TIME: 8 hours or more, mostly unattended
Ⓜ

The distinctive yeasty flavor and fluffy but chewy texture of these waffles mean they go with everything. Eat these traditionally with butter and syrup for breakfast, or serve them as a "bread" with virtually any meal. You could make your own vegetarian "chicken and waffles" by serving these with Deep-Fried Tofu (page 487) or Batter-Fried Vegetables (page 159).

2 teaspoons instant yeast
2 cups all-purpose flour
1 tablespoon sugar
½ teaspoon salt
1½ cups milk
8 tablespoons (1 stick) butter, melted and cooled
½ teaspoon vanilla extract (optional)
   Good-quality vegetable oil for brushing the waffle iron
2 eggs

1. The night before you want to serve the waffles, combine the yeast, flour, sugar, and salt in a large bowl. Stir in the milk, then the butter and the vanilla if you're using it. The mixture will be creamy and loose. Cover with plastic wrap and let sit overnight at room temperature. (You can do this in the morning if you want waffles for dinner.)
2. To start baking, brush the waffle iron lightly with oil and heat it (check the manufacturer's instructions). Separate the eggs and stir the yolks into the batter. Beat the egg whites in a medium bowl with a clean whisk or electric mixer until they hold soft peaks. Fold them gently into the batter.
3. Spread ½ cup or so batter onto the waffle iron and bake until the waffle is done (usually 3 to 5 minutes, depending on the iron). Serve or keep warm for a few minutes in a 200°F oven.

Overnight Waffles

French Toast

MAKES: 4 servings
TIME: 20 minutes

F M

French toast can be made with fresh or stale bread (the dish, obviously, was created to use leftover bread), quick breads, and even tortillas. European-style loaves require a bit more soaking to soften the crust; hearty whole grain breads make more substantial slices. Many people prefer French toast made from soft, thick slices of brioche or challah. Whatever you use, just be sure the bread is good quality; packaged sandwich slices make insipid French toast.

You can easily vary this recipe: Use any nondairy milk, or enrich the soaking liquid by using half-and-half, cream, or coconut milk. Season it with ground cardamom, cloves, allspice, nutmeg, or almond extract instead of the cinnamon or vanilla extract. To make an eggier French toast, increase the eggs and decrease the milk by a couple of tablespoons for each extra egg.

2 eggs
1 cup milk
Pinch salt
1 tablespoon sugar (optional)
1 teaspoon vanilla extract or ground cinnamon (optional)
Butter or good-quality vegetable oil, as needed
8 slices bread

1. Put a large griddle or skillet over medium-low heat while you prepare the egg batter. Heat the oven to 200°F if you won't be serving the French toast immediately.
2. Beat the eggs lightly in a wide, shallow bowl and stir in the milk, salt, and the sugar and vanilla, if you're using them.
3. Put about 1 teaspoon butter or oil on the griddle or in the skillet. When the butter is melted or the oil is hot, brush it over the surface. Dip each slice of bread into the batter, turn once or twice to coat both sides with batter, then put it on the griddle. Cook until nicely browned on each side, turning once after 3 to 5 minutes, adding more butter or oil as needed; you may find that you can raise the heat a bit. Serve or keep warm on an ovenproof plate in the oven for up to 30 minutes.

CRISP FRENCH TOAST There are two ways to give French toast a bit of a crust: Stir ½ cup flour into the

6 Tips for Perfect Waffles

1. The iron must be hot. Almost all have lights that let you know when they're ready for baking. Be patient while it heats.

2. The iron should be clean and lightly oiled, even if it's nonstick. Before turning it on, brush the iron lightly with good-quality vegetable oil, or use an oil-soaked paper towel. When it's fully heated, open the iron for a few seconds to let any smoke escape; close it until it reheats a bit, then start cooking.

3. If you have an extra 5 minutes, separate the eggs and beat the whites by themselves (see page 546), then fold them into the batter right before cooking. Great fluffiness.

4. Be patient and don't underbake waffles. After pouring or spreading the batter over the bottom plate, close the top and leave it alone for at least 2 minutes. Gently pull up on the top of the iron. If the lid resists, give it another minute or 2. Don't automatically trust the indicator light, and don't rely on the myth about waffles being ready when there's no more steam wafting. If you want your waffle crisp, you're probably going to have to wait an extra minute or so after the light goes on (or off, depending on your machine), then do the tug test.

5. Serve waffles straight from the iron. If you must hold them for a few minutes—5, tops—put them on a rack in a 200°F oven.

6. During those couple of minutes spent waiting for the waffles to bake, melt the butter and warm the syrup. I use the microwave set on low.

batter, or dip the bread in the batter, then dredge it in sweetened bread crumbs or crushed cornflakes. In either case, cook as directed.

NUT-CRUSTED FRENCH TOAST Add another egg and decrease the milk to ¾ cup. Spread about 1 cup sliced almonds or any chopped nuts on a plate; after dipping the bread in the egg batter, put the slice on the nuts and press gently to make the nuts stick; flip it over to coat the other side. Proceed with the recipe, taking care not to burn the nuts.

SAVORY FRENCH TOAST Opens up a whole new world of brunch (or dinner) possibilities: Omit the sugar and vanilla, and whisk ½ cup grated Parmesan cheese and lots of cracked black pepper into the batter. Proceed with the recipe.

THE BASICS OF DAIRY

The best-tasting, most useful dairy product may be cheese, which is why there's a whole section on cooking with it here. But almost all dairy products have great value, and dairy is an important part of most vegetarians' diets. It still pays to remember that, like all animal products, cheese, butter, and even yogurt are treats. Savor them, and don't take them for granted.

If you can't tolerate dairy, or if you're a vegan, you still have plenty of options for these recipes, but you shouldn't expect to duplicate the richness of whole milk, cream, or butter. See "Vegan Substitutions" (page 15) to get started.

A few words about storing dairy products: Refrigerate them in their original containers or in clean glass, ideally at 40°F or a little colder. Pour off what you need, then immediately return the rest to the fridge. Never put unused milk or cream back in the carton or jug; it's likely to spoil faster. When stored properly, a dairy product should stay good for a couple of days after its "sell-by" date. You can freeze unsalted butter for a month or so (and salted butter

somewhat longer) without noticeably affecting its flavor, but don't freeze milk or cream.

MILK

The vast majority of milk produced worldwide is cow's milk. You can find goat's milk more easily now, but it has a very distinctive flavor not appropriate for every dish. If you have a way to buy milk from a local dairy, that's your best bet. Failing that, locally produced organic milk is the way to go (When people ask me "What if I can only find local *or* organic?". . . it's a tough question, since much organic milk is from reconstituted powder shipped from abroad. I prefer principled local, which is not hard to determine but can be difficult to find.) Non-homogenized (the milk and cream can still separate) is great if you can find it.

Whole (3.25 percent fat), reduced-fat (2 percent fat); low-fat (1 percent fat); fat-free, skim, or nonfat (no fat): Unless otherwise noted, you can use reduced-fat, low-fat (but not fat-free), or whole milk in the recipes in this book, though I now use only whole milk or nondairy milk.

UHT MILK

Short for "ultra-high-temperature milk," this is the unrefrigerated stuff you see in aseptic (sterilized and vacuum-sealed) boxes on supermarket shelves. UHT milk keeps for at least three months after packaging and is always dated. I always have some in the pantry for emergencies; it has a distinctive flavor that you can get used to and even like.

BUTTERMILK

This tangy, thick, and sometimes lumpy liquid isn't at all what it used to be, which was the liquid that remained after churning butter. Now it's made from milk of any fat content, cultured with lactic acid–producing bacteria. It's more like thin yogurt than anything else, though the flavor is slightly different. It is usually labeled "cultured buttermilk" or "cultured low-fat buttermilk." Use it for baking, flavoring mashed potatoes, or making cold sauces, dips, and dressings.

It's easy to "sour" regular milk to quickly produce a substitute: Bring any volume of milk to room temperature (microwave it 10 seconds at a time to do this quickly), then stir in 1 tablespoon white vinegar or lemon juice per cup. Let the mixture sit until clabbered —thick and lumpy—about 10 minutes.

CREAM

There are all sorts of labels for cream, but mostly the kind you want is heavy (not "whipping") cream, without any additives or emulsifiers, and not ultra-pasteurized (this takes longer to whip and has a distinctive, definitely cooked, flavor). The fat content of whipping cream ranges from 30 percent to 36 percent; heavy cream is 36 percent fat or more. See page 701 for more information about the stages of whipping cream.

HALF-AND-HALF

Just like the name implies, this is half milk and half cream, with a fat content that ranges from 10.5 to 18 percent. It's nice in dishes when you don't need the richness of heavy cream, and it's certainly easy enough to blend your own.

SOUR CREAM

Sour cream is made much like yogurt, but starts with heavy cream and a little milk. It's cultured by adding lactic acid bacteria to make it thick and produce its characteristic tangy flavor. Sour cream can be tricky to cook with because it can curdle—though not as quickly as yogurt—so add it to other ingredients over very low heat, and incorporate it a little at a time. I don't recommend using reduced-fat sour cream.

CRÈME FRAÎCHE

Similar to sour cream except made entirely of cream. It's less sour than sour cream, and a little thinner, but rich and a decadent addition to many recipes.

Crème fraîche is easier to find these days, but can be expensive. Note that you can easily make your own: Put 1 cup cream in a small glass bowl and stir in 2 tablespoons buttermilk or yogurt. Cover and let sit at room temperature until thickened, anywhere from 12 to 24 hours. Cover tightly, refrigerate, and use within a week or so.

YOGURT

Cultured milk, made with different bacteria from buttermilk and sour cream, which produce its unique flavor and texture. Look for "live, active cultures" (or similar terminology) on the label and avoid any with gelatins, gums, or stabilizers. Yogurt is available in whole, low-fat, and nonfat versions, as well as yogurt products like kefir (a cultured milk drink), labneh (yogurt cheese), and the now ubiquitous Greek (strained) yogurt (which you can make yourself; see opposite).

Americans are coming around to unflavored yogurt, but you can still find all sorts of crazy flavors, some with more sugar than ice cream. So why bother? Just flavor yogurt yourself (see opposite) or make your own from scratch.

You can use yogurt in sweet and savory dishes. If you're not adding it to a batter, warm it gently and incorporate it a little at a time, or it will curdle. In recipes, whole-milk yogurt always gives the richest results.

Yogurt

MAKES: 1 quart
TIME: Overnight or longer, mostly unattended
Ⓜ

Though many excellent-quality yogurts are sold in stores, homemade yogurt has a uniquely sweet flavor; it's especially fabulous if you can get truly fresh milk. (It's also cheaper.) And though yogurt is a little trickier to make than fresh cheese (page 568)—mostly because the temperature must be controlled for a long time while it processes—it's easy enough to get the hang of. Once you make your first batch, reserve ½ cup so you have a starter for the next.

Whole milk makes the best yogurt, though you can use any kind of milk you like.

   4   **cups milk**
   ½   **cup natural yogurt ("with active cultures"),**
       ideally at room temperature

1. Put the milk in a small-to-medium saucepan and bring it just to a boil. Turn off the heat and cool to between 110° and 115°F (use an instant-read thermometer).

2. Whisk together the milk and yogurt. Put in a yogurt maker or a prewarmed thermos, or in a heated bowl, wrap in a towel or blanket, and set in a warm place. The idea is to keep the mixture at about 100°F.

3. Do not disturb the mixture for at least 6 hours. Then carefully check by tilting the container to see whether the milk has become yogurt. If not, leave it alone for another 6 hours. When the yogurt is done, let it cool to room temperature, transfer to an airtight container, refrigerate, and use within 1 week.

STRAINED YOGURT Most commonly known as "Greek yogurt," though there are variations from other countries, including Iceland: Once you make the yogurt, line a fine-meshed strainer with a coffee filter or several layers of cheesecloth. Put the strainer over a large bowl and pour in the yogurt. Let it drain in the refrigerator until it reaches the desired consistency, usually after 1 to 2 hours. (If you save the whey, check out "What to Do with All That Whey," page 568).

YOGURT CHEESE (LABNEH) You can make this with store-bought yogurt too. There are even filters available specifically for this purpose: Instead of refrigerating the yogurt, put it in a jelly bag, or in several layers of cheesecloth and tie with kitchen twine, and suspend it over the sink or a large bowl. Let drain for at least 6 hours, preferably longer, until the yogurt has a cream cheese–like consistency. Use as you would cream cheese for dips and spreads. Wonderful mixed with herbs or spices, especially Za'atar (page 652).

12 Ideas for Flavoring Yogurt

Stir any of these into yogurt to taste.

1. Honey
2. Maple syrup
3. Vanilla extract, with or without sugar
4. Chopped nuts
5. Preserves or jam
6. Chutneys (pages 668 to 670)
7. Salsas (pages 659 to 664)
8. Spice blends (pages 648 to 652)
9. Chopped fresh herbs
10. Any pickles, chopped
11. Chopped fresh or dried chiles
12. Minced garlic or fresh ginger

BUTTER

Butter is fat and water; higher fat is better. The supermarket standard is 80 percent fat, which means 20 percent is water. It doesn't matter much except for when you're baking delicate cookies or cakes, though higher-fat butter also tends to be higher quality and better tasting. Always buy unsalted butter (also called "sweet butter" or "sweet cream butter"), but know that it doesn't keep quite as long as the salted kind. Store extra sticks in the freezer, not the fridge; they'll keep there for about a month before they start to taste like your freezer. Never use whipped butter in recipes; its volume isn't the same as that of stick butter.

Cultured butter is made from cream that has live active cultures added back in after pasteurization, resulting in a fuller flavor than sweet cream butter, which is the vast majority of butter you'll find in stores.

Cultured Butter

MAKES: 2 cups
TIME: 20 minutes
Ⓜ Ⓕ

You can make your own crème fraîche (opposite) or buy it. What you'll have left after the first processing is real buttermilk, which you can use for baking or plenty of other uses. Cultured butter will keep for a few weeks in the refrigerator. This recipe can easily be scaled up.

> 2 **cups crème fraîche**
> ¼ **cup whole milk yogurt (not Greek-style)**
> 2 **cups ice, plus more as needed**
> **Salt**

1. Put the crème fraîche and yogurt in a large bowl and bring to room temperature. In a separate bowl, combine the ice and 2 cups of water and refrigerate until ready to use.

2. Put enough of the crème fraîche mixture in a food processor to fill it no more than halfway; you may need to work in batches. Turn the machine on and let it run until the mixture separates into liquid (buttermilk) and thick curds (butter), 1 to 3 minutes.

3. Pour out the buttermilk (store it in an airtight container in the refrigerator). Add ½ cup of the ice water to the food processor and let the machine run continuously for 30 seconds; again pour out the buttermilk but don't bother to save it. Repeat one or more times until the liquid runs clear. Add a large pinch salt and pulse the machine a few times to combine. Taste and adjust the seasoning.

4. Transfer the butter onto paper towels to drain; shape it however you like. Wrap tightly with plastic or wax paper and refrigerate. It will keep for a few weeks.

SWEET CREAM BUTTER Use the best cream you can find: Bring 2 cups heavy cream to room temperature. Proceed with the recipe. Salting is optional. Sweet cream butter will only keep about a week.

THE BASICS OF CHEESE

Cheese is a good source of protein, as well as calcium and other nutrients that can't be found in many other places for vegetarians. And from the perspectives of flavor and texture, there's nothing else like it. Just don't let cheese become a vegetarian crutch; think of it as a treat, not a major food group.

The variety of cheeses is staggering. They may be made from cow's, sheep's, or goat's milk (or for that matter, yak's, water buffalo's, or camel's), or a mixture; they may be fresh or aged from as little as 30 days to as long as several years. This is what makes shopping for cheese so much fun, especially in a good cheese shop.

For most of us, cooking with cheese is far more common than eating a cheese course, and the cheese itself is more common too. But the principles that determine which cheese works best in which dishes—strength of flavor, firmness, graininess, the ability to crumble or melt—also work for eating cheese plain.

Store cheese in the warmest part of the refrigerator—the door compartment is probably best—preferably in a resealable container. Specialty cheese paper also works, as does wax paper; and even though almost every retailer in the world uses it, plastic wrap is to be avoided as it doesn't allow the cheese to breathe and can transfer its smell to the cheese.

A bit of white or green mold doesn't mean cheese has gone bad; you can just trim it off. In general, if a cheese smells as it is supposed to, it's fine. And take a little nibble; if it tastes fine, it is fine. But if a bloomy rinded cheese (like brie or Camembert) develops a pinkish red mold, throw it out. Beyond those caveats, follow your nose and trust your instincts on whether a cheese is ready for the trash bin.

Most cheese is best eaten at room temperature, which can take several hours for a piece of cheese taken right from the fridge; keep it covered with paper or a clean cloth or place it in a cheese dome until ready to serve.

What follows is a rather idiosyncratic overview of the types of cheeses used in cooking, though it is hardly comprehensive. It's meant to illustrate the ways in which cheese can be incorporated into cooking and those I use most often. Feel free to branch out and experiment with others.

ALL-PURPOSE CHEESES
These are kitchen workhorses that can be used in recipes in a multitude of ways, from tangy dips to rich pasta dishes, from pancakes to desserts.

GRATING CHEESES Parmesan is king (see "Parmesan, the Ultimate All-Purpose Cheese," page 556) but there's also pecorino Romano, manchego, Grana Padano (the next closest thing to real Parmesan, and less expensive), dry Jack, and more. They can be sharp and strong, like Romano (which is also the saltiest), or mild enough to snack on, like manchego. Use them grated in pasta sauces, to garnish and enrich all sorts of dishes, and in combination with other dairy for delicious dips. You can hardly go wrong.

RICOTTA In between the best, which is made yourself (page 569), and the stuff sold in tubs, there are some decent options to be found. Wonderful spread on toast with a drizzle of olive oil or jam, or stirred into a sauce or grain dish to add richness, or used as a stuffing for pasta. A nice all-purpose cheese to have around, though it doesn't keep for more than a week, usually.

BLUE CHEESES Gorgonzola, Roquefort, Cabrales, other European blues, and American blue cheese like Maytag. Blue-veined cheeses, which intentionally cultivate flavorful but harmless molds, may be an acquired taste, but devotees (I'm one) crave them. Try sprinkling some strong blue cheese on plain cooked vegetables along with bread crumbs and running it under the broiler. Wonderful in sauces, dressings, and dips.

FETA Though many feta cheeses are now packed in airtight plastic, I prefer to buy those stored in brine. The flavor is fresh and milky, with salty rather than sharp notes, and the texture is dry and crumbly. If the feta you buy is too salty for you, rinse the cheese and pat it dry before using; next time, try a different variety. Use it crumbled into salads or grain dishes or mashed with lemon juice and fresh herbs and spread on crostini or crackers.

FRESH SOFT GOAT CHEESE Sometimes called chèvre (which is simply French for "goat"), this distinctive cheese is great used as part of creamy fillings and spreads or dolloped on top of a bowl of soup to be swirled in for a bit of tangy richness.

CREAM CHEESE Supermarket varieties only hint at the potential of cream cheese, which is tangy, rich, and creamy.

MELTING CHEESES

The best melting cheeses melt smoothly; it's best to grate or slice them thinly for quick, even melting. Use these types of cheeses to top dishes for a creamy finish, make into grilled cheese, or for quesadillas or other cheesy Mexican dishes like enchiladas.

SWISS-STYLE CHEESES — GRUYÈRE, FONTINA, EMMENTAL ("SWISS"), RACLETTE, APPENZELLER, COMTÉ Though each of these is unique, I'm grouping them together here because they share a velvety texture when melted and a complex, nutty taste that makes them good choices for combining with other ingredients.

MONTEREY JACK, QUESO ASADERO, AND QUESO OAXACA Mild, with good body when melted, these rindless cheeses are perfect for Mexican food as a creamy counterpoint to assertive seasoning.

CHEDDAR I prefer sharp cheddar cheeses with at least a little bit of age on them, because they are more

Cutting or Crumbling Parmesan

Real Parmesan has a granular, irregular texture; it's almost never sliced like other cheeses. There are two easy ways to cut it:

It's easy to shave Parmesan into small flakes, pulling a vegetable peeler toward you.

Use a small, not-too-sharp knife or other tool to break the Parmesan off chunks.

flavorful and melt better. Cheddars are also good stand-alone cheeses for snacking, especially when combined with apples, dried fruit, nuts, and whole grain toast.

MOZZARELLA Freshly made mozzarella (which often comes packed in water) is quite different from the drier, slightly aged brick kind. Fresh mozzarella tastes like milk, only with a little tang, and should never be rubbery or stringy. It's a great cheese to melt on pizza or pasta, obviously, or to eat raw in salads or sandwiches.

CHEESES THAT KEEP THEIR SHAPE DURING COOKING

These cheeses have a high melting point and will soften rather melt when heated. They can be thrown on the grill or fried or seared in a skillet, developing a delicious brown crust; with some cheeses, the interior will get creamy, with others, it will retain its structure while heating through.

HALLOUMI A semi-hard brined cheese usually made from a combination of goat and sheep's milk. It originated in Cyprus but is now made around the world and is particularly popular in Greece, Turkey, and the Middle East. It has a distinctive salty flavor.

PANEER A mild fresh cheese made from water buffalo or cow's milk that is a staple in the cooking of India, Pakistan, Nepal, and Bangladesh in dishes like saag paneer. Look for it in Indian food stores, or use Fresh Cheese, the Easy Way (page 568).

QUESO DE FREÍR (OR QUESO PARA FREÍR) A firm, mild cow's milk cheese with a salty taste. It is popular throughout Central America and the Caribbean, usually prepared by slicing, then frying or pan-searing. Look for it in the supermarket where other Hispanic dairy products are sold; it may simply be labeled "Grilling Cheese."

KASSERI, KEFALOTYRI, AND GRAVIERA These Greek cheeses, made from a combination of sheep, cow, and/or goat's milk, are great choices for pan-searing.

BREAD CHEESE This cheese finds its origins in Finland, where it is called juustoleipa or leipajuusto and is made from cow, goat, or reindeer milk. It's now produced in the U.S. (in Wisconsin) from cow's milk and it's sold already browned, with lovely golden spots all over it. It takes well to grilling, pan-searing, baking, or frying.

Blue Cheese Dip or Spread

MAKES: About 6 servings
TIME: 15 minutes
🄵 🄼

This recipe is a template for all kinds of dips and spreads; blue cheese, goat cheese, or cream cheese—just about any soft cheese can be used here. And you can adjust the texture however you like: For a dip, thin with sour cream or yogurt; for a thick spread, use cream cheese or yogurt cheese.

1 cup crumbled blue cheese
1 cup sour cream, yogurt, or cream cheese
2 tablespoons minced shallot or scallions
2 teaspoons chopped fresh sage
2 tablespoons fresh lemon juice
   Salt and pepper
   Milk or cream if needed

Combine all the ingredients in a bowl and mash with a fork or potato masher, or whirl in a food processor. Taste and adjust the seasoning, adding salt, pepper, and lemon juice if necessary. Thin the mixture with milk or cream if it's too thick. Serve or cover and refrigerate for up to 2 days.

TOFU DIP OR SPREAD Vegan and creamy: Replace the blue cheese and sour cream with 8 ounces soft silken tofu (for a dip) or firm tofu (for a spread). Use any of the flavorings in the main recipe or in the following list. Purée in a food processor until very smooth; add small amounts of soy milk to thin it, if necessary. **V**

11 Flavorings to Stir or Blend into Any Cheese or Tofu Dip or Spread

A single ingredient can add loads of flavor, but don't go overboard.

1. Any herbs, fresh or dried
2. Grated lemon zest or lemon juice
3. Dried or Oven-Dried Tomatoes (page 261), chopped
4. Chopped fresh chiles or chipotle chiles in adobo sauce, or any Chile Paste (page 664)
5. Spinach, cooked, squeezed dry, and chopped
6. Mushrooms, chopped and cooked
7. Caramelized Onions (page 222)
8. Roasted Garlic (page 205)
9. Chili powder (page 648) or Fragrant Curry Powder (page 649)
10. Za'atar (page 652)
11. Citrus Sprinkle (page 651)

Swiss-Style Cheese Bake

MAKES: 4 to 6 servings
TIME: 45 minutes
M

When you don't have time for full-on fondue or want to have something ready to pop into the oven after a day outside in the cold, this dish—essentially melted cheese with potatoes and vegetables—is perfect. Try layering the ingredients into small individual crocks if you have them. And consider that you can use virtually any kind of cooked vegetables here, which makes it a great use for leftovers.

   Butter or olive oil for greasing the baking dish(es)
2 cups grated fontina, Emmental, Gruyère, Cantal, cheddar, or Jack cheese
1 tablespoon cornstarch
3 cups cooked potato cubes (boiled or roasted, peeled or not)
   Salt and pepper
2 cups roughly chopped cooked asparagus, broccoli, or Brussels sprouts
¼ cup chopped walnuts (optional)
¼ cup grated Parmesan cheese
   Chopped fresh parsley for garnish (optional)

1. If you're baking immediately, heat the oven to 375°F. Grease an 8-inch square baking dish or four to six 8-ounce ovenproof crocks with a little butter or oil. Toss the grated cheese with the cornstarch until the cheese is coated evenly.
2. Spread the potatoes evenly in the pans. Sprinkle with salt and pepper and half of the cheese. Top with the vegetable, a little more salt and pepper, and the remaining cheese mixture. Sprinkle with the walnuts, if you're using them, and the Parmesan. Cover the pans tightly with aluminum foil. (You can assemble the dish to this point and refrigerate it for up to a day. Bring to room temperature and heat the oven before proceeding.)

3. Bake, covered, until the cheese melts and the vegetables are hot, 15 to 20 minutes. Remove the foil and continue baking until the cheese is golden and bubbly, another 10 minutes or so. Sprinkle with parsley, if you're using it, and let rest for a few minutes before serving.

ITALIAN-STYLE CHEESE BAKE Use Taleggio for the cheese; replace the potatoes with 3 cups chopped escarole, endive, or radicchio; and use sautéed fennel for the vegetable. You can mix up to 1 tablespoon chopped fresh thyme with the vegetables if you want. Garnish with chopped hazelnuts.

CHEDDAR CHEESE BAKE Use sharp cheddar for the cheese; replace the potatoes with 3 cups chopped cooked cauliflower; and replace the vegetable with 2 cups chopped raw apples. Garnish with walnuts and parsley, if you like.

SMOKED MOZZARELLA AND GREENS BAKE Use smoked mozzarella for the cheese and sautéed kale for the vegetable. Garnish with chopped almonds and a sprinkle of smoked paprika.

MUSHROOM CHEESE BAKE Use mozzarella for the cheese; replace the potatoes with 3 cups roasted mushrooms; and use chopped blanched broccoli raab for the vegetable. Garnish with walnuts and parsley.

EGGPLANT CHEESE BAKE Use mozzarella for the cheese; replace the potatoes with 3 cups chopped roasted eggplant; and use sliced roasted red peppers (page 228) for the vegetable. Garnish with toasted pine nuts and basil.

CHILE CHEESE BAKE Use Jack for the cheese and sliced roasted poblano peppers (see page 228) for the vegetable. Garnish with pepitas and cilantro.

PROVOLONE AND BROCCOLI BAKE Use provolone for the cheese (extra aged provolone is nice); replace the potatoes with 2 cups chopped drained canned tomatoes; and use chopped steamed broccoli for the vegetable. Garnish with toasted bread crumbs and parsley.

AUTUMN CHEESE BAKE Use Gruyère for the cheese; replace the regular potatoes with sweet potatoes; and replace the vegetable with 2 cups chopped sautéed apples. Garnish with pecans and parsley.

3 More Cheese Dip or Spread Ideas

CHEESE	FOR A DIP	FOR A SPREAD	AROMATICS	SEASONINGS
1 cup crumbled feta	1 cup sour cream or yogurt	1 cup cream cheese	2 tablespoons chopped scallions and 1 teaspoon minced garlic	1 teaspoon chopped fresh marjoram
1 cup goat cheese	1 cup sour cream	1 cup cream cheese	2 tablespoons minced shallot	¼ cup chopped mixed herbs (like parsley, chives, chervil, and thyme)
1½ cups finely grated Parmesan	1 cup sour cream	1 cup cream cheese	1 teaspoon finely grated lemon zest	Lots of pepper

Batter-Fried Cheese

Paneer Pakora
MAKES: 4 to 6 servings
TIME: 15 minutes with premade cheese
F

Refrigerate the cheese for about an hour; chilling it will help it keep its shape during cooking. Bear in mind that cooking cheese—whether you're frying, grilling, or broiling—must be quick. There's no need to actually cook the cheese; you just want to give it a quick flash of heat to brown the exterior or cook the coating.

Try it with some typical accompaniments, like Smooth Green Chile Sauce, Indian Style (page 666), any chutney (see pages 668 to 670), or Raita (page 674). If you use cornmeal, try serving the cheese with any tomato-based sauce or salsa.

> 2 **tablespoons chickpea flour (besan) or cornmeal, or more as needed**
> **Salt and pepper**
> **Good-quality vegetable oil for frying**
> 1 **pound paneer, queso de freír, halloumi, or other appropriate cheese (see "Cheeses That Keep Their Shape During Cooking," page 556) or 1 recipe Fresh Cheese, the Easy Way (page 568), cut into bite-sized pieces**

1. Put the flour and 6 tablespoons water in a medium bowl and whisk until combined. Sprinkle with salt and pepper. The consistency should be like a pancake batter; add flour or water as necessary and adjust the seasoning.
2. Put ½ to 1 inch oil in a large, deep skillet, preferably nonstick, over medium or medium-high heat. Heat until it's very hot but not smoking.
3. Toss the cheese cubes in the chickpea batter until well coated. Using a slotted spoon, carefully put batches of the cheese in the hot oil (first letting any excess batter drain off into the bowl), gently rotating them in the oil for even cooking and browning on all sides, 5 to 7 minutes. Put on paper towels to drain and immediately sprinkle with salt and pepper. Serve hot or at room temperature.

SPICED BATTER-FRIED CHEESE Add a pinch of cayenne for heat and any other ground spice or spice mixture you like: Add ½ teaspoon or so garam masala, Fragrant Curry Powder (page 649), or chili powder and a pinch cayenne and mix the into the chickpea batter in Step 1.

BATTER-FRIED CHEESE WITH SPICED YOGURT
A lovely dish; excellent served with basmati rice and Cilantro-Mint Chutney (page 668): Cook all the cheese cubes. Cook 1 large onion, sliced, in good-Zquality vegetable oil in a large skillet over medium-high heat until golden brown. Stir in 1 tablespoon minced garlic and 1 tablespoon garam masala or curry powder and cook for another minute, until fragrant. Stir in 2 cups yogurt and the fried cheese cubes, along with some salt and pepper; heat until barely bubbling. Adjust the seasoning and serve.

10 Dishes or Sauces for Batter-Fried Cheese

Stir the fried cheese cubes into the sauce or dish 5 to 10 minutes before it has finished cooking to heat it through and allow it to absorb the flavors without falling apart.
1. Spicy Indian Tomato Sauce (page 667)
2. Smooth Green Chile Sauce, Indian Style (page 666)
3. Spiced Tomato Sauce (page 313)
4. Simplest Dal (page 450) or any dal recipe (pages 450 to 454)
5. Skillet Eggplant or any of its variations (page 199)
6. Spinach with Paneer and Yogurt (page 250)
7. Leeks Braised in Olive Oil or Butter or any of its variations (page 215)
8. Stovetop Mixed Vegetables with Olive Oil (page 157)
9. Biryani (page 375)
10. Spicy Red Beans, Indian Style (page 443)

Cheese Enchiladas
with Red Mole

MAKES: 8 servings
TIME: About 3 hours, mostly unattended

M

Mole is a group of classic slow-cooked Mexican sauces that get their rich, deep flavor from a long list of ingredients (including chocolate, nuts, seeds, herbs, chiles, and more). This mole is loaded with nuts, and I've purposefully kept the cheese filling to a minimum so the sauce remains the star. It isn't time-consuming once everything is assembled, but I'd still consider this a special occasion dish. If you're looking for everyday enchiladas, see the first variation.

Serve with sliced white or red radishes, sliced avocado, chopped fresh tomatoes or tomatillos, shredded lettuce, sour cream or crema, and/or toasted pumpkin seeds.

12–15 mild to medium dried chiles (like New Mexico, mulatto, pasilla, guajillo, ancho, or a combination), toasted, soaked, and cleaned (see page 226)

2 cups assorted nuts (like peanuts, almonds, pecans, walnuts, pine nuts, and hazelnuts)

¼ cup tahini (to make your own, see page 305) or sesame seeds

¼ cup cocoa powder or chopped unsweetened chocolate

1 large onion, cut into large chunks

1 head garlic, cloves separated and peeled

4 plum tomatoes (canned are fine)

2 thick slices white bread (stale is fine)

4 cups vegetable stock (pages 97–100) or water, plus more as needed

¼ cup good-quality vegetable oil, plus more for frying

3 or 4 bay leaves

1 cinnamon stick

2 tablespoons ground cumin

1 tablespoon ground allspice

2 teaspoons anise seeds
Salt and pepper
Brown sugar (optional)

24 small corn tortillas, plus more if any break

3 cups shredded Monterey Jack cheese

½ cup crumbled queso fresco for garnish

½ cup chopped red onion or scallions for garnish

½ cup chopped fresh cilantro for garnish
Lime wedges for garnish

1. Put the chiles, nuts, tahini, cocoa, onion, garlic, tomatoes, and bread in a blender with just enough stock to get the machine running. (You may have to work in 2 batches.)

2. Put the oil in a large, deep pot over medium heat. Add the puréed mixture, bay leaves, cinnamon, cumin, allspice, and anise seeds. Sprinkle with salt and pepper. Cook, stirring frequently and scraping the bottom of the pan, until it begins to color and become fragrant, 3 to 5 minutes. Turn the heat to low and continue cooking, stirring occasionally, until the mixture is deeply colored, softened, and nearly dry, another 15 to 20 minutes.

3. Turn the heat back up to medium-high and slowly stir in the remaining stock. Bring to a boil, then lower the heat so the sauce barely bubbles. Cook, stirring occasionally and adding more liquid as needed, for an hour or so, until the sauce is thick and smooth. Taste and adjust the seasoning; add a tablespoon or so brown sugar if you like. (You can make the mole in advance up to this point. Cool, cover, and refrigerate for up to 3 days. Gently reheat before proceeding.) Remove the cinnamon stick and bay leaves and keep the sauce warm.

4. Heat the oven to 350°F. Spoon a thin layer of the mole in a 9 × 12-inch baking dish. Put about ½ inch oil in a large, deep skillet over medium-high heat. When it's hot, cook the tortillas, one at a time, until softened and pliable, about 10 seconds. Drain on paper towels. Add more oil to the pan as needed.

5. Sprinkle about 2 tablespoons of the Monterey Jack in the center of each tortilla, roll tightly, and put into the baking dish, seam side down. The enchiladas should be in a single layer, packed in snugly against one another. Cover the top with some more mole. Bake until the cheese is melted and hot, 25 minutes. When you take the enchiladas out of the oven, sprinkle with the queso fresco, onion, and cilantro. Serve with lime wedges on the side and pass the remaining mole at the table.

SIMPLE CHEESE ENCHILADAS Definitely easier: Instead of making the mole, prepare a double recipe of Red Enchilada Sauce (page 663). Proceed with the recipe from Step 4, substituting this sauce for the mole.

CHEESE ENCHILADAS WITH GREEN ENCHILADA SAUCE Also known as Enchiladas Suizas: Instead of making the mole sauce, prepare a double recipe of Green Enchilada Sauce (page 664). Increase the Monterey Jack to 5 cups and fill each tortilla with a heaping tablespoon. Sprinkle the remaining Monterey Jack on top of the enchiladas before baking.

SCRAMBLED EGG AND CHEESE ENCHILADAS Great with mole or Red Enchilada Sauce (page 663): Just before you're ready to assemble the enchiladas in Step 5, scramble 4 or 5 eggs according to the recipe on page 523. Stop cooking when the eggs are just holding together but still rather loose. Proceed with the recipe, using a spoonful of scrambled eggs along with the cheese to fill each enchilada.

HARD-BOILED EGG AND CHEESE ENCHILADAS Terrific texture: Hard-boil 6 eggs according to the recipe on page 521. When you're ready to assemble the enchiladas in Step 5, peel the eggs and mash them roughly with a fork. Proceed with the recipe, using a sprinkle of the eggs along with the cheese to fill each enchilada.

SQUASH OR SWEET POTATO ENCHILADAS Instead of Monterey Jack cheese, use 4 cups cooked, mashed, and seasoned winter squash or sweet potatoes to fill the tortillas in Step 5. Omit the queso fresco garnish to make these vegan. ◙

TOFU ENCHILADAS WITH RED MOLE Vegan and delicious: Make the sauce and tortillas as directed. Omit all the cheeses in the recipe and prepare a double recipe of Scrambled Tofu with Mushrooms (page 489). Use this to fill the enchiladas. **V**

Panfried Cheese

MAKES: 4 servings
TIME: 20 minutes
F **M**

Some form of panfried cheese exists in every dairy-consuming cuisine, with the technique remaining much the same and the cheese changing.

- 3 tablespoons all-purpose flour
- 1 teaspoon paprika
- 2 eggs
- ½ cup bread crumbs, preferably fresh (page 678)
- 1 pound paneer, queso de freír, halloumi, or other appropriate cheese (see "Cheeses That Keep Their Shape During Cooking," page 556) or 1 recipe Fresh Cheese, the Easy Way (page 568), cut into ½-inch slices
  Olive oil for frying

1. Mix together the flour and paprika on a plate. Beat the eggs in a shallow bowl, and put the bread crumbs on a plate. Dredge the cheese slices in the flour, then the beaten eggs, and finally the bread crumbs. If time allows, put the cheese on wax paper and refrigerate for an hour or longer.

2. Put at least ⅛ inch oil in a large skillet over medium-high heat. When it's hot, fry the cheese slices until golden brown, about 30 seconds, then turn and brown the other side. Drain on paper towels and serve as soon as possible.

Cheese "Burgers"

MAKES: 4 servings
TIME: 20 minutes
F M

You can always slip one of these rich cheese patties between 2 slices of toasted bread or into a hamburger bun, but I like them better as an entrée with Fast Tomato Sauce (page 312). Make them smaller and serve them as croutons on any green salad, or put in a shallow bowl with a ladle or 2 of Roasted Vegetable Stock (page 99) or just about any vegetable soup like Onion Soup or Wintertime Tomato Soup (page 100 or 107).

> 2 cups grated Parmesan cheese
> 1 cup chopped fresh parsley
> 1 cup bread crumbs (preferably fresh; see page 678)
> 2 eggs
> 2 tablespoons olive oil
>   Salt and pepper

1. Mix together the cheese, parsley, and bread crumbs in a large bowl. Add the eggs and use a fork to gently beat the eggs and blend everything into a semisolid mixture. The "dough" should be about the consistency of dumpling or biscuit dough. Carefully shape into 4 patties and set them on a plate or wax paper.

2. Put the oil in a large skillet over medium-high heat. When it's hot, add the patties (it's fine to cook them in one batch). Cook undisturbed until they start to look crisp around the edges, about 5 minutes. Carefully flip and cook the other side for 3 to 5 minutes, until golden brown. Drain briefly on paper towels. Sprinkle lightly with salt and heavily with pepper and serve.

COUSCOUS AND CHEESE "BURGERS" This is especially nice with whole wheat couscous: Instead of the bread crumbs, use 1 cup cooked couscous (page 407).

PESTO CHEESE "BURGERS" More substantial and nuttier: Use chopped fresh basil instead of parsley and increase to 3 eggs. In Step 1, add ½ cup chopped pine nuts or walnuts and 1 clove garlic, minced, to the cheese mixture. Proceed with the recipe.

BAKED CHEESE "BURGERS" Multiply the recipe and they're perfect for a crowd: Instead of cooking the burgers in a skillet, heat the oven to 375°F at the beginning of Step 1. Line a baking sheet with parchment paper or grease it well with olive oil. Set the shaped patties on the sheet. Bake until crisp and golden, about 15 minutes.

Curried Cheese

Paneer Masala
MAKES: 4 servings
TIME: 25 minutes
F M

Paneer, like tofu, is a wonderful mild yet rich main ingredient for curries and Indian-style stir-fries. It browns beautifully and holds its shape well when cooked. Try this dish and its better-known relative, Saag Paneer (page 250).

6 tablespoons butter or good-quality
vegetable oil
1 pound paneer, queso de freír,
halloumi, or other appropriate cheese
(see "Cheeses That Keep Their Shape
During Cooking," page 556) or
1 recipe Fresh Cheese, the Easy Way
(page 568), cut into bite-sized cubes
1 large onion, chopped
2 tablespoons minced garlic
2 tablespoons minced fresh ginger
1 tablespoon garam masala or
curry powder (to make your own,
see page 648 or 649)
2 cups (about 1 pound) chopped fresh tomatoes
(canned is fine; don't bother to drain)
Salt and pepper
½ cup cream, coconut milk, or yogurt
½ cup chopped fresh cilantro (optional)

1. Put 3 tablespoons of the butter or oil in a large skillet over medium-high heat. When the butter is melted or the oil is hot, add the cheese and cook until golden brown on all sides, a total of 6 to 10 minutes; remove from the pan and put on a paper towel–lined plate.

2. Put the remaining butter or oil in the same pan over medium-high heat. When the butter is melted or the oil is hot, add the onion and cook, stirring occasionally, until soft, 3 to 5 minutes. Add the garlic, ginger, and garam masala and cook for another minute, until fragrant. Add the tomatoes, sprinkle with some salt and pepper, stir, and cook until slightly thickened, about 10 minutes.

3. Add the cheese along with the cream and bring to a slow bubble. Cook for about 5 minutes, until everything is heated through. Adjust the seasoning, garnish with cilantro if you're using it, and serve.

CURRIED CHEESE WITH TOMATOES AND MINT Omit the garam masala and cream. Use only fresh tomatoes.

Substitute mint for the cilantro. In Step 2, add the tomatoes with the garlic and ginger, cook for a minute or 2, then add the cheese. Stir in the mint just before serving.

CURRIED CHEESE WITH CHILE PASTE Make this as hot as you like; for a less mouth-searing dish, mellow out the chile paste with a little tomato paste thinned with water: Omit the onion, garlic, ginger, garam masala, tomatoes, and cream. In Step 1, once the cheese has browned, stir in ¼ cup or so Indian-Style Chile Paste (page 665)—or whatever chile paste you have on hand—and a pinch garam masala or curry powder until it is well distributed in the pan. Cook for just a minute, adding a splash of water if it gets too dry. Garnish with cilantro and serve.

CURRIED CHEESE WITH CHILES Toss in some roasted cashews or peanuts for crunch: Omit the tomatoes and cream. In Step 2, add 2 cups chopped fresh mild green chiles with the onion. After adding the garlic and ginger, cook for 2 minutes, then stir in the cheese and finish as directed.

CURRIED TOFU Substitute 1 pound firm or extra-firm tofu, cut into cubes, for the fresh cheese, and use oil and coconut milk. **V**

Grilled Yogurt-Marinated Cheese and Vegetable Skewers

Paneer Tikka

MAKES: 4 servings
TIME: 40 minutes, mostly unattended
M

The spiced yogurt marinade adds loads of flavor. You can also grill or broil the cheese without the skewers. Just cut it into thick strips instead of cubes. The marinade can be made a day ahead.

½ cup yogurt

1 tablespoon fresh lemon juice

1 teaspoon minced garlic

1 teaspoon minced fresh ginger

1 teaspoon ground coriander

½ teaspoon ground cumin

¼ teaspoon cayenne

Salt

1 pound paneer, queso de freír, halloumi, or other appropriate cheese (see "Cheeses That Keep Their Shape During Cooking," page 556) or 1 recipe Fresh Cheese, the Easy Way (page 568), cut into 1½-inch cubes

2 small red or yellow onions, quartered

2 tomatoes, quartered

1 bell pepper (any color), cored, seeded, and cut into 1½-inch pieces

2 tablespoons butter, melted, or olive oil

Chopped fresh cilantro for garnish

1. Combine the yogurt, lemon juice, garlic, ginger, coriander, cumin, and cayenne in a large bowl. Sprinkle with some salt. Add the cheese cubes, toss to coat, and let marinate while you heat the grill, or refrigerate for up to 1 hour.

2. If using wooden skewers, soak them in water for 30 minutes before cooking. Prepare a charcoal or gas grill or turn on the broiler to moderate heat; adjust the rack to 4 inches away from the heat source. Thread the cheese cubes, onion and tomato quarters, and bell pepper pieces onto the skewers, leaving a little bit of space between the pieces. Brush with the butter.

3. Grill or broil, turning occasionally, until the cheese is lightly browned and the vegetables are tender, 8 to 10 minutes. Sprinkle with the cilantro and serve.

GRILLED TOFU AND VEGETABLE SKEWERS Substitute Cashew Cream (page 300) for the yogurt and firm tofu for the fresh cheese. **V**

Grilled Cheese and Watermelon Skewers

MAKES: 4 servings
TIME: 15 minutes

F

An unexpected and delicious summertime entrée.

1 pound paneer, queso de freír, halloumi, or other appropriate cheese (see "Cheeses That Keep Their Shape During Cooking," page 556) or 1 recipe Fresh Cheese, the Easy Way (page 568), cut into 1- to 1½-inch cubes

1 pound watermelon flesh, seeded and cut into 1- to 1½-inch pieces

½ pound cherry tomatoes

Olive oil

Salt and pepper

1 tablespoon fresh lemon juice

¼ cup chopped fresh mint for garnish

1. If using wooden skewers, soak them in water for 30 minutes before cooking. Prepare a charcoal or gas grill or turn on the broiler to moderate heat; adjust the rack to 4 inches away from the heat source.

2. Put a piece of cheese, then watermelon, then a cherry tomato on a skewer, and repeat in the same order. Put the finished skewers in a large baking dish. Drizzle with olive oil and sprinkle with salt and pepper.

3. Put the skewers on the grill and cook until one side has grill marks and the watermelon has charred a little, then flip and cook the other side, 6 to 8 minutes total. Put the skewers on a serving platter. Sprinkle lemon juice over all and garnish with the mint. Serve hot or at room temperature.

GRILLED FRESH CHEESE WITH FIGS Replace the watermelon with halved fresh figs (about 1 pound), and the cherry tomatoes with grapes. Replace the lemon juice and mint with 1 tablespoon honey and a pinch red chile flakes.

FRESH CHEESE

Making fresh cheese is almost as easy as boiling milk. All cheese begins by separating curds (milk solids) and whey (watery liquid). Most commercially made cheeses rely on rennet, a plant- or animal-based enzyme, to cause this chemical reaction (known as "curdling" or "coagulating"). But there are a couple of easy ways to do this at home. If you use an acid like vinegar or lemon juice, you will probably be able to taste it in the final product, a disadvantage. Buttermilk, which is a mild-tasting but effective coagulant, is nicer. The result is tender cheese with a pure milky flavor, akin to the Indian staple paneer, true queso fresco (the fresh white cheese common in Mexico), the fromage blanc of France, and a dozen other products made worldwide.

To use fresh cheese, just cut it into slices or cubes or gently crumble it by hand or with two forks (it's too soft to grate). It's delicious eaten on its own, and a wonderful enrichment for a variety of dishes, as you can see on page 570. Fresh cheese will keep for 3 to 4 days in the fridge. (Technically, you can freeze it, tightly wrapped, for up to 3 months, but I don't see the point.)

If you enjoy the process of making fresh cheese, you can branch out to other cheeses (see the variations),

---

What to Do with All That Whey

Depending on how much cheese-making (or yogurt-making) you do, you could end up with a lot of whey on your hands. There are plenty of uses for this nutritious byproduct; just make sure you've cooled it first.

1. Use whey instead of milk or water for bread or other baked goods

2. Use whey instead of or in addition to stock in soups and stews or when cooking grains or beans.

3. Add it to smoothies.

4. Use whey to water your plants or add to your pet's food bowl.

---

or try the slightly more complicated mozzarella, which requires slightly less common ingredients.

Fresh Cheese, the Easy Way

MAKES: About 1 pound
TIME: 2 hours, mostly unattended
M

The recipe—and all the variations—works with 1%, 2%, or whole milk, which makes the richest cheese. If you live near a farm and can get fresh whole milk, do it. That's the best.

8   **cups (½ gallon) milk**
4   **cups buttermilk**
    Salt (optional)

1. Put the milk in a large, heavy-bottomed pot over medium-high heat. Cook, stirring occasionally to keep it from scorching, until the milk bubbles up the sides of the pot, 10 to 15 minutes.
2. Line a fine-meshed strainer with 3 layers of cheesecloth or a piece of undyed cotton muslin. Place the colander in the sink, or over a deep bowl or pot if you want to keep the whey. Have a long piece of kitchen twine ready.
3. Add the buttermilk to the boiling milk all at once and stir constantly until the mixture separates into curds and whey. It will look like cooked egg whites suspended in a slightly thick yellowish liquid. Remove from the heat and stir in a large pinch salt if you're using it.
4. Carefully pour the mixture into the cloth so that the curds collect and the whey drains through. Gather up the corners of the cloth and twist the top to start working the curds into a ball. Run the bundle under cold water until you can handle it. Keep twisting and squeezing out the whey until the bundle feels firm and dry. Don't worry about handling it roughly; it can take it.
5. Tie the string around the top to hold it tight, then tie the string around a long spoon or stick to suspend the cheese over the sink or a colander or strainer set over a bowl to drain. Let it rest, undisturbed, until cool and

set, about 1½ hours. (If you save the whey, see "What to Do with All That Whey," opposite.) Remove the string, open the cloth, and serve the cheese immediately or wrap in plastic and refrigerate for up to 3 days.

FRESH COTTAGE CHEESE Drain as dry or as moist as you like: In Step 4, after you pour the curds and whey through the cheesecloth, simply leave the curds loose in the strainer until they've drained the amount of moisture you desire, anywhere from 30 to 60 minutes. Don't squeeze them dry. Scoop the curds into a container and store in the refrigerator.

FRESH RICOTTA Unbelievable, especially with top-quality milk: Reduce the buttermilk to 2 cups and proceed with the recipe through Step 3. The mixture will look like thickened buttermilk. In Step 4, after you pour it through the cheesecloth, simply leave the ricotta in the strainer until it reaches the texture you like, anywhere from 30 to 60 minutes. Then scoop the ricotta into a container and store in the refrigerator. To make the ricotta smooth, beat or whisk it after draining.

BRINED FRESH CHEESE Like a mild feta: After the cheese is set, mix a brine of 2 tablespoons salt and 2 cups water in a jar or plastic container. Submerge the cheese in the brine and refrigerate for at least 24 hours before eating.

4 Ways to Flavor Fresh Cheese

In Step 4 of the recipe for making fresh cheese, after pouring the curds and whey into the cloth-lined strainer, immediately stir any of the following ingredients into the curds and proceed with the recipe.

1. Up to 1 tablespoon finely grated citrus zest of your choice

2. Up to 2 tablespoons chopped fresh herbs

3. Up to ¼ cup minced nuts, like walnuts, almonds, or hazelnuts

4. Up to 1 tablespoon coarsely ground black or green peppercorns

Cheese Scramble

MAKES: 4 servings
TIME: 15 minutes

F

The mild flavor of the cheese goes well with just about any vegetable and can be spiced as much or as little as you like. Serve this with Paratha (page 592) or Chapati (page 591), or over basmati rice, or with toast.

Finishing Fresh Cheese

STEP 1 Pour the coagulated, lumpy mix into a cheesecloth-lined fine-meshed strainer.

STEP 2 Pull the corners together and twist and squeeze out excess moisture.

STEP 3 Tie into a sack with kitchen twine and hang from a wooden spoon or other implement over the sink or a colander or strainer set over a bowl.

1 tablespoon good-quality vegetable oil

1 small onion or 4 scallions, chopped

1 tablespoon minced garlic

1 teaspoon garam masala or curry powder (to make your own, see page 648 or 649)

½ cup fresh or thawed frozen peas or cooked edamame (page 433)

1 recipe Fresh Cheese, the Easy Way (page 568) or about 1 pound farmer cheese, paneer, halloumi, or queso fresco, crumbled

Salt and pepper

Chopped fresh cilantro for garnish (optional)

1. Put the oil in a large skillet over medium-high heat. When it's hot, add the onion and garlic and cook, stirring occasionally, until the onion is soft, 3 to 5 minutes. Add the garam masala and stir; cook for another 2 minutes, until fragrant.

2. Stir in the peas and cheese and sprinkle with salt and pepper. Cook, stirring often, until heated through, 2 to 3 minutes. Add a tablespoon or 2 of water if the cheese begins to stick to the pan. Taste and adjust the seasoning, sprinkle with cilantro, if you're using it, and serve.

FRESH CHEESE SCRAMBLE WITH CHILES Use any kind of fresh chile you like: Add 1 or 2 (or as many as you like) fresh chiles (like jalapeño, serrano, or Anaheim), seeded and sliced, or 1 tablespoon red chile flakes. Add with the onion in Step 1.

9 More Dishes or Sauces That Work with Fresh Cheese

Stir cubes of fresh cheese into the following dishes during the last few minutes of cooking, to heat the cheese through and allow it to absorb the flavors without falling apart. It won't melt but might get a little soft.

1. Curried Eggplant with Coconut Milk (page 199)

2. Spinach with Paneer and Yogurt (page 250)

3. Simplest Dal (page 450) or any dal recipe (pages 450 to 454)

4. Coconut-Lentil Soup with Vegetables (page 127)

5. Spicy Indian Tomato Sauce (page 667)

6. Smooth Green Chile Sauce, Indian Style (page 666)

7. Spicy Tomato Sauce (page 313)

8. Bulgur Chili (page 408)

9. Fast Tomato Sauce (page 312)

FRESH CHEESE SCRAMBLE WITH TOMATOES Add 1 cup chopped tomato (about ½ pound whole) or chopped drained canned tomatoes with the spices in Step 1.

FRESH CHEESE SCRAMBLE WITH EGGS Chopped Hard-Boiled Eggs (page 521) are also great here: Add 3 eggs, lightly beaten, in Step 2; stir often, cooking until the eggs are cooked but still moist and soft.

Breads, Muffins, Pizza, and Wraps

Quick breads and their close relatives, biscuits and scones, are leavened with baking powder, baking soda, or, in some cases, just eggs. No yeast means no waiting for a rise, so they are true to their name and offer near-instant gratification. They also offer reliability. While yeast breads can be temperamental, quick breads are practically foolproof and so are among the ideal baked goods for beginners. And because they are so forgiving, they're easy to customize, as you'll see.

Unleavened crackers and flatbreads are made from easy-to-mix, easy-to-handle doughs that don't contain baking powder, baking soda, or yeast. In the case of crackers (page 589), the results are crispy, almost shatteringly so. For Paratha (page 592) and other flatbreads, the heat of the oven is enough to cause the bread to puff up.

Warm and slathered with butter or dipped into olive oil or soup, served with cheese or a wide variety of dishes from all over the world, few foods are as important—or satisfying—as yeast bread. You'll find a wonderful collection here ranging from classic country style bread to yeasted flatbreads and other bread kin, like breadsticks and pizza.

And finally, the recipes I like to think of as "Bread Plus"—these take bread as their starting points:

Anatomy of a Wheat Kernel

A wheat kernel consists of three parts: the bran, germ, and endosperm. The bran is the outside layer and the source of most of wheat's fiber, along with a lot of nutrients, including niacin and iron. It comprises 14 percent of the kernel. The germ is the embryo, the part of the kernel from which a new plant would develop (the kernel is, after all, a seed) and like the bran contains niacin and zinc as well as vitamin E, protein, and a number of other nutrients. It makes up only 3 percent of the kernel. The endosperm is the food store for the germ, largely comprised of starch. It does contain other nutrients but not in the same concentrated way as the germ and the endosperm.

wrapping dough around savory stuffings in Calzones (page 615) and Samosas (page 617) or filling store-bought or homemade tortillas to make burritos, tacos, and quesadillas (page 620). The chapter concludes with what I think is one of the best ways to enjoy good crusty bread—sliced, toasted, and topped to make Bruschetta (page 623).

THE BASICS OF FLOUR

Virtually any grain, bean, nut, or starchy food can be ground, and, when it's fine enough, that product can be called "flour." But even if the name is appropriate, "flours" vary so much in different ways—flavor, texture, baking properties, color nutrition . . . really, everything—that you must understand the differences if you're going to cook with anything other than standard all-purpose white flour. Substitutions, even partial substitutions, are only rarely straightforward.

Having said that, this is a joyous and fun world to explore, filled with possibilities. To get you started, here's a run-down of the most common flours, as well as some specialty flours that are becoming more mainstream; see, too, the chart with some basic guidelines for substituting on page 576.

FLOURS CONTAINING GLUTEN

Wheat—especially hard wheat—contains the most gluten, and is therefore best for bread-baking. Barley, spelt, emmer, faro, and rye also contain gluten, in smaller amounts. (For a fuller discussion of gluten, see "The Magic of Gluten," opposite.)

ALL-PURPOSE FLOUR

The workhorse of flours, made from the endosperm of wheat, usually a combination of hard and soft. It may be enriched with vitamins and nutrients to compensate for those stripped away during the milling process. It contains 8 to 11 percent protein, and is a good choice for cakes, cookies, pastries, noodles, quick breads, and yeast breads. It should be said that for the most part this is a commodity product, varying little in quality (at least in predictable quality) and far from the highest-character flour you can use. But it *is* all-purpose; almost everyone uses it at some point.

BREAD FLOUR

Milled from hard wheat, bread flour has more protein than all-purpose (up to 14 percent), and greater gluten strength (see "The Magic of Gluten," below), which makes it the flour of choice for elastic, easy-to-handle doughs that produce a chewy crumb and sturdy crust. Typically unbleached, bread flour is sometimes conditioned with ascorbic acid, which can make the finished dough taste slightly sour.

CAKE AND PASTRY FLOURS

Milled from soft wheat, these flours have a low protein content (generally about 9 percent for pastry flour, and slightly less for cake flour). This means doughs and batters don't develop much elasticity, resulting in a tender,

Bleached versus Unbleached Flour

Freshly milled unbleached wheat flour has a yellowish tint that fades to a whitish color over a period of months. Bleached flour is treated with chemicals like chlorine and benzoyl peroxide to yield a whiter color than can be achieved through natural aging. Exposing flour to these chemicals reduces the amount of vitamin E it contains; it also has an effect on the flour's proteins, negatively affecting their ability to create gluten. I only use unbleached flour.

delicate crumb in cakes and flakier pastries. Minimal handling enhances those qualities. (You'll sometimes see something called self-rising flour, which is soft wheat flour mixed with salt and baking powder; it's used as a shortcut to make biscuits and quick breads, but you don't need it.)

The Magic of Gluten

You can't talk about flour without considering gluten, for two reasons: Some people can't eat it, and some types of baking can't happen without it.

Gluten gives people with celiac disease a variety of near-intolerable troubles, including keeping their bodies from absorbing nutrients. Some non-celiacs seem to have trouble with gluten also, for reasons that are less clear, but this isn't the place to discuss that. Let's just acknowledge that right now many people avoid gluten in their diets.

Gluten gives some doughs the structure needed to rise, as well as their characteristic chew. Bakers talk about a flour having low or high gluten strength, and about a dough or batter forming or developing gluten. When flour containing high amounts of gluten is mixed with water, an elastic, weblike structure is formed. It is this structure that captures the carbon dioxide bubbles produced by yeast or other leavening agents (like baking powder) while the dough rises. This structure becomes permanent—baked in, as it were—as the bread, cake,

muffin, or cookie bakes and moisture evaporates, leaving behind the nooks, crannies, and air pockets we call the "crumb."

All high-gluten flours are high-protein, but not all high-protein flours are high in gluten. Of all the grains, wheat is highest in gluten, with hard wheat containing more gluten than soft wheat. That's why, when you want to make a traditional, crusty, open-crumbed hearty loaf of bread, bread flour is your best choice, as it is milled from 100 percent hard wheat.

But the toughness contributed by gluten is not always desirable: Think of bread that you pull with your teeth, as opposed to a delicate muffin, where a fine, tender crumb is the goal. That's why pancake and cake and muffin batters sometimes use cake flour (which is low-protein and therefore low-gluten) and why recipes for these (and for pie doughs, biscuits, and the like) instruct you to stir or mix or otherwise handle minimally; handling develops gluten and therefore toughness in baked goods that should be just the opposite.

WHOLE WHEAT FLOUR

Made from red wheat, this is produced by grinding all three components of the wheat kernel—the bran, germ, and endosperm. This means more fiber and nutrients than all-purpose flour (and up to 14 percent protein), as well as way more flavor. Whole wheat flour produces heavier baked goods than white flour—the germ and bran have no gluten, and retard its development—so in most cases it's best to combine it with white flour in recipes. (Having said that, 100 Percent Whole Wheat Bread, page 602, is a revelation, and white whole wheat flour, below, is more forgiving.) Whole wheat flour can be milled from ultra-fine to coarse; though the most common supermarket types are relatively coarse, finer grinds produce a more even texture and behave more like all-purpose and bread flour.

WHOLE WHEAT PASTRY FLOUR

This is milled from soft wheat, with about 10 percent protein. Like its white flour counterpart, it produces a delicate crumb in cakes and pastries, but with the characteristics of whole wheat, meaning more flavor and more density.

WHITE WHOLE WHEAT FLOUR

Milled from white wheat instead of red wheat, which gives it a relatively mild flavor; but it's still whole wheat, so has the nutritional advantages and the baking characteristics of "regular" whole wheat, which means most baked goods relying on it are on the heavy side.

BARLEY FLOUR

Most barley flour is whole—it contains the germ, endosperm, and bran—and contains gluten, though much less than wheat flour. It has a slightly sweet, nutty flavor (and loads of soluble fiber), and has been relied on in bread baking for centuries. In bread-baking, use it with high gluten flours to make up for its low gluten levels.

RYE FLOUR

This is graded dark, medium, or light, depending on the strain of rye and how much bran and germ have been milled out. The darker the flour, the stronger the flavor and the higher the protein and dietary fiber. Pumpernickel flour (some brands sell it as pumpernickel meal) is coarsely ground rye flour, with much or all of the bran and germ included. Rye has a low gluten strength and a tendency to produce gumminess (it's tricky); for that reason, it's usually used in combination with a good gluten-forming flour, like bread flour.

SPELT FLOUR

A high-protein flour made from ground spelt, an ancient variety of wheat, with a pleasant nutty flavor and relatively low gluten levels. You can find both white and whole grain spelt flour.

GLUTEN-FREE FLOURS

There is a wide range of flours available that are gluten free, which is good news not only for those who are gluten intolerant but for everyone who wants to play with interesting ingredients. Some of these are new products but others—cornmeal and chickpea flour, for example—have been around for millennia, and as a result form the basis for some fantastic traditional dishes.

But be aware: There is nothing like wheat flour. If you intend to use any of these as a substitute for wheat flour, know that your results will always be different. Having said that, there are some specially formulated commercial gluten-free flour mixes but I prefer to make my own mixes from scratch; see opposite.

CORNMEAL AND CORN FLOUR

Ground dried corn, available in fine, medium, or coarse grinds and in yellow, white, or blue, depending on the color of the corn. Stone-ground cornmeal—which is generally what you want—retains the hull and germ, so it's more nutritious and flavorful than common steel-ground cornmeal, though also more perishable (store it in the freezer).

Corn flour is just another name for finely ground cornmeal. But be careful: In recipes written in the UK, it means cornstarch. You can make corn flour by grinding medium or coarse cornmeal in a food processor until it won't get any finer.

BUCKWHEAT FLOUR

Buckwheat flour, which has a distinctively sour and grassy (but not unpleasant!) taste, is milled from its seeds, called groats. Buckwheat itself contains no gluten but it is often milled with wheat, so if gluten is an issue for you, check the label.

RICE FLOUR

Sometimes sold as rice powder or cream of rice, this is sifted ground hulled rice. White rice flour is processed to remove the bran and germ and is mild flavored. Brown rice flour has had only the outer husk removed, so it's higher in protein, fiber, and other nutrients and nuttier in flavor. Both have a slightly grainy, gritty texture. It's best to combine them with other flours. (They are fabulous on their own in coatings for fried foods.) Glutinous (sweet) rice flour is entirely different, producing a stickier texture.

NUT FLOURS

Made by finely grinding nuts, nut flours (or meals as they're also called) are high in protein and fat. Grinding your own (see page 299) can be tricky, because a blender or food processor may turn nuts to paste before they're ground finely enough. Nut flours work well in quick breads, but you must mix them with gluten-rich flours in yeast breads.

Homemade Gluten-Free Flour Mixes

If you're an avid baker who's avoiding gluten, then you'd do well to learn how to make your own gluten-free flour mixes. The mixes below can be exchanged with wheat flours in equal part, but keep in mind that there is always some variation when it comes to substituting flours.

TYPE OF FLOUR	INGREDIENTS	YIELD
All-purpose	1½ cups brown rice flour ¾ cup potato flour ¼ cup tapioca flour 1 teaspoon xanthan gum (optional)	2½ cups
Pastry	1¾ cups white rice flour ¾ cup potato flour ¼ cup tapioca flour	2¾ cups
Bread* *Consider replacing 2 tablespoons of the water in the recipe with 1 egg white for extra protein to take the place of the gluten.	1½ cups brown rice flour ¾ cup potato flour ¾ cup sweet rice flour 2½ teaspoons xanthan gum	About 3 cups
Cake	1½ cups brown rice flour ½ cup potato starch ¼ cup tapioca flour ½ teaspoon xanthan gum	2¼ cups

OAT FLOUR

Milled from oats, oat flour produces baked goods that are moist, crumbly, and nutty tasting. You can grind your own coarse oat flour by giving rolled oats a whirl in the blender or food processor.

POTATO FLOUR

Made from ground dried potatoes. Use too much and it will add an obvious potato flavor; it can also make the end result gummy. When blended with other gluten-free flours, particularly relatively dry flours like coconut and rice, it can add moistness and depth, particularly to breads and any recipe that isn't too sweet.

BEAN FLOURS

Ground from dried beans, the most common bean flours used in baking are soy, chickpea (sometimes called garbanzo bean; as *besan*, it is particularly popular in Indian cooking), fava, and garfava (a mixture of chickpea and fava bean flours). Each carries its own distinctive beany flavor, so use them in recipes where that works well with the flavor profile of the item, or use them with a light hand in combination with other flours; the result will almost always be somewhat dense, moist, and crumbly.

SORGHUM FLOUR

Sorghum flour, which is whole grain, has a neutral or slightly sweet flavor. It grinds up very fine and is

Substituting Flours in Baking

Use this chart as a quick reference for replacing all-purpose flour in yeast and quick breads. (The results are generally better in quick breads, where you usually don't want too chewy a texture.) You can mix and match, but don't go over the maximum proportion for any one flour; generally, unless you're really experienced, you're never going to replace more than half the all-purpose flour, and often you'll do even less.

An easy way to measure these substitutions is to put the estimated amount of alternative flour (or flours) in the measuring cup first, then fill the remainder with all-purpose flour and level it off.

FLOUR	QUANTITY TO USE IN RECIPES	FLOUR	QUANTITY TO USE IN RECIPES
Whole wheat	Up to one half	Teff	Up to one quarter
Barley	Up to one half	Spelt	Up to one quarter
Sorghum	Up to one half	Nut	Between one quarter and one third
Quinoa	Up to one half	Oat	Between one quarter and one third
Light rye	Up to one half	Rice	Between one quarter and one third
Medium rye	Up to one third	Coconut	Up to one fifth, and increase the liquid used in the recipe by an equal amount
Dark rye	Up to one quarter		
Buckwheat	Up to one quarter	Cornmeal	Up to one sixth
Soy	Up to one quarter		

found in most prepackaged gluten-free flour blends and baking mixes.

TAPIOCA FLOUR

The ground dried starch of the cassava root, also sometimes labeled tapioca starch. Tapioca flour is mostly used as a thickener in puddings and fruit pies, but its gelatinous properties can also add some chewiness to baked foods. It's often included in gluten-free flour blends (no more than 10 percent or so).

COCONUT FLOUR

Ground from dried coconut meat, coconut flour is high in fiber and low in carbohydrates. It has a light coconut flavor, which makes it a nice addition to quick breads or muffins. Be aware that coconut flour is extremely absorbent and the liquid in any recipe you add it to will need to be adjusted upward, or the final product will be dry.

TEFF FLOUR

Teff is a grass native to Ethiopia, with grains the size of poppy seeds; ground, they make a mild, slightly sweet, nutty flour.

QUINOA FLOUR

Super-high in protein and mildly flavored. You can make your own quinoa flour by grinding the grains in your processor. They won't grind down to the same fineness of milled quinoa flour but it'll do in a pinch.

THE BASICS OF LEAVENING

Leavening gives baked goods lift. (The word *leaven* means "lighten.") And all leaveners work the same way: by producing carbon dioxide bubbles that are trapped by the dough's structure, and in turn, make the dough rise.

YEAST

Yeast is available in three forms: fresh yeast, active dry yeast, and instant yeast. Fresh yeast is usually sold in foil-wrapped cakes, and is the trickiest to use; it must be proofed—made active in liquid—before using. Active dry yeast is fresh yeast that has been pressed and dried. It is sold foil packets; you don't need to refrigerate it, because the packets are sealed for a shelf life of up to two years (check the expiration date before using, though). Instant yeast, also called fast-acting, fast-rising, rapid-rise, and bread machine yeast, is the yeast almost everyone uses now (it's what I use in all of my recipes calling for yeast). It can be added directly to the dough at almost any point. Neither active dry or instant yeast requires proofing to do their job, but you can proof them if you like to make sure they are still vital.

To proof any kind of yeast, mix it with a small amount of warm (not hot) water; if you like, add a pinch or so of sugar. If the mixture doesn't begin to foam or bubble up within 5 to 10 minutes, the yeast is dead and you need to try again with new yeast.

BAKING SODA

Baking soda (sodium bicarbonate) produces bubbles of carbon dioxide in the presence of moisture and acid, usually an acidic liquid like buttermilk, yogurt, or vinegar. This reaction occurs on contact, so once baking soda is added, whatever it is you are baking needs to get into the oven as soon as possible. You want those bubbles formed in the oven, not on the counter, so add it in last, mixed into the flour to ensure even distribution through the dough or batter. If you are tinkering with a recipe, be careful not to add too much baking soda, because it's quite salty. Plus, whenever you add more baking soda you must add more acid; too much of either or both, and the whole thing could become unpleasantly acidic.

BAKING POWDER

Baking powder is baking soda with a dry acid added to it, along with some starch that keeps the baking powder dry and inert until it's activated. Single-acting baking powder generally contains cream of tartar as the acid and is activated by moisture, so the batter or dough should be baked as soon as possible after being mixed.

Double-acting baking powder also contains slower-acting sodium aluminum sulfate, which releases the majority of its carbon dioxide when exposed to heat in the oven, for a second leavening. So batters using double-acting baking powder can sit at room temperature for a few minutes before being baked—but just a few. Too much baking powder can give baked goods a bitter taste and—if the air bubbles grow too big and break—cause them to collapse.

THE BASICS OF MIXING BATTERS AND DOUGHS

To get the texture or "crumb" you want, whether you're baking quick breads or a yeasted or unleavened bread, you need to pay attention to gluten—or its absence. Do you want to develop it fully? Retard it as much as possible? Or leave it out altogether?

MIXING QUICK BREAD BATTERS AND DOUGHS

Overmixing batter or dough for quick breads, muffins, scones, biscuits, pancakes, and the like will make them tough; since these are meant to be tender, your goal is to minimize or avoid any gluten development (see "The Magic of Gluten," page 573) when blending. To do this, combine the dry and wet ingredients in as few strokes as possible. When you see no more dry bits of flour, the job is done; don't worry about any remaining lumps. This is the reason I hand-mix these types of baked goods; it's much too easy to overmix if you are using a food processor or stand mixer.

MIXING AND KNEADING DOUGH FOR YEAST BREADS

By contrast, developing the gluten in a yeasted wheat bread dough, in which you want that elastic, weblike structure that gives bread its chewiness, is what making bread is all about. If you mix your dough in a food processor (which is a good technique, and with one

important exception, No-Knead Bread on page 601, all of the directions for the yeasted and unleavened bread recipes include instructions for using the food processor) or a stand mixer, that action will also largely take the place of kneading. You certainly can mix a bread dough by hand but these can be stiff doughs, requiring some elbow grease, and you will definitely have to knead the dough to finish developing the gluten to the proper point before letting it rise.

Here is a rundown on the three methods but remember, only use these methods when you are looking for a firm crumb and a chewy crust; these are too rough for tender baked goods:

FOOD PROCESSOR

Put the dry ingredients in the work bowl and pulse once or twice to combine. Add any butter, eggs, honey, molasses, or other semiliquid ingredients to the bowl and pulse a few more times. With the machine running, pour in the liquid through the feed tube, and let the machine run until the dough comes together in a doughy mass. If it looks too dry (this will take practice, because some doughs should be quite wet), add more liquid a tablespoon at a time and continue processing; if it looks too wet or loose, add flour a tablespoon at a time. Once the dough has come together, let the machine run for another 30 seconds or so. This takes the place of some (or all) of the kneading. Just take care not to overprocess; the sharp blades that develop the gluten can also break it apart, and friction can overheat the processor and the dough.

Turn the dough out onto a work surface and briefly knead by hand (see illustrations opposite) until the dough is ready; depending on the recipe, this part may take a few extra minutes or could be entirely unnecessary. If there are bulky ingredients like raisins, nuts, or seeds that you want to mix into the dough, knead them in by hand; they'd get pulverized by the food processor blade. Just scatter the add-ins on the work surface and turn the dough out on top of them. Knead until they are incorporated throughout the inside of the dough.

STAND MIXER

Put all the ingredients—including add-ins like raisins and nuts—in the mixer bowl. If your machine is not very powerful, you may want to add the flour a little bit at a time so it doesn't stall. For wet doughs, start with the paddle attachment just until the ingredients are thoroughly mixed. Then, using a dough hook, start mixing on low speed and gradually increase the speed to medium, scraping the side of the bowl as needed, until the dough is smooth and elastic. This takes around 8 to 10 minutes. Afterward, you can just leave the dough in the bowl to rise, or seal the deal with a few kneads by hand (not always necessary, but good for getting a feel for finished dough) and return it to the bowl.

Some things to be aware of while you're mixing: Sometimes the dough rides up onto the base of the hook and sort of flops around without really being kneaded. If this happens, stop the machine, pull the dough off the hook, and put it back at the bottom of the bowl. Plunge the hook back into the dough and continue mixing. Also, stand mixers sometimes move on the counter a bit as the dough thumps against the side of the bowl, so keep an eye out to stop it from walking over the edge.

BY HAND

Put half the flour with the salt and yeast (and sugar if it's included) in a large bowl and stir to blend. Add all the water, any butter, oil, eggs, or other liquids, and stir with a wooden spoon until smooth. Add the remaining flour a bit at a time. When the mixture becomes too stiff to stir with a spoon, begin kneading right in the bowl, adding as little flour as possible —just enough to keep the dough from being a sticky mess that clings to your hands and won't stay in the bowl. When the dough comes together into a ball, transfer it to a lightly floured work surface and knead until smooth, about 10 minutes, before proceeding with the recipe.

Kneading Dough by Hand

Kneading develops gluten, which gives bread its structure and chewiness. When doing it by hand, you can feel the dough go from a floury mass to a smooth, elastic ball. For many bread bakers, this is the most gratifying part of the process. If necessary, dust the work surface and dough with flour. How much you use depends on how sticky the dough is; you want to use just enough so that the dough doesn't stick to your fingers or the work surface when you try to work it. Turn the dough out of the bowl onto the work surface.

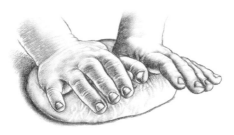

STEP 1 Use the heels of your hands to press the dough down.

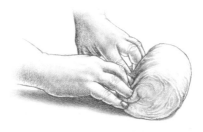

STEP 2 Fold the dough back over itself, then repeatedly press and fold the dough for 5 to 6 minutes, or until it becomes far less sticky and quite elastic, like a taut ball.

QUICK BREADS, MUFFINS, SCONES, AND BISCUITS

Making quick breads and their related kin is easy and satisfying. You don't need special techniques or equipment. They are generally leavened with either baking powder or soda or a combination of the two. The crumb is soft, moist, and airy, with a little chew but no crunch. The inclusion of fat, usually in the form of butter, makes them tender and flavorful.

Most of these recipes can be put together with ingredients you already have in your pantry, which means you can have banana bread or muffins or biscuits baking in the oven at almost a moment's notice. And nothing is better than enjoying a slice of toasted quick bread or a still warm biscuit split oven and topped with a bit of butter or jam or cream cheese, along with a cup of coffee, for breakfast or as an afternoon snack.

While yeast breads benefit from high-gluten (bread) flour and rough handling (kneading), the resulting gluten development makes the dough chewy and the crust thick. In quick breads, what you want is tenderness: Handle them gently, and that's what you'll get. For more details, see "Mixing Quick Bread Batters and Dough," page 578.

STORING AND FREEZING QUICK BREADS

Once cool, wrap quick breads, muffins, scones, etc., in wax or parchment paper and store at room temperature; they will keep for several days, though they taste best enjoyed fresh or within a day. Don't use plastic wrap; it will make the baked product soggy. You can also freeze these; in this case, do use plastic wrap, then also wrap with foil and freeze; they will keep for up to a month. Thaw in the refrigerator if time allows and remove the plastic. Rewrap in the foil if you want to warm them (in a 300°F oven), though you don't need to reheat them.

Corn Bread

MAKES: About 6 servings
TIME: About 45 minutes

Ⓜ

Corn bread people are divided into not-sweet and sweet camps, Southerners largely being of the not-sweet persuasion, Northerners seen as liking it sweeter. I like it both ways, as reflected in this recipe. The foundation recipe is without sugar; for those who prefer it with, check out the variation for Rich Sweet Corn Bread. Also try Corn and Bean Bread, which is an American classic (in some forms predating the arrival of Europeans) and really good.

2	tablespoons melted butter or olive oil, plus cold butter for greasing the pan
1½	cups cornmeal
½	cup all-purpose flour
1	teaspoon baking soda
1	teaspoon salt
1	egg
1¼	cups buttermilk or yogurt, plus more as needed

1. Heat the oven to 375°F. Grease a 9-inch square baking pan with butter.

2. Whisk the cornmeal, flour, baking soda, and salt together in a large bowl. Whisk the egg into the buttermilk. Stir the wet ingredients into the dry ingredients just enough to combine everything. If the batter is very dry and doesn't come together easily, add a few more tablespoons buttermilk, 1 tablespoon at a time, until it comes together.

3. Add the melted butter and stir until just incorporated; avoid overmixing. Pour the batter into the prepared pan and spread into an even layer. Bake for 25 to 30 minutes, until the top is lightly browned, the sides have pulled away from the pan, and a toothpick inserted into the center comes out clean. Cut into squares and serve hot or warm.

RICH SWEET CORN BREAD Use 4 tablespoons (½ stick) butter. Add ¼ cup sugar to the flour mixture. Use 2 eggs and separate them; whisk the yolks into the buttermilk and beat the whites in a small bowl with an electric mixer until stiff but not dry peaks form, then gently fold them into the batter.

CORNY CORN BREAD Add 1 cup fresh or frozen corn kernels along with the liquid ingredients.

WHOLE WHEAT QUINOA CORN BREAD Hearty whole grains create a great crumbly texture with a bit of crunch: Substitute whole wheat flour for the all-purpose flour. Stir 1 cup cooked quinoa (any color) into the flour mixture.

CORN AND BEAN BREAD Reduce the buttermilk to 1 cup; omit the flour. Stir 1½ cups well-cooked white beans (canned are fine), puréed and drained, into the wet mixture before adding it to the dry ingredients.

CHEDDAR-JALAPEÑO CORN BREAD Add ½ cup grated cheddar cheese and 1 tablespoon minced seeded jalapeño when you add the wet ingredients to the dry ingredients.

SCALLION CORN BREAD Add 6 chopped scallions when you add the wet ingredients to the dry ingredients.

GLUTEN-FREE CORN BREAD Be sure to buy cornmeal that states on the package that it is gluten-free (some brands may be processed in mills that also process wheat): Omit the all-purpose flour and increase the cornmeal to 2 cups.

Banana Bread

MAKES: 1 loaf
TIME: About 1 hour, largely unattended
Ⓜ

The best banana bread is a balancing act: It requires a fair amount of fat to keep it moist and lighten the crumb, and a little whole wheat flour to give it depth of flavor and more interesting texture. The final product should be sweet, but not overly so, crumbly, and tender, with an irresistible crust. Though coconut is my favorite secret ingredient, feel free to omit it, or the nuts. Or add more nuts, raisins, or other dried fruit instead. This bread keeps better than most quick breads, though it probably won't be around too long, especially since it makes the best toast in the world.

8	tablespoons (1 stick) butter, melted, plus softened butter for greasing
2	cups all-purpose flour
1	cup sugar
1½	teaspoons baking powder
1	teaspoon salt
3	very ripe bananas, mashed with a fork until smooth
2	eggs
1	teaspoon vanilla extract
½	cup chopped walnuts or pecans (optional)
½	cup shredded coconut (optional)

1. Heat the oven to 350°F. Grease a 9 × 5-inch loaf pan. Whisk the flour, sugar, baking powder, and salt together in a large bowl.
2. Mix the melted butter and bananas together in a medium bowl. Beat in the eggs and vanilla until well combined. Stir the wet ingredients into the dry ingredients just enough to combine everything. Gently fold in the nuts and coconut if you're using them.
3. Pour the batter into the prepared pan. Bake for 50 to 60 minutes, until the bread is golden brown and a toothpick inserted in the center of the bread comes out almost entirely clean. Cool in the pan on a rack for 15 minutes, then carefully turn it upside down to release the loaf. Serve warm or at room temperature. Or wrap and keep at room temperature for up to a couple of days.

Zucchini Bread

PLANTAIN BREAD A great use for overly ripe (read black) plantains: Substitute 1 cup mashed very ripe plantains for the bananas.

BANANA BREAD WITH CANDIED GINGER The ginger adds heat and sweetness: Omit the nuts and coconut. Add ¾ cup chopped candied ginger.

BANANA BREAD WITH CHOCOLATE AND ORANGE Omit the nuts and coconut. Add 2 ounces dark chocolate, chopped, and the grated zest of 1 navel orange.

PEANUT BUTTER BANANA BREAD Reduce the butter to 5 tablespoons. Add ⅓ cup peanut butter to the bananas.

PUMPKIN BREAD Substitute 1 cup pumpkin purée for the bananas. Whisk 1 teaspoon ground cinnamon, ¼ teaspoon each freshly grated nutmeg and ground ginger, and ⅛ teaspoon ground cloves into the dry ingredients.

Zucchini Bread

MAKES: 1 loaf
TIME: About 1¼ hours, largely unattended
M

Vegetables are the unsung heroes of the quick bread world; they bring subtle flavor and keep breads moist. This zucchini bread is made with olive oil and is only lightly sweet, which makes it a great bread to top with butter and a drizzle of honey for breakfast. Try combining two different vegetables in one loaf to add depth of flavor (see "Adding Grated Vegetables to Quick Breads," page 584).

½	**cup olive oil, plus more for greasing**
2	**cups all-purpose flour**
1	**cup sugar**
1½	**teaspoons baking powder**
½	**teaspoon baking soda**
1	**teaspoon salt**
1	**tablespoon grated orange zest**
¾	**cup fresh orange juice or milk**

2	**eggs**
1	**cup grated zucchini**
½	**cup chopped pecans**

1. Heat the oven to 350°F. Grease a 9 × 5-inch loaf pan with oil.

2. Whisk the flour, sugar, baking powder, baking soda, and salt together in a large bowl.

3. Beat the oil, zest, juice, and eggs together in a medium bowl. Pour the wet ingredients into the dry ingredients, stirring just enough to combine. Do not overmix; it's okay if the batter is not perfectly smooth. Fold in the zucchini and pecans.

4. Pour the batter into the prepared pan. Bake for 50 to 60 minutes, until the bread is golden brown and a toothpick inserted into the center comes out almost entirely clean. Cool in the pan on a rack for 15 minutes, then carefully turn it upside down to release the loaf. Serve warm or at room temperature. Or wrap in plastic and keep at room temperature for a couple of days.

VEGAN ZUCCHINI BREAD Substitute 2 tablespoons ground flaxseed mixed with 6 tablespoons water for the eggs; let sit for at least 3 minutes, until the mixture has a gel-like consistency. Use orange juice or substitute the milk with soy or almond milk. **V**

CHOCOLATE ZUCCHINI BREAD Sounds weird; tastes delicious: Replace ½ cup flour with Dutch process cocoa powder. Fold up to 1 cup chopped dark chocolate (about 6 ounces) into the batter.

5 Additions for Zucchini Bread

1. 1 teaspoon vanilla extract, added to the wet ingredients

2. Up to 1½ teaspoons mixed ground spices like cinnamon, cardamom, nutmeg, allspice, and/or cloves (cloves are powerful, so go easy on them), added to the dry ingredients

3. Up to ½ cup chopped candied ginger, folded into the finished batter

4. Up to 1 cup chopped toasted nuts, folded into the finished batter

5. Up to ½ cup dried fruit, chopped or sliced as needed, folded into the finished batter

Blueberry Muffins

MAKES: 12 standard or 8 large
TIME: About 40 minutes
Ⓜ

This low-maintenance recipe is a canvas for experimentation. Mix and match your fruit with chopped chocolate, nuts, seeds, or spices. If you're using frozen fruit, there's no need to thaw it. The only rule here is not to overmix—muffin batter must remain lumpy if you want the muffins themselves to be tender.

> 3   tablespoons good-quality vegetable oil, plus more for greasing (optional)
> 2   cups all-purpose flour
> ½   cup sugar
> 1½ teaspoons baking powder
> 1   teaspoon ground cinnamon
> ½   teaspoon salt
> 1   egg
> 1   cup milk, plus more if needed
> ½   teaspoon grated lemon zest
> 1   cup fresh or frozen blueberries

1. Heat the oven to 375°F. Grease a 12-cup muffin tin or 8-cup jumbo muffin tin with oil or line it with paper or foil muffin cups.

2. Whisk the flour, sugar, baking powder, cinnamon, and salt together in a large bowl.

3. Beat the egg, milk, lemon zest, and oil together in a medium bowl. Add the wet ingredients to the dry ingredients and stir just enough to combine everything. If the batter is very dry and doesn't come together easily, add 1 to 2 tablespoons more milk. Gently fold the blueberries into the batter.

4. Distribute the batter among the muffin cups, filling them about two-thirds full. Bake for 20 to 25 minutes, until the muffins are browned on top and a toothpick inserted in the center of a muffin comes out clean. Cool in the pan on a rack for 5 minutes before removing the muffins. Serve warm or at room temperature. Or cover

Adding Grated Vegetables to Quick Breads

Vegetables add flavor, color, moisture, and texture to muffins and quick breads. Shredded root vegetables work best; use about 1 cup per recipe. Each one favors its own seasonings, though it's fun to mix and match; here are a few of my favorite combinations:

VEGETABLE	ADD OR SUBSTITUTE
Beets	Substitute honey for up to half of the sugar
Carrots	Substitute brown sugar for the granulated sugar
Celery root	Add 1 tablespoon grated lemon zest; or use ½ cup shredded apple and ½ cup shredded celery root for more complex flavor overall

VEGETABLE	ADD OR SUBSTITUTE
Parsnips	Add 1 teaspoon ground cinnamon, ¼ teaspoon ground ginger, and ¼ teaspoon freshly grated nutmeg
Sweet potato	Substitute maple syrup for up to half of the sugar
Zucchini	Add 1 tablespoon grated orange zest

tightly and keep at room temperature for up to a couple of days.

VEGAN BLUEBERRY MUFFINS Substitute almond milk for the regular milk. Replace the egg with 1 tablespoon ground flaxseed mixed with 3 tablespoons water; let sit for at least 3 minutes, until the mixture has a gel-like consistency before adding it. **V**

CORNMEAL BLUEBERRY MUFFINS Cornmeal gives these muffins a great crumbly texture: Substitute cornmeal for ½ cup of the flour.

BLUEBERRY YOGURT MUFFINS Substitute ¾ cup yogurt or sour cream for the milk. Reduce the baking powder to 1 teaspoon and add ½ teaspoon baking soda.

WHOLE WHEAT BLUEBERRY MUFFINS Substitute 1½ cups whole wheat flour and ½ cup ground flaxseed for the all-purpose flour.

CRANBERRY-GINGER MUFFINS Substitute 2 teaspoons ground ginger or minced fresh ginger for the cinnamon. Replace the blueberries with fresh or frozen cranberries.

Bran Muffins

MAKES: 12 standard or 8 large
TIME: About 40 minutes
M

These bran muffins are hearty but still light in texture and not too sweet. Toast the bran first for maximum flavor. You can replace the raisins with any dried fruit, like cherries, chopped figs, or chopped apricots.

- ⅓ **cup good-quality vegetable oil, plus more for greasing (optional)**
- 2 **cups wheat bran**
- ½ **cup all-purpose flour**
- ¼ **cup light brown sugar**
- 1 **teaspoon baking powder**
- 1 **teaspoon baking soda**
- ½ **teaspoon salt**
- 1 **cup raisins**
- 1 **egg**
- 1 **cup buttermilk or yogurt**
- 1 **tablespoon grated orange zest**
- 1 **teaspoon vanilla extract**

1. Heat the oven to 350°F. Grease a 12-cup muffin tin or 8-cup jumbo muffin tin with oil or line it with paper or foil muffin cups. Toast the wheat bran on a baking sheet for 6 to 8 minutes. Set aside to cool and turn the oven up to 400°F.

2. Whisk the flour, brown sugar, baking powder, baking soda, salt, and cooled wheat bran together in a large bowl. Stir in the raisins.

3. Beat the egg, buttermilk, orange zest, vanilla, and oil together in a medium bowl. Add the wet ingredients to the dry ingredients and stir just enough to combine everything.

4. Distribute the batter among the muffin cups, filling them about two-thirds full. Bake for 18 to 20 minutes, until the muffins are browned on top and a toothpick inserted in the center of a muffin comes out clean. Cool in the pan on a rack for 5 minutes before removing the muffins. Serve warm or at room temperature. Or cover tightly and keep at room temperature for up to a couple of days.

DARKER BRAN MUFFINS Heat the raisins with ½ cup water in a saucepan over medium heat; simmer until all the water is absorbed, about 10 minutes. Purée the raisins in a blender or food processor until smooth. Reduce the buttermilk to ½ cup. Add the purée to the wet ingredients along with 3 tablespoons molasses.

MORNING GLORY MUFFINS Fruit and vegetables add moisture and sweetness to the muffins: Reduce the raisins to ½ cup; fold ½ cup each grated carrots, chopped apple, and chopped walnuts and ¼ cup shredded coconut into the batter.

BANANA CHOCOLATE CHIP BRAN MUFFINS Substitute 2 mashed bananas for ½ cup of the buttermilk. Substitute 1 cup chopped dark chocolate (about 6 ounces) for the raisins.

BERRY BRAN MUFFINS I like blueberries, raspberries, and blackberries: Substitute fresh or frozen mixed berries for the raisins. Sprinkle each muffin with a pinch of granulated sugar before baking.

HONEY–OAT BRAN MUFFINS Replace the light brown sugar with honey. Substitute rolled oats for 1 cup of the wheat bran.

PUMPKIN BRAN MUFFINS Substitute pumpkin purée for ½ cup of the buttermilk. Replace the raisins with ½ cup toasted pumpkin seeds.

Buttermilk Biscuits

MAKES: 6 to 12, depending on size
TIME: 20 to 30 minutes
Ⓜ

The best biscuits are made with cold butter, which produces flakiness, and buttermilk, which supplies a welcome tang and makes the baking soda leap. For an especially delicate crumb, use cake flour. These biscuits are easily adapted to lean sweet or savory; once you've mastered the basic technique, try one of the variations.

Newcomers to biscuits will be surprised at how easy these are, and how wonderful the results.

2 cups all-purpose or cake flour, plus
    more for shaping
1 tablespoon baking powder
1 teaspoon baking soda
1 teaspoon salt
5 tablespoons cold butter, cut into
    ½-inch slices
¾ cup plus 2 tablespoons buttermilk or yogurt

1. Heat the oven to 450°F. Whisk the flour, baking powder, baking soda, and salt together in a large bowl. Add the butter and work it into the flour mixture, breaking it into tiny pieces with your fingers until the mixture looks like coarse meal.

2. Add the buttermilk and stir just until the mixture comes together and forms a ball. Spread some flour (about ¼ cup) on a clean work surface and turn the dough onto the flour. Knead the dough a few times, adding a little more flour to your hands only if the dough is very sticky.

Making Biscuits

STEP 1 Work the butter into the flour mixture with your fingers until the mixture looks like coarse meal.

STEP 2 Stir in the buttermilk until the dough comes together.

STEP 3 Knead the dough a few times on a floured surface.

STEP 4 Pat the dough out to about ¾ inch thick and cut out rounds with a biscuit cutter or sturdy drinking glass.

3. Press the dough out ¾ inch thick and cut out 1½- to 2½-inch rounds with a biscuit cutter or sturdy drinking glass. Put the rounds on an ungreased baking sheet. Press together the scraps, pat them out ¾ inch thick, and cut out more biscuits. Repeat once more if you still have dough.

4. Bake for 5 to 10 minutes, depending on size, until the biscuits are golden brown. Transfer the biscuits to a rack to cool; serve within 15 minutes. Or wrap in foil and keep warm in a 200°F oven for up to an hour.

WHOLE WHEAT BISCUITS Whole wheat flour absorbs more liquid than all-purpose, so you may need to add an extra tablespoon or so of buttermilk: Substitute whole wheat pastry flour for the all-purpose flour.

CHEDDAR-CHIVE BISCUITS Toss ¾ cup shredded cheddar cheese and ¼ cup minced fresh chives in the flour and butter mixture before adding the buttermilk.

ORANGE-CURRANT BISCUITS Add 1 tablespoon grated orange zest and 3 tablespoons sugar to the dry ingredients. Toss ½ cup dried currants in the flour and butter mixture before adding the buttermilk.

STRAWBERRY AND CREAM BISCUITS Add 3 tablespoons sugar to the dry ingredients. Substitute ¾ cup cream for the buttermilk. Toss 1 cup chopped ripe strawberries and their juice with the flour and butter mixture before adding the cream.

SWEET POTATO BISCUITS Southern-style goodness: Grease the baking sheets. Stir 1 cup cooked, drained, and puréed sweet potato or winter squash into the butter and flour mixture. Add only enough buttermilk to form the dough into a ball, usually between ½ and ¾ cup; if your potatoes are very dry, you may need the whole amount. Roll the dough a little thinner, about ½ inch thick. Cut into biscuits as directed, and bake at 450°F for 12 to 15 minutes. The addition of the sweet potato will roughly double the yield.

7 Sweet and Savory Add-Ins for Buttermilk Biscuits

1. Up to 1 cup fresh corn kernels
2. Up to 1 cup shredded or cubed cheese
3. Up to ½ cup chopped dried or fresh fruit
4. Up to 1 tablespoon ground spices or spice blends, like chili or curry powder
5. Up to ¼ cup minced jalapeño chile
6. Up to ¼ cup chopped fresh herbs
7. Up to 1 tablespoon finely grated citrus zest

Scones

MAKES: 8 or 10
TIME: About 40 minutes
Ⓜ

A proper English scone is all about balance; it should be rich but not too sweet, with a surprisingly crisp and delightful crust wrapped around a meltingly tender crumb. Be delicate with the dough to maintain its light texture. If you have a food processor, just pulse the ingredients together and you're done.

2	**cups cake flour, plus more as needed**
1	**tablespoon baking powder**
½	**teaspoon salt**
3	**tablespoons sugar**
5	**tablespoons cold butter, cut into pieces**
1	**egg, beaten**
½–¾	**cup cream, plus more for brushing**

1. Heat the oven to 450°F. Whisk the flour, baking powder, salt, and 2 tablespoons of the sugar together in a large bowl. Add the butter and work it into the flour mixture, breaking it into tiny pieces with your fingers until the mixture looks like coarse meal.

2. Add the egg and just enough cream to form a slightly sticky dough. If the dough is very sticky, add a tiny bit of flour; the dough should still stick to your hands a little.

3. Sprinkle a little flour on a clean work surface and turn out the dough onto the flour. Knead the dough once or twice. Press it into a ¾-inch-thick circle; cut into 8 or 10 wedges with a sharp knife. Separate the wedges and put them on an ungreased baking sheet, not touching. Brush the top of each scone with a bit of cream and sprinkle with a little of the remaining sugar.

4. Bake for 9 to 11 minutes, until the scones are light golden brown. Serve immediately.

WHOLE WHEAT–OATMEAL SCONES If light and delicate isn't your thing, try this heartier version: Substitute 1¼ cups whole wheat flour for the cake flour. Add ¾ cup rolled oats to the flour mixture.

ORANGE-CARAWAY SCONES Mix 1 tablespoon caraway seeds and 1 tablespoon grated orange zest into the flour mixture.

LEMON-YOGURT SCONES Substitute yogurt for the cream, and stir 3 tablespoons fresh lemon juice and 1 tablespoon grated lemon zest into the yogurt before adding it to the flour mixture.

BERRY OR RAISIN SCONES If you like, add up to 1 tablespoon grated orange or lemon zest to the flour mixture. Stir ⅓ cup fresh or frozen raspberries or blueberries, dried cranberries, or raisins into the flour mixture before adding the cream.

PARMESAN SCONES Add ¾ cup grated Parmesan to the flour mixture before adding the cream. Omit the final sprinkle of sugar.

ROSEMARY-GRUYÈRE SCONES Mix ½ cup grated Gruyère cheese and 2 tablespoons chopped fresh rosemary into the flour mixture before adding the cream. Omit the final sprinkle of sugar.

5 Undeniably Good Flavor Combinations for Scones
1. Blueberries and grated lemon zest
2. Pears and chopped candied ginger
3. Blackberries and grated orange zest

4. Almonds and any chopped dried fruit, like fig, cherry, or apricot
5. Chopped chocolate and walnuts

UNLEAVENED CRACKERS AND FLATBREADS

Homemade crackers are a snap to make, with lots of room for improvising. You can blend pretty much whatever you'd like—cheese, nuts, garlic, herbs, and spices, for starters—directly into the dough or replace up to half of the all-purpose flour with whole wheat, rye, or cornmeal. Or, just before baking, dust the tops with coarse salt, poppy seeds, or your favorite spice blend.

Flatbreads are daily staples throughout much of the world—think, for instance, of tortillas and chapati—that are made with no yeast, baking powder, or soda to make the dough rise. But this doesn't mean they're dense: Each has a unique texture, and they're all unlike any of their leavened cousins. As an added plus, they're generally much quicker and easier to make: You can whip up a batch of tortillas, for example, in half an hour.

Simplest Crackers
MAKES: About 3 dozen
TIME: 20 to 30 minutes
F **M**

Crisp and easy to make, these are a blank canvas for anything you want to add to either the dough (see the list on page 590) or the finished crackers: herbs, coarse salt, cheeses, jams, and more.

   1 **cup all-purpose flour, plus more for rolling**
  ½ **teaspoon salt**
  2 **tablespoons cold butter, cut into pieces**

1. Put a large pizza stone on the center rack of the oven, if you have one. Heat the oven to 400°F.

2. Put the flour, salt, and butter in a food processor and pulse until combined, or cut them together in a bowl with 2 knives or your fingertips until the mixture looks like coarse meal. Add about ¼ cup water and continue to mix until the dough holds together but is not sticky, adding water 1 tablespoon at a time as needed.

3. Put a large piece of parchment paper on a clean work surface and lightly dust it with flour. Turn out the dough onto the parchment and knead it a few times to make a smooth ball. Divide the dough in half and set aside one piece. Roll out the dough to ⅛ inch thick or even thinner—it can't be bigger than your baking sheet or pizza stone, but aim to get it about that size—flipping it a few times to prevent sticking and sprinkling with more flour as needed. If it sticks, sweep a bench scraper under the dough to help you lift it. If at any point the dough shrinks back, let it rest, uncovered, for a few minutes. Score lightly with a sharp knife or pizza cutter if you want to break the crackers into neat squares or rectangles after baking. Repeat with the other half to bake both pieces at once or set it aside if you're baking in batches.

4. Transfer the parchment with the dough directly to the pizza stone, or to a baking sheet and put the sheet on the center rack. Bake for about 10 minutes, checking periodically to make sure the edges don't burn. Depending on your oven, the crackers may brown unevenly; you may want to trim or break off any darker parts along the edges and then let the rest finish. If the crackers brown before they've fully crisped up, crack the oven door, decrease the heat to 200°F, and continue baking until completely dried out and crisp, another 5 minutes or so. Cool completely on the parchment on a rack, then carefully break the crackers apart. Serve at room temperature or store in an airtight container for up to a couple of days.

CREAM CRACKERS Rich and delicious, they need nothing on top but a little salt: Increase the butter to 4 tablespoons (½ stick). Substitute cream or milk for the water.

VEGAN CRACKERS Substitute a good-quality vegetable oil for the butter. **V**

SODA CRACKERS Flakier and puffier: Mix 1½ teaspoons instant yeast and ½ teaspoon baking soda into the flour before working in the butter. Once the dough comes together, knead it until it's smooth and elastic, a few minutes. Put it in a greased bowl, cover, and refrigerate for at least 1 hour, or overnight if you have time. Proceed with Step 3. Before baking, prick each cracker once or twice with a fork and sprinkle them with salt.

12 Mix-Ins for Cracker Dough

Add these along with the flour when you're mixing the dough:

1. Up to ⅓ cup roasted garlic or caramelized onions

2. Minced fresh chiles (like jalapeño or Thai) or hot red pepper flakes to taste

3. Up to ½ cup finely chopped nuts

4. Up to ½ cup finely chopped dried fruit

5. Up to 1 teaspoon dried herbs, like thyme, marjoram, rosemary, or oregano

6. Up to ¼ cup soft, mild fresh herbs, like dill, parsley, cilantro, or tarragon; no more than 1 tablespoon stronger fresh herbs like rosemary, thyme, sage, or oregano

7. Up to 1 cup cooked greens, like spinach or kale, squeezed dry and chopped

8. Up to 1 cup grated hard cheese, like Parmesan, Manchego, or ricotta salata

9. Up to ½ cup grated medium-hard cheese, like cheddar, Asiago, or pepper Jack

10. Up to ½ cup bits of soft cheese, like goat, blue or Gorgonzola, feta, or cream cheese

11. 1 to 2 tablespoons ground spices, like cumin, cayenne, coriander, or paprika

12. Up to ½ cup chopped olives or dried tomatoes; if the tomatoes are very dry and tough, rehydrate in warm water for 10 minutes or so, then drain before using

Chapati

MAKES: 4 servings
TIME: At least 1 hour

M V

True chapati are made with a finely ground whole wheat flour (called *atta* or chapati flour) and then quickly twice-cooked—first on a dry griddle, then over an open flame—so that the dough traps steam and puffs up dramatically; you might try it sometime.

This recipe, however, is much simpler but makes a bread that is still delicious. The dough can be mixed in advance, but chapati must be eaten immediately after a batch is cooked. Line a basket or plate with a cloth napkin before starting, and as the chapati come off the griddle, pile them up and wrap loosely. This will keep them warm while you cook the rest. Chapati are best with stews and soups, especially bean dishes and their traditional accompaniment, dal (pages 450 to 454).

2¼ cups whole wheat flour
1 cup all-purpose flour, plus more for dusting
1 teaspoon salt

1. Use a fine-meshed strainer or a flour sifter to sift the flours into a food processor. Discard the coarse bran or save it for another use. Add the salt and, with the machine running, pour in 1 cup warm water. Process for about 30 seconds, then remove the cover. The dough should be a well-defined, barely sticky, easy-to-handle ball. If it's too dry, add more water 1 tablespoon at a time and process for 5 or 10 seconds after each addition. If it is too wet, which is unlikely, add a tablespoon or 2 of flour and process briefly. Turn out the dough onto a lightly floured work surface, cover, and let rest for at least 30 minutes or up to 2 hours. (At this point, you can wrap the dough tightly in plastic and refrigerate it for up to a day; bring to room temperature before proceeding.)

2. Pinch off pieces of dough; the recipe will make 8 to 12 chapati. Using flour as necessary, pat each piece into a 4-inch disk. Dust lightly with flour to keep them from sticking, cover with plastic or a damp cloth and set aside while you pat out the others. It's okay to overlap them a bit, but don't stack them.

3. Line a basket or plate with a cloth napkin. Put a griddle or cast-iron or stainless-steel skillet over medium heat. When it's hot, roll out a disk until it's fairly thin, about ⅛ inch, dusting with flour as necessary; the shape doesn't matter as long as it fits the griddle or pan. Tap off the excess flour and put the chapati on the griddle or pan, count to 15 or so, then use a spatula to flip it. Cook the other side until it starts to blister, char, and puff up a bit, about a minute. (Use this time to finish rolling out the next disk.) Flip the chapati and cook the first side again until dark and toasty smelling. Transfer to the basket and cover with the napkin. Repeat until all are cooked. Serve immediately.

GRILLED CHAPATI Rustic, smoky, and puffy—perfect for when you've already got a fire going and have some room on the grill: Heat a charcoal or gas grill until moderately hot and put the rack about 4 inches from the heat source. Oil the grates well. If you have the space, take the disks outside for the final rolling. If not, roll all the chapati out, flour them well, and stack between layers of wax or parchment paper. Cook the chapati, several at a time, as described in Step 3, only directly on the grill grates instead of the griddle.

4 Ways to Vary Chapati Dough

1. Replace up to ½ cup of the whole wheat flour with cornmeal, brown rice flour, or chickpea flour (besan; see page 576).
2. Replace the all-purpose flour with additional whole wheat; the dough will be slightly more difficult to handle, but the results are delicious.
3. Reduce the water to ½ cup and add ½ cup yogurt to the flour at the same time; you might need an additional ¼ cup water to get the correct consistency.
4. Brush the chapati with oil, coconut milk, or melted butter during cooking.

Paratha

MAKES: 8 to 12
TIME: At least 1 hour
Ⓜ Ⓥ

Unlike the chapati on page 591, this dough is enriched with oil, which gives it a lovely flaky texture. Like chapati, these must be eaten immediately after being cooked: Line a basket or plate with a cloth napkin before starting and, as they finish, pile them up and wrap loosely.

You can also grill these; follow the directions in the Grilled Chapati variation (page 591).

  1½ **cups whole wheat flour, plus more as needed**
  1½ **cups all-purpose flour, plus more for dusting**
  1 **teaspoon salt**
     About ¼ cup good-quality vegetable oil

1. Put the flours and salt in a food processor. Turn the machine on and pour ¾ cup water through the feed tube. Process for about 30 seconds, adding more water, a little at a time, until the mixture forms a ball and is slightly sticky to the touch. If it's dry, add another tablespoon or 2 water and process for another 10 seconds. (In the unlikely event that the dough is too sticky, add flour a tablespoon at a time.) Remove the dough and, dusting with flour as necessary, shape it into a ball; wrap in plastic and let rest at room temperature for at least 20 minutes or up to several hours. Or refrigerate for up to a day or freeze for up to a week; thaw if necessary and bring to room temperature before proceeding.

2. Pinch off pieces of dough; the recipe will make 8 to 12 paratha. Using flour as necessary, roll each piece into a 4-inch disk and brush with oil. Roll up like a cigar, then into a coil, like a cinnamon bun; set aside until you finish all the pieces.

3. Line a basket or plate with a cloth napkin. Heat a griddle or cast-iron or stainless-steel skillet over medium heat. When it's hot, press one of the coils flat, then roll it out into a thin disk. Put on the griddle or pan and cook until lightly browned on one side, 3 to 5 minutes; brush the top with oil, flip, and brown on the second side, another few minutes. Transfer to the basket and cover with the napkin. Continue until all the breads are done, then serve.

SPINACH PARATHA Almost as easy but with a great twist: Cook 1 pound fresh spinach (see page 153) and squeeze well to dry. In Step 1, add the spinach and a squeeze of lemon juice along with the water and process as directed, adding more water or flour as needed. Proceed with the recipe.

PARATHA WITH YOGURT Substitute yogurt for the water.

PARATHA WITH MINT AND BLACK PEPPER After combining the flours and salt, pulse ¼ cup chopped fresh mint and 1 teaspoon black pepper into the mixture before adding the water.

PARATHA WITH CILANTRO AND CHILES After combining the flours and salt, pulse ¼ cup chopped fresh cilantro and 2 hot green chiles, chopped (leave the seeds in if you want even more heat), into the mixture before adding the water.

PARATHA WITH GINGER AND SCALLION After combining the flours and salt, pulse ¼ cup chopped scallions and 2 tablespoons minced fresh ginger into the mixture before adding the water.

Aloo Paratha

MAKES: 8 to 12
TIME: At least 1 hour
Ⓜ Ⓞ

I adore this stuffed bread, especially when the filling is super-seasoned and bright with lemon.

Ajwain, or ajowan caraway, is the fruit of an annual herb also known as bishop's weed and carom. Primarily cultivated in Iran and India, its fruit look like small cumin seeds, and are very fragrant, with the aroma and flavor of thyme, which you can use instead; or use cumin if you prefer. As for the final brushing: Use butter for its rich flavor; use oil if you want to taste the potatoes.

Aloo Paratha

1½ cups whole wheat flour

1½ cups all-purpose flour, plus more for rolling

1 teaspoon ajwain, dried thyme, or ground cumin

2 teaspoons salt, plus more to taste

2 pounds baking potatoes, peeled and cut in half

2 tablespoons butter or good-quality vegetable oil

1 or 2 serrano, jalapeño, or other hot chiles, seeded and minced, or more to taste

2 tablespoons minced fresh ginger

2 teaspoons ground coriander

½ teaspoon turmeric

1½ tablespoons fresh lemon juice, plus more to taste

¼ cup chopped fresh mint

Pepper

8 tablespoons (1 stick) melted butter or ½ cup good-quality vegetable oil, or more as needed, for brushing

1. Put the whole wheat and all-purpose flours, ajwain, and 1 teaspoon of the salt in a food processor. Turn the machine on and pour the oil and ¾ cup water through the feed tube. Process for about 30 seconds, adding more water, a little at a time, until the mixture forms a ball and is slightly sticky to the touch. (If you add too much water, add all-purpose flour, a tablespoon at a time.) Remove the dough and, using flour as necessary, shape into a ball; wrap in plastic and let rest while you

make the potato mixture. Or refrigerate for up to a day or freeze for up to a week; thaw if necessary and bring to room temperature before proceeding.

2. Put the potatoes in a large saucepan and add water to cover and ½ teaspoon salt. Bring to a boil over high heat, then turn the heat down so the water simmers steadily. Cook until the potatoes are tender, 15 to 20 minutes, then drain. Return the pot to medium heat and melt 2 tablespoons of the butter. Add the chile, ginger, coriander, and turmeric and stir until fragrant, less than a minute. Remove the pot from the heat, add the potatoes, lemon juice, mint, the remaining ½ teaspoon salt, and some pepper, and mash. Taste and adjust the seasoning; you may want to add more chile or lemon juice.

3. Set out a bowl of flour. Lightly flour the work surface and a rolling pin. Break off a piece of dough about the size of a golf ball. Toss it in the bowl of flour and then roll it in your hands to make a ball. Flatten it into a 2-inch disk, then use the rolling pin to roll it into a thin round about 5 inches in diameter, dusting with flour as necessary.

4. Depending on how much stuffing you like, mound 2 or 3 heaping tablespoons of the filling into the center of a round of dough. Bring the edges of the round up over the top of the filling and press them together to make a pouch. Press down on the "neck" of the pouch with the palm of one hand to make a slightly rounded disk. Coat the disk in the bowl of flour and roll it out again into a round 6 to 7 inches in diameter. (It's okay if the filling busts the seams in places.) Pat it between your hands to brush off the excess flour. Put the paratha on a plate and cover with a sheet of plastic wrap. Continue to roll and fill all of the remaining dough into paratha; stack them on the plate with plastic wrap between them. You can keep the paratha stacked like this for an hour or 2 in the refrigerator before cooking them, if necessary.

5. Line a basket or plate with a cloth napkin. Set out a small bowl with the melted butter or oil and a spoon or brush. Heat a griddle or cast-iron or stainless-steel skillet over medium-high heat for a minute or 2, then put a paratha (or two if they'll fit) on and cook until

Shaping Aloo Paratha

STEP 1 Bring the edges of the dough up around the filling and pinch shut.

STEP 2 Press down on the filled dough pouch to flatten.

it darkens slightly, usually less than a minute. Flip the paratha with a spatula and cook for another 30 seconds on the second side. Use the back of a spoon or a brush to coat the top of the paratha with some butter or oil. Turn and coat the other side. Continue cooking the paratha until the bottom of the bread has browned, turn, and repeat. Do this a few times until both sides of the paratha are golden brown and very crisp, 2 to 3 minutes total for each paratha. Transfer to the basket and cover with the napkin. Continue until all the breads are done, then serve.

GOBI PARATHA Traditional and similar, but with that distinctive cauliflower flavor: Instead of the potatoes, use 1 small head cauliflower, trimmed of leaves and heavy stems, cut into pieces, and boiled until tender. Use mustard seeds instead of the ground coriander.

SWEET POTATO PARATHA Substitute 2 pounds sweet potatoes for the baking potatoes; you'll likely have to simmer it for 5 to 10 minutes longer to become tender.

Corn Tortillas

MAKES: 12 to 16
TIME: About 1½ hours, partially unattended
Ⓜ Ⓞ

An especially worthwhile DIY project given that supermarket corn tortillas are chalky and dry. Nothing about the process is difficult. You don't even need a tortilla press, although if you have one, here's a chance to use it.

    1½ cups masa harina or all-purpose flour,
         plus flour for dusting
    ¼   teaspoon salt
    2   tablespoons good quality vegetable oil,
         olive oil, or softened butter
         About ½ cup boiling water, or more as needed

1. In a medium bowl or food processor, mix the masa and salt together. Stir or pulse in the oil. Slowly add 1 cup very hot water (or more as needed) while mixing with a

wooden spoon or, after it's cooled down a bit, your hand, until the dough comes together into a ball (Or slowly stream it in through the feed tube with the food processor running until the dough holds together in a ball.)

2. Turn the dough out onto a lightly floured work surface and knead until it becomes smooth and elastic: 4 to 5 minutes if you're mixing by hand and about 1 minute if you're using a food processor. Wrap the dough in plastic and let it rest at room temperature for at least 30 minutes or up to a couple hours (or in the fridge for up to a few days; bring it back to room temperature before proceeding).

3. Divide the dough into twelve 2-inch pieces or sixteen 1½-inch pieces; the larger pieces will yield tortillas about 8 inches across, the smaller ones tortillas about 6 inches across.

IF YOU'RE ROLLING BY HAND Slightly flatten each piece into a disk on a lightly floured work surface, then cover and let rest for a few minutes. When you're ready to cook the tortillas, use a heavy rolling pin to roll each disk as thin as possible into a circle at least 8 inches in diameter, stacking them between sheets of plastic

When to Use a Tortilla Press

Most gadgets that are hauled out only once or twice in their lifetime, for just a small handful of recipes, are a waste of money (and counter space). Likewise, you shouldn't hurry to buy a tortilla press for your first attempt at homemade tortillas. But it's not a one-trick pony either: Because it flattens dough with firm, even pressure, it's a useful tool for any cracker or flatbread, particularly Chapati (page 591) and Naan (page 608), homemade pasta, pizza dough (page 609), and round dumpling wrappers. And, of course, it's a smart time-saver if you make a lot of tortillas. You can also approximate a press by putting the dough balls between 2 sheets of plastic wrap or parchment paper and smashing them down with a heavy skillet or pot. Rotate the dough and repeat a few times to apply even pressure. Finish, if necessary, by using the heels of your hands to spread the dough gently from its edges.

wrap or parchment paper as you work. To save time, you can continue to roll out the dough while the first pieces cook.

IF YOU'RE USING A TORTILLA PRESS Divide the dough into sixteen 1½-inch pieces (you need less dough because it will get thinner with a press). Shape each into a slightly flattened disk and let rest for a few minutes. Put a piece of plastic wrap or parchment on the inside of the press, add the dough, top with another piece of plastic, and close the press. Squeeze the clamp as hard as you can; if you'd like it thinner, rotate the dough and repeat.

4. Put a large skillet or griddle (preferably cast iron) over medium-high heat for 4 to 5 minutes. Cook the tortillas one at a time until brown spots begin to appear on the bottom, about a minute; turn and cook the other side for a minute. Wrap the finished tortillas in a towel to keep them warm while you cook the rest. Serve, or cool, wrap tightly, and refrigerate for up to several days or freeze for up to a few months.

FLOUR TORTILLAS There are plenty of halfway decent flour tortillas available at supermarkets these days, but eating a freshly rolled one right out of the skillet is a pleasure reserved for the home cook: Substitute all-purpose flour for the masa harina and ½ cup boiling water for the 1 cup very hot water in Step 1. If you want whole wheat tortillas, substitute whole wheat flour for 1 cup of the all-purpose.

BAKED TORTILLA CHIPS You get the best flavor using corn tortillas. Heat the oven to 400°F. Lightly brush or spray each cooked tortilla on both sides with a good quality vegetable oil. Stack the tortillas and cut them, pielike, into 4 to 8 wedges. Bake on ungreased baking sheets, shaking once or twice, until they just begin to color, 6 to 10 minutes. Sprinkle with salt and serve hot or at room temperature.

FRIED TORTILLA CHIPS Put at least 1 inch of good quality vegetable oil in a deep pan on the stove and turn the heat to medium-high; bring to 350°F. Stack the cooked tortillas and cut them, pielike, into 4 to 8 wedges. Fry in the oil as many at once as will fit without crowding, turning if necessary. Total cooking time will be about 2 minutes; the chips should just begin to darken in color but shouldn't totally brown. Remove with tongs or a slotted spoon and drain on paper towel–lined plates or racks. Sprinkle with salt and serve hot or at room temperature.

YEAST BREADS

You can make very good yeast bread even if you've never made it before—really. If you have a food processor, you can be pulling it from the oven two or three hours from now. And it'll be good, very good, better than what is served to you in most restaurants. This is not to say that there isn't technique and judgment involved, or that you won't get better: I've been baking bread for almost 50 years, and I'm still improving all the time. (And my bread is infinitely better than it was in 1970.) But the basics—flour, water, yeast, salt—are consistent, and the proportions don't change much.

One myth to dispel right off the bat: Bread is not hard work. Making it is simple, and once you have a favored technique, you can make it happen fast, slowly, or in between—at your pace. Just master the basics, a whole world will open up to you and, unless you're living in a city with a great bakery (there aren't many), you'll soon be making better bread than you can buy.

How you mix up bread dough is up to you—in a food processor, a stand mixer, or by hand—all three methods yield good results. I prefer the food processor, so that is how the directions are written. If you are going to mix the dough by hand or using a stand mixer, please read "Mixing and Kneading Dough for Yeast Breads" on page 578.

STORING AND FREEZING BREAD AND BREAD DOUGH

Once cool, wrap breads in wax or parchment paper and store at room temperature; they will keep for several days, though they taste best enjoyed fresh or within a day. Don't use plastic wrap; it will make the baked product soggy. Breads also freeze well: Wrap loaves in a couple of layers of foil, then wrap that in plastic, and freeze. Use them as soon as possible, within days is best: Thaw either on the counter or in the fridge, then recrisp them, unwrapped, in a 350°F oven for 10 minutes or so. Or unwrap and reheat while still frozen in a 400°F oven for about 20 minutes.

You can also freeze bread dough. After the first rising or after shaping, wrap tightly in foil or plastic wrap, then in a plastic bag; freeze for up to 3 months (but expect long-term freezing to negatively affect the quality). Thaw in the refrigerator, then finish any additional shaping and/or rising at room temperature. Bake as directed.

Rustic French Bread

MAKES: 1 boule, 3 or 4 baguettes, or 12 to 16 rolls
TIME: About 5 hours, largely unattended

Until I became a dedicated no-knead baker (see page 601), this was my go-to bread recipe, and I still use it a lot, especially for baguettes. It's reliable, easy (the dough comes together in seconds in the food processor), reasonably fast (the three-hour rise is pretty modest as far as breads go), and the crust is sensational. That last part

is achieved by a hot oven and an initial blast of steam created by adding water to a preheated skillet. You can shorten the rise time without sacrificing much, or slow it down for even better results; see the variations.

    4   cups all-purpose or bread flour, plus more
        as needed
    1¾ teaspoons salt
    1   teaspoon instant yeast

1. Put the flour salt, and yeast in a food processor and turn the machine on. With the machine running, pour 1½ cups water through the feed tube in a steady stream. Process until the dough forms a sticky ball. If the dough begins sticking to the side of the bowl, add more flour, 1 to 2 tablespoons at a time, and keep going. If it's too dry, add water 1 tablespoon at a time and process for 5 or 10 seconds after each addition. (If you prefer to mix the dough using a stand mixer or by hand, see page 579.)
2. Transfer the dough to a large bowl, cover with plastic wrap, and let rise on the counter until doubled in volume, 3 to 4 hours.
3. If you'll be baking the bread on a pizza stone, put it on the center rack of the oven; if not, line a baking sheet with parchment. Put an ovenproof skillet (preferably cast iron) on the lowest rack. Heat the oven to 450°F.

(continued on page 600)

Useful Equipment to Have for Making Bread or Pizza

If you're going to make bread and/or pizza from scratch on a regular basis, there are three items I recommend you get; they will make the experience a lot more enjoyable:

PIZZA STONE
Made from thick unglazed stone or ceramic, a pizza stone absorbs the heat of the oven and transfers it evenly to whatever is cooked on top of it; when that is pizza or bread, it results in a crisp crust. They are available in a variety of sizes; choose the size that best makes sense for you and what you're baking. My pizza stone lives in my oven, set on the lowest rack, even when I'm not baking directly on it; it helps keep the oven temperature steady.

PIZZA PEEL
If you're going to be baking a lot on the pizza stone, invest in a pizza peel as well; it's by far the easiest (and safest) way to slide dough onto a hot stone. It's looks like a large Ping-Pong paddle with a long handle.

INSTANT-READ THERMOMETER
You should have one anyway. Doneness for some of the breads in this chapter is measured by the internal temperature of the loaf.

Shaping Bread

You can make any shape you like with most basic bread doughs, though the most common are the easiest. But whenever you're shaping, *lightly* flour your work surface before putting the dough on it; you can use semolina or fine cornmeal if you prefer, which will add a little crunch to the bread. Here's how to make the most popular shapes, based on the recipe for Rustic French Bread, page 597.

Boule

A *boule* (ball) or free-form loaf is the simplest shape.

STEP 1 Use your hands to shape the risen dough into a round ball; you can make an oval if you prefer.

STEP 2 Continually tuck the dough underneath toward the center of the bottom, stretching the top slightly and creating surface tension. Pinch the seam at the bottom to smooth it over as much as possible. (Note that this process is different for No-Knead Bread, page 601.)

STEP 3 For the final rise, line a medium bowl or colander with a clean kitchen towel and sprinkle a bit of flour evenly over it. Put the dough ball, seam side down, in the towel; sprinkle with a little more flour and fold the towel over the top or loosely cover with another towel. Let rise, following the time range in the recipe.

Rolls

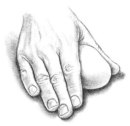

STEP 1 Divide the dough into 12 to 16 pieces and shape each as you would a boule, then roll on a lightly floured surface. Use your hands to smooth them over.

STEP 2 After they've risen, slash the tops with a razor or sharp knife, then bake.

Baguettes

Shaping baguettes is a little more complicated than the others, but easy enough with practice. I don't recommend using baguette pans because dough tends to get stuck in the holes in the pan.

STEP 1 Divide the dough into 3 or 4 pieces, depending on what size you want; figure that a baguette will be about one and a half times its original size after the final rise.

STEP 2 Roll each piece into a long, thin log and use your fingers to press the resulting seam together tightly.

STEP 3 You can create what's called a couche—a bed, essentially—for your baguettes to rise with a piece of heavy canvas, a towel, or a large tablecloth folded into quarters to give it extra stiffness. Sprinkle it lightly with flour and arrange the baguettes on top, pulling up the cloth between each loaf to hold it in place. Cover and let rise at room temperature.

Loaf

Loaf pans help keep the crust tender for softer loaves like sandwich bread. Beginners may find loaves a tad tricky to shape, but will get the hang of it quickly.

STEP 1 If the dough has risen in an oiled bowl, you need no flour; otherwise, work on a very lightly floured surface. Use the heel of your hand to form the dough into a rectangle.

STEP 2 Fold the long sides of the rectangle over to the middle. Pinch the seam closed, pressing tightly with your fingers.

STEP 3 Fold under the ends of the loaf.

STEP 4 Use the back of your hand to press the loaf firmly into the pan.

(continued from page 597)

4. Dust a work surface with a little flour. Turn the dough out onto the surface and knead it a few times. Shape the dough into a boule (see page 598), sprinkling with flour as necessary to prevent sticking, but keeping it to a minimum. Line a colander or large bowl with a clean kitchen towel, flour it well, put the dough in it, and cover with another towel (this keeps it from spreading too much). Let the dough rise for 40 minutes, until, when you press one of your fingers about ¼ inch into the dough, it springs back about halfway.

5. Slash the top of the loaf once or twice with a razor blade or sharp knife. If you're using a pizza stone, slide the boule, seam side down, onto a lightly floured peel or flexible cutting board, then onto the stone. If not, place the boule on the prepared baking sheet and put the sheet on the center rack. Partially pull out the rack with the skillet and very carefully pour in 1 cup hot water —it will create a lot of steam. Slide the rack back in and immediately close the oven door.

6. Bake, rotating the bread or the baking sheet after about 20 minutes, until the crust is beautifully browned and the internal temperature reaches 200°F, 40 to 45 minutes. Keep an eye on it; if it's browning too quickly, lower the temperature to 425°F. Remove the loaf from the oven, spray with a bit of water if you would like a shinier crust, and cool on a rack for at least an hour.

BAGUETTES OR FRENCH ROLLS Same dough, different shapes: Divide the kneaded dough into 3 or 4 pieces for baguettes or 12 to 16 pieces for rolls. Follow the shaping directions on page 599. Go light on the flour when you're shaping the dough; a little friction makes rolling easier. Place on a floured towel to rise and cover with another towel. Use the floured towel to transfer them to the pizza stone or sheet. Bake at 465°F until the center is 200°F, 20 to 25 minutes. Cool for at least 20 minutes.

FASTER FRENCH BREAD Here you sacrifice a little flavor and texture for speed, but you won't be disappointed with these results: In Step 2, shorten the rising time to 1 hour. Proceed with the recipe.

WHOLE GRAIN FRENCH BREAD Substitute whole wheat, rye, or barley flour for ¾ cup of the all-purpose flour. Proceed with the recipe. You can replace up to a third of the flour (1⅓ cups) without losing most the characteristic texture of the bread, but any more than that will produce a loaf with a softer crust and doughier crumb. Better, at that point, to make breads specifically designed for whole grains, like 100 Percent Whole Wheat Bread, page 602.

OVERNIGHT FRENCH BREAD Slower, and even better: This bread requires two mixings, one to make a "sponge" and one to finish the dough, and takes 12 hours or preferably overnight. Otherwise, nothing changes. In Step 1, put 2½ cups of the flour, the yeast, and 1 teaspoon of the salt in the food processor. With the machine running, pour 1½ cups water through the feed tube. Process until a smooth, pancake-like batter is formed. Cover and let rest in a cool place overnight or for at least 6 hours. Add the remaining flour and

Letting Dough Rise and "Room Temperature"

When dough rises, it means the yeast (a living thing until the heat of the oven kills it) is metabolizing the natural sugars in the dough and producing carbon dioxide. In recipes you will usually be given guidelines on just how much rise is wanted before moving to the next step—until the dough has doubled in volume, for example. Exactly how long this may take depends primarily on temperature, and "room temperature" is vague; seven or eight degrees difference in room temperature can double or halve the rising rate. The rough times given here assume that a room is comfortable for you. (Which, of course, varies from person to person, but let's say 68° to 70°F.) That temperature will give you a steady rise in enough time for subtle flavors to develop. But unquestionably timing is going to be a judgment call, which is why learning how to bake bread really well takes some time.

salt to the sponge, turn the machine on again, and, if necessary, add water, a little at a time, until a moist, well-defined ball forms. Proceed with Step 2.

No-Knead Bread

MAKES: 1 large loaf
TIME: Nearly 24 hours, almost completely unattended
V

This innovation—the word "recipe" does not do the technique justice—came from Jim Lahey, owner of Sullivan Street Bakery in New York City. Jim created a way for regular home cooks to nearly duplicate an artisan bakery loaf with its crackling crust, open-holed crumb, light texture, and fantastic flavor, all without kneading or special equipment. A wet dough and slow fermentation are the keys to success (see "The Science Behind No-Knead Bread," below), as is the baking method—a heated covered pot, which essentially creates an oven within an oven to trap steam as the bread bakes. This is the original, simplest version, though many people have tinkered with the formula since it was first published in 2006. I'm not kidding when I say the results will blow your mind.

The only thing required is forethought. Ideally, you will start the dough about 24 hours before you plan to eat the bread; you can cut that to 12 and even 9 hours (see the variation), but you'll be sacrificing some of the yeasty flavor and open crumb.

3 Ideas for No-Knead Bread

1. Replace up to one third of the flour with whole wheat or other whole grain flours. (After you get good at making this bread, you can experiment with higher ratios of whole grain flour; but often those doughs will require more water.)

2. To incorporate add-ins or seasonings (see "17 Ingredients to Add to Any Yeast Bread," page 604), adding them after you've mixed the dough is best. When the ingredients are perishable, like cheese, you have to wait until just before the second rising.

3. To change the shape of the loaf, use different pots. A fish poacher makes a nice baguette, for example.

4 cups all-purpose or bread flour, plus more for dusting (you can substitute up to 1 cup whole wheat, rye, spelt, or kamut flours with no other changes to the recipe)

2 teaspoons salt
Scant ½ teaspoon instant yeast

2 cups warm water (about 70°F)

2 tablespoons olive oil (optional)
Cornmeal, semolina, or wheat bran (optional)

The Science Behind No-Knead Bread

This bread puts time and moisture to work so you don't have to. The dough uses little yeast and compensates for this by fermenting very slowly; this delivers a more complex flavor than other yeast bread recipes. The dough is extremely wet, more than 40 percent water by weight, at the high end of the range professional bakers use to create crisp crust and well-structured crumb, both of which are evident in this loaf.

You couldn't knead this dough if you wanted to. And there truly is no need. The moisture in the dough, combined with the long fermentation time, gives the protein in the flour the environment it needs to develop the gluten that creates the distinctive elastic, weblike structure necessary to trap the carbon dioxide generated by the yeast as it feeds.

By starting this wet dough in a hot, covered pot, you develop a crunchy, chewy crust, since the moist enclosed environment of the pot is, in effect, an oven. That oven has plenty of steam in it, which is necessary to create that kind of surface. Once uncovered, the crust hardens and browns. And fear not: The dough does not stick to the pot, any more than it would to a heated pizza stone.

1. Mix the flour, salt, and yeast together in a large bowl. Add the water and stir until blended; you'll have a shaggy, sticky dough—add a little more water if it seems dry. Cover the bowl with plastic wrap. Or put the oil in a second large bowl, transfer the dough to that, turn it to coat with oil, and cover with plastic wrap. Let the dough rise for 12 to 18 hours at about 70°F. The dough is ready when its surface is dotted with bubbles. Rising time will be shorter at warmer temperatures, longer if your kitchen is cooler; you can get predictably good results by letting the bread rise for 24 hours in the fridge.

2. Lightly flour a work surface. Turn the dough out of the bowl onto the surface, and fold it over itself once or twice; it will be soft, but once sprinkled with flour, not terribly sticky. Cover loosely with plastic wrap and let rest for about 15 minutes.

3. Generously coat a cotton kitchen towel (not terry cloth) with cornmeal, semolina, or wheat bran (or use a silicone baking mat). Using just enough flour to keep the dough from sticking, gently and quickly shape the dough into a ball. Put the ball seam side down on the towel and dust with more flour or with cornmeal. Cover with another cotton towel or plastic wrap and let rise for about 2 hours; when it's ready, the dough will be more than doubled in size and won't spring back readily when poked with your finger.

4. After the dough has been rising for about 1½ hours, put a 3- to 4-quart pot with an ovenproof cover—cast iron or enameled cast iron—in the oven. Heat the oven to 450°F. When the dough is ready, carefully remove the pot from the oven and turn the dough over into the pot, seam side up. (Slide your hand under the towel and just turn the dough over into the pot; it's messy, and it probably won't fall in artfully, but it will straighten out as it bakes.) Cover with the lid and bake for 30 minutes, then remove the lid and bake for another 20 to 30 minutes, until the loaf is beautifully browned. (If at any point the bread starts to smell scorched, lower the heat a bit.) Remove the bread from the pot with a spatula or tongs and cool on a rack for at least 30 minutes before slicing.

NO-KNEAD BREAD, SPED UP Reduce the initial rise in Step 1 to 8 hours. Skip the 15-minute resting period in Step 2. Shape the dough in Step 3 but skip the second rise; proceed immediately to Step 4.

100 Percent Whole Wheat Bread

MAKES: 1 loaf
TIME: 14 to 28 hours, almost completely unattended

Ⓥ

The poufy supermarket bread that claims to be "whole wheat" is stretching the term to the point of meaninglessness. True whole wheat breads like this one—a variation of No-Knead Bread (page 601)—are dense, and so sturdy that some call it "travel bread." What the loaf lacks in airiness it makes up for with its intensely nutty flavor. Slices are perfect for topping with pungent cheeses, jams, or any spread, and the dough can accommodate all sorts of additional ingredients (see the variations).

You can also substitute rye, cornmeal, oat, or other whole grain flours for up to 1 cup of the wheat flour. For a softer, lighter loaf that's partially whole wheat, see the 50 Percent Whole Wheat Sandwich Bread variation on page 605.

> 3 **cups whole wheat flour**
> 2 **teaspoons salt**
> ½ **teaspoon instant yeast**
> **Good-quality vegetable oil for greasing and brushing**

1. Whisk the flour, salt, and yeast together in a large bowl. Add 1½ cups water and stir until blended; the dough should be very wet, almost like a batter; add more water if it's too thick. Cover the bowl with plastic wrap and let it rest in a warm place for about 12 hours, or in a cooler place (even the fridge) for up to 24 hours. The dough is ready when its surface is dotted with bubbles. Rising time will be shorter at warmer temperatures, a bit longer if your kitchen is chilly.

2. Use a little oil to grease a 9 × 5-inch loaf pan. Scoop the dough into the loaf pan and use a rubber spatula to gently spread it in evenly. Brush or drizzle the top with a little more oil. Cover with a towel and let rise until doubled in size, an hour or 2 depending on the warmth of your kitchen. (It won't reach the top of the pan, or will just barely.) When it's almost ready, heat the oven to 350°F. **3.** Bake until the bottom of the loaf sounds hollow when you tap it or the internal temperature is about 200°F on an instant-read thermometer, about 45 minutes. Remove from the pan and cool on a rack before slicing.

100 PERCENT WHOLE WHEAT BREAD WITH WALNUTS AND OLIVES Fold in ½ cup each chopped walnuts and chopped pitted olives (green are my favorite but you can use any kind) before putting the dough in the pan in Step 2.

HONEY–WHOLE WHEAT BREAD WITH GRAINS AND FRUIT A slightly sweeter take: Add 2 tablespoons honey in Step 1. Fold in ½ cup each cooked grains (like oatmeal, quinoa, brown rice, or wheat berries) and dried fruit (chopped if necessary) before putting the dough in the pan in Step 2.

100 PERCENT WHOLE WHEAT BREAD WITH PUMPKIN AND SAGE Reduce the water to ½ cup and add 1 cup puréed cooked pumpkin or squash and up to 2 teaspoons chopped fresh sage to the dough in Step 1.

Sandwich Bread, Eight Ways

MAKES: 1 large loaf
TIME: At least 3 hours, largely unattended
Ⓜ

Sandwich bread contains fat and is baked in a loaf pan. This combination makes it both richer than the rustic-style breads on pages 597 to 602, and more tender (which makes the sandwich easier to eat).

> 3½ cups all-purpose flour, plus more as needed
> 2 teaspoons salt

---

17 Ingredients to Add to Any Yeast Bread

Add any of these ingredients to the flour and yeast (before the water):

1. 1 to 2 tablespoons any spice blend, depending on pungency, toasted lightly in a dry pan if you like

2. Up to 1 tablespoon spices like caraway or cumin seeds, toasted lightly in a dry pan if you like

3. Up to ½ cup cooked whole grains

4. Up to ¼ cup finely ground coffee or tea

5. Up to ¼ cup wheat germ, toasted lightly in a dry pan if you like

Knead any of these ingredients into the dough during the final shaping:

6. Up to 1 cup chopped nuts or seeds, toasted if you like

7. Up to ½ cup chopped dried fruit (including dried tomatoes) or raisins

8. Up to 1 cup chopped bean or seed sprouts

9. Up to ½ cup chopped pitted olives

10. Up to 1 cup lightly mashed drained cooked beans

11. Up to 1 cup grated hard cheese, like Parmesan, manchego, or ricotta salata

12. Up to ½ cup grated medium-hard cheese, like cheddar, Asiago, or pepper Jack

13. Up to ½ cup bits of soft cheese like goat cheese, blue cheese like Gorgonzola, or cream cheese

14. Up to ¼ cup chopped fresh mild herbs like parsley, mint, cilantro, dill, or chives; no more than 1 tablespoon of strong ones like rosemary, sage, or oregano

15. 1 fresh chile (like jalapeño or Thai), seeded and minced, or 1 teaspoon red chile flakes or more to taste

16. Up to ½ cup Caramelized Onions (page 222)

17. Up to ½ cup Roasted Garlic (page 205), lightly mashed or coarsely chopped

1½ teaspoons instant yeast

1 tablespoon sugar or honey

2 tablespoons good-quality vegetable oil or butter (at room temperature if you're mixing by hand), plus more for greasing

Scant 1⅓ cups milk (preferably whole or 2 percent), warmed to at least 70°F if you're working by hand

1. Put the flour, salt, and yeast in a food processor and process for 5 seconds. With the machine running, add the sugar, oil, and most of the milk through the feed tube (you'll need a little less milk if you're using honey). Process for about 30 seconds, then stop the machine and remove the cover. The dough should be in a well-defined, barely sticky, easy-to-handle ball. If it's too dry, add milk a tablespoon at a time and process for 5 or 10 seconds after each addition. If too wet, which is unlikely, add 1 tablespoon flour at a time and process briefly. (If you prefer to mix the dough using a stand mixer or by hand, see page 579.)

2. Use a little oil to grease a large bowl. Shape the dough into a rough ball, place it in the bowl, and cover with plastic wrap or a damp kitchen towel. Let rise for at least 2 hours, until nearly doubled in size. Lightly flour the work surface and turn the dough out of the bowl onto the surface. Fold the dough a couple of times to deflate it, then shape it once again into a ball; let rest for about 15 minutes, covered.

3. Using only enough flour to keep the dough from sticking to your hands or the work surface, flatten it into a rectangle, then shape it into a loaf (see page 599 for illustrations). Use a little oil to grease a 9 × 5-inch loaf pan. Put the loaf in the pan, flattening the top of it with the back of your hand as shown on page 599. Cover and let rise for about 1 hour, until the top of the dough is nearly level with the top of the pan.

4. Heat the oven to 350°F. Uncover the pan and brush the top of the loaf lightly with water. Bake for 45 to 50 minutes, until the bottom of the loaf sounds hollow when you tap it (it will fall easily from the pan) or the

internal temperature reads about 210°F. Remove the loaf from the pan and cool on a rack before slicing.

50 PERCENT WHOLE WHEAT SANDWICH BREAD Something more like what you get in the supermarket, though not fluffy: Substitute 1¾ cups whole wheat flour for half of the flour. Use honey for the sweetener, increasing it to 2 tablespoons. Proceed as directed.

BRAN AND OAT SANDWICH BREAD Reduce the flour to 2 cups. Add ½ cup wheat bran or oat bran and ¾ cup whole wheat flour. Use about ¼ cup honey or maple syrup for the sweetener and decrease the milk to about 1 cup. Knead ¾ cup rolled oats into the dough until evenly distributed before shaping the loaf in Step 2. (If you wet your hands, it will be easier to handle.) Proceed with the recipe.

ANADAMA BREAD A New England classic: Substitute ½ cup cornmeal for ½ cup of the flour. You may also substitute whole wheat flour for 1 cup of the flour. Replace the sugar or honey with ½ cup molasses and use a little less milk.

RYE BREAD Substitute 1 cup rye flour for 1 cup of the flour. Knead 1 tablespoon caraway seeds into the dough until evenly distributed before shaping the loaf in Step 2.

SUNFLOWER SEED OAT BREAD Increase the honey to 2 tablespoons. Knead ½ cup each raw shelled sunflower seeds and rolled oats into the dough until evenly distributed before shaping the loaf in Step 2.

VEGAN SANDWICH BREAD Use sugar instead of honey and oil instead of butter. For the milk, substitute any nondairy milk. **V**

ENGLISH MUFFINS Really lovely: Use the main recipe or any of the variations. In Step 3, cut the dough into 12 roughly equal pieces; if you want perfectly sized muffins, use a scale. Using just enough flour to enable you to handle the dough, shape each into a 3- to 4-inch-diameter disk. Dust with flour and let rise for 30 to 45 minutes, until puffy. Heat a griddle or large skillet over low heat for about 10 minutes; do not oil it. Sprinkle it with cornmeal, then pan-bake the muffins, a few at a time, turning occasionally, until lightly browned on both sides, a total of about 15 minutes. Cool on a rack and split with a fork before toasting. Store in an airtight container for up to a couple days.

Breadsticks

MAKES: 50 to 100
TIME: A day or so, largely unattended
Ⓜ Ⓥ

You won't believe how good these are. In Piedmont, Italy—where breadsticks are called *grissini*—you would never adorn these with anything. But their slightly sweet flavor is good with a sprinkling of poppy seeds or sea salt right before baking.

- 3 **cups all-purpose or bread flour**
- 2 **teaspoons instant yeast**
- 2 **teaspoons salt**
- 1 **teaspoon sugar**
- 2 **tablespoons olive oil, plus more as needed**
- ½ **cup semolina or cornmeal**

1. Put the flour, yeast, salt, and sugar in a food processor; pulse once or twice. Add the oil and pulse a couple of times. With the machine running, add 1 cup warm (not hot) water through the feed tube. Continue to add water, 1 tablespoon at a time and processing briefly after each addition, until the mixture forms a ball. It should be a little shaggy and quite sticky. (If you prefer to mix the dough using a stand mixer or by hand, see page 579.)
2. Put a little oil in a large bowl and transfer the dough to it, turning to coat it well. Cover with plastic wrap and let it rise for 1 hour in a warm place. Lightly flour the work surface and turn the dough out of the bowl onto the surface. Fold the dough a couple of times to deflate

it, then shape it once again into a ball. Put it back in the bowl, cover again, and let rise in the refrigerator for several hours or preferably overnight, until doubled in volume.
3. Heat the oven to 400°F. Lightly grease 2 baking sheets with oil and sprinkle very lightly with semolina or cornmeal.
4. Cut the dough into 3 pieces; keep 2 covered while you work with the other. To roll by hand: On a well-floured surface, roll 1 piece of dough out as thinly as possible into a large rectangle about a foot long. Use a sharp knife or pastry wheel to cut the dough into roughly ¼-inch-thick strips (slightly smaller is better than slightly bigger) along the long side.
5. Transfer the strips to the prepared baking sheets, spacing them 1 inch apart, and brush with oil. Bake until crisp and golden, 10 to 20 minutes, then cool completely on racks. Repeat with the remaining dough. Serve or store in an airtight container for up to 1 week.

HERBED BREADSTICKS Add 2 teaspoons chopped fresh rosemary, thyme, or sage to the dough along with the oil.

PARMESAN BREADSTICKS Try dipping these in tomato sauce: Add up to ¾ cup grated Parmesan cheese to the flour mixture at the start of Step 1.

CHEDDAR-JALAPEÑO BREADSTICKS Add ½ cup grated Cheddar cheese and 1 jalapeño chile, seeded and chopped, to the flour at the start of Step 1.

OLIVE OR DRIED TOMATO BREADSTICKS Darkly colored and full flavored: Before beginning to make the dough in Step 1, purée ½ cup pitted olives (green or black) or dried tomatoes with the oil in the food processor. Add the dry ingredients and proceed with the recipe.

SESAME RICE BREADSTICKS Replace 1 cup of the flour with brown rice flour. Sprinkle the breadsticks with light or black sesame seeds before baking.

PESTO BREADSTICKS Brush the dough with ¼ cup Pesto (page 634) before cutting into strips.

BREADSTICKS WITH PINE NUTS AND CARAWAY SEEDS
By hand, knead ½ cup pine nuts and 1 tablespoon caraway seeds into the dough at the end of Step 1 until well distributed.

Naan

MAKES: About 12
TIME: 2 hours, largely unattended

While the subtle sourness of this north Indian staple comes through most in the plain main recipe, naan also takes especially well to garlic (see the variation). For a slightly warmer, more savory flavor, substitute ½ cup whole wheat flour for some of the all-purpose.

> 2   **teaspoons instant yeast**
> 2   **tablespoons milk**
> 2   **tablespoons yogurt**
> 1   **tablespoon sugar**
> 3½ **cups all-purpose flour plus ½ cup whole wheat flour, or 4 cups all-purpose flour, plus more for dusting**
> 1   **egg**
> 2   **teaspoons salt**
>   **Good-quality vegetable oil for greasing**
> 4   **tablespoons (½ stick) butter, melted and still warm (optional)**

1. Stir the yeast, milk, yogurt, and sugar together in a small bowl.

2. Put the flour(s), egg, and salt in a food processor. Turn the machine on and add the yeast mixture through the feed tube. Process for about 30 seconds, adding 1½ cups water, a little at a time, until the mixture forms a ball and is slightly sticky to the touch. If it is dry, add another tablespoon or 2 water and process for another 10 seconds. In the unlikely event that the mixture is too sticky, add flour, a tablespoon at a time.

(If you prefer to mix the dough using a stand mixer or by hand, see page 579.)

3. Sprinkle a little flour on a clean work surface and turn out the dough onto the surface. Knead by hand for a few seconds to form a smooth, round ball. Lightly oil a large bowl and put the dough in it; cover with plastic wrap. Let rise until the dough doubles in size, 1 to 2 hours. You can cut this rising time short if you are in a hurry, or you can let the dough rise in the refrigerator for up to 6 or 8 hours.

4. Put a pizza stone or baking sheet on the lowest rack in your oven (remove the other racks) and heat the oven to 500°F. Fold and press the dough a couple of times to deflate it. Using as much flour as necessary to keep the dough from sticking to the work surface or your hands, roll it into a snake, then tear the snake into 12 equal-size balls. Let them rest for 10 minutes, covered with plastic wrap or a damp kitchen towel.

5. Roll out each ball into an oval roughly 6 to 8 inches long and 3 to 4 inches wide. Open the oven door, grab one oval with a hand on each end, give it a little tug with one hand to shape it into a teardrop, then toss it onto the stone or baking sheet. Close the oven door. Flip the naan after 3 minutes. The naan is ready when it's puffed, mottled, and browned around the edges, 6 to 8 minutes in total. You can cook as many naan as will comfortably fit at once.

6. Wrap the freshly baked naan in a kitchen towel to keep them warm and pliable. Serve as soon as possible, brushed on one side with melted butter if you like.

GARLIC NAAN Make a paste of 1 tablespoon minced garlic and 2 teaspoons fresh lemon juice. If you like, add some minced fresh green chile for heat and a pinch of cumin seeds. Add in Step 2 along with the yeast mixture.

VEGAN NAAN Omit the egg. Replace the milk and yogurt with ¼ cup soy milk mixed with 1 teaspoon white vinegar; give it time to curdle before adding it in Step 1. **V**

PIZZA

There are people who devote their lives to home-baked pizza, and even your first try at it will give you a sense of why it's so easy to obsess over: It's not only different from anything you can buy in the frozen food section of the supermarket, or have delivered, or eat in a restaurant, it's better. Not only that, you have complete control over ingredients.

Topping pizza is much like saucing pasta: Too many ingredients, and the tastes get muddled; too much sauce, and the flavor of the crust is overwhelmed; too much cheese and the crust gets soggy and sags. It may be difficult to resist, but be restrained and you'll be rewarded with great taste and texture. (That's why pizza is in the bread chapter: It's about the crust!)

That being said, have fun: Try classic combinations like tomatoes, basil, and Parmesan; tomato sauce and mozzarella; or roasted peppers and olives. Experiment with different vegetables and cheeses, like grilled eggplant and feta or caramelized onions and Gorgonzola. After the pizza comes out of the oven, try adding a sprinkle of minced fresh herbs or dust the pie with a spice blend or finely ground nuts. There's nothing wrong with being untraditional (though one could argue that traditional combinations are best); pizza is a wonderful vehicle for enjoying your favorite ingredients.

Pizza Dough

MAKES: 1 large or 2 or more small pies
TIME: 1 hour or more
Ⓜ Ⓥ

You won't believe how easy it is to make pizza at home. And because pizza dough freezes well for at least a couple of weeks, it's completely practical to whip up a batch for one or two people, wrap half of the dough tightly in plastic wrap or a resealable plastic bag, and tuck it away for another day.

> 3 cups all-purpose or bread flour, plus more as needed
> 2 teaspoons instant yeast
> 2 teaspoons sea salt
> 3 tablespoons olive oil, plus more if needed

Pizza on the Grill

Grilled pizza is fun to make and easier than you'd think, especially if your grill has a cover. Wood fires are the trickiest fuel to control but impart distinctive flavor to the crust; gas grills are the easiest for baking pizzas, and charcoal lies somewhere in between. Use what you have and what you have the patience for.

You'll want a fire that is hot enough to brown the dough but not so hot as to scorch it before the interior cooks; a good fire is one you can hold your hand a few inches above for three or four seconds. An ideal fire is one where part of the grill is fairly hot and part of it relatively cool. On a gas grill, this means setting one side on high and the other on low, or some similar arrangement. With a charcoal grill, build your fire on only one side. Use the hot side to initially brown the dough, the cool side to heat the toppings. If you're making smaller pizzas, you can turn them with tongs as soon as they firm up a bit; if the pizza is larger, you may need a peel or a spatula, and your fingers, to turn it.

The process is straightforward: Grill one side of the pizza just enough to firm it up and brown it a bit, then flip it (again, if the pizzas are small, you can use tongs; otherwise a spatula aided by your fingers does the trick) and add the toppings. If you want the toppings to get very hot, cover the grill. If you don't care whether they actually cook, but just want them to warm up a bit, you can leave the grill open.

It's even more important to use flavorful toppings and to keep them to a minimum when you're grilling pizza. Fully loaded pizzas won't cook properly on the grill, and will be impossible to handle. One way around this is to grill pizzas with one or two ingredients, then top them with another after you remove them from the fire.

1. Put the flour, yeast, and salt in a food processor. Turn the machine on and pour 1 cup water and 2 tablespoons of the oil through the feed tube. (If you prefer to mix the dough using a stand mixer or by hand, see page 579.)

2. Process for about 30 seconds, adding more water, a tablespoon or so at a time, until the mixture forms a ball and is slightly sticky to the touch. If it's dry, add another tablespoon or 2 water (but no more than a total of ¼ cup in this step) and process for another 10 seconds. In the unlikely event that the mixture is too sticky, add flour a tablespoon at a time.

3. Knead the dough by hand for a few seconds to form a smooth, round ball, using a tiny bit of flour or oil if necessary to keep it from sticking to your hands. Put the remaining oil in a bowl, turn the dough in it, and cover the bowl with plastic wrap. Let rise until the dough doubles in size, 1 to 2 hours. (You can cut this rising time short if you're in a hurry, or you can let the dough rise more slowly, in the refrigerator, for up to 6 or 8 hours.)

At this point, you can wrap the dough tightly in plastic wrap or a resealable plastic bag and freeze for up to a month. Thaw in the bag or a covered bowl in the refrigerator or at room temperature; bring to room temperature before shaping.

4. When the dough is ready, form it into a ball. Divide it into 2 or more pieces if you like, and roll each piece into a round ball. Place each ball on a lightly floured surface, sprinkle with a little flour, and cover with plastic wrap or a kitchen towel. Let rise until they puff slightly, about 20 minutes. Proceed with any of the pizza recipes that follow on pages 611 to 614.

WHOLE WHEAT PIZZA DOUGH Still chewy and light but a little heartier, with a nutty taste and a bit more fiber: Use 1½ cups whole wheat flour and 1½ cups all-purpose or bread flour. You'll probably need to use closer to 1½ cups water, or maybe even a little more.

CRUNCHIER PIZZA DOUGH This dough may be a little more difficult to handle, but it has superior flavor and a pleasant crunch: Substitute cornmeal for ½ cup of the flour.

6 Quick Ideas for More Flavorful Pizza Dough

You can mix and match as long as you don't overdo it and overpower the natural flavor of the crust or make it soggy. Before adding the water, try the following, alone or in combination:

1. Add ½ to 1 teaspoon cracked black pepper

2. Add 1 teaspoon to 1 tablespoon chopped fresh herbs

3. Add ¼ to ½ cup chopped nuts or seeds

4. Substitute ½ to 1 cup rice flour or other alternative flour for the white flour

5. Add 1 tablespoon puréed cooked garlic (roasted is best; see page 205) or ½ teaspoon minced raw garlic (or to taste)

6. Use flavored olive oil, like garlic or rosemary oil, in place of regular olive oil (to make your own, see page 627)

White Pizza

MAKES: 1 large or 2 or more small pies
TIME: About 3 hours, largely unattended

Ⓜ Ⓥ

In a way, *pizza bianca* is the mother of all pizzas. It may seem spare compared to what we're used to, but I urge you to try it and experiment with some of the possible additions and tweaks that follow the recipe, because it's among the best breads you'll ever eat.

I always use a good coarse salt for white pizza, because salt is almost a primary ingredient.

> 1 recipe Pizza Dough (page 609), mixed and risen
> All-purpose flour or semolina for shaping
> Olive oil
> Kosher or coarse sea salt
> 1 tablespoon or more roughly chopped fresh rosemary
> Several fresh rosemary sprigs (optional)

1. When the dough is ready, knead it lightly, form it into a ball, and divide it into 2 if you like; roll each piece into a ball and place each ball on a lightly floured work surface. Sprinkle with a little more flour, cover with plastic wrap or a kitchen towel, and let rest while you heat the oven.

2. If you'll be baking the pizza on a pizza stone, put the stone on the lowest rack of the oven; if not, lightly oil a baking sheet or 2. Heat the oven to 500°F or higher. Roll or lightly press each dough ball into a disk, lightly flouring the work surface and the dough as necessary (do not use more flour than you need to). Let the disks sit for a few minutes; this will let the dough relax and make it easier to roll out. If you have a peel and pizza stone, roll or pat out the dough on the peel, as thin as you like, turning it occasionally and sprinkling it with flour or semolina as necessary. If you're using baking sheets, press each dough ball into a flat round directly on a baking sheet.

3. Sprinkle the top with some salt and the chopped rosemary and drizzle with a little oil; if you have some rosemary sprigs, decorate the top with them. Slide the pizza from the peel onto the stone, or put the baking sheet on the center rack in the oven. Bake for 6 to 12 minutes,

---

Shaping Dough for Pizza

Your goal is to coax the dough into shape by pressing or rolling and stretching. It's easiest if you allow the dough to rest between steps: when you divide it, when you flatten it, and even during stages of rolling or stretching.

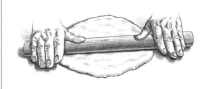

STEP 1 Stretch the dough with your hands. If at any point the dough becomes very resistant, cover and let it rest for a few minutes.

STEP 2 Press the dough out with your hands. Use a little flour or olive oil to keep it from sticking.

OR STEP 2 Alternatively, roll it out with a pin; either method is effective.

Pizza with Tomato Sauce, Mozzarella, and Broccoli (page 614); Red, White, and Green Pizza (page 614)

depending on the oven heat, until nicely browned. Serve immediately. Or cool on a rack and serve at room temperature; this will keep for a few hours.

MARGHERITA PIZZA The ultimate summertime treat: Top the pies with sliced fresh tomatoes, olive oil, a little mozzarella (preferably fresh), and grated Parmesan cheese before putting them in the oven. Top with fresh basil leaves after it's cooked (otherwise, they'll turn black).

POMODORO PIZZA All tomatoes, no cheese: Top the pies with sliced fresh tomatoes, thinly sliced garlic, olive oil, and, if you like, a few chopped black olives or whole capers before putting them in the oven. V

WHITE PIZZA WITH MINT Unexpected and refreshing: Instead of the chopped rosemary, scatter about ¼ cup chopped fresh mint on top and press it down into the dough a bit. V

WHITE PIZZA WITH MUSHROOMS Earthy and satisfying: Omit the rosemary; instead top the pies with some Sautéed Mushrooms (page 217) and sprinkle with lots of minced fresh parsley before baking; sage is also good. V

WHITE PIZZA WITH BALSAMIC CARAMELIZED ONIONS Omit the rosemary. Make Caramelized Onions (page 222), cooked fairly dark. Season to taste with salt and pepper, then stir in 1 tablespoon balsamic vinegar (or to taste). Top each pizza with a portion of the onions and a generous sprinkling of minced fresh thyme or sage before baking. A sprinkling of plain bread crumbs is also good. V

WHITE PIZZA WITH POTATOES AND ROSEMARY Slice 8 to 12 ounces waxy potatoes into very thin rounds; sauté in a skillet with some olive oil and a sprinkle of salt and pepper until they are just tender, about 10 minutes. Arrange over the dough, then sprinkle with the rosemary and bake. V

Pizza with Tomato Sauce and Mozzarella

MAKES: 1 large or 2 or more small pies
TIME: About 3 hours if you need to make sauce, largely unattended
M

This recipe is more like American-style pizza than the White Pizza on page 611, with a smear of tomato sauce and a fair amount of mozzarella. It's a little too loaded to grill, but the good news is that the cheese helps other unwieldy toppings—like broccoli, bell peppers, or olives—stick to the pie. For more variations, see "11 Ideas for Pizza Toppings" (page 614).

1 recipe Pizza Dough (page 609), mixed and risen
  All-purpose flour or semolina for shaping
  About 2 tablespoons olive oil
2 cups Fast Tomato Sauce (page 312) or other tomato sauce
2 cups grated mozzarella (about 8 ounces)
  Salt and pepper

1. When the dough is ready, knead it lightly, form it into a ball, and divide it in 2 if you like; roll each piece into a ball and place each ball on a lightly floured surface. Sprinkle with a little more flour, cover with plastic wrap or a kitchen towel, and let rest while you heat the oven.
2. If you'll be baking the pizza on a pizza stone, put the stone on the lowest rack of the oven; if not, lightly oil a baking sheet or 2. Heat the oven to 500°F or higher. Roll or lightly press each dough ball into a disk, lightly flouring the work surface and the dough as necessary (do not use more flour than you need to). Let the disks sit for a few minutes; this will let the dough relax and make it easier to roll out. If you have a peel and pizza stone, roll or pat out the dough on the peel, as thin as you like, turning it occasionally and sprinkling it with flour or semolina as necessary. If you're using baking sheets, press each dough ball into a flat round directly on the baking sheets.
3. Drizzle the dough with the oil, then top the pizza(s) with the sauce and cheese; sprinkle with salt and pepper.

Put the baking sheet on the center rack in the oven or slide the pizza directly onto the stone. Bake until the crust is crisp and the cheese melted, 8 to 12 minutes. Let stand for several minutes before slicing for the cheese to set up.

PIZZA WITH TOMATO SAUCE, MOZZARELLA, AND BROCCOLI
Best with broccoli raab: Sauté ½ pound broccoli florets or broccoli raab spears in 1 tablespoon olive oil with some chopped or sliced garlic and red chile flakes to taste over medium-high heat just until tender. After you put the cheese on the pizza, distribute the broccoli over the top and press gently into the cheese. Bake as directed.

RED, WHITE, AND GREEN PIZZA Decrease the tomato sauce and mozzarella each to 1 cup. Spread the tomato sauce over the pizza, scatter over the mozzarella, then dollop ½ cup Pesto (page 634) over everything. Bake as directed.

GREEK-STYLE PIZZA Substitute 1 cup crumbled feta for 1 cup of the mozzarella. Scatter some thinly sliced red onion, chopped kalamata olives, and chopped fresh oregano over the cheese. Bake as directed. If you like, grate a little lemon zest on top after the pizza comes out of the oven.

SUMMER PIZZA Reduce the mozzarella to 1 cup. Cut the kernels off 2 ears fresh corn and scatter them over the cheese along with half a small red onion, sliced, and 4 ounces crumbled goat cheese. Bake as directed.

FILLED BREADS, WRAPS, AND BRUSCHETTA

Beyond quick breads, flatbreads, and yeast breads there is a world of stuffed breads and doughs like calzones and samosas, and wraps like summer rolls and burritos, as well as one of the best reasons in the world to toast bread, bruschetta. These can be served as appetizers, snacks, or the centerpiece of a larger meal.

11 Ideas for Pizza Toppings

Use the following ingredients alone or in combination on any of the pizzas in this section.

1. Small amounts of Gorgonzola or other blue cheese, or fontina or other semisoft cheese; gratings of Parmesan are almost always welcome, as are dollops of ricotta

2. Mashed Roasted Garlic (page 205)

3. Minced fresh chiles (like jalapeño or Thai) or red chile flakes or cayenne to taste

4. Pitted black olives, especially the oil-cured

kind (good on White Pizza with Balsamic Caramelized Onions, page 222), or green olives

5. Reconstituted dried tomatoes (or Oven-Dried Tomatoes, page 261)

6. Well-washed and dried tender greens, especially spicy ones like arugula and watercress, added after baking or grilling; they will wilt from the heat from the crust in about 1 minute.

7. Sautéed spinach, strewn around in a thin layer

8. Marinated roasted red peppers (page 228)

9. Grilled or Broiled Eggplant (page 201) or the pan-cooked eggplant slices from Eggplant Parmesan (page 202)

10. Slices of grilled zucchini (see page 167)

11. Farm-fresh eggs. Make a breakfast pizza

with coddled eggs: After the pizza has baked for about 5 minutes (or after you have turned it, if you are grilling the pizza), break eggs on top of the crust (no more than 4 on a large crust or 2 on a smaller crust), spacing them nicely. Return to the oven and bake until the whites are opaque, the yolks are still runny, and the crust is crisp, about another 5 minutes.

Calzones

MAKES: 2 calzones, enough for 4 main-dish servings
TIME: About 3 hours, largely unattended
Ⓜ

You can make calzones using any pizza topping as a filling (see "11 Ideas for Pizza Toppings," page 614, for suggestions), but they're best with a combination of cheese and vegetables. The filling should be substantial but also be fairly dry; liquid fillings will leak or make the dough soggy. That's why drained ricotta, which is moist but not wet, is the ideal base.

Serve calzones plain, or with Fresh Tomato Sauce (page 313), or any other tomato sauce, for dipping or topping.

- 1 recipe Pizza Dough (page 609), mixed and risen
- 2 cups ricotta cheese
- 1 cup chopped cooked spinach or other greens, such as chard or broccoli (see page 153)
- 1 cup chopped or grated mozzarella
- 1 cup freshly grated Parmesan cheese
   Salt and pepper

1. When the dough is ready, knead it lightly and cut it in half. Form 2 balls and place them on a lightly floured work surface. Sprinkle with a little more flour, cover with plastic wrap or a kitchen towel, and let them rest for 20 minutes.

2. If the ricotta is very wet, drain it in a fine-meshed strainer for 10 minutes or so to remove excess moisture. Transfer to a large bowl, add the vegetable, mozzarella, and Parmesan, and mix until well combined. Taste and add salt, if necessary, and pepper.

3. If you'll be baking the calzones on a pizza stone, put the stone on the lowest rack of the oven; if not, lightly oil a baking sheet. Heat the oven to 350°F. Roll or lightly press each dough ball into a disk, lightly flouring the work surface and the dough as necessary (do not use more flour than you need to). Let the

disks sit for a few minutes; this will allow the dough to relax, and make it easier to roll out. Roll or pat out each ball of dough into an 8- to 10-inch round, not too thin, on a floured pizza peel or the prepared baking sheet.

4. Put half the filling into the center of each dough round. Moisten the edges with a little water. Fold one edge over onto the other and press closed with your fingertips.

5. Bake the calzones directly on the pizza stone or on the baking sheet on the center rack of the oven for 30 to 40 minutes, until nicely browned. Serve hot or warm.

SPINACH-ARTICHOKE CALZONES Substitute ½ cup room-temperature cream cheese for 1 cup of the ricotta. Use spinach for the green and add ¾ cup chopped cooked artichoke hearts and 1 clove garlic, minced, to the filling mixture in Step 2.

VEGAN SPINACH CALZONES Increase the chopped greens to 2 cups. Whirl them together in a food processor with a 14- to 16-ounce package extra firm tofu, drained and cut into several pieces, 2 cloves garlic, and salt and pepper until smooth and fully combined. Continue with Step 3. Ⓥ

9 Dishes for Filling Calzones

Calzones are perfect for using up leftovers. Reduce the ricotta to 1 cup and use 1 cup of the following, drained of any excess liquid, instead of the spinach.

1. Gigantes with Brussels Sprouts (page 441)
2. White Beans, Tuscan Style (page 444)
3. Shortcut Roasted Chickpeas with Rosemary and Lemon Zest (page 472)
4. Roasted or Grilled Asparagus (page 171)
5. Eggplant Slices with Garlic and Parsley (page 201)
6. Leeks Braised in Olive Oil or Butter (page 215)
7. Sautéed Mushrooms (page 217)
8. Roasted red peppers (see page 228)
9. Winter Squash, Roasted (page 266)

Calzones (page 615)

Lentil Samosas

MAKES: 24
TIME: 1½ hours, partially unattended
Ⓜ

Samosas are filled pastries found almost everywhere in the world, sometimes under different names (think of empanadas, for example). This recipe makes a nice big batch for party food. You can use virtually any thick dal or bean dish instead of the quickly prepared lentils, or see the variations. See The Simplest Yogurt Sauce (page 673), which makes a fine dip for these.

> 2 tablespoons good-quality vegetable oil
> 1 small onion, minced
>   Salt and pepper
> 1 medium carrot, minced
> 1 stalk celery, minced
> 2 tablespoons minced garlic
> 2 tablespoons minced fresh ginger
> 1 cup dried lentils (any kind), rinsed
>   and picked over
> 2 cups vegetable stock (pages 97–100) or water
> 2 tablespoons garam masala or curry powder
>   (to make your own, see page 648 or 649)
> 2 cups all-purpose flour, plus more as needed
> 2 tablespoons cold butter, plus more for greasing
> 2 tablespoons yogurt

1. Put the oil in a deep skillet or medium saucepan over medium heat. When it's hot, add the onion, sprinkle with salt and pepper, and cook, stirring occasionally, until soft, 3 to 5 minutes. Add the carrot, celery, garlic, and ginger and keep cooking and stirring until all the vegetables start to wilt and are fragrant, another 3 to 5 minutes.

2. Add the lentils, stock, and garam masala, along with enough water to cover the lentils by about ½ inch. Turn the heat to high. When the mixture begins to boil, lower the heat so it bubbles gently. Cover and cook, stirring every so often, until the lentils and vegetables are very soft, about 45 minutes or more. Add more stock or water during cooking only if needed to keep the lentils from scorching. The lentils should be fairly stiff and dry when they're done; if not, remove the lid, turn up the heat a bit, and let some of the liquid bubble away. Taste, adjust the seasoning, and set aside to cool.

3. While the lentils are cooking, put the flour with a large pinch salt, the butter, and yogurt in a food processor; turn on the machine. A few seconds later, pour about ½ cup water through the feed tube. Let the machine run, adding a little more water if necessary, until a dough ball forms. Turn the dough out onto a lightly floured work surface and knead a few times, adding a little more flour if necessary. Wrap the dough in plastic and refrigerate for at least 30 minutes. (You can make both the lentils and the dough to this point up to a day in advance. Cover or wrap tightly and refrigerate, bring to room temperature before proceeding.)

4. Heat the oven to 350°F. Lightly grease a couple of baking sheets or line them with parchment paper. Sprinkle a work surface with flour. Divide the dough into quarters; cover 3 of the quarters and divide the fourth into 6 pieces. Roll each piece into a round ball, then roll each ball out to a 3-inch-diameter round. Put about 1 tablespoon of the filling on one side of each round. Brush the rim with a little water (you can use your fingertip), then fold over into a half-moon and press to seal.

5. Put the samosas, about 1 inch apart, on the prepared baking sheets. Keep covered with plastic wrap while you repeat with the remaining dough. Bake the samosas, turning as needed, until golden brown, about 30 minutes, and serve hot.

FRIED LENTIL SAMOSAS Use this technique for the main recipe or any of the other variations: Put at least 3 inches peanut or good-quality vegetable oil in a countertop deep-fryer or in a deep pan on the stove and turn the heat to medium-high; bring to 350°F (see "Deep-Frying," page 26). Put as many samosas as will fit without crowding in the hot oil and fry, turning once or twice, until lightly browned, about 5 minutes. Drain on paper towels and serve hot. Or keep them warm in a 200°F oven, or serve at room temperature, but in any case serve within an hour.

POTATO AND PEA SAMOSAS Made rich with coconut milk: Instead of the lentils, peel 1 pound potatoes and cut into cubes (you should have 3 to 4 cups). Thaw about ½ cup frozen peas (or shell fresh peas). Prepare the recipe through Step 1, substituting 1 tablespoon each mustard seeds and cumin seeds for the garam masala if you like. In Step 2, use the potatoes instead of the lentils and coconut milk instead of the stock. Proceed with the recipe, cooking the potatoes until very tender, 20 minutes or so, checking to make sure they're not too dry or too wet. Mash the potatoes coarsely; stir in the peas and set aside to cool. Proceed with the recipe from Step 3.

SPINACH AND CHEESE SAMOSAS Crumble or shred about 1 cup fresh cheese (see page 568), paneer, mozzarella, queso fresco, or feta. Blanch and shock 1 pound spinach (see page 150), trimmed, or use a 10-ounce package thawed frozen spinach; drain well, squeeze dry, and coarsely chop. Mix with the cheese and sprinkle with salt and pepper. Taste and adjust the seasoning. Proceed with the recipe from Step 3, using this mixture to fill the samosas.

Summer Rolls

MAKES: 4 to 8 servings (8 rolls)
TIME: 40 minutes
V

This classic Vietnamese preparation, with its pliable white rice paper wraps, salad-like filling, and flavorful dipping sauces, takes a little practice, but not much— you'll get good at it pretty quickly. Think of this recipe as an outline for any kind of summer roll you like; the filling can be anything from tofu to shredded vegetables to slices of fruit.

Working with rice paper wrappers is not rocket science. All they need is a dip in hot water to soften up and become pliable; they'll continue to soften a bit after they've been rolled. The two most common mistakes people make with rice paper is letting it soak too long (it'll become mushy and tear easily) and making the

rolls too far in advance, which results in the wrapper drying out. So remember to keep the hot water dip short and to serve the rolls immediately or wrap well with plastic and serve within an hour.

For dipping, try Peanut Sauce, Four Ways (page 657), Fishless Fish Sauce (page 656), Ponzu (page 657), Basil Dipping Sauce (page 654), Vietnamese-Style or Thai-Style Chile Pastes (page 664), Chile-Garlic Paste (page 665), or just soy sauce with vinegar or water.

8	sheets rice paper, 10 or 12 inches in diameter
8–10	tender lettuce leaves, like Boston, washed, dried, and torn
1	4-ounce bundle rice vermicelli, soaked in hot water until softened (about 10 minutes) and drained
2	scallions, cut into 2-inch pieces and then thinly sliced lengthwise
2	carrots, thinly julienned or grated
½	cup lightly packed fresh mint leaves
½	cup lightly packed fresh cilantro leaves
½	cup lightly packed fresh basil leaves, preferably Thai basil
	Lime wedges for garnish

1. Set up a work station: Lay out a damp kitchen or paper towel on the work surface and a wide, shallow bowl of hot water (110° to 120°F, which is about what hot water measures from most taps). Line up a stack of rice paper and the containers of the remaining ingredients (except the lime wedges), in order. At the end, put a plate or baking sheet large enough to hold the completed rolls in one layer.

2. Dip a sheet of the rice paper in the hot water, turning once, until soft, about 10 seconds. Lay it flat on the towel. On the bottom third of the rice paper, spread an eighth of each of the remaining ingredients in a line. Fold in the bottom edge and both sides, then roll tightly into a cylinder, like a burrito (see page 622). The rice paper will adhere to itself. Put the roll on the plate, seam side down. Repeat this process with the remaining ingredients.

3. Serve with the lime wedges and your choice of dipping sauce. Or wrap in damp paper towels and plastic wrap and serve within an hour or so with the lime wedges.

10 Fabulous Fillings for Summer Rolls

Not all of these are traditional, but they are all good.

1. Pressed or smoked tofu slices (see page 483 or 486)
2. Deep-Fried, Crisp Panfried, or Marinated Tofu (pages 486 or 494)
3. Daikon, peeled and thinly julienned or grated
4. Spinach leaves
5. Asparagus, steamed (see page 171)
6. Green or wax beans, cooked and shocked (page 150)
7. Hothouse cucumber, peeled and thinly julienned or grated
8. Green papaya, peeled and thinly julienned or grated
9. Mango or ripe papaya, peeled and thinly julienned
10. Steamed Sticky Rice (page 370) or Coconut Rice (page 368), warm or at room temperature

FILLED TORTILLAS

Whether you make them yourself or buy them, tortillas are a fantastic convenience food, the basis of burritos, tacos, and quesadillas. (Vegetarians should beware that some traditionally made tortillas sold in Mexican or Latin markets may contain lard.) Flour tortillas are soft and subtle, almost neutral in flavor, and range in size from small (2 or 3 inches) to very large (12 inches or so, ideal for burritos). Corn tortillas are a bit harder to handle but better in every other way: They have better texture, more flavor, and are whole-grain. The best corn tortillas have a fresh corn flavor and a soft and pliable texture when raw. Both flour and corn tortillas are a breeze to make yourself (see page 595).

FILLINGS AND TOPPINGS FOR TACOS, BURRITOS, AND QUESADILLAS

Beans are are the most traditional filling for wraps using tortillas, like tacos; rice is a modern but common

addition. Be sure the beans are well seasoned and not too soupy. Add more texture by using firmer grains, like wheat berries, instead of rice.

Vegetables are another option, especially grilled or breaded and fried, giving tacos and burritos an irresistible crunchy-soft texture. You can use just about any vegetable you like (see "Grilling Vegetables," page 166, and "Batter-Fried Vegetables," page 159).

The least traditional fillings are not Mexican at all: tofu, seitan, and tempeh. Frying, baking, and grilling tofu or tempeh give them a meaty texture, and seitan offers a pleasantly chewy texture.

Then there are the toppings: Check out the raw and cooked salsas on pages 659 to 664 but consider, too, Crunchy Corn Guacamole (page 174) or Mexican-Style Quickest Pickled Vegetables (page 89). Shredded lettuce or radish, chopped tomatoes, grated cheese, sour cream or yogurt, and hot sauces are givens; serve them in bowls on the table for everyone to dress their own tacos and burritos as they like.

Quesadillas

MAKES: 4 main-dish or 8 appetizer servings
TIME: 15 minutes

Quesadillas are essentially grilled cheese sandwiches made with tortillas; few hot dishes are easier or make better use of teeny amounts of leftovers. Try to resist overstuffing: too much cheese, and they ooze all over the place; too many extra ingredients, and the cheese never melds the tortillas together.

> Good-quality vegetable oil as needed
> 8 8-inch flour tortillas
> 2 cups grated Cotija, queso blanco, mild cheddar, or Monterey Jack, or a combination
> ¼ cup salsa (pages 659 to 664), guacamole (page 174), and/or sour cream or yogurt for serving (optional)

10 Taco and Burrito Ideas

Here are some suggestions for filling tacos and burritos; mix and match as you like. Sprinkle on Crunchy Crumbled Tempeh (page 512) or any other crumble (page 679) for extra texture, especially in combination with soft tofu or bean fillings or in soft tortillas.

Also see Breakfast Burritos (page 533) for some delicious ideas using scrambled eggs.

TACO OR BURRITO	FILLINGS	SALSAS, TOPPINGS, AND EXTRAS
Taco (corn or flour tortilla) or burrito (any tortilla)	Any tofu (pages 484 to 487); Beer-Glazed Black Beans (page 440; optional)	Corn Salsa (page 662) or Super-Spicy Chile-Garlic Paste (page 665); Crunchy Corn or Minimalist Guacamole (page 174)
Taco (corn tortilla) or burrito (whole wheat flour tortilla)	Spicy Scrambled Tofu (page 489)	Garlic-Scallion Sauce (page 631); Bean Salsa (page 660) or Fresh Tomatillo Salsa (page 660); bean or nut crumbles (page 679)
Taco (corn or flour tortilla) or burrito (flour tortilla)	Refried Beans (page 460); Mexican Rice with Vegetables (page 373; optional)	Radish Salsa (page 662) or Jícama Salsa (page 662)
Burrito (whole wheat or flavored tortilla)	White Rice and Black Beans (page 367); Coconut-Fried Plantains (page 162; optional)	Minimalist Guacamole (page 174); Cooked Tomatillo Salsa (page 663)
Taco (corn or flour tortilla)	The Simplest Bean Burgers (page 502), crumbled	Charred Salsa Roja (page 663)
Taco (corn or flour tortilla) or burrito (flour or whole wheat tortilla)	Spicy Black Bean Croquettes (page 475), crumbled	Radish Salsa (page 662)
Taco (corn or flour tortilla) or burrito (whole wheat or flavored tortilla)	Breaded and fried eggplant, zucchini, yellow squash, or any vegetable (see chart on page 160)	Fresh Tomato Salsa (page 660)
Taco (corn tortilla)	Grilled or Broiled or Pan-Seared Seitan (pages 510-512)	Salsa Borracha (page 663) or Smoky and Hot Salsa Roja (page 663)
Burrito (whole wheat or flavored)	Tempeh Chili with Black Beans (page 517)	Cooked Tomatillo Salsa (page 663) or Fresh Tomatillo Salsa (page 660)
Taco (corn or flour tortilla)	Batter-Fried Squash Blossoms (page 160)	Crunchy Corn Guacamole (page 174); Fresh Tomatillo Salsa (page 660)

1. Set a skillet over medium-low heat. Add just enough oil to coat the bottom lightly. Put a tortilla on the skillet and sprinkle over ½ cup cheese. Top with another tortilla, pressing down a bit with a spatula. When the cheese begins to melt and the bottom tortilla begins to brown, after about 2 minutes, use the spatula to flip the quesadilla over.

2. Cook just until the bottom tortilla is warm and lightly toasted, about another 2 minutes. Transfer the quesadilla to a cutting board if you're serving them as they are done. Otherwise, transfer the quesadilla to a baking sheet and keep warm in a 200°F oven. Repeat with the remaining tortillas and filling.

3. Cut the quesadillas into wedges and serve with salsa, guacamole, or sour cream.

GRILLED QUESADILLAS Prepare a charcoal or gas grill for moderately heat; adjust the rack to about 4 inches from the heat source. Brush one side of a tortilla with oil and set it on the grill. Build your quesadilla as instructed in Step 1 and brush oil on the top tortilla. Proceed as directed.

CHILE-BEAN QUESADILLAS Hearty enough to enjoy for dinner: Reduce the cheese to 1 cup. Mash 1 cup drained well-cooked beans of your choice until mostly smooth. Season with salt and pepper and stir in 1 teaspoon each ground cumin and ancho chile powder. To build each quesadilla, spread the bottom tortilla with ¼ cup of the mashed beans, then sprinkle with chopped or very thinly sliced jalapeños to taste, 1 tablespoon chopped fresh cilantro, and ¼ cup crumbled or shredded cheese. Cook as directed.

ROASTED VEGETABLE QUESADILLAS This takes a little longer but is worth it: Reduce the cheese to 1½ cups. Cut your choice of vegetables (you want a combination: zucchini, yellow summer squash, onions, bell peppers, green beans, asparagus, broccoli, cauliflower are all good choices) into small pieces or dice, no more than ½ inch across; you want to have about 3 cups, as the pieces will shrink a bit as they roast. If you like, include shelled edamame and/or corn kernels. Place in a bowl and toss with 1½ tablespoons olive oil, 2 teaspoons fresh thyme or ½ teaspoon dried, and salt and pepper until coated.

Rolling a Burrito

Rolling a burrito doesn't take too much skill. The biggest obstacle to success is overstuffing. To keep the burrito together after rolling, place it seam side down on a plate or wrap the bottom half in foil or wax paper until you're ready to eat.

STEP 1 Put the filling on the third of the tortilla closest to you.

STEP 2 Fold in the sides a little bit.

STEP 3 Roll up, tucking in the sides and the top edge to form a fairly tight roll.

Arrange in a single layer on a baking sheet and roast at 450°F until tender, about 15 minutes. To build each quesadilla, arrange a quarter of the roasted vegetables over the bottom tortilla, sprinkle with 6 tablespoons cheese, top with the other tortilla, and cook as directed.

QUINOA AND KALE QUESADILLAS Greens and grains all in one. This is best made using leftover quinoa or any other grain, including rice: Reduce the cheese to 1½ cups. Remove the stems from 3 to 5 kale leaves and very thinly slice them crosswise into ribbons; you want about 1½ cups. Toss the kale with 1 tablespoon balsamic vinegar. To build each quesadilla, arrange about ¼ cup quinoa over the bottom tortilla, then 6 tablespoons kale, 6 tablespoons cheese, and the other tortilla. Cook as directed.

AVOCADO AND SCALLION QUESADILLAS No need for cheese here; the avocado provides all the creaminess you'll need: Depending on their size, you will need 1 or 2 ripe Hass avocadoes for every 2 quesadillas. Peel, pit, and mash the avocados into a coarse purée. Depending on how many avocados you're using, stir in up to 2 tablespoons fresh lime juice (the juice of 1 lime). To build each quesadilla, spread the bottom tortilla with one quarter of the avocado, then sprinkle with 2 tablespoons chopped scallions and some torn fresh basil leaves. Cook as directed, until the avocado is warm. V

MANGO AND CABBAGE SLAW QUESADILLAS WITH SWEET THAI CHILI SAUCE Sweet, crunchy, and gooey all at once: You'll need 1 ripe mango for every 2 quesadillas. Peel the mango, slice the flesh off the seed, and cut into ½-inch dice. Toss with 1 tablespoon fresh lime juice and ¼ cup chopped fresh cilantro. Very thinly slice green cabbage into ribbons to equal 1 cup. To build each quesadilla, sprinkle one quarter of the mango mixture over the bottom tortilla, then ¼ cup cabbage and ½ cup cheese. Spread one side of the other tortilla with 1 tablespoon sweet Thai chili sauce, place it sauce side down on the quesadilla, and cook as directed.

9 More Fillings for Tacos and Burritos

With some of these ingredients—like bean or veggie burgers—you'll be crumbling or chopping them up before filling.

1. Winter squash slices, roasted (page 266)

2. My Mom's Pan-Cooked Peppers and Onions (page 228)

3. Sautéed Ripe Plantains (page 278) or Fried Plantain Chips (page 280)

4. Sautéed chayote (page 154)

5. Bulgur Chili (page 408) or any chili with rice or grains

6. Any grilled or roasted vegetable, like eggplant, mushrooms, any summer squash, peppers or chiles, and onions (pages 166 to 167)

7. Pinto Beans with Red Bell Pepper (page 444)

8. Chili non Carne (page 455) or Espresso Black Bean Chili (page 456)

9. Black Bean Cakes with Queso Fresco (page 440)

Bruschetta

MAKES: 4 servings
TIME: About 20 minutes
F V

At its simplest, bruschetta is crisp, hot bread rubbed gently with a clove of garlic, drizzled with lots of good olive oil, and sprinkled with salt: a snack or a starter. But with more toppings it can become a light meal; see the variations and the list on page 624.

Use the best rustic bread you can get your hands on (or make it: see page 597), and slice it thick, so that the outside gets crunchy while the inside stays moist.

8 thick slices rustic bread
1–4 garlic cloves, halved, or peeled and crushed
Olive oil as needed
Salt and pepper

1. Prepare a charcoal or gas grill or turn on the broiler for moderate heat; adjust the rack about 4 inches from the heat source. Grill or broil the bread until lightly browned on both sides, ideally with some grill marks or light charring.

2. While the bread is still hot, rub the slices with the garlic on one or both sides. Put on a plate, drizzle with oil (a tablespoon or so should do it) and sprinkle with salt and pepper. Serve warm.

BRUSCHETTA WITH TOMATOES AND BASIL Excellent with an assortment of summer tomatoes: Coarsely chop about 1 pound fresh tomatoes. If you have time, put them in a strainer for a few minutes to drain the excess water. When the bread is ready to cook, combine the tomatoes and about 1 cup torn fresh basil leaves in a bowl, along with a drizzle of olive oil and a sprinkle of salt. Toss to combine. After rubbing the garlic on the bread in Step 2, put the tomato mixture on top each slice. Sprinkle with pepper and serve.

CROSTINI Thinly sliced and ultra-crisp, these Italian-style crouton-like toasts until recently were known in America as "toast points": Slice the bread thinner and into smaller pieces so you have between 16 and 24 pieces. Crisp them on a grill, under a broiler, or in a 400°F oven until golden on all sides. Rub them with garlic if you like and top them in any of the ways described in the sidebar and list below.

5 Great Spreads for Bruschetta or Crostini

After toasting the bread, you might think about topping each piece with one of these:
1. Blue Cheese Dip or Spread or its variations (page 556)
2. Egg Salad or its variations (page 541)
3. Tapenade or its variations (page 291)
4. Bean dips and Hummus (pages 462 to 466)
5. Virtually any puréed vegetable (page 150 to 153)

22 Unexpected Toast Toppers

You have a lot of options when it comes to topping bruschetta and crostini beyond the usual open-face sandwich ideas. And don't forget that you can slice virtually any other bread—whole grain, sandwich, or even corn bread or focaccia— and give it the toast-and-top treatment. For each of the following suggestions, put the bread on a plate immediately after toasting, without the garlic and oil, and top.

1. Any vinaigrette (page 628), with or without a green salad

2. Balsamic Strawberries with Arugula (page 39)

3. Parsley and Herb Salad (page 40)

4. Shaved Artichoke Salad (page 44)

5. Seaweed Romaine Salad (page 55)

6. Tomato Salad with Hard-Boiled Eggs (page 57)

7. Ratatouille Salad or its variation (page 66)

8. Chopped Whole Roasted Cauliflower with Balsamic Glaze and Raisins (page 190)

9. Corn Salad with Tomatoes, Feta, and Mint or its variation (page 52)

10. Mushroom Salad, Italian-American Style (page 62)

11. Bean Salad, Many Ways (page 71)

12. Warm Chickpea Salad with Arugula (page 73)

13. Lemony Lentil Salad (page 73)

14. Fresh Cottage Cheese or Fresh Ricotta (page 569)

15. Beans and Greens (page 444)

16. Beans and Mushrooms or its variations (page 447)

17. Chickpea Fondue or its variations (page 465)

18. White Bean Purée or its variations (page 459)

19. Mashed Favas (page 466)

20. Skillet Eggplant with Tomatoes (page 199)

21. Leeks Braised in Olive Oil or Butter or its variations (page 215)

22. Sautéed Mushrooms or its variations (page 217)

Sauces, Condiments, Herbs, and Spices

CHAPTER AT A GLANCE

This chapter is all about quick ways to add flavor, from its most basic building blocks—oil, vinegar, herbs, and spices—to the sauces, toppings, chutneys, chile pastes, and vinaigrettes you can make from them. In a trend that was starting when the first edition of this book came out, the movement toward vibrant, fresh flavor continues and the recipes in this chapter will serve as a flavoring arsenal to put spectacular finishing touches on most anything you make.

THE BASICS OF OILS

When you cook with oils, their differences affect the flavor and texture of the food. But when you use them raw, whether in dressings or as a last-minute drizzle, the strongest-tasting ones act as a true seasoning.

WHAT TO LOOK FOR WHEN BUYING OIL

Unless it states otherwise on the label, assume that the oil was chemically extracted. This means that the raw materials (seeds, corn, soybeans, etc.) were crushed, washed in a petroleum solvent called hexane, then put through a complicated refining process that includes high heat. A residue of hexane remains, even though you won't find it listed on the label as an ingredient. The FDA deems this residue insignificant and harmless, but I prefer to avoid it.

Instead, I look for oils that are expeller pressed or, better yet, cold pressed. Expeller-pressed oils are extracted using a screw press; heat is also involved, caused by the friction produced by the tremendous pressure needed for extraction, though it is much less than the heat used in chemical extraction. The same process is used for cold pressing, which should take place in a temperature-controlled environment. Unfortunately the term is not regulated in this country, so it's hard to know how much it's worth. (In Europe, "cold-pressed" olive oil can't be heated above 80°F—barely warm— during extraction.)

Other terms to look for on labels to avoid chemically extracted oil are: unrefined, mechanically pressed, and organic. By law, neither hexane nor GMO products may be used in the extraction of oil labeled organic.

OILS, FATS, AND HEALTH

All oils contain a combination of monounsaturated, polyunsaturated, and saturated fats, in differing ratios. Olive oil, for example, is the best known for being high in monounsaturated fats; avocado and canola oil are also largely monounsaturated. Walnut oil and flaxseed oil contain a higher percentage of polyunsaturated fats, and coconut and palm oil are mostly saturated fat.

Both monounsaturated and polyunsaturated fats are viewed by the health community as being beneficial or "good" fats. Multiple studies have drawn correlations between diets high in monounsaturated fats (the Mediterranean diet) and a low rate of heart disease. Polyunsaturated fats (there are two types: omega-3 fatty acids and omega-6 fatty acids) are considered "essential" fats, meaning they are necessary for life function. Studies indicate that these two types of polyunsaturated fats can protect against heart disease and stroke, as well as provide other health benefits. However, in general, we Americans eat way more omega-6 than omega-3s—largely because omega-6 oils are used in most frying—and that's thought to be a problem. If this concerns you, avoid soy, corn, cottonseed, safflower, and sunflower oils, especially the chemically refined varieties.

Saturated fats (which are also found in cheese, whole-milk dairy products, and red meat) are controversial. For the longest time, they were thought to promote heart disease, but the most recent evidence is conflicted. I prefer using and eating saturated fats over highly processed vegetable oils (like soy or corn oil), but for the most part I use olive and peanut oils.

Trans fats, found in hydrogenated or partially hydrogenated fats (liquid fats that have been processed to be solid at room temperature, including most vegetable shortening and margarine) and in many highly processed foods, have been shown to increase bad cholesterol, reduce good cholesterol, and contribute to the onset of diabetes, stroke, and heart disease. Avoid them. This is becoming easier as regulations against using them become stronger and manufacturers become wiser. However, according to the FDA rule presently in effect, foods labeled "zero trans fat" may still contain less than 0.5 gram of trans fat per serving; this will continue to be the case until 2018 when the FDA's full ban on trans fats is supposed to go into effect.

OILS HIGH IN MONOUNSATURATED FAT

All of these oils contain a greater percentage of monounsaturated fat than polyunsaturated or saturated fat:

- Olive oil
- Avocado oil
- Canola oil
- Peanut oil

OILS HIGH IN POLYUNSATURATED FAT

These oils contain more polyunsaturated fat than monounsaturated or saturated fat:

- Sesame oil
- Walnut oil
- Corn oil
- Soybean oil
- Grapeseed oil
- Sunflower oil

OILS HIGH IN SATURATED FAT

These oils are more than 50 percent saturated fat:

- Coconut oil (more than 90 percent saturated fat)
- Palm oil

STORING OILS

Rancid oil tastes bad, and might even be bad for you. When oil starts to turn, it oxidizes, a process that converts some of its components into free radicals, which can cause cell damage when consumed. Since cold-pressed oils—which are the best oils—spoil fastest, you have to watch out for this.

But it's easy to keep oil fresh: Keep oil in a dark, cool place, preferably not in clear glass. If you buy large quantities, put a pint or so in a bottle and keep the rest in a dark place or, even better, in the refrigerator. If you do store your oil at room temperature, smell it after a month or 2 before using it. You'll know when it's rancid; if it is, toss it.

A Note About the Oils I Use in My Recipes

I use a variety of oils in cooking: extra virgin olive oil (inexpensive for sautéing, better for drizzling and salads); peanut oil (the best for stir-frying); toasted sesame oil for flavor. When I call for a "good-quality vegetable oil," use a neutral-flavored oil of your choosing, preferably, as I have argued for here, expeller or cold pressed.

SMOKE POINTS

If oil gets hot enough, it will smoke (this temperature is called its "smoke point") and if heated enough, will eventually catch fire. The smoke point can vary from 225° to 450°F, depending on the oil. Obviously you want to avoid starting a kitchen fire, but beyond that, oil heated to smoking has off flavors, loses its potential health benefits, and may even be higher in free radicals. When cooking with any oil, watch the pan carefully and adjust the heat as needed.

Knowing an oil's exact smoke point is helpful, but in reality few home cooks ever use a thermometer for anything other than deep-frying. Let your senses be your guide. Oil becomes more fragrant as it gets hot, and when it's ready for cooking the surface begins to ripple and shimmer. Tilt the pan a bit and you'll notice that the oil is thinner than it was straight from the bottle. Those are the signals that it's ready for cooking, and nearing its smoke point. Adding food automatically lowers the temperature of the oil, especially if your ingredients are cold.

Flavored Oil

MAKES: ½ cup
TIME: 20 minutes, plus time to cool
F M V

Flavored oils have three major uses: in vinaigrettes, in cooking, and as a last-minute drizzle. In each of these cases they will save you a step and a few moments, but since they take almost no time to prepare, in most cases you'll have the time to make one while you're cooking, so you don't need to sweat in advance.

It's almost impossible to use too much of the flavoring ingredients in this preparation, but if you do—if your oil becomes too strong—simply dilute it with a little fresh oil. You can certainly mix or match among the flavor options here, but remember that combinations—especially the more creative ones—will limit the range of the oil's usefulness and reduce the distinct impact of each flavor.

Be sure to rinse the leaves and dry them well before starting.

Possible Flavor Ingredients

- ¼ cup lightly packed fresh herb leaves, (like rosemary, thyme, bay leaf, tarragon, marjoram, or oregano)
- 2 cloves garlic, lightly crushed
- 1 inch fresh ginger, thinly sliced
- 2 tablespoons chopped shallots or scallions
- 2 tablespoons celery leaves
- 1 tablespoon black peppercorns, allspice berries, or whole cloves
- 4 star anise pods
- 2 dried chiles
- 1 nutmeg, broken into pieces (hit it with a hammer)

Pinch salt
½ cup extra virgin olive oil or good-quality vegetable oil

1. Stir the flavor ingredient or ingredients of your choosing, the salt, and oil together in a small saucepan and turn the heat to low. Warm gently until the mixture sizzles, then continue to cook until the oil is very fragrant, another minute or 2.

2. Cool, then strain into a clean bottle or other container. Refrigerate and use within a month or 2 at the most.

Vinaigrette

MAKES: About ¾ cup
TIME: 5 minutes

F M V

Try this experiment: Put vegetable oil and water together in a blender and turn it on. The mixture will turn white and creamy; add salt, pepper, and a few other flavorings; you now have something you can sell for $3 for 8 ounces, as long as you're a multinational food company. Because that's what most bottled dressing is: an emulsion of inferior oil (usually soy or "vegetable"), liquid (often water, with some vinegar), seasonings (often artificial, or at least far from fresh), and preservatives.

I emphasize this because I'm trying to convince you to make your own rather than buy bottled dressing. Do it in a blender or by shaking the ingredients in a jar, beating them with a fork or whisk, or with an immersion blender. It doesn't matter: It will be superior to *any* dressing you've ever bought in a bottle.

The standard ratio for a vinaigrette is three parts oil to one part vinegar, but many people prefer more oil; a ratio of four to one can be delicious. If you use a mild vinegar and strong-tasting olive oil, you may prefer two parts oil to one part vinegar or something even a little more acidic. Somewhere in that range, between four-to-one and one-to-one, you're going to find a home for your own taste. But that's the key: Taste your vinaigrette, then taste it some more. Eventually your palate will find a home it loves.

My everyday dressing almost always includes a bit of mustard (see the second variation), which helps emulsify the dressing while adding tang. I often add a bit of shallot and tarragon, but the options are endless, as you'll see when you get into the variations.

½ cup extra virgin olive oil
3 tablespoons good wine vinegar, or more to taste
Salt and pepper
1 tablespoon chopped shallot (optional)

Mustard Vinaigrette, left, and Real Ranch Dressing (page 672)

20 Simple Additions to Vinaigrette

1. **Any fresh herb:** For tender, milder herbs like parsley, basil, or dill, use as much as ¼ cup lightly packed leaves; add them with the shallot. For stronger, tougher herbs like rosemary, tarragon, or thyme, add 1 teaspoon chopped at the end, whizzing briefly just to combine.

2. **Any dried herb or spice:** Here it's harder to offer general guidelines, but start with as little as a pinch—⅛ teaspoon or so—and work your way up from there. Be careful not to blow away the vinaigrette; dried herbs and spices can be quite strong.

3. **Minced garlic:** Start with a small clove. For milder garlic flavor, let a crushed clove sit in the vinaigrette for a few minutes, then fish it out. Or wipe your salad bowl with a crushed garlic clove, then discard. Roasted Garlic (page 205) makes a terrific addition and emulsifies like crazy; because it's mild, you can use 5 cloves or more.

4. **Minced red onion, scallions, mild white onion, or white part of a leek:** Start with 1 tablespoon or so and substitute for the shallot.

5. **Honey, maple syrup, pomegranate molasses, or other sweeteners, within reason:** Don't use more than a tablespoon or so.

6. **Freshly grated Parmesan (or other hard cheese; see page 554) or crumbled blue cheese, feta, or goat cheese:** Anything from a tablespoon to ¼ cup will add flavor. Add after processing the shallot, giving the blender just a quick whiz to incorporate it.

7. **Sour cream, yogurt, or silken tofu:** A couple of tablespoons will add incredible creaminess to your vinaigrette. Whiz in at the end, just until creamy and fully incorporated.

8. **Prepared or freshly grated horseradish:** Use at least 1 teaspoon and add with the shallot.

9. **A tablespoon or 2 minced tomato (seeded and preferably skinned) or bits of reconstituted sun-dried tomato** added with the shallot.

10. **Roasted Vegetable Stock (page 99):** Add just a tablespoon or 2 along with the shallot.

11. **Minced nuts or seeds, especially peanuts, almonds, walnuts, hazelnuts, pecans, or pumpkin seeds:** A small handful will do it; add with the shallot.

12. **Avocado:** Blend in the flesh of 1 small or medium avocado along with the shallot.

13. **Poppy seeds:** 2 tablespoons is a wonderful addition to Lemon Vinaigrette in particular.

14. **Roasted and peeled bell pepper (see page 228):** One is usually enough; add with the shallot.

15. **Canned chipotle:** 1 chile is plenty, with just a tiny bit of its adobo, added along with the shallot.

16. **Soaked and softened sea greens, like arame, hijiki, or wakame:** ½ cup is about right; add with the shallot.

17. **Peach, pear, or apple:** Peel, seed, and cut 1 small one into chunks; add with the shallot.

18. **Dried fruit, like blueberries, cherries, raisins, apricots, pineapple, or mango:** Add up to ¼ cup with the shallot.

19. **Any pitted black or green olives:** ¼ cup or even more if you'd like, but be sure to add these before you salt the vinaigrette; add with the shallot.

20. **Flavored Oil (page 627):** Once you have one on hand, it's such a simple way to make a vibrant vinaigrette. Use for the oil (or, if it's very strong, use half flavored oil and half regular olive oil). Consider your flavorings when you choose the vinegar; some flavorings work with all sorts of vinegars, others might pair better with a more or less assertive vinegar. Part of the fun is experimenting.

1. Put the oil, vinegar, and a pinch each salt and pepper in a blender and turn the machine on; a creamy emulsion will form within 30 seconds. Taste and add more vinegar a teaspoon or 2 at a time until the balance tastes right to you.

2. Add the shallot if you're using it, and turn the machine on and off a few times until the shallot is minced within the dressing. Taste, adjust the seasoning, and serve. This is best made fresh but will keep, refrigerated, for a few days. (Bring it back to room temperature and whisk briefly before using.)

LEMON VINAIGRETTE Light, fresh tasting, and all purpose: Use ¼ cup or so fresh lemon juice for the acid and plenty of black pepper. A tablespoon of warm water will help the mixture emulsify. You can change this up by using other citrus juices like lime, orange, or grapefruit.

MUSTARD VINAIGRETTE Add 1 heaping teaspoon (or more) of any good prepared mustard to the blender. It doesn't have to be Dijon; whole grain is fine too. You can also use dry mustard; start with about ½ teaspoon.

SOY VINAIGRETTE One of my favorite quick dressings: Add 1 tablespoon soy sauce to the mix, along with sesame oil to taste (about 1 teaspoon). Lemon juice, lime juice, and vinegar are all just fine here.

GINGER VINAIGRETTE Use a mixture of 1 tablespoon each sherry vinegar, fresh lime juice, and lukewarm water for the liquid. Add a 1-inch piece fresh ginger, sliced, to the blender in Step 2 with the shallot, if using. Taste and adjust the seasoning, using plenty of black pepper.

SWEET BALSAMIC VINAIGRETTE Strong, sweet, and delicious (but no longer vegan): Use balsamic vinegar for the acid. Add about 1 clove garlic and 1 tablespoon honey.

COCONUT CURRY VINAIGRETTE Instead of olive oil, use coconut milk. Use rice vinegar or coconut vinegar for the acid. Blend in 1 tablespoon curry powder.

Ginger-Scallion Sauce

MAKES: About 1 cup
TIME: 15 minutes
F M V

The fresh, bright combination of ginger and scallions is the traditional and perfect accompaniment to Steamed Dumplings (page 356). It's also a fabulous addition to soups and, with a bit more oil, a convenient way to start a stir-fry. Finally (well, probably not finally—you'll think of other uses), it's terrific on top of plain, thin, Chinese-style egg noodles.

Pouring the hot oil over the scallion-ginger-garlic mixture releases their fabulous flavor. If chopping and mincing isn't your thing, just throw a big chunk of ginger and 3 or 4 scallions into the food processor, along with the garlic, and pulse until finely chopped but not puréed.

½	cup chopped scallions
¼	cup minced fresh ginger
1	clove garlic, minced
1	teaspoon salt, or more to taste
½	cup peanut or grapeseed oil

1. Stir the scallions, ginger, garlic, and salt together thoroughly in a heatproof bowl.

2. Put the oil in a small saucepan or skillet over high heat until almost smoking. Carefully pour the oil over the ginger-scallion mixture, and mix well. Serve, or cool, cover, and refrigerate for up to 3 days. Bring to room temperature before serving.

GARLIC-SCALLION SAUCE Less complex but more powerful: Omit the ginger and increase the minced garlic to ¼ cup.

CHILE-SCALLION SAUCE A little heat: Add 3 tablespoons (or to taste) of your favorite minced fresh chile. Reduce the ginger to 1 tablespoon or omit it entirely, and increase the garlic to 2 large cloves.

THE BASICS OF VINEGARS

Vinegar, with its savory tartness, plays an essential supporting role in dozens of recipes in this chapter. Here you'll find two recipes, Balsamic Syrup (page 633) and Worcestershire Sauce, Hold the Anchovies (opposite), in which vinegar is the main player. (And of course there's Vinaigrette, page 628.)

I urge you to keep at least a couple of vinegars on hand; they are valuable additions—beyond their use in dressings—to many kinds of cooked dishes, as well as in pickling (see the recipes on pages 89 to 94) and marinades.

I think sherry vinegar is the best value in vinegar these days; that's why you'll find it at the top of the list. The rest are listed in order of a combination of personal preference and availability. Near the bottom are vinegars that are interesting and good but have limited uses; they may be hard to find but are still of interest and worth picking up if you come across them or order them online.

SHERRY VINEGAR The best and most flavorful vinegar for the money (the bottle must say Vinagre de Jerez for it to be genuine). Very acidic (8 percent), so start by using less than of other vinegars.

RICE VINEGAR A must-have in Asian cooking but also welcome in vinaigrettes. Check the ingredients—you don't want "seasoned" rice vinegar. Its acidity is among the lowest of the vinegars, 4.5 percent.

BALSAMIC VINEGAR Most is distilled vinegar flavored with caramel syrup, but even that may have a pleasant taste, and is fine in salads and perfect for Balsamic Syrup (page 633). Aceto Balsamico Tradizionale di Modena— real balsamic vinegar—is expensive, and arguably worth it. Look for one made from wine vinegar and aged at least a little while—10 years is not uncommon—in wood barrels.

CHINESE BLACK VINEGAR Made from glutinous rice, with a delicious, almost haunting flavor. Look for one with a short list of ingredients and the word Chinkiang (or something similar) on the label; that's the province in which it's traditionally made. Add it to fried rice (page 380) or use it on its own as a dipping sauce or to make Worcestershire Sauce, Hold the Anchovies (opposite).

CIDER VINEGAR Real cider vinegar can have a distinctively fruity flavor, and good ones are now easier to find than good wine vinegars. Look for a good domestic variety.

PLUM/UMEBOSHI VINEGAR The rather salty, slightly fruity flavor of this Japanese vinegar can be addictive. It's made from umeboshi, dried and pickled stone fruit similar to plums. Use as a dipping sauce for cold soba noodles (page 338).

RED WINE VINEGAR Unless you're going to spend the money ($8 to $30) for a good one, sherry vinegar is a better bet.

WHITE WINE VINEGAR/CHAMPAGNE VINEGAR Like white wine, white wine vinegar can be dull or delightful. Real Champagne vinegar is among the best, but in general, these are disappointing—buy neither the cheapest nor most expensive.

MALT VINEGAR Made from malted grain, this tastes malty, with a slight lemon aroma and flavor. Get real brewed malt vinegar, not a "nonbrewed condiment," which is nothing more than water, acetic acid, and coloring. Delicious splashed onto fried or roasted foods.

CANE VINEGAR Ranges in color from golden to deep brown. An all-purpose vinegar with a slightly syrupy taste.

COCONUT VINEGAR Has a cloudy white color with a tangy bite; works best in Southeast Asian–style dishes.

Balsamic Syrup

MAKES: ¼ cup
TIME: About 20 minutes
F **M** **V**

Inexpensive balsamic vinegar is both sweet (it usually contains sugar) and sour, so it naturally goes well with both savory and sweet foods. And this simple reduction, which begins with inexpensive balsamic vinegar, is a nice substitute for the high-priced stuff. Just be sure to start with a clean-tasting balsamic vinegar, because reducing it will concentrate both good and bad aspects.

1 cup balsamic vinegar

Put the vinegar in a small nonreactive pan over medium-low heat. Bring to a boil, then immediately lower the heat so it bubbles gently. Reduce at a low simmer to ¼ cup, about 20 minutes; it should be thickened and syrupy. It will thicken a little more as it cools. Serve warm or let cool, then store in an airtight container indefinitely.

8 Great Additions to Balsamic Syrup

For more flavor, slip any of the following ingredients into the pan while the vinegar is reducing. When you're done, strain the syrup or fish out the solids with a slotted spoon.

1. Raw or Roasted Garlic (page 205), to taste
2. ½ cup Caramelized Onions or shallots (page 222)
3. Herbs: a sprig of the stronger ones like rosemary, tarragon, or thyme; a few sprigs of the milder ones like parsley, mint, or basil
4. ¼ cup fresh, fruity red wine

7 Things to Drizzle with Balsamic Syrup

1. Basic Green Salad (page 36)

2. Roasted or grilled veggies, especially roasted red peppers (see page 228) with toasted pine nuts

3. Grilled, roasted, or broiled fruit, especially figs, peaches, or nectarines

4. A slice of aged goat cheese, blue cheese, Parmesan, or manchego or a dollop of mascarpone

5. Fresh strawberries

6. Cubes of watermelon

7. Vanilla ice cream or fruit sorbets, especially raspberry or strawberry

5. ½ cup chopped fruit or berries like raspberries, apples, figs, strawberries, blackberries, pears, grapes, or cherries
6. ⅓ cup chopped dried fruits like dates, apricots, pears, cherries, strawberries, or figs
7. 2 tablespoons molasses (or pomegranate molasses), maple syrup, or honey
8. ½ cup fresh orange juice

Worcestershire Sauce, Hold the Anchovies

MAKES: About 1½ cups
TIME: 30 minutes
F **M** **V**

Having a vegan Worcestershire sauce in the fridge enlivens everything from Vegetarian Caesar Dressing (page 672) to meatless "meat" balls (see page 506) to Seitan (page 508). The combination of ingredients may seem wacky, but if you've ever read the label on the real stuff, you'll see where I'm coming from. Tamarind paste is important to get the precise Lea & Perrins flavor and color, but apricot preserves make a fine alternative.

1½ cups Chinese black vinegar
   2 tablespoons crumbled or ground dulse or
     chopped rehydrated kombu (see page 244)
   2 tablespoons brown sugar
   2 teaspoons tamarind paste or apricot preserves
   1 teaspoon black peppercorns
   1 teaspoon whole cloves
   ½ teaspoon red chile flakes, or more to taste
   1 tablespoon soy sauce
   1 tablespoon molasses
   1 1-inch piece real black licorice (optional)

1. Put the vinegar, dulse, brown sugar, tamarind paste, peppercorns, cloves, and chile flakes in a small nonreactive saucepan over medium-high heat. Bring it to a boil, stirring once or twice.

2. Once the mixture starts boiling, immediately take it off the heat and add the soy sauce, molasses, and licorice if you're using it. Set aside to steep until completely cool, 20 to 25 minutes. Strain into a glass jar or bottle with a tight-fitting lid and refrigerate for up to 6 months.

THE BASICS OF HERBS

Herbs, both fresh and dried, are essential to cooking; if you have fresh herbs on hand, you'll use them, and appreciate them. (Few dried herbs are worth keeping around, with oregano, marjoram, thyme, rosemary, and tarragon the notable exceptions.) Because of their distinctive flavors, no herb is a direct substitute for any other. There are many situations, however, in which you're not necessarily looking for a distinct flavor but rather a certain freshness that an herb will provide. In these cases, of course, you can substitute parsley for basil, or cilantro for mint, and so on. Just don't expect the end result to taste the same.

STORING HERBS

Fresh herbs keep best when stored in the refrigerator. For most, wrap them in damp paper towels and slip them into a plastic bag. For those with fragile leaves, like basil, chervil, dill, mint, or parsley, set them stem down in a jar of water with a plastic bag over the leaves, and change the water every couple of days. They'll keep a few days or longer if they were very fresh to begin with.

Store dried herbs in tightly sealed jars, away from sunlight, for up to a year, but after six months or so, taste them before using to make sure they haven't gotten musty.

Pesto

MAKES: About 1 cup
TIME: 10 minutes
F M

The best pesto is made with a mortar and pestle, and in Genoa, where pesto originated, few people will admit to using a food processor. But when you get into their kitchens, that's just what they do. And so do I.

Don't add the Parmesan until you're ready to use the pesto. And to help retain its bright green color, drizzle a layer of olive oil over the top once you've put the pesto in a container. Herb pastes made with less oil do not keep as well, so eat them sooner rather than later. If you have a garden filled with basil, by all means make as much pesto as you can and throw it into the freezer. But if you're using store-bought basil, unless it's incredibly cheap you might as well just make pesto in the quantities given here and enjoy it fresh.

Although it is not traditional, you can substitute parsley or any other tender-leafed herb for all of some of the basil, with fine but distinctively different results.

   2 lightly packed cups fresh basil leaves
     Salt
   ½ clove garlic, or more to taste
   2 tablespoons pine nuts or walnuts
   ½ cup extra virgin olive oil, or more as needed,
     plus extra for topping for storage
   ½ cup freshly grated Parmesan, pecorino Romano,
     or other hard cheese

(continued on page 638)

The Herb Lexicon

HERB	DESCRIPTION	USES
Basil	The most familiar varieties, like Genovese, have flavors of licorice and cloves; Thai and holy basil are peppery and more minty.	Best raw or cooked only briefly. Use the leaves whole or tear them; chop if you don't mind the leaves turning black. The flowers are edible and great thrown into salads.
Bay leaves Sweet bay Sweet laurel Bay laurel	Glossy, green, and leathery when fresh; grayed and brittle when dried. Fresh are much stronger than dried; whole dried leaves are far better than ground. Turkish are superior to Californian.	In stocks, soups, sauces, poaching liquids, to flavor vinegars. Throw a few leaves in the next time you're roasting vegetables. Remove them from the dish before serving.
Chervil	Looks like parsley, with lacy leaves and an anise flavor. Fresh only; dried is useless.	Best used raw or tossed in at the end of cooking. Delicious in omelets, sauces, salads, and with vegetables.
Chives	Bright green, hollow, and grass-like, with a mild onion flavor. Garlic chives have a more garlicky taste, but aren't as common.	Best raw or cooked only briefly. An assertive addition to soft cheese spreads and compound butter.
Cilantro Fresh coriander Chinese parsley Mexican parsley	Tender and parsley-like in appearance, but distinctive (some say soapy) in aroma and flavor. Only fresh is desirable; dried is useless. (The seeds are considered a spice; see "Coriander," page 643.)	Best added at the last minute. Associated with the flavors of Mexican, Thai, and Indian cooking. Use the roots in stews or other long-cooked dishes.
Dill Dill weed	Stalks with blue-green, feathery, tender leaves. Fresh is superior to dried, which has less flavor but at least retains the character of the fresh leaves. Dill seeds are often included in pickling spice mixes.	Use at the end of cooking, as its flavor is diminished by hot temperatures (though tying stems in a bundle and cooking with stews gives a nice flavor). Tasty in dishes made with sour cream, yogurt, or mustard, or tossed into a green salad.
Epazote	Bright green, jagged, and pointed leaves, usually sold in bunches when fresh. Its aroma is unusual, its taste powerful, so use it carefully. Fresh is better, but dried is more common in this country. Sold in Mexican and Latin American markets.	Use chopped or whole fresh or dried leaves in small quantities; 1 tablespoon fresh or 1 teaspoon dried is sufficient for most recipes serving 4 to 6 people. Traditionally used with beans, and some moles; also good with corn and other summer vegetables, in quesadillas, and in scrambled eggs.

HERB	DESCRIPTION	USES
Lavender	Narrow gray-green leaves with long purple or pink flower spikes; only the flower buds are commonly available dried. The scent and flavor are minty and floral.	Use sparingly; it's strong and can be bitter. Mince fresh leaves and flowers and toss into salads and fruit dishes or add to sauces, candies, and pastries.
Lemongrass Citronella root Sereh	A stiff, narrow stalk with a strong citrus flavor and aroma—think citronella candles. Best fresh; dried is acceptable. The powdered form, called sereh, is not as good. Sold in supermarkets and Asian markets.	Cut off woody tops and peel away tough outer layers; mince or pound the tender inner pieces to release their flavor and aroma. Soak dried lemongrass in hot water for at least 30 minutes before using.
Lime leaves Makrut lime leaves	Tough, shiny green leaves that often look like two conjoined leaves. Very aromatic, with unusually floral and limey flavor. Fresh is best, but dried is good. Sold in most Asian markets.	Used in Southeast Asian dishes of all types. Mince or toss in whole leaves during cooking; use double the amount of dried leaves for fresh. Or use 1 teaspoon grated lime zest for each leaf called for.
Marjoram	Light green, fuzzy, oval leaves. Often confused and interchangeable with oregano, but superior. Dried isn't too bad, though it's far more pungent than fresh.	Add fresh toward the end of cooking; crumble dried leaves. Wonderful with green salads, vinaigrettes, eggs, beans, all sorts of vegetables, and tomato sauces.
Mint	Bright green, wrinkled leaves (spearmint), or smooth ones (peppermint and other varieties). Best fresh; dried is decent, at least in savory dishes.	Fresh leaves should be chopped or crushed to release their flavor. Traditional with peas or potatoes, goes well with many vegetables and fruits; perfect in yogurt-based sauces, as well as in chutneys and many Southeast Asian dishes. Ideal for herbal teas and cocktails.
Oregano Greek oregano Wild marjoram	Dark green, fuzzy, spade-shaped leaves. Stronger and spicier than marjoram, especially Mexican oregano. Dried is especially pungent. Fresh is infinitely better, but dried is acceptable.	Fresh and dried can be cooked or used as a garnish in small amounts. Good with tomatoes, cheeses, pizza, vegetables, beans, and vinaigrettes.

HERB	DESCRIPTION	USES
Parsley	Dark leaves with fresh flavor. Dried is not worth buying. There are two varieties: curly and flat-leaf (Italian) parsley; the latter is somewhat better, but it's not worth making a big deal about.	Inexpensive and versatile, used in just about everything: soups, salads, vinaigrettes, sauces, vegetables, eggs, pasta, and as a garnish. Especially valuable in winter for its freshness.
Rosemary	Grayish-green needles on woody branches, with crisp, piney aroma and flavor. Dried leaves are also flavorful.	Wonderful with beans, most vegetables, egg dishes, pasta, and breads. The woody branches make perfect skewers for broiling or grilling.
Sage	Soft, woolly, oval-shaped grayish-green or multicolored leaves. Sharply flavored, slightly bitter, and very aromatic. Fresh leaves are best; dried are stronger and somewhat mustier, but not bad.	Use fresh leaves whole or chopped. Crumble dried leaves. Wonderful with beans, stuffings, breads, biscuits, and pasta.
Shiso Perilla Japanese basil or mint Beefsteak plant	Flat, bright green or reddish purple leaves with a jagged edge. Combination of basil, mint, and cinnamon flavors. Dried is less flavorful but somewhat useful. Sold in many Asian (especially Japanese) and some Mexican markets.	Use as you would use basil or mint. Traditionally served with sashimi and sushi, as well as with cucumbers, pickles, tempura; in salads, soups; when dried, sprinkled over rice.
Tarragon	Narrow, lance-shaped, bright to dark green leaves, with strong, complex flavor and aroma, faintly licoricelike. Fresh is always best; dried is less flavorful but usable.	Whole or minced fresh leaves can be cooked; flavor is not at all tamed by heat, so use it sparingly. Crumble dried tarragon to release essential oils.
Thyme	Tiny green or gray-green leaves that can be minty, lemony, or earthy, depending on the variety. Fresh is more pungent and aromatic than dried, though dried thyme is useful.	The classic French cooking herb, often used in long-simmering or braising recipes. Use fresh leaves and tips as a garnish, but very sparingly—thyme's strong flavor easily overwhelms everything else. Perfect teamed with olive oil and garlic at the beginning of many sautés.

(*continued from page 634*)

1. Put the basil with a pinch salt, the garlic, nuts, and about half the oil in a food processor or blender. Process, stopping to scrape down the side of the container if necessary and adding the rest of the oil gradually.

2. Add more oil if you prefer a thinner mixture. Serve or transfer to an airtight container and top with a thin layer of olive oil. Store in the refrigerator for a week or 2 or in the freezer for several months. Stir in the Parmesan by hand just before serving.

MINT OR DILL "PESTO" Try it on pasta or grilled vegetables: Substitute mint or dill for the basil; the garlic is optional. Use a good-quality vegetable oil and omit the cheese. Finish, if you'd like, with a squeeze of lemon juice. Use within a day. **V**

ARUGULA "PESTO" Terrific with grilled vegetables or plain rice: Substitute arugula (tough stems removed) for the basil. Omit the cheese. Use within a day. **V**

Parsley "Pesto"

MAKES: About 1 cup
TIME: 10 minutes
F **M** **V**

Simpler, purer, less complex than traditional pesto, parsley purée is—to me at least—even more useful. For one thing, you can find decent parsley year-round. For another, it's a brighter, fresher purée and therefore less specific in its uses. And, as you can see from the variations, different herbs work equally well.

> 2   **cups lightly packed fresh parsley leaves (thin stems are okay)**
>   **Salt**
> ½   **clove garlic, or more to taste**
> ½   **cup extra virgin olive oil, or more as needed**
> 1   **tablespoon sherry vinegar or fresh lemon juice**

1. Put the parsley with a pinch salt, the garlic, and about half the oil in a food processor or blender. Process,

stopping to scrape down the side of the container if necessary, and adding the rest of the oil gradually.

2. Add the vinegar, then a little more oil or some water if you prefer a thinner mixture. Taste and adjust the seasoning. Serve or cover and refrigerate for up to a couple of days.

CILANTRO PURÉE, DILL PURÉE, BASIL PURÉE, OR MINT PURÉE These are good; they're especially great with grilled vegetables: Substitute any of these herbs (leaves only or very thin stems too) for the parsley.

CHIMICHURRI Very strong: Use 3 or more cloves garlic, 2 tablespoons vinegar or lemon juice, and at least 1 teaspoon red chile flakes. Do not refrigerate.

GREEN OLIVE MOJO Intense: Reduce the olive oil to ¼ cup; use ¼ cup fresh lime juice, or to taste, in place of the vinegar. After puréeing, use the food processor to pulse in 1 cup pitted green olives; or chop the olives by hand and add them. In any case, do not purée them.

THE BASICS OF SALT AND SPICES

Along with herbs, fresh and dried, salt and spices (which include black pepper) are indispensable for adding flavor or enhancing flavor in almost any dish you can think of.

SALT

Salt is basically sodium chloride. But it's not as simple as that. Though all salts are created naturally—in the rock and seas of the earth—they are not created equal. Common table salt is mined, milled, refined, and sometimes "enhanced" with iodine and other ingredients into small, free-flowing grains that dissolve faster than most other salts. But consistency has a downside: the flavor of table salt is harsh, with iodine the predominant mineral taste. Kosher salt, a relatively inexpensive alternative,

Parsley "Pesto"

has a clean, slightly minerally taste, and is my go-to salt for most everything.

Then there is sea salt, which contains subtler flavors (usually described as "briny," "metallic," or "earthy"), from the famous fleur de sel from Brittany in France and Maldon from England to literally thousands of kinds made all over the world, most locally. (And then there are the absurdly expensive boutique salts, which should send you running in the other direction.) Generally, in salt, the more trace minerals (mostly magnesium, calcium, and potassium) there are, the less sodium chloride there is, which is why many sea salts taste less "salty" than table and kosher salt. It's worth a quick side-by-side taste test to see which salts you prefer; if you doubt you can tell the difference, you'll probably be surprised.

SALT IN MY RECIPES

Because the quantity of salt in food is largely a matter of personal taste, my recipes almost always call for simply "salt" in the ingredient list. This frees you to use whichever salt you like best, in whichever quantity you enjoy. But I don't totally leave you in the dark. The instructions suggest when to season with salt—usually more than once during the process and definitely at the end —and give you an idea how much to add with words like "pinch" or "sprinkle."

I do specify exact measurements in rare dishes where a precise amount of salt really makes a difference.

SPICES

The average American eats more than 3 pounds of

Grinding Salt

Some very coarse salts require additional grinding. Use a salt mill designed for this purpose or crush small amounts with a mortar and pestle. The idea is to avoid metal parts, which will corrode and rust.

spices a year, twice as much as twenty years ago, with significant upticks in the purchase of once-exotic spices like paprika, anise, cumin, fennel, turmeric, and dried and ground chiles (see pages 226 to 227 for more on chiles). And I'm glad to say, there's no end in sight.

BUYING, TOASTING, GRINDING, AND STORING SPICES

I suggest you buy spices from somewhere that either specializes in them or sells them in bulk, where they'll be cheaper and fresher. That generally means Asian, Indian, or Latin markets, gourmet shops, or online.

Whole spices have huge advantages over preground: They tend to be of higher quality to begin with. They keep much better. You can toast them at the last minute, which helps bring out their flavor. And the last-minute grinding means you get all that flavor; it doesn't dry out over the course of months (or, if you're like most of us, years) of storage.

Having said that, we have to acknowledge that almost everyone uses preground spices; they're just too convenient not to. Still, I'd say toast and grind whole spices when you can. Even if "when you can" means every fifth time, even if it means every tenth time, it's worth it.

When I can, I toast whole spices just before grinding, or when they're used as a finishing seasoning. Gentle warming activates and releases their oils and makes the spices aromatic. If your spices are big, like cinnamon sticks or nutmeg, break them up or crush into pieces in whatever way you need to—with your fingers, the back of a knife, a hammer, the bottom of a pan, whatever. If they're encased in pods, like cardamom, lightly crush the pods and remove the seeds; discard the husks.

Set a dry skillet over medium-high heat. Add the spices and cook, swirling the pan or stirring constantly with a wooden spoon, for just a minute or 2; you'll know when they're ready because their aroma will become far more pronounced. Remove them from the pan immediately, because the spices will easily burn and turn bitter. If they do, toss them out and start again.

(continued on page 648)

Clockwise from top left:
Za'atar (page 652), Fragrant Curry
Powder (page 649), Nori "Shake"
(page 650), Japanese Seven-Spice Mix
(page 650), Citrus Sprinkle (page 651)

The Spice Lexicon

SPICE	DESCRIPTION	USES
Allspice Pimento	Berries that come from the aromatic evergreen pimento tree. They look like large reddish brown peppercorns, smell a bit like a combination of cloves and nutmeg, and taste slightly peppery. Jamaican allspice is the best. Available as whole berries and ground.	By the pinch; a little goes a long way. Delicious with grains like bulgur, couscous, rice, and with polenta and vegetables like beets, carrots, parsnips, winter squash, and sweet potatoes. Good in mulled wines or sprinkled into tomato or cranberry juice.
Anise seeds Aniseed	Tiny, crescent-shaped, greenish-brown seeds from the anise plant, with a sweet licorice flavor. Star anise or fennel can usually fill in for these and vice versa. Available whole or ground.	Common in desserts, anise also works well in savory dishes that include apples, cucumbers, carrots, turnips, or cabbage, and in fruit salads, pickles, stuffings, and sauerkraut.
Annatto Achiote	The triangular, brick-colored seeds of the annatto tree smell earthy or musky and taste slightly peppery, but their flavor is subtle. Traditionally used in Latin American dishes. Available whole, ground, or, less frequently, as a prepared paste.	The seeds are too hard to crush easily and must be soaked for 10 minutes in boiling water first. Once cool and drained, grind them with a mortar and pestle or in a spice mill. Whole seeds are used to color and flavor oil as a first step in cooking dishes; be sure to fish them out before adding the other ingredients.
Asafetida Hing	Made from the dried sap exuded from the stem of giant fennel. The lumps are a waxy brownish black, and the powder is a beige color. Its high-sulfur odor is transformed into a haunting aroma and flavor a bit like onion. Available in lumps or ground. The powder is easier to use, but it's generally less pure, so go for the lump form if possible. Asafetida doesn't have its characteristic odor until it is ground.	Indian cuisine primarily, especially vegetables, beans, potatoes, and in chutney, pickles, and sauces, usually in spice mixtures. Very potent, so use only by the pinch. Try adding a tiny amount to plain boiled rice. To minimize the smell, double-pack powdered asafetida in a jar inside another jar, or it will stink up your pantry. A lump will keep indefinitely and should be pulverized just before use.
Caraway	Slender, ridged, whole brown seeds from a parsley-related plant; its flavor is reminiscent of both anise and cumin.	Traditionally used in rye bread, caraway is delicious in cabbage and potato dishes and hearty soups and stews.
Cardamom	Whole pods may be green, brown-black, or whitish. Each contains about 10 brown-black seeds, which are slightly sticky. Cardamom has a rich spicy scent, a bit like ginger mixed with pine and lemon. You may find whole pods, or "hulled," meaning the seeds. Ground cardamom is the most commonly sold form, but also the least potent. I buy whole pods (mostly white).	A staple in Indian and some Middle Eastern cooking. Sometimes pods are cooked whole, especially in braised dishes. Otherwise, crush the pods with the flat side of a knife, remove the seeds, and grind or crush as required. Often combined with other spices, as in curry powder and garam masala. Also used (especially in Scandinavia) in cakes, pastries, and sweets.

SPICE	DESCRIPTION	USES
Celery seeds	Tiny tan-colored seeds, usually from lovage, a relative of celery that has an intense celery flavor.	A little goes a long way. Use in pickling brines, cheese spreads, and salad dressings, or baked into breads and biscuits.
Cinnamon Canela, Ceylon or Sri Lanka cinnamon	The aromatic bark of a tropical laurel tree. Cassia—cinnamon's less expensive cousin—is often sold as cinnamon; it's the bark from a laurel tree native to China. The bark dries into long, slender, curled sticks that are a reddish-light brown color. Ground cinnamon is useful, though it's easy enough to grind sticks. Cassia is redder; its flavor is more biting and bitter, making it better suited to savory dishes than sweet ones.	Use whole cinnamon sticks or pieces of cassia in soups, stews, chilis, and curries or add to rice or other grains. True cinnamon is excellent in pastries, as well as in rice pudding and French toast. Delicious paired with apples, and in mulled cider and cold fruit soups.
Cloves	The unripe flower buds of a tree native to the islands of Southeast Asia. Pink when picked, they are dried to a reddish brown color, separated from their husks, and dried again. Whole cloves should be dark brown, oily, and fat, not shriveled. They have a sweet, warm aroma and a piercing flavor. Both whole and ground forms are common, and both are useful.	Use cloves sparingly—the flavor can be overwhelming—and try to remove whole cloves before serving. To make this easier, you can stud an onion with cloves and then remove the onion; or wrap them in cheesecloth. Ground cloves—just a pinch, usually—are good in spice blends, batters and doughs, fruit pie fillings, and stewed fruit.
Coriander	Seeds of the cilantro plant, they are small, round, and vary in color from pale green when fresh to light or dark brown when dried. The lemony flavor is somewhat like cilantro leaves, but the overall taste is much more complex, with hints of cumin, fennel, and even cloves. Both whole seeds and ground are common.	Coriander seeds can be cooked whole into dishes (and are quite pleasant to eat) or ground first; if you're grinding, consider toasting first for a bit more flavor. Often used in conjunction with other spices, especially cumin and cardamom. Used in Asian- and Latin American–style stews, soups, and some breads and pastries.
Cumin	The highly aromatic seeds of the cumin plant, a relative of parsley. Because they look similar, brown cumin and caraway are often confused, though they taste nothing alike. If you find cumin bitter, seek out the black seeds, which are more peppery and sweet. Whole seeds and ground are available in brown (the most common), black, and white varieties. Black and white cumin can usually be found in Indian markets.	Lightly toasting the seeds before use enhances their flavor. Like coriander, frequently included in spice mixtures like garam masala and chili powder. Also used solo a great deal in Latin American and Middle Eastern cooking.

The Spice Lexicon *(cont.)*

SPICE	DESCRIPTION	USES
Dill	Seeds are light brown, oval, and flat. They have a stronger taste than the fresh or dried herb. Seeds and leaves are both common, though the leaves are considered an herb (see page 635).	Often used whole, though occasionally ground. Excellent with cucumbers, radishes, potatoes, and sauces made with sour cream, yogurt, or mustard. Also featured in pickling spice.
Fennel seeds	From bulbless fennel, these seeds are small, pale greenish-brown ovals with tiny ridges and an aromatic, warm, sweet taste reminiscent of licorice. Not as strong as anise. Whole seeds are most common but also available ground.	Delicious in salad dressings, yogurt sauces; used in Indian dishes, as well as many pilafs; one of the five ingredients in five-spice powder and some curry powders. A popular flavor in Italy and southern France. When ground, fennel seeds make an interesting addition to spice cookies, shortbread, and quick breads.
Fenugreek seeds Methi	The distinctive rectangular seeds are small, brownish yellow, and very hard. They have a pungent, almost acrid aroma and an earthy, somewhat bitter taste that is found in many Indian dishes. Available whole and ground.	Fenugreek is used mainly in the cuisines of India and northern Africa, in chutneys, dals (lentils), and curries. Goes especially well with eggplant and potatoes. An essential ingredient in many curry powders, giving them their distinctive aroma.
Ginger	Ground dried ginger (see page 206 for more on fresh ginger) is yellowish tan and has the distinctive aroma of ginger. Crystallized (candied) ginger is delicious out of hand and can also be used in cooking.	Ground ginger is often used in sweets like cakes, cookies, quick breads.
Juniper berries	The berry-like seed cones from the evergreen juniper tree; the size of dried peas, blue-black in color. They taste like a mix of pine, fruit, and lemon peel; the dominant flavor in gin.	Juniper berries are very pungent, so use in moderation. Toasting them briefly in a dry skillet will bring out their aroma, and crushing releases their flavor. Can also use them whole, in a cheesecloth bag or tea ball, removing them before serving. A classic flavoring for stuffings, sauerkraut, sauces, and pickling.
Mace	Mace is the hard, lacy coating—or aril—that covers the nutmeg kernel. When the fruit first opens, mace is bright red. After drying and pressing, it becomes yellow-brown. Its flavor is very similar to that of nutmeg, though more bitter. Usually available ground; called "blades" when whole.	Add ground mace to savory dishes toward the end of cooking for best flavor. Whole blades can be used as is in soups or stews, then removed before eating. Commonly used ground in cakes and other sweets, traditional in doughnuts and pumpkin pie. Nutmeg is almost always an acceptable substitute.

SPICE	DESCRIPTION	USES
Nutmeg	Nutmeg is the kernel inside the seed of the fruit of a tropical evergreen tree; it's dark brown and about 1 inch long. It is sometimes a whitish color, the result of being dusted with lime to discourage insects; wash this off before grating or grinding. Available whole or ground; since the whole nutmeg keeps nearly forever and is easily grated, there's no reason to buy ground.	Nutmeg is very strong, so use sparingly, by grating it; put the unused portion back in the jar or bag. Lovely with fruit dishes, custards, cakes and other sweets, as well as vegetables, especially spinach. Also works well with cream and cheese sauces for pasta. Used in many spice mixtures, including jerk seasoning and some curry powders.
Paprika Pimentón	Light red-orange powder with a spicy-sweet aroma; if it's brown, it's too old. Varies in heat from mild (sweet) to hot. The best paprika comes from Spain (pimentón is smoked paprika, and really good) or Hungary (Szegedi is a good word to look for). California paprika is usually quite mild and not as good.	Use as you would any ground dried chile (that's what it is). Delicious with grains, eggs, cheese, and many vegetables and in soups, stews, sauces, rice, and potato dishes. You can substitute a ground mild chile like ancho for paprika with no problem.
Pepper	Peppercorns are the fruit of a vine native to India but now also grown in Indonesia, Malaysia, Vietnam, and elsewhere. They are harvested ripe as they begin to mature from green to red or yellow-green fruit. After curing in the sun, they shrivel and turn black. Black pepper has a range of flavors from citrusy to woodsy to piney, depending on where it is grown, along with pungent heat. For white peppercorns, the fruit are skinned before drying, while the just-ripe green peppercorns are freeze-dried or preserved in brine. True red, fully mature peppercorns are not widely available. Available whole, cracked, and ground.	White pepper is milder than black and perfect for everything from cream sauces to fruit desserts, anytime you're looking for pepper flavor with a little less punch or want to avoid dark specks. I prefer green peppercorns packed in brine. Refrigerate brined green peppercorns after opening. Don't bother with freeze-dried unless they are very high quality and you plan on reconstituting them in hot water like dried mushrooms. Ground, I don't think you'll notice much difference from black pepper.
Poppy seeds	Poppy seeds come from the same plant as opium but contain no traces of the drug. The teeny seeds, the size of a pinhead, come from inside the flower's pods. Poppy seeds add a nutty flavor and subtle crunch to foods. Available whole or crushed into a paste; black is the most common variety, though there are also white poppy seeds.	More like a seasoning than a nut or seed. For a nuttier flavor, lightly toast them, carefully so they don't burn. Used in Europe and the Middle East in sweets and baked goods. Good in salad dressings, fruit salads, and with Eastern European–style noodle dishes. In India, poppy seeds are toasted, ground, and used to flavor and thicken curries. The paste is used as a filling for strudel-type pastries and in other baked goods.

The Spice Lexicon (*cont.*)

SPICE	DESCRIPTION	USES
Saffron	Very expensive but worth having around. Really. Threads should be strong, long, and a brilliant orange-red color. Highly aromatic, warm, and spicy, with a slightly bitter taste; gives food a distinctive yellow color and exotic, wonderful flavor. To approximate its color use annatto or turmeric, but nothing tastes like saffron or has the same glow. Buy only threads; ground is useless.	Use sparingly—a good pinch is about right; too much can give food a medicinal taste. Add threads directly to the dish or steep in some of the cooking liquid or oil or a bit of boiling water for a few minutes first. Used in many traditional breads and cakes, as well as in rice, pasta, and cheese dishes.
Sichuan peppercorns Chinese peppercorns, Sansho	The seed pod of a small tree native to China. Flavor is unique, and essential to Sichuan cooking: a flowery, slightly smoky aroma combined with a somewhat lemony medicinal flavor and a tongue-numbing, unhot "spiciness" that feels almost like local anesthesia. (This is how Sichuan food can contain so many chiles without being overwhelmingly hot.) Available whole or infused in oil.	One of the spices in five-spice powder. When used alone, generally added at the end of cooking. Used in Chinese, Indonesia, Tibetan, and Korean cooking.
Star anise	The fruit of an evergreen tree native to China; the pod is a dark brown, eight-pointed star, about 1 inch in diameter, with seeds in each point—perhaps the strangest-looking spice you'll ever buy, and quite lovely. Although it has a licorice-like flavor, it is botanically unrelated to anise. Available whole.	Both pod and seeds are used. Whole pods make an attractive garnish. If less than a whole star is required, break the pod into individual points. Wrap the points in cheesecloth and remove before serving. Use in soups, marinades, and spice mixtures; part of five-spice powder.
Sumac	The dried fruit of a type of sumac; used as a souring agent, much like lemon, in Middle Eastern cooking. The brick-red (though sometimes deep purple) berries also lend a bit of color. Available as dried whole berries or ground, which is more common.	To use whole, crack them and soak in water for 15 to 20 minutes, then wrap in cheesecloth and squeeze to extract the juice, which can be used much like lemon juice. Powder is usually added during the last few minutes of cooking for the best flavor or as a last-minute sprinkle. Used with grilled items, on salads, or in dips like hummus or baba ghanoush. Mixed with thyme and toasted sesame seeds in the spice mix za'atar.

SPICE	DESCRIPTION	USES
Turmeric Indian saffron	A rhizome like ginger, but darker skinned, with thin fingers; flesh is bright orange-red and difficult to grind. Available ground (most common), in dried pieces, or occasionally fresh.	Turmeric is most frequently used ground dried in spice blends, but if you see some fresh, try mincing it into pickles. Typical in Indian vegetarian cooking, where its deep flavor is welcome in dal and curries; also good with rice and other grain dishes like couscous. It has gained great popularity over the past five years largely for its touted health benefits and can be added to juice drinks and smoothies.
Vanilla bean	The dried seed pod of an orchid native to the tropical forests of Central and South America, vanilla is also grown in Madagascar and Tahiti. Pods are 4 to 5 inches long, dark chocolate brown, tough but pliant, and sometimes covered with white crystals, called *givre* ("frost") in French. They contain hundreds of tiny black seeds (seen in top-quality vanilla ice cream). Good vanilla is expensive, so be suspicious of cheap beans. Wrap tightly in foil or seal in a glass jar and store in a cool place or the refrigerator. Available in whole pods (superior) and extract (convenient).	Steep pods whole in sauces or syrups, but usually best to split the pod lengthwise, scrape the seeds into the liquid, and add the pod as well. Make vanilla sugar by burying a couple of whole beans in a jar of sugar, which will absorb their aroma after a few days. Replenish the sugar in the jar as you use it. Exceptional with chocolate and coffee; used to flavor all kinds of desserts. Good with fruits: try poaching pears, apples, figs, or pineapple in a syrup flavored with vanilla.
Wasabi powder	Wasabi, also known as Japanese horseradish, belongs to the same family as horseradish (Brassica) but is an entirely different genus. In this country, it is usually only to be found in jars, the rhizomes dried and reduced to a dark green powder. Most wasabi powder found on supermarket or even specialty food shelves is actually ground horseradish mixed with mustard and green food coloring. For the real deal, 100% ground wasabi, it should be labeled "pure namida"; your best bet for finding it is online. Wasabi packs tremendous punch—heat that will clear your sinuses and make your eyes water. Store it in the refrigerator or freezer.	Heat destroys the flavor compounds in wasabi, so it is best used in cold or room temperature preparations. To keep it from clumping, mix it with just a little bit of water to make a paste, then stir that into whatever you are adding it to.

(continued from page 640)

Whiz the spice or spices in a clean coffee or spice grinder. (You can use a cheap one, which costs ten bucks; purists use a mortar and pestle.) Unplug it, then wipe it out as best you can. If you're feeling really energetic (or you want no lingering trace of that spice), grind a little rice to a powder after removing the spices; the rice powder will remove the seasonings when you dump it out.

Ground spices stay potent for a few weeks while the flavor of whole spices will remain vibrant for months, up to a year, sometimes even longer. Keep both away from sunlight, moisture, and heat in a tightly covered opaque container or in a jar in a dark place. The cooler, the better, though the refrigerator is not ideal because it's too humid. Some people recommend storing spices in the freezer, though I've never had the need to.

Chili Powder

MAKES: About ¼ cup
TIME: 5 minutes
F M V

Do yourself and everyone you cook for a favor and toss out any taco seasoning or packaged chili powder you may have tucked away. Not only will this version blow anything you can buy out of the water, it's easy to make.

2	tablespoons ground ancho, New Mexico, or other mild chile
1	tablespoon dried Mexican oregano
2	teaspoons cumin seeds
2	teaspoons coriander seeds
½	teaspoon cayenne, or to taste
½	teaspoon black peppercorns

1. Put all the ingredients in a small skillet over medium heat. Toast, shaking the pan occasionally, until the mixture is fragrant, 3 to 5 minutes.
2. Cool, then grind to a fine powder in a spice or coffee grinder. Store in a tightly covered container for up to several weeks.

Grinding and Cracking Peppercorns

When I call for black pepper in my recipes, I simply ask for pepper, recognizing that a lot of folks use preground. But do know that pepper that you grind fresh for immediate use doesn't taste at all like what you shake out of a can or jar. I guarantee you: Buy a peppermill and you'll never go back to preground. You may not use it all the time, but it's especially valuable at the table.

There are many different types of peppermills. Ideally you want a sturdy metal or wooden mill with a screw at the top or bottom to adjust the grind. You can also grind pepper in a spice or coffee grinder. For recipes that call for cracked peppercorns, crack them with the flat side of a big knife. Or put them in a plastic bag and take a hammer to them.

Garam Masala

MAKES: About ¼ cup
TIME: 15 minutes
F M V

Literally "warm mixture," this North Indian spice blend can be customized to your taste and used wherever a recipe calls for curry powder.

10	cardamom pods, seeds only (discard the hulls)
1	3-inch cinnamon stick
1	tablespoon cumin seeds
1	tablespoon fennel seeds
1	teaspoon whole cloves
½	teaspoon freshly grated nutmeg

1. Put all the ingredients in a medium skillet over medium heat. Cook, shaking the pan occasionally, until lightly browned and fragrant, just a few minutes.
2. Cool, then grind to a fine powder in a spice or coffee grinder. Store in a tightly covered opaque container for up to several months.

Hot Curry Powder

MAKES: About ¼ cup
TIME: 10 minutes
F M V

Curry powders are generally quite personalized—no two ever taste quite the same—so definitely adjust this recipe to your taste. If this one sounds too hot for you (the black peppercorns alone pack quite a punch), try the one that follows, or just reduce the number of chiles.

2   small dried Thai or other hot chiles
1   tablespoon black peppercorns
1   tablespoon coriander seeds
1   teaspoon cumin seeds
1   teaspoon fennel seeds
1   tablespoon ground turmeric
1   tablespoon ground ginger
1   teaspoon ground fenugreek
    Cayenne (optional)

1. Put the chiles, peppercorns, coriander, cumin, and fennel in a medium skillet over medium heat. Cook, shaking the pan occasionally, until lightly browned and fragrant, just a few minutes; for the last minute of cooking, add the turmeric, ginger, and fenugreek.
2. Cool, then grind to a fine powder in a spice or coffee grinder. Add the cayenne at this stage if you're using it. Store in a tightly covered opaque container for up to several months.

Fragrant Curry Powder

MAKES: About ¼ cup
TIME: 10 minutes
F M V

A mild and complex spice mix, perfect when you're looking for loads of flavor without heat.

5   white cardamom pods, seeds only
    (discard the hulls)
3   whole cloves
2   bay leaves
2   dried curry leaves (optional)
1   3-inch cinnamon stick
¼   cup coriander seeds
2   tablespoons cumin seeds
1   teaspoon black peppercorns
¼   teaspoon freshly grated nutmeg
1   teaspoon ground fenugreek

1. Put the cardamom seeds, cloves, bay leaves, curry leaves if you're using them, cinnamon, coriander, cumin, peppercorns, and nutmeg in a medium skillet over medium heat. Cook, shaking the pan occasionally, until lightly browned and fragrant, just a few minutes; for the last minute of cooking, add the fenugreek.
2. Cool, then grind to a fine powder in a spice or coffee grinder. Store in a tightly covered opaque container for up to several months.

Five-Spice Powder

MAKES: About ¼ cup
TIME: 5 minutes
F M V

Sichuan peppercorns make this spice blend unusual and unforgettable. Once banned from import due to a contagious disease they can carry, these have now happily returned, thanks to a flash-heat treatment that kills the nasty little virus. This tiny fruit pod (it's not really a peppercorn) has an unusual smoky, citrusy flavor.

Use this classic Chinese spice blend in stir-fries, for spiced nuts, or sprinkled on desserts like ice cream or poached pears.

6   star anise pods
1   3-inch stick cinnamon
2   tablespoons fennel seeds
1   tablespoon Sichuan or black peppercorns
1½ teaspoons whole cloves

Put all the ingredients in a spice or coffee grinder and grind to a fine powder. Store in a tightly covered opaque container for up to several months.

Japanese Seven-Spice Mix

Shichimi Togarashi

MAKES: About ¼ cup
TIME: 5 minutes
F M V

This spice mix is a perfect last-minute addition to soba or udon noodles, soups, salads, vegetables, and anything grilled.

You can make your own dried tangerine peels—or those of any citrus—by removing the outer skin with a zester or vegetable peeler (avoid getting too much of the bitter white pith) and dehydrating in a 200°F oven for an hour, or leaving the pieces on a paper towel overnight or until dry.

    1 tablespoon Sichuan peppercorns or
       black peppercorns
    2 teaspoons white sesame seeds
    1 tablespoon crumbled dried nori
    1 tablespoon dried tangerine or orange peel
    1 tablespoon chili powder
    1 teaspoon black sesame seeds
    1 teaspoon poppy seeds

1. Put the peppercorns and white sesame seeds in a spice or coffee grinder and grind to a coarse powder. Add the nori and tangerine peel and grind quickly, about 5 seconds.

2. Mix in the chili powder, black sesame seeds, and poppy seeds. Store in a tightly covered opaque container and refrigerate for up to 3 months.

Nori "Shake"

MAKES: About ¼ cup
TIME: 20 minutes
F M V

This seaweed "shake" is not a green smoothie, but an American translation of the ubiquitous family of Japanese seasonings that you sprinkle on food as a last-minute condiment, either with your fingers, with a spoon, or out of some kind of big-holed shaker (thus the name). Sushi Rice (page 384) is a good place to use nori shake; so are bowls of broth with soba or udon noodles, and Vegan Tempura (page 161).

I like to make shakes in small batches because they stay fresh for only a little while. This recipe makes enough for four 1-tablespoon servings. But if you're going to use it all within a week or so, go ahead and double or triple the recipe.

    2 sheets nori
    1 tablespoon sesame seeds
    1 teaspoon salt, preferably sea salt
       Cayenne (optional)

1. Set a large skillet (preferably cast-iron) over medium heat. When it's hot, put a nori sheet in the pan and toast until it turns slightly green, which will take only a few seconds. Turn and quickly toast on the other side. Set aside to cool and repeat with the other nori sheet.

2. While the pan is still hot, toast the sesame seeds, stirring or swirling the pan constantly to keep them from burning. When they are fragrant and beginning to turn golden, put them in a small bowl, sprinkle with the salt, and stir.

3. Crumble the nori into the bowl with the sesame seeds and salt. If you want a finer shake, whir the nori in a spice grinder for a few pulses and then add. Stir in the cayenne if you're using it. Store in a tightly covered opaque container for up to a week.

DULSE "SHAKE" Instead of the nori, toast 3 tablespoons crumbled dulse.

Jerk Seasoning

MAKES: About ¼ cup
TIME: 5 minutes
F M V

In Jamaica, jerk seasoning is typically used as a rub or in a marinade for grilled chicken or pork, but there's really no reason you can't use this on your grilled vegetables or tofu. It's also an easy way to spice up Quesadillas (page 620) or grilled Fresh Cheese (page 568).

    1   tablespoon allspice berries
    2   teaspoons dried thyme
    1   teaspoon black peppercorns
    2   tablespoons salt
    1   tablespoon paprika
    1   tablespoon sugar
    1   teaspoon cayenne, or to taste
    ¼   teaspoon freshly grated nutmeg
    2   teaspoons ground ginger or
        minced fresh ginger
    2   teaspoons minced garlic

1. Put the allspice, thyme, and peppercorns in a spice or coffee grinder and grind to a fine powder.
2. Mix in the salt, paprika, sugar, cayenne, nutmeg, ginger (ground or fresh), and garlic and use immediately. Or mix in the salt, paprika, sugar, cayenne, nutmeg, and ground ginger, if that's what you're using, and store in a tightly covered opaque container for up to several weeks; add the garlic and fresh ginger when you are ready to use it.

Citrus Sprinkle

MAKES: About ¼ cup
TIME: 2 hours, largely unattended
Ⓜ Ⓥ

Sun-dried citrus peels or leaves from citrus trees are popular seasonings throughout the Middle East, Southeast Asia, and the Mediterranean, where they're often blended with other so-called warm seasonings like cardamom, cinnamon, and coriander seeds. Unfortunately, these citrus ingredients are often tough to find in the United States and their quality is often suspect.

Here, then, is an easy and versatile substitute, a tangy blend that works on everything from egg dishes to fresh fruit to rice pudding. And because it's mostly citrus, you can also use it to add character to other spice blends, like Za'atar (page 652) or Japanese Seven-Spice Mix (page 650).

    4   limes
    3   lemons
    2   oranges (not navel; blood, Valencia,
        or bitter oranges are best)
    1   tablespoon freshly ground black
        peppercorns (optional)
    1   tablespoon coriander seeds

1. Preheat the oven to 200°F. Use a vegetable peeler or zester to remove the peels from all the citrus; take care to remove only the peel, leaving the white pith behind. Spread the peels on a baking sheet and toast in the oven until dry, curled, and slightly golden, about 1 hour. Shake the pan occasionally to promote even drying.
2. When cool, put the peels, the pepper if you're using it, and coriander in a spice or coffee grinder and grind into a coarse powder. Store in a tightly covered opaque container for up to a month.

Pickling Spice

MAKES: About 1 cup
TIME: 10 minutes
Ⓕ Ⓜ Ⓥ

A traditional spice blend that gives a pickled flavor to virtually anything; see the pickle recipes in the salad chapter (pages 89 to 94).

    2   3-inch cinnamon sticks
    10 bay leaves
    2   small hot dried red chiles, or 1 tablespoon
        red chile flakes or to taste
    ¼   cup mustard seeds
    2   tablespoons allspice berries
    2   tablespoons black peppercorns
    2   tablespoons coriander seeds
    2   tablespoons dill seeds
    2   teaspoons whole cloves
    2   teaspoons cardamom seeds

1. Break the cinnamon sticks, bay leaves, and chiles into pieces.

2. Roughly chop the remaining spices, or crush them by pressing on the spices with a heavy skillet, leaving most of the seeds whole.

3. Stir to combine all the spices and store in a tightly sealed opaque container for several months.

Za'atar

MAKES: About ½ cup
TIME: 10 minutes
F M V

A tangy, nutty seasoning used throughout the Middle East, this herb and seed blend is a good addition to Hummus (page 463) and can be sprinkled over olives, vegetables, rice, slices of feta cheese, or toasted pita bread drizzled with olive oil. For a fast dip, mix it with some plain yogurt and extra virgin olive oil (see The Simplest Yogurt Sauce, page 673).

Sesame seeds turn rancid quickly, so keep this in the fridge for longer storage.

    2   tablespoons dried thyme
    2   tablespoons ground sumac
    ¼   cup toasted sesame seeds (see page 299)
        Salt and pepper

1. Use your fingers to crumble the thyme into a small jar or bowl.

2. Stir in the sumac and sesame seeds. Season with a little salt and pepper. Store in a tightly covered opaque container in the refrigerator for up to a month.

THE BASICS OF MISO

Miso, which we think of as Japanese, probably originated in China. The base is made from soybeans or other beans, grain (usually rice or barley), and salt.

Then a starter (*koji*)—usually one that includes a mold called *Aspergillus oryzae*—is added to begin fermentation. High-quality, naturally made miso may go through a cycle of fermentation and aging that lasts as long as three years, sometimes in wood barrels that add flavor (just as they do in winemaking). With more industrial or "quick" miso, this process is hurried and usually includes pasteurization.

BUYING AND STORING

Like good-quality yogurt, traditionally made miso is a living food, full of enzymes, micronutrients, and active cultures. Since pasteurization kills beneficial microorganisms along with undesirable ones, and at least some of the taste, it's best to buy unpasteurized miso whenever possible; these may be Japanese or, increasingly, domestic.

There are dozens of subcategories of miso, but most fall into three depending on the main ingredients. (Miso is also sometimes identified by color, regardless of ingredients.) When soybeans are fermented with white or brown rice the result is *kome-miso,* usually white or light beige in color and smooth in texture, with a hint of sweetness. You may also see it labeled "mellow miso" or "sweet white miso." This is best used in dressings and light sauces, and as a dairy substitute.

Mugi-miso is made from barley and soybeans and is often referred to as yellow, medium, or mild miso. It is usually smooth textured and ranges from golden to reddish brown; the flavor varies a bit but is best described as earthy. Consider this an all-purpose miso.

Hatcho miso contains all soybeans; these are the richest, darkest, deepest-flavored misos. Some are chunky; some are smooth. Either way, this is the best type of miso for heartier soups and stews, full-bodied sauces, and glazes.

Miso must be stored refrigerated, where it will keep for months. To keep it from spoiling, always use a clean spoon when you remove some from the container.

COOKING WITH MISO

Unless you are a miso aficionado, you'll probably have just one miso in the fridge at a time. It may not be traditional, but all may be used interchangeably in recipes calling for miso. There is one rule, however, that should not be broken: Don't boil it. You will not only deactivate the beneficial cultures, but you will dramatically reduce the complex flavor.

Simple Miso Dipping Sauce

MAKES: 4 servings (about 1 cup)
TIME: 15 minutes
F M O

Richer and subtler than Ponzu (page 657) or other soy-based dipping sauces, this is perfect for dunking or for dressing heartier foods like boiled or grilled potatoes, whole wheat pastas, and "meat" balls (see page 506). Serve it in small bowls for dipping.

The type of miso you choose (see opposite) will make this sauce lighter or heavier, but it's good all ways. Warm the sauce gently on the stove if you'd like, but don't let it come to a boil or you'll weaken the flavor.

- 6 tablespoons any miso
- ¾ cup warm water or sake
- 1 teaspoon sugar
- 1 tablespoon mirin or honey
- 1 tablespoon rice vinegar, or more to taste
  Salt

1. Whisk the miso, water, sugar, mirin, and vinegar together in a small bowl. Taste and adjust the vinegar and add salt if needed.
2. Serve, heat gently, or cover and refrigerate for up to a week.

SIMPLE MISO-HERB DIPPING SAUCE Lots of bang for your buck: Add ½ cup minced fresh cilantro, basil, Thai basil, or mint, or a combination. For a smooth green sauce, combine everything in the blender.

SIMPLE MISO-CITRUS DIPPING SAUCE Brighter and fresher: Instead of the rice vinegar, add a tablespoon or 2 fresh lemon, lime, orange, or tangerine juice. If you like, finely grate some zest and float a sprinkle on top of each little bowl.

SIMPLE MISO-SOY DIPPING SAUCE Add a tablespoon or 2 soy sauce to the main recipe or either of the preceding variations.

Nutty Miso Sauce

MAKES: 4 servings (about 1 cup)
TIME: About 15 minutes
F M V

When the Japanese chef Yumiko Kano showed me this sauce, she used it to dress blanched and shocked green beans. Now I toss it on all sorts of vegetables, from grilled eggplant or mushrooms to steamed kale or broccoli. Try a dollop on thickly sliced tomatoes, use a bowlful as a dip for raw celery, or spoon it on boiled rice or soba, somen, or udon noodles.

Virtually any unsalted roasted nut and most seeds will work here. For starters, try almonds, cashews, hazelnuts, peanuts, or pumpkin or sunflower seeds.

- 1 1-inch piece fresh ginger
- ¼ cup light miso (white or sweet)
- 1 cup walnuts
- 1 teaspoon soy sauce, or to taste (optional)

Grate the ginger into a small fine-meshed strainer over a bowl and press out the juice, about a teaspoon. Put the ginger juice, miso, nuts, and soy sauce if you're using it in a blender and blend until smooth, scraping down the side if necessary. Add a little water or more soy sauce until the mixture is the desired thickness. Serve or cover and refrigerate for up to 3 days.

TAHINI MISO SAUCE Faster and easier; just use a whisk: Instead of the walnuts, use ½ cup each tahini and water.

Sweet Miso Glaze

MAKES: About ¾ cup
TIME: 10 minutes
F M O

Miso glaze works well as a basting sauce for grilling, broiling, or roasting vegetables or tofu. (I especially like this sauce made with red miso on mushrooms.) You can use any miso for the base, but it's best to pair stronger-tasting red miso with full-flavored vegetables so as not to overpower them. The converse is also true, as strong-tasting miso can drown out subtler tastes.

The sugar in the mirin helps promote browning and gives a deep sheen to whatever you're preparing. But if you don't have mirin, or if you can find only mirin that is essentially corn syrup, use honey, a sweet and fruity after-dinner-style wine, or—for that matter—sugar.

> ½ **cup any miso**
> ¼ **cup mirin, or 2 tablespoons honey mixed with**
> **2 tablespoons water**
> **Salt**

Whisk the miso and mirin together in a small bowl until smooth. Taste and add salt if needed. Serve or cover and refrigerate for up to 2 days.

SWEET AND HOT MISO GLAZE Mince 1 clove garlic and 1 small hot or medium fresh chile, like Thai or serrano; add them to the finished glaze.

Miso-Carrot Sauce with Ginger

MAKES: About 1¼ cups
TIME: 15 minutes
F M V

This colorful dressing is the high-quality version of the goopy stuff they put on salads in many Japanese restaurants. I make it in the food processor, but if you prefer something smoother, just throw everything in a blender.

Use this as a salad dressing, but also on warm or chilled chickpeas or edamame. Or toss a few spoonfuls into any plain cooked whole grain.

> ¼ **cup peanut oil**
> ¼ **cup rice vinegar**
> 3 **tablespoons mild or sweet miso**
> **(like yellow or white)**
> 1 **tablespoon sesame oil**
> 2 **carrots, cut into big pieces**
> 1 **1-inch piece fresh ginger, cut into coins**
> **Salt and pepper**

1. Put the peanut oil, vinegar, miso, sesame oil, carrots, and ginger in a food processor and pulse a few times to chop the carrots. Then let the machine run for a minute or so until the mixture is chunky-smooth.

2. Taste and adjust the seasoning with salt and pepper if necessary. Serve or cover and refrigerate for up to several days.

SOY SAUCE–BASED SAUCES

Soy sauce's distinctive combination of savory and salty plays a part in all of these sauces, most of which find their origins or inspiration in Asia. Though they all include soy sauce, these sauces present a wide range of flavors, playing off soy's characteristic umami-ness with bright citrus, vibrant fresh herbs, and/or chile heat. You can use these as dipping sauces, marinades, or an ingredient in other recipes. And please, use best-quality soy sauce, with no added caramel coloring or flavoring.

Basil Dipping Sauce

MAKES: About ½ cup
TIME: 15 minutes
F M V

This dead-easy sauce is incredibly useful, especially considering that you can completely change its nature by replacing the basil with cilantro or mint, or using them in combination.

Miso-Carrot Sauce
with Ginger

Any of the variations would make a fantastic dipping sauce for Summer Rolls (page 618).

- 1 clove garlic, minced
- 2 tablespoons soy sauce, plus more to taste
- 2 tablespoons rice vinegar
- 1 tablespoon sugar
- 1 or 2 fresh Thai chiles, seeded and thinly sliced
- ¼ cup thinly sliced fresh basil, preferably Thai

Whisk all the ingredients with 2 tablespoons water in a small bowl until the sugar is dissolved. Let sit for 5 minutes for the flavors to meld, then serve.

LEMONGRASS DIPPING SAUCE Replace the basil with 1 stalk lemongrass, peeled, trimmed, and minced.

LIME LEAF DIPPING SAUCE Replace the basil with 1 lime leaf, minced, or the grated zest of a lime.

Fishless Fish Sauce

MAKES: About ½ cup
TIME: 15 minutes
F M V

Based on the classic fish sauces of Southeast Asia (Thai *nam pla* and Vietnamese *nuoc cham* are the best known) but without the fish. The dulse adds a salty pungency like the original, but if you don't have any handy you won't go far wrong by combining the remaining ingredients.

- 1 tablespoon crumbled or ground dulse (see page 244; optional)
- 1 clove garlic, minced
- 2 tablespoons soy sauce
- 4 limes
- 1 tablespoon palm sugar or brown sugar

1. Whisk the dulse, garlic, and soy sauce with 2 tablespoons water in a small bowl.

2. Grate the zest of 2 of the limes into the bowl. Juice all 4 limes and add the juice. Add the sugar and stir well. Let sit for 5 minutes for the flavors to meld, then serve.

THAI-STYLE DIPPING SAUCE Based on nam prik and ideal for spring rolls or grilled tofu, or drizzled over steamed vegetables: Add anywhere from 1 to 10 hot fresh chiles (preferably Thai), minced, or red chile flakes to taste, and 1 tablespoon or so finely shredded carrot.

VIETNAMESE-STYLE DIPPING SAUCE Aka nuoc cham gung: Add 1 or 2 hot fresh chiles (preferably Thai), minced, or red chile flakes to taste, and 1 tablespoon minced fresh ginger. Squeeze in the juice of another lime too.

Korean-Style Soy and Sesame Dipping Sauce and Marinade

MAKES: About 1½ cups
TIME: 15 minutes
F M V

This finger-licking-good sauce is quintessentially Korean, with its soy, sesame, sugar, and garlic. It just might be the perfect marinade for grilled tofu, and is also wonderful for saucing Sushi Bowls (page 384) and as a dip for crudités.

- ½ cup soy sauce
- 2 tablespoons sake or rice vinegar
- 2 tablespoons sesame oil
- ¼ cup toasted sesame seeds (see page 299)
- 1 tablespoon sugar
- 2 large cloves garlic, minced
- 1 tablespoon minced or grated fresh ginger
- ¼ cup minced scallions

Stir all the ingredients together in a small bowl until the sugar is dissolved. Serve or cover and refrigerate for up to 2 days.

TAHINI SOY SAUCE Thicker and richer: Substitute ¼ cup mirin (or 2 tablespoons honey mixed with 2 tablespoons water) for the sake and tahini for the toasted sesame seeds. Omit the ginger and scallions. Add a pinch of red chile flakes if you like. ☐

Ponzu

MAKES: About 2 cups
TIME: 10 minutes, plus time to cool
☐ ☐ ☐

The famous Japanese dipping sauce usually contains shavings of dried bonito, a relative of tuna. In this version, seaweed replaces the fish more than adequately.

- 1 3- to 5-inch piece kombu or about 1 tablespoon crumbled or ground dulse
- 1 cup soy sauce
- ⅓ cup mirin, or 2½ tablespoons honey mixed with 2½ tablespoons water
- 1 cup fresh yuzu juice, or ½ cup fresh lemon juice and ½ cup fresh lime juice

1. Put the kombu, soy sauce, and mirin in a small saucepan. Heat gently over medium-low heat (do not boil), then turn off the heat and let cool to room temperature.
2. Remove the kombu or strain out the dulse and stir in the yuzu juice. Serve or cover and refrigerate; it will keep indefinitely. Bring to room temperature to serve.

LEMONGRASS PONZU Reduce the soy sauce to ¼ cup, increase the mirin to ¾ cup, and add ½ cup water or Kombu Dashi (page 100) and a stalk of lemongrass, peeled, trimmed, and crushed, to the pan with the kombu. Simmer for 15 minutes, then strain. Omit the yuzu juice. Serve warm or at room temperature.

Dashi Dipping Sauce

MAKES: About 1 cup
TIME: 5 minutes, plus time to cool
☐ ☐ ☐

A complex, delicious sauce that couldn't be easier to prepare, especially if you already have dashi on hand. It's wonderful with tempura (page 161).

- 1 cup Kombu Dashi (page 100)
- ¼ cup mirin, or 2 tablespoons honey mixed with 2 tablespoons water
- 2 tablespoons soy sauce

Put the dashi, mirin, and soy sauce in a small saucepan and bring to a boil. Turn off the heat and let cool. Serve or cover and refrigerate for up to 3 days.

7 Quick Additions to Dashi Dipping Sauce

This stuff is so easy to spice you won't believe it—once it's cooked, you can stir in almost anything. Use the amounts here as guidelines; really, you can just add to taste.
1. 1 tablespoon minced or grated fresh ginger or 1 teaspoon ground
2. ¼ cup grated daikon
3. 1 tablespoon wasabi paste
4. 1 tablespoon toasted sesame seeds (see page 299) or tahini
5. 1 teaspoon minced raw garlic or 1 tablespoon roasted (see page 205)
6. ¼ cup minced scallions or shallots
7. 1 teaspoon minced fresh or dried chile

Peanut Sauce, Four Ways

MAKES: 2 cups
TIME: 35 minutes
☐ ☐

Best tossed with Chinese egg noodles (see page 331) or pooled on the bottom of a plate and topped with slices of grilled or fried vegetables or tofu. It also makes

Teriyaki Sauce

a fine dip for celery, red bell pepper, cherry tomatoes, and rice crackers. If you want a smooth sauce, use peanut butter instead of chopped peanuts.

    3   hot fresh red chiles, seeded, or cayenne or
        red chile flakes to taste
    3   cloves garlic, peeled
    2   shallots, peeled
    1   stalk lemongrass, white part only,
        thinly sliced (optional)
    2   teaspoons ground turmeric
    1   tablespoon peanut or grapeseed oil
    1   cup coconut milk (to make your own,
        see page 304)
    2   tablespoons soy sauce, plus more to taste
    2   tablespoons fresh lime juice
    1   tablespoon brown sugar
    ½   cup chopped roasted peanuts or crunchy
        peanut butter
        Salt

1. Put the chiles, garlic, shallots, lemongrass if you're using it, and turmeric in a food processor and grind until fairly smooth; scrape down the side of the container once or twice if necessary.

2. Put the oil in a medium saucepan or skillet over medium heat. When it's hot, add the chile-garlic mixture and cook until fragrant, about 1 minute. Add the coconut milk, soy sauce, lime juice, sugar, and peanuts and whisk until fully combined. Simmer, stirring occasionally, until the sauce thickens, about 15 minutes. Taste and add a sprinkle of salt or a little more soy sauce if necessary. Serve or cool, cover, and refrigerate for up to a week. Gently rewarm before using.

CURRY PEANUT SAUCE Another layer of flavor: Omit the chiles, lemongrass, and turmeric. Instead, put one 2-inch piece fresh ginger and 2 tablespoons curry powder in the food processor along with the garlic and shallots.

SWEET PEANUT SAUCE Indonesian in spirit: Add ¼ cup ketchup along with the coconut milk.

SIMPLER PEANUT SAUCE More peanutty (and makes less): Use only the chiles, sugar, soy sauce, and peanuts. Blend in a food processor, adding a little water or more soy sauce to get the consistency you like. Gently heat the sauce in a small saucepan over low heat or in the microwave. Stir in ¼ cup sliced scallions and ¼ cup minced fresh cilantro and serve.

Teriyaki Sauce
MAKES: About 1 cup
TIME: 15 minutes
F M O

Familiar and widely loved, teriyaki sauce is also fast and simple. You can slather it on broiled or deep-fried tofu, add it to stir-fried vegetables (which in turn can be served over rice or noodles), or use it as a ketchup replacement on any of the veggie burgers on pages 502 to 508—or anywhere else, for that matter.

    ½   cup soy sauce
    ½   cup mirin, or ¼ cup honey mixed
        with ¼ cup water
    1   tablespoon minced or grated fresh ginger
    1   clove garlic, minced
    ¼   cup minced scallions

Put the soy sauce and mirin in a small saucepan. Heat over medium-low heat until bubbling, about 2 minutes. Turn off the heat and stir in the ginger, garlic, and scallions. Serve, or cool, cover, and refrigerate for up to a day. Bring to room temperature before serving.

SALSAS

The building blocks for America's favorite condiment (ketchup is now second) are simple and flavorful. Of course tomatoes are a staple, but so are fruits, green tomatoes, and tomatillos. All can be combined with herbs, and onions and garlic, oil, citrus, and chiles—mild or hot—usually play a role as well. The final product may be left chunky and loose or puréed.

Fresh Tomato Salsa

Salsa Fresca
MAKES: About 2 cups
TIME: 15 minutes
F M V

Salsa fresca (or *pico de gallo*) is easy, fast, really tasty, and invaluable. Keep it around all the time, and you'll serve it with chips as well as grilled vegetables, simply cooked grains, any kind of eggs, and things you never imagined. If you double the recipe, you can serve it like a chunky gazpacho and eat it with a spoon, or purée it for a smoother texture.

If you prefer a milder onion flavor, soak the minced onion in cold water for a couple of minutes (or even just rinse it for a few seconds), before adding it to the salsa. Or use 2 or 3 minced scallions instead.

- 2 **large fresh tomatoes, chopped**
- ½ **large white onion, minced**
- 1 **teaspoon minced garlic, or to taste**
- 1 **habanero or jalapeño chile, seeded and minced, or to taste (leave the seeds in if you like it hotter)**
- ½ **cup chopped fresh cilantro**
- 2 **tablespoons fresh lime juice or 1 tablespoon red wine vinegar**
   Salt and pepper

Combine the tomatoes, onion, garlic, chile, cilantro, and lime juice in a bowl. Taste, and adjust the seasoning with salt and pepper. If possible, let the flavors develop for 15 minutes or so before serving, but by all means serve within a couple of hours.

CHILEAN SALSA A little more assertive, but less acidic: Increase the garlic to 1 tablespoon; add 1 teaspoon chopped fresh oregano and 1 to 2 tablespoons olive oil; omit the lime juice.

SALSA CRUDA This makes a good pasta sauce: Eliminate the onion and chile; substitute basil for the cilantro and balsamic vinegar for the lime juice. Add 1 tablespoon or more good extra virgin olive oil.

BEAN SALSA Black beans are most traditional, but pintos or even chickpeas work well too: Add a cup of your favorite cooked beans, substitute red onion for the white, and add 1 teaspoon ground cumin. Let sit for about 30 minutes for the flavors to develop.

Fresh Tomatillo Salsa

Pico de Gallo Verde
MAKES: About 2 cups
TIME: 10 minutes
F M V

Super-fresh tasting, acidic, and bright. Look for firm, unshriveled tomatillos with tight, papery husks; then remove them and rinse off the sticky residue. (If fresh tomatillos are not available, canned are not bad.) You can substitute green tomatoes if you'd like.

Poblanos and some other fresh chiles have tough skins that are best removed. The easiest way is to char the skin, which has the added benefit of giving the salsa a light smoky flavor. You can, however, skip this step.

- 2 **poblano or other mild green fresh chiles**
- 2 **cups chopped husked tomatillos**
- 3 **scallions, minced**
- 2 **teaspoons minced garlic, or to taste**
- ¼ **cup chopped fresh cilantro**
- 3 **tablespoons fresh lime juice, or to taste**
   Salt and pepper

1. If you like, roast and clean the chiles according to the directions on page 228. Mince the chiles.
2. Stir the tomatillos, scallions, garlic, cilantro, and lime juice together in a medium bowl with the chiles. If serving immediately, taste and adjust the seasoning with salt and pepper. Or cover and refrigerate for up to 2 days.

Clockwise from top:
Fresh Tomatillo Salsa,
Salsa Roja (page 662),
Radish Salsa (page 662)

(Bring back to room temperature, taste, and adjust again before serving.)

CORN SALSA Distinctive and delicious: Substitute 2 cups corn kernels from Corn on the Cob, Grilled or Roasted (page 195) for the tomatillos.

JÍCAMA SALSA Very crunchy: Replace the tomatillos with chopped peeled jícama and substitute minced fresh ginger for the garlic. Add 2 tablespoons chopped fresh mint along with the cilantro. Let sit for about 30 minutes before serving.

Radish Salsa

MAKES: About 2 cups
TIME: 30 minutes
F M V

Serve this colorful salsa with any tamale (page 394) or quesadilla (page 620), or simply a big bowl of tortilla chips; it also makes a fine garnish for almost any dish.

- 2 **cups chopped radish (like daikon, red, or a combination; about 1 pound)**
- ½ **English cucumber, peeled and diced**
- ½ **small red onion, minced**
- 1 **scallion, thinly sliced**
- 1 **teaspoon minced garlic**
- 1 **tablespoon minced fresh chile (like jalapeño or Thai), or to taste, or red chile flakes or cayenne to taste**
- 2 **tablespoons fresh lemon juice, or more to taste**
- ¼ **cup chopped fresh cilantro**
  Salt and pepper

Stir all the ingredients together in a medium bowl. Taste and adjust the seasoning, adding more chile, lemon juice, or salt as needed. Serve immediately or cover and refrigerate for up to a day.

CUCUMBER SALSA Replace the radish with additional diced cucumber and carrot (about 1 medium each), the red onion with 1 large shallot, and the lemon juice with lime. Omit the garlic. Add 1 tablespoon rice vinegar.

GREEN PAPAYA SALSA Substitute peeled, seeded, and shredded green papaya for the radishes; replace the scallions and red onion with 1 thinly sliced large shallot; use lime juice instead of lemon. Add 1 tablespoon rice vinegar.

Salsa Roja

MAKES: About 2 cups
TIME: 45 to 50 minutes
M V

This classic cooked tomato and chile sauce can be served as is or puréed and used for enchiladas or tacos. The guajillo chiles lend a complex, smoky flavor, as well as moderate heat. If you want a milder salsa, substitute ancho or another mild chile.

Save the chile soaking water to thin the salsa if it gets too thick, or use it in Tortilla Soup (page 111). But use it judiciously; it can become quite fiery.

- 2 **large guajillo or other medium-hot dried chiles, toasted, soaked, and cleaned (see page 226)**
- ¼ **cup good-quality vegetable oil**
- 2 **large onions, chopped**
- 4 **cloves garlic, minced**
- 2 **pounds tomatoes, peeled, seeded, and chopped, with their liquid (about 3 cups; canned are fine)**
- 1 **tablespoon sugar**
  Salt and pepper
- ¼ **cup chopped fresh cilantro**
- 3 **tablespoons fresh lime juice**

1. Mince the chiles. Put the oil in a medium saucepan or deep skillet with a lid over medium-high heat. When it's hot, add the chiles, onions, and garlic and cook, stirring

occasionally, until the onions soften, about 5 minutes. Add the tomatoes, sugar, some salt, and plenty of pepper.
2. Adjust the heat so the mixture bubbles gently and cook, stirring occasionally, until it thickens and comes together, about 20 minutes.
3. Stir in the cilantro and lime juice. Taste and adjust the seasoning. Serve hot or at room temperature, or cover and refrigerate for up to 2 days.

RED ENCHILADA SAUCE Essential on enchiladas (page 561): Use an immersion blender to purée the sauce in the pan. Or cool the mixture slightly, pour it into a blender or food processor, and purée carefully, scraping down the sides as necessary.

SALSA BORRACHA Translates as "drunken salsa" because it's cooked with beer and finished with tequila: In Step 1, add a 12-ounce bottle or can of beer with the tomatoes. Once it thickens (it might take a little longer), use an immersion blender to purée the sauce in the pan. Or cool the mixture slightly, pour it into a blender or food processor, and purée carefully, scraping down the side as necessary. Finish with 2 tablespoons (about a shot) of tequila if you like.

CHARRED SALSA ROJA If you have the grill going already, why not? Cut the tomatoes and onions into thick slices and grill on both sides until charred, about 10 minutes total. Proceed with the recipe. Add 2 tablespoons or so chopped fresh mint, if you like, in Step 3 along with the cilantro.

SMOKY AND HOT SALSA ROJA Toast, soak, and clean a dried chipotle chile along with the others. Or add a canned chipotle chile, chopped, with adobo to taste along with the tomatoes.

SALSA SOFRITO Substitute roasted red or yellow bell peppers (see page 228) for the guajillos; replace the cilantro with a tablespoon or so chopped fresh oregano; and use red wine vinegar instead of the lime juice.

Cooked Tomatillo Salsa

Salsa Verde
MAKES: About 2 cups
TIME: 30 minutes
F M V

Salsa verde is an all-purpose salsa that keeps in the fridge for at least a week. Spoon it onto scrambled eggs and roll in a flour tortilla with a little cheese, or serve a bowlful with tamales (page 394), or, of course, chips.

To keep it on the mild side, substitute another poblano for the hot chile. But if in-your-face heat is what you're looking for, add even more hot chiles and/or some of their seeds.

10–12	tomatillos, husked and rinsed
2	medium poblano or other mild fresh green chiles, roasted and cleaned (see page 228)
1 or 2	serrano or other hot fresh green chiles, roasted and cleaned (optional)
3	tablespoons good-quality vegetable oil
2	large onions, diced
5	cloves garlic, minced
1	teaspoon dried oregano (preferably Mexican)
1	cup vegetable stock (pages 97–100) or water
	Salt and pepper
½	cup chopped fresh cilantro
¼	cup fresh lime juice

1. Preheat the oven to 400°F. Put the tomatillos on a baking sheet and roast until the skins are lightly browned and blistered, about 20 minutes. Remove the tomatillos; when they're cool enough to handle, chop them finely, along with the chiles, saving their juices.
2. While the tomatillos are roasting, put the oil in a large deep skillet over medium heat. When it's hot, add the onions and garlic and cook, stirring occasionally, until very soft and lightly browned, about 10 minutes. Add the tomatillos, chiles, oregano, stock, and a large pinch of salt and pepper; stir and bring to a low simmer. Cook, stirring occasionally, until the mixture is slightly thickened, 10 to 15 minutes.

3. Stir in the cilantro and lime juice, taste, and adjust the seasoning. Serve at room temperature or cover and refrigerate for up to 2 days. (Bring back to room temperature before serving.)

GREEN ENCHILADA SAUCE For Cheese Enchiladas (page 561): Use an immersion blender to purée the finished sauce in the pan. Or cool the mixture slightly, pour into a blender or food processor, and purée carefully.

GREEN CHILE SALSA Milder and simpler: Omit the tomatillos and serranos; increase the chiles to 5 poblanos. Decrease the stock to ¼ cup, more or less, as needed. Proceed with Steps 1 and 2; then use an immersion blender to purée the salsa. Or cool the mixture slightly, pour into a blender, and purée carefully. Proceed with Step 3. This salsa will keep in the refrigerator, covered, for a couple of days.

PUMPKIN SEED SAUCE Thick, with a toasted nut flavor like green mole, only much easier: Toast or roast 1 cup pumpkin seeds (pepitas; see page 299) and pulse them several times in a food processor until finely chopped. Add them to the onion-garlic mixture in Step 2 along with 1 tablespoon minced fresh epazote if you like.

CHILE PASTES AND SAUCES

Chiles are indigenous to Mexico, Central, and South America and were unknown to the rest of the world until the latter part of the fifteenth century, an astonishing fact considering how key the chile is to so many cuisines today. While these pastes and sauces are based on chiles, which particular chiles are used and what other ingredients are included determines the final flavor and heat. You'll find a range of choices in this section, representing the classic preparations from around the world. They can be stirred into stews, soups, curries, bean and lentil dishes, eggs—almost anything you can think of. For more information on the different types of chiles, see "The Chile Pepper Lexicon" on page 227.

Chile Paste, 8 Ways

MAKES: About ½ cup
TIME: 45 minutes, largely unattended
Ⓜ Ⓥ

Like spice blends and rubs, chile pastes are not exactly sauces, but cooking ingredients that are useful in dressings, sauces, and marinades and for smearing on foods before grilling or roasting.

The base ingredient here: dried chiles. You can use a relatively mild one like ancho; guajillo or chipotle will be much hotter. The best, though, is a combination that includes both heat and complexity (my favorite is mostly ancho with a hit of chipotle). The variations simply build additional flavors into the chile paste. Whichever kind you make, if fresh herbs or aromatics are involved, refrigerate and use within a day or so for maximum freshness and oomph. (Chile paste made with dried seasonings will last a couple of weeks.)

> 2 **ounces dried whole chiles (6 to 12 total, depending on size)**
> **Salt**
> 2 **tablespoons good-quality vegetable oil**

1. Toast and clean the chiles (see page 226). For a hotter paste, set aside some of the seeds. Put the chiles in a bowl and cover with boiling water and a small plate to keep them submerged. Soak for about 30 minutes, until soft.
2. Drain the chiles, saving the soaking liquid. Put the chiles, any seeds you might be using, and a pinch of salt in a blender or food processor. Purée until smooth, adding a spoonful of soaking water at a time, until you reach the desired consistency.
3. Put the oil in a small skillet and turn the heat to medium-high. When it's hot, add the paste and cook, stirring constantly, until deeply colored and fragrant, about 2 minutes. Serve or cool, cover, and refrigerate for up to 2 days. Just before serving, taste and adjust the seasoning.

THAI-STYLE CHILE PASTE Quite complex: Use 2 or 3 dried Thai chiles along with the mild chiles. To the blender or processor, add 1 inch lemongrass, cleaned (see page 636) and chopped, and ¼ cup lightly packed fresh cilantro or basil leaves (preferably Thai).

VIETNAMESE-STYLE CHILE PASTE Use 2 or 3 dried Thai chiles along with the mild chiles. To the blender or processor, add 3 or 4 cloves garlic, 2 tablespoons Fishless Fish Sauce (page 656), and ¼ cup lightly packed fresh mint leaves. After cooking, squeeze in the juice of a lime.

INDIAN-STYLE CHILE PASTE To the blender or processor, add 1 tablespoon garam masala.

HARISSA Quite complex: To the blender or processor, add 1 tablespoon ground coriander, 2 teaspoons ground cumin, and 1 to 3 cloves garlic. Use extra virgin olive oil.

MEXICAN-STYLE CHILE PASTE Use all guajillo chiles: To the blender or processor, add 2 cloves garlic, 1 teaspoon ground cumin, and 2 tablespoons chopped fresh epazote, Mexican oregano, or regular oregano.

CHIPOTLE PASTE Hot. Hot. Hot: Use some or all chipotle chiles. Or skip Step 1 and use ⅓ cup canned chipotle chiles with adobo sauce.

CHILE AND BLACK BEAN PASTE To the blender or processor, add 2 tablespoons fermented black beans; taste the paste before adding any salt.

Chile-Garlic Paste

MAKES: About 2 cups
TIME: 10 minutes
F **M** **V**

Globally, chile-garlic paste is almost ubiquitous; certainly nothing is more versatile. Customize the heat level by using milder chiles (like New Mexico) or hotter ones (Thai or habanero). Remove the seeds and stems from the chiles before crushing them unless you like things really hot.

---

6 Ways to Use Chile Pastes

1. Toss a spoonful or 2 of any chile paste with cooked vegetables, pasta, grains, or more complex dishes.

2. To turn chile paste into a "real" sauce, heat a batch with ¼ cup or so oil, butter, cream, stock, tomato sauce, or even water.

3. Stir chile paste into yogurt, sour cream, or mayonnaise for a quick chilled sauce or dip.

4. Mix with extra virgin olive or good-quality vegetable oil and brush on vegetables as they come off the grill.

5. Stir a little into nut pastes for a spicy spread for toasted bread.

6. Smear on sandwiches (especially grilled cheese!).

---

1   cup dried red chiles (like red Thai, chile de árbol, pequín, or red New Mexico)
¼   cup chopped garlic
¼   cup white wine vinegar or distilled vinegar
2   teaspoons sugar
1   teaspoon salt, or to taste

Put the chiles, garlic, vinegar, sugar, and salt in a blender or food processor with ¼ cup hot water and purée to a smooth paste. Add additional hot water by the tablespoon if necessary to achieve the consistency you want. Serve or cover and refrigerate for up to 3 months.

SUPER-SPICY CHILE-GARLIC PASTE Based on fresh chiles instead of dried, and blistering hot—really: Put 3 to 5 habaneros and 5 cloves garlic in a small skillet over medium heat. Cook, shaking the skillet occasionally, until the garlic and chiles are brown (or partially wrap the garlic and chiles in foil and roast in a 400°F oven for about 30 minutes). Stem and seed the chiles (wear gloves, if you have them). Put the chiles, garlic, ½ cup chopped fresh cilantro, and ¼ cup fresh lime juice in a food processor or blender and purée until pasty.

Red Curry Paste

MAKES: About ¾ cup
TIME: 25 minutes
F M V

Cilantro roots, which are often attached to the bunch of cilantro you buy in the supermarket, have as much flavor as the leaves. Just be sure to rinse them very well to get all the sand and dirt off before using. Use the remaining cilantro for garnish or in Cilantro-Mint Chutney (page 668).

10	Thai or other medium to hot dried red chiles or to taste, seeded
4	dried lime leaves, fresh lime leaves, minced, or 1 tablespoon minced or grated lime zest
1	½-inch piece fresh galangal or 4 quarter-sized dried pieces, or one 1-inch piece fresh ginger, coarsely chopped
1	teaspoon coriander seeds
1	teaspoon cumin seeds
2	stalks lemongrass, cleaned (see page 636) and roughly chopped
2	shallots, roughly chopped
4	cloves garlic, smashed
2	tablespoons chopped cilantro roots (see headnote), or 3 tablespoons chopped fresh cilantro stems
3	tablespoons peanut oil

1. Soak the chiles, along with the lime leaves and galangal if you're using dried, in warm water for about 15 minutes.
2. Put the coriander and cumin seeds in a small skillet over medium heat. Cook, shaking the pan occasionally, until lightly browned and fragrant, about 3 minutes. Cool, then grind to a powder in a spice or coffee grinder.
3. Drain the chiles, lime leaves, and galangal and transfer to a blender or food processor along with the ground coriander and cumin, lemongrass, shallots, garlic, and cilantro (if not using dried lime leaves or galangal, add the fresh now; if not using lime leaves or galangal, add the lime zest and ginger now). Grind to a paste, stopping the machine to scrape down the side as necessary.

Gradually add the oil while blending; you're looking for a fairly smooth, thick paste. Serve or cover and refrigerate for up to 2 weeks.

GREEN CURRY PASTE Substitute 10 fresh green chiles for the dried red chiles; no need to soak them in Step 1. Add 1 tablespoon ground turmeric before blending in Step 3.

Smooth Green Chile Sauce, Indian Style

MAKES: 4 to 6 servings
TIME: 20 minutes
F M V

Nothing about this chile sauce is subtle; the color is deep green, the aroma mouthwatering, and the flavors intense. Add some yogurt (see the first variation) if you'd like to mellow the sauce a bit.

If the relatively mild poblanos aren't strong enough for you, increase the heat by adding some serrano or other hot chiles. And for a quicker, somewhat milder sauce, you can use a small can or 2 of green chiles instead.

6	poblano or other mild fresh green chiles, roasted and cleaned (see page 228)
1	tablespoon minced fresh ginger
2	teaspoons cumin seeds
¼	cup chopped fresh cilantro
	Pinch asafetida (optional)
¼	cup good-quality vegetable oil
	Salt and pepper
3	tablespoons fresh lime juice

1. Put the chiles, ginger, cumin seeds, cilantro, and asafetida if you're using it in a blender or food processor; purée until smooth, adding a tablespoon or so of water if necessary.
2. Put the oil in a medium saucepan over medium-high heat. When it's hot, add the chile purée and cook, stirring frequently, for about 2 minutes. (Be careful when

adding the chile purée—it will splatter when it hits the hot oil.) Reduce the heat and cook, stirring occasionally, until thickened, another 2 to 3 minutes.

3. Season with salt and pepper and stir in the lime juice. Serve hot, or cool, cover, and refrigerate for up to 3 days.

CHILE-YOGURT SAUCE A wonderful combo of cool and hot, ideal with Samosas (page 617) or as a dip: Let the chile sauce cool, then stir in ½ cup or more yogurt. Serve at room temperature.

CHILE AND COCONUT SAUCE Rich, spicy, creamy, and delicious: In Step 2, stir a 14-ounce can coconut milk into the thickened chile purée and heat until simmering.

RED CHILE SAUCE, INDIAN STYLE Lovely color, deep flavor: Replace the poblanos with 6 New Mexico or other mild red fresh chiles, roasted and cleaned.

RED CHILE SAUCE, NORTH AFRICAN STYLE Replace the poblanos with 6 New Mexico or other mild red fresh chiles. Substitute 2 cloves garlic for the ginger; add ½ teaspoon each caraway seeds, coriander seeds, and fennel seeds; omit the asafetida.

Spicy Indian Tomato Sauce

Makhani

MAKES: 2 cups
TIME: About 40 minutes
Ⓜ Ⓞ

A tomato-based sauce from the Punjabi region, almost sweet, a little hot, and rich with spice. The butter roasting of the cumin and mustard seeds—used essentially as a garnish—is an Indian technique called *tarka*, sometimes translated as "tempering." You can also add some minced garlic or ginger to the mix.

I love using this sauce with Hard-Boiled Eggs (page 521), cubes of fried tofu (page 486) or fresh cheese, and green peas or another vegetable. I also like it as a dipping sauce for Aloo Paratha (page 592).

4 tablespoons (½ stick) butter or good-quality vegetable oil
1 onion, chopped
2 cloves garlic, minced
1 1-inch piece fresh ginger, minced
1 tablespoon minced fresh chile (like jalapeño or Thai) or to taste, or red chile flakes or cayenne to taste
2 teaspoons garam masala or curry powder (to make your own, see page 648 or 649)
½ teaspoon chili powder
Large pinch sugar
Salt and pepper
2 cups chopped fresh tomatoes (about 1 pound whole), preferably peeled and seeded, or drained canned tomatoes
½ cup cream or coconut milk (to make your own, see page 304)
½ cup chopped fresh cilantro
1 teaspoon cumin seeds
1 teaspoon mustard seeds

1. Put 3 tablespoons of the butter or oil in a deep skillet over medium-high heat. When the butter is melted or the oil is hot, add the onion, garlic, ginger, and chile. Cook, stirring occasionally, until the onion is soft, about 5 minutes. Stir in the garam masala, chili powder, and sugar and sprinkle with salt and pepper; cook and stir until the spices become fragrant, a minute or 2.

2. Add the tomatoes and cook, stirring frequently, until they start to release their liquid, about 3 minutes. Add the cream and cilantro and keep stirring until the sauce comes to a boil.

3. Turn the heat down so that the sauce bubbles gently and cook, stirring occasionally, until the tomatoes break up and the sauce comes together and thickens, about 30 minutes. Taste and adjust the seasoning. The sauce can be made ahead to this point, cooled, covered, and refrigerated for up to 3 days. Reheat gently before proceeding.

4. Put the remaining 1 tablespoon butter or oil in a small pan over medium-high heat. When the butter is melted or the oil is hot, add the cumin and mustard seeds and toast them until they begin to pop. Spoon over the sauce just before serving.

CHUTNEYS

Although chutneys rely on many of the same (tropical) ingredients as salsas—lime, cilantro, chile, mango, and so on—and are used the same way, as dips, condiments, dressings, and relishes, there are differences. Chutney is a bit denser, often crunchier or nuttier, and used more as a condiment than a sauce. And instead of tasting bright with acidity and chile, it's usually a more complex combination of sweet, sour, and salty that is best described as piquant.

Raw Onion Chutney

MAKES: About ¾ cup
TIME: About 1 hour, largely unattended
M V

I love chutneys bursting with chiles and ginger and herbs, but when you're pairing a chutney with richly flavored legumes like the dals on pages 450 to 453, sometimes a simpler, more directly assaultive accompaniment is in order. This onion-based chutney— a standard in India—certainly fits that bill: It's fresh, bright, pungent, and mind-bogglingly easy. White onions, shallots, or scallions work equally well here.

> 2 small-to-medium or 1 large red or sweet (Vidalia, Bermuda, etc.) onion, quartered and thinly sliced or chopped
> 1 teaspoon salt, or more to taste
> ½ teaspoon coarsely cracked black peppercorns
> ¼ cup red wine vinegar
> 1 teaspoon or more paprika
> Pinch cayenne, or to taste (optional)
> Pinch chaat masala, or to taste (optional)

1. Thoroughly combine the onion with the salt, peppercorns, vinegar, and paprika in a small bowl; let sit for an hour.
2. Stir in the cayenne and/or chaat masala if using them. Serve, or cover and refrigerate for up to a month. Bring to room temperature to serve.

HOT PEPPER CHUTNEY Replace the onion with 4 to 5 hot fresh red chiles. Substitute 2 cloves garlic for the black peppercorns. Pulse in a food processor until coarsely chopped (do not purée). This will keep in the refrigerator, covered, for at least 2 weeks.

Cilantro-Mint Chutney

MAKES: 1½ cups
TIME: 15 minutes
F M V

This recipe plays up the wonderful affinity of cilantro and mint. Made with either herb alone, the chutney will still be worthwhile, but with both it's almost magical, as it would be with Thai or regular basil substituted for the mint.

Depending on your tolerance for heat, you may adjust the number of chiles in the recipe. But remember that raw garlic and ginger pack a punch too.

> 1½ cups firmly packed fresh cilantro leaves
> ½ cup firmly packed fresh mint leaves
> 1 or 2 Thai or other hot fresh green chiles, to taste, or red chile flakes to taste
> 1 2-inch piece fresh ginger, cut into chunks
> ½ large or 1 small-to-medium red onion, cut into chunks
> 2 cloves garlic
> ¼ cup fresh lime juice
> ½ teaspoon salt, or more to taste

1. Put the cilantro, mint, chiles, ginger, onion, and garlic in a food processor and pulse until finely ground.
2. Add the lime juice and salt and process until nearly smooth; you may need to add up to ¼ cup water to help

Clockwise from top: Raw Onion
Chutney. Cilantro-Mint Chutney,
Coconut Chutney (page 670)

the food processor get going. Taste and adjust the seasoning. Serve, or cover and refrigerate for up to a day. Bring to room temperature to serve.

CREAMY CILANTRO-MINT CHUTNEY Yogurt cools the whole thing down a bit and makes it closer to a Raita (page 674): Add ½ cup or more good-quality yogurt, then taste, adjust the seasoning, and serve.

LONG-LASTING CILANTRO-MINT CHUTNEY Increase the garlic to 5 cloves and use ½ cup white wine vinegar instead of the lime juice. Covered and refrigerated, this will last up to several weeks.

Coconut Chutney

MAKES: About 1 cup
TIME: 10 minutes
F M V

This fresh, chewy chutney goes well with just about any Indian-inspired rice dish. In a pinch, you can make it with ingredients from the pantry, and if you don't have coconut, it's equally interesting and delicious (and more colorful) when made with chopped carrots or beets.

½ cup shredded coconut
1 1-inch piece fresh ginger, chopped, or 1 teaspoon ground ginger
1 hot fresh green or red chile, or red chile flakes to taste
½ bunch fresh cilantro, leaves only
¼ teaspoon ground cumin
2 tablespoons fresh lime juice
Salt

1. Put the coconut, ginger, chile, cilantro, and cumin in a food processor or blender and pulse until finely ground.
2. Add the lime juice and a pinch salt and pulse again, until nearly but not quite smooth. Taste and adjust the seasoning. Serve at room temperature. This is best enjoyed the day it is made.

MAYONNAISE AND MAYONNAISE-STYLE SAUCES

Homemade mayo is a zillion times better than anything you'll ever eat out of a jar. It won't keep as long, but it will stay good for at least a week.

Most beginning cooks find the whole idea of making mayonnaise from scratch downright perilous. If failure is your phobia, there's a cure: practice. While a separated or "broken" mayonnaise may not be very appetizing, it's certainly not the end of the world (basically, it's vinaigrette with an egg in it). You'll do better next time. (Alternatively, make a new batch, using the failed mayonnaise in place of oil.)

Then there's the fear of getting food poisoning from raw eggs, a fear you either have or don't. If you do, then use pasteurized eggs, or choose from the eggless recipes that follow, or buy the best mayo you can find and doctor it up with some of the suggestions in this section.

Mayonnaise

MAKES: 1 cup
TIME: 10 minutes
F M

Homemade mayos usually fail because you add the oil to the egg too fast. Temperature fluctuations can cause some instability, so try to make sure your eggs aren't too cold and your oil is at room temperature.

To help you add the oil in a slow, steady stream, put it in a squeeze bottle or a liquid measuring cup with a spout. (Blender or food processor feed tubes with a tiny drizzle hole in them solve this problem; you can jerry-rig one of those with a drill and a fine bit.)

1 egg yolk
1 tablespoon fresh lemon juice, sherry vinegar, or white wine vinegar
2 teaspoons Dijon mustard
1 cup good-quality vegetable oil or extra virgin olive oil
Salt and pepper

1. TO MAKE BY HAND Put the yolk, lemon juice or vinegar, and mustard in a medium bowl. Beat together with a wire whisk. Begin to add the oil as you beat, a little at a time, adding more as each bit is incorporated. You'll notice when a thick emulsion forms, and then you can add the oil a little faster. Depending on how fast you beat, the whole process will take about 5 minutes.

TO MAKE BY MACHINE Put the yolk, lemon juice or vinegar, and mustard in a blender or food processor and turn the machine on. While it's running, add the oil in a slow, steady stream. When an emulsion forms, you can add it a little faster, until all the oil is added and the mixture is smooth.

2. Add salt and pepper, to taste. Serve or cover and refrigerate for up to a week.

GARLIC MAYONNAISE (AÏOLI) Strong and addictive: Replace at least half the oil with olive oil. Peel 3 to 8 cloves garlic, to taste. Mince and stir in along with the salt and pepper.

CHILE MAYONNAISE Use mild chiles like ancho, or hot like Thai or dried chipotle: Soak 1 or 2 dried chiles in warm water until soft. Drain and pat dry. Or use 1 canned chipotle and a little of its adobo sauce. Mince the chiles and stir in along with the salt and pepper.

ROASTED PEPPER MAYONNAISE Pretty and more complex: Roast and clean 1 medium red, yellow, or orange bell pepper (see page 228). Mince and stir in along with the salt and pepper.

COLD MUSTARD SAUCE Delicious sandwich spread: Omit the mustard in Step 1. Add 1 heaping tablespoon Dijon or whole grain mustard along with the salt and pepper. Thin with a tablespoon or 2 of cream—fresh, fraîche, or sour—to the desired consistency.

GREEN SAUCE, FRENCH STYLE Easier by machine: After the emulsion is made, add 1 sprig fresh

---

12 Ideas for Flavoring Mayonnaise

After the mayo is done, stir, blend, or process in any of the following ingredients, alone or in combination. If working by hand, there will always be bits and pieces of the stir-ins for a more rustic sauce. By machine, the mayonnaise will be smooth and evenly colored.

1. A pinch of saffron threads infused in 1 tablespoon boiling water for 10 minutes

2. Up to 1 tablespoon minced strong fresh herb leaves like rosemary, oregano, tarragon, marjoram, epazote, or thyme

3. Up to ¼ cup minced mild fresh herb leaves like parsley, cilantro, chives, chervil, or basil

4. Up to ¼ cup minced sweet pickle

5. 2 tablespoons soy sauce, or to taste

6. 1 teaspoon wasabi powder, or to taste

7. 1 teaspoon grated citrus zest, or to taste

8. At least 1 teaspoon prepared horseradish

9. A few dashes Tabasco sauce, Worcestershire Sauce, Hold the Anchovies (page 633), or other prepared sauce

10. Up to ½ cup chopped toasted almonds, walnuts, or pecans

11. 1 tablespoon minced fresh ginger

12. Up to 2 tablespoons chili powder

---

tarragon, about 10 sprigs watercress (thick stems removed), 10 chives, and the leaves from 5 sprigs parsley to the blender or processor along with the salt and pepper. Process until not quite puréed but definitely green.

RÉMOULADE SAUCE Omit the mustard in Step 1, then stir these additions into the finished mayonnaise: ¼ cup each chopped fresh parsley and chopped scallions, 3 tablespoons Dijon or coarse-grain mustard, 1 tablespoon ketchup, and grated horseradish and cayenne to taste.

Vegannaise

MAKES: Almost 1 cup
TIME: 10 minutes
F M V

If you crave a vegan sandwich spread, salad dressing, or dip base, something you can use in place of traditional mayonnaise, you can stop buying commercially made substitutes now. In fact, you can whip this up in the time it takes to pull the jar from the store shelf and walk to the checkout counter.

A few tips: Cider vinegar lends a more mayonnaise-like flavor; lemon juice is brighter. For a slightly golden tint, add the pinch of turmeric or saffron. Don't skimp on the blending time; your reward will be a creamy consistency. All the variations to Mayonnaise (page 670) and the add-ins work for this recipe too.

> 6 ounces extra-firm silken tofu (about ¾ cup)
> ¼ cup olive oil
> 2 tablespoons cider vinegar or fresh lemon juice
> 2 teaspoons Dijon mustard
> ¼ teaspoon salt, plus more to taste
> Pinch ground turmeric (optional)

1. Put all the ingredients in a blender. Turn the machine to medium speed and let it run for a minute or 2, then turn it off.
2. Scrape the side of the container down with a rubber spatula, turn the blender back on, and let it run for 3 minutes. Stop and scrape again, then run the blender for a minute or so more. Taste and add more salt if necessary. Serve or cover and refrigerate for up to 3 days.

SWEETER VEGANNAISE, SALAD DRESSING STYLE Like really good Miracle Whip, if that makes sense: Add 1 tablespoon sugar along with the other ingredients.

THICKER VEGANNAISE The consistency will be more like store-bought: Reduce the oil to 2 tablespoons and the vinegar to 1 tablespoon. You will have to stop and scrape the side down more frequently.

VEGETARIAN CAESAR DRESSING It's no longer vegan, but it still doesn't contain eggs: Add ¼ cup finely grated Parmesan cheese, 1 tablespoon Worcestershire Sauce, Hold the Anchovies (page 633), and several grinds of pepper.

Real Ranch Dressing

MAKES: 2 cups
TIME: 10 minutes
F M

The big secret to ranch dressing is buttermilk powder, which you can find in the baking section of your supermarket. Nothing else delivers that characteristic buttermilk tang, and it works as a thickener to boot.

> 1 cup mayonnaise (to make your own, see page 670)
> 1 cup buttermilk
> ¼ cup buttermilk powder
> Salt and pepper
> ¼ cup chopped fresh chives or parsley (optional)

1. Put the mayonnaise, buttermilk, and buttermilk powder in a medium jar with a tight-fitting lid. Sprinkle with a little salt and lots of pepper. Add the chives or parsley if you like, put on the lid, and shake vigorously for 30 seconds or so.
2. Taste and adjust the seasoning. Serve or cover and refrigerate for up to 3 days. (It will keep longer if you don't add the fresh herbs.)

CHILE RANCH DRESSING Add 2 teaspoons chili powder.

CURRY RANCH DRESSING Add 1 tablespoon curry powder.

PARMESAN RANCH DRESSING Add 2 tablespoons freshly grated Parmesan cheese and taste first before adding any salt.

"BLEU" RANCH DRESSING Add ¼ cup finely crumbled blue cheese.

Seaweed "Mayo"

MAKES: About ¾ cup
TIME: About 40 minutes, largely unattended
Ⓜ Ⓥ

Like eggs, seaweed has the ability to thicken liquids naturally, which is why it makes such a stable vegan "mayonnaise"; it also makes one with a distinctive and very good flavor. The color will vary depending on which type of seaweed you use. For a vibrant green, use instant wakame. Hijiki "mayo" will be mocha colored with little dark brown flecks, while arame is greenish brown.

Use this as a dip for crudités or as a sandwich spread. It's terrific with Grilled or Broiled Tofu (page 486) and grilled vegetables, or tossed with hot or cold rice, udon, or soba noodles.

> 1 cup arame or hijiki, or ¼ cup instant wakame (see page 244)
> 2 tablespoons sesame, peanut, or grapeseed oil, or a combination
> 1 tablespoon sake or rice vinegar
> Salt

1. Put the arame or hijiki in a medium bowl and cover with warm water. Let soak until very soft, about 30 minutes. Drain, reserving the soaking liquid.
2. Put the seaweed, oil, and sake in a blender with a sprinkle of salt and 2 tablespoons of the soaking water (or tap water, if you're using instant wakame). Turn the machine on; a creamy emulsion will form in about 30 seconds. Stop and push down any stray seaweed that didn't make it into the dressing and blend again to incorporate. Taste and add more salt if needed. Serve or cover and refrigerate for up to 3 days. (If any liquid separates out, just stir it back in before using.)

YOGURT SAUCES

Good yogurt (you can make your own; see page 552) is sour and rich and practically a sauce on its own; add a little salt and you're set. The group of recipes here builds on that, taking yogurt and adding various seasonings or chopped vegetables to it, in the traditions of (mostly) the Middle East and India, where yogurt sauces are called *raitas*.

There is so much good yogurt around these days—including goat and sheep yogurt—that you can easily avoid inferior varieties, including those that contain gelatin or pectin and those that don't contain live cultures. The best yogurt may be thick or thin; it may have a hard, almost cream cheese–like layer on top, or it may not. But what it does have is a fresh, sweet-sour smell and delicious flavor.

---

6 Uses for Yogurt Sauce

Any of the yogurt sauces can be used in myriad different ways.

1. Thin with a little lemon juice and olive oil and use as a salad dressing.

2. Top grilled or steamed vegetables or baked potatoes.

3. Use as a dip for raw veggies or chips.

4. Stir into cooked rice or other grains for extra creaminess, body, flavor, and protein.

5. Cook on top of roasted vegetables as you might cheese (don't overcook; add during the last 5 or 10 minutes of cooking).

6. Stir into chopped or sliced raw fruit for a more complex fruit salad.

The Simplest Yogurt Sauce

MAKES: 1 cup
TIME: 3 minutes
Ⓕ Ⓜ

You might not even think of this as sauce, but I swear, if you use it on grilled or roasted vegetables or as a dip, people will think you're a genius. Add a few drops of lemon juice if your yogurt isn't quite sour enough, which is sometimes the case.

1 cup yogurt (preferably whole milk)

1 teaspoon minced garlic

Salt and pepper

A few drops fresh lemon juice (optional)

Stir the yogurt, garlic, a pinch salt, and a grind or 2 of pepper together in a small bowl. Taste and adjust the seasoning, adding the lemon juice if necessary. Serve or cover and refrigerate for up to a few hours; bring back to near room temperature before serving.

BUTTER-BASED SAUCES

For many people, butter has ceased to be a staple. But when viewed as a luxury, butter takes on a new dimension.

Here, then, are a few simple butter-based sauces:

compound butters, which are butter flavored with herbs or other ingredients, and the classic hollandaise and béchamel sauces. None is likely to be daily fare for you, but all are good to have in your repertoire, especially when you want to treat yourself or your guests to something special.

Hollandaise Sauce

MAKES: About 1 cup
TIME: 10 minutes

F

You can make hollandaise in a blender (see the variation opposite), but the stovetop version is perhaps a little finer and pretty much foolproof. Depending on how you're using it, you can stir about 1 teaspoon minced fresh tarragon, 1 tablespoon fresh dill or chervil, or some other herb into the finished sauce.

The Simplest Yogurt Sauce, Unleashed

Without much work, you can turn this simple sauce into a number of different sauces or condiments. Here are a few ideas that can be used alone or in combination.

HERBED YOGURT SAUCE
Add ¼ cup chopped fresh mint, or to taste. Or use parsley, dill, cilantro, or any other tender herb. Dried mint or dill, about 1 teaspoon, is also acceptable; other dried herbs are not as good.

ONION YOGURT SAUCE
Add 1 tablespoon or more minced onion, shallot, or scallion; you can omit the garlic or not, as you like.

RAITA
The classic Indian yogurt sauce. Add about 1 cup chopped cucumber (peeled if you'd like, and seeded) and/or peeled, seeded, and

diced tomato or any mixture of vegetables, like those you'd use in Chopped Salad (page 36).

RICHER YOGURT SAUCE
Top with 1 tablespoon or so good extra virgin olive oil, along with a sprinkle of paprika, cumin, or garam masala, if you like.

AVOCADO YOGURT SAUCE
Stir in half or more of a ripe avocado, mashed or puréed in a food processor, along with a little extra lemon juice.

FIERY YOGURT SAUCE
Add red chile flakes, chili powder, or minced fresh chile, to taste.

GINGER YOGURT SAUCE
Stir in 1 tablespoon or so of minced fresh ginger.

SPICY YOGURT SAUCE
Stir in any of these, alone or in combination, to taste: ground cumin, paprika, cayenne, dry mustard, saffron threads (mix them first with 1 tablespoon boiling water and let stand for 10 minutes before stirring in) or turmeric (which will give the same color, though not the same flavor), or ground ginger.

YOGURT SAUCE WITH BEANS
Add a cup drained cooked or canned beans; chickpeas work especially well;

Roasted Chickpeas (page 472) work nicely this way also.

SWEET YOGURT SAUCE
A spoonful of honey—either alone or in combination with any of the suggestions above—goes great with heavily seasoned food. And the sweetness helps round out yogurt's natural acidity. Or try pomegranate molasses.

BLUE CHEESE DRESSING
Good with sour cream too: Omit the garlic. Add about ½ cup crumbled blue cheese (Roquefort, for example) along with a bit of fresh lemon juice.

3 egg yolks
Salt
6 tablespoons (¾ stick) butter, softened and cut into tablespoons
1 teaspoon fresh lemon juice
Pinch cayenne (optional)

1. Put the yolks in a small saucepan with 2 tablespoons water and a pinch salt; turn the heat to very low and cook, whisking constantly, until light, foamy, and slightly thickened. (If at any point during this process the yolks begin to curdle, immediately remove from the heat and continue to whisk for a minute before returning the pan to the stove.)
2. Remove from the heat and stir in the butter, a tablespoon or 2 at a time. Return to the heat and continue to whisk until the mixture is thick and bright yellow. Whisk in the lemon juice, then taste and adjust the seasoning (add the cayenne now if you're using it) and serve. (If you like, you can keep the finished sauce warm over extremely low heat or—better—over very hot water, for 15 or even 30 minutes, whisking occasionally.)

BLENDER HOLLANDAISE Melt the butter in a small saucepan over low heat or in the microwave; do not let it brown. Combine the egg yolks, salt, lemon juice, and cayenne if you're using it in the blender and turn on the machine. Slowly drizzle in the butter; the mixture will thicken. Taste and add more lemon juice or other seasonings if necessary.

4 Dishes That Hollandaise Will Turn into Luxurious Affairs

1. Steamed broccoli or asparagus

2. Poached Eggs (page 525)

3. Boiled potatoes

4. Barley Pilaf (page 406) or any plain grain dish

Béchamel Sauce, Eight Ways

MAKES: About 1 cup
TIME: 10 to 20 minutes
F

These creamy sauces all begin with flour and butter (or use oil, when making one of the vegan variations), cooked together to make a thickening paste (roux). To guarantee success, cook the roux long enough to rid the flour of its raw taste; this takes just a couple of minutes but requires nearly constant stirring. And add the milk or other liquid slowly enough, whisking all the while, so that no lumps form. If they do form, you can beat or blend them out, but that's more work.

2 tablespoons butter or extra virgin olive oil
2 tablespoons all-purpose flour
1–1½ cups milk
Salt and pepper

1. Put the butter or oil in a small saucepan over medium-low heat. When the butter melts or the oil is hot, use a wire whisk to incorporate the flour. Turn the heat to low and cook, whisking almost constantly, until the roux turns tan, about 3 minutes.
2. Stir in the milk, a little bit at a time, whisking all the while. When about a cup of the liquid has been stirred in, the mixture will be fairly thick. Add more milk, a little at a time, until the consistency is just a little thinner than you like, then cook, still over low heat, until the mixture thickens up again.
3. Sprinkle with salt and pepper and serve immediately. Or keep warm over gently simmering water for up to an hour, stirring occasionally.

VEGAN BÉCHAMEL SAUCE You can use this to make any of the variations that follow, except for the Mornay. Use oil instead of butter. Substitute oat or rice milk for the cow's milk, and whisk constantly to prevent lumps. Thin the sauce if you'd like with more of the milk, especially if you're going to add flavorings. **V**

BROWN SAUCE A pinch of thyme is good here: In Step 1, use oil instead of butter and cook the roux until brown. Use Roasted Vegetable Stock (page 99) in place of the milk. ⓥ

MUSTARD AND/OR CAPER SAUCE Whisk in 1 tablespoon or more prepared mustard, capers, or both during the last minute of cooking.

PIQUANT SAUCE Season to taste with lemon juice (at least a tablespoon) or vinegar during the last minute of cooking.

MUSHROOM SAUCE Soak a few dried mushrooms in warm water until soft. Remove the mushrooms from the soaking liquid with a slotted spoon and mince them; you'll need 1 to 2 tablespoons. Use oil instead of butter and Roasted Vegetable Stock or Mushroom Stock (page 99) instead of milk, including the strained mushroom soaking liquid when measuring it. Add the mushrooms during the last minute of cooking. ⓥ

LIGHT TOMATO SAUCE Add about 1 tablespoon tomato paste about a minute before removing the sauce from the heat.

CURRY SAUCE Add 1 tablespoon curry powder, or to taste, along with the flour.

MORNAY (CHEESE) SAUCE Stir ½ to 1 cup grated Emmental, Gruyère, or other good cheese into the sauce after it has thickened.

Compound Butter

MAKES: About 5 tablespoons
TIME: 10 minutes
Ⓕ Ⓜ

Compound butter is nothing more than butter mixed with a flavorful ingredient: an herb, like parsley; a spice, like cumin; an aromatic, like garlic; a bit of fruit, like lemon; or a prepared ingredient, like mustard or soy

sauce. The possibilities for use are endless, though traditionally it's been used as a finishing ingredient in sauces and to top grilled or broiled items. But those limits need not concern you. Since it can be made in advance, compound butter is a handy way to add flavor and a luxurious texture to pasta, grains, beans, veggies—whatever.

Compound butter can be refrigerated for days or frozen for a month or so. Make it, roll it into a log, and wrap in two or three layers of plastic before storing. When you need some, cut off a piece and return the rest to the freezer.

> 2 **tablespoons minced fresh herbs (like parsley, chervil, cilantro, chives, dill, or sage), or a smaller amount of tarragon, rosemary, or thyme, or a combination**
> 4 **tablespoons (½ stick) butter, just below room temperature**
> **Salt**
> **Pepper (optional)**
> **Juice of ½ lemon (optional)**

1. Use a fork to cream the herbs with the butter. Taste and add salt as needed, and pepper and lemon juice if you'd like.

2. Use or form into a log, wrap, and refrigerate or freeze until needed.

11 Add-Ins for Compound Butter

These can be used in conjunction with an herb or not, as you prefer (same with the lemon juice) or combined with one another. Amounts are approximate to be added to 4 tablespoons (½ stick) butter and should be adjusted to suit your taste.

1. 2 tablespoons minced scallions

2. 1 tablespoon minced fresh ginger; for a sweet compound butter, also add a tablespoon or 2 of honey or minced candied ginger

3. 1 teaspoon grated lemon or lime zest, along with 1 tablespoon fresh lemon or lime juice

4. 1 tablespoon capers, rinsed and mashed, with 1 teaspoon minced or grated lemon zest

Compound butters, made
with, top to bottom: dill,
wasabi, smoked paprika

5. 1 tablespoon balsamic vinegar, with 1 tablespoon minced shallot if you'd like

6. 1 tablespoon Dijon mustard or 1 teaspoon wasabi powder

7. 2 teaspoons smoked paprika

8. 2 tablespoons minced pitted green or black olives

9. 1 teaspoon minced garlic or 2 or more cloves Roasted Garlic (page 205)

10. Mashed flesh of ½ peach, plum, or pear

11. 1 to 2 teaspoons soy sauce

CRISP TOPPINGS AND GARNISHES

Before grated cheese and fresh herbs became so widely available, many people frequently used stale bread—always on hand—as a garnish. With affluence, less reliance on bread (and generally worse bread), we don't use this garnish much, but its crunch is so appealing that it's due for a comeback.

When you make your own bread crumbs you're not only linking to an ancient tradition, you're not only reusing something you'd otherwise toss, but you're improving vastly on any bread crumbs you've ever purchased. Check it out, as well as the other crunchies here.

Fresh Bread Crumbs

MAKES: About 2 cups
TIME: 10 minutes

F M V

Bread crumbs instantly add texture and substance to almost anything. Sometimes they work like a seasoning or garnish, other times, as in stuffings, they become the main attraction. Make your own whenever possible —the coarse texture is preferable to finely ground store-bought—starting with homemade bread or a good bakery loaf. The difference is stark.

That said, it's a good idea to stock the pantry with

a package of panko crumbs, the Japanese-style bread crumbs; they work in all types of cuisines.

About ½ large loaf French or Italian bread, preferably a day or two old

1. Tear the bread into pieces and put about half in a food processor. Pulse a few times, then let the machine run for a few seconds, until coarsely chopped.

2. Remove and repeat with the remaining bread. Use or store in an airtight container for up to a month.

TOASTED BREAD CRUMBS Crumbs are less likely to become too fine if you toast them after grinding: After grinding, put the bread crumbs on a baking sheet and bake in a 350°F oven, shaking the pan occasionally, until lightly browned, about 15 minutes. These may be stored like fresh, though it makes more sense to store untoasted bread crumbs and toast just before using.

FRIED BREAD CRUMBS These are delicious, and seasoning sticks to them better than uncoated bread crumbs —but they don't keep as well, so use them immediately after frying: Heat ¼ cup extra virgin olive oil in a large skillet and add the bread crumbs; cook, stirring occasionally, until lightly browned, about 5 minutes. Season with salt or any spice blend and drain on paper towels; use immediately.

Croutons

MAKES: 4 to 6 servings
TIME: 15 minutes

F M V

The difference between homemade croutons and the packaged variety cannot be overstated; homemade are delicious and contain no additives. Start with good bread and good olive oil, try some of the variations, and you'll be a convert.

Remember that you can make croutons from any good bread. Corn bread, olive bread, whole grain and whole wheat breads, even raisin or other specialty breads are all excellent candidates.

¼ cup olive oil, or more as needed
1 clove garlic, smashed (optional)
4–6 ½-inch-thick slices good bread
Salt
Pepper (optional)

1. Put the oil and garlic if you're using it in a skillet large enough to hold the bread in a single layer and turn the heat to medium (you may need to do this in batches, depending on the size of the slices). When the oil shimmers or the garlic sizzles, add the bread. Sprinkle it with salt and pepper if you'd like.

2. When the bread browns lightly, after about 5 minutes, turn and brown the other side. If the pan dries out (which it likely will), you can add more olive oil if you like. When the second side is browned, after another 5 minutes or so, remove the croutons. Use or store in an airtight container or wrapped in wax paper for up to a day.

CUBED CROUTONS Before beginning, cut the bread into ½- to 1-inch cubes. Cook them in the oil, tossing occasionally, until lightly browned all over.

HERBED CROUTONS Best with cubes: As the bread browns, stir in about ¼ cup minced fresh parsley, dill, or chervil, or a combination.

Crumbles

Think of crumbles as crisp crumbs or small croutons, made from things other than bread. The idea is to turn common foods—cooked beans or noodles or nuts—into toppings for anything from soups and salads to mashed potatoes and grilled vegetables. There's a tradition of this technique in Japan, where fried bits of tempura batter—*agedama*—are used as a final garnish.

You can handle them all the same way: Start with a large, deep skillet and enough good-quality olive or vegetable oil to cover the pan to a depth of ⅛ to ¼ inch. Turn the heat to medium-high while you prepare your ingredient (see the list below). When the oil is hot, cook the crumbles, turning them gently, stirring, and breaking the pieces up so that they brown and crisp on all sides. Use a slotted spoon to remove them when they are done and set them on paper towels to drain. While they're still hot, sprinkle with salt and pepper or your favorite spice blend (see pages 648 to 652). Each of these is enough for 4 or so servings.

FALAFEL CRUMBLES
Next time you make Falafel (page 472), save ½ cup of batter to make crumbles. (It'll keep in the fridge for a day or 2.) Use a small fork to distribute the batter in the hot oil, and when it starts to set, stir carefully to form small bits.

BEAN CRUMBLES
Start with 1 cup cooked or canned chickpeas, beans, or lentils. Make sure they're well drained. Use a fork to mash them a bit, then put them in the hot oil. As they cook, carefully break them up even more.

NUT CRUMBLES
Pulse ½ cup of your favorite nuts in a food processor a couple of times, or chop by hand, until they're about the size of split peas. Put them in the hot oil and fry until deeply golden, stirring constantly to keep them from burning. They'll be ready in just a minute or so.

NOODLE CRUMBLES
Start with 1 cup cooked long noodles, like spaghetti, angel hair, or thin Asian noodles. Whole grain kinds give you the most flavor and texture. Chop the strands into ½-inch pieces. Add them to the hot oil and cook, stirring occasionally, until crisp, browned, and wavy.

CRUMBLED GRAINS
Take ½ cup large cooked whole grains like wheat or rye berries, hominy, fregola, or farro (page 398). Cook them in the hot oil, stirring occasionally, until golden.

POTATO SKIN CRUMBLES
Coarsely chop the peels from 2 well-scrubbed potatoes. Add them to the hot oil and stir gently to keep them separate while they cook.

HIGHLY SEASONED CROUTONS Use plenty of pepper, along with about 1 teaspoon chili or curry powder.

DRY-BAKED CROUTONS Perfect for large batches; when kept in an airtight container, these will stay crunchy for at least a week. Plus, there's no fat: Preheat the oven to 400°F. Omit the oil and garlic. Slice or cube the bread, spread on a rimmed baking sheet, and bake, undisturbed, until the croutons begin to turn golden, about 15 minutes. Turn the slices or shake the pan to roll the cubes around a bit. Continue baking until they're the desired color, anywhere from 5 to 15 minutes more. Sprinkle with salt and pepper or other seasoning if you like.

Desserts

CHAPTER AT A GLANCE

Almost all desserts are vegetarian—even if you're a strict vegetarian, you pretty much have to watch out only for gelatin (though see "Sugar: The Vegetarian's Dilemma," opposite), which is animal based. So for this collection of recipes, instead of doing a greatest hits of every type of sweet, I've focused on adding more recipes that are vegan and fruit forward, plus many gluten-free options, with some classics thrown in for good measure. You'll find cookies, cakes, pies, puddings, and all sorts of frozen desserts in these pages, all sweetly satisfying.

THE BASICS OF SWEETENERS

Different types of sweeteners have different levels of sweetness and solubility, which dictate how each will behave during cooking. Here's a rundown of both more and less common sweeteners and some ideas for how to use them.

GRANULATED SWEETENERS

WHITE SUGAR

White sugar, the most common granulated sweetener, is processed from sugar cane or sugar beets. It's the equivalent of all-purpose flour; you can use it almost everywhere when recipes call for sugar, and usually it'll work fine. It doesn't add much in the way of flavor, just a kind of neutral sweetness (it does wonders for texture, too, as we'll discuss). The grains are medium size and dissolve well when heated or combined with a relatively large proportion of liquid, or with liquid that's been warmed. All of the following are forms of white sugar.

- Powdered sugar—also called confectioners', icing, 10X, 6X, or 4X sugar (the number indicates the degree of fineness; the higher the number, the finer the sugar)—is just regular sugar ground to a fine powder, with cornstarch added to prevent caking and crystallization. It's used mostly in icings (it dissolves very easily, which also makes it convenient for cold drinks) or for sifting over desserts.

- Superfine sugar—also called castor, caster, or baking sugar—is somewhere between white sugar and powdered sugar in its fineness. It's great to use in anything that won't be cooked but that has some liquid, because the fine crystals dissolve quickly. You can make your own by grinding granulated sugar in a food processor for a few seconds.
- Coarse sugar—decorator's, pearl, or sanding sugar— has a crystal size larger than that of regular sugar, which means it is much slower to dissolve. Use it as a garnish on cookies, cakes, or sweet breads.

BROWN SUGAR

The light and dark brown sugar that most all of us are familiar with (the soft stuff that needs to be packed down when measuring it for a recipe) is refined white sugar to which molasses has been added. Light brown sugar is about 3.5 percent molasses, dark brown is about 6.5 percent molasses. I use light and dark more or less interchangeably so if I call for one and you don't have it, feel free to use the other instead. In most dessert recipes, you can substitute brown sugar for white, as long as you remember the color and flavor will be different.

RAW SUGAR

To make what is marketed as "raw sugar," the sugar is not fully refined; some of the molasses is left in (the "raw" is a misnomer, since this sugar is refined, just not as refined as white sugar). There are several different types of raw sugar; their flavors and textures reflect how much molasses remains:

- **Turbinado** Light brown crystals, with a mild molasses flavor
- **Demerara** Amber or lighter in color, with a large grain and toffee-like flavor
- **Muscovado** Dark brown (darker than dark brown sugar) and very moist, with an assertive molasses flavor

COCONUT SUGAR

This is the product of the sap of the flower buds of the coconut palm, boiled down to a syrup and then dehydrated into a granular sugar. It does not taste like coconut at all, rather, the flavor is closer to brown sugar (and like brown sugar, the granules have a brown tint and are moister than white sugar). You can substitute it 1:1 for granulated or brown sugar. Depending on how much you are using, substituting coconut sugar for white sugar can give the final baked good a darker color and moister texture; it also can result in the item cooking through faster, so if using it for the first time, check on your baked good much earlier than you normally would.

OTHER GRANULATED SUGARS

Date sugar is made from finely ground dehydrated dates. It's tasty and nutritious, but doesn't dissolve easily and varies in sweetness from one batch to the next. Fun for improvised desserts but not a good choice when accurate measures matter.

Fructose is a simple sugar found in honey, fruit, berries, and some root vegetables. It's super-concentrated and loses power when heated or mixed into liquids, so it's tricky to use; I don't mess with it.

Stevia is a no-calorie sweetener, nearly 300 times sweeter than sugar, that's derived from the plant of the same name. Only highly purified stevia (called rebaudioside, or rebiana, or reb A) is approved for use as an ingredient by the FDA. To me, it's in the same category as artificial sweeteners like saccharin, aspartame, and sucralose, and should be avoided as a sweetener and an ingredient in baking unless you have medical reasons to use it.

LIQUID SWEETENERS

HONEY

Because the source of the nectar determines the flavor of the honey, there are more than 300 varieties of honey sold in the United States alone, including orange blossom, clover, and eucalyptus. Many commercially produced honeys are blends from different plant sources. All are about 25 percent sweeter than cane or beet sugar, so you use less of it to achieve the same sweetness. Start by replacing just some of the sugar in your favorite recipe and see what happens; cookies, for example, are

Sugar: The Vegetarian's Dilemma

Part of the process of removing impurities when refining cane sugar (not sugar derived from beets) involves carbonization, and some U.S. sugar manufacturers still use bone char for the carbonization. None of this ends up in the sugar but its use in the process is an issue for some vegetarians. To avoid this conflict, use only beet sugar. (An alternative is to check online for the current lists of cane sugar manufacturers not using bone char.) And remember, this is a possible issue for all products containing cane sugar, not just the white sugars: brown sugar, raw sugar, and molasses, and anything made with these.

tricky because honey causes them to spread more than cookies baked with sugar. And remember that the color of honey will darken foods slightly. Some guidelines for baking with honey:

- Reduce the liquid by ¼ cup for each cup of honey used.
- For every cup of honey, add ½ teaspoon baking soda to balance the honey's acidity.
- When you substitute honey for sugar in quick breads, cookies, and cakes, reduce the oven temperature by 25 degrees to prevent overbrowning.

MAPLE SYRUP

Made from the sap of maple trees, maple syrup is the most American of sweeteners. It varies in color and flavor, depending on the time of year it's collected. There's a grading system that's meant to help you choose, although it often causes confusion. Until relatively recently, it consisted of Grade A (Fancy, Medium Amber, or Dark Amber), Grade B (darker, thicker, with a stronger flavor), and Grade C (darkest, with the most pronounced flavor; this was usually not sold retail). Now, it's all Grade A—rendering the grade meaningless —but accompanied with descriptors. Grade A, Fancy, is now Grade A, Golden Color with Delicate Taste; Grade B is now Grade A, Very Dark with Robust Taste. Whatever you call it, the thicker, darker syrup is better for baking since its flavor is more pronounced.

You can substitute ⅔ cup maple syrup for every 1 cup of sugar; for every 1 cup of maple syrup added, reduce the liquid in the recipe by ¼ cup and add ¼ teaspoon baking soda to balance the syrup's acidity. Finally, reduce the oven temperature by 25 degrees to prevent overbrowning. You can also substitute it for honey in a 1:1 ratio with no other changes to the recipe. In both cases, be aware that its distinctive flavor will have an impact on the final taste of the baked good.

MOLASSES

A brown, heavy syrup produced during the sugar-making process. The first boiling produces light molasses, which can be used like honey; the second produces dark molasses, a thick, full-flavored, not-so-sweet syrup for cooking; and the third yields blackstrap molasses, the darkest, thickest, most nutritious, and, from the cook's perspective, least useful of the bunch. You can cook and bake with blackstrap, though it's best to blend it with light molasses or honey, and you'll still find the flavor surprising at best.

AGAVE NECTAR

This is made by boiling down the sap of several types of agave, including the blue agave plant (the source plant for tequila); it is much sweeter than sugar or honey. You can substitute it for no more than half the granulated sugar in a recipe; for every 1 cup sugar, use ⅔ cup agave nectar and reduce the other liquids in the recipe by ¼ cup.

RICE SYRUP (RICE HONEY)

When the starches in whole grain rice are processed, they become the complex sugars maltose and glucose. Rice syrup has a mildly sweet butterscotch taste, and generally produces baked goods that are crisper than those made with cane sugar. Because rice syrup is half

---

12 Ways to Infuse Simple Syrup

Heat makes infusion a breeze. Add your flavoring (or mix and match any of the following) to the sugar and water for Simple Syrup (opposite), heat until the sugar is dissolved, then simmer over very low heat for 5 to 10 minutes unless otherwise noted. Leave in larger items, or strain them out just before you transfer the syrup to a container.

The following are suggested amounts for one batch of simple syrup, but you can and should feel free to adjust the quantities to your taste.

1. Use brown sugar or raw sugar in place of the granulated sugar

2. 2 tablespoons minced citrus zest or 2 to 3 strips, plus ¾ cup juice

3. The scraped seeds from 1 or 2 vanilla beans, with the scraped pod if you like

4. 6 cinnamon sticks; 6 to 8 crushed cardamom pods; and/or 2 tablespoons whole cloves or allspice berries.

Feel free to combine; these are especially excellent with brown sugar and citrus

5. ¼ cup black peppercorns, whole or cracked (don't be skeptical—pepper contributes a wonderfully fragrant, complex flavor)

6. ¼ pound (about 10 inches) fresh ginger, cut into thin rounds. Steep off the heat for 30 to 45 minutes

7. 2 tablespoons culinary-grade lavender buds. Be careful adding more; it can end up tasting soapy

8. 2 to 4 stalks fresh lemongrass, coarsely chopped

9. 1½ cups lightly packed fresh mint or basil leaves, 1 cup lemon verbena or lemon balm leaves, or 6 to 8 sprigs thyme or rosemary. Simmer for 5 minutes, then cover and steep off the heat for another 5 minutes

10. 2 tea bags or 2 tablespoons loose leaves, like chamomile, green tea, or Earl Grey. Add to the syrup after the sugar has dissolved and steep for no more than 5 minutes.

11. ½ cup chopped or ground coffee beans

12. 3 to 5 coarsely chopped fresh hot chiles, like Thai, jalapeño, or habanero

as sweet as cane sugar, substituting it in recipes calling for cane sugar can be challenging. As a guideline, for each 1 cup cane sugar substitute 1¼ cups rice syrup, decrease the liquid by ¼ cup, and add ¼ teaspoon baking soda to balance the syrup's acidity. You can use it as a direct substitute for honey.

OTHER LIQUID SWEETENERS

Corn syrup (not to be confused with the controversial high-fructose version, which isn't sold in supermarkets) is a thick, sticky sweetener processed from corn starch. Light corn syrup is clarified; dark is flavored with caramel, which makes it sweeter and (duh) darker.

Cane syrup is made by boiling sugar cane juice until golden and thickened. It has a distinctive caramel flavor and is sweeter than molasses because the sugar hasn't been removed. It's popular in the South, particularly Louisiana, where it is used like maple syrup, poured over pancakes and waffles.

Malt syrup, made from sprouted barley, is most often used in the home production of beer; it has a mild, sweet flavor. (Made into a powder, it's used to make malted milk shakes.)

Treacle, popular in Europe, is similar in flavor to molasses; the light variety is called "golden syrup," the dark type "black treacle."

Sorghum syrup is another molasses-like sweetener made from an African grain; use it as you would honey or molasses.

Palm syrup is made by boiling the sap of the date palm tree (palm sugar has the same source); it's sweet and dark, and is often added to desserts in Asia.

Simple Syrup

MAKES: 2 cups
TIME: 10 minutes
F M V

This is perfect for instantly adding sweetness with no worry of remaining undissolved sugar granules. It comes in handy when making sorbets, granitas, and cold drinks including tea, coffee, and cocktails. Make this syrup in any quantity you need; the ratio—equal parts water and sugar—is always the same.

2 cups sugar

Put the sugar and 2 cups water in a small saucepan. Bring to a boil and cook until the sugar is dissolved, stirring occasionally. Set aside to cool to room temperature. Use immediately or refrigerate in an airtight container for up to 6 months.

THE BASICS OF CHOCOLATE

I approach chocolate the same way I do cheese or wine: No matter how many variables there are, you want to start with a delicious ingredient, the best quality that you can afford and find without hassle. If the chocolate tastes great when you bite into it, it's certainly good enough for cooking; it if doesn't, remember that cooking won't fix or hide off flavors or strange textures. This is why I avoid mass-produced chocolate chips and premade sauces; they're usually not delicious when eaten straight, and it's simple enough to chunk, chop, or melt a good eating chocolate. Your desserts will be much better for that small bit of extra work.

And it's increasingly easy to find good chocolate; even supermarkets carry better brands than they did just a few years ago. One thing many people don't know is that you can use good "candy-bar" chocolate for cooking—you're not limited to whatever happens to be on the shelf next to the flour. Go by quality first, then the type of chocolate. For most desserts—and for eating, actually—I turn to bittersweet or semisweet chocolate.

Chocolate production is not a simple thing: It begins with the seeds of the tropical cacao tree. The cacao beans (as they're called) are fermented, then dried, sorted, roasted, and shelled. All this produces what is called a nib, which is ground and refined into chocolate liquor, which consists of the cocoa solids and cocoa butter. The cocoa butter isn't butter in the way you would normally think about it; it's the natural fat of the cacao bean. It is responsible for the mouthfeel of chocolate.

To get to edible chocolate, the liquor is mixed with other ingredients—at the very least, sugar, but it can also include vanilla or other flavorings, additional cocoa butter, milk solids, vegetable oils, emulsifiers like lecithin—then stirred or "conched." Before chocolate can be molded, it is tempered—a heating and cooling process that yields chocolate that is hard, smooth, and glossy. High-quality beans and careful production distinguishes good chocolate from bad, as does avoiding the addition of ingredients that detract from quality; I look for chocolate made with cocoa solids, cocoa butter, and sugar, period. The types of chocolate are defined by the percentage of chocolate liquor they contain.

UNSWEETENED CHOCOLATE
Also known as baking chocolate, this is a chocolate liquor—cocoa solids and cocoa butter—with no sugar added. Unsweetened chocolate is too bitter to eat, but useful for home chocolate making, cooking, and baking.

DARK CHOCOLATE
This is the type of chocolate I use for cooking and baking. The chocolate liquor content ranges from 35 to 99 percent, with less than 12 percent milk solids (in fact, it doesn't have to include any milk solids). It is sold as sweet dark, semisweet, extra dark, bittersweet, or extra bittersweet, depending on how much sugar and/or milk solids are added. Try a few brands before settling on your favorites for cooking. First listen to the snap when you break a piece in two; it should sound crisp. Many good-quality bittersweet chocolates taste almost chalky if you're not used to them, but they coat your mouth evenly without any waxiness or grittiness—that's the cocoa butter at work. As the chocolate melts on your tongue, you should register all sorts of flavors, from coffee-like roasted notes to fruit and acidic tones.

MILK CHOCOLATE
This must contain a minimum of 10 percent chocolate liquor, 12 percent milk solids, and 3.39 percent milk fat. If you like sweet, melt-in-your mouth chocolate, this is it. Look for a brand that tastes rich, almost buttery, with no cloying or greasy aftertaste. Good quality milk chocolate should be as complex as bittersweet or dark chocolate, with the flavors muted against a backdrop of creaminess.

COCOA POWDER
Be sure to use unsweetened cocoa powder, not the sweetened stuff used for making hot chocolate. Cocoa powder has had the cocoa butter removed. "Dutched," "Dutch process," or "alkalized" cocoa has been treated with an alkali to reduce acidity and darken the color. "Natural" cocoa powder is light brown and more acidic but also carries more chocolate flavor, if you possess discriminating taste buds. Basically, they are interchangeable in the recipes here. The only potential problem is in leavening; if you use natural cocoa and there's no baking soda in the recipe, add a pinch to balance the acidity.

WHITE CHOCOLATE
White chocolate is not technically chocolate, but a confection made from cocoa butter, butterfat, milk solids, sugar, and flavorings; it contains no cocoa solids. It must contain at least 20 percent cocoa butter, 14 percent milk solids, and 3.39 percent milk fat. Although it's a completely different ingredient, it substitutes well for "regular" chocolate in most recipes.

There's a huge difference between good white chocolate and the cheap stuff. Scan the label; cocoa butter should be the first ingredient; do not buy a white chocolate that contains vegetable fat. Always taste it before you cook with it. Good white chocolate has a subtle flavor and should never be waxy, gritty, or bland. At its best, white chocolate melts very slowly in your mouth and is something like eating straight vanilla, if it could be made into chocolate.

White chocolate doesn't keep nearly as long as chocolate, only a few weeks.

CAROB

Not chocolate at all, but made from a legume; commonly used as a cocoa substitute for people who are allergic to chocolate. It tastes grassy and vegetative and, because it has none of the fat of cocoa butter, it's grainier. Few people prefer it to chocolate.

STORING CHOCOLATE

There's no need to refrigerate chocolate, but since it keeps best in a cool, dry place, the fridge is just fine. Stored properly, chocolate can last for at least a year; bittersweet chocolate can even improve as it ages.

Sometimes chocolate develops a white or gray sheen or thin coating. The chocolate hasn't gone bad; it's "bloomed," a condition caused by exposure to too much moisture or fluctuating temperatures that have caused the fat or sugar to come to the surface and crystallize. The chocolate is still perfectly fine for cooking, as long as you're not making coated candy. It's also okay to eat bloomed chocolate out of hand, too, though the texture may be grainy.

CHOPPING OR SHAVING CHOCOLATE

Chop chocolate with a chef's knife on a cutting board, pressing down firmly but carefully to cut it into first big pieces, then smaller, until you get the size you want. This will go better if the chocolate is cold to start.

To make chocolate shavings, put the chocolate on a clean cloth towel and carefully pull the knife toward you, or use a vegetable peeler. It might take a couple passes to get the hang of it, but they're surprisingly easy to make. Again, cold chocolate is easier to work with.

MELTING CHOCOLATE

Be careful when you melt chocolate, because it scorches easily. First, chop the chocolate (small pieces melt faster than big chunks). Then boil a pot of water, take it off the heat, set a small glass bowl with your chocolate over it,

and stir until melted (or use a double boiler). You can also melt the chocolate directly over the lowest possible heat, keeping a very close eye on it. Or microwave the chocolate for a minute or two at the lowest setting; watch it like a hawk and interrupt to stir once or twice. Melting chocolate with liquids is trickier, so I always melt the chocolate alone, then work with it.

COOKIES AND BARS

Cookies and bars can be whipped up at a moment's notice, and are one of life's greatest pleasures. Not much is required beyond two mixing bowls—and sometimes just one—a wooden spoon, and a cookie sheet or a baking pan (for bars). Here are a few tips for success.

- You can avoid greasing pans if you line them with parchment paper or use a silicone baking mat to prevent sticking. (On the other hand, "greasing" pans with butter adds flavor.)
- For drop cookies, space the cookies at least 2 inches apart to allow for spread.
- Because most ovens have hot spots, rotate pans halfway through the estimated bake time to promote even browning. If you are baking multiple sheets of cookies

at the same time, rotate cookie sheets and—for added promotion of even cooking—move the sheet on the bottom rack up and vice versa.

- Don't bake more than two sheets of cookies at one time, even if your oven has three racks; it will impede the airflow too much and interfere with browning.
- Let the cookies rest for a few minutes before removing them from the sheet. Straight-from-the-oven cookies are soft and may fall apart or stick to one another on a plate. (But don't wait too long or they will stick to the pan.)

Chocolate Chunk Cookies

MAKES: 2 to 3 dozen
TIME: About 30 minutes
Ⓜ

Chewy in the middle, crisp at the edges, and full of real chocolate flavor, these cookies will make you forget all about waxy, bland chocolate chips. Use whatever chocolate you like best; I always go dark. This recipe has almost infinite variations; some favorites follow.

½	**pound (2 sticks) butter, softened**
¾	**cup granulated sugar**
¾	**cup brown sugar**
2	**eggs**
1	**teaspoon vanilla extract**
2	**cups all-purpose flour**
1	**teaspoon salt**
¾	**teaspoon baking soda**
8	**ounces chocolate, chopped**

1. Heat the oven to 375°F.

2. Cream together the butter and sugars in a large bowl until light and fluffy. Add the eggs one at a time and beat until well blended, then stir in the vanilla. Stir together the flour, salt, and baking soda in a medium bowl. Gradually add the dry ingredients to the butter mixture and stir until just incorporated. Stir in the chocolate.

3. Drop tablespoon-size mounds of dough onto ungreased baking sheets about 2 inches apart. Bake for

8 to 10 minutes, until lightly browned. Cool for 3 to 5 minutes on the sheets before transferring the cookies to a wire rack to finish cooling. Store in an airtight container for a day or two.

VEGAN CHOCOLATE CHUNK COOKIES Use any neutral-tasting vegetable oil, or coconut oil for a little extra flavor: Add 1 teaspoon baking powder to the flour mixture. Replace the butter and eggs with ⅔ cup oil and ¼ cup water or unsweetened nondairy milk; beat them both with the sugars until everything is smooth. Use vegan chocolate (see page 687). You can also use these substitutions to make any of the other variations. Ⓥ

OATY CHOCOLATE CHUNK COOKIES For subtle oat flavor and softer texture: Substitute 1 cup oat flour (to make your own, pulse rolled oats in a food processor) for 1 cup of all-purpose. These can also be gluten free and even oatier if you substitute 2 cups oat flour for all of the all-purpose flour and increase the baking soda to 1 teaspoon.

CHOCOLATE–CHOCOLATE CHUNK COOKIES Melt 1 ounce each semisweet and unsweetened chocolate, let cool, and add to the dough before adding the flour mixture.

MEXICAN CHOCOLATE CHUNK COOKIES These are barely spicy; I think of them as toasty, warm, and slightly savory: Add 1 teaspoon ground cinnamon, ½ teaspoon cayenne, and ¼ teaspoon freshly grated nutmeg to the dry ingredients.

Oatmeal Raisin Cookies

MAKES: 2 to 3 dozen
TIME: About 30 minutes
Ⓜ

One of the most accommodating doughs, these cakey cookies beg for add-ins. Just about any dried fruit can be used in place of the raisins, but don't stop there; try adding crushed nuts, nut butters, or chocolate. The dough can handle up to 1½ cups of extras.

        12 tablespoons (1½ sticks) butter, softened

        1 cup brown sugar

        ½ cup granulated sugar

        2 eggs

        1 teaspoon vanilla extract

        2 cups rolled oats (not instant)

    1½ cups all-purpose flour

        2 teaspoons ground cinnamon

        1 teaspoon baking soda

        1 teaspoon salt

        ¼ cup milk

    1½ cups raisins

1. Heat the oven to 375°F.

2. Cream together the butter and sugars in a large bowl until light and fluffy. Add the eggs one at a time, beating after each addition until just combined, then stir in the vanilla. Stir together the oats, flour, cinnamon, baking soda, and salt in a medium bowl. Gradually add the dry ingredients and the milk to the butter mixture. Stir in the raisins.

3. Drop tablespoon-size mounds of dough onto un-greased baking sheets about 2 inches apart. Bake for 12 to 15 minutes, until lightly browned. Cool for about 2 minutes on the sheets before transferring the cookies to racks to finish cooling. Store in an airtight container for a day or 2.

VEGAN OATMEAL COOKIES Instead of butter, use ½ cup melted coconut oil. Mix 2 tablespoons ground flaxseeds with 6 tablespoons water until smooth; let sit for a few minutes, until the mixture is gelatinous, and use this in place of the eggs. Use your favorite nondairy milk. You can also use these substitutions to make any of the variations. V

CHEWY OATMEAL RAISIN COOKIES Omit the milk and add 1 tablespoon molasses with the vanilla.

OATMEAL-CHOCOLATE CHUNK COOKIES Chop 8 ounces dark chocolate into chunks and substitute for the raisins.

CHERRY-CHOCOLATE CHUNK OATMEAL COOKIES
Swap ¾ cup dried cherries for the raisins.

OATMEAL APPLE COOKIES Substitute unsweetened applesauce for the milk and 1½ cups chopped dried apples (about 5 ounces) for the raisins.

OATMEAL CARROT COOKIES Add a pinch freshly grated nutmeg and/or ground cloves along with the cinnamon, and substitute 1½ cups grated carrots for the raisins.

OATMEAL-RUM RAISIN COOKIES Soak the raisins in ½ cup dark rum until plump, a couple of hours. Discard (or drink) whatever rum is left over. Include a handful of chopped pecans if you like.

Peanut Butter Cookies

MAKES: 3 dozen
TIME: About 30 minutes
M

Like all good peanut butter cookies, these sport chewy centers, crunchy edges, and big peanut flavor, all the more so if you add chopped peanuts. Creamy or crunchy peanut butter is your call, but do make sure it contains nothing other than peanuts and salt.

        8 tablespoons (1 stick) butter, softened

        1 cup light brown sugar

        ½ cup granulated sugar

        1 cup peanut butter

        2 eggs

        1 teaspoon vanilla extract

        1 cup all-purpose flour

        ½ teaspoon baking soda

        ¼ teaspoon salt

        1 cup roasted peanuts, chopped (optional)

1. Heat the oven to 350°F.

2. Cream together the butter and sugars until light and fluffy, then beat in the peanut butter. Add the eggs and vanilla. Stir together the flour, baking soda, and salt in

a small bowl. Gradually add the dry ingredients to the butter mixture and mix until just combined. If you're using them, stir in the peanuts.

3. Drop tablespoon-size mounds of dough onto ungreased baking sheets about 2 inches apart. Use the back of a fork to press lines into the top of each cookie, rotating it to make a crosshatch pattern. If the fork gets too sticky, dip it in a bit of water. Bake for 8 to 10 minutes, until lightly browned. Cool for about 2 minutes on the sheets before transferring the cookies to racks to finish cooling. Store in an airtight container for a day or 2.

VEGAN PEANUT BUTTER COOKIES Replace the butter and eggs with ⅓ cup good-quality neutral-tasting vegetable oil or coconut oil (which will have a bit more flavor), and ¼ cup unsweetened almond milk or water. Add an extra ¼ cup peanut butter. You can also use these substitutions to make any of the variations (for the Peanut Butter–Honey, use maple syrup instead of honey). 🅥

FLOURLESS PEANUT BUTTER COOKIES These cookies have only 5 ingredients, so even if you aren't avoiding gluten, they're irresistibly convenient: Increase the peanut butter to 2 cups and mix it with the sugars, eggs, and vanilla until fully combined; omit all other ingredients.

PEANUT BUTTER–CHOCOLATE CHIP COOKIES Chop 6 ounces chocolate and stir it into the finished dough in place of the chopped peanuts.

PEANUT BUTTER–HONEY COOKIES Replace the brown sugar with 1 cup honey and add 1 teaspoon baking powder to the dry ingredients.

PB&J COOKIES Like a peanut butter thumbprint: When the dough is finished, cover the bowl and refrigerate until firm, about 2 hours. Scoop the dough and roll it by hand into tablespoon-size balls, then place on the sheets about 2 inches apart. Use your thumb to make a shallow indentation in the top of each cookie, then fill the indentations with about a teaspoon of the fruit jam or jelly of your choice and bake.

Fig Bittmans

MAKES: About 2 dozen
TIME: About 45 minutes, plus time to chill
Ⓜ

You won't believe how much better these are than the packaged versions most of us have eaten all of our lives. The fig filling is so simple but has an irresistibly caramel-like texture, and the pop of citrus is not only surprising but exciting.

12	tablespoons (1½ sticks) butter, softened
¾	cup brown sugar
1½	teaspoons vanilla extract
1	egg
3	tablespoons grated orange zest
2	cups all-purpose flour
½	teaspoon baking powder
½	teaspoon baking soda
½	teaspoon salt
8	ounces dried figs, chopped
1	cup fresh orange juice

1. Beat together the butter and sugar in a large bowl with an electric mixer until fluffy. Beat in 1 teaspoon of the vanilla and the egg until well blended, then the zest.
2. In a separate bowl, stir together the flour, baking powder, baking soda, and salt. Gradually mix the dry ingredients into the butter mixture until just combined. Shape the dough into a disk, wrap in plastic, and chill for at least 1 hour, until firm.
3. Make the filling while the dough chills. Combine the figs and orange juice in a small saucepan and bring to a simmer over medium heat. Cook until the figs are soft, 5 to 15 minutes, depending on how dry the figs are. Drain and purée with the remaining ½ teaspoon vanilla. Set aside to cool.
4. Heat the oven to 375°F. On a lightly floured work

surface, divide the dough into quarters and roll each piece into a long rectangle about 4 inches wide; square off the edges of the dough as needed to keep it relatively even. Spoon the fig filling lengthwise evenly down the middle of each piece of dough; fold up the sides of the dough around it and press gently to seal. Bake on ungreased cookie sheets, seam side down, for about 15 minutes, until the logs are evenly golden. Cut into squares while they are still warm. Store in a tightly covered container for up to 1 week.

Flourless Brownies

MAKES: About 1 dozen
TIME: About 45 minutes
Ⓜ

If you love chocolate, you've probably had flourless chocolate cake. Flourless brownies are just as satisfying —fudgy and rich with a double dose of chocolate. Powerful stuff.

½	**pound (2 sticks) butter, plus more for greasing**
8	**ounces dark chocolate, chopped**
4	**large eggs**
1	**cup sugar**
1	**teaspoon vanilla extract**
¼	**cup cocoa powder**

1. Heat the oven to 350°F. Grease an 8- or 9-inch square baking pan, or line it with parchment paper and grease the parchment.
2. Put the chocolate and butter in a small saucepan over low heat, stirring frequently until melted and smooth. Cool.
3. Beat together the eggs and sugar in a large bowl with an electric mixer until thick. Add the vanilla and gradually add the chocolate mixture; mix until fully incorporated. Fold in the cocoa powder.
4. Pour the batter into the prepared pan, using a spatula to spread it into an even layer if necessary. Bake for

about 35 minutes, until the center is barely set. Cool completely in the pan on a wire rack before cutting. These will keep in an airtight container for no more than a day or 2.

NUTTY FLOURLESS BROWNIES Here nuts are both a flour substitute and a crunchy add-in: Use 3 eggs rather than 4 and substitute 1 cup almond flour for the cocoa powder. Fold 1 cup chopped nuts (toasted, see page 299, or raw) into the batter before pouring it into the pan.

No-Bake Granola Bars

MAKES: About 1 dozen
TIME: About 15 minutes
Ⓕ Ⓜ Ⓞ

There's been plenty of disputing granola's status as a health food, and for good reason, since much of what you buy is loaded with sweeteners. When you make your own, and use it to make these snack bars, the results are immeasurably superior. You can also make these with raw oats—the result will be chewier and simpler.

¼	**cup good-quality olive oil, plus more for greasing**
3	**cups The Best Granola (page 421) or rolled oats**
¾	**cup honey or maple syrup**
¼	**cup brown sugar**
	Pinch salt

1. Lightly grease an 8- or 9-inch square baking pan with oil. If using oats, toast them if you like: Spread in a rimmed baking sheet and toast in a 350°F oven for 15 to 20 minutes, until golden.
2. Put the granola in a large heatproof bowl. Bring the honey, brown sugar, ¼ cup oil, and salt to a boil in a small saucepan. Pour this over the granola and mix until everything is well coated, working quickly while the liquid is still warm.
3. Press the mixture evenly into the prepared pan and let chill completely in the fridge. Cut into squares

or rectangles. Store in an airtight container for up to 4 days.

PEANUT BUTTER GRANOLA BARS Your own power bar: Substitute ½ cup peanut butter (or any other nut butter) for the brown sugar and oil; heat only the honey or maple syrup and whisk in the nut butter immediately after you remove it from the heat.

COCONUT GRANOLA BARS Toast the coconut beforehand for a warmer, sweeter flavor: Stir the granola with ¾ cup shredded coconut, then toss to coat in the brown sugar mixture.

MAPLE-CINNAMON GRANOLA BARS Stir 1½ teaspoons ground cinnamon into the granola. Use maple syrup. Add up to 1¼ cups chopped pecans if you like. **V**

BAKED OAT BARS Like a cross between a granola bar and a cookie: Heat the oven to 375°F and grease a rimmed baking sheet. Melt 12 tablespoons (1½ sticks) butter and let cool before mixing with the granola, honey, sugar, and 2 egg whites; omit the oil. Bake until golden brown, about 30 minutes.

No-Bake Fruit and Cereal Bars

MAKES: About 1 dozen
TIME: About 15 minutes
F **M** **O**

This snack bar is so simple that you can almost put it together in the time it takes to buy a junky version at the store. Between the fruit and cereal, there's a lot of room for variation. Keep it relatively light with puffed rice or shredded wheat; bulk it up with granola or whole grain flakes. Dried dates, figs, and apricots are particularly nice.

    2 tablespoons good-quality vegetable oil, plus
       more for greasing
    1½ cups dried fruit
    2 tablespoons honey or maple syrup
       Fruit juice or water as needed
    3 cups The Best Granola (page 421) or high-
       quality ready-to-eat cereal

1. Lightly grease an 8- or 9-inch square baking pan. Put the dried fruit, oil, and honey in a food processor and pulse until sticky; if necessary, add juice or water 1 tablespoon at a time to break up the fruit. In a large bowl, fold the fruit mixture into the cereal until the cereal is well coated.
2. Press the mixture evenly into the prepared pan and chill in the fridge until set. Cut into squares or rectangles. Store in an airtight container for up to 4 days.

CAKES

Cakes come in all shapes, textures, and flavors. For the selection here, I've focused on a few classics, some creative twists, and some vegan and gluten-free offerings that are good enough to satisfy non-vegan gluten eaters as well.

Baking times in these recipes are approximate and will vary a little—or even a lot—depending on the accuracy of your oven, the size of pan or pans you use, even the temperature of your batter. But since you don't want to open the oven to check on things more than is necessary, start by getting an oven thermometer; then, when you're baking a cake, wait until about three-quarters of the estimated time has expired, then take a peek, check for doneness (rotate the pan if the cake is cooking unevenly) and judge accordingly how to proceed.

I like to use my nose to judge when a cake is nearing doneness: When you start to smell it, take that first look; then stick a toothpick or cake tester (a thin metal skewer) into the center; if it comes out clean, it's done. (You can also press gently in the center of the cake with one finger. It should immediately spring back. If it leaves a mark, let the cake bake a bit longer.)

Chocolate Cake

MAKES: At least 10 servings
TIME: About 1 hour
M

This is a basic chocolate cake—fantastic with anything from your favorite frosting to whipped cream, a layer of jam, or just a dusting of confectioners' sugar—made extra light with whipped egg whites and cake flour. You can also use this to make cupcakes (see page 697); it'll yield about two dozen.

- 8 tablespoons (1 stick) butter, softened, plus more for greasing
- 2 cups cake or all-purpose flour, plus more for dusting
- 3 ounces unsweetened chocolate, coarsely chopped
- 2 teaspoons baking powder
- ½ teaspoon baking soda
- ½ teaspoon salt
- ¾ cup sugar
- 2 eggs, separated
- 1 teaspoon vanilla extract
- 1¼ cups milk

1. Heat the oven to 350°F. Grease and flour the bottom and sides of two 9-inch or three 8-inch layer cake pans, or a 13 × 9-inch sheet cake pan.

2. Melt the chocolate in a small saucepan over very low heat or in a double boiler over hot—not boiling—water, stirring occasionally. When the chocolate is just about melted, remove from the heat and continue to stir it until smooth.

3. Stir together the flour, baking powder, baking soda, and salt in a medium bowl. Use an electric mixer to cream the butter in a large bowl until smooth, then gradually add the sugar. Beat until light in color and fluffy, 3 or 4 minutes. Beat in the egg yolks, one at a time, then the vanilla, and finally the chocolate. Gradually stir the dry ingredients into the batter a little at a time, alternating with the milk. Stir just until smooth.

4. Wash and dry the beaters thoroughly, then beat the egg whites in a medium bowl until they hold soft peaks. Use a rubber spatula to fold them gently but thoroughly into the batter. Turn it into the pan(s) and bake until a toothpick inserted into the center of the cake(s) comes out clean, about 30 minutes for layers or 20 minutes for a sheet cake. Let the cake cool in the pan(s) for 5 minutes, then invert onto a rack to finish cooling.

5. Frost or glaze or sprinkle with confectioners' sugar if you like and store at room temperature. If you're not frosting right away, you can wrap each layer tightly with plastic wrap and store at room temperature for up to 2 days or with plastic wrap and foil and store in the freezer for up to a few months.

VEGAN CHOCOLATE CAKE Use ½ cup cocoa powder instead of the chopped chocolate; whisk it with the other dry ingredients. Swap the butter for ½ cup good-quality neutral-tasting vegetable oil and the sugar for 1 cup maple syrup. Omit the eggs. Substitute 1½ cups unsweetened almond or soy milk for the dairy milk; add 1 tablespoon cider vinegar to the milk and let the mixture sit for 10 minutes before using. You can also use these substitutions to make any of the variations. **V**

CHOCOLATE-ORANGE CAKE This cake is especially decadent with rich ganache: Beat 2 tablespoons grated orange zest into the butter mixture. To assemble the cake, spread a thin layer of Orange Glaze (page 703) on the first layer of the cake. Frost the remaining cake with Chocolate Ganache or Vegan Chocolate Ganache (page 705) flavored with 1 tablespoon grated orange zest.

CHOCOLATE-ESPRESSO CAKE Beat 3 tablespoons instant espresso powder into the butter mixture. Frost the cake with Chocolate Ganache or Vegan Chocolate Ganache (page 705). If you like, decorate the cake with chopped chocolate-covered espresso beans.

Chocolate Cake
with Cream Cheese
Frosting (page 702)

Yellow Cake

MAKES: One 8- or 9-inch or 13 × 9-inch cake (at least 10 servings)
TIME: About 1 hour

Ⓜ

Because this is a great base for lots of frosting and filling combinations, it's my go-to cake for birthdays and special occasions. You can also use this recipe to make cupcakes (opposite); it'll yield about two dozen.

10	tablespoons (1¼ sticks) butter, softened, plus more for greasing
2	cups cake or all-purpose flour, plus more for dusting
2½	teaspoons baking powder
¼	teaspoon salt
1¼	cups sugar
8	egg yolks
2	teaspoons vanilla extract or 1 tablespoon grated or minced orange zest
¼	teaspoon almond extract (optional)
¾	cup milk

1. Heat the oven to 350°F. Grease and flour the bottom and sides of two 9-inch or three 8-inch layer cake pans or a 13 × 9-inch sheet cake pan.

2. Stir together the flour, baking powder, and salt in a medium bowl. Use an electric mixer to cream the butter in a large bowl until smooth, then gradually add the sugar. Beat until light in color and fluffy, 3 or 4 minutes. Beat in the yolks, one at a time, then add the vanilla and almond extract if you're using it. Gradually add the flour mixture to the batter, mixing by hand and alternating with the milk. Stir just until smooth.

3. Divide the batter evenly between the pans or pour into the sheet pan and bake until a toothpick inserted into the center comes out clean or with a few moist crumbs, about 35 minutes for layers or about 25 minutes for a sheet cake. Cool in the pan for 5 minutes, run a knife around the edge of the cake to loosen it, then invert onto a rack to finish cooling.

4. Frost or glaze if you like and store at room tempera-ture. If you're not frosting right away, you can wrap each layer tightly with plastic and store at room temperature for up to 2 days or wrap in plastic and foil and store in the freezer for up to a few months.

VEGAN YELLOW CAKE Substitute 1 cup soy or almond milk for the dairy milk; stir in 1 tablespoon cider vinegar and let the mixture sit for 10 minutes. Reduce the baking powder to 2 teaspoons and add ½ teaspoon baking soda. Omit the eggs and replace the butter with ¾ cup canola oil. Optional: Whisk ¼ teaspoon ground turmeric into the flour mixture to supply the cake's signature yellow color. Ⓥ

PISTACHIO-SAFFRON CAKE Try it with Orange Glaze (page 703) or Whipped Cream (page 700) infused with rose water: Heat the milk to steaming and steep ½ teaspoon crumbled saffron threads in it until it's cool, at least 20 minutes. Substitute finely ground pistachios for 1 cup of the flour.

CARAMEL CAKE A southern classic: Omit the almond extract and use 2 teaspoons vanilla extract. Substitute buttermilk for the milk. Reduce the baking powder to 2 teaspoons and add ½ teaspoon baking soda.

Carrot Cake

MAKES: One 8- or 9-inch or 13 × 9-inch cake (12 servings)
TIME: About 1 hour

Ⓜ

As close to a perfect carrot cake as I know, bursting with spices, nuts, and coconut. This one also features pineapple, which lends a tropical note. Fabulous for snacking. You can also turn this into cupcakes (opposite); it'll yield about two dozen.

	Butter or oil for greasing
2	cups all-purpose flour, plus more for dusting
2	teaspoons baking soda
1	teaspoon baking powder

        1   teaspoon salt
        1   teaspoon ground cinnamon
        1   teaspoon ground ginger
        ½   teaspoon freshly grated nutmeg
        1   cup good-quality vegetable oil
     1¾   cups sugar
        4   eggs
        2   teaspoons vanilla extract
        2   cups grated carrots (about 4 carrots)
        1   cup canned crushed pineapple, drained
        1   cup chopped walnuts or pecans
        ½   cup shredded coconut
            Cream Cheese Frosting (page 702; optional)

1. Heat the oven to 350°F. Grease and flour the bottom and sides of two 9-inch or three 8-inch layer cake pans or a 13 × 9-inch sheet cake pan.

2. Whisk together the flour, baking soda, baking powder, salt, cinnamon, ginger, and nutmeg in a large bowl. In a separate bowl, whisk the oil, sugar, eggs, and vanilla together. Stir the wet ingredients into the dry ingredients, then fold in the carrots, pineapple, nuts, and coconut until just combined.

3. Turn the batter into the pan(s) and bake until a toothpick inserted into the center comes out clean or with a few moist crumbs, about 30 minutes for layers and 40 minutes for a sheet cake. Cool in the pans for

5 minutes, then invert onto a rack to finish cooling. For a sheet cake, leave it in the pan.

4. Frost the cake if you like. Store at room temperature, covered or wrapped well in plastic wrap, for no more than a few days.

SWEET POTATO COCONUT CAKE Substitute 2 cups grated sweet potato (about 1 sweet potato) for the carrots and swap out the nuts for an additional ½ cup shredded coconut.

BEET CAKE For beautiful color and subtle flavor: Substitute 2 cups grated beets (about 3 beets) for the carrots.

Orange-Almond Cake

MAKES: One 8-inch cake (8 to 10 servings)
TIME: About 3 hours, largely unattended
M

Try this unusual recipe from cookbook author Claudia Roden and you'll keep returning to it. It not only has an unbelievably short ingredient list and produces wonderfully tender results, it's also gluten free. It needs nothing for garnish but goes well with all kinds of fresh fruit or whipped cream. The batter comes together in a food processor; the only time-consuming part is simmering the oranges, but that much is hands-off.

Making Cupcakes and Babycakes

Cupcakes turn cake into a portable, fun food that always elicits a smile, while larger babycakes are elegant dinner party fare. (The major difference between the two is size: Cupcakes are baked in muffin tins, while babycakes are baked in greased ramekins.) The recipes for Yellow Cake (page 696), Chocolate Cake (page 694), and Carrot Cake (page 696) all can used to make cupcakes or babycakes.

To make cupcakes, either set a paper cup into each well of a standard muffin tin or generously grease the inside; fill each cup two-thirds full. Since the cakes are small, start checking about halfway through the original recipe's bake time. Any of the above recipes will yield

about two dozen regular size cupcakes. You can also use mini muffin tins, which produce two-bite cakes that many people find irresistible. Prep them exactly the same way, although of course bake time will be significantly shorter.

For babycakes, grease 4- or 6-ounce ramekins and dust each with flour or cocoa powder, thoroughly tapping out any excess. Fill them two-thirds full and check for doneness halfway through the suggested bake time. Allow babycakes to cool in their ramekins and serve as is (if you have enough of them) or invert onto a plate, as you would a cake. Depending on the size of ramekin you use, the above recipes will yield one to two dozen babycakes.

2 jumbo seedless navel oranges
Butter for greasing
2 cups raw almonds (about 1 pound)
6 eggs
1 cup sugar
1 teaspoon baking powder

1. Wash the oranges and put them in a saucepan. Cover completely with water and simmer for about 2 hours, until they are very soft. Drain and cut into pieces.
2. Heat the oven to 400°F and liberally grease an 8-inch baking pan.
3. Put the almonds in a food processor and pulse into a rough meal. Don't overprocess; you want the mixture to remain dry (not grind it into nut butter). It's fine to have little chunks of almond in the mix. Transfer to a bowl.
4. Put the oranges in the food processor (no need to wipe it out) and pulse into a not-entirely-smooth purée. Add the eggs, almond meal, sugar, and baking powder and process until thoroughly combined.
5. Pour the batter into the prepared pan and bake for 35 to 50 minutes, until a tester inserted in the middle comes out clean; check on it as soon as you detect its delicious aroma from the oven. Cool completely in the pan before removing.

Plum-Rosemary Upside-Down Cake

MAKES: One 9-inch cake (at least 8 servings)
TIME: About 1 hour
Ⓜ

Juicy, ripe plums caramelize beautifully to create a rich, syrupy topping when the cake is inverted. (Use a cast-iron skillet to maximize browning.) You could also use apples, blackberries, pitted cherries, or cranberries.

8 tablespoons (1 stick) unsalted butter, melted
½ cup dark brown sugar
1 teaspoon minced fresh rosemary
4 or 5 ripe sweet plums, halved, pitted, and cut into chunks

1 cup buttermilk
2 eggs
½ cup sugar
2 cups all-purpose flour
1 teaspoon baking soda
¼ teaspoon salt
Ice cream for serving

1. Heat the oven to 350°F. Liberally grease a 9-inch round cake pan or cast-iron skillet with half of the butter. Sprinkle the brown sugar and rosemary evenly over the bottom of the pan and spread the plums in the pan in a single layer.
2. Whisk together the remaining butter, the buttermilk, eggs, and sugar in a large bowl until foamy. In a separate bowl, stir together the flour, baking soda, and salt. Gradually add the wet ingredients to the dry ingredients and stir until well incorporated.
3. Carefully spread the batter over the plums, using a spatula to make sure it's evenly distributed. Bake until the top of the cake is golden brown and a toothpick inserted in the center comes out clean, 50 to 60 minutes. Cool in the pan for just 5 minutes.
4. Run a knife around the edge of the pan. Invert the serving plate on the top of the pan and flip the pan so that the serving plate is now on the bottom and the pan is upside down and on top. The cake should fall out onto the serving plate. If the cake sticks, turn it right side up and run the knife along the edge again, then use a spatula to lift gently around the edge. Invert the cake again and tap on the bottom of the pan. If any of the fruit sticks to the pan, don't worry; use a knife to remove the pieces and fill in any gaps on the top of the cake. Serve warm with ice cream.

FRESH PINEAPPLE UPSIDE-DOWN CAKE Use the sweetest pineapple you can find: Omit the rosemary. Substitute six ½-inch-thick slices peeled fresh pineapple, or as many as will fit in the pan, for the plums and ½ cup cornmeal for half the all-purpose flour.

BERRY UPSIDE-DOWN CAKE Use 3 to 4 cups fresh berries, like blackberries, blueberries, or raspberries, in place of the plums, enough to cover the bottom of the pan in a single, even layer. If you use strawberries, quarter them first.

APPLE UPSIDE-DOWN CAKE Substitute 3 or 4 medium peeled, cored, and sliced apples for the plums. Add 1 teaspoon ground cinnamon to the flour mixture if you like.

GINGERY PEACH UPSIDE-DOWN CAKE Sweet meets spicy: Substitute 3 or 4 medium pitted and sliced ripe peaches for the plums. Substitute 2 tablespoons minced candied ginger for the rosemary. Whisk 1 teaspoon ground ginger into the dry ingredients.

PEAR AND ALMOND UPSIDE-DOWN CAKE Small Seckel pears look elegant, but full-size pears work too: Substitute ¼ cup chopped almonds for the rosemary; 3 to 4 small ripe pears, peeled, cored, and halved, for the plums; and ½ cup ground almonds for half the flour. Mix 3 tablespoons almond paste in with the butter.

Sweet Rice and Coconut Cake

Bibingka
MAKES: One 9-inch cake (8 to 10 servings)
TIME: 1¼ hours
Ⓜ

This easy, gluten-free Filipino cake is traditionally baked in a clay pot lined with a banana leaf, and sold at Christmas markets. The banana leaf—you can find them frozen at Mexican and Asian grocers—adds a subtle and unusual earthiness to the flavor and makes for a knockout presentation, but it's certainly not necessary; the cake is equally delicious made using parchment paper.

- 1½ cups rice flour
- 2 teaspoons baking powder
- ¼ teaspoon salt
- ¾ cup light brown sugar, plus more for sprinkling
- 3 eggs
- 4 tablespoons (½ stick) butter, melted, plus more for brushing

- 1½ cups coconut milk (to make your own, see page 304)
- ¼ cup shredded coconut, plus more for sprinkling

1. Heat the oven to 350°F. Line the bottom and side of a 9-inch cake pan with banana leaves cut to fit the pan. If you can't find banana leaves, use parchment paper.
2. Whisk together the rice flour, baking powder, and salt in a large bowl. Whisk together the brown sugar, eggs, butter, and coconut milk until combined in a medium bowl. Add the wet ingredients to the dry ingredients and mix until combined; stir in the coconut.
3. Pour the batter into the prepared pan and bake until a toothpick inserted into the center comes out clean or with a few moist crumbs, about 1 hour. Cool in the pan for 5 minutes, then invert onto a rack to finish cooling; remove the banana leaves or pieces of parchment. While the cake is still warm, brush it with melted butter and sprinkle additional sugar or shredded coconut on top. This is best eaten the day it's made, but covered with plastic wrap, it will keep at room temperature for up to 3 days.

SWEET RICE AND COCONUT LIME CAKE Add 1 tablespoon grated lime zest to the wet ingredients.

SWEET RICE AND COCONUT SPICE CAKE Whisk 1 teaspoon ground cinnamon, ½ teaspoon ground ginger, and ¼ teaspoon freshly grated nutmeg into the dry ingredients.

Cheesecake

MAKES: At least 12 servings
TIME: About 1½ hours
Ⓜ

Maybe everyone has a favorite cheesecake recipe; this is mine, a basic iteration I've been making since I first started cooking. It reminds me of the simple cheesecakes of my childhood.

Butter for greasing

4 eggs

3 8-ounce packages cream cheese, softened

1¼ cups sugar

2 teaspoons vanilla extract

1 cup sour cream

1. Heat the oven to 325°F and grease the bottom and sides of a 9-inch springform pan. Line with a circle of parchment paper.

2. Use an electric mixer to beat the eggs in a large bowl until light. Add the cream cheese, 1 cup of the sugar, and 1 teaspoon of the vanilla; beat until smooth.

3. Turn the batter into the prepared pan and put the pan into a larger baking pan that will hold it comfortably. Add enough warm water to the baking pan to come to within an inch of the top of the springform pan. Transfer carefully to the oven and bake until the cake is just set and very lightly browned, about 1 hour. Remove the pan from the water bath.

4. Turn the oven up to 450°F. Stir together the sour cream and the remaining ¼ cup sugar and 1 teaspoon vanilla in a small bowl; spread on the top of the cake. Return the cake to the oven for 10 minutes without the water bath; turn off the oven and let it cool inside for 30 minutes before removing it, running a knife around the edge of the cake to prevent sticking to the pan, and cooling it completely on a rack. Cover and refrigerate until well chilled before removing from the pan, slicing, and serving. It will keep in the refrigerator for several days.

VEGAN CHEESECAKE Cashews make this version as creamy as the original: Grease the pan with melted coconut oil. Put 3 cups raw cashews in a large bowl, cover with water, and soak for at least 4 hours or overnight. Drain the nuts and add to a blender or food processor with ⅔ cup maple syrup, ⅓ cup fresh lemon juice, ⅓ cup melted coconut oil, ⅓ cup nondairy milk of your choice, 2 teaspoons vanilla, and ½ teaspoon salt. Blend until very smooth, as long as a few minutes, scraping down the side occasionally. Pour into the prepared pan

and freeze until set. Serve frozen or thawed at room temperature for 15 minutes. Store in the freezer or refrigerator. V

FROSTINGS AND TOPPINGS

There are six recipes here, but literally dozens of variations, enough to put the icing on the cake for any occasion for the rest of your baking life. And they're all amenable to change-ups in flavorings, tailored to your preferences. Vegan Whipped Cream, by the way (opposite) is a revelation.

Whipped Cream

MAKES: About 2 cups (4 to 6 servings)
TIME: 5 minutes
F M

Probably the most useful, versatile, and ubiquitous topping of all, whipped cream is so easy there's absolutely no need to ever buy the canned stuff. (Well, it's fun to use; but most of it tastes awful.)

If you're making a lot of whipped cream, it's easier and faster to use an electric mixer, but you'll do fine whipping smaller amounts by hand. Either way, start with well-chilled cream with no additives and a clean glass or metal mixing bowl. Add the sugar or flavorings just as the cream starts to hold its shape.

1 cup cream

Up to ¼ cup sugar (optional)

1. Use a whisk or an electric mixer to beat the cream to the desired texture in a medium bowl. To check this, dip the whisk or beater into the cream and pull up; see the illustrations, opposite, for more info about soft and stiff peaks.

2. Once the cream starts to hold its shape, gradually fold in the sugar if you're using it. Finish whipping to the consistency you like. It's best to use fresh whipped cream immediately since it will start to "weep," or separate, but you can cover and refrigerate it for a few hours without much trouble. If you're working more in advance, see "How to Make Whipped Cream Ahead of Time" on page 702 for tips.

VEGAN WHIPPED CREAM A revelation: Instead of cream, use one 14-ounce can coconut cream or full-fat coconut milk. (Don't confuse coconut cream with cream of coconut, a processed food that is sometimes used in cocktails.) Refrigerate the can overnight. When you're ready to make the cream, carefully open the can, scoop out the solids, and put them into a bowl. Add up to 3 tablespoons confectioners' sugar and/or 1 tablespoon vanilla extract if you like and beat until soft peaks form. V

8 Ways to Flavor Whipped Cream
Start with 1 cup cream and beat until it holds shape before adding any of the following.

1. Vanilla Whipped Cream: Scrape the seeds from ½ pod into the cream or use 1 teaspoon good-quality vanilla extract.
2. Honey Whipped Cream: Use honey instead of sugar.
3. Maple Whipped Cream: Use some maple syrup in place of sugar. Add just enough to flavor the whipped cream; if you want it sweeter, add sugar so you don't liquefy the whipped cream.
4. Cinnamon or Nutmeg Whipped Cream: Sprinkle in ground cinnamon, nutmeg, cardamom, or any finely ground sweet spice.
5. Boozy Whipped Cream: Add 1 to 2 tablespoons bourbon, brandy, Kahlúa, Grand Marnier, framboise, amaretto, etc.
6. Citrus Whipped Cream: Add ½ teaspoon or so grated citrus zest.
7. Ginger Whipped Cream: Add ½ teaspoon finely grated or very finely minced fresh ginger.
8. Rose or Orange Blossom Whipped Cream: Add 1 to 2 teaspoons rose water or orange blossom water.

The Stages of Whipping Cream

Before you start whipping, be sure you have well-chilled cream, a clean metal or glass bowl and a balloon whisk or a mixer fitted with the whisk attachment. Add the sweetener or flavorings when the cream is just starting to hold a shape. To check what stage you're at (you don't want to overbeat), just pull the whisk out from the cream and look at the peak it forms. (If it doesn't form any peak, just keep going.)

SOFT PEAKS **The cream will just make a low peak with a tip that readily folds onto itself.**

STIFF PEAKS **A fairly firm peak with a tip that hardly bends; dragging your finger through the cream will leave a distinct mark. It should not be clumpy, though. Sometimes medium peaks are called for, a solid peak with a tip that folds over but not onto itself.**

OVERWHIPPED **The cream will be clumpy and rough looking. To fix, add a couple tablespoons more cream and stir it in to smooth it out. Or keep whipping; you'll get butter.**

Cream Cheese Frosting

MAKES: Enough frosting and filling for one 9-inch layer cake or 2 dozen cupcakes
TIME: About 15 minutes
F

A classic partner for Carrot Cake (page 696). Cream cheese lends tang and brightness that balances any sugary, heavily spiced, or dark-chocolaty cake.

- 1 pound cream cheese
- 12 tablespoons (1½ sticks) butter, softened
- 3 cups confectioners' sugar
- 2 teaspoons vanilla extract

1. Use an electric mixer to beat the cream cheese until fluffy, about 3 minutes. Add the butter and beat until incorporated and smooth, another 3 minutes.
2. Continue to beat as you add the sugar gradually, about a cup at a time, until the frosting is smooth and well combined. Add the vanilla and beat until light and fluffy, about 3 minutes.

LEMONY CREAM CHEESE FROSTING Cream cheese and citrus complement each other brilliantly: Beat 1 table-spoon grated lemon zest into the cream cheese and butter mixture. Add 2 tablespoons fresh lemon juice with the vanilla.

Vegan Icing

MAKES: About 2½ cups, enough to frost a 9 × 13-inch sheet cake or about 1½ dozen cupcakes
TIME: 10 minutes, plus 8 to 24 hours for chilling
V

Duplicating the texture and flavor of buttercream is impossible. But these two vegan spins let you have your cake—and frost it, too. The main recipe takes the semi-solid cream from coconut milk and turns it into a smooth, pleasantly nutty, shiny, and rich spreadable icing. (You can buy the coconut cream separately, too. Whatever you use, the important thing is that the coconut cream is solid when you start.) The variation is more like birthday cake frosting—fluffy and not too sweet. Use it to ice or frost Vegan Yellow Cake (page 696) or Vegan Chocolate Cake (page 694).

- 2 14-ounce cans full-fat coconut milk
- 2–3 cups confectioners' sugar
- 1 teaspoon vanilla extract
   Pinch salt

1. Refrigerate the cans of coconut milk overnight. When you're ready to make the icing, carefully open the cans, scoop out the solids, and put them into a bowl. (If you're working with a stand mixer, fit it with the paddle attachment and use that bowl.) You should have about 2 cups cream; save the liquid to drink or for another recipe.
2. Using an electric mixer, beat the chilled coconut cream on medium to combine. Increase the speed to high and gradually beat in 2 cups of the sugar, ½ cup at a time, beating well after each addition. Stir in the vanilla and salt. Taste and gradually add more sugar to get the taste and consistency you want. Use immediately, or cover and refrigerate for up to 3 days. To avoid separa-

tion, refrigerate the frosted cake until ready to serve and keep leftovers chilled, too.

CREAMY VEGAN FROSTING The new palm oil blends are good replacements for hydrogenated vegetable shortening since they're naturally solid at room temperature: Substitute 1½ cups all-vegetable shortening for the coconut cream. Proceed with the recipe, adding oat or other nondairy milk 1 tablespoon at a time until you've reached your desired frosting consistency; you might need as much as ½ cup. (After refrigerating this frosting, you'll need to let it sit on the counter for a few minutes to make it spreadable again.)

Lemon Glaze

MAKES: Enough for any size cake
TIME: 10 minutes
F M V

The perfect something extra for all kinds of desserts, from cakes to cookies to quick breads. You can replace the lemon with nearly any other citrus. For a thicker glaze that can be spread on cookies, decrease the total amount of lemon juice and water by a tablespoon or two.

> 1 tablespoon grated lemon zest
> ¼ cup fresh lemon juice, plus more as needed
> ½ teaspoon vanilla extract (optional)
> 3 cups confectioners' sugar, plus more as needed

Put the lemon zest and juice, ¼ cup water, vanilla if you're using it, and sugar in a medium bowl and beat until smooth; it should be about the consistency of thick maple syrup—just pourable. Adjust the consistency by adding a little more juice or a little more sugar. Use immediately or cover and refrigerate for up to 2 weeks.

VANILLA GLAZE An all-purpose sweet but simple glaze: Substitute ½ cup nondairy or dairy milk for the lemon juice and water and omit the lemon zest. Increase the vanilla to 2 teaspoons. O

ORANGE GLAZE A milder citrus that pairs easily with a variety of cakes and quick breads: Substitute orange zest for the lemon zest and ½ cup orange juice for the lemon juice and water. V

CREAMY LEMON GLAZE A touch of cream and some butter make for a richer glaze, though, of course, no longer vegan: Substitute ¼ cup cream for the water and add 3 tablespoons very soft butter. Whisk until smooth and glossy.

COCONUT GLAZE Drizzle this over Banana Bread (page 581): Substitute ½ cup coconut milk for the lemon juice and water and ¼ cup shredded coconut for the zest. Omit the vanilla. V

CINNAMON GLAZE Substitute ¾ cup nondairy or dairy milk for the lemon juice and water and 1½ teaspoons ground cinnamon for the zest. Omit the vanilla. O

GINGER GLAZE Follow the previous variation, using ground ginger instead of cinnamon. O

Jam Glaze

MAKES: Enough for any size cake
TIME: 15 minutes
F M V

This is the easiest glaze recipe of them all, fantastic not just for its fruit flavor but also for the extra punch of color and sheen that it adds to fruit desserts. Simply thin jam with water and tune the flavor with spices, liqueur, or extracts as desired. If using berries, you can strain the seeds from the glaze if you like; do this while it's still warm.

> 1 cup fruit jam (to make your own, see page 722)

Put the jam and 1 cup water in a small saucepan over medium heat. Bring to a low bubble and cook to a syrupy consistency, 10 to 15 minutes. Set aside to cool; use immediately or cover and refrigerate for up to 2 weeks.

APRICOT-VANILLA JAM GLAZE A bright, elegant pairing for most baked goods, including Yellow Cake (page 696): Use apricot jam and add 1 teaspoon vanilla extract.

CHERRY-PORT JAM GLAZE A seriously decadent adult treat—especially on Chocolate Cake (page 694): Use cherry jam; in a small saucepan, reduce 1 cup port wine by half, then add ½ cup water and the jam. Proceed as instructed.

ORANGE-GINGER JAM GLAZE Sweet and spicy: Use orange marmalade and add 1 teaspoon ground ginger.

Chocolate Ganache

MAKES: About 1½ cups
TIME: 15 minutes
F

This luscious mixture of chocolate and cream is a breeze to make. At different consistencies, it can become a glaze, a dense filling for truffles, a frosting, or a mousse-like whipped cream. You can make this with white, milk, or dark chocolate.

- 1 **cup cream**
- 8 **ounces chocolate, chopped**

Put the cream in a small saucepan and heat it until it's steaming. Put the chocolate in a heatproof bowl, pour on the hot cream, and whisk until the chocolate is melted and incorporated into the cream. Use right away as a sauce or coating; as it cools down, it will start to set and get stiffer and harder to spread. See the variations to whip it into a smooth, rich frosting or turn it into a creamy glaze.

VEGAN CHOCOLATE GANACHE Substitute coconut milk for the cream and use vegan chocolate (see page 687). You can also make ganache with nut, grain, or soy milks. (Rice milk will be too thin). All will impart their subtle flavors, but since coconut milk has the most fat, it yields the richest and smoothest ganache. You can use this substitution for all the variations. **V**

WHIPPED GANACHE FROSTING Simply whipping the ganache will transform its texture; its light, fluffy consistency is perfect for frosting cakes, cupcakes, or brownies or piping or filling a variety of confections: Use an electric mixer to beat the cooled ganache on low, gradually increasing the speed to medium-high until the mixture turns light and fluffy. If you like it sweeter, gradually add confectioners' sugar to taste, ¼ cup at a time (up to 1½ cups), as you beat.

CHOCOLATE GANACHE GLAZE As a midpoint between ganache and chocolate sauce, this is an especially lavish sauce for dipping fresh fruit or cookies; you can also use it to glaze cakes or top ice cream: Thin the still-warm ganache with additional cream, about 2 tablespoons at a time, until it's easily pourable and doesn't harden too much when cooled to room temperature. To test the consistency, spread a small spoonful on a plate; it should thicken but remain very soft.

FLAVORED GANACHE You can use the guidelines for "12 Ways to Infuse Simple Syrup" on page 684 to change up the taste of your ganache. Add the flavorings to the cold cream, and by the time it's warm enough to pour over the chocolate, it will carry the flavor beautifully. You'll need to strain out the solids before pouring the cream over the chocolate.

QUICK GANACHE TRUFFLES One of the richest yet easiest treats you can make; see "12 Ways to Infuse Simple Syrup" (page 684) for more flavor ideas: Chill the ganache in the fridge until it's solid all the way through, 1 to 2 hours depending on quantity. Scoop out a tablespoonful and quickly roll it into a 1-inch ball (wearing latex gloves helps to prevent melting); repeat, lining up the truffles on a plate or baking sheet as you work. If the truffles become too soft to handle, stick them in the fridge or freezer for a few minutes. Roll them in cocoa powder, confectioners' sugar, or cinnamon sugar. Serve immediately or refrigerate, wrapped in plastic, for a day or so.

PIES, COBBLERS, AND CRISPS

What all of these have in common is some form of crust or topping, a universally loved treat that almost always depends on a fair amount of fat—usually butter—to make it light, flaky, and delicious. (But check out the Vegan Piecrust on page 710.) What distinguishes pies and tarts from cobblers and crisps is the composition of the crust, how it is formed, and whether it's on top or on bottom.

THE BASICS OF MAKING A CRUST

A crust can make or break a pie or tart. I'm here to tell you that you can make a really good crust your first time out, and you'll improve quickly and steadily.

MIXING THE DOUGH

I routinely use my food processor to mix the dough for crusts, and I recommend you do too. You can mix the dough by hand, of course, pinching the butter with flour between your fingers, or using various utensils like a pastry blender or two forks. However you do it, the idea is to get small bits of fat coated in flour, which will make for a flaky and light crust. The dough should be handled minimally, because you don't want gluten to develop, as it does in bread dough; for crusts you want tenderness, not chew.

Once you make a dough, let it rest in the refrigerator (or even the freezer, but not too long—you want to chill it, not freeze it) to relax the gluten and to firm up the fat. Relaxing the gluten will make rolling easier and chilling the fat will result in flakiness in the oven.

ROLLING THE DOUGH

Be patient, and practice, and you'll soon be routinely transforming dough from a ball or disk to a fairly uniform ¼-inch-thick round crust. Although at first you may need more than one try, ideally, you'll roll out the dough only once, because rerolling will make it tough.

Rolling Pie Dough

STEP 1 Roll with firm, steady, but not overly hard pressure, from the center out, sprinkling the dough with tiny amounts of flour if necessary.

STEP 2 You can also roll between two sheets of plastic wrap. If at any point during rolling the dough becomes sticky, refrigerate it for 15 minutes or so.

STEP 3 Patch any holes with pieces of dough from the edges.

STEP 4 When the dough is ready, pick it up using the rolling pin (flour the dough and pin very lightly first).

STEP 5 Then drape the dough over your pie plate.

Here are some tips that will make rolling dough easier.

- Start with dough that is firm but not frozen. It should yield a bit to pressure, but your fingers shouldn't sink in; if they do, refrigerate or freeze for a while longer.
- Flour the work surface and the top of the dough to prevent it from sticking to the counter and the rolling pin. Beginners should use flour liberally; as you get the hang of it, you'll use less and less. Alternatively, put the dough between two pieces of plastic wrap and roll it in there; as long as the dough is not too sticky, this will work just fine.
- Roll from the middle of the disk outward, rotating the rolling pin and the dough to make sure it's rolled evenly. Apply even and firm but gentle pressure to the rolling pin.
- Fix any holes with pieces that break off at the edges; add a dab of water to help seal your patches in place. Don't try to pinch the hole closed.
- If the dough becomes sticky, slide it onto a baking sheet or a piece of plastic wrap or parchment paper and freeze it for a few minutes.
- When the dough is rolled out, move it to the pie plate or tart pan by draping it over the rolling pin and moving it into the plate or by removing the plastic wrap on one side, gently flipping the dough onto the plate, then removing the other piece of plastic wrap.
- Press the dough firmly into the plate all over. Refrigerate for about an hour before filling; if you're in a hurry, freeze for a half-hour or so.

CRIMPING THE CRUST

Once the dough is in the pan, you can trim it and make the edge more attractive.

Tarts typically have a simple edge: Just use a knife to cut away the excess dough. Fluted tart pans make a pretty, ruffled-looking edge without any extra work on your part.

Piecrusts, on the other hand, can have more elaborate edges. Trim the excess dough away making sure to leave enough so that you can fold the edge underneath itself all the way around, then crimp the edge. Here are three ways to do that (also see the illustrations below).

- Pinching method: Pinch the edges of the dough between the side of your forefinger and your thumb.
- Knuckle method: Use the thumb and forefinger of one

Crimping the Crust

PINCHING METHOD Pinch the edges of the dough between the side of your forefinger and your thumb.

KNUCKLE METHOD Use the thumb and forefinger of one hand to hold the dough in place. Press a knuckle from your other hand against the crust, pushing it into the space made by your thumb and forefinger.

FORK METHOD Simply press down with the tines of a fork along the edges of the dough.

hand to hold the dough in place from the inside. Then press a knuckle from your other hand against the crust, pushing it into the space made by your thumb and forefinger.

- Fork method: Simply press down with the tines of a fork along the edges of the dough.

PRE-BAKING A CRUST

There are several reasons to prebake—"blind bake"—a pie or tart crust. Prebaking minimizes shrinking and helps produce a nicely shaped crust. It also ensures that the crust cooks through (without overcooking the filling), giving it ideal flavor and color; browned crusts look and taste better than pale ones. And a prebaked crust is less likely to become soggy when the filling is particularly moist. Finally, when the filling is precooked or served raw, you have no other choice than to prebake. Both Flaky Piecrust (page 709) and Vegan Piecrust (page 710) recipes and all their variations can be prebaked.

To prebake, you need butter or oil, foil, and a cup or 2 of raw rice, dried beans, or pie weights. (All of these can be reused for this purpose.) The weight helps prevent the crust from shrinking and bubbling with air pockets while it's baking. They aren't absolutely essential—you can prick the bubbles with a fork as they appear throughout the baking—but they make things easier, and your crust will look better.

Preheat the oven to 425°F. Be sure the crust is pressed firmly into the pan, adequately pricked with a fork, and well chilled before baking.

Butter or oil one side of a piece of foil large enough to cover the crust; press the foil onto the crust, greased side down. Weight the foil with a pile of rice, dried beans, or pie weights. Bake for 12 minutes; remove from the oven and remove the weights and foil. Reduce the oven temperature to 350°F and continue baking the crust until it starts to turn golden brown, another 10 minutes or so. Continue baking until the crust is completely golden brown if the pie's filling requires no

Decorating a Crust

Once the dough is in the pan, you'll want to trim it, and you can also make the edge more attractive or add a top crust or other embellishments.

SIMPLE TOP CRUST **Use a paring knife or cookie cutter to trim simple shapes from the crust if you want. Place the crust over the filling, trim the edge, and crimp the top and bottom crust edges to seal. If you didn't cut out shapes, cut a few slits in the crust to let steam escape.**

BRAIDED EDGE **Cut the dough into ¼-inch-wide strips and braid three strips snugly together. Repeat until you have four braids; set them on a plate to chill. Brush egg wash or water around the sides and "glue" the braids all along the perimeter, braiding the loose ends together so they make one continuous braid. Prebake or fill and bake as directed.**

additional baking; cool on a rack before filling. Or cool, fill, and finish baking according to the individual recipe.

BAKING FILLED PIES, COBBLERS, AND CRISPS

To keep fruit juices from bubbling over and onto the floor of your hot oven, place the dish on a baking sheet; it'll catch any spillovers as well as encourage bottom browning.

If the crust edges start to get too dark, loosely wrap a ring of foil around them.

Flaky Piecrust

MAKES: 1 double crust for a 9-inch pie
TIME: About 20 minutes, plus time to chill

F M

Because piecrust uses so few ingredients, quality and technique make all the difference in getting a flaky, delicious result. Don't overwork the dough and do keep it cool (see pages 706 to 708 for details). It's important for the water to truly be ice cold; add several ice cubes to it before measuring.

> 2¼ **cups all-purpose flour, plus more for dusting**
> 2 **teaspoons sugar**
> 1 **teaspoon salt**
> ½ **pound (2 sticks) very cold butter, cut into chunks**
> 6 **tablespoons ice water, plus more if necessary**

1. Use a food processor to pulse together the flour, sugar, and salt to combine. Add the butter and pulse until it is just barely blended with the flour and the butter is broken down to the size of peas. If you prefer to make the dough by hand, combine all the dry ingredients and butter in a large bowl. With your fingertips, 2 knives or forks, or a pastry cutter, work the butter pieces into the flour, being sure to incorporate all of the butter evenly, until the mixture has the texture of small peas.

2. Add 6 tablespoons ice water to the flour mixture. Process for about 5 seconds or mix by hand with a wooden spoon, just until the dough begins to clump together,

adding 1 or 2 tablespoons more ice water if necessary (or a little more flour if you add too much water).

3. Divide the dough in half and put each half into a quart-size plastic zipper bag. Press the dough into a disk by mushing along the outside of the bag until you have a thick disk shape. It's important not to overheat, overwork, or knead the dough; squeeze it with enough pressure just to hold it together. Freeze the disks of dough for 10 minutes or refrigerate for at least 30 minutes before rolling. If you're making a single-crust pie, freeze one disk for another time.

4. Dust a large pinch of flour over a clean work surface. Sprinkle a little more flour on top of the dough and dust the rolling pin with flour. Too much flour will dry out the dough; you can always sprinkle on a little more if the dough starts to stick. Using firm but not too hard pressure on the pin, start rolling the first disk of dough from the center outward to form a circle. If the dough feels too hard or is cracking a lot, let it rest for a few minutes. As you roll, add flour as needed and rotate and turn the dough with a spatula to form an even circle.

5. When the dough circle is about 2 inches larger than the pie plate and less than ⅛ inch thick, it's ready. Roll the dough up halfway onto the pin so it's easy to move, then center it over the pie plate and unroll it into place. Press the dough into the contours of the dish without squishing or stretching it; patch any tears with a small scrap of dough, sealed with a drop of water. Trim any excess dough to about ½ inch all around.

6. If you're making a single-crust pie, tuck the edges under themselves so the dough is thicker on the rim than it is inside; if you're making a double-crust pie, leave the edges untucked for now. Put the pie plate in the fridge until the crust feels cool to the touch before filling or prebaking. For a top crust or embellished crust, roll the second disk into a circle on a flat baking sheet (dusted with flour) and put that in the fridge too; then, when you're ready to assemble, follow the directions for decorative crusts (page 708).

WHOLE WHEAT PIECRUST Whole wheat flour absorbs more water than white, so take care: Substitute whole wheat pastry flour for the all-purpose flour. Increase the water to ½ cup, adding more, a tablespoon at a time, until the dough forms.

NUT PIECRUST Substitute nut flour of your choice for 1 cup of the all-purpose flour. Toast the nut flour on a baking sheet in a 350°F oven for 5 minutes or until fragrant and lightly browned. Proceed as directed.

OAT PIECRUST Crumbly and homey: Substitute ground rolled oats for 1 cup of the flour; run the oats in a food processor until they have the consistency of a fine meal.

SAVORY PIECRUST The piecrust to use for quiches: Omit the sugar.

Vegan Piecrust

MAKES: 1 double crust for a 9-inch pie
TIME: About 20 minutes, plus time to chill
F M V

Coconut oil produces a flaky, tender crust, and the usual rules apply: Work quickly, keep the oil cool and firm, and don't overwork the dough. Refined coconut oil has a far more neutral, versatile flavor than unrefined.

> 2¼ **cups all-purpose flour, plus more for dusting**
> 2 **teaspoons sugar**
> 1 **teaspoon salt**
> ½ **cup coconut oil, chilled**
> 6 **tablespoons ice water, plus more if necessary**

1. Put the flour, sugar, and salt in a food processor and pulse to combine. Add the oil and pulse until it is just barely blended and crumbly. If you prefer to make the dough by hand, combine all the dry ingredients in a large bowl. Use your fingers to work the oil into the flour mixture until it's just barely blended.

2. Add 6 tablespoons ice water. Process for about 5 seconds, or mix by hand, just until the dough begins to clump together, adding 1 or 2 tablespoons more ice

water if necessary (or a little more flour if you add too much water).

3. Divide the dough in half and put each half into a quart-size plastic zipper bag. Press the dough into a disk, taking care not to overheat, overwork, or knead the dough; use just enough pressure to hold it together. Freeze the dough for 10 minutes or refrigerate for at least 30 minutes before rolling. If you're making a single-crust pie, freeze one disk for another time; wrapped tightly, the dough will keep for several months. Defrost it overnight in the refrigerator before proceeding.

4. Sprinkle a clean work surface with a large pinch of flour. Sprinkle a bit more flour on top of the dough. Use a rolling pin to firmly and evenly roll the dough, starting in the center and working outward, rotating a quarter-turn each time to make an even circle. If the dough is too stiff, let it rest for a few minutes. Sprinkle a bit of flour on the dough and rolling pin as needed to prevent sticking.

5. When the dough circle is about 2 inches larger than the pie plate and less than ⅛ inch thick, it's ready. Roll the dough up halfway onto the pin so it's easy to move, then center it over the pie plate and unroll it into place. Press the dough into the contours of the dish without squishing or stretching it. Trim the excess dough to about ½ inch all around.

6. If you're making a single-crust pie, tuck the edges under themselves so the dough is thicker on the rim than it is inside; if you're making a double-crust pie, leave the edges untucked for now. Put the pie plate in the fridge until the crust feels cool to the touch before filling or prebaking, at least 15 minutes. For a top crust or embellished crust, roll the second disk into a circle on a flat baking sheet (dusted with flour) and put that in the fridge too; then, when you're ready to assemble, follow the directions for decorative crusts (page 708).

SAVORY VEGAN PIECRUST Perfect for Mostly Vegetable Vegan Quiche (page 539): Omit the sugar and increase the ice water to 8 tablespoons. Substitute ¾ cup olive oil for the coconut oil; no need to chill it.

No-Bake Fruit and Nut Crust

MAKES: 1 single crust for an 8- to 10-inch pie or tart
TIME: 10 minutes
F M V

There's no messing up this sweet, chewy, crunchy—and gluten- and dairy-free—crust; it's so straightforward. Use any nuts and any dried fruit you want; the nuts add great flavor and texture, while the dried fruit provides sweetness and a pliable, chewy texture to form a pasty dough that is simply pressed into the pan.

    1   cup almonds or any nuts
    ¾   cup pitted and packed dried fruit
        (like dates, raisins, cherries, figs, or apricots)

1. Put the nuts in a food processor and pulse until ground, but not puréed into nut butter; transfer to a bowl. Put the dried fruit in the food processor, add a teaspoon or so of water, and pulse until minced and a bit pasty (some fruit will need a bit more water than others); add to the nuts. Mix the nuts and dried fruit until well combined. (At this point, you can form the crust into a disk, wrap it in plastic, and refrigerate or freeze until about 30 minutes before you're ready to use it; thaw if necessary and proceed with the recipe.)
2. Press the mixture into the bottom and sides of a pie or tart pan and add the filling.

NO-BAKE FRUIT AND COCONUT CRUST Substitute 1½ cups shredded coconut for the nuts. You can skip pulsing the coconut if you like, though doing so will create a more finely textured crust.

Sweet Crumble Topping

MAKES: About 2 cups
TIME: 10 minutes
F M

Essentially a streusel, this topping is like a delicate nut cookie. It's lovely on any crisp (page 717), as well as sprinkled on quick breads, muffins, or tarts and pies before baking. Use the whole wheat flour for a more robust flavor; change the nuts and spices to vary the flavor or complement a particular flavor in the dish in which it's being used. Add about 3 tablespoons cocoa powder to make a chocolate crumble.

    8   tablespoons (1 stick) butter
    1   cup brown sugar
    1   cup all-purpose or whole wheat flour,
        plus more as needed
    ½   cup chopped walnuts or pecans
    1   tablespoon fresh lemon juice
    ½   teaspoon ground cinnamon, or to taste
        Pinch salt

1. Cream together the butter and brown sugar using an electric mixer, food processor, or fork. Stir or pulse in the flour, nuts, lemon juice, cinnamon, and salt until combined and crumbly; it won't hold together like a dough. (You can make this in advance; pile onto a piece of plastic and wrap, then refrigerate or freeze until about 30 minutes before you're ready to use it. Thaw if necessary, then use.)
2. Crumble the mixture over a crisp, quick bread, or muffins as directed in the specific recipe.

GLUTEN-FREE CRUMBLE TOPPING Rice flour makes this very delicate and gluten free: Substitute rice flour for the all-purpose flour.

VEGAN CRUMBLE TOPPING Decrease the flour to ¾ cup and add ½ cup almond flour. Decrease the brown sugar to ¼ cup. Instead of butter, use ¼ cup chilled coconut oil and 2 tablespoons good-quality vegetable oil. V

CITRUS-SPICE CRUMBLE TOPPING Perfect with Cherry Crisp (page 717): Add 1 tablespoon grated or minced mixed citrus zest, like lemon, lime, orange, or grapefruit. Substitute ½ teaspoon each ground coriander and black pepper for the cinnamon.

OAT CRUMBLE TOPPING The classic for crisps: Substitute ½ cup rolled oats (or other rolled grain) for half of the flour. If you like, substitute maple syrup for the brown sugar.

CRACKED WHEAT CRUMBLE TOPPING Bulgur, wheat berries, or brown rice will work just as well: Substitute cooked cracked wheat (see page 398) for the nuts.

COCONUT CRUMBLE TOPPING Substitute shredded coconut for the walnuts. You can omit the cinnamon, if you like.

HAZELNUT OR ALMOND CRUMBLE TOPPING A delicious sweet, nutty flavor: Substitute hazelnuts or almonds, preferably blanched, for the walnuts or pecans, and 3 tablespoons hazelnut or almond paste for the flour. Reduce the brown sugar to ½ cup if the paste is very sweet.

Apple Pie

MAKES: One 9-inch pie, enough for about 8 servings
TIME: 1½ hours
Ⓜ Ⓞ

Pretty close to the all-American standard, a recipe you'll turn to again and again, especially once you get into the variations.

- ¼ cup all-purpose flour
- ¾ cup sugar, plus more for sprinkling
- ½ teaspoon ground cinnamon
- ½ teaspoon freshly grated nutmeg
- ¼ teaspoon salt
- 3 pounds firm, sweet apples, like Honeycrisp, Pink Lady, or Northern Spy, peeled, cored, and sliced into wedges about ¼ inch thick
- 1 tablespoon fresh lemon juice
- 2 tablespoons butter, cut into pieces (optional)
  Flaky Piecrust (page 709) or Vegan Piecrust (page 710), bottom crust fitted into a 9-inch

pie plate, top crust transferred to a rimless baking sheet, both chilled
Dairy or nondairy milk as needed

1. Heat the oven to 450°F. Whisk together the flour, sugar, spices, and salt in a small bowl. Mix together the apples and lemon juice in a large bowl. Add the dry ingredients to the apples and toss to coat.

2. Layer the apple mixture in the rolled-out pie shell (make sure to pour in any excess juices), then dot with the butter if you're using it. Cover with the top crust, crimp the edges of the 2 crusts together, then decorate the edges with a fork or your fingers as illustrated on page 707.

3. Put the pie on a baking sheet and brush the top lightly with milk; sprinkle with sugar. Use a sharp paring knife to cut two or three 2-inch-long slits in the top crust; this will allow steam to escape. Bake for 10 minutes; reduce the heat to 350°F and bake for another 40 to 50 minutes, until the crust is golden brown. Check on the pie when it has been cooking for a total of 35 minutes and tent the edges of the crust with foil to prevent burning. Cool on a rack before serving warm or at room temperature.

CIDER APPLE PIE Intensify the apple flavors for a pie with oomph: Omit the lemon juice. Place the apples and ⅔ cup apple cider in a large pot. Bring the cider to a boil, cover, and cook over high heat for about 5 minutes, stirring occasionally. Drain the apples and reserve the cider. Transfer the cider to a small saucepan and, over medium-high heat, reduce it to about ⅓ cup. Add the reduced apple cider back to the apples, let cool completely, then proceed with the recipe.

APPLE PIE WITH CHEDDAR CRUST For a sweet and savory twist—many people swear by this combination; try it with fresh herbs as in the list at right: Mix 1 cup shredded sharp cheddar cheese into the dry ingredients of Savory Piecrust (page 710).

8 Additions to Apple Pie

Apples are well complemented by ingredients added to the filling that emphasize their warmth, like nuts, booze, or spices, as well as brighter flavors like berries and citrus:

1. Chopped nuts, ½ to 1 cup

2. Warm spices, like minced fresh, candied, or ground ginger, cardamom, allspice, or cloves, 1 teaspoon or more to taste

3. Bourbon or rum, about 2 tablespoons sprinkled over the fruit

4. Whole cranberries, about 1 cup, plus an extra ¼ cup sugar

5. Pitted stone fruit, like plums or cherries, cut up, or whole raspberries, blueberries, or blackberries, 1 cup or more, the amount of apples reduced accordingly

6. Dried fruit, like raisins, dried cherries, cranberries, pineapple, mango, or blueberries or some dried apple slices to intensify the apple flavor, ½ to 1 cup

7. Grated lemon or orange zest, 1 tablespoon

8. Finely minced fresh herbs, like rosemary, thyme, or sage, up to 1 tablespoon

Blueberry Pie

MAKES: One 9-inch pie, enough for about 8 servings
TIME: About 1½ hours
M O

If your berries are perfectly ripe and in season, use the lesser amount of sugar, keep the spices to a minimum, and let the berries shine.

> 5 **cups blueberries, picked over, rinsed briefly, and dried lightly**
>
> ½–1 **cup sugar, to taste, plus more for sprinkling**
>
> 2 **tablespoons plus 1 teaspoon cornstarch**
> **Pinch salt**
>
> ¼ **teaspoon ground cinnamon**
> **Pinch ground allspice or freshly grated nutmeg**
>
> 1 **teaspoon grated lemon zest (optional)**
>
> 1 **tablespoon fresh lemon juice**

> **Flaky Piecrust (page 709) or Vegan Piecrust (page 710), bottom crust fitted into a 9-inch pie pan, top crust transferred to a rimless baking sheet, both chilled**
>
> 2 **tablespoons butter, cut into bits (optional)**
> **Dairy or nondairy milk as needed**

1. Heat the oven to 450°F. Gently toss the blueberries with the sugar, cornstarch, salt, and spices in a large bowl. Stir in the lemon zest if you're using it and the juice and pile the berries into the rolled-out shell, making the pile a little higher in the center than at the sides. Dot with the butter if you're using it.

2. Cover with the top crust. Crimp and decorate the edges with a fork or your fingers, using any of the methods illustrated on page 707.

3. Put the pie on a baking sheet and brush the top lightly with milk; sprinkle with sugar. Use a sharp paring knife to cut two or three 2-inch-long slits in the top crust to allow steam to escape. Bake for 10 minutes; reduce the heat to 350°F and bake for another 40 to 50 minutes, until the crust is golden brown. Do not underbake. Cool on a rack entirely, about 1 hour, before serving to let the filling set.

BLUEBERRY-LEMON PIE For a bit more zing: Use all the zest and juice from the lemon.

MIXED BERRY PIE Use a total of 5 cups of berries, in any combination you like, making sure to remove stems when needed. Use 3½ tablespoons cornstarch. If your berries aren't very sweet, be sure to add a bit more sugar too.

STRAWBERRY, RHUBARB, OR STRAWBERRY-RHUBARB PIE Use a total of 5 cups of fruit, in any combination you like. String the rhubarb, then cut it into 1-inch pieces. Hull the strawberries; slice in half or leave whole. If you're using rhubarb, use at least 1 cup sugar. Use 3 tablespoons cornstarch or ¼ cup instant tapioca as thickener. Omit the lemon juice and zest.

RASPBERRY-LIME PIE Substitute raspberries for the blueberries and 2 tablespoons fresh lime juice and 1 tablespoon grated lime zest for the lemon juice and zest.

Pear Galette

MAKES: 6 to 8 servings
TIME: 1 hour

Galettes are free-form, rustic, no-fuss tarts; they look imperfect, but their taste more than makes up for that. See the illustrations below for a visual guide.

½	recipe Flaky Piecrust (page 709), prepared through Step 3
2–3	large pears, peeled, cored, and cut into thin wedges (about ¼ inch thick)
2	tablespoons butter, melted
	Milk as needed
1	tablespoon sugar

1. On a lightly floured work surface, roll the dough out into a 10-inch round. Transfer the dough to a baking sheet and refrigerate for at least 15 minutes or until you're ready to assemble the galette.

2. Heat the oven to 425°F. Working around the center, arrange the pear slices in an overlapping pattern to end up with a flower petal effect. Reserve a couple pear slices and cut into smaller pieces to fill the center.

3. Brush or drizzle the pears with the melted butter, then fold the outer edge over the filling and brush the crust with milk. Dust everything with sugar.

4. Bake for 25 to 30 minutes, until the crust is golden brown and the pears have softened. Cool the galette to room temperature before serving.

PEAR GALETTE WITH BALSAMIC SYRUP Play with sweet and a little bit of savory: While the galette is baking, make Balsamic Syrup (page 633). Let the galette cool slightly before drizzling the syrup over it.

PEACH-RASPBERRY GALETTE Omit the pears and melted butter. Pit and slice 3 medium peaches. In a medium bowl, combine them with 1 cup raspberries, 1 teaspoon fresh lemon juice, 1 tablespoon flour, and ¼ cup sugar. Place the filling in the center of the piecrust and proceed with the recipe.

Making a Galette

STEP 1 Roll out your chilled dough. Don't worry about making it perfect, as long as it's evenly thick; uneven edges are part of the appeal. Chill for at least 15 minutes.

STEP 2 Add the filling, arranging or spreading it to just an inch or two from the edge.

STEP 3 Fold the edges over part of the filling, pleating it so it remains in place to contain any errant juices.

JAM GALETTE As easy as it gets: Omit the pears, butter, and sugar. Spread 1½ cups jam over the center of the pie-crust. If you like, sprinkle a handful of chopped nuts on top for a bit of crunch. You can also spread a thin layer of a complementary jam flavor under any of the preceding galette recipes for an extra layer of sweetness.

Apricot Cobbler

MAKES: 6 to 8 servings
TIME: About 1 hour

An old-fashioned dessert with virtually limitless fruit filling options. The filling isn't thickened, so the topping absorbs the fruit juices as it bakes. Serve with ice cream or whipped cream.

Any of the fruit fillings in the Cherry Crisp (opposite) main recipe and its variations can be used in this cobbler, and vice versa.

   8 tablespoons (1 stick) cold butter, cut into bits, plus more for greasing
   2 pounds apricots, pitted and sliced
   1 cup sugar, or to taste
  ½ cup all-purpose flour
  ½ teaspoon baking powder
     Pinch salt
   1 egg
  ½ teaspoon vanilla extract

1. Preheat the oven to 375°F. Grease an 8- or 9-inch square or round baking dish with some butter.
2. Put the apricots in a bowl and toss with half of the sugar. Spread the apricots in the prepared dish and let sit while you prepare the biscuit topping.
3. Put the flour, baking powder, salt, and remaining ½ cup sugar in a food processor and pulse once or twice. Add the butter and process for 10 seconds, until the mixture is well blended. By hand, beat in the egg and vanilla.
4. Drop this mixture onto the fruit by tablespoonfuls; do not spread it out. Bake until golden yellow and just starting to brown, 35 to 45 minutes. Serve immediately.

PEAR-BOURBON COBBLER Substitute 2 pounds pears for the apricots. Pour ¼ cup bourbon evenly over the pears in the pan before adding the topping.

CHERRY-ALMOND COBBLER Among the best-tasting cobblers you can make: Instead of apricots, use 6 cups pitted sweet cherries. Toss them with ⅓ cup chopped almonds. Substitute almond flour for ¼ cup of the all-purpose flour.

APPLE-RHUBARB COBBLER Slightly pink and tangy: Use 2 pounds apples and 1 pound rhubarb instead of the apricots. String the rhubarb, cut it into 1-inch pieces, and toss with the sliced apples.

7 Easy Additions to Cobbler Toppings

The thicker, biscuit-like dough can handle more substantial additions than a crumb topping, so you can use it as a springboard for new flavors and textures.

1. 1 teaspoon ground cinnamon, 1 teaspoon ground ginger, ½ teaspoon ground cardamom, ¼ teaspoon ground cloves, ¼ teaspoon ground allspice, and/or ¼ teaspoon freshly grated nutmeg added along with the flour

2. Up to 1 tablespoon minced fresh herbs, like thyme, rosemary, or sage added with the egg and vanilla

3. 1 tablespoon grated citrus zest, rubbed into the sugar before the butter is added

4. Cornmeal, substituted for up to half of the flour

5. Up to ½ cup molasses or honey, folded into the finished dough

6. Up to 1 cup grated hard cheese, like cheddar, Gouda, or Parmesan; an especially good complement to apples. Add with the egg and vanilla

7. Up to 1 cup toasted chopped nuts or seeds stirred in at the end

Cherry Crisp

MAKES: 6 to 8 servings
TIME: About 60 minutes
◙

Fresh tart cherries have a brief season in midsummer, and this is one of the best ways to use them. But you can use frozen tart cherries throughout the year too. You can also make this crisp with Bing and other cherries, though the flavor will not be quite so complex.

I like crisps and cobblers naturally juicy, but if you want to thicken the filling a bit, add 2 tablespoons flour or cornstarch to the sugar you use to toss the fruit in Step 2. Or better still, toss in a handful of dried cherries.

Any of the fruit fillings in the Apricot Cobbler (opposite) main recipe and its variations can be used in this crisp, and vice versa.

> Butter or oil for greasing
> **3** pounds tart cherries
> ½ cup granulated sugar, or more to taste

Sweet Crumble Topping (page 711) or Vegan Crumble Topping (page 711)

1. Heat the oven to 400°F. Grease an 8- or 9-inch square or round baking dish. Pit the cherries. You should have about 6 cups fruit.

2. Put the cherries in a large bowl and toss with the sugar. Transfer to the prepared dish and crumble on the topping. Bake until the topping is golden and just starting to brown, 30 to 40 minutes. Serve immediately or warm.

APPLE CRISP Substitute 6 cups peeled, cored, and sliced apples (2 to 3 pounds) for the cherries, 1 tablespoon brown sugar for the granulated sugar, and add the juice of ½ lemon when tossing the apples and sugar.

CRANBERRY-ORANGE CRISP Intense flavors, gorgeous color, and a treat in winter: Substitute 2 pounds oranges (about 6) and 2 cups cranberries for the cherries. Peel and segment the oranges or cut them into wheels (see page 292). Add 1 teaspoon minced fresh ginger to the filling.

RASPBERRY-PEACH CRISP With ripe peaches and good raspberries, a real treat: Substitute 3 cups raspberries and 3 cups sliced pitted peaches for the cherries, 1 tablespoon brown sugar for the granulated sugar, and add the juice of ½ lemon when tossing the fruit together. Toss the mixture with 2 tablespoons flour or cornstarch to help thicken the juices as they bake.

BLUEBERRY-LEMON CRISP Sweet, tart, and lovely: Substitute 6 cups blueberries for the cherries and 1 tablespoon brown sugar for the granulated sugar. Toss the blueberries with 1 tablespoon grated lemon zest and the juice of 1 whole lemon, then toss with 2 tablespoons flour or cornstarch to help thicken the juices as they bake.

GINGER-PLUM CRISP Spicy and juicy: Substitute sliced pitted plums for the cherries, 1 tablespoon brown sugar for the granulated sugar, and add the juice of ½ lemon and 1 tablespoon grated fresh ginger when tossing the plums and sugar together. Add 1 teaspoon ground ginger to the food processor when making the topping.

FRUIT DESSERTS, SAUCES, AND JAMS

These are the most fruit-forward recipes in the chapter —whole fruits roasted, baked, or poached; fruits sweetly stewed to be enjoyed topped with a dollop of ice cream or whipped cream, or to have the roles reversed and spooned over ice cream or a slice of cake; raw or cooked fruit reduced to a purée to drizzle over all manner of desserts as you like; and finally, an easy fruit jam that can become a part of a post-dinner cheese board.

Poached Pears

MAKES: 4 servings
TIME: About 20 minutes
Ⓜ Ⓥ

Poached pears make a dramatically beautiful dessert, especially when you use red wine (see the variation). Your fruit doesn't need to be perfectly ripe for this to be delicious; just adjust the sugar level accordingly.

- 2½ **cups sugar**
- ½ **vanilla bean, split lengthwise**
- 4 **pears (Anjou, Bosc, and Seckel are good choices)**

1. Stir the sugar and vanilla together with 5 cups water in a medium saucepan (large enough to accommodate the pears) over high heat and bring to a boil. Peel the pears, leaving their stems on. Core them by digging into the blossom end with a melon baller, spoon, or paring knife.
2. Lower the pears into the boiling syrup and adjust the heat so that the syrup simmers gently. Cook, turning the pears every 5 minutes or so, until they meet little resistance when prodded with a thin-bladed knife, usually 10 to 20 minutes. Turn off the heat and cool in the

liquid. (At this point you can cover and refrigerate the pears in their poaching liquid for up to a day; bring to room temperature before serving.) Remove the vanilla bean and pears and reduce the poaching liquid to a cup or less (this can also be stored for a day).
3. Transfer the pears to serving plates. Spoon a little of the reduced syrup over each pear before serving.

POACHED PEARS WITH GINGER AND STAR ANISE Add 3 star anise pods, 5 slices fresh ginger, and 2 whole cloves to the poaching liquid.

RED WINE–POACHED PEARS The best: Use 1½ cups water, 1½ cups red wine, ¾ cup sugar, one 3-inch cinnamon stick, and 1 lemon, sliced, for the poaching liquid.

CINNAMON POACHED APPLES A nice alternative, and unexpected: Substitute apples for the pears and swap a cinnamon stick for the vanilla bean.

Baked Apples

MAKES: 4 servings
TIME: 1¼ hours, largely unattended
Ⓜ Ⓥ

Simple and elegant, especially considering it's almost no work. For more indulgent options, try one of the variations that follow. This recipe is also lovely with Bosc pears.

- 4 **large round baking apples, preferably Cortland or Ida Red**
  About 1 cup water, sweet white wine, or apple juice
  Granulated or brown sugar as needed (optional)
- 1 **teaspoon ground cinnamon, or ½ teaspoon freshly grated nutmeg and ½ teaspoon ground cardamom (optional)**

1. Heat the oven to 350°F. With an apple corer or sharp paring knife, carefully core each apple from the stem end down, leaving about 1 inch of core intact at the

bottom. If you don't have an apple corer, a melon baller, grapefruit spoon, or small metal spoon is useful for scooping out the core. Peel the top half of each apple. Put the apples stem end up in a baking dish with about ½ inch of liquid on the bottom.

2. If using sugar, put about 1 teaspoon in the cavity of each apple and sprinkle another teaspoon or so on top. If you are using spices, dust them over the apples.

3. Bake the apples, uncovered, for about 1 hour, until very tender. If the apples look like they are drying out after the first 30 minutes, tent with foil for the rest of the cooking time and baste them with the cooking liquid a couple of times. Serve warm or at room temperature or cool, cover, and refrigerate for up to a few days (it's best to bring the apples back to room temperature before serving).

BUTTERY BAKED APPLES Richer, of course: Cream the sugar or spices with 2 tablespoons butter before adding it.

MAPLE OR HONEY BAKED APPLES Substitute maple syrup or honey for the sugar. ◙

JAM-FILLED BAKED APPLES Pick a flavor to complement apple, like quince or apricot: Fill the apple cavities with jam about 10 minutes before the end of baking.

CHEESE-STUFFED BAKED APPLES Savory: Skip the sugar and fill the apple cavities with grated cheddar or crumbled blue cheese before baking.

Broiled Peaches

MAKES: 4 servings
TIME: 20 minutes or less
F

This simple, sophisticated dessert is so obvious yet somehow unexpected. Best made with ripe freestone peaches; serve with whipped cream or ice cream.

  4 **peaches**
     About 2 tablespoons butter
     About 2 tablespoons honey

1. Heat the broiler and put the rack about 4 inches from the heat source.

2. Cut the peaches in half and remove the pits. Set each half on its "back" and fill the cavities with about a teaspoon each butter and honey. Broil for 3 to 5 minutes, until the edges just begin to brown or a little longer. Serve hot or warm.

BROILED PEACHES WITH MOLASSES Substitute molasses for the honey for a richer, more intense flavor.

BROILED PEACHES WITH HONEY AND ROSEMARY A really nice balance of flavors: Add a pinch of minced fresh rosemary to the cavity of each peach.

BROILED GRAPEFRUIT Breakfast turned dessert: Replace the peaches with 2 grapefruits and omit the honey and butter. Sprinkle the pulp of each grapefruit half with 1 tablespoon brown sugar and broil until brown and bubbling. **V**

Roasted Figs with Mascarpone

MAKES: 4 servings
TIME: 25 minutes
F

A last-minute dessert, and an easy way to take advantage of fig season. For extra sweetness, dissolve a tablespoon of sugar in the butter for drizzling. Whipped cream is a nice alternative to mascarpone.

  8 **fresh figs, halved**
  3 **tablespoons butter, melted**
     Mascarpone for serving

Heat the oven to 400°F. Arrange the figs, cut side up, on a baking sheet and drizzle with the melted butter. Roast until the figs become very tender, about 10 minutes. Cool slightly and serve with a dollop of mascarpone.

HONEY-ROASTED FIGS For a bit more sweetness and caramelization: Decrease the butter to 2 tablespoons and melt with 2 tablespoons honey. Drizzle over the figs before baking.

ROASTED PINEAPPLE Heat the oven to 425°F. Arrange eight ½-inch-thick pineapple slices on a baking sheet. If you like, melt a tablespoon or 2 of granulated sugar with the butter. Bake until the pineapple is soft and begins to turn color, 10 to 15 minutes per side.

Fruit Compote

MAKES: About 1½ cups
TIME: 10 to 20 minutes
F M V

Fruit compote is a fancy way of saying "stewed fruit." This is incredibly easy and goes with everything, from pancakes and waffles (pages 542 to 547) to Yellow Cake (page 696) or Chocolate Cake (page 694); or serve as the main dessert with a dollop of Whipped Cream or Vegan Whipped Cream (page 700 or 701) or vanilla ice cream.

2½ cups berries or other fruit, peeled as needed
    and chopped or sliced
2   tablespoons sugar
    Pinch salt

Put the fruit, sugar, salt, and a couple of tablespoons of water in a small saucepan. Cover tightly with a lid, turn the heat to medium-low, and cook, stirring occasionally, until some of the juice is released and the fruit begins to soften. This can take anywhere from 5 to 20 minutes, depending on the fruit. Serve warm or at room temperature or cool and refrigerate in an airtight container for up to 2 weeks.

APPLE OR PEAR COMPOTE WITH RAISINS AND CINNAMON An autumn treat for toast or pancakes: Use sliced apples or pears and add ½ cup raisins and 1½ teaspoons ground cinnamon.

PLUM, STAR ANISE, AND BLACK PEPPER COMPOTE A complex flavor combination punctuated by a hint of black pepper: Use sliced plums and add 1 star anise pod and ½ teaspoon freshly ground black pepper.

PINEAPPLE, LEMONGRASS, AND BASIL COMPOTE Incredibly vibrant and fresh: Use chopped pineapple and add 1 stalk lemongrass, split, and 2 tablespoons chopped fresh basil. Pick out the lemongrass before serving.

ORANGE-CRANBERRY SPICE COMPOTE Use 1½ cups peeled orange slices and 1 cup fresh cranberries. Add ½ teaspoon freshly grated nutmeg and ¼ teaspoon each ground cardamom and cloves.

PEACH, GINGER, AND MAPLE COMPOTE Maple lends a lovely caramel flavor to the compote: Use peach slices and add 1 teaspoon ground ginger or 1 tablespoon minced fresh ginger. Substitute maple syrup for the sugar.

BLUEBERRY-LAVENDER COMPOTE Use blueberries and add 1 teaspoon chopped dried lavender.

STRAWBERRY, ROSE WATER, AND VANILLA COMPOTE A delicate flavor combination: Use quartered strawberries and add 1 tablespoon rose water and 1 vanilla bean, split and scraped. Remove the vanilla bean before serving.

RASPBERRY, THYME, AND HONEY COMPOTE Use raspberries and add 1 tablespoon chopped fresh thyme. Substitute honey for the sugar.

DRIED FRUIT COMPOTE Use what you have on hand: Chop dried fruit into ½-inch pieces to make 1¼ cups total; cover them with water and soak for 1 hour. Transfer the fruit and its soaking liquid to a small saucepan and add 2 more cups water. Bring the mixture to a boil, then reduce the heat and simmer until soft and thickened, about 45 minutes. Remove from the heat, flavor as you like, and cool.

Fruit Sauce, Two Ways

MAKES: About 2 cups
TIME: 5 to 10 minutes

F M O

Recipes don't get much easier than fruit sauce. The first method requires practically no work at all and gives you a pure flavor with a very saucy consistency; it works best with soft fruits and berries. The second yields a thicker, more luxurious sauce and is best made with apples and pears.

Raw Fruit Method

2 cups berries or other soft ripe fruit (peaches, cherries, nectarines, mangoes) picked over, pitted, and/or peeled as necessary
Confectioners' sugar
Water, fruit juice, or fruity white wine as needed

1. Purée the fruit in a blender. If using fruit with tiny seeds, like raspberries or blackberries, or tough fibers like mangoes, pass the purée through a fine-meshed strainer, using a wooden spoon or the back of a ladle to press down on the pulp and extract as much purée as possible.

2. Add confectioners' sugar to taste. If necessary, thin with a little water, orange juice, lemon juice, or fruity white wine. Serve warm or at room temperature or cover and refrigerate for a day or two.

Cooked Fruit Method

½ cup sugar
3 tablespoons butter
2 cups any ripe fruit (apples, pears, bananas, peaches, cherries, nectarines, berries, mangoes, melon, pumpkin), picked over, pitted or seeded, and/or peeled as necessary

1. Put the sugar, butter, and ½ cup water in a heavy-bottomed medium saucepan over medium-high heat and cook, shaking and stirring, until the mixture is thick and syrupy but not browned.

2. Toss in the fruit and cook over low heat until the fruit begins to break up and release its juices, about 2 minutes for berries, longer for other fruit; some fruits, like apples, may also require a little more water. Press the fruit through a fine-meshed strainer or run it through a food mill to purée and remove any skins or seeds. Serve warm or at room temperature, or cover and refrigerate for up to a week.

RUSTIC FRUIT SAUCE Cook the fruit as directed in the second method, but don't bother pressing it through a strainer or puréeing it.

MELBA SAUCE Simmer 2 cups fresh or thawed frozen raspberries by themselves in a medium saucepan until soft and broken up. Put them through a fine-meshed strainer, pressing to extract as much juice as possible. Discard the seeds and pulp and add enough water to the juice to make ¾ cup. Return the juice to the saucepan and add ⅔ cup red currant jelly, 1 tablespoon fresh lemon juice, ½ teaspoon grated lemon zest, and the sugar. Omit the butter. Simmer until the sugar is dissolved and the sauce is smooth.

Fruit Jam

MAKES: About 1½ cups
TIME: About 45 minutes

M V

You'll be hard-pressed to come up with a reason not to make your own jam with a method as simple as this.

1 pound fruit, peeled, pitted or seeded, and chopped as necessary
¼ cup sugar, or more to taste
2 tablespoons fresh lemon juice, vinegar, booze, or other acidic liquid

Put the fruit in a medium saucepan over medium heat. After a minute or so, add the sugar and juice. Adjust the heat so that the mixture bubbles steadily, using a higher heat if the mixture looks too soupy; lower the heat if it seems dry. Cook, stirring occasionally, until the mixture is thick, 10 to 30 minutes. Taste as you go and add more sugar if needed. Cool completely, cover, and refrigerate; it will thicken more as it cools. Store in the refrigerator, where it will keep for at least a week. Freeze for longer storage.

THICKER FRUIT JAM For fruit low in pectin, like blueberries, raspberries, strawberries, and peaches, adding pectin will yield a thicker jam in a shorter time; it also helps preserve the fruit's natural flavor and color: Add 1 tablespoon pectin powder to the fruit along with the sugar and juice.

CHIA SEED FRUIT JAM Chia seeds become incredibly gelatinous when you combine them with liquid, creating a jammy consistency: Decrease the sugar to 1 tablespoon. Cook the fruit just until it starts to break down, 5 to 15 minutes, depending on the fruit. Remove from the heat, and stir in 2 tablespoons chia seeds; let it sit for 5 to 10 minutes, then check on the consistency. If it's looser than you would like, stir in another ¼ teaspoon seeds and let sit another 5 to 10 minutes. Continue to add seeds in this way till you get the thickness you like.

PUDDINGS AND GELÉES

Few things are more comforting or appealing than pudding—sweet, smooth, and satisfying. You'll find my favorite basic stove-top pudding here, as well as rice pudding (both of which you can veganize), as well as a chocolaty tofu-based pudding and a no-cook chia pudding made with coconut milk.

Another childhood favorite is Jell-O, but since it's made with gelatin (which is animal-based), it's off limits to vegetarians. I've included a version here (called a *gelée*, after the word for jelly in French) that uses plant-based agar instead. Because almost any liquid—from fruit juice to tea—can be turned into the base for gelée, you can let your imagination run wild. And gelées need not only be eaten with a spoon: You increase the amount

of thickener to make them stiffer, then cut them up once set and eat out of hand, or dice and add to anything from iced tea or juice to a dessert soup (pages 739 to 742).

Vanilla Pudding

MAKES: 4 to 6 servings
TIME: 20 minutes, plus time to chill
F M O

This pudding is thickened with cornstarch rather than eggs, which makes it less rich but just as thick and creamy as eggy pudding (which, of course, is one of the variations). It's also more forgiving, and easier for beginners.

2½	cups half-and-half, whole milk, or nondairy milk of your choice
⅔	cup sugar
	Pinch salt
1	vanilla bean or 1 teaspoon vanilla extract
3	tablespoons cornstarch
2	tablespoons butter, softened (optional)

1. Put 2 cups of the half-and-half, the sugar, and salt in a medium saucepan over medium-low heat. If you're using a vanilla bean, split it in half lengthwise and use a small sharp knife to scrape the seeds into the half-and-half; add the pod. Cook just until it begins to steam.
2. Stir together the cornstarch and the remaining half-and-half in a small bowl; there should be no lumps. Fish the pod out of the steaming cream and add the cornstarch mixture. Cook, stirring occasionally, until the mixture thickens and just starts to boil, about 5 minutes. Reduce the heat to very low and continue to cook, stirring, for another 5 minutes or so. Stir in the butter if you're using it and the vanilla if you're using extract.
3. Pour the mixture into a 1-quart dish or into 4 to 6 small ramekins or bowls. Put plastic wrap directly on top of the pudding to prevent a "skin" from forming, or leave uncovered if you like skin. Refrigerate until chilled and serve within a day.

TRADITIONAL VANILLA PUDDING Nothing beats traditional egg-enriched pudding: Substitute 2 eggs and 4 yolks for the cornstarch. In Step 2, whisk or beat the eggs with the sugar and salt; add one-third of the heated half-and-half gradually while whisking constantly, then whisk the egg mixture into the remaining half-and-half. Cook, whisking constantly, until the mixture is thick enough to coat the back of a spoon (see below), about 10 minutes, then stir in the butter, if you're using, and vanilla extract.

CHOCOLATE PUDDING In Step 2, add 2 ounces chopped bittersweet chocolate to the thickened pudding, stirring until entirely melted and mixed in.

TEMBLEQUE (COCONUT PUDDING) A Caribbean staple that's easy and delicious: Substitute coconut milk for the half-and-half and ½ teaspoon ground cinnamon for the vanilla. Increase the cornstarch to ⅓ cup. Omit the butter and stir 2 cups shredded coconut into the thickened pudding. **V**

Coating the Back of a Spoon

When you're stirring an egg-based pudding on top of the stove, this is the easiest way to know when it's done: Dip a large spoon (the larger the spoon, the more surface area you have to judge the coating) into the liquid and drag the tip of your finger across the back of the spoon. If there is a good layer of the liquid clinging to the back of the spoon and a distinct trail from where your fingertip was, it's properly thickened. If the liquid just slides right off the spoon, or your finger trail is covered quickly by runny liquid, keep cooking.

REAL BANANA PUDDING Guaranteed to be the best you've ever had: Use whole or nondairy milk, reduce the sugar to ¼ cup, and add 3 very ripe bananas, peeled and cut into ½-inch pieces. In Step 1, steep the bananas in the warm milk for about 20 minutes. Strain out the bananas and vanilla pod; discard them and return the milk mixture to the pot. Proceed with the recipe.

APRICOT OR PEACH PUDDING You must use ripe and flavorful fruit here or it's not worth the effort: Replace 1¼ cups of the half-and-half with fresh apricot or peach purée (page 271).

GREEN TEA OR EARL GREY PUDDING Omit the vanilla bean and steep a couple of tablespoons loose green or Earl Grey tea in the half-and-half after it steams in Step 1. Strain the liquid and return it to the pot before proceeding.

Piña Colada Chia Pudding

MAKES: 4 servings
TIME: 5 minutes, plus soaking time
M **V**

Chia seeds have the capacity to absorb ten times their weight in liquid, while creating a gel-like texture. This chia seed–liquid combo can be used as a substitute for eggs (see page 303) but here I use them to make a no-cook vegan pudding.

Leave the seeds whole, and your pudding will have a delightful, slightly bumpy texture, like a thick bubble tea; it also looks fantastic—serve it in glass bowl or small Mason or Ball jar if you can. If you prefer a velvety texture, whir the ingredients in a blender until smooth.

Use this recipe as a template, changing the liquid or combination of liquids to whatever you prefer; just keep the ratio of 2 cups liquid to ⅓ cup chia seeds. Chia seeds are forgiving, so if you find that your pudding is thicker than you like, add more liquid and stir; the pudding won't break. Use any kind of nondairy liquid you like.

1½ **cups coconut milk (to make your own,**
     see page 304)
½ **cup pineapple juice**
⅓ **cup chia seeds**
1 **cup chopped fresh pineapple**
½ **cup shredded coconut, toasted (see page 299)**

1. Put the coconut milk, pineapple juice, and chia seeds in a medium bowl or blender. Whisk to combine or process until smooth, depending on the final texture you prefer. If blending, transfer to a bowl. If leaving the seeds whole, stir the mixture after 30 minutes, as the seeds can drop to the bottom of the bowl before the gelling action starts to take effect. Cover and refrigerate for at least 4 hours or overnight.

2. Spoon the pudding into individual bowls and top each with the pineapple, then sprinkle with the coconut and serve. Best enjoyed within a day or two of making it.

LAYERED CHIA PUDDING To add more flavor and visual pow, layer the pudding with the fruit sauce of your choice, creating bands of color; I think the raw fruit method for making the sauce works best (page 722). One cup fruit sauce should be sufficient for four servings. Mango would work wonderfully with the main recipe, but feel free to change up the liquid you use for the pudding to best match the fruit you are using for sauce.

CHOCOLATE CHIA PUDDING This would still taste wonderful with the pineapple and coconut toppings, but you can change it up with shaved vegan chocolate (see page 687) or dollop with Vegan Whipped Cream (page 701): Omit the pineapple juice, increase the coconut milk to 2 cups (or use any other nondairy milk you prefer) and add ⅓ cup cocoa powder and 2 tablespoons maple or agave syrup to the mixture before combining. Taste and add up to another tablespoon sweetener if you'd like.

MATCHA CHIA PUDDING Delicious (and beautiful) topped with blueberries. And since the matcha flavor grows as the pudding sits, taste just before serving; you might find that you need more sweetener: Omit the pineapple juice and increase the coconut milk to 2 cups (or use any other nondairy milk you prefer). Stir 1 tablespoon green matcha powder with 1 tablespoon hot water in a small bowl until smooth, then add that and 1 to 2 tablespoons maple or agave syrup to the chia mixture before combining.

Mexican Chocolate Tofu Pudding

MAKES: 4 to 6 servings
TIME: 10 minutes, plus time to chill

F M V

This pudding has blown the minds of more dinner guests than anything else I've ever made, and all it takes is a blender. The tofu is the thickener, and it needs no cooking. Use the best chocolate you can find here, because it is by far the dominant flavor.

¾ **cup Simple Syrup (page 685) or sugar**
1 **pound silken tofu**
8 **ounces vegan chocolate (see page 687),**
    melted
1 **teaspoon vanilla extract**
1½ **teaspoons ground cinnamon**
½ **teaspoon chili powder, or more to taste**
    Shaved vegan chocolate for garnish (optional)

1. If you're using sugar, combine it with ¾ cup water in a small saucepan and heat until the sugar dissolves. Set aside to cool.

2. Put the simple syrup, tofu, chocolate, vanilla, cinnamon, and chili powder in a blender and purée until completely smooth, stopping to scrape down the side if necessary. Divide the pudding among 4 to 6 ramekins and chill for at least 30 minutes before serving. If you like, use a vegetable peeler to shave some curls of chocolate on top.

CHOCOLATE-ORANGE TOFU PUDDING Citrus adds bright flavor: Substitute 1 tablespoon grated orange zest for the vanilla, cinnamon, and chili powder.

CHOCOLATE-RASPBERRY TOFU PUDDING Decrease the simple syrup to ½ cup or dissolve ½ cup sugar in ½ cup water. If you don't mind seeds, blend ½ cup fresh or thawed frozen raspberries with the other ingredients; otherwise, purée and strain 1 cup raspberries to make about ½ cup purée and add that to the blender. Omit the vanilla, cinnamon, and chili powder.

PEANUT BUTTER–BANANA TOFU PUDDING Use ¼ cup simple syrup or dissolve ¼ cup sugar in ¼ cup water. Blend it with the tofu, vanilla, 2 ripe bananas, and ½ cup creamy peanut butter. Omit the cinnamon and chili powder.

Cinnamon-Nut Rice Pudding

MAKES: 4 servings
TIME: 2½ hours, largely unattended
M O

There are dozens of rice puddings, but this is the one I like best. The rice almost melts into the milk, creating a custard-like consistency with a subtle rice flavor. If you prefer a more rice-intense pudding, use the larger quantity of rice.

¼–⅓	cup white rice
⅓–½	cup sugar, or to taste
	Small pinch salt
4	cups nut milk or whole milk
2	3-inch cinnamon sticks
	Ground cinnamon for garnish
	Toasted chopped nuts (see page 299) for garnish

1. Heat the oven to 325°F. Put the rice, sugar, salt, milk, and cinnamon sticks in a 3- or 4-quart casserole (an ovenproof saucepan will do), stir a couple of times, and put, uncovered, in the oven. Cook for 2 hours, stirring every 30 minutes.
2. The pudding should almost be done. Begin to check it every 10 minutes, stirring gently each time you check. The pudding will be done anywhere from 10 to 30 minutes later, when the grains of rice are swollen and the

pudding is thick but still pourable; it will thicken considerably as it cools. (If the mixture is silky-creamy and thick, the rice suspended perfectly in a rich custard, it is overcooked; it will be too hard when it cools, though still quite good to eat.) Remove the cinnamon sticks while it's cooling.
3. Serve warm, at room temperature, or cold, garnished with a bit of ground cinnamon and chopped nuts.

COCONUT RICE PUDDING Rich: Substitute coconut milk for the nut milk and shredded coconut for the nuts. Omit the cinnamon. V

Lemon-Lime Gelée

MAKES: 4 to 6 servings
TIME: 25 minutes, plus time to chill
F M V

All sorts of flavors are possible here, from sweet-tart lemon-lime to coffee to coconut, and they're all perfect on a summer day or when you want something light and refreshing. Freshly squeezed juice is the best, of course; otherwise, use nectar if it's available. Try unexpected juices like cherry, peach, nectarine, plum, apricot, mango, or passion fruit. To adjust the sweetness of the gelée, replace some of the simple syrup with water, juice, fruit purée, or other liquid.

I tend to like my gels set on the loose side, more like a flan. It still holds its shape on the spoon, but it's delicate and melts immediately in your mouth. If that sounds appealing, use 3 tablespoons agar flakes. For a jiggle akin to Jell-O, use 4 tablespoons. Then you can make cubes or cookie-cutter shapes—great for kids.

3–4	tablespoons agar flakes
1	tablespoon mixed grated lemon and lime zest
¼	cup fresh lemon juice
¼	cup fresh lime juice
1½	cups Simple Syrup (page 685)

1. Put 2 cups water in a small saucepan and add the agar flakes; let it sit for about 10 minutes to soften, then

Clockwise from top:
Lemon-Lime Gelée,
Champagne Gelée with
Berries, Raspberry Gelée
(pages 727 and 729)

bring the water to a boil. Put the zests, juices, and simple syrup in a medium heatproof bowl, then stir in the agar water.

2. Strain the liquid into individual ramekins, small bowls, cups, or a single larger dish (keep in mind you probably want the gelée to be at least 1 inch thick). Let the gelée set at room temperature, then refrigerate until chilled and firm, another hour or so.

RASPBERRY (OR ANY BERRY) GELÉE Use 1 cup water to dissolve the agar. Substitute 1½ cups raspberry or any berry purée, strained to remove the seeds, for the citrus zests and juices.

POMEGRANATE GELÉE Drop fresh pomegranate seeds into the cooling gelée if you like: Use 2½ cups pomegranate juice to dissolve the agar. Omit the citrus zests and juices.

HONEY GELÉE Good-quality honey is essential here; don't shy away from some of the bolder-flavored varieties available: Omit the citrus zests and juices. Substitute 1½ cups honey for the simple syrup. In Step 1, when the agar water has boiled, immediately stir in the honey and keep stirring until it's dissolved.

COFFEE GELÉE Use 1 cup water to dissolve the agar. Substitute 1½ cups freshly brewed coffee or espresso for the citrus zests and juices.

CHAMPAGNE GELÉE WITH BERRIES Pretty with the berries suspended in it; serve it in clear glass: Substitute 3 cups chilled Champagne or sparkling wine for the citrus zests and juices and the water. In Step 1, mix the agar with the simple syrup in a saucepan and bring it to a boil. Cool it only slightly, about 5 minutes, then carefully stir in the Champagne. Transfer to the serving dish(es) and put in the fridge for about 5 minutes so, just until it's starting to set; drop in the berries (they should suspend in the semi-set gelée) and return to the fridge to fully chill.

FROZEN DESSERTS

There's nothing like fresh ice cream, straight from the machine—it's soft-serve at its best, with ideal texture and the freshest flavors. Tangy home-made frozen yogurt will also put store-bought to shame.

Don't have an ice cream maker? Try No-Machine Banana-Mango Ice Cream (page 731)—no dairy, no machine necessary! Or granita, kind of like an uber-slushie. Sorbet and ice milk are light and full of fruit. Finally, there are ice pops, totally kid-friendly but sophisticated enough for adults.

Vanilla Custard Ice Cream

MAKES: About 1 quart
TIME: About 30 minutes, plus time to chill and churn
Ⓜ

Eggs add luxurious thickness and a mellow, round flavor, making for a rich ice cream that's fabulous on its own and also serves as a base for any flavor you can dream up (see page 730 for a slew of ideas). As long as you have 3 cups of liquid, you can play around with the number of eggs (three yolks produces very good ice cream), but know that higher fat makes for better texture.

- 6 **egg yolks**
- ½ **cup sugar**
- 2 **cups half-and-half**
- 1 **cup heavy cream**
- ¼ **teaspoon salt**
- 2 **teaspoons vanilla extract**

1. Put the egg yolks and sugar in a large saucepan and use a whisk or electric mixer to beat them until thick and pale yellow, about 5 minutes.
2. Whisk the half-and-half, cream, and salt into the yolk mixture until thoroughly combined. Put the saucepan over medium-low heat and cook, stirring constantly,

until thick; if the custard ever starts to simmer, turn down the heat. It's ready when it coats the back of a spoon and a line drawn with your finger remains intact (see the illustration on page 724); this should take 5 minutes or so.

3. Strain the custard into a bowl and stir in the vanilla. Cover and refrigerate until it is completely cool, at least 2 hours and preferably overnight. Transfer to an ice cream maker and churn according to the manufacturer's directions. Serve or transfer to an airtight container and freeze.

VANILLA BEAN ICE CREAM Real vanilla beans add warmth and depth of flavor: Use a paring knife to split a vanilla bean down the middle and scrape out the seeds. In a large saucepan, combine the seeds and pod with the half-and-half and cream; heat the mixture over medium-low heat, stirring occasionally, until steam rises from the mixture, about 5 minutes. Remove from the heat and let cool completely to allow the vanilla to steep; remove the pod. Beat the egg yolks and sugar in a bowl as directed, whisk them into the cooled cream mixture, and proceed with the recipe.

14 More Ice Cream Flavors

The base ratio always remains the same: 6 egg yolks with 3 cups liquid total; only the type of liquid and flavorings change. And, remember, cream or dairy milk can always be replaced with nondairy milk. For any variation that requires steeping, add it to the half-and-half and cream before heating, then let the mixture cool.

ICE CREAM	FLAVORING(S)	HOW TO ADD
Chocolate	5 ounces dark chocolate, chopped	Add to the ice cream base with the half-and-half and cream.
Strawberry (or any berry)	1 cup berry purée, strained	Stir into the ice cream base before chilling.
Coffee	2 to 3 shots freshly brewed espresso or ½ cup ground coffee	Swap liquid coffee for ½ cup of the half-and-half, or steep ground coffee in the hot base and strain.
Coconut	1 cup coconut milk; ½ cup shredded coconut; toast in a dry skillet until lightly browned if you like	Replace the cream with the coconut milk and fold the coconut into the ice cream base before chilling.
Pumpkin	1 cup canned pumpkin purée; ½ teaspoon each ground cinnamon and ground ginger	Whisk 1 cup of the hot ice cream base with the pumpkin to thin it, then combine it and the spices with the base before chilling.
Rum-Raisin	½ to ¾ cup raisins; ¼ cup dark rum; ½ cup light brown sugar	Soak the raisins in the rum at room temperature for an hour or so, or bring to a boil and set aside to cool. Use the brown sugar instead of white. Add the rum-raisin mixture to the ice cream base for the last minute or 2 of cooking, before chilling.

No-Machine Banana-Mango Ice Cream

MAKES 4 servings
TIME: 20 minutes, plus freezing time for fruit and ice cream
Ⓜ Ⓥ

You actually do need a machine for this, but not an ice cream machine: Either a blender (it should be powerful enough to handle ice) or a food processor will work. It doesn't get any simpler than this, or closer to the real fruit flavor of whichever fruits you decide to use.

2 ripe bananas
2 ripe mangoes
   Nondairy milk of your choice, as needed

1. Peel and slice the bananas ½ inch thick. Peel and slice the mangoes off the pit into 1-inch pieces. Put them in a resealable plastic bag and freeze solid; this will take at least a few hours.

2. Put the frozen fruit in a food processor or a blender and process, adding the milk as needed to get a smooth, creamy texture; add just 1 or 2 tablespoons at a time.

ICE CREAM	FLAVORING(S)	HOW TO ADD
Maple-Nut	¾ cup maple syrup; 1 cup chopped, lightly toasted nuts, like pecans or walnuts	Swap out the sugar for the maple syrup and add the nuts to the base before chilling.
Buttermilk	1 cup buttermilk	Substitute the buttermilk for the cream.
Mascarpone	1 cup mascarpone	Substitute the mascarpone for the cream.
Banana	2 ripe bananas, chopped	Peel and steep the bananas in the hot ice cream base, then strain them out before chilling the base.
Ginger	2 tablespoons chopped fresh ginger; ½ cup minced candied ginger	Steep the fresh ginger in the hot ice cream base, then strain it out and stir in the candied ginger before chilling.
Green Tea	1 tablespoon matcha powder or 2 tablespoons leaf green tea	Stir the matcha into the base before chilling, or infuse the hot ice cream base with the leaf green tea, then strain out.
Avocado	1 large avocado puréed with the juice of 1 lime	Whisk the avocado with a bit of the hot ice cream base until smooth, then stir it into the base before chilling.
Miso-Peach	½ cup light brown sugar; 2 peaches (or nectarines), peeled, puréed to make about 1 cup, and whisked with 1 tablespoon white miso	Use the brown sugar instead of white. Add the peach mixture to the ice cream base before chilling.

You'll need to stop the machine to scrape down the sides of the container several times.

3. You can eat the ice cream at this point, but it will be very soft. I prefer to transfer it to an airtight container and freeze until solid, which will take about 2 hours.

ORANGE-BANANA-MANGO ICE CREAM When you've finished processing the ice cream, stir in the grated zest of 2 oranges (cold can mute flavor—that's why you're adding so much zest).

ALMOND-BANANA-MANGO ICE CREAM Add 1 teaspoon almond extract to the food processor along with the fruit.

BANANA-CHOCOLATE ICE CREAM Make it all about the banana. Omit the mangoes and use 4 bananas. Once you've finished processing, stir in 1 cup chopped vegan bittersweet chocolate (see page 687).

Frozen Yogurt

MAKES: About 1 quart
TIME: 5 minutes, plus time to chill and churn
Ⓜ

With just two ingredients and hardly any prep work, this is one of the easiest desserts there is. Whole-milk yogurt produces the creamiest results. (Greek yogurt, which is much thicker, often becomes too hard in the freezer but is an excellent complement to fruit purées, as in the variation.)

3½	cups yogurt
¾	cup granulated or superfine sugar

Whisk together the yogurt and sugar until combined. Chill for 30 minutes, then churn in an ice cream maker according to the manufacturer's instructions. Serve or transfer to an airtight container and freeze.

HONEY FROZEN YOGURT Yes, this can pass as breakfast: Reduce the sugar to 3 tablespoons and add ⅔ cup honey.

FRUITY FROZEN YOGURT Any fruit is wonderful here, as is a combination: Replace the yogurt with 2 cups Greek yogurt and add 1½ cups fruit purée.

COCONUT FROZEN YOGURT Replace 1 cup of the yogurt with 1 cup coconut milk. Add 1 cup shredded coconut just before churning.

7 Mix-Ins for Frozen Yogurt

Stir these to the yogurt before chilling; use as many as you like.

1. 1 cup chopped fresh or dried fruit
2. 1 tablespoon grated citrus zest
3. 2 teaspoons vanilla extract
4. 4 ounces chopped dark chocolate
5. ¼ cup balsamic vinegar or Balsamic Syrup (page 633)
6. 1 tablespoon minced fresh ginger
7. 1 teaspoon ground cardamom or cinnamon

Fresh Fruit Sorbet

MAKES: About 3 cups
TIME: About 10 minutes, plus time to chill and churn
Ⓜ Ⓥ

Sorbet is simple and light, with little to distract you from the main ingredient's flavor. If, at the peak of the season, you find yourself with an overabundance of overripe fruit, this is a perfect use. But remember that not all sorbets are fruit-based; see the chart on pages 734 to 735 for options.

4	cups ripe soft fruit, peeled, pitted, and chopped as necessary
¾	cup granulated sugar, superfine sugar, or Simple Syrup (page 685)
1	tablespoon fresh lemon juice, or more to taste

1. Purée together the fruit, sugar, and lemon juice in a blender. Taste and add more sugar and/or lemon juice if necessary; err on the sweeter side, as the sorbet will taste less sweet than the purée after being chilled. If

(continued on page 736)

**Frozen Yogurt with
Raw Fruit Sauce** (page 722)

19 More Ways to Make Sorbet or Ice Milk Flavors

The Fresh Fruit Sorbet (page 732) and its ice milk variation are the jumping-off points for these variations.

SORBET OR ICE MILK	FLAVORING(S)	LIQUID	SWEETENER
Lemon–Lime Sorbet	1½ teaspoons each grated lemon and lime zest	1 cup each fresh lemon and lime juice	2 cups Simple Syrup (page 685)
Blood Orange, Orange, or Grapefruit Sorbet	1½ teaspoons grated blood orange, regular orange, or grapefruit zest; ½ teaspoon grated fresh ginger (optional)	2 cups fresh blood orange, regular orange, or grapefruit juice	1 cup superfine sugar or Simple Syrup (page 685)
Raspberry–Red Wine Sorbet	1 cup raspberries	1 cup red wine (cook all ingredients for 10 minutes, then strain)	1 cup Simple Syrup (page 685)
Espresso Sorbet or Ice Milk	3 to 4 shots freshly brewed espresso; ¼ cup crushed chocolate-covered espresso beans (optional)	2 cups water, nondairy or dairy milk, or cream	1 cup superfine sugar or Simple Syrup (page 685)
Honey Sorbet		2 cups hot water (dissolve the honey in the water)	1 cup good-quality honey
Spicy Melon Sorbet	1 tablespoon minced jalapeño chile	2 cups any melon purée	¾ cup superfine sugar or Simple Syrup (page 685)
Goat Ice Milk	1½ teaspoons grated lemon zest	2 cups goat's milk	½ cup superfine sugar or Simple Syrup (page 685)
Tomato Sorbet		2 cups peeled ripe red, orange, or yellow tomatoes, puréed and strained; ½ cup water	½ cup superfine sugar or Simple Syrup (page 685)
Papaya-Lime Sorbet	1½ teaspoons grated lime zest; 3 tablespoons fresh lime juice, or to taste	2 cups papaya purée	½ cup superfine sugar or Simple Syrup (page 685)
Pear-Rosemary Sorbet	1 sprig fresh rosemary steeped in hot simple syrup, then strained out	2 cups chopped peeled pear, puréed with lemon juice	¾ cup superfine sugar or Simple Syrup (page 685)

SORBET OR ICE MILK	FLAVORING(S)	LIQUID	SWEETENER
Orange-Thyme Sorbet	3 sprigs fresh thyme steeped in hot simple syrup, then strained out; ½ teaspoon minced fresh thyme	2 cups fresh orange juice	¾ cup Simple Syrup (page 685)
Pineapple-Lavender Sorbet	1 teaspoon culinary-grade lavender buds; ½ cup chopped pineapple	2 cups pineapple juice	¾ cup superfine sugar or Simple Syrup (page 685)
Chamomile-Tangerine Sorbet	2 tablespoons culinary-grade chamomile buds or tea steeped in hot simple syrup, then strained out	2 cups fresh tangerine juice	1 cup Simple Syrup (page 685)
Cherry-Chocolate Sorbet	¾ cup cocoa powder; 1 cup pitted and halved cherries	2 cups boiling water (mix ½ cup of it with the cocoa until smooth, then add remaining ingredients)	¾ cup superfine sugar or Simple Syrup (page 685)
Fennel-Lemon Sorbet	2 teaspoons grated lemon zest; 2 tablespoons fresh lemon juice	2 cups shaved fennel bulb, cooked in simple syrup until soft, puréed, and strained	1 cup superfine sugar or Simple Syrup (page 685)
Horchata Ice Milk	2 cinnamon sticks steeped in hot rice milk, then strained out; 1 teaspoon grated lime zest; 1 tablespoon fresh lime juice or to taste	2 cups rice milk	1 cup superfine sugar or Simple Syrup (page 685)
Strawberry–Pink Peppercorn Sorbet or Ice Milk	1 tablespoon crushed pink peppercorns	2 cups strawberry purée, or 1 cup strawberry purée and 1 cup nondairy or dairy milk or cream	½ cup superfine sugar or Simple Syrup (page 685)
Cucumber-Honey Sorbet		3 cups cucumber purée, strained (you should have about 2 cups)	½ cup honey
Thai Basil Lemon-Lime Sorbet	2 sprigs fresh Thai basil steeped in hot simple syrup, then strained out; 2 tablespoons minced fresh Thai basil leaves; 2 teaspoons mixed grated lemon and lime zest	1 cup each fresh lemon and lime juice	1 cup Simple Syrup (page 685)

(*continued from page 732*)

necessary, add water 2 tablespoons at a time to help the fruit mix. If you're using mango or seedy berries, strain the purée through a fine-meshed strainer, stirring and pressing on the mixture with a rubber spatula to leave any fibers or seeds behind; be sure to scrape all the purée from the underside of the strainer.

2. Cover and refrigerate until completely cool, then churn in an ice cream maker according to the manufacturer's directions. Serve or transfer to an airtight container and freeze.

FRESH FRUIT ICE MILK In terms of richness, somewhere in between sorbet and ice cream: Substitute 1 cup dairy or nondairy milk (or cream if you want it really rich) for 1 cup of the fruit and omit the lemon juice. ◘

Food Processor Fruit Sorbet

MAKES: About 1 quart
TIME: 10 minutes
F M O

You don't need an ice cream maker, or even fresh fruit, to make this sorbet—it comes together in a matter of minutes in a food processor and can go straight to the table. You can use juice or water instead of the yogurt or tofu, adding just enough to break down the fruit. Feel free to double the recipe, for entertaining or stashing away, and serve with whipped cream (or Vegan Whipped Cream, page 701) to give it some richness.

    1   **pound frozen fruit**
    ½   **cup yogurt or silken tofu**
    ¼   **cup sugar**

1. Put the fruit, yogurt, sugar, and 2 tablespoons water in a food processor. Process until just puréed and creamy, scraping down the side of the container as needed. If the fruit isn't breaking apart, add more water 1 or 2 tablespoons at a time. Be careful not to overprocess.

2. Serve or transfer to an airtight container and freeze. It gets very hard in the freezer, so thaw at room tem-

perature for 15 minutes or in the refrigerator for about 1 hour before serving.

CREAMY ALL-FRUIT SORBET Frozen bananas break down into a soft-serve-like creaminess; add a bit more frozen fruit to minimize the banana flavor if you like: Replace the yogurt or tofu with 1 chopped frozen banana. Process it on its own until creamy before adding the fruit and sugar; use fruit juice or water as needed to keep the machine working.

MANGO-COCONUT SORBET Use frozen mangoes for the fruit and coconut milk instead of the yogurt or tofu.

CHERRY-CHOCOLATE SORBET Use frozen pitted cherries for the fruit. In Step 1, add 4 ounces chopped chocolate to the food processor along with the rest of the ingredients.

PEACH-GINGER SORBET Use frozen peaches for the fruit. In Step 1, add 1 teaspoon minced fresh ginger to the food processor with the rest of the ingredients.

Fruit Granita

MAKES: About 3 cups
TIME: 10 minutes, plus time to chill
M V

This is a no-special-equipment-needed, minimal-effort dessert that can be made with almost any fruit imaginable. The crunchy, icy texture is similar to a snow cone but with a much better, lighter flavor. Perfectly ripe fruit stands on its own; herbs and spices add sophistication. The best part: You can make it with any liquid—juice, coconut milk, coffee, or any sorbet recipe or variation; use about 2 cups total.

    2   **cups chopped ripe fruit**
    ¼   **cup Simple Syrup (page 685; optional)**
        Fresh lemon juice (optional)

1. Purée the fruit in a blender or food processor with the syrup (or if you're not using it, add some water if necessary to get the machine going). Strain the purée through a fine-meshed strainer if there are lots of seeds or fibers, stirring and pressing on the mixture with a rubber spatula; be sure to scrape all the purée from the underside of the strainer. (You should end up with a little less than 2 cups purée, but don't stress about the exact quantity.) Add lemon juice if you're using it or some simple syrup to taste.

2. Pour into a large shallow pan or baking dish and freeze, using a fork to break up the ice every 30 minutes (see illustrations below), until completely frozen, about 2 hours. It should be slushy and crunchy with ice crystals. Serve or pack loosely in an airtight container. If at any point it becomes too hard, pulse it just once or twice in a food processor.

SWEET CITRUS GRANITA Substitute 2 cups juice from any sweet citrus (such as orange, tangerine, or grapefruit) and 1 tablespoon grated zest for the fruit.

LEMON OR LIME GRANITA Substitute 2 cups fresh lemon or lime juice (or a combination) and 1 tablespoon grated zest for the fruit; start with ½ cup simple syrup and add more to taste if you like.

GREEN APPLE GRANITA Wonderfully tart: Peel, core, and chop 3 large Granny Smith apples. Purée in a blender with the simple syrup, lemon juice, and a little more water to get the machine going. Strain; if you like, add ½ teaspoon ground cinnamon or a splash of bourbon.

WATERMELON-MINT GRANITA This couldn't be more refreshing: Purée 2 cups chopped seeded watermelon with ¼ cup lightly packed fresh mint leaves; strain.

TROPICAL GRANITA Use any combination of chopped pineapple, peach, mango, papaya, or any other tropical fruit to make 2 cups total. Purée and strain; if you like, stir in ¼ cup coconut milk or a splash rum.

COFFEE GRANITA The simplest; serve as the Italians do with a dollop of Whipped Cream or Vegan Whipped Cream (pages 700 to 701): Whisk ½ cup sugar into 2 cups hot freshly brewed coffee until dissolved. Cool to room temperature, then proceed with Step 2.

GREEN TEA GRANITA Steep 2 green tea bags or 2 tablespoons loose green tea in 2 cups water brought almost to a boil for 10 minutes. Strain or remove the tea bags, stir in ¼ cup honey or to taste, and 2 tablespoons fresh lemon juice. Cool to room temperature, then proceed with Step 2.

Fruit Ice Pops

MAKES: 4 to 8 pops, depending on size
TIME: 5 minutes, plus time to freeze
M O

This is an easy, refreshing summer dessert that requires no churning, scraping, or multitasking. You don't even need a mold—paper cups will do the job. Think of this recipe as a template for nearly any fruit or vegetable combination you can think of, and see the variations for some jumping-off points or try it with any of the sorbet and granita recipes or variations.

2 cups chopped ripe fruit
3 tablespoons sugar or honey
2 teaspoons fresh lemon juice (optional)

Making Granita

STEP 1 Use a fork to scrape the granita every 30 minutes as it freezes.

STEP 2 After about 2 hours, the finished granita should be slushy with crunchy ice crystals.

Clockwise from top left:
Cucumber-Melon Pops,
Mango-Coconut Pops,
Avocado-Lime Pops,
Watermelon-Basil Pops

1. Use a blender or food processor to purée the fruit, sugar, and lemon juice if you're using it; add 1 tablespoon water at a time as needed to get the machine going.

2. Divide the liquid evenly among plastic molds or small paper cups. Freeze for about 45 minutes, then insert a wooden stick into each; the pops will have frozen enough that the stick will stay upright. Freeze for another 2 hours or until solid. These can stay in the freezer for up to 2 weeks; any longer and they may get freezer burn. Run the molds or cups under cool running water for a few seconds to loosen the pops and serve.

WATERMELON-BASIL POPS Purée 2 cups chopped seeded watermelon and ¼ cup lightly packed fresh basil leaves with the sugar and lemon juice.

CUCUMBER-MELON POPS Purée 1 peeled and seeded small cucumber and 1 cup chopped honeydew melon with the sugar and lemon juice.

MANGO-COCONUT POPS Purée 1½ cups chopped mango (push it through a fine-meshed strainer if you want to remove any fibers) and ½ cup coconut milk with the sugar and lemon juice.

BANANA–PEANUT BUTTER POPS Purée 2 bananas, 1 cup dairy or nondairy milk, ¼ cup peanut butter, 2 tablespoons sugar, and ½ teaspoon vanilla extract. Sprinkle 1 tablespoon chopped roasted peanuts into each mold or cup before adding the purée.

AVOCADO-LIME POPS Purée 2 large ripe avocados, ¼ cup fresh lime juice, and 1½ cups water. Add the sugar for sweet ice pops or salt and pepper to taste for something more savory.

CAMPARI POPS Booze is great in ice pops, but don't use more than ½ cup or the liquid won't freeze: Combine 1½ cups grapefruit juice with ½ cup Campari and ¼ cup Simple Syrup (page 685).

MOJITO POPS Purée ½ cup lightly packed fresh mint leaves, ⅓ cup white rum, ⅓ cup fresh lime juice, ¼ cup Simple Syrup, and 1 cup water.

---

9 More Ice Pop Combinations

Use 2 cups chopped ripe fruit, puréed, or 100% juice for the fruit.

1. Peach and 1 tablespoon grated fresh ginger

2. Cherry and 1 teaspoon vanilla extract

3. Apple and 1 teaspoon ground cinnamon

4. Pineapple and ¼ cup lightly packed fresh mint leaves

5. Lime and ¼ cup lightly packed fresh cilantro leaves; add sugar to taste

6. Strawberry (strain to remove seeds) and 2 tablespoons balsamic vinegar

7. Raspberry (strain to remove seeds) and 2 tablespoons rose water

8. Blueberry and ½ cup almond milk

9. Grape (use seedless, or strain to remove seeds) and ¼ cup peanut butter, layered into the pop molds

---

DESSERT SOUPS

Dessert soups are a fantastic way to showcase deliciously ripe fruit while ending the meal on the light side.

Because the idea is to capture the fruits' wonderful flavors, the majority of these are uncooked, and since fruit is the highlight, getting what's in season and delicious is key; this is no place to compromise on quality or flavor.

Dessert soups, like their savory cousins, can be either brothy, chunky, or puréed. All styles are equally easy to make. Here are a few pointers.

- Keep the flavors simple; let the fruit or other base ingredient speak for itself.
- Make the soup no more than a day in advance, if not just a couple hours before serving; these flavors are fleeting.

- In most recipes, you can substitute just about any ripe and flavorful fruit for any other.
- For puréed soups, the consistency should be like that of heavy cream, neither watery nor overly thick.
- If you like, add a scoop of ice cream, sour cream, crème fraîche, yogurt, Vegan Whipped Cream (page 701), sorbet, or granita; it adds another layer of flavor, texture, and temperature. Or, cut a fruit gelée (page 727) into cubes and add that as a garnish.

Rhubarb-Orange Soup

MAKES: 4 to 6 servings
TIME: 30 minutes, plus time to chill
M O

Since first having this soup in England, where rhubarb is much more popular than in the United States, I can't help making it at the first sight of rhubarb in the market.

1 medium orange
2 pounds rhubarb stalks, trimmed
1 cup sugar
   Whipped Cream (page 700) or Vegan Whipped Cream (page 701), sour cream, crème fraîche, or lightly sweetened yogurt for garnish (optional)

1. Grate the zest of the orange and juice the orange. String the rhubarb, then cut it into roughly 2-inch lengths.
2. Put the rhubarb, sugar, 4 cups water, orange juice, and half the zest in a large saucepan and bring to a boil. (Wrap and refrigerate the remaining zest.) Turn the heat down to medium and cook until the rhubarb begins to fall apart, 10 to 15 minutes.
3. Chill; if you're in a hurry, pour the mixture into a large bowl and set that bowl in an even larger bowl filled with ice water. When cool, whisk briefly to break up the rhubarb, adding the reserved zest at the same time. Cover and refrigerate until cold. Serve cold, garnished as you like.

CRANBERRY-ORANGE SOUP Lovely after a filling Thanksgiving or any meal: Substitute 1 pound cranberries for the rhubarb. Thin the soup with more orange juice if necessary.

QUINCE-GINGER SOUP Another sweet-tart soup: Substitute 2 teaspoons grated or minced fresh ginger for the orange zest and 2 pounds quince, roughly chopped (skin, core, and all), for the rhubarb. Proceed with the recipe, cooking the quince until the orange juice has a pinkish red tinge and the flesh is soft; strain, discard the flesh, and chill the soup.

Watermelon and Mint Soup

MAKES: 4 servings
TIME: 20 minutes
F M V

This light and refreshing soup is an ideal summertime dessert—add more rum and turn it into a cocktail you can either sip in a glass or eat with a spoon. Cantaloupe, honeydew, and other melons work here too, but since they aren't as watery as watermelon you'll have to press the purée more in Step 2, and may have to add a little water to the blender. For a classic berry soup—the kind you'd get at a fancy brunch—try the first variation.

½ cup Simple Syrup (page 685)
4 sprigs fresh mint
2 pounds ripe watermelon, rind and seeds removed
3 tablespoons fresh lemon or lime juice
¼ cup rum (optional)
1 teaspoon grated lemon or lime zest
   Chopped fresh mint for garnish

1. Put the syrup and mint in a small saucepan and bring to a boil. Turn off the heat and steep for about 10 minutes, then discard the sprigs and let the mint syrup cool to room temperature.
2. Cut enough of the watermelon into ½-inch cubes to measure 2 cups; set aside. Put the remaining watermelon in a blender; add the lemon juice, the rum if you're using it, and mint syrup. Purée until liquefied.

Rhubarb-Orange Soup

Line a fine-meshed strainer with a clean kitchen towel and set it over a large bowl; strain the watermelon purée, pressing on the pulp to squeeze as much juice out as you can. You can cover and refrigerate the soup at this point for up to several hours.

3. Divide the watermelon soup among 4 bowls, add the watermelon cubes and zest and garnish with mint.

SPARKLING WINE WITH BERRIES So simple and lovely: Omit the rum and use lemon juice and zest. Substitute 3 cups mixed berries (whole or sliced as necessary) for the watermelon and add 3½ cups sparkling white wine; increase the simple syrup to 1 cup. Infuse the syrup in Step 1; skip Step 2. Divide the berries among the bowls, pour over the mint syrup, then pour on the sparkling wine. Garnish with mint.

VANILLA-APRICOT SOUP Slice the apricots and float them in the sweet soup, or purée together: Increase the simple syrup to 1 cup. Substitute 1 vanilla bean for the mint, ripe apricots for the watermelon, Cointreau or sweet white wine for the rum, and use whipped cream or crème fraîche for garnish. Use lemon juice and zest. Split the vanilla bean in half lengthwise, use a small sharp knife to scrape the seeds into the simple syrup (save the pod for another use), add 1 cup water and the lemon juice and zest, and infuse. Skip Step 2; slice the apricots, put in the bowls, and pour the vanilla soup over the top. Macerate for up to 2 hours if you have the time.

Sweet Coconut Soup

MAKES: 4 servings
TIME: 15 minutes with cooked beans
F M V

Combining jasmine tea and coconut milk makes for an unusual, light, and delicious soup. Mung beans—a common ingredient in Asian desserts—add a mild flavor and texture, but since some people find them too gritty, I make them optional. The fruit adds more layers of flavor, texture, and color; keep the pieces bite-sized for easier eating.

2 teaspoons jasmine tea
¼ cup sugar, or to taste
2 cups coconut milk (to make your own, see page 304)
1 cup cooked mung or adzuki beans (see page 435; optional)
1 cup sliced or chopped fresh fruit, like mango, kiwi, papaya, melon, lychees, or any tropical fruit
  Shaved or shredded coconut, preferably fresh, for garnish

1. Bring 1½ cups water to a boil and brew the tea for about 5 or 6 minutes (you want it to be strong); strain out the tea leaves. Stir in the sugar until it's dissolved; set the tea aside and let it cool (quicker in the fridge). Shake or whisk the coconut milk to blend the thick "cream" with the juice (especially if you're using canned). Chill the coconut milk as well (to quickly chill the tea and/or coconut milk, put a cup or two of ice in a medium bowl and pour the tea or milk over the top; stir for about 30 seconds, then strain out the ice). Combine the tea and coconut milk.

2. Divide the beans if you're using them and the fruit among 4 bowls and pour over the coconut-tea mixture. Garnish with coconut and serve.

SWEET COCONUT SOUP WITH GRAINS OR TAPIOCA Use cooked grains in place of the beans: Substitute 1 cup cooked pearl couscous, pearled barley, rice, or pearl tapioca for the mung or adzuki beans.

SWEET ALMOND SOUP Light and delicious; serve it chilled or warm: Omit the tea and beans. Substitute almond milk for the coconut milk; berries, pomegranate seeds, apricots, or peaches for the fruit; and sliced almonds for the shaved coconut. Add 1 teaspoon almond extract, rose water, or vanilla extract if you like. Mix the sugar and extracts, if you're using any, into the almond milk, stirring until the sugar is dissolved. Chill or warm the almond milk and pour it over the fruit; serve the soup cold or warm.

Beverages

Hot and cold drinks satisfy us in many ways—they can quench our thirst, deliver a jolt of eye-opening caffeine, supply breakfast or an energy pick-me-up in a drinkable form, and/or give us the opportunity to take a welcome bit of respite from our busy lives to pause and sip.

Beverages can also be a vehicle for added nutrition. Let liquefied fruits and vegetables fly solo or combine them for delicious, fresh juices and ades or filling smoothies. Enjoy a decadent mug of bittersweet hot chocolate and get some beneficial antioxidants at the same time. A cup of tea can provide warming comfort as well as a raft of health benefits. And it turns out that coffee, long (and wrongly) maligned for its caffeine, may also contribute to good health, with studies showing positive effects of moderate consumption.

Many of these beverages can be purchased but then might also contain lots of sugar or high fructose corn syrup plus all kinds of additives. Making them at home allows you full control over what goes into your drink and into your body. You can use local and/or organic produce, you can use (or not) the sweetener of your choice in just the amount you prefer, and you can customize your drink as you like, experimenting with different flavorings or combinations of fruits and vegetables. It's a great time to be thirsty!

FRESH FRUIT AND VEGETABLE JUICES

I don't own a juicer so the recipes in this section don't assume you do either. One reason is cost: To buy a quality machine means spending upwards of $200 or more. But more importantly, I don't "juice" because the process removes the fiber from fruits and vegetables, which is an important component of overall good nutrition. If you have a juicer, follow the directions in your owner's manual. Otherwise, follow the directions on page 748 for using a blender as a juicer.

A word about quantity: The recipes in this section produce a relatively small amount of juice, because fresh juices have really concentrated flavors—and calories—and can be quite filling.

COMBINING PRODUCE FOR SWEET OR SAVORY JUICES

Both fruits and vegetables can make sweet juice. Mixing oranges, apples, pears, or grapes with vegetables like carrots, celery, bell peppers, or zucchini gives the resulting juice a naturally sweet taste without overwhelming the vegetables' flavor. Tropical fruits like coconut, papaya, and mango add a bit of body. For more intense sweetness, consider combining vegetables with berries or cherries, melons, kiwi, or plums. Lemons, limes, and even grapefruits are the natural choices to add a refreshing hit of acidity (though make sure to remove the pithy rind, which is bitter, and any seeds). Then consider the flavors brought by fruits like pineapple and tomato, which are both sweet and acidic.

Sweet juices have an affinity for the spices and aromatics used in baking: cinnamon, vanilla, nutmeg, allspice, ginger, cardamom, anise (including star

---

7 Vegetables *Not* to Use for Fresh Juice

Some people juice everything, but these are my exceptions and conditions:

1. Potatoes: Raw potatoes may upset your stomach. In any case, they don't taste good and they make juices thick and cloudy.

2. Sweet potatoes: Muddy.

3. Cabbage: I prefer milder leafy greens like spinach, watercress, bok choy, or kale.

4. Mushrooms: I don't like the flavor; also, raw shiitake mushrooms contain a compound that can cause a rash in people sensitive to it.

5. Fresh shell beans: Edamame, peas, and green beans are fine, but fresh black-eyed peas, chickpeas, and limas are too woody when raw.

6. Eggplant: Way too bitter.

7. Turnips: Too strong.

anise), and citrus zest. You can enhance the natural sweetness of juice with honey, sugar, or Simple Syrup (page 685).

Savory juices don't have to taste like Bloody Mary mix, though tomatoes are a perfect starting point for all sorts of savory juices, as are strong-flavored vegetables like beets, radishes, and hearty greens. Don't forget fresh herbs, parsley, basil, chives, mint, cilantro, thyme, rosemary, and so on (these can be nice complements to sweet juices as well). You can even add aromatic ingredients like garlic, ginger, shallots, chiles, or leeks, with the rest of the produce or seasonings like salt, pepper, soy sauce, spices, or spice blends to the juice after it's in the glass or pitcher.

Cucumber-Ginger Seltzer

MAKES: 2 servings (2 cups)
TIME: 10 minutes
F **V**

A really fabulous hot-weather drink: refreshing, light, and zinged up with ginger. It makes a chic cocktail too; see the variation.

> 3   medium cucumbers, peeled
> 1   1-inch piece fresh ginger, peeled
> 2   lemons or 3 limes, peeled and seeded if necessary
> 1   cup seltzer
>   Lemon or lime zest for garnish

1. Juice the cucumbers, ginger, and lemons.
2. Combine the juices in a pitcher and pour over ice. Add the seltzer, garnish with zest, and serve immediately.

CUCUMBER-GINGER COCKTAIL Put the juice mixture in a chilled shaker with plenty of ice. In Step 2, replace ½ cup of the seltzer with vodka, gin, or sake; shake well. Pour into 4 martini glasses, add an extra splash of seltzer, and garnish with the lemon zest. Serve immediately.

CELERY-GINGER SELTZER Substitute 4 or 5 celery stalks for the cucumber.

GRAPE-GINGER SELTZER Sweeter: Add a little wine for a great sangria: Substitute 2 cups seedless grapes for the cucumber.

CUCUMBER-MINT SELTZER Also great as a cocktail mixer with vodka, rum, gin, or tequila: Substitute 2 tablespoons chopped fresh mint leaves for the ginger.

17 Fabulous Seasonal Juice Combinations

SPRING

1. Green apple, strawberry, and rhubarb

2. Radish, lettuce, and chive

3. Green pea, orange, and mint

SUMMER

4. Carrot, apricot, and ginger

5. Fennel, cherry, and orange

6. Tomato, celery, carrot, parsley, beet, spinach, cucumber, and red bell pepper

7. Beet, raspberry, and lime

8. Pineapple, carrot, and orange

9. Pear, blueberry, and ginger

10. Mango, pineapple, kiwi, and coconut

11. Cucumber, red bell pepper, and watercress

12. Cherry, raspberry, and honeydew

13. Nectarine, apricot, and mango

FALL

14. Pomegranate (use 100% bottled juice for this; juicing pomegranate seeds instead of enjoying their juicy crunchiness is a waste of a seasonal fruit

that isn't around all that long) and tangerine or orange

15. Grape and celery

WINTER

16. Tangerine, cranberry, and apple

17. Beet, carrot, apple, lemon, and ginger

Tomato, Carrot, and Celery Juice

Tomato, Carrot, and Celery Juice

MAKES: 2 servings (2 cups)
TIME: 10 minutes

F V

This three-vegetable blend is refreshing and slightly sweet. Add some parsley, basil, or even garlic for a stronger drink.

    4 large fresh tomatoes, cut into chunks
    2 medium carrots, peeled
    2 celery stalks
       Splash hot sauce (optional)

1. Juice the tomatoes, carrots, and celery.
2. Stir the juices together in a pitcher and serve at room temperature or over ice, with hot sauce if you like.

BLOODY MARY This could be the best Bloody Mary you've ever had: Omit the carrots. Juice 2 peeled 1-inch cubes fresh horseradish with the tomatoes and celery, or stir 1 tablespoon prepared horseradish into the juice. Add ¼ cup vodka (or leave it virgin). Serve over ice with a stick of cucumber or a celery stalk for garnish, plus hot sauce if you like.

Pumpkin, Carrot, and Orange Juice

MAKES: 2 servings (2 cups)
TIME: 15 minutes

F V

Intensely orange and loaded with vitamins, this juice is a great fall beverage. It's good chilled, hot and infused with spices (see the variations), or used for cooking, especially for pilafs, risotto, baking, or reduced to make a sauce.

    1½ pounds pumpkin, peeled, seeded,
        and cut into chunks

    3 medium carrots, peeled
       Juice of 4 oranges (about 1 cup)

1. Juice the pumpkin and carrots.
2. Put the juices in a pitcher, stir in the orange juice, and serve at room temperature or over ice.

SPICED PUMPKIN, CARROT, AND ORANGE JUICE
A wonderful autumn drink: Heat the combined juices with a cinnamon stick and a whole clove or 2. Strain into mugs and serve with a dollop of Whipped Cream (page 700) or Vegan Whipped Cream (page 701) and a grating of nutmeg.

GINGERY PUMPKIN, CARROT, AND ORANGE JUICE
Add a 1- or 2-inch piece fresh ginger when juicing.

PUMPKIN AND APPLE CIDER Perfect for fall, and it can be spiced and heated like the first variation: Replace the carrots with 4 or 5 apples and omit the orange juice.

Lemony Spinach-Parsley Juice

MAKES: 2 servings (2 cups)
TIME: 15 to 20 minutes

F O

The bright green color of this juice looks almost unnatural, but beautifully so. Leave out the sweetener and you have a terrific juice for cooking.

    1 pound spinach, rinsed well
    1 bunch fresh parsley
    1 lemon, peeled
       Honey or Simple Syrup (page 685)

1. Juice the spinach, parsley, and lemon.
2. Put the juices in a pitcher and stir in honey to taste. Serve over ice.

5 Ways to Cook with Juice

Fresh juices are good for cooking. They work virtually anywhere water or wine will, and add unexpected and often delightful flavors. Some juices are better to cook with than others: Those containing tomatoes, carrots, beets, fennel, spinach, bell peppers, and pumpkin, to name just a few, work well. The juice from cucumbers, lettuce, cabbage, and greens like kale or collards can become dull, musty, or unpleasantly bitter when cooked. (Remember that the juice will taste just like the vegetable, only more concentrated, so it's not that hard to figure out.) Here are some ideas:

1. For a sweet or savory sauce or dip Put the juice in a pan over high heat and bring to a boil; turn the heat down so the juice bubbles gently. Simmer until it is reduced by about one-third of its original volume. For sweet sauces, whisk in butter or cream and a little sugar or honey if necessary (taste first). For savory sauces, whisk in extra virgin olive oil, butter, and/or cream and season with salt and pepper.

2. As the cooking liquid for grains and beans Substitute juice for some or all of the cooking liquid for just about any grain or bean dish. This is especially good for pilaf, risotto, and polenta.

3. As a soup base Combine juice with stock or water or use it on its own.

4. For a glaze Add juice when sautéing vegetables, legumes, or tofu, or brush it on food you're baking or roasting. Juices with a higher sugar content, like carrot, beet, or fruit juices, will create a delicious glaze.

5. In baking and desserts Substitute juice for water—or up to half of the milk or cream—in recipes for quick breads, cakes, yeast breads, ice creams, custards, and puddings (especially rice pudding). If you're using sweet juices, be sure to account for this—you might want to slightly reduce the amount of sugar in the recipe.

Juicing with a Blender

1. Prepare the fruit and vegetables as necessary: Trim away tough skins; remove hard seeds and cores. Cut the produce into manageable chunks.

2. Working in batches if necessary, put the prepared fruit or vegetables in a blender and start blending at the lowest setting. Add only enough water to get the blender going.

3. Purée until completely smooth, stopping the machine as necessary to scrape down the sides. If it's too thick, add water in small increments and keep blending.

4. Pour the purée into a fine-meshed strainer set over a bowl or pitcher; stir and press with a large spoon to extract the juice, discarding the solids as necessary to clear the sieve. For a more watery juice, you can line the strainer with cheesecloth, or clean muslin, or use a nut milk or jelly bag. Expect to use more elbow grease, have less juice, and leave behind the nutritious pulp.

Using the Pulp

The pulp that remains behind when you juice can have a productive second life. Carrot, parsnip, turnip, beet, tomato, summer squash, and bell pepper pulps all make nice additions to stocks, soups, purées, and savory breads. Fruit pulps like apple, pear, peach, nectarine, and apricot, as well as carrot pulp, are great in pancake and quick bread batters and in oatmeal cookies. Discard the pulp from fibrous vegetables like celery or leafy greens, but try any of the others mentioned above in The Best Granola (page 421), or the quick bread and muffin recipes on pages 580 to 587.

SMOOTHIES AND OTHER BLENDER DRINKS

If you want a hand-held breakfast or snack, few things beat a blended beverage, whether it be a smoothie, shake, or horchata. If you want it sweet, opt for syrupy sweeteners like honey, maple syrup, or Simple Syrup (page 685) to keep the consistency as silky as possible. (Granulated sugar tends to remain undissolved and gritty.) For drinks that include fruit, using frozen fruit will yield a thicker, ice-cold drink. The inclusion of banana, mango, and/or avocado will add creaminess to a smoothie, as will silken tofu, yogurt, or nut butter.

Banana-Nut Smoothie

MAKES: 6 or 7 servings (about 7 cups)
TIME: 10 minutes
F O

Nuts add body, flavor, and nutrition to smoothies. To turn this into dessert, use half-and-half or ice cream instead of milk.

2 bananas, peeled
1 cup raw nuts like almonds, walnuts, peanuts, cashews, or macadamias
2 tablespoons honey, Simple Syrup (page 685), or maple syrup (optional)
1 cup milk or nondairy milk, plus more as needed
¾ cup crushed ice

Put the ingredients, in the order listed, in a blender. Purée until smooth. Add more milk if you want a thinner consistency. Serve immediately.

BANANA SPLIT SMOOTHIE A great dessert, too: Use only ½ cup nuts. Replace the milk with frozen yogurt or ice cream and omit the ice. Add ¼ cup chocolate syrup.

Honey Avocado Smoothie

MAKES: 4 servings (about 4 cups)
TIME: 10 minutes
F O

Avocados have a natural affinity for honey, and together they give this shake a velvety texture.

1 ripe medium or large avocado, pitted, peeled, and cut into chunks
1½ cups milk or nondairy milk
2 tablespoons honey, maple syrup, or Simple Syrup (page 685), or more to taste
1 tablespoon fresh lemon juice
2 cups ice cubes

Put the ingredients, in the order listed, in a blender. Purée until smooth. Add more honey if you like and blend again. Serve immediately.

HONEY GRAPEFRUIT SHAKE Tangy and very refreshing: Replace the avocado with ½ cup fresh grapefruit juice.

Almond Shake

MAKES: 4 servings (about 4 cups)
TIME: 10 minutes
F O

The combination of almond milk and whole almonds makes this shake wildly almondy. But you can use regular milk here; the resulting drink will have a milder taste.

1½ cups almond milk
½ cup raw almonds
2 cups ice cubes
   Honey, maple syrup, or Simple Syrup (page 685)

Put the milk, almonds, and ice in a blender. Add a tablespoon or so honey. Purée until smooth. Add more honey if you like and blend again.

From left to right:
Berry-Banana Smoothie,
Peach-Orange Smoothie,
Kale-Banana Smoothie

HAZELNUT SHAKE Use hazelnut milk and hazelnuts instead of almonds.

NUT "NOG" You can make this with either almonds or hazelnuts: Omit the ice and increase the almond milk to 2 cups. Blend until smooth, then pour into a small saucepan or microwave-safe bowl and heat gently until warmed through. Add some rum or bourbon if you like and garnish with sprinkling of freshly grated nutmeg.

Peach-Orange Smoothie

MAKES: 3 servings (about 3 cups)
TIME: 10 minutes
F O

Thick and filling.

    1   cup chopped pitted peaches, peeled if you like
    1   orange, peeled and segmented
    1   banana, peeled and cut into chunks
    ½   cup fresh orange juice, plus more as needed
    ½   cup crushed ice
    1   cup yogurt or silken tofu

Put the ingredients, in the order listed, in a blender. Purée until smooth. Add more juice if you want a thinner consistency. Serve immediately.

PINEAPPLE-COCONUT SMOOTHIE Super-rich and very tropical: Replace the peaches with chopped peeled pineapple. Substitute coconut milk for the orange juice, or add ½ cup shredded coconut with the orange juice.

BERRY-BANANA SMOOTHIE A beautiful color: Substitute blueberries, raspberries, or hulled and halved strawberries for the peaches, and omit the orange.

CARROT-ORANGE SMOOTHIE Still sweet: Omit the peaches and banana and add another orange. Substitute 1 cup carrot juice for the orange juice and increase the yogurt to 1½ cups.

Ripe Bananas Anytime

Bananas are a staple in smoothies because they add body, creaminess, and distinctive flavor that goes with just about anything. I keep a few super-ripe ones in the freezer at all times: Whenever I have the last couple in a bunch that are starting to go over the top, I pop them—skin and all—into a resealable plastic bag in the freezer for up to several months. They'll get black and frosty on the outside, but the flesh will remain perfect. For smoothies, I break peeled frozen bananas into pieces and toss them into a blender with the rest of the ingredients; they'll thicken and chill whatever I combine them with. Or I thaw them in a strainer to drain extra water and use them in Banana Bread (page 581) or any other recipe.

AVOCADO-ORANGE SMOOTHIE Very creamy and rich: Replace the peaches and orange with 1 medium or large avocado, pitted, peeled, and chopped.

KALE-BANANA SMOOTHIE Drink your greens! Replace the peaches and orange with 2 cups chopped stemmed kale. If you like, substitute coconut milk or pineapple juice for the orange juice.

Watermelon-Mint Agua Fresca

MAKES: 4 servings (6 cups)
TIME: 15 minutes
F O

This refreshing Mexican drink (*agua fresca* translates as "fresh water") is a snap to put together.

    4   cups chopped peeled and seeded watermelon
    ¼   cup lightly packed fresh mint leaves
        Pinch salt
    1   tablespoon Simple Syrup (page 685), honey, or turbinado sugar, or to taste (optional)

Put the watermelon, 2 cups cold water, the mint, and salt in a blender and process on high speed until smooth. Sweeten if you like. Enjoy as is or pour through a fine-meshed strainer to remove any fibers.

PEACH-BASIL AGUA FRESCA Replace the watermelon with 3 cups chopped pitted peaches (peeled if you like) and use basil instead of mint. Increase the water to 3 cups.

STRAWBERRY-RASPBERRY AGUA FRESCA Replace the watermelon with 2 cups raspberries and 2 cups halved hulled strawberries. The mint is optional.

MANGO-LIME AGUA FRESCA Replace the watermelon with 3 cups chopped peeled mango. Increase the water to 3 cups and add 2 tablespoons fresh lime juice (or to taste).

SINGLE-SERVE CHIA FRESCA A unique texture and delicious way to get a boost of protein. No need for a blender: For a traditional chia fresca, in a large glass combine 1½ cups cold water, 2 tablespoons fresh lemon or lime juice, and 1 teaspoon sugar or 1 tablespoon liquid sweetener like honey or any syrup. Stir in 2 teaspoons chia seeds. Give the seeds about 10 minutes to absorb liquid, stirring to keep the seeds in suspension if any of them fall to the bottom. Taste and add more citrus juice or sweetener if you'd like.

SINGLE-SERVE FRUITY CHIA FRESCA This drink will be a little thicker than the previous variation. Start with 1½ cups agua fresca from the main recipe or a variation. Stir in 2 teaspoons chia seeds and wait and stir as directed for Chia Fresca.

Horchata

MAKES: 4 servings
TIME: 45 minutes, plus time to soak
Ⓜ Ⓥ

The horchata most Americans know is the Mexican rice-based beverage that's widely available in bottles and in restaurants, but there are also Spanish horchatas made with nuts or *chufa*, a hazelnutlike root sometimes sold as tiger nuts. Traditionally horchatas were made with a mortar and pestle to grind the rice into a paste, but a blender takes most of the work out of it.

You can make horchata with milk instead of water if you like. And it's lovely with a bit of garnish, like chopped walnuts or almonds, and fruit like melon, papaya, mango, peaches, nectarines, or grapes. (Try prickly pear if you can find it.)

Adding Protein to Smoothies and Shakes

If you want an extra hit of protein, you can certainly add a tablespoon or 2 of commercial protein powder to any of these blender drinks. But be warned that not all protein powders are created equal. Before buying a can or package, be sure to check out the list of ingredients—you may be surprised what's in there along with the protein. Some brands contain corn syrup solids, cellulose gum, anticlumping additives, emulsifiers, and/or artificial and natural flavoring agents and sweeteners. Select one with the shortest possible ingredient list, preferably only a single item, like 100% ground flaxseed, chia seed, or hemp seed, or pea meal. (And for flaxseed, chia seeds, and hemp seeds, you can grind your own in a spice grinder if you like.)

Another option is to stir whole chia seeds into your smoothie: 1 tablespoon contains 4 grams protein. However, because of chia's amazing ability to absorb liquid (up to ten times its own weight), it's best to mix it with additional liquid (¼ cup liquid for every 1 tablespoon ground—if you prefer a smooth consistency—or whole seeds) and let it sit for about 10 minutes before stirring it into your drink. Otherwise, you might find yourself eating your smoothie with a spoon rather than drinking it. Also, see variations above for recipes for Single-Serve Chia Fresca and Fruity Chia Fresca.

From left to right:
Single-Serve Fruity Chia Fresca,
Watermelon-Mint Agua Fresca
(page 751), Mango-Lime Agua Fresca,
Strawberry-Raspberry Agua Fresca

1 lime
1½ cups uncooked long-grain rice
2 4-inch cinnamon sticks
½ cup sugar or Simple Syrup (page 685), plus more to taste

1. Remove the zest from the lime in large pieces. Juice the lime and reserve the juice. Put the lime zest, rice, and cinnamon sticks in a large bowl. Pour 4 cups warm water over the mixture and let it sit overnight. If the weather is hot, cover the bowl and refrigerate.

2. Remove and discard the cinnamon sticks and zest. Working in batches if necessary, pour the rice and soaking liquid into a blender. Blend, pouring in 2 cups cold water (total) while the machine is running, until almost smooth. Pour through a fine-meshed strainer into a large pitcher or clean bowl; discard the solids.

3. Stir in the sugar until dissolved, adding more if you like. Chill in the fridge. Flavor to taste with the reserved lime juice and serve.

FAST HORCHATA It's the cheater's way, but cuts the time down to 15 minutes: Omit the rice. Instead of the soaking described in Step 1, put 4 cups plain rice milk in a medium saucepan with the zest and cinnamon sticks. Warm gently over medium heat, stirring occasionally until the milk is fragrant. Add 2 cups cold water and proceed with the recipe from Step 3.

ALMOND HORCHATA The almond flavor blends with the rice wonderfully—nutty, fruity, and sweet: Add 1 cup almonds to the blender in Step 2; proceed with the recipe.

MELON HORCHATA Any melon—cantaloupe, honeydew, Crenshaw, or watermelon—works nicely: Add 2 cups chopped peeled seeded melon to the blender in Step 2 and proceed with the recipe.

PEACH HORCHATA Nectarines are great too: Add 2 cups chopped pitted peaches (peeled if you like) to the blender in Step 2 and proceed with the recipe.

ADES AND HOT CHOCOLATE

Both of these iconic drinks have been bastardized by the food industry to the point that we forget just how good they can be. They're easy to make and infinitely better than the store-bought versions marketed to us as "convenient."

Lemonade or Limeade

MAKES: 4 servings (about 4½ cups)
TIME: 10 minutes

F M V

Lemonade is the stuff of summer, and from-scratch has a fabulous balance of sweet and sour that is incredibly refreshing—no cloying aftertaste. The same is true of limeade. Make either with still or sparkling water (which is known as a rickey) and as sweet or tart as you like. I like mine mouth-puckeringly tart.

1 cup fresh lemon or lime juice (4–6 lemons or 6–8 limes)
½ cup Simple Syrup (page 685) or sugar, plus more to taste

1. Stir together 3 cups cold water, the juice, and simple syrup in a pitcher. If using sugar, stir well until it dissolves. Taste and slowly add more sweetener if you like.

2. Serve over crushed ice or ice cubes.

SALTY LEMONADE OR LIMEADE Surprisingly refreshing, and perfect with anything spicy. Save the rinds from the lemons or limes when you juice them. Boil the water in Step 1, then remove the pot from the heat and add the lemon or lime rinds. Cover and steep for 10 minutes. Strain and combine with the juice and ½ teaspoon or so salt. Add simple syrup or sugar to taste (you may not need it all) and serve over ice.

GINGER LEMONADE A nice kick of ginger makes this a lively thirst quencher: Grate about an inch of fresh ginger into the finished lemonade.

ORANGEADE Use 1 cup fresh orange juice and ¼ cup lemon juice. You will need less simple syrup or sugar.

PINEAPPLEADE Peel, core, and chop 1 ripe pineapple. Purée the pineapple in a blender with enough water to cover (you many need to do this in batches). Strain through a fine-meshed strainer, pressing on the solids to extract as much juice as possible. Combine the pineapple juice with ½ cup lime juice, 1 cup simple syrup, and enough water (still or sparkling) to make about 4 cups. Chill. Serve garnished with mint.

RASPBERRYADE This is even more perfect with a little mint puréed with the raspberries and a sprig or two of mint as a garnish: Roughly purée a cup or more raspberries and push the purée through a fine-meshed strainer to remove the seeds. Stir into the lemonade or limeade and adjust the sweetness as necessary.

Hot Chocolate

MAKES: 4 servings (about 4 cups)
TIME: 10 minutes
F **O**

Forget instant, this hot chocolate is rich, dark, and so satisfying. If you want it vegan, remember to check the ingredients on the chocolate to make sure it doesn't contain milk solids. Many quality dark chocolates (which may not be labeled vegan) don't include them.

> 4 **ounces good-quality dark chocolate or vegan chocolate, chopped**
> 4 **cups milk or nondairy milk**
> 2 **tablespoons sugar**
> **Whipped Cream or Vegan Whipped Cream (page 700 or 701) or marshmallows for garnish (optional)**

1. Put the chocolate, milk, and sugar in a heavy saucepan over low heat. Whisk slowly until the chocolate melts and the sugar dissolves.

2. When the mixture is smooth and steamy, pour it into mugs, top with a dollop of whipped cream or marshmallows if you like, and serve.

MEXICAN HOT CHOCOLATE Traditionally made frothy with a *molinillo* (a wooden chocolate-stirring utensil), but you can use a whisk, an immersion blender, egg beater, electric mixer, or even a blender. If you can't find Mexican drinking chocolate, use bittersweet chocolate and add 1 teaspoon ground cinnamon: Replace the chocolate with 2 disks Mexican drinking chocolate (about 6 ounces), chopped, and add 2 split vanilla beans or 2 teaspoons vanilla extract to the pot in Step 1. For Step 2, remove from the heat and whisk or blend the chocolate mixture vigorously until it's frothy. Reheat if necessary and serve immediately.

SPANISH HOT CHOCOLATE Seriously rich and thick: Double the amount of chocolate and add ground cinnamon to taste, about 1 teaspoon, in Step 1.

SPICY HOT CHOCOLATE A bit of extra heat: Add a cinnamon stick or 1 teaspoon ground cinnamon and a small dried hot red chile or about ½ teaspoon red chile flakes to the saucepan in Step 1. Strain out the cinnamon stick and chile before serving.

HOT WHITE CHOCOLATE Nice looking, but not as rich: Replace the dark chocolate with white chocolate and omit the sugar. Garnish with a sprinkle of grated orange zest before serving.

7 More Flavored Hot Chocolates

1. Mocha: Add a shot of espresso before serving, or replace half the milk with coffee.
2. Minty: Add 1 teaspoon mint or peppermint extract before serving.
3. Vanilla: Add 2 teaspoons extract before serving.
4. Cardamom: Stir in 1 teaspoon ground cardamom before serving.
5. Bergamot: Add ½ teaspoon bergamot extract before

serving, or add 2 bags Earl Grey tea to the mixture as it heats up.

6. Nutty: Whisk ¼ cup nut butter into the hot mixture until it dissolves, then let it heat another minute or two before serving.

7. Boozy: Add ¼ cup brandy, whisky, bourbon, or dark rum before serving.

TEA

All tea comes from just one species of evergreen bush, *Camellia sinensis*, a native of Southeast Asia, and largely falls into one of four categories: black, oolong, green, and white. These categories are determined by how the leaves are harvested and processed. Once the tea leaves meant for black and oolong tea are harvested (by hand or mechanically), they are allowed to "wither," or begin the process of drying to reduce their moisture content a bit. The leaves may be left whole or be broken up. The leaves then go through a process called oxidation, which exposes the leaves to a flow of oxygen-rich air whose temperature and humidity is precisely controlled. The degree to which the leaves are allowed to oxidize determines the tea's ultimate flavor and is what differentiates black (completely oxidized) and oolong (less oxidized). After oxidation, the leaves are dried to stop the process.

BLACK TEA

You are drinking a form of black tea when you drink Lipton or most other plain tea-bag tea, or English breakfast or Earl Grey teas. Black tea is graded by the leaf's size and whether the leaf is whole or broken. Within these grades are multiple classifications, like orange pekoe, souchong, and complex names like Fine Tippy Golden Flowery Orange Pekoe (FTG-FOP). All the regions, estates, and grades give you a lot to think about; the trick is to find what you like and stick with it. Many people who appreciate good black teas prefer Assam and Darjeeling; Keemun is

also delicious. (All three are named for their regions of origin.)

OOLONG TEA

Oolong tea is most familiar to Americans as the tea served at Chinese restaurants, but it represents a mere 2 percent of the overall world tea consumption. The most revered oolong is from Taiwan; it is called Formosa oolong although it originated in the Fujian province of China, where fine oolongs are still produced. This tea is graded by quality, where "choice" is the best, then "finest," "good," and on down to "standard."

GREEN TEA

Green tea leaves are briefly steamed then dried; this results in minimal oxidation, fixes their green color, and yields the freshest taste. This process produces a brew that's high in antioxidants and lower in caffeine than black and oolong tea. China, Taiwan, and Japan are huge producers and consumers of green tea. Green tea is graded by leaf size and age; gunpowder (young leaves rolled into tight pellets) is the best, then young hyson (older, twisted leaves), imperial (older still and rolled into pellets), and dust (the oldest and broken into small pieces). Matcha is made from tea leaves that are shaded from the sun for the three weeks before harvest, which causes the leaves to overproduce chlorophyll, resulting in its characteristic vibrant green color. The leaves are hand picked, and then ground into a fine powder after drying (top quality matcha is stone-ground).

WHITE TEA

White tea is made from tea leaves that are hand picked before they fully unfurl; the "white" of white tea refers to the fine white hairs that are on the leaf buds. Once picked, they are allowed to wither and fully dry in a controlled environment, minimizing oxidation (it's the least oxidized of all the teas). This results in a tea with a delicate, sweet taste, with flavor notes that can include peach, honey, melon, and more.

THE BASICS OF BREWING TEA

Beyond the quality of the tea you choose, five factors affect the tea you drink: the water, the quantity of tea, the strainer (mesh tea ball, tea bag, etc.), the water temperature, and the steeping time.

WATER

Use fresh, filtered for best taste. Water that's reheated or reboiled has less oxygen in it and doesn't brew the tea as well.

QUANTITY OF TEA

There is no hard and fast rule for how much tea you should use, since it depends on whether you like your tea strong or weak. But as a general guideline, 1 teaspoon (a large pinch) tea leaves per ¾ cup water is the place to start.

STRAINER

The more room you allow your tea to expand when steeping, the more the tea will develop color, flavor, and aroma, so it makes sense to use a large strainer, or to add the loose tea to your pot and then strain out the leaves when you pour it.

WATER TEMPERATURE

Different teas like different temperatures of water. Black tea brews best with water that is at a full, rolling boil, while oolongs, greens, and white teas prefer the water "off the boil"—somewhere between steaming and boiling. Here are the ideal temperature ranges:
- Black tea: Full boil
- Oolong tea: 180–190°F
- Green tea: 160–180°F
- White tea: 175–180°F

STEEPING TIME

In general, the longer you steep, the stronger the tea—up to a point; steeping for too long causes tea to become bitter. If you want stronger tea, use more tea

Loose Tea or Bags?

Tea bags are undeniably convenient, and the quality of bagged tea is getting better all the time. But loose tea is not exactly challenging to deal with, and is preferable for a couple of reasons: Most bag tea is of low quality, and if it's not, it's relatively expensive.

Additionally, tea leaves need room to expand and unfold to steep properly and make a full-flavored cup of tea. Typical bags are too cramped. Using loose tea and a strainer large enough to allow the wetted leaves to expand properly (or adding the water to loose leaves and straining afterward) ensures that you get the most flavor from a smaller quantity of tea leaves.

If you must use tea bags, remember that the smaller the pieces of tea, the faster it will steep. Some bagged tea could be ready in as little as 30 to 60 seconds.

instead of more time. If you're using bagged or broken tea, crumbled bits and pieces (see "Loose Tea or Tea Bags?" above), use the shortest time listed below or even less; whole leaves take longer, and tightly rolled or compressed teas take the longest.

Though only you can decide how strong you like your tea, each tea has a more-or-less standard steeping time. Here are some guidelines to get you started with loose leaf tea:
- Black tea: 3 to 6 minutes
- Oolong tea: 3 to 5 minutes
- Green tea: 2 to 4 minutes
- White tea: 2½ to 5 minutes

Masala Chai

MAKES: 4 servings (4 cups)
TIME: 15 minutes
F M O

Most "chai" sold at American coffee shops is made from a syrupy sweet liquid concentrate and bears little resemblance to the real thing. Real masala chai is made with tea and a spice mixture that varies from one place to another—and, like all spice mixtures, from one person to another—along with milk and sugar.

> 5 **teaspoons black tea (preferably Assam)**
> 4 **teaspoons sugar, or to taste**
>   **About ⅓ cup milk or nondairy milk**
> 5 **green cardamom pods, lightly crushed**
> 1 **tablespoon fennel seeds**
>   **Pinch pepper**

1. Brew the tea according to the directions on page 757, using 4 cups boiling water and allowing the tea to steep for 3 to 5 minutes. Strain. This may be done as far in advance as you like.

2. Reheat the tea slowly over low heat with the sugar, milk, cardamom, fennel, and pepper. When it is very hot, strain again. Taste, adjust the sweetness, and serve immediately.

SERIOUSLY SPICY CHAI Lots of spices for a complex and wonderful chai: In Step 2, also add 2 or 3 whole cloves, 1 cinnamon stick, 5 nickel-size slices fresh ginger (don't bother to peel), and 1 star anise pod, lightly crushed.

MILKIER CHAI Instead of the ⅓ cup milk, replace half or all of the 4 cups water with milk—regular or nondairy—taking care not to boil the milk.

CHAI LATTE Add the spices to the tea leaves before steeping. Decrease the water to 2 cups. After straining, for each serving add ½ cup spiced tea to ¼ cup steamed milk (see page 766) and add sugar to taste.

HERBAL CHAI Replace the black tea with yerba mate, chamomile, or just 5 nickel-size slices fresh ginger (don't bother to peel) and a pinch saffron threads.

THAI CHAI If Thai tea isn't available, see Thai Iced Tea on page 762 to make your own blend: Replace the black tea with Thai tea; use 1 stalk lemongrass, crushed, instead of the cardamom; and substitute 5 nickel-size

slices fresh ginger (don't bother to peel) for the fennel seeds. Use coconut milk if you like.

7 Different Ways to Spice or Flavor Masala Chai

1. Throw in a tiny pinch red chile flakes.
2. Use a smoky tea like Lapsang Souchong.
3. Add a pinch grated orange, tangerine, or lemon zest.
4. Replace the milk with coconut milk or any nondairy milk.
5. Use other spices: allspice berries, coriander seeds, grated nutmeg, anise seed.
6. Add a piece of vanilla bean or ½ teaspoon vanilla extract.
7. Add 1 teaspoon cocoa or carob powder.

Matcha

MAKES: 1 serving
TIME: 5 minutes
🄵 🆅

When you make a cup of matcha tea, you are not steeping the leaves but rather dissolving them in water and drinking the tea itself, not an infusion. When buying, seek out matcha powder imported from Japan to ensure the best quality.

> 1–2 **teaspoons matcha powder, to taste**

Pour the matcha powder through a tea strainer (to keep any clumps from forming) into a tea bowl, then add ¼ cup hot water (just short of boiling). With a special bamboo whisk used just for matcha (called a *chasen*) or a frother or small whisk, whisk the water with the tea until it is foamy on top. Enjoy immediately.

FLAVORED AND HERBAL TEAS

Call this "tea plus"—adding flavorings to the cup or pot to infuse along with the tea leaves, or using juices or milk (regular or nondairy) instead of water to brew your tea. Or, forgo the tea entirely—use fresh herbs and you'll never buy those dried herbal tea packets again.

There are just a few brewing guidelines for these teas:

Matcha

- When using water, bring the water to a full boil before adding the flavorings with the tea leaves. (The exceptions to this are cinnamon and ginger; let them come to a boil with the water, then let them simmer for a few minutes before continuing.)
- When brewing with juice or milk, follow the directions for Orange-Ginger Tea below.
- These teas require a longer steeping time than regular tea, from 5 to 15 minutes.

Orange-Ginger Tea

MAKES: 4 servings (4 cups)
TIME: 15 to 25 minutes
F M V

Replacing some of the water with fruit juice—or adding chopped fruit—is an easy way to flavor tea. Apples, pears, berries, peaches, apricots, and cherries all work really well. The possibilities are many; take a look at the variations for more ideas. These fruit teas are excellent hot or iced. See "The Basics of Making Iced Tea" on page 761.

> 2 cups fresh orange juice
> 1 tablespoon any good black tea or Earl Grey tea
> 5 nickel-size slices fresh ginger (don't bother to peel)
> 1 3-inch cinnamon stick
> Sugar

1. Put the orange juice in a small pot with 2 cups water and add the tea, ginger, and cinnamon. Turn the heat to medium and heat until steam rises from the surface. Turn off the heat and cover; let steep for 5 to 15 minutes, to your taste.
2. Strain; return to the pan and reheat gently. Add sugar to taste. Serve immediately, or refrigerate and serve cold.

MINT-CITRUS TEA Reduce the orange juice to 1 cup and add ½ cup each fresh lemon juice and grapefruit or lime juice. Replace the ginger and cinnamon with 1 cup lightly packed fresh mint leaves.

JASMINE-APPLE TEA Replace the orange juice with apple juice, or with 1 cup chopped apple and 2 additional cups water. Use jasmine tea instead of black tea. Substitute a large pinch grated lemon zest for the ginger and cinnamon if you prefer.

CRANBERRY-ORANGE TEA Substitute cranberry juice for the orange juice. Omit the ginger and cinnamon if you prefer. Grate the zest from 1 orange, add 1 tablespoon, and squeeze the juice into the pot in Step 1.

APRICOT-CARDAMOM TEA Replace the orange juice with apricot juice and use Earl Grey tea. Add 1 teaspoon ground cardamom or 3 or 4 lightly crushed whole pods in Step 1.

RASPBERRY GREEN TEA Replace the orange juice with 1 cup fresh raspberries, use green tea, and omit the ginger and cinnamon. When you strain the tea, press on the raspberries to get all their juice.

Mint Tea

MAKES: 4 servings (4 cups)
TIME: 20 to 25 minutes
F M V

Herbal teas can be made from any herb, root, flower, spice, and/or fruit. Depending on what you're brewing, some may take as long as 15 minutes to develop full flavor; others may need a bit of simmering, especially if you're including cinnamon or ginger.

> 1 cup lightly packed fresh mint (leaves and stems okay)
> Sugar

1. Bring 4 cups water to a boil in a small pot. Add the mint, cover, and steep for 10 to 15 minutes, to taste.
2. Strain, then add sugar to taste and stir until it is completely dissolved. Reheat to serve hot, or serve over ice.

Roasted Barley Tea

MAKES: 4 servings (3½ to 3¾ cups)
TIME: 30 minutes
F M V

Very big in Korea, and for good reason: The flavor is nutty and sweet, and it's good hot or cold.

¼ cup hulled (not pearled) barley
Sugar (optional)

1. Put the barley in a dry skillet over medium heat. Toast for about 10 minutes, shaking the pan occasionally, until browned and fragrant. Meanwhile, bring 4 cups water to a boil in a small pot.
2. Add the barley to the water. Cover, turn the heat to very low, and simmer for 15 minutes. Strain the liquid and serve hot, at room temperature, or chilled. You can add sugar to taste if you like, but it isn't necessary.

ROASTED RICE TEA Popular in Japan: Substitute brown or white rice for the barley.

THE BASICS OF MAKING ICED TEA

It's easy enough to pour hot brewed tea or herbal tea over ice and call it iced tea, but you'll get better results with one of the following methods. These days just about anything hot is also served cold, but I think the traditional choices—good black tea or Thai tea—are the best places to start. Green and oolong teas are lovely when served over ice too.

THE HOT WATER METHOD, TWO WAYS

FAST This isn't recommended for herbal teas. Double the amount of loose tea or tea bags you usually use and brew normally (see "The Basics of Brewing Tea," page 757). Strain out the tea leaves or remove the bags and let the tea cool until it's no longer steaming, then pour it over lots of ice.

NO HURRY Brew your tea as usual, let it cool to room temperature, and then pour it over ice or chill it further in the refrigerator.

11 Terrific Herbal Teas

Nothing tastes like your own herbal tea, especially if you have access to an herb garden. Use the following quantities with 4 cups liquid. You can include the herb stems along with the leaves. And be sure to steep everything longer than you would regular tea—10 to 15 minutes total, or longer, to taste.

1. Ginger ½ cup chopped or sliced fresh ginger (don't bother to peel)

2. Ginger-Lemongrass 10 nickel-size slices fresh ginger (don't bother to peel) and 2 stalks lemongrass, trimmed and crushed

3. Sage-Lemon ½ cup or so lightly packed fresh sage leaves and 2 tablespoons grated lemon zest

4. Lavender-Mint or Lavender-Verbena 1 tablespoon culinary-grade lavender flowers and ½ cup lightly packed fresh mint or 10 or so lemon balm or verbena leaves

5. Cinnamon five 3-inch cinnamon sticks

6. Rosemary-Orange or Rosemary-Lemon 3 sprigs fresh rosemary

and 1 tablespoon grated orange or lemon zest

7. Rose-Herb 10 lemon balm or verbena leaves, ½ cup lightly packed fresh mint leaves, and the petals of a fragrant unsprayed red rose or 1 to 2 tablespoons rose water (to taste); add the rose water just before serving

8. Lemon Balm and/or Lemon Verbena about 20

lemon balm or verbena leaves

9. Bay 6 to 8 fresh or 3 or 4 dried bay leaves and a couple black peppercorns if you like

10. Mint or Basil about 1 cup lightly packed fresh leaves

11. Angelica about ½ cup lightly packed fresh leaves

THE COLD WATER METHOD

Again, not recommended for herbal teas. Double the amount of loose tea or tea bags and put them in cold water; cover tightly and let the tea steep on the counter, in the refrigerator, or in direct sun (for "sun tea") until it's as strong as you like it—usually between 6 and 8 hours.

SWEETENING ICED TEA

Getting sugar or honey to dissolve in cold tea is almost impossible. Sweeten the tea while it's still hot or warm or use Simple Syrup (page 685).

UNCLOUDING ICED TEA

When tea cools too rapidly, it can become cloudy, which affects only its appearance. But to make your cloudy tea clear, try pouring a bit of boiling water into it or add a squeeze of citrus juice. To prevent clouding, let your tea cool a bit longer at room temperature before you chill or ice it, or use the cold water method. Hard water can also cause cloudy tea, so if you live in a hard-water area, try using spring water.

Thai Iced Tea

Cha Yen

MAKES: 4 to 6 servings (about 6 cups)
TIME: 15 to 20 minutes
F

A creamy treat, which—surprisingly—nicely accompanies spicy food. Thai tea is a blend of black tea, orange flowers, star anise, vanilla, cloves, and cinnamon, and is sold at most Asian markets. But you can also use any black tea with a whole star anise, 2 whole cloves, a cinnamon stick, and a tiny dash vanilla extract.

1¼	**cups Thai tea or the tea blend outlined above**
4–6	**tablespoons sweetened condensed milk**
	Sugar
	Milk

1. Bring 6 cups water to a boil. Put the tea in a heatproof pitcher and pour in the hot water. Allow the tea to steep for 5 to 10 minutes, to taste.
2. Put 1 tablespoon of the condensed milk in each of 4 to 6 heatproof glasses. Carefully strain the hot tea into the glasses and stir well. Add sugar and milk to taste. Add ice cubes to chill and serve.

HOT THAI TEA Omit the ice and serve in tea cups.

CHA DUM YEN Omit the sweetened condensed milk and milk. **V**

COFFEE

Coffee has come a long way over the past two decades, with a stunning range of coffee varieties available, even in supermarkets, as well as ways to brew. Today, there is no reason not to be able to brew a good cup of coffee at home.

GRINDING COFFEE BEANS

For the best flavor, you want to start with whole beans and grind them yourself. It takes only a minute and you'll immediately taste the difference between freshly ground and already ground coffee. There are two kinds of grinders, the blade grinder and burr grinder. The difference between the two is that the burr grinder is much better at grinding the beans to a uniform size, from coarse to a fine powder; for that reason, burr grinders are preferred by coffee aficionados. But they're also a lot more expensive than blade grinders. For me, the important thing is that you make the switch to grinding your own beans, so if a blade grinder is what fits in your budget, go for it.

For espresso, grind the coffee as finely as you can. For drip coffee, grind anywhere from medium to fine. Plungers (French presses) and percolators need a medium to coarse grind.

I recommend buying whole beans in quantities that you will use within a couple of weeks. If you buy larger amounts of beans at one time, keep out what you need for the week and store the rest in the freezer—preferably in a freezer bag for extra protection—for up to 3 or 4 months. This practice is scorned by coffee fanatics, but, well, I'm not one.

THE BASICS OF BREWING COFFEE

The vast majority of coffee in the United State is brewed using the drip method, which works perfectly well, especially if you make your coffee using a Chemex, Melitta, or similar system. (The currently fashionable term for this is "pourover"; see "Filter Brewers," right, for instructions.)

There have been advances made in more expensive models of automatic drip coffee makers. Some presoak the ground coffee before starting the brewing process; many meet the temperature and brewing time standards recommended by the Specialty Coffee Association of America (195° to 205°F and 4 to 8 minutes).

I don't recommend the single-serve coffee makers that require little more than sticking in a coffee pod and turning it on; I find they yield pretty bad results. But there are other options:

DRIP MAKERS

The most consistent and best way to brew American-style coffee. Use a fine-to-medium grind (not too fine, or the water will have a hard time filtering through them and back up), 1½ level tablespoons ground coffee per 6-ounce cup; for stronger coffee, use more. Freshly brewed coffee is always best; letting your coffee sit on the machine's hot plate to keep warm is a sure way to kill the subtler aromas and flavors. A better method is to brew only what you'll serve immediately or, if you need to, keep the rest hot in a thermos. Coffee makers that brew directly into a thermal carafe work well.

FILTER BREWERS

This simple manual coffee maker consists of a metal, ceramic, or glass filter cone and a glass or ceramic carafe, and can range from a single generous (10-ounce) serving to 10-cup capacity. To use, bring water to just shy of boiling, or let the water boil and then cool for a minute before starting. Fit a paper filter in the cone, set it on the carafe, and pour in a little of the hot water to wet the paper. Pour out any water that drips through into the carafe. Put fine-to-medium grind coffee in the filter, 3 level tablespoons for a single-serving carafe, and about 2 tablespoons for each additional cup. (I like strong coffee; if you like it less so, start with 2 tablespoons for a single-serving carafe and add 1 tablespoon per additional cup, and then fine-tune the amounts from there.) Pour in enough of the hot water to fully wet the grounds and let sit for a few seconds before slowing pouring in the rest of the water. Let the coffee drip through to the top of the carafe, then remove the filter cone and put it in the sink to finish dripping.

FRENCH PRESS

The French press is as simple as it gets. Put medium-to-coarse grounds in the carafe (1½ tablespoons per 6 ounces water). Add enough boiling hot water to fully wet the grounds and wait a couple of seconds before slowly pouring in the rest of the water to fill the carafe to just below the top. Stir—it's best to use wood; you run the risk of cracking the carafe with a metal implement—and put the top on without pushing down the plunger. Let it sit for 3 minutes, then slowly push the plunger all the way down. Serve the coffee immediately. A word of caution: Sometimes the plunger will initially resist going down at all, or stop midplunge (this usually means that the coffee was too finely ground). If this happens, don't press hard on it, as hot coffee may squirt out the spout of the carafe; instead, let it sit another minute or so. At that point, it should go down easily.

PERCOLATORS

This is basically boiled coffee and not recommended by me or anyone else, but when you need to make a large

Cold Brew Coffee,
Thai Iced Tea (page 762)

quantity of coffee for twenty or more people, you have no choice. For the best results, use a fairly coarse grind, 1½ tablespoons ground coffee per 6 ounces water, set the perking time to about 5 minutes, and turn off the heat when it's done perking. If your crowd is fewer than twenty, you're better off making a couple of batches of drip coffee and keeping it hot in thermoses.

Cold Brew Coffee

MAKES: About 2 cups
TIME: 5 minutes, plus soaking/brewing time
M V

For lovers of iced coffee, this is the perfect way to get undiluted flavor. Yes, it does take time, but next to no effort—plan for it and you'll always have a jar in the fridge ready to go when you thirst for it. You can scale this recipe however you want; you can also experiment with the coffee-to-water ratio as well as brewing time. Where you end up all depends on how strong you like your coffee: If you'd like your cold brew to function more as a concentrate—if, for example, you like your iced coffee really milky—then bring the ratio of grounds to water closer to 1:1 than 1:2, and/or extend the brewing time.

1 cup coarse-ground coffee

1. Put the coffee grounds in a pitcher or other large glass container, like a 1-quart mason jar. Add 2 cups cold filtered water. Stir to make sure the grounds are fully saturated. Cover and let sit at room temperature for at least 12 and up to 24 hours. Give it a taste periodically to see if it is strong enough for you; when it is, you're ready for Step 2.
2. Line a fine-meshed strainer with 2 layers of dampened cheesecloth and set it over a bowl. Very slowly pour the coffee and grounds into the strainer. Let the coffee fully drain into the bowl. Transfer the coffee to a clean pitcher or airtight glass container and refrigerate until cold before enjoying over ice.

QUICKER ICED COFFEE If you don't have the patience for cold brew or aren't willing to foot the expense—it does require an awful lot of coffee—you have other options. The simplest is to brew a pot a coffee as you normally would, then refrigerate it and serve it cold. If you like your iced coffee full strength, pour some coffee into an ice cube tray, freeze, and use the frozen coffee cubes to chill your coffee with no flavor dilution. You can also pour hot coffee over ice; assuming you're using normal ice cubes, not the coffee cubes described above, brew the coffee extra strong, as it will be diluted when it hits the ice in the glass.

THE BASICS OF MAKING ESPRESSO

Espresso machines range from stovetop pots (which make a coffee-like substance many people like but I don't) to junky countertop models to super-duper versions that cost many hundreds or even thousands of dollars. Only the good ones are worth using, and if you're that into espresso, you probably don't need advice from me. But if you're a beginner, here are my two cents on the subject. Following these tips will get you the best possible espresso with the machine you have:

- **The beans** Use fresh, oily-looking dark-roasted beans, preferably Italian or French roast.
- **The grind** Espresso grinds are very fine, like superfine sugar or slightly grainy powder. A burr grinder (see page 762) isn't essential, but it helps.
- **Water temperature** The ideal temperature is 192°F. If your machine is electric, make sure it is that hot; most have built-in thermostats. Stovetop makers work by building pressure from boiling water, and you can't control the water temperature.
- **Packing the grinds** The grounds should be packed (called "tamping") into the metal cup using the tamper for even distribution. The packing will affect the brew time: Too soft and the water goes through too

quickly; too hard and the water doesn't go through quickly enough. Mostly, if you have a fine grind, fill the basket and tamp just about as hard as you can; you'll be on the right track.

- The cups: Make sure they're hot before you start brewing.
- Brew time: Ideally it's 25 to 30 seconds for the perfect aroma, flavor, and crema (the foam that forms on the surface of a shot of espresso).
- Serving: Serve immediately; the longer the espresso sits, the more the aroma and flavor dissipate.
- Cleaning: Clean your machine often and thoroughly using an espresso machine cleaning solution or a 50:50 vinegar-water solution, and always follow the manufacturer's instructions.

STEAMING AND FROTHING MILK

Getting beautiful frothy milk is not difficult; it just requires a bit of practice. Two percent or whole regular milk gives the best results, but you can steam skim milk or soy milk pretty nicely.

- Start with fresh, cold milk. Use a stainless-steel pitcher if possible. Make sure the espresso machine is ready per the manufacturer's instructions.
- Submerge the steam wand deep into the milk to heat it. As it warms, lower the pitcher so the tip of the wand is just below the milk's surface—this is how you build foam. Continue to lower the pitcher as the foam rises.
- Steam until the pitcher is almost too hot to handle and the milk has doubled in volume; the froth should be thick and hold soft peaks. Pour into your coffee.
- Immediately clean the wand by running a couple quick spurts of steam out of it to force any milk out. Wipe the exterior of the wand with a damp cloth or sponge.

12 Ways to Enjoy Coffee or Espresso

1. Cappuccino Put a shot of espresso in a coffee cup and fill with steamed milk foam.

2. Latte Put a shot of espresso in a large heat-proof glass or a cup and fill with steamed milk.

3. Caramel latte Add 1 to 2 tablespoons caramel syrup to the milk before steaming it.

4. Café au lait Combine brewed coffee with hot (preferably steamed) milk; usually half coffee, half milk, but use whatever ratio you like. Steam the milk using the steam wand on your espresso machine or heat it in a pot over medium heat until tiny bubbles appear on the sides.

5. Caffè breve Top a shot of espresso with steamed half-and-half.

6. Espresso macchiato Steam as small an amount of milk as your machine can handle and "stain" an espresso with a spoonful or so of the steamed milk foam.

7. Mocha Add 1 to 2 tablespoons chocolate syrup to your coffee, along with milk and sugar if you like.

8. Espresso con panna Top a shot of espresso with a dollop of whipped cream.

9. Viennese espresso Mix a shot of espresso with a pinch each ground cinnamon and cloves and top with a dollop of whipped cream.

10. Coffee soda Pour a shot of espresso into a glass filled with ice and add seltzer. For a less potent version, follow the recipe for Cold Brew Coffee (page 765) and add seltzer.

11. Frappé Combine 1 cup brewed coffee, cold, 1 teaspoon or more sugar, cream or milk to taste, and about ½ cup crushed ice in a blender. Purée until frothy and serve immediately. For a frozen mocha, add chocolate syrup.

12. Iced Vietnamese coffee Grind Vietnamese or Thai coffee (or any robust coffee) as finely as possible. Use about 2 tablespoons coffee per 8 ounces water. Brew the coffee using a drip brewer (see page 763). Put a couple of tablespoons sweetened condensed milk in a heatproof glass; fill with ice and pour the coffee over. Stir; add more condensed milk if you like.

Appendix

76 Great Appetizers

When it comes to entertaining, you've got lots of wonderful vegetarian choices for starters, from dips and skewers to all sorts of delicious help-yourself appetizers. Many of these can also be combined for a meal of small plates. For a sit-down dinner, you can also opt for a first-course salad or soup; take a look at the recipes in those particular chapters for ideas.

1. Endive and Blue Cheese Salad (page 42)

2. Mushroom Salad, Italian-American Style (page 62)

3. Quickest Pickled Vegetables (page 89) and variations

4. Marinated Garden Vegetables (page 91) and variations

5. Spicy Korean-Style Pickles (page 91) and variation

6. Crudités (page 92)

7. Korean Vegetable Pancakes (page 157) and variations

8. Batter-Fried Vegetables (page 159) and variations

9. Coconut-Fried Plantains (page 162)

10. Fried Onion Rings, Streamlined Ⓥ (page 162)

11. Vegetable Crisps Ⓥ (page 163)

12. Crunchy Corn Guacamole Ⓥ (page 174) and variations

13. Crisp-Fried Bean Sprouts Ⓥ (page 176)

14. Manchurian Cauliflower (page 189)

15. Corn Pancakes, Thai Style (page 196)

16. Corn Fritters (page 196)

17. Portobello "Bacon" (page 218)

18. Fried Okra (page 221) and variation

19. Roasted Red Peppers Ⓥ (page 228)

20. Potato Chips Ⓥ (page 242)

21. Potato Croquettes (page 242) and variations

22. Texas Caviar with Sea Greens Ⓖ (page 246)

23. Nori Chips Ⓥ (page 247)

24. Japanese Egg Crêpes with Nori (page 248)

25. Zucchini Pancakes with Pesto (page 254) and variations

26. Broiled Cherry Tomatoes with Herbs Ⓥ (page 258)

27. Stuffed Tomatoes (page 262) and variations

28. Crisp Squash Seeds Ⓥ (page 268)

29. Fried Plantain Chips Ⓥ (page 280)

30. Tapenade Ⓥ (page 291)

31. Cashew Cheese Ⓥ (page 302)

32. Chestnuts Ⓥ (page 303)

33. Cold Sesame or Peanut Noodles (page 332) and variations

34. Steamed Dumplings (page 356) and variations

35. Fried Tofu Wontons with Chives and Ginger (page 359)

36. Potato-Stuffed Pierogi (page 361) and variations

37. Nigiri Sushi Ⓥ (page 384)

38. Rice Balls (page 389) and variation, served with Simple Miso Dipping Sauce (page 653) or Dashi Dipping Sauce (page 657)

100 Essential Recipes

Here's a list of what I consider essential recipes, and they really make up a kind of basic mini-cookbook on their own.

⊽ Vegan   ▣ Vegan Optional

Ⓥ Vegan   Ⓞ Vegan Optional

Index

Page numbers in *italics* indicate illustrations. **V** indicates a vegan entry.

Crunchy granola
  no-bake fruit and cereal
    bars, 693
  no-bake granola bars,
    692–693
Cuban style, chickpeas in their
  own broth, 455
Cubed croutons, 679
Cucumber(s)
  adding marinated to sushi
    bowls, 385
  in chopped salad, 37
  cold sesame or peanut noo-
    dles, 332
  cool, -yogurt soup with nuts,
    144
  as crudité, 92
  farro, salad, 80
  farro salad with, and yogurt-
    dill dressing, 77, 80
  in fried rice, 381
  as garnish for soba with dip-
    ping sauce, 338
  -ginger seltzer, 745 V
    variations on, 745
  -honey sorbet, 735
  in Japanese-style summer-
    time pasta salad, 85
  -melon ice pops, 739
  -mint seltzer, 745
  quickest pickled, 89, 90, 91
  salad, Korean style, 49
  salad with soy and ginger,
    49 V
    variations on, 49
  salsa, 662
  salting, as salad addition, 48
  scallion marinated, 47
  sea slaw, 54, 55
  seeding, 49, 49
  in simplest seaweed salad, 53
  spicy Korean-style pickles,
    91, 93
    variation on, 93
  for summer rolls, 620
  vegetable noodles, 310
  wild rice salad with, and
    yogurt, 80

Cultured butter, 553–554
Cumin, 643
  in applesauce, 275
  carrot salad with, 43
    variation on, 43
  in cracker dough, 590
  root vegetable salad
    with, 43
  in yeast bread, 604
Cupboard, setting up, 12, 14
Cupcakes, making, 697
Currant(s)
  orange-, biscuit, 588
  rice pilaf with, 372
  spinach with, and nuts,
    250 V
Curried amaranth griddlecakes,
  406
Curried baked beans, 469
Curried carrot-coconut soup,
  120
Curried cheese, 564–565
  variations on, 565
Curried lentils with potatoes,
  chickpeas, and spin-
  ach, 453
Curried pearl couscous pilaf,
  410
Curried rice cakes, 341
Curried rice with chickpeas,
  370
Curried stir-fried potatoes,
  239, 240, 241 V
  variations on, 241
Curried tofu jerky, 497
Curry
  buttery lentils and potatoes
    with, 453
  coconut, vinaigrette, 631
  green, paste, 666
  lentils and potatoes with,
    451, 453
  peanut sauce, 659
  ranch dressing, 672
  red, paste, 666 V
  sauce, 676
  winter squash with coconut
    milk and, 264, 265

Curry powder
  with chickpea fries, 480
  in cooked beans, 434
  fragrant, 641, 649
  in fried rice, 381
  hot, 649
  in mashed potatoes, 234
  twice-baked potatoes, 232
  in vegetable crisps, 163
  in waffle batter, 548
Curry tahini sauce, 305
Customizing granola, 421
Cutting, basics of, 18, 21–23
Cutting boards, 16–17
Cutting lettuce, 32

D

Daikon radish. See also
  Radishes
  in Korean-style vegetable
    soup, 115
  in pho, 130
  purée, 152
  in stir-fried vegetables, 155
  in summer rolls, 620
  as topping for Japanese-
    style summertime
    pasta salad, 86
Dairy, 551–554
  buttermilk, 551–552
  cream, 552
  crème fraîche, 552
  half-and-half, 552
  milk, 551
  pasta with, 316–317
    butter, sage, and
      Parmesan, 316–317
      variations on, 317
    creamy, lemony,
      variations on, 317
  sour cream, 552
  UHT milk, 551
Dal(s)
  cooking and eating, 450
  mixed whole-bean, with
    walnuts, 451
    variations on, 451

mung bean
  with apples, coconut, and
    mint, 452, 453
    variations on, 452, 453
  simplest, 450
    variations on, 450–451
Dandelions
  in green salad, 33
  in mashed favas, 466
Dark chocolate, 686
  in flourless brownies, 692
  in frozen yogurt, 732
Darker bran muffins, 586
Dashi, 100
  -boiled tofu, 485
  dipping sauce, 657
    additions to, 657
Dates, 282
  in balsamic syrup, 633
  in bulgur beet burgers with
    ginger, 502, 504, 505
  buying and storing, 282
  cooking, 282
  in kale salad, 44
  preparing, 282
  in roasted carrots or pars-
    nips with, and raisins,
    188 V
Date sugar, 683
Deep-fried tofu, 487, 488 V
  variation on, 487, 489
Deep-frying, 26–27, 157
Deglazing, 27
Demerara, 682
Desserts
  cakes, 693–700
    baby, 697
    carrot, 696–697
      variations on, 697
    cheese, 699–700
      variation on, 700
    chocolate, 694, 695
      variations on, 694
    cup, 697
    orange-almond, 697–698
    plum-rosemary upside-
      down, 698–699
      variations on, 698–699

Home fries, 235 V

  dishes made with, 236

Homemade tofu, 484–485 V

Hominy, 390, 398, 399

  posole with beans, 394

Honey, 683

  in avocado smoothie, 749

  in baked apples, 720

  in broiled peaches with
      rosemary and, 720

  cucumber-, sorbet, 735

  in customizing granola, 421

  in frozen yogurt, 732

  gelée, 729

  -oat bran muffins, 587

  peanut-butter-, cookies, 690

  raspberry, thyme, and com-
      pote, 721

  -roasted figs, 721

  sorbet, 734

  vegan substitutions for, 15

  in vinaigrette, 42, 630

  whipped cream, 701

  -whole wheat bread with
      grains and fruits, 604

  in yogurt, 553

Honeydew in fruit, cheese, and
    nut combos, 39

Hoppin' john with smoked tofu,
    457, 458, 459 V

  variations on, 459

Horchata, 752, 754 V

  ice cream, 735

  variations on, 754

Horse beans, 431

Horseradish

  in crunchy amaranth
      griddlecakes, 406

  in egg salad or deviled eggs,
    542

  in mashed potatoes, 234

  in mayonnaise, 671

  sautéed kohlrabi with cream
    and, 214

  in vinaigrette, 630

  in wheat berry salad with
    cabbage and mustard,
    85

Hot and sour braised tempeh,
    513

Hot and sour soup, 112–113 V

  egg drop, 113

Hot chocolate, 755–756

  flavored, 755–756

  variations on, 755

Hot curry powder, 649 V

  in potato salad, 70

Hot sauce, 16

  for huevos rancheros, 533

  for topping baked potatoes,
    233

Hot Thai tea, 762

Hot water, 98

Hot white chocolate, 755

Huevos rancheros, 533, 534,
    535

  with red mole, 535

  simplest, 535

Hulled barley, 403, 407

Hummus, 463, 464, 465 V

  as crudité dip, 92

  fondue, 466

  as spread for bruschetta or
    crostini, 624

  variations on, 465

Hush puppies, okra, 221

Hydrogenated fats, 621

I

Iceberg lettuce, 32

Ice cream

  flavors, 730–731

  no-machine banana-mango,
    731–732 V

  vanilla custard, 729–730

Iced Vietnamese coffee, 766

Ice milk

  flavors, 734–735

  fresh fruit, 736

Ice pops

  combinations, 739

  variations on, 739

Immersion blender in making a
    purée, 120

Indian rice, 402

Indian saffron, 647

Indian style

  chile paste, 665

  potato croquettes, 243

  pumpkin soup, 121

  rice salad, 77

  smooth green chile sauce,
    666–667 V

Instant-read thermometer,
    597

Inverno pasta, 320

Italian style

  bean salad, 72

  cauliflower soup, 102, 103

  cheese bake, 558

  egg drop soup, 142

  lentil soup with rice, 129

  tofu pancakes, 499

Italian tofu crumbles, 499

J

Jack cheese

  in mashed potatoes, 234

  for topping baked potatoes,
    233

  in waffle batter, 548

Jackfruit, 283–284

  BBQ, sandwiches, 284 V,
    295

  buying and storing, 283

  cooking, 283

  preparing, 283

Jalapeño(s), 227

  in applesauce, 275

  in buttermilk biscuits, 588

  cheddar-
    breadsticks, 606

    corn bread, 581

  in cooked beans, 434

  in cracker dough, 590

  in egg salad or deviled eggs,
    542

  in five-layer avocado salad,
    51–52

  in mashed potatoes, 234

  pan-grilled corn with chile,
    198 V

  in potato salad, 70

  in roasted sweet potato with
    red pepper vinaigrette,
    71

  in scrambled eggs, 524

  in yeast bread, 604

Jam(s)

  -filled baked apples, 720

  fruit, 722–723 V

    variations on, 723

  galettes, 716

  glaze, 703, 705

    variations on, 705

  in oatmeal and other cooked
    grains, 420

  in yogurt, 553

Japanese basil, 637

Japanese egg crêpes with nori,
    248, 249

Japanese flavors, marinated
    tofu with, 496

Japanese mint, 637

Japanese pickles, in sushi
    bowls, 385

Japanese rice with shiitakes
    edamame, and sea greens,
    387–388 V

  variations on, 388

Japanese seven-spice mix, 641,
    650

  in seasoning vegetable
    crisps, 163

  sprinkling on popcorn, 390

Japanese style

  bean salad, 72

  potato croquettes, 243

  rice salad, 77

  summertime pasta salad, 82,
    85–86 V

  toppings for, 86

Japanese vegetable pancakes,
    159

Jasmine-apple tea, 760

Jerk seasoning, 650–651 V

  for vegetable crisps,
    163

Jerky tofu, 496–497 V

  variations on, 496–497

Olives, 290–291
  bitter greens with maple
    -onion dressing,
    40, *41*
  bok choy with capers, and
    garlic, 179
  braised celery with tomato,
    capers, and, 192
  braised leeks with, 216 V
  breaded sautéed cauliflower
    with onion and, 189
  buying and storing, 291
  cauliflower salad with,
    and bread crumbs,
    65–66 V
  chopped, for twice-baked
    potatoes, 232
  in compound butter, 678
  cooking, 291
  couscous salad with, feta
    and, 89
  couscous-stuffed tomatoes
    with harissa and, 262
  in cracker dough, 590
  edamame with tomatoes
    and, 437
  in egg salad or deviled eggs,
    542
  garlicky kale or collards
    with, pine nuts and,
    211–212 V
  in kale salad, 44
  100 percent whole wheat
    bread with walnuts
    and, 604
  or dried tomato breadsticks,
    606
  pearl couscous pilaf with
    almonds and, 410 V
  as pizza topping, 614
  in potato salad, 70
  preparing, 291
  tapenade, 291–292 V
  types of, 291
  in vinaigrette, 630
  in yeast bread, 604
Omega-3 fatty acids, 626
Omega-6 fatty acids, 626

Omelet(s)
  caramelized onions in, 223
  cheese, 528–529
  flat
    with cauliflower or broc-
      coli, 530–531
    cheesy, 530
    filling combinations for,
      530
    Greek style, 531
    Mexican style, 531
    frozen vegetables in, 531
    ideas for filling, 529
    paneer and Spanish, Indian
      style, 529
    simplest, 528–529
    Spanish, 529
    vegan, 529–530 V
    Vietnamese, 532
  100 percent whole wheat
    bread, 602, *603*, 604 V
  variations on, 604
One-pot gumbo, 459
One-pot pasta, 314, *315*
  variation on, 314
Onion(s), 14, 221–224
  adding marinated to sushi
    bowls, 385
  baked eggs with cheese and,
    525
  in balsamic syrup, 633
  biryani, *374*, *375*
  bitter greens with maple-,
    dressing, 40, *41*
  braised tofu and peas in
    curried coconut milk,
    493–494 V
  breaded sautéed cauliflower
    with olives and, 189
  buying and storing, 222
  caramelized, 224–225
    in cheese or tofu dip or
      spread, 557
    in cracker dough, 590
    dressing cabbage salad
      with, 40
    in omelets, 223
    pasta with, 320, *321*

  variations on, 320
  in stuffing pasta, 349
  uses for, 223
  in yeast bread, 604
  cooking, 224
  doneness, 224
  filling omelets with, 525
  fried rings, streamlined,
    162 V
  frying, 160
  in green salad, 36
  grilling, 167
  home fries with, 235–236
  kasha with golden brown,
    413–414
  in mashed potatoes, 234
  my mom's pan-cooked,
    228–229
  pan-cooking, 221
  pasta with caramelized, 320,
    321 V
    variations on, 320
  precooked grains with, 399,
    404
  preparing, 222–223
  raw, chutney, 668, *669* V
    variation on, 668
  roasted halves, 223–224 V
    variations on, 224
  salting, as salad addition, 48
  in scrambled eggs, 524
  simplest, gratin, 171
  simplest bean burgers, 502,
    503
  soup, 100–101
    variations on, 101
  stir-fried ramen with vegeta-
    bles, 338–339
  types of, 221–222
  vegetable stock, 97
  in vinaigrette, 630
  white pizza with balsamic
    caramelized, 613
  yogurt sauce, 674
Oolong tea, 756
Orange(s), 292
  adding sliced, to green
    salad, 36

  -almond cake, 697–698
  avocado-, smoothie, 751
  banana bread with chocolate
    and, 583
  -banana-mango ice cream,
    732
  blossom whipped cream,
    701
  -caraway scones, 589
  carrot-, smoothie, 751
  -chive biscuits, 588
  chocolate-
    cake, 694
    tofu pudding, 726
  citrus sprinkle, *641*, 651
  cranberry-
    crisp, 717
    soup, 740
    tea, 760
  cranberry relish with, and
    ginger, 281–282 V
  cranberry sauce with, and
    ginger, 281–282
  -cranberry spice compote,
    721
  -currant biscuits, 588
  five-layer avocado salad,
    51–52
  in fruit, cheese and nut com-
    bos, 39
  -ginger jam glaze, 705
  glaze, 703 V
  peach-, smoothie, *750*, 751
    variation on, 751
  raw beet salad with cabbage
    and, 51
  rosemary-, tea, 761
  sorbet, 734
  -thyme sorbet, 735
Orangeade, 755
Orange juice
  in balsamic syrup, 633
  -ginger tea, 760 V
    variations on, 760
  lima bean purée with fennel,
    460
  pumpkin, carrot, and, 747 V
    variations on, 747

Sweet laurel, 635
Sweet miso-cured vegetables, 94
Sweet miso glaze, 654
    variation on, 654
Sweet peanut sauce, 659
Sweet potato(es), 254–255
    baked pinto beans and, enchilada style, 470
    biscuits, 588
    boiled or steamed, 153–154
    buying and storing, 255
    and cashew gratin, 239
    coconut cake, 697
    cooking, 255
    and cream cheese gratin, 239
    doneness, 255
    French-fried, 243
    frying, 160
    gnocchi, 353
    grilling, 167
    in jook, 424
    mashed gratin, 255–256
    paratha, 595
    pasta with, 322
    preparing, 255
    and quinoa salad, 80, 82
        variation on, 80
    ravioli, 349–350
    roasted quinoa with cheese and, 412
    salads
        roasted, with red pepper vinaigrette, 71 **V**
        variations on, 71
    simply cooked, 255
    spicy stir-fried, 241
    vegetable noodles, 310
Sweet rice and coconut cake, 699
    variations on, 699
Sweet Thai chili sauce, 623
Sweet yogurt sauce, 674
Swiss chard. See Chard
Swiss cheese, 555
    fried eggs with, 525
    simplest asparagus gratin, 171

in waffle batter, 548
Swiss-style cheese bake, 557–558
    variations on, 558
Syrup
    cane, 685
    malt, 685
    maple, 683–684
    palm, 685
    rice, 684–685
    simple, 685 **V**
        infusing, 684–685
    sorghum, 685

T

Tabasco sauce, in mayonnaise, 671
Tabbouleh, 40, 76 **V**
    variation on, 76
Tacos
    fillings and toppings for, 620, 623
    ideas for, 621
    potato, 236
Tagine, pearl couscous, 411 **V**
Tahini, 16, 306 **V**
    chickpeas in their own broth with, 455
    in crunchy amaranth griddlecakes, 406
    miso sauce, 653
    roasted broccoli salad with, dressing, 68, 69 **V**
    sesame glaze, grilled or broiled eggplant with, 201
Tahini sauce, 306
    changing up, 305
    with chickpea fries, 480
    as crudité dip, 92
Tahini soy sauce, 659
Tamale(s)
    cornhusk, 395, 395
    dishes that make great fillings, 397
    naked, with chile-cheese filling, 394–395, 396

Tamarind, beer-glazed black beans with, 440
Tamping, 765
Tangerine(s), 292
    chamomile-, sorbet, 735
    zest, in anything-scented peas, 226
Tanginess, addition of acidity to raw vegetable salads, 52
Tangy orange-black bean soup, 125
Tapenade, 291–292 **V**
    in pasta with broccoli, cauliflower, or broccoli raab, 322
    as spread for bruschetta or crostini, 624
Tapioca, sweet coconut soup with, 742
Tarbais, 433
Tarbaises, 433
Tarragon, 637
    in anything-scented peas, 226
    for boiled potatoes, 233
    with chickpea fries, 480
    in cooked beans, 434
    in cracker dough, 590
    in endive and blue cheese salad, 42
    in fluffy cracked wheat with and mustard, 416–417
    in mayonnaise, 671
    in sautéed mushrooms, 218
Tatsoi, in making salad, 34
Tea, 756–762
    black, 756
    brewing, 757
    flavored and herbal, 758, 760
        variations on, 761
    green, 756
    iced, 761–762
        sweetening, 762
        Thai, 762, 764
            variations on, 762
    unclouding, 762
    in infusing simple syrup, 684
    loose, or bags, 757

masala chai, 757–758
    variations on, 758
    matcha, 758, 759
    mint, 760 **V**
    oolong, 756
    orange-ginger, 760 **V**
        variations on, 760
    roasted barley, 761 **V**
        variation on, 761
    white, 756
Teff, 398, 401, 4040
Tembleque, 724 **V**
Tempeh, 14, 482
    basics of, 512–518
    bean threads with coconut milk and mint, 334, 335, 336
    braised, three ways, 513 **V**
    chili con, 456
    chili with black beans, 517–518
    crunchy crumbled, 512–513 **V**
    in fried rice, 381
    "goulash," 140
    hash, 515, 516, 517 **V**
        variations on, 517
    in pasta with broccoli, cauliflower, or broccoli raab, 323
    in pho, 130
    quinoa salad with crunchy, 82–83
    with rice and spinach, 514, 515 **V**
        variation on, 515
    smoked, 487
    in stuffing pasta, 349
    tofu burgers, 507
    as topping for Japanese-style summertime pasta salad
    as topping for paella, 378
    in twice-fried green beans, 209
Tempeh water, 98
Tempura fried vegetables, 161

spicy, 313
with wine, 313
Tomato water, 98
Tongs, 17
Tools, 16–18, *19–20*
Toovar dal, 432
Toppings. *See also* Frostings
    for baked potatoes, 233
    for cobblers, 717
    crisp, 678–680
    for crostini, 624
    for grilled watermelon
        steak, 290
    for jook, 424
    for pizza, 610, 614
    for precooked tofu or
        seitan, 490
    sweet crumble, 711–712
        variations on, 711–712
Tortellini
    making, *347*
    spinach-ricotta, 349
Tortilla(s)
    corn, 595–596
        variations on, 596
    filled, 620–624
        fillings and topping for, 620
    scrambled, with scallions
        and chiles, 536
    Spanish, 531–532
        variations on, 531–532
Tortilla chips
    baked, 596
    fried, 596
Tortilla paisana, 532
Tortilla press, using, 595, 596
Tortilla soup, 111–112 🔽
    garnishes for, 112
Tossed salads, 35
Traditional pesto
    as crudité dip, 92
    in egg salad or deviled eggs,
        542
    with fried, grilled, or broiled
        cheese, 564
    pasta frittata, 532
    red, white, and green pizza,
        614

Trans fats, 626–627
Treacle, 685
Tremocos, 432
Triticale, 403
Tropical granita, 737
Truffles, quick ganache,
    705–706
Turbinado, 682
Turmeric, 647
Turnips, 262–263
    braised and glazed, 263
    in braised tofu and peas
        in curried coconut
        milk, 493
    cooking, 263
    doneness, 263
    French-fried, 243
    Korean-style vegetable soup,
        115
    leafy tops of, in salads, 34
    in minestrone, 109–110
    in pasta primavera, 319
    in pho, 130
    preparing, 263
    purée, 152
    in risotto, 379
Turtle beans, 430
Tuscan-style whole grain
    soup, 137

U

Udon noodles, 331
    in improvising noodle bowl,
        333
    green tea broth with,
        132
    additions to, 132
UHT milk, 551
Ultimate vegan chili, 410 🔽
Ultra-fast avocado soup, 146
    variations on, 146
Unleavened crackers and
    flatbreads, 589–596
    aloo paratha, 592, *593*,
        594–595
    shaping, *594*
    variations on, 595

chapati, 591 🔽
    variations on, 591
    corn tortillas, 595–596
        variations on, 596
    paratha, 592 🔽
        variations on, 592
Unleavened crackers and
    flatbreads (*cont.*)
    simplest crackers, 589–590
        mix-ins for dough, 590
        variations on, 590
Unsweetened chocolate, 686
    chocolate cake, 694
Upside-down cake, plum-
    rosemary, 698–699
    variations on, 698–699
Urad beans, 433

V

Vanilla
    apricot-, jam glaze, 705
    -apricot soup, 742
    custard ice cream, 729–730
    glaze, 703
    hot chocolate, 755
    ice cream, balsamic syrup
        with, 633
    pudding, 723–724
        variations on, 724
    strawberry, rose water, and,
        compote, 721
    whipped cream, 701
Vanilla beans, 647
Vaquero beans, 433
Vegan béchamel sauce, 675 🔽
Vegan blueberry muffins,
    586 🔽
Vegan breaded and panfried
    eggplant, 162 🔽
Vegan breakfast burritos,
    533 🔽
Vegan cheesecake, 700 🔽
Vegan chocolate cake, 694 🔽
Vegan chocolate chunk cook-
    ies, 688 🔽
Vegan chocolate ganache,
    705 🔽

Vegan cream of tomato soup,
    107 🔽
Vegan creamy corn chowder,
    121 🔽
Vegan crumble topping, 711 🔽
Vegan grilled eggplant salad,
    68 🔽
Vegan icing, 702–703 🔽
    variation on, 703 🔽
Vegan mashed potatoes,
    235 🔽
Vegan mushroom stew, 108 🔽
Vegan naan, 608 🔽
Vegannaise, 672 🔽
    in sea slaw, 55
    variations on, 672 🔽
Vegan oatmeal cookies, 689 🔽
Vegan oatmeal pancakes,
    544 🔽
Vegan omelet, 529–530 🔽
Vegan pancake, 543 🔽
Vegan peanut butter cookies,
    690 🔽
Vegan piecrust, 710 🔽
    variations on, 710 🔽
Vegan roasted beet borscht,
    105 🔽
Vegans, chocolate for, 687
Vegan sandwich bread, 605 🔽
Vegan spinach calzones, 615 🔽
Vegan substitutions, 15
Vegan tempura, 161 🔽
Vegan ultra-fast avocado soup,
    146 🔽
Vegan whipped cream, 701 🔽
Vegan yellow cake, 696 🔽
Vegan zucchini bread, 583 🔽
Vegetable(s). *See also specific
    by name*
    adding grated, to quick
        breads, 584
    aromatic, in stuck-pot red
        rice with potato crust,
        383
    barley soup with seasonal,
        134–135
    batter-fried, 159–161
        variations on, 160, 161

Worcestershire sauce, hold the
anchovies, 633–634 **V**
in mayonnaise, 671
for topping baked potatoes,
233
Wrappers
dumpling, 355–356
store-bought, 355

Y

Yams, 254–255. *See also* Sweet
potatoes
Yankee beans, 432
Yeast
in leavening, 577
nutritional, 390
Yeast breads, 596–608
additions for, 603
breadsticks, 606, *607,* 608
variations on, 608
equipment for making, 597
letting rise and "room temperature," 600
mixing and kneading dough
for, 578–579
naan, 608
variations on, 608
no-knead bread, 601–602
ideas for, 601
science behind, 601
variation on, 602
100 percent whole wheat
bread, 602, *603,*
604 **V**
variations on, 604
rustic French bread, 597,
600–601**V**
variations on, 600

sandwich bread, eight ways,
603–605
variations on, 605–606
shaping
baguettes, 599
boule, 598
loaf, 599
rolls, 598
storing and freezing dough,
596–597
Yellow cake, 696
variations on, 696
Yellow or red split pea soup
with ginger, 124
Yellow rice, 373
variations on, 373
Yogurt, 552–553. *See also*
Greek yogurt
biryani, *374, 375*
blueberry, muffins, 586
cheese, 553
chile-, sauce, 667
collard or kale with, 211
cool, soup with nuts, 144
variations on, 144
corn bread, 580–581
cucumber salad with, 49
-dill dressing, farro salad
with cucumber and,
77, 80
food processor fruit sorbet,
736
frozen, 732, *733*
mix-ins for, 732
variations on, 732
grilled, -marinated cheese
and vegetable skewers,
565–566
variation on, 566

grilled or broiled eggplant
salad with, *200,* 201
ideas for flavoring, 553
lemon- scones, 589
paratha with, 592
pasta with caramelized
onions, 320
peach-orange smoothie, 751
raw beet salad with dressing, 51
sauces, 673–674
simplest, 673–674
variations on, 674
uses for, 673
strained, 553
tahini sauce, 305
in vinaigrette, 630
Yogurt cheese, 553
Yogurt pancakes, 543
Yogurt sauce, 673–674
with chickpea fries, 480
in cooked beans, 434
simplest, 673–674
uses for, 673
Yuba noodles, 332

Z

Za'atar, *641,* 652 **V**
in cheese or tofu dip or
spread, 557
falafel with, 473
sprinkling on popcorn, 390
for vegetable crisps, 163
Ziti, baked, 330
variations on, 330
Zucchini
bread, *582,* 583–584
additions for, 583–584

bread pancakes, 543
coconut-lentil soup with
vegetables, 127
in fried rice, 381
frying, 160
green gumbo, 113
grilling, 167
marinated, 91
in minestrone, 109–110
miso-cured vegetables, 94
pancakes with pesto, 254
variations on, 254
pearl couscous tagine, 411
as pizza topping, 614
quickest pickled, 89, *90,* 91
ratatouille, 156–157 **V**
salads, ratatouille, 66–67
smoky eggplant and, soup,
110–111 **V**
variations on, 110–111
in stir-fried vegetables, 155
vegetable noodles, 310

Converting Measurements

Essential Conversions

VOLUME TO VOLUME

3 teaspoons	1 tablespoon
4 tablespoons	¼ cup
5 tablespoons plus 1 teaspoon	⅓ cup
4 ounces	½ cup
8 ounces	1 cup
1 cup	½ pint
2 cups	1 pint
2 pints	1 quart
4 quarts	1 gallon

VOLUME TO WEIGHT

¼ cup liquid or fat	2 ounces
½ cup liquid or fat	4 ounces
1 cup liquid or fat	8 ounces
2 cups liquid or fat	1 pound
1 cup sugar	7 ounces
1 cup flour	5 ounces

Metric Approximations

MEASUREMENTS

¼ teaspoon	1.25 milliliters
½ teaspoon	2.5 milliliters
1 teaspoon	5 milliliters
1 tablespoon	15 milliliters
1 fluid ounce	30 milliliters
¼ cup	60 milliliters
⅓ cup	80 milliliters
½ cup	120 milliliters
1 cup	240 milliliters
1 pint (2 cups)	480 milliliters
1 quart (4 cups)	960 milliliters (0.96 liter)
1 gallon (4 quarts)	3.84 liters
1 ounce (weight)	28 grams
¼ pound (4 ounces)	114 grams
1 pound (16 ounces)	454 grams
2.2 pounds	1 kilogram (1,000 grams)
1 inch	2.5 centimeters

OVEN TEMPERATURES

Description	°Fahrenheit	°Celsius
Cool	200	90
Very slow	250	120
Slow	300–325	150–160
Moderately slow	325–350	160–180
Moderate	350–375	180–190
Moderately hot	375–400	190–200
Hot	400–450	200–230
Very hot	450–500	230–260